General Biology I, II, III
Biology 101/102/103 at MHCC

Eleventh Edition

Cecie Starr / Ralph Taggart

THOMSON
™
BROOKS/COLE

Australia · Canada · Mexico · Singapore · Spain · United Kingdom · United States

General Biology I, II, III
Starr / Taggart

Executive Editors:
Michele Baird, Maureen Staudt &
Michael Stranz

Project Development Manager:
Linda de Stefano

Marketing Coordinators:
Lindsay Annett and Sara Mercurio

Production/Manufacturing Supervisor:
Donna M. Brown

Pre-Media Services Supervisor:
Dan Plofchan

Kalina Hintz and Bahman Naraghi

Cover Image
Getty Images*

The Adaptable Courseware Program
consists of products and additions to
existing Brooks/Cole products that are
produced from camera-ready copy.
Peer review, class testing, and
accuracy are primarily the responsibility
of the author(s).

General Biology I, II, III / Starr, Taggart
– Eleventh Edition

ISBN-13: 978-0-495-29465-8
ISBN-10: 0-495-29465-9

International Divisions List

Asia (Including India):
Thomson Learning
(a division of Thomson Asia Pte Ltd)
5 Shenton Way #01-01
UIC Building
Singapore 068808
Tel: (65) 6410-1200
Fax: (65) 6410-1208

Australia/New Zealand:
Thomson Learning Australia
102 Dodds Street
Southbank, Victoria 3006
Australia

Latin America:
Thomson Learning
Seneca 53
Colonia Polano
11560 Mexico, D.F., Mexico
Tel (525) 281-2906
Fax (525) 281-2656

Canada:
Thomson Nelson
1120 Birchmount Road
Toronto, Ontario
Canada M1K 5G4
Tel (416) 752-9100
Fax (416) 752-8102

UK/Europe/Middle East/Africa:
Thomson Learning
High Holborn House
50-51 Bedford Row
London, WC1R 4L$
United Kingdom
Tel 44 (020) 7067-2500
Fax 44 (020) 7067-2600

Spain (Includes Portugal):
Thomson Paraninfo
Calle Magallanes 25
28015 Madrid
España
Tel 34 (0)91 446-3350
Fax 34 (0)91 445-6218

CUSTOM CONTENTS

INTRODUCTION
1. Invitation to Biology   2

Unit I: PRINCIPLES OF CELLULAR LIFE
2. Life's Chemical Basis   18
3. Molecules of Life   32
4. Cell Structure and Function   50
5. A Closer Look at Cell Membranes   74
6. Ground Rules of Metabolism   90
7. Where It Starts—Photosynthesis   106
8. How Cells Release Chemical Energy   122

Unit II: PRINCIPLES OF INHERITANCE
9. How Cells Reproduce   140
10. Meiosis and Sexual Reproduction   154
11. Observing Patterns in Inherited Traits   168
12. Chromosomes and Human Inheritance   186
13. DNA Structure and Function   206
14. From DNA to Protein   218
15. Controls Over Genes   230
16. Studying and Manipulating Genomes   242

Unit III: PRINCIPLES OF EVOLUTION
17. Evidence of Evolution   260
18. Microevolutionary Processes   282
19. Evolutionary Patterns, Rates, and Trends   300
20. Life's Origin and Early Evolution   318

Unit VII: PRINCIPLES OF ECOLOGY
45. Population Ecology   800
46. Community Structure and Biodiversity   820
47. Ecosystems   842
48. The Biosphere   866
49. Behavioral Ecology   898

Epilogue
Appendix I   Classification System
Appendix II   Answers to Self-Quizzes
Appendix III   Answers to Genetics Problems
Appendix IV   Periodic Table of the Elements
Appendix V   The Amino Acids
Appendix VI   Units of Measure

Appendix VII   Closer Look at Some Major Metabolic Pathways
Appendix VIII   Restless Earth – Life's Changing Geological Stage
Appendix IX   Annotations to A Journal Article
Glossary
Index

ROMANO, FRANK A., III, *Jacksonville State University*
RUPPERT, ETTA *Clemson University*
SHOFNER, MARCIA *University of Maryland, College Park*
SIEVERT, GREG *Emporia State University*
SIMS, THOMAS L. *Northern Illinois University*
SONGER, STEPHANIE R. *Concord University*
SPRENKLE, AMY B. *Salem State College*
ST. CLAIR, LARRY *Brigham Young University*
TEMPLET, ALICE *Nicholls State University*
TURELL, MARSHA *Houston Community College*
WALSH, PAT *University of Delaware*
WILKINS, HEATHER DAWN *University of Tennessee at Martin*
WINDELSPECHT, MICHAEL *Appalachian State University*
WYGODA, MARK *McNeese State University*
ZAHN, MARTIN D. *Thomas Nelson Community College*
ZANIN, KATHY *The Citadel*

CONTRIBUTORS: INFLUENTIAL CLASS TESTS AND REVIEWS

ADAMS, DARYL *Minnesota State University, Mankato*
ANDERSON, DENNIS *Oklahoma City Community College*
BENDER, KRISTEN *California State University, Long Beach*
BOGGS, LISA *Southwestern Oklahoma State University*
BORGESON, CHARLOTTE *University of Nevada*
BOWER, SUSAN *Pasadena City College*
BOYD, KIMBERLY *Cabrini College*
BRICKMAN, PEGGY *University of Georgia*
BROWN, EVERT *Casper College*
BRYAN, DAVID W. *Cincinnati State College*
BURNETT, STEPHEN *Clayton College*
BUSS, WARREN *University of Northern Colorado*
CARTWRIGHT, PAULYN *University of Kansas*
CASE, TED *University of California, San Diego*
COLAVITO, MARY *Santa Monica College*
COOK, JERRY L. *Sam Houston State University*
DAVIS, JERRY *University of Wisconsin, LaCrosse*
DENGLER, NANCY *University of California, Davis*
DESAIX, JEAN *University of North Carolina*
DiBARTOLOMEIS, SUSAN *Millersville University of Pennsylvania*
DIEHL, FRED *University of Virginia*
DONALD-WHITNEY, CATHY *Collin County Community College*
DUWEL, PHILIP *University of South Carolina, Columbia*
EAKIN, DAVID *Eastern Kentucky University*
EBBS, STEPHEN *Southern Illinois University*
EDLIN, GORDON *University of Hawaii, Manoa*
ENDLER, JOHN *University of California, Santa Barbara*
ERWIN, CINDY *City College of San Francisco*
FOREMAN, KATHERINE *Moraine Valley Community College*
FOX, P. MICHAEL *SUNY College at Brockport*
GIBLIN, TARA *Stephens College*
GILLS, RICK *University of Wisconsin, La Crosse*
GREENE, CURTIS *Wayne State University*
GREGG, KATHERINE *West Virginia Wesleyan College*
HARLEY, JOHN *Eastern Kentucky University*
HARRIS, JAMES *Utah Valley Community College*
HELGESON, JEAN *Collin County Community College*
HESS, WILFORD M. *Brigham Young University*
HOUTMAN, ANNE *Cal State, Fullerton*
HUFFMAN, DAVID *Southwestern Texas University*
HUFFMAN, DONNA *Calhoun Community College*
INEICHER, GEORGIA *Hinds Community College*
JOHNSTON, TAYLOR *Michigan State University*
JUILLERAT, FLORENCE *Indiana University, Purdue University*
KENDRICK, BRYCE *University of Waterloo*
KETELES, KRISTEN *University of Central Arkansas*
KIRKPATRICK, LEE A. *Glendale Community College*
KREBS, CHARLES *University of British Columbia*
LANZA, JANET *University of Arkansas, Little Rock*
LEICHT, BRENDA *University of Iowa*
LOHMEIER, LYNNE *Mississippi Gulf Coast Community College*
LORING, DAVID *Johnson County Community College*
MACKLIN, MONICA *Northeastern State University*

MANN, ALAN *University of Pennsylvania*
MARTIN, KATHY *Central Connecticut State University*
MARTIN, TERRY *Kishwaukee College*
MASON, ROY B. *Mount San Jacinto College*
MATTHEWS, ROBERT *University of Georgia*
MAXWELL, JOYCE *California State University, Northridge*
McCLURE, JERRY *Miami University*
McNABB, ANN *Virginia Polytechnic Institute and State University*
MEIERS, SUSAN *Western Illinois University*
MEYER, DWIGHT H. *Queensborough Community College*
MICKLE, JAMES *North Carolina State University*
MILLER, G. TYLER *Wilmington, North Carolina*
MINOR, CHRISTINE V. *Clemson University*
MITCHELL, DENNIS M. *Troy University*
MONCAYO, ABELARDO C. *Ohio Northern University*
MOORE, IGNACIO *Virginia Tech*
MORRISON-SHETTLER, ALLISON *Georgia State University*
MORTON, DAVID *Frostburg State University*
NELSON, RILEY *Brigham Young University*
NICKLES, JON R. *University of Alaska, Anchorage*
NOLD, STEPHEN *University of Wisconsin- Stout*
PADGETT, DONALD *Bridgewater State College*
PENCOE, NANCY *State University of West Georgia*
PERRY, JAMES *University of Wisconsin, Center Fox Valley*
PITOCCHELLI, DR. JAY *Saint Anselm College*
PLETT, HAROLD *Fullerton College*
POLCYN, DAVID M. *California State University, San Bernardino*
PURCELL, JERRY *San Antonio College*
REID, BRUCE *Kean College of New Jersey*
RENFROE, MICHAEL *James Madison University*
REZNICK, DAVID *California State University, Fullerton*
RICKETT, JOHN *University of Arkansas, Little Rock*
ROHN, TROY *Boise State University*
ROIG, MATTIE *Broward Community College*
ROSE, GRIEG *West Valley College*
SANDIFORD, SHAMILI A. *College of Du Page*
SCHREIBER, FRED *California State University, Fresno*
SELLERS, LARRY *Louisiana Tech University*
SHAPIRO, HARRIET *San Diego State University*
SHONTZ, NANCY *Grand Valley State University*
SHOPPER, MARILYN *Johnson County Community College*
SIEMENS, DAVID *Black Hills State University*
SMITH, BRIAN *Black Hills State University*
SMITH, JERRY *St. Petersburg Junior College, Clearwater Campus*
STEINERT, KATHLEEN *Bellevue Community College*
SUMMERS, GERALD *University of Missouri*
SUNDBERG, MARSHALL D. *Emporia State University*
SVENSSON, PETER *West Valley College*
SWANSON, ROBERT *North Hennepin Community College*
SWEET, SAMUEL *University of California, Santa Barbara*
SZYMCZAK, LARRY J. *Chicago State University*
TAYLOR, JANE *Northern Virginia Community College*
TERHUNE, JERRY *Jefferson Community College, University of Kentucky*
TIZARD, IAN *Texas A&M University*
TRAYLER, BILL *California State University at Fresno*
TROUT, RICHARD E. *Oklahoma City Community College*
TURELL, MARSHA *Houston Community College*
TYSER, ROBIN *University of Wisconsin, LaCrosse*
VAJRAVELU, RANI *University of Central Florida*
VANDERGAST, AMY *San Diego State University*
VERHEY, STEVEN *Central Washington University*
VICKERS, TANYA *University of Utah*
VOGEL, THOMAS *Western Illinois University*
WARNER, MARGARET *Purdue University*
WEBB, JACQUELINE F. *Villanova University*
WELCH, NICOLE TURRILL *Middle Tennessee State University*
WELKIE, GEORGE W. *Utah State University*
WENDEROTH, MARY PAT *University of Washington*
WINICUR, SANDRA *Indiana University, South Bend*
WOLFE, LORNE *Georgia Southern University*
YONENAKA, SHANNA *San Francisco State University*
ZAYAITZ, ANNE *Kutztown University of Pennsylvania*

Introduction

Current configurations of the Earth's oceans and land masses—the geologic stage upon which life's drama continues to unfold. This composite satellite image reveals global energy use at night by the human population. Just as biological science does, it invites you to think more deeply about the world of life—and about our impact upon it.

What Am I Doing Here?

Leaf through a newspaper on any given Sunday and you might get an uneasy feeling that the world is spinning out of control. There is a lot about the Middle East, where great civilizations have come and gone. You will not find much on the spectacular coral reefs of the surrounding seas, especially at the northern end of the Red Sea. Now the news is about oil and politics, bioterrorists and war.

Think back on the 1991 Persian Gulf conflict, when an Iraqi dictator ordered 460 million gallons of crude oil to be dumped into the Gulf and oil fields to be set on fire. Thick smoke blocked out sunlight, and black rain fell. Today, the human population in neighboring Kuwait shows a spike in cancer rates, which may have been caused by dangerous particles in the smoke. Similarly, New Yorkers who breathed in the dense, noxious dust that billowed through the air after the 2001 World Trade Center attack are still reporting chronic health problems.

Besides terrorists, nature itself seems to have it in for us. Cholera, the flu, and SARS pose global threats. A long-term AIDS pandemic is unraveling the fabric of African societies. Monstrous storms, droughts, heat waves, and fires batter the land (Figure 1.1). Once-vast glaciers and the polar ice caps are melting fast, the atmosphere is warming up, and living conditions may change just about everywhere.

It is enough to make you throw down the paper and go sit in a park. It is enough to make you wish you lived in the good old days, when things were so much simpler.

Of course, read up on the good old days and you will find they weren't so good. Bioterrorists were around in 1346, when soldiers catapulted the corpses of bubonic plague

Figure 1.1 Biology is a way of thinking critically about life, one that helps us understand nature and our place in it. It starts with the premise that any aspect of nature—including this forest fire in Montana—has one or more underlying causes. To the right, an oil field burning out of control during the Persian Gulf War, an example of human impact on nature.

victims into a walled city under siege. Infected people and rats fled the city and helped fuel the Black Death, a plague that left 25 million dead all across Europe. Later, in 1918, the Spanish flu raced around the world and left between 30 million and 40 million people dead. Like today, many felt helpless in a world that seemed out of control.

What it boils down to is this: For at least a couple of million years, we humans and our immediate ancestors have been trying to make sense of the natural world. We observe it, we come up with ideas, and we test the ideas. However, the more pieces of the puzzle we fit together, the bigger the puzzle gets. We are now smart enough to know that it is almost overwhelmingly big.

You might choose to walk away from the challenge and simply let others tell you what to think. Or you might choose to develop your own understanding of the puzzle. Maybe you are interested in the pieces that affect your health, the food you eat, or your home or family. Maybe you simply find organisms and their environment fascinating. Regardless of the focus, the scientific study of life—*biology*—can deepen your perspective on the world.

Throughout this book, you will come across examples of how organisms are constructed, how they function, where they live, and what they do. The examples support concepts which, when taken together, convey what "life" is. This chapter is an overview of the basic concepts. It also sets the stage for forthcoming descriptions of scientific observations, experiments, and tests that help show how you can develop, modify, and refine your views of life.

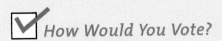

Watch the video online!

How Would You Vote?

The warm seas of the Middle East support some of the world's most spectacular coral reef ecosystems. Should the United States provide funding to help preserve these reefs? See BiologyNow for details, then vote online.

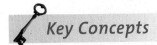

Key Concepts

LEVELS OF ORGANIZATION

The world of life has levels of organization that extend from atoms and molecules to the biosphere. The quality called "life" emerges at the level of cells. Section 1.1

LIFE'S UNDERLYING UNITY

The world of life shows unity, for all organisms are alike in key respects. They require inputs of energy and materials to function and maintain their complex organization. They work to keep their internal operating conditions within a tolerable range. They all sense and respond to conditions inside and outside themselves. They inherit DNA from parents, which gives them a capacity to survive and reproduce. Section 1.2

LIFE'S DIVERSITY

Millions of diverse kinds of organisms, or species, have appeared and disappeared over time. Each species is unique in some traits—that is, in some aspects of its body plan, functioning, and behavior. Section 1.3

EXPLAINING UNITY IN DIVERSITY

Theories of evolution, especially a major theory of evolution by way of natural selection, help explain the link between life's unity and diversity. The theories are a useful foundation for research in all fields of biological inquiry. Section 1.4

HOW WE KNOW

Biologists engage in systematic observations, hypotheses, predictions, and experimental tests in the outside world and in the laboratory. Well-designed tests can be repeated by others and yield the same results each time. Sections 1.5–1.7

Links to Earlier Concepts

This book parallels nature's levels of organization, from atoms to the biosphere. Learning about the structure and function of atoms and molecules primes you to understand the structure of living cells. Learning about protein synthesis, active transport, and other processes that keep a single cell alive can help you understand how large organisms survive, because their trillions of living cells use the same processes. Knowing what it takes to survive can help you sense why and how organisms interact with one another and the environment.

At the start of each chapter, we will be reminding you of such structural and functional connections. Within chapters, you will come across keychain icons with cross-references that will link you to relevant sections in earlier chapters.

1.1 Levels of Organization in Nature

The world of life shows increasingly inclusive levels of organization. Take time to see how the levels connect to get a sense of how the topics of this book are organized and where they will take you.

MAKING SENSE OF THE WORLD

If we are interpreting the distant past correctly, the first humans lived in small bands that did not venture far from home. Safety, danger, and resources that did not extend beyond the immediate horizon comprised their world. Much later in time, human populations dispersed all around the globe. They soon had a lot more to observe, think about, and explain.

Today, even the far reaches of the known universe hold clues to our world. Scientists, clerics, farmers, astronauts, and anyone else who is of a mind to do so try to make sense of things. Interpretations differ, for no one person can be expert in everything learned so far or have foreknowledge of all that remains hidden. If you are reading this book, then you are starting to explore how a subset of scientists, the biologists, think about things, what they found out, and what they are up to now. Alternative ways of explaining the world are available in books for nonscience classes, such as those dealing with philosophy and religion. As you read this book, keep an open mind. Doing so can help you make more enlightened decisions about which explanations work for you.

A PATTERN IN BIOLOGICAL ORGANIZATION

What do we call the external world in its entirety? *Nature*. Biologists are interested in its forms of life, past and present. They have studied life all the way down to interacting atoms and all the way up to the impacts of organisms on a global scale. In doing so, they discovered a great pattern of organization.

That pattern starts at the level of atoms, which are the smallest units of nature's fundamental substances (Figure 1.2*a*). At the next level, atoms have combined into larger units called molecules (Figure 1.2*b*).

The pattern reaches the threshold of life as certain molecules are assembled as cells (Figure 1.2*c*). Complex

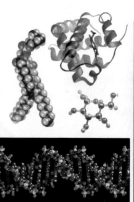
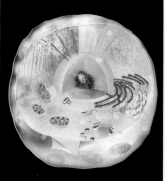
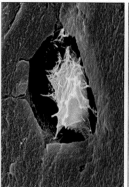
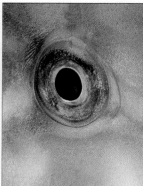
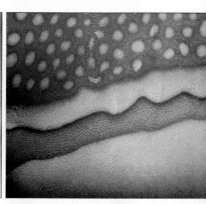

ⓑ molecule ⟶ **ⓒ cell** ⟶ **ⓓ tissue** ⟶ **ⓔ organ** ⟶ **ⓕ organ system**

two or more joined atoms of the same or different elements. "Molecules of life" are complex carbohydrates, lipids, proteins, DNA, and RNA. Only living cells now make them.

Smallest unit that can live and reproduce on its own or as part of a multicelled organism. It has an outer membrane, DNA, and other components.

Organized array of cells and substances that are interacting in some task. Many cells (*white*) made this bone tissue from their own secretions.

Structural unit made of two or more tissues interacting in some task. A parrotfish eye is a sensory organ used in vision.

Organs interacting physically, chemically, or both in some task. Parrotfish skin is an integumentary system with tissue layers, organs such as glands, and other parts.

ⓐ atom

Elements are fundamental forms of matter. Atoms are the smallest units that retain an element's properties. Electrons, protons, and neutrons are its building blocks. This hydrogen atom's electron zips around a proton in a spherical volume of space.

Figure 1.2 *Animated!* Levels of organization in nature.

carbohydrates, complex fats and other lipids, proteins, DNA, and RNA—these are the "molecules of life." In nature, only living cells can make them. A **cell** is the smallest unit of life; it has a capacity to survive and reproduce on its own, given raw materials, an energy source, information encoded in its DNA, and suitable environmental conditions.

Each kind of organism, or **species**, consists of one or more cells. In multicelled species, cells form tissues, organs, and organ systems. Often there are trillions of specialized cells that interact directly or indirectly in the task of keeping the whole multicelled body alive. Figure 1.2*d–g* defines these levels of organization.

The population is the next level of organization. It is a group of the same species in some specified area. Fields of poppies in a valley or schools of fish in a lake are such groups (Figure 1.2*h*). The next level is the community. It includes all populations of all species in a specified area (Figure 1.2*i*). A community inside an underwater cave in the Red Sea, a forest in Argentina, or populations of tiny organisms that live, reproduce, and die quickly inside a flower are examples.

The next level of organization is the ecosystem, or a community interacting with its physical and chemical environment. The highest level, the biosphere, includes all regions of Earth's crust, waters, and atmosphere in which organisms live.

Bear in mind, life is more than the sum of its parts. At each successive level of organization, new properties emerge that are not inherent in any part by itself, as when living cells emerge from "lifeless" molecules. The interactions among parts generate **emergent properties**.

This book is a journey through the globe-spanning organization of life. Take a moment to study Figure 1.2. You can use it as a road map of where each part fits in the great scheme of nature.

> Nature shows levels of organization, from the simple to the increasingly complex. Life's unique characteristics emerge as atoms and molecules interact and form cells. They extend from interactions among cells to populations, communities, ecosystems, and the biosphere.

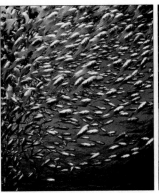

g multicelled organism

Individual made of different types of cells. Cells of most multicelled organisms, including this Red Sea parrotfish, are organized as tissues, organs, and organ systems.

h population

Group of single-celled or multicelled individuals of the same species occupying a specified area. This is a fish population in the Red Sea.

i community

All populations of all species occupying a specified area. This is part of a coral reef in the Gulf of Aqaba at the northern end of the Red Sea.

j ecosystem

A community that is interacting with its physical environment. It has inputs and outputs of energy and materials. Reef ecosystems flourish in warm, clear seawater throughout the Middle East.

k the biosphere

All regions of Earth's waters, crust, and atmosphere that hold organisms. In the vast universe, Earth is a rare planet. Without its abundance of free-flowing water, there would be no life.

1.2 Overview of Life's Unity

"Life" is not easy to define. It is just too big, and it has been changing for 3.8 billion years! Even so, you can characterize it in terms of its unity and diversity. Here's the unity part: All living things require inputs of energy and materials; they sense and respond to change, as when they adjust conditions inside their body; and they reproduce with the help of DNA. But they differ in the details of their traits. That's the diversity part—variation in traits.

ENERGY AND LIFE'S ORGANIZATION

Cells, remember, are the smallest units that are alive. To stay alive, they get energy from the environment and convert it to forms that help them do work, such as constructing and organizing molecules into cell parts. **Energy** is the capacity for doing work. Whether a cell is free-living or a tiny bit of a multicelled organism, its organization would end without continuous inputs of energy. Higher levels of organization—populations, communities, and ecosystems—also would fall apart in the absence of energy inputs from the environment.

Producers make their food from simple materials in the environment. Plants and other photosynthetic types use sunlight energy to construct sugars from carbon dioxide and water molecules. They use the sugars as packets of energy and as building blocks for making complex carbohydrates, fats, and proteins. Animals and decomposers are **consumers**. They cannot make food; they eat producers and other organisms. Decomposers break down the remains of organisms to simpler raw materials, some of which become cycled back to the producers.

We are outlining a series of energy transfers from the environment, through producers, then on through consumers, and back to the environment. It is a one-way flow of energy, because all the energy that enters the world of life in a given interval eventually leaves it. Why? At each transfer step, a small amount escapes as an unorganized form of energy: heat. All organisms are participants in this continuous, directional flow of energy (Figure 1.3).

ORGANISMS SENSE AND RESPOND TO CHANGE

All organisms are alike in another way. They sense changes in their surroundings and make controlled, compensatory responses to them. They do so with the assistance of **receptors**. Receptors are molecules and structures that detect stimuli, which are specific kinds of energy. Different receptors can respond to different stimuli. A stimulus may be sunlight energy, chemical energy, or the mechanical energy of a bite (Figure 1.4).

Activated receptors trigger changes in the activities of organisms. As a simple example, after you finish eating an apple, sugars leave your small intestine and enter blood. Think of blood and the fluid around cells as the body's *internal* environment. The composition and volume of that fluid must be kept within a range that your cells can tolerate. Too much or too little sugar changes the composition of blood, as happens with diabetes and other medical problems. Normally, when there is too much sugar, your pancreas secretes more insulin. Most living cells in your body have receptors for this hormone. It stimulates cells to take up sugar.

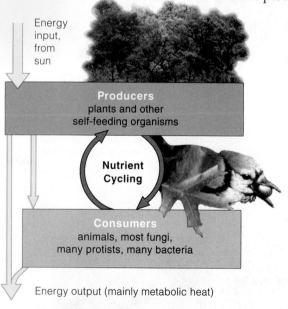

Energy input, from sun

Producers
plants and other self-feeding organisms

Nutrient Cycling

Consumers
animals, most fungi, many protists, many bacteria

Energy output (mainly metabolic heat)

Figure 1.3 *Animated!* The one-way flow of energy and cycling of materials in the world of life.

Figure 1.4 A roaring response to signals from pain receptors, activated by a lion cub flirting with disaster.

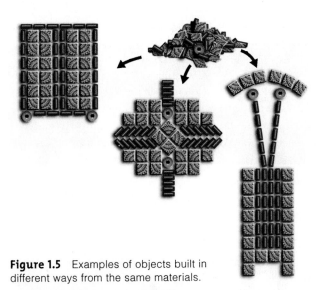

Figure 1.5 Examples of objects built in different ways from the same materials.

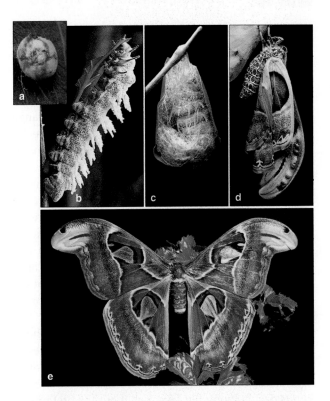

Figure 1.6 "The insect"—actually a series of stages of development guided largely by instructions in DNA. Here, a silkworm moth, from a fertilized egg (**a**), to a larval stage called a caterpillar (**b**), to a pupal stage (**c**), to the winged form of the adult (**d,e**).

When enough cells are doing so, the blood sugar level returns to the normal range.

As conditions in the internal environment change in potentially harmful ways, receptor-driven mechanisms kick in and return conditions to the state that cells can tolerate. **Homeostasis** is the name for this state, and it is a defining feature of life.

ORGANISMS GROW AND REPRODUCE

Organisms grow and reproduce based on information in **DNA**, a nucleic acid. DNA is *the* signature molecule of life. No chunk of granite or quartz has it.

DNA holds the information about building proteins from a few kinds of amino acids. Each protein has a particular amino acid sequence, which is the start of its particular shapes and properties.

By analogy, if you access suitable instructions and apply energy to the task, you might organize a pile of a few kinds of ceramic tiles into diverse patterns. Figure 1.5 has examples.

Protein-building information is vital for cell growth and reproduction. Proteins have many structural and functional roles. Important kinds function as enzymes, the cell's main worker molecules. With enzymes, cells build, split, and rearrange molecules exceedingly fast. Without enzymes, there could be no more complex carbohydrates, complex lipids, proteins, and nucleic acids. There could be no cells, no life.

In nature, an organism inherits DNA—the basis of its traits—from its parents. *Inheritance* is the acquisition of traits after parents transmit their DNA to offspring. Think about it. Why do baby storks look like storks and not like pelicans? Because they inherited stork DNA, which is different from pelican DNA.

Reproduction refers to actual mechanisms by which parents transmit DNA to offspring. For trees, humans, and other large organisms, the information in DNA is used in ways that guide growth and *development*—the transformation of the first cell of the new individual through orderly stages. The outcome is a multicelled adult, typically with tissues and organs (Figure 1.6).

Life's levels of organization start with a one-way flow of energy from the environment, through producers and consumers, then back to the environment.

Organisms interact through this one-way flow of energy and through a cycling of raw materials.

Organisms maintain their organization by sensing and responding to change. Many responses return conditions in the body's internal environment to a range that cells can tolerate, a state called homeostasis.

Organisms grow and reproduce based on information encoded in DNA, which they inherit from their parents.

1.3 If So Much Unity, Why So Many Species?

Although unity pervades the world of life, so does diversity. Organisms differ enormously in body form, the functions of their body parts, and behavior.

Superimposed on life's unity is tremendous diversity. How many species are with us today? Estimates range as high as 100 million. And 99.9 percent of all species that ever lived are extinct. So far, we have named approximately 1.8 million species.

For centuries, many scholars have been organizing information about life's diversity. Carolus Linnaeus, a naturalist, came up with the strategy of giving each species a two-part name. The first part designates the **genus** (plural, genera). A genus is a grouping of one or more species characterized by certain traits, at least one of which is unique to them. The second part of the name designates a particular species within the genus that has at least one trait no other species has.

Scarus gibbus is the formal name for the humphead parrotfish shown in Figure 1.2*g*. A different species in its genus is named *S. coelestinus* (midnight parrotfish). This example also shows that you can abbreviate the genus designation after you spell it out the first time.

Later, ever more inclusive groupings were devised, such as phylum (plural, phyla), order, kingdom, and domain. These are rankings of classification systems, which simply are ways to organize knowledge about relationships among species. Observable traits are still markers, but so is a richly expanding base of molecular evidence of descent from a shared ancestor.

Most biologists now favor a classification system having three domains: Bacteria, Archaea, and Eukarya (Figure 1.7 and Table 1.1). Protists, plants, fungi, and animals make up domain Eukarya (Figure 1.8).

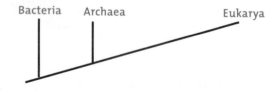

Figure 1.7 Three domains of life.

— Bacteria —

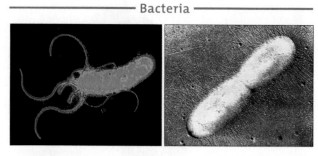

The most common prokaryotes; collectively, these single cells are the most metabolically diverse species on Earth.

— Archaea —

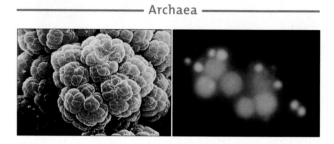

These prokaryotes are evolutionarily closer to eukaryotes than to bacteria. *Left*, a colony of methane-producing cells. *Right*, two species from a hydrothermal vent on the seafloor.

Figure 1.8 A few representatives of life's diversity.

Bacteria (singular, bacterium) and **archaeans** are *prokaryotic* cells. These single-celled organisms do not have a nucleus, which is a membrane-bound sac that, in all other species, encloses DNA. Of all organisms, they show the greatest metabolic diversity. Different species are producers and consumers in near-boiling water, frozen desert rocks, sulfur-clogged lakes, and other exceptionally harsh environments. Experimental evidence suggests that the first cells on Earth faced similarly hostile challenges to survival.

Structurally, the **protists** are the simplest organisms that are *eukaryotic*, which means their cells contain a nucleus. Different kinds are producers or consumers. Many are single cells, larger and more complex than prokaryotes. Some are tree-size, multicelled seaweeds. Actually, the protists are so diverse that they are being reclassified into a number of separate major lineages.

Cells of species we call fungi, plants, and animals are eukaryotic. Most **fungi** are multicelled, and not all of them form mushrooms (the reproductive structures for species that grow mostly underground). Many are decomposers. They secrete enzymes that digest food outside their body, then individual cells absorb the bits. Nearly all **plants** are multicelled and photosynthetic.

Table 1.1	Comparison of Life's Three Domains
Bacteria	Single cells, prokaryotic (no nucleus). Most ancient lineage.
Archaea	Single cells, prokaryotic. Evolutionarily closer to eukaryotes.
Eukarya	Eukaryotic cells (with a nucleus). Single-celled and multicelled species categorized as protists, plants, fungi, and animals.

Protists Single-celled and multicelled eukaryotic species that range from the microscopic to giant seaweeds. Many biologists are now viewing the "protists" as many major lineages.

Plants Generally, photosynthetic, multicelled eukaryotes, many with roots, stems, and leaves. Plants are the primary producers for ecosystems on land. Redwoods and flowering plants are examples.

Fungi Single-celled and multicelled eukaryotes; different kinds are decomposers, parasites, or pathogens. Without decomposers, communities would become buried in their own wastes.

Animals Multicelled eukaryotes that ingest tissues or juices of other organisms. Like this basilisk lizard, most actively move about during at least part of their life.

They make all of their own food by using sunlight as an energy source, and atoms of carbon dioxide and water as building blocks.

All **animals** are multicelled consumers that ingest tissues or juices of other organisms. Herbivores are grazers, carnivores eat meat, scavengers eat almost anything edible, and parasites pilfer nutrients from a host's tissues. All animals grow and develop through a series of stages. Most of them actively move about during at least part of their lives.

Pulling this information together, are you getting a sense of what it means when someone says that life shows unity *and* diversity?

On the basis of observable traits and molecular evidence of shared ancestry, we rank species in ever more inclusive groupings. The largest groupings are domains: archaea, bacteria, and eukarya (protists, fungi, plants, and animals).

1.4 An Evolutionary View of Diversity

How can organisms be so much alike and still show tremendous diversity? A theory of evolution by way of natural selection is one explanation.

Individuals of a species share certain traits, which are aspects of their physical form, function, and behavior. Rarely are individuals exactly alike; they differ in the details. Except for identical twins, for instance, the 6.4 billion individuals of our species (*Homo sapiens*) vary in height, hair color, and other traits.

Variation in most traits arises through **mutations**, or changes in DNA, which offspring inherit from their parents. Most mutations have neutral or bad effects. Some cause a trait to change in a way that makes one individual of a population better adapted than others to prevailing conditions. That is, its bearer might have an easier time securing food, a mate, and so on—so it has a better chance of reproducing and passing on the mutation to offspring. What is the outcome? Consider how a naturalist, Charles Darwin, expressed it:

First, a natural population tends to increase in size until its individuals compete more and more for food, shelter, and other dwindling environmental resources.

Second, those individuals differ from one another in the details of their shared, heritable traits.

Third, bearers of adaptive forms of traits are more likely to survive and reproduce, so those forms tend to become more common over successive generations. This outcome is called **natural selection**.

Consider how pigeons vary in feather color, size, and other traits (Figure 1.9). Say that pigeon breeders prefer black, curly-tipped feathers. They select captive birds having the darkest, curliest-tipped feathers and

WILD ROCK DOVE

let only those birds mate. In time, no birds in their captive populations have light, uncurly feathers. By culling through many traits, breeders have developed well over 300 varieties of domesticated pigeons.

Pigeon breeding is a case of *artificial* selection. One form of a trait is favored over others in an artificial environment under contrived, manipulated conditions. Darwin saw that breeding practices could be an easily understood model for *natural* selection, a favoring of some forms of a given trait over others in nature.

Just as breeders are "selective agents" that promote reproduction of certain pigeons, different agents act on the range of variation in the wild. Among them are pigeon-eating peregrine falcons, as in Figure 1.9. The swifter or better camouflaged pigeons are more likely to avoid falcons and live long enough to reproduce, compared with not-so-swift or too-flashy pigeons.

When different forms of a trait are becoming more or less common over successive generations, evolution is under way. In biology, **evolution** simply means that heritable change is occurring in a line of descent. Later chapters get into actual mechanisms of evolution. For now, it is enough to remember these preview points.

Body form, function, and behavior are mostly heritable traits. Different forms of a trait arise through DNA mutations. One may be more adaptive than others to prevailing conditions.

Natural selection is an outcome of differences in survival and reproduction among individuals of a population that vary in one or more heritable traits. Evolution, or change in lines of descent, gives rise to life's diversity.

Figure 1.9 Outcome of artificial selection: just a few of the hundreds of varieties of domesticated pigeons, all descended from captive populations of wild rock doves. At right, peregrine falcons are agents of natural selection in the wild.

1.5 The Nature of Biological Inquiry

The preceding sections introduced some big concepts. Consider approaching this or any other collection of "facts" with a critical attitude. "Why should I accept that they have merit?" The answer requires a look at how biologists make inferences about observations, then test their inferences against actual experience.

OBSERVATIONS, HYPOTHESES, AND TESTS

To get a sense of "how to do science," you might start with practices that are common in scientific research:

1. Observe some aspect of nature and research what others have found out about it, then frame a question or identify a problem related to your observation.

2. Develop a **hypothesis**: a testable explanation of the observed phenomenon or process.

3. Using the hypothesis as a guide, make a **prediction** —a statement of what you should find in nature if you were to go looking for it. This is often called the "if–then" process. *If* gravity does not pull objects toward Earth, *then* it should be possible to observe an apple falling up, not down, from a tree.

4. Devise ways to **test** the accuracy of predictions, as by making systematic observations, building models, and conducting experiments. **Models** are theoretical, detailed descriptions or analogies that might help us visualize an object or event that has not been, or cannot be, directly observed.

5. If your tests do not confirm the prediction, check to see what might have gone wrong. It may be that you overlooked a factor that had impact on the results. Or maybe the hypothesis is not a good one.

6. Repeat the tests or devise new ones—the more the better, because hypotheses that withstand many tests have a higher probability of being useful.

7. Objectively analyze and report the test results, as well as the conclusions you drew from them.

You might hear someone refer to these practices as "the scientific method," as if all scientists march to the drumbeat of an absolute, fixed procedure. They do not. Many observe and describe some aspect of nature and leave the hypothesizing to others. A few are lucky; they stumble onto information that they are not even looking for. Of course, it isn't always a matter of luck. Chance seems to favor a mind that has already been prepared, by education and experience, to recognize what the information might mean.

However, scientists do have something in common. It is a critical attitude about testing ideas in rigorous ways that are designed to disprove them.

Careful observations are a logical way to test the predictions that flow from a hypothesis. So are **experiments**, or tests carried out under controlled conditions that researchers manipulate. Such tests are carried out in nature and in laboratories, and they remove irrelevant factors that might skew the results. You will find two examples in the section to follow.

ABOUT THE WORD "THEORY"

Suppose a hypothesis has not been disproved after years of rigorous tests. Scientists use it to interpret more data or observations, which often involve more hypotheses. When a hypothesis meets these criteria, it may become accepted as a **scientific theory**.

You may hear people apply the word "theory" to a speculative idea, as in the phrase, "It's just a theory." However, a scientific theory differs from speculation in a big way. *After testing a scientific theory's predictive power many times and in many ways in the natural world, researchers have yet to find evidence that disproves it.* That is why the theory of evolution by natural selection is respected. It has been used successfully to explain a diverse number of questions about the natural world, such as how life diversified, how river dams can alter ecosystems, and why antibiotics can stop working.

Perhaps a well-tested theory is as close to the truth as we can get. For instance, after more than a century of many thousands of tests, Darwin's theory holds, with only minor modification. Yet we cannot prove it holds under all possible conditions, because doing so would take an infinite number of tests. We *can* say that a theory has a high probability of not being wrong. Even then, biologists keep on looking for information and devising tests that may disprove its premises. This willingness to modify even an entrenched theory is a strength of science, not a weakness.

Scientific inquiry into nature involves asking questions, formulating hypotheses, making predictions, testing predictions, and objectively reporting the results.

A scientific theory is a time-tested intellectual framework that is used to interpret a broad range of observations and data. Scientific theories remain open to rigorous tests, revision, and tentative acceptance or rejection.

1.6   The Power of Experimental Tests

Experiments are tests that can simplify observation in nature, because conditions under which observations are made can be controlled. Well-designed experiments test predictions about what you will find in nature when a hypothesis is correct—or won't find if it is wrong.

AN ASSUMPTION OF CAUSE AND EFFECT

A scientific experiment starts with this premise: *Any aspect of nature has an underlying material cause that can be tested through controlled experiments.* This premise sets science apart from faith in the supernatural ("beyond nature"). It means a hypothesis must be testable in the natural world in ways that might well disprove it.

Most aspects of nature are outcomes of interacting variables. A **variable** is a feature of an object or event that may differ over time or among the representatives of that object or event.

Researchers design experiments to test one variable at a time. They establish a **control group**, a standard used for comparison against one or more **experimental groups**. One type of control group is *identical* with an experimental group, but the test conditions are not. Those conditions differ by one variable. Another type of control group *differs* from an experimental group in one variable, but the test conditions are identical for both groups.

EXAMPLE OF AN EXPERIMENTAL DESIGN

In 1996 the FDA approved Olestra®, a type of synthetic fat replacement made from sugar and vegetable oil, as a food additive. Potato chips were the first Olestra-laced food product on the market in the United States. Controversy raged. After eating the chips, some people complained of bad cramps. Two years later, researchers at Johns Hopkins University designed an experiment. If Olestra causes gastrointestinal cramps, then people who eat food that contains Olestra are more likely to get cramps than people who do not.

To test this prediction, they used a Chicago theater as the "laboratory." They asked more than 1,100 people between ages thirteen and thirty-eight to watch a movie and eat their fill of potato chips. Each person got an unmarked bag that held thirteen ounces of chips. The individuals who received a bag of Olestra-laced potato chips were the experimental group. Individuals who got a bag of regular chips were the control group.

Afterward, researchers contacted the subjects and tabulated reports of gastrointestinal cramps. Of 563 people in the experimental group, 89 (or 15.8 percent) complained of problems. But so did 93 of 529 people

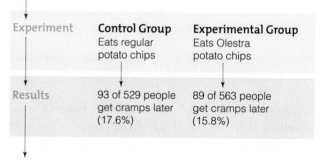

Hypothesis
Olestra® causes intestinal cramps.

Prediction
People who eat potato chips made with Olestra will be more likely to get intestinal cramps than those who eat potato chips made without Olestra.

Experiment	Control Group Eats regular potato chips	Experimental Group Eats Olestra potato chips
Results	93 of 529 people get cramps later (17.6%)	89 of 563 people get cramps later (15.8%)

Conclusion
Percentages are about equal. People who eat potato chips made with Olestra are just as likely to get intestinal cramps as those who eat potato chips made without Olestra. These results do not support the hypothesis.

Figure 1.10 *Animated!* Example of a typical sequence of steps taken in a scientific experiment.

(17.6 percent) in the control group, who had munched on regular chips! The experiment yielded no evidence that eating Olestra-laced potato chips, at least in one sitting, causes gastrointestinal problems (Figure 1.10).

EXAMPLE OF A FIELD EXPERIMENT

Many toxic or unpalatable species are vividly colored and often have distinct patterning. Predators learn to avoid individuals that display these visual cues after eating a few of them and getting sick.

In some cases, two bad-tasting species of butterflies resemble each other. **Mimicry** is a case of looking like something else and confusing predators (or prey). The naturalist Fritz Müller wondered why such a visual similarity persists. As he hypothesized, it may benefit both species. He knew that young birds catch and eat butterflies before learning to avoid eating bad-tasting ones. If both of the butterfly species are sampled, then each would lose fewer individuals to predatory birds.

Durrell Kapan, an evolutionary biologist, tested the hypothesis with *Heliconius cydno* in a rain forest. There are two forms of these bad-tasting butterflies. One has yellow markings on its wings, and the other does not (Figure 1.11*a*). Moreover, the yellow-marked butterfly resembles *H. eleuchia*, another bad-tasting species in a different part of the forest. The wings of *H. eleuchia* also have yellow markings (Figure 1.11*b*).

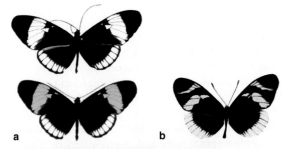

Figure 1.11 *Heliconius* butterflies. (**a**) Wing markings of the two forms of *H. cydno*. (**b**) Wing markings of *H. eleuchia*.

(**c**) Kapan's experiment with *Heliconius* butterflies in Ecuador. *H. cydno* butterflies with white or yellow wing markings were captured and transferred to habitats of *H. eleuchia*, a species that resembles yellow-marked *H. cydno*. Predatory birds (**d**), familiar with bad-tasting *H. eleuchia*, avoided yellow-marked *H. cydno* butterflies but ate most of those with yellow-free wings.

Experimental Group
34 yellow
H. cydno butterflies

Control Group
46 white
H. cydno butterflies

Experiment
Both groups are introduced into isolated habitats of yellow *H. eleuchia*. Resighted individuals are counted every day for two weeks.

Results
Control group (white *H. cydno*) is selected against: 37 of 46 (80%) disappear, compared with 20 of 34 (59%) of the experimental butterfly group.

Kapan predicted: If birds have learned to avoid *H. eleuchia* in their part of the forest, then they also will avoid imports of yellow-marked *H. cydno* butterflies. For the control group, Kapan used captured *H. cydno* butterflies with yellow-free wings. *H. cydno* butterflies with yellow-marked wings made up the experimental group. He released both of the groups into isolated *H. eleuchia* habitats. For two weeks, the approximate life span of the butterflies, he counted the survivors.

Kapan found that butterflies of the experimental group were less likely to survive in the new forest habitat. Because they did not display the visual cue recognized by the local birds—yellow markings—they were more likely to be eaten. The control group did better, as the test results in Figure 1.11*c* indicate. We can expect that predatory birds recognized this batch of imports as bad tasting and avoided them. Besides confirming Kapan's prediction, these test results also provide evidence of natural selection in action.

BIAS IN REPORTING RESULTS

Experimenters run a risk of interpreting data in terms of what they wish to prove or dismiss. That is why they prefer *quantitative* reports, with actual counts or some other precise measurements. With such reports, researchers get a chance to repeat an experimental test and check conclusions. Appendix IX gives an example.

This last point gets us back to the value of thinking critically. Scientists must keep asking themselves: *Will my observations or experiments show that a hypothesis is false?* They are expected to put aside pride or bias by testing ideas in ways that might prove them wrong. Even if someone won't do so, others will, for science works as a community that is both cooperative and competitive. Ideally, individuals will share their ideas, knowing that it is as useful to expose errors as it is to applaud insights. They can and often do change their mind when shown contradictory evidence.

Experiments simplify observations in nature by restricting a researcher's focus to one variable at a time. A variable is any feature of an object or event that may differ over time or among representatives of the object or event.

Tests are based on the premise that any aspect of nature has one or more underlying causes. Scientific hypotheses can be tested in ways that might disprove them.

1.7 The Limits of Science

Beyond the realm of scientific inquiry, some events are unexplained. Why do we exist, for what purpose? Why do we have to die at a particular moment? Such questions lead to *subjective* answers, which come from within, as an outcome of all the personal experiences and mental connections that shape our consciousness. People differ enormously in this regard, which is why subjective answers do not readily lend themselves to scientific analysis and experiments.

This is not to say subjective answers are without value. No human society can function for long unless its individuals share a commitment to standards for making judgments, even if they are subjective. Moral, aesthetic, philosophical, and economic standards vary from one society to the next. But they all guide people in deciding what is important and good, and what is not. All attempt to give meaning to what we do.

Every so often, scientists stir up controversy when they explain something that was thought to be beyond natural explanation, or belonging to the supernatural. This is often the case when a society's moral codes are interwoven with religious interpretations of the past. Exploring a long-standing view of the natural world from a scientific perspective might be misinterpreted as questioning morality, even though the two are not the same thing.

As one example, centuries ago in Europe, Nikolaus Copernicus studied the planets and decided that Earth circles the sun. Today this seems obvious. Back then, it was heresy. The prevailing belief was that the Creator made Earth—and, by extension, humans—as the fixed center of the universe. Galileo Galilei, another scholar, thought the Copernican model of the solar system was a good one and said so. He was forced to retract his statement, on his knees, and put Earth back as the fixed center of things. Word has it that he muttered, "Even so, it *does* move." Later on, Darwin's theory of evolution also ran up against prevailing beliefs.

Today, as then, society has sets of standards. Those standards might be questioned when a new, natural explanation runs counter to supernatural beliefs. This does not mean that scientists who raise questions are less moral, less lawful, less sensitive, or less caring than anyone else. It means a specific standard guides their work: *Explanations about nature must be testable in the external world, in ways that others can repeat.*

> *Science does not address subjective questions. The external world, not internal conviction, is the testing ground for the theories generated in science.*

Summary

Section 1.1 Nature has increasingly inclusive levels of organization, with life emerging at the cellular level. All organisms consist of one or more cells. In most multicelled species, the cells are organized as tissues, organs, and organ systems. Individuals of the same species in a specified area form a population, and all populations in the same area form a community. An ecosystem is a community and its environment. The biosphere includes all regions of Earth's atmosphere, waters, and land that hold systems of life.

Distinctive properties emerge at each successive level of organization. It takes interactions among the parts to generate these emergent properties of life.

Biology Now
Explore levels of biological organization with the interaction on BiologyNow.

Section 1.2 Life shows unity. All organisms require energy and raw materials from the environment to grow, maintain their organization, and reproduce, based on information encoded in DNA. All sense and respond to change. They work to counter changes in their internal environment so that conditions remain tolerable for cell activities, a state called homeostasis (Table 1.2).

Biology Now
Using instructions with the animation on BiologyNow, view how different objects are assembled from the same materials. Also view energy flow and materials cycling.

Section 1.3 As in the past, species now show great diversity. Each species has unique aspects of body form, function, and behavior. Species are ranked in ever more inclusive groupings in classification systems, starting with a two-part name (genus and species name). One classification system assigns all species to three domains: Bacteria, Archaea, and Eukarya. Protists, plants, fungi, and animals make up Domain Eukarya.

Biology Now
Explore the characteristics of the three domains of life with the interaction on BiologyNow.

Section 1.4 Life's diversity arises through mutation: change in the structure of DNA molecules. Mutations are the basis for variation in heritable traits, which are the traits that parents bestow on offspring. Such traits include most details of body form and function.

Individuals of a population differ in the details of their shared heritable traits. Variant forms of traits may affect the ability to survive and reproduce. The adaptive forms give their bearers a competitive edge, so they tend to become more common among successive generations; less adaptive traits become less common or are lost. Thus the traits that help define the population (and species) may change over successive generations; that is, the population may evolve. The outcome of differences in reproduction among individuals that differ in one or more heritable traits is called natural selection.

Biology ⑧ Now

Learn more about natural selection and evolution with InfoTrac readings on BiologyNow.
Read the InfoTrac article "Will We Keep Evolving?"
Ian Tattersall, Time, April 2000.

Section 1.5 Scientific methods differ, but they all are based on the premise that any aspect of nature has one or more underlying causes. Researchers observe some object or event, form hypotheses (testable explanations about it), make predictions about what they can expect to find if the hypothesis is not wrong, and then test the predictions. Their tests may involve making more observations, building models, or doing experiments.

Scientists analyze and share test results. A hypothesis that does not hold up under repeated testing is modified or discarded. A scientific theory is a set of hypotheses that can be used to explain a broad range of observations and data. Many diverse tests have supported it.

Sections 1.6, 1.7 Supernatural explanations cannot be tested. Science deals only with aspects of nature that lend themselves to systematic observation, hypotheses, predictions, and experimental tests. Most aspects are outcomes of many interacting variables that differ among individuals and over time. A scientific experiment can simplify observations in nature and in the laboratory because the variables can be precisely manipulated and controlled. A scientist changes one variable at a time and observes what happens. A typical experiment is designed so that one or more experimental groups can be compared with a control group.

Table 1.2 Summary of Life's Characteristics

Shared characteristics that reflect life's unity

1. Life emerges at the level of cells. All organisms consist of one or more cells.

2. In nature, only organisms make complex carbohydrates and lipids, proteins, and nucleic acids. They all use these molecules of life as building blocks and energy sources, and for the preservation of heritable information.

3. Organisms require ongoing inputs of energy to maintain their complex organization. All obtain energy from the environment and convert it to forms that can be used for growth, survival, and reproduction.

4. Organisms sense and make controlled responses to conditions in their external and internal environments.

5. Organisms grow and reproduce based on heritable information in DNA.

6. The traits that define a population of organisms can change over the generations; the population can evolve.

Foundations for life's diversity

1. Mutations (heritable changes in the structure of DNA) give rise to variation in heritable traits, which are most details of body form, function, and behavior.

2. Diversity is the sum total of variations that accumulated in different lines of descent over the past 3.8 billion years, as by natural selection and other processes of evolution.

Self-Quiz

Answers in Appendix II

1. The smallest unit of life is the _____ .

2. _____ is required to maintain levels of biological organization, from cells to populations, communities, and even entire ecosystems.

3. _____ is a state in which the internal environment is being maintained within a tolerable range.

4. Researchers assign all species to one of three _____ .

5. DNA _____ .
   a. contains instructions for building proteins
   b. undergoes mutation
   c. is transmitted from parents to offspring
   d. all of the above

6. _____ is the acquisition of traits from parents who transmit their DNA to offspring.
   a. Reproduction   c. Homeostasis
   b. Development   d. Inheritance

7. Differences in heritable traits arise through _____ .

8. A trait is _____ if it improves an organism's ability to survive and reproduce in the prevailing environment.

9. A control group is _____ .
   a. the standard against which experimental groups can be compared
   b. the experiment that gives conclusive results

10. Match the terms with the most suitable description.
   ___c___ emergent properties
   ___e___ natural selection
   ___b___ scientific theory
   ___a___ hypothesis
   ___d___ prediction

   a. statement of what you expect to find in nature based on hypotheses
   b. testable explanation about what causes an event or aspect of nature
   c. requires interaction of parts that make up a new level of organization
   d. a time-tested, related set of hypotheses that explains a broad range of observations and data
   e. outcome of differences in survival and reproduction among individuals of a population that differ in the details of one or more traits

Additional questions are available on Biology ⑧ Now™

Critical Thinking

1. Assess your bedroom. Is the bed made? Are the sheets clean? Are socks and underwear folded and put away? Are clothes strewn all over the floor? Now explain what the bedroom has in common with a living cell.

2. It is often said that only living things respond to the environment. Yet even a rock shows responsiveness, as when it yields to gravity's force and tumbles down a hill or changes its shape slowly under the repeated batterings of wind, rain, or tides. So how do living things differ from rocks in their responsiveness?

3. Witnesses in a court of law are asked to "swear to tell the truth, the whole truth, and nothing but the truth." What are some of the problems inherent in the question? Can you think of a better alternative?

a Natalie, blindfolded, randomly plucks a jelly bean from a jar of 120 green and 280 black jelly beans; a ratio of 30 to 70 percent.

b The jar is hidden before she removes her blindfold. She observes a single green jelly bean in her hand and assumes the jar holds only green jelly beans.

c Still blindfolded, Natalie randomly picks 50 jelly beans from the jar and ends up with 10 green and 40 black ones.

d The larger sample leads her to assume one-fifth of the jar's jelly beans are green and four-fifths are black (a ratio of 20 to 80). Her larger sample more closely approximates the jar's green-to-black ratio. The more times Natalie repeats the sampling, the greater the chance she will come close to knowing the actual ratio.

Figure 1.12 A simple demonstration of sampling error.

4. The Olestra potato chip experiment in Section 1.6 was a *double-blind* study: Neither the subjects of the experiment nor the researchers who made the follow-up phone calls knew which potato chips were in which bag. What are some of the challenges a researcher must consider when performing a double-blind study?

5. Suppose an outcome of some event has been observed to happen with great regularity. Can we predict that the same thing will always happen again? Not really, because there is no way for us to account for all of the possible variables that might affect the outcome. To illustrate this point, Garvin McCain and Erwin Segal offer a parable:

Once there was a highly intelligent turkey. The turkey lived in a pen, attended by a kind, thoughtful master. It had nothing to do but reflect on the world's wonders and regularities. It observed some major regularities.

Morning always started out with the sky turning light, followed by the clop, clop, clop of the master's footsteps, which was always followed by the appearance of delicious food. Other things varied—sometimes the morning was warm and sometimes cold—but food always followed footsteps. The sequence of events was so predictable that it eventually became the basis of the turkey's theory about the goodness of the world.

One morning, after more than 100 confirmations of the goodness theory, the turkey listened for the clop, clop, clop, heard it, and had its head chopped off.

Scientists understand that all well-tested theories about nature have a high probability of not being wrong. They realize, however, that any theory is subject to modification if and when contradictory information becomes available. The absence of absolute certainty has led some people to conclude that "facts are irrelevant—facts change." If that is so, should we just stop doing scientific research? Why or why not?

6. Many magazines are loaded with articles on exercise, diet, and many other health-related topics. Some authors recommend a specific diet or dietary supplement. What kinds of evidence should the articles include so that you can decide whether to accept the recommendations?

7. Rarely can experimenters observe all individuals of a group. They select subsets or samples of populations, events, and other aspects of nature. However, they must try to avoid bias, which means risking a test by using subsets that are not really representative of the whole. *Sampling error* can occur when estimates are based on a limited sample rather than the whole population (Figure 1.12). Test results are less likely to be distorted when a sampling is large and the test is repeated. Explain how sampling error could have affected results of the potato chip experiment described in Section 1.6 if the experimenters had not been careful.

8. In 1988 Dr. Randolph Byrd and his colleagues started a study of 393 patients admitted to the San Francisco General Hospital Coronary Care Unit. In the experiment, born-again Christian volunteers were asked to pray daily for a patient's rapid recovery and for prevention of complications and death.

None of the patients knew if he or she was being prayed for. None of the volunteers or patients knew each other. Byrd categorized how each patient fared in the hospital as "good," "intermediate," or "bad." He determined that patients who had been prayed for fared a little better than those who had not. His was the first experiment that had documented statistically significant results that seemed to support the prediction that prayer might have beneficial effects for seriously ill patients.

His published results engendered a storm of criticism, mostly from scientists who cited bias in the experimental design. For instance, Byrd had categorized the patients after the experiment was over. Think about how bias might play a role in interpreting medical data. Why do you suppose the experiment generated a heated response from many in the scientific community?

I Principles of Cellular Life

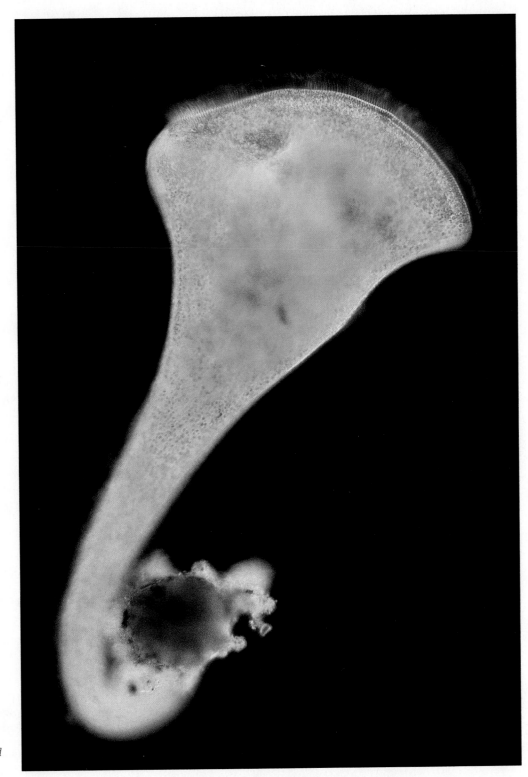

Staying alive means securing energy and raw materials from the environment. Shown here, a living cell of the genus Stentor. This protist has hairlike projections around the opening to a cavity in its body, which is about two millimeters long. Its "hairs" of fused-together cilia beat the surrounding water. They create a current that wafts food into the cavity.

2 LIFE'S CHEMICAL BASIS

What Are You Worth?

Hollywood thinks Leonardo DiCaprio is worth $20 million per movie, the Yankees think shortstop Alex Rodriguez is worth $217 million per decade, and the United States thinks the average teacher is worth $44,367 per year. Chemically, though, how much is the human body really worth (Figure 2.1a)?

Each of us is a collection of **elements**, or fundamental substances that each consist of only one kind of atom. An **atom** is the smallest unit of an element that still retains the element's properties. It occupies space, has mass, and cannot be broken down into something else, at least by everyday means.

Oxygen, carbon, hydrogen, nitrogen, and calcium are the main elements in organisms. Next are phosphorus, potassium, sulfur, sodium, and chlorine. There are a lot of *trace* elements, each making up less than 0.01 percent of the body's weight. Selenium and lead are examples.

Wait a minute! Selenium, lead, mercury, arsenic, and many other elements are toxic, right? So how can they be part of the collection? We're finding that trace amounts

Mass of Elements in a 70-Kilogram Human Body		Cost (Retail)
Oxygen	43.00 kilograms (kg)	$0.021739
Carbon	16.00 kg	6.400000
Hydrogen	7.00 kg	0.028315
Nitrogen	1.80 kg	9.706929
Calcium	1.00 kg	15.500000
Phosphorus	780.00 grams (g)	68.198594
Potassium	140.00 g	4.098737
Sulfur	140.00 g	0.011623
Sodium	100.00 g	2.287748
Chlorine	95.00 g	1.409496
Magnesium	19.00 g	0.444909
Iron	4.20 g	0.054600
Fluorine	2.60 g	7.917263
Zinc	2.30 g	0.088090
Silicon	1.00 g	0.370000
Rubidium	0.68 g	1.087153
Strontium	0.32 g	0.177237
Bromine	0.26 g	0.012858
Lead	0.12 g	0.003960
Copper	72.00 milligrams (mg)	0.012961
Aluminum	60.00 mg	0.246804
Cadmium	50.00 mg	0.010136
Cerium	40.00 mg	0.043120
Barium	22.00 mg	0.028776
Iodine	20.00 mg	0.094184
Tin	20.00 mg	0.005387
Titanium	20.00 mg	0.010920
Boron	18.00 mg	0.002172
Nickel	15.00 mg	0.031320
Selenium	15.00 mg	0.037949
Chromium	14.00 mg	0.003402
Manganese	12.00 mg	0.001526
Arsenic	7.00 mg	0.023576
Lithium	7.00 mg	0.024233
Cesium	6.00 mg	0.000016
Mercury	6.00 mg	0.004718
Germanium	5.00 mg	0.130435
Molybdenum	5.00 mg	0.001260
Cobalt	3.00 mg	0.001509
Antimony	2.00 mg	0.000243
Silver	2.00 mg	0.013600
Niobium	1.50 mg	0.000624
Zirconium	1.00 mg	0.000830
Lanthanum	0.80 mg	0.000566
Gallium	0.70 mg	0.003367
Tellurium	0.70 mg	0.000722
Yttrium	0.60 mg	0.005232
Bismuth	0.50 mg	0.000119
Thallium	0.50 mg	0.000894
Indium	0.40 mg	0.000600
Gold	0.20 mg	0.001975
Scandium	0.20 mg	0.058160
Tantalum	0.20 mg	0.001631
Vanadium	0.11 mg	0.000322
Thorium	0.10 mg	0.004948
Uranium	0.10 mg	0.000103
Samarium	50.00 micrograms (µg)	0.000118
Beryllium	36.00 µg	0.000218
Tungsten	20.00 µg	0.000007
Grand Total		**$118.63**

Figure 2.1 (a) What are you worth, chemically speaking? (b) Proportions of the most common elements in a human body, Earth's crust, and seawater. How are they similar? How do they differ?

a

Human		Earth's Crust		Seawater	
Oxygen	61.0%	Oxygen	46.0%	Oxygen	85.7%
Carbon	23.0	Silicon	27.0	Hydrogen	10.8
Hydrogen	10.0	Aluminum	8.2	Chlorine	2.0
Nitrogen	2.6	Iron	6.3	Sodium	1.1
Calcium	1.4	Calcium	5.0	Magnesium	0.1
Phosphorus	1.1	Magnesium	2.9	Sulfur	0.1
Potassium	0.2	Sodium	2.3	Calcium	0.04
Sulfur	0.2	Potassium	1.5	Potassium	0.03

b

of at least some of them have vital functions. For instance, even a little selenium is toxic, but *too* little can cause heart problems and thyroid disorders.

Superficially, then, the human body can be viewed as a balanced collection of elements. The amounts are worth no more than $118.63, and the kinds are not even unique; they occur in Earth's crust and even seawater (Figure 2.1*b*). However, the *proportions* of elements in humans and other organisms are unique relative to nonliving things. Look at all of that carbon, for instance! Also, you will never find a clod of dirt or a volume of seawater that comes close to the *structural and functional organization* of a living body. Assembling that collection of elements into an organized, operational body takes a fabulous molecular library (DNA), enzymes and other metabolic workers, and large, ongoing inputs of energy (just ask any pregnant woman).

Remember this when someone tries to say "chemistry" has nothing to do with you. It has everything to do with you. People, toothpaste, turkeys, refrigerators, jet fuel, health, disease, corsages, acid rain, nerve gas, old-growth forests—name any living or nonliving bit of the universe, and chemistry is part of it.

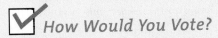
Watch the video online!

How Would You Vote?

Fluoride helps prevent tooth decay. But too much wrecks bones and teeth, and causes birth defects. A lot can kill you. Many communities in the United States add fluoride to their supply of drinking water. Do you want it in yours? See BiologyNow for details, then vote online.

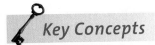
Key Concepts

ATOMS AND ELEMENTS

An element is a fundamental substance made of one type of atom. The atom is the smallest unit of an element that still retains the element's properties, and its building blocks are protons, electrons, and neutrons. Isotopes are atoms of an element that vary in the number of neutrons. Sections 2.1, 2.2

WHY ELECTRONS MATTER

Atoms acquire, share, and give up electrons. Whether one atom will bond with others depends on the number and arrangement of its electrons. Section 2.3

ATOMS BOND

The bonding behavior of biological molecules starts with the number and arrangement of electrons in each type of atom. Ionic, covalent, and hydrogen bonds are the main categories of bonds between atoms in biological molecules. Section 2.4

NO WATER, NO LIFE

Life originated in water and is adapted to its properties. Water has temperature-stabilizing effects. Many kinds of substances dissolve easily in it. Water also shows cohesion. Section 2.5

HYDROGEN IONS RULE

Life depends on precise controls over the formation, use, and buffering of hydrogen ions. Section 2.6

Links to Earlier Concepts

With this chapter, we start at the base of life's levels of organization, so take a moment to review the simple chart in Section 1.1. It all starts with atoms and energy. Life's organization requires tapping into a great one-way flow of energy and storing it in bonds between atoms (1.2).

The chapter also has a simple example of how the body's built-in mechanisms help return the internal environment to a homeostatic state when conditions shift beyond ranges that cells can tolerate (1.2).

2.1 Start With Atoms

LINK TO SECTION 1.1

Know a bit about protons, neutrons, and electrons, and you have a clue to why the elements that make up the body behave as they do. Each element's unique properties start with the number of protons in its atoms.

An element, again, is a fundamental substance made of only one kind of atom. Atoms are built from three kinds of subatomic particles: protons, electrons, and neutrons. Each **proton** carries a positive *charge*, which is a defined amount of electricity. You can symbolize a proton as p^+. An atom's nucleus, or core region, holds one or more protons. Except for the hydrogen atom, it also holds **neutrons**, which carry no charge. Moving around the atomic nucleus are one or more **electrons**, which carry a negative charge (e^-). Figure 2.2 shows a few simple models for atomic structure.

The positive charge of one proton and the negative charge of one electron balance each other. Therefore, an atom that has the same number of electrons and protons has no net electrical charge.

Each element has a unique *atomic number*, which is the number of protons in the nucleus of its atoms. A hydrogen atom has one proton, so the atomic number is 1. For carbon, with six protons, it is 6.

Protons and neutrons contribute to an atom's mass. (Electrons are too tiny to do so.) We can assign each element a *mass number*, or the total number of protons *and* neutrons in the atomic nucleus. For carbon, with six protons and six neutrons, the mass number is 12.

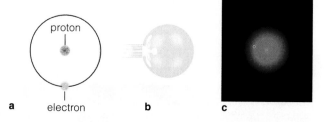

Figure 2.2 Different ways to represent atoms, using hydrogen (H) as the example. (**a**) The shell model, good for showing the number of electrons and their organization around the nucleus. (**b**) Ball models show the sizes of atoms relative to one another. (**c**) Electron density clouds are best at conveying the distribution of electrons around the nucleus.

Why bother with the number of electrons, protons, and neutrons? Knowing them can help you predict how each kind of element will behave under a variety of conditions inside and outside the body.

Elements were being classified in terms of chemical similarities long before their subatomic particles were discovered. In 1869, Dmitry Mendeleev, known more for his extravagant hair than his discoveries (he cut it only once a year), arranged the known elements in a repeating pattern, based on their chemical properties. By using gaps in this **periodic table of the elements**, Mendeleev correctly predicted the existence of many elements that had not yet been discovered.

Elements fall into order in the table according to their atomic number (Figure 2.3). All elements in each vertical column have the same number of electrons that are available for interaction with other atoms. As a result, they behave in similar ways. For example, helium, neon, radon, and other gases in the farthest right column of the periodic table are *inert* elements. Not one of the electrons in their atoms is available for chemical interactions. Such elements rarely do much; they occur mostly as solitary atoms.

You won't find all of the elements in nature. Those after atomic number 92 are extremely unstable. Some have been formed in exceedingly small quantities in laboratories—sometimes no more than a single atom —and they wink out of existence fast.

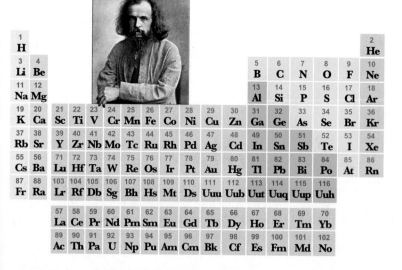

Figure 2.3 Periodic table of the elements and Dmitry Mendeleev, who created it. Some symbols for elements are abbreviations for their Latin names. For instance, Pb (lead) is short for *plumbum*; the word "plumbing" is related, because ancient Romans used lead to make their water pipes.

An element is a fundamental substance consisting of only one kind of atom. Atoms are the smallest units that retain an element's properties.

An atom consists of one or more positively charged protons, negatively charged electrons, and (except for hydrogen) neutrons. Whether any given atom will interact with others depends on how many electrons it has.

2.2 Putting Radioisotopes To Use

*All elements are defined by the number of protons in their atoms—but an element's atoms can differ in their number of neutrons. We call such atoms **isotopes** of the same element. Some are radioactive.*

In 1896, Henri Becquerel made a chance discovery. He had placed some uranium crystals in a desk drawer, next to a coin and metal screen on top of some sheets of opaque black paper. Underneath that paper was a photographic plate. A day later, the physicist used the film and developed it. Oddly, a negative image of the coin and the metal screen showed up. Becquerel hypothesized that energy radiating from the uranium salts had passed through the paper— which was impenetrable to light—and exposed the film around both metal objects.

As we now know, uranium has isotopes—fifteen of them. Most naturally occurring elements do. Carbon has three isotopes, nitrogen has two, and so on. A superscript number to the left of an element's symbol is the isotope's mass number. For instance, carbon's three natural isotopes are ^{12}C (carbon 12, the most common form, with six protons, six neutrons), ^{13}C (with six protons, seven neutrons), and ^{14}C (with six protons, eight neutrons).

Some isotopes are unstable, or radioactive. A radioactive isotope, or **radioisotope**, spontaneously emits energy in the form of subatomic particles and x-rays when its nucleus disintegrates. This process is called **radioactive decay**, and it can transform one element into another. As an example, ^{13}C and ^{14}C are radioisotopes of carbon. Each predictably decays with a particular amount of energy into a more stable product. After 5,700 years, about half of the atoms in a sample of ^{14}C will have turned into ^{13}N (nitrogen) atoms. Researchers use radioactive decay to estimate the age of rocks and biological remains, as Section 17.5 explains.

The different isotopes of an element are still the same element. For the most part, carbon is carbon, regardless of how many neutrons it has. Living systems use ^{12}C the same way as ^{14}C. Knowing this, researchers or clinicians who want to track a particular substance construct a **tracer**. Tracers are molecules in which a radioisotope has been substituted for a more stable isotope. They can be delivered into a cell or multicelled body, even into populations used in laboratory experiments. The energy from radioactive decay is like a shipping label. It helps researchers track the pathway or destination of a substance of interest with the help of radioactivity-detecting instruments.

For example, Melvin Calvin and his colleagues used a tracer to discover specific reaction steps of photosynthesis. They let growing plants take up a radioactive gas (carbon dioxide made with ^{14}C). By using radioactivity-detecting instruments, they tracked the carbon radioisotope through steps by which plants produce simple sugars and starches.

Radioisotopes also are used in medicine. *PET* (short for Positron-Emission Tomography) uses radioisotopes to study metabolism. Clinicians attach a radioisotope to glucose or another sugar. They inject this tracer into a patient, who is moved into a PET scanner (Figure 2.4a). Cells in different parts of the body absorb the tracer at different rates. The scanner detects radiation caused by energy from the decay of the radioisotope. That radiation is used to form an image on a monitor, as in Figure 2.4. Such images reveal variations and abnormalities in metabolic activity.

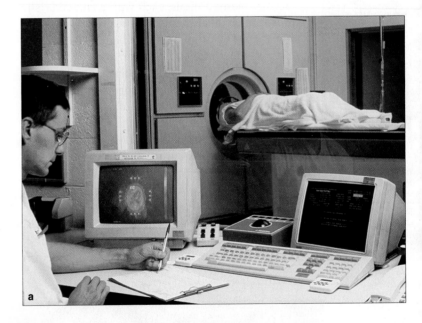

Figure 2.4 *Animated!* (**a**) Patient whose brain is being probed in a PET scanner. (**b,c**) A ring of detectors intercepts radioactive emissions from tracers that had been injected into the patient. The body region of interest is scanned. Computers analyze and color-code the number of emissions from each location in the scanned region. Results are converted into digital images and displayed on computer screens.

(**d**) Different colors in a scan signify differences in metabolic activity. Cells in the left half of this brain absorbed and used labeled molecules at expected rates. Cells in the right half showed little activity. This patient has a neurological disorder.

portion of the patient's body being scanned

detector ring inside the PET scanner

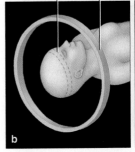

The ring intercepts emissions from the labeled molecules

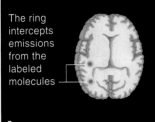

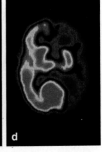

2.3 What Happens When Atom Bonds With Atom?

Atoms acquire, share, and donate electrons. The atoms of some elements do this quite easily; others do not. Why is this so? To come up with an answer, look to the number and arrangement of electrons in atoms.

LINK TO
SECTION
1.1

ELECTRONS AND ENERGY LEVELS

In our world, simple physics explains the motion of an apple falling from a tree. Tiny electrons belong to a strange world where everyday physics does not apply. (If electrons were as big as apples, you would be 3.5 times taller than our solar system is wide.) Different forces bring about the motion of electrons, which can get from here to there without going in between!

We can calculate where an electron is, although not exactly. The best we can do is say that it is somewhere in a fuzzy cloud of probability density. Where it can go in the cloud depends on how many other electrons belong to the atom. The electrons become arranged in orbitals, or volumes of space around the atomic nucleus. Many orbitals, each with a characteristic three-dimensional shape, are possible.

An atom has the same number of electrons as protons. Most atoms have many electrons. How are they all arranged, given that electrons repel each other? Think of each atom as a multilevel apartment building with lots of vacant rooms to rent to electrons, and a nucleus in the basement. Each "room" is one orbital, and it rents out to two electrons at most. An orbital holding one electron only has a vacancy; another electron can move in.

Each floor in that atomic apartment building corresponds to an energy level. There is only one room on the first floor (one orbital at the lowest energy level, closest to the nucleus). It fills first. For hydrogen, the simplest atom, a lone electron

occupies the room (Figure 2.5). Helium, with its two electrons, has no vacancies at the first (lowest) energy level. In larger atoms, more electrons rent the second-floor rooms. If the second floor is filled, then more electrons rent third-floor rooms, and so on. *Electrons fill orbitals at successively higher energy levels.*

The farther an electron is from the basement (the nucleus), the greater its energy. An electron in a first-floor room can't move to the second or third floor, let alone the penthouse, unless a boost of energy puts it there. Suppose the electron absorbs just enough energy from, say, sunlight, to get excited about moving up. Move it does. If nothing fills that lower room, though, the electron will quickly return to it, emitting extra energy as it does. Later on, you will see how cells in plants and in your eyes harness and use that energy.

FROM ATOMS TO MOLECULES

In shell models for atoms, nested "shells" correspond to energy levels. They give us an easy way to check for electron vacancies, as in Figure 2.6. Bear in mind, atoms do not look like these flat diagrams. The shells are not three-dimensional volumes of space, and they certainly don't show the electron orbitals.

The atoms with vacancies in their outermost shell tend to give up, acquire, or share electrons. Actually, what we call **chemical bonds** are just a case of atoms sharing their electrons with one another. An atom with no vacancies rarely bonds with others. But the most common atoms in organisms—such as oxygen, carbon, hydrogen, nitrogen, and calcium—do have vacancies in orbitals at their outermost energy level. They tend to participate in bonds.

A **molecule** is simply two or more atoms of the same or different elements joined in a chemical bond.

vacancy

no
vacancy

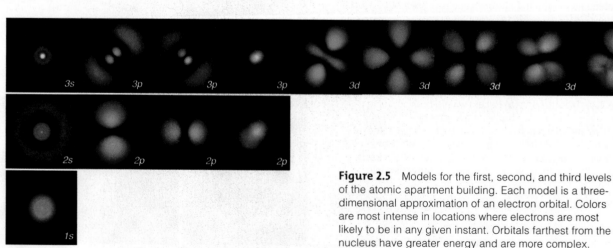

third
energy level
(second floor)

second
energy level
(first floor)

first
energy level
(closest to the
basement)

Figure 2.5 Models for the first, second, and third levels of the atomic apartment building. Each model is a three-dimensional approximation of an electron orbital. Colors are most intense in locations where electrons are most likely to be in any given instant. Orbitals farthest from the nucleus have greater energy and are more complex.

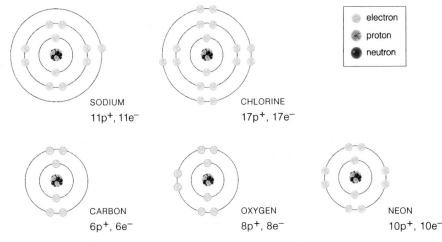

c **Third shell** This shell corresponds to the third energy level. It has nine orbitals (one *s*, three *p*, and five *d* orbitals), or room for eighteen electrons. Sodium has one electron in the third shell of orbitals, and chlorine has seven. Both have vacancies, so they both are receptive to chemical bonding.

SODIUM
11p⁺, 11e⁻

CHLORINE
17p⁺, 17e⁻

electron
proton
neutron

b **Second shell** This shell, which corresponds to the second energy level, has one *s* orbital and three *p* orbitals—room for a total of eight electrons. Carbon has six electrons, two in the first shell and four in the second shell. It has four vacancies. Oxygen has two vacancies. Both carbon and oxygen form chemical bonds.

CARBON
6p⁺, 6e⁻

OXYGEN
8p⁺, 8e⁻

NEON
10p⁺, 10e⁻

a **First shell** A single shell corresponds to the first energy level, which has a single orbital (*1s*) that can hold two electrons. Hydrogen has only one electron in this shell and gives it up easily. A helium atom has two electrons (no vacancies) and usually does not enter into chemical bonds.

HYDROGEN
1p⁺, 1e⁻

HELIUM
2p⁺, 2e⁻

Figure 2.6 *Animated!* Shell models, which help us visualize vacancies in an atom's outermost orbitals. Each circle, or shell, represents all orbitals at one energy level. Larger circles correspond to higher energy levels. Such models are highly simplified. A more realistic rendering would show electrons as fuzzy clouds of probability density about 10,000 times larger than the nucleus.

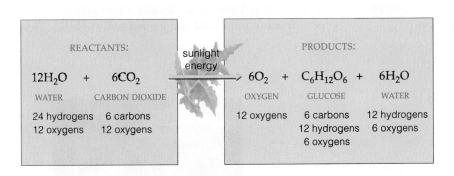

REACTANTS:

$$12H_2O \quad + \quad 6CO_2$$

WATER \qquad CARBON DIOXIDE

24 hydrogens \quad 6 carbons
12 oxygens \quad 12 oxygens

sunlight energy

PRODUCTS:

$$6O_2 \quad + \quad C_6H_{12}O_6 \quad + \quad 6H_2O$$

OXYGEN \qquad GLUCOSE \qquad WATER

12 oxygens \quad 6 carbons \quad 12 hydrogens
\qquad\qquad 12 hydrogens \quad 6 oxygens
\qquad\qquad 6 oxygens

Figure 2.7 Chemical bookkeeping. We use formulas when writing out chemical equations, which represent reactions between atoms and molecules. Substances entering a reaction (reactants) are written to the left of a reaction arrow, and products to the right. How many molecules (or atoms) enter as reactants or form as products are indicated by a number that precedes their formula. *The same number of atoms that enter a reaction must be there at the end.* The atoms get shuffled around, but they never vanish. To be sure you wrote an equation correctly, count the atoms.

You can write a molecule's chemical composition as a formula, which uses symbols for the elements present and subscripts for the number of atoms of each kind of element (Figure 2.7). For example, one molecule of water has the chemical formula H_2O. The subscript number shows that there are two hydrogen (H) atoms for each oxygen (O) atom. If you have six molecules of water, then you would write $6H_2O$.

Compounds are molecules that consist of two or more different elements in proportions that never do vary. Water is an example. All water molecules have one oxygen atom bonded to two hydrogen atoms. The ones in rain clouds, the seas, a Siberian lake, flower petals, your bathtub, or anywhere else have twice as many hydrogen atoms as oxygen atoms. In a **mixture**, two or more substances intermingle without bonding.

For example, when you swirl sugar into water, you make a mixture. The proportions of elements in this mixture, or any other kind of mixture, can vary.

Electrons occupy orbitals, or defined volumes of space around an atom's nucleus. Successive orbitals correspond to levels of energy, which become higher with distance from the atomic nucleus.

One or at most two electrons can occupy any orbital. The atoms with vacancies in orbitals at their highest level tend to interact and form bonds with other atoms.

A molecule is two or more atoms joined in a chemical bond. In compounds, atoms of two or more elements are bonded together. A mixture consists of intermingled substances.

2.4 Major Bonds in Biological Molecules

Electrons of one type of atom interact with electrons of others in specific ways. Those interactions give rise to the distinctive properties of biological molecules.

ION FORMATION AND IONIC BONDING

An electron, recall, has a negative charge equal to a proton's positive charge. When an atom contains as many electrons as protons, these charges balance each other, so the atom has a net charge of zero. When an atom *gains* an extra electron, it acquires a net negative charge. When an atom *loses* an electron, it acquires a net positive charge. Either way, it has become an **ion**.

Consider: A chlorine atom has seven protons. It has seven electrons (one vacancy) in the third orbital level—which is most stable when filled with eight. This atom tends to attract an electron from someplace else. With that extra electron, it becomes a chloride ion (Cl^-), with a net negative charge.

Also consider: A sodium atom has eleven protons and eleven electrons. Its second orbital level is full of electrons, and only one electron is in the third orbital level. Giving up the one electron is easier than getting seven more. When it does so, the atom still has eleven protons. But now it has ten electrons. It has become a sodium ion, with a net positive charge (Na^+).

Remember that opposite charges attract each other. When a positively charged ion encounters a negatively charged ion, the two may associate closely with each other. A close association of ions is an **ionic bond**. For example, Figure 2.8a shows a crystal of table salt, or NaCl. In such crystals, ionic bonds hold ions of sodium and chloride in an orderly, cubic arrangement.

COVALENT BONDING

In an ionic bond, an atom that has lost one or more electrons associates with an atom that gained one or more electrons. What if both atoms have room for an extra electron? They can *share* one in a hybrid orbital that spans both atomic nuclei. The vacancy in each atom becomes filled with the shared electrons.

When atoms share two electrons, they are joined in a single **covalent bond** (Figure 2.8b). Such bonds are stable and are much stronger than ionic bonds.

We can represent covalent bonds as single lines in structural formulas, which show how the atoms of a molecule are physically arranged. A line between two atoms represents a pair of electrons that are being shared in a single covalent bond. To give examples of this bonding pattern, molecular hydrogen (H_2) has one covalent bond and can be written as H—H. Two

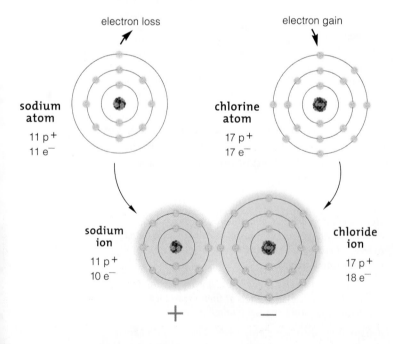

electron loss   electron gain

sodium
atom
11 p$^+$
11 e$^-$

chlorine
atom
17 p$^+$
17 e$^-$

sodium
ion
11 p$^+$
10 e$^-$

chloride
ion
17 p$^+$
18 e$^-$

+   −

Figure 2.8 *Animated!* Important bonds in biological molecules.

1 mm

a Example of ongoing interactions called ionic bonding. In each crystal of table salt, or NaCl, many sodium ions and chloride ions are staying close together because of the mutual attraction of their opposite charges.

atoms share two electron pairs in a *double* covalent bond. Molecular oxygen (O=O) is like this. Others share three electron pairs in a *triple* covalent bond, as in molecular nitrogen (N≡N). Each time you take a breath, O_2 and N_2 molecules flow toward your lungs.

In a *nonpolar* covalent bond, two atoms are sharing electrons equally, so the molecule shows no difference in charge between the two "ends" of the bond. We find such bonds in molecular hydrogen (H_2), oxygen (O_2), and nitrogen (N_2).

In a *polar* covalent bond, two atoms do not share electrons equally. Why not? The atoms are of different elements, and one has more protons than the other. The one with the most protons exerts more of a pull on the electrons, so its end of the bond ends up with a slight negative charge. We say it is "electronegative." The atom at the other end of the bond ends up with a slight positive charge. For instance, a water molecule (H—O—H) has two polar covalent bonds. The oxygen atom carries a slight negative charge, and each of its two hydrogen atoms carries a slight positive charge.

HYDROGEN BONDING

A **hydrogen bond** is a weak attraction that has formed between a covalently bound hydrogen atom and an electronegative atom in a different molecule or in a different region of the same molecule.

Because hydrogen bonds are weak, they form and break easily. Collectively, however, many hydrogen bonds contribute to the properties of liquid water, as you will see next.

Hydrogen bonds also play important roles in the structure and function of biological molecules. They often form between different parts of large molecules that have folded over on themselves and hold them in particular shapes. Many of these bonds hold DNA's two nucleotide strands together. Figure 2.8c hints at the number of these interactions in DNA.

Ions form when atoms acquire a net charge by gaining or losing electrons. Two ions of opposite charge attract each other. They can associate in an ionic bond.

In a covalent bond, atoms share a pair of electrons. When atoms share the electrons equally, the bond is nonpolar. When the sharing is not equal, the bond is polar—slightly positive at one end, slightly negative at the other.

In a hydrogen bond, a covalently bound hydrogen atom attracts a small, negatively charged atom in a different molecule or in a different region of the same molecule.

Two hydrogen atoms, each with one proton, share two electrons in a single nonpolar covalent bond.

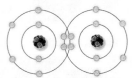

molecular hydrogen (H_2)
H—H

Two oxygen atoms, each with eight protons, share four electrons in a nonpolar double covalent bond.

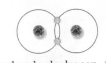

molecular oxygen (O_2)
O=O

Oxygen has vacancies for two electrons in its highest energy level orbitals. Two hydrogen atoms can each share an electron with oxygen. The resulting two polar covalent bonds form a water molecule.

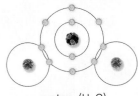

water (H_2O)
H—O—H

b Covalent bonding. Each atom becomes more stable by sharing electron pairs in hybrid orbitals.

Two molecules interacting weakly in one H bond, which can form and break easily.

hydrogen bond

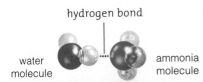

water molecule   ammonia molecule

H bonds helping to hold part of two large molecules together.

Many H bonds hold DNA's two strands together along their length. Individually each one is weak, but collectively they can stabilize DNA's large structure.

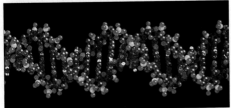

c Hydrogen bonds. Such bonds can form at a hydrogen atom that is already covalently bonded in a molecule. The atom's slight positive charge weakly attracts an atom with a slight negative charge that is already covalently bonded to something else. As shown, this can happen between one of the hydrogen atoms of a water molecule and the nitrogen atom of an ammonia molecule.

2.5 Water's Life-Giving Properties

No sprint through basic chemistry is complete unless it leads to the collection of molecules called water. Life originated in water. Organisms still live in it or they cart water around with them inside cells and tissue spaces. Many metabolic reactions use water. A cell's structure and shape absolutely depend on it.

POLARITY OF THE WATER MOLECULE

Figure 2.9*a* shows the structure of a water molecule. Two atoms of hydrogen have formed polar covalent bonds with an oxygen atom. The molecule has no net charge. Even so, the oxygen pulls the shared electrons more than the hydrogen atoms do. Thus, the molecule of water has a slightly negative "end" that is balanced out by its slightly positive "end."

The water molecule's polarity attracts other water molecules. Also, the polarity is so attractive to sugars and other polar molecules that hydrogen bonds form easily between them. That is why polar molecules are known as **hydrophilic** (water-loving) substances.

That same polarity repels oils and other nonpolar molecules, which are **hydrophobic** (water-dreading) **substances.** Shake a bottle filled with water and salad oil, then set it on a table. Soon, new hydrogen bonds replace the ones that the shaking broke. The reunited water molecules push out oil molecules, which cluster as oil droplets or as an oily film at the water's surface.

The same kinds of interactions proceed at the thin, oily membrane between the water inside and outside cells. Membrane organization—and life itself—starts with such hydrophilic and hydrophobic interactions. You will read about membrane structure in Chapter 5.

WATER'S TEMPERATURE-STABILIZING EFFECTS

Cells are mostly water, and they also release a lot of metabolic heat. The many hydrogen bonds in water keep cells from cooking in their own juices. How? All bonds vibrate nonstop, and they move more as they absorb heat. **Temperature** is a measure of molecular motion. Compared to most other fluids, water absorbs more heat energy before it gets measurably hotter. So water serves as a heat reservoir, and its temperature remains relatively stable. Over time, increases in heat step up the motion within water molecules. Before that happens, however, much of the heat will go into disrupting hydrogen bonds between molecules.

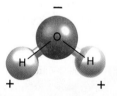

slight negative charge on the oxygen atom

The + and − ends balance each other; the whole molecule carries no net charge, overall.

slight positive charge on the hydrogen atoms

a

Figure 2.9 *Animated!* Water, a substance essential for life.

(**a**) Polarity of an individual water molecule.

(**b**) Hydrogen bonding pattern among water molecules in liquid water. Dashed lines signify hydrogen bonds, which break and re-form rapidly.

(**c**) Hydrogen bonding in ice. Below 0°C, every water molecule hydrogen-bonds with four others, in a rigid three-dimensional lattice. The molecules are farther apart, or less densely packed, than they are in liquid water. As a result, ice floats on water.

Thanks partly to rising levels of methane and other greenhouse gases that are contributing to global warming, the Arctic ice cap is melting. At current rates, it will be gone in fifty years. So will the polar bears. Already their season for hunting seals is shorter, bears are thinner, and they are giving birth to fewer cubs.

Figure 2.10 Spheres of hydration around two ions.

Figure 2.11 Examples of water's cohesion. (**a**) When a pebble hits liquid water and forces molecules away from the surface, the individual water molecules do not fly every which way. They stay together in droplets. Why? Countless hydrogen bonds exert a continuous inward pull on individual molecules at the surface.

(**b**) And just how does water rise to the very top of trees? Cohesion, and evaporation from leaves, pulls it upward.

a

b

When water temperature is stable, hydrogen bonds form as fast as they break. When water gets hotter, the increase in molecular motion can keep the bonds broken, so individual molecules at the water's surface can escape into air. By this process, **evaporation**, heat energy converts liquid water to gaseous form. The increased energy has overcome the attraction between water molecules, which break free. Water's surface temperature decreases during evaporation.

Evaporative water loss helps you and some other mammals cool off when you sweat on hot, dry days. Sweat, about 99 percent water, evaporates from skin.

Below 0°C, water molecules do not move enough to break their hydrogen bonds, so they become locked in the latticelike bonding pattern of ice (Figure 2.9c). Ice is less dense than water. During winter freezes, ice sheets may form near the surface of ponds, lakes, and streams. The ice "blanket" insulates the liquid water beneath it and helps protect many fishes, frogs, and other aquatic organisms against freezing.

WATER'S SOLVENT PROPERTIES

Water is an excellent *solvent*, meaning ions and polar molecules easily dissolve in it. A dissolved substance is known as a **solute**. In general, a substance is said to be *dissolved* after water molecules cluster around ions or molecules of it and keep them dispersed in fluid.

A clustering of water molecules around a solute is called a *sphere of hydration*. Such spheres form around any solute in cellular fluids, tree sap, blood, the fluid in your gut, and every other fluid associated with life. Watch it happen after you pour table salt (NaCl) into a cup of water. In time, the crystals of salt separate into ions of sodium (Na^+) and chloride (Cl^-). Each Na^+ attracts the negative end of some water molecules even as Cl^- attracts the positive end of others (Figure 2.10). Spheres of hydration formed this way keep the ions dispersed in fluid.

WATER'S COHESION

Still another life-sustaining property of water is its cohesion. **Cohesion** means something is showing a capacity to resist rupturing when it is stretched, or placed under tension. You see its effect when a tossed pebble breaks the surface of a lake, a pond, or some other body of liquid water (Figure 2.11a). At or near the surface, uncountable numbers of hydrogen bonds are exerting a continuous, inward pull on individual molecules. Bonding creates a high surface tension.

Cohesion is working inside organisms, too. Plants, for example, absorb nutrient-laden water when they grow. Columns of liquid water rise inside pipelines of vascular tissues, which extend from roots to leaves. Water evaporates from leaves when molecules break free and diffuse into air (Figure 2.11b). The cohesive force of hydrogen bonds pulls replacements into the leaf cells, in ways explained in Section 30.3.

Being polar, water molecules hydrogen-bond to one another and to other polar (hydrophilic) substances. They tend to repel nonpolar (hydrophobic) substances.

The unique properties of liquid water make life possible. Water has temperature-stabilizing effects, cohesion, and a capacity to dissolve many substances easily.

2.6 Acids and Bases

LINK TO SECTION 1.2

Ions dissolved in fluids inside and outside each living cell influence its structure and function. Among the most influential are hydrogen ions. They have far-reaching effects largely because they are chemically active and because there are so many of them.

THE pH SCALE

At any instant in liquid water, some water molecules split into ions of hydrogen (H^+) and hydroxide (OH^-). These ions are the basis of the **pH scale**. The scale is a way to measure the concentration of hydrogen ions in solutions such as seawater, blood, or sap. The greater the H^+ concentration, the lower the pH. Pure water (not rainwater or tap water) always has as many H^+ as OH^- ions. This state is neutrality, or pH 7.0 (Figure 2.12).

A decrease in pH by just one unit from neutrality corresponds to a tenfold increase in H^+ concentration, and an increase by one unit corresponds to a tenfold decrease in H^+ concentration. One way to get a sense of the range is to taste dissolved baking soda (pH 9), water (pH 7), and lemon juice (pH 2).

HOW DO ACIDS AND BASES DIFFER?

When dissolved in water, substances called **acids** *donate* hydrogen ions and **bases** *accept* hydrogen ions. *Acidic* solutions, such as lemon juice, gastric fluid, and coffee, release H^+; their pH is below 7. *Basic* solutions, such as seawater and egg white, easily combine with H^+. Basic solutions, which also are known as alkaline solutions, have a pH above 7.

Nearly all of life's chemistry occurs near pH 7. Most of your body's internal environment (tissue fluids and blood) is between pH 7.3 and 7.5. Seawater is more basic than body fluids of the organisms living in it.

Acids and bases can be weak or strong. The weak acids, such as carbonic acid (H_2CO_3), are stingy H^+ donors. Strong acids readily give up H^+ in water. An example is the hydrochloric acid that dissociates into H^+ and Cl^- inside your stomach. The H^+ makes your gastric fluid far more acidic, which in turn activates protein-digesting enzymes.

Too much HCl can cause an *acid stomach*. Antacids taken for this condition, including milk of magnesia, release OH^- ions that combine with H^+ to reduce the pH of stomach contents.

Actually, strong acids and bases can cause severe chemical burns. That is why we are supposed to read the labels on containers of ammonia, drain cleaner, and many other common household products. That is why we are not supposed to let a car battery's sulfuric acid drip on skin.

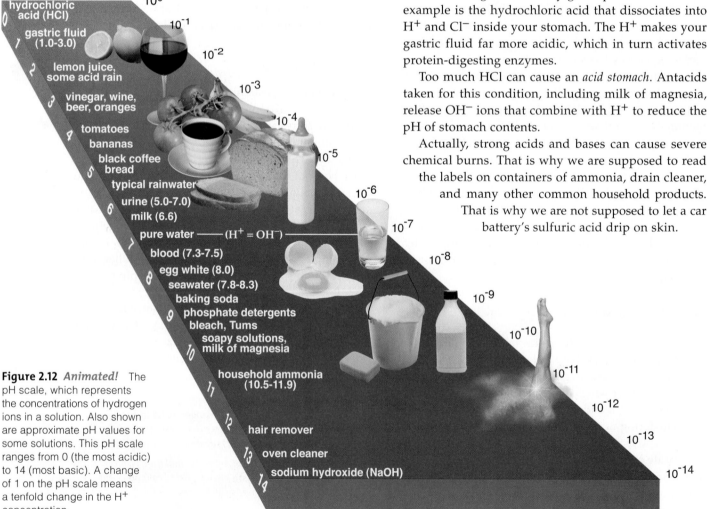

Figure 2.12 *Animated!* The pH scale, which represents the concentrations of hydrogen ions in a solution. Also shown are approximate pH values for some solutions. This pH scale ranges from 0 (the most acidic) to 14 (most basic). A change of 1 on the pH scale means a tenfold change in the H^+ concentration.

Figure 2.13 Emissions of sulfur dioxide from a coal-burning power plant. Airborne pollutants such as sulfur dioxide dissolve in water vapor to form acidic solutions. They are a component of acid rain.

At high concentrations, strong acids or bases that enter an ecosystem can kill organisms. For instance, fossil fuel burning and nitrogen-containing fertilizers release strong acids that lower the pH of rainwater (Figure 2.13). Some regions are sensitive to this *acid rain*. Alterations in the chemical composition of soil and water harm fishes and other organisms in these regions. We return to this topic in Section 48.2.

SALTS AND WATER

A **salt** is any compound that dissolves easily in water and releases ions *other than* H^+ and OH^-. It commonly forms when an acid interacts with a base. For example:

$$HCl \text{ (acid)} + NaOH \text{ (base)} \rightleftharpoons NaCl \text{ (salt)} + H_2O$$

HYDROCHLORIC ACID   SODIUM HYDROXIDE   SODIUM CHLORIDE

NaCl, the salt product of this reaction, dissociates into sodium ions (H^+) and chloride ions (Cl^-) when it is dissolved in water. Many of the ions that are released when salts dissolve in fluid are important components of cellular processes. For example, ions of sodium, potassium, and calcium are essential for nerve and muscle cell functions. They also help plant cells take up water from soil.

BUFFERS AGAINST SHIFTS IN pH

Cells must respond fast to even slight shifts in pH, because excess H^+ or OH^- can alter how biological molecules function. Responses are rapid with **buffer systems**. Think of such a system as a dynamic chemical partnership between a weak acid and its salt. These two related chemicals work in equilibrium to counter slight shifts in pH. For example, if a small amount of a strong base enters a buffered fluid, the weak acid partner can neutralize excess OH^- ions by donating some H^+ ions to the solution.

Most body fluids are buffered. Why? Enzymes, receptors, and all other essential biological molecules work most efficiently within a narrow range of pH. Deviation from the range disrupts cellular processes.

Carbon dioxide, a by-product of many reactions, becomes part of a buffer system as it combines with water to form carbonic acid and bicarbonate. When the pH of human blood rises slightly, carbonic acid can neutralize the excess OH^- by releasing hydrogen ions, which combine with OH^- to form water:

$$OH^- + H_2CO_3 \longrightarrow HCO_3^- + H_2O$$

CARBONIC ACID   BICARBONATE (salt)   WATER

When blood becomes more acidic, bicarbonate mops up excess H^+ and thus shifts the balance of the buffer system toward the acid:

$$HCO_3^- + H^+ \longrightarrow H_2CO_3$$

BICARBONATE   CARBONIC ACID

Buffer systems can neutralize only so many excess ions. With even a slight excess above that point, the pH swings widely. When the blood pH (7.3–7.5) falls even to 7, buffering fails, and the consequences can be severe. An individual may fall into a *coma*, an often irreversible state of unconsciousness. This happens in *respiratory acidosis*. Carbon dioxide accumulates, too much carbonic acid forms, and blood pH plummets. By contrast, when the blood pH increases even to 7.8, *tetany* may occur; skeletal muscles cannot be released from contraction. *Alkalosis* is a rise in blood pH that, if not reversed by medical treatment can be lethal.

Ions dissolved in fluids on the inside and outside of cells have key roles in cell function. Acidic substances release hydrogen ions, and basic substances accept them. Salts are compounds that release ions other than H^+ and OH^-.

Acid–base interactions help maintain pH, which is the H^+ concentration in a fluid. Buffer systems help maintain the body's acid–base balance at levels suitable for life.

Summary

Introduction   Chemistry can help us understand the composition and behavior of the substances that make up cells, organisms, and all components of the biosphere. Table 2.1 summarizes some key chemical terms that you will encounter throughout this book.

Section 2.1   All substances consist of one or more elements. Atoms are the smallest units that still retain

the element's properties. An uncharged atom consists of one or more positively charged protons, an equal number of negatively charged electrons, and (except for hydrogen) one or more neutrons, which carry no charge. Protons and neutrons occupy an atom's core region, or nucleus, and essentially account for its mass.

Section 2.2   Atoms of an element typically differ in the number of neutrons; they are isotopes. Radioisotopes are unstable, and their nucleus spontaneously decays.

Biology ⊜ Now
Learn about how radioisotopes are used in a PET scan with the animation on BiologyNow.

Section 2.3   Whether one atom will interact with others depends on the number and arrangement of its electrons. Electrons occupy orbitals (volumes of space) around the atomic nucleus. The shell model for atomic structure is a diagram with successively larger circles, or shells, that keep track of all electrons in the orbitals at a given energy level.

When an atom has one or more vacancies in orbitals, it interacts with other atoms by donating, accepting, or sharing electrons (forming chemical bonds).

Biology ⊜ Now
Use the animation and interaction on BiologyNow to investigate electron distribution and the shell model.

Section 2.4   Each chemical bond is an interaction between the electron structures of atoms. The main types are called ionic, covalent, and hydrogen bonds.

When an atom loses or gains one or more electrons, it becomes an ion, with a positive or a negative charge. In an ionic bond, a positive ion and a negative ion stay together by mutual attraction of their opposite charges.

Atoms often fill vacancies in their outermost orbitals by sharing one or more pairs of electrons. Two atoms share electrons equally in a *nonpolar* covalent bond. The sharing is unequal in a *polar* covalent bond, so the bond has a slight negative charge at one end and a slight positive charge at the other. The charges balance, so the participating atoms carry no net charge, overall.

In a hydrogen bond, a covalently bound hydrogen atom weakly attracts an electronegative atom that is bound in a different molecule or a different region of the same molecule.

Biology ⊜ Now
Compare the types of chemical bonds in biological molecules using the animation on BiologyNow.

Section 2.5   Polar covalent bonds join three atoms in **a water molecule (two hydrogen atoms and one oxygen).** The polarity of the water molecule invites extensive hydrogen bonding between molecules in bodies of water. The polarity is the basis of hydrogen bonding, which gives liquid water a notable ability to resist temperature changes, to show internal cohesion, and to easily dissolve diverse polar or ionic substances. These properties of water help make life possible.

Biology ⊜ Now
Explore the structure and properties of water with the animation on BiologyNow.

Table 2.1	Summary of Important Players in the Chemical Basis of Life
Element	Fundamental substance consisting of one kind of atom
Atom	Smallest unit of an element that still retains element's properties. Occupies space, has mass, and cannot be broken apart by ordinary physical or chemical means.
Proton (p^+)	Positively charged particle of the atomic nucleus
Electron (e^-)	Negatively charged particle that can occupy a volume of space (orbital) around the nucleus
Neutron	Uncharged particle of the atomic nucleus
Isotope	One of two or more forms of an element's atoms that differ in the number of neutrons in the nucleus
Radioisotope	An unstable isotope that emits particles and energy; has an unstable combination of protons and neutrons
Tracer	Molecule that incorporates one or more atoms of a radioisotope. Used with tracking devices to identify the movement or destination of the molecule or atom in a metabolic pathway, the body, or some other system
Ion	An atom that has gained or lost an electron and carries a positive or negative charge. A proton without an electron zipping around it is a hydrogen ion (H^+)
Molecule	Unit of matter in which two or more atoms of the same element, or different ones, are bonded together
Compound	Molecule of two or more different elements in unvarying proportions (e.g., water)
Mixture	Intermingling of two or more elements or compounds in proportions that usually vary
Solute	Any molecule or ion dissolved in some solvent
Hydrophilic substance	Polar molecule or molecular region that can readily dissolve in water
Hydrophobic substance	Nonpolar molecule or molecular region that strongly resists dissolving in water
Acid	Substance that releases H^+ when dissolved in water
Base	Substance that accepts H^+ when dissolved in water
Salt	Compound that releases ions other than H^+ or OH^- when dissolved in water

Section 2.6 The pH scale is used to measure the hydrogen ion (H^+) concentration of a solution. A typical pH range is from 0 (highest H^+ concentration; most acidic) to 14 (lowest H^+ concentration; the most basic or alkaline). At pH 7, or neutrality, H^+ and OH^- concentrations are equal.

Salts are compounds that dissolve easily in water and release ions other than H^+ and OH^-. Acids release H^+ ions in water. Bases combine with them. A buffer system is a dynamic chemical partnership between a weak acid or base and its salt. The two go back and forth donating and accepting ions to counter slight shifts in pH and thus maintain a favorable pH. Most biological processes operate within a narrow pH range.

Biology⊜Now
Investigate the pH of common solutions with the interaction on BiologyNow.

Figure 2.14 Laboratory of a typical alchemist.

Self-Quiz
Answers in Appendix II

1. Is this statement false: Every type of atom consists of protons, neutrons, and electrons.

2. Electrons carry a _____ charge.
   a. positive   b. negative   c. zero

3. A(n) _____ is any molecule to which a radioisotope has been attached for research or diagnostic purposes.
   a. ion   b. isotope   c. element   d. tracer

4. Atoms share electrons unequally in a(n) _____ bond.
   a. ionic   c. polar covalent
   b. hydrogen   d. nonpolar covalent

5. In a hydrogen bond, a covalently bound hydrogen atom weakly attracts an _____ atom in a different molecule or a different region of the same molecule.
   a. electronegative   b. electropositive

6. Liquid water shows _____ .
   a. polarity   d. cohesion
   b. hydrogen-bonding capacity   e. b through d
   c. notable heat resistance   f. all of the above

7. Hydrogen ions (H^+) are _____ .
   a. the basis of pH values   d. dissolved in blood
   b. unbound protons   e. both a and b
   c. targets of certain buffers   f. a through d

8. When dissolved in water, a(n) _____ donates H^+, and a(n) _____ accepts H^+.

9. A(n) _____ is a dynamic chemical partnership between a weak acid and its salt.
   a. ionic bond   c. buffer system
   b. solute   d. solvent

10. Match the terms with their most suitable description.
   ____ trace element   a. atomic nucleus components
   ____ salt   b. two atoms sharing electrons
   ____ covalent   c. any polar molecule that readily
        bond   dissolves in water
   ____ hydrophilic   d. releases ions other than H^+ and
        substance OH^- when dissolved in water
   ____ protons,   e. makes up less than 0.001
        neutrons   percent of body weight

Additional questions are available on **Biology⊜Now™**

Critical Thinking

1. Some molecules consist of atoms of a single element, but others are compounds. Explain which type of molecule you would expect to be more abundant in living things.

2. *Ozone* is a chemically active form of oxygen gas. High in Earth's atmosphere, a vast layer of it absorbs about 98 percent of the sun's harmful rays. Normally, oxygen gas consists of two oxygen atoms joined in a double nonpolar covalent bond: $O=O$. Ozone has three covalent bonds in this arrangement: $O=O-O$. It is highly reactive with a variety of substances, and it gives up an oxygen atom and releases gaseous oxygen ($O=O$). Using what you know about chemistry, explain why you think it is so reactive.

3. Some undiluted acids are less corrosive than when diluted with a little water. In fact, lab workers are told to wipe off splashes with a towel before washing. Explain.

4. Medieval scientists and philosophers called alchemists were predecessors of modern-day chemists (Figure 2.14). Many tried to transform lead (atomic number 82) into gold (atomic number 79). Why didn't they succeed?

5. David, an inquisitive three-year-old, poked his fingers into warm water in a metal pan on the stove and didn't sense anything hot. Then he touched the pan itself and got a nasty burn. Explain why water in a metal pan heats up far more slowly than the pan itself.

6. Why can water striders (Figure 2.15) and the basilisk lizard shown in Figure 1.8 walk on water?

7. Why do you think H^+ is often written as H_3O^+?

Figure 2.15 Water strider, not sinking.

3 MOLECULES OF LIFE

Science or the Supernatural?

About 2,000 years ago in the mountains of Greece, the oracle of Delphi made rambling, cryptic prophecies after inhaling sweet-smelling fumes that had collected in the sunken floor of her temple. She actually was babbling in a hydrocarbon-induced trance. We now know her temple was perched on intersecting, earthquake-prone faults. When the faults slipped, methane, ethane, and ethylene seeped out from the depths. All three gases are colorless hallucinogens.

Ancient Greeks thought Apollo spoke to them through the oracle; they believed in the supernatural. Scientists looked for a natural explanation, and they found carbon compounds behind her words. Why is their explanation more compelling? It started with tested information about the structure and effects of natural substances, and it was based on analysis of gaseous substances at the site.

All three gases consist only of carbon and hydrogen atoms; hence the name, hydrocarbons. Thanks to scientific inquiry, we now know a lot about them. Consider methane. It was present when Earth first formed. It is released when volcanoes erupt, when we burn wood or peat or fossil fuels, and when termites and cattle pass gas. Methane collects in the atmosphere and in ocean depths along the continental shelves. Methane also is one of the greenhouse gases and a contributing factor in global warming.

And methane all by itself may be big trouble. Long ago, organic remains of marine organisms sank to the bottom of the ocean. Today, a few kilometers below the sediments that slowly accumulated on top of them, the remains have become food for methane-producing archaeans. Collectively, their metabolic activity produces tremendous quantities of methane. All of that gas bubbles upward and seeps from the seafloor (Figure 3.1*b*). At these methane seeps, the low temperature and high water pressure "freeze" methane into icy methane hydrate.

There may be a thousand billion tons of frozen methane hydrate on the seafloor. It is the world's largest reservoir of natural gas, but we do not have a safe, efficient way to retrieve it. Why not? The icy crystals are unstable. They instantaneously fall apart into methane gas and liquid water as soon as the temperature goes up or the pressure goes down. It does not take much, only a few degrees.

Methane hydrate can disintegrate explosively. It can cause an irreversible chain reaction that may vaporize neighboring deposits on the seafloor. We see plenty of evidence of small methane hydrate explosions in the past that pockmarked the ocean floor. Immense explosions have caused underwater landslides that stretched, almost unbelievably, from one continent to another.

methane

Figure 3.1 *Left,* ruins of the Temple of Apollo, where hydrocarbon gases seep out from the ground. *Right,* microorganisms and bubbles of methane gas almost 230 meters (750 feet) below sea level in the Black Sea. The methane is produced by archaeans far beneath the seafloor, then seeps into deep ocean water.

Watch the video online!

Also consider this: The greatest of all mass extinctions occurred 250 million years ago and marked the end of the Permian period. All but about 5 percent of the species in the seas and about 70 percent of the known plants, insects, and other species on the land abruptly vanished. Scientists, who are not given to hyperbole, call it The Great Dying.

Chemical clues locked in fossils dating from that time point to a sharp spike in the atmospheric concentration of carbon dioxide—not just any carbon dioxide, but molecules that had been assembled by living things. Methane hydrate disintegrated abruptly, and in a gargantuan burp, millions of tons of methane exploded from the seafloor. Methane-eating bacteria converted nearly all of it to carbon dioxide—which displaced most of the oxygen in the seas and sky.

Too much carbon dioxide, too little oxygen. Imagine being transported abruptly to the top of Mount Everest and trying to jog in the "thin air," with its lower oxygen concentration. You would pass out and die. Before The Great Dying, free oxygen made up about 35 percent of the atmosphere. After the burp, its concentration plummeted to 12 percent. We can expect that most animals on land and in the seas suffocated.

The methane problem is closer than you might think. Not long ago, researchers found vast methane hydrate deposits 96 kilometers (60 miles) or so off the coast of Newport, Oregon, and off the Atlantic seaboard. What is to become of us if there is another methane burp?

In short, knowledge about lifeless substances can tell you a lot about life, including your own. It will serve you well when you turn your mind to just about any topic concerning the past, present, and future—from ancient myths, to health or disease, to forests, to physical and chemical conditions that affect life everywhere.

How Would You Vote?

Should we work toward developing the vast undersea methane deposits as an energy source, given that the environmental costs and risks to life are unknown? See BiologyNow for details, then vote online.

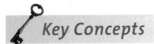

Key Concepts

NO CARBON, NO LIFE

We define cells partly by their capacity to assemble the organic compounds called complex carbohydrates and lipids, proteins, and nucleic acids. These large molecules of life have a backbone of carbon atoms, and functional groups attached to the backbone influence their properties. All are assembled from cellular pools of simple sugars, fatty acids, amino acids, and nucleotides. Sections 3.1, 3.2

CARBOHYDRATES

Carbohydrates are the most abundant biological molecules in nature. The simple sugars function as quick energy sources or transportable forms of energy. Complex carbohydrates are structural materials or energy reservoirs. Section 3.3

LIPIDS

Some kinds of complex lipids function as the body's energy reservoirs, others as structural components of cell membranes, as waterproofing or lubricating substances, and as signaling molecules. Section 3.4

PROTEINS

Structurally and functionally, proteins are the most diverse molecules of life. They include enzymes, structural materials, signaling molecules, and transporters. Sections 3.5, 3.6

NUCLEOTIDES AND NUCLEIC ACIDS

Both DNA and RNA are nucleic acids made of a few kinds of nucleotide subunits. They interact as the cell's system of storing, retrieving, and translating heritable information about building all the proteins necessary for life. Section 3.7

Links to Earlier Concepts

You are about to enter the next level of organization in nature, as represented by the molecules of life. Keep the big picture in mind by quickly scanning Section 1.1 once again.

You will be building on your understanding of how electrons are arranged in atoms (2.3) as well as the nature of covalent bonding and hydrogen bonding (2.4). Here again, you will be considering one of the consequences of mutation in DNA (1.4), this time with sickle-cell anemia as the example.

LINK TO
SECTIONS
1.1, 2.4

3.1 Molecules of Life—From Structure to Function

Under present-day conditions in nature, only living cells make complex carbohydrates, lipids, proteins, and nucleic acids. Different classes of these biological molecules are a cell's instant energy sources, structural materials, metabolic workers, cell-to-cell signals, and libraries and translators of hereditary information.

WHAT IS AN ORGANIC COMPOUND?

The molecules of life are **organic compounds**, which are defined as containing the element carbon and at least one hydrogen atom. The term is a holdover from a time when chemists thought "organic" substances were the ones made naturally in living organisms only, as opposed to the "inorganic" substances that formed abiotically. The term persists, although scientists now synthesize organic compounds in laboratories and have reason to believe that organic compounds were present on Earth before organisms were.

The **hydrocarbons** consist only of hydrogen atoms covalently bonded to carbon. Examples are gasoline and other fossil fuels. Like other organic compounds, each has a specific number of atoms that are arranged in specific ways. Each organic compound has one or more **functional groups**, which are particular atoms or clusters of atoms covalently bonded to carbon.

In this book we use the following color code for the main atoms of organic compounds:

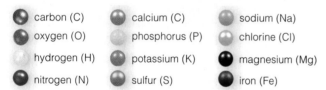

- carbon (C)
- oxygen (O)
- hydrogen (H)
- nitrogen (N)
- calcium (C)
- phosphorus (P)
- potassium (K)
- sulfur (S)
- sodium (Na)
- chlorine (Cl)
- magnesium (Mg)
- iron (Fe)

START WITH CARBON'S BONDING BEHAVIOR

Living things consist mainly of oxygen, hydrogen, and carbon (Figure 2.1). Their oxygen and hydrogen are primarily in the form of water. Put water aside, and carbon makes up more than half of what is left.

Carbon's importance to life starts with its versatile bonding behavior. *Each carbon atom can covalently bond with as many as four other atoms.* Such bonds, in which two atoms share one, two, or three pairs of electrons, are relatively stable. They join carbon atoms together as a backbone to which hydrogen, oxygen, and other elements are attached. In those configurations—in the arrangement of atoms and the distribution of electric charge—we find clues to how the different molecules of life will function and what their three-dimensional shapes will be.

WAYS TO REPRESENT ORGANIC COMPOUNDS

Methane is the simplest organic compound to think about. This colorless, odorless gas is present in the atmosphere, sea sediments, termite colonies, stagnant swamps, and stockyards. Its four hydrogen atoms are covalently bonded to one carbon atom (CH_4). You can use a ball-and-stick model to depict bond angles and show how the mass of this molecule or any other is distributed (in atomic nuclei). A space-filling model is better at conveying a molecule's size and surfaces:

structural formula for methane   ball-and-stick model   space-filling model

Let's use a ball-and-stick model to depict an organic compound with six covalently bonded carbon atoms from which hydrogen *and* oxygen atoms project:

ball-and-stick model for the linear structure of glucose

This type of carbon backbone sometimes forms chains inside cells. But most of the time it coils back on itself, and its two ends connect to form a ring structure:

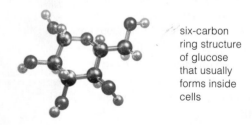

six-carbon ring structure of glucose that usually forms inside cells

We typically depict carbon ring structures in simpler ways. A flat structural model may show the carbons but not other atoms bonded to them. If an icon for the ring shows no atoms at all, it is understood that one carbon atom occupies each "corner" of the ring:

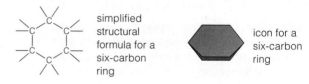

simplified structural formula for a six-carbon ring

icon for a six-carbon ring

Figure 3.2 shows ways to represent hemoglobin, a much larger molecule. You and all other vertebrates make this protein, which transports oxygen to tissues throughout your body. The ball-and-stick and space-filling models can give you an idea of this molecule's mass and structural complexity. But neither will tell you much about its oxygen-transporting function.

Now look at Figure 3.2c. This ribbon model shows how a hemoglobin molecule consists of four chains. As you will see later, each chain is a string of subunits called amino acids. Different regions of each chain are straight, folded, and coiled. For now, it is enough to know hemoglobin's three-dimensional shape includes four pockets, each containing a small cluster of atoms called a heme group. A heme group binds or releases oxygen in different body regions in response to how concentrated this gas is in different tissues.

More sophisticated models are now in use. Certain computer models, for instance, show local differences in electric charge across molecular surfaces. The areas color-coded, say, red on one molecule's surface might be attractive to a blue surface on another part of the same molecule or a different one (Figure 3.3).

Ultimately, such insights into the three-dimensional structure of molecules help us understand how cells and multicelled organisms function. For instance, virus particles can infect a cell when they dock at specific proteins located at the cell surface. Like Lego blocks, the proteins have ridges, clefts, and charged regions at their surface that can fit precisely into ridges, clefts, and charged regions of a protein at the surface of the virus. If a researcher can design a drug molecule that matches up with a viral protein and figure out how to deliver enough copies of it into a patient, then a lot of virus particles may be tricked into binding with the decoys instead of infecting body cells.

You will come across different kinds of molecular models throughout this book. In each case, the model selected gives you a glimpse into the structure and function of the molecule being described.

Carbohydrates, lipids, proteins, and nucleic acids are the main biological molecules—the organic compounds that only living cells assemble under present-day conditions in nature.

Organic compounds have diverse, three-dimensional shapes and functions that start with a carbon backbone and the bonding arrangements that arise from it.

Insights into the structure of molecules ultimately help us understand how cells, and multicelled organisms, function.

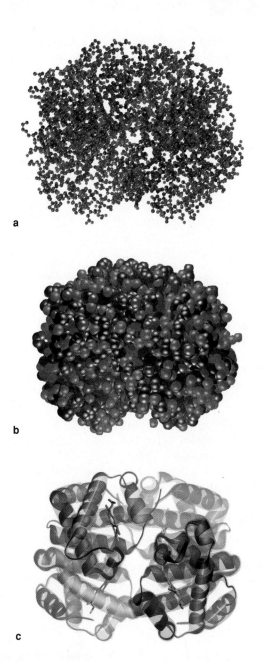

Figure 3.2 Visualizing the structure of hemoglobin, the oxygen-transporting molecule in red blood cells. (**a**) Ball-and-stick model, (**b**) space-filling model, and (**c**) ribbon model, with four heme groups (*red-orange*). Unlike the color coding for atoms, colors used for ribbon models and simple icons for complex molecules vary, depending on the context.

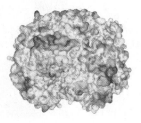

Figure 3.3 Model for the charged surface regions of a hemoglobin molecule. In this case, *blue* indicates positive charge and *red* indicates negative charge.

3.2 How Do Cells Build Organic Compounds?

Before taking a run through the characteristics of the main biological molecules, get acquainted with their building blocks and how they are put together.

LINK TO
SECTION 2.3

Hydroxyl	—OH	In alcohols (e.g., sugars, amino acids); water soluble
Methyl	$\begin{array}{c} H \\ | \\ -C-H \\ | \\ H \end{array}$	In fatty acid chains; insoluble in water
Carbonyl	$-\overset{\mid}{\underset{O}{C}}-H$ (—CHO, aldehyde) $\quad$ $-\overset{\mid}{\underset{O}{C}}-$ (>CO, ketone)	In sugars, amino acids, nucleotides; water soluble. An *aldehyde* if at end of a carbon backbone; a *ketone* if attached to an interior carbon of backbone
Carboxyl	$-\overset{\mid}{\underset{O}{C}}-OH$ (—COOH, non-ionized) $\quad$ $-\overset{\mid}{\underset{O}{C}}-O^-$ (—COO⁻, ionized)	In amino acids, fatty acids; water soluble. Highly polar; acts as an acid (releases H^+)
Amino	$\begin{array}{c} -N-H \\ | \\ H \end{array}$ (—NH₂, non-ionized) $\quad$ $\begin{array}{c} -N-H^+ \\ | \\ H \end{array}$ (—NH₃⁺, ionized)	In amino acids and certain nucleotide bases; water soluble; acts as a weak base (accepts H^+)
Phosphate	$-O-\overset{\overset{O^-}{\mid}}{\underset{\underset{O}{\parallel}}{P}}-O^-$ $\quad$ ⓟ icon	In nucleotides (e.g., ATP), also in DNA, RNA, many proteins, phospholipids; water soluble, acidic
Sulfhydryl	—SH $\quad$ —S—S— (disulfide bridge)	In amino acid cysteine; helps stabilize protein structure (at disulfide bridges)

Figure 3.4 *Animated!* Common functional groups in biological molecules, with examples of their occurrences.

FOUR FAMILIES OF BUILDING BLOCKS

What is your favorite flower? Cells in the plant that made it turned carbon (from carbon dioxide), water, and the sun's energy into small organic compounds. The four main families of these small compounds are called simple sugars, fatty acids, amino acids, and nucleotides. Many kinds of molecules in each family contain two to thirty-six carbon atoms, at most.

Cells maintain and replenish pools of small organic compounds, which collectively account for about 10 percent of all organic material in a cell. They use up some molecules as ongoing sources of energy. They use others as individual subunits, or **monomers**, of the larger molecules necessary for their structure and functioning. The larger molecules—**polymers**—consist of three to millions of subunits that may or may not be identical. When they are broken apart, the released monomers might be used at once for energy, or they might reenter the cellular pools as free molecules.

A VARIETY OF FUNCTIONAL GROUPS

Functional groups, again, are lone atoms or clusters of atoms covalently bonded to carbon atoms of organic compounds. Each has specific chemical and physical properties that are consistent from one molecule to the next. How do such groups differ from hydrocarbon regions? They are more reactive. Important features of carbohydrates, lipids, proteins, and nucleic acids arise from the number, kind, and arrangement of functional groups, such as those shown in Figure 3.4.

Consider: Sugars in your diet belong to a class of organic compounds, the **alcohols**, which have one or more *hydroxyl* groups (—OH). Enzyme action can split

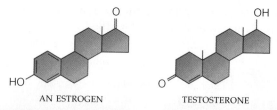

AN ESTROGEN $\qquad$ TESTOSTERONE

Figure 3.5 Observable differences in traits between the male and female wood duck (*Aix sponsa*). Two sex hormones govern the development of feather color and other traits that help males and females recognize each other and so promote reproductive success. Both hormones—testosterone and one of the estrogens—have the same carbon ring structure. They differ in the position of functional groups attached to the ring.

FEMALE WOOD DUCK $\qquad$ MALE WOOD DUCK

molecules or join them at such groups. Also, small alcohols dissolve swiftly because water molecules hydrogen-bond with them. Larger alcohols do not dissolve quickly because they have hydrocarbon chains, which are water insoluble. Such chains are also part of fatty acids, which is why lipids with fatty acid tails resist dissolving in water.

We find *carbonyl* groups—highly reactive and prone to electron transfers—in carbohydrates and fats, and *carboxyl* groups in amino acids and fatty acids. ATP activates other molecules by giving up *phosphate* groups. This group also combines with sugars to form the backbones of DNA and RNA. *Sulfhydryl* groups help stabilize many proteins.

How much can one functional group do? Look at a seemingly minor difference in the functional groups of two structurally similar sex hormones (Figure 3.5). Early on, an embryo of a wood duck, human, or any other vertebrate is neither male nor female. If it starts making testosterone (a hormone), a set of tubes and ducts will develop into male sex organs and later govern male traits. In the *absence* of testosterone, the ducts and tubes will develop into female sex organs. In that case, estrogens will guide the development of female traits.

FIVE CATEGORIES OF REACTIONS

So how do cells actually do the construction work? It will take more than one chapter to sketch out answers (and best guesses) to that question. For now, simply be aware that the reactions by which the cell builds, rearranges, and splits up organic compounds require more than energy inputs. They also require **enzymes**, a class of proteins that cause metabolic reactions to proceed much faster than they would on their own. Different enzymes mediate different reactions. In later chapters, you will come across specific examples of these five categories of reactions:

1. *Functional-group transfer.* One molecule gives up a functional group entirely, and a different molecule immediately accepts it.

2. *Electron transfer.* One or more electrons stripped from one molecule are donated to another molecule.

3. *Rearrangement.* Juggling of internal bonds converts one type of organic compound into another.

4. *Condensation.* Covalent bonds join two molecules into a larger molecule.

5. *Cleavage.* A molecule splits into two smaller ones.

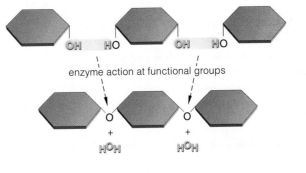
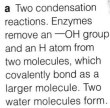

a Two condensation reactions. Enzymes remove an —OH group and an H atom from two molecules, which covalently bond as a larger molecule. Two water molecules form.

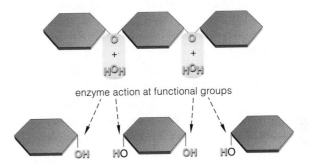

b Hydrolysis, a water-requiring cleavage reaction. Enzyme action splits a molecule into three parts, then attaches an —OH group and an H atom derived from a water molecule to each exposed site.

Figure 3.6 *Animated!* Examples of the metabolic reactions by which most biological molecules are synthesized, rearranged, or broken apart.

To get a sense of these cell activities, think about a **condensation reaction**. Enzymes split an —OH group from one molecule and an H atom from another, and a covalent bond forms at the exposed sites on both of the fragments. The discarded atoms often form water (Figure 3.6a). Starch and other large polymers form by way of repeated condensation reactions.

Another example: A type of cleavage reaction called **hydrolysis** is like condensation, but in reverse (Figure 3.6b). Enzymes split molecules at specific groups, then attach one —OH group and an H atom derived from a water molecule to the exposed sites. Cells can cleave polymers into smaller molecules when these are required for building blocks or for energy.

Cells build large molecules mainly from four families of small organic compounds called simple sugars, fatty acids, amino acids, and nucleotides.

Functional groups covalently bonded to carbon backbones add enormously to the structural and functional diversity of organic compounds, cells, and multicelled organisms.

Cells continually assemble, rearrange, and degrade organic compounds by enzyme-mediated reactions involving the transfer of functional groups or electrons, rearrangement of internal bonds, and a combining or splitting of molecules.

3.3 The Most Abundant Ones—Carbohydrates

Which biological molecules are most plentiful in nature? Carbohydrates. Most carbohydrates consist of carbon, hydrogen, and oxygen in a 1:2:1 ratio. Cells use them as structural materials and transportable or storable forms of energy. Monosaccharides, oligosaccharides, and polysaccharides are the main classes.

THE SIMPLE SUGARS

"Saccharide" is from a Greek word that means sugar. The *mono*saccharides (one sugar unit) are the simplest carbohydrates. They have at least two —OH groups bonded to their carbon backbone and one aldehyde or ketone group. Most dissolve easily in water. Common types have a backbone of five or six carbon atoms that tends to form a ring structure when dissolved.

Ribose and deoxyribose are the sugar monomers of RNA and DNA, respectively; each has five carbon atoms. Glucose has six (Figure 3.7*a*). Cells use glucose as an instant energy source, as a building block, and

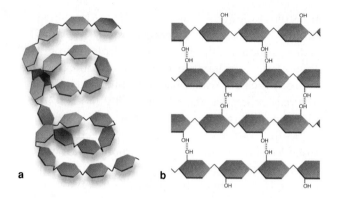

Figure 3.8 Bonding patterns for glucose units in (**a**) starch, and (**b**) cellulose. In amylose, a form of starch, a series of covalently bonded glucose units form a chain that coils. In cellulose, bonds form between glucose chains. The pattern stabilizes the chains, which can become tightly bundled.

as a precursor (parent molecule). For instance, glucose might be remodeled into vitamin C (a sugar acid) or into glycerol, an alcohol with three —OH groups.

SHORT-CHAIN CARBOHYDRATES

Unlike the simple sugars, an *oligo*saccharide is a short chain of covalently bonded sugar monomers. (*Oligo*– means a few.) The *di*saccharides consist of two sugar monomers. Lactose, a disaccharide in milk, consists of one glucose and one galactose unit. Sucrose, the most plentiful sugar in nature, has a glucose and a fructose unit (Figure 3.7*c*). Table sugar is sucrose extracted from sugarcane and sugar beets. Many proteins and lipids have oligosaccharide side chains. Later in the book, you will learn about oligosaccharide side chains that function in self-recognition, immunity, and other tasks. They are components of diverse molecules that are like docks and flags at the cell surface.

COMPLEX CARBOHYDRATES

The "complex" carbohydrates, or *poly*saccharides, are straight or branched chains of many sugar monomers —often hundreds or thousands. Different kinds have one or more types of monomers. The most common kinds are cellulose, starch, and glycogen. All three consist of glucose but differ in their properties (Figures 3.8 and 3.9). Why? The answer starts with differences in the covalent bonding patterns between their glucose units, which are joined together in chains.

In starch, the pattern of covalent bonding puts each glucose unit at an angle relative to the next unit in line. The chain ends up coiling like a spiral staircase

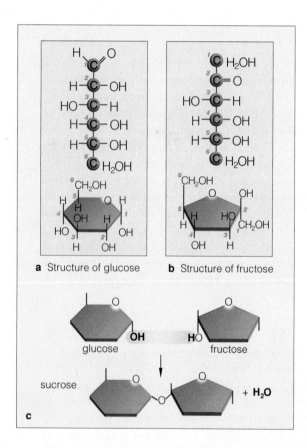

a Structure of glucose   **b** Structure of fructose

Figure 3.7 (**a,b**) Straight-chain and ring forms of glucose and fructose. For reference purposes, carbon atoms of these simple sugars are numbered in sequence, starting at the end closest to the molecule's aldehyde or ketone group. (**c**) Condensation of two monosaccharides into a disaccharide.

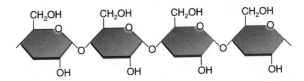

a Structure of amylose, a soluble form of starch. Cells inside tree leaves briefly store excess glucose monomers as starch grains in their chloroplasts, which are tiny, membrane-bound sacs that specialize in photosynthesis.

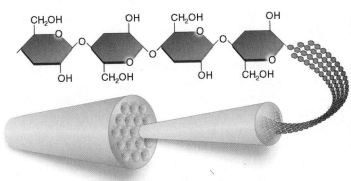

b Structure of cellulose. In cellulose fibers, chains of glucose units stretch side by side and hydrogen-bond at —OH groups. The many hydrogen bonds stabilize the chains in tight bundles that form long fibers. Few organisms produce enzymes that can digest this insoluble material. Cellulose is a structural component of plants and plant products, such as wood and cotton dresses.

c Glycogen. Animal cells build this polysaccharide as a storage form when the body has excess glucose. It is especially abundant in the liver and muscles of highly active animals, including fishes and people.

Figure 3.9 Molecular structure of (**a**) starch, (**b**) cellulose, and (**c**) glycogen, and their typical locations in a few organisms. All three carbohydrates consist only of glucose units.

(Figure 3.8*a*). Many —OH groups project out from the coils, which makes the chains accessible for cleavage reactions. This is important. For example, plants store much of their photosynthetically produced glucose in the form of starch. When free glucose is in short supply, enzymes can quickly hydrolyze the starch.

In cellulose, glucose chains stretch side by side and hydrogen-bond to one another, as in Figure 3.8*b*. The bonding arrangement stabilizes the chains in a tightly bundled pattern, which can resist hydrolysis by most enzymes. Long fibers of cellulose are a structural part of plant cell walls (Figure 3.9*b*). Like the steel rods in reinforced concrete, these fibers are tough, insoluble, and resistant to weight loads and mechanical stress, as when stems are buffeted by strong winds.

In animals, glycogen is the sugar-storage equivalent of starch in plants (Figure 3.9*c*). Muscle and liver cells store a lot of it. When the sugar level in blood falls, liver cells degrade glycogen, and the released glucose enters the blood. Exercise strenuously but briefly, and muscle cells tap glycogen for a burst of energy.

Chitin is a modified polysaccharide, with nitrogen-containing groups attached to its glucose monomers.

Figure 3.10 Molecular structure of chitin, a polysaccharide that occurs in protective body coverings of many animals, including this tick, as well as fungi. You may "hear" chitin when big spider legs clack across a metal oil pan on a garage floor.

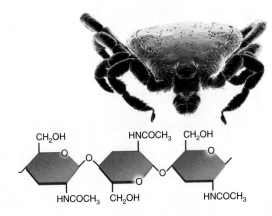

Chitin strengthens the external skeleton and other hard parts of many animals, including crabs, earthworms, insects, spiders, and ticks of the sort shown in Figure 3.10. It also strengthens the cell walls of fungi.

Carbohydrates include simple sugars (such as glucose), oligosaccharides (such as sucrose), and polysaccharides (such as starch). Cells use some carbohydrates as structural materials, others as packets of instant energy, and others as transportable or storable forms of energy.

3.4 Greasy, Oily—Must Be Lipids

Lipids are greasy or oily to the touch. Cells use different lipids as energy reservoirs, structural materials, and signaling molecules. Fats, phospholipids, and waxes have fatty acid tails. Sterols have a backbone of four carbon rings.

FATS AND FATTY ACIDS

Being nonpolar hydrocarbons, **lipids** do not dissolve in water, but they mix with other nonpolar substances —for instance, as butter does in warm cream sauce.

Fats are lipids with one, two, or three fatty acids dangling like tails from a glycerol molecule. A **fatty acid** starts as a carboxyl group attached to a backbone of as many as thirty-six carbon atoms. Each carbon in the backbone has one, two, or three hydrogen atoms covalently bonded to it (Figure 3.11). *Unsaturated* fatty acids contain one or more double covalent bonds. The *saturated* fatty acids have single bonds only.

Weak interactions keep many saturated fatty acids tightly packed in animal fats. These fats are solid at room temperature. Most plant fats stay liquid at room temperature, as "vegetable oils." Their packing is not as stable because of rigid kinks in their fatty acid tails. That is why vegetable oils flow freely.

Neutral fats such as butter, lard, and vegetable oils are mostly **triglycerides**. Each has three fatty acid tails linked to one glycerol (Figure 3.12). Triglycerides are the most abundant lipids in your body and its richest reservoir of energy. Gram for gram, they yield more than twice as much energy as complex carbohydrates such as starches. All vertebrates store triglycerides as droplets in fat cells that make up adipose tissue.

Layers and patches of adipose tissue insulate the body and cushion some of its parts. Like many other

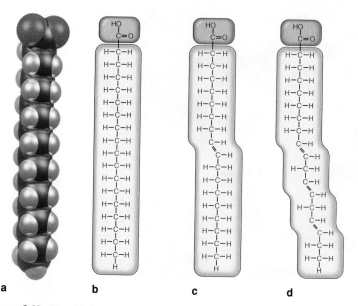

Figure 3.11 Three fatty acids. (**a,b**) Space-filling model and structural formula for stearic acid. The carbon backbone is fully saturated with hydrogen atoms. (**c**) Oleic acid, with a double bond in its backbone, is an unsaturated fatty acid. (**d**) Linolenic acid, also unsaturated, has three double bonds.

Figure 3.12 *Animated!* Condensation of (**a**) three fatty acids and one glycerol molecule into (**b**) a triglyceride. The photograph shows triglyceride-protected emperor penguins during an Antarctic blizzard.

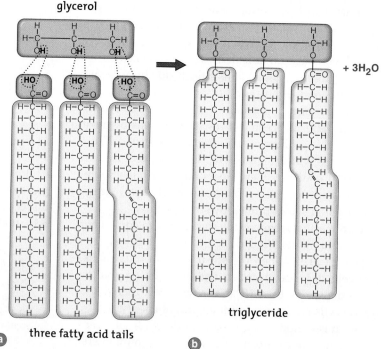

glycerol

$+ 3H_2O$

triglyceride

three fatty acid tails

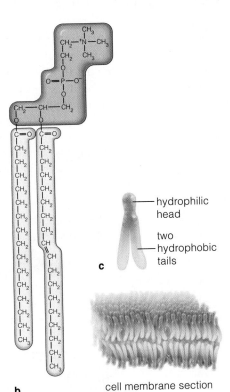

Figure 3.13 (**a**) Space-filling model, (**b**) structural formula, and (**c**) an icon for a phospholipid. This is the most common type in animal and plant cell membranes. Are its two tails saturated or unsaturated?

hydrophilic head

two hydrophobic tails

cell membrane section

Figure 3.14 (**a**) Honeycomb—food warehouses and bee nurseries. Bees construct these compartments from their own water-repellent, waxy secretions. (**b**) Sterol backbone. (**c**) Structural formula for cholesterol, the main sterol of animal tissues. Your liver makes enough cholesterol for your body. A fat-rich diet may lead to clogged arteries.

animals, penguins of the Antarctic can keep warm in extremely cold winter months thanks to a thick layer of triglycerides beneath their skin (Figure 3.12).

PHOSPHOLIPIDS

Phospholipids have a glycerol backbone, two nonpolar fatty acid tails, and a polar head (Figure 3.13). They are the main component of cell membranes, which consist of two layers of lipids. Phospholipid heads of one layer are dissolved in the cell's fluid interior, and phospholipid heads of the other layer are dissolved in the fluid surroundings. Sandwiched between the two are all of the hydrophobic tails. You will read about membrane structure and function in Chapter 5.

WAXES

Waxes have long-chain fatty acids tightly packed and bonded to long-chain alcohols or carbon rings. All have a firm consistency; all repel water. Surfaces of plants have a cuticle that contains waxes and another lipid, cutin. A plant cuticle restricts water loss and thwarts some parasites. Waxes also protect, lubricate, and lend pliability to skin and to hair. Birds secrete waxes, fats, and fatty acids that waterproof feathers. Bees use beeswax for honeycomb, which houses each new bee generation as well as honey (Figure 3.14a).

CHOLESTEROL AND OTHER STEROLS

Sterols are among the many lipids with no fatty acids. The sterols differ in the number, position, and type of their functional groups, but all have a rigid backbone of four fused-together carbon rings (Figure 3.14b).

Every eukaryotic cell membrane contains sterols. Cholesterol (Figure 3.14c) is the most common type in animal tissues. It is remodeled into compounds as diverse as bile salts, steroids, and vitamin D, which is required for strong bones and teeth. Bile salts play a part in fat digestion inside the small intestine. The steroids called sex hormones are essential for gamete formation and the development of secondary sexual traits. Such traits include the amount and distribution of hair in mammals, and feather color in birds.

Being largely hydrocarbon, lipids can intermingle with other nonpolar substances, but they resist dissolving in water.

Triglycerides, or neutral fats, have a glycerol head and three fatty acid tails. They are the major energy reservoirs. Phospholipids are the main component of cell membranes.

Sterols such as cholesterol are membrane components and precursors of steroid hormones and other compounds. Waxes are firm yet pliable components of water-repelling and lubricating substances.

3.5 Proteins—Diversity in Structure and Function

Of all large biological molecules, proteins are the most diverse. Some kinds speed reactions; others are the stuff of spider webs or feathers, bones, hair, and other body parts. Nutritious types abound in seeds and eggs. Many proteins move substances, help cells communicate, or defend against pathogens. Amazingly, cells assemble thousands of different proteins from only twenty kinds of amino acids.

An **amino acid** is a small organic compound with an amino group ($-NH_3^+$), a carboxyl group ($-COO^-$, the acid), a hydrogen atom, and one or more atoms called its R group. In most cases, these components are attached to the same carbon atom (Figure 3.15a). Appendix V shows all of the biological amino acids.

When a cell constructs a protein, it strings amino acids together, one after the other. Instructions coded

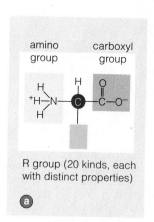

amino group   carboxyl group

R group (20 kinds, each with distinct properties)

a

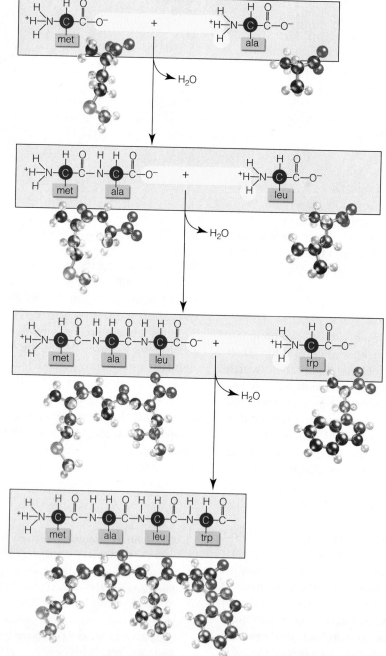

b Instructions encoded in DNA specify the order of amino acids to be joined in a polypeptide chain. The first amino acid is usually methionine (met). Alanine (ala) comes next in this example.

c In a condensation reaction, a peptide bond forms between the methionine and alanine. Leucine (leu) is next in line.

d A peptide bond forms between the alanine and the leucine. Tryptophan (trp) is next.

e Part of the newly formed polypeptide chain. The sequence of amino acids in this part is met–ala–leu–trp. The reactions may continue until there are hundreds or thousands of amino acids in the chain.

Figure 3.15 *Animated!*
(**a**) Generalized formula for amino acids. The *green* box highlights the R group, one of the side chains that include functional groups. Appendix V shows ball-and-stick models for twenty amino acids.

(**b–e**) Peptide bond formation during protein synthesis. Section 14.4 offers a closer look at protein synthesis.

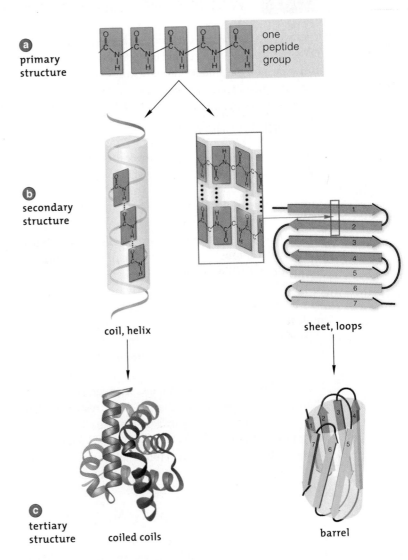

Figure 3.16 The first three of four levels of protein structure. (**a**) Primary structure is a linear sequence of amino acids. (**b**) Many hydrogen bonds (dotted lines) along a polypeptide chain result in a helically coiled or sheetlike secondary structure. (**c**) Coils and sheets packed into stable domains represent a third structural level.

a primary structure — one peptide group

b secondary structure — coil, helix — sheet, loops

c tertiary structure — coiled coils — barrel

in DNA specify the order in which any of the twenty kinds of amino acids will occur. A *peptide* bond forms as a condensation reaction joins the amino group of one amino acid and the carboxyl group of the next in line (Figure 3.15*b–e*). Each **polypeptide chain** consists of three or more amino acids. The carbon backbone of this chain incorporates nitrogen atoms in this regular pattern: —N—C—C—N—C—C— .

A protein's sequence of amino acids is known as its *primary* structure (Figure 3.16*a*). Its *secondary* structure emerges as the chain twists, bends, loops, and folds. Hydrogen bonding between certain R groups makes some stretches of amino acids coil helically, a bit like a spiral staircase, or makes them form sheets or loops as in Figure 3.16*b*. Bear in mind, part of the primary structure for each type of protein is unique in certain respects, but you will come across similar patterns of coils, sheets, and loops among different proteins.

Much as an overly twisted rubber band coils back on itself, the coils, sheets, and loops of a protein fold up even more, into compact domains. A "domain" is a polypeptide chain or a part of it that has become organized as a structurally stable unit. This third level of organization is a protein's *tertiary* structure. The shape of domains and the charge distribution around that shape determines protein function. For instance, the barrel-shaped domains of some proteins function as tunnels through membranes (Figure 3.16*c*).

Many proteins are two or more polypeptide chains bonded together or associating intimately with one another. This is the fourth level of organization, or *quaternary* protein structure. Many enzymes and other proteins are globular, with several polypeptide chains folded into rounded shapes. Hemoglobin, described shortly, is a classic example of such a protein.

Protein structure doesn't stop here. Enzymes often attach short, linear, or branched oligosaccharides to a new polypeptide chain, making a *glyco*protein. Many glycoproteins occur at the cell surface or are secreted from cells. Lipids also get attached to many proteins. The cholesterol, triglycerides, and phospholipids that your body absorbs after a meal are transported about as components of *lipo*proteins.

Many proteins are fibrous, with polypeptide chains organized as strands or sheets. They contribute to cell shape and organization, and help cells and cell parts move about. Other fibrous proteins make up cartilage, hair, skin, and parts of muscles and brain cells.

A protein's primary structure is a sequence of covalently bonded amino acids that make up a polypeptide chain.

Local regions of a polypeptide chain become twisted and folded into helical coils, sheetlike arrays, and loops. These arrangements are the protein's secondary structure.

A polypeptide chain or parts of it become organized as structurally stable, compact, functional domains. Such domains are a protein's tertiary structure.

Many proteins show quaternary structure; they consist of two or more polypeptide chains.

A protein's shape and charge distribution around that shape dictate protein function.

3.6 Why Is Protein Structure So Important?

LINK TO
SECTION
1.4

Cells are good at making proteins that are just what their DNA specifies. But mistakes and mutations happen, and they may alter the protein's primary structure in bad ways. The consequences are sometimes far-reaching.

JUST ONE WRONG AMINO ACID . . .

Four tightly packed polypeptides called globins make up each hemoglobin molecule. Each globin chain is folded into a pocket that cradles a **heme** group, a large organic molecule with an iron atom at its center (Figure 3.17). Heme is an oxygen transporter. During its life span, each of the red blood cells in your body transports billions of oxygen molecules, all bound to the heme in globin molecules.

Globin comes in two slightly different forms, alpha and beta. Two of each form make up one hemoglobin molecule in adult humans. Glutamate is normally the sixth amino acid in the beta globin chain, but a DNA mutation sometimes puts a different amino acid—valine—in the chain's sixth position (Figure 3.18*b*). Unlike glutamate, which carries an overall negative charge, valine has no net charge. As a result of that one substitution, a tiny patch of the protein changes from polar to nonpolar—which in turn causes globin's behavior to change slightly. Hemoglobin that has this mutation in its beta chain is designated HbS.

. . . AND SICKLE-CELL ANEMIA MAY FOLLOW!

Every human inherits two genes for beta globin, one from each of two parents. (Genes are units of DNA that encode heritable traits.) Cells access both genes when they make beta globin. If one gene is normal and the other has the valine mutation, a person makes enough normal hemoglobin and can lead a relatively normal life. Someone who inherits two mutant genes can only make hemoglobin HbS. The outcome, *sickle-cell anemia*, is a severe genetic disorder.

As blood moves through lungs, hemoglobin in red blood cells binds oxygen and then gives it up in body regions where oxygen levels are low. After the oxygen is released, red blood cells quickly return to the lungs and pick up more. In the few moments when they have no bound oxygen, hemoglobin molecules clump together just a bit. However, HbS molecules do not form such clusters in regions where oxygen levels are low. They form large, stable, rod-shaped aggregates.

Red blood cells containing these aggregates become distorted into sickle shapes (Figure 3.18*c*). These cells clog tiny blood vessels and disrupt blood circulation. Tissues become oxygen-starved. Figure 3.18*d* lists the far-reaching effects of sickle-cell anemia.

PROTEINS UNDONE—DENATURATION

Environmental conditions, too, can skew a protein's functioning. Globin cradles heme, an enzyme speeds some reaction, a receptor transduces an energy signal. These proteins and others cannot function unless they stay coiled, folded, and packed in a precise way. Their shape depends on many hydrogen bonds and other interactions that heat, shifts in pH, or detergents can disrupt. At such times, polypeptide chains unwind and change shape in an event called **denaturation**.

Consider albumin, a protein in the white of an egg. When you cook eggs, the heat does not disrupt the covalent bonds of albumin's primary structure. But it destroys albumin's weaker hydrogen bonds, and so the protein unfolds. When the translucent egg white turns opaque, we know albumin has been altered. For a few proteins, denaturation might be reversed if and

Figure 3.17 *Animated!*
(**a**) Globin, a coiled polypeptide chain. The chain cradles heme, a functional group that contains an iron atom. (**b**) Hemoglobin, an oxygen-transport protein in red blood cells. This is one of the proteins with quaternary structure. It consists of four globin molecules held together by hydrogen bonds. To help you distinguish among them, the two alpha globin chains are color-coded yellow and orange, and the two beta globins are color-coded blue and green.

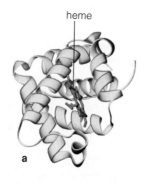

heme

a

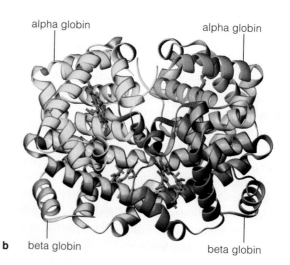

alpha globin   alpha globin

b   beta globin   beta globin

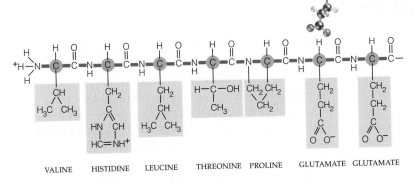

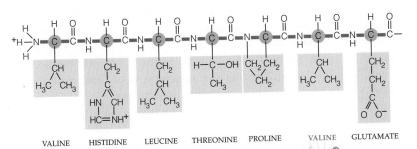

VALINE HISTIDINE LEUCINE THREONINE PROLINE GLUTAMATE GLUTAMATE

a Normal amino acid sequence at the start of a beta chain for hemoglobin.

VALINE HISTIDINE LEUCINE THREONINE PROLINE VALINE GLUTAMATE

b One amino acid substitution results in the abnormal beta chain in HbS molecules. Valine was added instead of glutamate at the sixth position of the growing polypeptide chain.

c Glutamate has an overall negative charge; valine has no net charge. This difference gives rise to a water-repellent, sticky patch on HbS molecules. They stick together because of that patch, forming rod-shaped clumps that distort normally rounded red blood cells into sickle shapes. (A sickle is a farm tool that has a crescent-shaped blade.)

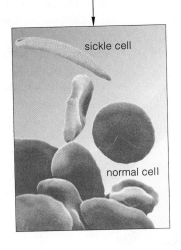

sickle cell

normal cell

Clumping of cells in bloodstream

Circulatory problems, damage to brain, lungs, heart, skeletal muscles, gut, and kidneys

Heart failure, paralysis, pneumonia, rheumatism, gut pain, kidney failure

Spleen concentrates sickle cells

Spleen enlargement

Immune system compromised

Rapid destruction of sickle cells

Anemia, causing weakness, fatigue, impaired development, heart chamber dilation

Impaired brain function, heart failure

d Melba Moore, celebrity spokesperson for sickle-cell anemia organizations. *Right,* range of symptoms for a person with two mutated genes (Hb^S) for hemoglobin's beta chain.

Figure 3.18 *Animated!* Sickle-cell anemia's molecular basis and its symptoms. Section 18.6 explores evolutionary and ecological aspects of this genetic disorder.

when normal conditions return, but albumin isn't one of them. There is no way to uncook an egg.

What is the take-home lesson? *A protein's structure dictates its function.* Hemoglobin, hormones, enzymes, transporters—such proteins help us survive. Twists and folds in their polypeptide chains form anchors, or membrane-spanning barrels, or jaws that grip enemy agents in the body. Mutations can alter the chains enough to block or enhance an anchoring, transport, or defensive function. Sometimes the consequences are awful. Yet changes in sequences and functional domains also give rise to variation in traits—the raw material for evolution. *Learn about protein structure and function and you are on your way to comprehending life in its richly normal and abnormal expressions.*

The structure of proteins dictates function. Mutations that alter a protein's structure sometimes have drastic consequences for its function, and for the health of organisms harboring them.

3.7 Nucleotides, DNA, and the RNAs

Certain small organic compounds called nucleotides are energy carriers, enzyme helpers, and messengers. Some are the building blocks for DNA and RNA. They are central to metabolism, survival, and reproduction.

Nucleotides have one sugar, at least one phosphate group, and one nitrogen-containing base. Deoxyribose or ribose is the sugar. Both sugars have a five-carbon ring structure; ribose has an oxygen atom attached to carbon 2 of the ring and deoxyribose does not. The bases have a single or double carbon ring structure.

The nucleotide **ATP** (adenosine triphosphate) has a row of three phosphate groups attached to its sugar (Figure 3.19). ATP can readily transfer the outermost phosphate group to many other molecules and make them reactive. Such transfers are vital for metabolism.

Other nucleotides have different metabolic roles. Some are **coenzymes**, necessary for enzyme function. They move electrons and hydrogen from one reaction site to another. NAD$^+$ and FAD are major kinds.

Still other nucleotides act as chemical messengers within and between cells. Later in the book, you will read about one of these messengers, which is known as cAMP (cyclic adenosine monophosphate).

Certain nucleotides also function as monomers for single- and double-stranded molecules called **nucleic acids**. In such strands, a covalent bond forms between the sugar of one nucleotide and the phosphate group of the next (Figure 3.20). The nucleic acids DNA and RNA store and retrieve heritable information.

All cells start life and then maintain themselves with instructions in their double-stranded molecules of deoxyribonucleic acid, or **DNA**. This nucleic acid is made of four kinds of deoxyribonucleotides. Figure 3.20*a* shows their structural formulas. As you can see, the four differ only in their component base, which is adenine, guanine, thymine, or cytosine.

Figure 3.21 shows how hydrogen bonds between bases join the two strands along the length of a DNA molecule. Think of every "base pairing" as one rung of a ladder, and the two sugar–phosphate backbones as the ladder's two posts. The ladder twists and turns in a regular pattern, forming a double helical coil.

The sequence of bases in DNA encodes heritable information about all the proteins that give each new cell the potential to grow, maintain itself, and even to reproduce. Part of that sequence is unique for each species. Some parts are identical, or nearly so, among many species. We return to DNA's structure and its functions in Chapter 13.

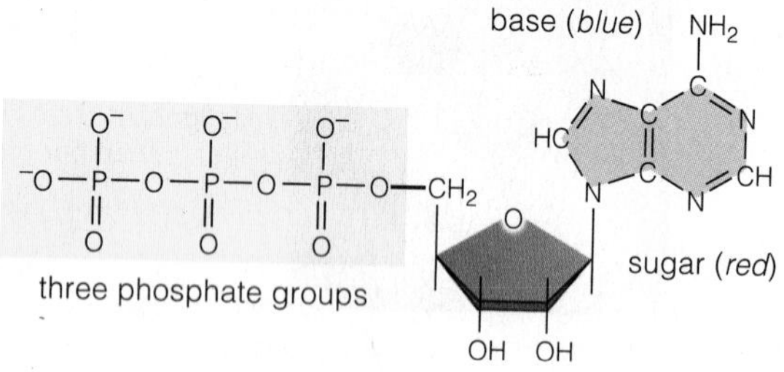

Figure 3.19
The structural formula for an ATP molecule.

base (*blue*) NH₂

three phosphate groups

sugar (*red*)

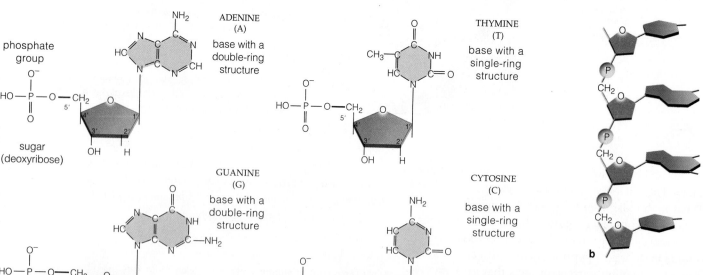

Figure 3.20 *Animated!* (**a**) Nucleotides of DNA. Two nucleotide bases, adenine and guanine, have a double-ring structure. The two others, thymine and cytosine, have a single-ring structure. (**b**) Bonding pattern between successive bases in nucleic acids.

ADENINE (A) — base with a double-ring structure

THYMINE (T) — base with a single-ring structure

GUANINE (G) — base with a double-ring structure

CYTOSINE (C) — base with a single-ring structure

phosphate group

sugar (deoxyribose)

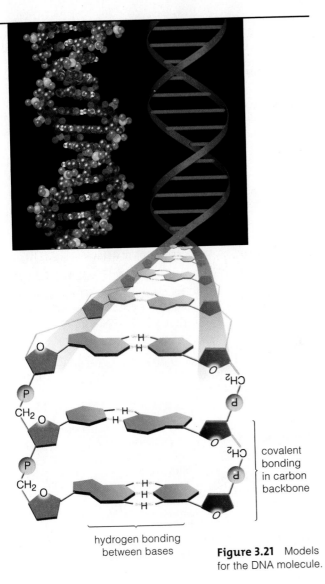

hydrogen bonding between bases

covalent bonding in carbon backbone

Figure 3.21 Models for the DNA molecule.

The **RNAs** (ribonucleic acids) have four kinds of ribonucleotide monomers. Unlike DNA, most RNAs are single strands, and one base is uracil instead of thymine. One type of RNA is a messenger that carries eukaryotic DNA's protein-building instructions out of the nucleus and into the cytoplasm, where they are translated into proteins by other RNAs. Chapter 14 returns to RNA and its role in protein synthesis.

Different nucleotides function as coenzymes, energy carriers such as ATP, chemical messengers, and building blocks for the nucleic acids DNA and the RNAs.

DNA consists of two nucleotide strands joined by hydrogen bonds and twisted as a double helix. Its nucleotide sequence encodes heritable protein-building information.

RNA usually is a single-stranded nucleic acid. Different RNAs have roles in processes by which a cell retrieves and uses genetic information in DNA to build proteins.

Summary

Section 3.1 Under present-day conditions in nature, only living cells can synthesize complex carbohydrates and lipids, proteins, and nucleic acids—the molecules of life. These molecules differ in their three-dimensional structure and function, starting with the carbon backbone and functional groups. Their structure affords clues to how cells, and multicelled organisms, function.

Biology⊛Now
Read the InfoTrac article "The Form Counts: Proteins, Fats, and Carbohydrates," Beatrice Trum, Consumer's Research Magazine, August 2001.

Section 3.2 All organic compounds have carbon and at least one hydrogen atom. Carbon atoms bond covalently with as many as four other atoms, often in long chains or rings. Functional groups attached to a carbon backbone influence an organic compound's properties. Enzyme-driven reactions synthesize all of the molecules of life from smaller organic molecules. Table 3.1 on the next page summarizes these compounds.

Biology⊛Now
Explore functional groups and view the animation of condensation and hydrolysis on BiologyNow.

Section 3.3 The main carbohydrates are simple sugars, oligosaccharides, and polysaccharides. Cells use carbohydrates as instant energy sources, transportable or storage forms of energy, and structural materials.

Section 3.4 Lipids are greasy or oily compounds that tend not to dissolve in water but mix easily with nonpolar compounds, such as other lipids. Neutral fats (triglycerides), phospholipids, waxes, and sterols are lipids. Cells use lipids as major sources of energy and as structural materials, as in cell membranes.

Biology⊛Now
Watch an animation showing how a triglyceride forms by condensation on BiologyNow.

Section 3.5 Structurally and functionally, proteins are the most diverse molecules of life. Their primary structure is a sequence of amino acids—a polypeptide chain. Such chains twist, coil, and bend into functional domains. Many proteins, including hemoglobin and most enzymes, consist of two or more chains. Certain aggregations of proteins form hair, muscle, connective tissue, and other body parts.

Biology⊛Now
Explore amino acid structure and learn about peptide bond formation with the animation on BiologyNow.
Read the InfoTrac article "Protein Folding and Misfolding," David Gossard, American Scientist, September 2002.

Section 3.6 A protein's overall structure determines its function. Sometimes a mutation in DNA results in an amino acid substitution that alters the protein's structure in ways that cause genetic diseases, including sickle-cell anemia. Weak bonds that hold a protein's

Table 3.1 Summary of the Main Organic Compounds in Living Things

Category	Main Subcategories	Some Examples and Their Functions	
CARBOHYDRATES . . . contain an aldehyde or a ketone group, and one or more hydroxyl groups	**Monosaccharides** (simple sugars) **Oligosaccharides** (short-chain carbohydrates) **Polysaccharides** (complex carbohydrates)	Glucose Sucrose (a disaccharide) Starch, glycogen Cellulose	Energy source Most common form of sugar; the form transported through plants Energy storage Structural roles
LIPIDS . . . are mainly hydrocarbon; generally do not dissolve in water but do dissolve in nonpolar substances, such as other lipids	**Lipids with fatty acids** *Glycerides:* Glycerol backbone with one, two, or three fatty acid tails *Phospholipids:* Glycerol backbone, phosphate group, one other polar group, and (often) two fatty acids *Waxes:* Alcohol with long-chain fatty acid tails **Lipids with no fatty acids** *Sterols:* Four carbon rings; the number, position, and type of functional groups differ among sterols	Fats (e.g., butter), oils (e.g., corn oil) Phosphatidylcholine Waxes in cutin Cholesterol	Energy storage Key component of cell membranes Conservation of water in plants Component of animal cell membranes; precursor of many steroids and vitamin D
PROTEINS . . . are one or more polypeptide chains, each with as many as several thousand covalently linked amino acids	**Fibrous proteins** Long strands or sheets of polypeptide chains; often tough, water-insoluble **Globular proteins** One or more polypeptide chains folded into globular shapes; many roles in cell activities	Keratin Collagen Enzymes Hemoglobin Insulin Antibodies	Structural component of hair, nails Structural component of bone Great increase in rates of reactions Oxygen transport Control of glucose metabolism Tissue defense
NUCLEIC ACIDS (AND NUCLEOTIDES) . . . are chains of units (or individual units) that each consist of a five-carbon sugar, phosphate, and a nitrogen-containing base	**Adenosine phosphates** **Nucleotide coenzymes** **Nucleic acids** Chains of nucleotides	ATP cAMP (Section 36.2) NAD^+, $NADP^+$, FAD DNA, RNAs	Energy carrier Messenger in hormone regulation Transfer of electrons, protons (H^+) from one reaction site to another Storage, transmission, translation of genetic information

shape can be disrupted by temperature, pH shifts, or exposure to detergent. Usually, the disruptions make the protein unfold permanently.

Biology⌇Now

Learn more about hemoglobin structure and sickle-cell mutation by viewing the animation on BiologyNow.

Section 3.7 There are different kinds of nucleotides, but all consist of a sugar, a phosphate group, and a nitrogen-containing base. They have essential roles in metabolism, survival, and reproduction. ATP energizes many kinds of molecules by phosphate-group transfers. Other nucleotides function as coenzymes or chemical messengers. DNA and RNA are nucleic acids, each composed of four kinds of nucleotide subunits.

DNA's nucleotide bases encode information on the primary structure of all of the cell's proteins. Different kinds of RNA molecules interact with DNA and with one another in the translation of that information.

Biology⌇Now

Explore DNA with the animation on BiologyNow.

Self-Quiz

Answers in Appendix II

1. Name the molecules of life and the families of small organic compounds from which they are built.

2. Each carbon atom can share pairs of electrons with as many as _____ other atoms.
   a. one   b. two   c. three   d. four

3. Sugars are a class of _____ , which have one or more _____ groups.
   a. proteins; amino   c. alcohols; hydroxyl
   b. acids; phosphate   d. carbohydrates; carboxyl

4. _____ is a simple sugar (a monosaccharide).
   a. Glucose   c. Ribose   e. both a and b
   b. Sucrose   d. Chitin   f. both a and c

5. The fatty acid tails of unsaturated fats incorporate one or more _____ .
   a. single covalent bonds   b. double covalent bonds

6. Sterols are among the many lipids with no _____ .
   a. saturation   c. hydrogens
   b. fatty acids   d. carbons

7. Which of the following is a class of molecules that encompasses all of the other molecules listed?
   a. triglycerides   c. waxes   e. lipids
   b. fatty acids   d. sterols   f. phospholipids

8. _____ are to proteins as _____ are to nucleic acids.
   a. Sugars; lipids   c. Amino acids; hydrogen bonds
   b. Sugars; proteins   d. Amino acids; nucleotides

9. A denatured protein has lost its _____ .
   a. hydrogen bonds   c. function
   b. shape   d. all of the above

10. Nucleotides occur in _____ .
    a. ATP   b. DNA   c. RNA   d. all are correct

11. Which of the following nucleotides is *not* found in DNA?
    a. adenine   b. uracil   c. thymine   d. guanine

12. Match the molecule with the most suitable description.
    _____ long sequence of amino acids   a. carbohydrate
    _____ energy carrier in cells   b. phospholipid
    _____ glycerol, fatty acids, phosphate   c. polypeptide
    _____ two strands of nucleotides   d. DNA
    _____ one or more sugar monomers   e. ATP

Additional questions are available on Biology ⊛ Now™

Critical Thinking

1. In the following list, identify which is the carbohydrate, the fatty acid, the amino acid, and the polypeptide:

   a. $^+NH_3$—CHR—COO$^-$ c. (glycine)$_{20}$

   b. $C_6H_{12}O_6$ d. $CH_3(CH_2)_{16}COOH$

2. A clerk in a health-food store tells you that "natural" vitamin C extracts from rose hips are better than synthetic tablets of this vitamin. Given what you know about the structure of organic compounds, how would you respond?

3. It seems there are "good" and "bad" unsaturated fats. The double bonds of both put a bend in their fatty acid tails. The bend in *trans* fatty acid tails keeps them aligned in the same direction along their length. The bend in *cis* fatty acid tails makes them zigzag (Figure 3.22).

   Some *trans* fatty acids occur naturally in beef. But most form by industrial processes that solidify vegetable oils for margarine, shortening, and the like. These substances are widely used in prepared foods (such as cookies) and in french fries and other fast-food products. *Trans* fatty acids are linked to heart attacks. Speculate on why the body handles *cis* fatty acids better than *trans* fatty acids.

4. The shapes of a protein's domains often give us clues to functions. For example, Figure 3.23 is a model for one of the HLAs, a type of recognition protein perched above the surface of all vertebrate body cells. Certain cells of the immune system use HLAs to distinguish self (the body's own cells) from nonself. Each HLA has a jawlike region that can bind bits of an invader or some other threat. It thus alerts the immune defenders that the body has been invaded or otherwise threatened. Speculate on what may happen if a mutation makes the jawlike region misfold.

5. Cholesterol from food or synthesized in the liver is too hydrophobic to circulate in blood; complexes of protein and lipids ferry it around. Low density lipoprotein, or *LDL*, transports cholesterol out of the liver and into cells.

cis fatty acid

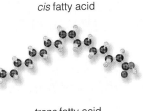

trans fatty acid

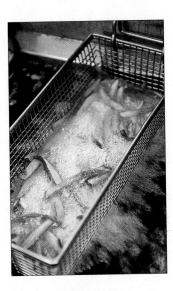

Figure 3.22 Maybe rethink the french fries?

High density lipoprotein, or *HDL*, ferries the cholesterol that is released from dead cells back to the liver.

High LDL levels are implicated in atherosclerosis, heart problems, and strokes. The main protein in LDL is called ApoA1. A mutant form of ApoA1 has the wrong amino acid (cysteine instead of arginine) at one place in its primary sequence. Carriers of this LDL mutation have very low levels of HDL, which is typically predictive of heart disease. Yet the carriers have no heart problems.

Some heart patients received injections of the mutant LDL, which acted like a drain cleaner. It quickly reduced the size of cholesterol deposits in the patients' arteries.

A few years from now, such a treatment may reverse years of damage. However, many researchers caution that a low-fat, low-cholesterol diet is still the best assurance of long-term health. Would you choose artery-cleansing treatments over a healthy diet?

where the molecule binds and displays "enemies" (*arrow*)

one of the chains spans the plasma membrane and anchors the molecule

Figure 3.23 From structure to function—a protein that helps your body defend itself against bacteria and other foreign agents. HLA-A2 has two polypeptide chains that are like jaws. Another protein anchors it to the plasma membrane.

4 CELL STRUCTURE AND FUNCTION

Animalcules and Cells Fill'd With Juices

Do you ever think of yourself as being close to 1/1,000 of a kilometer tall? Probably not. Yet that is how we refer to cells. We measure them in micrometers—in millionths of a millimeter, which is a thousandth of a meter, which is a thousandth of a kilometer. The bacterial cells in Figure 4.1 are a few micrometers "tall."

Before those cells were fixed on the head of a pin so someone could take their picture, they were the living descendants of a lineage far more ancient than yours. Their line of descent goes back so far they do not even have their DNA housed in a nucleus. They are prokaryotes, which are, at least structurally, the simplest cells of all. Your cells are eukaryotic. Somewhere in time, a nucleus developed in their single-celled ancestors, along with a variety of other internal compartments that help keep metabolic activities organized.

Nearly all cells are invisible to the naked eye. No one knew about them until the seventeenth century, when the first microscopes were being put together in Italy, then in France and England. These were not much to speak of. Galileo Galilei, for instance, simply used two glass lenses inside a cylinder, but the arrangement was good enough to reveal details of an insect's eyes. At midcentury, Robert Hooke focused a microscope on thinly sliced cork from a

mature tree and saw tiny compartments (Figure 4.2). He gave them the Latin name *cellulae*, meaning small rooms—hence the origin of the biological term "cell." Actually they were dead plant cell walls, which is what cork is made of, but Hooke did not think of them as being dead because neither he nor anyone else knew cells could be alive. He observed cells "fill'd with juices" in green plant tissues but didn't have a clue to what they were, either.

Given the simplicity of their instruments, it is amazing that the pioneers in microscopy observed as much as they did. Antoni van Leeuwenhoek, a Dutch shopkeeper, had exceptional skill in constructing lenses and possibly the keenest vision. By the late 1600s, he was spying on such wonders as sperm, protists, a bacterium, and "many very small animalcules, the motions of which were very pleasing to behold," in scrapings of tartar from his teeth.

In the 1820s, improved lenses brought cells into sharper focus. Robert Brown, a botanist, was the first to identify a plant cell nucleus. Later, the botanist Matthias Schleiden wondered if a plant cell develops as an independent unit even though it is part of the plant. By 1839, after years of studying animal tissues, the zoologist Theodor Schwann reported that cells and their products make up animals as well as plants. He also reported that cells have an individual

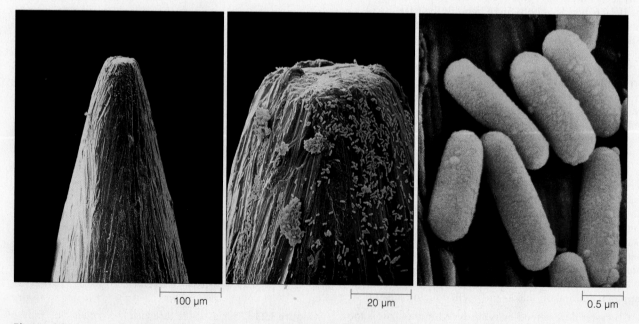

100 μm   20 μm   0.5 μm

Figure 4.1 How small are cells? This example will give you an idea. Shown here at increasingly higher magnifications, a population of rod-shaped bacterial cells peppering the tip of a household pin.

IMPACTS, ISSUES

Figure 4.2 Robert Hooke's microscope and his sketch of cell walls from cork tissue.

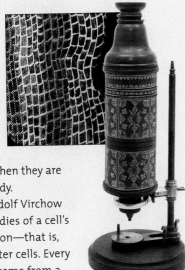

life of their own even when they are part of a multicelled body.

The physiologist Rudolf Virchow completed his own studies of a cell's growth and reproduction—that is, its division into daughter cells. Every cell, he decided, must come from a cell that already exists.

So microscopic analysis yielded three generalizations, which together constitute the **cell theory**. First, organisms consist of one or more cells. Second, the cell is the smallest unit of organization that still displays the properties of life. Third, the continuity of life arises directly from the growth and division of single cells.

This chapter introduces defining features of prokaryotic and eukaryotic cells. It is not meant for memorization. Read it simply to gain an overview of current understandings of cell structure and function. In later chapters, you might refer back to it as a road map through the details. With its images from microscopy, this chapter and others invite you into otherwise invisible worlds. Why bother to travel there? We are close to creating the simplest form of life in test tubes. That is something worth thinking about.

 How Would You Vote?

Researchers are modifying prokaryotes to identify what it takes to be alive. They are creating "new" organisms by removing genes from living cells, one at a time. What are the potential advantages or bioethical pitfalls of this kind of research? See BiologyNow for details, then vote online.

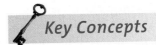 **Key Concepts**

WHAT ALL CELLS HAVE IN COMMON

A plasma membrane is a boundary between the interior of a cell and the surroundings, where the inputs and outputs of substances are controlled. Eukaryotic DNA is enclosed in a nucleus. Prokaryotic DNA is concentrated in a nucleoid. Cytoplasm is everything between the plasma membrane and the region of DNA. Section 4.1

MICROSCOPES

Microscopes employ rays of light or beams of electrons to reveal details at the cellular level of organization. They offer evidence of the cell theory: Each organism consists of one or more cells and their products, a cell has a capacity for independent life, and since the time of life's origin, all cells have arisen from cells that already exist. Section 4.2

PROKARYOTIC CELLS

Structurally, prokaryotic cells are the simplest and most ancient forms of life. Archaeans and bacteria are the only groups. Collectively, they show great metabolic diversity. Different kinds live in or on other organisms and in Earth's waters, soils, sediments, and rocky layers. Section 4.3

EUKARYOTIC CELLS

Organelles—small, membrane-bounded sacs—divide the interior of eukaryotic cells into functional compartments. All cells of protists, plants, fungi, and animals start out life with a nucleus; they are eukaryotic. They differ in the type and number of organelles, in cell structures, and in surface specializations. Sections 4.4–4.9

THE CYTOSKELETON

Arrays of a variety of protein filaments reinforce cell shape and keep its parts organized. Some filaments assemble and disassemble in dynamic ways that can move cells or their inner components to new locations. Sections 4.10–4.11

Links to Earlier Concepts

Look back on your road map through the levels of organization in nature (Section 1.1). With this chapter you arrive at the level of living cells. You will start to see how lipids are structurally organized as cell membranes (3.4), where DNA and RNA reside in cells (3.7), and where carbohydrates are built and broken apart (3.2–3.3). You will expand your view of how cell structure and function depend on proteins (3.5–3.6).

4.1 So What Is "A Cell"?

LINK TO
SECTION
3.4

*Structurally, bacteria and archaeans are the simplest cells. They are **prokaryotic**, with no nucleus. Cells of all other organisms are **eukaryotic**. They contain a nucleus and other membrane-bound internal compartments.*

THE BASICS OF CELL STRUCTURE

The **cell** is the smallest unit with the properties of life: a capacity for metabolism, controlled responses to the environment, growth, and reproduction. Cells differ in size, shape, and activities, yet are all alike in three respects. They start out life with a plasma membrane, a region of DNA, and cytoplasm (Figure 4.3).

A **plasma membrane** defines the cell as a distinct entity. This thin, outer membrane separates metabolic activities from random events outside, but it does not isolate the cell interior. It is like a house with many doors that do not open for just anyone. Water, carbon dioxide, and oxygen enter and leave freely. Nutrients, ions, and other substances must be escorted.

In eukaryotic cells, the DNA occupies a **nucleus**, a membrane-bound, internal sac. In prokaryotic cells, it occupies a **nucleoid**, a region of the cytoplasm that is not enclosed in a membranous sac.

Cytoplasm is everything in between the plasma membrane and the region of DNA. It has a semifluid matrix and structural components that have roles in protein synthesis, energy conversions, and other vital tasks. For instance, cytoplasm holds many **ribosomes**, the molecular structures on which proteins are built.

PREVIEW OF CELL MEMBRANES

A **lipid bilayer** is a continuous, oily boundary that prevents the free passage of water-soluble substances across it (Figure 4.4). It is the structural basis of the plasma membrane and of various membranes inside

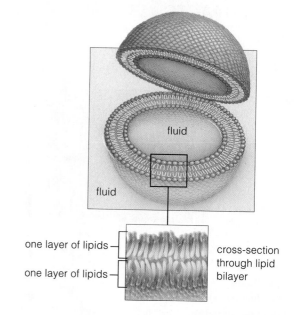

fluid

fluid

one layer of lipids

one layer of lipids

cross-section through lipid bilayer

Figure 4.4 Simplified model for the lipid bilayer of all cell membranes. Remember the phospholipids (Section 3.4)? They are the most abundant lipids in cell membranes. Their hydrophobic tails are sandwiched between their hydrophilic heads, which are dissolved in cytoplasm on one side of the bilayer and in extracellular fluid on the other side.

eukaryotic cells. Membranes in the cytoplasm form channels or sacs that compartmentalize the tasks of transporting, synthesizing, modifying, stockpiling, or digesting substances.

Diverse proteins embedded in the lipid bilayer or positioned at one of its surfaces carry out most of the membrane functions (Figure 4.5). For instance, some proteins are channels and others are pumps across the bilayer. Others are receptors; they are like docks for hormones and other signaling molecules that trigger required changes in cell activities. You will read more about membrane proteins in chapters to follow.

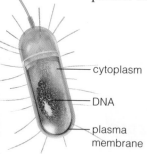

cytoplasm

DNA

plasma membrane

a Bacterial cell (prokaryotic)

Figure 4.3 Overview of the general organization of prokaryotic cells and eukaryotic cells. The three examples are not drawn to the same scale.

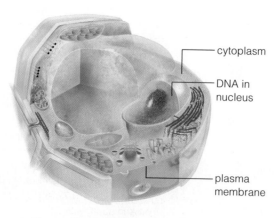

cytoplasm

DNA in nucleus

plasma membrane

b Plant cell (eukaryotic)

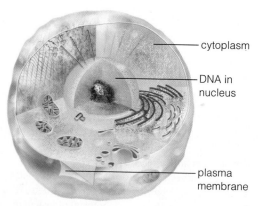

cytoplasm

DNA in nucleus

plasma membrane

c Animal cell (eukaryotic)

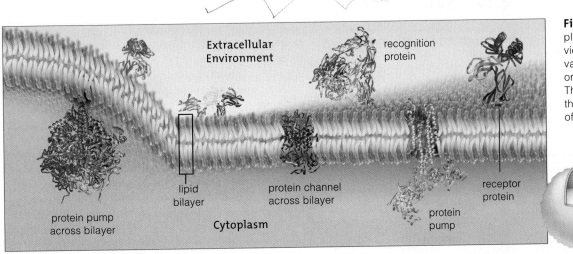

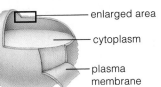

Figure 4.5 Model for a plasma membrane, cutaway view. The lipid bilayer has a variety of proteins spanning or attached to its surfaces. The next chapter focuses on the structure and function of cell membranes.

Labels on figure: Extracellular Environment; recognition protein; lipid bilayer; protein channel across bilayer; Cytoplasm; receptor protein; protein pump; protein pump across bilayer; enlarged area; cytoplasm; plasma membrane

WHY AREN'T CELLS BIGGER?

Are any cells big enough to be seen without the help of a microscope? A few. They include "yolks" of bird eggs, cells in watermelon tissues, and amphibian and fish eggs. These cells can be large because they are not doing too much, metabolically speaking, at maturity. Most of their volume is a nutrient warehouse. If a cell has to perform many tasks, you can expect it to be too tiny to be seen by the unaided eye.

So why aren't all cells big? A physical relationship called the **surface-to-volume ratio** constrains increases in cell size. By this relationship, an object's volume increases with the cube of its diameter, but the surface area increases only with the square.

Apply this constraint to a round cell. As Figure 4.6 shows, *when a cell expands in diameter during growth, its volume increases faster than its surface area.* Suppose you could make a round cell increase four times in diameter. Its volume would increase 64 times (4^3), but its surface area would increase just 16 times (4^2). Each unit of its plasma membrane would now be required to service four times as much cytoplasm as before.

When the girth of any cell becomes too great, the inward flow of nutrients and outward flow of wastes will not be fast enough to keep up with the metabolic activity that keeps the cell alive. The outcome will be a dead cell.

Besides, a big, round cell also would have trouble moving materials through its cytoplasm. The random motion of molecules can distribute substances through tiny cells. When a cell is not tiny, you can expect it to be long or thin, or to have outfoldings or infoldings that increase its surface area relative to its volume. When a cell is smaller, narrower, or frilly surfaced, substances cross its surface and become distributed through the interior with greater efficiency.

Surface-to-volume constraints also shape the body plans of multicelled species. For example, small cells attach end to end in strandlike algae, so each interacts directly with its surroundings. Cells in your muscles are as long as the muscle itself, but each one is thin enough to efficiently exchange substances with fluids in the tissue surrounding them.

diameter (cm):	0.5	1.0	1.5
surface area (cm^2):	0.79	3.14	7.07
volume (cm^3):	0.06	0.52	1.77
surface-to-volume ratio:	13.17:1	6.04:1	3.99:1

Figure 4.6 *Animated!* One example of the surface-to-volume ratio. This physical relationship between increases in volume and surface area puts constraints on the sizes and shapes that are possible in cells.

All living cells have an outermost plasma membrane, an internal region called cytoplasm, and an internal region where DNA is concentrated.

Bacteria and archaeans are two groups of prokaryotic cells. Unlike eukaryotic cells, they do not have an abundance of organelles, particularly a nucleus.

Two layers of lipids are the structural framework for cell membranes. Proteins in the bilayer or positioned at one of its surfaces carry out diverse membrane functions.

A physical relationship called the surface-to-volume ratio constrains increases in cell size. The relationship also influences the shape of individual cells and the body plans of multicelled organisms.

4.2   How Do We "See" Cells?

Like their centuries-old forerunners, modern microscopes are our best windows on the cellular world.

path of light rays (bottom to top) to eye

Ocular lens enlarges primary image formed by objective lenses.

prism that directs rays to ocular lens

Objective lenses (those closest to specimen) form the primary image. Most compound light microscopes have several.

stage (holds microscope slide in position)

Condenser lenses focus light rays through specimen.

illuminator

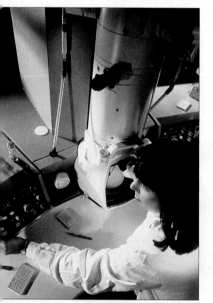

source of illumination (housed in the base of the microscope)

Figure 4.7 *Animated!* Generalized diagram and photograph of one kind of compound light microscope.

Research with modern microscopes still supports the three generalizations of the cell theory. In essence, all organisms consist of one or more cells, the cell is the smallest unit that still retains the characteristics of life, and since the time of life's origin, each new cell is descended from a cell that is already alive.

Like earlier instruments, many microscopes still use waves of light, and the light's wavelengths dictate their capacity to make images. Visualize a series of waves moving across an ocean. Each **wavelength** is the distance from the peak of one wave to the peak behind it.

In *compound light microscopes* (Figure 4.7), two or more sets of glass lenses bend waves of light passing through a cell or some other specimen. The shapes of lenses bend the waves at angles that disperse them in ways that form an enlarged image. *Micrographs* are simply photographs of images that emerge with the help of a microscope.

Cells become visible when they are thin enough for light to pass through them, but most cells are nearly colorless and look uniformly dense. Certain colored dyes can stain cells nonuniformly and make their component parts show up, but stains kill cells. Dead cells break down fast, which is why most cells are preserved before staining.

At present, the best light microscopes can enlarge cells about 2,000 times. Beyond that, cell structures appear larger but they are not clearer. Structures smaller than one-half of a wavelength of light are too small to resolve, so they cannot be distinguished.

Electron microscopes use magnetic lenses to bend and diffract beams of electrons, which cannot be diffracted through a glass lens. Electrons travel in wavelengths about 100,000 times shorter than those of visible light. Hence electron microscopes can resolve details that are 100,000 times smaller than you can see with a light microscope.

In *transmission* electron microscopes, electrons pass through a specimen and are used to make images of its internal details (Figure 4.8). *Scanning* electron microscopes direct a beam of electrons back and forth across a surface of a specimen, which has been given a thin metal coating. The metal responds by emitting electrons and x-rays, which can be converted into an image of the surface.

Figure 4.9 compares the resolving power of microscopes and of the human eye. Figure 4.10 compares the kinds of images that different microscopes offer.

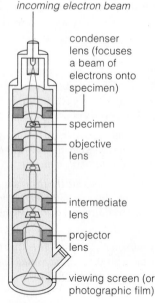

incoming electron beam

condenser lens (focuses a beam of electrons onto specimen)

specimen

objective lens

intermediate lens

projector lens

viewing screen (or photographic film)

Figure 4.8 *Animated!* Generalized diagram of an electron microscope. The photograph gives an idea of the lens diameters for a transmission electron microscope (TEM). When a beam of electrons from an electron gun moves down the microscope column, magnets focus them. With a transmission electron microscope, electrons pass through a thin slice of specimen and illuminate a fluorescent screen on a monitor. Shadows cast by the specimen's internal details appear, as in Figure 4.10c.

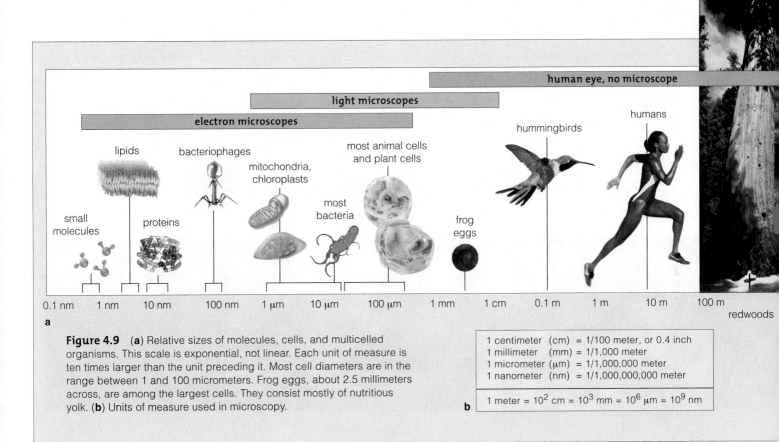

Figure 4.9 (a) Relative sizes of molecules, cells, and multicelled organisms. This scale is exponential, not linear. Each unit of measure is ten times larger than the unit preceding it. Most cell diameters are in the range between 1 and 100 micrometers. Frog eggs, about 2.5 millimeters across, are among the largest cells. They consist mostly of nutritious yolk. (b) Units of measure used in microscopy.

1 centimeter (cm)	= 1/100 meter, or 0.4 inch
1 millimeter (mm)	= 1/1,000 meter
1 micrometer (μm)	= 1/1,000,000 meter
1 nanometer (nm)	= 1/1,000,000,000 meter

1 meter = 10^2 cm = 10^3 mm = 10^6 μm = 10^9 nm

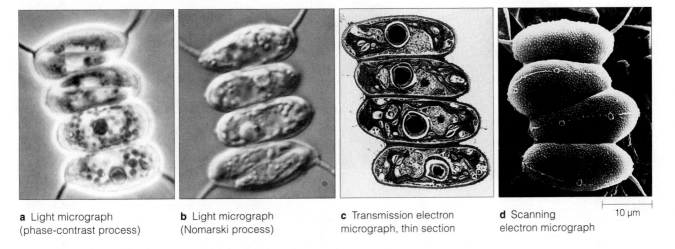

a Light micrograph (phase-contrast process)

b Light micrograph (Nomarski process)

c Transmission electron micrograph, thin section

d Scanning electron micrograph

10 μm

Figure 4.10 How different microscopes reveal different aspects of the same organism: a green alga (*Scenedesmus*). All four images are at the same magnification. (**a,b**) Light micrographs. (**c**) Transmission electron micrograph. (**d**) Scanning electron micrograph. A horizontal bar below a micrograph, as in (**d**), provides a visual reference for size. One micrometer (μm) is 1/1,000,000 of 1 meter. Using the scale bar, can you estimate the length and width of a *Scenedesmus* cell?

4.3 Introducing Prokaryotic Cells

LINKS TO
SECTIONS
1.1, 1.3, 3.5

The word prokaryote is taken to mean "before the nucleus." The name reminds us that bacteria and then archaeans originated before cells with a nucleus evolved.

Prokaryotes are the smallest known cells. As a group they are the most metabolically diverse forms of life on Earth. Different kinds exploit energy sources and raw materials in nearly all environments, including dry deserts, deep ocean sediments, and mountain ice.

We recognize two domains of prokaryotic cells— **Bacteria** and **Archaea** (Sections 1.3 and 19.5). Cells of both groups are alike in outward appearance and in size. However, the two groups differ in major ways.

Bacteria start making each new polypeptide chain with formylmethionine, a modified amino acid. Archaeans start a chain with methionine—as eukaryotic cells do (Section 3.5). Eukaryotic cells make many histones, a type of protein that structurally stabilizes the DNA. Archaeans make a few histones. Bacteria make a few histone-like proteins that stabilize the nucleoid.

Most prokaryotic cells are not much wider than one micrometer. The rod-shaped species are no more than a few micrometers long (Figures 4.11 and 4.12). Structurally, these are the simplest cells. A semirigid or rigid wall outside the plasma membrane imparts shape to most species. As Section 4.10 explains, arrays

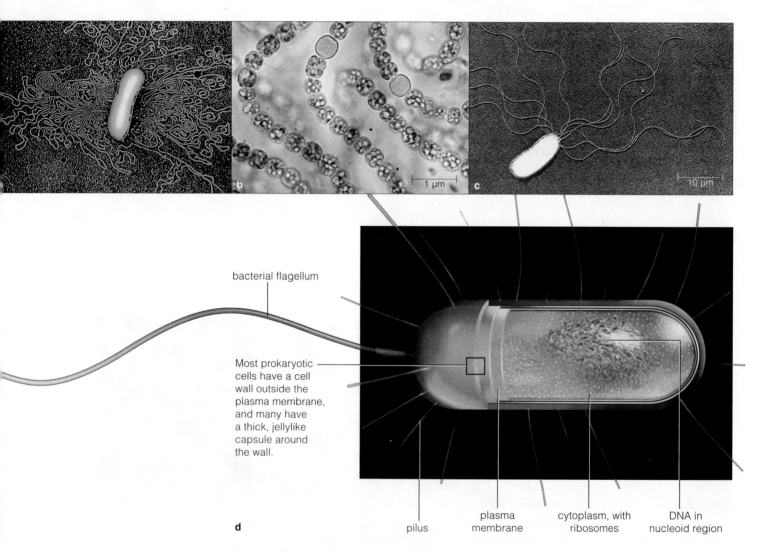

bacterial flagellum

Most prokaryotic cells have a cell wall outside the plasma membrane, and many have a thick, jellylike capsule around the wall.

pilus

plasma membrane

cytoplasm, with ribosomes

DNA in nucleoid region

d

Figure 4.11 *Animated!* (**a**) Micrograph of *Escherichia coli*. Researchers manipulated this bacterial cell to release its single, circular molecule of DNA. (**b**) Different bacterial species are shaped like balls, rods, or corkscrews. Ball-shaped cells of a photosynthetic bacterium (*Nostoc*) stick together in a thick, jellylike sheath of their own secretions. Chapter 21 offers more examples. (**c**) Like this *Pseudomonas marginalis* cell, many species have one or more bacterial flagella that propel the cell body through fluid environments. (**d**) Generalized sketch of a typical prokaryotic cell.

Figure 4.12 From Bitter Springs, Australia, fossilized bacteria dating to about 850 million years ago, in precambrian times. (**a**) A colonial form, most likely *Myxococcoides minor.* (**b**) Cells of a filamentous species (*Palaeolyngbya*).

(**c**) One of the structural adaptations seen among archaeans. Many of these prokaryotic species live in extremely hostile habitats, such as the ones thought to have prevailed when life originated. Most archaeans and some bacteria have a dense lattice of proteins that are anchored to the outer surface of their plasma membrane. In some species, the unique composition of the lattice may help the cell withstand extreme conditions in the environment. For instance, we find such lattices on archaeans living in near-boiling, mineral-rich water spewing from hydrothermal vents on the ocean floor.

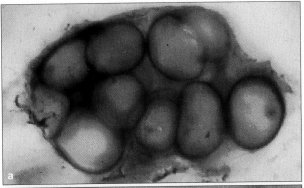

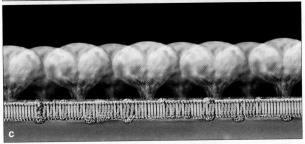

of protein filaments just under the plasma membrane reinforce the cell's shape.

Sticky polysaccharides often envelop bacterial cell walls. They let cells attach to such interesting surfaces as river rocks, teeth, and the vagina. Many disease-causing (pathogenic) bacteria have a thick protective capsule of jellylike polysaccharides around their wall.

Cell walls are permeable to dissolved substances, which cross them on the way to and from the plasma membrane. Some eukaryotic cells also have a wall, but it differs structurally from prokaryotic cell wall.

Many species have one or more bacterial flagella (singular, flagellum). These motile structures do not have a core of microtubules, as eukaryotic cells do (Section 4.11). They start at a tiny rotary motor in the plasma membrane and extend past the cell wall. They help move cells through fluid habitats, such as body fluids of host animals. Many bacteria also have pili (singular, pilus). These protein filaments help the cell cling to surfaces. A "sex" pilus latches on to another cell, then shortens. The attached cell is reeled in, and genetic material is transferred into it (Section 21.3).

As in eukaryotic cells, the plasma membrane of bacteria and archaeans selectively controls the flow of substances into and out of the cytoplasm. Its lipid bilayer bristles with protein channels, transporters, and receptors, and it incorporates built-in machinery for reactions. For example, the plasma membrane in photosynthetic bacterial species has organized arrays of proteins that capture light energy and convert it to bond energy of ATP, which helps build sugars.

The cytoplasm contains many ribosomes on which polypeptide chains are built. DNA is concentrated in an irregularly shaped region of cytoplasm called the nucleoid. Prokaryotic cells inherit one molecule of DNA that is circular, not linear. We call it a bacterial chromosome. The cytoplasm of some species also has plasmids: far smaller circles of DNA that carry just a

few genes. Typically, plasmid genes confer selective advantages, such as antibiotic resistance.

One more intriguing point: In cyanobacteria, part of the plasma membrane projects into the cytoplasm and is repeatedly folded back on itself. As it happens, pigments and other molecules of photosynthesis are embedded in the membrane—as they are in the inner membrane of chloroplasts. Is this a sign that ancient cyanobacteria were the forerunners of chloroplasts? Section 20.4 looks at this possibility. It is one aspect of a remarkable story about how prokaryotes gave rise to all protists, plants, fungi, and animals.

Bacteria and archaeans are two major groups of prokaryotic cells. These cells do not have a nucleus. Most have a cell wall around their plasma membrane. The wall is permeable, and it reinforces and imparts shape to the cell body.

Although structurally simple, prokaryotic cells as a group show the most metabolic diversity. Metabolic activities that are similar to ones occurring in eukaryotic organelles occur at the bacterial plasma membrane or in the cytoplasm.

4.4 Introducing Eukaryotic Cells

All cells synthesize, store, degrade, and transport diverse substances, but eukaryotic cells compartmentalize these operations. Their interior is subdivided into a nucleus and other organelles that have specialized functions.

Like prokaryotes, eukaryotic cells have ribosomes in their cytoplasm. Unlike prokaryotes, they have a well-developed, dynamic "skeleton" of proteins. They all start out life with a nucleus and other membrane-bounded sacs called **organelles**. *Eu–* means true; and *karyon*, meaning kernel, is taken to mean a nucleus. Figures 4.13 and 4.14 show two eukaryotic cells.

What advantages do organelles offer? Their outer membrane encloses and sustains a microenvironment for cell activities. Membrane components control the types and amounts of substances entering or leaving. They concentrate some substances for reactions and isolate or dispose of incompatible or toxic types.

For instance, organelles called mitochondria and chloroplasts concentrate hydrogen ions in a sac, then let them flow out in a way that forms ATP. Enzymes in lysosomes digest large organic compounds. They would even digest the cell if they were to escape.

Also, just as organ systems interact in controlled ways that can keep a whole body running smoothly, specialized organelles interact in ways that help keep a whole cell functioning as it should.

As another example, substances are modified and transported in a specific direction through an entire series of organelles. One series, the *secretory* pathway, moves new polypeptide chains from some ribosomes through ER and Golgi bodies, then on to the plasma membrane for release from the cell. Another series, an *endocytic* pathway, moves ions and molecules into the cytoplasm. In both cases, tiny sacs called **vesicles** act like taxis and move substances from one organelle to the next in line. The sacs form by pinching off from organelle membranes or the plasma membrane.

Figure 4.15 is a visual overview of components that are typical of plant and animal cells.

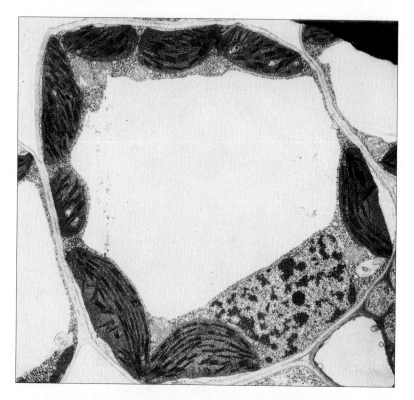

Figure 4.13 Transmission electron micrograph of a plant cell, cross-section. This is a photosynthetic cell from a blade of timothy grass.

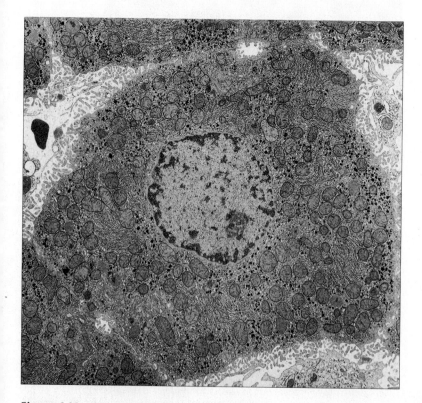

Figure 4.14 Transmission electron micrograph of an animal cell, cross-section. This is one cell from a rat liver.

All eukaryotic cells start out life with a nucleus, ribosomes, and a cytoskeleton. Specialized cells typically incorporate many more kinds of organelles as well as cell structures.

Organelles physically separate chemical reactions, many of which are incompatible.

Organelles organize metabolic events, as when different kinds interact in assembling, storing, or moving substances along pathways to and from the plasma membrane or to specific destinations in the cytoplasm.

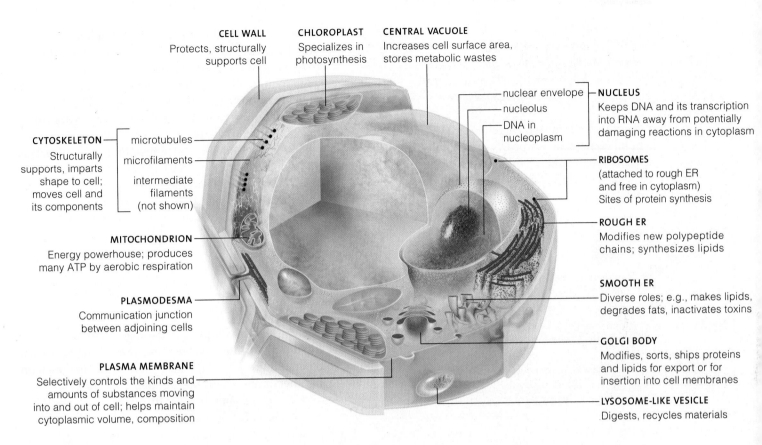

CELL WALL
Protects, structurally supports cell

CHLOROPLAST
Specializes in photosynthesis

CENTRAL VACUOLE
Increases cell surface area, stores metabolic wastes

nuclear envelope
nucleolus
DNA in nucleoplasm

NUCLEUS
Keeps DNA and its transcription into RNA away from potentially damaging reactions in cytoplasm

CYTOSKELETON
Structurally supports, imparts shape to cell; moves cell and its components

microtubules
microfilaments
intermediate filaments (not shown)

RIBOSOMES
(attached to rough ER and free in cytoplasm)
Sites of protein synthesis

ROUGH ER
Modifies new polypeptide chains; synthesizes lipids

MITOCHONDRION
Energy powerhouse; produces many ATP by aerobic respiration

SMOOTH ER
Diverse roles; e.g., makes lipids, degrades fats, inactivates toxins

PLASMODESMA
Communication junction between adjoining cells

GOLGI BODY
Modifies, sorts, ships proteins and lipids for export or for insertion into cell membranes

PLASMA MEMBRANE
Selectively controls the kinds and amounts of substances moving into and out of cell; helps maintain cytoplasmic volume, composition

LYSOSOME-LIKE VESICLE
Digests, recycles materials

a Typical plant cell components.

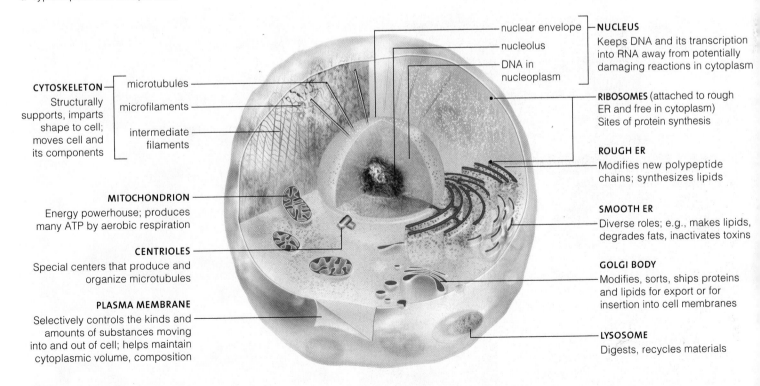

nuclear envelope
nucleolus
DNA in nucleoplasm

NUCLEUS
Keeps DNA and its transcription into RNA away from potentially damaging reactions in cytoplasm

CYTOSKELETON
Structurally supports, imparts shape to cell; moves cell and its components

microtubules
microfilaments
intermediate filaments

RIBOSOMES (attached to rough ER and free in cytoplasm)
Sites of protein synthesis

ROUGH ER
Modifies new polypeptide chains; synthesizes lipids

MITOCHONDRION
Energy powerhouse; produces many ATP by aerobic respiration

SMOOTH ER
Diverse roles; e.g., makes lipids, degrades fats, inactivates toxins

CENTRIOLES
Special centers that produce and organize microtubules

GOLGI BODY
Modifies, sorts, ships proteins and lipids for export or for insertion into cell membranes

PLASMA MEMBRANE
Selectively controls the kinds and amounts of substances moving into and out of cell; helps maintain cytoplasmic volume, composition

LYSOSOME
Digests, recycles materials

b Typical animal cell components.

Figure 4.15 *Animated!* Organelles and structures typical of (**a**) plant cells and (**b**) animal cells.

4.5 The Nucleus

Constructing, operating, and reproducing cells cannot be done without carbohydrates, lipids, proteins, and nucleic acids. It takes a class of proteins—enzymes—to build and use these molecules. Instructions for building those proteins are encoded in DNA.

Eukaryotic cells have their genetic material distributed among some number of DNA molecules of different lengths. For instance, the nucleus of a human body cell normally holds forty-six DNA molecules. If you could stretch them out end to end, the line would be about 2 meters (6–1/2 feet) long. That is a lot of DNA—a lot more than the one circular molecule found in prokaryotic cells, which are smaller and less complex.

The nucleus has two main functions. First, it keeps the DNA from getting tangled with the cytoplasmic machinery and isolates it from potentially damaging reactions. Second, the outer membranes of a nucleus are a boundary where cells control the movement of substances to and from the cytoplasm. This structural and functional separation makes it far easier to keep DNA molecules organized and to copy them before a cell divides.

Figure 4.16 shows the components of the nucleus. Table 4.1 lists their functions.

NUCLEAR ENVELOPE

The **nuclear envelope** is a double-membrane system in which two lipid bilayers are pressed against each other (Figure 4.17). Its outer membrane merges with the membrane of ER, an organelle in the cytoplasm. Like rough ER membranes, this outer membrane has a profusion of ribosomes bound to it.

Table 4.1 Components of the Nucleus

Nuclear envelope	Pore-riddled double-membrane system that selectively controls which substances enter and leave the nucleus
Nucleoplasm	Semifluid interior portion of the nucleus
Nucleolus	Rounded mass of proteins and copies of genes for ribosomal RNA used to construct ribosomal subunits
Chromosome	One DNA molecule and the many proteins that are intimately associated with it
Chromatin	Total collection of all DNA molecules and their associated proteins in the nucleus

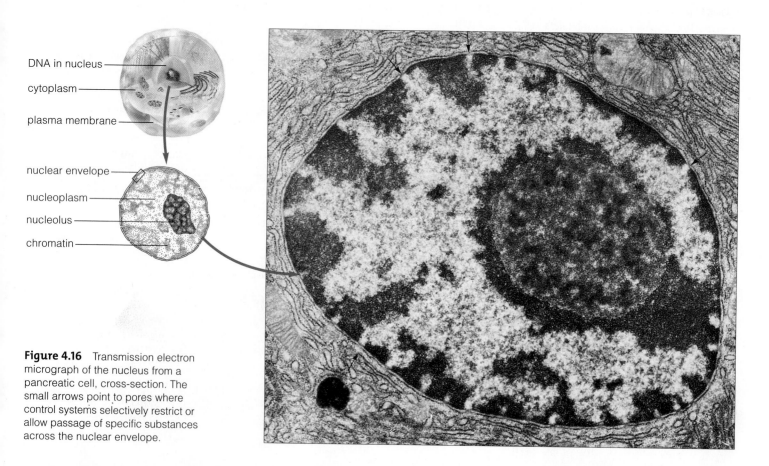

DNA in nucleus
cytoplasm
plasma membrane

nuclear envelope
nucleoplasm
nucleolus
chromatin

Figure 4.16 Transmission electron micrograph of the nucleus from a pancreatic cell, cross-section. The small arrows point to pores where control systems selectively restrict or allow passage of specific substances across the nuclear envelope.

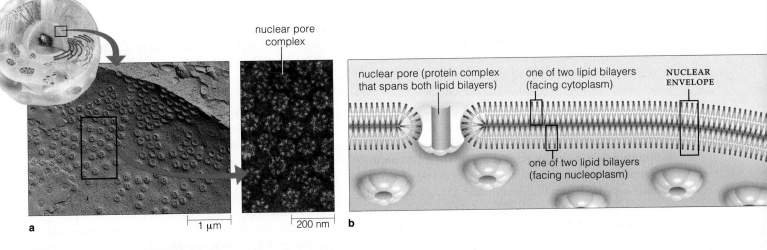

nuclear pore complex

nuclear pore (protein complex that spans both lipid bilayers)

one of two lipid bilayers (facing cytoplasm)

NUCLEAR ENVELOPE

one of two lipid bilayers (facing nucleoplasm)

1 μm   200 nm

a   b

Figure 4.17 *Animated!* Proteins of the nuclear envelope. (**a**) *Left*, the outer surface of a nuclear envelope was frozen and then fractured. The envelope split apart, revealing the pores that span the two lipid bilayers. *Right*, each pore across the envelope is an organized cluster of membrane proteins. It permits the selective transport of substances into and out of the nucleus. (**b**) Sketch of the nuclear envelope's structure.

The inner surface of the nuclear envelope is bathed in a semifluid matrix called nucleoplasm. The surface has attachment sites for fibrous proteins that anchor the DNA molecules and help keep them organized.

Membrane proteins that span both bilayers have diverse functions. Many are receptors or transporters; many others form pore complexes (Figure 4.17). Ions and small, water-soluble molecules cross the nuclear envelope only at the pores, which span both bilayers.

NUCLEOLUS

The ribosomes mentioned earlier consist of subunits that are constructed in the nucleus from ribosomal RNA and proteins. The construction site is a **nucleolus** (plural, nucleoli). At least one occurs in all nuclei. It is a dense mass of proteins and multiple copies of genes coding for ribosomal RNA. The subunits do not join together until after they move out through pores and enter the cytoplasm. One large and one small subunit join as an intact ribosome during protein synthesis.

GRAINY, THREADLIKE, RODLIKE—NUCLEAR DNA'S CHANGING APPEARANCE

When a eukaryotic cell is not dividing, you cannot see individual DNA molecules, nor can you see that each consists of two strands twisted together. The nucleus just looks grainy, as in Figure 4.16. When the cell is preparing to divide, however, it copies all of its DNA. Soon, the duplicated molecules become visible as long threads that condense further into compact structures.

Early microscopists named that seemingly grainy substance chromatin and called the condensed forms chromosomes. Today we define **chromatin** as the cell's collection of DNA and all proteins associated with it. A **chromosome** is a double-stranded DNA molecule and its associated proteins, regardless of whether it is in dispersed or condensed form:

one chromosome (one dispersed DNA molecule + proteins; not duplicated)

one chromosome (threadlike and now duplicated; two DNA molecules + proteins)

one chromosome (duplicated and also condensed tightly)

In other words, a chromosome's appearance changes over the life of a eukaryotic cell. In chapters to come, you will be looking at different aspects of eukaryotic chromosomes, so you may find it useful to remember that chromosome structure is dynamic, not fixed.

The nucleus has an outer envelope of two lipid bilayers. The envelope keeps DNA molecules separated from the cytoplasmic machinery and controls access to a cell's hereditary information.

With this separation, DNA is easier to keep organized and to copy before a parent cell divides into daughter cells.

Pores across the nuclear envelope help control the passage of many substances between the nucleus and cytoplasm.

At different stages in the life of a eukaryotic cell, nuclear DNA looks different; its structural organization changes.

4.6 The Endomembrane System

*New polypeptide chains fold and twist into proteins. Some proteins are used at once or stockpiled in the cytoplasm. Others enter the **endomembrane system**—ER, Golgi bodies, and vesicles. All proteins to be exported or inserted into cell membranes pass through this system (Figure 4.18).*

ENDOPLASMIC RETICULUM

Endoplasmic reticulum, or **ER**, is a flattened channel that starts at the nuclear envelope and folds back on itself repeatedly in the cytoplasm. At various points inside the channel, many polypeptide chains become modified into final proteins, and lipids are assembled.

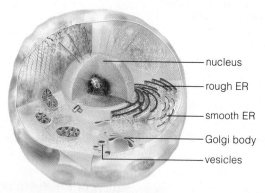

nucleus

rough ER

smooth ER

Golgi body

vesicles

Vesicles that pinch off from ER membranes deliver many of the proteins and lipids to Golgi bodies.

Rough ER has many ribosomes attached to its outer surface (Figure 4.18c). Many of the polypeptide chains being translated on ribosomes have an entry code—a sequence of fifteen to twenty amino acids—that lets them cross the ER membrane and enter the channel, where enzymes may modify them. Other chains do not get all the way across; they become inserted into the ER membrane, as diverse membrane proteins.

Cells that make, store, and secrete proteins have a lot of rough ER. For instance, your pancreas has ER-rich cells that make and secrete digestive enzymes.

Smooth ER is ribosome-free (Figure 4.18d). It makes lipid molecules that become part of cell membranes. The ER also takes part in fatty acid breakdown and degrades some toxins. Sarcoplasmic reticulum, a type of smooth ER, functions in muscle contraction.

GOLGI BODIES

Patches of ER membrane bulge and break away as vesicles, each with proteins inside or incorporated in

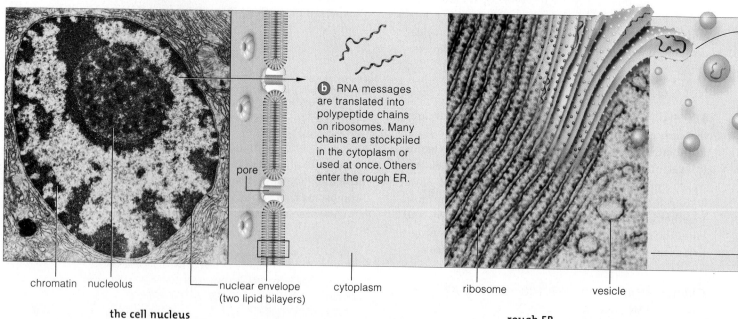

b RNA messages are translated into polypeptide chains on ribosomes. Many chains are stockpiled in the cytoplasm or used at once. Others enter the rough ER.

pore

chromatin   nucleolus

nuclear envelope (two lipid bilayers)

cytoplasm

ribosome

vesicle

the cell nucleus

rough ER

a DNA instructions for making proteins are transcribed in the nucleus and moved to the cytoplasm. RNAs are the messengers and protein builders.

c Flattened sacs of rough ER form one continuous channel between the nucleus and smooth ER. Polypeptide chains that enter the channel undergo modification. They will be inserted into organelle membranes or will be secreted from the cell.

Figure 4.18 *Animated!* Endomembrane system. With this system's components, many proteins are processed, lipids are assembled, and both products are sorted and shipped to cellular destinations or to the plasma membrane for export.

its membrane. Many vesicles fuse with **Golgi bodies**, organelles in which the membrane channel folds back on itself like a stack of pancakes (Figure 4.18*e*). Golgi bodies attach sugar side chains to proteins and lipids that they received from the ER. They also cleave some proteins. Finished products are packaged in vesicles.

DIVERSE MEMBRANOUS SACS

Vesicles, again, are tiny sacs that form as buds from the ER, Golgi bodies, and plasma membrane. Many act as storage sacs in the cytoplasm. Others transport substances to or from another organelle or the plasma membrane. As Section 5.6 explains, *exocytic* vesicles release substances to the outside. *Endocytic* ones form at the plasma membrane. They enclose substances at the surface, then sink through the cytoplasm.

Lysosomes are vesicles that bud from Golgi bodies and take part in intracellular digestion. They store inactive forms of diverse hydrolytic enzymes that can digest almost all biological molecules. The enzymes are activated when another vesicle moves through the cytoplasm and fuses with the lysosome. The contents of the vesicle are digested into bits. As you will see in Section 5.6, that is what happens after macrophages have engulfed cells, particles, and assorted debris.

Peroxisomes hold enzymes that digest fatty acids, amino acids, and hydrogen peroxide (H_2O_2), a toxic metabolic product. Enzymes convert H_2O_2 to water and oxygen or use it in reactions that degrade alcohol and other toxins. Drink alcohol, and peroxisomes in liver and kidney cells usually degrade nearly half of it.

Vesicles also fuse and form larger membranous sacs, or vacuoles. The central vacuole of mature plant cells, described in Section 4.8, is one of them.

Inside the highly folded channel formed by ER membranes, many new polypeptide chains are modified and lipids are assembled. In the channels formed by Golgi membranes, many of the proteins and lipids are further modified and packaged for export or shipment to locations in the cell.

Vesicles are small sacs that help integrate cell activities. Many kinds store or transport substances. Lysosomes and peroxisomes start out as vesicles and become organelles of digestion in the cytoplasm.

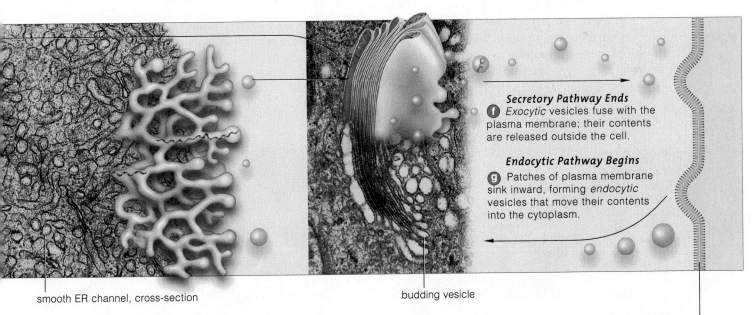

smooth ER channel, cross-section

budding vesicle

smooth ER

d Some proteins in the channel continue on to smooth ER, becoming membrane proteins or smooth ER enzymes. Some of these enzymes make lipids and inactive toxins.

Golgi body

e A Golgi body receives, processes, and repackages substances that arrive in vesicles from the ER. Different vesicles transport the substances to other parts of the cell.

Secretory Pathway Ends
f *Exocytic* vesicles fuse with the plasma membrane; their contents are released outside the cell.

Endocytic Pathway Begins
g Patches of plasma membrane sink inward, forming *endocytic* vesicles that move their contents into the cytoplasm.

plasma membrane

h Exocytic vesicles release cell products and wastes to the outside. Endocytic vesicles move nutrients, water, and other substances into the cytoplasm from outside (Section 5.6).

4.7 Mitochondria

LINK TO
SECTION
3.7

Recall, from Section 3.7, that ATP is an energy carrier. It delivers energy, in the form of phosphate-group transfers, that drives reactions at sites throughout the cell. Without energy deliveries from ATP, cells could not grow, survive, or reproduce. ATP formation is essential for life.

The **mitochondrion** (plural, mitochondria) is a type of organelle that specializes in ATP formation. Reactions in this organelle help cells extract more energy from organic compounds than they can get by any other means. The reactions, called *aerobic* respiration, require free oxygen. With each breath, you take in oxygen mainly for mitochondria in your trillions of cells.

Typical mitochondria are 1 to 4 micrometers long; a few are 10 micrometers long. Some are branching. These organelles change shape, split in two, and fuse together. Figure 4.19 shows an example.

Each mitochondrion has an outer membrane and another one inside that most often is highly folded (Figure 4.19). The membrane arrangement creates two compartments. Hydrogen ions become stockpiled in the outer compartment. The ions then flow to the inner compartment in a controlled way. The energy inherent in the flow drives ATP formation.

No prokaryotic cells have mitochondria. Nearly all eukaryotic cells do. A single-celled yeast might have only one. Cells that have huge demands for energy may have a thousand or more. Skeletal muscle cells are one example. Liver cells, too, have a profusion of mitochondria. Take a closer look at Figure 4.14. That micrograph alone should tell you that the liver is an energy-demanding organ.

In size and biochemistry, mitochondria resemble bacteria. Like bacteria, they have their own DNA, and they divide on their own. They have some ribosomes. Did mitochondria evolve by way of endosymbiosis in ancient prokaryotic cells? By this theory, one cell was engulfed by another cell, or entered it as an internal parasite, but it escaped digestion. That cell and its descendants kept their plasma membrane intact and reproduced in the host. In time, they became protected, permanent residents. Structures and functions once required for independent life were no longer essential and were lost. Later descendants evolved into double-membraned mitochondria. We return to their possible endosymbiotic origins in Section 20.4.

All organisms require ATP, which carries energy (in the form of phosphate bonds) from one reaction site to another. ATP drives nearly all cell activities.

The organelles called mitochondria are the ATP-producing powerhouses of all eukaryotic cells.

Energy-releasing reactions proceed at the compartmented, internal membrane system of mitochondria. The reactions, which require oxygen, produce far more ATP than can be produced by any other cellular reaction.

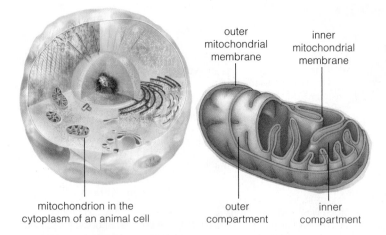

outer
mitochondrial
membrane

inner
mitochondrial
membrane

mitochondrion in the
cytoplasm of an animal cell

outer
compartment

inner
compartment

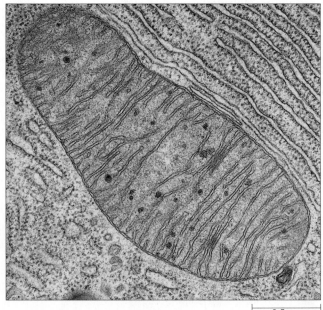

0.5 µm

Figure 4.19 Sketch and transmission electron micrograph, thin section, of a typical mitochondrion. This organelle specializes in forming large quantities of ATP, the main carrier of energy between reaction sites in cells. ATP formation in mitochondria cannot occur without free oxygen.

4.8 Specialized Plant Organelles

Two kinds of organelles are prominent in many plant cells. They are plastids, such as chloroplasts, and central vacuoles.

CHLOROPLASTS AND OTHER PLASTIDS

Plastids are organelles that function in photosynthesis or storage in plants. Three types are common in plant tissues: chloroplasts, chromoplasts, and amyloplasts.

Chloroplasts are organelles that are specialized for photosynthesis. Most have oval or disk shapes. Two outer membranes enclose their semifluid interior, the stroma (Figure 4.20). In the stroma, a third membrane forms a single compartment that is commonly folded in intricate ways. Often the folds resemble a stack of flattened disks, called a granum (plural, grana).

Photosynthesis proceeds at the innermost, *thylakoid* membrane, which incorporates light-trapping pigments and other proteins. The most abundant photosynthetic pigments are chlorophylls, which reflect green light. Many kinds of accessory pigments assist chlorophylls in capturing light energy. The energy drives reactions in which ATP and an enzyme helper, NADPH, form. The ATP and NADPH are then used at sites in the stroma where sugars, starch, and other compounds are assembled. The new starch molecules may briefly accumulate in the stroma, as starch grains.

In many ways, chloroplasts are like photosynthetic bacteria. Like mitochondria, they may have evolved by endosymbiosis (Section 20.4).

Chromoplasts have no chlorophylls. They have an abundance of carotenoids, the source of red-to-yellow colors of many flowers, autumn leaves, ripe fruits, and carrots and other roots. The colors attract animals that pollinate the plants or disperse seeds.

Amyloplasts are pigment-free. They typically store starch grains. They are notably abundant in cells of stems, potato tubers (underground stems), and seeds.

CENTRAL VACUOLES

Many mature, living plant cells contain a fluid-filled **central vacuole**. This organelle stores amino acids, sugars, ions, and toxic wastes. Also, it expands during growth and increases fluid pressure on the pliable cell wall. The cell surface area is forced to increase, which favors absorption of water and other substances. Often the central vacuole takes up 50 to 90 percent of the cell's interior, with cytoplasm confined to a narrow zone in between this large organelle and the plasma membrane (Figures 4.15*a* and 4.20).

Photosynthetic cells of plants and many protists contain chloroplasts and other plastids that function in food production and storage.

Many plant cells have a central vacuole. When this storage vacuole enlarges during growth, cells are forced to enlarge, which increases the surface area available for absorption.

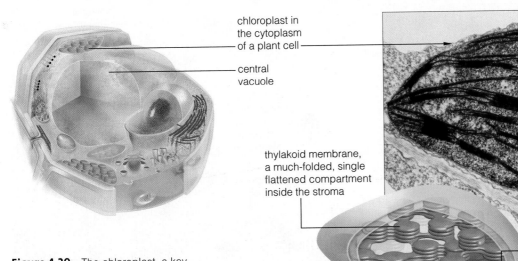

chloroplast in the cytoplasm of a plant cell

central vacuole

thylakoid membrane, a much-folded, single flattened compartment inside the stroma

two outer membranes

stroma (semifluid interior)

Figure 4.20 The chloroplast, a key defining character of all photosynthetic eukaryotic cells. *Right*, transmission electron micrograph of a chloroplast from corn (*Zea mays*), thin section.

4.9 Cell Surface Specializations

Turn now to a brief glimpse into some specialized surface structures of eukaryotic cells. Many of these architectural marvels are made primarily of cell secretions. Others are clusters of membrane proteins that connect neighboring cells, structurally and functionally.

EUKARYOTIC CELL WALLS

Single-celled eukaryotic species are directly exposed to the environment. Many have a **cell wall** around the plasma membrane. A cell wall protects and physically supports a cell, and imparts shape to it. The wall is porous, so water and solutes easily move to and from the plasma membrane. Any cell would die without these exchanges. Different plant cells form one or two walls around their plasma membrane. Cells of many protists and fungi have a wall. Animal cells do not.

Consider the growing parts of multicelled plants. New cells are secreting molecules of pectin and other gluelike polysaccharides, which form a matrix around them. They also secrete ropelike strands of cellulose molecules into the matrix. These materials make up the plant cell's **primary wall** (Figure 4.21). The sticky primary wall cements abutting cells together. Being thin and pliable, it allows the cell to enlarge under the pressure of incoming water.

Cells that have only a thin primary wall retain the capacity to divide or change shape as they grow and develop. Many types stop enlarging when they are mature. Such cells secrete material on the primary wall's inner surface. These deposits form a lignified, rigid **secondary wall** that reinforces cell shape (Figure 4.21d). The secondary wall deposits are extensive and contribute more to structural support.

In woody plants, up to 25 percent of the secondary wall is made of lignin. This organic compound makes plant parts more waterproof, less susceptible to plant-attacking organisms, and stronger.

At plant surfaces exposed to air, waxes and other cell secretions build up as a protective cuticle. This semitransparent surface covering limits water losses on hot, dry days (Figure 4.22a).

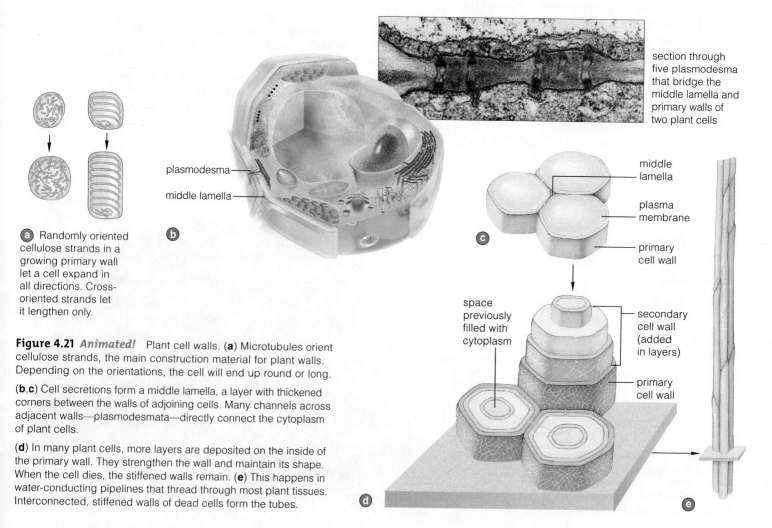

section through five plasmodesma that bridge the middle lamella and primary walls of two plant cells

plasmodesma

middle lamella

(a) Randomly oriented cellulose strands in a growing primary wall let a cell expand in all directions. Cross-oriented strands let it lengthen only.

middle lamella

plasma membrane

primary cell wall

space previously filled with cytoplasm

secondary cell wall (added in layers)

primary cell wall

Figure 4.21 *Animated!* Plant cell walls. **(a)** Microtubules orient cellulose strands, the main construction material for plant walls. Depending on the orientations, the cell will end up round or long.

(b,c) Cell secretions form a middle lamella, a layer with thickened corners between the walls of adjoining cells. Many channels across adjacent walls—plasmodesmata—directly connect the cytoplasm of plant cells.

(d) In many plant cells, more layers are deposited on the inside of the primary wall. They strengthen the wall and maintain its shape. When the cell dies, the stiffened walls remain. **(e)** This happens in water-conducting pipelines that thread through most plant tissues. Interconnected, stiffened walls of dead cells form the tubes.

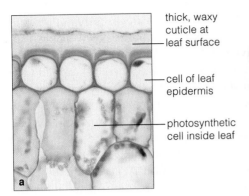

thick, waxy
cuticle at
leaf surface

cell of leaf
epidermis

photosynthetic
cell inside leaf

a

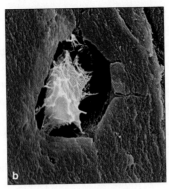

b

Figure 4.22 (**a**) Section through a plant cuticle, a surface covering made of cell secretions.

(**b**) A living cell imprisoned in hardened bone tissue, the stuff of vertebrate skeletons.

MATRIXES BETWEEN ANIMAL CELLS

Animal cells have no cell walls. Intervening between many of them are matrixes made of cell secretions and of materials absorbed from the surroundings. For example, the cartilage at the knobby ends of leg bones contains scattered cells and protein fibers embedded in a ground substance of firm polysaccharides. Living cells also secrete the extensive, hardened matrix that we call bone tissue (Figure 4.22*b*).

CELL JUNCTIONS

Even when a wall or some other structure imprisons a cell in its own secretions, the cell interacts with the outside world at its plasma membrane. In multicelled species, structures extend into neighboring cells or into a matrix. **Cell junctions** are molecular structures where a cell sends or receives signals or materials, or recognizes and glues itself to cells of the same type.

In plants, for instance, channels extend across the primary wall of adjacent living cells and interconnect the cytoplasm of both (Figure 4.21*b*). Each channel is a plasmodesma (plural, plasmodesmata). Substances flow quickly from cell to cell across these junctions.

In most tissues of animals, three types of cell-to-cell junctions are common (Figure 4.23). *Tight* junctions link the cells of most body tissues, including epithelia that line outer surfaces, internal cavities, and organs. These junctions seal abutting cells together so water-soluble substances cannot leak between them. That is why gastric fluid does not leak across the stomach lining and damage internal tissues. *Adhering* junctions occur in skin, the heart, and other organs subjected to continual stretching. At *gap* junctions, the cytoplasm of certain kinds of adjacent cells connect directly. Gap junctions function as open channels for a rapid flow of substances, most notably in heart muscle.

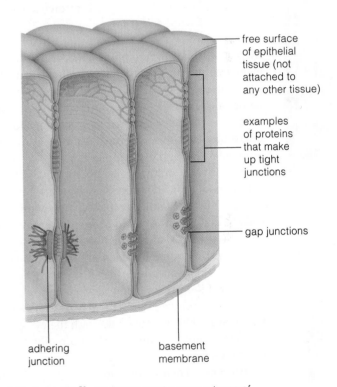

free surface
of epithelial
tissue (not
attached to
any other tissue)

examples
of proteins
that make
up tight
junctions

gap junctions

adhering
junction

basement
membrane

Figure 4.23 *Animated!* The three most common types of cell junctions in animal tissues.

A variety of protist, plant, and fungal cells have a porous wall that surrounds the plasma membrane.

Young plant cells have a thin primary wall pliable enough to permit expansion. Some mature cells also form a lignin-reinforced secondary wall that provides structural support.

Animal cells have no walls, but they and many other cells often secrete substances that form matrixes between cells. In multicelled species, different junctions commonly serve as structural and functional connections between cells.

4.10 Even Cells Have a Skeleton

What does the word "skeleton" mean to you? A collection of bones, such as a rib cage? That is one kind of skeleton in nature. However, anything that forms a structural framework is a skeleton—and cells, too, have one.

COMPONENTS OF THE CYTOSKELETON

The **cytoskeleton** of eukaryotic cells is an organized system of protein filaments that extends between the nucleus and plasma membrane. Different portions of it reinforce, organize, and move internal cell parts or the cell body. Many parts are permanent, and others form only at certain times in the life of a cell.

Microtubules and **microfilaments** are two classes of cytoskeletal elements in nearly all eukaryotic cells. Some cells also have ropelike **intermediate filaments** (Figures 4.24 and 4.25).

Microtubules   Microtubules, the largest cytoskeletal elements, help keep organelles and cell structures in place or move them to new locations. For instance, before a cell divides, microtubules form a spindle that harnesses chromosomes and moves them about. Other microtubules move chloroplasts, vesicles, and other organelles through the cytoplasm.

In plant and animal cells, microtubules are hollow cylinders of tubulin monomers (Figure 4.24a). Tubulin consists of two chemically distinct polypeptide chains, each folded into a rounded shape. As a microtubule is being assembled, all of its monomers are oriented in the same direction. The assembly pattern puts slightly different chemical properties at opposite ends of the cylinder. Like bricks being stacked into a new wall, monomers join the cylinder's *plus* (fast-growing) end, which at first grows freely through the cytoplasm.

Microtubules of animal cells normally grow in all directions from small patches of dense material called centrosomes. Their *minus* (slow-growing) ends remain

anchored in it. Microtubules can abruptly fall apart in controlled ways; they are not permanently stable.

In any given interval, some of the microtubules are being allowed to disassemble. Others get capped with proteins that stabilize them. For instance, microtubules in the advancing end of an amoeba stay intact when the cell is hot on a chemical trail to a potential meal. Nothing is stimulating microtubules to grow in that cell's trailing end, so they are allowed to fall apart.

Some plants make poisons that act on microtubules of plant-eating animals. By binding to tubulins, the poisons make microtubules fall apart and stop new ones from forming. For instance, the autumn crocus (*Colchicum autumnale*) makes colchicine (Figure 4.26a). The plant has an evolved insensitivity to colchicine, which can't bind well to its own tubulins. The western yew (*Taxus brevifolia*) makes the microtubule poison taxol (Figure 4.26b). A synthetic taxol stops the growth of certain tumors. It keeps microtubule spindles from forming, and thereby suppresses the uncontrolled cell divisions that form abnormal tissue masses. Taxol has the same effect on normal cells; it is just that tumor cells divide far more often than most of them.

Microfilaments   Microfilaments are the thinnest of all cytoskeletal elements inside eukaryotic cells (Figure 4.24b). Two helically coiled polypeptide chains of actin monomers make up each filament.

Microfilaments are assembled and disassembled in controlled ways. Often they are organized in bundles or networks. As an example, just beneath the plasma membrane is a **cell cortex**: bundled up, crosslinked, and gel-like meshes of microfilaments. Some parts of the cortex reinforce a cell's shape. Others reconfigure the surface. For instance, during animal cell division, a ring of microfilaments around the cell's midsection contracts and pinches the cell in two. Microfilaments also anchor membrane proteins and are components of muscle contraction. In some large cells, *cytoplasmic streaming* gets under way as microfilament meshes loosen up. Local gel-like regions become more fluid and flow strongly, thereby redistributing substances and cell components through the cell interior.

Myosin and Other Accessory Proteins   Genes for tubulin and actin were not drastically modified over time; they have been highly conserved in the DNA. All eukaryotic cells make similar forms of these monomers for microtubules and microfilaments. In spite of the structural uniformity, microtubules and microfilaments have different functions, thanks to other proteins that associate with them.

tubulin subunits

a   25 nm

actin subunit

b   5–7 nm

one polypeptide chain

8–12 nm

c

Figure 4.24 Structural arrangement of subunits in (**a**) microtubules, (**b**) microfilaments, and (**c**) one of the intermediate filaments.

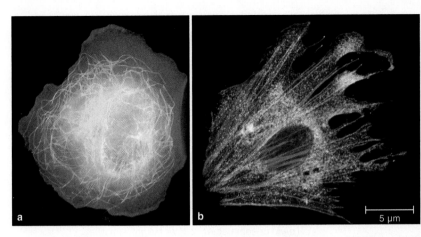

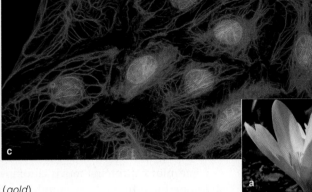

Figure 4.25 Cells stained to reveal the cytoskeleton. (**a**) Distribution of microtubules (*gold*) and actin filaments (*red*) in a pancreatic epithelial cell. This cell secretes bicarbonate, which functions in digestion by neutralizing stomach acid. The *blue* region is DNA. (**b**) Actin filaments (*red*) and accessory proteins (*green, blue*) help new epithelial cells such as this one migrate to proper locations in tissues as human embryos are developing. (**c**) Intermediate filaments of keratin (*red*) of cultured kangaroo rat cells. Each *blue*-stained organelle is a nucleus.

Figure 4.26 Two sources of microtubule poisons: (**a**) Autumn crocus, *Colchicum autumnale*. (**b**) Western yew, *Taxus brevifolia*.

For example, as you will read in the next section, kinesin and myosin are two kinds of *motor* proteins. Inputs of ATP energy make them move along tracks of cytoskeletal elements and put cell components in new locations. As another example, the *crosslinking* proteins interconnect microfilaments at the cell cortex.

Intermediate Filaments Intermediate filaments are between microtubules and microfilaments in size. They are eight to twelve nanometers wide and are the most stable elements of some cytoskeletons (Figure 4.25c). Six known groups strengthen and maintain the shape of cells or cell parts. For example, lamins help form a basketlike mesh that reinforces the nucleus. They anchor adjoining actin and myosin filaments as units of contraction inside muscle cells. Desmins and vimentins help hold these contractile units in position. Different cytokeratins reinforce cells that make nails, claws, horns, and hairs. Intermediate filaments may reinforce the nuclear envelope of all eukaryotic cells.

Different animal cells have different intermediate filaments in their cytoplasm. Because each type of cell contains one or at most two kinds, researchers can use these intermediate filaments to identify which type of cell it is. This typing is a useful tool in diagnosing the tissue origin of different forms of cancerous cells.

WHAT ABOUT PROKARYOTIC CELLS?

Unlike eukaryotic cells, bacteria and archaeans do not have a well-developed cytoskeleton. Until recently, we thought they did not have any cytoskeletal elements. However, reinforcing filaments have been identified in certain bacteria. What is more, the filaments are made of protein subunits that are a lot like tubulin and actin. Also, their repetitive pattern of assembly is similar to the assembly patterns for microtubules and microfilaments in eukaryotic cells.

For instance, just beneath the plasma membrane of rod-shaped bacterial cells, protein monomers (MreB) form filaments that help determine cell shape. These filaments, which are structurally like one of the actins, suggest that the eukaryotic cytoskeleton had its origin in ancestral prokaryotes.

A cytoskeleton is the basis of cell shape, internal structure, and movement. In eukaryotic cells, its components are microtubules, microfilaments, and in some cell types, intermediate filaments. Accessory proteins associate with these filaments and extend their range of functions.

Microtubules, cylinders of tubulin monomers, organize the cell interior and have roles in moving cell components.

Microfilaments consist of two helically coiled polypeptide chains of actin monomers. They form flexible, linear bundles and networks that reinforce or restructure the cell surface.

Intermediate filaments strengthen and maintain cell shapes. Some are present only in certain animal cells. Others may help reinforce the nuclear envelope of all eukaryotic cells.

Cytoskeletal elements similar to the microtubules and microfilaments have been identified in prokaryotic cells.

4.11 How Do Cells Move?

The skeleton of eukaryotic cells differs notably from your skeleton in a key respect. The cytoskeleton has elements that are not permanently rigid. At prescribed times, they assemble and disassemble.

MOVING ALONG WITH MOTOR PROTEINS

Think of a train station at the busiest holiday season, and you get an idea of what goes on in cells. Many of the cell's microtubules and microfilaments are like train tracks. The kinesins, dyneins, myosins, and other motor proteins function as the freight engines (Figure 4.27). Energy from ATP fuels the movement.

Some motor proteins move chromosomes. Others slide one microtubule over another; still others inch along tracks inside nerve cells that extend from your spine to your toes. Many engines are organized one after another, and each moves a vesicle partway along the track before giving it up to the next engine in line. From dawn to dusk, kinesins inside plant cells drag chloroplasts to new positions, the better to intercept light as the angle of the sun changes overhead.

Different kinds of myosins can move structures along microfilaments or slide one microfilament over another. As Sections 37.5 and 37.6 show, muscle cells form long fibers that are functionally divided into many contractile units along their length. Each unit has many parallel rows of microfilaments and myosin filaments. Myosin activated by ATP shortens the unit by sliding the microfilaments toward the unit's center. When all units shorten, the cell shortens; it contracts.

Figure 4.27 *Animated!* Kinesin (*brown*). This motor protein inches along a microtubule and drags a vesicle (*pink*) or some other cellular freight with it.

CILIA, FLAGELLA, AND FALSE FEET

Besides moving internal parts, many cells move their body or extend parts of it. Consider **flagella** (singular, flagellum) and **cilia** (singular, cilium). Both are motile structures that project from the surface of many types of cells. Both are completely sheathed by a membrane that is an extension of the plasma membrane.

Ciliated protists swim by beating their many cilia in synchrony. Cilia in certain airways to your lungs beat nonstop. Their coordinated movement sweeps out the airborne bacteria and particles that otherwise might cause disease (Figure 4.28a). Eukaryotic flagella usually are longer and not as profuse as cilia. Many single eukaryotic cells, such as sperm, swim with the help of whiplike flagella (Figure 4.28b).

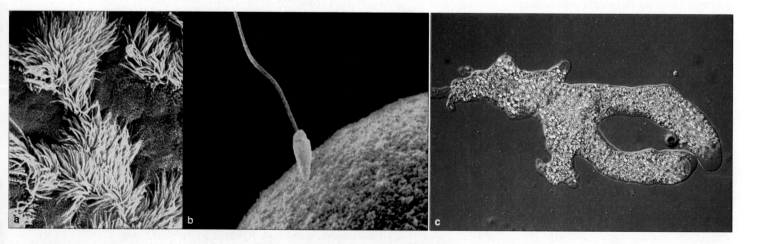

Figure 4.28 Cilia, a flagellum, and false feet. (**a**) Light micrograph of cilia (*gold*) projecting from the surface of some of the cells that line an airway to human lungs. (**b**) Scanning electron micrograph of a human sperm about to penetrate an egg. (**c**) Light micrograph of a predatory amoeba (*Chaos carolinense*) extending two pseudopods around a single-celled green alga (*Pandorina*).

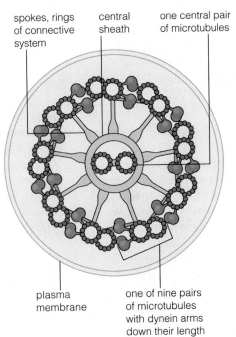

spokes, rings of connective system
central sheath
one central pair of microtubules

plasma membrane

one of nine pairs of microtubules with dynein arms down their length

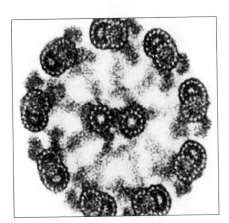

cross-section through one cilium

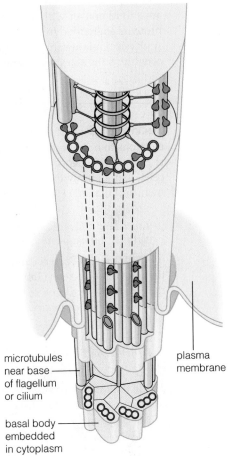

microtubules near base of flagellum or cilium

basal body embedded in cytoplasm

plasma membrane

Figure 4.29 Internal organization of cilia and flagella. Both motile structures have a 9+2 array, an internal ring of nine pairs of microtubules around one pair at the core. Spokes and linking elements connected to the array stabilize it and keep it from slipping sideways, out of alignment.

Dynein arms projecting from microtubules in the ring incorporate ATPases. Repeated phosphate-group transfers from ATP cause them to bind briefly and reversibly to the microtubule pair in front of them. Each time, the arms force the pair to slide down a bit. The short, sliding strokes occur all around the ring, down the length of the microtubule, and it makes the motile structure bend.

Extending down the length of a cilium or flagellum is a *9+2 array*. Nine pairs of microtubules form a ring around a central pair, all stabilized by protein spokes and links. First a centrosome gives rise to a **centriole**. This barrel-shaped structure produces and organizes microtubules into the 9+2 array, then it remains below the finished array as a **basal body** (Figure 4.29).

Flagella and cilia move by a sliding mechanism. All pairs of microtubules extend the same distance into the motile structure's tip. Stubby dynein arms project from each pair in the outer ring. When ATP energizes them, the arms grab the microtubule pair in front of them, tilt in a short, downward stroke, then let go. As the bound pair slides down, its arms bind the pair in front of it, forcing it to slide down also— and so on around the ring. The microtubules cannot slide too far, but each *bends* a bit. Their sliding motion is converted to a bending motion.

As one more example, macrophages and amoebas form **pseudopods**, or "false feet." These temporary, irregular lobes bulge out from the cell. They move the cell and also engulf prey or some other target (Figure 4.28c). The pseudopods advance in a steady direction as microfilaments inside them are elongating. Motor proteins that are attached to the microfilaments are dragging the plasma membrane along with them in the direction of interest.

Cell contractions and migrations, chromosome movements, and other forms of cell movements arise by interactions among organized arrays of microtubules, microfilaments, and accessory proteins.

When energized by ATP, motor proteins move in specific directions, along tracks of microtubules and microfilaments. They deliver cell components to new locations.

Interactions among cytoskeletal elements bring about the movement of the motile structures called cilia and flagella, as well as the dynamic movements of pseudopods.

Summary

Section 4.1 Cells start life with a plasma membrane, cytoplasm that contains ribosomes and other structures, and DNA in a nucleus or nucleoid. Their membranes are a lipid bilayer with diverse kinds and numbers of proteins embedded in it or positioned at its surfaces. A physical relationship, the surface-to-volume ratio, constrains the sizes and shapes of cells.

Biology Now
Use the interaction on BiologyNow to investigate the physical limits on cell size.

Section 4.2 Different microscopes use light or electrons to reveal cell shapes and structures. Microscopy reinforces the theory that all organisms are made of cells, that an individual cell has a capacity to live on its own, and that all cells now arise from preexisting cells.

Biology Now
Learn how different types of microscopes function with the animation on BiologyNow.

Section 4.3 Bacteria and archaeans are prokaryotic; they have no nucleus (Table 4.2). They are structurally the simplest cells known, but collectively they show great metabolic diversity.

Biology Now
View the animation about prokaryotic cell structure on BiologyNow.

Section 4.4 Organelles are membranous sacs that divide the interior of eukaryotic cells into functional compartments. Table 4.2 lists the major types.

Biology Now
Introduce yourself to the major types of eukaryotic organelles with the interaction on BiologyNow.

Section 4.5 The nucleus keeps DNA molecules separated from metabolic reactions in the cytoplasm and controls access to a cell's hereditary information. It helps keep the DNA organized and easier to copy before a cell divides into daughter cells.

Biology Now
Take a close-up look at the nuclear membrane with the animation on BiologyNow.

Section 4.6 In the endomembrane system's ER and Golgi bodies, new polypeptide chains are modified and lipids are assembled. Many proteins and lipids become part of membranes or packaged inside vesicles that function in transport, storage, and other cell activities.

Biology Now
Follow a path through the endomembrane system with the animation on BiologyNow.

Section 4.7 The mitochondrion is the organelle that specializes in forming many ATP by aerobic respiration.

Section 4.8 The chloroplast is an organelle that specializes in photosynthesis.

Biology Now
Look inside a chloroplast with the animation on BiologyNow.

Section 4.9 Most prokaryotic cells, cells of many protists and fungi, and all plant cells have a porous wall around their plasma membrane. In multicelled species, structural and functional connections link cells.

Biology Now
Study the structure of cell walls and junctions with the animation on BiologyNow.

Sections 4.10, 4.11 Microtubules, microfilaments, and intermediate filaments make up a cytoskeleton in eukaryotic cells. They reinforce cell shapes, organize parts, and often move cells or structures, as by flagella.

Biology Now
Learn more about cytoskeletal elements and their actions with the animation on BiologyNow.

Self-Quiz

Answers in Appendix II

1. Cell membranes consist mainly of a _____ .
   a. carbohydrate bilayer and proteins
   b. protein bilayer and phospholipids
   c. lipid bilayer and proteins

2. Identify the components of the cells shown in the two sketches at the bottom of the next page.

3. Organelles _____ .
   a. are membrane-bound compartments
   b. are typical of eukaryotic cells, not prokaryotic cells
   c. separate chemical reactions in time and space
   d. All of the above are features of organelles.

4. You will not observe _____ in animal cells.
   a. mitochondria   c. ribosomes
   b. a plasma membrane   d. a cell wall

5. Is this statement false: The plasma membrane is the outermost component of all cells. Explain your answer.

6. Unlike eukaryotic cells, prokaryotic cells _____ .
   a. lack a plasma membrane   c. have no nucleus
   b. have RNA, not DNA   d. all of the above

7. Match each cell component with its function.
   ____ mitochondrion   a. protein synthesis
   ____ chloroplast   b. initial modification of new
   ____ ribosome   polypeptide chains
   ____ rough ER   c. modification of new proteins;
   ____ Golgi body   sorting, shipping tasks
                         d. photosynthesis
                         e. formation of many ATP

Additional questions are available on **Biology Now™**

Critical Thinking

1. Why is it likely that you will never meet a two-ton amoeba on a sidewalk?

2. Your professor shows you an electron micrograph of a cell with many mitochondria, Golgi bodies, and a lot of rough ER. What kinds of cellular activities would require such an abundance of the three kinds of organelles?

3. *Kartagener syndrome* is a genetic disorder caused by a mutated form of the protein dynein. Affected people have chronically irritated sinuses, and mucus builds up in the

Table 4.2 Summary of Typical Components of Prokaryotic and Eukaryotic Cells

Cell Component	Function	Prokaryotic Bacteria, Archaea	Eukaryotic Protists	Eukaryotic Fungi	Eukaryotic Plants	Eukaryotic Animals
Cell wall	Protection, structural support	✔*	✔*	✔	✔	None
Plasma membrane	Control of substances moving into and out of cell	✔	✔	✔	✔	✔
Nucleus	Physical separation and organization of DNA	None	✔	✔	✔	✔
DNA	Encoding of hereditary information	✔	✔	✔	✔	✔
RNA	Transcription, translation of DNA messages into polypeptide chains of specific proteins	✔	✔	✔	✔	✔
Nucleolus	Assembly of subunits of ribosomes	None	✔	✔	✔	✔
Ribosome	Protein synthesis	✔	✔	✔	✔	✔
Endoplasmic reticulum (ER)	Initial modification of many of the newly forming polypeptide chains of proteins; lipid synthesis	None	✔	✔	✔	✔
Golgi body	Final modification of proteins, lipids; sorting and packaging them for use inside cell or for export	None	✔	✔	✔	✔
Lysosome	Intracellular digestion	None	✔	✔*	✔*	✔
Mitochondrion	ATP formation	**	✔	✔	✔	✔
Photosynthetic pigments	Light–energy conversion	✔*	✔*	None	✔	None
Chloroplast	Photosynthesis; some starch storage	None	✔*	None	✔	None
Central vacuole	Increasing cell surface area; storage	None	None	✔*	✔	None
Bacterial flagellum	Locomotion through fluid surroundings	✔*	None	None	None	None
Flagellum or cilium with 9+2 microtubular array	Locomotion through or motion within fluid surroundings	None	✔*	✔*	✔*	✔
Complex cytoskeleton	Cell shape; internal organization; basis of cell movement and, in many cells, locomotion	Rudimentary***	✔*	✔*	✔*	✔

* Known to be present in cells of at least some groups.

** Many groups use oxygen-requiring (aerobic) pathways of ATP formation, but mitochondria are not involved.

*** Protein filaments form a simple scaffold that helps support the cell wall in at least some species.

airways to their lungs. Bacteria form huge populations in the thick mucus. Their metabolic by-products and the inflammation they trigger combine to damage tissues. Males affected by the syndrome can produce sperm, but they are infertile (Figure 4.30). Some have still become fathers with the help of a procedure that injects sperm cells directly into eggs. Explain how an abnormal dynein molecule could cause the observed effects.

4. As they grow and develop, many kinds of plant cells form a secondary wall on the *inner* surface of the primary wall that formed earlier. Speculate on the reason why the secondary wall does not form on the outside.

5. Reflect on Table 4.2. Notice how most prokaryotes, all plant cells, and many protist and fungal cells have walls, and that animal cells have none. Why do you suppose animal cells alone do not form walls?

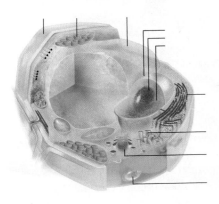
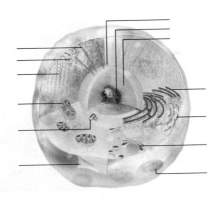
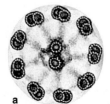
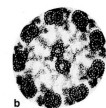

Figure 4.30 Cross-section through the flagellum of a sperm cell from (**a**) a male affected by Kartagener syndrome and (**b**) an unaffected male. Check the dynein arms projecting from the microtubule pairs.

One Bad Transporter and Cystic Fibrosis

Each living cell is engaged in risky business. Think of how it has to move something as ordinary as water in one direction or the other across its plasma membrane. If all goes well, it takes in or sends out water in just the right amounts—not too little, not too much. But who is to say life always goes well?

CFTR is one of the protein channels across the plasma membrane of epithelial cells. Sheets of these cells line sweat glands, airways and sinuses, and ducts in the digestive and reproductive systems. Chloride ions move through them, and water follows to form a thin film on the free surface of the linings. Mucus, which lubricates tissues and helps prevent infection, slides freely on the watery film.

Sometimes mutation changes how CFTR works. Not enough chloride and water reach the lining's free surface, so the film does not form. Mucus dries out and thickens. Among other things, it clogs ducts from the pancreas, so digestive enzymes cannot get to the small intestine where most food is digested and absorbed. Weight loss follows. Sweat glands secrete too much salt and alter the water–salt balance for the internal environment, which affects the heart and other organs. Males become sterile.

Problems also develop in airways to the lungs, where ciliated cells are supposed to sweep away bacteria and other particles stuck in mucus. Now the mucus makes cilia too sticky, and **biofilms** form. Biofilms are microbial populations anchored to one epithelial lining or another by stiff, sticky polysaccharides of their own making. They resist the body's defenses and antibiotics. *Pseudomonas aeruginosa*, the most efficient of the colonizers, cause low-grade infections that may last for years. Most patients can expect to live no longer than thirty years, at which time their lungs usually fail. At present there is no cure.

These symptoms—outcomes of mutation in the CFTR protein—characterize *cystic fibrosis* (CF), the most common fatal genetic disorder in the United States. More than 10 million people carry a mutant form of the gene. CF develops when they inherited a mutated gene from both parents. This happens in about 1 of every 3,300 live births (Figure 5.1).

CFTR is one of the ABC transporters in all prokaryotic and eukaryotic cells (Figure 5.2). Some of these proteins, including CFTR, are channels that let hydrophobic substances cross a membrane. Others pump substances across. By their action, some types affect what other membrane proteins are doing.

In all but 10 percent of CF patients, loss of a single amino acid during protein synthesis causes the disorder. Before a new CFTR protein is shipped to the plasma membrane, it is supposed to be modified in that endomembrane system you read about in Chapter 4. Copies of the mutant protein do enter the ER, but enzymes destroy 99 percent of them before they reach Golgi bodies. Thus few chloride channels reach their normal destinations.

Mutant CFTR may also contribute to the sinus problems of an estimated 30 million people in the United States

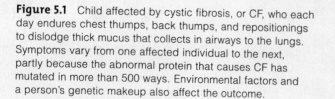

Figure 5.1 Child affected by cystic fibrosis, or CF, who each day endures chest thumps, back thumps, and repositionings to dislodge thick mucus that collects in airways to the lungs. Symptoms vary from one affected individual to the next, partly because the abnormal protein that causes CF has mutated in more than 500 ways. Environmental factors and a person's genetic makeup also affect the outcome.

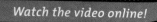

Watch the video online!

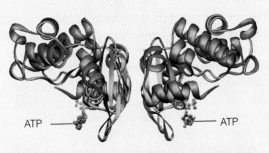

Figure 5.2 Model for part of an ABC transporter, a category of membrane proteins that includes CFTR. The parts shown here are ATP-driven motors that can widen an ion channel across the plasma membrane.

alone. In *sinusitis*, the linings of cavities inside the skull (around the nose) are chronically inflamed. In one study at Johns Hopkins University, researchers found a single copy of a mutant CFTR gene in 10 of 147 sinusitis patients. And they were only looking for 16 of more than 500 known mutant forms of the CFTR gene!

Think about it. A startling percentage of the human population can develop problems when the copies of even one kind of membrane protein don't work.

Your life depends on the functions of thousands of kinds of proteins and other molecules. Breathing, eating, moving, sleeping, crying, thinking—whatever you might be doing starts at the level of individual cells. And each cell functions properly only if it can be responsive to conditions in the microenvironments on both sides of its plasma membrane. Each eukaryotic cell also has to be responsive to conditions on both sides of its organelle membranes. *Cell membranes—* these thin boundary layers make the difference between organization and chaos.

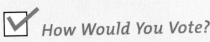

How Would You Vote?

The ability to detect mutant genes that cause severe disorders raises bioethical questions. Should we encourage the mass screening of prospective parents for mutant genes that cause cystic fibrosis? Should society encourage women to give birth only if their child will not develop severe medical problems? See BiologyNow for details, then vote online.

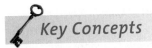

Key Concepts

MEMBRANE STRUCTURE AND FUNCTION

Cell membranes have a thin, oily, water-insoluble lipid bilayer that functions as a boundary between the outside environment and the cell interior.

The lipid bilayer consists primarily of phospholipids. Many diverse proteins are embedded in the bilayer or are positioned at one of its surfaces. The proteins carry out most membrane functions, such as transport across the bilayer and cell-to-cell recognition. Sections 5.1, 5.2

DIFFUSION ACROSS MEMBRANES

Metabolism requires concentration gradients that drive the directional movements of substances. Cells have built-in mechanisms for increasing or decreasing water and solute concentrations across the plasma membrane and internal cell membranes. Section 5.3

TRANSPORT ACROSS MEMBRANES

In passive transport, a solute crosses a membrane by diffusing through a channel inside a transport protein. In active transport, a different kind of transport protein pumps the solute across a membrane, against its concentration gradient. An input of energy, typically from ATP, jump-starts active transport. Section 5.4

OSMOSIS

By a molecular behavior called osmosis, water diffuses across any selectively permeable membrane to a region where its concentration is lower. Section 5.5

MEMBRANE TRAFFIC

Larger packets of substances and, in some cases, engulfed cells move across the plasma membrane by processes of endocytosis and exocytosis. Membrane cycling pathways extend from the plasma membrane to organelles of the endomembrane system. Section 5.6

Links to Earlier Concepts

Reflect again on the road map in Section 1.1. Here you will see how complex lipids and proteins become organized in cell membranes (3.4, 4.1). Remember the different levels of protein organization? You will consider some examples of how protein structure translates into specific functions (3.6). You will be applying your knowledge of the properties of water molecules to the movement of water across membranes (2.5). You will see how the endomembrane system (4.6) helps cycle membranes.

5.1 Organization of Cell Membranes

LINKS TO
SECTIONS
3.4, 4.1

*Cell membranes consist of a lipid bilayer in which
many different kinds of proteins are embedded. The
membrane is a continuous boundary layer that
selectively controls the flow of substances across it.*

REVISITING THE LIPID BILAYER

Think back on the phospholipids, the most abundant
components of cell membranes (Section 3.4 and Figure
5.3*a*). Each has a phosphate-containing head and two
fatty acid tails attached to one glycerol backbone. The
head is hydrophilic, meaning it dissolves fast in water.
The tails are hydrophobic; water repels them.

Immerse a lot of phospholipids in water, and they
interact with water molecules and with one another
until they spontaneously cluster into a sheet or film at
the water's surface. Some line up as two layers, with
all fatty acid tails sandwiched between the outward-
facing hydrophilic heads. This is a **lipid bilayer**, the
basic framework for cell membranes (Figure 5.3*c*).

THE FLUID MOSAIC MODEL

By the **fluid mosaic model**, every cell membrane has
a mixed composition—or a *mosaic*—of phospholipids,
glycolipids, sterols, and proteins. The lipids form an
oily bilayer that serves as a barrier to water-soluble
substances. Diverse proteins are either embedded in
the bilayer or attached to one of its surfaces. They
carry out most membrane functions.

The membrane is *fluid* because of interactions and
motions of its components. The phospholipids differ in
their heads and the length of their fatty acid tails. At
least one of the tails is usually kinked, or unsaturated.
Remember, an unsaturated fatty acid has one or more
double covalent bonds in its carbon backbone; a fully
saturated type has none. Also, most phospholipids
drift sideways, spin around their long axis, and flex
their tails, so they do not bunch up as a solid layer.

Figure 5.4 shows the fluid mosaic model. Section
5.2 is an overview of the membrane proteins that you
will be reading about in many chapters to come.

DO MEMBRANE PROTEINS STAY PUT?

Some time ago, researchers figured out how to split a
frozen plasma membrane down the middle of its
bilayer. They found that proteins were not spread like
a coat on the bilayer, as some had thought, but rather
that many were embedded in it (Figure 5.5*a*). Were
those proteins rigidly positioned in the membrane?
No one knew until researchers designed an ingenious

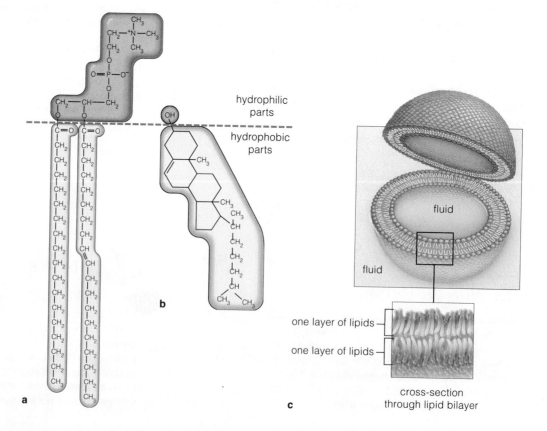

Figure 5.3 (**a**) Structural formula for
phosphatidylcholine. This phospholipid
is one of the most common molecules
of animal cell membranes. *Orange*
signifies its hydrophilic head, and
yellow, its hydrophobic tails.

(**b**) Structural formula for cholesterol,
the main sterol in animal tissues.
Phytosterols are its equivalent in
plant tissues.

(**c**) Spontaneous organization of lipid
molecules into two layers (a bilayer
structure). When immersed in liquid
water, their hydrophobic tails become
sandwiched between their hydrophilic
heads, which dissolve in the water.

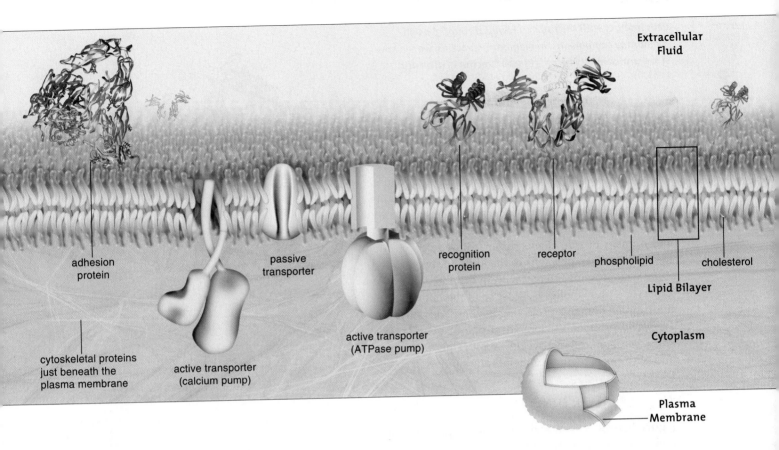

Figure 5.4 *Animated!* Fluid mosaic model for the plasma membrane of an animal cell.

adhesion protein

passive transporter

recognition protein

receptor

phospholipid

cholesterol

Extracellular Fluid

Lipid Bilayer

cytoskeletal proteins just beneath the plasma membrane

active transporter (calcium pump)

active transporter (ATPase pump)

Cytoplasm

Plasma Membrane

experiment. They induced an isolated human cell and an isolated mouse cell to fuse. The plasma membranes from the two species merged to form one continuous membrane in a new, hybrid cell. Most of the proteins mixed together in less than an hour (Figure 5.5*b*).

As we now know, many proteins are free to move laterally through the lipid bilayer, but others stay put. Some unite in complexes and do not move relative to one another. Receptors for acetylcholine, a signaling molecule, are like this. Cytoskeletal elements tether other proteins and restrict their lateral movements. For instance, a mesh of cross-lined spectrin proteins anchor glycophorin, a type of recognition protein, to the surface of all red blood cells. A transport protein that moves chloride one way and bicarbonate the other across the plasma membrane is similarly anchored.

All cell membranes consist of two layers of lipids—mainly phospholipids—and diverse proteins. Hydrophobic parts of the lipids are sandwiched between hydrophilic parts, which are dissolved in cytoplasmic fluid or in extracellular fluid.

All cell membranes have protein receptors, transporters, and enzymes. The plasma membrane also incorporates adhesion, communication, and recognition proteins.

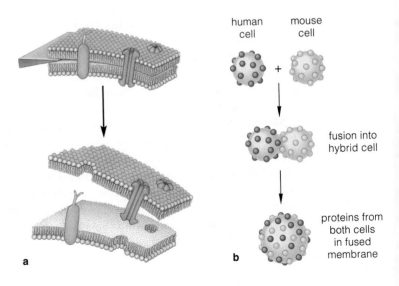

human cell   mouse cell

fusion into hybrid cell

proteins from both cells in fused membrane

a   b

Figure 5.5 *Animated!* Studying membranes. (**a**) Researchers split the two layers of a cell membrane's lipid bilayer apart, which revealed that proteins are embedded in the bilayer. (**b**) Result of an experiment in which plasma membranes from cells of two species were induced to fuse. Membrane proteins from both drifted laterally and became mixed.

5.2 Overview of the Membrane Proteins

LINK TO
SECTION
3.6

Cells interact with their surroundings through plasma membrane components. In membrane proteins, we see how structural diversity translates into functional diversity.

HOW ARE THE PROTEINS ORIENTED?

The fluid mosaic model is a good starting point for exploring membranes. But membranes differ in their composition and organization. Even the two surfaces of the same bilayer differ. For instance, many proteins (and lipids) of a plasma membrane have side chains of oligosaccharides and other carbohydrates, but only on the outward-facing surface (Figure 5.6). The kinds and number of side chains differ from one species to the next, even among cells of the same individual.

Integral proteins interact with hydrophobic parts of a bilayer's phospholipids. Most span the bilayer, with hydrophilic domains projecting beyond both surfaces. *Peripheral* proteins are located at one of the bilayer's surfaces. They interact weakly with integral proteins and with polar regions of membrane lipids.

WHAT ARE THEIR FUNCTIONS?

Figure 5.6 shows the main membrane proteins, lists their defining features, and gives some examples. The **transport proteins** either passively let specific solutes diffuse through a membrane-spanning channel in their interior or actively pump them through. Transporters are incorporated into all cell membranes.

The other proteins shown are typical of the plasma membrane. The **receptor proteins** bind extracellular substances, such as hormones, that can trigger change in cell activities. For example, certain enzymes control cell growth and division. They are switched on when somatotropin binds with receptors for it. Cells differ in their combinations of receptors.

Multicelled organisms have **recognition proteins** that are unique identity tags for each species; they are like molecular fingerprints. **Adhesion proteins** help cells of the same type locate each other and remain in the proper tissues. The **communication proteins** form channels that match up across the plasma membranes of two cells. They let signals and substances rapidly flow from the cytoplasm of one into the other.

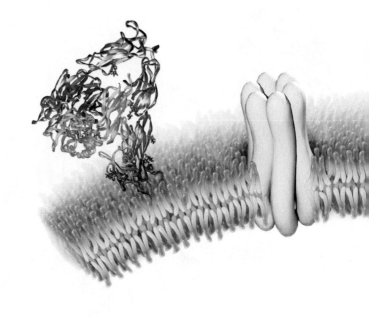

Adhesion Proteins

These proteins are embedded in the plasma membrane. They help one cell adhere to another or to a protein, such as collagen, that is part of an extracellular matrix.

Integrins, including this one, relay signals across the cell membrane. Cadherins of one cell bind with identical cadherins in adjoining cells. Selectins, which hold cells together, are abundant in endothelium, the special lining of blood vessels and the heart.

Communication Proteins

Communication proteins of one cell match up with identical proteins in the plasma membrane of an adjoining cell. Fingerlike projections of both intertwine in the space between the two cells. The result is a channel that directly connects the cytoplasm of both. Chemical and electrical signals flow fast through the channel.

This protein is one-half of a cardiac gap junction in heart muscle. The other half is in the lipid bilayer of another heart muscle cell (not shown) positioned above it. Signals flow so fast across such channels that heart muscle cells contract as a single functional unit.

All cell membranes have transporters that passively and actively assist water-soluble substances across the lipid bilayer. The plasma membrane, especially of multicelled species, has diverse receptors and proteins that function in self-recognition, adhesion, and communication.

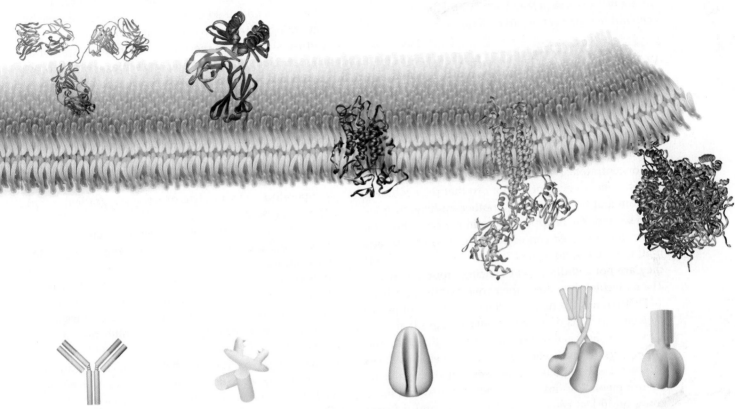

Receptor Proteins

Receptors embedded in a membrane are docks for hormones and other signaling molecules that may cause target cells to change their activities.

A signal might make a cell synthesize a certain protein, block or speed a reaction, secrete a substance, or get ready to divide.

Shown above, an antibody, a type of receptor made only by the type of white blood cell known as the B lymphocytes. These receptors are vital for all immune responses (Chapter 39).

Recognition Proteins

Certain glycoproteins (and glycolipids) project above the plasma membrane and identify a cell as *nonself* (foreign) or *self* (belonging to one's own body or a tissue).

Some, such as the HLAs (page 49), function in tissue defense. Foreign fragments bound to HLA sound the alarm for cells that defend the body. Other recognition proteins help cells stick to one another in tissues.

Passive Transporters

Passive transporters have a channel through their interior. Different kinds assist solutes or water simply by letting them diffuse through the channel, down concentration or electric gradients (Section 5.4). They do not require activation by energy inputs.

Shown here, GluT1; when its channel changes shape, glucose can cross a membrane. Aquaporins are open channels for water (page 89).

One cotransporter helps chloride and bicarbonate ions across a membrane at the same time, in opposite directions.

Ion-selective channels have molecular gates. Some gates open or close fast if a small molecule binds to them or if the charge distribution across the membrane shifts. Nerve and muscle cells have gated channels for sodium, calcium, potassium, and chloride ions.

Active Transporters

Active transport proteins pump a solute across the membrane to the side where it is more concentrated and less likely to move on its own. They require energy inputs to do this. Some are cotransporters that let one kind of solute flow passively "downhill" even as they pump a different kind "uphill."

Left, a calcium pump. Like the sodium–potassium pump, it is one of the ATPases.

Right, a type of ATPase that pumps H^+ through its interior channel, against gradients. It also can let H^+ diffuse back through the channel in a way that drives ATP synthesis. Hence its more precise name, ATP synthase (Chapters 7 and 8).

Figure 5.6 *Animated!* Major categories of membrane proteins. Included are simple icons and descriptions for membrane proteins that you will encounter in later chapters. The transporters span the lipid bilayer of all cell membranes. The other proteins shown are components of plasma membranes. Bear in mind, cell membranes also incorporate additional kinds of proteins, including some enzymes.

5.3 Diffusion, Membranes, and Metabolism

LINKS TO
SECTIONS
2.3, 2.5, 3.4

What determines whether a substance will move one way or another to and from a cell, across that cell's membranes, or through the cell itself? Diffusion down concentration gradients is part of the answer.

WHAT IS A CONCENTRATION GRADIENT?

A **concentration gradient** is a difference in the number per unit volume of molecules (or ions) of a substance between two adjoining regions. In the absence of other forces, the molecules move from a region where they are more concentrated to a region where they are not as concentrated. Why? Their inherent thermal energy keeps them in constant motion, so that they collide at random and bounce off one another millions of times each second. This happens more in regions where the molecules are most concentrated, and when you add it all up, the *net* movement is toward the region where they are not colliding and bouncing around as much. The molecules flow down their concentration gradient.

Diffusion is the name for the net movement of like molecules or ions down a concentration gradient. It is a factor in how substances move into, through, and out of cells. In multicelled species, it moves substances between body regions and between the body and its environment. For instance, when photosynthesis is going on in leaf cells, oxygen builds up and diffuses out of the cells and into air spaces in the leaf, where its concentration is lower. It then diffuses into the air outside the leaf, where its concentration is lower still.

Like other substances, oxygen tends to diffuse in a direction set by its *own* concentration gradient, not by gradients of other solutes. You can see the outcome by squeezing a drop of dye into water. The dye molecules diffuse slowly into the region where they are not as concentrated, and the water molecules move into the region where *they* are not as concentrated. Figure 5.7 shows simple examples of diffusion.

WHAT DETERMINES DIFFUSION RATES?

How fast a particular solute diffuses depends on the steepness of its concentration gradient, its size, the temperature, and electric or pressure gradients that may be present.

First, rates are high with steep gradients, because more molecules are moving out of a region of greater concentration compared with the number moving into it. Second, more heat energy makes molecules move faster and collide more often in warmer regions. Third, smaller molecules diffuse faster than large ones do.

Fourth, an electric gradient may alter the rate and direction of diffusion. An **electric gradient** is simply a difference in electric charge between adjoining regions. For example, each ion dissolved in fluids bathing a cell membrane contributes to a local electric charge. Opposite charges attract. Therefore, the fluid having more negative charge overall exerts the greatest pull on positively charged substances, such as sodium ions. Later chapters explain how many cell activities, such as ATP formation and the sending and receiving of signals in nervous systems, require the driving force of electric and concentration gradients.

Fifth, diffusion also may be affected by a **pressure gradient**. This is a difference in pressure exerted per unit volume (or area) between two adjoining regions.

MEMBRANE CROSSING MECHANISMS

Now think about the water bathing the surfaces of a cell membrane. Plenty of substances are dissolved in it, but the kinds and amounts close to its two surfaces

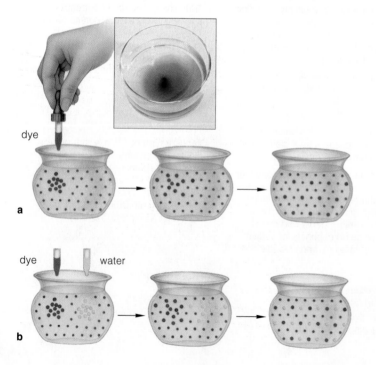

Figure 5.7 *Animated!* Two examples of diffusion. (**a**) A drop of dye enters a bowl of water. Gradually, the dye molecules become evenly dispersed through the molecules of water. (**b**) The same thing happens with the water molecules. Here, dye (*red*) and water (*yellow*) are added to the same bowl. Each substance will show a net movement down its own concentration gradient.

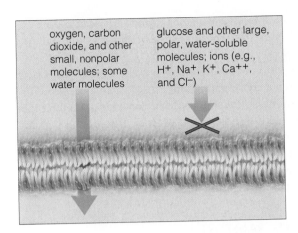

oxygen, carbon dioxide, and other small, nonpolar molecules; some water molecules

glucose and other large, polar, water-soluble molecules; ions (e.g., H^+, Na^+, K^+, Ca^{++}, and Cl^-)

Figure 5.8 *Animated!* Selective permeability of cell membranes. Small, nonpolar molecules and some water molecules cross the lipid bilayer. Ions and large, polar, water-soluble molecules and the water dissolving them cross with the help of transport proteins. Also, proteins called aquaporins specifically enhance the diffusion of water across the plasma membrane of certain cells.

differ. The membrane itself helps set up and maintain these differences. How? Its diverse lipid and protein components show **selective permeability**. They allow some substances but not others to enter and leave a cell. They also control when each substance can cross and how much crosses at a given time (Figure 5.8).

Membrane barriers and crossings are vital, because metabolism depends on the cell's capacity to increase, decrease, and maintain concentrations of substances required for reactions. That capacity also supplies the cell or organelles with raw materials, removes wastes, and maintains the cell volume and pH within ranges that favor reactions.

Lipids of a membrane's bilayer are mostly nonpolar, so they let small, nonpolar molecules such as O_2 and CO_2 slip across. Water molecules are polar, but some can slip through gaps that form when hydrophobic tails of lipids flex and bend (Section 5.1).

The lipid bilayer is impermeable to ions and large, polar molecules, including glucose. These substances cross a membrane by diffusing through the interior of transport proteins that span the bilayer. In many cells, proteins called aquaporins allow molecules of water to quickly cross the plasma membrane.

The passive transporters help specific solutes move down their concentration gradients but do not expend energy doing so. The mechanism, described shortly, is called *passive transport* or "facilitated" diffusion.

The active transporters help specific solutes diffuse across membranes, but they are not passive about it.

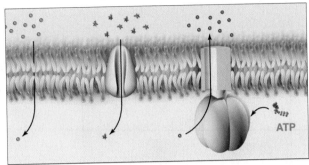

High

Concentration gradient across cell membrane

Low

| Diffusion of lipid-soluble substances across bilayer | Passive transport of water-soluble substances through channel protein; no energy input needed | Active transport through ATPase; requires energy input from ATP |

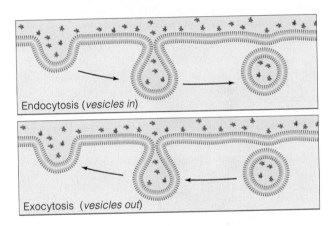

Endocytosis (*vesicles in*)

Exocytosis (*vesicles out*)

Figure 5.9 Overview of membrane crossing mechanisms.

They move solutes against concentration and electric gradients, and they require an input of energy to do so. We call this mechanism *active transport*.

Other mechanisms move large particles into or out of cells. In *endocytosis* a vesicle forms around particles when a patch of plasma membrane sinks inward and seals back on itself. In *exocytosis*, a vesicle that formed in the cytoplasm fuses with the plasma membrane, so that its contents are released to the outside.

Before getting into these diverse mechanisms, you may wish to study the overview in Figure 5.9.

Diffusion is the net movement of molecules or ions of a substance into an adjoining region where they are not as concentrated. The steepness of such a concentration gradient as well as temperature, molecular size, and electric and pressure gradients affect diffusion rates.

Cellular mechanisms increase and decrease concentration gradients across cell membranes.

5.4 Working With and Against Gradients

LINK TO SECTION 4.6

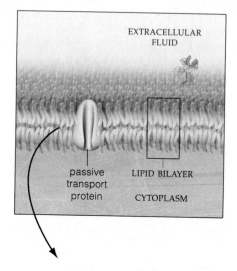

EXTRACELLULAR FLUID

passive transport protein

LIPID BILAYER

CYTOPLASM

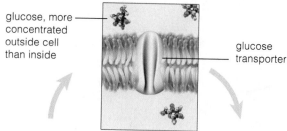

glucose, more concentrated outside cell than inside

glucose transporter

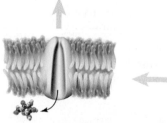

d When the glucose binding site is again vacant, the protein resumes its original shape.

a Glucose binds to a vacant site inside the channel through the transport protein.

c Glucose becomes exposed to fluid on other side of the membrane. It detaches from the binding site and diffuses out of the channel.

b Bound glucose makes the protein change shape. Part of the channel closes behind the solute. Another part opens in front of it.

Figure 5.10 *Animated!* Passive transport. This model shows one of the glucose transporters that span the plasma membrane. Glucose crosses in both directions. The *net* movement of this solute is down its concentration gradient.

Large, polar molecules and ions cannot diffuse across a lipid bilayer. They require the help of transport proteins.

Many kinds of solutes cross a membrane by diffusing through a channel or tunnel inside transport proteins. When one solute molecule or ion enters the channel and weakly binds to the protein, the protein's shape changes. The channel closes behind the solute and opens in front of it, which exposes the solute to fluid on the other side of the membrane. Now the solute is released; the binding site reverts to its original shape.

PASSIVE TRANSPORT

In **passive transport**, a concentration gradient, electric gradient, or both drive diffusion of a substance across a cell membrane, through the interior of a transport protein. The protein does not require an energy input to assist the directional movement. That is why this mechanism is also known as facilitated diffusion.

Some passive transporters are open channels; others open or close as conditions change. Figure 5.10 shows how a glucose transporter works. When one end of its channel is shut, the other is open and invites glucose in. The channel closes behind the glucose and opens in front of it, on the other side of the membrane.

The *net* direction of a solute's movement depends on how many of its molecules or ions are randomly colliding with the transporters. Encounters simply are more frequent on the side of the membrane where its concentration is greatest. The solute's *net* movement tends to be toward the side of the membrane where it is less concentrated.

If nothing else were going on, passive transport would continue until concentrations on both sides of a membrane were equal. However, other events affect the outcome. For example, the bloodstream moves glucose to all tissues. There, glucose transporters help molecules of glucose get into cells. But as fast as some glucose molecules are diffusing into the cells, others are being used as building blocks and energy sources. By *using* glucose, then, cells help maintain a gradient that favors the uptake of *more* glucose molecules.

ACTIVE TRANSPORT

Solute concentrations continually shift across the cell membrane. Living cells never stop expending energy to pump solutes into and out of their interior. With **active transport**, energy-driven protein motors help a particular kind of solute cross a cell membrane *against* its concentration gradient.

Only specific solutes can bind to functional groups that line the interior channel of an active transporter, which is activated by a phosphate group from an ATP molecule. The phosphate-group transfer changes the transporter's shape in a way that releases the solute on the other side of the membrane.

Figure 5.11 focuses on a **calcium pump**. This active transporter helps keep the concentration of calcium in a cell at least a thousand times lower than outside. What is so great about that? You will find out later, but for now think of how one of your muscle moves. The nervous system commands calcium ions to flood out from a specialized ER compartment that threads around muscle fibers inside the muscle. Calcium ions clear the way for trillions of motor proteins (myosins) to interact with actin filaments in ways that bring about contraction (Section 37.7). That muscle will go on contracting until staggering numbers of calcium pumps move those ions back inside the compartment, against their concentation gradient.

The **sodium–potassium pump** is a cotransporter that moves two kinds of ions in opposite directions. Sodium ions (Na^+) from the cytoplasm diffuse into the pump's channel and bind to functional groups. A phosphate-group transfer by ATP activates the pump, which changes shape. The change opens the channel on other side of the membrane, where Na^+ is released and potassium (K^+) diffuses in—down *its* gradient. The phosphate group is released. The channel closes behind the K^+, which is released to the other side of the membrane. As you will see, the nervous, digestive, and urinary systems of vertebrates cannot function without cellular pumps that respond to signals and to chemical changes (Sections 34.3, 41.5, and 42.3).

All cells incorporate membrane pumps. In Section 32.3, you will read about an H^+ pump that controls the transport of a hormone in growing plant parts.

Many membrane transport proteins act as open or gated channels across cell membranes. They undergo reversible changes in shape that assist solutes across the membrane.

In passive transport, a transporter allows a solute to cross a cell membrane simply by diffusing through its interior.

In active transport, the net diffusion of a specific solute is against its gradient. The transporter must be activated, usually by an energy input from ATP, which counters the force inherent in the gradient.

Passive and active transport continually help lower or raise gradients across a membrane, which helps the cell respond to signals and to chemical changes.

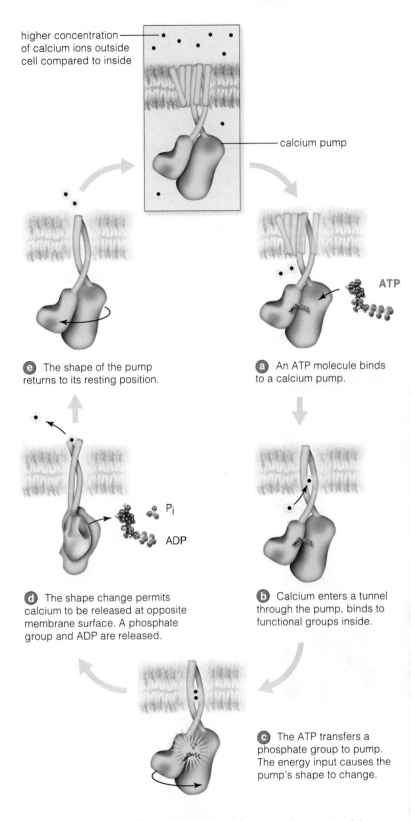

higher concentration of calcium ions outside cell compared to inside

calcium pump

e The shape of the pump returns to its resting position.

a An ATP molecule binds to a calcium pump.

ATP

d The shape change permits calcium to be released at opposite membrane surface. A phosphate group and ADP are released.

P_i

ADP

b Calcium enters a tunnel through the pump, binds to functional groups inside.

c The ATP transfers a phosphate group to pump. The energy input causes the pump's shape to change.

Figure 5.11 *Animated!* Active transport. This example uses a calcium pump that spans the plasma membrane. This sketch shows its channel for calcium ions. After two calcium ions bind to the pump, ATP transfers a phosphate group to it, thus providing energy that drives the movement of calcium *against* a concentration gradient across the cell membrane.

5.5 Which Way Will Water Move?

LINKS TO
SECTIONS
2.5, 4.8, 4.9

By far, more water diffuses across cell membranes than any other substance, so the main factors that influence its directional movement deserve special attention.

MOVEMENT OF WATER

Something as gentle as a running faucet or as mighty as Niagara Falls demonstrates **bulk flow**, or the mass movement of one or more substances in response to pressure, gravity, or another external force. Bulk flow accounts for some movement of water in multicelled organisms. A beating heart generates fluid pressure that pumps blood, which is mostly water. Sap flows inside tubes in trees, and this, too, is bulk flow.

What about the movement of water into and out of cells and organelles? If the concentration of water is not equal on both sides of a membrane, osmosis will probably occur. **Osmosis** is the diffusion of water across a selectively permeable membrane, to a region where the water concentration is lower.

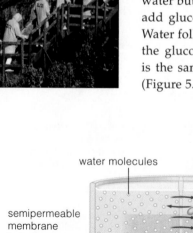

You might be wondering: How can water —a liquid—be more or less concentrated? For the answer, you have to think of water in terms of its concentration relative to the amounts of solutes that may be dissolved in it. The greater the solute concentration, the lower the water concentration.

Visualize yourself pouring some glucose or another solute to a glass of water, so that you increase the volume of liquid. The glass has the same number of water molecules but in a greater volume of liquid.

Now visualize yourself using a membrane to divide the inside of another glass of water into two compartments. The membrane lets water but not glucose diffuse across it. Next, add glucose on one side of the membrane. Water follows its concentration gradient into the glucose solution until its concentration is the same on both sides of the membrane (Figure 5.12).

In cases of osmosis, "solute concentration" refers to the total number of molecules or ions in a volume of a solution. It does not matter whether the dissolved substance is glucose, urea, or anything else. The type of solute does not dictate water concentration.

EFFECTS OF TONICITY

Suppose you decide to test the statement that water tends to move into a region where solutes are more concentrated. You make three sacs from a membrane that water but not sucrose can cross, and fill each one with a solution that is 2 percent sucrose. You immerse the first sac in a liter of distilled water, the second sac in a solution that is 10 percent sucrose, and the third sac in a solution that is 2 percent sucrose.

In each experiment, tonicity dictates the extent and direction of water movement across the membrane, as Figure 5.13 shows. *Tonicity* refers to the relative solute concentrations of two fluids. When two fluids that are on opposing sides of a membrane differ in their solute concentrations, the **hypotonic solution** is the one with fewer solutes. The one having more solutes is a **hypertonic solution**. Water tends to diffuse from a hypotonic fluid into a hypertonic fluid. **Isotonic solutions** show no net osmotic movement.

Most cells have built-in mechanisms that counter shifts in tonicity. Red blood cells do not. Figure 5.13 shows what would happen to them if tonicity were to change. Normally, fluid in red blood cells is isotonic with tissue fluid. If the tissue fluid became hypotonic, too much water would diffuse into the cells, which would burst. If that tissue fluid became hypertonic, water would diffuse out, and the cells would shrivel.

EFFECTS OF FLUID PRESSURE

Most cells do not swell and burst from an influx of water by osmosis. For one thing, they can selectively transport solutes out. For another thing, the cells of plants and many protists, fungi, and bacteria have a

water molecules   protein molecules

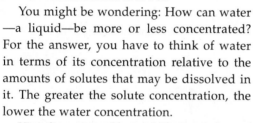

semipermeable membrane between two compartments

Figure 5.12 Solute concentration gradients and osmosis. A membrane divides this container into two compartments. Water but not proteins can cross it. Pour 1 liter of water in the left compartment and 1 liter of a protein-rich solution in the right compartment. The proteins occupy some of the space available, and the net diffusion of water in this case is from left to right (large *gray* arrow).

wall that helps keep them from rupturing when they become turgid, or swollen with fluid.

In later chapters, you will see how osmosis affects the water and solutes inside plants and animals. For now, just think about the hypotonic and hypertonic solutions in Figure 5.14. Water molecules move back and forth until the water concentration is equal on both sides of a membrane that separates them. But the volume of the formerly hypertonic solution has now increased, because its solutes cannot diffuse out.

The same thing happens in plant cells, which tend to be hypertonic relative to soil water. When a young plant cell grows, water moves into it by osmosis and exerts fluid pressure on its primary wall (Section 4.9). Up to a point, this pliable wall expands under fluid pressure, and the cell increases in volume. Continued expansion ends when the wall shows enough resistance to stop the further inward movement of water.

Any volume of fluid exerts **hydrostatic pressure**, or *turgor* pressure, against the wall or membrane that contains it. The **osmotic pressure** of any fluid is one measure of the tendency of water to follow its water concentration gradient and move into that fluid. When hydrostatic pressure and osmotic pressure are equal in magnitude, osmosis stops completely.

Plant cells also are vulnerable to the loss of water, which can occur when soil dries or becomes too salty. Water stops diffusing in and starts diffusing out, so hydrostatic pressure falls and the cytoplasm shrinks.

Osmosis is a net diffusion of water between two solutions that differ in solute concentration and are separated by a selectively permeable membrane. The greater the number of molecules and ions dissolved in a given amount of water, the lower the water concentration will be.

Water tends to move osmotically to regions of greater solute concentration (from hypotonic to hypertonic solutions). There is no net diffusion between isotonic solutions.

Fluid pressure that a solution exerts against a membrane or wall influences the osmotic movement of water.

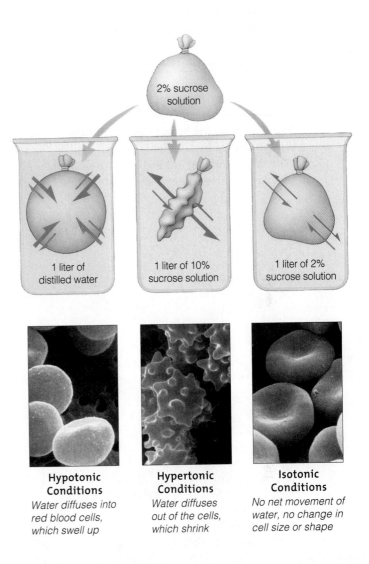

Hypotonic Conditions	Hypertonic Conditions	Isotonic Conditions
Water diffuses into red blood cells, which swell up	*Water diffuses out of the cells, which shrink*	*No net movement of water, no change in cell size or shape*

Figure 5.13 *Animated!* Tonicity and the direction of water movement between two adjoining regions. In each of three containers, arrow widths signify the direction and the relative amounts of flow. The micrographs below each sketch show the shape of a human red blood cell that is immersed in fluids of higher, lower, or equal concentrations of solutes. The solutions inside and outside red blood cells are normally balanced. This type of cell has no way to adjust to drastic change in solute levels in its fluid surroundings.

Figure 5.14 *Animated!* Experiment showing an increase in fluid volume as an outcome of osmosis. A selectively permeable membrane separates two compartments. Over time, the net diffusion will be the same in both directions across the membrane, but the fluid volume in the second compartment will be greater because there are more solute molecules in it.

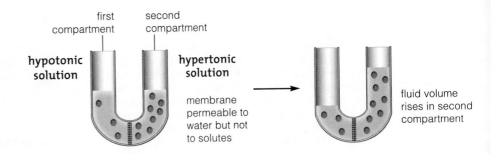

5.6 Membrane Traffic To and From the Cell Surface

LINKS TO
SECTIONS
4.6, 4.11

We leave this chapter with another look at exocytosis and endocytosis. By these mechanisms, vesicles move substances to and from the plasma membrane. Vesicles help the cell take in and expel materials in larger packets than transport proteins would be able to handle.

ENDOCYTOSIS AND EXOCYTOSIS

Think back on the lipid bilayer and how it minimizes the number of hydrophobic groups exposed to water. When the arrangement is disrupted—as when part of the plasma membrane or an organelle pinches off as a vesicle—the bilayer becomes self-sealing. Why? The disruption exposes too many of hydrophobic groups to the surroundings. When a patch of membrane is budding off, its phospholipids are being repelled by water on both sides of it. The water molecules "push" the phospholipids together, which rounds off the bud as a vesicle and also seals the rupture.

The lipid bilayer's self-sealing behavior is the basis of membrane traffic to and from a cell surface (Figure 5.15). That traffic moves in two directions.

By **endocytosis**, a small patch of plasma membrane balloons inward and pinches off inside the cytoplasm. It forms an endocytic vesicle that moves its contents to some organelle or stores them in a cytoplasmic region. By **exocytosis**, a vesicle moves to the cell surface, and then the protein-studded lipid bilayer of its membrane fuses with the plasma membrane. While this exocytic vesicle is losing its identity, its contents are released to the outside (Figure 5.15).

There are three endocytic pathways. With *receptor-mediated* endocytosis, a hormone, vitamin, mineral, or another substance binds to receptors at the plasma membrane. A slight depression, or pit, forms in the plasma membrane beneath the receptors. The pit sinks into the cytoplasm as hydrophobic interactions cause a vesicle to form (Figure 5.16).

Phagocytosis ("cell eating") is a common endocytic pathway. Phagocytes such as amoebas engulf microbes, food particles, or cellular debris. In multicelled species, macrophages and some other white blood cells engulf pathogenic viruses and bacteria, cancerous body cells, and other threats. Receptors play a different role in phagocytosis. When they bind to a specific substance, they cause microfilaments to become rearranged into a mesh just beneath the phagocyte's plasma membrane. The microfilaments contract and a bulging volume of cytoplasm is squeezed toward the cell periphery. The bulge, still enclosed in the plasma membrane, extends outward as a pseudopod (Section 4.11 and Figure 5.17).

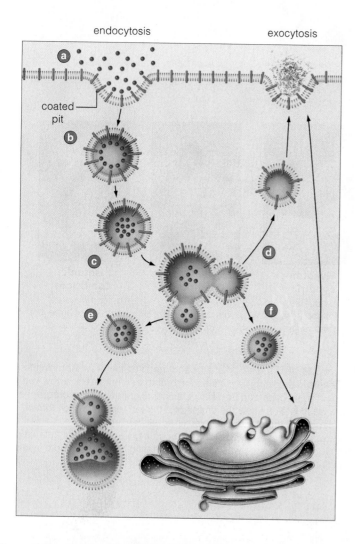

Figure 5.15 *Animated!* Endocytosis and exocytosis. This sketch starts with receptor-mediated endocytosis. (**a**) Molecules get concentrated inside coated pits at the plasma membrane. (**b**) The pits sink inward and become endocytic vesicles. (**c**) The vesicle contents are sorted and often released from receptors. (**d**) Many sorted molecules are cycled back to the plasma membrane. (**e,f**) Many others are delivered to lysosomes and stay there or are degraded. Still others are routed to spaces in the nuclear envelope and inside ER membranes, and others to Golgi bodies.

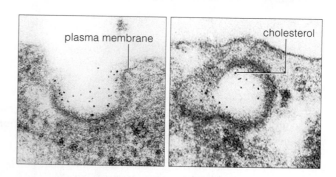

Figure 5.16 Endocytosis of cholesterol molecules.

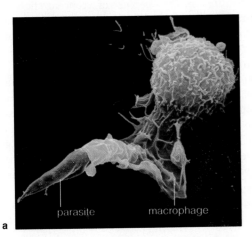

a

b   bacterium   phagocytic vesicle

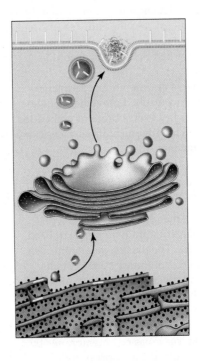

Figure 5.18 Example of how the asymmetric distribution of proteins, carbohydrates, and lipids in cell membranes originates. Proteins of the plasma membrane start out as new polypeptide chains, which become modified inside the channels of the ER and Golgi bodies. Many depart in vesicles that bud off, move to the plasma membrane, and fuse with it. The proteins inside automatically become oriented in the proper direction in the plasma membrane.

Figure 5.17 (**a**) A macrophage engulfing *Leishmania mexicana*. This parasitic protozoan causes leishmaniasis, an often-fatal disease. Bites from infected sandflies can transmit the parasite to humans. (**b**) Phagocytosis. Lobes of an amoeba's cytoplasm surround a target. The plasma membrane of the extensions fuses to form a phagocytic vesicle. In the cytoplasm, this endocytic vesicle fuses with lysosomes, which digest its contents.

Pseudopods flow completely around their target and then form a cytoplasmic vesicle. The vesicle sinks into the cytoplasm and fuses with lysosomes (Section 4.6). Lysosomal enzymes digest the vesicle's contents into fragments and smaller, reusable molecules.

Bulk-phase endocytosis is not as selective. A vesicle forms around a small volume of the extracellular fluid regardless of the kinds of substances dissolved in it.

MEMBRANE CYCLING

As long as a cell is alive, exocytosis and endocytosis are continually replacing and withdrawing patches of its plasma membrane, as in Figure 5.15. Apparently they do so at rates that maintain the total surface area of the plasma membrane. Steady losses in the form of endocytic membranes are balanced by replacements in the form of exocytic membranes.

For example, neurons release neurotransmitters in bursts of exocytosis. Each neurotransmitter is a type of signaling molecule that acts on neighboring cells.

An intense burst of endocytosis counterbalances each major burst of exocytosis.

The membranes are not shipped any which way. As an example, the composition and organization of the plasma membrane start inside the ER membranes, where many polypeptide chains become modified before being packaged and moved on to their final destinations (Section 4.6). Proteins that will become part of the plasma membrane are shipped in vesicles that fuse with a Golgi body. There, they are further modified, then sent off in other vesicles that fuse with the plasma membrane. As Figure 5.18 shows, fusion releases the proteins to the membrane surface that faces outside. There they will perform their functions.

Whereas transport proteins in a plasma membrane deal with ions and small molecules, exocytosis and endocytosis move large packets of materials in bulk across a plasma membrane.

By exocytosis, a cytoplasmic vesicle fuses with the plasma membrane, and its contents are released outside the cell.

By endocytosis, a small patch of plasma membrane sinks into the cytoplasm and pinches off as a vesicle. Membrane receptors often activate cytoskeletal elements that take part in endocytosis.

Phagocytosis is a form of endocytosis by which predatory amoebas engulf prey and certain white blood cells actively engulf tissue invaders, tissue debris, and cancer cells.

Summary

Section 5.1 Animal cell membranes consist mainly of phospholipids, along with glycolipids and sterols. The lipids are organized as a double layer, with all of their hydrophobic tails sandwiched between hydrophilic heads at both surfaces.

The lipid bilayer gives a cell membrane its primary structure and prevents uncontrolled movement of water-soluble substances across it. Diverse proteins embedded in the bilayer or associated with one of its surfaces carry out most membrane functions.

Biology Now
Learn about membrane structure and the experiments that elucidated it with the animation on BiologyNow.

Section 5.2 Each cell membrane associates with cytoplasmic proteins that structurally reinforce it. Each has receptors at its surface. The plasma membrane also contains adhesion proteins, communication proteins, recognition proteins, and diverse receptors (Figure 5.19). Differences in the number and types of proteins affect responsiveness to substances at the membrane, as well as cell metabolism, pH, and volume.

Water-soluble substances cross cell membranes by passing through the interior of transport proteins, which open to both sides of the membrane.

Receptor proteins bind extracellular substances, and binding triggers alterations in cell activities.

Recognition proteins are molecular fingerprints; they identify cells as being of a given type. Adhesion proteins help cells of tissues adhere to one another and to proteins of the extracellular matrix.

Communication junctions extend across the plasma membranes of adjoining cells; they let substances and signals travel swiftly from one into the other.

Biology Now
Use the animation on BiologyNow to familiarize yourself with the functions of receptor proteins.

Section 5.3 A concentration gradient is a difference in the number per unit volume of molecules (or ions) of a substance between two regions. The molecules tend to show a net movement down such a gradient, to the region where they are less concentrated. This behavior is called diffusion. The steepness of a concentration gradient, temperature, molecular size, and gradients in electrical charge and pressure influence diffusion rates.

Built-in cellular mechanisms work with and against gradients to move solutes across membranes.

Molecular oxygen, carbon dioxide, and other small, nonpolar molecules easily diffuse across a membrane's lipid bilayer. Ions and large, polar molecules such as glucose cross it through the interior of transport proteins that span the bilayer. Water molecules slip through gaps that briefly open in the bilayer. Aquaporins selectively assist water molecules across certain cell membranes.

Biology Now
Investigate diffusion across membranes with the interaction on BiologyNow.

Section 5.4 Many solutes cross membranes through transport proteins that act as open or gated channels or that reversibly change shape. Passive transport does not require energy input; a solute is free to follow its own concentration gradient across the membrane. Active transport requires an energy input from ATP to move a specific solute against its concentration gradient.

Biology Now
Compare the processes of passive and active transport, using the animation on BiologyNow.

Section 5.5 Osmosis is the diffusion of water across a selectively permeable membrane. The water molecules move down a water concentration gradient, which is influenced by solute concentrations and pressure.

Biology Now
Explore the effects of osmosis with the interaction and animation on BiologyNow.

Section 5.6 By exocytosis, a cytoplasmic vesicle fuses with the plasma membrane, and its contents are released outside. By endocytosis, a patch of plasma membrane forms a vesicle that sinks into the cytoplasm.

Biology Now
Use the animation on BiologyNow to discover how membrane components are cycled.

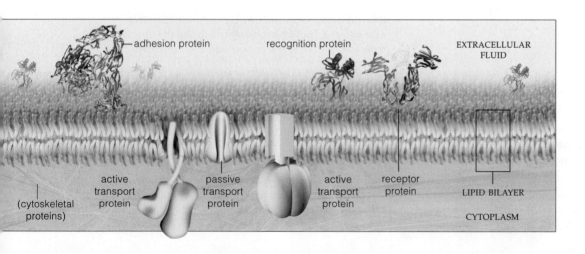

adhesion protein · recognition protein · EXTRACELLULAR FLUID

(cytoskeletal proteins) · active transport protein · passive transport protein · active transport protein · receptor protein · LIPID BILAYER · CYTOPLASM

Figure 5.19 Summary of major types of membrane proteins.

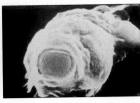

Figure 5.20 Go ahead, name the mystery membrane mechanism.

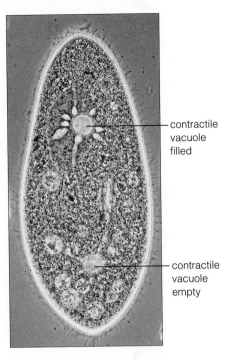

Figure 5.21 Light micrograph of one of the ciliated protozoans (*Paramecium*). This tiny single-celled body is crammed with diverse organelles, including contractile vacuoles.

— contractile vacuole filled

— contractile vacuole empty

Self-Quiz

Answers in Appendix II

1. Cell membranes consist mainly of a _____ .
   a. carbohydrate bilayer and proteins
   b. protein bilayer and phospholipids
   c. lipid bilayer and proteins

2. In a lipid bilayer, _____ of all of the lipid molecules are sandwiched between all of the _____ .
   a. hydrophilic tails; hydrophobic heads
   b. hydrophilic heads; hydrophilic tails
   c. hydrophobic tails; hydrophilic heads
   d. hydrophobic heads; hydrophilic tails

3. Most membrane functions are carried out by _____ .
   a. proteins   c. nucleic acids
   b. phospholipids   d. hormones

4. Plasma membranes incorporate _____ .
   a. transport proteins   c. recognition proteins
   b. adhesion proteins   d. all of the above

5. Diffusion is the movement of ions or molecules from one region to another where they are less concentrated. The rate of diffusion is affected by _____ .
   a. temperature   c. molecular size
   b. electrical gradients d. all of the above

6. _____ can readily diffuse across a lipid bilayer.
   a. Glucose   c. Carbon dioxide
   b. Oxygen   d. b and c

7. Some sodium ions cross a cell membrane through transport proteins that first must be activated by an energy boost. This is an example of _____ .
   a. passive transport   c. facilitated diffusion
   b. active transport   d. a and c

8. Immerse a living cell in a hypotonic solution, and water will tend to _____ .
   a. move into the cell   c. show no net movement
   b. move out of the cell d. move in by endocytosis

9. Vesicles form by way of _____ .
   a. membrane cycling d. halitosis
   b. exocytosis   e. a through c
   c. phagocytosis   f. all of the above

10. Match the term with its most suitable description.
    ____ phagocytosis   a. molecular fingerprint
    ____ passive transport b. basis of diffusion
    ____ recognition protein c. big in membranes
    ____ active   d. one cell engulfs another
        transport   e. requires energy boost
    ____ phospholipid   f. docks for signals and
    ____ concentration   substances at cell surface
        gradient   g. no energy boost required
    ____ receptors   to move solutes

Additional questions are available on **Biology❂Now™**

Critical Thinking

1. Is the white blood cell shown in Figure 5.20 disposing of a worn-out red blood cell by endocytosis, phagocytosis, or both?

2. Water moves osmotically into *Paramecium*, a single-celled aquatic protist. If unchecked, the influx would bloat the cell and rupture its plasma membrane, and the cell would die. An energy-requiring mechanism that involves contractile vacuoles expels excess water (Figure 5.21). Water enters the vacuole's tubelike extensions and collects inside. A full vacuole contracts and squirts water out of the cell through a pore. Are *Paramecium*'s surroundings hypotonic, hypertonic, or isotonic?

3. Water crosses cell membranes by diffusing past lipids that are jostling apart from one another in the bilayer. In many tissues, it also crosses faster through the interior channels of *aquaporins* (*white* arrow in Figure 5.22). As many as 3 billion water molecules per second flow through an aquaporin. Researchers already have found similar aquaporins in bacteria, plants, and insects.

Different aquaporins help different tissues respond to shifting conditions in the internal environment. They have roles in how the kidneys conserve or get rid of excess water. They play a part in producing and maintaining the fluid that bathes the spinal cord and brain, in producing saliva and tears, in keeping the lining of the lungs moist, and in keeping red blood cells from bursting or shriveling as the body's water–solute balance shifts.

If the gene for one of these water channels mutates, the outcome may be serious. Mutation in *aquaporin–0* results in cataracts, and mutation in *aquaporin–2* leads to a form of diabetes insipidus. Yet *aquaporin–1* seems less essential. In its absence, affected adults tend to produce unusually dilute urine but remain in good health as long as they drink plenty of water. Even so, affected individuals are rare. Speculate on the reasons why.

extracellular fluid

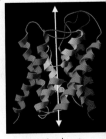

cytoplasm

Figure 5.22 Model for one of the four aquaporin subunits.

Alcohol, Enzymes, and Your Liver

The next time someone asks you to have a drink or two, or three, stop for a moment and think about the challenge confronting the cells that are supposed to keep a drinker alive—especially heavy drinkers. It makes little difference whether someone gulps down 12 ounces of beer, 5 ounces of wine, or 1–1/2 ounces of eighty-proof vodka. Each of these drinks has the same amount of "alcohol" or, more precisely, ethanol.

Ethanol molecules—CH_3CH_2OH—have water-soluble and fat-soluble components. Once they reach the stomach and the small intestine, they are quickly absorbed into the internal environment. The bloodstream transports more than 90 percent of ethanol's components to liver cells. There, enzymes speed their breakdown to a nontoxic form called acetate, or acetic acid. The liver has great numbers of alcohol-metabolizing enzymes, but they can detoxify only so much in a given hour.

One of the enzymes you will read about in this chapter is catalase, a foot soldier against toxins that can attack the body (Figure 6.1). Catalase assists another enzyme, alcohol dehydrogenase. When alcohol circulates through the liver, these enzymes convert it to acetaldehyde. The reactions cannot end there, because acetaldehyde becomes toxic

when it accumulates in high concentrations. In healthy people at least, still another kind of enzyme speeds its breakdown to nontoxic forms.

Given the liver's central role in alcohol metabolism, habitually heavy drinkers gamble with alcohol-induced liver diseases. Over time, the capacity to tolerate alcohol diminishes because there are fewer and fewer liver cells —hence fewer enzymes—for detoxification.

What are some of the possible outcomes? A big one is *alcoholic hepatitis*, an all-too-common disease characterized by inflammation and destruction of liver tissue. Another disease, *alcoholic cirrhosis*, permanently scars the liver. In time, the liver stops working, with devastating effects.

The liver is the largest gland in the human body, and its activity impacts everything else. You would have a really hard time digesting and absorbing food without it. Your cells would have a hard time synthesizing and taking up carbohydrates, lipids, and proteins, and staying alive.

There is more to think about. The liver gets rid of a lot more toxic compounds than just acetaldehyde. It also makes certain plasma proteins that circulate freely in blood. In their absence, your body would not be able to defend itself well from attacks or to stop bleeding even from small cuts.

Figure 6.1 Something to think about—ribbon model for catalase, an enzyme that helps detoxify many substances that can damage the body, such as the alcohol in beer, martinis, and other drinks.

It would not be able to maintain the fluid volume of the internal environment that all of your cells depend upon.

Now think about a self-destructive behavior known as *binge drinking*. The idea is to consume large amounts of alcohol in a brief period. Binge drinking is now the most serious drug problem on campuses throughout the United States. Consider this finding from one study: Of nearly 17,600 students surveyed at 140 colleges and universities, 44 percent said they are caught in the culture of drinking. They report having five alcoholic drinks a day, on average.

Binge drinking can do far more than damage the liver. Put aside the related 500,000 injuries from accidents, the 70,000 cases of date rape, the 400,000 cases of (whoops) unprotected sex among students in an average year. Binge drinking can kill before you know what hit you. Drink too much, too fast, and you can abruptly end the beating of your heart.

With this example, we turn to **metabolism**, the cell's capacity to acquire energy and use it to build, degrade, store, and release substances in controlled ways. At times, the activities of your cells may be the last thing you want to think about. But they help define who you are and what you will become, liver and all.

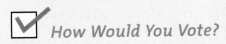
Watch the video online!

How Would You Vote?

Some people have damaged their liver because they drank too much alcohol. Others have a diseased liver. There are not enough liver donors for all the people waiting for liver transplants. Should life-style be a factor in deciding who gets a transplant? See BiologyNow for details, then vote online.

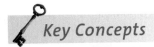
Key Concepts

THE NATURE OF ENERGY FLOW

Energy cannot be created or destroyed. It can only be converted from one form to another. Concentrated forms of energy tend to spread out, or disperse, spontaneously to less concentrated and less usable forms, such as dispersed heat. Collectively, chemical bonds resist this tendency and help organisms maintain their complex organization. Section 6.1

ENERGY CHANGES AND ATP

Metabolic reactions require an energy input before they can run spontaneously to completion. Some end with products that have more energy than the reactants. Others release more usable energy than the amount invested to start the reactions. ATP couples reactions that can release usable energy with reactions that require it. Section 6.2

ENERGY CHANGES AND ENZYMES

On their own, chemical reactions proceed too slowly to sustain life. Enzymes increase reaction rates enormously. They lower the amount of energy it takes to align reactive groups, destabilize electric charges, and break bonds so that products can form from reactants.

Temperature, pH, salinity, and other environmental factors influence enzyme activity. So does the availability of cofactors, or enzyme helpers. Sections 6.3, 6.4

THE NATURE OF METABOLISM

Metabolic pathways are enzyme-mediated sequences of reactions. By controlling enzymes that govern key steps in these pathways, cells build up, maintain, and decrease amounts of thousands of substances. ATP-forming pathways require redox reactions, or electron transfers. Section 6.5

FROM CONCEPT TO APPLICATION

We can simply absorb information about nature, including how enzymes work. We also can interpret information in novel ways that may have practical application. Section 6.6

Links to Earlier Concepts

Reflect again on the road map for life's organization (Section 1.1). Here you will gain insight into how organisms tap into a grand, one-way flow of energy to maintain that organization (1.2). You will start thinking about how cells use the chemical behavior of electrons and protons in ways that help make ATP (2.3). Remember what you learned about acids and bases (2.6)? Here you will see how pH influences enzyme activity.

6.1 Energy and Time's Arrow

LINK TO
SECTION
1.2

You know, almost without thinking about it, that your life does not stand still and will not start all over again. You have a sense of time's arrow—that everything we have observed and experienced, and all we expect will happen, goes forward. But <u>why</u> does it go forward?

WHAT IS ENERGY?

A dictionary definition of **energy** is "the capacity to do work," which doesn't say much. It is no more than a clue to two of the most sweeping laws of nature we humans have ever tried to wrap our minds around. In itself, the **first law of thermodynamics** seems simple enough: *Energy cannot be created or destroyed.*

Basically, this law deals with the *quantity* of energy in the universe. There is a finite amount distributed in different forms. However, one form may be converted to another.

One form, *potential* energy, is a capacity to do work because of something's location and the arrangement of its parts. While the skydivers shown in Figure 6.2 were still inside the plane, each had a store of potential energy because of their position above the ground. ATP and other molecules in their body had potential energy because of how their atoms were held together in particular arrangements by chemical bonds.

When the skydivers jumped, potential energy was transformed into *kinetic* energy, or energy of motion. ATP in muscle cells gave up some potential energy to molecules of contractile units and set them in motion. The motion of many thousands of muscle cells made whole muscles move. With each energy transfer from ATP, a bit of energy slipped off into the surroundings as *thermal* energy, or heat.

Figure 6.2 Forms of energy. How many can you identify?

The potential energy of molecules has its own name, *chemical* energy. It is measurable, as in kilocalories. A **kilocalorie** is the same as 1,000 calories, or the amount of energy it takes to heat 1,000 grams of water from 14.5°C to 15.5°C at standardized pressure.

THE ONE-WAY FLOW OF ENERGY

Now imagine all the energy changes going on inside the skydivers, between their hot bodies and molecules of air they are falling through, between the sun and those plants in the fields below them. Zoom out past the sun, past our solar system, and all the way to the boundary of the known universe, and you will pass staggeringly diverse energy conversions.

Amazingly, another law of thermodynamics helps explain every conversion by dealing with the *quality* of energy. It tells us why the sun will eventually burn out, why animals eat plants and one another, why nitroglycerin spontaneously explodes but you don't, why it rains, why skydivers fall down instead of up and splat if their parachutes don't open, and why your life can't start over again.

The **second law of thermodynamics** sounds simple enough: *Energy tends to flow from concentrated to less concentrated forms—so the cost of concentrating it in one area comes at a greater cost of energy dispersal or dilution somewhere else.* This tendency gives us our sense of "time's arrow." Skydivers in free fall do not have a concentrated form of energy that can get them back to the plane. A hot pan gives off heat as it cools, and that heat cannot diffuse back from the air to the pan. You can't rewind the winds flowing around the eye of a hurricane. You can't take back a scream.

The second law says only that concentrated energy tends to disperse spontaneously. It does not say when or how slowly or fast that might happen. In our own world, *the collective strength of chemical bonds resists the spontaneous direction of energy flow.* Think of the energy in uncountable numbers of chemical bonds between all the atoms making up the Rocky Mountains. Millions of years will pass before attacks by winds, rain, ice, and other assaults will break enough bonds to return the mountains to the seas. Or think of all the chemical bonds in your skin, heart, liver, and other body parts. The concentration of energy definable as "you" stays together as long as they do.

Entropy is the measure of how much and how far a concentrated form of energy has been dispersed after an energy change. It is not a measure of order versus disorder. In 2004, at one of the most active subduction zones on the seafloor, a major earthquake generated a

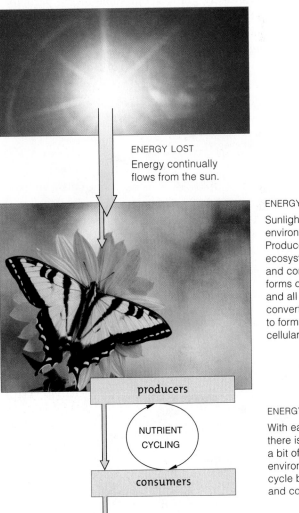

Figure 6.3 Aftermath of an appalling change in entropy. Gleebruk village, Indonesia, shown before and after a tsunami struck in December 2004. A major earthquake on the seafloor generated giant ocean waves—a form of concentrated mechanical energy that spread out after the waves hit land.

tsunami that spread across the Indian Ocean. Few of us missed the images of monstrous waves lashing at coasts all the way from Indonesia to Africa (Figure 6.3). Orderly rows of houses, hotels, and crops were ripped apart and washed away. But this horrific mess was not an increase in entropy; *it was its aftermath*. The earthquake had generated waves of pressure—a form of mechanical energy—in ocean water. There was a huge concentration of pressure that dissipated as the waves slammed against shorelines. The before/after difference in mechanical energy—from the original concentration on the seafloor to the last fingers of surf that fizzled away on land—was the entropy change.

The point is, *energy tends to flow in one direction, from concentrated to less concentrated forms.* The world of life is responsive to the flow. Photosynthetic cells of plants and other producers tap into a concentrated store of energy: light from the sun. They convert it to chemical bond energy in sugars and other organic compounds. Consumers as well as producers access that stored energy by breaking and rearranging chemical bonds. With each conversion, though, some energy is lost as heat, a dispersed form of energy that cells can't gather up again. The inevitable losses mean that the world of life must maintain its complex organization through ongoing replenishments of energy—which is being lost from someplace else (Section 1.2 and Figure 6.4).

Energy is the capacity to do work, and it cannot be created or destroyed. It can be converted from one form to another.

Energy concentrated in one place tends to spread out, or disperse, on its own. The collective strength of chemical bonds resists this spontaneous direction of energy flow.

Life continues as long as organisms tap into concentrated energy sources and use them to build complex molecules even as they continually lose energy in the form of heat.

ENERGY LOST
Energy continually flows from the sun.

ENERGY GAINED

Sunlight energy reaches environments on Earth. Producers of nearly all ecosystems secure some and convert it to stored forms of energy. They and all other organisms convert stored energy to forms that can drive cellular work.

producers

NUTRIENT CYCLING

consumers

ENERGY LOST

With each conversion, there is a one-way flow of a bit of energy back to the environment. Nutrients cycle between producers and consumers.

Figure 6.4 A one-way flow of energy into an ecosystem compensates for the one-way flow of energy out of it.

6.2 Time's Arrow and the World of Life

LINKS TO
SECTIONS
1.5, 3.7, 5.4

Once the two laws of thermodynamics were just hypotheses. They became accepted as theories so powerful and wide-ranging that they became known as laws. Remember, the best theories—and laws—are supported by predictions based on them (Section 1.5). With respect to metabolism, the key prediction is this: It takes net inputs of energy to force small molecules to combine into larger ones, such as glucose, that are more concentrated forms of energy.

The molecules of life do not form spontaneously, and they are not that stable in the presence of free oxygen, which reacts with them and disrupts their structure. Cellular mechanisms safeguard these molecules. They control when and where energy changes will occur; that is, when energy will flow from one substance to another during chemical reactions.

You already know about some of the participants in metabolic reactions. Starting substances are called *reactants*. Substances formed before a reaction ends are *intermediates*, and those remaining are *products*. ATP

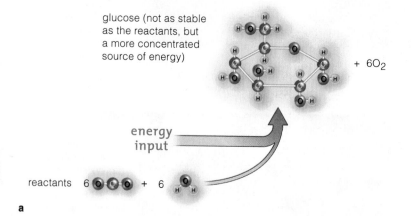

glucose (not as stable as the reactants, but a more concentrated source of energy)

$+ 6O_2$

energy input

reactants 6 ⬤⬤⬤ $+ 6$ H⬤H

a

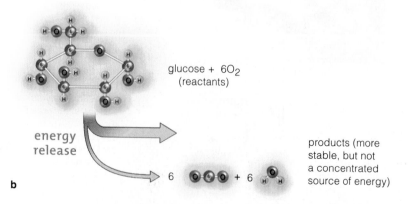

glucose + $6O_2$ (reactants)

energy release

products (more stable, but not a concentrated source of energy)

6 ⬤⬤⬤ $+ 6$ H⬤H

b

Figure 6.5 Animated! Two categories of energy changes in chemical work. (**a**) Endergonic reactions require a net input of energy. (**b**) Exergonic reactions end with a net release of usable energy.

and other *energy carriers* activate enzymes and other molecules by phosphate-group transfers. *Enzymes* are catalysts; they speed specific reactions enormously. *Cofactors* are metal ions or coenzymes. They assist the enzymes by accepting and donating electrons, atoms, and functional groups. *Transport proteins* help solutes across membranes. Their action affects concentrations of substances, which in turn affects how, when, and whether a reaction can proceed.

ACTIVATION ENERGY—WHY THE WORLD DOESN'T GO UP IN SMOKE

When substances react, some of the chemical energy required to break bonds is conserved as new bonds form. Some energy is lost as heat, light, or both. Think of what happens after a spark from a campfire ignites tinder-dry plants. Plants are mostly cellulose—which has three reactive hydroxyl groups *in each one of many repeating units*: $C_6H_7O(OH)_3$. Once this reaction starts, it proceeds swiftly on its own. Most of the cellulose breaks down fully to carbon dioxide (CO_2) and water (H_2O), with the release of light and heat. Remember Figure 1.1? A single match can start a firestorm.

Why doesn't the world go up in flames on its own? It takes a boost of energy to overcome the strength of chemical bonds in reactants. The boost has to be big for some reactions but not much for others. Like other explosives, nitroglycerin has a lot of oxygen atoms. A hard shake or jarring is all it takes for nitroglycerin to start falling apart—explosively fast—into hot gases.

Each kind of reaction has a characteristic **activation energy**, the minimum amount of energy that can get the reaction to the point that it will run on its own. By controlling the energy inputs into reactions, cells are able to control when and how fast the reactions occur.

UP AND DOWN THE ENERGY HILLS

Let's see how this works when photosynthetic cells build glucose and other carbohydrates. An input of energy from the sun triggers two stages of reactions. Ultimately, six CO_2 and six H_2O molecules are used in the formation of one glucose molecule ($C_6H_{12}O_6$) and six oxygen molecules (O_2). Figure 6.5*a* is a simple way to think about these reactants and products.

The synthesis of glucose is an example of a series of reactions that just will not happen on their own. Why not? Carbon dioxide and water do have energy stored in their covalent bonds, but the bonds are so stable that it is as if they are at the base of an "energy hill." It takes inputs of energy to break those bonds

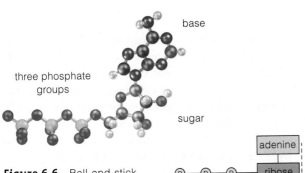

base

three phosphate groups

sugar

Figure 6.6 Ball-and-stick model for ATP. Successive phosphate-group transfers turn ATP into ADP (adenosine diphosphate), then into AMP (adenosine monophosphate).

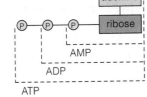

adenine
ribose
AMP
ADP
ATP

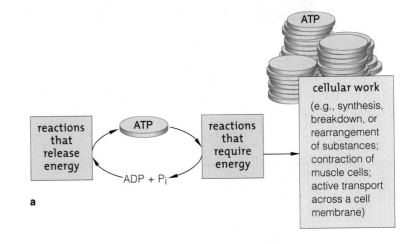

ATP

cellular work

(e.g., synthesis, breakdown, or rearrangement of substances; contraction of muscle cells; active transport across a cell membrane)

reactions that release energy → ATP → reactions that require energy

ADP + P$_i$

a

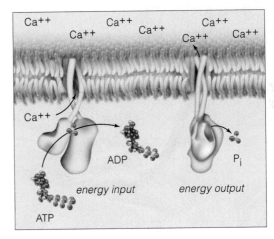

Ca++ Ca++ Ca++ Ca++ Ca++ Ca++

Ca++

Ca++

ADP

P$_i$

energy input

energy output

ATP

b A case of cellular work. ATP transfers a phosphate group to a transport protein spanning a plasma membrane. As you read in Section 5.4, the energy boost causes this active transport protein to change its shape in ways that pump calcium ions out of the cell, against their concentration gradient.

Figure 6.7 *Animated!* (**a**) ATP function. Recurring phosphate-group transfers convert ATP into ADP, and back to ATP. (**b**) Example of ATP-driven cellular work.

and convert them to something higher up on the hill. Any reactions that require a net input of energy are said to be *endergonic* (meaning energy in).

Glucose is a concentrated source of energy. When it is broken apart, energy is released. Cells capture some of the energy to do cellular work. Energy also ends up in covalent bonds of smaller, more stable products. With aerobic respiration, those products are six CO_2 and six H_2O molecules (Figure 6.5*b*).

Aerobic respiration releases energy bit by bit, with many conversion steps, so cells can capture some of it efficiently. This metabolic process is like a downhill run, from a concentrated form of energy (glucose) to less concentrated forms. Any reactions that end with a net release of energy are *exergonic* (meaning energy out). They, too, require an energy boost to get past the activation energy barrier. However, the net amount of energy released is more than the amount invested.

ATP—THE CELL'S ENERGY CURRENCY

It doesn't take a huge leap of the imagination to sense that cells stay alive by *coupling* reactions that require energy with reactions that release it. For nearly all metabolic reactions, adenosine triphosphate, or **ATP**, is the energy carrier, or coupling agent. All cells make this nucleotide, which consists of a five-carbon sugar (ribose), the base adenine, and three phosphate groups (Figure 6.6). ATP easily gives up phosphate groups to other molecules and thus primes them to react. Any phosphate-group transfer is called **phosphorylation**.

ATP is the currency in a cell's economy. Cells spend it in energy-requiring reactions and also invest it in energy-releasing reactions that help keep them alive. We use a cartoon coin to symbolize ATP (Figure 6.7*a*). Because ATP is the main energy carrier for so many reactions, you might infer—correctly—that cells have

ways of renewing it. When ATP gives up a phosphate group, ADP (adenosine diphosphate) forms. ATP can re-form when ADP binds to inorganic phosphate (P$_i$) or to a phosphate group that was split from a different molecule. Regenerating ATP by this **ATP/ADP cycle** helps drive most metabolic reactions (Figure 6.7*b*).

Activation energy is the minimum amount of energy required to get any reaction to the point where it will run spontaneously, with no further energy input. The amount differs for different reactions.

Reactions that build large organic compounds from smaller ones cannot run without a net input of energy. Reactions that degrade large molecules to smaller ones end with a net output of usable energy.

ATP, the main energy carrier in all cells, couples energy-releasing and energy-requiring reactions. It primes other molecules to react by phosphate-group transfers.

6.3 How Enzymes Make Substances React

If you left a cupful of glucose out in the open, years would pass before you would see its conversion to carbon dioxide and water. Yet that same conversion takes just a few seconds in your body. Enzymes make the difference.

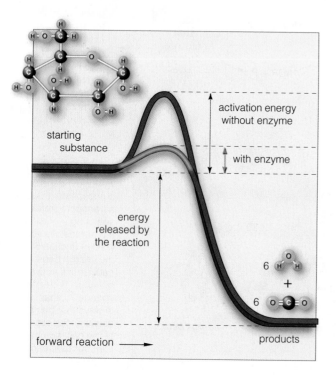

Enzymes are catalysts that can make reactions occur hundreds to millions of times faster than they would on their own. Enzyme molecules can work again and again; a reaction does not use them up or irreversibly alter them. Each type of enzyme chemically recognizes, binds, and alters specific reactants only. For instance, thrombin recognizes and cleaves only a peptide bond between arginine and glycine in a particular protein, thereby converting the protein into a factor that helps clot blood. Finally, nearly all enzymes are proteins. (A few kinds of RNAs also show enzymatic activity.)

Reactions cannot proceed until the reactants have a minimum amount of internal energy—the activation energy. Visualize activation energy as a barrier—a hill or brick wall (Figures 6.8 and 6.9). Enzymes lower it. How? *Compared with the surrounding environment, they offer a stable microenvironment, more favorable for reaction.*

Consider: Enzymes are far larger than **substrates**, another name for the reactants that bind to a specific enzyme. Their polypeptide chains are folded in ways that afford structural stability. Certain folds also form one or more chemically stable **active sites**: pockets or crevices where the substrates bind and where specific reactions can proceed rapidly and repeatedly.

Part of a substrate is complementary in shape, size, solubility, and charge to the active site. Because of the

Figure 6.8 *Animated!*
Activation energy: the minimum amount of internal energy that reactants must have before a reaction will run to products. An enzyme enhances the reaction rate by lowering the required amount; it lowers the energy hill.

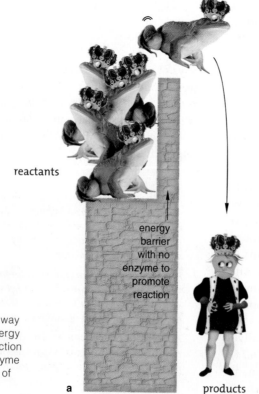

Figure 6.9 Simple way to think about the energy required to get a reaction going without an enzyme (**a**) and with the help of an enzyme (**b**).

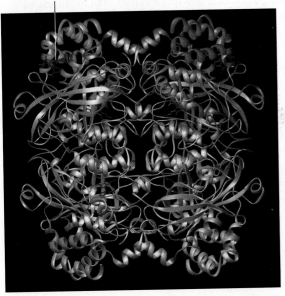
one of four heme groups cradled in one of four polypeptide chains

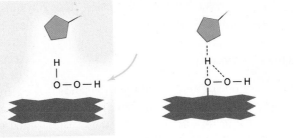

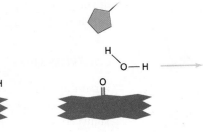

a Hydrogen peroxide (H_2O_2) enters a cavity in catalase. It is the substrate for a reaction aided by an iron molecule in a heme group (*red*).

b A hydrogen of the peroxide is attracted to histidine, an amino acid projecting into the cavity. One oxygen binds the iron.

c This binding destabilizes the peroxide bond, which breaks. Water (H_2O) forms. In a later reaction, another H_2O_2 will pull the oxygen from iron, which will then be free to act again.

Figure 6.10 *Animated!* How catalase works. This enzyme has four polypeptide chains and four heme groups (coded *red*).

fit, each enzyme chemically recognizes and binds its substrate among thousands of substances in cells.

Think back on the main types of enzyme-mediated reactions (Section 3.2). With *functional group transfers*, one molecule gives up a functional group to another. With *electron transfers*, one or more electrons stripped away from a molecule are donated elsewhere. With *rearrangements*, a juggling of internal bonds converts one kind of molecule to another. With *condensation*, two or more molecules become covalently bound into a larger molecule. Finally, with *cleavage* reactions, a larger molecule splits into smaller ones.

When we talk about activation energy, *we really are talking about the energy it takes to align reactive chemical groups, destabilize electric charges, and break bonds*. These events put a substrate at its **transition state**. Then, its bonds are at the breaking point, and the reaction can run easily to product (Figure 6.10).

The binding between an enzyme and its substrate is weak and temporary (that is why the reaction does not change the enzyme). However, energy is released when these weak bonds form. This "binding energy" stabilizes the transition state long enough to keep the enzyme and its substrate together for the reaction to be completed.

With enzymes, four mechanisms work alone or in combination to lower the activation energy and move substrates to the transition state:

Helping substrates get together. When they are at low concentrations, molecules of substrates rarely react. Binding at an active site is as effective as a localized boost in concentration, by as much as ten millionfold.

Orienting substrates in positions favoring reaction. On their own, substrates collide from random directions. By contrast, the weak but extensive bonds at an active site put reactive groups close together.

Shutting out water molecules. Because of its capacity to form hydrogen bonds so easily, water can interfere with the breaking and formation of chemical bonds in reactions. Certain active sites have an abundance of nonpolar amino acids with hydrophobic groups, which repel water and keep it away from the reactions.

Inducing a fit between enzyme and substrate. By the **induced-fit model**, a substrate is almost but not quite complementary to an active site. An enzyme restrains the substrate and stretches or squeezes it into a certain shape, often next to another molecule or to a reactive group. By optimizing the fit between them, it moves the substrate to the transition state.

On their own, chemical reactions occur too slowly to sustain life. Enzymes greatly increase reaction rates by lowering the activation energy. That is the minimum amount of energy required to align reactive groups, destabilize electric charges, and break bonds so that products can form from reactants.

In an enzyme's active site, substrates move to a transition state, when their bonds are at the breaking point and the reaction can run spontaneously to completion.

The transition state is reached by various mechanisms that concentrate and orient substrates, exclude water from the active site, and induce an optimal fit between the active site and substrate.

6.4 Enzymes Don't Work In a Vacuum

LINK TO
SECTION
2.6

Many factors influence what an enzyme molecule does at any given time or whether it is built in the first place. Here we highlight a few of the major factors.

CONTROLS OVER ENZYMES

What happens when one or another of the thousands of substances in cells becomes too abundant or scarce? Many controls over enzymes help cells respond fast by adjusting specific reactions. Feedback mechanisms can activate or inhibit enzymes in ways that conserve energy and resources. Cells produce what conditions require—no more, no less.

Controls maintain, lower, or raise concentrations of substances. They adjust how fast enzyme molecules are synthesized, and they activate or inhibit the ones already built. In multicelled species, enzyme controls keep individual cells functioning in ways that benefit the whole body.

In some cases, a molecule that acts as an activator or inhibitor can reversibly bind to an *allosteric* site on the enzyme, not to the active site (*allo*– other; *steric*, structure). Binding alters the enzyme's shape in a way that hides or exposes the active site (Figure 6.11).

Visualize a bacterial cell making tryptophan and other amino acids—the building blocks for proteins. Even when it has made enough proteins, tryptophan synthesis continues until its increasing concentration causes **feedback inhibition**. This means a change that results from a specific activity *shuts down the activity*.

A feedback loop starts and ends at many allosteric enzymes. In this case, unused tryptophan binds to an allosteric site on the first enzyme in the tryptophan biosynthesis pathway. Binding makes the active site change shape, so less tryptophan can be made (Figure 6.12). At times when not many tryptophan molecules are around, the allosteric sites are unbound. Thus the active sites remain functional, and the synthesis rate picks up. In such ways, feedback loops quickly adjust the concentrations of substances.

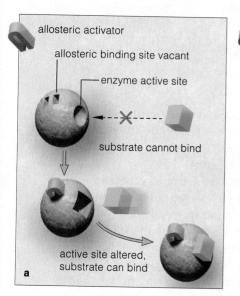
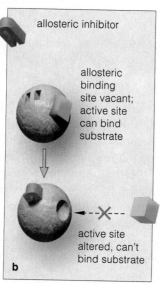

Figure 6.11 *Animated!* Allosteric control over enzyme activity. (**a**) An active site is unblocked when an activator binds to a vacant allosteric site. (**b**) An active site is blocked when an inhibitor binds to a vacant allosteric site.

EFFECTS OF TEMPERATURE, pH, AND SALINITY

What an enzyme molecule actually does also depends on conditions in the environment. Temperature, pH, and salinity all have impact on it.

Temperature is a measure of molecular motion. As it rises, it boosts reaction rates both by increasing the likelihood that a substrate will bump into an enzyme and by raising a substrate molecule's internal energy. Remember, the more energy a reactant molecule has, the closer it gets to jumping that activation energy barrier and taking part in a reaction.

Above the range of temperatures that an enzyme can tolerate, weak bonds are broken. The shape of the enzyme changes, so substrates no longer can bind to the active site. The reaction rate falls sharply (Figure 6.13). Such declines typically occur with fevers above 44°C (112°F), which people usually cannot survive.

Also, remember how the pH of solutions can vary (Section 2.6)? In the human body, most enzymes work best at pH 6–8. For instance, trypsin is active in the small intestine (pH of about 8). The enzyme pepsin is one of the exceptions. This nonspecific protease can digest any protein. It is produced in inactive form and

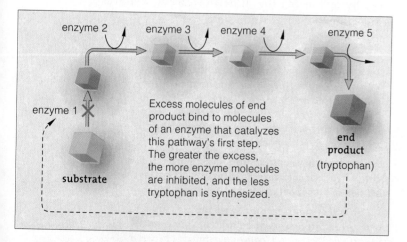

Figure 6.12 *Animated!* Feedback inhibition of a metabolic pathway. Five kinds of enzymes act in sequence to convert a substrate to tryptophan.

normally becomes activated only in gastric fluid, in the stomach. Gastric fluid is highly acidic, with a pH of 1–2. If activated pepsin were to leak out of the stomach, it would digest the proteins in your tissues instead of those in food. Figure 6.14 shows the effects of pH on pepsin and two other kinds of enzymes.

Also, most enzymes stop working effectively when the fluids in which they are dissolved are saltier or less salty than their range of tolerance. Too much or too little salt interferes with the hydrogen bonds that help hold an enzyme in its three-dimensional shape. By doing so, it inactivates the enzyme.

HELP FROM COFACTORS

Finally, don't forget the cofactors. These metal ions or coenzymes help at the active site of enzymes or taxi electrons, H^+, or functional groups to other reactions. **Coenzymes** are a class of organic compounds that may or may not have a vitamin component.

One or more metal ions assist nearly a third of all known enzymes. Metal ions easily give up and accept electrons. As part of coenzymes, they help products form by shifting electron arrangements in substrates or intermediates. That is what goes on at the hemes in catalase. Heme has an organic ring structure, with an iron atom at the center of the ring. As you saw in Figure 6.10, the iron atoms assist catalase in speeding the breakdown of hydrogen peroxide to water.

Like vitamin E, catalase is an **antioxidant**. It helps neutralize free radicals. *Free radicals*, or atoms with at least one unpaired electron, are leftovers of reactions. They attack the structure of DNA and other biological molecules. As we age, we make less and less catalase, so free radicals accumulate (Section 43.6).

Some coenzymes are tightly bound to an enzyme. Others, such as NAD^+ and $NADP^+$, can diffuse freely through the cytoplasm. Either way, they participate intimately in a metabolic reaction. Unlike enzymes, many become modified during the reaction, but they are regenerated elsewhere.

Controls over enzymes enhance or inhibit their activity. By doing so, they maintain, lower, or raise concentrations of many thousands of substances in coordinated ways.

Enzymes work best when the cellular environment stays within limited ranges of temperature, pH, and salinity. The actual ranges differ from one type of enzyme to the next.

Many enzymes are assisted by cofactors, which are specific metal ions or coenzymes.

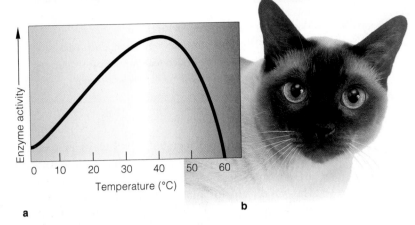

Figure 6.13 Enzymes and the environment. (**a**) How increases in temperature affect one enzyme's activity.

(**b**) The air temperature outside the body affects the fur color of Siamese cats. Epidermal cells that give rise to the cat's fur produce a brownish-black pigment, melanin. Tyrosinase, an enzyme in the melanin production pathway, is heat-sensitive in the Siamese. It becomes less active in warmer parts of the cat's body, which end up with less melanin, and lighter fur. Put this cat's feet in booties for a few weeks and its warm feet will become light.

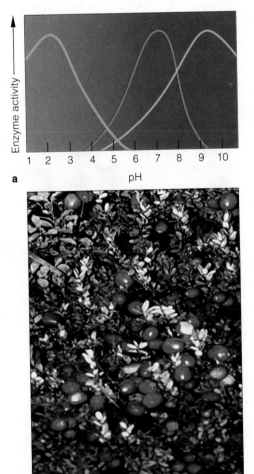

Figure 6.14 Enzymes and the environment. (**a**) How pH values affect three enzymes. The *blue* graph line shows the activity for pepsin. (**b**) Cranberry plants grow best in acidic bogs. Unlike most plants, they have no nitrate reductase. This enzyme converts nitrate (NO_3) found in most soils to metabolically useful ammonia (NH_3). In highly acidic soils, nitrogen is already in the form of ammonia (NH_4^+).

6.5 Metabolism—Organized, Enzyme-Mediated Reactions

LINK TO
SECTION
2.3

How cells use energy changes is one aspect of metabolism. Another is the concentration, conversion, and disposal of materials by energy-driven reactions. Most reactions in cells are part of stepwise metabolic pathways.

TYPES OF METABOLIC PATHWAYS

We have mentioned metabolic pathways in passing. Now let's formally define them. **Metabolic pathways** are enzyme-mediated sequences of reactions in cells. The *biosynthetic* (or anabolic) kinds require a net input of energy to produce glucose, starch, and other large molecules from small ones. Photosynthesis is the main biosynthetic pathway for the world of life (Figure 6.15).

Degradative (or catabolic) pathways are exergonic, overall, in that they end with a net release of usable energy. In degradative pathways, unstable molecules typically are broken down into smaller, more stable products, with the release of energy in forms that cells may use. Aerobic respiration is the main degradative pathway in the biosphere, and energy released during the reactions is used to form many ATP (Figure 6.15).

Many metabolic pathways are linear, a straight line from reactants to the products. In cyclic pathways, the last reaction regenerates the type of reactant molecule that is used in the first step of the reaction sequence. For instance, in the second stage of photosynthesis, a molecule known as RuBP is the entry point for cyclic reactions, and the cycle's last intermediate undergoes internal jugglings that convert it to RuBP. In branched pathways, reactants or intermediates are channeled into two or more different sequences of reactions.

THE DIRECTION OF METABOLIC REACTIONS

Bear in mind, metabolic reactions do not always run from reactants to products. They might start out in this "forward" direction. But most also run in reverse, with products being converted back to reactants.

Reversible reactions tend to run spontaneously toward **chemical equilibrium**, when the reaction rate is about the same in either direction. In most cases, the amounts of reactant and product molecules are not identical; they differ at that time (Figure 6.16). It is like a party where people drift between two rooms. The number in each room stays the same—say, thirty in one and ten in the other—even as individuals move back and forth.

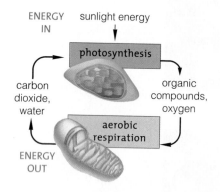

Figure 6.15 The main metabolic pathways in ecosystems. Energy from the sun drives the formation of glucose in photosynthesis, and aerobic respiration yields a great deal of usable energy from glucose breakdown.

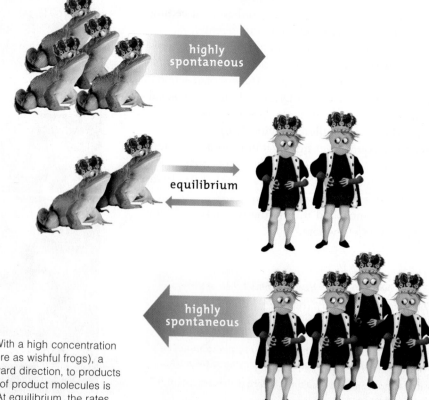

Figure 6.16 Chemical equilibrium. With a high concentration of reactant molecules (represented here as wishful frogs), a reaction runs most strongly in the forward direction, to products (the princes). When the concentration of product molecules is high, it runs most strongly in reverse. At equilibrium, the rates of the forward and reverse reactions are the same.

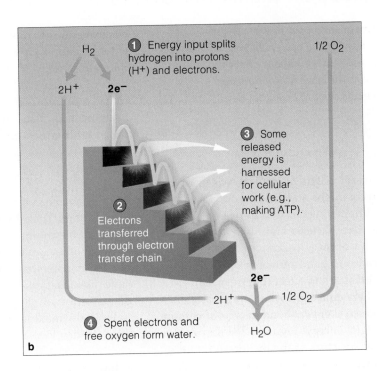

Figure 6.17 *Animated!* Uncontrolled versus controlled energy release. (**a**) Free hydrogen and oxygen exposed to an electric spark react and release energy all at once. (**b**) Electron transfer chains allow the same reaction to proceed in small, more manageable steps that can handle the released energy.

Labels in figure a:
H₂   1/2 O₂
electric spark
Explosive release of energy as heat that cannot be harnessed for cellular work
H₂O
a

Labels in figure b:
H₂   1/2 O₂
① Energy input splits hydrogen into protons (H⁺) and electrons.
2H⁺   2e⁻
③ Some released energy is harnessed for cellular work (e.g., making ATP).
② Electrons transferred through electron transfer chain
2e⁻
2H⁺   1/2 O₂
④ Spent electrons and free oxygen form water.
H₂O
b

Why bother to think about this? *Each cell can bring about big changes in activities by controlling the enzymes that mediate a few steps of reversible metabolic pathways.*

For instance, when your cells need a quick bit of energy, they rapidly split glucose into two pyruvate molecules. They do so by a sequence of nine enzyme-mediated steps of a pathway called glycolysis. When glucose supplies are too low, cells quickly reverse this pathway and build glucose from pyruvate and other substances. How? Six steps of the pathway happen to be reversible, and the other three are bypassed. An input of energy from ATP drives the bypass reactions in the uphill (energetically unfavorable) direction.

What if cells did not have this reverse pathway? They would not be able to build glucose fast enough to compensate for episodes of starvation, when glucose supplies in blood become dangerously low.

REDOX REACTIONS IN THE MAIN PATHWAYS

You may be wondering: Why don't cells break down glucose all at once? Glucose, recall, is not as stable as the products of its full breakdown. Toss a cupful of glucose into a campfire, and its carbon and hydrogen atoms will explosively combine with oxygen in air. All of the released energy will be lost as heat.

Cells release energy efficiently by stepwise electron transfers, or **oxidation–reduction reactions**. In these "redox" reactions, one molecule gives up electrons (it is oxidized) and another gains them (it is reduced).

Commonly, hydrogen atoms are released at the same time. Remember, we represent free hydrogen atoms (naked protons) as H⁺. Being attracted to the opposite charge of the electrons, H⁺ tags along with them.

Start thinking about redox reactions, because they are central to photosynthesis and aerobic respiration. In the next two chapters, you will follow coenzymes as they pick up the electrons and H⁺ stripped from substrates and then deliver them to **electron transfer chains**. Such chains are membrane-bound arrays of enzymes and other molecules that accept and give up electrons in sequence. Electrons are at a higher energy level when they enter a chain than when they leave.

Think of these electrons as descending a staircase and stingily losing a bit of energy at each step, as in Figure 6.17. In the case of photosynthesis and aerobic respiration, the stepwise electron transfers concentrate energy—in the form of H⁺ electrochemical gradients—in ways that contribute to ATP formation.

> *Metabolic pathways are orderly, enzyme-mediated reaction sequences, some biosynthetic, others degradative.*
>
> *Control over a key step of a metabolic pathway can bring about rapid shifts in cell activities.*
>
> *Many aspects of metabolism involve electron transfers, or oxidation–reduction reactions. Electron transfer chains are important sites of energy exchange in both photosynthesis and aerobic respiration.*

6.6 Light Up the Night—And the Lab

LINK TO
SECTION
2.3

You can always think about organisms from a "gee-whiz-ain't-nature-grand" point of view. Or you can come up with novel ways to think about what they do and how they do it. The latter way of thinking puts you squarely in the camp of biologists. Here is a case in point.

ENZYMES OF BIOLUMINESCENCE

At night, in the warm waters of tropical seas or in the summer air above gardens and fields, you may catch sight of abrupt shimmerings or flashes of light. Many species, ranging from bacteria and algae to fishes to fireflies, flash with orange, yellow, yellow-green, or blue light. In seawater, great numbers of them often flash together with startling effect (Figure 6.18*a*).

All of the flashers emit light when enzymes called luciferases transduce chemical bond energy of certain molecules into light energy. Figure 6.18*c* shows the three-dimensional structure of the luciferase found in fireflies. Remember, electrons can be excited to higher energy levels with an input of energy. In this case, reactions start when ATP, in the presence of oxygen, transfers a phosphate group to luciferin. An array of electrons in this molecule become excited enough to enter reactions. At a certain reaction step, they release the extra energy in the form of *fluorescent* light. Any kind of destabilized molecule that reverts to a more stable configuration may emit such light. When the reactions take place in organisms, the emitted light is called **bioluminescence**.

A RESEARCH CONNECTION

People have been marveling over bioluminescence for a long time. Then biologists thought to borrow the genes for bioluminescence from fireflies and use them to make other organisms light up. Through methods of gene transfers, as sketched out in Chapter 16, they have now inserted copies of those genes into bacteria, plants, and mice (Figure 6.19).

In itself, making mice glow seems like a bizarre thing to do. However, some biologists immediately saw the potential for using bioluminescence genes as a diagnostic tool. For example, every year, 3 million people die from a lung disease caused by different strains of the bacterium *Mycobacterium tuberculosis*. No single antibiotic is effective against all the strains.

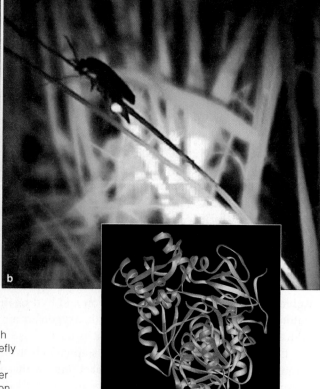

Figure 6.18 (**a**) Stirring up bioluminescent marine organisms near Vieques Island, Puerto Rico. As many as 5,000 free-living cells called dinoflagellates may be in each liter of water, and each flashes with blue light when agitated. (**b**) North American firefly (*Photinus pyralis*) emitting a flash from its light organ. Peroxisomes in this organ are packed with luciferase molecules. Firefly flashes help potential mates find each other in the dark. (**c**) Ribbon model for firefly luciferase. This enzyme catalyzes the reaction that releases light. Its single polypeptide chain is folded into multiple domains.

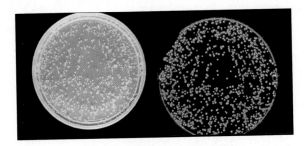

Figure 6.19 Colonies of bioluminescent bacteria in daylight (*left*) and glowing in a culture dish in the dark (*right*).

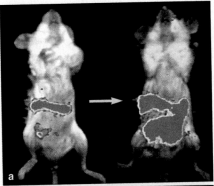
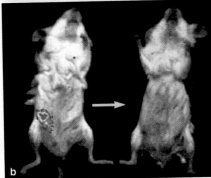

Figure 6.20 Utilizing bioluminescent bacterial cells to chart the location of infectious bacteria inside living laboratory mice and their spread through body tissues. (**a**) False-color images in this pair of photographs show how the infection spread in a control group that had not been given a dose of antibiotics. (**b**) This pair shows how antibiotics had killed most of the infectious bacterial cells.

If an infection has progressed to a dangerous stage, there is no time to waste, but there is no guarantee a treatment will be effective unless the particular strain causing a patient's infection is identified.

One way to do this is to take a sample of bacterial cells from the patient, then expose them to luciferase genes. In some cells, the genes get incorporated into the bacterial DNA. Those cells are isolated, and then colonies of their descendants are exposed to different antibiotics. When an antibiotic does *not* work, colonies glow; the cells are alive. When an antibiotic works, there is no glow; all of the bacterial cells are dead.

Christopher and Pamela Contag, two postdoctoral students at Stanford University, thought about using gene transfers to light up *Salmonella* cells in mice. As they knew, researchers who study viral or bacterial diseases had to infect dozens to hundreds of mice for experiments. Then they had to kill the mice and study their tissues to see whether infection had occurred. The practice was costly and tedious, and it meant the loss of a lot of infection-free experimental animals.

First the Contags approached a medical imaging researcher, David Benaron, with this hypothesis: If we make live, infectious bacteria bioluminescent, then flashes of light will shine through tissues of infected, living animals. As an early test of their prediction, the researchers put glowing *Salmonella* cells into a thawed chicken breast from a market. It glowed from inside.

The Contags transferred the bioluminescence genes into three *Salmonella* strains, which were injected into three experimental groups of laboratory mice. The Contags used a digital imaging camera to track and record whether infections developed in each group.

The first strain was weak; the mice fought off the infection in less than six days and did not glow. The second strain was not as weak but could not spread through the mouse body; it was localized. The third strain was dangerous. It spread rapidly through the entire mouse gut—which glowed.

Thus bioluminescent gene transfer, combined with imaging of enzyme activity, can track the course of infection. It is now used to evaluate the effectiveness of drugs in living organisms (Figure 6.20). It also may have use in gene therapy, which involves replacing one or more defective or cancer-causing genes in a patient with functional copies of the genes.

In short, people thought to use bioluminescence as visible evidence of metabolism—of the cell's capacity to acquire energy and use it to build, break apart, store, and release substances in controlled ways. Each flash reminds us that living cells are taking in energy-rich solutes, constructing membranes, storing things, replenishing enzymes, and checking out their DNA. A constant supply of energy drives these activities. The flashes remind us of how modern-day biologists are busy putting knowledge to use in practical ways.

> *Bioluminescence is an outcome of enzyme-mediated reactions that release energy as fluorescent light.*
>
> *Biologists have transferred genes for bioluminescence, the luciferases, into a variety of organisms. The gene transfers have research applications and practical uses.*

Summary

Section 6.1 Cells require energy for metabolism, or chemical work. The first law of thermodynamics tells us that energy cannot be created from scratch or destroyed. Energy can only be converted from one form to another. Examples are potential energy, such as that stored in chemical bonds, and kinetic energy (energy of motion).

The second law of thermodynamics tells us that energy tends to spread out or disperse spontaneously from concentrated to less concentrated forms, such as dispersed heat. Entropy is the measure of how much and how far a concentrated form of energy has been dispersed after an energy change.

The collective strength of the chemical bonds that hold together systems of life resists the spontaneous direction of energy flow. Those systems maintain their complex organization by being resupplied with energy lost from someplace else. Sunlight is the original source of energy for nearly all webs of life.

Section 6.2 Table 6.1 summarizes the functions of the key players in metabolism: reactants, intermediates, products, enzymes, cofactors, energy carriers, and transporters. The second law of thermodynamics lets us make this prediction about metabolism: It takes net inputs of energy to force stable molecules to combine into forms that are less stable but more concentrated sources of energy.

All reactants require a minimum amount of internal energy before they will enter into a reaction, although the amount differs among them. That amount is the activation energy for the reaction.

Some reactions are endergonic; they require a net energy input to run to completion. The formation of glucose from carbon dioxide and water is an example. Other reactions are exergonic; the net amount of energy they release is greater than the amount invested. Aerobic respiration is an example.

Cells couple reactions that require energy with other reactions that release energy. ATP is the main energy carrier between reaction sites. It jump-starts reactions by donating one or more of its phosphate groups to a reactant. It is regenerated when ADP binds to inorganic phosphate or to a phosphate group.

Biology⊗Now
Learn about energy changes in chemical reactions and the role of ATP with the animation on BiologyNow.

Section 6.3 Enzymes are catalysts, which means they enormously enhance the rates of specific reactions. Nearly all are proteins that are much larger than their substrates (some RNAs also are catalytic). Folds in their polypeptide chains form active sites, or small clefts that create favorable microenvironments for reaction.

Enzymes speed reactions by lowering the activation energy. For each kind of reaction, that is the energy it takes to align reactive chemical groups, destabilize electric charges, and break chemical bonds. Enzymes move substrates faster to a transition state, when the reaction can proceed most easily to products.

Four mechanisms help get substrates to the transition state: Binding in an active site effectively boosts local concentrations of substrates, it orients substrates, it shuts out most or all water molecules that could interfere with the reaction, and it induces an optimum fit with the substrate that pulls it to the transition state.

Biology⊗Now
Investigate how enzymes facilitate reactions with the animation and interaction on BiologyNow.

Section 6.4 Many factors influence enzyme action and, through it, metabolic pathways. Each type of enzyme functions best within a characteristic range of temperature, pH, and salinity. Controls over enzyme activity, including negative feedback mechanisms, influence the kinds and amounts of substances available in a given interval. Also, most enzymes require the assistance of cofactors. These metal ions and coenzymes help out at an active site by ferrying electrons, hydrogen ions, or functional groups to some other reaction site.

Biology⊗Now
Observe mechanisms of enzyme control with the animation on BiologyNow.

Section 6.5 Cells modify concentrations of many thousands of substances, often by coordinating outputs of orderly, enzyme-mediated reaction sequences called metabolic pathways. The energy-requiring, *biosynthetic* pathways build large, unstable molecules from smaller, more stable ones. Photosynthesis is an example. The energy-releasing, *degradative* pathways break down large molecules to smaller products. Aerobic respiration is the main degradative pathway. Most metabolic reactions are reversible. Cells rapidly shift rates of metabolism by controlling a few steps of reversible pathways.

Table 6.1	Summary of the Main Participants in Metabolic Reactions
Reactant	Substance that enters a metabolic reaction or pathway; also called the substrate of a specific enzyme
Intermediate	Any substance that forms in a reaction or pathway, between the reactants and the end products
Product	Substance at the end of a reaction or pathway
Enzyme	A protein that greatly enhances reaction rates; a few RNAs also do this
Cofactor	Coenzyme (such as NAD^+) or metal ion; assists enzymes or move electrons, hydrogen, or functional groups to other reaction sites
Energy carrier	Mainly ATP; couples energy-releasing reactions with energy-requiring ones
Transport protein	Protein that passively assists or actively pumps specific solutes across a cell membrane

Cells release energy most efficiently by way of oxidation–reduction reactions, which simply are electron transfers. In both photosynthesis and aerobic respiration, redox reactions occur at electron transfer chains that are components of cell membranes.

Biology⑤Now
Compare the effects of controlled and uncontrolled energy release with the animation on BiologyNow.

Section 6.6 Bioluminescence is one outcome of enzyme-mediated reactions that release energy in the form of fluorescent light. The transfer of genes for bioluminescence into organisms has research and practical applications.

Biology⑤Now
Read the InfoTrac article, "An Enlightening Food Safety Tool," Lynn Petrak, The National Provisioner, October 2004.

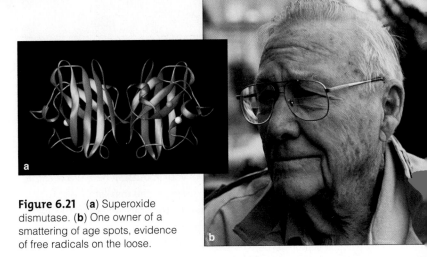

Figure 6.21 (a) Superoxide dismutase. (b) One owner of a smattering of age spots, evidence of free radicals on the loose.

Self-Quiz
Answers in Appendix II

1. _____ is life's primary source of energy.
   a. Food   b. Water   c. Sunlight   d. ATP

2. Energy _____ .
   a. cannot be created or destroyed
   b. can change from one form to another
   c. tends to flow spontaneously in one direction
   d. all of the above

3. Entropy is a measure of _____ .
   a. order versus disorder in a system
   b. how much and how far a form of energy has been dispersed after an energy change
   c. the forerunner of an energy change
   d. all of the above

4. Enzymes _____ .
   a. are proteins, except for a few RNAs
   b. lower the activation energy of a reaction
   c. are destroyed by the reactions they catalyze
   d. a and b

5. Enzyme function is influenced by _____ .
   a. changes in temperature
   b. changes in pH
   c. changes in salinity
   d. all of the above

6. Which of the following statements is *incorrect*?
   A metabolic pathway _____ .
   a. has an orderly sequence of reaction steps
   b. is mediated by only one enzyme that starts it
   c. may be biosynthetic or degradative, overall
   d. all of the above

7. Match the substance with its suitable description.
   ____ coenzyme or metal ion   a. reactant
   ____ adjusts gradients at membrane b. enzyme
   ____ substance entering a reaction c. cofactor
   ____ substance formed during   d. intermediate
        a reaction   e. product
   ____ substance at end of reaction   f. energy carrier
   ____ enhances reaction rate   g. transport
   ____ mainly ATP   protein

Additional questions are available on **Biology⑤Now™**

Critical Thinking

1. State the law of thermodynamics that deals with the *quantity* of energy in the universe. State the law that deals with the *quality* of energy.

2. Cyanide, a toxic compound, binds irreversibly to an enzyme that is a component of electron transfer chains. The outcome is *cyanide poisoning*. Binding prevents the enzyme from donating electrons to a nearby acceptor molecule in the system. What effect will this have on ATP formation? From what you know of ATP's function, what effect will this have on a person's health?

3. Why does applying lemon juice to sliced apples keep them from turning brown?

4. One molecule of catalase can break down 6 million hydrogen peroxide molecules every minute. It is found in most organisms that live under aerobic conditions because hydrogen peroxide is toxic—cells must dispose of it fast or risk being damaged. Peroxide is catalase's substrate; but by a neat trick, catalase also can inactivate other toxins, including alcohol. Can you guess what the trick is?

5. Hydrogen peroxide bubbles if dribbled on an open cut but does not bubble on unbroken skin. Explain why.

6. *Free radicals* are unbound molecular fragments that have the wrong number of electrons. They form during many enzyme-catalyzed reactions, including the digestion of fats and amino acids. They slip out of electron transfer chains. They also form when x-rays and other kinds of ionizing radiation bombard water and other molecules. Free radicals are highly reactive. When they dock with a molecule, they alter its structure and function.

Superoxide dismutase (Figure 6.21a) is an enzyme that works with catalase to keep free radicals and hydrogen peroxide from accumulating in cells. As we age, cells make copies of enzymes in ever diminishing numbers, in altered form, or both. When this happens to superoxide dismutase and catalase, free radicals and hydrogen peroxide build up. Like loose cannonballs, they careen through cells and blast away at the structural integrity of proteins, DNA, lipids, and other molecules. For instance, look at the "age spots" on an older person's skin (Figure 6.21b). Each spot is a mass of brownish-black pigments that have accumulated in skin cells. Do some research and identify other problems that arise when free radicals take over.

Sunlight and Survival

Think about the last bit of apple, lettuce, chicken, pizza, or any other food you put in your mouth. Where did it come from? Look past the refrigerator, the market or restaurant, and the farm. Look to plants, the starting point for nearly all of the food—the carbon-based compounds—you eat.

Plants are among the **autotrophs**, or "self-nourishing" organisms. Autotrophs get energy and carbon from the physical environment and use it to make their own food. Most bacteria, many protists, and all fungi and animals are like you; they cannot obtain energy and carbon from the physical environment. They are **heterotrophs**, which feed on autotrophs, one another, and organic wastes. *Hetero–* means other, as in "being nourished by others."

Plants are a type of *photo*autotroph. By the process of **photosynthesis**, they make sugars and other compounds by using sunlight as an energy source and carbon dioxide as their source of carbon. Each year, plants around the world produce 220 billion tons of sugar, enough to make 300 quadrillion sugar cubes. That is a LOT of sugar. They also release great amounts of oxygen (Figure 7.1).

It wasn't always this way. The first prokaryotic cells on Earth were *chemo*autotrophs. Like the existing archaeans, they did not have the enzymes for complicated metabolic magic. They extracted energy and carbon from simple organic and inorganic compounds, such as methane and hydrogen sulfide, that happened to be around. Both gases were part of the chemical brew that made up the early atmosphere. Carbon dioxide also was present, but it takes special enzymes to harness it. There was little free oxygen.

Things did not change much for about a billion years. Then light-sensitive molecules evolved in a few lineages, which became the first *photo*autotrophs. Life had tapped into an immense supply of energy. Not long afterward, parts of the photosynthetic machinery became modified

Figure 7.1 Photosynthesis—the main pathway by which energy and carbon enter the web of life. This orchard of photosynthetic autotrophs is producing apples and oxygen at the Jerzy Boyz organic farm in Chelan, Washington.

in some photoautotrophs. Water molecules could now be split apart as a source of electrons for the reactions, and supplies of water were essentially unlimited. Over time, oxygen atoms released from uncountable water molecules diffused out of uncountable numbers of cells —and the world of life would never be the same.

Free oxygen reacts fast with metals, including metal ions that help enzymes. The reactions release free radicals which, as you know, are toxic to cells. So oxygen that had accumulated in the atmosphere put selection pressure on prokaryotic populations all over the world. Prokaryotes that could not neutralize toxic oxygen radicals vanished or were marginalized in muddy sediments, deep water, and other anaerobic (oxygen-free) habitats.

As you will read in this chapter, pathways that could detoxify the oxygen radicals evolved in some lineages. One pathway, aerobic respiration, lets cells *use* oxygen's reactive properties in highly beneficial ways.

Another bonus for life: As oxygen accumulated high in the atmosphere, many atoms combined to form ozone (O_3). An ozone layer formed and became a shield against lethal ultraviolet radiation from the sun. Life could now move out of the deep ocean, out from mud, out from under rocks, and diversify under the open sky.

As you read this chapter on photosynthesis, keep in mind that its emergence and its continuity are big reasons why *you* can exist, and read this book, and think about what it takes to stay alive.

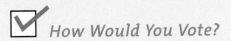

How Would You Vote?

The oxygen in Earth's atmosphere is a sure indicator that photosynthetic organisms flourish here. New technologies will allow astronomers in search of life to measure the oxygen content of the atmosphere of planets too far away for us to visit. Should public funds be used to continue this research? See BiologyNow for details, then vote online.

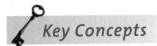

Key Concepts

THE RAINBOW CATCHERS

A one-way flow of energy through the world of life starts after chlorophylls and other pigments absorb wavelengths of visible light from the sun's rays. In plants, some bacteria, and many protists, that energy ultimately drives the synthesis of glucose and other carbohydrates. Sections 7.1, 7.2

OVERVIEW OF PHOTOSYNTHESIS

In plant cells and many protists, photosynthesis proceeds through two stages inside organelles called chloroplasts. At a membrane system in the chloroplast, the sun's energy is first converted to chemical energy. Then carbohydrates are synthesized in the chloroplast's semifluid matrix. Section 7.3

MAKING ATP AND NADPH

In the first stage of photosynthesis, sunlight energy becomes converted to chemical bond energy in ATP. NADPH forms, and free oxygen escapes into the air. Sections 7.4, 7.5

MAKING SUGARS

The second stage is the "synthesis" part of photosynthesis. Enzymes assemble sugars from atoms of carbon and oxygen obtained from carbon dioxide. The reactions use the ATP and NADPH that formed in the first stage of photosynthesis. The ATP delivers energy, and the NADPH delivers electrons and hydrogens to the reaction sites. Sections 7.6, 7.7

GLOBAL IMPACTS OF AUTOTROPHS

The emergence of the world's main energy-releasing pathway, aerobic respiration, was an evolutionary consequence of photosynthesis—the world's main energy-acquiring pathway. Collectively, photoautotrophs and chemoautotrophs make the food that sustains all of life. They also have enormous impact on the global climate. Section 7.8

Links to Earlier Concepts

Before considering the chemical basis of photosynthesis, you may wish to review the nature of electron energy levels (Section 2.3), particularly how photons and electrons interact. You will be using your knowledge of carbohydrate structure (3.4), chloroplasts (4.8), active transport proteins (5.2, 5.4), and concentration gradients (5.3).

Remember the concepts of energy flow and the underlying organization of life (6.1 and 6.2)? They help explain how energy flows through photosynthesis reactions. You also will expand your understanding of how cells harvest energy through the operation of electron transfer chains (6.5).

7.1 Sunlight as an Energy Source

LINKS TO
SECTIONS
2.3, 6.1, 6.2

Remember how energy flows in one direction through the world of life? In nearly all cases, the flow starts when photoautotrophs intercept energy, in the form of wavelengths of visible light, from the sun.

PROPERTIES OF LIGHT

An understanding of photosynthesis requires a bit of knowledge of the properties of energy that radiates from the sun. That energy undulates across space in a manner analogous to the waves moving across a sea. The term **wavelength** refers to the horizontal distance between the crests of every two successive waves of radiant energy.

Although energy travels in waves, it has a particle-like quality. When absorbed, it can be measured as if it were organized in discrete packets, or **photons**. A photon consists of a fixed amount of energy. The least energetic photons travel in longer wavelengths, and the most energetic ones travel in shorter wavelengths.

Photoautotrophs only capture light of wavelengths between 380 and 750 nanometers. Humans and other organisms see light of these wavelengths as different colors, from deep violet through blue, green, yellow, orange, and red. Figure 7.2 shows where the spectrum of visible light fits in the **electromagnetic spectrum**—the range of all wavelengths of radiant energy, from shortest (gamma rays) to longest (radio waves).

Shorter wavelengths are energetic enough to alter or break chemical bonds in DNA and proteins. That is why UV (ultraviolet) light, x-rays, and gamma rays are a threat to all organisms. That is why early life evolved away from sunlight—deep in the ocean, or in

sediments, or under rocks. Life did not move onto dry land until after the ozone layer formed high above Earth. The ozone layer absorbs much of the dangerous UV light (Sections 48.1 and 48.2).

Visible light of all wavelengths combined appears white. White light separates into its individual colors when it passes through a prism or water droplets in moisture-laden air. The prism or droplets bend light of longer wavelengths (yellow to red) more than they bend shorter wavelengths (violet to blue), the result being the band of colors we see in rainbows.

FROM SUNLIGHT TO PHOTOSYNTHESIS

Pigments are a class of molecules that absorb photons in particular wavelengths only. Certain kinds are the molecular bridges from sunlight to photosynthesis.

Photons that a specific pigment does not absorb are reflected by it or continue traveling right on through it. **Chlorophyll *a***, the major pigment in all but one group of photoautotrophs, absorbs violet and red light. It reflects green and yellow light, which is why plant parts with an abundance of chlorophylls appear green. *Accessory* pigments harvest additional wavelengths. The most common accessory pigment, **chlorophyll b**, reflects green and blue light. **Carotenoids** reflect red, orange, and yellow light. Besides their photosynthetic role, carotenoids impart color to many flowers, fruits, and vegetables. **Xanthophylls** reflect yellow, brown, blue or purple light. The **anthocyanins** reflect red and purple light, as they do in cherries and many flowers. In many deciduous plants, chlorophylls in green leaves mask accessory pigments until autumn (Figure 7.3*a*).

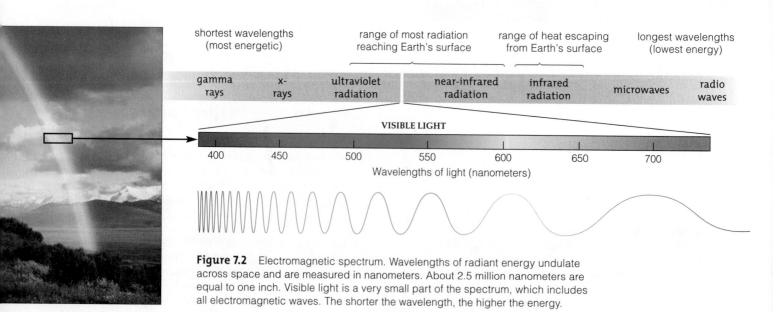

Figure 7.2 Electromagnetic spectrum. Wavelengths of radiant energy undulate across space and are measured in nanometers. About 2.5 million nanometers are equal to one inch. Visible light is a very small part of the spectrum, which includes all electromagnetic waves. The shorter the wavelength, the higher the energy.

a

The **phycobilins** reflect red or blue-green light. Red algae and cyanobacteria have notable amounts of these accessory pigments. A few bacteria of ancient lineages have unique pigments. Purple bacteriorhodopsin is the main kind in the archaean *Halobacterium halobium*.

Collectively, different photosynthetic pigments can absorb nearly all wavelengths across the spectrum of visible light. What happens next? You have to zoom into a pigment for the answer. As Figure 7.3*b,c* shows, a pigment molecule has at least one array of atoms in which single covalent bonds alternate with double covalent bonds. Remember electron orbitals (Section 2.3)? Electrons of these atoms share one orbital that spans the entire array. That array lets the pigment act like an antenna for receiving photon energy.

Each pigment absorbs light of specific wavelengths, which correspond to photon energy. Energy inputs, remember, boost electrons to higher energy levels. A photon is absorbed by a pigment only if it has exactly enough energy to boost an electron of the pigment's antenna region to a higher energy level.

An excited electron returns to a lower energy level almost immediately and emits its extra energy as heat or as a photon. As you will see shortly, that energy bounces back and forth like a fast volleyball among a team of photosynthetic pigments. It quickly reaches the team captain—a special chlorophyll that can *give up* excited electrons and so start the reactions.

Radiation from the sun travels in waves, which differ in length and energy content. We perceive visible light of different wavelengths as different colors and measure their energy content in packets called photons.

In plants, chlorophyll a and accessory pigments absorb specific wavelengths of visible light. They are molecular bridges between the sun's energy and photosynthesis.

Pigment molecules absorb photons at their arrays of alternating single and double covalent bonds. The arrays let the pigments act like energy-receiving antennas.

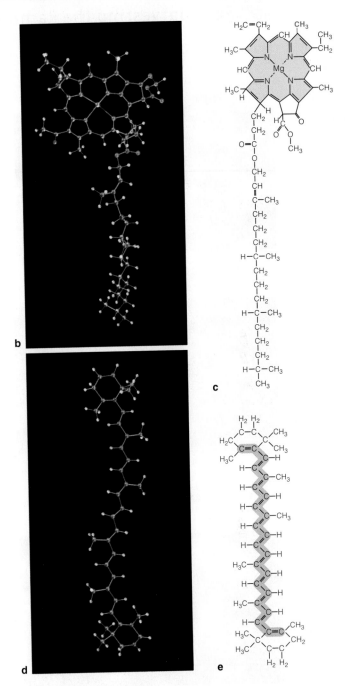

b

c

d

e

Figure 7.3 (**a**) Evidence of pigments in the changing leaves of autumn. In bright green leaves, photosynthetic cells continuously make chlorophyll, which masks accessory pigments. In autumn, chlorophyll synthesis lags behind its breakdown in many species. Accessory pigments then show through and give leaves characteristic red, orange, and yellow fall colors.

Ball-and-stick models and structural formulas for (**b,c**) chlorophyll *a* and (**d,e**) beta-carotene. The light-catching region of each pigment is tinted the specific color of light it transmits. Each pigment has a hydrocarbon backbone that readily dissolves in the lipid bilayer of cell membranes.

Chlorophylls *a* and *b* differ only in one functional group at the position shaded *red* (—CH_3 for chlorophyll *a* and —COO^- for chlorophyll *b*). The light-catching portion is the flattened ring structure, which is similar to a heme (Section 3.1). It holds a magnesium atom instead of iron.

LINK TO
SECTION
4,8

7.2 Harvesting the Rainbow

Different kinds of photosynthetic pigments work together. How efficient are these pigments at harvesting light of different wavelengths in the sun's rays?

At one time, people thought that plants used substances in soil to make food. By 1882, a few chemists had an idea that plants use sunlight, water, and something in the air. The botanist Wilhelm Theodor Engelmann wondered: *What parts of sunlight do plants favor?* He already knew that photosynthesis releases free oxygen. He came up with a hypothesis. If photosynthesis involves certain colors of light, then photosynthesizers will release more or less oxygen in response to different colors.

Engelmann also knew that certain bacteria use oxygen during aerobic respiration, and he predicted that they would gather in places where a photosynthetic organism was releasing the most oxygen. He directed a spectrum of visible light across a drop of water that contained bacterial cells (Figure 7.4a). The droplet also contained a strand of *Cladophora*, a photosynthetic alga (Figure 7.5).

Most of the bacterial cells gathered where violet and red light fell across the algal strand. More free oxygen had to be diffusing away from parts of the strand that were illuminated by the violet and red light—a sign that those colors are best at driving photosynthesis.

Engelmann did identify the wavelengths. But molecular biology was far in the future, so he did not know about the pigments that absorb the light.

Today, an **absorption spectrum** conveys how efficiently a given pigment absorbs light of different wavelengths. As Figure 7.4b shows, chlorophylls are best at absorbing red and violet light, but they transmit much of the yellow and green light. What if you combined absorption spectra for chlorophylls and all of the accessory pigments, including those in Figure 7.4b,c? You would see that, collectively, they respond to almost the full spectrum of wavelengths from the sun. They are efficient at what they do.

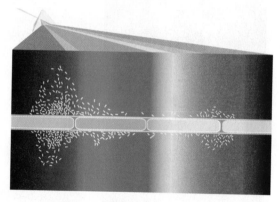

a Outcome of Engelmann's experiment

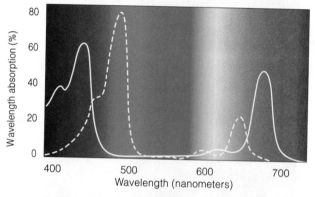

b Absorption spectra for chlorophyll *a* (solid graph line) and chlorophyll *b* (dashed line)

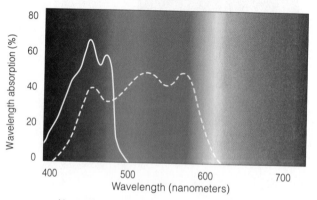

c Absorption spectra for beta-carotene (solid line) and one of the phycobilins (dashed line)

Figure 7.4 *Animated!* (a) One of the early photosynthesis experiments. W. T. Engelmann directed a ray of sunlight—broken into its component colors by a crystal prism—across a water droplet on a microscope slide. The droplet held an algal strand (*Cladophora*) and aerobic bacterial cells. As shown here, nearly all of the cells gathered under violet and red light, the most efficient wavelengths for photosynthesis.

(b,c) Later research revealed that all photosynthetic pigments combined absorb most wavelengths in the spectrum of visible light with remarkable efficiency. These graphs show absorption spectra for only four of many pigments: chlorophylls *a* and *b*, beta-carotene, and a phycobilin.

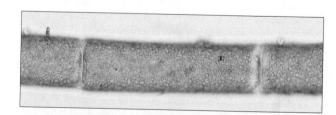

Figure 7.5 Light micrograph of the type of cells making up one algal strand.

7.3 Overview of Photosynthesis Reactions

Plants do something you never will do. They can make their own food from no more than light, water, and carbon dioxide.

Photosynthesis proceeds in two reaction stages. In the first stage—the **light-dependent reactions**—sunlight energy is converted to chemical bond energy of ATP. Water molecules are split, and typically the coenzyme NADP+ accepts the released hydrogen and electrons, thus becoming NADPH. The oxygen atoms released from water molecules escape into the surroundings.

The second stage, the **light-independent reactions**, runs on energy delivered by ATP. That energy drives the synthesis of glucose and other carbohydrates. The building blocks are the hydrogen atoms and electrons from NADPH, as well as carbon and oxygen atoms stripped from carbon dioxide and water.

Photosynthesis is often summarized this way:

$$12H_2O + 6CO_2 \xrightarrow[\text{enzymes}]{\text{light energy}} 6O_2 + C_6H_{12}O_6 + 6H_2O$$

water   carbon   oxygen   glucose   water
         dioxide

We will focus on what goes on inside **chloroplasts**, the organelles of photosynthesis in plants and many protists. A chloroplast has two outer membranes that enclose a semifluid matrix called the **stroma**. A third membrane—the **thylakoid membrane**—is folded up inside the stroma. In many cells, it looks like stacks of flattened sacs (thylakoids) connected by channels. But the space inside all the sacs and channels forms one continuous compartment, as in Figure 7.6*b*. Sugars are synthesized outside the compartment, in the stroma.

As you will see in the next section, the thylakoid membrane is studded with pigments. Most pigments are packed together as light-harvesting complexes. A number of **photosystems**, or reaction centers, also are embedded in the membrane, and each is surrounded by hundreds of light-harvesting complexes that pass on energy to it. With enough energy, its electrons get excited. That excitation sets in motion the first stage of reactions, as sketched out in Figure 7.6*c*.

In the first stage of photosynthesis, sunlight energy drives ATP and NADPH formation, and oxygen is released. In chloroplasts, this stage occurs at the thylakoid membrane.

The second stage proceeds in the stroma of chloroplasts. Energy from ATP drives the synthesis of sugars from water and carbon dioxide.

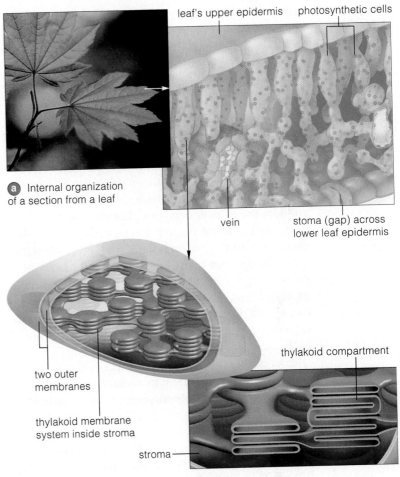

a Internal organization of a section from a leaf

leaf's upper epidermis   photosynthetic cells

vein   stoma (gap) across lower leaf epidermis

two outer membranes

thylakoid membrane system inside stroma

thylakoid compartment

stroma

b Cutaway view of a chloroplast inside the cytoplasm of one photosynthetic cell, and a close-up of its thylakoid compartment.

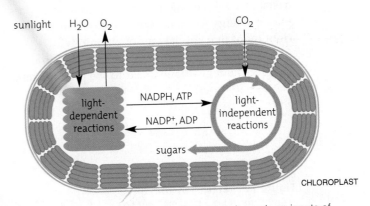

sunlight H_2O O_2 CO_2

light-dependent reactions   NADPH, ATP →   light-independent reactions

NADP+, ADP

sugars

CHLOROPLAST

c Two stages of photosynthesis. The first stage depends on inputs of sunlight. It occurs at the thylakoid membrane system. ATP and NADPH form; free oxygen diffuses away. In the second stage, enzymes in the stroma catalyze the assembly of sugars. Energy from ATP starts the reactions. Building blocks are hydrogen atoms and electrons (from NADPH) and carbon atoms (from carbon dioxide).

Figure 7.6 *Animated!* Zooming in on sites of photosynthesis inside the leaf of a typical plant.

7.4 Light-Dependent Reactions

LINKS TO
SECTIONS
5.2, 6.5

In the first stage of photosynthesis, photons absorbed at photosystems drive ATP formation. Water molecules are split. Their oxygen diffuses away, but the coenzyme NADP⁺ picks up the released electrons and hydrogen.

WHAT HAPPENS TO THE ABSORBED ENERGY?

Visualize a lone photon as it collides with a pigment molecule. One of the pigment's electrons can absorb that photon's energy, which boosts the electron to a higher energy level. If nothing else were to happen, the electron would drop back to its unexcited state and lose the extra energy as a photon or as heat.

In the thylakoid membrane, however, energy that excited electrons give up is kept in play. Embedded in the membrane are many hundreds of light-harvesting complexes: circular clusterings of pigments and other proteins (Figure 7.7a). The pigments in light-harvesting complexes do not waste absorbed photons. Instead, their electrons hold on to photon energy by passing it back and forth, like a volleyball.

Energy released from one complex gets passed to another, which passes it on to another, and so on until the energy reaches a photosystem. Chloroplasts have two kinds of photosystems, *type I* and *type II*. The two have slightly different chlorophyll *a* molecules. Each contains other molecules, including different pigments. Hundreds of light-harvesting complexes surround it.

Look back on Figure 7.3, which shows the structure of chlorophyll. Two molecules of chlorophyll *a* are at the center of a photosystem. Their flat rings face each other so closely that the electrons in *both* rings are destabilized. When light-harvesting complexes pass on photon energy to a photosystem, electrons are popped right off of that special pair of chlorophylls.

The freed electrons immediately enter an electron transfer chain positioned next to the photosystem. As

you know, **electron transfer chains** are components of cell membranes. Each is an orderly array of enzymes, coenzymes, and other proteins that transfer electrons step-by-step (Section 6.5). *The entry of electrons from a photosystem into an electron transfer chain is the first step in the light-dependent reactions*—in the conversion of photon energy to chemical energy for photosynthesis.

MAKING ATP AND NADPH

Figure 7.8 tracks electrons from a type II photosystem on through an electron transfer chain in the thylakoid membrane. As certain components of the chain accept and donate the electrons, they pick up hydrogen ions (H⁺) from the stroma and release them into the inner thylakoid compartment. They do so again and again. Soon, concentration and electric gradients are built up across the membrane, and the combined force of the gradients attracts H⁺ back toward the stroma.

But H⁺ cannot diffuse across the membrane's lipid bilayer. It can cross only through channels inside **ATP synthases**, a type of transport protein you read about in Section 5.2. In this case, the knoblike portion of the protein projects into the stroma. Ion flow through the channel makes the knob turn, which forces inorganic phosphate to become attached to an ADP molecule. In this way, ATP forms in the stroma.

As long as electrons flow through transfer chains, the cell can keep on producing ATP. But how are the electrons from photosystem II replaced? By a process called *photolysis*, new electrons are pulled away from water molecules, which then dissociate into hydrogen ions and molecular oxygen. The free oxygen diffuses out of the chloroplast, then out of the cell and into the surroundings. Hydrogen ions remain in the thylakoid compartment. They contribute to the concentration and electric gradients that drive ATP formation.

Figure 7.7 (a) Ringlike array of pigment molecules that intercept rays of sunlight coming from any direction. (b) One of the many photosystems (represented as a *green* sphere) embedded in a chloroplast's thylakoid membrane. Each photosystem collects energy from hundreds of light-harvesting complexes that surround it; only eight complexes are shown here.

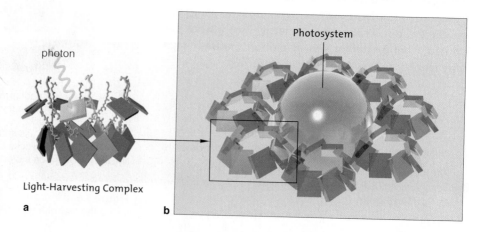

photon

Light-Harvesting Complex

a

b

Photosystem

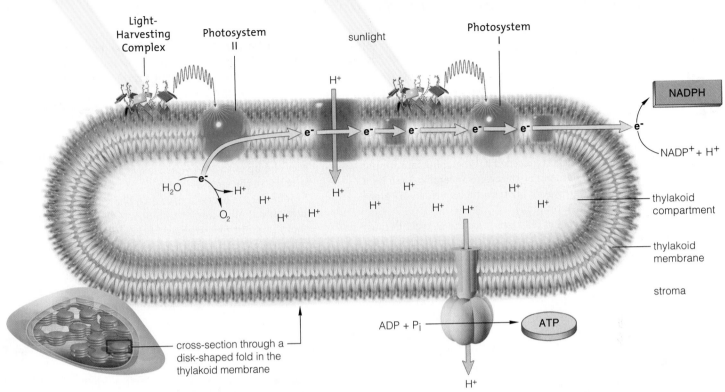

a Light-harvesting complexes absorb photon energy (*red*), which drives electrons out of photosystem II. Replacement electrons are pulled from water molecules, which then split into oxygen and hydrogen ions (H+). Oxygen leaves the cell as O_2.

b The electrons released from photosystem II enter an electron transfer chain (*brown*), which also moves H+ from the stroma into the thylakoid compartment. The electrons continue on to photosystem I.

c H+ concentration and electric gradients build up across the thylakoid membrane. The force of the gradients propels H+ through ATP synthases. The flow causes this membrane protein to move in a way that forces the attachment of P_i to ADP, thus forming ATP.

d Photon energy (*red*) drives electrons from photosystem I. An intermediary molecule (*brown*) adjacent to the photosystem in the membrane accepts and then transfers the electrons to NADP+, which picks up H+ at the same time and becomes NADPH.

Figure 7.8 *Animated!* How ATP and NADPH form during the first stage of photosynthesis. The drawing represents a cross-section through one of the disk-shaped folds of the thylakoid membrane. This entire sequence is called the *noncyclic* pathway of photosynthesis, because electrons that originally left photosystem II are not cycled back to it. They end up in NADPH.

But where do the electrons end up? After they pass through the electron transfer chain, they enter a type I photosystem where the light-harvesting complexes are volleying energy to a special pair of chlorophylls at the reaction center. The chlorophylls release electrons, which an intermediary molecule transfers to NADP+. When this coenzyme accepts the electrons, it attracts hydrogen ions and thereby becomes NADPH.

We have been describing the *noncyclic* pathway of ATP formation in chloroplasts, so named because the electrons that leave photosystem II do not get cycled back to it; they end up in NADPH.

When too much NADPH forms, it accumulates in the stroma, so the photosystem II pathway backs up. At such times, photosystem I may run independently so that cells can continue to make ATP. It is a *cyclic* pathway of ATP formation, because the electrons that leave photosystem I get cycled back to it. Before they

return, they pass through an electron transfer chain that moves H+ into the thylakoid compartment. The resulting H+ gradients drive ATP formation, but no NADPH forms in this shorter pathway.

Two kinds of photosystems, type I and type II, are embedded in the thylakoid membrane. Hundreds of light-harvesting complexes surround and transfer photon energy to each one.

In a noncyclic pathway of photosynthesis, photon energy forces electrons out of photosystem II and on to an electron transfer chain, which sets up H+ gradients that drive ATP formation. Electrons continue on through photosystem I and end up in a reduced coenzyme, NADPH.

ATP also can form by a cyclic pathway, in which electrons leave photosystem I and are cycled back to it. However, NADPH cannot form by this pathway.

7.5 Energy Flow in Photosynthesis

FOCUS ON
SCIENCE

LINKS TO
SECTIONS
6.1–6.3

One of the recurring themes in biology is that organisms convert one form of energy to another in highly controlled ways. The energy exchanges during the light-dependent reactions, outlined in Figure 7.9, are a classic example.

The preceding section focused on a photosynthetic pathway that starts at photosystem II and ends with the formation of ATP and NADPH. However, a simpler pathway that was less energy efficient preceded it. When photoautotrophs first evolved, remember, they were anaerobic. Their light-dependent pathway of photosynthesis yielded ATP alone, and it still operates today.

Again, this set of reactions is said to be cyclic because excited electrons flow out of photosystem I, through an electron transfer chain, then back to photosystem I.

Later, the photosynthetic machinery in some kinds of photoautotrophs was remodeled. Photosystem II became part of it. That was the start of a combined sequence of reactions powerful enough to oxidize—that is, to strip hydrogen atoms from—water molecules. Free oxygen is a by-product of this pathway.

Remember, the combined pathway is noncyclic; the electrons that leave photosystem II are not returned to it. They end up in NADPH, which delivers them to the sugar factories in the stroma.

Today, some bacteria have only photosystem I. Others have only photosystem II. Cyanobacteria, plants, and all photosynthetic protists have photosystems of both types and carry out both cyclic and noncyclic pathways. Which pathway dominates depends on conditions at the time.

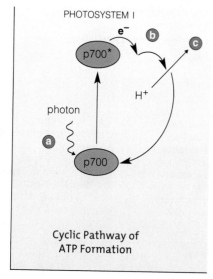

Cyclic Pathway of ATP Formation

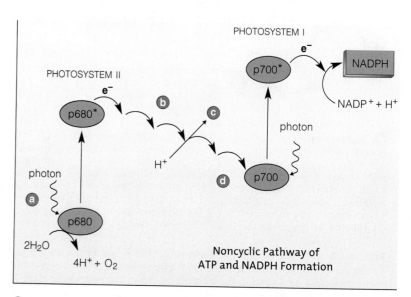

Noncyclic Pathway of ATP and NADPH Formation

a Photosystem I receives photon energy from a light-harvesting complex. It loses an electron.

b The electron passes from one molecule to another in an electron transfer chain that is embedded in the thylakoid membrane. It loses a little energy with each transfer, and ends up being reused by photosystem I (thus the pathway is considered "cyclic").

c Molecules in the transfer chain carry H+ across the thylakoid membrane into the inner compartment. Hydrogen ions accumulating in the compartment create an electrochemical gradient across the membrane that drives ATP synthesis, as shown in Figure 7.8.

a Photosystem II receives photon energy from a light-harvesting complex, then loses an electron. The electron moves through a different electron transfer chain. It loses a little energy with each transfer and ends up at photosystem I.

b Photosystem I receives photon energy from a light-harvesting complex, then loses an electron. Released electrons and hydrogen ions are used in the formation of NADPH from NADP+.

c As in the cyclic pathway, operation of the electron transfer chain pulls hydrogen ions into the thylakoid compartment. In this case, hydrogens released from dissociated water molecules also enter the compartment. The H+ concentration and electric gradient across the membrane are tapped for ATP formation (Figure 7.8).

d Electrons lost from photosystem I are replaced by the electrons lost from photosystem II. Electrons lost from photosystem II are replaced by electrons obtained from water. (Photolysis pulls water molecules apart into electrons, H+, and O_2.)

Figure 7.9 Animated! Using energy in the light-dependent reactions. The pair of chlorophyll *a* molecules at the center of photosystem I is designated p700. The pair in photosystem II is designated p680. The pairs respond most efficiently to wavelengths of 700 and 680 nanometers, respectively.

7.6 Light-Independent Reactions: The Sugar Factory

In the chloroplast's stroma, cyclic, enzyme-mediated reactions build sugars from hydrogen, carbon, and oxygen. These light-independent reactions run on energy that became conserved in ATP during the first stage of photosynthesis. NADPH that formed in the first stage donates the hydrogen and electrons. Plants get the carbon and oxygen from carbon dioxide (CO_2) in the air; algae get them from CO_2 dissolved in water.

The light-independent reactions proceed from carbon fixation, to PGAL formation, then RuBP regeneration. In **carbon fixation**, a carbon atom from CO_2 becomes attached to an organic compound. **Rubisco** (ribulose bisphosphate carboxylase/oxygenase) mediates this step in most plants. When it transfers the carbon to five-carbon RuBP (ribulose biphosphate), it opens the sugar factory—a series of enzyme-mediated reactions called the **Calvin–Benson cycle** (Figure 7.10).

The six-carbon intermediate that forms is unstable and splits at once into two PGA (phosphoglycerate) molecules, each with a three-carbon backbone (Figure 7.10*a*). Next, ATP energy and the reducing power of NADPH convert each PGA to a different three-carbon compound, PGAL (phosphoglyceraldehyde, or G3P).

How? ATP transfers a phosphate group to each PGA, and NADPH donates hydrogen and electrons to it.

Glucose, remember, has six carbon atoms. *Six CO_2 must be fixed and twelve PGAL must form to produce one glucose molecule and also to keep the Calvin–Benson cycle running.* Two PGAL combine to form one six-carbon glucose molecule with a phosphate group attached. The other ten PGAL undergo internal rearrangements in ways that regenerate RuBP (Figure 7.10*c–f*).

Most of the glucose is converted at once to sucrose or starch by other pathways that conclude the light-independent reactions. Sucrose is a transportable form of carbohydrate in plants. Excess glucose is converted to starch and briefly stored, as starch grains, in the stroma. Starch is converted to sucrose for export to leaves, stems, and roots. Plants can use photosynthetic products and intermediates as energy sources and as building blocks for all required organic compounds.

> *Driven by ATP energy, the light-independent reactions make sugars with hydrogen and electrons from NADPH, and with carbon and oxygen from carbon dioxide.*

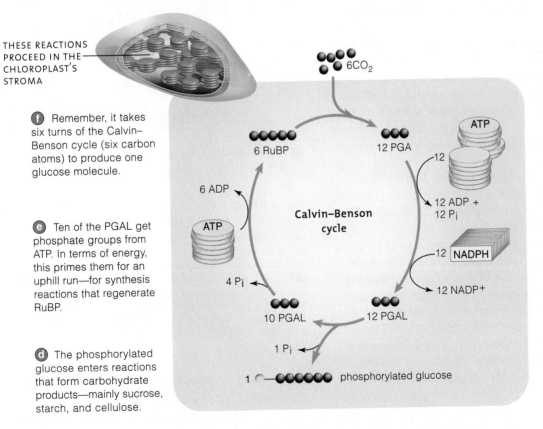

THESE REACTIONS PROCEED IN THE CHLOROPLAST'S STROMA

f Remember, it takes six turns of the Calvin–Benson cycle (six carbon atoms) to produce one glucose molecule.

e Ten of the PGAL get phosphate groups from ATP. In terms of energy, this primes them for an uphill run—for synthesis reactions that regenerate RuBP.

d The phosphorylated glucose enters reactions that form carbohydrate products—mainly sucrose, starch, and cellulose.

6CO₂

6 RuBP

12 PGA

ATP

Calvin–Benson cycle

6 ADP

ATP

4 Pᵢ

10 PGAL

12 PGAL

1 Pᵢ

12 ADP + 12 Pᵢ

12 NADPH

12 NADP⁺

1 — phosphorylated glucose

a CO_2 in air spaces inside a leaf diffuses into a photosynthetic cell. Six times, rubisco attaches a carbon atom of CO_2 to the RuBP that starts the Calvin–Benson cycle. Each time, the resulting intermediate splits to form two PGA molecules, for a total of twelve PGA.

b Each PGA molecule gets a phosphate group from ATP, plus hydrogen and electrons from NADPH. The resulting intermediate, PGAL, is thus primed for reaction.

c Two of the twelve PGAL molecules combine to form one molecule of glucose with an attached phosphate group.

Figure 7.10 *Animated!* Light-independent reactions of photosynthesis. The sketch is a summary of all six turns of the Calvin–Benson cycle and its product, one glucose molecule. *Brown* circles signify carbon atoms. Appendix VII details the reaction steps.

7.7 Different Plants, Different Carbon-Fixing Pathways

If sunlight intensity, air temperature, rainfall, and soil composition never varied, photosynthesis might be the same in all plants. But environments differ, and so do details of photosynthesis, as you can see by comparing what happens on hot, dry days when water is scarce.

C4 VERSUS C3 PLANTS

All plant surfaces exposed to air have a waxy, water-conserving cuticle. The only way for gases to diffuse into or out of a plant is at **stomata** (singular, stoma). These are tiny openings across the surface of leaves and green stems (Figure 7.11*a*). Stomata close on hot, dry days. Water stays inside the plant, but the CO_2 required for photosynthesis cannot diffuse in, and the O_2 by-product of photosynthesis cannot diffuse out.

That is why basswood, beans, peas, and many other plants do not grow well in hot, dry climates without steady irrigation. We call them **C3 plants**, because the *three*-carbon PGA is the first stable intermediate of the Calvin–Benson cycle. When their stomata are closed and the photosynthetic reactions are running, oxygen builds up in leaves and triggers a process that lowers a plant's sugar-making capacity. Remember rubisco, the enzyme that fixes carbon for the Calvin–Benson cycle? When O_2 levels rise, *photorespiration* dominates; rubisco attaches oxygen—not carbon—to RuBP. This reaction yields one molecule of PGA instead of two. The lower yield slows sugar production and growth of the plant. Compare Figure 7.11*a* with Figure 7.10.

C4 plants, such as corn, also close stomata on hot, dry days. But the CO_2 level does not decline as much because these plants fix carbon twice, in two types of photosynthetic cells (Figure 7.11*b*). In *mesophyll* cells, a four-carbon molecule, oxaloacetate, forms when CO_2 donates a carbon to PEP. The enzyme catalyzing this step will not use oxygen no matter how much there is. Oxaloacetate is converted to malate, which moves into *bundle-sheath cells* through plasmodesmata. The malate releases CO_2, which enters the Calvin–Benson cycle.

The C4 cycle keeps the CO_2 level near rubisco high enough to stop photorespiration. It requires one more ATP than the C3 cycle. However, less water is lost and more sugar can be made on hot, bright, dry days.

Photorespiration hampers the growth of many C3 plants. So why hasn't natural selection eliminated it? Rubisco evolved when the atmosphere held little O_2 and a great deal of CO_2. Perhaps the gene coding for rubisco's structure cannot mutate without disruptive effects on rubisco's primary role—carbon fixation.

Over the past 50 to 60 million years, the C4 cycle evolved independently in many lineages. Before then,

Leaves of basswood (*Tilia americana*)

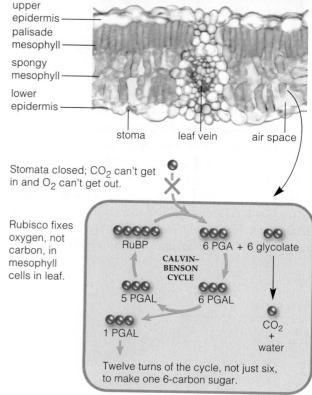

upper epidermis
palisade mesophyll
spongy mesophyll
lower epidermis

stoma   leaf vein   air space

Stomata closed; CO_2 can't get in and O_2 can't get out.

Rubisco fixes oxygen, not carbon, in mesophyll cells in leaf.

RuBP   6 PGA + 6 glycolate

CALVIN–BENSON CYCLE

5 PGAL   6 PGAL

1 PGAL CO_2 + water

Twelve turns of the cycle, not just six, to make one 6-carbon sugar.

(a) Carbon fixation in C3 plants during hot, dry weather, when there is too little CO_2 and too much O_2 in leaves.

Figure 7.11 Comparison of carbon-fixing adaptations in three kinds of plants that evolved in different environments.

(a) The Calvin–Benson cycle, which also is called the C3 cycle, is common in evergreens and many nonwoody plants of temperate zones, such as basswood and bluegrass. **(b)** A C4 cycle is common in grasses, corn, and other plants that evolved in the tropics and that fix CO_2 twice. **(c)** Prickly pear (*Opuntia*), a CAM plant. These plants, which open stomata and fix carbon at night, include orchids, pineapples, and many succulents besides cacti.

atmospheric CO_2 levels were higher, so C3 plants had the selective advantage in hot climates. Which cycle will be most adaptive in the future? The CO_2 levels have been rising for decades and may double in the next fifty years. If so, C3 plants will yet again be at an advantage—and many vital crop plants may benefit.

Leaves
of corn
(*Zea mays*)

Beavertail
cactus
(*Opuntia
basilaris*)

upper
epidermis —

mesophyll
cell

leaf vein —

bundle-
sheath cell —

lower
epidermis —

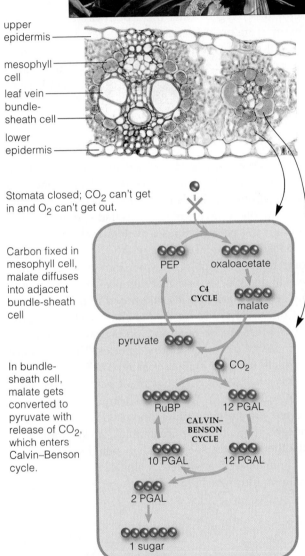

stoma

epidermis with
thick cuticle —

mesophyll cell —

air space —

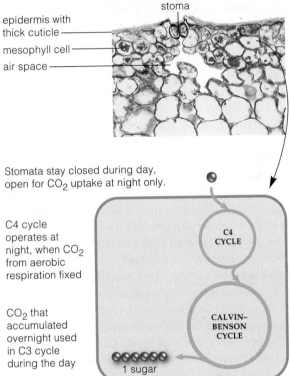

Stomata closed; CO_2 can't get
in and O_2 can't get out.

Carbon fixed in
mesophyll cell,
malate diffuses
into adjacent
bundle-sheath
cell

PEP   oxaloacetate

**C4
CYCLE**
         malate

In bundle-
sheath cell,
malate gets
converted to
pyruvate with
release of CO_2,
which enters
Calvin–Benson
cycle.

pyruvate

CO_2

RuBP   12 PGAL

**CALVIN–
BENSON
CYCLE**

10 PGAL   12 PGAL

2 PGAL

1 sugar

b Carbon fixation in C4 plants during hot, dry weather,
when there is too little CO_2 and too much O_2 in leaves.

Stomata stay closed during day,
open for CO_2 uptake at night only.

C4 cycle
operates at
night, when CO_2
from aerobic
respiration fixed

CO_2 that
accumulated
overnight used
in C3 cycle
during the day

**C4
CYCLE**

**CALVIN–
BENSON
CYCLE**

1 sugar

c Carbon fixation in CAM plants, adapted to hot, dry climates.

night, when mesophyll cells use a C4 cycle. Each cell
stores malate and other organic acids until the next
day, when stomata close. Malate releases CO_2, which
the cell uses in the Calvin–Benson cycle (Figure 7.11*c*).

Some CAM plants survive prolonged drought by
keeping stomata shut even at night. They fix CO_2 from
aerobic respiration. Not much forms, but it is enough
to maintain low metabolic rates and very slow growth.
Try growing cacti in mild climates, and you will see
that they compete poorly with C3 and C4 plants.

*C3 plants, C4 plants, and CAM plants respond differently to
hot, dry conditions. At such times, stomata close to conserve
water, and so photosynthetic cells must deal with too much
oxygen and not enough carbon dioxide in leaves.*

CAM PLANTS

We see a carbon-fixing adaptation to desert conditions
in a cactus. This plant, a type of succulent, has juicy,
water-storing tissues and thick surface layers that limit
loss of water. It is one of many **CAM plants** (short for
Crassulacean Acid Metabolism). A cactus will not open
stomata on hot days; it opens them and fixes CO_2 *at*

7.8 Autotrophs and the Biosphere

We conclude this chapter by reflecting on the mind-boggling numbers of single-celled and multicelled photosynthesizers and other autotrophs. We find them on land and in the water provinces, and they profoundly influence the biosphere.

THE ENERGY CONNECTION

This chapter opened with a brief look at the origin of photosynthesis and its impact on the world of life. All organisms require ongoing supplies of energy and carbon-based compounds for growth and survival. Autotrophs get them from the physical environment. Energy-rich carbon compounds become concentrated in single-celled kinds and in the tissues of multicelled kinds. In this way, autotrophs become concentrated stores of food tempting to heterotrophs.

Autotrophs are more than carbon-rich food baskets for the biosphere. Early practitioners of the noncyclic pathway of photosynthesis enriched the atmosphere with oxygen, and their descendants still replenish it.

Early photoautotrophs lived when iron and other metals were abundant both above and below the seas. As fast as oxygen was released, it swiftly latched onto (oxidized) the metals. Over time, it rusted them out, as evidenced by the bands of red iron deposits on the seafloor. Once that happened, oxygen bubbled out of vast populations of photoautotrophs, unimpeded.

In a wink of geologic time, maybe a few hundred thousand years, oxygen levels rose in the seas and the sky. Most anaerobic species had no means of adapting to the change, and they perished in a mass extinction. Other chemoautotrophs that could not tolerate oxygen endured in seafloor sediments, hot springs, and other anaerobic habitats. Some still live near hydrothermal vents, where superheated water spews out from big fissures in the seafloor. Archaeans near the vents get hydrogen and electrons from hydrogen sulfide in the mineral-rich water. Chemoautotrophs live in oxygen-free soils, where they extract energy from nitrogen-rich wastes and remains of other organisms.

However, among some ancient species of bacteria, metabolic pathways became modified in ways that detoxified oxygen. Later on, a pathway that released energy from organic compounds became modified in ways that allowed it to *use* oxygen as a final electron acceptor. As a direct outcome of the selection pressure exerted by oxygen—a by-product of photosynthesis—aerobic respiration had evolved (Figure 7.12).

PASTURES OF THE SEAS

Today, aerobic species are all around us. Each spring, the renewed growth of photoautotrophs is evident as trees leaf out and fields turn green. At the same time, uncountable numbers of single-celled species drifting through the ocean's surface waters make a seasonal response. You can't see them without a microscope. In some regions, a cup of seawater may hold 24 million cells of one species, and that number does not include any other aquatic species suspended in the cup.

Collectively, these cells are the "pastures of the seas." Most are bacteria and protists that ultimately feed nearly all other marine species. Their primary productivity is the start of vast aquatic food webs.

Imagine zooming in on a small patch of "pasture" in an Antarctic sea. There, tiny shrimplike crustaceans are feeding on even tinier photosynthesizers. Dense concentrations of these crustaceans, or krill, are food for other animals, such as fishes, penguins, seabirds, and immense blue whales. A single, mature whale is straining four tons of krill from the water. Before they

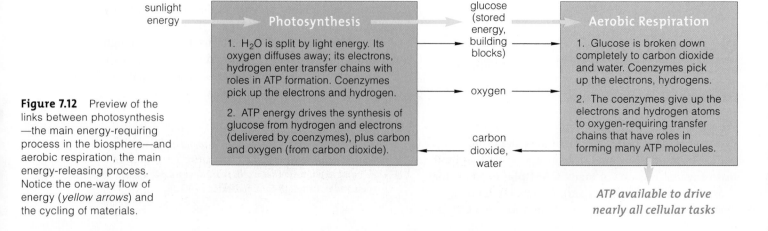

Figure 7.12 Preview of the links between photosynthesis—the main energy-requiring process in the biosphere—and aerobic respiration, the main energy-releasing process. Notice the one-way flow of energy (*yellow arrows*) and the cycling of materials.

sunlight energy

Photosynthesis

1. H₂O is split by light energy. Its oxygen diffuses away; its electrons, hydrogen enter transfer chains with roles in ATP formation. Coenzymes pick up the electrons and hydrogen.

2. ATP energy drives the synthesis of glucose from hydrogen and electrons (delivered by coenzymes), plus carbon and oxygen (from carbon dioxide).

glucose (stored energy, building blocks)

oxygen

carbon dioxide, water

Aerobic Respiration

1. Glucose is broken down completely to carbon dioxide and water. Coenzymes pick up the electrons, hydrogens.

2. The coenzymes give up the electrons and hydrogen atoms to oxygen-requiring transfer chains that have roles in forming many ATP molecules.

ATP available to drive nearly all cellular tasks

themselves became food for the whale, the four tons' worth of krill had munched their way through 1,200 tons of the pasture!

The pastures "bloom" in spring, when the seawater becomes warmer and greatly enriched with nutrients that currents churn up from the deep. The conditions favor huge increases in population sizes.

Until NASA gathered data from space satellites, we had no idea of the size and distribution of these marine pastures. Figure 7.13a shows the near-absence of photosynthetic activity one winter in the Atlantic Ocean. Figure 7.13b shows a springtime bloom that stretched from North Carolina all the way past Spain!

Collectively, these cells affect the global climate, because they deal with staggering numbers of gaseous reactant and product molecules. For instance, they sponge up nearly half of the carbon dioxide used in carbon fixation. Without them, atmospheric carbon dioxide would accumulate more rapidly and possibly accelerate global warming (Sections 47.9 and 47.10).

Although drastic global change is a real possibility, human activities release more carbon dioxide to the atmosphere than photoautotrophs can take up. Such activities include burning fossil fuels and setting fire to vast tracts of forests to clear land for farming.

There is more. Each day, tons of industrial wastes, raw sewage, and fertilizers in runoff from croplands enter the ocean and change its chemical composition. How long can we expect the marine photoautotrophs to function in this chemical brew? The answer may affect your life in more ways than one. It may affect populations and ecosystems throughout the world.

In sum, autotrophs exist in tremendous numbers. They nourish themselves and all other living things, and they are major players in the cycling of oxygen, nitrogen, phosphorus, and other elements all through the biosphere. Later chapters focus on their impact on the environment. In this unit, we turn next to major pathways by which all cells release the chemical bond energy that is stored in glucose and other biological molecules—the legacy of autotrophs everywhere.

Energy flow and the cycling of carbon and other nutrients through the biosphere starts with autotrophs.

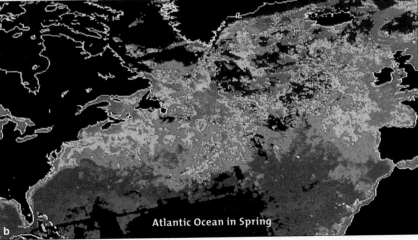

Figure 7.13 Two satellite images that convey the sheer magnitude of photosynthetic activity during springtime in the surface waters of the North Atlantic Ocean. Sensors in equipment launched with the satellite recorded concentrations of chlorophyll, which were greatest in regions coded *red*.

Take a deep breath while looking at these images. You just took in free oxygen that originated with some photoautotroph, somewhere in the world. Poison the autotrophs and how long will oxygen-dependent heterotrophs last?

Summary

Section 7.1 Photosynthesis runs on energy obtained when pigment molecules absorb wavelengths of visible light from the sun. Chlorophyll *a*, the main pigment, is best at absorbing violet and red wavelengths. Diverse photosynthetic pigments are accessory pigments. They form light-harvesting complexes that capture photons of particular wavelengths. Photons not captured are reflected as the characteristic color of each pigment.

Section 7.2 Collectively, photosynthetic pigments absorb most of the full range of wavelengths in the spectrum of visible light with impressive efficiency.

Section 7.3 Photosynthesis has two stages: light-dependent and light-independent reactions. Figure 7.14 and the following equation summarize the process:

$$12H_2O + 6CO_2 \xrightarrow[\text{enzymes}]{\text{light energy}} 6O_2 + C_6H_{12}O_6 + 6H_2O$$

water carbon   oxygen glucose water
      dioxide

In chloroplasts, the light-dependent reactions occur at a thylakoid membrane that forms a single compartment in the semifluid interior (stroma).

Biology⊛Now
View the sites where photosynthesis takes place with the animation on BiologyNow.

Sections 7.4, 7.5 Accessory pigments arrayed in clusters in the thylakoid membrane absorb photons and pass energy to many photosystems. Light-dependent

reactions use electrons released from photosystems in a noncyclic or a cyclic pathway of ATP formation.

In the noncyclic pathway, electrons are released from photosystem II and enter an electron transfer chain. Their flow through the chain causes hydrogen ions to accumulate in the thylakoid compartment. They flow on to photosystem I where photon absorption also causes the release of electrons. An intermediary molecule next to photosystem I accepts the electrons and transfers them to $NADP^+$, which attracts hydrogen ions (H^+) at the same time and becomes a reduced coenzyme, NADPH.

The electrons lost from photosystem II are replaced by way of photolysis—a reaction that pulls electrons from water molecules, with the release of H^+ and O_2.

In the cyclic pathway, electrons from photosystem I enter an electron transfer chain, then are cycled back to the same photosystem. NADPH does not form.

In both pathways, the H^+ buildup in the thylakoid compartment forms concentration and electric gradients across the thylakoid membrane. H^+ flows in response to the gradients, through ATP synthases. The flow causes P_i to be attached to ADP in the stroma, forming ATP.

Biology⊛Now
Review the pathways by which light energy is used to form ATP with the animation on BiologyNow.

Section 7.6 The light-independent reactions proceed in the stroma. In C3 plants, the enzyme rubisco attaches carbon from CO_2 to RuBP to start the Calvin–Benson cycle. In this cyclic pathway, energy from ATP, carbon and oxygen from CO_2, and hydrogen and electrons from NADPH are used to make phosphorylated glucose, which quickly enters reactions that form the products of photosynthesis (mainly sucrose, cellulose, and starch). It takes six turns of the Calvin–Benson cycle to fix the six CO_2 required to make one glucose molecule.

Biology⊛Now
Read the InfoTrac article "Robust Plants' Secret? Rubisco Activase!" Marcia Wood, Agricultural Research, November 2002.

Section 7.7 Environments differ, and so do details of sugar production. On hot, dry days, plants conserve water by closing stomata, but O_2 from photosynthesis cannot escape. In C3 plants, high O_2/low CO_2 levels cause the enzyme rubisco to use O_2 in an alternate pathway that does not make as much sugar. In C4 plants, carbon fixation occurs in one cell type, and the carbon enters the Calvin–Benson cycle in a different cell type. CAM plants close stomata in the day and fix carbon at night.

Biology⊛Now
Read the InfoTrac article "Light of Our Lives," Norman Miller, Geographical, January 2001.

Section 7.8 Photoautotrophs and chemoautotrophs produce the food that sustains themselves and all other organisms. Also, staggering numbers of diverse aerobic and anaerobic autotrophs live in the seas as well as on land. They have impact on the global cycling of oxygen, carbon, nitrogen, and other substances, and the global climate. Human activities are having impact on them.

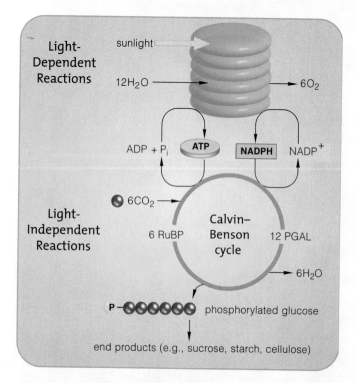

Figure 7.14 Visual summary of photosynthesis.

Figure 7.15 Leaves of *Elodea*, an aquatic plant.

Figure 7.16 (**a**) Red alga from a tropical reef. (**b**) Coastal green alga (*Codium*).

Self-Quiz

Answers in Appendix II

1. Photosynthetic autotrophs use _____ from the air as a carbon source and _____ as their energy source.

2. Chlorophyll *a* absorbs violet and red light, and it reflects light of _____ and _____ wavelengths.
   a. violet; red   c. green only
   b. yellow; green   d. white; orange

3. Light-*dependent* reactions in plants occur at the _____ .
   a. thylakoid membrane   c. stroma
   b. plasma membrane   d. cytoplasm

4. In the light-*dependent* reactions, _____ .
   a. carbon dioxide is fixed   c. CO_2 accepts electrons
   b. ATP and NADPH form   d. sugars form

5. What accumulates inside the thylakoid compartment during the light-*dependent* reactions?
   a. glucose   b. RuBP   c. hydrogen ions   d. CO_2

6. When a photosystem absorbs light, _____ .
   a. sugar phosphates are produced
   b. electrons are transferred to ATP
   c. RuBP accepts electrons
   d. light-dependent reactions begin

7. Light-*independent* reactions proceed in the _____ .
   a. cytoplasm   b. plasma membrane   c. stroma

8. The Calvin–Benson cycle starts when _____ .
   a. light is available
   b. carbon dioxide is attached to RuBP
   c. electrons leave photosystem II

9. What substance is *not* part of the Calvin–Benson cycle?
   a. ATP   d. carotenoids
   b. NADPH   e. O_2
   c. RuBP   f. CO_2

10. Match each event with its most suitable description.
    ____ ATP formation only   a. rubisco required
    ____ CO_2 fixation   b. ATP, NADPH required
    ____ PGAL formation   c. electrons cycled back
                                  to photosystem II

Additional questions are available on **Biology ⊜ Now™**

Critical Thinking

1. About 200 years ago, Jan Baptista van Helmont did experiments on the nature of photosynthesis. He wanted to know where growing plants get the materials necessary for increases in size. He planted a tree seedling weighing 5 pounds in a barrel filled with 200 pounds of soil. He watered the tree regularly. Five years passed. Then van Helmont weighed the tree and the soil. The tree weighed 169 pounds, 3 ounces. The soil weighed 199 pounds, 14 ounces. Because the tree gained so much weight and the soil lost so little, he concluded the tree had gained all of its additional weight by absorbing water he had added to the barrel. Given what you know about biological molecules, why was he misguided? Knowing what you do about photosynthesis, what really happened?

2. A cat eats a bird, which earlier ate a caterpillar that chewed on a weed. Which organisms are autotrophs? Which are the heterotrophs?

3. Imagine walking through a garden of red, white, and blue petunias. Explain each of the colors in terms of which wavelengths of light the flower is absorbing.

4. Krishna exposes pea plants to a carbon radioisotope ($^{14}CO_2$), which they absorb. In which compound will the labeled carbon appear first if the plants are C3? C4?

5. While gazing into an aquarium, you observe bubbling from an aquatic plant (Figure 7.15). What is happening?

6. Only about eight classes of pigment molecules are known, but this limited group gets around in the world. For example, photoautotrophs make carotenoids, which move through food webs, as when tiny aquatic snails graze on green algae and then flamingos eat the snails. Flamingos modify the ingested carotenoids. Their cells split beta-carotene to form two molecules of vitamin A. This vitamin is the precursor of retinol, a visual pigment that transduces light into electric signals in eyes. Beta-carotene gets dissolved in fat reservoirs under the skin. Cells that give rise to bright pink feathers take it up.

   Select a similar organism and do some research to identify sources for pigments that color its surfaces.

7. Most pigments respond to only part of the rainbow of visible light. If acquiring energy is so vital, then why doesn't each kind of photosynthetic pigment absorb the whole spectrum? *Why isn't each one black?*

   If early photoautotrophs evolved in the seas, then so did their pigments. Ultraviolet and red wavelengths do not penetrate water as deeply as green and blue wavelengths do. Possibly natural selection favored the evolution of different pigments at different depths. Many relatives of the red alga in Figure 7.16*a* live deep in the sea. Some are nearly black. Green algae, such as the one in Figure 7.16*b*, live in shallow water. Their chlorophylls absorb red wavelengths, and accessory pigments harvest others. Some accessory pigments also function as shields against ultraviolet radiation.

   Speculate on how natural selection may have favored the evolution of different pigments at different depths, starting at hydrothermal vents. You might start at Richard Monasterky's article in *Science News* (September 7, 1996) on Cindy Lee Dover's work at hydrothermal vents.

8 HOW CELLS RELEASE CHEMICAL ENERGY

When Mitochondria Spin Their Wheels

In the early 1960s, Swedish physician Rolf Luft mulled over some odd symptoms of a patient. The young woman felt weak and too hot all the time. Even on the coldest winter days she could not stop sweating, and her skin was always flushed. She was thin in spite of a huge appetite.

Luft inferred that his patient's symptoms pointed to a metabolic disorder. Her cells seemed to be spinning their wheels. They were active, but much of their activity was being dissipated as metabolic heat. So he ordered tests designed to detect her metabolic rates. The patient's oxygen consumption was the highest ever recorded!

Microscopic examination of a tissue sample from the patient's skeletal muscles revealed mitochondria, the cell's ATP-producing powerhouses. But there were far too many of them, and they were abnormally shaped. Other studies showed that the mitochondria were engaged in aerobic respiration—yet they were making very little ATP.

The disorder, now called *Luft's syndrome*, was the first to be linked directly to a defective organelle. By analogy, someone with this mitochondrial disorder functions like a city with half of its power plants shut down. Skeletal and heart muscles, the brain, and other hardworking body parts with the highest energy demands are hurt the most.

More than a hundred other mitochondrial disorders are now known. One, a heritable disease called *Friedreich's ataxia*, causes loss of coordination (ataxia), weak muscles, and visual problems. Many affected people die when they are young adults because of heart muscle irregularities. Figure 8.1 shows two affected individuals.

A mutant gene causes Friedreich's ataxia. Its abnormal protein product makes iron accumulate in mitochondria. Iron is vital for electron transfers that drive ATP formation, but too much favors the concentration of free radicals that can attack the structural integrity of all molecules of life.

Defective mitochondria also contribute to many age-related problems, including Type 1 diabetes, atherosclerosis, amyotrophic lateral sclerosis (Lou Gehrig's disease), as well as Parkinson's, Alzheimer's, and Huntington's diseases.

Clearly, human health depends on mitochondria that are structurally and functionally sound. However, zoom out from our characteristically human focus and you will find that every kind of animal, every kind of plant and fungus, and nearly every protist depend on them.

Remember how ATP forms at a membrane system inside chloroplasts? Similar events happen at a membrane system inside mitochondria. In both photosynthesis and aerobic respiration, electrons are released when an energy input breaks chemical bonds, and they are sent step-by-step through transfer chains in the membrane. Photosynthesis splits bonds in water molecules; aerobic respiration splits bonds in glucose and other organic compounds.

In mitochondria, too, energy harnessed as electrons go through transfer chains helps concentrate hydrogen ions on one side of the membrane. Here again, potential energy

Figure 8.1 Sister, brother, and broken mitochondria. Both of these individuals show symptoms of Friedreich's ataxia, a heritable genetic disorder that prevents them from making enough ATP to keep their body structurally and functionally sound. At age five, Leah started to lose her sense of balance and coordination. Six years later she was in a wheelchair and is now diabetic and partially deaf. Her brother Joshua was three when problems started. Eight years later he could not walk. He is now blind. Both sister and brother have heart problems; both had spinal fusion surgery. Special equipment allows them to attend school and work part-time. Leah is a professional model.

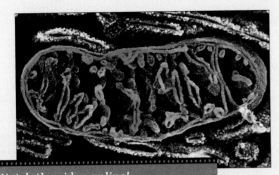

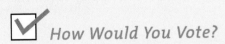

is briefly stored as concentration and electric gradients across that membrane. That stored energy is converted to the bond energy of ATP. And ATP is a transportable form of energy; it can jump-start nearly all of the metabolic reactions that keep cells, and organisms, going.

The point is, you already have a sense of how operation of electron transfer systems can concentrate energy in a form that can be tapped to make ATP. Even prokaryotic cells make ATP by operating simpler electron transfer systems, which are built into their plasma membrane. As you will see, the details differ from one group to the next. Yet even these variations do not obscure life's unity at the biochemical level.

How Would You Vote?

Developing new drugs is costly. There is little incentive for pharmaceutical companies to target ailments, such as Friedreich's ataxia, that affect relatively few individuals. Should the federal government allocate some funds to private companies that search for cures for diseases affecting a relatively small number of people? See BiologyNow for details, then vote online.

Key Concepts

THE MAIN ENERGY-RELEASING PATHWAYS

All organisms release chemical bond energy from glucose and other organic compounds to drive ATP formation. The main energy-releasing pathways all start in the cytoplasm. Only aerobic respiration, which uses free oxygen, ends in mitochondria. It has the greatest energy yield.   Section 8.1

GLYCOLYSIS—FIRST STAGE OF THE PATHWAYS

Glycolysis is the first stage of aerobic respiration. It also is the first stage of anaerobic pathways, such as alcoholic and lactate fermentation. Enzymes partially break down glucose to pyruvate, and they can do so in the presence of oxygen or in its absence.   Section 8.2

HOW AEROBIC RESPIRATION ENDS

Aerobic respiration continues through two more stages. In the second stage, pyruvate from glycolysis is broken down to carbon dioxide. Electrons and hydrogen that coenzymes picked up during the first two stages enter electron transfer chains. In the third stage, transfer chains set up conditions that favor ATP formation. Free oxygen accepts the spent electrons.   Sections 8.3, 8.4

HOW ANAEROBIC PATHWAYS END

Fermentation also starts with glycolysis, but substances other than oxygen are the final electron acceptor. The net energy yield is always small.   Section 8.5

WHAT IF GLUCOSE IS NOT AVAILABLE?

When required, molecules other than glucose can enter the aerobic pathway as alternative energy sources.   Section 8.6

PERSPECTIVE AT UNIT'S END

We see evidence of life's unity in its molecular and cellular organization and in the utter dependence of all organisms on the one-way flow of energy.   Section 8.7

Links to Earlier Concepts

This chapter expands the picture of life's dependence on energy flow by showing how all organisms tap energy stored in glucose and convert it to transportable forms, ATP especially (Sections 6.1, 6.2). You may wish to review the structure of glucose (3.1, 3.3). You will see more examples of controlled energy release at electron transfer chains (6.4). You will reflect once more on global connections between photosynthesis and aerobic respiration (7.8).

8.1 Overview of Energy-Releasing Pathways

LINKS TO
SECTIONS
6.1, 6.2

Plants make ATP during photosynthesis and use it to synthesize glucose and other carbohydrates. But all organisms, plants included, can make ATP by breaking down carbohydrates, lipids, and proteins.

Organisms stay alive only as long as they get more energy to replace the energy they use up (Section 6.1). Plants and all other photoautotrophs get energy from the sun; heterotrophs get energy by eating plants and one another. Regardless of its source, the energy must be converted to some form that can drive thousands of diverse life-sustaining reactions. Energy that becomes converted into chemical bond energy of adenosine triphosphate—ATP—serves that function.

COMPARISON OF THE MAIN TYPES OF ENERGY-RELEASING PATHWAYS

The first energy-releasing metabolic pathways were operating billions of years before Earth's oxygen-rich atmosphere evolved, so we can expect that they were *anaerobic*; the reactions did not use free oxygen. Many prokaryotes and protists still live in places where oxygen is absent or not always available. They make ATP by fermentation and other anaerobic pathways. Many eukaryotic cells still use fermentation, including skeletal muscle cells. However, the cells of nearly all eukaryotes extract energy efficiently from glucose by **aerobic respiration**, an oxygen-dependent pathway. Each breath you take provides your actively respiring cells with a fresh supply of oxygen.

Make note of this point: *In every cell, all of the main energy-releasing pathways start with the same reactions in the cytoplasm.* During the initial reactions, **glycolysis**, enzymes cleave and rearrange a glucose molecule into two molecules of **pyruvate**, an organic compound that has a three-carbon backbone.

After glycolysis, energy-releasing pathways differ. Only the aerobic pathway ends inside mitochondria. There, free oxygen accepts and removes electrons after they indirectly help the formation of ATP (Figure 8.2).

As you examine the energy-releasing pathways in sections to follow, keep in mind that enzymes catalyze each step, and intermediates formed at one step serve as substrates for the next enzyme in the pathway.

OVERVIEW OF AEROBIC RESPIRATION

Of all energy-releasing pathways, aerobic respiration gets the most ATP for each glucose molecule. Whereas anaerobic routes have a net yield of two ATP, aerobic respiration typically yields thirty-six or more. If you were a bacterium, you would not require much ATP. Being far larger, more complex, and highly active, you

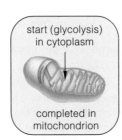

Anaerobic Energy-
Releasing Pathways
Aerobic
Respiration

Figure 8.2 *Animated!* Where the main energy-releasing pathways of ATP formation start and end. Only aerobic respiration ends in mitochondria. This pathway alone delivers enough ATP to build and maintain big multicelled organisms, including redwoods and highly active animals, such as people and Canada geese.

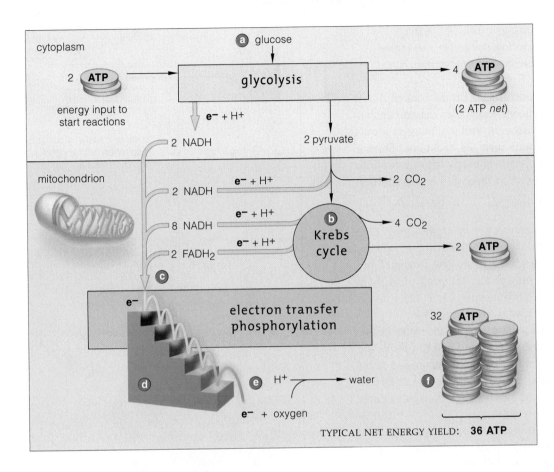

Figure 8.3 *Animated!* Overview of aerobic respiration. The reactions start in the cytoplasm, but they end inside mitochondria.

(a) In the first stage, glycolysis, enzymes partly break down glucose to pyruvate.

(b) In the second stage, enzymes break down pyruvate to carbon dioxide.

(c) NAD$^+$ and FAD pick up the electrons and hydrogen stripped from intermediates in both stages.

(d) The last stage is electron transfer phosphorylation. NADH and FADH$_2$, which are reduced coenzymes, deliver electrons to electron transfer chains. H$^+$ accompanies these electrons. Electron flow through the chains sets up H$^+$ gradients, which are tapped to make ATP.

(e) Oxygen accepts electrons at the end of the third stage, forming water.

(f) From start to finish, a typical net energy yield from a single glucose molecule is thirty-six ATP.

depend on the aerobic pathway's high yield. When a molecule of glucose is the starting material, aerobic respiration can be summarized this way:

$$C_6H_{12}O_6 \; + \; 6O_2 \longrightarrow 6CO_2 \; + \; 6H_2O$$

glucose   oxygen   carbon   water
                           dioxide

However, as you can see, the summary equation only tells us what the substances are at the start and finish of the pathway. In between are three reaction stages.

As you track the reactions, you will encounter two coenzymes, abbreviated **NAD$^+$** (nicotinamide adenine dinucleotide) and **FAD** (flavin adenine dinucleotide). Both accept electrons and hydrogen derived from intermediates that form during glucose breakdown. Unbound hydrogen atoms are hydrogen ions (H$^+$), or naked protons. When the two coenzymes are carrying electrons and hydrogen, they are in a reduced form and may be abbreviated NADH and FADH$_2$.

Figure 8.3 is your overview of aerobic respiration. Glycolysis, again, is the first stage. The second stage is a cyclic pathway, the **Krebs cycle**. Enzymes break down pyruvate to carbon dioxide and water. These reactions release many electrons and hydrogen atoms.

Few ATP form during glycolysis or the Krebs cycle. The big energy harvest comes in the third stage, after reduced coenzymes give up electrons and hydrogen to electron transfer chains—the machinery of **electron transfer phosphorylation**. Operation of these chains sets up H$^+$ concentration and electric gradients. The gradients drive ATP formation at nearby membrane transport proteins. During this final stage, many ATP molecules form. It ends when free oxygen accepts the "spent" electrons from the last portion of the transfer chain. The oxygen picks up H$^+$ at the same time and thereby forms water, a by-product of the reactions.

Nearly all metabolic reactions run on energy released from glucose and other organic compounds. The main energy-releasing pathways start in the cytoplasm with glycolysis, a series of reactions that break down glucose to pyruvate.

Anaerobic pathways have a small net energy yield, typically two ATP for each glucose molecule metabolized.

Aerobic respiration, an oxygen-dependent pathway, runs to completion in mitochondria. From start (glycolysis) to finish, it typically has a net energy yield of thirty-six ATP.

8.2 Glycolysis—Glucose Breakdown Starts

LINKS TO
SECTIONS
2.4, 3.3

Let's track what happens to a glucose molecule in the first stage of aerobic respiration. Remember, these same steps occur in anaerobic energy-releasing pathways.

Any of several six-carbon sugars can be broken down in glycolysis. Each glucose molecule, remember, has six carbon, twelve hydrogen, and six oxygen atoms (Section 3.3). The carbons form its backbone. During glycolysis, this one molecule is partly broken down to two molecules of pyruvate, a three-carbon compound:

glucose ⟶ (P)–glucose ⟶ 2 pyruvate

The initial steps of glycolysis are *energy-requiring*. One ATP molecule primes glucose to rearrange itself by donating a phosphate group to it. The intermediate that forms, fructose-6-phosphate, accepts a phosphate group from another ATP molecule. Thus, cells invest two ATP to jump-start glycolysis (Figure 8.4a).

The resulting intermediate is split into one PGAL (phosphoglyceraldehyde) and one DHAP, a molecule that has the same number of atoms arranged a bit differently. An enzyme can reversibly convert DHAP into PGAL. It does so, and two PGAL molecules enter the next reaction (Figure 8.4b).

In the first *energy-releasing* step of glycolysis, the two PGAL are converted to intermediates that give up a phosphate group to ADP, so two ATP form. In later reactions, two more intermediates do the same thing. Thus, four ATP have formed by **substrate-level phosphorylation**. We define this metabolic event as a direct transfer of a phosphate group from a substrate of a reaction to another molecule—in this case, to ADP.

Meanwhile, the two PGAL give up electrons and hydrogens to two NAD^+, which becomes NADH.

Even though four ATP are now formed, remember that two ATP were invested to start the reactions. The *net* yield of glycolysis is two ATP and two NADH.

To summarize, glycolysis converts bond energy of glucose to bond energy of ATP—a transportable form of energy. The electrons and hydrogen stripped from glucose and picked up by NAD^+ can enter the next stage of reactions. So can the products of glycolysis—two pyruvate molecules.

> *Glycolysis is a series of reactions that partially break down glucose or other six-carbon sugars to two molecules of pyruvate. It takes two ATP to jump-start the reactions.*
>
> *Two NADH and four ATP form. However, when we subtract the two ATP required to start the reactions, the net energy yield of glycolysis is two ATP from one glucose molecule.*

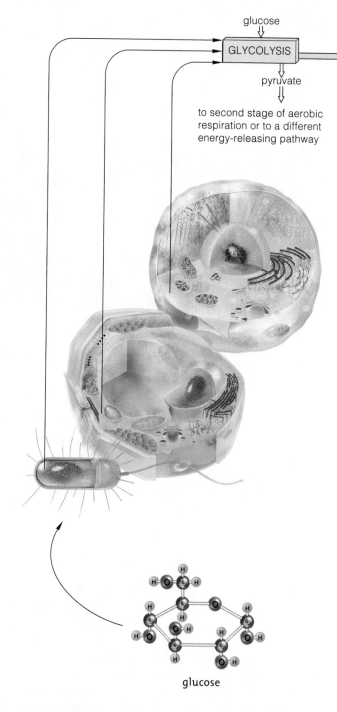

Figure 8.4 *Animated!* Glycolysis. This first stage of the main energy-releasing pathways occurs in the cytoplasm of all prokaryotic and eukaryotic cells. Glucose is the reactant in this example. Appendix VII gives the structural formulas of reaction intermediates and products. Two pyruvate, two NADH, and four ATP form in glycolysis. Cells invest two ATP to start the reactions, however, so the *net* energy yield is two ATP.

Depending on the type of cell and environmental conditions, the pyruvate may enter the second set of reactions of the aerobic pathway, including the Krebs cycle. Or it may be used in other reactions, such as those of fermentation.

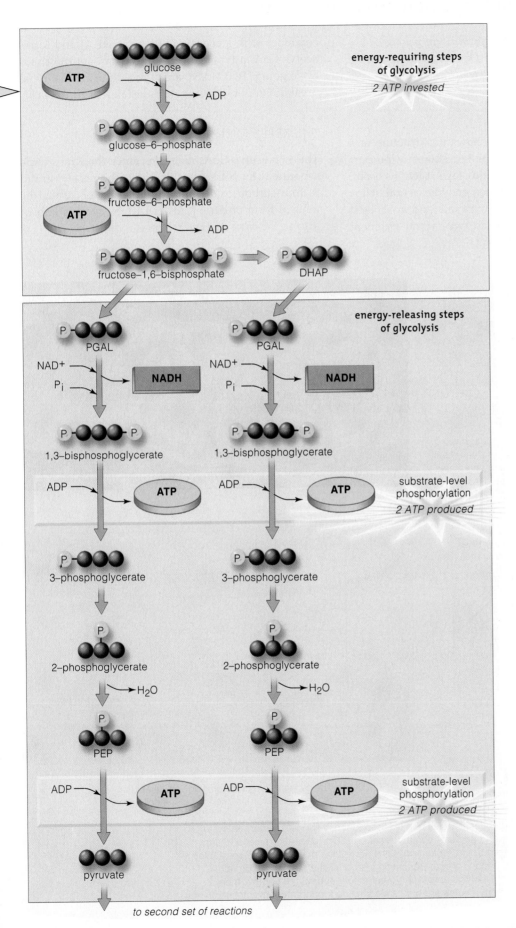

Track the six carbon atoms (*brown circles*) of glucose. Glycolysis requires an energy investment of two ATP:

a One ATP transfers a phosphate group to glucose, jump-starting the reactions.

b Another ATP transfers a phosphate group to an intermediate, causing it to split into two three-carbon compounds: PGAL and DHAP (dihydroxyacetone phosphate). Both have the same atoms, arranged differently, and they are interconvertible. But only PGAL can continue on in glycolysis. DHAP gets converted, so two PGAL are available for the next reaction.

c Two NADH form when each PGAL gives up two electrons and a hydrogen atom to NAD^+.

d Two intermediates each transfer a phosphate group to ADP. *Thus, two ATP have formed by direct phosphate group transfers.* The original energy investment of two ATP is now paid off.

e Two more intermediates form. Each gives up one hydrogen atom and an —OH group. These combine as water. Two molecules called PEP form by these reactions.

f Each PEP transfers a phosphate group to ADP. *Once again, two ATP have formed by substrate-level phosphorylation.*

In sum, glycolysis has a net energy yield of two ATP for each glucose molecule. Two NADH also form during the reactions, and two molecules of pyruvate are the end products.

8.3   Second Stage of Aerobic Respiration

LINKS TO
SECTIONS
1.1, 2.4

The two pyruvate molecules that form during glycolysis may be completely dismantled in a mitochondrion. Many coenzymes pick up the released electrons and hydrogens.

ACETYL–CoA FORMATION

Start with Figure 8.5, which shows the structure of a typical mitochondrion. Figure 8.6a zooms in on part of the interior where the second-stage reactions occur. At the start of these reactions, enzyme action strips one carbon atom from each pyruvate and attaches it to oxygen, forming CO_2. Each two-carbon fragment combines with a coenzyme (designated A) and forms acetyl–CoA, a type of cofactor that can get the Krebs cycle going. Two NAD^+ are reduced during the initial breakdown of two pyruvate molecules (Figure 8.7a,b).

THE KREBS CYCLE

The two acetyl–CoA molecules enter the Krebs cycle separately. Each transfers its two-carbon acetyl group to four-carbon oxaloacetate, which forms citrate, the ionized form of citric acid. The Krebs cycle is known also as the *citric acid cycle*, after its first step.

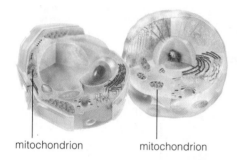

mitochondrion   mitochondrion

Figure 8.5   Scanning electron micrograph of a mitochondrion, sliced crosswise. Remember, nearly all eukaryotic species, including plants and animals, contain these organelles.

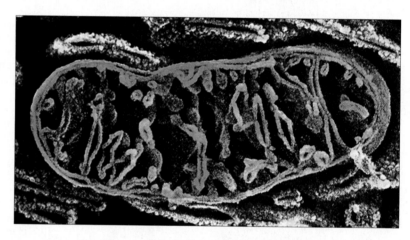

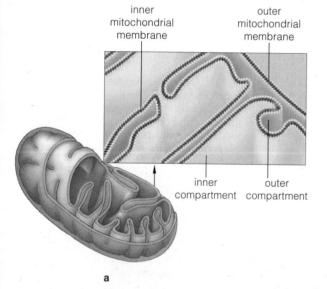

inner mitochondrial membrane   outer mitochondrial membrane

inner compartment   outer compartment

a

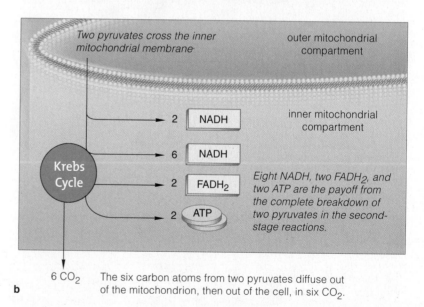

Two pyruvates cross the inner mitochondrial membrane·   outer mitochondrial compartment

inner mitochondrial compartment

Krebs Cycle → 2 NADH

→ 6 NADH

→ 2 FADH₂

→ 2 ATP

Eight NADH, two FADH₂, and two ATP are the payoff from the complete breakdown of two pyruvates in the second-stage reactions.

6 CO_2 The six carbon atoms from two pyruvates diffuse out of the mitochondrion, then out of the cell, in six CO_2.

b

Figure 8.6 *Animated!* (**a**) Functional zones of a mitochondrion. An inner membrane system divides the interior into an inner and an outer compartment. Aerobic respiration's second and third stages take place at this membrane system. (**b**) Overview of the number of ATP molecules and coenzymes that form in the second stage. Reactions start after the membrane proteins transport the two pyruvate from glycolysis across the outer mitochondrial membrane, then across the inner membrane. Both pyruvates are dismantled inside the inner compartment.

a One carbon atom is stripped from each pyruvate and is released as CO_2. The remaining fragment binds with coenzyme A, forming acetyl–CoA.

Acetyl-CoA Formation

pyruvate

coenzyme A

NAD^+

(CO_2)

NADH

—CoA

acetyl-CoA

b NAD^+ picks up hydrogen and electrons, forming one NADH.

- -

Krebs Cycle

CoA

h The final steps regenerate oxaloacetate. NAD^+ picks up hydrogen and electrons, forming NADH. *At this point in the cycle, three NADH and one $FADH_2$ have formed.*

oxaloacetate

citrate

c In the first step of the Krebs cycle, acetyl–CoA transfers two carbons to oxaloacetate, forming citrate.

NAD^+

NADH

NADH

d In rearrangements of intermediates, another carbon atom is released as CO_2, and NADH forms as NAD^+ picks up hydrogen and electrons.

NAD^+

g $FADH_2$ forms as the coenzyme FAD picks up electrons and hydrogen.

FADH₂

FAD

NAD^+

NADH

e Another carbon atom is released as CO_2. Another NADH forms. *The three carbon atoms that entered the second-stage reactions in each pyruvate have now been released.*

ATP

ADP + phosphate group

f A phosphate group is attached to ADP. At this point, one ATP has formed by substrate-level phosphorylation.

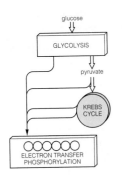

glucose

GLYCOLYSIS

pyruvate

KREBS CYCLE

ELECTRON TRANSFER PHOSPHORYLATION

Figure 8.7 *Animated!* Aerobic respiration's second stage: formation of acetyl–CoA and the Krebs cycle. The reactions proceed in a mitochondrion's inner compartment. *It takes two turns of the cycle to break down the two pyruvates from glucose.* A total of two ATP, eight NADH, two $FADH_2$, and six CO_2 molecules form. Organisms release the CO_2 from the reactions into their surroundings. For details, see Appendix VII.

The second-stage reactions run twice, one for each pyruvate molecule. The remaining carbon atoms are released in the form of CO_2 (Figure 8.7d,e). Only two ATP form during the two turns, which does not add much to the small net yield from glycolysis. However, in addition to the two NAD^+ that were reduced when the acetyl–CoA formed, six more NAD^+ and two FAD molecules are reduced. With their cargo of electrons and hydrogen, these coenzymes—*eight NADH and two FADH₂*—are a big potential payoff for the cell. All of the electrons have potential energy, which coenzymes can deliver to the final reaction sites.

As you can see from Figure 8.7, a total of *six* carbon atoms (from two pyruvates) depart during the second stage of aerobic respiration, in six molecules of CO_2. Therefore, the glucose from glycolysis has lost all of its carbons; it has become fully oxidized.

A final note: Figure 8.7 is a simplified version of these second-stage reactions. For interested students, Figure B in Appendix VII offers more details.

Aerobic respiration's second stage starts after two pyruvate molecules from glycolysis move from the cytoplasm, across the outer and inner mitochondrial membranes, and then into the inner mitochondrial compartment.

During these reactions, pyruvate is converted to acetyl–CoA, which starts the Krebs cycle. Two ATP and ten coenzymes (eight NADH, two FADH₂) form. All of pyruvate's carbons depart, in the form of carbon dioxide.

Together with two coenzymes (NADH) that formed during glycolysis, the ten coenzymes from the second stage will deliver electrons and hydrogen to the third and final stage.

8.4 Third Stage of Aerobic Respiration—A Big Energy Payoff

LINKS TO
SECTIONS
5.2, 6.4

In the aerobic pathway's third stage, energy release goes into high gear. Coenzymes from the first two stages provide the hydrogen and electrons that drive the formation of many ATP. Electron transfer chains and ATP synthases function as the machinery.

ELECTRON TRANSFER PHOSPHORYLATION

The third stage starts as coenzymes donate electrons to electron transfer chains in the inner mitochondrial membrane (Figure 8.8a). The flow of electrons through the chains drives the attachment of phosphate to ADP molecules. That is what the name of the event, *electron transfer phosphorylation*, means.

Incremental energy release, recall, is more efficient than one burst of energy, nearly all of which would be lost as unusable heat (Section 6.4). As electrons flow through the chains, they transfer energy bit by bit, in tiny amounts, to molecules that briefly store it. The two NADH that formed in the cytoplasm (by glycolysis) cannot directly reach the ATP-forming machinery. They must give up their electrons and hydrogen to transport proteins, which shuttle them across the inner membrane, into the innermost compartment. There, NAD$^+$ or FAD

pick them up. The eight NADH and two FADH$_2$ from the second stage are already inside.

All of the coenzymes turn over electrons to transfer chains and at the same time give up hydrogen, which now has a positive charge (H$^+$). Again, electrons lose a bit of energy at each transfer through the chain. At three transfers, that energy drives the pumping of H$^+$ into the outer compartment (Figure 8.8b). There, many ions accumulate—which sets up concentration and electric gradients across the inner membrane.

H$^+$ cannot cross a lipid bilayer. Instead, it follows its gradients by flowing through ATP synthases (Section 5.2 and Figure 8.8c). The ion flow causes parts of the ATP synthase molecules to change their shape in a reversible way. The change promotes the attachment of unbound phosphate to ADP, thus forming ATP.

The last components of the electron transfer chains pass electrons to oxygen, which combines with H$^+$ and thereby forms water. *Oxygen is the final acceptor of electrons originally stripped from glucose.*

In oxygen-starved cells, the electrons have nowhere to go. The whole chain backs up with electrons all the way to NADPH, so no H$^+$ gradients form, and no ATP forms, either. Without oxygen, cells of complex organisms do not survive long. They cannot produce enough ATP to sustain life processes.

glucose
↓
GLYCOLYSIS
↓
pyruvate
↓
KREBS
CYCLE
↓
ELECTRON TRANSFER
PHOSPHORYLATION

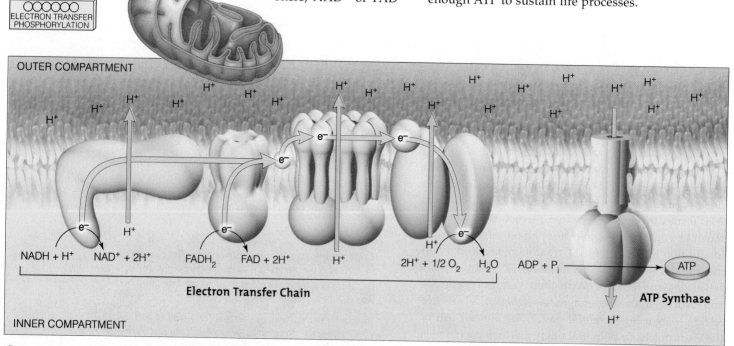

OUTER COMPARTMENT

NADH + H$^+$ NAD$^+$ + 2H$^+$ FADH$_2$ FAD + 2H$^+$ H$^+$ 2H$^+$ + 1/2 O$_2$ H$_2$O   ADP + P$_i$ → ATP

Electron Transfer Chain   **ATP Synthase**

INNER COMPARTMENT   H$^+$

(a) At the inner mitochondrial membrane, NADH and FADH$_2$ give up electrons to transfer chains. When electrons are transferred through the chains, unbound hydrogen (H$^+$) is shuttled across the membrane to the outer compartment.

(b) Free oxygen is the final acceptor of electrons at the end of the transfer chain.

(c) H$^+$ concentration and electric gradients now exist across the membrane. H$^+$ follows the gradients through the interior of ATP synthases, to the inner compartment. The flow drives the formation of ATP from ADP and unbound phosphate (P$_i$).

Figure 8.8 Electron transfer phosphorylation, the third and final stage of aerobic respiration.

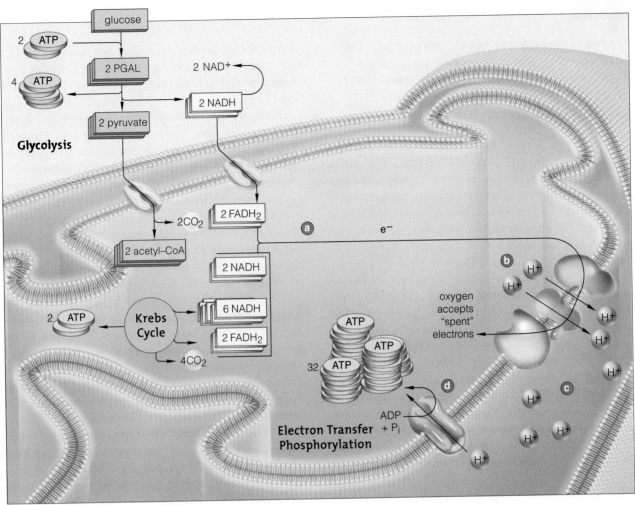

(a) Electrons and hydrogen from NADH and FADH$_2$ that formed during the first and second stages enter electron transfer chains.

(b) As electrons are being transferred through these chains, H$^+$ ions are shuttled across the inner membrane, into the outer compartment.

(c) More H$^+$ accumulates in the outer compartment than in the inner one. Chemical and electric gradients have been established across the inner membrane.

(d) Hydrogen ions follow the gradients through the interior of ATP synthases, driving ATP formation from ADP and phosphate (P$_i$).

Figure 8.9 *Animated!* Summary of the transfers of electrons and hydrogen from coenzymes involved in ATP formation in mitochondria.

SUMMING UP: THE ENERGY HARVEST

Thirty-two ATP typically form in the third stage. Add the four ATP from the earlier stages, and the net yield from a glucose molecule is *thirty-six ATP* (Figure 8.9). By contrast, anaerobic pathways may use up eighteen glucose molecules to get the same net yield.

The yield varies. First, reactant, intermediate, and product concentrations can change it. Second, the two NADH from glycolysis cannot enter a mitochondrion. They give up electrons and hydrogen to transport proteins in the outer mitochondrial membrane, which shuttle them across. NAD$^+$ or FAD that are already inside accept them, forming NADH or FADH$_2$.

When NADH inside delivers electrons to a certain entry point into a transfer chain, enough H$^+$ gets pumped across the membrane to make three ATP.

FADH$_2$ delivers them to a different entry point. Less H$^+$ is pumped across, and only two ATP form.

In liver, heart, and kidney cells, the electrons and hydrogen enter the first entry point, and the energy harvest is thirty-eight ATP. More commonly, as in skeletal muscle and brain cells, they are transferred to FAD, so the harvest is thirty-six ATP.

In aerobic respiration's third stage, electrons from NADH and FADH$_2$ flow through transfer chains and H$^+$ is shuttled across the mitochondrion's inner membrane, into the outer compartment. H$^+$ concentration and electric gradients form across the inner membrane. H$^+$ flows back outside through ATP synthases, which drives the formation of many ATP.

8.5 Anaerobic Energy-Releasing Pathways

LINK TO
SECTION
7.8

Unlike aerobic respiration, the anaerobic pathways do not use oxygen as the final acceptor of electrons. Their final steps have an important function: they regenerate NAD⁺.

FERMENTATION PATHWAYS

Fermenters are diverse. Many are protists and bacteria in marshes, bogs, mud, deep sea sediments, the animal gut, canned foods, sewage treatment ponds, and other oxygen-free places. When exposed to oxygen, some die. Bacteria that cause botulism are examples. Other fermenters are indifferent to oxygen's presence. Still other kinds use oxygen, but they also can switch to fermentation when oxygen becomes scarce.

Glycolysis is the first stage of fermentation, just as it is in aerobic respiration (Figure 8.4). Here again, two pyruvate, two NADH, and two ATP form. But the last steps do not degrade glucose to carbon dioxide and water. They get no more ATP beyond the small yield from glycolysis. *The final steps in fermentation pathways regenerate the essential coenzyme NAD⁺.*

Fermentation yields enough energy to sustain many single-celled anaerobic species. It helps some aerobic cells when oxygen levels are stressfully low. But it isn't enough to sustain large, multicelled organisms, this being why you will never see anaerobic elephants.

Alcoholic Fermentation In **alcoholic fermentation**, the three-carbon backbone of two pyruvate molecules from glycolysis is split. The reactions result in two

molecules of acetaldehyde (an intermediate with a two-carbon backbone), and two of carbon dioxide. Acetaldehyde accepts electrons and hydrogen from NADH to form ethyl alcohol, or ethanol (Figure 8.10).

Some yeasts are famous fermenters. Bakers mix *Saccharomyces cerevisiae* cells and sugar into dough. The bubbles of carbon dioxide that form expand the dough (make it rise). Oven heat forces bubbles out of the dough, and the alcohol product evaporates away.

Wild and cultivated strains of *Saccharomyces* help produce alcohol in wine. Crushed grapes are left in vats along with the yeast, which converts sugar in the juice to ethanol. Ethanol is toxic to microbes. When a fermenting brew's ethanol content nears 10 percent, yeast cells start to die, and fermentation ends.

Lactate Fermentation With **lactate fermentation**, the NADH gives up electrons and hydrogen to the pyruvate. The transfer converts pyruvate to lactate, a three-carbon compound (Figure 8.11). You probably have heard of lactic acid, the non-ionized form of this compound. But lactate is by far the most common form in living cells, which is our focus here.

Lactate fermentation by *Lactobacillus* and certain other bacteria can spoil food, yet some species have commercial uses. Huge populations in vats of milk give us cheeses, yogurt, buttermilk, and other dairy products. Fermenters also help in curing meats and in pickling some fruits and vegetables, such as sauerkraut. Lactate is an acid; it gives these foods a sour taste.

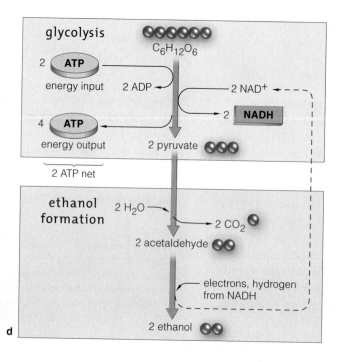

glycolysis
$C_6H_{12}O_6$

2 ATP
energy input   2 ADP   2 NAD⁺
                             2 NADH

4 ATP
energy output   2 pyruvate

2 ATP net

ethanol
formation   2 H₂O
             2 CO₂
2 acetaldehyde

electrons, hydrogen
from NADH

2 ethanol

Figure 8.10 *Animated!* Steps of alcoholic fermentation. (**a**) Yeasts, which are single-celled fungi, use this anaerobic pathway to make ATP.

(**b**) A vintner examining the color and clarity of one fermentation product of *Saccharomyces*. Strains of this yeast live on the sugar-rich tissues of ripe grapes.

(**c**) Carbon dioxide released from cells of *S. cerevisiae* is making bread dough rise in this bakery.

(**d**) Alcoholic fermentation. The intermediate acetaldehyde functions as the final electron acceptor. The end product of the reactions is ethanol (ethyl alcohol).

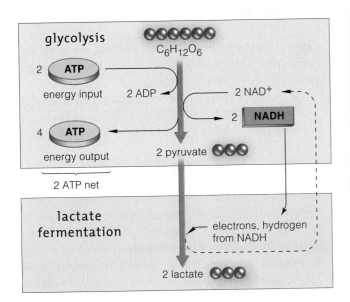

Figure 8.11 *Animated!* Steps of lactate fermentation. In this anaerobic pathway, the product (lactate) is the final acceptor of electrons originally stripped from glucose. These fermentation reactions have a net energy yield of two ATP (from glycolysis).

Figure 8.12 Sprinters, calling upon lactate fermentation in their muscles. The micrograph, a cross-section through part of a muscle, reveals three types of fibers. The lighter fibers sustain short, intense bursts of speed; they make ATP by lactate fermentation. The darker fibers contribute to endurance; they make ATP by aerobic respiration.

Lactate fermentation as well as aerobic respiration yields ATP for muscles that are partnered with bones. These skeletal muscles contain a mixture of cell types. Cells fused together inside *slow-twitch* muscle fibers support light, steady, prolonged activity, as during marathon runs or bird migrations. Cells of slow-twitch muscle fibers make ATP only by aerobic respiration, and they have many mitochondria. They are dark red because they hold large amounts of myoglobin. This pigment, which is related to hemoglobin, binds and stores oxygen for aerobic respiration (Figure 8.12).

By contrast, cells of pale *fast-twitch* muscle fibers have few mitochondria and no myoglobin. They use lactate fermentation to make ATP. They function when energy needs are immediate and intense, as during weight lifting or sprints (Figure 8.12). The pathway produces ATP quickly but not for very long; it does not support sustained activity. That is one reason you do not see chickens migrating. The flight muscles in a chicken contain mostly fast-twitch fibers, which make up the "white" breast meat.

Short bursts of flight evolved in the ancestors of chickens, perhaps as a way to flee from predators or improve agility during territorial battles. Chickens do walk and run; hence the "dark meat" (slow-twitch muscle) in their thighs and legs. Would you expect to see light or dark breast muscles in a migratory duck or in an albatross that skims ocean waves for months?

Section 37.5 offers more information on alternative energy pathways in skeletal and cardiac muscle cells.

ANAEROBIC ELECTRON TRANSFERS

Especially among prokaryotes, we see less common but more diverse energy-releasing pathways, some of which are topics of later chapters. Many assist in the global cycling of sulfur, nitrogen, and other elements. Collectively, the practitioners of these pathways affect nutrient availability in ecosystems everywhere.

Some bacteria and archaeans engage in **anaerobic electron transfers**. Electrons from organic compounds flow through transfer chains in the plasma membrane and H+ flows out of the cell through ATP synthases. Inorganic compounds are often used as final electron acceptors. The net energy yield is variable but small.

Some anaerobic species in waterlogged soil give up electrons to sulfate, forming a putrid gas (hydrogen sulfide). Other anaerobes live in the nutrient-rich mud of some aquatic habitats. Still others are the basis of food webs at hydrothermal vents (Sections 7.8, 48.15).

> In alcoholic fermentation, the final acceptor of electrons from glucose is acetaldehyde, a reaction intermediate. In lactate fermentation, it is pyruvate.
>
> Both pathways have a net energy yield of two ATP, which forms in glycolysis. The remaining reactions regenerate the coenzyme NAD+, without which glycolysis would stop.
>
> Some bacteria and archaeans generate ATP by anaerobic electron transfers across the plasma membrane.

8.6 Alternative Energy Sources in the Body

LINKS TO
SECTIONS
3.3, 3.4

So far, you have looked at what happens after glucose molecules enter an energy-releasing pathway. Now start thinking about what cells can do when they have too much or too little glucose.

THE FATE OF GLUCOSE AT MEALTIME AND BETWEEN MEALS

What happens to glucose at mealtime? While you and all other mammals are eating, glucose and other small organic molecules are being absorbed across the gut lining, and your blood is transporting them through the body. The rising glucose concentration in blood prompts an organ, the pancreas, to secrete insulin. This hormone makes cells take up glucose faster.

Cells trap the incoming glucose by converting it to glucose–6–phosphate. This intermediate of glycolysis forms as ATP transfers a phosphate group to glucose (Figures 8.4 and 8.13). Phosphorylated glucose cannot be transported out of the cell.

When a cell takes in more glucose than it requires for energy, its ATP-forming machinery goes into high gear. Unless it is using ATP rapidly, the cytoplasmic concentration of ATP rises, and glucose–6–phosphate is diverted into a biosynthesis pathway. The glucose gets converted to glycogen, a storage polysaccharide in animal cells (Section 3.3). Liver cells and muscle cells especially favor the conversion. Together, these two types of cells maintain the body's largest stores of glycogen molecules.

Between meals, the blood level of glucose declines. If the decline were not countered, that would be bad news for the brain, your body's glucose hog. At any time, your brain is taking up more than two-thirds of the freely circulating glucose. Why? The brain's many hundreds of millions of nerve cells (neurons) use this sugar as their preferred energy source.

The pancreas responds to low glucose levels by secreting glucagon. This hormone causes liver cells to convert stored glycogen to glucose and send it back to the blood. Only liver cells do this; muscle cells will not give it up. The glucose level in blood rises, so brain cells keep on functioning. Thus, *hormones control whether your cells use free glucose as an energy source or tuck it away.*

Don't let this explanation lead you to believe that your cells store enormous amounts of glycogen. Glycogen makes up only 1 percent or so of the total energy reserves of the average adult's body—the energy equivalent of two cups of cooked pasta. Unless you eat on a regular basis, you will deplete your liver's small glycogen stores in less than twelve hours.

Of the total energy reserves in, say, a typical adult who eats well, 78 percent (about 10,000 kilocalories) is concentrated in body fat and 21 percent in proteins.

ENERGY FROM FATS

How does a human body access its fat reservoir? A fat molecule, recall, has a glycerol head and one, two, or three fatty acid tails (Section 3.4). The body stores most fats as triglycerides, which have three tails each. Triglycerides accumulate in fat cells of adipose tissue. This tissue is strategically located beneath the skin of buttocks and other body regions.

When the blood glucose level falls, triglycerides are tapped as an energy alternative. Enzymes in fat cells cleave bonds between glycerol and fatty acids, which both enter the blood. Enzymes in the liver convert the glycerol to PGAL. As you know, PGAL is one of the key intermediates in glycolysis (Figure 8.4). Nearly all cells of your body take up circulating fatty acids, and enzymes inside them cleave the fatty acid backbones. The fragments become converted to acetyl–CoA, which can enter the Krebs cycle.

Compared with glucose, a fatty acid tail has more carbon-bound hydrogen atoms, so it yields more ATP. Between meals or during steady, prolonged exercise, fatty acid conversions supply about half of the ATP that muscle, liver, and kidney cells require.

What happens if you eat too many carbohydrates? Aerobic respiration converts the glucose subunits to pyruvate, then to acetyl–CoA, which enters the Krebs cycle. When too much glucose is circulating through the body, acetyl–CoA is diverted to a pathway that synthesizes fatty acids. *Too much glucose ends up as fat.*

ENERGY FROM PROTEINS

Some enzymes in your digestive system split dietary proteins into their amino acid subunits, which are then absorbed into the bloodstream. Cells use amino acids to make proteins or other nitrogen-containing compounds. Even so, when you eat more protein than your body needs, amino acids are further degraded. Their $-NH_3^+$ group is pulled off, so ammonia (NH_3) forms. Depending on the types of amino acids, the leftover carbon backbones are split, and acetyl–CoA, pyruvate, or an intermediate of the Krebs cycle forms. Your cells can divert any of these organic compounds into the Krebs cycle (Figure 8.13).

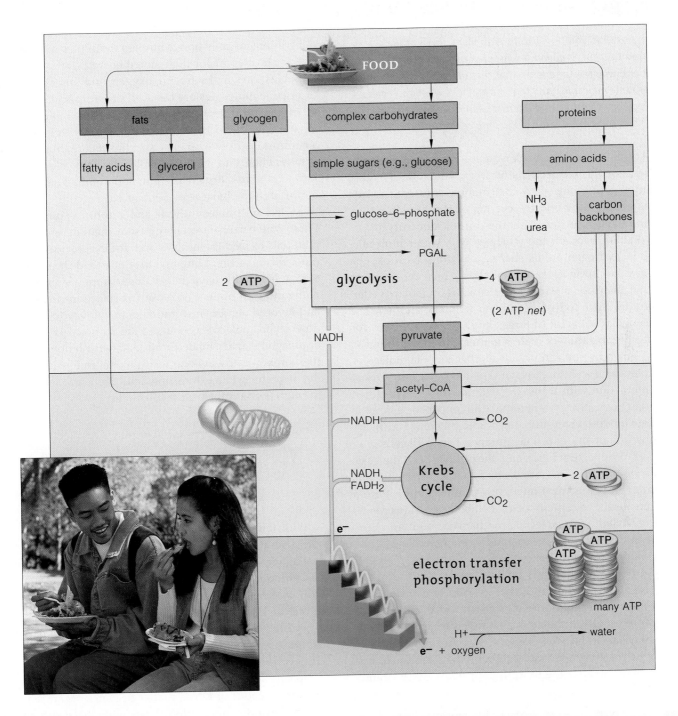

Figure 8.13 *Animated!* Reaction sites where different organic compounds can enter the stages of aerobic respiration. The compounds shown are alternative energy sources in humans and other mammals. Notice how complex carbohydrates, fats, and proteins cannot enter the aerobic pathway directly. First the digestive system, then individual cells, must break apart these molecules to simpler compounds.

As you can see, maintaining and accessing energy reserves is complicated business. Controlling the use of glucose is special because it is the fuel of choice for the brain. However, providing all of your cells with energy starts with the kinds of food you eat.

In humans and other mammals, the entrance of glucose or other organic compounds into an energy-releasing pathway depends on the kinds and proportions of carbohydrates, fats, and proteins in the diet.

8.7 Reflections on Life's Unity

In this unit, you traveled through many levels of life's organization. You have a sense that all organisms tap into a one-way flow of energy, that they alone make certain organic molecules, and that life emerges when molecules become organized and interact as units called cells. In short, you have a sense of life's molecular unity.

At this point in the book, you still may have difficulty sensing the connections between yourself—a highly intelligent being—and such remote-sounding events as energy flow and the cycling of carbon, hydrogen, and oxygen. Is this really the stuff of humanity?

Think back on the structure of a water molecule. Two hydrogen atoms sharing electrons with oxygen may not seem close to your daily life. Yet, through that sharing, water molecules show a polarity that invites them to hydrogen-bond with one another. The chemical behavior of three simple atoms is a start for the organization of lifeless matter into living things.

For now you can visualize other diverse molecules interspersed through water. The nonpolar kinds resist interaction with water; polar kinds dissolve in it. On their own, the phospholipids among them assemble into a two-layered film. Such lipid bilayers, recall, are the framework of cell membranes, hence all cells.

From the very beginning, the cell has been the basic *living* unit. The essence of life is not some mysterious force. It is organization and metabolic control. With a membrane to contain them, metabolic reactions *can* be controlled. With molecular mechanisms built into their membranes, cells can respond to energy changes and to shifts in solute concentrations in the environment. Response mechanisms operate by "telling" proteins —enzymes—when and what to build or tear down.

And it is not some mysterious force that creates proteins. DNA, the double-stranded treasurehouse of inheritance, has the chemical structure—*the chemical message*—that helps molecule reproduce molecule, one generation after the next. In your body, DNA strands

tell trillions of cells how countless molecules must be built or torn apart for their stored energy.

So yes, carbon, hydrogen, oxygen, and other atoms of organic molecules are the stuff of you, and us, and all of life. Yet it takes far more than organic molecules to complete the picture. Life continues only as long as a continuous flow of energy sustains its organization. It takes energy to assemble molecules into cells, cells into organisms, organisms into communities, and so on through the biosphere (Section 1.1).

Reflect on photosynthesis and aerobic respiration. Photosynthesizers use energy from the sun and raw materials to feed themselves and, indirectly, nearly all other forms of life. Long ago they enriched the whole atmosphere with oxygen, a leftover from a noncyclic pathway. That atmosphere exerted selection pressure and favored aerobic respiration, a novel way to break down food molecules by using the free oxygen. And photosynthesizers made more food with leftovers of the aerobic pathway—carbon dioxide and water. In this way the cycling of carbon, hydrogen, and oxygen through living things came full circle.

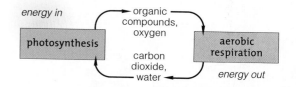

With few exceptions, infusions of energy from the sun sustain life's sweeping organization. And energy, remember, flows through time in one direction—from concentrated to less concentrated forms (Section 6.1). Only as long as more energy flows into the great web of life can life continue in all its rich expressions.

So life is no more *and no less* than a marvelously complex system for prolonging order. Sustained with energy transfusions from the sun, life continues by a capacity for self-reproduction. With energy and the hereditary codes of DNA, matter becomes organized, generation after generation. Even with the death of individuals, life elsewhere is prolonged. With each death, molecules are released and may be cycled as raw materials for new generations.

With this flow of energy and cycling of materials through time, each birth is affirmation of our ongoing capacity for organization, each death a renewal.

The diversity of life, and its continuity through time, arises from unity at the bioenergetic and molecular levels.

Summary

Section 8.1 All organisms, including photosynthetic types, access the chemical bond energy of glucose and other organic compounds, then use it to make ATP. They do so because ATP is a transportable form of energy that can jump-start nearly all metabolic reactions. They break apart compounds and release electrons and hydrogen, both of which have roles in ATP formation.

Glycolysis, the partial breakdown of one glucose to two pyruvate molecules, takes place in the cytoplasm of all cells. It is the first stage of all the main energy-releasing pathways, and it does not use free oxygen.

Anaerobic pathways end in the cytoplasm, and the net yield of ATP is small. An oxygen-requiring pathway called aerobic respiration continues in mitochondria. It releases far more usable energy from glucose.

Biology⊜Now
Get an overview of aerobic respiration with the animation on BiologyNow.

Section 8.2 It takes two ATP molecules to jump-start glycolysis. One activates six-carbon glucose; the other primes an intermediate to split into two three-carbon molecules (PGAL). The two PGAL give up electrons and hydrogen to coenzymes (NAD^+), forming two NADH. Two intermediates each give up a phosphate group to ADP, forming two ATP. Two more intermediates do the same.

Thus, during glycolysis, four ATP form by substrate-level phosphorylation, but the *net* yield is two ATP (because two ATP had to be invested up front). The end products of glycolysis are two molecules of pyruvate, each with a three-carbon backbone.

Biology⊜Now
Take a step-by-step journey through glycolysis with the animation on BiologyNow.

Section 8.3 The second and third stages of aerobic respiration get under way when the two pyruvates from glycolysis enter a mitochondrion.

The second stage consists of the Krebs cycle and a few preparatory steps before it. It takes two full turns of these cyclic reactions to break down both of the pyruvates.

Before the cycle, each pyruvate is stripped of a carbon atom (which departs in CO_2) as well as electrons and hydrogen (which NAD^+ picks up, forming NADH). A coenzyme (acetyl–CoA) picks up the two-carbon leftover.

The Krebs cycle starts when acetyl–CoA transfers the leftover to oxaloacetate, forming citrate. During stepwise rearrangements, intermediates give up two carbon atoms (which depart in CO_2) and electrons and hydrogen (which three NAD^+ and one FAD accept). An ATP forms.

In total, then, the second stage of aerobic respiration —including preparatory steps and two full turns of the Krebs cycle—results in the formation of six CO_2, two ATP, eight NADH, and two $FADH_2$.

Biology⊜Now
Explore a mitochondrion and observe the reactions inside with the animation on BiologyNow.

Section 8.4 The third stage of aerobic respiration takes place at electron transfer chains and ATP synthases in the inner mitochondrial membrane.

The electron transfer chains accept electrons and hydrogen from NADH and $FADH_2$ that formed during the first two stages of the aerobic pathway. Electron flow through the chains causes H^+ to accumulate in the inner mitochondrial compartment, so H^+ concentration and electric gradients build up across the inner membrane.

H^+ follows its gradients and flows back to the outer mitochondrial compartment, through the interior of ATP synthases. This ion flow causes reversible changes in the shape of parts of the ATP synthase. Those changes force ADP to combine with unbound phosphate, thus forming ATP. This happens repeatedly, so many ATP molecules are produced.

Free oxygen picks up the electrons at the end of the transfer chains and combines with H^+, forming water.

Aerobic respiration has a typical net energy yield of thirty-six ATP for each glucose molecule metabolized.

Biology⊜Now
Study how each step in aerobic respiration contributes to energy harvests with the animation on BiologyNow.

Section 8.5 Anaerobic energy-releasing pathways do not use free oxygen and occur only in cytoplasm. The net energy yield is small.

Fermentation pathways follow glycolysis and add no more to the two ATP net yield from glycolysis. They function only to regenerate NAD^+.

In alcoholic fermentation, the two pyruvates from glycolysis are converted to two acetaldehyde and two CO_2 molecules. When NADH transfers electrons and hydrogen to acetaldehyde, two ethanol (ethyl alcohol) molecules form and NAD^+ is regenerated.

In lactate fermentation, NAD^+ is regenerated when NADH gives up electrons and hydrogen to the two pyruvates. Two lactate molecules are end products.

Slow-twitch and fast-twitch skeletal muscle fibers support different levels of activity. Aerobic respiration and lactate fermentation occur in different fibers that make up these muscles.

Many prokaryotes make ATP by anaerobic electron transfers. They have electron transfer chains and ATP synthases in their plasma membrane. Sulfate or some other inorganic substance in the environment is often the final electron acceptor.

Biology⊜Now
Compare alcoholic and lactate fermentation with the animation on BiologyNow.

Section 8.6 In the human body, simple sugars from carbohydrates, glycerol and fatty acids from fats, and carbon backbones of amino acids from proteins can enter the aerobic pathway as alternative energy sources.

Biology⊜Now
Follow the breakdown of different organic molecules with the interaction on BiologyNow.

Section 8.7 Life's diversity and continuity arise from its unity at the bioenergetic and molecular levels.

Self-Quiz

Answers in Appendix II

1. Glycolysis starts and ends in the _____ .
   - a. nucleus
   - b. mitochondrion
   - c. plasma membrane
   - d. cytoplasm

2. Which of the following molecules does not form during glycolysis?
   - a. NADH
   - b. pyruvate
   - c. $FADH_2$
   - d. ATP

3. Aerobic respiration is completed in the _____ .
   - a. nucleus
   - b. mitochondrion
   - c. plasma membrane
   - d. cytoplasm

4. In the third stage of aerobic respiration, _____ is the final acceptor of electrons from glucose.
   - a. water
   - b. hydrogen
   - c. oxygen
   - d. NADH

5. Fill in the blanks in the diagram below.

6. In alcoholic fermentation, _____ is the final acceptor of electrons stripped from glucose.
   - a. oxygen
   - b. pyruvate
   - c. acetaldehyde
   - d. sulfate

7. Fermentation makes no more ATP beyond the small yield from glycolysis. The remaining reactions _____ .
   - a. regenerate FAD
   - b. regenerate NAD^+
   - c. regenerate NADH
   - d. regenerate $FADH_2$

8. In certain organisms and under certain conditions, _____ can be used as an energy alternative to glucose.
   - a. fatty acids
   - b. glycerol
   - c. amino acids
   - d. all of the above

9. Match the event with its most suitable description.
   - ____ glycolysis
   - ____ fermentation
   - ____ Krebs cycle
   - ____ electron transfer phosphorylation
   - a. ATP, NADH, $FADH_2$, CO_2, and water form
   - b. glucose to two pyruvates
   - c. NAD^+ regenerated, two ATP net
   - d. H^+ flows through ATP synthases

Additional questions are available on Biology Now™

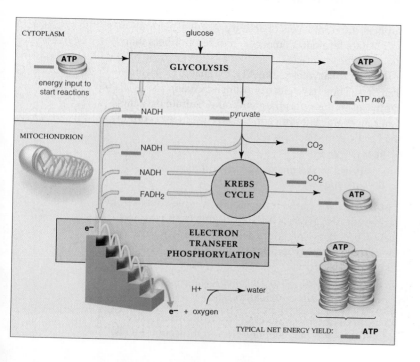

Critical Thinking

1. Living cells of your body absolutely do not use their nucleic acids as alternative energy sources. Suggest why.

2. Suppose you start a body-building program. You are already eating plenty of carbohydrates. Now a qualified nutritionist recommends that you start a protein-rich diet that includes protein supplements. Speculate on how extra dietary proteins will be put to use, and in which tissues.

3. Each year, Canada geese lift off in precise formation from their northern breeding grounds. They head south to spend the winter months in warmer climates, then make the return trip in spring. As is the case for other migratory birds, their flight muscle cells are efficient at using fatty acids as an energy source. Remember, the carbon backbone of fatty acids can be cleaved into small fragments that can be converted to acetyl–CoA for entry into the Krebs cycle.

   Suppose a lesser Canada goose from Alaska's Point Barrow has been steadily flapping along for about three thousand kilometers and is approaching Klamath Falls, Oregon. It looks down and notices a rabbit sprinting from a coyote with a taste for rabbit.

   With a stunning burst of speed, the rabbit reaches the safety of its burrow.

   Which energy-releasing pathway predominated in muscle cells in the rabbit's legs? Why was the Canada goose relying on a different pathway for most of its journey? And why wouldn't the pathway of choice in goose flight muscle cells be much good for a rabbit making a mad dash from its enemy?

4. At high altitudes, oxygen levels are low. Mountain climbers risk altitude sickness, which is characterized by shortness of breath, weakness, dizziness, and confusion.

   Oddly, early symptoms of *cyanide poisoning* resemble altitude sickness. This highly toxic poison binds tightly to a cytochrome, the last molecule in mitochondrial electron transfer chains. When cyanide becomes bound to it, the cytochrome can't transfer electrons to the next component of the chain. Explain why cytochrome **shutdown might** cause the same symptoms as altitude sickness.

5. ATP forms in mitochondria. In warm-blooded animals, so does a lot of heat, which is circulated in ways that help control body temperature. Cells of *brown adipose tissue* make a protein that disrupts the formation of electron transfer chains in mitochondrial membranes. H^+ gradients are affected, so fewer ATP form; electrons in the transfer chains give up more of their energy as heat. Because of this, some researchers hypothesize that brown adipose tissue may not be like white adipose tissue, which is an energy (fat) reservoir. Brown adipose tissue may function in thermogenesis, or heat production.

   Mitochondria, recall, contain their own DNA, which may have mutated independently in human populations that evolved in the Arctic and in the hot tropics. If that is so, then mitochondrial function may be adapted to climate.

   How do you suppose such a mitochondrial adaptation might affect people living where the temperature range no longer correlates with their ancestral heritage? Would you expect people whose ancestors evolved in the Arctic to be more or less likely to put on a lot of weight than those whose ancestors lived in the tropics? See *Science*, January 9, 2004: 223–226 for more information.

II Principles of Inheritance

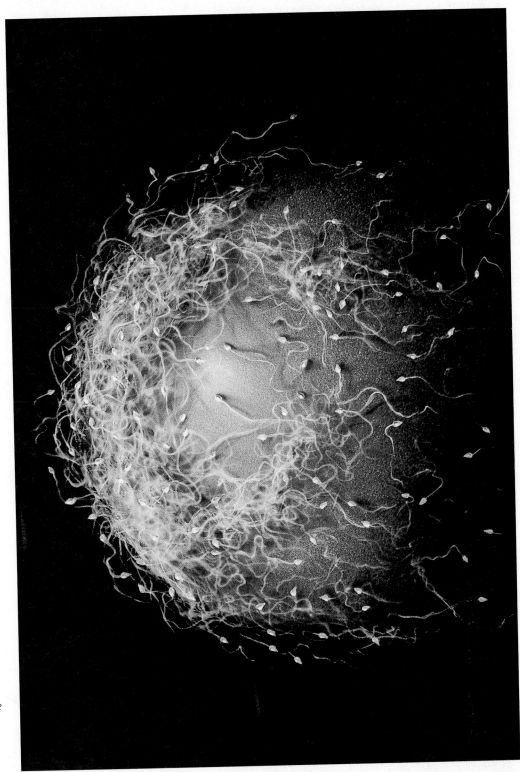

Human sperm, one of which will penetrate this mature egg and so set the stage for the development of a new individual in the image of its parents. This exquisite art is based on a scanning electron micrograph.

Henrietta's Immortal Cells

Each human starts out as a fertilized egg. By the time of birth, the body consists of about a trillion cells, all descended from that single cell. Even in an adult, billions of cells still divide every day and replace their damaged or worn-out predecessors.

In 1951, George and Margaret Gey of Johns Hopkins University were trying to develop a way to keep human cells dividing outside the body. An "immortal" cell lineage could help researchers study basic life processes as well as cancer and other diseases. Using cells to study cancer would be a better alternative than experimenting with patients and risking their already vulnerable lives.

For almost thirty years, the Geys tried to grow normal and diseased human cells. But they could not stop the cellular descendants from dying within a few weeks.

Mary Kubicek, a lab assistant, tried again and again to establish a self-perpetuating lineage of cultured human cancer cells. She was about to give up, but she prepared one last sample. She named them *HeLa* cells, a code for the first two letters of the patient's first and last names.

The HeLa cells began to divide. They divided again and again. Four days later, the researchers had to subdivide the cells into more culture tubes. The cell populations increased at a phenomenal rate; cells were dividing every twenty-four hours and coating the inside of the tubes within days.

Sadly, cancer cells in the patient were dividing just as frequently. Six months after she had been diagnosed with cancer, malignant cells had invaded tissues throughout her body. Two months after that, Henrietta Lacks, a young woman from Baltimore, was dead.

Although Henrietta passed away, her cells lived on in the Geys' laboratory (Figure 9.1). In time, HeLa cells were shipped to research laboratories all over the world. The Geys used HeLa cells to identify viral strains that cause polio, which at the time was epidemic. They developed the tissue culture techniques that were used to grow a vaccine. Other researchers used HeLa cells to investigate cancer, viral growth, protein synthesis, the effects of radiation on cells, and more. Some HeLa cells even traveled into space for experiments on the *Discoverer XVII* satellite. Even now, hundreds of important research projects move forward annually, thanks to Henrietta's immortal cells.

Figure 9.2 shows a photograph of Henrietta. She was only thirty-one when the runaway cell divisions killed her. Decades later, her legacy continues to help humans everywhere, through cellular descendants that are still dividing day after day.

Understanding cell division—and, ultimately, how new individuals are put together in the image of their parents—starts with answers to three questions. *First*, what kind of

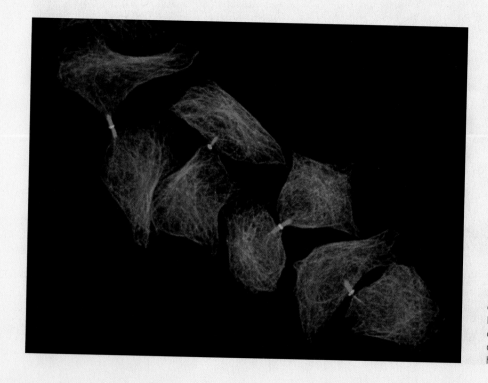

Figure 9.1 The terrifying beauty of dividing HeLa cells—a legacy of Henrietta Lacks, who was a young casualty of cancer. Her cellular contribution to science is still helping others every day.

Figure 9.2 Henrietta Lacks.

information guides inheritance? *Second*, how is information copied in a parent cell before being distributed to each daughter cell? *Third*, what kinds of mechanisms actually parcel out the information to daughter cells?

We will require more than one chapter to survey the nature of cell reproduction and other mechanisms of inheritance. In this chapter, we introduce the structures and mechanisms that cells use to reproduce.

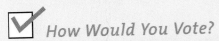

Watch the video online!

 How Would You Vote?

It is illegal to sell your organs, but you can sell your cells, including eggs, sperm, and blood cells. HeLa cells are still being sold all over the world by cell culture firms. Should the family of Henrietta Lacks share in the profits? See BiologyNow for details, then vote online.

 **Key Concepts**

CHROMOSOMES AND DIVIDING CELLS

Individuals of a species have a characteristic number of chromosomes in their cells. Those chromosomes differ in length and shape, and they carry different parts of the cell's hereditary information. Division mechanisms parcel out the information to each daughter cell, along with enough cytoplasm to start up its own operation. Section 9.1

WHERE MITOSIS FITS IN THE CELL CYCLE

A cell cycle starts when a daughter cell forms and ends when that cell completes its own division. A typical cycle goes through interphase, mitosis, and cytoplasmic division. In interphase, a cell increases its mass and number of components, and copies its DNA. Section 9.2

STAGES OF MITOSIS

Mitosis divides the nucleus, not the cytoplasm. It has four continuous stages: prophase, metaphase, anaphase, and telophase. A microtubular spindle forms. It moves the cell's duplicated chromosomes into two parcels, which end up in two genetically identical nuclei. Section 9.3

HOW THE CYTOPLASM DIVIDES

After nuclear division, the cytoplasm divides and typically puts a nucleus in each daughter cell. The cytoplasm of an animal cell is simply pinched in two. In plant cells, a cross-wall forms in the cytoplasm and divides it. Section 9.4

THE CELL CYCLE AND CANCER

Built-in mechanisms monitor and control the timing and rate of cell division. On rare occasions, the surveillance mechanisms fail, and cell division becomes uncontrollable. Tumor formation and cancer are the outcome. Section 9.5

Links to Earlier Concepts

Before reading, review the description about the changing appearance of chromosomes in the nucleus of eukaryotic cells (Section 4.6). You may wish to review the introduction to microtubules and the motor proteins associated with them (4.10, 4.11). Doing so will help you understand the nature of the mitotic spindle and the potential value of cancer research that is zeroing in on it. A look back at the walls of plant cells (4.9) will help give you a sense of why they cannot divide by pinching their cytoplasm in two parcels, as animal cells do.

9.1 Overview of Cell Division Mechanisms

LINK TO
SECTION
4.5

*The continuity of life depends on **reproduction**. By this process, parents produce a new generation of cells or multicelled individuals like themselves. Cell division is the bridge between generations.*

A dividing cell faces a challenge. Each of its daughter cells must get information encoded in the parental DNA and enough cytoplasm to start up its own operation. DNA "tells" it which proteins to build. Some of the proteins are structural materials; others are enzymes that speed construction of organic compounds. If the cell does not inherit all of the required information, it will not be able to grow or function properly.

In addition, the parent cell's cytoplasm already has enzymes, organelles, and other metabolic machinery. When a daughter cell inherits what looks like a blob of cytoplasm, it actually is getting start-up machinery that will keep it running until it can use information in DNA for growing on its own.

MITOSIS, MEIOSIS, AND THE PROKARYOTES

Eukaryotic cells cannot simply split in two, because their DNA is housed in a single nucleus. They do split the cytoplasm into daughter cells, but not until *after* DNA has been copied and packaged into more than a single nucleus by way of mitosis or meiosis.

Mitosis is a nuclear division mechanism that occurs in *somatic* cells (body cells) of multicelled eukaryotes. It is the basis of increases in body size during growth, replacements of worn-out or dead cells, and tissue repair. Many plants, animals, fungi, and single-celled protists also reproduce asexually, or make copies of themselves, by way of mitosis (Table 9.1).

Meiosis is a different nuclear division mechanism. It precedes the formation of gametes or spores, and it is the basis of sexual reproduction. The type of gametes known as sperm and eggs develop from *germ* cells, or immature reproductive cells. Spores form in the life cycle of many protists as well as plants and fungi.

As you will discover in this chapter and the next, meiosis and mitosis have much in common. Even so, their outcomes differ.

What about prokaryotes—bacteria and archaeans? All of these cells reproduce asexually by prokaryotic fission, an entirely different mechanism. We consider prokaryotic fission later, in Section 21.2.

KEY POINTS ABOUT CHROMOSOME STRUCTURE

In Section 4.5, you read that a eukaryotic chromosome is one double-stranded DNA molecule with a lot of proteins attached to it. Each eukaryotic species has a characteristic number of chromosomes inside its cells, and before a cell enters nuclear division, it duplicates every one of them. Each chromosome and its copy stay attached to each other as **sister chromatids** until late in the division process. Figure 9.3 is a simple way to think about what an unduplicated chromosome and a duplicated chromosome look like.

During an early stage of mitosis or meiosis, each duplicated chromosome coils back on itself again and

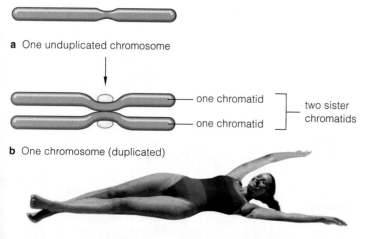

a One unduplicated chromosome

one chromatid
one chromatid
} two sister chromatids

b One chromosome (duplicated)

Figure 9.3 A simple way to visualize a eukaryotic chromosome in the unduplicated state and duplicated state. Eukaryotic cells are duplicated before mitosis or meiosis. Each becomes two sister chromatids. Students sometimes have trouble visualizing which is which. Think of a chromatid as one arm and leg of a sunbather.

Table 9.1	Comparison of Cell Division Mechanisms
Mechanisms	Functions
Mitosis, cytoplasmic division	In *all* multicelled eukaryotes, the basis of the following three processes: 1. Increases in body size during growth 2. Replacement of dead or worn-out cells 3. Repair of damaged tissues In single-celled and many multicelled species, *also* the basis of asexual reproduction
Meiosis, cytoplasmic division	In single-celled and multicelled eukaryotes, the basis of sexual reproduction; precedes gamete formation or spore formation (Chapter 10)
Prokaryotic fission	In bacteria and archaeans, the basis of asexual reproduction (Section 21.2)

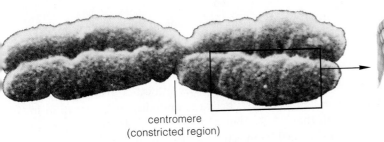

centromere
(constricted region)

a A duplicated chromosome in its most condensed form.

again, into a highly condensed form. Figure 9.4a gives an example of a duplicated human chromosome when it is most condensed. The orderly coiling arises from interactions between the DNA molecule and proteins associated with it. At regular intervals, the double-stranded DNA winds twice around tiny "spools" of proteins called **histones**. The repeating histone–DNA spools look like beads on a string when microscopists loosen them up (Figure 9.4d). Each of the "beads" is a **nucleosome**, which is the smallest unit of structural organization in eukaryotic chromosomes (Figure 9.4e).

While each duplicated chromosome is condensing, it becomes constricted at a predictable location along its length in a pronounced way. This constriction is a **centromere** (Figure 9.4a). The centromere's location is different for each type of chromosome and is one of its defining characteristics. During nuclear division, we find a kinetochore at the centromere of each chromatid. A kinetochore is a docking site for microtubules that will help move the chromatids to prescribed locations during nuclear division.

What is the point of this structural organization? The tight packaging probably keeps the chromosomes from getting tangled up while they are moved and sorted out into parcels *during* nuclear division. Also, *between* cell divisions, nucleosome packaging can be loosened in specific regions. In many cases, enzymes thereby gain access to the precise bits of hereditary information that a cell requires at that time.

When a cell divides, each daughter cell receives a required number of chromosomes and some cytoplasm. Eukaryotic cells divide their nucleus first, then the cytoplasm.

In eukaryotes, a nuclear division mechanism called mitosis is the basis of bodily growth, cell replacements, tissue repair, and often asexual reproduction.

Also in eukaryotes, a nuclear division mechanism called meiosis precedes the formation of gametes and, in many species, spores. Meiosis is the basis of sexual reproduction.

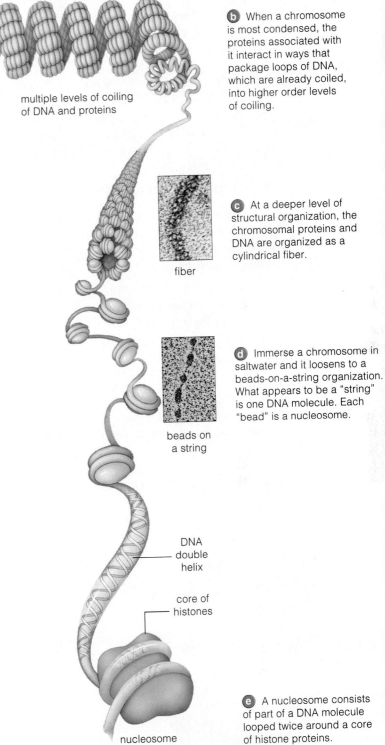

multiple levels of coiling of DNA and proteins

b When a chromosome is most condensed, the proteins associated with it interact in ways that package loops of DNA, which are already coiled, into higher order levels of coiling.

fiber

c At a deeper level of structural organization, the chromosomal proteins and DNA are organized as a cylindrical fiber.

beads on a string

d Immerse a chromosome in saltwater and it loosens to a beads-on-a-string organization. What appears to be a "string" is one DNA molecule. Each "bead" is a nucleosome.

DNA double helix

core of histones

nucleosome

e A nucleosome consists of part of a DNA molecule looped twice around a core of histone proteins.

Figure 9.4 *Animated!* (a) Scanning electron micrograph of a duplicated human chromosome in its most condensed form. (b,c) Proteins package many loops of coiled DNA into the coiled array of a cylindrical fiber. (d,e) The smallest unit of structural organization is the nucleosome: part of a DNA molecule looped twice around a core of histone molecules. The transmission electron micrographs correspond to organizational levels (c) and (d).

9.2 Introducing the Cell Cycle

Start by thinking of reproduction in terms of a cell's life, from the time it forms until it divides. This interval is not the same as a life cycle—the sequence of stages through which individuals of a species pass during their lifetime.

A **cell cycle** is a series of events from one cell division to the next (Figure 9.5). It starts when a new daughter cell forms by mitosis and cytoplasmic division. It ends when that cell divides. Mitosis, cytoplasmic division, and interphase constitute one turn of the cycle.

THE WONDER OF INTERPHASE

During **interphase**, the cell increases in mass, roughly doubles the number of components in its cytoplasm, and duplicates its DNA. For most cells, interphase is the longest portion of the cell cycle. Biologists divide it into three stages:

G1 Interval ("Gap") of cell growth and functioning before the onset of DNA replication

S   Time of "Synthesis" (DNA replication)

G2 Second interval (Gap), after DNA replication when the cell prepares for division

G1, S, and G2 are code names for some events that are just amazing, considering how much DNA is packed in a nucleus. Remember, if you could stretch out all the DNA molecules from one of your somatic cells in a single line, they would extend past the fingertips of both outstretched arms. A line of all the DNA from one salamander cell would stretch about 540 feet.

The wonder is, enzymes and other proteins in cells *selectively* access, activate, and silence information in all that DNA. They also make base-by-base copies of every DNA molecule before cells divide. Most of this cellular work is completed in interphase.

G1, S, and G2 of interphase have distinct patterns of biosynthesis. Most of your cells remain in G1 while they are making proteins, carbohydrates, and lipids. Cells destined to divide enter S, when they copy their DNA as well as the proteins attached to it. During G2, they make proteins that will drive mitosis.

The length of the cycle is about the same for cells of the same type. However, it can differ from one cell type to the next. All of the neurons (nerve cells) inside your brain are stuck in G1 of interphase and normally will not divide again. Yet 2 million to 3 million cells in your red bone marrow are dividing every second. They give rise to new red blood cells, which will last only a few months before they wear out. As another example, when a new sea urchin is developing, the number of cells doubles every two hours.

Once S begins, DNA replication usually proceeds at a predictable rate and ends before a cell prepares to divide. The rate holds for all cells of a species, so you may well wonder if the cell cycle has built-in molecular brakes. It does. Apply the brakes that are supposed to work in G1, and the cycle stalls in G1. Lift the brakes, and the cell cycle runs to completion. Said another way, *control mechanisms govern the rate of cell division.*

Imagine a car losing its brakes just as it starts down a steep mountain road. As you will read later in the chapter, cancer begins this way. The crucial controls over the cell cycle are lost.

One more point: Stressful conditions often interrupt the cell cycle. For instance, when deprived of a vital nutrient, the free-living cells known as amoebas remain in interphase. They will remain there as long as they have not moved past a certain checkpoint. However, past that point, the cycle normally continues regardless of outside conditions, because built-in control mechanisms have lifted the brakes.

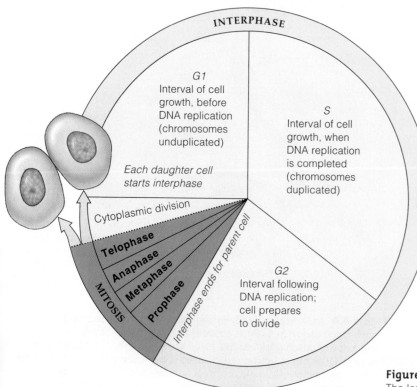

INTERPHASE

G1
Interval of cell growth, before DNA replication (chromosomes unduplicated)

Each daughter cell starts interphase

S
Interval of cell growth, when DNA replication is completed (chromosomes duplicated)

Cytoplasmic division

Telophase
Anaphase
Metaphase
Prophase
MITOSIS

Interphase ends for parent cell

G2
Interval following DNA replication; cell prepares to divide

Figure 9.5 *Animated!* Eukaryotic cell cycle, generalized. The length of each interval differs among different cell types.

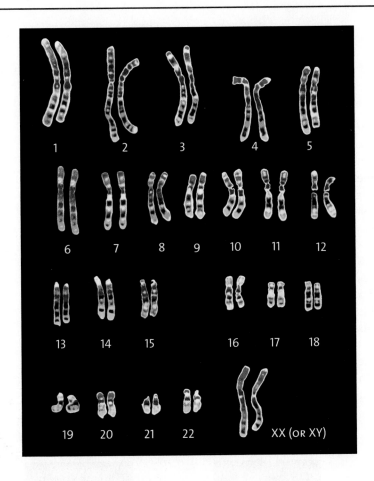

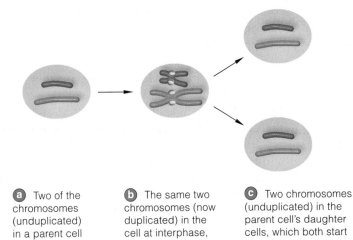

a Two of the chromosomes (unduplicated) in a parent cell at interphase

b The same two chromosomes (now duplicated) in the cell at interphase, prior to mitosis

c Two chromosomes (unduplicated) in the parent cell's daughter cells, which both start life in interphase

Figure 9.6 Preview of how mitosis maintains a parental chromosome number, one generation to the next. Human diploid cells have twenty-three pairs of metaphase chromosomes, for a total of forty-six (*left*). (The last ones in the lineup are a pair of sex chromosomes. In human females, they are two X chromosomes; in males, they are XY.)

The sketches above track what happens to just two of the forty-six. When all goes well, each time a human somatic cell undergoes mitosis and cytoplasmic division, daughter cells end up with an unduplicated set of twenty-three pairs of chromosomes. The icon below shows the bipolar mitotic spindle that helps bring about this outcome.

MITOSIS AND THE CHROMOSOME NUMBER

Mitosis follows G2, and it maintains the parent cell's chromosome number. The **chromosome number** is the sum of all chromosomes in cells of a given type. Body cells of gorillas and chimpanzees have 48, pea plants have 14, and humans have 46 (Figure 9.6).

Actually, your cells have a **diploid number** (*2n*) of chromosomes; there are two of each type. Those 46 are like volumes of two sets of books numbered from 1 to 23. You have two volumes of, say, chromosome 22—*a pair of them*. Except for one sex chromosome pairing (XY), both have the same length and shape, and carry the same hereditary information about the same traits.

Think of them as two sets of books on how to build a house. Your father gave you one set. Your mother had her own ideas about wiring, plumbing, and so on. She gave you an alternate edition on the same topics, but it says slightly different things about many of them.

With mitosis, a diploid parent cell can produce two diploid daughter cells. This doesn't mean each merely gets forty-six or forty-eight or fourteen chromosomes. If only the total mattered, then one cell might get, say, two pairs of chromosome 22 and no pairs whatsoever of chromosome 9. But neither cell could function like its parent *without two of each type of chromosome*.

Mitosis has four stages—*prophase, metaphase, anaphase,* and *telophase*—which require a **bipolar mitotic spindle**. This dynamic structure consists of microtubules that grow or shrink as tubulin subunits are added to or lost from their ends. Its microtubules extend from both spindle poles. Some overlap midway between the two poles, and others tether the duplicated chromosomes.

The next section will explain how the microtubules extending from one pole connect to one chromatid of each chromosome, and microtubules from the other pole connect to its sister. As you will see, the spindle moves the two chromatids apart, to opposite poles. The result is two complete sets of now-unduplicated chromosomes, one for each forthcoming daughter cell. Figure 9.6 is a preview of how mitosis maintains the parental chromosome number.

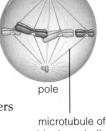

pole

pole

microtubule of bipolar spindle

Interphase, mitosis, and cytoplasmic division constitute one turn of the cell cycle. During interphase, a new cell increases its mass, doubles the number of its components, and duplicates its chromosomes. The cycle ends after the cell undergoes mitosis and then divides its cytoplasm.

9.3 A Closer Look at Mitosis

LINKS TO
SECTIONS
4.10, 4.11

Focus now on a "typical" animal cell to see how mitosis can keep the chromosome number constant, division after division, from one cell generation to the next.

We know that a cell is in **prophase**, the first stage of mitosis, when its chromosomes become visible in light microscopes as threadlike forms. ("Mitosis" is from the Greek *mitos,* meaning thread.) Each chromosome was duplicated earlier, in interphase; each is two sister chromatids joined at the centromere. Now they twist and fold. By late prophase, they will be condensed in thicker, compact, rod-shaped forms (Figure 9.7a–c).

Also before prophase, two barrel-shaped centrioles and two centrosomes started duplicating themselves next to the nucleus. A centriole, recall, gives rise to a flagellum or cilium (Section 4.11). If you observe this structure, you can bet that flagellated or ciliated cells develop during the organism's life cycle.

In animal cells, each centriole helps organize one **centrosome**, a center where microtubules originate. In prophase, one set of the duplicated centrioles and centrosomes moves to the other side of the nucleus, then microtubules grow out of each centrosome. *These are the microtubules that form the bipolar spindle.*

During the transition from prophase to metaphase, the nuclear envelope breaks up completely into many tiny, flattened vesicles. The microtubules are now free to interact with chromosomes and with one another. Many dock at kinetochores; others keep on growing from centrosomes until they overlap midway between the two spindle poles. Remember the motor proteins associated with microtubules (Section 4.11)? Energy from ATP activates dyneins and kinesins, which then generate the force to assemble the mitotic spindle, and to bind and move the chromosomes.

Again, some microtubules extending from one pole tether one chromatid of each chromosome, and some from the opposite pole tether the sister chromatid. The opposing sets of microtubules engage in a tug-of-war. They add and lose tubulin subunits, so they grow and shrink until they are the same length. At that point, **metaphase**, all duplicated chromosomes are aligned midway between the spindle poles (*meta–,* midway). The alignment is crucial for the next stage of mitosis.

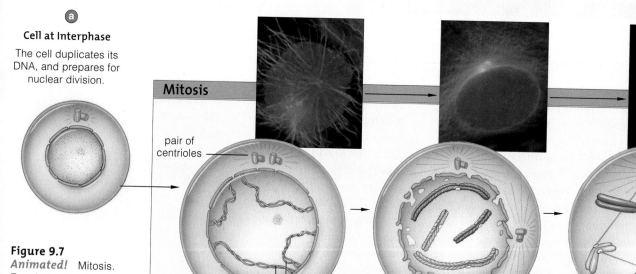

a Cell at Interphase

The cell duplicates its DNA, and prepares for nuclear division.

Mitosis

pair of centrioles

nuclear envelope — chromosomes

b Early Prophase

Mitosis begins. The DNA and its associated proteins have started to condense. The two chromosomes color-coded *purple* were inherited from the female parent. The other two (*blue*) are their counterparts, inherited from a male parent.

c Late Prophase

The duplicated chromosomes continue to condense. New microtubules form. They move one of two pairs of centrioles and centrosomes to the opposite side of the nucleus. The nuclear envelope starts to break up.

d Transition to Metaphase

Now microtubules penetrate the nuclear region. Collectively, they form a bipolar spindle. Some tether one sister chromatid of each chromosome to one or the other spindle pole. Others overlap at the spindle equator.

Figure 9.7
Animated! Mitosis. For clarity, these generalized sketches track only two pairs of chromosomes from a diploid (2*n*) animal cell. Cells of nearly all eukaryotic species have more pairs than this. The micrographs track a mouse cell through mitosis. The mouse cell's DNA is stained *blue,* and its microtubules are stained *green.*

At **anaphase**, sister chromatids of each chromosome are moved toward opposite spindle poles. How? Motor proteins attached to each chromatid's kinetochore are inching along microtubular tracks that lead to one or the other spindle pole. The microtubules themselves are shrinking at both ends even as motor proteins are dragging the chromatids with them. And so the sister chromatids end up at opposite poles (Figure 9.7f).

At the same time, the spindle poles themselves are being pushed farther apart! Different microtubules, the ones that overlap midway between the spindle poles, are ratcheting past one another. Motor proteins drive this interaction and push the poles apart.

One sister chromatid is a duplicate of the other. So once they detach from each other at anaphase, there are two separate chromosomes, one at each pole.

Telophase gets under way when one of each type of chromosome reaches a spindle pole. Two genetically identical clusters of chromosomes are now located at opposite "ends" of the cell. All of the chromosomes decondense and become threadlike. Vesicles derived from old nuclear envelope fuse and form patches of

membrane around each cluster. Patch joins with patch until a new nuclear envelope encloses each cluster. And so two nuclei form (Figure 9.7g). In our example, the parent cell had a diploid number of chromosomes. So does each nucleus. Once two nuclei have formed, telophase is over—and so is mitosis.

Prior to mitosis, each chromosome in a cell's nucleus is duplicated, so it consists of two sister chromatids.

In prophase, chromosomes condense to rodlike forms, and microtubules form a bipolar spindle. The nuclear envelope breaks up. Some microtubules harness the chromosomes.

At metaphase, all duplicated chromosomes are aligned midway between the spindle's poles, at its equator.

At anaphase, microtubules move the sister chromatids of each chromosome apart, to opposite spindle poles.

At telophase, a new nuclear envelope forms around each of two clusters of decondensing chromosomes.

Thus two daughter nuclei have formed. Each has the same chromosome number as the parent cell's nucleus.

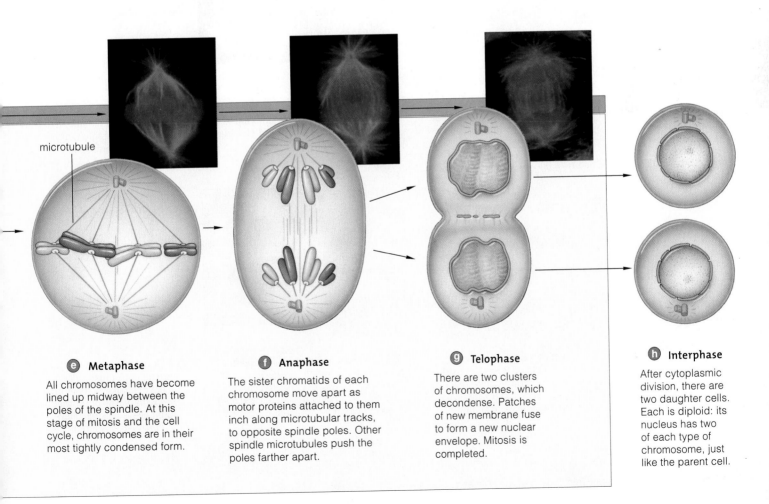

microtubule

e Metaphase

All chromosomes have become lined up midway between the poles of the spindle. At this stage of mitosis and the cell cycle, chromosomes are in their most tightly condensed form.

f Anaphase

The sister chromatids of each chromosome move apart as motor proteins attached to them inch along microtubular tracks, to opposite spindle poles. Other spindle microtubules push the poles farther apart.

g Telophase

There are two clusters of chromosomes, which decondense. Patches of new membrane fuse to form a new nuclear envelope. Mitosis is completed.

h Interphase

After cytoplasmic division, there are two daughter cells. Each is diploid: its nucleus has two of each type of chromosome, just like the parent cell.

9.4 Cytoplasmic Division Mechanisms

LINKS TO
SECTIONS
4.9, 4.11

In most cell types, the cytoplasm usually divides at some time between late anaphase and the end of telophase. The mechanism of cytoplasmic division—or, more formally, cytokinesis—differs among species.

HOW DO ANIMAL CELLS DIVIDE?

Dividing animal cells partition their cytoplasm by a **contractile ring mechanism**. Most often, the plasma membrane starts to sink inward as a thin indentation about halfway between the cell's poles (Figure 9.8a). This is a cleavage furrow, the first visible sign that the cytoplasm is dividing. It advances until it extends all around the cell. As it does so, it deepens along a plane corresponding to the former spindle's equator.

What is going on? Part of the cell cortex, that mesh of cytoskeletal elements under the plasma membrane,

is a ring of actin filaments organized as a thin band around the cell's midsection. The band is anchored to the plasma membrane. When energized by ATP, all the filaments contract and slide past one another in a way that shrinks the band diameter (compare Section 4.11). Being attached to the plasma membrane, the band drags it inward until the cytoplasm is pinched in two (Figures 9.8a and 9.9). Two daughter cells form this way. Each ends up with a nucleus and cytoplasm, enclosed within a plasma membrane.

HOW DO PLANT CELLS DIVIDE?

The contractile ring mechanism that works for animal cells could not work for plant cells. The contractile force could not pinch through plant cell walls, which are stiff with cellulose and often lignin. Microtubules

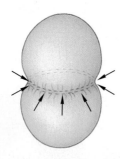
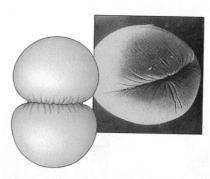

1 Mitosis is completed, and the bipolar spindle is starting to disassemble.

2 At the former spindle equator, a ring of actin filaments attached to the plasma membrane contracts.

3 The diameter of the contractile ring continues to shrink and pull the cell surface inward.

4 The contractile mechanism continues to operate until the cytoplasm is partitioned.

a Contractile Ring Formation

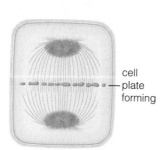
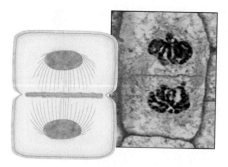

cell plate forming

1 The plane of division and of a future cross-wall was established by a band of microtubules and actin filaments that formed and broke up before mitosis. Vesicles cluster here when mitosis ends.

2 Vesicle membranes fuse. The wall material is sandwiched between two new membranes that lengthen along the plane of a newly forming cell plate.

3 Cellulose is deposited inside the sandwich. In time, these deposits will form two cell walls. Others will form the middle lamella between the walls and cement them together.

4 A cell plate grows at its margins until it fuses with the parent cell plasma membrane. The primary wall of growing plant cells is still thin. New material is deposited on it.

b Cell Plate Formation

Figure 9.8 *Animated!* Cytoplasmic division of an animal cell (**a**) and a plant cell (**b**).

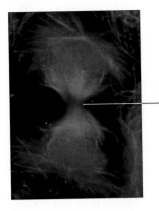

ring of microfilaments midway between the two spindle poles, in the same plane as the spindle equator

Figure 9.9 Micrograph capturing the contractile ring action inside an animal cell.

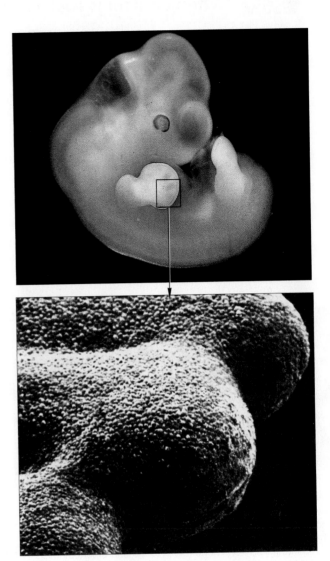

Figure 9.10 The paddlelike structure of a human embryo that develops into a hand by mitosis, cytoplasmic divisions, and other processes. The scanning electron micrograph shows individual cells.

just beneath the plasma membrane help orient the fibers of cellulose in the wall. Before prophase, these microtubules disassemble and new ones assemble in a narrow band around the nucleus—a band that also includes actin filaments. As other microtubules form the bipolar spindle, the narrow band disappears, and an actin-depleted zone is left behind. *The zone marks the plane of cytoplasmic division* (Figure 9.8b).

Along that plane, tiny vesicles packed with wall-building materials from Golgi bodies fuse with one another. Together, deposits of these materials form a disk-shaped structure known as a cell plate. Deposits of cellulose accumulate at the plate. In time, they are thick enough to form a cross-wall through the cell. New plasma membrane extends across both sides of it. The wall grows until it bridges the cytoplasm and partitions the parent cell. This cytoplasmic division mechanism is known as **cell plate formation**.

APPRECIATE THE PROCESS!

Take a moment to look closely at your hands. Visualize the cells making up your palms, thumbs, and fingers. Now imagine the mitotic divisions that produced all of the cell generations that preceded them while you were developing, early on, inside your mother (Figure 9.10). And be grateful for the astonishing precision of mechanisms that led to their formation at prescribed times, in prescribed numbers, for the alternatives can be terrible indeed.

Why? Good health and survival itself depend on the proper timing and completion of cell cycle events. Some genetic disorders arise as a result of mistakes during the duplication or distribution of even one chromosome. In other cases, unchecked cell divisions often destroy surrounding tissues and, ultimately, the

individual. Such losses can start in body cells. They can start in the germ cells that give rise to sperm and eggs, although rarely. The last section of this chapter can give you a sense of the consequences.

After mitosis, a separate mechanism partitions the cytoplasm into two daughter cells, each with a nucleus.

A contractile ring mechanism partitions a dividing animal cell. A band of actin filaments around the cell midsection contracts and pinches the cytoplasm in two.

A mechanism called cell plate formation partitions plant cells. Golgi-derived vesicles deposit material at a plane of cytoplasmic division to form a cross-wall, which connects to the parent cell wall.

9.5 When Control Is Lost

LINKS TO
SECTIONS
4.10, 6.5

Controls over cell division affect growth and reproduction. On rare occasions, something goes wrong in a somatic cell or reproductive cell. Cancer may be the outcome.

THE CELL CYCLE REVISITED

Every second, millions of cells in your skin, bone marrow, gut lining, liver, and elsewhere are dividing and replacing their worn-out, dead, and dying predecessors. They do not divide willy-nilly. Many mechanisms control cell growth, DNA replication, and division. They also control when the division machinery is put to rest.

What happens when something goes wrong? Suppose, for instance, that sister chromatids do not separate as they should during mitosis. As a result, one daughter cell ends up with too many chromosomes and the other with too few. Or suppose the wrong nucleotide gets added to a growing strand of DNA during the replication process. Suppose free radicals, peroxides, or ultraviolet radiation attack and disrupt the structure of chromosomal DNA (Section 6.5). Such problems are frequent but inevitable, and a cell may not function properly unless they are quickly countered.

The cell cycle has built-in checkpoints where specific proteins monitor the structure of chromosomal DNA. At different points, these proteins monitor whether the preceding phase of the cycle was successfully completed. Other kinds sense whether conditions favor cell division. All of these proteins—the products of checkpoint genes—form the mechanisms that can advance, delay, or block the cell cycle.

For example, **kinases** are a class of enzymes that can activate other molecules by transferring a phosphate group to them. When DNA is broken or incomplete, they activate certain proteins in a cascade of signaling events that ultimately stop the cell cycle or induce cell death. As another example, the checkpoint proteins called **growth factors** promote transcription of genes that have roles in the body's growth. One of these, epidermal growth factor, activates a kinase by binding to receptors on target cells in epithelial tissues. Binding is a signal to start mitosis.

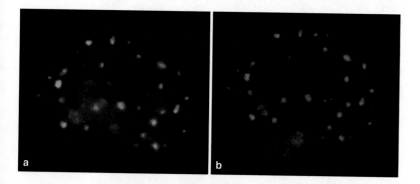

Figure 9.11 Protein products of checkpoint genes in action. A form of radiation damaged the DNA inside this nucleus. (**a**) *Green* dots pinpoint the location of *53BP1*, and (**b**) *red* dots pinpoint the location of *BRCA1*. Both proteins have clustered around the same chromosome breaks in the same nucleus. The integrated action of these proteins and others blocks mitosis until the DNA breaks are fixed.

CHECKPOINT FAILURE AND TUMORS

Sometimes a checkpoint gene mutates and its protein product no longer functions properly. When all checkpoint mechanisms fail, the cell loses control over the cell cycle. Figures 9.11 through 9.14 show a few of the outcomes.

In some cases, the cycle gets stuck in mitosis. Mitotic cell divisions occur over and over again, with no transition into or out of interphase. In other cases, chromosomal DNA that has been damaged is replicated. In still other cases, signaling mechanisms that can make an abnormal cell commit suicide are disabled. You will read more about this mechanism in Section 28.5. Regardless of the cause, the cell's continually dividing descendants form an abnormal mass—a **tumor**—in the surrounding tissue.

Usually, several checkpoint proteins are absent in tumor cells. That is why checkpoint gene products that inhibit mitosis are called *tumor suppressors*. Checkpoint genes encoding proteins that stimulate mitosis are known as *proto-oncogenes*. Mutations that alter their products or the rate at which they are synthesized help transform a normal cell into a tumor cell. Mutant checkpoint genes are linked with an increased risk of tumor formation, and sometimes they run in families.

Moles and other tumors are **neoplasms**, or abnormal masses of cells that lost controls over how they grow and divide. Ordinary skin moles are among the noncancerous, or *benign*, neoplasms. They grow very slowly, and their cells retain the surface recognition proteins that keep them in

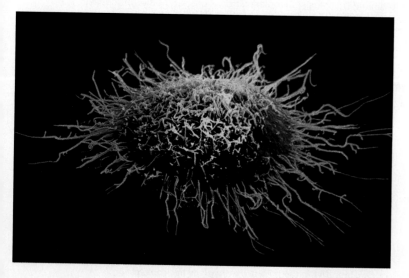

Figure 9.12 Scanning electron micrograph of the surface of a cervical cancer cell, the kind of malignant cell that killed Henrietta Lacks.

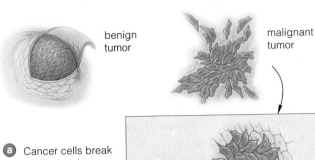

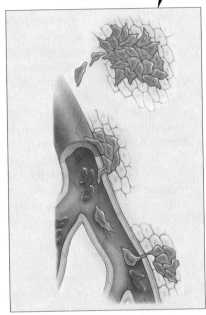

a Cancer cells break away from their home tissue.

b The metastasizing cells become attached to the wall of a blood vessel or lymph vessel. They release digestive enzymes onto it. Then they cross the wall at the breach.

c Cancer cells creep or tumble along inside blood vessels, then leave the bloodstream the same way they got in. They start new tumors in new tissues.

Figure 9.13 *Animated!* Comparison of benign and malignant tumors. Benign tumors typically are slow-growing and stay put in their home tissue. Cells of a malignant tumor migrate abnormally through the body and establish colonies even in distant tissues.

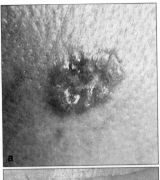

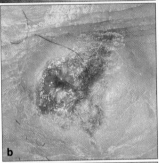

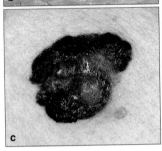

Figure 9.14 Skin cancers. (**a**) A *basal cell carcinoma* is the most common type. This slow-growing, raised lump is typically uncolored, reddish-brown, or black.

(**b**) The second most common form of skin cancer is called a *squamous cell carcinoma*. This pink growth, firm to the touch, grows fast under the surface of skin exposed to the sun.

(**c**) *Malignant melanoma* spreads fastest. Cells form dark, encrusted lumps. They may itch like an insect bite or bleed easily.

their home tissue (Figure 9.13). Unless a benign neoplasm grows too large or becomes irritating, it poses no threat to the body.

CHARACTERISTICS OF CANCER

Cancers are the abnormally growing and dividing cells of a *malignant* neoplasm. They disrupt surrounding tissues, both physically and metabolically. Cancer cells are grossly disfigured. They can break loose from home tissues, slip into and out of blood vessels and lymph vessels, and invade other tissues where they do not belong (Figure 9.13).

Cancer cells typically display four characteristics. *First*, they grow and divide abnormally. Controls on overcrowding in tissues are lost and cell populations reach extremely high densities. The number of small blood vessels, or capillaries, that transport gases and other substances to and from the growing cell mass also increases abnormally.

Second, the cytoplasm and plasma membrane of cancer cells become grossly altered. The membrane becomes leaky and has altered or missing proteins. The whole cytoskeleton shrinks, becomes disorganized, or both. Enzyme action shifts, as in amplified reliance on ATP formation by glycolysis.

Third, cancer cells often have a weakened capacity for adhesion. Because their recognition proteins are altered or lost, they cannot stay anchored in proper tissues. They break away and may establish growing colonies in distant tissues. *Metastasis* is the name for this process of abnormal cell migration and tissue invasion.

Fourth, cancer cells may have lethal effects. Unless they are eradicated by surgery, chemotherapy, or some other procedures, their uncontrollable divisions can put the individual on a painful road to death.

Each year in the developed countries alone, cancers cause 15 to 20 percent of all deaths. And cancer is not just a human problem. Cancers are known to occur in most of the animal species studied to date.

Cancer is a multistep process. Researchers have already identified many of the mutant genes that contribute to it. They also are working to identify drugs that specifically target and destroy cancer cells or stop them from dividing.

HeLa cells, for instance, were used in early tests of taxol, an anticancer drug that stops spindles from disassembling. With this kind of research, we may one day have drugs that can put the brakes on cancer cells. We return to this topic in later chapters.

Summary

Section 9.1 By processes of reproduction, parents produce a new generation of individuals like themselves. Cell division is a bridge between generations. When a cell divides, its daughter cells each receive a required number of DNA molecules and some cytoplasm.

Only eukaryotic cells undergo mitosis, meiosis, or both. These nuclear division mechanisms partition the duplicated chromosomes of a parent cell into daughter nuclei. A separate mechanism divides the cytoplasm. Prokaryotic cells divide by a different mechanism.

Mitosis is the basis of multicellular growth, cell replacements, and tissue repair. Also, many singled-celled and multicelled species reproduce asexually by mitosis.

Meiosis, the basis of sexual reproduction, precedes the formation of gametes or spores.

A eukaryotic chromosome is a molecule of DNA and many histones and other proteins associated with it. The proteins structurally organize the chromosome and affect access to genes. The smallest unit of organization, the nucleosome, consists of a stretch of double-stranded DNA looped twice around a spool of histones.

When duplicated, the chromosome consists of two sister chromatids, each with a kinetochore (a docking site for microtubules). Until late in mitosis (or meiosis), the two remain attached at their centromere region.

Biology❸Now
Explore the structure of a chromosome with the animation on BiologyNow.

Section 9.2 Each cell cycle starts when a new cell forms, runs through interphase, and ends when that cell reproduces by nuclear and cytoplasmic division. A cell carries out most functions in interphase: it increases in mass, roughly doubles the number of its cytoplasmic components, then duplicates each of its chromosomes.

Biology❸Now
Investigate the stages of the cell cycle with the interaction on BiologyNow.

Section 9.3 The sum of all chromosomes in cells of a given type is the chromosome number. Human body cells have a diploid chromosome number of 46 (pairs of 23 types of chromosomes). Mitosis, which maintains the chromosome number, has four continuous stages:

Prophase. The duplicated, threadlike chromosomes start to condense. With the help of motor proteins, new microtubules start forming a bipolar mitotic spindle. The nuclear envelope starts to break apart. Some of the microtubules extending from one spindle pole tether one chromatid of each chromosome; others extending from the opposite pole tether the sister chromatid. Microtubules extending from both poles grow until they overlap at the spindle's midpoint.

Metaphase. At metaphase, all chromosomes have become aligned at the spindle's midpoint.

Anaphase. Sister chromatids detach from each other. The kinetochore of each drags it along microtubules, which are shortening at both ends. The microtubules that overlap ratchet past each other, pushing the spindle poles farther apart. Different motor proteins drive the movements. One of each type of parental chromosome ends up clustered together at each spindle pole.

Telophase. The chromosomes decondense to threadlike form. A new nuclear envelope forms around each cluster. Both nuclei have the parental chromosome number.

Fill in the blanks of the diagram below to check your understanding of the four stages of mitosis, and how it maintains the chromosome number.

Biology❸Now
Observe how mitosis occurs with the animation on BiologyNow.

Section 9.4 The mechanisms of cytoplasmic division differ. In animal cells, a microfilament ring that is part of the cell cortex contracts and pulls the cell surface inward until the cytoplasm is partitioned. In plant cells, a band of microtubules and microfilaments forms around the nucleus before mitosis starts. It marks the site where a cell plate will form from Golgi-derived material. The cell plate will enlarge and become a cross-wall that will partition the cytoplasm.

Biology❸Now
Compare the cytoplasmic division of plant and animal cells with the animation on BiologyNow.

Section 9.5 Checkpoint gene products are part of the controls over the cell cycle. Mutant checkpoint genes cause tumors by disrupting normal controls. Cancer is a multistep process involving altered cells that grow and divide abnormally. Malignant cells may metastasize, or break loose and colonize distant tissues.

Biology❸Now
See how cancers spread throughout a body with the animation on BiologyNow.

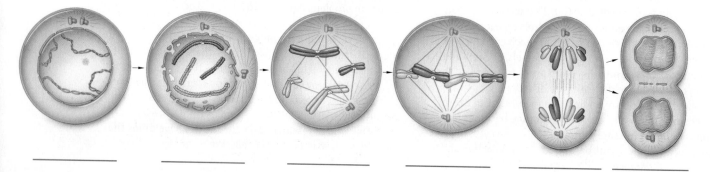

Self-Quiz

Answers in Appendix II

1. Mitosis and cytoplasmic division function in _____ .
   a. asexual reproduction of single-celled eukaryotes
   b. growth, tissue repair, often asexual reproduction
   c. gamete formation in prokaryotes
   d. both a and b

2. A duplicated chromosome has _____ chromatid(s).
   a. one   b. two   c. three   d. four

3. The basic unit that structurally organizes a eukaryotic chromosome is the _____ .
   a. higher order coiling   c. nucleosome
   b. bipolar mitotic spindle   d. microfilament

4. The chromosome number is _____ .
   a. the sum of all chromosomes in cells of a given type
   b. an identifiable feature of each species
   c. maintained by mitosis
   d. all of the above

5. A somatic cell having two of each type of chromosome has a(n) _____ chromosome number.
   a. diploid   b. haploid   c. tetraploid   d. abnormal

6. Interphase is the part of the cell cycle when _____ .
   a. a cell ceases to function
   b. a germ cell forms its spindle apparatus
   c. a cell grows and duplicates its DNA
   d. mitosis proceeds

7. After mitosis, the chromosome number of a daughter cell is _____ the parent cell's.
   a. the same as   c. rearranged compared to
   b. one-half   d. doubled compared to

8. Only _____ is not a stage of mitosis.
   a. prophase   b. interphase   c. metaphase   d. anaphase

9. Match each stage with the events listed.
   ____ metaphase   a. sister chromatids move apart
   ____ prophase   b. chromosomes start to condense
   ____ telophase   c. daughter nuclei form
   ____ anaphase   d. all duplicated chromosomes are aligned at the spindle equator

Additional questions are available on Biology⊗Now™

Critical Thinking

1. Figure 9.15 shows a cell going through stages of mitosis. Notice the barrel-shaped spindle that is quite evident at anaphase. Also notice the dense array of short microtubules midway between the two clusters of chromosomes at telophase. From these clues, would you say that this is a plant cell or an animal cell?

2. Pacific yews (*Taxus brevifolius*) are among the slowest growing trees, which makes them vulnerable to extinction. People started stripping their bark and killing them when they heard that *taxol*, a chemical extracted from the bark, may work against breast and ovarian cancer. It takes bark from about six trees to treat one patient. Do some research and find out why taxol has potential as an anticancer drug and what has been done to protect the trees.

3. X-rays emitted from some radioisotopes damage DNA, especially in cells undergoing DNA replication. Humans

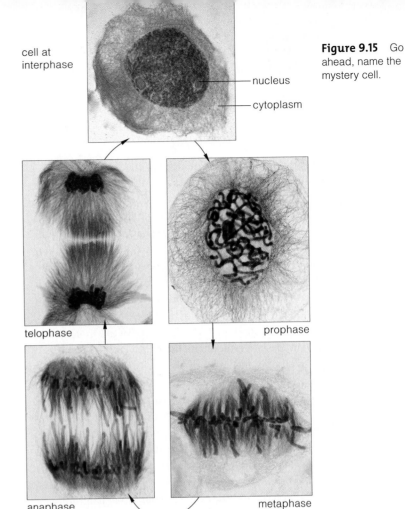

cell at interphase

nucleus

cytoplasm

Figure 9.15 Go ahead, name the mystery cell.

telophase

prophase

anaphase

metaphase

exposed to high levels of x-rays face *radiation poisoning*. Hair loss and a damaged gut lining are early symptoms. Speculate why. Also speculate on why radiation exposure is used as a therapy to treat some cancers.

4. Suppose you have a way to measure the amount of DNA in a single cell during the cell cycle. You first measure the amount at the G1 phase. At what points during the remainder of the cycle would you predict changes in the amount of DNA per cell?

5. The cervix is part of the uterus, a chamber in which embryos develop. The *Pap smear* is a screening procedure that can detect *cervical cancer* in its earliest stages.

Treatments range from freezing precancerous cells or killing them with a laser beam to removal of the uterus (a hysterectomy). The treatments are more than 90 percent effective when this cancer is detected early. Survival chances plummet to less than 9 percent after it spreads.

Most cervical cancers develop slowly. Unsafe sex increases the risk. A key risk factor is infection by human papillomaviruses (HPV), which cause genital warts. Viral genes coding for the tumor-inducing proteins get inserted into the DNA of cervical cells. Of one group of cervical cancer patients, 91 percent had been infected with HPV.

Not all women request Pap smears. Many wrongly believe the procedure is costly. Many do not recognize the importance of abstinence or "safe" sex. Others don't want to think about whether they have cancer. Knowing about the cell cycle and cancer, what would you say to a woman who falls in one or more of these groups?

Why Sex?

Single-celled eukaryotes started to engage in sex many hundreds of millions of years ago, although no one knows how. An unsolved puzzle is why they did it at all.

Asexual reproduction by way of mitotic cell division is easier and faster. Evolutionarily speaking, one individual alone parcels out its DNA to offspring, which are just like their parent. Without sex, that one individual has all of its DNA represented in the new generation. The advantages are evident among most of the protists and fungi, which reproduce asexually most of the time. They quickly give rise to huge populations of cells just like themselves. The advantages are evident among many plants and many invertebrates, including corals, sea stars, and flatworms. Even after bits of these organisms bud or break off, or if the body splits in two, the parts grow into complete copies of the parent. How can the costs of sexual reproduction—such as all of the energy required to construct and use special mate-attracting body parts—beat that?

Sexual reproduction can be an alternative adaptation in changing environments. Consider the plant-sucking insects called aphids. In spring and summer, when plant juices are plentiful, a female aphid reproduces by parthenogenesis. In one day she can give birth to as many as five females, all from unfertilized eggs (Figure 10.1a). Aphid population sizes soar until autumn, when food dwindles. Males now form from eggs, aphids engage in sex, and large fertilized eggs are laid that can withstand winter conditions. Next spring, the eggs develop into asexually oriented females.

Alternative adaptations to the environment also may be why we find a few all-female species of fishes, reptiles, and birds—not mammals—in nature. Not content to let it go at that, University of Tokyo researchers recently fused two mouse eggs in a test tube and made an embryo with no DNA from a male. The embryo developed into Kaguya, the world's first fatherless mammal (Figure 10.1b). The female mouse grew up, engaged in sex with a male mouse, and gave birth to offspring. But back to the big picture:

Sexual reproduction also has advantages when other organisms change. This is especially apparent when we consider the interactions between predators and prey, or between hosts and the parasites or pathogens that infect them. An intriguing idea, the Red Queen hypothesis, may explain the connection between these interactions and sexual reproduction.

In Lewis Carroll's book *Through the Looking Glass,* the Queen of Hearts tells Alice, "Now here, you see, it takes all the running you can do, to keep in the same place." When mutation introduces a better defense against a predator, parasite, or pathogen, we can comfortably predict that natural selection will favor it. However, we also can predict that selection will favor individual predators, parasites, or pathogens that have a novel means to overcome the new defense. The interacting species coevolve; each is running as fast as it can to keep up with the ongoing changes in the other. Talk about an evolutionary treadmill.

Applying the Red Queen hypothesis to our questions, sexual reproduction endures because individuals that practice it can come up with far more variety in heritable defenses compared to the ones that do not. Remember the chromosomes? Sexual reproducers typically have a diploid chromosome number; they inherit two of each type, from two parents. Their two sets of chromosomes

Figure 10.1 Reproductive moments. (**a**) Aphid giving birth. Like females of some other sexually reproducing species, this one reproduces asexually in spring but engages in sex before winter. (**b**) A fatherless mouse. (**c**) Poppy plant being helped by a beetle, which makes pollen deliveries for it. (**d**) Mealybugs mating.

generally hold information about the same traits, but the information about a given trait is not always *exactly* the same on both of them. Some of it might even be bad under prevailing conditions but might be useful in the future. As you will see shortly, meiosis and fertilization mix up information, so that a tremendous variety of novel traits is tried out among the offspring of each new generation. The capacity for rapid, adaptive responses to abiotic and biotic conditions may well be present somewhere in the expressed range of variation.

Asexual reproduction cannot shuffle information into novel combinations. It puts out the same versions of traits again and again into the environmental testing ground. Doing so works well enough—as long as the organism is already equipped to handle change.

With this chapter, we turn to mechanisms of sexual reproduction. Three interconnected events—meiosis, the formation of gametes, and fertilization—are hallmarks of this reproductive mode. The outcome is the production of offspring that display novel combinations of traits. As you will see throughout the book, that outcome has contributed immensely to the range of diversity, past and present.

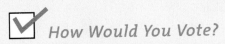

Watch the video online!

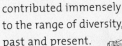

How Would You Vote?

Japanese researchers have successfully created a "fatherless" mouse that contains the genetic material from the eggs of two females. The mouse is healthy and fully fertile. Do you think researchers should be allowed to try the same process with human eggs? See BiologyNow for details, then vote online.

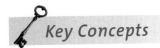

Key Concepts

SEXUAL VERSUS ASEXUAL REPRODUCTION

By asexual reproduction, one parent alone transmits genetic information to offspring. By sexual reproduction, offspring inherit novel combinations of information from more than one parent, because those parents typically differ in their alleles. Alleles are slightly different molecular forms of a gene that specify different versions of the same trait.   Section 10.1

OVERVIEW OF MEIOSIS

Meiosis, a nuclear division mechanism, divides the parental chromosome number by half. It occurs only in cells set aside for sexual reproduction.   Section 10.2

STAGES OF MEIOSIS

Meiosis sorts out a reproductive cell's chromosomes into four new nuclei. After it ends, gametes form by way of cytoplasmic division and other events.   Section 10.3

CHROMOSOME RECOMBINATIONS AND SHUFFLINGS

During meiosis, each pair of chromosomes swaps segments and exchanges alleles. Also, one of each pair is randomly aligned for distribution into a new nucleus. Which ends up in a given gamete is a matter of chance. Chromosomes are shuffled again at fertilization. These events contribute to variation in traits among offspring.   Section 10.4

SEXUAL REPRODUCTION IN THE LIFE CYCLES

In animals, gametes form by different mechanisms in males and females. In most plants, spore formation and other events intervene between meiosis and gamete formation. Spores store and protect hereditary information through times that predictably do not favor survival of offspring.   Section 10.5

MITOSIS AND MEIOSIS COMPARED

Recent molecular evidence suggests that meiosis originated through mechanisms that already existed for mitosis and, before that, for repairing damaged DNA.   Section 10.6

Links to Earlier Concepts

For this chapter, you will be drawing on your sense of the dynamic nature of microtubule assembly and disassembly (Sections 4.10, 4.11, 9.2). Be sure you have a clear picture of the structural organization of chromosomes (9.1) and that you can define chromosome number (9.2). Reflect on how a bipolar spindle made of microtubules moves chromosomes during nuclear division (9.3), and how the cytoplasm gets divided following nuclear division (9.4). You will be revisiting the checkpoint gene products that monitor and repair chromosomal DNA during the cell cycle (9.5).

10.1 Introducing Alleles

Asexual reproduction produces genetically identical copies of a parent. Sexual reproduction introduces variation in the details of traits among offspring.

When an orchid or aphid reproduces by itself, what sort of offspring does it get? By the process of **asexual reproduction**, all offspring inherit the same number and kinds of genes from a single parent. **Genes** are sequences of chromosomal DNA. The genes for each species contain all the heritable information necessary to make new individuals. Rare mutations aside, then, asexually produced individuals can only be *clones*, or genetically identical copies of the parent.

Inheritance gets far more interesting with **sexual reproduction**, a process involving meiosis, formation of gametes, and fertilization—a union of two gametes. In most sexual reproducers, such as humans, the first cell of a new individual holds *pairs of genes* on pairs of chromosomes. Usually, one of each pair is maternal and the other paternal in origin (Figure 10.2).

If information in all pairs of genes were identical down to the last detail, sexual reproduction would also produce clones. Just imagine—you, every person you know, the entire human population might be a clone, with everybody looking alike. But the two genes of a pair might *not* be identical. Why not? The molecular structure of any gene can change permanently; it can mutate. So two genes that happen to be paired in an individual's cells may "say" slightly different things about a trait. Each unique molecular form of the same gene is called an **allele**.

Such tiny differences affect thousands of traits. For instance, whether your chin has a dimple depends on which pair of alleles you inherited at one chromosome location. One kind of allele at that location says "put a dimple in the chin." Another kind says "no dimple." Alleles are one reason why the individuals of sexually reproducing species do not all look alike. *With sexual reproduction, offspring inherit new combinations of alleles, which lead to variations in the details of their traits.*

This chapter gets into the cellular basis of sexual reproduction. More importantly, it starts you thinking about far-reaching effects of gene shufflings at certain stages of the process. The process introduces variations in traits among offspring that are typically acted upon by agents of natural selection. Thus, *variation in traits is a foundation for evolution.*

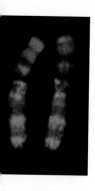

Figure 10.2
A maternal and a paternal chromosome. Any gene on one might be slightly different structurally than the same gene on the other.

Sexual reproduction introduces variation in traits by bestowing novel combinations of alleles on offspring.

10.2 What Meiosis Does

Meiosis is a nuclear division process that divides a parental chromosome number by half in specialized reproductive cells. Sexual reproduction will not work without it.

THINK "HOMOLOGUES"

Think back to the preceding chapter and its focus on mitotic cell division. Unlike mitosis, meiosis sorts out chromosomes into parcels not once but *twice*. Unlike mitosis, it is the first step leading to the formation of gametes. Male and female gametes—such as sperm and eggs—fuse to form a new individual. In most multicelled eukaryotes, cells that form in specialized reproductive structures or organs are the forerunners of gametes. Figure 10.3 gives three examples of where cells that give rise to gametes originate.

As you know, the **chromosome number** is the sum total of chromosomes in cells of a given type. If a cell has a **diploid number** ($2n$), it has a *pair* of each type of chromosome, often from two parents. Except for a pairing of nonidentical sex chromosomes, each pair has the same length, shape, and assortment of genes, and they line up with each other at meiosis. We call them **homologous chromosomes** (*hom–* means alike).

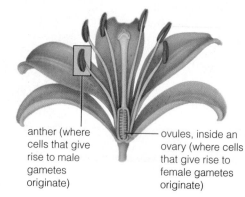

anther (where cells that give rise to male gametes originate)

ovules, inside an ovary (where cells that give rise to female gametes originate)

a Flowering plant

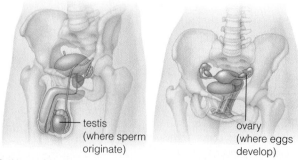

testis (where sperm originate)

ovary (where eggs develop)

b Human male   **c** Human female

Figure 10.3 Examples of reproductive organs, where cells that give rise to gametes originate.

The body cells of humans are diploid, with 23 + 23 homologous chromosomes (Figure 10.4). So are human germ cells that give rise to gametes. Following meiosis, every gamete normally gets 23 chromosomes—one of each type. Meiosis reduced the parental chromosome number by half, to a **haploid number** (*n*).

TWO DIVISIONS, NOT ONE

Bear in mind, meiosis *is* similar to mitosis in certain respects. As in mitosis, a germ cell duplicates its DNA in interphase. The two DNA molecules and associated proteins stay attached at the centromere, the notably constricted region along their length. For as long as they remain attached, we call them **sister chromatids:**

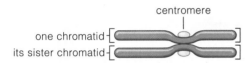

one chromosome in the duplicated state

As in mitosis, the microtubules of a spindle apparatus move the chromosomes in prescribed directions.

With meiosis, however, *chromosomes go through <u>two</u> consecutive divisions that end with the formation of four haploid nuclei*. The germ cell does not enter interphase between the two nuclear divisions, which are known as meiosis I and meiosis II:

	Meiosis I		Meiosis II
Interphase (DNA is replicated prior to meiosis I)	Prophase I Metaphase I Anaphase I Telophase I	*No* interphase (DNA is *not* replicated prior to meiosis II)	Prophase II Metaphase II Anaphase II Telophase II

In meoisis I, each duplicated chromosome aligns with its partner, *homologue to homologue*. After the two chromosomes of every pair have lined up with each other, they are moved apart:

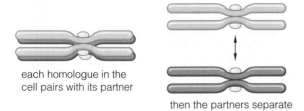

each homologue in the cell pairs with its partner

then the partners separate

The cytoplasm typically starts to divide at some point after each homologue detaches from its partner. The two daughter cells formed this way are haploid, with *one* of each type of chromosome. Don't forget, these chromosomes are still in the duplicated state.

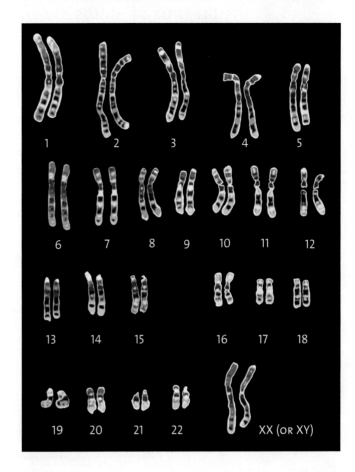

Figure 10.4 Another look at the twenty-three pairs of homologous human chromosomes. This example is from a human female, with two X chromosomes. Human males have a different pairing of sex chromosomes (XY). These chromosomes have been labeled with fluorescent markers.

Next, during meiosis II, *the two sister chromatids of each chromosome are separated from each other:*

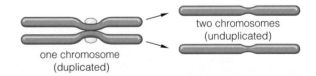

one chromosome (duplicated)

two chromosomes (unduplicated)

There are now four parcels of 23 chromosomes, and each has one chromosome of each type. New nuclear envelopes enclose them, as four nuclei. Typically the cytoplasm divides once more, so the outcome is four haploid (*n*) cells. Figure 10.5 on the next two pages puts these chromosomal movements in the context of the sequential stages of meiosis.

Meiosis, a nuclear division mechanism, reduces a parental cell's chromosome number by half—to a haploid number (n).

10.3 Visual Tour of Meiosis

Meiosis I

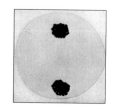

plasma
membrane

newly forming
microtubules in
the cytoplasm

spindle equator
(midway between
the two poles)

one pair of
homologous
chromosomes

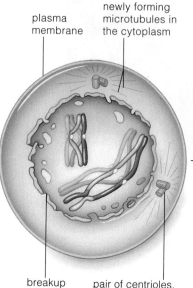
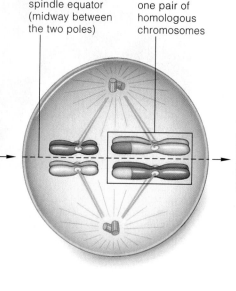
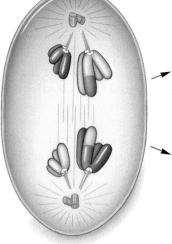
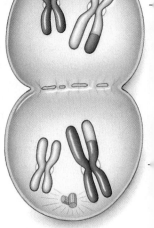

breakup
of nuclear
envelope

pair of centrioles,
and a centrosome,
moving to opposite
sides of nucleus

ⓐ Prophase I

As prophase I begins, chromosomes become visible as threadlike forms. Each pairs with its homologue and usually swaps segments with it, as indicated by the breaks in color in the large chromosomes. Microtubules are forming a bipolar spindle (Section 9.3). If two pairs of centrioles are present, one pair is moved to the opposite side of the nuclear envelope, which is starting to break up.

ⓑ Metaphase I

Microtubules from one spindle pole have tethered one of each type of chromosome; microtubules from the other pole have tethered its homologue. By metaphase I, a tug-of-war between the two sets of microtubules has aligned all chromosomes midway between the poles.

ⓒ Anaphase I

Microtubules attached to each chromosome shorten and move it toward a spindle pole. Other microtubules, which extend from the poles and overlap at the spindle equator, ratchet past each other and push the two poles farther apart. Motor proteins drive the ratcheting.

ⓓ Telophase I

One of each type of chromosome has now arrived at the spindle poles. For most species, the cytoplasm divides at some point, forming two haploid cells. All chromosomes are still duplicated.

Figure 10.5 *Animated!* Meiosis in one type of animal cell. This is a nuclear division mechanism. It reduces the parental chromosome number in immature reproductive cells by half, to the haploid number, for forthcoming gametes. To keep things simple, we track only two pairs of homologous chromosomes. Maternal chromosomes are shaded *purple* and paternal chromosomes *blue*.

Of the four haploid cells that form by meiosis and cytoplasmic divisions, one or all may develop into gametes and function in sexual reproduction. In plants, the cells that form may develop into spores, a stage that precedes gamete formation in the life cycle.

Meiosis II

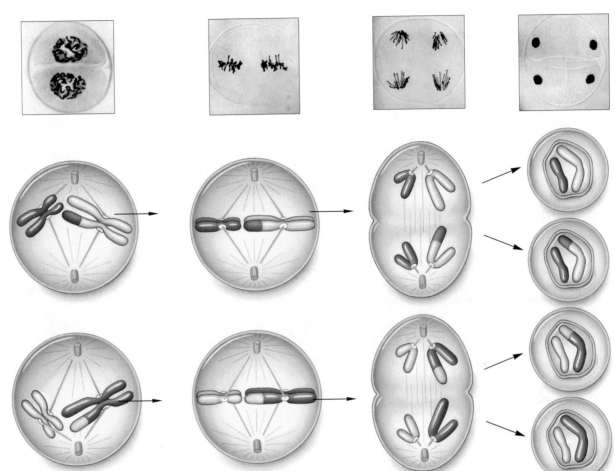

There is no DNA replication between the two nuclear divisions.

e Prophase II

A new bipolar spindle forms in each haploid cell. Microtubules have moved one member of the pair of centrioles to the opposite end of each cell. One chromatid of each chromosome becomes tethered to one spindle pole, and its sister chromatid becomes tethered to the opposite pole.

f Metaphase II

Microtubules from both spindle poles have assembled and disassembled in a tug-of-war that ended at metaphase II, when all chromosomes are positioned midway between the poles.

g Anaphase II

The attachment between sister chromatids of each chromosome breaks. Each is now a separate chromosome but is still tethered to microtubules, which move it toward a spindle pole. Other microtubules push the poles apart. A parcel of unduplicated chromosomes ends up near each pole. One of each type of chromosome is present in each parcel.

h Telophase II

In telophase II, four nuclei form as a new nuclear envelope encloses each cluster of chromosomes. After cytoplasmic division, each of the resulting daughter cells has a haploid (*n*) number of chromosomes.

10.4   How Meiosis Introduces Variations in Traits

As Sections 10.2 and 10.3 make clear, the basic function of meiosis is the reduction of a parental chromosome number by half. In evolutionary terms, two other functions are as important: Prophase I crossovers and the random alignment of chromosomes at metaphase I contribute greatly to the variation in traits among offspring.

The preceding section mentioned in passing that pairs of homologous chromosomes swap parts of themselves during prophase I. It also showed how a homologous chromosome becomes aligned with its partner during prophase I. Both events introduce new combinations of alleles into the gametes that form at some point *after* meiosis. Along with the chromosome shufflings that occur during fertilization, they contribute to variation in traits that occur among new generations of offspring in sexually reproducing species. Later in the book, you will explore how variation in traits has evolutionary and ecological consequences. We suggest that you read this section closely. It will serve you well later on.

CROSSING OVER IN PROPHASE I

Figure 10.6*a* is a simple sketch of a pair of duplicated chromosomes, early in prophase I of meiosis. Notice how they are in threadlike form. All chromosomes in a germ cell condense this way. When they do, each is drawn close to its homologue. The chromatids of one become stitched point by point along their length to the chromatids of the other, with little space between them. This tight, parallel orientation favors **crossing over**, a molecular interaction between a chromatid of one chromosome and a chromatid of the homologous partner. DNA strands break and seal in complex ways, but the outcome is that the two "nonsister" chromatids exchange corresponding segments; they swap genes.

a This maternal chromosome (*purple*) and paternal chromosome (*blue*) were duplicated in interphase. They appear in microscopes early in prophase I, when they are starting to condense to threadlike form. Sister chromatids of each chromosome are positioned so close together that they look like a single thread. (We pulled them apart a bit in this sketch so you can distinguish between them.)

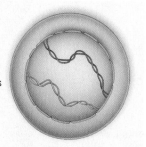

b Each chromosome now becomes zippered up with its homologous partner, so all four chromatids are tightly aligned. If the two sex chromosomes have different forms (such as X paired with Y), they still get tightly aligned, but only in a tiny region at their ends.

c Here is the simplest way to think about crossing over. However, don't forget that the chromosomes are not really rod-shaped during early prophase I. They are still condensing to threadlike form, and each is tightly aligned with its homologous partner.

d The intimate contact encourages crossovers at various intervals along the length of nonsister chromatids. Here we show the location of just one crossover.

e Nonsister chromatids exchange segments at the crossover site. They keep on condensing into thicker, rodlike forms. They will be fully unzipped from each other by metaphase I.

f Crossing over breaks up the old combinations of alleles and puts new ones together in homologous chromosomes. It mixes up maternal and paternal information about traits.

Figure 10.6 *Animated!*   Key events of prophase I, the first stage of meiosis. For clarity, we show only one pair of homologous chromosomes and one crossover. More than one crossover usually occurs in each chromosome pair. *Blue* signifies a paternal chromosome, and *purple*, its maternal homologue.

Gene swapping would be pointless if each type of gene never varied. But remember, a gene can come in slightly different forms—alleles. You can predict that a number of the alleles on one chromosome will *not* be identical to their partner alleles on the homologous chromosome. Each crossover event is a chance to swap slightly different versions of heritable information on gene products.

We will look at the mechanism of crossing over in later chapters. For now, just remember this: *Crossing over leads to recombinations among genes of homologous chromosomes, and eventually to variation in traits among offspring.*

METAPHASE I ALIGNMENTS

Major shufflings of intact chromosomes start during the transition from prophase I to metaphase I. Suppose this is happening right now in one of your germ cells. Crossovers have already made genetic mosaics of the chromosomes, but put this aside in order to simplify tracking. Just call the twenty-three chromosomes you inherited from your mother the *maternal* chromosomes and the twenty-three you inherited from your father the *paternal* chromosomes.

At metaphase I, microtubules from both poles have now aligned all of the duplicated chromosomes at the spindle equator (Figure 10.5*b*). Have they tethered all maternal chromosomes to one pole and all paternal chromosomes to the other? Maybe, but probably not. When the microtubules were growing, they latched on to the first chromosome they contacted. Because the tethering was random, there is no particular pattern to the metaphase I positions of maternal and paternal chromosomes.

Now carry this thought one step further. During anaphase I, when a duplicated chromosome is moved away from its homologous partner, *either partner* can end up at either spindle pole.

Think of the possibilities while tracking just three pairs of homologues. By metaphase I, these three pairs may be arranged in any one of four possible positions (Figure 10.7). This means that eight combinations (2^3) are possible for forthcoming gametes.

Cells that give rise to human gametes have twenty-three pairs of homologous chromosomes, not three. Thus, every time a human sperm or egg forms, there is a total of *8,388,608* (or 2^{23}) possible combinations of maternal and paternal chromosomes! Moreover, in a sperm or an egg, many hundreds of alleles inherited from the mother might not "say" the exact same thing about hundreds of different traits as alleles inherited

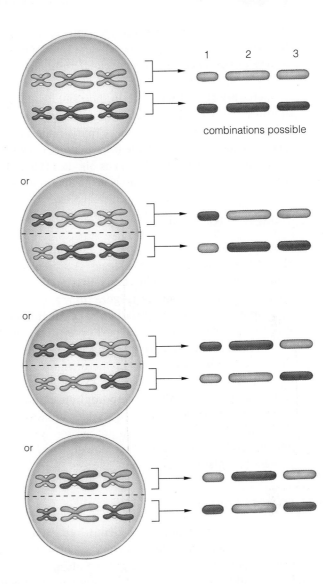

combinations possible

Figure 10.7 *Animated!* Possible outcomes for the random alignment of merely three pairs of homologous chromosomes at metaphase I. The three types of chromosomes are labeled 1, 2, and 3. With four alignments, eight combinations of maternal chromosomes (*purple*) and paternal chromosomes (*blue*) are possible in gametes.

from the father. Are you getting an idea of why such fascinating combinations of traits show up among the generations of your own family tree?

Crossing over, an interaction between a pair of homologous chromosomes, breaks up old combinations of alleles and puts new ones together during prophase I of meiosis.

The random tethering and subsequent positioning of each pair of maternal and paternal chromosomes at metaphase I lead to different combinations of maternal and paternal traits in each new generation.

10.5 From Gametes to Offspring

LINK TO
SECTION
9.4

What happens to the gametes that form after meiosis? Later chapters have specific examples. Here, simply focus on where they fit in the life cycles of plants and animals.

Gametes are not all the same in their details. Human sperm have one tail, opossum sperm have two, and roundworm sperm have none. Crayfish sperm look like pinwheels. Most eggs are microscopic in size, yet an ostrich egg inside its shell is as big as a football. A flowering plant's male gamete is just a sperm nucleus.

GAMETE FORMATION IN PLANTS

The life cycle of most plant species alternates between sporophyte and gametophyte stages. A *sporophyte* is a multicelled spore-producing body that makes sexual spores by way of meiosis (Figure 10.8a). In plants, each **spore** is a haploid reproductive cell that is not a gamete and that does not take part in fertilization. At some point, the spore undergoes mitotic cell divisions that give rise to a *gametophyte*. One or more gametes do form inside this multicelled haploid body.

Pine trees are examples of sporophytes, and their female gametophytes form on the scales of pinecones. Rose bushes and fuschias also are sporophytes, and gametophytes form inside their flowers. You will be focusing on plant life cycles in Chapters 23 and 32.

GAMETE FORMATION IN ANIMALS

In animals, diploid germ cells give rise to gametes. In a male reproductive system, a germ cell develops into a primary spermatocyte. This large, immature cell enters meiosis and cytoplasmic divisions. Four haploid cells result and develop into spermatids (Figure 10.9). Each

cell undergoes changes, such as the formation of a tail, and becomes a **sperm**, a type of mature male gamete.

In female animals, a germ cell becomes a primary oocyte, which is an immature egg. Unlike sperm, the primary oocyte increases in size and stockpiles many cytoplasmic components. In addition, its four daughter cells differ in size and function (Figure 10.10).

When the primary oocyte divides after meiosis I, one daughter cell—the secondary oocyte—gets nearly all of the cytoplasm. The other cell, a first polar body, is exceedingly small. Later, both of these haploid cells enter meiosis II, then cytoplasmic division. One of the secondary oocyte's daughter cells becomes the second polar body. The other daughter cell gets most of the cytoplasm and develops into a gamete. The mature female gamete is an ovum (plural, ova). An ovum also is known informally as an **egg**.

And so we have one egg. The three polar bodies that formed don't function as gametes and aren't rich in nutrients or plump with cytoplasm. In time they degenerate. But their formation assures that the egg will have a haploid chromosome number. Also, by getting most of the cytoplasm, the egg holds enough metabolic machinery to support early cell divisions of the new individual, as Chapters 43 and 44 explain.

MORE SHUFFLINGS AT FERTILIZATION

The chromosome number characteristic of the parents is restored at **fertilization**, a time when a female and male gamete unite and their haploid nuclei fuse. If meiosis did not precede fertilization, the chromosome number would double in each generation. Doublings would disrupt hereditary information, usually for the worse. Why? That information is like a fine-tuned set

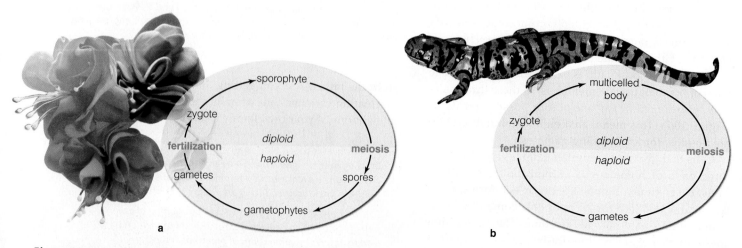

Figure 10.8 (**a**) Generalized life cycle for most plants. (**b**) Generalized life cycle for animals. The zygote is the first cell to form when the nuclei of two gametes fuse at fertilization.

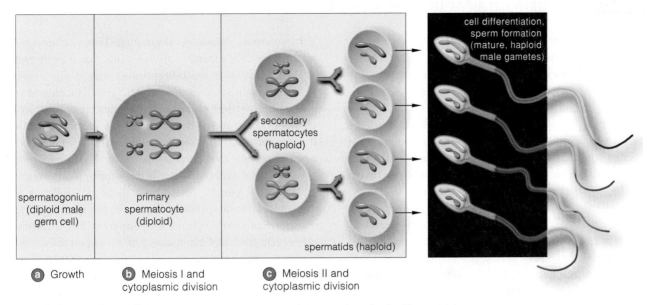

spermatogonium (diploid male germ cell)

primary spermatocyte (diploid)

secondary spermatocytes (haploid)

spermatids (haploid)

cell differentiation, sperm formation (mature, haploid male gametes)

a Growth

b Meiosis I and cytoplasmic division

c Meiosis II and cytoplasmic division

Figure 10.9 *Animated!* Generalized sketch of sperm formation in animals. Figure 44.4 shows a specific example (how sperm form in human males).

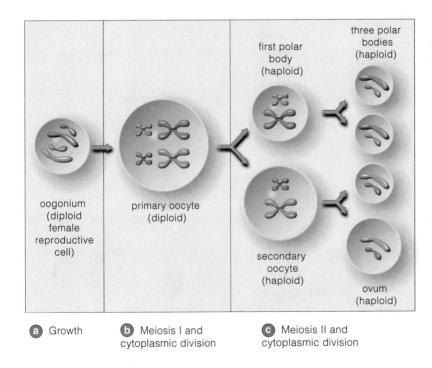

oogonium (diploid female reproductive cell)

primary oocyte (diploid)

first polar body (haploid)

three polar bodies (haploid)

secondary oocyte (haploid)

ovum (haploid)

a Growth

b Meiosis I and cytoplasmic division

c Meiosis II and cytoplasmic division

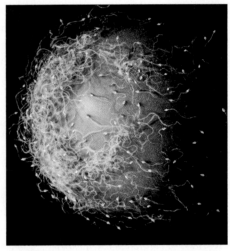

Figure 10.10 *Animated!* Animal egg formation. Eggs are far larger than sperm and larger than the three polar bodies. The painting above, based on a scanning electron micrograph, depicts human sperm surrounding an ovum.

of blueprints that must be followed exactly, page after page, to build a normal individual.

Fertilization also adds to variation among offspring. Reflect on the possibilities for humans alone. During prophase I, every human chromosome undergoes an average of two or three crossovers. In addition to the crossovers, random positioning of pairs of paternal and maternal chromosomes at metaphase I results in one of millions of possible chromosome combinations in each gamete. And of all male and female gametes that form, *which* two actually get together is a matter of chance. The sheer number of combinations that can exist at fertilization is staggering!

The distribution of random mixes of chromosomes into gametes, random metaphase chromosome alignments, and fertilization contribute to variation in traits of offspring.

10.6 Mitosis and Meiosis—An Ancestral Connection?

LINKS TO
SECTIONS
9.2, 9.5

This chapter opened with hypotheses about the survival advantages of asexual and sexual reproduction. It seems like a giant evolutionary step from producing clones to producing genetically varied offspring. But was it?

Figure 10.11 shows an obvious parallel between the four stages of mitosis and meiosis II. The same kind of bipolar spindle assorts duplicated chromosomes into parcels in very similar ways. Recent studies also reveal striking similarities at the molecular level.

In all organisms, from prokaryotes to mammals, certain genes code for proteins that can recognize and repair breaks in the double-stranded DNA molecules of chromosomes. Such damage, recall, is monitored by products of checkpoint genes while DNA is being replicated during the cell cycle (Sections 9.2 and 9.5). If they detect a problem, there is a pause in the cycle until it is repaired. Even in bacteria—the most ancient lineages on Earth—a mechanism exists that may well have been recruited for mitosis and meiosis.

Some highly conserved gene products often repair breaks and odd rearrangements in chromosomal DNA that occur during mitosis. They also put chromosomal DNA back together in prophase I, after homologous chromosomes exchange segments. This outcome—a form of genetic recombination—could have been part of the evolution of sexual reproduction.

Is *Giardia intestinalis* one model? This descendent of one of the earliest eukaryotic lineages does not have mitochondria, and it does not form a bipolar spindle during mitosis. This single-celled parasite has never been observed to reproduce sexually. Yet it has gene products that serve in meiosis in higher eukaryotes.

We invite you to think about these possibilities as you read later chapters in the book. We invite you to explore likely connections on your own. For instance, when you look at *Chlamydomonas*, a single-celled alga of freshwater habitats, mull over the fact that haploid *Chlamydomonas* cells reproduce asexually by mitotic cell division. But two cells of different mating strains also can function as *gametes*; they can fuse and form a diploid individual. Do such cells offer more clues to the origin of sexual reproduction? Maybe.

> *Recombination mechanisms that are vital for reproduction of eukaryotic cells might have evolved from DNA repair mechanisms in prokaryotic ancestors.*

Figure 10.11 Comparative summary of key features of mitosis and meiosis, starting with a diploid cell. Only two paternal and two maternal chromosomes are shown. Both were duplicated in interphase, prior to nuclear division. Both use a bipolar spindle made of microtubules to sort out and move the chromosomes.

Mitosis maintains the parental chromosome number. Meiosis halves it, to the haploid number.

Mitotic cell division is the basis of asexual reproduction among eukaryotes. It is the basis of growth and tissue repair of multicelled eukaryotic species.

Meiotic cell division is a required step before the formation of gametes or sexual spores.

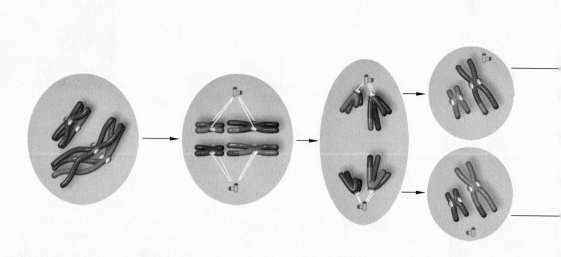

Meiosis I

Prophase I
Chromosomes duplicated earlier in diploid (2n) germ cell during interphase. They condense. Bipolar spindle forms, tethers them to its poles. Crossovers between each pair of homologous chromosomes.

Metaphase I
Each maternal chromosome and its paternal homologue randomly aligned at the spindle equator; either one may get attached to either pole.

Anaphase I
Homologues separate from their partner, are moved to opposite poles.

Telophase I
Two haploid (n) clusters of chromosomes. New nuclear envelopes may form. Cytoplasm may divide before meiosis II gets under way.

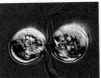

Giardia intestinalis

Chlamydomonas cells mating

Mitosis

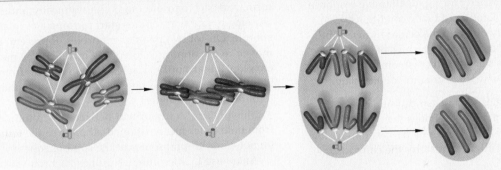

Prophase

Chromosomes duplicated earlier in diploid (*2n*) body cell, in interphase. They condense. A spindle forms; chromosomes tethered to its poles.

Metaphase

All chromosomes aligned at the spindle equator.

Anaphase

Sister chromatids of each chromosome moved to opposite spindle poles.

Telophase

Two diploid (*2n*) nuclei form. After cytoplasmic division, two diploid body cells.

Meiosis II

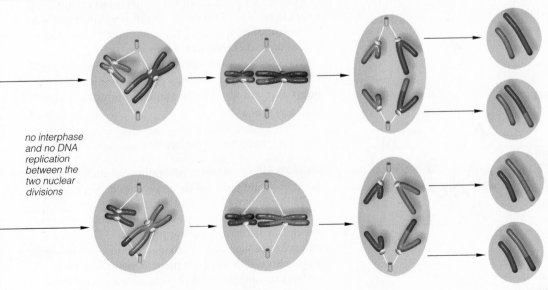

no interphase and no DNA replication between the two nuclear divisions

Prophase II

All chromosomes still duplicated. New spindle forms in each nucleus, tethers chromosomes to spindle poles.

Metaphase II

All chromosomes aligned at the spindle equator.

Anaphase II

Sister chromatids of each chromosome moved to opposite spindle poles.

Telophase II

Four haploid (*n*) nuclei form. After cytoplasmic division, haploid cells function as gametes or spores.

Summary

Section 10.1 Life cycles of eukaryotic species often have asexual and sexual phases.

Asexual reproduction by way of mitosis yields a clone, or offspring that are genetically the same as one parent. Compared with sexual modes, it is easier, requires less energy, and gives rise to huge populations in far less time.

Sexual reproduction involves two parents that engage in meiosis, gamete formation, and fertilization. It leads to novel allele combinations in offspring. Compared to asexual reproduction, the expressed range of variation offers a far greater capacity for rapid, adaptive response to novel changes in abiotic and biotic conditions.

Alleles are slightly different molecular forms of the same gene that specify different versions of the same gene product. Meiosis and fertilization mix up the alleles (and forms of traits) in each generation of offspring.

Section 10.2 Meiosis, a nuclear division process, precedes gamete formation. It divides the chromosome number characteristic of a species by half, so that fusion of two gametes at fertilization restores the chromosome number (Figure 10.12).

Offspring of most sexual reproducers inherit pairs of chromosomes, one from a maternal and one from a paternal parent. Except in individuals that have inherited nonidentical sex chromosomes (e.g., X with Y), the pairs are homologous (alike); each pair has the same length, shape, and mostly the same gene sequence. All pairs interact at meiosis. Meiosis parcels out one chromosome of each type for forthcoming gametes.

Section 10.3 All chromosomes in a reproductive cell are duplicated in interphase, prior to meiosis. Meiosis sorts out duplicated chromosomes twice, in two divisions (meiosis I and II) that are not separated by interphase.

In meiosis I, the first nuclear division, homologous chromosomes are partitioned into two clusters, both with one of each type of chromosome.

Prophase I. Chromosomes condense into threadlike form, and each pair of homologues typically undergoes crossing over. Microtubules start forming a bipolar spindle. One of two pairs of centrioles, if present, is moved to the opposite side of the nucleus. The nuclear envelope breaks up, so microtubules growing from both spindle poles can penetrate the nuclear region and tether the chromosomes.

Metaphase I. A tug-of-war between microtubules from both poles has positioned all pairs of the tethered homologous chromosomes at the spindle equator.

Anaphase I. Microtubules pull each chromosome away from its homologue, to opposite spindle poles. Other microtubules that overlap at the spindle equator ratchet past each other to push the poles farther apart. There are now two parcels of duplicated chromosomes, one near each spindle pole.

Telophase I. Two haploid nuclei form around the parcels. Cytoplasmic division typically follows.

In meiosis II, the second nuclear division, the sister chromatids of each chromosome are pulled away from each other and partitioned into two clusters. This occurs in both haploid nuclei that formed in meiosis I. By the end of telophase II, there are four nuclei, each with a haploid chromosome number.

When the cytoplasm divides, there are four haploid cells. One or all may serve as gametes or, in plants, as spores that will give rise to gamete-producing bodies.

Biology⊜Now
Explore what happens during each stage of meiosis with the animation on BiologyNow.

Section 10.4 Novel combinations of alleles and of maternal and paternal chromosomes arise through events in prophase I and metaphase I.

*Non*sister chromatids of homologous chromosomes undergo crossing over during prophase I. They break and exchange segments, so that each ends up with allelic combinations that were not present in either parent.

Maternal and paternal chromosomes get tethered randomly to one spindle pole or the other. Thus they are positioned at random when they are aligned at the spindle equator at metaphase I, so alleles of either one may end up in a new nucleus, then in a gamete.

Biology⊜Now
Study how crossing over and metaphase I alignments affect allele combinations with the animation on BiologyNow.

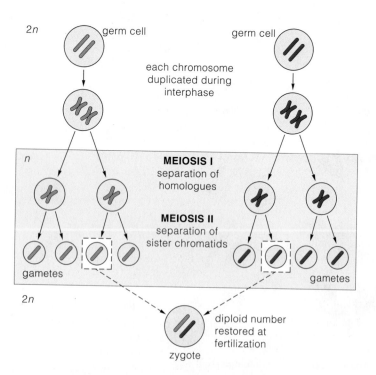

Figure 10.12 Summary of changes in chromosome number at different stages of sexual reproduction, using two diploid (2*n*) germ cells as the example. During two nuclear divisions, meiosis reduces the chromosome number by half (*n*). The union of haploid nuclei of two gametes at fertilization restores the diploid number.

Section 10.5 Life cycles of plants and animals have sexual phases. Sporophytes are a multicelled plant body that produces sexual spores. Such plant spores give rise to gametophytes, in which haploid gametes form.

In most animals, germ cells in reproductive organs give rise to sperm or eggs. Fusion of a sperm and egg nucleus at fertilization results in a zygote, the first cell of a new individual.

Learn how gametes form with the animation on BiologyNow.

Section 10.6 Like mitosis, meiosis uses a bipolar spindle to move and sort duplicated chromosomes. But meiosis occurs only in sex cells and does not produce clones of the parent; it reduces the parental chromosome number by half. Crossing over and random alignments of different mixes of maternal and paternal chromosomes for distribution to gametes occur only in meiosis. These events, and the chance of any two gametes meeting at fertilization, contribute to enormous variation in traits among offspring.

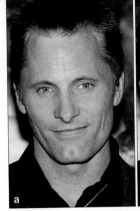

Figure 10.13
Bdelloid rotifer.

 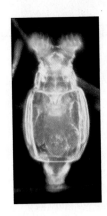

Figure 10.14 Viggo Mortensen (**a**) with and (**b**) without a chin dimple.

11. Match each term with its description.
_____ chromosome   a. different molecular forms
          number   of the same gene
_____ alleles   b. none between meiosis I, II
_____ metaphase I   c. all chromosomes aligned
_____ interphase   at spindle equator
                              d. sum total of all chromosomes
                                 in cells of a given type

Additional questions are available on **Biology Now™**

Self-Quiz   *Answers in Appendix II*

1. Meiosis and cytoplasmic division function in _____ .
   a. asexual reproduction of single-celled eukaryotes
   b. growth, tissue repair, often asexual reproduction
   c. sexual reproduction
   d. both b and c

2. A duplicated chromosome has _____ chromatid(s).
   a. one   b. two   c. three   d. four

3. A somatic cell having two of each type of chromosome has a(n) _____ chromosome number.
   a. diploid   b. haploid   c. tetraploid   d. abnormal

4. Sexual reproduction requires _____ .
   a. meiosis   c. spore formation
   b. fertilization   d. a and b

5. Generally, a pair of homologous chromosomes _____ .
   a. carry the same genes   c. interact at meiosis
   b. are the same length, shape d. all of the above

6. Meiosis _____ the parental chromosome number.
   a. doubles   b. halves   c. maintains   d. corrupts

7. Meiosis ends with the formation of _____ .
   a. two cells   c. eight cells
   b. two nuclei   d. four nuclei

8. The cell in the diagram below is in anaphase I rather than anaphase II. I know this because _____ .

9. Sister chromatids of each duplicated chromosome separate during _____ .
   a. prophase I   c. anaphase I
   b. prophase II   d. anaphase II

10. Sexual reproducers bestow variation in traits on offspring by _____ .
   a. crossing over   c. fertilization
   b. metaphase I   d. both a and b
      random   e. All of the above
      orientations   are factors.

Critical Thinking

1. Why can you predict that meiosis will give rise to genetic variation between parent cells and daughter cells in fewer cell cycles than mitosis?

2. The bdelloid rotifer lineage started at least 40 million years ago (Figure 10.13). About 360 known species of these tiny animals live in many aquatic habitats worldwide. All are female. Do some research to identify conditions in the physical and biological environments to which they might be reproductively adapted.

3. Actor Viggo Mortensen inherited a gene that makes his chin dimple. Figure 10.14*b* shows what he might have looked like if he inherited a different form of that gene. What is the name for alternative forms of the same gene?

4. Assume you can measure the amount of DNA in the nucleus of a primary oocyte, and then in the nucleus of a primary spermatocyte. Each gives you a mass *m*. What mass of DNA would you expect to find in the nucleus of each mature gamete (egg and sperm) that forms after meiosis? What mass of DNA will be (1) in the nucleus of a zygote that forms at fertilization and (2) in that zygote's nucleus after the first DNA duplication?

5. The diploid chromosome number for the somatic cells of several eukaryotic species are listed at right. Write down the number of chromosomes that normally end up in gametes of each species. Then write what the number would be after three generations if meiosis did not occur before gamete formation.

Fruit fly, *Drosophila melanogaster*	8
Garden pea, *Pisum sativum*	14
Corn, *Zea mays*	20
Frog, *Rana pipiens*	26
Earthworm, *Lumbricus terrestris*	36
Human, *Homo sapiens*	46
Chimpanzee, *Pan troglodytes*	48
Amoeba, *Amoeba*	50
Horsetail, *Equisetum*	216

In Pursuit of a Better Rose

Researchers at Texas A&M and Clemson universities are breathing new life into *rose breeding*. People have been practicing this form of artificial selection for thousands of years. Starting with small, simple, five-petaled wild roses, they patiently cross-bred plants and in time were rewarded with a profusion of petals, fabulous fragrances, exquisite colors, and other compelling traits. Today, rose fanciers in thirty-six countries all over the world claim membership in the World Federation of Rose Societies. In any given year, people from all walks of life buy billions of dollars' worth of rosebuds and blooms. On Valentine's Day in the United States alone, 110 million cut roses are offered as symbols of love and romance. Roses are now big business.

Fossils in Colorado tell us that roses have been around for at least 40 million years. When rose breeding started, the ancestral stock had a diploid chromosome number—two sets of seven chromosomes. A great variety of cultivars now have four, seven, fourteen, even twenty-one sets of chromosomes! Within those chromosomes are genes that specify the size, number, and shape of petals and thorns, genes that deal with floral scents and colors, and genes that dictate whether plants bloom once or all year long. Other genes influence resistance to diseases and pests.

Unlike many wild roses, most of the cultivated varieties are susceptible to black spot, powdery mildew, and other diseases (Figure 11.1). The fungus that causes black spot is notably active in rainy, humid regions; the one that causes powdery mildew thrives in greenhouses. Fungicides work against pathogenic fungi, but they are costly, and many kinds also kill beneficial microorganisms.

Possibly a safer approach would be to cross-breed a wild plant known to have disease resistance with a plant known to be susceptible. However, traditional breeding practices are hit-or-miss, and they are tedious. Breeders have to wait for plants to form seeds, then plant the seeds, then observe whether any or all plants of the new generation, and the next, and the one after that show disease resistance.

Enter the new researchers. They are working to make genetic maps for all seven of the rose chromosomes. Just as road maps pinpoint cities along a highway, genetic maps can pinpoint where genes that influence specific traits are located along the length of chromosomes. By pinpointing a gene that influences a desired trait, breeders will be able to speed up their artificial selection practices.

For example, remember those radioisotopes described in Chapter 2? Researchers use them to make a DNA probe, a bit of radioactive DNA. They use it to test offspring from a cross for a specific DNA region—say, one near a gene that affects disease resistance. If the probe does not bind to the DNA of offspring, a breeder can assume the new plant has

Figure 11.1 One representative of a long history of artificial selection. Like most of the modern cultivars and unlike many wild roses, this one is vulnerable to black spot, a disease that results in the telltale destruction of leaves. Researchers are working to develop faster, more efficient ways to breed roses that have disease resistance and other desired traits.

not inherited the resistance gene and can try a new cross. Such *marker-assisted selection* is useful when several genes control a trait, as for disease resistance. A plant lineage that inherits all the genes may be the least vulnerable to attack.

In time, the maps being pieced together at Texas A&M, Clemson, and elsewhere will become consolidated into a permanent genetic map for roses. Its information will be retrieved for breeding programs. It also will be put to use for actual transfers of desirable genes into roses by way of biotechnology and genetic engineering. But these are cutting-edge topics that will not make much sense without in-depth knowledge of the structure and function of DNA, genes, and their protein products. We reserve them for later chapters in this unit. For now, start with something you already know about—the chromosomes and alleles introduced in the preceding chapter. This will be enough for you to follow the classical breeding practices that gave us our first glimpses of the principles of inheritance.

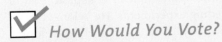

How Would You Vote?

The federal government helps support some agricultural extension programs that offer homeowners advice on gardens and ornamental plants. Do you consider this to be an appropriate use of government resources? See BiologyNow for details, then vote online.

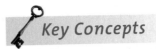

Key Concepts

WHERE MODERN GENETICS STARTED

Gregor Mendel gathered the first experimental evidence of the genetic basis of inheritance: Each gene has a specific location on a chromosome. Organisms that have a diploid chromosome number have *pairs* of genes, at equivalent locations on pairs of homologous chromosomes. Alleles that are nonidentical may affect a trait differently. One allele is often dominant, in that its effect on a trait masks the effect of a recessive allele paired with it.   Section 11.1

INSIGHTS FROM MONOHYBRID EXPERIMENTS

Some experiments yielded evidence of gene segregation: When one chromosome is separated from its homologous partner during meiosis, their pairs of alleles also separate and end up in different gametes.   Section 11.2

INSIGHTS FROM DIHYBRID EXPERIMENTS

Other experiments yielded evidence of independent assortment: During meiosis, each pair of homologous chromosomes is sorted out for distribution into one gamete or another independently of how all of the other pairs of homologous chromosomes are assorted.   Section 11.3

VARIATIONS IN GENE EXPRESSION

Not all traits have clearly dominant or recessive forms. One allele of a pair may be fully or partially dominant over its partner or codominant with it. Two or more gene pairs often influence the same trait, and some single genes influence many traits. The environment introduces more variation in gene expression.   Sections 11.4–11.7

Links to Earlier Concepts

Before starting this chapter, review the definitions of genes, alleles, and diploid versus haploid chromosome numbers (Sections 10.1 and 10.2). As you read, you may wish to refer to the earlier introduction to natural selection (1.4) and to the visual road map for the stages of meiosis (10.3). You will be considering experimental evidence of two major topics that were introduced earlier—the effects that crossing over and metaphase I alignments have on inheritance (10.4).

11.1 Mendel, Pea Plants, and Inheritance Patterns

LINKS TO
SECTIONS
1.4, 10.1

We turn now to recurring inheritance patterns among humans and other sexually reproducing species. You already know meiosis halves the parental chromosome number, which is restored at fertilization. Here the story picks up with some observable outcomes of these events.

More than a century ago, people wondered about the basis of inheritance. Most had an idea that two parents contribute hereditary material to offspring, but few even suspected that it is organized in units, or genes.

Figure 11.2 Gregor Mendel, the founder of modern genetics.

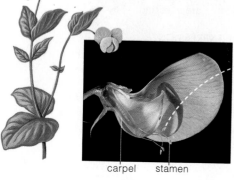

carpel   stamen

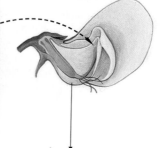

a Garden pea flower, cut in half. Sperm form in pollen grains, which originate in male floral parts (stamens). Eggs develop, fertilization takes place, and seeds mature in female floral parts (carpels).

b Pollen from a plant that breeds true for purple flowers is brushed onto a floral bud of a plant that breeds true for white flowers. The white flower had its stamens snipped off. This is one way to assure cross-fertilization of plants.

c Later, seeds develop inside pods of the cross-fertilized plant. An embryo within each seed develops into a mature pea plant.

d Each new plant's flower color is indirect but observable evidence that hereditary material has been transmitted from the parent plants.

Figure 11.3 *Animated!* Garden pea plant (*Pisum sativum*), which can self-fertilize or cross-fertilize. Experimenters can control the transfer of its hereditary material from one flower to another.

Rather, according to the prevailing view, hereditary material was fluid, with the fluids from both parents blending at fertilization like milk into coffee.

The idea of "blending inheritance" failed to explain the obvious. For example, many children who differ in eye color or hair color have the same two parents. If parental fluids blended, then the eye or hair color of children should be a blend of the parental colors. If neither parent had freckles, freckled children would never pop up. A white mare bred with a black stallion should consistently give birth to gray offspring, but as horse breeders knew, this was not always the case. Blending inheritance could scarcely explain much of the obvious variation in traits that people could see with their own eyes.

Even Charles Darwin accepted the blending notion until he and his cousin conducted experiments that disproved it. According to Darwin's theory of natural selection, individuals of a population show variation in traits. Over the generations, variations that help an individual survive and reproduce show up among more and more offspring, and less helpful variations become less frequent and might even disappear. Thus blending inheritance *seemed* to support the theory of natural selection. As it turned out, the idea of discrete units of information—genes—explain it better.

Even before Darwin presented his theory, someone was gathering evidence that eventually would help support it. A monk, Gregor Mendel (Figure 11.2), had already guessed that sperm and eggs carry distinct units of information about **heritable traits**. After he analyzed specific traits of pea plants, one generation after another, he found indirect but *observable* evidence of how parents transmit genes to offspring.

MENDEL'S EXPERIMENTAL APPROACH

Mendel spent most of his adult life in Brno, a city near Vienna that is now part of the Czech Republic. Yet he was not a man of narrow interests who accidentally stumbled onto dazzling principles.

Mendel's monastery was close to European capitals that were centers of scientific inquiry. Having been raised on a farm, he was keenly aware of agricultural principles and their applications. He kept abreast of literature on breeding experiments. He belonged to an agricultural society and won awards for developing improved varieties of vegetables and fruits. Shortly after entering the monastery, Mendel **took courses** in mathematics, physics, and botany at the University of Vienna. Few scholars of his time showed interest in both plant breeding *and* mathematics.

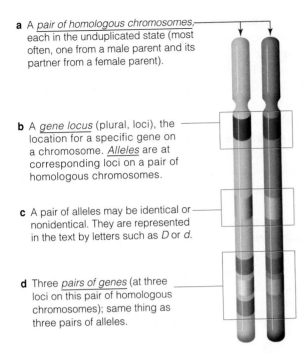

a A *pair of homologous chromosomes,* each in the unduplicated state (most often, one from a male parent and its partner from a female parent).

b A *gene locus* (plural, loci), the location for a specific gene on a chromosome. *Alleles* are at corresponding loci on a pair of homologous chromosomes.

c A pair of alleles may be identical or nonidentical. They are represented in the text by letters such as *D* or *d.*

d Three *pairs of genes* (at three loci on this pair of homologous chromosomes); same thing as three pairs of alleles.

Figure 11.4 *Animated!* A few genetic terms. Garden peas and other species with a diploid chromosome number have pairs of genes, on pairs of homologous chromosomes. Most genes come in slightly different molecular forms called alleles. Different alleles specify different versions of the same trait. An allele at any given location on a chromosome may or may not be identical to its partner on the homologous chromosome.

Shortly after his university training, Mendel started to study *Pisum sativum*, the garden pea plant (Figure 11.3). This plant is self-fertilizing. Its flowers produce both male and female gametes—call them sperm and eggs—that can come together and give rise to a new plant. One lineage of pea plants can "breed true" for certain traits. This means that successive generations will be like parents in one or more traits, as when all offspring grown from seeds of self-fertilized, white-flowered parent plants also have white flowers.

Pea plants also cross-fertilize when plant breeders transfer pollen from one plant to the flower of another plant. As Mendel knew, breeders open a floral bud of a plant that bred true for white flowers or some other trait and snip out its stamens. (Pollen grains, in which sperm develop, start forming in stamens.) The buds can be brushed with pollen from a plant that bred true for a *different* version of the trait—say, purple flowers.

As Mendel hypothesized, such clearly observable differences might help him track a given trait through many generations. If there were patterns to the trait's inheritance, *then those patterns might tell him something about heredity itself.*

TERMS USED IN MODERN GENETICS

In Mendel's time, no one knew about genes, meiosis, or chromosomes. As we follow his thinking, we will clarify the picture by substituting some modern terms used in inheritance studies, as stated here and in Figure 11.4:

1. **Genes** are units of information on heritable traits, which parents transmit to offspring. Each gene has a specific location (locus) in chromosomal DNA.

2. Cells with a **diploid** chromosome number ($2n$) have pairs of genes, on pairs of homologous chromosomes.

3. **Mutation** alters a gene's molecular structure and its message about a trait. It may cause a trait to change, as when a gene for flower color specifies yellow and a mutant form of the gene specifies white. All molecular forms of the same gene are known as **alleles**.

4. When offspring inherit a pair of *identical* alleles for a trait generation after generation, they typically are a true-breeding lineage. Offspring of a cross between two individuals that breed true for different forms of a trait are **hybrids**; each one has inherited *nonidentical* alleles for the trait.

5. A pair of identical alleles on a pair of homologous chromosomes is a *homozygous* condition. A pairing of nonidentical alleles is a *heterozygous* condition.

6. An allele is *dominant* when its effect on a trait masks the effect of any *recessive* allele paired with it. Capital letters signify dominant alleles, and lowercase letters signify recessive ones. *A* and *a* are examples.

7. Pulling this all together, a **homozygous dominant** individual has a pair of dominant alleles (*AA*) for the trait under study. A **homozygous recessive** individual has a pair of recessive alleles (*aa*), and a **heterozygous** individual has a pair of nonidentical alleles (*Aa*).

8. Two terms help keep the distinction clear between genes and the traits they specify. *Genotype* refers to the particular alleles that an individual carries. *Phenotype* refers to an individual's observable traits.

9. P stands for true-breeding parents, F_1 for the first-generation offspring, and F_2 for the second-generation offspring of self-fertilized or intercrossed F_1 individuals.

Mendel hypothesized that tracking clearly observable differences in forms of a given trait might reveal patterns of inheritance. He recognized patterns of dominance and recessiveness in certain traits, which later were connected with pairs of alleles on pairs of homologous chromosomes.

11.2 Mendel's Theory of Segregation

Mendel used monohybrid experiments to test a hypothesis: Pea plants inherit two "units" of information (genes) for a trait, one from each parent.

In **monohybrid experiments**, two homozygous parents differ in a trait that is governed by alleles of one gene. They are crossed to produce F_1 offspring that are all heterozygous ($AA \times aa \longrightarrow Aa$). Next, depending on the species, F_1 individuals are allowed to self-fertilize or mate in order to produce an F_2 generation.

MONOHYBRID EXPERIMENT PREDICTIONS

Mendel tracked seven traits for two generations. In one set of experiments, he crossed plants that bred true for purple *or* white flowers. All F_1 offspring had purple flowers, but in the next generation, some F_2 offspring had white flowers! So what was going on? Pea plants have pairs of homologous chromosomes. Assume one

plant is homozygous dominant (AA) and another is homozygous recessive (aa) at the locus that governs flower color. Following meiosis, each sperm or egg that forms has only one of these alleles (Figure 11.5). Therefore, when a sperm fertilizes an egg, only one outcome is possible: $A + a \longrightarrow Aa$.

With his background in mathematics, Mendel knew about sampling error (Figure 1.12). He crossed seventy plants. He also counted and recorded the number of dominant and recessive forms of traits in thousands of offspring. On average, three of every four F_2 plants were dominant, and one was recessive (Figure 11.6).

The ratio hinted that fertilization is a chance event having a number of possible outcomes. Mendel knew about probability—*which applies to chance events and thus could help him predict possible outcomes of genetic crosses.* **Probability** means this: The chance that each outcome of an event will occur is proportional to the number of ways in which the outcome can be reached.

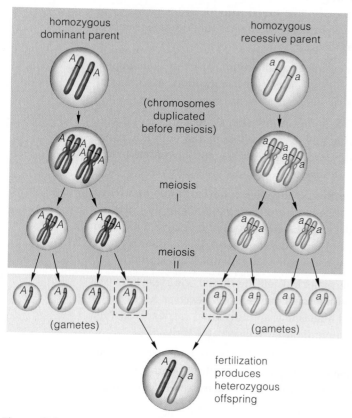

Figure 11.5 One gene of a pair segregating from the other gene in a monohybrid cross. Two parents that breed true for two versions of a trait produce only heterozygous offspring.

Figure 11.6 *Right*, from some of Mendel's monohybrid experiments with pea plants, counts of F_2 offspring having dominant or recessive hereditary "units" (alleles). On average, the 3:1 phenotypic ratio held for traits.

Trait Studied	Dominant Form	Recessive Form	F_2 Dominant-to-Recessive Ratio
SEED SHAPE	5,474 round	1,850 wrinkled	2.96:1
SEED COLOR	6,022 yellow	2,001 green	3.01:1
POD SHAPE	882 inflated	299 wrinkled	2.95:1
POD COLOR	428 green	152 yellow	2.82:1
FLOWER COLOR	705 purple	224 white	3.15:1
FLOWER POSITION	651 along stem	207 at tip	3.14:1
STEM LENGTH	787 tall	277 dwarf	2.84:1

A **Punnett-square method**, explained and applied in Figure 11.7, shows the possibilities. If half of a plant's sperm or eggs are *a* and half are *A*, then we can expect four outcomes with each fertilization:

POSSIBLE EVENT	PROBABLE OUTCOME
sperm *A* meets egg *A*	1/4 *AA* offspring
sperm *A* meets egg *a*	1/4 *Aa*
sperm *a* meets egg *A*	1/4 *Aa*
sperm *a* meets egg *a*	1/4 *aa*

Each F$_2$ plant has 3 chances in 4 of inheriting at least one dominant *A* allele (purple flowers). It has 1 chance in 4 of inheriting two recessive *a* alleles (white flowers). That is a probable phenotypic ratio of 3:1.

Mendel's observed ratios were not *exactly* 3:1. Yet he put aside the deviations. To understand why, flip a coin several times. As we all know, a coin is as likely to end up heads as tails. But often it ends up heads, or tails, several times in a row. If you flip the coin only a few times, the observed ratio might differ greatly from the predicted ratio of 1:1. Flip it many times, and you are more likely to approach the predicted ratio.

That is why Mendel used rules of probability and counted so many offspring. He minimized sampling error deviations in the observed results.

TESTCROSSES

Testcrosses supported Mendel's prediction. In such experimental tests, an organism shows dominance for a specified trait but its genotype may be unknown, so it is crossed with a homozygous recessive individual. The test results may reveal whether it is homozygous dominant or heterozygous.

For example, Mendel crossed F$_1$ purple-flowered plants with true-breeding white-flowered plants. If all were homozygous dominant, then F$_2$ offspring would all be purple flowered. If heterozygous, only about half would be. As it happened, about half of the testcross offspring had purple flowers (*Aa*) and half had white (*aa*). To predict outcomes of this testcross, construct a Punnett square.

The results from Mendel's monohybrid experiments became the basis of a theory of **segregation**, which we state here in modern terms:

> MENDEL'S THEORY OF SEGREGATION *Diploid cells have pairs of genes, on pairs of homologous chromosomes. The two genes of each pair are separated from each other during meiosis, so they end up in different gametes.*

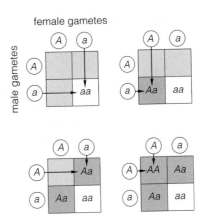

a Step-by-step construction of a Punnett square. Circles signify gametes. *A* and *a* signify a dominant and recessive allele, respectively. Possible genotypes among offspring are written in the squares.

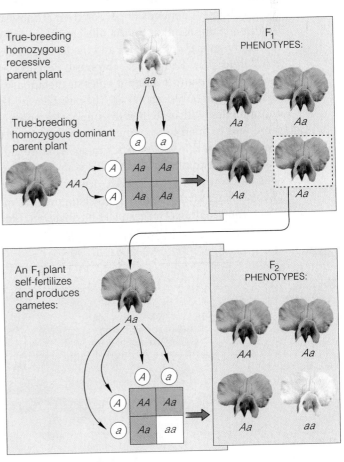

b Cross between two plants that breed true for different forms of a trait, followed by a monohybrid cross between their F$_1$ offspring.

Figure 11.7 *Animated!* (**a**) Punnett-square method of predicting probable outcomes of genetic crosses. (**b**) Results from one of Mendel's monohybrid experiments. On average, the ratio of dominant-to-recessive that showed up among second-generation (F$_2$) plants was 3:1.

11.3 Mendel's Theory of Independent Assortment

Mendel used dihybrid experiments to explain how two pairs of genes are sorted into gametes.

Dihybrid experiments start with a cross between true-breeding homozygous parents that differ in two traits governed by alleles of two genes. The F_1 offspring are all heterozygous for the alleles of both genes.

Let's duplicate one of Mendel's dihybrid crosses for flower color (alleles *A* or *a*) and for height (*B* or *b*):

True-breeding parents: AABB X aabb

Gametes: AB AB   ab ab

F_1 hybrid offspring: AaBb

As Mendel would have predicted, F_1 offspring from this cross are all purple-flowered and tall (*AaBb*).

How will genes that control these traits assort in the F_1 plants? It depends in part on their chromosome locations. Suppose that the *Aa* alleles are on one pair of homologous chromosomes and the *Bb* alleles are on a different pair. Remember, chromosome pairs align midway between the spindle poles at metaphase I of meiosis (Figures 10.5 and 11.8). The pair bearing the *A* and *a* alleles will be tethered to opposite poles. The same will happen to the other chromosome pair that bears the *B* and *b* alleles. After meiosis, there can be four possible combinations of alleles in the sperm or eggs that form: 1/4 *AB*, 1/4 *Ab*, 1/4 *aB*, and 1/4 *ab*.

Given the alternative metaphase I alignments, many allelic combinations can result at fertilization. Simple

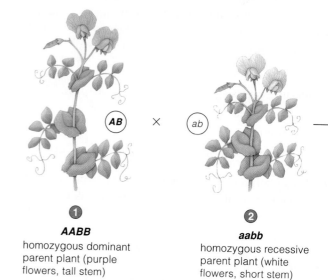

①
AABB
homozygous dominant parent plant (purple flowers, tall stem)

②
aabb
homozygous recessive parent plant (white flowers, short stem)

Figure 11.9 *Animated!* Results from one of Mendel's dihybrid experiments with the garden pea plant. The parent plants were true-breeding for different versions of two traits: flower color and plant height. *A* and *a* signify the dominant and recessive alleles for flower color. *B* and *b* signify dominant and recessive alleles for height. The Punnett square on the facing page shows all of the allelic combinations possible in the F_2 generation.

Adding up the corresponding F_2 phenotypes, we get:

▢ 9/16 or 9 purple-flowered, tall
▢ 3/16 or 3 purple-flowered, dwarf
▢ 3/16 or 3 white-flowered, tall
▢ 1/16 or 1 white-flowered, dwarf

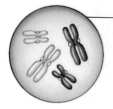

Nucleus of a diploid (2n) reproductive cell with two pairs of homologous chromosomes

Figure 11.8 An example of independent assortment at meiosis. Either chromosome of a pair may get tethered to either spindle pole. When just two pairs are tracked, two different metaphase I alignments are possible.

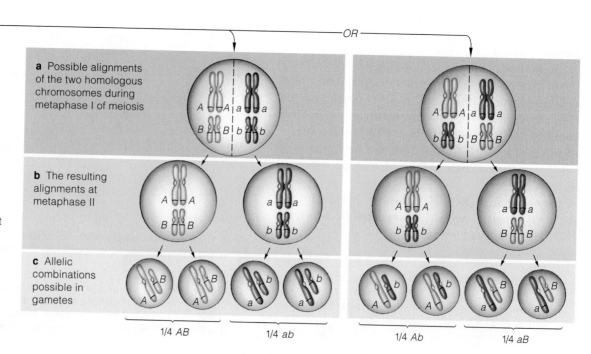

—OR—

a Possible alignments of the two homologous chromosomes during metaphase I of meiosis

b The resulting alignments at metaphase II

c Allelic combinations possible in gametes

1/4 AB   1/4 ab   1/4 Ab   1/4 aB

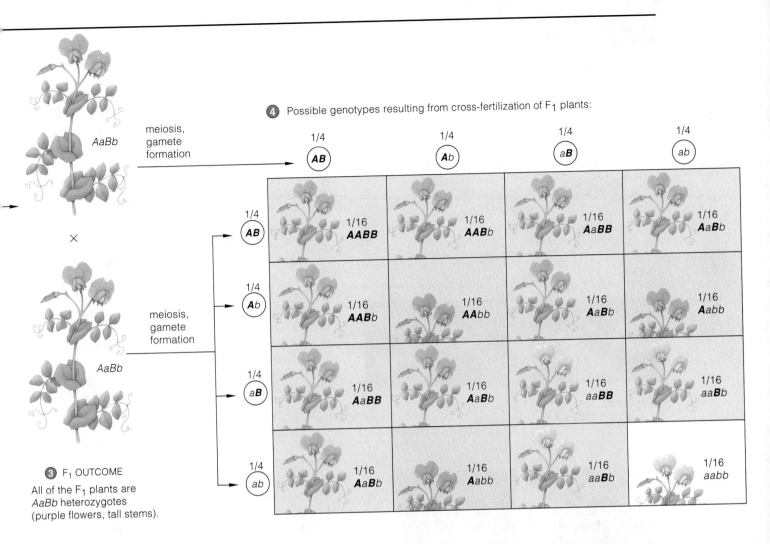

4 Possible genotypes resulting from cross-fertilization of F$_1$ plants:

AaBb — meiosis, gamete formation

	1/4 AB	1/4 Ab	1/4 aB	1/4 ab
1/4 AB	1/16 **AABB**	1/16 **AABb**	1/16 **AaBB**	1/16 **AaBb**
1/4 Ab	1/16 **AABb**	1/16 **AAbb**	1/16 **AaBb**	1/16 **Aabb**
1/4 aB	1/16 **AaBB**	1/16 **AaBb**	1/16 **aaBB**	1/16 **aaBb**
1/4 ab	1/16 **AaBb**	1/16 **Aabb**	1/16 **aaBb**	1/16 **aabb**

× AaBb — meiosis, gamete formation

3 F$_1$ OUTCOME
All of the F$_1$ plants are
AaBb heterozygotes
(purple flowers, tall stems).

multiplication (four sperm types × four egg types) tells us that sixteen combinations of gametes are possible among F$_2$ offspring of a dihybrid cross (Figure 11.9).

Adding all possible phenotypes gives us a ratio of 9:3:3:1. We can expect to see 9/16 tall purple-flowered, 3/16 dwarf purple-flowered, 3/16 tall white-flowered, and 1/16 dwarf white-flowered F$_2$ plants. The results from the dihybrid experiment that Mendel reported were close to this ratio.

Mendel analyzed the numerical results from such experiments, but he did not know that seven pairs of homologous chromosomes carry a pea plant's "units" of inheritance. He could only hypothesize that two units for flower color were sorted out into gametes independently of the two units for height.

In time, his hypothesis became known as the theory of **independent assortment**. In modern terms, after meiosis ends, the genes on each pair of homologous chromosomes are sorted into gametes independently of how genes on other pairs of homologues are sorted out. Independent assortment and segregation give rise to genetic variation. In a monohybrid cross for one gene pair, three genotypes are possible: *AA*, *Aa*,

and *aa*. We represent this as 3^n, where n is the number of gene pairs. The more pairs, the more combinations are possible. If, say, the parents differ in twenty gene pairs, the number approaches 3.5 billion!

In 1866 Mendel published his work. Apparently his article was read by few and understood by no one. In 1871 he became monastery abbot, and his pioneering experiments ended. He died in 1884, never to know that his experiments would be the starting point for modern genetics. Mendel's theory of segregation still stands for most genes in most organisms: the units of hereditary material (genes) do retain their identity all through meiosis. However, his theory of independent assortment requires qualification, because the alleles of gene pairs do not *always* assort independently into gametes, as Section 11.5 explains.

MENDEL'S THEORY OF INDEPENDENT ASSORTMENT *As meiosis ends, genes on pairs of homologous chromosomes have been sorted out for distribution into one gamete or another, independently of gene pairs on other chromosomes.*

11.4 More Patterns Than Mendel Thought

LINKS TO
SECTIONS
4.6, 6.6

Mendel happened to focus on traits that have clearly dominant and recessive forms. However, expression of genes for some traits is not as straightforward.

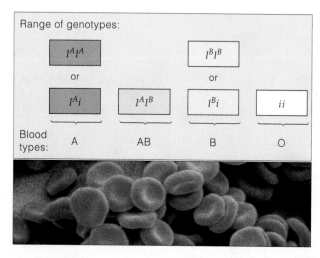

Figure 11.10 *Animated!* Possible allelic combinations that are the basis for ABO blood typing.

homozygous parent   x   homozygous parent

All F₁ offspring heterozygous for flower color:

Cross two of the F₁ plants, and the F₂ offspring will show three phenotypes in a 1:2:1 ratio:

Figure 11.11 Incomplete dominance in heterozygous (*pink*) snapdragons, in which an allele that affects red pigment is paired with a "white" allele.

CODOMINANCE IN ABO BLOOD TYPES

In *codominance*, a pair of nonidentical alleles affecting two phenotypes are both expressed at the same time in heterozygotes. For example, red blood cells have a type of glycolipid at the plasma membrane that helps give them their unique identity. The glycolipid comes in slightly different forms. An analytical method, *ABO blood typing*, reveals which form a person has.

An enzyme dictates the glycolipid's final structure. Three alleles for this enzyme are present in all human populations. Two, I^A and I^B, are codominant when paired. (These superscripts represent two dominant alleles for the gene.) The third allele, *i*, is recessive when paired with I^A or I^B. The occurrence of three or more alleles for a single gene locus among individuals of a population is called a **multiple allele system**.

Each of these glycolipid molecules was assembled in the endomembrane system (Section 4.6). First, an oligosaccharide chain was attached to a lipid, then a series of sugars was attached to the chain. But alleles I^A and I^B specify different forms of the enzyme that attaches the last sugar. The two attach *different* sugars, which gives the glycolipid a different identity: A or B.

If you have I^AI^A or I^Ai, your blood is type A. With I^BI^B or I^Bi, it is type B. With codominant alleles I^AI^B, it is AB; you have both versions of the sugar-attaching enzyme. If you are (*ii*), the glycolipid molecules never did get a final sugar on the side chain, so your blood type is not A or B. It is O. Figure 11.10 is a simple way to think about these combinations.

INCOMPLETE DOMINANCE

In *incomplete* dominance, one allele of a pair is not fully dominant over its partner, so the heterozygote's phenotype is *somewhere between* the two homozygotes. Cross true-breeding red and white snapdragons and their F₁ offspring will be pink-flowered. Cross two F₁ plants and you can expect to see red, white, and *pink* flowers in a particular ratio (Figure 11.11). Why? Red snapdragons have two alleles that let them make a lot of molecules of a red pigment. White snapdragons have two mutant alleles and are pigment-free. Pink snapdragons have a "red" allele and a "white" allele; these genotypes have not "blended." Heterozygotes make enough pigment to color flowers pink, not red.

Two interacting gene pairs also can give rise to a phenotype that neither produces by itself. In chickens, interactions among alleles at the *R* and *P* gene loci specify walnut, rose, pea, and single combs, as shown in Figure 11.12.

EPISTASIS

Traits also arise through **epistasis**: interactions among products of two or more gene pairs. Two alleles might mask expression of another gene's alleles, and some expected phenotypes might not appear at all.

As an example, several gene pairs govern whether a Labrador retriever has black, yellow, or brown fur (Figure 11.13). Its coat color depends on how enzymes and other products of alleles at more than one gene locus make a dark pigment, melanin, and deposit it in tissues. Allele B (black) is dominant to b (brown). At a different locus, allele E promotes melanin deposition but two recessive alleles (ee) reduce it. In this case, fur appears yellow regardless of alleles at the B locus.

SINGLE GENES WITH A WIDE REACH

Alleles at one locus on a chromosome may affect two or more traits in good or bad ways, an outcome called **pleiotropy**. Many genetic disorders, including cystic fibrosis, sickle-cell anemia, and Marfan syndrome, are examples. *Marfan syndrome* arises from an autosomal dominant mutation of the gene for fibrillin, a protein in the most abundant, widespread vertebrate tissues —connective tissues. Thin, loose or crosslinked strands of fibrillin passively recoil after being stretched, as by the beating heart.

Altered fibrillin weakens the connective tissues in 1 of 10,000 men and women and puts the heart, blood vessels, skin, lungs, and eyes at risk. One mutation disrupts the synthesis of fibrillin 1, its secretion from cells, and its tissue deposition. It alters the structure and function of smooth muscle cells inside the wall of the aorta, a big vessel carrying blood out of the heart. Immune cells infiltrate and multiply inside the wall's lining. Calcium deposits accumulate and inflame the wall. Elastic fibers split into fragments. The aorta wall, thinned and weakened, can rupture abruptly during strenuous exercise. Until recent advances in medicine, Marfan syndrome killed most affected people before their fifties. Flo Hyman was one of them (Figure 11.14).

> An allele at a given gene locus may be fully dominant, incompletely dominant, or codominant with its partner on a homologous chromosome.
>
> Some gene products may interact with each other and influence the same trait through epistasis.
>
> A single gene's product may have pleiotropic effects, or positive or negative impact on two or more traits.

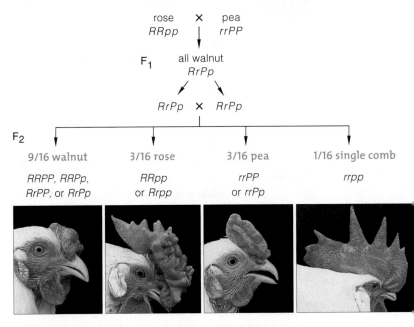

| rose | × | pea |
| $RRpp$ | | $rrPP$ |

F$_1$ all walnut $RrPp$

$RrPp$ × $RrPp$

F$_2$

| 9/16 walnut | 3/16 rose | 3/16 pea | 1/16 single comb |
| $RRPP$, $RRPp$, $RrPP$, or $RrPp$ | $RRpp$ or $Rrpp$ | $rrPP$ or $rrPp$ | $rrpp$ |

Figure 11.12 Polygenic inheritance in chickens. Interactions among alleles at two gene loci have variable effects on the comb on a chicken's head. The first cross is between a Wyandotte (rose comb) and a Brahma (pea comb).

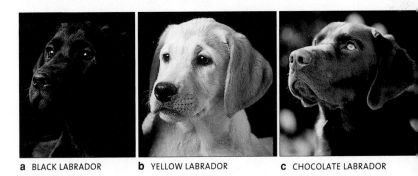

a BLACK LABRADOR   **b** YELLOW LABRADOR   **c** CHOCOLATE LABRADOR

Figure 11.13 Coat color among Labrador retrievers. The trait arises through epistatic interactions among alleles of two genes.

Figure 11.14 Flo Hyman, left, captain of the United States volleyball team that won an Olympic silver medal in 1984. Two years later, at a game in Japan, she slid to the floor and died. A dime-sized weak spot in the wall of her aorta had burst. We know at least two affected college basketball stars also died abruptly as a result of Marfan syndrome.

11.5 Impact of Crossing Over on Inheritance

LINKS TO
SECTIONS
3.2, 10.3, 10.4

Crossing over between homologous chromosomes is one of the main pattern-busting events in inheritance.

We now know there are many genes on each type of autosome and sex chromosome. All the genes on one chromosome are called a **linkage group**. For instance, the fruit fly (*Drosophila melanogaster*) has four linkage groups, corresponding to its four pairs of homologous chromosomes. Indian corn (*Zea mays*) has ten linkage groups, corresponding to its ten pairs, and so on.

If genes on the same chromosome stayed together through meiosis, then there would be no surprising mixes of parental traits. You could expect parental phenotypes among, say, the F_2 offspring of dihybrid experiments to show up in a predictable ratio. As early experiments with fruit flies showed, however, that ratio was often predictably different for linked genes. In one dihybrid experiment, 17 percent of the F_2 offspring inherited a new combination of alleles that did not occur in either of their parents.

Many genes on the same chromosome do not stay linked through meiosis, but some stay together more often than others. Why? They are closer together on the chromosome, and so they are separated less often by crossing over. *The probability that crossing over will disrupt the linkage between any two genes is proportional to the distance between the two genes.*

If genes *A* and *B* are twice as far apart as genes *C* and *D* on a chromosome, then we can expect crossing over to disrupt the linkage between genes *A* and *B* more frequently than between the other two genes:

Two genes are very closely linked when the distance between them is small. Their combinations of alleles nearly always end up in the same gamete. Linkage is more vulnerable to crossing over when the distance between two gene loci is greater (Figure 11.15). When two loci are far apart, crossing over is so frequent that the genes assort independently into gametes.

Human gene linkages were identified by tracking DNA inheritance in families over the generations. One thing is clear from such studies: Crossovers are not rare. For most eukaryotes, meiosis cannot even be completed properly until at least one crossover occurs between each pair of homologous chromosomes.

All of the genes at different locations along the length of a chromosome belong to the same linkage group.

Crossing over between homologous chromosomes disrupts gene linkages and results in nonparental combinations of alleles in chromosomes.

The farther apart two genes are on a chromosome, the greater will be the frequency of crossing over and genetic recombination between them.

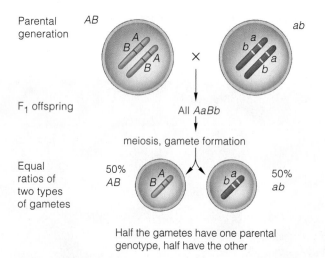

a Full linkage between two genes; no crossing over. Genes very close together along the length of the same chromosome typically stay together during gamete formation.

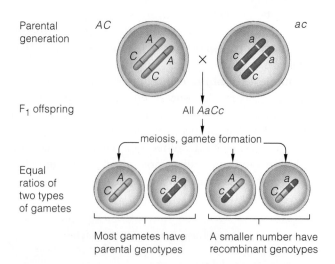

b Incomplete linkage; crossing over affected the outcome. Any two genes that are far apart along the length of a chromosome are more vulnerable to crossing over.

Figure 11.15 *Animated!* Examples of outcomes of crossing over between two gene loci: (**a**) full linkage and (**b**) incomplete linkage.

11.6 Genes and the Environment

The environment often contributes to variable gene expression among a population's individuals.

Possibly you have noticed a Himalayan rabbit's coat color. Like a Siamese cat, this mammal has dark hair in some parts of its body and lighter hair in others. The Himalayan rabbit is homozygous for the c^h allele of the gene specifying tyrosinase. Tyrosinase is one of the enzymes involved in melanin production. The c^h allele specifies a heat-sensitive form of this enzyme. This form is active only when the temperature around body cells is below 33°C, or 91°F.

When cells that give rise to this rabbit's hair grow under warmer conditions, they cannot make melanin, so hairs appear light. This happens in body regions that are massive enough to conserve a fair amount of metabolic heat. The ears and other slender extremities tend to lose metabolic heat faster, so they are cooler. Figure 11.16 shows one experiment that demonstrated how the environmental temperature can influence the production of melanin.

One classic experiment identified environmental effects on yarrow plants. These plants can grow from cuttings, so they are a useful experimental organism. Why? Cuttings from the same plant all have the same genotype, so experimenters can discount genes as a basis for differences that show up among them.

In this study, cuttings (clones) from each of several yarrow plants were grown at three elevations. The researchers periodically observed the growth of the plants in their habitats. They found that cuttings from the same parent plants grew differently at different altitudes. For example, cuttings from one plant grew tall at the lowest and the highest elevation, but a third cutting remained short at mid-elevation (Figure 11.17). Even though these plants were genetically identical, their phenotypes differed in different environments.

Similarly, plant a hydrangea in a garden and it may have pink flowers instead of the expected blue ones. Soil acidity affects the function of gene products that color hydrangea flowers.

What about humans? One of our genes codes for a transporter protein that moves serotonin across the plasma membrane of brain cells. This gene product has several effects, one of which is to counter anxiety and depression when traumatic events challenge us. For a long time, researchers have known that some people handle stress without getting too upset, while others spiral into a deep and lasting depression.

Mutation of the gene for the serotonin transporter compromises responses to stress. It is as if some of us are bicycling through life without an emotional helmet.

Figure 11.16 *Animated!* Observable effect of an environmental factor that alters gene expression. A Himalayan rabbit normally has black hair only on its long ears, nose, tail, and leg regions farthest from the body mass. In one experiment, a patch of a rabbit's white coat was removed and an icepack was placed over the hairless patch. Where the colder temperature had been maintained, the hairs that grew back were black.

Himalayan rabbits are homozygous for an allele that encodes a mutant version of tyrosinase, an enzyme required to make melanin. As described in the text, this allele encodes a heat-sensitive form of the enzyme, which functions only when air temperature is below about 33°C.

a Mature cutting at high elevation (3,060 meters above sea level)

b Mature cutting at mid-elevation (1,400 meters above sea level)

c Mature cutting at low elevation (30 meters above sea level)

Figure 11.17 Experiment demonstrating the impact of environmental conditions of three different habitats on phenotype in yarrow (*Achillea millefolium*). Cuttings from the same parent plant were grown in the same kind of soil at three different elevations.

Only when we take a fall does the phenotypic effect—depression—appear. Other genes also affect emotional states, but mutation of this particular gene reduces our capacity to snap out of it when bad things happen.

> *Variation in traits arises not only from gene mutations and interactions, but also in response to variations in environmental conditions that each individual faces.*

11.7 Complex Variations in Traits

For most populations or species, individuals show rich variation for many of the same traits. Sometimes the phenotypes cannot be predicted, and most of the time they are part of a continuous range of variation.

REGARDING THE UNEXPECTED PHENOTYPE

Think back on Mendel's dihybrid crosses. Nearly all of the traits that he tracked occurred in predictable ratios because the two genes happened to be on different chromosomes or far apart on the same chromosome. They tended to segregate cleanly. Track two or more different pairs of genes—as Mendel did—and you might observe phenotypes that you would not have predicted at all. And not all of the variation is a result of tight linkage or crossing over.

As one example, *camptodactyly*, a rare abnormality, affects the shape and movement of fingers. Some of the people who carry a mutant allele for this heritable trait have immobile, bent fingers on both hands. Others have immobile, bent fingers on the left or right hand only. Fingers of still other people who have the mutant allele are not affected in any obvious way at all.

What causes such odd variation? Remember, most organic compounds are synthesized by a sequence of metabolic steps. *Different enzymes, each a gene product, control different steps.* One gene may have mutated in a number of ways. A gene product might be blocking some pathway or making it run nonstop or not long enough. Perhaps poor nutrition or some other variable factor in the individual's environment is influencing the activity of one of the pathway's enzymes. Such variable factors can introduce big or small variations even in otherwise expected phenotypes.

CONTINUOUS VARIATION IN POPULATIONS

Another point: Individuals of populations generally show a range of small differences in most traits. This feature of natural populations is known as **continuous variation**. It arises through **polygenic inheritance**, or the inheritance of multiple genes that affect the same trait. The distribution of all forms of a trait becomes more and more continuous when greater numbers of genes and environmental factors are involved.

Look in a mirror at your eye color. The colored part is the iris, a doughnut-shaped, pigmented structure just under the cornea (Figure 11.18). The color results from several gene products. Some products help make and distribute different kinds and amounts of melanins, which are similar to the light-absorbing pigment that affects coat color in mammals. Almost black irises have

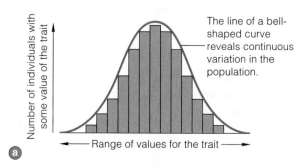

The line of a bell-shaped curve reveals continuous variation in the population.

a Range of values for the trait

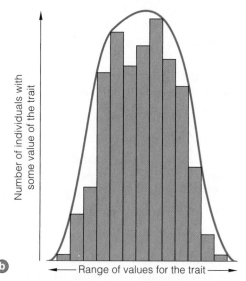

b Range of values for the trait

Figure 11.19 *Animated!* Continuous variation. (**a**) A bar graph can reveal continuous variation in a population. The proportion of individuals in each category is plotted against the range of measured phenotypes. (**b**) The curved line above this particular set of bars is a real-life example of a bell-shaped curve that emerged for the population in Figure 11.20. It reflects continuous variation in body height, one of the traits that help characterize human populations.

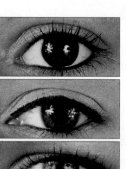
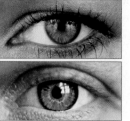
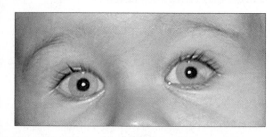

Figure 11.18 Sampling of the range of continuous variation in human eye color. Products of different gene pairs interact in making and distributing the pigment melanin, which helps color the iris. Small color differences arise from different combinations of alleles. The frequency distribution for the eye-color trait is continuous over a far larger range than this, from black to light blue.

dense melanin deposits, which can absorb most of the incoming light. Deposits are not as extensive in brown eyes, so some unabsorbed light is reflected out. Light brown or hazel eyes have even less melanin.

Green, gray, or blue eyes have lesser amounts of the pigments. Many or most of the blue wavelengths of light that enter the eyeball are simply reflected out.

How can you describe the continuous variation of some trait in a group? Divide the range of phenotypes for a trait—say, height—into measurable categories, such as numbers of inches. Next, do a count of how many individuals fall into each category; this will give you the relative frequencies of phenotypes across the range of measurable values. Finally, plot out the data as a bar chart, such as the one in Figure 11.19a.

In this figure, the shortest bars represent categories having the fewest individuals. The tallest bar signifies the category that has the most individuals. In this case, a graph line skirting the top of all of the bars will be a bell-shaped curve. Such **bell curves** are typical of any trait showing continuous variation. Figure 11.19b is a bell curve based on real-life measurements at the University of Florida (Figure 11.20).

And so we conclude this chapter, which introduces heritable and environmental factors that give rise to great variation in traits. What is the take-home lesson? Simply this: An individual's phenotype is an outcome of complex interactions among its genes, enzymes and other gene products, and the environment. Chapter 18 will consider some of the evolutionary consequences.

Enzymes and other gene products control each step of most metabolic pathways. Mutations, interactions among genes, and environmental conditions typically affect one or more steps in ways that contribute to variation in phenotypes.

Individuals of populations or species show continuous variation—a range of small differences. Usually, the more genes and environmental factors that influence a trait, the more continuous the distribution of phenotypes.

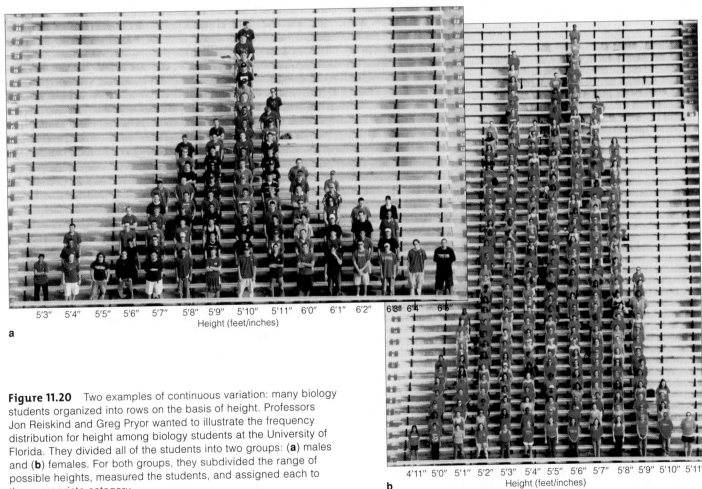

Figure 11.20 Two examples of continuous variation: many biology students organized into rows on the basis of height. Professors Jon Reiskind and Greg Pryor wanted to illustrate the frequency distribution for height among biology students at the University of Florida. They divided all of the students into two groups: (**a**) males and (**b**) females. For both groups, they subdivided the range of possible heights, measured the students, and assigned each to the appropriate category.

Summary

Section 11.1 Genes are heritable units of information about traits. Each gene has its own locus, or location, along the length of a particular chromosome. Different molecular forms of the same gene are known as alleles.

By experimenting with garden pea plants, Mendel was the first to gather evidence of patterns by which genes are transmitted from parents to offspring.

Offspring of a cross between two individuals that breed true for different forms of a trait are hybrids; each inherited nonidentical alleles for a trait being studied.

An individual with two dominant alleles for a trait (*AA*) is homozygous dominant. A homozygous recessive has two recessive alleles (*aa*). A heterozygote has two nonidentical alleles (*Aa*) for a trait. A dominant allele may mask the effect of a recessive allele partnered with it on the homologous chromosome.

Genotype refers to the particular alleles at any or all gene locations on an individual's chromosomes. *Phenotype* refers to an individual's observable traits.

Biology⊛Now
Learn how Mendel crossed garden pea plants and the definitions of important genetic terms on BiologyNow.

Section 11.2 A cross between parents of different genotypes yields hybrid offspring. For monohybrid experiments, two parents that bred true for different forms of a trait produce F_1 heterozygotes that are identical for one pair of genes. Mendel's monohybrid experiments gave indirect evidence that some forms of a gene may be dominant over recessive forms.

All F_1 offspring of a parental cross *AA* x *aa* were *Aa*. Crosses between F_1 monohybrids resulted in these allelic combinations among the F_2 offspring:

	A	*a*
A	*AA*	*Aa*
a	*Aa*	*aa*

AA (dominant)
Aa (dominant)
Aa (dominant) } the expected phenotypic ratio of 3:1
aa (recessive)

Mendel's monohybrid experiment results led to a theory of segregation: Diploid organisms have pairs of genes, on pairs of homologous chromosomes. Genes of each pair segregate from each other at meiosis, so each gamete formed gets one or the other gene.

Biology⊛Now
Carry out monohybrid experiments with the interaction on BiologyNow.

Section 11.3 Dihybrid experiments start with a cross between true-breeding heterozygous parents that differ for alleles of two genes (*AABB* x *aabb*). All F_1 offspring are heterozygous for both genes (*AaBb*). In Mendel's dihybrid experiments, phenotypes of the F_2 offspring of F_1 hybrids were close to a 9:3:3:1 ratio:

9 dominant for both traits
3 dominant for *A*, recessive for *b*
3 dominant for *B*, recessive for *a*
1 recessive for both traits

His results support a theory of independent assortment: Before gamete formation, meiosis assorts gene pairs of homologous chromosomes independently of how gene pairs of all the other chromosomes are sorted. Random alignment of all pairs of homologous chromosomes at metaphase I is the basis of this outcome.

Biology⊛Now
Observe the results of a dihybrid cross with the interaction on BiologyNow.

Section 11.4 Inheritance patterns are not always straightforward.

Some alleles are not fully dominant over their partner allele on the homologous chromosomes, and both are expressed at the same time. The phenotype that results from this allelic combination is somewhere between the two homozygous conditions.

Some alleles are codominant and are expressed at the same time in heterozygotes. An example occurs in the multiple allele system underlying ABO blood typing.

Also, products of one or more genes commonly interact in ways that influence the same trait, and a single gene may have effects on two or more traits.

Biology⊛Now
Explore patterns of non-Mendelian inheritance with the interactions on BiologyNow.

Section 11.5 A linkage group consists of all genes along the length of one chromosome. Crossing over between pairs of homologous chromosomes disrupts expected inheritance patterns by breaking linkages. Its outcome is nonparental combinations of alleles in gametes. The farther apart two genes are on a chromosome, the greater will be the frequency of crossing over and genetic recombination between them.

Section 11.6 Environmental factors also can alter how genes are expressed in individuals of a population. An example is a difference in temperature that affects the activity of a heat-sensitive form of an enzyme—a gene product—that helps produce a coat color pigment.

Biology⊛Now
See how the environment can affect phenotype with animation on BiologyNow.

Section 11.7 Gene interactions and environmental factors influence many enzymes differently among individuals, and many phenotypes result. They also contribute to small, incremental differences—a range of continuous variation—in a population.

Biology⊛Now
Plot the continuous distribution of height for a class with the interaction on BiologyNow.

Self-Quiz   *Answers in Appendix II*

1. Alleles are _____ .
   a. different molecular forms of a gene
   b. different phenotypes
   c. self-fertilizing, true-breeding homozygotes

2. A heterozygote has a _____ for a trait being studied.
  a. pair of identical alleles
  b. pair of nonidentical alleles
  c. haploid condition, in genetic terms

3. The observable traits of an organism are its _____ .
  a. phenotype   c. genotype
  b. sociobiology   d. pedigree

4. Second-generation offspring of a cross between parents who are homozygous for different alleles are the _____ .
  a. F_1 generation   c. hybrid generation
  b. F_2 generation   d. none of the above

5. F_1 offspring of the cross $AA \times aa$ are _____ .
  a. all AA c. all Aa
  b. all aa d. 1/2 AA and 1/2 aa

6. Refer to Question 5. Assuming complete dominance, the F_2 generation will show a phenotypic ratio of _____ .
  a. 3:1   b. 9:1   c. 1:2:1   d. 9:3:3:1

7. Crosses between two dihybrid F_1 pea plants, which are offspring from a parental cross $AABB \times aabb$, result in F_2 phenotypic ratios close to _____ .
  a. 1:2:1   b. 3:1   c. 1:1:1:1   d. 9:3:3:1

8. The probability of a crossover occurring between two genes on the same chromosome is _____ .
  a. unrelated to the distance between them
  b. increased if they are close together
  c. increased if they are far apart

9. Two genes that are close together on the same chromosome are _____ .
  a. linked   c. homologous   e. all of the
  b. identical alleles d. autosomes   above

10. Match each example with the most suitable description.
  _____ dihybrid experiment   a. bb
  _____ monohybrid experiment   b. $AABB \times aabb$
  _____ homozygous condition   c. Aa
  _____ heterozygous condition   d. $Aa \times Aa$

Additional questions are available on **Biology⟨⟩Now**™

Genetics Problems
Answers in Appendix III

1. A gene encodes the second enzyme in a melanin-synthesizing pathway. An individual who is homozygous for a recessive mutant allele of this gene cannot produce or deposit melanin in body tissues. *Albinism*, the absence of melanin, is the result.

  Humans and a number of other organisms can have this phenotype. Figure 11.21 shows two examples. In the following situations, what are the possible genotypes of the father, the mother, and their children?

  a. Both parents have normal phenotypes; some of their children are albino and others are unaffected.

  b. Both parents are albino and have albino children.

  c. The woman is unaffected, the man is albino, and they have one albino child and three unaffected children.

2. As rose breeders know, several alleles influence specific traits, such as long, symmetrical, urn-shaped buds, double flowers, glossy leaves, and resistance to mildew (Figure 11.22). Alleles of a single gene govern whether a plant will

Figure 11.21 Two albino organisms. By not posing his subjects as objects of ridicule, the photographer of human albinos is attempting to counter the notion that there is something inherently unbeautiful about them.

dominant   dominant

recessive   recessive

Figure 11.22 (**a**) Climbing rose and (**b**) shrub rose. (**c**) Globe-shaped buds versus (**d**) urn-shaped buds.

be a climber (dominant) or shrubby (recessive). When a true-breeding climber is crossed with a shrubby plant, all F_1 offspring are climbers. If an F_1 plant is crossed with a shrubby plant, about 50 percent of the offspring will be shrubby and 50 percent will be climbers. Using symbols A and a to represent the dominant and recessive alleles, make a Punnett-square diagram of the expected genotypic and phenotypic outcomes in the F_1 offspring and the offspring of the cross between an F_1 plant and a shrubby plant.

Figure 11.23 The Manx, a breed of cat that has no tail.

3. One gene has alleles *A* and *a*. Another has alleles *B* and *b*. For each of the following genotypes, what type(s) of gametes will form, assuming independent assortment during meiosis occurs?

a. *AABB*   c. *Aabb*

b. *AaBB*   d. *AaBb*

4. Refer to Problem 3. What will be the genotypes of offspring from the following matings? Indicate the frequencies of each genotype among them.

a. *AABB* × *aaBB*   c. *AaBb* × *aabb*

b. *AaBB* × *AABb*   d. *AaBb* × *AaBb*

5. Return to Problem 3. Assume you now study a third gene having alleles *C* and *c*. For each genotype listed, what type(s) of gametes will be produced, assuming that independent assortment occurs?

a. *AABBCC*   c. *AaBBCc*

b. *AaBBcc*   d. *AaBbCc*

6. Certain alleles are so essential for normal development that an individual who is homozygous recessive for a mutant form cannot survive. Such recessive, *lethal alleles* can be perpetuated in the population by heterozygotes.

Consider the allele *Manx* (M^L) in cats. Homozygous cats ($M^L M^L$) die when they are still embryos inside the mother cat. In heterozygotes ($M^L M$), the spine develops abnormally. The cats end up with no tail (Figure 11.23).

Two $M^L M$ cats mate. What is the probability that any one of their *surviving* kittens will be heterozygous?

7. In one experiment, Mendel crossed a pea plant that bred true for green pods with one that bred true for yellow pods. All the F_1 plants had green pods. Which form of the trait (green or yellow pods) is recessive? Explain how you arrived at your conclusion.

8. Mendel crossed a pea plant that produced plump and rounded seeds with a pea plant that produced wrinkled seeds. In the F_1 generation, all seeds were round. Mendel planted the F_1 seeds, which grew into plants that, when self-fertilized, produced 5,474 round seeds and 1,850 wrinkled seeds in the F_2 generation. The alleles that govern seed shape are designated *R* and *r*.

a. What are the genotypes of the parents?

b. What are the possible outcomes of a cross between a homozygous round-seeded plant and a wrinkle-seeded plant?

9. Mendel crossed a true-breeding tall, purple-flowered pea plant with a true-breeding dwarf, white-flowered plant. All F_1 plants were tall and had purple flowers. If an F_1 plant self-fertilizes, then what is the probability that a randomly selected F_2 offspring will be heterozygous for the genes specifying height and flower color?

10. Suppose you identify a new gene in mice. One of its alleles specifies white fur. A second allele specifies brown fur. You want to determine whether the relationship between the two alleles is one of simple dominance or incomplete dominance. What sorts of genetic crosses would give you the answer? What types of observations would you require to form conclusions?

11. In sweet pea plants, an allele for purple flowers (*P*) is dominant to an allele for red flowers (*p*). An allele for long pollen grains (*L*) is dominant to an allele for round pollen grains (*l*). Bateson and Punnett crossed a plant having purple flowers/long pollen grains with one having white flowers/round pollen grains. All F_1 offspring had purple flowers and long pollen grains. In the F_2 generation, the researchers observed the following phenotypes:

296 purple flowers/long pollen grains

19 purple flowers/round pollen grains

27 red flowers/long pollen grains

85 red flowers/round pollen grains

What is the best explanation for these results?

12. A dominant allele *W* confers black fur on guinea pigs. A guinea pig that is homozygous recessive (*ww*) has white fur. Fred would like to know whether his pet black-furred guinea pig is homozygous (*WW*) or heterozygous (*Ww*). How might he determine his pet's genotype?

13. Red-flowering snapdragons are homozygous for allele R^1. White-flowering snapdragons are homozygous for a different allele (R^2). Heterozygous plants ($R^1 R^2$) bear pink flowers. What phenotypes should appear among first-generation offspring of the crosses listed? What are the expected proportions for each phenotype?

a. $R^1 R^1 \times R^1 R^2$ c. $R^1 R^2 \times R^1 R^2$

b. $R^1 R^1 \times R^2 R^2$ d. $R^1 R^2 \times R^2 R^2$

(In cases of incomplete dominance, alleles are usually designated by superscript numerals, as shown here, not by the uppercase letters for dominance and lowercase letters for recessiveness.)

For each cross, list which of these F_1 phenotypes show up as well as the proportion of each:

a. _____red   _____ pink   _____ white

b. _____red   _____ pink   _____ white

c. _____red   _____ pink   _____ white

d. _____red   _____ pink   _____ white

14. Two pairs of genes affect comb type in chickens (Figure 11.12), and they assort independently. When both are homozygous for recessive alleles, a chicken has a single comb. But a dominant allele of one gene, *P*, gives rise to a pea comb, and a dominant allele of the other gene (*R*) gives rise to a rose comb. An *epistatic* interaction occurs when a chicken has at least one of both dominant alleles, *P__ R __*, which gives rise to a walnut comb.

Predict the ratios resulting from a cross between two walnut-combed chickens that are heterozygous for both genes (*PpRr*) and list them below:

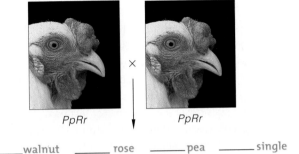

PpRr × PpRr

_____ walnut _____ rose _____ pea _____ single

15. As Section 3.6 explains, a single mutant allele gives rise to an abnormal form of hemoglobin (*Hb^S* instead of *Hb^A*). Homozygotes (*Hb^{S}Hb^S*) develop the genetic disease sickle-cell anemia. Heterozygotes (*Hb^{A}Hb^S*) show few obvious symptoms.

A couple who are both heterozygous for the *Hb^A* allele plan to have children. For *each* of the pregnancies, state the probability that this couple will have a child who is:
   a. homozygous for the *Hb^S* allele
   b. homozygous for the *Hb^A* allele
   c. heterozygous *Hb^{A}Hb^S*

16. Watermelons (*Citrullus*) are important crops around the world (Figure 11.24). A single gene determines the density of green pigment that colors the rind, with solid light green (*g*) recessive to solid dark green (*G*). When a true-breeding plant having a dark-green rind is crossed with a plant having a light-green rind, what fraction of the dark-green F$_2$ offspring is expected to be heterozygous for this trait?

17. The rind of a watermelon that is homozygous for recessive allele *e* bursts, or splits explosively, when cut. Genotype *EE* results in a "nonexplosive" rind that is better for shipping watermelons to market. The rind of a watermelon that is homozygous for the recessive allele *f* has a furrowed surface. A furrowed rind has less market appeal than a smooth rind, which results from expression of dominant allele *F*.

For one testcross, a dihybrid plant that produces melons with a smooth, nonexplosive rind is crossed with a plant that produces melons with a furrowed, explosive rind. Make a Punnett square of the following results:

   118 smooth, nonexplosive
   112 smooth, explosive
   109 furrowed, nonexplosive
   121 furrowed, explosive

What is the smooth rind/furrowed rind ratio among the testcross offspring? What is the ratio of nonexplosive

Figure 11.24 A sampling of the variation in the rind characteristics of watermelon (*Citrullus*).

rind/explosive rind? Are the two gene loci assorting independently of each other?

18. Two pairs of genes determine kernel color in wheat plants. Alleles of one pair show incomplete dominance over the other pair. The product of allele *A^1* at one locus produces enough pigment to add a dose of red color to the kernels, but that of allele *A^2* does not. The product of allele *B^1* at the second locus also adds a dose of red color to the kernels, but that of allele *B^2* does not.

The chart shown below lists the numbers of different wheat kernel colors observed during a recent harvest, together with their corresponding genotypes. Using the information in this table, draw a graph showing the percentage of kernels in the wheat population that inherited each of the five kernel colors.

Explain why the kernel color in wheat plants shows a varied phenotypic distribution.

Genotype	Phenotype	Number Displaying the Trait	Percentage of Population
A^{1}A^{1}B^{1}B^1	Dark red	181	
A^{1}A^{1}B^{1}B^2 or A^{1}A^{2}B^{1}B^1	Red	360	
A^{1}A^{2}B^{1}B^2 or A^{1}A^{1}B^{2}B^2 or A^{2}A^{2}B^{1}B^1	Salmon	922	
A^{1}A^{2}B^{2}B^2 or A^{2}A^{2}B^{1}B^2	Pink	358	
A^{2}A^{2}B^{2}B^2	White	179	
Totals		2,000	

12 CHROMOSOMES AND HUMAN INHERITANCE

Strange Genes, Richly Tortured Minds

"This man is brilliant." That was the extent of a letter of recommendation from Richard Duffin, a mathematics professor at Carnegie Mellon University. Duffin wrote the line in 1948 on behalf of John Forbes Nash, Jr. (Figure 12.1). Nash was twenty years old at the time and applying for admission to Princeton University's graduate school.

Over the next decade, Nash made his reputation as one of America's foremost mathematicians. He was socially awkward, but so are many highly gifted people. Nash showed no symptoms of paranoid schizophrenia, a mental disorder that eventually debilitated him.

Full-blown symptoms emerged in his thirtieth year. Nash had to abandon his position at the Massachusetts Institute of Technology. Two decades passed before he was able to return to his pioneering work in mathematics.

Of every hundred people worldwide, one is affected by *schizophrenia*. This neurobiological disorder (NBD) is characterized by delusions, hallucinations, disorganized speech, and abnormal social behavior. As researchers know, exceptional creativity often accompanies schizophrenia. It also accompanies other NBDs, including autism, chronic depression, and bipolar disorder, which manifests itself as jarring swings in mood and social behavior.

Compared to the general population, highly intelligent individuals are *less* likely to develop NBDs—unless they also happen to be outside-the-box creative thinkers. Disturbingly creative writers alone are eighteen times more suicidal, ten times more likely to be depressed, and twenty times more likely to have bipolar disorder. Virginia Woolf's suicide after a prolonged mental breakdown is a tragic example.

We now have evidence that even emotionally healthy people who show creative brilliance have more personality traits in common with the mentally impaired than they do with individuals closer to the norm. For instance, they, too, are hypersensitive to environmental stimuli. Some may be on a razor's edge between mental stability and instability. Those who do go on to develop NBDs become part of a crowd that includes Socrates, Newton, Beethoven, Darwin, Lincoln, Poe, Dickens, Tolstoy, van Gogh, Freud, Churchill, Einstein, Picasso, Woolf, Hemingway, and Nash.

We have not yet identified all of the interactions among genes and the environment that might tip such individuals one way or the other. But we do know about several mutant genes that predispose them to develop NBDs.

Creatively gifted people, as well as those affected by NBDs, often turn up in the same family tree—which points

Figure 12.1 John Forbes Nash, Jr., a prodigy who solved problems that had baffled some of the greatest minds in mathematics. His early work in economic game theory won him a Nobel Prize. He is shown here at a premier of *A Beautiful Mind*, an award-winning film based on his battle with schizophrenia. His neural disorder places him in the ranks of other highly creative, distinguished, yet troubled individuals, including Abraham Lincoln, Virginia Woolf, and Pablo Picasso.

to a genetic basis for their special traits. Also, those affected by bipolar disorder and schizophrenia show altered gene expression in certain brain regions. Cells make too many or too few of the enzymes of electron transfer phosphorylation. Remember, this stage of aerobic respiration yields the bulk of the body's ATP. Does its disruption alter brain cells in ways that boost creativity but also invite illness? Perhaps.

With this intriguing connection, we invite you to reflect on how far you have come in this unit of the book. You first surveyed mitotic and meiotic cell divisions. You looked at how chromosomes and genes become shuffled during meiosis and then during fertilization. You also became acquainted with Gregor Mendel's discovery of major patterns of inheritance. This knowledge is your portal to the chromosomal basis of human inheritance.

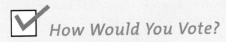

Watch the video online!

How Would You Vote?

Diagnostic tests for predisposition to neurobiological disorders will soon be available. Individuals might use knowledge of their susceptibility to modify choices in life-styles. Insurance companies and employers might also use that information to exclude predisposed but otherwise healthy individuals. Would you support legislation governing these tests? See BiologyNow for details, then vote online.

Key Concepts

AUTOSOMES AND SEX CHROMOSOMES

Sexually reproducing species have pairs of autosomes, which are chromosomes that are the same in length, shape, and which genes they carry. Nearly all animals also have a pair of sex chromosomes.

Karyotyping, a diagnostic tool, helps reveal changes in the structure or number of an individual's chromosomes. Section 12.1, 12.2

AUTOSOMAL INHERITANCE

Many alleles on autosomes are expressed in Mendelian patterns of simple dominance and recessiveness. Sections 12.3, 12.4

SEX-LINKED INHERITANCE

The pairing of sex chromosomes in human females (XX) differs from the pairing in males (XY). One of the genes on the Y chromosome dictates gender. Many alleles on the X chromosome are expressed in Mendelian patterns of simple dominance and recessiveness. Sections 12.5–12.7

CHANGES IN CHROMOSOME STRUCTURE

On rare occasions, a chromosome may undergo permanent change in its structure, as when a segment of it is deleted, duplicated, inverted, or translocated. Section 12.8

CHANGES IN CHROMOSOME NUMBER

Also on rare occasions, the parental number of autosomes or sex chromosomes changes. In humans, the change usually results in problems. Section 12.9

HUMAN GENETIC ANALYSIS AND OPTIONS

Various analytical and diagnostic procedures often reveal genetic disorders. Risks and benefits are associated with what individuals as well as society at large do with the information. Sections 12.10, 12.11

Links to Earlier Concepts

You will be drawing on your knowledge of chromosome structure (Sections 9.1, 9.3), meiosis (10.3, 10.4), and gamete formation (10.5). Be sure you understand dominance, recessiveness, and the homozygous and heterozygous conditions (11.1). Remember, environmental factors influence gene expression (11.6). Colchicine (4.10) will turn up again. So will glycolysis (8.2), this time in the context of a genetic disorder. You also will consider whether the hemoglobin family evolved after changes in chromosome structure (3.6).

12.1 Human Chromosomes

LINKS TO
SECTIONS
4.10, 9.1, 9.5, 10.3

You already know quite a bit about chromosomes and their roles in inheritance. Let's now focus on human autosomes and sex chromosomes.

Like nearly all animals, humans normally are male or female. Also like many species, they have a diploid chromosome number ($2n$), meaning that body cells have pairs of homologous chromosomes. Remember, all but one of the pairs are alike in their length, shape, and gene sequence. One member of the last pairing is a unique sex chromosome that is present in males or females, but not in both.

For instance, a diploid cell in a human female has two X chromosomes (XX). A diploid cell in a human male has one X and one Y chromosome (XY). This is a common inheritance pattern among mammals, fruit flies, and many other animals. It is not the only one, however. Among butterflies, moths, birds, and certain fishes, the males have two identical sex chromosomes and females do not.

Human X and Y chromosomes differ physically and in which genes they carry. Recall, from Section 10.3, that each pair of homologous chromosomes synapses (zippers together tightly) in prophase I of meiosis. An X chromosome and Y chromosome synapse in a small region along their length, but that is enough to allow the two to interact as homologues during meiosis.

Human X and Y chromosomes fall into the general category of **sex chromosomes**. As you will see later, when sex chromosomes are inherited in certain combinations, they dictate the gender of the new individual—that is, whether it will become a male or a female.

All of the other chromosomes in our body cells are the same in both sexes. We categorize them as **autosomes**.

The duplicated human chromosome shown in Figure 12.2 has a targeted band (*yellow*), an artistic way of introducing a key point: Molecular biology increased the power of diagnostic tools that were already in use to analyze chromosomes —as with fluorescent dyes that can label DNA regions linked to genetic disorders. In the next section, you will read about two of the diagnostic procedures.

Figure 12.2 Long before the spectacular discoveries of molecular biology, researchers started identifying regions on chromosomes that probably held the genes responsible for certain genetic disorders.

> *Autosomes are pairs of chromosomes that are the same in males and females of a species. One other pairing, of sex chromosomes, differs between males and females.*

12.2 What Is Karyotyping?

With karyotyping, a diagnostic tool, images are constructed to analyze the structure and number of chromosomes in an individual's cells.

How do we know about an individual's autosomes and sex chromosomes? *Karyotyping* is one of the earliest diagnostic tools. A typical **karyotype** is a preparation of an individual's metaphase chromosomes, sorted out by length, shape, centromere location, and other defining features. Gross abnormalities in chromosome structure or an altered chromosome number can be pinpointed by comparing the individual's karyotype against a standard karyotype for the species.

Making a Karyotype   Human chromosomes are in their most condensed form and easiest to identify when a cell is at metaphase of mitosis (Sections 9.1 and 9.3). Technicians do not count on finding dividing cells in the body. They culture cells and induce mitosis artificially. They place a sample of cells, usually from blood, into a solution that stimulates growth and mitotic cell division. They add colchicine to the sample to arrest the cell cycle at metaphase. Colchicine, remember, is a poison that blocks spindle formation by preventing microtubules from forming (Section 4.10).

As Figure 12.3 explains, the cell culture is centrifuged to isolate all the metaphase cells. A hypotonic solution makes the cells swell, by way of osmosis, and move away from each other. The chromosomes inside them move away from each other, also. Then the cells are mounted on slides, fixed, and stained for microscopy.

Once the chromosomes are brought into focus, they are photographed. The photograph is cut with scissors or with a computer's cut-and-paste tools to separate the chromosomes. Then the chromosomes are lined up by size and shape, as in Figure 12.3*f*.

Spectral Karyotypes   *Spectral karyotyping*, a more recent diagnostic tool, uses a range of colored fluorescent dyes that bind to specific parts of chromosomes. Analysis of the resulting rainbow-hued karyotype often reveals abnormalities that would not otherwise be discernible.

Figure 12.4 shows a spectral karyotype. The Philadelphia chromosome in this karyotype, named after the city where someone discovered it, was the first chromosome to be specifically correlated with cancer—one of the leukemias. The Philadelphia chromosome was already known to be longer than human chromosome 9, which is its normal counterpart. But spectral karyotyping identified the extra length as a piece of chromosome 22.

By chance, both chromosomes broke inside a stem cell in bone marrow. Such cells give rise to blood cells. Enzymes reattached the pieces—but on the wrong chromosomes. You can identify the translocated parts in the Figure 12.4 karyotype. We will be returning to this type of change in the structure of chromosomes in Section 12.8.

Figure 12.3 *Animated!* Karyotyping, in which an image of metaphase chromosomes is cut apart. Individual chromosomes are aligned by their centromeres and arranged according to size, shape, and length.

(**a**) A sample of cells from an individual is put in a medium that stimulates cell growth and mitotic division. Colchicine is added to arrest the cell cycle at metaphase. (**b**) The culture is subjected to *centrifugation*, which works because cells have greater mass and density than the solution bathing them. A centrifuge's spinning force moves the cells farthest from the center of rotation, so they collect at the base of the centrifuge tubes.

(**c**) The culture medium is removed; a hypotonic solution is added. The cells swell, and chromosomes move apart. (**d**) The cells are mounted on a microscope slide and stained to make the chromosomes show up.

(**e**) A photograph of one cell's chromosomes is cut up and organized, as in the human karyotype in (**f**), which shows 22 pairs of autosomes and 1 pair of sex chromosomes—XX *or* XY. Scissors or computer tools do the cuts.

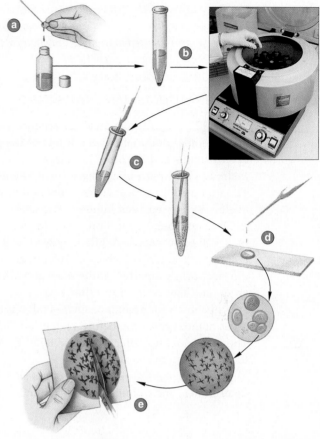

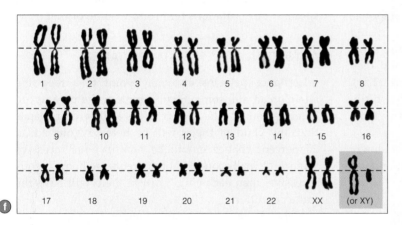

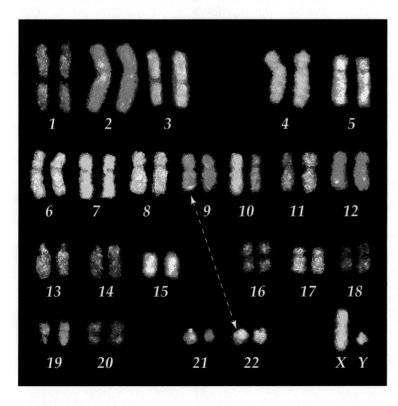

Figure 12.4 Image of a killer—the Philadelphia chromosome, as revealed by the artificial colors of spectral karyotyping. Its normal counterpart is human chromosome 9.

This chromosome exchanged a segment of itself with the nonhomologous chromosome 22. The broken end of chromosome 9 contained a gene that affects mitotic cell division. This gene fused with a DNA sequence in chromosome 22 that controls expression of another gene.

The fused gene is transcribed far more than it should be, and the cell cycle spins out of control (Section 9.5). The phenotypic outcome is *chronic myelogenous leukemia* (CML)—a rare form of leukemia in which the body produces far too many white blood cells. Uncontrolled divisions give rise to masses of malignant cells in bone tissues, where stem cells that give rise to white blood cells originate.

12.3 Examples of Autosomal Inheritance Patterns

LINKS TO
SECTIONS
8.2, 8.6

Most human traits arise from complex gene interactions, but many can be traced to autosomal dominant or recessive alleles that are inherited in simple Mendelian patterns. Some of these alleles cause genetic disorders.

AUTOSOMAL DOMINANT INHERITANCE

Figure 12.5a shows a typical inheritance pattern for an autosomal dominant allele. If one of the parents is heterozygous and the other homozygous, any child of theirs has a 50 percent chance of being heterozygous. The trait usually appears every generation. Why? The allele is expressed even in heterozygotes.

One autosomal condition, *achondroplasia*, affects 1 in 10,000 or so people. While they were still embryos, the cartilage model on which a skeleton is constructed did not form properly. Adults have abnormally short arms and legs relative to other body parts and they are only about four feet, four inches tall (Figure 12.5a). Most homozygotes die before or not long after birth. The allele does not affect the capacity of the survivors to grow and reproduce.

In *Huntington's disease*, the nervous system slowly deteriorates, and involuntary muscle action increases.

Symptoms often do not start until past age thirty, and those affected die during their forties or fifties. Many unknowingly transmit the mutant allele to children before then. The mutation causing the disorder alters a protein required for normal brain cell development. It is one of the *expansion* mutations, in which three nucleotides are repeated in series along the length of DNA. Hundreds of thousands of repeats occur within and between genes on human chromosomes, but this one (CAG) disrupts a gene product's function.

A few dominant alleles that cause severe problems persist in populations because expression of the allele may not interfere with reproduction, or affected people reproduce before the symptoms become severe. Also, spontaneous mutations reintroduce some of them.

AUTOSOMAL RECESSIVE INHERITANCE

Inheritance patterns also may point to a recessive allele on an autosome. First, if both of the parents are heterozygous for the allele, there is a 50 percent chance that any child of theirs will be heterozygous and a 25 percent chance it will be homozygous recessive (Figure 12.5b). Second, if both parents are homozygous recessive, then each child born to them will have the same condition.

Galactosemia is a heritable metabolic disorder that affects about 1 in every 100,000 newborns. This case of autosomal recessive inheritance involves alleles for an enzyme that helps digest the lactose in milk or milk products. The body normally converts lactose to glucose and galactose, then three enzymes convert the galactose to glucose–1–phosphate (Figure 12.6). This intermediate can enter glycolysis or be converted to glycogen (Sections 8.2 and 8.6). But galactosemics do not have functional copies for one of these three enzymes; they are homozygous recessive for a mutant

Figure 12.5 *Animated!* (**a**) Example of autosomal dominant inheritance. One dominant allele (*red*) is fully expressed in carriers. Achondroplasia, an autosomal dominant disorder, affects the three males shown above. At center, Verne Troyer (or Mini Me in the Mike Myers spy movies), stands two feet, eight inches tall.

(**b**) An autosomal recessive pattern. In this example, both of the parents are heterozygous carriers of the recessive allele (*red*).

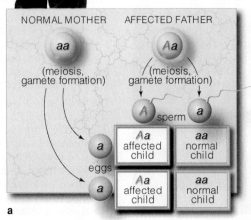

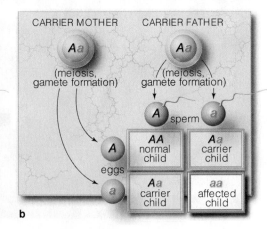

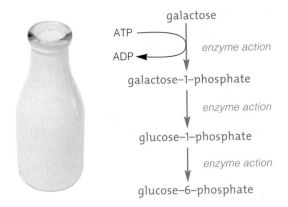

$$galactose$$

ATP —
ADP ◄— *enzyme action*

$$galactose-1-phosphate$$

↓ *enzyme action*

$$glucose-1-phosphate$$

↓ *enzyme action*

$$glucose-6-phosphate$$

Figure 12.6 How galactose is normally converted to a form that can enter the breakdown reactions of glycolysis. A mutation that affects the second enzyme in the conversion pathway gives rise to galactosemia.

allele that encodes it. Galactose–1–phosphate builds up to toxic levels in their body. High levels of this intermediate can be detected in urine. The excess leads to malnutrition, diarrhea, vomiting, and damage to the eyes, liver, and brain.

When they do not receive treatment, galactosemics typically die young. When they are quickly placed on a diet that excludes all dairy products, the symptoms may not be as severe.

WHAT ABOUT NEUROBIOLOGICAL DISORDERS?

Those human neurobiological disorders introduced at the start of the chapter do not follow simple patterns of Mendelian inheritance. In most cases, a lone gene does not give rise to depression, schizophrenia, or bipolar disorder. Still, it is useful to search for mutations that make some people more vulnerable, as long as we recognize that many genes and environmental factors contribute in individually small ways to the outcome.

For example, researchers who conducted extensive family studies and twin studies have predicted that mutant alleles in specific regions of autosomes 1, 3, 5, 6, 8, 11 through 15, 18, and 22 increase the chance of developing schizophrenia. Similarly, several mutant alleles have been reportedly linked to bipolar disorder and depression.

Some traits can be traced to dominant or recessive alleles on autosomes because they are inherited in simple Mendelian patterns. Certain alleles on these chromosomes give rise to genetic abnormalities and genetic disorders.

Sometimes textbook examples of the human condition seem a bit abstract, so take a moment to think about two boys who were too young to be old.

Imagine being ten years old with a mind trapped in a body that is getting a bit more shriveled, more frail—*old*—every day. You are barely tall enough to peer over the top of the kitchen counter. You weigh less than thirty-five pounds. Already you are bald and have a crinkled nose. Possibly you have a few more years to live. Would you, like Mickey Hays and Fransie Geringer, still be able to laugh?

On average, of every 8 million newborn humans, one will grow old far too soon. On one of its autosomes, that rare individual carries a mutant allele that gives rise to *Hutchinson–Gilford progeria syndrome*. While that new individual was still an embryo in its mother, billions of DNA replications and mitotic cell divisions distributed the information encoded in that gene to each newly formed body cell. Its legacy will be an accelerated rate of aging and a sharply reduced life span.

The mutation grossly disrupts gene interactions that are essential for growth and development. Observable symptoms start before age two. Skin that should be plump and resilient starts to thin. Skeletal muscles weaken. Limb bones that should lengthen and grow stronger soften. Premature baldness is inevitable (Figure 12.7). There are no documented cases of progeria running in families, so spontaneous mutation must be the cause. In one recent study, researchers examined twenty affected children. All the children carried a mutant gene that specifies lamin A, a structural protein that helps organize the nucleus.

Most progeriacs can expect to die in their early teens as a result of strokes or heart attacks. These final insults are brought on by a hardening of the wall of arteries, a condition typical of advanced age. Fransie was seventeen when he died. Before Mickey died at age twenty, he was the oldest living progeriac.

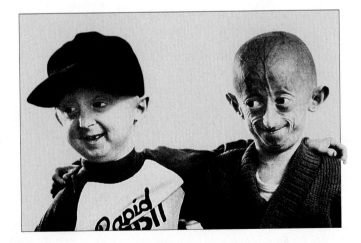

Figure 12.7 Two boys who met at a gathering of progeriacs at Disneyland, California, when they were not yet ten years old.

12.5 Sex Determination in Humans

Expression of one of the genes on the Y chromosome—that is what it takes to become a human male.

Every normal egg produced by a human female has one X chromosome. Half of the sperm cells formed in a male carry an X chromosome, and half carry a Y. If an X-bearing sperm fertilizes an X-bearing egg, then the resulting zygote will develop into a female. If the sperm carries a Y chromosome, it will develop into a male (Figure 12.8a).

With only 255 genes, the human Y chromosome might seem relatively puny. But one of them is the *SRY* gene—which happens to be the master gene for male sex determination. Its expression in XY embryos triggers the formation of testes, or male gonads, as shown in Figure 12.8b. What do these primary male reproductive organs do? For one thing, some of their cells make testosterone, a sex hormone that controls the emergence of male secondary sexual traits.

An XX embryo has no Y chromosome, no *SRY* gene, and much less testosterone. Therefore, primary female reproductive organs—ovaries—form instead. Ovaries make estrogens and other sex hormones that govern the development of female secondary sexual traits.

The human X chromosome carries 1,141 genes. Like other chromosomes, it includes some genes associated with sexual traits, such as the distribution of body fat and hair. But most of its genes deal with *nonsexual* traits, such as blood-clotting functions. Such genes can be expressed in males as well as in females. Males, remember, also inherit one X chromosome.

Expression of the SRY gene on the human Y chromosome triggers testosterone synthesis, which makes a developing embryo become a male. In the absence of the Y chromosome (and the SRY gene), a developing embryo becomes a female.

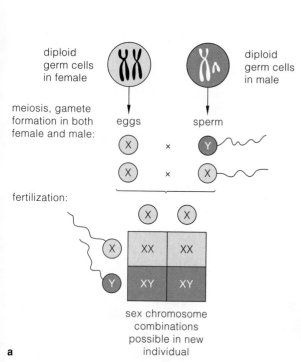

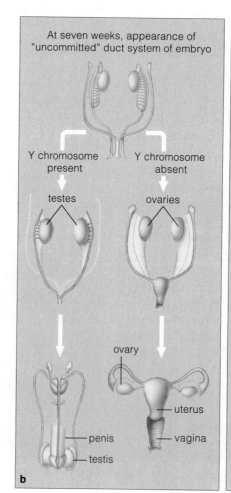

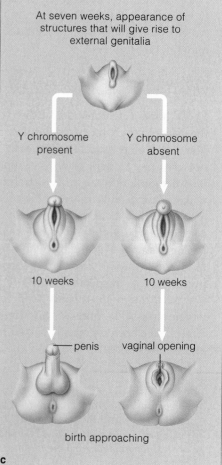

Figure 12.8 *Animated!* (**a**) Punnett-square diagram showing the sex determination pattern in humans.

(**b**) Early on, a human embryo is neither male nor female. Then tiny ducts and other structures that can develop into male *or* female reproductive organs start forming. In an XX embryo, ovaries form *in the absence of the Y chromosome and its SRY gene.* In an XY embryo, the gene product triggers the formation of testes. A hormone secreted from testes calls for development of male traits. (**c**) External reproductive organs in human embryos.

12.6 What Mendel Didn't Know: X-Linked Inheritance

After Mendel passed away in 1884, his paper on pea plants gathered dust in a hundred libraries. Then microscopists discovered chromosomes, and interest in the cellular basis of inheritance was rekindled. In 1900 researchers came across Mendel's paper while checking literature on genetic crosses. Their results confirmed what Mendel had already found out. Later, other researchers went on to discover something Mendel did not know about—genes on sex chromosomes.

By the early 1900s, researchers suspected that each gene has a specific location on a chromosome. Thomas Morgan and his coworkers confirmed it through their hybridization experiments with mutant forms of a fruit fly, *Drosophila melanogaster*. For instance, they found evidence that this fly's X chromosome has a gene for eye color and another gene for body color. They asked: Were the two genes linked on the same chromosome? That is, do they stay together during meiosis and end up in the same gamete?

Thomas Morgan, an embryologist, already had come across a relationship between sex determination and some *nonsexual* traits. For instance, human males and females both have blood-clotting factors. And yet, males are far more likely to develop hemophilia, which is a blood-clotting disorder. This sex-linked outcome was probably related to recessive forms of genes. But it was not like anything that Mendel identified in the results from his experimental crosses of pea plants. For pea plants, it made no difference which parent carried a recessive allele.

Morgan decided to study eye color and other nonsexual traits in *D. melanogaster*. This type of fruit fly has since become a favorite experimental organism. It can live in small bottles on nothing more expensive than a bit of agar, cornmeal, molasses, and yeast. A female lays hundreds of eggs in a few days, and her offspring reproduce in less than two weeks. Morgan knew that in a single year, he could use experimental tests to track observable traits for nearly thirty generations of thousands of fruit flies.

At first, all of the fruit flies in Morgan's bottles were wild type for eye color; they had brick-red eyes (Figure 12.9). Then Morgan got lucky. A gene that controls eye color mutated, and a white-eyed male appeared in a bottle, and Morgan quickly conducted **reciprocal crosses**. In the second of such paired crosses, a trait of each sex is reversed compared to the original cross to determine the role of parental sex on inheritance. In this case:

First cross: white-eyed male × red-eyed female
Second cross: red-eyed male × white-eyed female

White-eyed males mated with homozygous red-eyed females. All of the F_1 offspring had red eyes, and after the F_1 individuals had mated with each other, some of their F_2 offspring were males with white eyes (Figure 12.9c).

Then Morgan allowed true-breeding red-eyed males to mate with white-eyed females. *Half* of the F_1 offspring of this cross turned out to be red-eyed females, and *half* were white-eyed males. Later, the phenotypes of F_2 offspring were 1/4 red-eyed females, 1/4 white-eyed females, 1/4 red-eyed males, and 1/4 white-eyed males. The results did not fit with the straightforward inheritance patterns of pea plants. Could Mendel's theories explain them?

They could if the locus of an eye-color gene were on a sex chromosome. But which one? Because females (XX) could be white-eyed, the recessive allele had to be on one of their X chromosomes. What if white-eyed males (XY) had the recessive allele on their X chromosome and their Y chromosome had no corresponding eye-color allele? In that case, they would have white eyes. They would have no dominant allele to mask the effect of the recessive one, as the Punnett-square diagram in Figure 12.9c shows.

And so Morgan's idea of an X-linked gene dovetailed with Mendel's concept of segregation. By proposing that a specific gene is located on an X chromosome but not on the Y chromosome, Morgan explained his reciprocal crosses. His experimental results matched predicted outcomes.

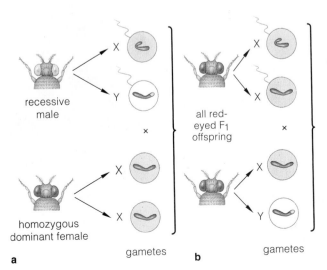

recessive male × homozygous dominant female

gametes **a**

all red-eyed F_1 offspring × gametes **b**

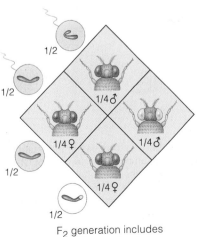

F_2 generation includes white-eyed males **c**

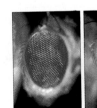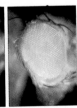

Figure 12.9 One of the experiments that pointed to sex-linked genes in *Drosophila melanogaster*. In this fruit fly, a wild-type allele specifies red eyes, and a mutant allele for the same locus specifies white eyes. *Wild-type* refers to a gene's most common form (either in nature or in standardized, laboratory-bred strains of a species) compared to less common, *mutant* alleles.

12.7 Examples of X-Linked Inheritance Patterns

LINK TO
SECTION
4.10

Alleles on an X chromosome give rise to phenotypes that also reflect simple Mendelian patterns of inheritance. Many of the recessive ones cause problems.

A recessive allele on an X chromosome often leaves certain clues when it causes a genetic disorder. First, more males than females are affected. Heterozygous females still have a dominant allele on their other X chromosome that masks the recessive allele's effects.

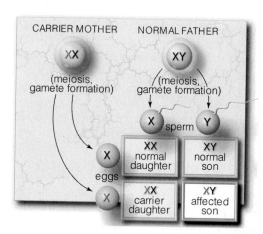

Figure 12.10 *Animated!* One pattern for X-linked recessive inheritance. In this case, the mother carries a recessive allele on one of her X chromosomes (*red*).

Males are not protected, because they inherit only one X chromosome along with one Y chromosome. Figure 12.10 reinforces this point. Second, a heterozygous female must be the bridge between an affected male and an affected grandson; an affected father cannot pass on the recessive allele to his son.

HEMOPHILIA A

Hemophilia A, a type of blood-clotting disorder, is one of the classic cases of X-linked recessive inheritance. Most of us have a functional clotting mechanism that quickly puts a stop to bleeding from minor injuries, in the manner explained in Section 38.9. The mechanism involves the synthesis of proteins that are products of genes on the X chromosome. Bleeding is prolonged in males who carry a mutant form of one of these X-linked genes. The affected males bruise easily, and the internal bleeding can cause problems in their muscles and joints.

This disorder affects 1 in 7,000 males, on average, but new mutations may account for a third of them. In heterozygous females, clotting time is close to normal. The disorder's frequency was relatively high among royal families of Europe and Russia in the nineteenth century. Figure 12.11 is a classic example of a pedigree for hemophilia A.

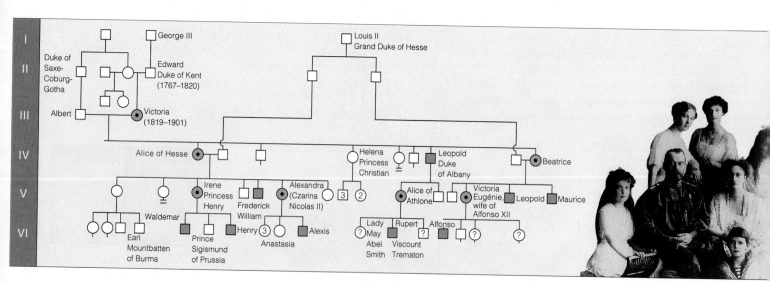

Figure 12.11 A classic case of X-linked recessive inheritance. This is a partial pedigree, or a chart of genetic connections, among descendants of Queen Victoria of England. It focuses on carriers and affected males who inherited the X-linked allele for hemophilia A (*white* circles and squares). At one time, the recessive allele was present in eighteen of Victoria's sixty-nine descendants, who sometimes intermarried. Of the Russian royal family members shown, the mother was a carrier. Through her obsession with the vulnerability of Crown Prince Alexis, a hemophiliac, she was sucked into political intrigue that helped trigger the Russian Revolution of 1917.

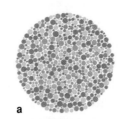 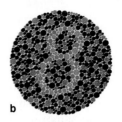

Figure 12.12 *Left*, what red–green color blindness means, using ripe red cherries on a green-leafed tree as an example. In this case, the perception of blues and yellows is normal, but the affected individual has difficulty distinguishing red from green.

Above, two of many Ishihara plates, which are standardized tests for different forms of color blindness. (**a**) You may have one form of red–green color blindness if you see the numeral "7" instead of "29" in this circle. (**b**) You may have another form if you see a "3" instead of an "8."

RED–GREEN COLOR BLINDNESS

The pattern of X-linked recessive inheritance shows up among individuals who have some degree of *color blindness*. The term refers to a range of conditions in which an individual cannot distinguish among some or all of the colors in the spectrum of visible light. Mutant gene products alter the structure and function of photoreceptors (light-sensitive receptors) in eyes.

Normally, humans can sense the differences among 150 colors. A person who is *red–green* color blind sees fewer than 25 because some or all of the receptors that respond to red and green wavelengths are weakened or absent. Other people confuse red and green colors. Still others see shades of gray instead of green but see blues and yellows quite well. Figure 12.12*a* represents this condition. Figure 12.12*b* is part of a standardized set of tests for color blindness.

Color blindness is more common in men, who are about twelve times more likely than women to develop the condition. Heterozygous women show symptoms as well. Can you explain why?

DUCHENNE MUSCULAR DYSTROPHY

Duchenne muscular dystrophy (DMD) is one of a group of X-linked recessive disorders characterized by rapid degeneration of muscles, starting early in life. About 1 in every 3,500 boys is affected.

The recessive allele encodes dystrophin. This is the protein that structurally supports fused-together cells in muscle fibers. It anchors much of the cell cortex to the plasma membrane (Section 4.10). In cases where

dystrophin is abnormal or absent, the cell cortex weakens and muscle cells die. The debris left behind in tissues triggers inflammation that becomes chronic.

Most individuals are diagnosed between ages three and seven. The progression of the disorder cannot be stopped. When the affected boy is about twelve years old, he will start using a wheelchair. His heart muscles will start to break down. Even with the best managed care, he usually will die before age twenty-five, most often as a result of respiratory failure.

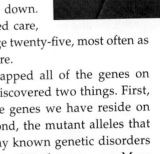

Recently, researchers mapped all of the genes on the X chromosome. They discovered two things. First, only 5 percent of all of the genes we have reside on this sex chromosome. Second, the mutant alleles that cause or contribute to many known genetic disorders can occur at locations along this chromosome. More than 300 such connections have been identified.

Diverse recessive alleles on the human X chromosome are implicated in more than 300 genetic disorders.

A heterozygous female may not show symptoms if she has a dominant allele on her other X chromosome, which masks the effect of the recessive allele. Males (XY) cannot transmit any X-linked allele to their sons.

12.8 Heritable Changes in Chromosome Structure

LINK TO
SECTION
10.3

On rare occasions, a chromosome's structure changes.
Many of the alterations have severe or lethal outcomes.

MAIN CATEGORIES OF STRUCTURAL CHANGE

One or more changes in the physical structure of a chromosome may give rise to a genetic disorder or abnormality. Such changes are rare, but they do occur spontaneously in nature. Some also can be induced by exposure to certain chemicals or irradiation. Either way, the alteration may be detected by microscopic examination and karyotype analysis of cells during mitosis or meiosis. Four kinds of structural changes are chromosomal duplications, deletions, inversions, and translocations.

Duplication Even normal chromosomes have DNA sequences that are repeated two or more times. These are called **duplications**:

normal chromosome

one segment repeated

Duplications can occur through unequal crossovers at prophase I. Homologous chromosomes align side by side, but their DNA sequences misalign at some point along their length. The probability of this happening is greater in regions where DNA has long repeats of the same series of nucleotides. A stretch of DNA gets deleted from one chromosome and is spliced into the partner chromosome. Some duplications cause neural problems and physical abnormalities. As you will see, others apparently were important in the evolution of primates that were ancestral to humans.

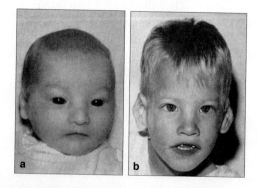

Figure 12.13 (**a**) A male infant who developed cri-du-chat syndrome. His ears are low on the side of the head relative to the eyes. (**b**) Same boy, four years later. By this age, affected humans stop making the mewing sounds typical of the syndrome.

Deletion A **deletion** is the loss of some portion of a chromosome, as by unequal crossovers, inversions, or chemical attacks:

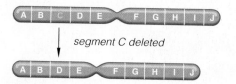

segment C deleted

In mammals, most deletions cause serious disorders or death. Missing or broken genes disrupt the body's growth, development, and metabolism. For instance, a tiny deletion from human chromosome 5 results in an abnormally shaped larynx and mental impairment. Crying infants sound like cats meowing (Figure 12.13). Hence the name of the disorder, *cri-du-chat* (cat-cry in French). Inversions and deletions often occur together as an outcome of unequal recombination events.

Inversion With an **inversion**, part of the sequence of DNA within the chromosome becomes oriented in the reverse direction, with no molecular loss:

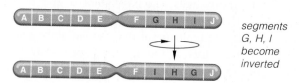

segments G, H, I become inverted

An inversion is not a problem for a carrier if it does not alter a crucial gene region. It can cause problems in meiosis. Chromosomes may mispair, and deletions may occur that can reduce the viability of gametes. Some individuals do not even know that they have an inverted chromosome region until a genetic disorder or abnormality surfaces in one or more children.

Translocation In Section 12.2, you came across a case of a broken part of one chromosome becoming attached to another chromosome. This type of change in chromosome structure is known as a **translocation**. Most translocations are reciprocal, in that both of the two chromosomes exchange broken parts:

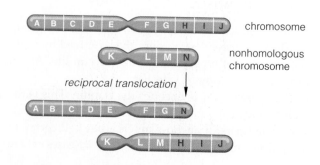

chromosome

nonhomologous chromosome

reciprocal translocation

Translocations often cause reduced fertility, because affected chromosomes have difficulty segregating in meiosis. Severe problems are rare, but they do arise. They include some sarcomas, lymphomas, myelomas, and leukemias.

DOES CHROMOSOME STRUCTURE EVOLVE?

Alterations in the structure of chromosomes generally are not good and may be selected against. Even so, many alterations with neutral effects have been built into the DNA of all species over evolutionary time.

Duplicates of genes could have bestowed adaptive advantages on descendants of their original bearers. Two or more copies of some gene means that one is free to mutate while the other continues to carry out its normal function. The slightly modified products of mutant genes can behave in slightly different or novel ways, some of which are beneficial.

Some duplications have proved adaptive. Reflect on the four globin chains of hemoglobin (Section 3.6). In humans and other primates, several genes for these polypeptide chains are strikingly similar. Apparently they evolved through duplications, mutations, and transpositions. They have slightly different molecular structures and slightly different capacities to bind and transport oxygen under a range of cellular conditions.

Alterations in chromosome structure might have contributed to the differences among closely related organisms, such as apes and humans. Eighteen of the twenty-three pairs of human chromosomes are almost identical with chimpanzee and gorilla chromosomes. The other five differ only at inverted and translocated regions. Figure 12.14 shows the striking similarities between some gibbon and human chromosomes that may have arisen by duplications and translocations.

To give one more example, human body cells have twenty-three pairs of chromosomes, but those of a chimpanzee, gorilla, or orangutan have twenty-four. Compare the banding patterns of these chromosomes. During human evolution, two chromosomes in an early ancestor fused, end to end, to form chromosome 2. In the fused region, researchers have discovered remnants of a telomere—the signature DNA sequence that caps the *ends* of all chromosomes (Figure 12.15).

A segment of a chromosome may be duplicated, deleted, inverted, or moved to a new location. Such changes can be harmful or lethal. Others have been conserved over time; they confer advantages or have had neutral effects.

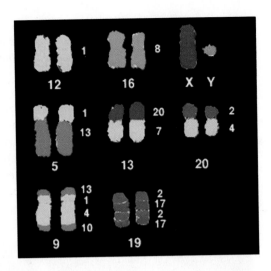

Figure 12.14 Spectral karyotype of duplicated chromosomes of the gibbon, one of the apes. The colors identify regions of gibbon chromosomes that are structurally identical with human chromosomes.

Top row: Chromosomes 12, 16, X, and Y are structurally the same in both primates. *Second row:* Translocations are present in gibbon chromosomes 5, 13, and 20, and they correspond to regions of human chromosomes 1, 13, 20, 7, 2, and 4.

Third row: Gibbon chromosome 9 corresponds to several human chromosome regions. In addition, duplications in gibbon chromosome 19 are present in human chromosomes 2 and 17.

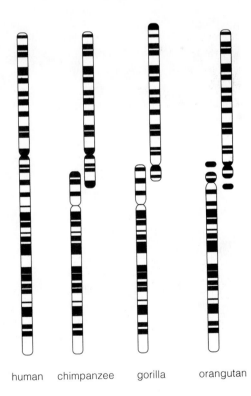

human   chimpanzee   gorilla   orangutan

Figure 12.15 Banding patterns of human chromosome 2 (*left*), compared with the patterns on two of the chromosomes in cells of the chimpanzee, gorilla, and orangutan. Such bands appear because different chromosome regions preferentially take up different kinds of stains. Their response to a given stain depends on their base composition and packing organization.

12.9 Heritable Changes in the Chromosome Number

LINKS TO
SECTIONS
9.3, 10.3

Occasionally, abnormal events occur before or during cell division, and gametes and new individuals end up with the wrong chromosome number. Consequences range from minor to lethal changes in form and function.

In **aneuploidy**, cells usually have one extra or one less chromosome. Autosomal aneuploidy is usually fatal for humans and is linked to most miscarriages. Aneuploidy typically arises through **nondisjunction**, whereby one or more pairs of chromosomes do not separate as they should during mitosis or meiosis. Figure 12.16 shows an example. In **polyploidy**, cells have three or more of each type of chromosome. Half of all species of flowering plants, some insects, fishes, and other animals are polyploid.

Such changes affect the chromosome number at fertilization. Suppose a normal gamete fuses with an $n+1$ gamete, with one extra chromosome. The new individual will be trisomic ($2n+1$), with three of one type of chromosome and two of every other type. Or what if an $n-1$ gamete and a normal n gamete fuse? In this case, the new individual will be monosomic, or $2n-1$. Mitotic divisions perpetuate such mistakes when an embryo is growing in size and developing.

AUTOSOMAL CHANGE AND DOWN SYNDROME

A few trisomics are born alive, but only trisomy 21 individuals reach adulthood. A newborn with three chromosomes 21 will develop *Down syndrome*. This autosomal disorder is the most frequent type of altered chromosome number in humans; it occurs once in every 800 to 1,000 births. It affects more than 350,000 people in the United States. Figure 12.16*a* shows a karyotype for a trisomic 21 female. About 95 percent of all cases arise through nondisjunction at meiosis. Affected individuals have upward-slanting eyes, a fold of skin that starts at the inner corner of each eye, a deep crease across each palm and foot sole, one (not two) horizontal furrows on their fifth fingers, and somewhat flattened facial features.

Not all of the outward symptoms develop in every individual. That said, trisomic 21 individuals do have moderate to severe mental impairment and heart problems. Also, their skeleton develops abnormally, so older children have shortened body parts, loose joints, and misaligned bones in hips, fingers, and toes. Their muscles and reflexes are weak. Motor skills, including speech, develop very slowly. With medical care, individuals can live for fifty-five years, on average.

The incidence of nondisjunction rises with increasing age of potential mothers (Figure 12.17). Nondisjunction might occur in the father, although less often. Trisomy 21 is just one of hundreds of conditions that can be detected through prenatal diagnosis (Section 12.11). With early training and medical intervention, individuals still can take part in normal activities. As a group, trisomics 21 tend to be cheerful and sociable.

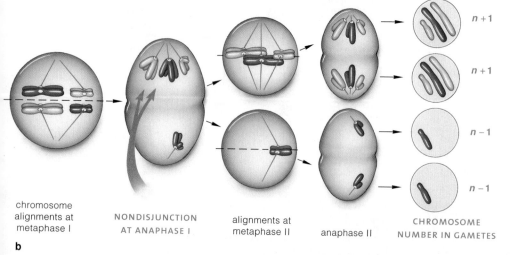

chromosome alignments at metaphase I

b

NONDISJUNCTION AT ANAPHASE I

alignments at metaphase II

anaphase II

CHROMOSOME NUMBER IN GAMETES

$n+1$

$n+1$

$n-1$

$n-1$

Figure 12.16 (**a**) A case of nondisjunction. This karyotype reveals the trisomic 21 condition of a human female. (**b**) One example of how nondisjunction arises. Of the two pairs of homologous chromosomes shown here, one fails to separate during anaphase I of meiosis. The chromosome number is altered in the gametes that form after meiosis.

CHANGE IN THE SEX CHROMOSOME NUMBER

Nondisjunction also causes most of the alterations in the number of X and Y chromosomes. The frequency of such changes is 1 in 400 live births. Usually, they lead to difficulties in learning and motor skills, such as speech, although problems can be so subtle that the underlying cause is not even diagnosed.

Female Sex Chromosome Abnormalities *Turner syndrome* individuals have an X chromosome and no corresponding X or Y chromosome (XO). About 1 in 2,500 to 10,000 newborn girls are XO. Nondisjunction originating with the father accounts for 75 percent of the cases. Yet cases are few, compared with other sex chromosome abnormalities. At least 98 percent of XO embryos may spontaneously abort early in pregnancy.

Despite the near lethality, XO survivors are not as disadvantaged as other aneuploids. On average, they are well proportioned, as shown here, but only four feet, eight inches tall. Most cannot make enough sex hormones; they do not have functional ovaries. The condition affects the development of secondary sexual traits, such as breast development. A few eggs form in the ovaries but degenerate by the time the girls are two years old.

A few females inherit three to five X chromosomes. An *XXX syndrome* occurs in about 1 of 1,000 live births. Adults are fertile. Except for slight learning difficulties, most fall in the normal range of social behavior.

Male Sex Chromosome Abnormalities About 1 of every 500 males has an XXY karyotype, with an extra chromosome inherited from the mother. Two-thirds of the cases are an outcome of nondisjunction at meiosis. Among the remainder, failure of the Y chromosome to separate at mitosis gave rise to a mosaic karyotype (XY in some cells and XXY in other cells).

The resulting *Klinefelter syndrome* develops during puberty. XXY males tend to be overweight and tall. The testes and the prostate gland usually are smaller than average. Many XXY males are within the normal range of intelligence, although some have short-term memory loss and learning disabilities. They make less testosterone and more estrogen than normal males, with feminizing effects. Sperm counts are low. Hair is sparse, the voice is pitched high, and the breasts are enlarged somewhat. When affected individuals enter

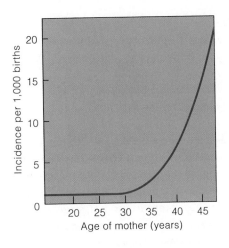

Figure 12.17 Relationship between the frequency of Down syndrome and mother's age at childbirth. The data are from a study of 1,119 affected children. The risk of having a trisomic 21 baby rises with the mother's age. This may seem odd, because about 80 percent of trisomic 21 individuals are born to women not yet thirty-five years old. But these women are in the age categories with the highest fertility rates, and they simply have more babies.

puberty, they can receive testosterone injections that can reverse the feminized traits.

About 1 in 500 to 1,000 males has one X and two Y chromosomes, an *XYY condition*. They tend to be taller than average, with mild mental impairment, but most fall in the normal phenotypic range. They were once thought to be genetically predisposed to a life of crime. This misguided view was based on a sampling error (too few cases of narrowly chosen groups, such as prison inmates) and were biased (the same researchers gathered karyotypes *and* personal histories). Fanning the stereotype was a report that a mass murderer of young nurses was XYY. He wasn't.

In 1976 a Danish geneticist reported results from his study of 4,139 tall males, all twenty-six years old, who had registered at their draft board. Besides their data from physical examinations and intelligence tests, the draft records offered clues to social and economic status, education, and criminal convictions, if there were any. Twelve of the males studied were XYY, which meant the "control group" had more than 4,000 males. The only finding was that mentally impaired, tall males who engage in criminal deeds are just more likely to get caught—irrespective of karyotype.

The majority of XXY, XXX, and XYY children may not even be diagnosed. Some are dismissed unfairly as being underachievers.

Nondisjunction in germ cells, gametes, or early embryonic cells changes the number of autosomes or the number of sex chromosomes. The change affects development and the resulting phenotypes.

Nondisjunction at meiosis causes most sex chromosome abnormalities, which typically lead to subtle difficulties with learning, and speech and other motor skills.

12.10 Human Genetic Analysis

Some organisms, including pea plants and fruit flies, are ideal for genetic analysis. They do not have very many chromosomes. They can grow and reproduce fast in small spaces, under controlled conditions. It does not take long to track a trait through many generations. Humans, however, are another story.

Unlike the flies in laboratory bottles, we humans live under variable conditions in diverse environments, and we live as long as the geneticists who study us. Most of us select our own mates and reproduce if and when we want to. Most families are not large, which means that there are not enough offspring available for researchers to make easy inferences.

Geneticists often gather information from several generations to increase the numbers for analysis. If a trait follows a simple Mendelian inheritance pattern, geneticists can be more confident about predicting the probability of its showing up again. The pattern also can be a clue to the past (Figure 12.18).

Such information is often displayed in **pedigrees**, or charts of genetic connections among individuals. Standardized methods, definitions, and symbols that

Figure 12.18 An intriguing pattern of inheritance. Eight percent of the men in Central Asia carry nearly identical Y chromosomes, which implies descent from a shared ancestor. If so, then 16 million males living between northeastern China and Afghanistan—close to 1 of every 200 men alive today—belong to a lineage that started with the warrior and notorious womanizer Genghis Khan. In time, his offspring ruled an empire that stretched from China all the way to Vienna.

represent different kinds of individuals are used to construct these charts. You already came across one in Section 12.7. Figures 12.19 and 12.20 are two more.

Those who analyze pedigrees rely on knowledge of probability and patterns of Mendelian inheritance that may yield clues to a trait. Such researchers have traced many genetic abnormalities and disorders to a dominant or recessive allele and often to its location on an autosome or a sex chromosome. Table 12.1 is a list of the ones used as examples in this book.

As individuals and as members of society, what do we do with the information? The next section gets into options. When considering them, keep in mind some important distinctions. First, a genetic *abnormality* is only a rare or uncommon version of a trait, as when a person is born with six digits on each hand or foot instead of the usual five. Whether you view such an abnormality as disfiguring or merely interesting is subjective only; there is nothing inherently life-threatening about it. By contrast, a genetic *disorder* is a heritable condition that sooner or later gives rise to mild to severe medical problems. Each

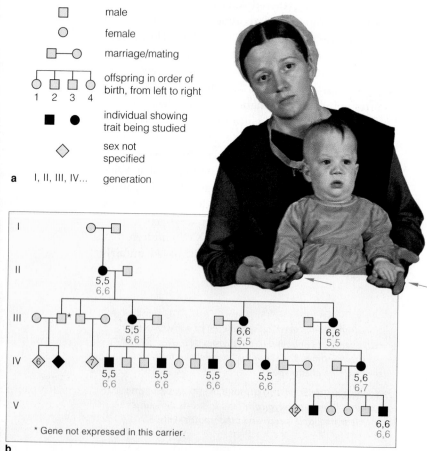

□	male
○	female
□─○	marriage/mating
	offspring in order of birth, from left to right
■ ●	individual showing trait being studied
◇	sex not specified
I, II, III, IV...	generation

a

* Gene not expressed in this carrier.

b

Figure 12.19 *Animated!* (**a**) Standardized symbols used in pedigrees. (**b**) A pedigree for *polydactyly*, characterized by extra fingers, toes, or both. *Black* numerals signify the number of fingers on each hand; *blue* numerals signify the number of toes on each foot. This condition recurs as one symptom of Ellis–van Creveld syndrome.

Table 12.1 Examples of Human Genetic Disorders and Genetic Abnormalities

Disorder or Abnormality	Main Symptoms
Autosomal recessive inheritance	
Albinism	Absence of pigmentation
Blue offspring	Bright blue skin coloration
Cystic fibrosis	Abnormal glandular secretions leading to tissue, organ damage
Ellis–van Creveld syndrome	Extra fingers, toes, short limbs
Fanconi anemia	Physical abnormalities, bone marrow failure
Galactosemia	Brain, liver, eye damage
Phenylketonuria (PKU)*	Mental impairment
Sickle-cell anemia	Adverse pleiotropic effects on organs throughout body
Autosomal dominant inheritance	
Achondroplasia	One form of dwarfism
Camptodactyly	Rigid, bent fingers
Familial hypercholesterolemia	High cholesterol levels in blood; eventually clogged arteries
Huntington's disease	Nervous system degenerates progressively, irreversibly
Marfan syndrome	Abnormal or no connective tissue
Polydactyly	Extra fingers, toes, or both
Progeria	Drastic premature aging
Neurofibromatosis	Tumors of nervous system, skin

Disorder or Abnormality	Main Symptoms
X-linked recessive inheritance	
Androgen insensitivity syndrome	XY individual but having some female traits; sterility
Red–green color blindness	Inability to distinguish among some or all shades of red and green
Fragile X syndrome	Mental impairment
Hemophilia	Impaired blood-clotting ability
Muscular dystrophies	Progressive loss of muscle function
X-linked anhidrotic dysplasia	Mosaic skin (patches with or without sweat glands); other effects
Changes in chromosome structure	
Chronic myelogenous leukemia (CML)	Overproduction of white blood cells in bone marrow; organ malfunctions
Cri-du-chat syndrome	Mental impairment; abnormally shaped larynx
Changes in chromosome number	
Down syndrome	Mental impairment; heart defects
Turner syndrome	Sterility; abnormal ovaries, abnormal sexual traits
Klinefelter syndrome	Sterility; mild mental impairment
XXX syndrome	Minimal abnormalities
XYY condition	Mild mental impairment or no effect

genetic disorder is characterized by a specific set of symptoms—a **syndrome**.

One more point to keep in mind: Alleles that give rise to severe genetic disorders are generally rare in populations, because they put their bearers at risk. Why don't they disappear entirely? Rare mutations introduce new ones. In addition, in heterozygotes, a normal allele masks harmful effects that may result from expression of the mutant recessive allele. This means that heterozygotes can transmit harmful alleles to their offspring. The next section addresses how we may address the consequences.

Pedigree analysis may reveal simple patterns of Mendelian inheritance. From such patterns, specialists can infer the probability that offspring will inherit certain alleles.

A genetic abnormality is a rare or less common version of a heritable trait. A genetic disorder is a heritable condition that results in mild to severe medical problems.

Figure 12.20 Pedigree for Huntington's disease, a progressive degeneration of the nervous system. Researcher Nancy Wexler and her team constructed this extended family tree for nearly 10,000 Venezuelans. Their analysis of unaffected and affected individuals revealed that a dominant allele on human chromosome 4 is the culprit. Wexler has a special interest in the disease; it runs in her family.

12.11 Prospects in Human Genetics

With the arrival of their newborn, parents typically ask, "Is our baby all right?" Quite naturally, they want their baby to be free of genetic disorders, and most babies are. But what are the options when something goes wrong?

Many prospective parents have difficulty coming to terms with the possibility that a child of theirs might develop a severe genetic disorder. What are their options?

Phenotypic Treatments   Surgery, prescription drugs, hormone replacement therapy, and often dietary controls can minimize and in some cases eliminate the symptoms of many genetic disorders.

For instance, strict dietary controls work in cases of *phenylketonuria*, or PKU. Individuals affected by this genetic disorder are homozygous for a recessive allele on an autosome. They cannot make a functional form of an enzyme that catalyzes the conversion of the amino acid phenylalanine to tyrosine. Because the conversion is blocked, phenylalanine accumulates and is diverted into other metabolic pathways. The outcome is an impairment of brain function.

Affected people who restrict phenylalanine intake can lead essentially normal lives. They must avoid soft drinks and other products that are sweetened with aspartame, a compound that contains phenylalanine.

Genetic Screening   The idea behind genetic screening is to detect alleles that cause genetic disorders, provide information on reproductive risks, and help families who are already affected. Often, carriers or affected individuals are detected early enough to start countermeasures for minimizing the damage before symptoms develop.

A few large-scale screening programs are operational. Besides helping individuals, the information they generate is being used to estimate the prevalence and distribution of harmful alleles in populations. In the United States, for instance, most hospitals routinely screen newborns for PKU, so we now see fewer individuals with symptoms of the disorder.

There are social risks that must be considered. How would you feel if you were labeled as someone with "bad" alleles? Would the knowledge invite chronic anxiety? Would potential employers or insurance companies turn you down? How would you interact with an affected child that you brought into the world if you had known about the risk in advance? No easy answers here.

Prenatal Diagnosis   Doctors and clinicians commonly use methods of *prenatal diagnosis* to determine the sex of embryos or fetuses and to screen for more than 100 known genetic problems. *Prenatal* means before birth. *Embryo* is a term that applies until eight weeks after fertilization, after which the term *fetus* is appropriate.

image on the
ultrasound screen

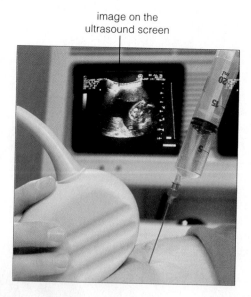

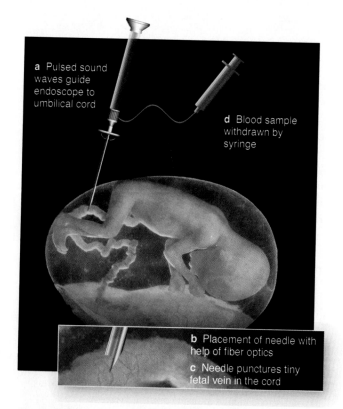

a Pulsed sound waves guide endoscope to umbilical cord

d Blood sample withdrawn by syringe

b Placement of needle with help of fiber optics

c Needle punctures tiny fetal vein in the cord

Figure 12.21 *Animated!*   Amniocentesis, a prenatal diagnostic tool. A pregnant woman's doctor holds an ultrasound emitter against her abdomen while drawing a sample of amniotic fluid into a syringe. He monitors the path of the needle with an ultrasound screen, in the background. Then he directs the needle into the amniotic sac that holds the developing fetus and withdraws twenty milliliters or so of amniotic fluid. The fluid contains fetal cells and wastes that can be analyzed for genetic disorders.

Figure 12.22   Fetoscopy for prenatal diagnosis.

Suppose a forty-five-year-old woman is pregnant and worries about Down syndrome. Between eight and twelve weeks after conception, she might opt for *amniocentesis* (Figure 12.21). By this diagnostic procedure, a clinician uses a syringe to withdraw a small sample of fluid from the amniotic cavity. The "cavity" is a fluid-filled sac, bounded by a membrane—the amnion—that encloses the fetus. The fetus normally sheds some cells into the fluid. Cells suspended in the fluid sample can be analyzed for many genetic disorders, including Down syndrome, cystic fibrosis, and sickle-cell anemia.

Chorionic villi sampling (CVS) is a similar diagnostic procedure. A clinician withdraws a few cells from the chorion, a membrane that surrounds the amnion and helps form the placenta. Unlike amniocentesis, however, CVS can be requested to find out information as early as eight weeks into pregnancy.

It is now possible to see a live, developing fetus with the aid of an endoscope, a fiber-optic device. In *fetoscopy*, sound waves are pulsed across the mother's uterus. Images of parts of the fetus, umbilical cord, or placenta show up on a computer screen that is connected to the endoscope (Figure 12.22). A sample of fetal blood is often drawn at the same time. This procedure can be used to diagnose many blood cell disorders, such as sickle-cell anemia and hemophilia.

There are risks to a fetus associated with all three procedures, including punctures or infections. Also, if the amnion does not reseal itself quickly, too much fluid can leak out of the amniotic cavity and endanger the fetus. Amniocentesis increases the risk of miscarriage by 1 to 2 percent. CVS may disrupt the placenta's development, which can cause missing or underdeveloped fingers and toes in 0.3 percent of newborns. Fetoscopy raises the risk of a miscarriage by 2 to 10 percent.

Genetic Counseling   Parents-to-be commonly ask genetic counselors to compare the risks associated with diagnostic procedures against the likelihood that their future child will be affected by a severe genetic disorder. At the time of counseling, they also should discuss the small overall risk (3 percent) that complications can affect *any* child during the birth process. They should talk about how old they are. The older either prospective parent is, the greater the risk may be.

As a case in point, suppose a first child or a close relative has a severe disorder. Genetic counselors come up with a program of diagnosis of parental genotypes, pedigrees, and genetic testing for known disorders. Using this information, counselors can predict risks for disorders in future children. They should remind prospective parents that the same risk usually applies to each pregnancy.

Regarding Abortion   What happens after prenatal diagnosis reveals a severe problem? Do prospective parents opt for an induced abortion? An *abortion* is an expulsion

Figure 12.23   Eight-cell and multicelled stages of human development.

of a pre-term embryo or fetus from the uterus. We can only say here that individuals must weigh awareness of the severity of the genetic disorder against their ethical and religious beliefs. Worse, today they must play out their personal tragedy on a larger stage that is dominated by a nationwide battle between highly vocal "pro-life" and "pro-choice" factions. We return to this volatile topic in Section 44.15, after explaining the stages of human embryonic development.

Preimplantation Diagnosis   This procedure relies on *in vitro fertilization*. Sperm and eggs from prospective parents are mixed in a sterile culture medium. One or more eggs may get fertilized. If this happens, mitotic cell divisions can turn an egg into a ball of eight cells within forty-eight hours (Figure 12.23).

According to one view, the tiny, free-floating ball is a pre-pregnancy stage. Like all of the unfertilized eggs that a woman's body discards monthly during her reproductive years, it has not attached to the uterus. All of its cells have the same genes. However, its cells are not yet committed to being specialized one way or another. Doctors carefully remove one of these undifferentiated cells and analyze its genes. If it has no detectable genetic defects, the ball is inserted into the uterus. The withdrawn cell will not be missed. Many of the resulting "test-tube babies" are born in good health.

Some couples who are at risk of passing on the alleles for cystic fibrosis, muscular dystrophy, or some other genetic disorder have opted for this procedure.

Summary

Section 12.1 Of twenty-three pairs of homologous chromosomes in human body cells, one is a pairing of sex chromosomes. The other chromosomes are called autosomes; in both sexes, they are the same length and shape, have the same centromere location, and carry the same genes along their length.

Section 12.2 In karyotyping, a diagnostic tool, an individual's metaphase chromosomes are prepared for microscopy, photographed, and arranged in sequence in a chart on the basis of their defining features.

Biology Now
Learn how to create a karyotype with the animation on BiologyNow.

Sections 12.3, 12.4 Some dominant and recessive alleles on autosomes are inherited in simple Mendelian patterns that can be predictably connected with specific phenotypes. Some mutant forms of these alleles give rise to genetic abnormalities or genetic disorders.

Biology Now
Investigate autosomal inheritance with the interaction on BiologyNow.

Sections 12.5, 12.6 Human females have identical sex chromosomes (XX) and males have nonidentical ones (XY). The *SRY* gene on the Y chromosome is the basis of sex determination. Its expression starts the synthesis of testosterone, a hormone that causes a human embryo to develop into a male. If an embryo has no Y chromosome (no *SRY* gene), it develops into a female.

Experiments with fruit flies yielded the first evidence that specific genes that give rise to nonsexual traits are located on the X chromosome.

Biology Now
See how gender is determined in humans with the interaction on BiologyNow.

Section 12.7 Certain dominant and recessive alleles on the X chromosome are inherited in simple patterns. A number of alleles on the X chromosome contribute to more than 300 known genetic disorders. Males cannot transmit a recessive X-linked allele to their sons; an affected female must be the bridge of inheritance.

Biology Now
Investigate X-linked inheritance with the interaction on BiologyNow.

Section 12.8 On rare occasions, a chromosome's physical structure undergoes abnormal alterations. Part of it may be duplicated, deleted, inverted, or moved to a new location (translocated) in the same chromosome or a different one.

Most alterations are harmful or lethal. Even so, many have accumulated in the chromosomes of all species over evolutionary time. Either they had neutral effects or they later proved to be useful. Many duplications, inversions, and translocations are built into primate chromosomes. They are strikingly similar among human, chimpanzee, gorilla, orangutan, and gibbon chromosomes, which is strong evidence of divergences from a common ancestor.

Section 12.9 The parental chromosome number can change permanently. Most often, this is an outcome of nondisjunction: the failure of one or more pairs of duplicated chromosomes to separate from each other, most often during meiosis.

Aneuploids have inherited one extra or one less chromosome than their parents. In the human population, trisomy 21, the most well-known form of aneuploidy, results in Down syndrome. Most human autosomal aneuploids die before birth.

Polyploids inherited three or more of each type of chromosome from their parents. About half of all flowering plants and some insects, fishes, and other animals are polyploid.

Changes in the number of sex chromosomes usually cause problems with learning and motor skills. Problems can be so subtle that the underlying cause may not be diagnosed, as among XXY, XXX, and XYY children.

Sections 12.10, 12.11 Traditionally, geneticists have constructed pedigrees, or charts of genetic connections among individuals, to estimate the probability that offspring will inherit a trait of interest. Phenotypic treatments, genetic screening, genetic counseling, prenatal diagnosis, and preimplantation diagnosis are options available for potential parents who are at risk of transmitting a harmful allele to offspring.

Biology Now
Examine a human pedigree with the animation on BiologyNow.
Explore amniocentesis with the animation on BiologyNow.

Self-Quiz
Answers in Appendix II

1. The _____ of chromosomes in a cell are compared to construct karyotypes.
   a. length and shape   c. gene sequence
   b. centromere location   d. both a and b

2. The _____ determines gender in humans.
   a. X chromosome   c. *SRY* gene
   b. *Dll* gene   d. both b and c

3. If one parent is heterozygous for a dominant allele on an autosome and the other parent is homozygous, any child of theirs has a _____ chance of being heterozygous.
   a. 25 percent   c. 75 percent
   b. 50 percent   d. no chance; it will die

4. Expansion mutations occur _____ within and between genes in human chromosomes.
   a. only rarely   c. not at all
   b. frequently   d. only in multiples of ten

5. Galactosemia is a case of _____ inheritance.
   a. autosomal dominant   c. X-linked dominant
   b. autosomal recessive   d. X-linked recessive

6. Is this statement true or false: A son can inherit an X-linked recessive allele from his father.

7. Color blindness is a case of _____ inheritance.
   a. autosomal dominant   c. X-linked dominant
   b. autosomal recessive   d. X-linked recessive

8. A (An) _____ can alter chromosome structure.
   a. deletion   c. inversion   e. all of the
   b. duplication   d. translocation   above

9. Nondisjunction may occur during _____ .
   a. mitosis   c. fertilization
   b. meiosis   d. both a and b

10. Is this statement false: Body cells sometimes inherit three or more of each type of chromosome characteristic of the species, a condition called aneuploidy.

11. The karyotype for Klinefelter syndrome is _____ .
    a. XO   c. XXY
    b. XXX   d. XYY

12. A recognized set of symptoms that characterize a specific disorder is a _____ .
    a. syndrome   b. disease   c. pedigree

13. Match the chromosome terms appropriately.
    ____ polyploidy   a. number and defining
    ____ deletion   features of an individual's
    ____ nondisjunction   metaphase chromosomes
    ____ translocation   b. segment of a chromosome
    ____ karyotype   moves to a nonhomologous
    ____ aneuploidy   chromosome
                           c. extra chromosome sets
                           d. one outcome: gametes with
                              wrong chromosome number
                           e. a chromosome segment lost
                           f. change by one chromosome

Additional questions are available on Biology ⑤Now™

Genetics Problems   *Answers in Appendix III*

1. Human females are XX and males are XY.
   a. Does a male inherit the X from his mother or father?
   b. With respect to X-linked alleles, how many different types of gametes can a male produce?
   c. If a female is homozygous for an X-linked allele, how many types of gametes can she produce with respect to that allele?
   d. If a female is heterozygous for an X-linked allele, how many types of gametes might she produce with respect to that allele?

2. In Section 11.4, you read about a mutation that causes a serious genetic disorder, *Marfan syndrome*. A mutant allele responsible for the disorder follows a pattern of autosomal dominant inheritance. What is the chance that any child will inherit it if one parent does not carry the allele and the other is heterozygous for it?

3. Somatic cells of individuals with Down syndrome usually have an extra chromosome 21; they contain forty-seven chromosomes.
   a. At which stages of meiosis I and II could a mistake alter the chromosome number?
   b. A few individuals with Down syndrome have forty-six chromosomes, two of which are normal-appearing

Figure 12.24 A case of Klinefelter syndrome. Until his teenage years, Stefan was shy, reserved, and prone to rage for no apparent reason. Psychologists and doctors assumed he had learning disabilities that affected comprehension, auditory processing, memory, and abstract thinking. One told Stefan he was stupid and lazy, and would be lucky to graduate from high school. In time, Stefan was graduated from college with degrees in business administration and sports management. He never discussed his learning disabilities. Instead, he took pride in doing the work on his own and not being treated differently.

Stefan was twenty-five years old before laboratory tests as well as karyotyping revealed a 46XY/47XXY mosaic condition. That same year, he started a job as a software engineer. Having a full-time position helped him open doors to volunteer work with the Klinefelter syndrome network. During his volunteer work, he met his future fiancée, whose son also has the syndrome.

chromosomes 21 and a longer-than-normal chromosome
14. Speculate on how this chromosome abnormality may have arisen.

4. As you read earlier, *Duchenne muscular dystrophy* is a genetic disorder that arises through the expression of a recessive X-linked allele. Usually, symptoms start in childhood. Gradual, progressive loss of muscle function leads to death, usually by age twenty or so. Unlike color blindness, the disorder is nearly always restricted to males. Suggest why.

5. In the human population, mutation of two genes on the X chromosome causes two types of X-linked *hemophilia* (A and B). In a few cases, a woman is heterozygous for both mutant alleles (one on each of the X chromosomes). All of her sons should have either hemophilia A or B.
   However, on very rare occasions, one of these women gives birth to a son who does not have hemophilia, and his one X chromosome does not have either mutant allele. Explain how such an X chromosome could arise.

6. Does the phenotype indicated by red circles and squares in this pedigree show a Mendelian inheritance pattern that is autosomal dominant, autosomal recessive, or X-linked?

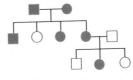

7. When it comes to acceptance of a genetic condition that is out of the ordinary, people tend to be subjective. As an example, consider the individual described in Figure 12.24. How would you have categorized him without knowing the genetic basis of his early behavior? How would you categorize him now in terms of what we as a society consider to be "ideal" phenotypes?

13 DNA STRUCTURE AND FUNCTION

Goodbye, Dolly

In 1997 in Scotland, geneticist Ian Wilmut made headlines when he did not bother with the union of sperm and eggs to produce a new lamb. He wanted to make a genetic copy —a **clone**—of a fully grown sheep. He thought he could do so by slipping the nucleus of an adult's body cell into an unfertilized egg that had its own nucleus gently sucked out beforehand. He succeeded. One egg that his team modified developed into a cloned lamb, which they named Dolly.

Dolly grew up and later gave birth to six lambs of her own (Figure 13.1). Since then, researchers all over the world have been using adult DNA to make identical copies of other adult mammals. Mice, rabbits, pigs, cattle, goats, mules, deer, horses, and cats have all been cloned.

Sheep normally do not show symptoms of old age until they are about ten years old. By age five, Dolly had become arthritic and overweight. Less than a year later, an infection in her lungs proved irreversible and she was put to sleep.

Did Dolly develop health problems simply because she was a clone? Earlier studies of her telomeres had raised suspicions. Telomeres are short segments that cap the ends of chromosomes and stabilize them. They become shorter and shorter as an animal ages. When Dolly was only two years old, telomeres in some of her cells were as short as those of a six-year-old sheep—the exact age of the adult animal that was her genetic donor.

Using adult DNA to clone mammals is challenging. Most clones die before birth or shortly afterward. It took almost seven hundred attempts to get a clone of a guar, a wild ox on the endangered species list. Less than two days after his birth, he died of complications following an infection.

The clones that do survive often have health problems. Like Dolly, many become unusually overweight as they age. Other clones are exceptionally large from birth or have some enlarged organs. Cloned mice develop lung and liver problems, and almost all die prematurely. Cloned pigs have heart problems, they limp, and one never did develop a tail or, worse still, an anus.

Physically moving the DNA from an adult's cell into an egg stripped of its own nucleus is only part of the challenge. Most genes in a mature cell are inactive. To guide the reproductive process, they have to be reprogrammed or switched on in controlled ways. Apparently, not all of the genes in all clones are being properly activated.

Some people want to put a stop to adult cloning because the risk of bringing defective mammals into the world troubles them deeply. Other people want research into reprogramming DNA to continue. For instance, they point to patients who are desperate for organ transplants. People are already cloning pigs that were genetically modified to produce organs that human donors are less likely to reject. A few people on the fringes of bioethical common sense are toying with the idea of reprogramming DNA to clone an adult human.

Is DNA amazing? It certainly is. Are we amazing in our capacity to use and abuse its potential? You bet.

Figure 13.1 Dolly and one of her lambs. Dolly was the first mammal to be formed by way of adult DNA cloning. She awakened society to the goings-on of the molecular revolution by jarring our notions of what it takes to reproduce a complex animal.

Watch the video online!

IMPACTS, ISSUES

Figure 13.2 Watson, Crick, and the model for DNA that brought about a revolution in molecular biology.

With this chapter, we move past the chromosomal basis of inheritance and turn to the investigations and models that led to our current understanding of DNA (Figure 13.2). The story is more than a march through the details of how its molecular structure encodes hereditary information. *It also is revealing of how ideas are generated in science.*

On the one hand, having a shot at fame and fortune quickens the pulse of men and women in any profession, and scientists are no exception. On the other hand, science proceeds as a community effort, with individuals sharing not only what they can explain but also what they do not understand. Even when an experiment fails to produce the anticipated results, it may turn up information that others can use or lead to questions that others can answer. Unexpected results, too, might be clues to something important about the natural world.

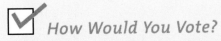

How Would You Vote?

Abnormal animals often form during animal cloning experiments, but cloning research may also result in new drugs and organ replacements for human patients. Should animal cloning be banned? See BiologyNow for details, then vote online.

Key Concepts

DISCOVERY OF DNA'S FUNCTION

In all living cells, DNA molecules are storehouses of information that governs heritable traits. Section 13.1

THE DNA DOUBLE HELIX

DNA is a double-stranded molecule consisting of four kinds of nucleotides: adenine, thymine, guanine, and cytosine. The two strands coil together helically, like a spiral stairway.

Each nucleotide base of one strand is hydrogen-bonded to a base of the other strand. As a rule, adenine pairs with thymine, and guanine with cytosine.

The order in which one kind of base follows the next in a strand encodes heritable information. The DNA of each species has at least some unique base sequences that are not found in the DNA of any other species. Section 13.2

HOW CELLS DUPLICATE THEIR DNA

Before a cell divides, enzymes and other proteins replicate the DNA; they make a copy of it. Different kinds unwind the double helix and construct a new, complementary strand on the exposed bases of each parent strand. They do so according to the base-pairing rule for DNA.

Repair enzymes monitor mismatched base pairings and other changes in the DNA strands. Section 13.3

DNA AND THE CLONING CONTROVERSIES

What does it mean when we say that DNA holds heritable information? The answer hits home when the messages encoded in its base sequences are tapped to make an exact copy of an adult animal. Section 13.4

THE FRANKLIN FOOTNOTE

As in any profession, some were winners and some losers in the DNA chase. Some players might have taken less-than-noble shortcuts. Section 13.5

Links to Earlier Concepts

This chapter builds on your understanding of hydrogen bonding (Section 2.4), condensation reactions (3.2), and the earlier overview of DNA structure and function (3.7). Your knowledge of chromosomes, mitosis, and meiosis will help you understand the nuclear transfers that are part of cloning procedures (9.3, 10.3). Keep the image of the eight-cell stage of human development in mind when you read about embryo cloning, because the cells used are no more developed than this (12.11).

13.1 The Hunt for Fame, Fortune, and DNA

*Why, in the spring of 1868, was Johann Miescher collecting cells from the pus of open wounds and, later, from sperm of a fish? This physician wanted to identify the chemical composition of the nucleus. Such cells have little cytoplasm, which makes it easier to isolate the nuclear material. In time he isolated an acidic compound that contains nitrogen and phosphorus. He had discovered what came to be known many years later as **deoxyribonucleic acid**, or **DNA**.*

EARLY AND PUZZLING CLUES

At the time Miescher made his discovery, no one knew much about the physical basis of inheritance. That is, *which substance encodes the information about reproducing parental traits in offspring?* Few researchers thought that DNA might hold the answer. For a long time, most were thinking PROTEINS! Because heritable traits are so diverse, they assumed that molecules of inheritance had to be structurally diverse, too. Proteins, they said, consist of unlimited combinations of twenty kinds of amino acids. Other molecules just seemed too simple.

Now fast-forward to 1928. An army medical officer, Frederick Griffith, wanted to develop a vaccine against the bacterium *Streptococcus pneumoniae*, a major cause of pneumonia. He did not succeed, but he isolated and cultured two strains that unexpectedly shed light on inheritance. The colonies of one strain had a rough surface appearance; colonies of the other appeared smooth. Griffith designated the strains *R* and *S*, and he used them in a series of experiments (Figure 13.3).

First, he injected mice with live *R* cells. The mice did not develop pneumonia. *The R strain was harmless.*

Second, he injected other mice with live *S* cells. The mice died. Blood samples from them teemed with live *S* cells. *The S strain was pathogenic; it caused the disease.*

Third, he killed *S* cells by exposing them to high temperature. *Mice injected with dead S cells did not die.*

Fourth, he mixed live *R* cells with heat-killed *S* cells. He injected them into mice. The mice died—*and blood samples drawn from them teemed with live S cells!*

What went on in the fourth experiment? Maybe heat-killed *S* cells in the mix were not really dead. But if that were so, then the mice injected with heat-killed *S* cells in experiment 3 would have died. Or maybe the harmless *R* cells had mutated into a killer strain. But if that were so, then the mice injected with the *R* cells only in experiment 1 would have died.

The simplest explanation was this: *Heat had killed the S cells but did not destroy their hereditary material—including the part that specified "how to cause infection."* Somehow, that material had been transferred from the dead *S* cells into living *R* cells, which put it to use.

Further tests made it clear that the transformation was permanently heritable. Even after a few hundred generations, *S* cell descendants were still infectious.

What was the hereditary material that caused the transformation? Scientists started looking in earnest, but most were still thinking PROTEINS!

Still, Griffith's results intrigued Oswald Avery, who began to transform harmless bacteria by mixing them with extracts of killed pathogenic cells. Avery asked: What part of the extracts caused the transformation? He found that adding protein-digesting enzymes to the extracts had no effect; cells were still transformed. However, adding a DNA-digesting enzyme to extracts prevented transformation. DNA was looking good.

CONFIRMATION OF DNA FUNCTION

By the 1950s, Max Delbrück, Alfred Hershey, Martha Chase, Salvador Luria, and other molecular sleuths were using viruses for experiments. These infectious particles hold information on substances required to make new virus particles. After viruses infect a host cell, their enzymes trick its metabolic machinery into synthesizing those substances. **Bacteriophages**, which only infect certain bacteria, were the viruses of choice for the early experiments.

As researchers knew, some bacteriophages consist only of DNA and a coat, probably of protein. Also, as

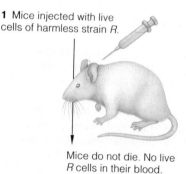

Figure 13.3
Animated!
Summary of results from Fred Griffith's experiments with *Streptococcus pneumoniae* and laboratory mice.

1 Mice injected with live cells of harmless strain *R*.

Mice do not die. No live *R* cells in their blood.

2 Mice injected with live cells of killer strain *S*.

Mice die. Live *S* cells in their blood.

3 Mice injected with heat-killed *S* cells.

Mice do not die. No live *S* cells in their blood.

4 Mice injected with live *R* cells *plus* heat-killed *S* cells.

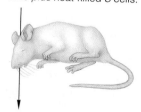

Mice die. Live *S* cells in their blood.

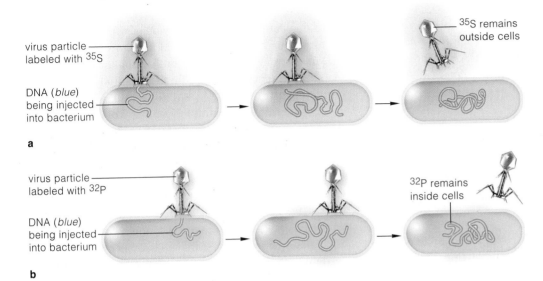

virus particle labeled with 35S

DNA (*blue*) being injected into bacterium

35S remains outside cells

a

virus particle labeled with 32P

DNA (*blue*) being injected into bacterium

32P remains inside cells

b

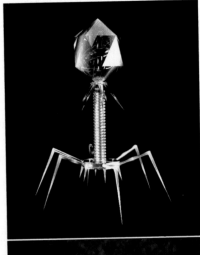

Figure 13.4 *Animated!* Example of the landmark experiments that tested whether genetic material resides in bacteriophage DNA, proteins, or both. Alfred Hershey and Martha Chase knew that sulfur (S) but not phosphorus (P) is a component of bacteriophage proteins. They also knew that phosphorus but not sulfur is a component of DNA.

(**a**) In one experiment, bacteria were grown in a culture medium with a tracer, the radioisotope 35S. The cells used the 35S when they built proteins. Bacteriophages infected the labeled cells, which started to make viral proteins. So the proteins of new virus particles became labeled with the 35S. The labeled virus particles infected a new batch of unlabeled cells. The mixture was whirred in a kitchen blender. Whirring dislodged the viral coats from infected cells. Chemical analysis revealed the presence of labeled protein in the solution but only traces of it inside the cells.

(**b**) In another experiment, bacteriophages infected cells that had taken up the radioisotope 32P. Later, the cells used 32P when they built viral DNA. This labeled the DNA and new virus particles. The labeled viruses were used to infect bacteria in solution, then were dislodged from them. Most labeled viral DNA stayed in the cells—evidence that DNA is the genetic material of this virus.

c *Above*, model for a bacteriophage. *Below*, micrograph of virus particles injecting their DNA into an *E. coli* cell.

micrographs revealed, the coat remains on the *outer surface* of infected cells. Did viruses inject hereditary material only into cells? If so, then was the material protein, DNA, or both? Figure 13.4 outlines just two of many experiments that pointed to DNA.

Then Linus Pauling did something no one had done before. With his training in biochemistry, a talent for model building, and a dose of intuition, he deduced the structure of a protein—collagen. His discovery was electrifying. If someone could pry open the secrets of proteins, then why not DNA? And if DNA's structural details were deduced, would those details hold clues to how DNA functions in inheritance? *Someone could go down in history as having discovered the secret of life!*

ENTER WATSON AND CRICK

Scientists started to scramble after the prize. Among them were Francis H. Crick, a Cambridge University researcher, and James Watson, a postdoctoral fellow recently arrived from Indiana University. They spent

hours arguing over everything they had read about DNA's size, shape, and bonding requirements. They fiddled with cardboard cutouts, and they badgered chemists to help them identify possible bonds they might have overlooked. They built models from thin bits of metal connected with wire "bonds."

In 1953, Watson and Crick built a model that fit all the pertinent biochemical rules and all the clues they had gleaned from other sources. They had discovered the structure of DNA. The molecule has breathtaking simplicity, and it helped Crick answer another riddle —*how life can show unity at the molecular level and still give rise to such spectacular diversity at the level of whole organisms.* Turn now to high points in the community effort that gave us these insights.

DNA functions as the cell's treasurehouse of inheritance. The cumulative efforts of many scientists, building on one another's work, resulted in the discovery of that function.

13.2 The Discovery of DNA's Structure

LINKS TO
SECTIONS
3.2, 3.7

Long before the bacteriophage studies were under way, biochemists knew that DNA contains only four kinds of nucleotides that are the building blocks of nucleic acids. But how were the nucleotides arranged in DNA?

DNA'S BUILDING BLOCKS

Recall, from Section 3.7, that a **nucleotide** in DNA has a five-carbon sugar (deoxyribose), a phosphate group, and one of the following nitrogen-containing bases:

adenine	guanine	thymine	cytosine
A	G	T	C

T and C are pyrimidines, with a backbone of carbon and nitrogen that forms a single ring. A and G are purines—larger, bulkier molecules having two rings. Overall, the four types of nucleotides have the same bonding pattern, as Figure 13.5 indicates.

By 1949, the biochemist Erwin Chargaff had shared with the scientific community two insights about the proportions of nucleotides in DNA. First, the amount of adenine relative to guanine differs among species. Second, the amounts of thymine and adenine in DNA are identical, and so are the amounts of cytosine and guanine. We may show this as A=T and G=C.

These symmetrical proportions had to mean something. As biochemists already knew, the nucleotides in DNA are joined to one another by way of condensation reactions that form long chains (Section 3.2). But how were the four kinds arranged in a chain, and in what order?

The first convincing clue to the actual arrangement emerged from Maurice Wilkins's research laboratory at Cambridge, England. Researcher Rosalind Franklin made exceptional **x-ray diffraction images** of DNA. Such images form after a beam of x-rays is directed at a molecule, which scatters the x-rays in a pattern that can be captured on film. The pattern consists only of dots and streaks; in itself, it is not the structure of the molecule. However, researchers can use it to calculate the positions of the molecule's atoms.

Before Franklin, researchers had been working with dehydrated DNA molecules. Franklin was the first to put DNA into a "wet" form—which is the form that occurs in cells—and make an exceptionally clear image of it. With that image, she painstakingly calculated that the DNA molecule is long and thin, and that it has a 2-nanometer diameter. She also found repeats of some molecular configuration every 0.34 nanometer along its length, and another repeat every 3.4 nanometers. These were crucial clues, but her part in the discovery process was downplayed until recently (Section 13.5).

What did the repeating variation in DNA mean? Could DNA be coiled along its length, like a circular stairway? Certainly Pauling thought so. After all, he had calculated that collagen is helically coiled. Like

nitrogen-containing
base

A *nucleoside* is one nitrogenous base plus one sugar

A *nucleotide* is one nucleoside plus one or more phosphate groups

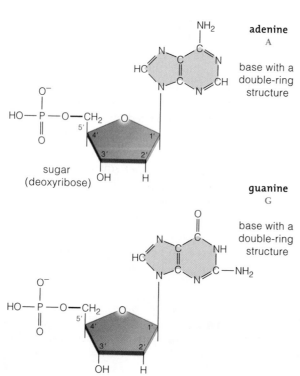

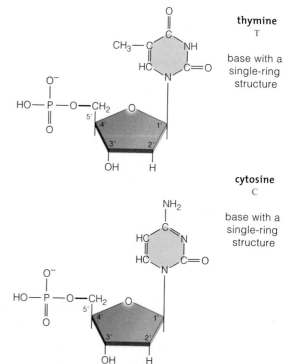

adenine
A

base with a
double-ring
structure

thymine
T

base with a
single-ring
structure

sugar
(deoxyribose)

guanine
G

base with a
double-ring
structure

cytosine
C

base with a
single-ring
structure

Figure 13.5 Four kinds of nucleotides in the DNA molecule.

many others—including Wilkins, Watson, and Crick—he was thinking "helix." As Watson later wrote, "We thought, why not try it on DNA? We were worried that *Pauling* would say, why not try it on DNA? Certainly he was a clever man. He was a hero of mine. But we beat him at his own game. I still can't figure out why."

Pauling, it turned out, made a big chemical mistake. His model had all the negatively charged phosphate groups facing the interior of the DNA helix instead of facing outward. If they were that close together, they would repel each other too much to remain stable.

PATTERNS OF BASE PAIRING

Franklin filed away her image of wet DNA, but it still came to the attention of Watson and Crick. From all the clues that had accumulated, they perceived that DNA must consist of two strands of nucleotides, held together at their bases by hydrogen bonds (Figure 13.6). Such bonds form when the two strands run in opposing directions and twist to form a double helix. Only two kinds of base pairings typically form along the molecule's length: A—T and G—C.

This bonding pattern accommodates variation in the order of bases. For instance, a stretch of DNA from a rose, a human, or any other organism might be:

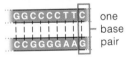
one base pair

or

All DNA molecules show the same bonding pattern. Many stretches of base sequences are the same in all of them. But some are unique for each species and even vary among individuals of a species! *The constancy in DNA's bonding pattern is the basis for life's unity—and variation in base sequences is the basis for life's diversity.*

Intriguingly, computer simulations show that if you want to pack a string into the least space, coil it into a helix. Was this space-saving advantage a factor in the molecular origin of the DNA double helix? Maybe.

The pattern of base pairing between the two strands in DNA is constant for all species—A with T, and G with C. However, each species has a number of unique sequences of base pairs along the length of its DNA molecules.

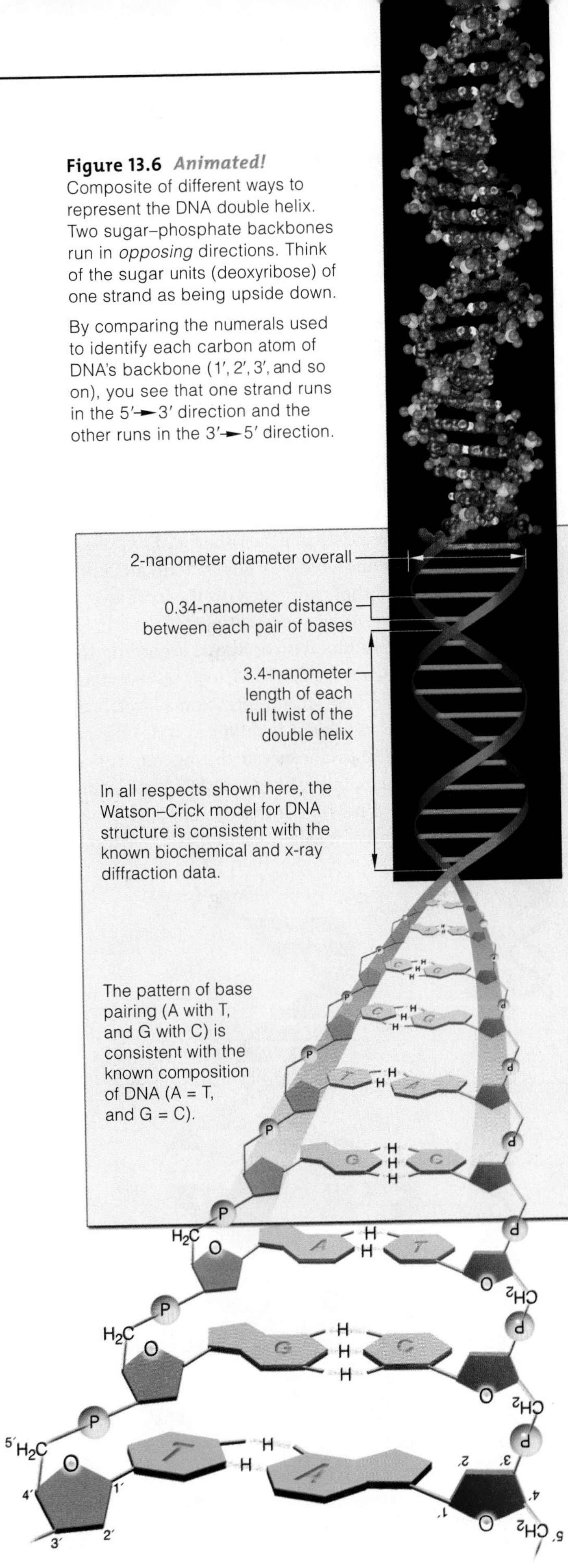

Figure 13.6 *Animated!*
Composite of different ways to represent the DNA double helix. Two sugar–phosphate backbones run in *opposing* directions. Think of the sugar units (deoxyribose) of one strand as being upside down.

By comparing the numerals used to identify each carbon atom of DNA's backbone (1′, 2′, 3′, and so on), you see that one strand runs in the 5′→3′ direction and the other runs in the 3′→5′ direction.

2-nanometer diameter overall

0.34-nanometer distance between each pair of bases

3.4-nanometer length of each full twist of the double helix

In all respects shown here, the Watson–Crick model for DNA structure is consistent with the known biochemical and x-ray diffraction data.

The pattern of base pairing (A with T, and G with C) is consistent with the known composition of DNA (A = T, and G = C).

13.3 DNA Replication and Repair

LINKS TO
SECTIONS
9.2, 9.5, 12.8

The discovery of DNA structure was a turning point in the studies of inheritance. Crick saw at once how a parent cell could make copies of that molecule for its daughter cells.

HOW DNA IS DUPLICATED

Semiconservative Replication Until Watson and Crick presented their model, no one could explain **DNA replication**, or how the molecule of inheritance is duplicated before a cell divides. Such replication takes place in interphase of the cell cycle.

Enzymes easily break the hydrogen bonds between the two nucleotide strands of a DNA molecule. When enzymes and other proteins act on the molecule, one strand unwinds from the other and exposes stretches of its nucleotide bases. Cells contain stockpiles of free nucleotides that can pair with the exposed bases.

Each parent strand stays intact, and a companion strand is assembled on each one according to the base-pairing rules **A** to **T**, and **G** to **C**. As soon as a stretch of a new, partner strand forms on a stretch of a parent strand, the two twist together in a double helix. Each parent strand is conserved during replication, so that half of every double-stranded DNA molecule is "old" and half is "new." Figures 13.7 and 13.8 offer a look into this process, called *semiconservative* replication.

Replication Enzymes DNA replication uses a team of molecular workers; Table 13.1 lists important ones. Signaling molecules that are part of the controls over the cell cycle activate replication enzymes. Starting at certain regions along the length of the DNA double helix, enzymes called **helicases** unzip the hydrogen bonds, which are individually weak and easy to break (Section 2.4). The two strands of the double helix now unwind from each other in both directions from the unzipped sites. The two parent strands are prevented from winding back together because small proteins temporarily bind with them.

Next, **DNA polymerases** catalyze the formation of two brand-new strands of DNA from free nucleotides. These enzymes also catalyze the hydrogen bonding of each new strand to the unwound region of one of the two parent DNA strands. But they can assemble new strands only in the $5' \rightarrow 3'$ direction.

Check out Figure 13.5 to see what this directional strand assembly means. A free nucleotide has a tail of three phosphate groups dangling from the 5' carbon of their sugar component. DNA polymerase splits off two. The energy released drives the attachment of the last phosphate to an —OH group dangling from the 3' carbon of a sugar—which belongs to the most recent nucleotide addition to the growing strand.

What about the parent strand that runs the other way? Nucleotides are assembled in short stretches on the parent strand, then **DNA ligases** seal the stretches

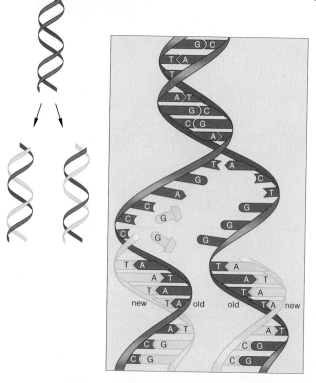

Figure 13.7 The semiconservative nature of DNA replication. The original two-stranded DNA molecule is coded *blue*. Each parent strand remains intact. One new strand (*gold*) is assembled on each of the parent strands.

Table 13.1 Three of the Enzymes With Roles in DNA Replication and Repair
Helicases
Catalyze the breaking of hydrogen bonds between base pairs in the DNA molecule, which unzips in two directions from double-stranded to single-stranded form. Protein factors work with helicases to keep the two parent strands unwound. The helicases are ATP-driven motors, similar to ATP synthases.
DNA polymerases
Catalyze the additions of free nucleotides to each new strand of deoxyribonucleases on a parent DNA template. Also proofread; some DNA polymerases can reverse direction by one base pair and correct mismatches, which occur once in every thousand or so additions.
DNA ligases
Catalyze the sealing-together of short stretches of new nucleotides, which are assembled discontinuously on one of the parent DNA strands. Also can seal strand breaks.

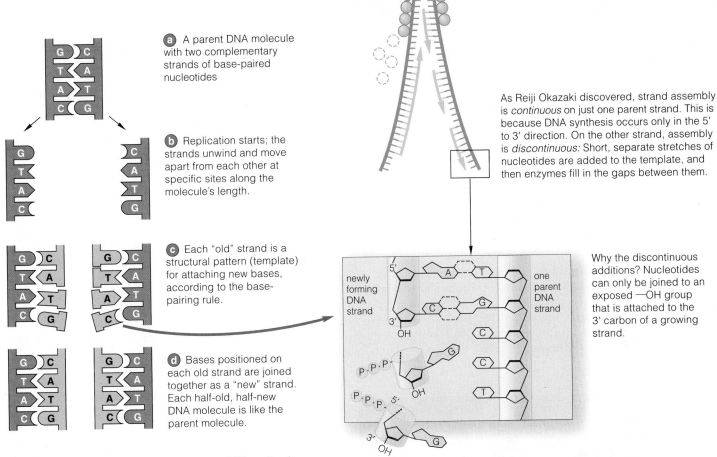

a A parent DNA molecule with two complementary strands of base-paired nucleotides

b Replication starts; the strands unwind and move apart from each other at specific sites along the molecule's length.

c Each "old" strand is a structural pattern (template) for attaching new bases, according to the base-pairing rule.

d Bases positioned on each old strand are joined together as a "new" strand. Each half-old, half-new DNA molecule is like the parent molecule.

As Reiji Okazaki discovered, strand assembly is *continuous* on just one parent strand. This is because DNA synthesis occurs only in the 5' to 3' direction. On the other strand, assembly is *discontinuous*: Short, separate stretches of nucleotides are added to the template, and then enzymes fill in the gaps between them.

Why the discontinuous additions? Nucleotides can only be joined to an exposed —OH group that is attached to the 3' carbon of a growing strand.

Figure 13.8 *Animated!* A closer look at DNA replication.

together into a continuous strand. A complementary strand now winds up with the parent strand that was its template. Two DNA double helixes are the result.

As you will read in Chapter 16, DNA polymerases and DNA ligases also have been put to good use as tools in recombinant DNA technology.

FIXING MISMATCHES AND BREAKS

Over the long term, changes in chromosomal DNA can give rise to variations in traits that help define a species (Section 12.8). However, in terms of a lifetime, the individual may not survive if something changes its DNA. For instance, on rare occasions, the wrong nucleotide is base-paired to a parent template (Table 13.1). Unless such mistakes are reversed, they might alter or weaken the functions of genes or the protein products. Chapter 12 has a number of examples of the kinds of genetic disorders that can follow changes.

DNA proofreading mechanisms swiftly fix most errors in replication and most of the strand breaks. For example, some DNA polymerases proofread new base pairings. They can reverse catalytic additions by one base and correct a mismatch. When they cannot,

replication is arrested, and controls over the cell cycle come into play (Sections 9.2 and 9.5).

Mismatches that slip past the proofreaders are only one type of DNA damage. One or both backbones of the double helix may break, as by ionizing radiation and some chemicals (Section 14.5). Also, a base in one strand may become covalently bonded to a base in the same strand or the partner strand.

Specialized sets of **repair enzymes** can repair some changes; they recognize and snip out a damaged site or mismatches. For instance, some glycosylases excise a mismatched base and replace it with a suitable one in a tiny burst of DNA synthesis.

DNA is replicated prior to cell division. At certain sites, helicases unzip hydrogen bonds between its two strands, so the double helix unwinds. Each strand remains intact —it is conserved—and DNA polymerases assemble a new, complementary strand on each parent strand.

DNA proofreading mechanisms and special sets of repair enzymes fix nearly all mismatched base pairs. Different kinds also seal or bypass most breaks.

13.4 Using DNA To Duplicate Existing Mammals

LINKS TO SECTIONS
9.3, 10.2, 12.11

Here we return to a topic introduced at the start of this chapter. Researchers can now isolate DNA from an adult mammal and use it to bypass meiosis, gamete formation, and fertilization. Unlike sexual reproduction, which gives rise to mixes of traits from two parents, adult DNA cloning produces an exact genetic copy of a single adult.

"Cloning" can be a confusing word. It can apply to a method in recombinant DNA technology that makes multiple copies of DNA fragments. It also applies to natural and manipulated interventions in the steps of reproduction and development. These interventions are called embryo cloning, adult cloning, and therapeutic cloning (Table 13.2).

Embryo Cloning   Embryo cloning occurs all the time in nature. For instance, soon after fertilized human eggs start dividing, a tiny ball of cells has formed. You saw one of these early developmental stages in Section 12.11. Once in every seventy-five or so pregnancies, the ball splits, and the two parts grow and develop into identical twins. A laboratory

procedure, "artificial twinning," simply simulates what goes on in nature. For instance, the balls of cells grown from fertilized cattle eggs in petri dishes are encouraged to split into identical-twin embryos. Then they are implanted in surrogate mothers, which give birth to cloned calves.

Embryo cloning has been practiced for decades. However, embryo clones inherit DNA from two parents, not one. If breeders are looking for a particularly valued trait, such as better milk production or mating vigor, they have to wait for clones to grow up to see if they display the trait.

Adult Cloning   Because it takes so long to observe the outcome, some researchers were looking for an alternative to embryo cloning of cattle and other complex animals. It seemed that cloning a differentiated cell would be far more efficient, because the desired phenotype was already there, right in front of them.

You may wonder what "differentiated" means. As you already know after reading about mitosis and meiosis, all cells descended from a fertilized egg inherit the same chromosomal DNA (Sections 9.3 and 10.2). However, as the new embryo develops, different cells inside it start to select and use DNA's information in different ways. Their selections commit them to becoming liver cells,

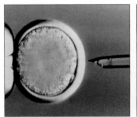 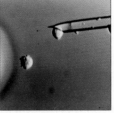 

1 A microneedle is about to remove the nucleus from an unfertilized sheep egg (*center*).

2 The microneedle has now emptied the sheep egg of its own nucleus, which held the DNA.

3 A nucleus from a donor cell (in the microneedle) is about to be deposited in the egg that was stripped of its nucleus.

4 An electric current will stimulate the egg to enter mitotic cell division. After a few rounds of divisions, the ball of cells will be implanted in the womb of a female sheep (ewe).

the first sheep cloned from adult DNA

Figure 13.9 *Animated!*   Transfer of an adult nucleus that led to Dolly.

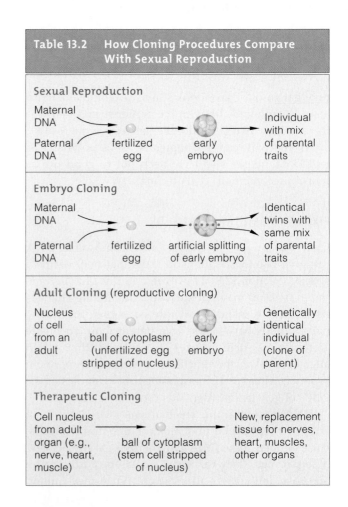

Table 13.2	How Cloning Procedures Compare With Sexual Reproduction

Sexual Reproduction

Maternal DNA + Paternal DNA → fertilized egg → early embryo → Individual with mix of parental traits

Embryo Cloning

Maternal DNA + Paternal DNA → fertilized egg → artificial splitting of early embryo → Identical twins with same mix of parental traits

Adult Cloning (reproductive cloning)

Nucleus of cell from an adult + ball of cytoplasm (unfertilized egg stripped of nucleus) → early embryo → Genetically identical individual (clone of parent)

Therapeutic Cloning

Cell nucleus from adult organ (e.g., nerve, heart, muscle) + ball of cytoplasm (stem cell stripped of nucleus) → New, replacement tissue for nerves, heart, muscles, other organs

Figure 13.10 *Left*, DNA donor Tahini, a Bengal cat. *Right*, Tabouli and Baba Ganoush, two of her clones. Eye color changes as a Bengal cat matures; in both clones, it will in time be the same as Tahini's. All three are household pets of the founder of a pet cloning company that, precisely because of its success, is at the center of a cloning controversy.

blood cells, or other specialists in structure, composition, and function in the adult. The mechanisms by which this happens are topics of later chapters.

With respect to adult cloning, a "grown-up" cell—one already differentiated—must be tricked into rewinding the developmental clock. Each of its descendants will have to start using a different subset of its DNA all over again to form a clone of its original owner.

Nuclear transfer is one way to trick a differentiated cell. A researcher with a good microscope and a very steady hand replaces the nucleus of an unfertilized egg with one from a differentiated cell of an adult animal, as in Figure 13.9. Small doses of chemicals or electric shocks may induce the cell to divide. If all goes well, then a cluster of embryonic cells forms and can be implanted inside a surrogate mother. In Dolly's case, the donor nucleus came from a cell from the lining of a sheep's udder.

A recipient egg is not always tricked into using the DNA as it is supposed to. For example, researchers studied many genes in the first cloned mice and found that 4 percent or so were being abnormally expressed. The cloning procedure had disrupted when and how mouse cells were supposed to use their genes. Even so, researchers around the world are becoming better at rewinding the developmental clock.

For instance, Genetic Savings and Clone is a company that uses adult DNA to clone beloved pet cats that are old and dying. So far, the pet owners who have requested the procedure report that their clones are healthy, lively, and uncannily like the DNA donor, not only in appearance but also in behavior. Figure 13.10 shows an example. Compare the markings on the top of the head, the face, the legs, and the tail of the donor and of the two clones.

Some people are deeply offended by the idea of spending tens of thousands of dollars to clone a cat when so many lost or orphaned cats are awaiting adoption in animal shelters. Some owners say that they have bonded deeply with their particular pet, that they would grieve mightily over its loss, and that it is, after all, their money.

The real issue, of course, is that *humans*—like cats, mice, and pigs—are mammals. Not very long ago, mammalian cloning was fraught with technical problems. It still is. As researchers get better at what they do, however, the use of adult DNA cloning to make a genetic copy of a human no longer seems in the realm of science fiction. That is why most countries recently banned the use of federal funding for any research into adult human cloning.

Therapeutic Cloning   *Therapeutic* cloning also uses nuclear transfers. In this case, the idea is to transplant DNA of a somatic cell from the heart, liver, muscles, or nerves into a stem cell. A *stem cell*, recall, is one that has not yet differentiated and retains the capacity to divide (Section 12.2). The descendant cells go on to differentiate into cell types of specific tissues and organs. The process is known as *somatic cell nuclear transfer* (SCNT).

SCNT already has produced stem cells that are an exact genetic match to an individual. This is not reproduction; no sperm are used. However, descendants of the modified cells may be able to regenerate a tissue for transplant back into a patient affected by an incurable disease or a spinal cord injury. Potentially, SCNT could regenerate organs. There are long waiting lists for organ transplants, and those who receive them have to take drugs to suppress the immune system for the rest of their lives.

We will return to some of these issues later on, after you learn more about the molecular basis of life. Make your own informed decisions about them, and remember this: For better or worse, our capacity to manipulate DNA started with Watson, Crick, and so many others who shared knowledge that became the underpinnings of a brave new world.

13.5 Rosalind's Story

FOCUS ON BIOETHICS

There is a saying among researchers in any discipline— publish or perish. As soon as Watson and Crick's structural model of DNA fell into place, they immediately published a one-page paper that dazzled the world. All others who had helped fill in crucial pieces of the puzzle, including Franklin, received little or no recognition. Franklin's contribution is now receiving more attention.

Rosalind Franklin arrived at King's Laboratory in London with impressive credentials (Figure 13.11). She developed a refined x-ray diffraction method while studying the structure of coal in Paris. She took a new mathematical approach to interpreting x-ray diffraction images and, like Pauling, had built three-dimensional molecular models. Now she was asked to create and run a state-of-the-art x-ray crystallography laboratory. Her assignment was to investigate the structure of DNA.

No one bothered to tell Franklin that, just down the hall, Maurice Wilkins was already working on the puzzle. Even a graduate student assigned to assist her failed to mention it. No one bothered to tell Wilkins about Franklin's assignment; he assumed that she was a technician hired to do his x-ray crystallography work because he didn't know how to do it himself. And so a clash began. To Franklin, Wilkins seemed inexplicably prickly. To Wilkins, Franklin was appalling in her lack of deference to him.

Wilkins had a prized cache of DNA, which he gave to his "technician." Five months later, Franklin gave a talk on what she had learned so far. DNA, she said, may have two, three, or four parallel chains twisted into a helix, with phosphate groups projecting outward.

With his crystallography background, Crick would have recognized the significance of her report—*if* he had been there. (A *pair* of chains oriented in opposing directions would be the same even if flipped 180 degrees. Two pairs of chains? No. DNA's density ruled that out. But one pair of chains? Yes!) Watson was in the audience but did not know what Franklin was talking about.

Later on, Franklin produced her superb x-ray diffraction image of wet DNA fibers (Figure 13.12). The image fairly screamed *HELIX!* Franklin also worked out the length and the diameter of DNA. However, she had been working with dry fibers for a long time, and she chose not to dwell on the meaning of her new data. Wilkins did.

In 1953, without Franklin's knowledge, he let Watson see that image and reminded him of what she had reported more than a year before. When Watson and Crick did focus on her data, they had the final bit of information that they needed to build a plausible model of DNA— one with two helically twisted chains running in opposing directions.

Figure 13.11 Portrait of Rosalind Franklin arriving at Cambridge in style, from Paris.

Figure 13.12 Franklin's best x-ray diffraction image of DNA fibers.

Summary

Section 13.1 Experimental tests that used bacteria and bacteriophages offered the first solid evidence that DNA is the hereditary material in living organisms.

Biology Now
Learn about experiments that revealed the function of DNA with the animation on BiologyNow.

Section 13.2 The nucleotide monomers of DNA have a five-carbon sugar (deoxyribose), a phosphate group, and one of four kinds of nitrogen-containing bases: adenine, thymine, guanine, or cytosine.

A DNA molecule consists of two nucleotide strands coiled together into a double helix. The bases of one strand hydrogen-bond with bases of the other.

Bases of the two DNA strands pair in a constant way. Adenine pairs with thymine (A–T), and guanine with cytosine (G–C). Which base follows another along a strand varies among species. The DNA of each species incorporates some number of unique sequences of base pairs that set it apart from the DNA of all other species.

Biology Now
Investigate the structure of DNA with the animation on BiologyNow.

Section 13.3 In DNA replication, enzymes called helicases unwind the DNA double helix, and small proteins hold the two strands apart. DNA polymerases covalently bond free nucleotides into chains in a base sequence complementary to the parent strand that serves as its template. Two double-stranded DNA molecules result. One strand of each is old (is conserved); the other strand is new.

Strand assembly occurs only at an exposed —OH group at the 3' end of a growing nucleotide strand. DNA ligases seal tiny gaps between short stretches of nucleotides in one of the growing strands.

Proofreading mechanisms fix most base-pairing mistakes and strand breaks. Special repair enzymes recognize and snip out damaged sites in the DNA as well as mismatches.

Biology Now
See how a DNA molecule is replicated with the animation on BiologyNow.

Section 13.4 "Cloning" means copying fragments of DNA in recombinant DNA work. It also refers to three other procedures: Embryo cloning results in genetically identical twins. Adult cloning results in a genetically identical copy of an existing adult. Therapeutic cloning is a proposed method of producing stem cells that are an exact genetic match of a patient, the idea being to regenerate tissues and possibly organs.

Biology Now
Observe the procedure used to create Dolly and other clones with animation on BiologyNow.

Section 13.5 Science advances as a community effort that is both cooperative and competitive. Ideally, individuals share their work and recognition for honors that come their way. As in all human endeavors, some fail to receive suitable recognition for their contribution.

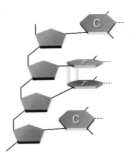

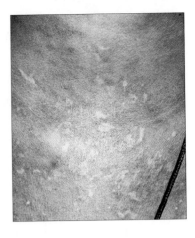

Figure 13.13 *Above,* a thymine dimer in a DNA strand. It can lead to xeroderma pigmentosum (*right*), a genetic disorder.

Self-Quiz

Answers in Appendix II

1. Which is *not* a nucleotide base in DNA?
   a. adenine   c. uracil   e. cytosine
   b. guanine   d. thymine   f. All are in DNA.

2. What are the base-pairing rules for DNA?
   a. A–G, T–C   c. A–U, C–G
   b. A–C, T–G   d. A–T, G–C

3. One species' DNA differs from others in its _____ .
   a. sugars   c. base sequence
   b. phosphates   d. all of the above

4. When DNA replication begins, _____ .
   a. the two DNA strands unwind from each other
   b. the two DNA strands condense for base transfers
   c. two DNA molecules bond
   d. old strands move to find new strands

5. DNA replication requires _____ .
   a. free nucleotides   c. many enzymes
   b. new hydrogen bonds   d. all of the above

6. _____ is the basis for the life's diversity.
   a. constancy in DNA's   b. variation in the base
      bonding pattern   sequences in DNA

7. Adult cloning starts with _____ .
   a. an early embryo   c. artificial twinning
   b. nuclear transfers   d. both b and c

8. Match the terms appropriately.
   ____ bacteriophage   a. nitrogen-containing base
   ____ clone   bonded to a sugar and one
   ____ nucleotide   or more phosphate groups
   ____ helicase   b. breaks hydrogen bonds,
   ____ DNA ligase   starts unwinding of DNA
   ____ DNA polymerase   during replication
                         c. only DNA and protein
                         d. fills in gaps, seals breaks
                            in a DNA strand
                         e. carbon copy of dad or mom
                         f. adds nucleotides to a
                            growing DNA strand

Additional questions are available on Biology✑Now™

Critical Thinking

1. A pathogenic strain of *E. coli* has acquired an ability to produce a dangerous toxin that causes medical problems and fatalities. It is especially dangerous to young children who eat undercooked or raw contaminated beef. Develop hypotheses to explain how a normally harmless bacterium such as *E. coli* can become a pathogen.

2. Matthew Meselson and Franklin Stahl's experiments supported a semiconservative model of DNA replication. These researchers obtained "heavy" DNA by growing *Escherichia coli* in a medium enriched with ^{15}N, a nitrogen radioisotope. They prepared "light" DNA by growing *E. coli* in the presence of ^{14}N, the more common isotope. An available technique helped them identify which replicated molecules were heavy, light, or hybrid (one heavy strand and one light). Use pencils of two colors, one for heavy strands and one for light. Assuming a DNA molecule has two heavy strands, arrange pencils to show how daughter molecules form after replication in a medium with ^{14}N. Represent four DNA molecules that form if the daughter molecules are replicated in the ^{14}N medium.

3. If you are part of a biology class, split into groups. See which one writes up the clearest, most concise description of the component parts and organization of this molecule:

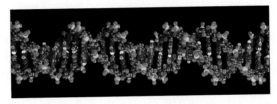

4. Mutations, remember, are permanent changes in DNA base sequences—the original source of genetic variation and the raw material of evolution. Yet how can mutations accumulate, given that cells have repair systems that fix changes or breaks in DNA strands?

5. In 1999, scientists discovered a woolly mammoth that had been frozen in glacial ice for the past 20,000 years. They thawed it very carefully so they could use its DNA to clone a woolly mammoth. It turns out there was not enough preserved material to work with. They plan to try again the next time a frozen woolly mammoth comes along. Reflect on Section 13.4, then speculate on the pros and cons of cloning an extinct animal.

6. *Xeroderma pigmentosum* (XP) is an autosomal recessive disorder that is characterized by the rapid formation of skin sores that can develop into cancers (Figure 13.13). Affected individuals have no mechanism for dealing with the damage that ultraviolet (UV) light can inflict on skin cells. They must avoid all forms of radiation—including sunlight and fluorescent lights.

Affected individuals do not have functioning DNA repair mechanisms. James Cleaver discovered this when he studied what happens in cells when DNA's nitrogen-containing bases absorb UV light. A covalent bond can form between two thymine bases in the same DNA strand. The resulting thymine dimer puts a kink in the strand. Propose what some of the consequences might be during interphase, when most proteins are synthesized, and then during DNA replication.

14 FROM DNA TO PROTEIN

Ricin and Your Ribosomes

In 2003, police acted on an intelligence tip and stormed a London apartment, where they found laboratory glassware and castor oil beans (Figure 14.1). They arrested a few young men and reminded the world that unconscionable people still view ricin as a bioweapon.

The castor oil plant (*Ricinus communis*) has ricin in all of its tissues, but its oil is valued as an ingredient in many plastics, paints, cosmetics, textiles, and adhesives. The oil —and ricin—is most concentrated in the seeds (beans), but the ricin is discarded when the oil is extracted.

A dose of ricin as small as a grain of salt can kill you; only plutonium and botulism toxin are more deadly. Researchers knew about ricin's lethal effects as long ago as 1888. During World War I, when deadly chlorine and mustard gases were wafting across battlefields, England and the United States investigated ricin's potential use as a weapon. Both countries shelved the research when the war ended.

Now fast-forward to 1969, at the height of the Cold War between Russia and the West. Georgi Markov, a Bulgarian writer, had defected to England. As he strolled down a busy London street, an assassin jammed the tip of a modified umbrella into one of Markov's legs. The tip held a tiny ball laced with ricin. Markov died in agony three days later.

Ricin is on stage once again. In 2004, traces were found in a United States Senate mailroom and State Department building, and in an envelope addressed to the White House. In 2005, the FBI arrested a man who had castor oil beans, substances consistent with ricin production, and an AK-47 stashed in a home in Florida.

How does ricin exert its deadly effects? *It inactivates ribosomes, the protein-building machinery of all cells.*

Ricin is a protein with two polypeptide chains. One chain helps ricin insert itself into cells. The other chain serves as an enzyme. Its catalytic action wrecks part of the ribosome where amino acids are assembled into proteins. It yanks adenine subunits out of an RNA molecule that is a crucial component of the ribosome's three-dimensional structure. Once that happens, the ribosome's shape unravels, protein synthesis stops, and cells spiral toward death. So does the individual. There is no antidote.

You can go about your business without ever knowing what a ribosome is or what it does. However, you also can recognize that protein synthesis is not a topic invented to torture biology students. It is something worth knowing about and appreciating for how it keeps us alive—and for appreciating anti-terrorism researchers who are working to keep us that way.

Watch the video online!

Figure 14.1 *Left*, castor oil plant seeds, source of the ribosome-busting ricin. *Right*, model for one of ricin's two polypeptide chains. This chain helps ricin penetrate living cells. The other one destroys the capacity for protein synthesis, and for life.

Start with what you already know about DNA, the book of protein-building information in cells. The alphabet used to write the book seems simple enough—just A, T, G, and C, for the four nucleotide bases adenine, thymine, guanine, and cytosine. But how do you get from an alphabet to a "word"— a protein? The answer starts with the order, or sequence, of the four nucleotide bases in a DNA molecule.

As you know, when a cell replicates its DNA, the two nucleotide strands of the DNA double helix unwind from each other completely. At other times, however, enzymes selectively unwind the two strands in certain regions, which exposes the base sequences of genes. Most genes encode information about specific proteins.

It takes two big steps, **transcription** and **translation**, to get from the sequence of nucleotide bases in genes to the sequence of amino acids in a protein. In eukaryotic cells, the first step occurs inside the nucleus. A newly exposed DNA base sequence functions as a structural pattern, or a template, for making a strand of ribonucleic acid (RNA) from the cell's pool of free ribonucleotides.

The RNA moves into the cytoplasm, where it becomes translated. In this second step of protein synthesis, the RNA guides the assembly of amino acids into a new polypeptide chain. These are the chains that twist and fold into the three-dimensional shapes of proteins.

In short, RNA is transcribed on DNA templates, then RNA is translated into proteins:

$$\text{DNA} \xrightarrow{\text{transcription}} \text{RNA} \xrightarrow{\text{translation}} \text{PROTEIN}$$

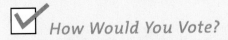

How Would You Vote?

Ricin is difficult to disperse through the air and is unlikely to be used in a large-scale terrorist attack. However, ricin powder did turn up in a Senate office building. Scientists are working to develop a vaccine against ricin. If mass immunizations were to be offered, would you sign up to be vaccinated? See BiologyNow for details, then vote online.

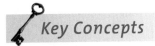

Key Concepts

INTRODUCTION

Life depends on enzymes and other proteins. All proteins consist of polypeptide chains. The chains are sequences of amino acids that correspond to genes—sequences of nucleotide bases in DNA. The path leading from genes to proteins has two steps: transcription and translation.

TRANSCRIPTION

During transcription, the two strands of the DNA double helix are unwound in a gene region. Exposed bases of one strand become the template for assembling a single strand of RNA. Only one type of RNA transcript encodes the message that gets translated into protein. It is called messenger RNA.   Section 14.1

CODE WORDS IN THE TRANSCRIPTS

The nucleotide sequence in DNA is read three bases at a time. Sixty-four base triplets correspond to specific amino acids and represent the genetic code.

The code words have been highly conserved through time. Only a few simple eukaryotes, prokaryotes, and prokaryote-derived organelles have slight variations on the genetic code.   Section 14.2

TRANSLATION

During translation, amino acids are bonded together into a polypeptide chain in a sequence specified by base triplets in messenger RNA. Transfer RNA delivers amino acids one at a time to ribosomes. An RNA component of ribosomes catalyzes the chain-building reaction.   Sections 14.3, 14.4

MUTATIONS IN THE CODE WORDS

Gene mutations introduce changes in protein structure, protein function, or both. The changes may lead to small or large variation in the shared traits that characterize individuals of a population.   Section 14.5

Links to Earlier Concepts

Once again you will meet up with the nucleic acids DNA and RNA (Section 3.7). Gene transcription has features in common with DNA replication, so you may wish to review Section 13.3 before you start. You will again consider how protein primary structure emerges (3.5), this time in the context of RNA interactions. The last section of this chapter will expand your knowledge of DNA repair mechanisms (13.3) and gene mutation (1.4, 3.6, 12.3, 12.8).

14.1 How Is RNA Transcribed From DNA?

LINKS TO
SECTIONS
3.7, 13.2, 13.3

*In **transcription**, the first step in protein synthesis, a sequence of nucleotide bases is exposed in an unwound region of a DNA strand. That sequence is the template upon which a single strand of RNA is assembled from adenine, cytosine, guanine, and uracil subunits.*

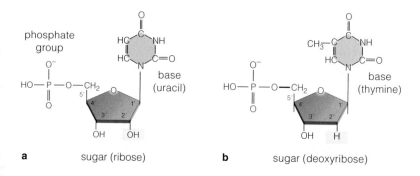

a sugar (ribose) **b** sugar (deoxyribose)

phosphate group

base (uracil)

base (thymine)

c Example of base pairing between a DNA strand and a new RNA strand assembled on it during *transcription*:

DNA template

RNA transcript

d Example of base pairing between an old DNA strand and a new strand forming on it during *DNA replication*:

DNA template

new DNA strand

Figure 14.2 (**a**) Uracil, one of four ribonucleotides in RNA. The other three—adenine, guanine, and cytosine—differ only in their bases. Uracil compared with (**b**) thymine, a DNA nucleotide. (**c**) Base pairing of DNA with RNA during transcription, compared with (**d**) base pairing during DNA replication.

The chapter introduction may have left you with the impression that protein synthesis requires one class of RNA molecules. It actually requires three. When genes that specify proteins are transcribed, the outcome is **messenger RNA** (mRNA). *This is the only class of RNA that carries the protein-building codes.* **Ribosomal RNA** (rRNA) and **transfer RNA** (tRNA) are transcribed from different genes. The rRNA becomes a component of ribosomes, the structures in which polypeptide chains are assembled. The tRNA delivers amino acids one by one to ribosomes in the order specified by mRNA.

THE NATURE OF TRANSCRIPTION

An RNA molecule is almost but not quite like a single strand of DNA. It has four kinds of ribonucleotides, each with the five-carbon sugar ribose, one phosphate group, and one base. Three bases—adenine, cytosine, and guanine—are the same as those in DNA. In RNA, though, the fourth base is **uracil**, not thymine. Uracil, too, can pair with adenine, which means that a new RNA strand can base-pair with a DNA strand. Figure 14.2 is a simple way to think about this pairing.

Transcription *differs* from DNA replication in three respects. Only part of one DNA strand, not the whole molecule, is unwound and used as the template. The enzyme **RNA polymerase**, not DNA polymerase, adds ribonucleotides one at a time to the end of a growing strand of RNA. Also, transcription results in one free RNA strand, not a hydrogen-bonded double helix.

DNA contains many protein-coding regions. Each is transcribed separately, and each has its own START

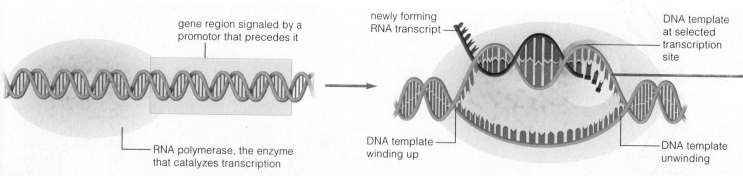

gene region signaled by a promotor that precedes it

newly forming RNA transcript

DNA template at selected transcription site

RNA polymerase, the enzyme that catalyzes transcription

DNA template winding up

DNA template unwinding

a RNA polymerase initiates transcription at a promoter in DNA. After binding to a promoter, RNA polymerases recognize a base sequence in DNA as a template for making a strand of RNA from free ribonucleotides, which have the bases adenine, cytosine, guanine, and uracil.

b All through transcription, the DNA double helix becomes unwound in front of the RNA polymerase. Short lengths of the newly forming RNA strand briefly wind up with its DNA template strand. New stretches of RNA unwind from the template (and the two DNA strands wind up again).

Figure 14.3 *Animated!* Gene transcription. By this process, an RNA molecule is assembled on a DNA template. (**a**) Gene region of DNA. The base sequence along one of DNA's two strands (not both) is used as the template. (**b–d**) Transcribing that region results in a molecule of RNA.

and STOP signal. A **promoter** is a START signal, a base sequence in DNA to which RNA polymerases bind and prepare for transcription. After binding, an RNA polymerase recognizes a gene region and moves along it. It uses the gene's base sequence as a template for covalently bonding free ribonucleotides together in a complementary sequence, as in Figure 14.3. When it reaches a sequence that signals "the end" of the gene region, the new RNA is released as a free transcript.

FINISHING TOUCHES ON THE mRNA TRANSCRIPTS

In eukaryotic cells, mRNA transcripts are modified before leaving the nucleus. Just as a dressmaker may snip off some threads or put bows on a dress before it leaves the shop, so do cells tailor their "pre-mRNA." For instance, some enzymes attach a modified guanine "cap" to the start of a pre-mRNA transcript. Others attach about 100 to 300 adenine ribonucleotides as a tail to the other end. Hence its name, poly-A tail.

Later, the pre-mRNA's cap will bind to a ribosome. Enzymes will nibble off the tail from the tip on back. Thus each tail's length dictates how long a particular protein-building message will last in the cytoplasm.

A transcript's message gets processed even before it leaves the nucleus. Eukaryotic genes contain **exons**: protein-coding base sequences that are interrupted by noncoding sequences, or **introns**. Both are transcribed, but all introns are snipped out before the transcript reaches the cytoplasm (Figure 14.4). Either all exons are retained in a mature mRNA transcript or some are

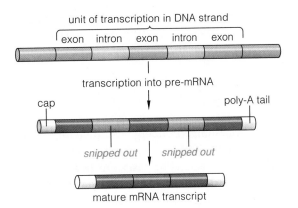

Figure 14.4
Animated! How pre-mRNA transcripts are processed into final form. Inside the nucleus, some or all introns are removed, and the transcript gets a cap and a tail.

removed and the rest are spliced together in various combinations. By this **alternative splicing**, one gene can specify two or more proteins that differ slightly in form and function! Cells use different combinations of exons at different times. Alternative splicing was once considered to be a rare event. However, it may occur in half (or all) genes of the human genome. It helps explain how human cells can make hundreds of thousands of proteins from only 21,500 or so genes.

In gene transcription, a sequence of exposed bases on one of the two strands of a DNA molecule serves as a template for synthesizing a complementary strand of RNA.

RNA polymerases assemble the RNA from four kinds of ribonucleotides that differ in their bases: A, U, C, and G.

Before leaving the nucleus, each new mRNA transcript, or pre-mRNA, undergoes modification into final form.

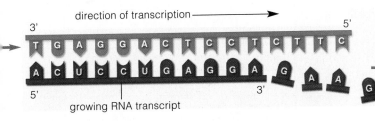

c What happened in the gene region? RNA polymerase catalyzed the covalent bonding of ribonucleotides to one another to form an RNA strand. The base sequence in the new strand is complementary to the exposed bases on the DNA as a template. Many other proteins assist in transcription; compare Section 13.3.

d At the end of the gene region, the last stretch of the new transcript is unwound and released from the DNA template. Shown below it is a model for a transcribed strand of RNA.

14.2 The Genetic Code

The correspondence between genes and proteins is encoded in protein-building "words" in mRNA transcripts. Three nucleotide bases make up each three-letter word.

Figure 14.5*a* shows a bit of mRNA transcribed from a DNA template. To translate it, you have to know how many letters (bases) make each word (amino acid). That is what Marshall Nirenberg, Philip Leder, Severo Ochoa, and Gobind Korana figured out. After mRNA has docked at a ribosome, its bases are "read" *three at a time*. The base triplets in mRNA are **codons**. Figure 14.5*b* shows how their sequence corresponds to the amino acid sequence in a growing polypeptide chain.

There are sixty-four different codons even though there are only twenty amino acids in proteins (Figure 14.6). Why so many? Think it through. If the codon were only one nucleotide, mRNA could specify only four kinds of amino acids. Codons of two nucleotides could code for sixteen kinds of amino acids—still not enough. Mixes of three nucleotides could code for sixty-four kinds—more than enough.

Certain codons actually do specify more than one kind of amino acid. For instance, both GAA and GAG specify glutamate. Also, in most species, the first AUG in the transcript is a START signal for translating "three-bases-at-a-time." It also means methionine is the first amino acid in all new polypeptide chains. UAA, UAG, and UGA do not specify any amino acid. They are STOP signals that block further additions of amino acids to a new chain.

The set of sixty-four different codons is the **genetic code**, and it has been highly conserved through time. Prokaryotes, a few organelles derived from them, and some protists of ancient lineages have a few slightly variant codons. For instance, a few unique codons give mitochondria their own "mitochondrial code." We can predict that they are outcomes of gene mutations that did not alter the mix of proteins in adverse ways. The near-universal use of the genetic code indicates that there is little tolerance for variation.

> *The genetic code is a set of sixty-four different codons, which are nucleotide bases in mRNA that are "read" in sets of three. Different codons (base triplets) specify different amino acids.*

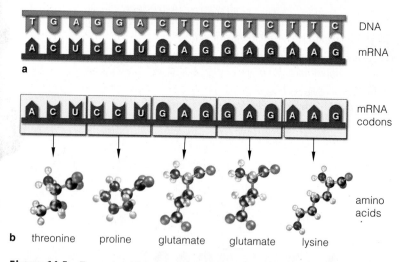

b threonine   proline   glutamate   glutamate   lysine

Figure 14.5 Example of the correspondence between genes and proteins. (**a**) An mRNA transcript of a gene region of DNA. Three nucleotide bases, equaling one codon, specify one amino acid. This series of codons (base triplets) specifies the sequence of amino acids shown in (**b**).

Figure 14.6 *Animated!* *Right*, the near-universal genetic code. Each codon in mRNA is a set of three ribonucleotide bases. Sixty-one of these base triplets encode specific amino acids. Three are signals that stop translation.

The *left* vertical column (*brown*) lists choices for the first base of a codon. The *top* horizontal row (*light tan*) lists the second choices. The *right* vertical column (*dark tan*) lists the third. To give three examples, reading left to right, the triplet U G G corresponds to tryptophan. Both U U U and U U C correspond to phenylalanine.

first base	second base				third base
	U	C	A	G	
U	phenylalanine	serine	tyrosine	cysteine	U
	phenylalanine	serine	tyrosine	cysteine	C
	leucine	serine	STOP	STOP	A
	leucine	serine	STOP	tryptophan	G
C	leucine	proline	histidine	arginine	U
	leucine	proline	histidine	arginine	C
	leucine	proline	glutamine	arginine	A
	leucine	proline	glutamine	arginine	G
A	isoleucine	threonine	asparagine	serine	U
	isoleucine	threonine	asparagine	serine	C
	isoleucine	threonine	lysine	arginine	A
	methionine (or START)	threonine	lysine	arginine	G
G	valine	alanine	aspartate	glycine	U
	valine	alanine	aspartate	glycine	C
	valine	alanine	glutamate	glycine	A
	valine	alanine	glutamate	glycine	G

14.3 The Other RNAs

Let's take stock. The codons in an mRNA transcript are the words in protein-building messages. Without translators, words that originated in DNA mean nothing; it takes the other two classes of RNA to synthesize proteins. Before getting into the mechanisms of translation, reflect on this overview of their structure and function.

Figure 14.7 shows the molecular structure for one of the tRNAs. All cells have pools of tRNAs and amino acids in their cytoplasm. Each tRNA has a molecular "hook," an attachment site for an amino acid. It has an **anticodon**, a ribonucleotide base triplet that can base-pair with a complementary codon in an mRNA transcript. When tRNAs bind to mRNA on a ribosome, the amino acid attached to each becomes positioned automatically in the order that the codons specify.

There are sixty-four codons but not as many kinds of tRNAs. How do tRNAs match up with more than one type of codon? According to base-pairing rules, adenine pairs with uracil, and cytosine with guanine. However, in codon–anticodon interactions, these rules can loosen for the third base in a codon. This freedom in codon–anticodon pairing at a base is known as the "wobble effect." For example, AUU, AUC, and AUA specify isoleucine. All three codons can base-pair with one type of tRNA that hooks on to isoleucine.

Again, interactions between the tRNAs and mRNA take place at ribosomes. A ribosome has two subunits made of rRNA and structural proteins (Section 4.5 and Figure 14.8). In eukaryotic cells, they are built in the nucleus and moved to the cytoplasm. There, a large and small subunit converge as an intact, functional ribosome only when mRNA is to be translated.

LINK TO SECTION 4.5

> *Only mRNA carries DNA's protein-building instructions from the nucleus into the cytoplasm.*
>
> *tRNAs deliver amino acids to ribosomes. Their anticodons base-pair with codons in the order specified by mRNA.*
>
> *Polypeptide chains are built on ribosomes, each consisting of a large and small subunit made of rRNA and proteins.*

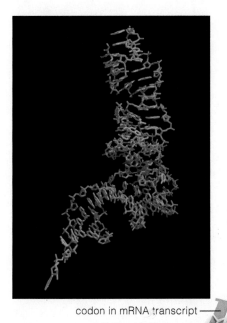

Figure 14.7 Model for a tRNA. The icon shown to the right is used in following illustrations. The "hook" at the lower end of this icon represents the binding site for a specific amino acid.

codon in mRNA transcript

anticodon in tRNA

amino acid

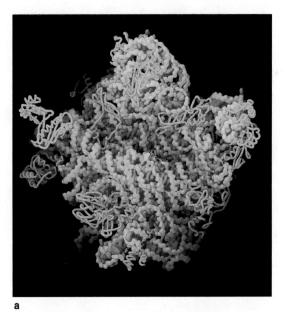

Figure 14.8 (a) Ribbon model for the large subunit of a bacterial ribosome. It has two rRNA molecules (*gray*) and thirty-one structural proteins (*gold*), which stabilize the structure. At one end of a tunnel through the large subunit, rRNA catalyzes polypeptide chain assembly. This is an ancient, highly conserved structure. Its role is so vital that the corresponding subunit of the eukaryotic ribosome, which is larger, may be similar in structure and function. (b) Model for the small and large subunits of a eukaryotic ribosome.

a

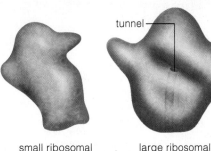

tunnel

small ribosomal subunit + large ribosomal subunit ⟶ intact ribosome

b

14.4 The Three Stages of Translation

LINKS TO
SECTIONS
3.5, 4.6

An mRNA transcript that encodes DNA's information about a protein enters an intact ribosome. There, its codons are translated into a polypeptide chain—a protein's primary structure (Section 3.5). Translation of the protein-building message proceeds through three continuous stages called initiation, elongation, and termination.

Only one kind of tRNA can start the *initiation* stage of translation. It alone has the anticodon UAC—which is complementary to the START codon of every mRNA transcript. The anticodon and codon meet up when this initiator tRNA binds to a small ribosomal subunit. Next, a large ribosomal subunit joins with the small subunit. Together, the initiator tRNA, the ribosome, and the mRNA transcript form an initiation complex (Figure 14.9a–c). The next stage can begin.

During the *elongation* stage, a polypeptide chain is synthesized while the mRNA passes between the two ribosomal subunits, a bit like a thread being moved through the eye of a needle. Many tRNA molecules deliver amino acids to the ribosome, and each binds to the mRNA in the order specified by their codons. One region of an rRNA molecule located at the center of the large ribosomal subunit is highly acidic, and it functions as an enzyme. It catalyzes the formation of peptide bonds between amino acids (Figure 14.9d–f).

Figure 14.9g shows how one peptide bond forms between the most recently attached amino acid and the next one brought to the ribosome. Here, you might wish to look once more at Section 3.5, which includes a step-by-step description of peptide bond formation during protein synthesis.

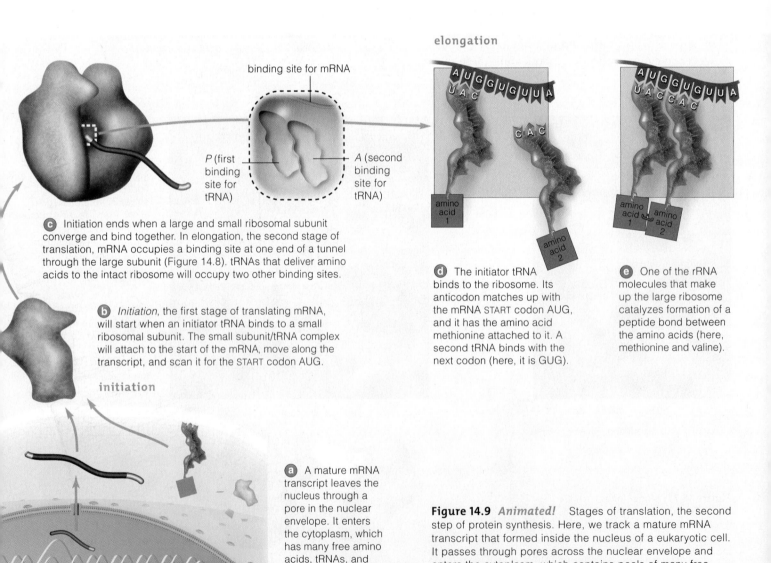

elongation

binding site for mRNA

P (first binding site for tRNA) *A (second binding site for tRNA)*

c Initiation ends when a large and small ribosomal subunit converge and bind together. In elongation, the second stage of translation, mRNA occupies a binding site at one end of a tunnel through the large subunit (Figure 14.8). tRNAs that deliver amino acids to the intact ribosome will occupy two other binding sites.

b *Initiation*, the first stage of translating mRNA, will start when an initiator tRNA binds to a small ribosomal subunit. The small subunit/tRNA complex will attach to the start of the mRNA, move along the transcript, and scan it for the START codon AUG.

initiation

a A mature mRNA transcript leaves the nucleus through a pore in the nuclear envelope. It enters the cytoplasm, which has many free amino acids, tRNAs, and ribosomal subunits.

d The initiator tRNA binds to the ribosome. Its anticodon matches up with the mRNA START codon AUG, and it has the amino acid methionine attached to it. A second tRNA binds with the next codon (here, it is GUG).

e One of the rRNA molecules that make up the large ribosome catalyzes formation of a peptide bond between the amino acids (here, methionine and valine).

Figure 14.9 *Animated!* Stages of translation, the second step of protein synthesis. Here, we track a mature mRNA transcript that formed inside the nucleus of a eukaryotic cell. It passes through pores across the nuclear envelope and enters the cytoplasm, which contains pools of many free amino acids, tRNAs, and ribosomal subunits.

During *termination*, the last stage of translation, the mRNA's STOP codon enters the ribosome. No tRNA has a corresponding anticodon. Proteins called release factors bind to the ribosome. Binding triggers enzyme activity that detaches the mRNA *and* the polypeptide chain from the ribosome (Figure 14.9*i–k*).

In cells that are quickly using or secreting proteins, you often see many clusters of ribosomes (polysomes) on an mRNA transcript, all translating it at the same time. This is what happens in unfertilized eggs, which usually stockpile mRNA transcripts in the cytoplasm in preparation for the cell divisions that lie ahead.

Many newly formed polypeptide chains carry out their functions in the cytoplasm. Others have a special sequence of amino acids. The sequence is a shipping label that gets them into ribosome-studded, flattened sacs of rough ER (Section 4.6). In the organelles of the endomembrane system, the chains will take on final form before shipment to their ultimate destinations as structural or functional proteins.

> *Translation is initiated when a small ribosomal subunit and an initiator tRNA arrive at an mRNA transcript's START codon, and a large ribosomal subunit binds to them.*
>
> *tRNAs deliver amino acids to a ribosome in the order dictated by the linear sequence of mRNA codons. A polypeptide chain lengthens as peptide bonds form between the amino acids.*
>
> *Translation ends when a STOP codon triggers events that cause the polypeptide chain and the mRNA to detach from the ribosome.*

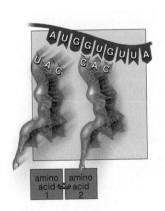

f The first tRNA is released, and the ribosome moves to the next codon position.

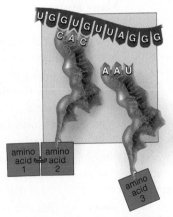

g A third tRNA binds with the next codon (here it is UUA). The ribosome catalyzes peptide bond formation between amino acids 2 and 3.

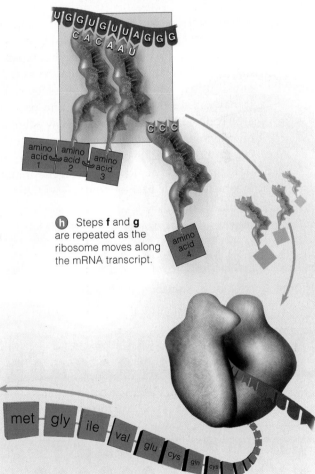

h Steps **f** and **g** are repeated as the ribosome moves along the mRNA transcript.

termination

i A STOP codon moves into the area where the chain is being built. It is the signal to release the mRNA transcript from the ribosome.

j The new polypeptide chain is released from the ribosome. It is free to join the pool of proteins in the cytoplasm or to enter rough ER of the endomembrane system.

k The two ribosomal subunits now separate, also.

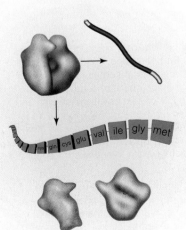

14.5 Mutated Genes and Their Protein Products

LINKS TO
SECTIONS
2.3, 3.6, 7.1

When a cell taps its genetic code, it is making proteins with precise structural and functional roles that keep it alive. If a gene changes, the mRNA transcribed from it may change and specify an altered protein. If the protein has a crucial role, the outcome will be a dead or abnormal cell.

Gene sequences can change. Sometimes one base gets substituted for another in the nucleotide sequence. At other times, an extra base is inserted or one is lost. Such small-scale changes in the nucleotide sequence of a DNA molecule are **gene mutations**, and they can alter the message that becomes encoded in mRNA. Cells have some leeway, because more than one codon can specify the same amino acid. For example, if UCU replaced UCC in an mRNA transcript, this might not be bad, because both codons specify serine. However, as the next examples show, many mutations result in proteins that function in an altered way or not at all.

COMMON GENE MUTATIONS

During DNA replication, recall, the wrong nucleotide may become paired with an exposed base on the DNA template and slip by proofreading and repair enzymes (Section 13.3). This type of mutation is a **base-pair substitution**. When the altered message is translated, it may call for the wrong amino acid or a premature STOP codon. Figure 14.10b shows how adenine *replaced* one thymine in the gene for beta hemoglobin, which can give rise to sickle-cell anemia (Section 3.6).

Figure 14.10c depicts another gene mutation, one in which a single base—thymine—was *deleted*. Again,

DNA polymerases read base sequences in blocks of three. A deletion is one of the *frameshift* mutations; it shifts the "three-bases-at-a-time" reading frame. An altered mRNA is transcribed from the mutant gene, so an altered protein is the result.

Frameshift mutations fall in the broader categories of **insertions** and **deletions**. One or more base pairs become inserted into DNA or are deleted from it.

Other mutations arise from transposable elements, or **transposons**, that can jump around in the genome. Geneticist Barbara McClintock found that these DNA segments or copies of them move spontaneously to a new location in a chromosome or even to a different chromosome. When transposons land in a gene, they alter the timing or duration of its activity, or block it entirely. Their unpredictability can give rise to odd variations in traits. Figure 14.11 gives an example.

HOW DO MUTATIONS ARISE?

Many mutations happen spontaneously while DNA is being replicated. This is not surprising, given the swift pace of replication (about twenty bases per second in humans and a thousand bases per second in certain bacteria). DNA polymerases and DNA ligases can fix most mistakes (Section 13.3). But sometimes they go on assembling a new strand right over an error. The bypass can result in a mutated DNA molecule.

Not all mutations are spontaneous. A number arise after DNA is exposed to mutation-causing agents. To give an example, x-rays and other high-energy forms of **ionizing radiation** break chromosomes into pieces (Figure 14.12). Ionizing radiation damages DNA indirectly, also. When it penetrates living tissues, it leaves behind a long trail of destructive free radicals. Doctors and

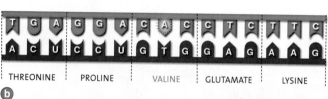

part of DNA template

mRNA transcribed from DNA

THREONINE | PROLINE | GLUTAMATE | GLUTAMATE | LYSINE — resulting amino acid sequence

a

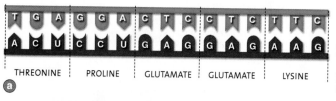

base substitution in DNA

altered mRNA

THREONINE | PROLINE | VALINE | GLUTAMATE | LYSINE — altered amino acid sequence

b

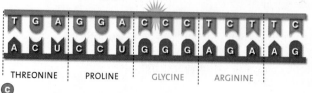

deletion in DNA

altered mRNA

THREONINE | PROLINE | GLYCINE | ARGININE — altered amino acid sequence

c

Figure 14.10 *Animated!* Example of gene mutation. (**a**) Part of a gene, the mRNA, and the specified amino acid sequence of the beta chain in hemoglobin. (**b**) A base-pair substitution in DNA replaces a thymine with an adenine. When the altered mRNA transcript is translated, valine replaces glutamate as the sixth amino acid of the new polypeptide chain. Sickle-cell anemia is the eventual outcome.

(**c**) Deletion of the same thymine would be a frameshift mutation. The reading frame for the rest of the mRNA shifts, a different protein product forms, and it causes thalassemia—a different type of red blood cell disorder.

Figure 14.11 Barbara McClintock, who won a Nobel Prize for her research. She proved that transposons slip into and out of different locations in DNA. The curiously nonuniform coloration of kernels in strains of Indian corn (*Zea mays*) sent her on the road to discovery.

Several genes govern pigment formation and deposition in corn kernels, which are a type of seed. Mutations in one or more of these genes produce yellow, white, red, orange, blue, and purple kernels. However, as McClintock realized, *unstable* mutations can cause streaks or spots in *individual* kernels.

All of a corn plant's cells have the same pigment-encoding genes. But a transposon invaded a pigment-encoding gene before the plant started growing from a fertilized egg. While a kernel's tissues were forming, its cells could not make pigment, but the same transposon jumped out of the pigment-encoding gene in some of its cells. Descendants of *those* cells could make pigment. The spots and streaks in individual kernels are visual markers for those cell lineages.

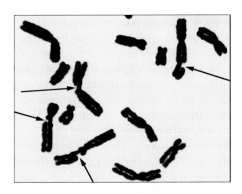

Figure 14.12 Chromosomes from a human cell after exposure to gamma rays, a form of ionizing radiation. We can expect such broken pieces (*arrows*) to be lost during interphase, when DNA is being replicated. The extent of the chromosome damage in an exposed cell typically depends on how much radiation it absorbed.

dentists both use the lowest possible doses of x-rays to minimize the damage to a patient's DNA.

Nonionizing radiation excites electrons to a higher energy level. DNA absorbs one form, ultraviolet (UV) light. Two nucleotide bases in DNA—cytosine and thymine—are most vulnerable to excitation that can change base-pairing properties. UV light can induce adjacent thymine bases in a DNA strand to pair *with each other*, as a bulky dimer (page 217). At least seven gene products interact as a DNA repair mechanism to remove the dimer, which wrinkles the DNA. If DNA polymerase encounters a thymine dimer, it will make replication errors. Exposing unprotected skin to the sun invites thymine dimer formation in skin cells.

When thymine dimers are not repaired, they cause DNA polymerases to make even more errors during the next replication cycle. They are the original source of mutations that lead to certain cancers.

Natural and synthetic chemicals accelerate rates of gene mutations. For instance, **alkylating agents** can transfer charged methyl or ethyl groups to reactive sites in DNA. At these sites, DNA is more vulnerable to mistakes in base pairing and to mutation. Cancer-causing agents in cigarette smoke and many other substances exert their effects by alkylating DNA.

THE PROOF IS IN THE PROTEIN

When a mutation arises in a somatic cell of a sexually reproducing individual, its good or bad effects will not endure; it is not passed on to offspring. If it arises in a germ cell or a gamete, however, it may enter the evolutionary arena. It also may do so when it is passed on to offspring by asexual reproduction. Either way, *the protein product of such heritable mutations will have harmful, neutral, or beneficial effects on the individual's capacity to function in the prevailing environment.* The effects of uncountable mutations in millions of species have had spectacular evolutionary consequences—and that is a topic of later chapters.

A gene mutation is a permanent change in one or more bases in the nucleotide sequence of DNA. The most common types are base-pair substitutions, insertions, and deletions.

Exposure to harmful radiation and to chemicals in the environment can cause mutations in DNA.

A protein specified by a mutated gene may have harmful, neutral, or beneficial effects on the individual's capacity to function in the environment.

Summary

Introduction   All enzymes and other proteins that are essential for life consist of polypeptide chains. Each chain, a linear sequence of amino acids, corresponds to nucleotide base sequences in DNA that form genes. The path from genes to proteins has two steps: transcription and translation (Figure 14.13).

Section 14.1   In eukaryotic cells, genes are transcribed in the nucleus and then translated cytoplasm. Both steps occur in the cytoplasm of prokaryotic cells, which have no nucleus. Enzymes unwind the two strands of a DNA double helix in a specific gene region. RNA polymerases covalently bond ribonucleotides one after another into a new RNA transcript, in an order complementary to the exposed bases on the DNA template. Adenine, guanine, cytosine, and uracil are the bases in ribonucleotides.

The mRNA transcript gets modified before it leaves the nucleus. Its 5' end gets capped, and its 3' end gets a poly-A tail, which paces how long the mRNA will stay intact in the cytoplasm. The introns between exons (the protein-coding portions of genes) are snipped out. The exons can be spliced together in different combinations.

Biology⊘Now
Learn how genes are transcribed and transcripts are processed with the animation on BiologyNow.

Sections 14.2, 14.3   Only messenger RNA (mRNA) carries the protein-building information in DNA to ribosomes for translation. Its genetic message is written in codons, or sets of three nucleotides along an mRNA strand that specify an amino acid. There are sixty-four codons, a few of which act as START or STOP signals for translation. That set constitutes a highly conserved genetic code. A few variations in code words evolved among prokaryotes and prokaryote-derived organelles (e.g., mitochondria) and in a few ancient lineages of single-celled eukaryotes.

Translation requires three classes of RNAs. Transfer RNA (tRNA) molecules have anticodons that can bind briefly to complementary codons in mRNA. They also have a binding site for a free amino acid, which they deliver to ribosomes during protein synthesis. Different tRNAs reversibly bind different amino acids. Ribosomal RNA (rRNA) and proteins that stabilize it make up the two subunits that form ribosomes.

Biology⊘Now
Explore the genetic code with the interaction on BiologyNow.

Section 14.4   During translation, peptide bonds form between amino acids in the order specified by codons in mRNA. Translation has three stages. In initiation, an initiator tRNA, two ribosomal subunits, and an mRNA converge as an initiation complex. In the elongation stage, tRNAs deliver amino acids to the intact ribosomes. Part of an rRNA molecule located in the ribosome's central region catalyzes peptide bond formation between amino acids. In the termination stage, a STOP codon and other factors trigger the release of mRNA and the new polypeptide chain. They also cause the ribosome's subunits to separate from each other.

Biology⊘Now
Observe the translation of an mRNA transcript with the animation on BiologyNow.

Section 14.5   Gene mutations are heritable, small-scale changes in the base sequence of DNA. Major types are base-pair substitutions, insertions, and deletions. Many arise spontaneously as DNA is being replicated. Some arise after transposons jump to new locations in chromosomes; others arise after DNA is exposed to ionizing radiation or to chemicals in the environment. Mutations may cause changes in protein structure, protein function, or both.

Biology⊘Now
Investigate the effects of mutation with the animation on BiologyNow.

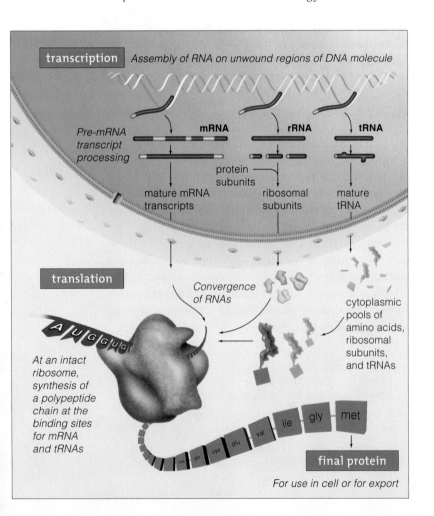

transcription   *Assembly of RNA on unwound regions of DNA molecule*

Pre-mRNA transcript processing

mRNA   **rRNA**   **tRNA**

protein subunits

mature mRNA transcripts   ribosomal subunits   mature tRNA

translation

Convergence of RNAs

cytoplasmic pools of amino acids, ribosomal subunits, and tRNAs

At an intact ribosome, synthesis of a polypeptide chain at the binding sites for mRNA and tRNAs

A U G G U G

ile   gly   met

val

glu

cys

final protein

For use in cell or for export

Figure 14.13 *Animated!*   Summary of protein synthesis in eukaryotic cells. DNA is transcribed into RNA in the nucleus. RNA is translated in the cytoplasm. Prokaryotic cells do not have a nucleus; transcription and translation proceed in their cytoplasm.

1. DNA contains many different gene regions that are transcribed into different _____ .
   a. proteins
   b. mRNAs only
   c. mRNAs, tRNAs, rRNAs
   d. all of the above

2. An RNA molecule is typically _____ .
   a. a double helix
   b. single-stranded
   c. double-stranded
   d. triple-stranded

3. An mRNA molecule is synthesized by _____ .
   a. replication
   b. duplication
   c. transcription
   d. translation

4. Each codon specifies a(n) _____ .
   a. protein
   b. polypeptide
   c. amino acid
   d. mRNA

5. _____ different codons represent a near-universal genetic code.
   a. Twelve
   b. Twenty
   c. Thirty-four
   d. Sixty-four

6. Anticodons pair with _____ .
   a. mRNA codons
   b. DNA codons
   c. RNA anticodons
   d. amino acids

7. _____ can cause gene mutations.
   a. replication errors
   b. transposons
   c. ionizing radiation
   d. non-ionizing radiation
   e. b and c are correct
   f. all of the above

8. Match the terms with the most suitable description.
   ____ alkylating agent
   ____ chain elongation
   ____ exons
   ____ genetic code
   ____ anticodon
   ____ introns
   ____ codon

   a. protein-coding parts of a mature mRNA transcript
   b. base triplet for amino acid
   c. second stage of translation
   d. base triplet; pairs with codon
   e. one environmental agent that induces mutation in DNA
   f. set of 64 codons for mRNA
   g. noncoding part of pre-mRNA transcript, removed before translation

Additional questions are available on Biology ⑤ Now™

Critical Thinking

1. Using Figure 14.6, translate this nucleotide sequence in part of an mRNA transcript into an amino acid sequence:

   5'—GGTTTCTTCAAGAGA—3'

2. Briefly review Section 13.3. Now suppose that DNA polymerase made a wrong base pairing while a crucial gene region of DNA was being replicated. DNA repair mechanisms did not kick in to fix the mistake. Here is the part of the DNA strand that contains the error:

After the DNA molecule is replicated, two daughter cells form. One daughter cell is carrying the mutation and the other cell is normal. Develop a hypothesis to explain this observation.

Figure 14.14 Soft skin tumors on an individual affected by the autosomal dominant disorder called neurofibromatosis.

3. *Neurofibromatosis* is a human autosomal dominant disorder caused by mutations in the *NF1* gene. It is characterized by the formation of soft, fibrous tumors in the peripheral nervous system and skin as well as abnormalities in muscles, bones, and internal organs (Figure 14.14).

Because the mutant allele is dominant, an affected child usually has an affected parent. Yet in 1991, scientists reported that a boy developed neurofibromatosis even though his parents did not. When they examined both copies of the boy's *NF1* gene, they found that the gene on the chromosome he inherited from his father contained a transposon. Neither father nor mother had a transposon in any of the copies of their *NF1* genes. Explain the cause of neurofibromatosis in the boy and how it arose.

4. Cigarette smoke is mostly carbon dioxide, nitrogen, and oxygen. The rest contains at least fifty-five different chemicals identified as carcinogenic, or cancer-causing, by the International Agency for Research on Cancer (IARC). When these carcinogens enter the bloodstream, enzymes convert them to a series of chemical intermediates that are easier to excrete. Some of the intermediates bind irreversibly to DNA. Propose one mechanism by which smoking cigarettes can cause cancer.

5. *Antisense drugs* may help us fight cancer and viral diseases, including SARS. These short mRNA strands are complementary to mRNAs that have been linked to these illnesses. Speculate on how these drugs work.

6. In some cases, the termination of transcription of prokaryotic DNA depends on the structure of the newly forming RNA transcript. The terminal end of an mRNA transcript often folds back tightly on itself and makes a hairpin-looped structure, like the one shown at right.

Why do you suppose that a "stem-loop" structure such as this stops transcription of prokaryotic DNA when the RNA polymerases reach it?

```
        C
      U—C
      G—C
      A—U
      C—G
      C—G
      G—C
      C—G
      C—G
...CCCACAG—CAUUUUU...
```

Between You and Eternity

You are in college, your whole life ahead of you. Your risk of developing cancer is as remote as old age, an abstract statistic that is easy to forget.

"There is a moment when everything changes—when the width of two fingers can suddenly be the total distance between you and eternity." Robin Shoulla wrote those words after being diagnosed with breast cancer. She was seventeen. At an age when most young women are thinking about school, parties, and potential careers, Robin was dealing with *radical mastectomy*—the removal of a breast, all lymph nodes under the arm, and skeletal muscles in the chest wall under the breast. She was pleading with her oncologist not to use her jugular vein for chemotherapy and wondering if she would survive through the next year (Figure 15.1).

Robin became an annual statistic—one of 10,000 or so females and, to a lesser extent, males who develop breast cancer before they are forty years old. About 180,000 new cases are diagnosed each year in the United States.

Cancers are as diverse as their underlying causes, but several gene mutations predispose individuals to developing certain kinds. Either the mutant genes are inherited or they mutate spontaneously in individuals after attacks by environmental agents, including some viruses, toxic chemicals, and ultraviolet radiation.

One gene on chromosome 17 encodes *ERBB2*, a type of membrane receptor. *ERBB2* is part of a control pathway that governs the cell cycle—that is, when and how often cells divide. It also is one of the proto-oncogenes. When such genes are mutated or overexpressed, they help trigger cancerous transformations. The cells of about 25 percent of breast cancer patients have too many of these receptors or extra copies of the gene itself. The cells do not stop dividing, and abnormal masses of cells are the outcome.

Two different genes, *BRCA1* and *BRCA2*, encode two of the proteins that can act as tumor suppressors. They help prevent the formation of benign or cancerous cell masses, as explained in Section 9.5. Such proteins usually function as part of DNA repair mechanisms. That is why mutation in *BRCA1* or *BRCA2* compromises the cell's capacity to fix damaged DNA. Other mutations are free to accumulate throughout the DNA and set the stage for cancer.

BRCA1 and *BRCA2* are called *breast cancer genes*, because their mutated forms often occur in cancerous breast cells. If a *BRCA* gene mutates in one of three especially dangerous ways, the individual has about an 80 percent chance of developing breast cancer before reaching age seventy.

Robin Shoulla survived. Although radical mastectomy is rarely performed today—a modified procedure is just as

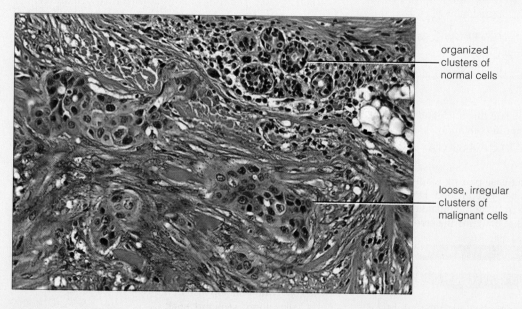

organized clusters of normal cells

loose, irregular clusters of malignant cells

Figure 15.1 Breast cancer. This light micrograph shows irregular clusters of carcinoma cells that infiltrated the ducts in breast tissue. On the facing page, Robin Shoulla. Diagnostic tests revealed cells like this in her body.

effective and less disfiguring—it is the only option when cancer cells infiltrate muscles under the breast. It was Robin's only option. She may never know which mutation caused her cancer. Thirteen years later, she has what she calls a normal life—a career, husband, children. Her goal is to grow very old with gray hair and spreading hips, smiling.

Robin's story lends immediacy to the world of **gene controls**. By these molecular mechanisms, all cells control when and how fast specific genes will be transcribed and translated, and whether gene products will be switched on or silenced. You will consider the impact of such controls in chapters throughout the book—and in many chapters of your life.

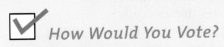

How Would You Vote?

Some females at high risk of developing breast cancer opt for prophylactic mastectomy, the surgical removal of one or more breasts even before cancer develops. Many of them would never have developed cancer. Should the surgery be restricted to cancer treatment? See BiologyNow for details, then vote online.

Key Concepts

OVERVIEW OF THE CONTROLS

Control mechanisms govern when, how, and to what extent an individual's genes are expressed. They respond to signaling molecules and to changing conditions.

Diverse control elements work before, during, and after gene transcription or translation. They interact with DNA, RNA, and protein products.

In multicelled species, long-term controls guide the stage-by-stage development of new individuals. Selective gene expression in embryos results in cell differentiation, whereby different cell lineages become specialized in composition, structure, and function. Section 15.1

EXAMPLES FROM EUKARYOTES

Precise controls govern an embryo's development. As examples, the orderly, regional expression of certain genes causes animal organs and limbs to form where they are supposed to. In the embryos of mammals, controls also compensate for sex chromosome imbalances. A female inherits twice as many X chromosomes as a male, but controls shut down most of the genes on one of her two X chromosomes in each cell. Section 15.2

CASE STUDY: FRUIT FLY DEVELOPMENT

Drosophila research revealed how a complex body plan emerges as different cells in a developing embryo activate or suppress shared genes in different ways. Section 15.3

WHAT ABOUT THE PROKARYOTES?

Prokaryotic gene controls deal mainly with short-term changes in nutrient availability and other aspects of the environment. The main gene controls bring about fast adjustments in rates of transcription. Section 15.4

Links to Earlier Concepts

You will be applying your knowledge of the organization of chromosomal DNA (Section 9.1) and of mRNA transcript processing (14.1). You may wish to review the mechanism that governs the activity of the key enzyme in tryptophan synthesis (6.4). Your understanding of the characteristics of autosomal recessive inheritance (12.3) and of the basis of sex determination in humans (12.1, 12.5) will come in handy.

15.1 When Controls Come Into Play

LINKS TO
SECTIONS
6.4, 9.1, 14.1

*Ultimately, **gene expression** refers to controls over the kinds and amounts of proteins that are in a cell in any specified interval. Tremendous coordination goes into synthesizing, stockpiling, using, exporting, and degrading thousands of types of proteins.*

SOME CONTROL MECHANISMS

Regulatory elements interact with DNA, RNAs, new polypeptide chains, and final proteins. Different kinds respond to shifts in concentrations of substances or to outside signals, such as hormones. Many responses exert *negative* control; they slow or stop some activity. Others exert *positive* control; they enhance it.

For instance, **promoters** are short stretches of base sequences in DNA where regulatory proteins gather and control transcription of specific genes, often in response to a hormonal signal. **Enhancers** are binding sites where such proteins increase transcription rates.

Chemical modification also can exert control. Many methyl groups ($-CH_3$) are "painted" on parts of newly replicated DNA to block access to genes. Acetyl groups ($-CH_3CO^-$) are attached to DNA to make genes accessible. **Methylation** and **acetylation** are the names for the addition of such groups to DNA or any other molecule.

When, how, and to what extent any of these controls come into play depends on the type of cell, its functions, its chemical environment, and signals from the outside. Later chapters provide rich examples. For now, become familiar with the points at which control is exerted.

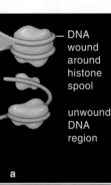

— DNA
wound
around
histone
spool

unwound
DNA
region

a

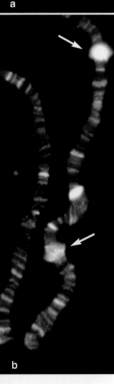

b

POINTS OF CONTROL

Controls Before Transcription The *access* to genes is under control. Remember how histones and other proteins help keep eukaryotic chromosomes organized (Section 9.1)? Where a DNA molecule is wound up tightly, polymerases cannot access genes. Acetylation can make histones loosen their grip (Figure 15.2a). As another example, a maternal *or* paternal allele at any locus in a diploid cell may become methylated, which can block the gene's influence on a trait.

Controls also affect *how* a gene will be transcribed. For instance, some gene sequences can be rearranged or multiplied. In immature amphibian eggs and gland cells of certain insect larvae, the chromosomal DNA is copied repeatedly in interphase. The copying results in *polytene* chromosomes, which contain hundreds or thousands of side-by-side copies of genes. The repeats allow these cells to churn out copious amounts of the gene products necessary for survival (Figure 15.2b).

Control of Transcript Processing Many controls influence mRNA transcript processing. Remember, the pre-mRNA transcripts are modified in ways that affect whether, when, and how they are translated (Section 14.1). Consider what happens in different muscle cells. Exons of the gene for troponin, a contractile protein, are put together in different combinations in different muscle cells. As a result, each type of muscle cell gets mRNA transcripts that are unique in a small region. The structure and functioning of the troponin product vary in subtle ways among them.

Also, the nuclear envelope helps control when the mRNA transcript reaches a ribosome. The transcript cannot pass through a nuclear pore complex unless proteins become attached to it. A base sequence in the untranslated end of mRNA is like a zip code. Controls "read" the code and attach proteins to it. The bound proteins help move the transcript to the region where it is supposed to be translated or stored. Destinations are vital. Which mRNAs—and, in time, gene products—end up in different regions of an immature egg's cytoplasm are "maternal messages" on how to start to construct the body plan of a new embryo.

Unfertilized eggs that stockpile maternal messages keep them silent with the help of controls called Y-box proteins. When phosphorylated, Y-box proteins bind and help stabilize mRNA. When many of the proteins bind to a transcript, they block its translation. In other words, phosphorylation of Y-box proteins is a control mechanism in mRNA inactivation. You will read about such controls in later sections of the book.

Figure 15.2 Examples of gene control mechanisms.
(**a**) Loosening a chromosome's DNA–histone units may expose genes for transcription. Attaching an acetyl group to a histone makes it loosen its grip on the DNA wound around it. Transcription enzymes attach and detach these groups.

(**b**) *Drosophila* polytene chromosomes. To sustain a rapid growth rate, *Drosophila* larvae eat continuously and use a lot of saliva. Giant chromosomes in their salivary glands form by repeated DNA replications. Each has hundreds or thousands of the same DNA molecule, aligned side by side.

An insect hormone, ecdysone, serves as a regulatory protein; it promotes gene transcription. In response to the hormonal signal, these chromosomes loosen and puff out in regions where genes are being transcribed. Puffs are largest and most diffuse where transcription is most intense (*arrows*).

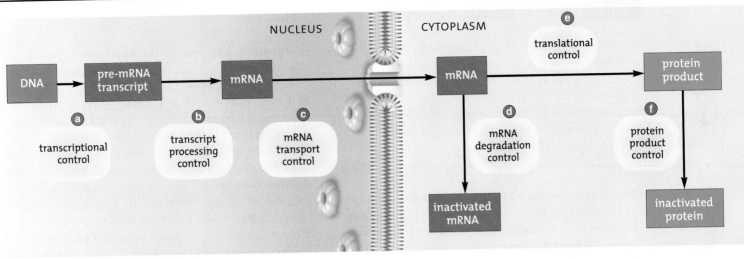

a DNA may be chemically modified, which can influence access to genes. In some species, genes become duplicated or rearranged.

b Pre-mRNA spliced in alternative ways can lead to different forms of a protein. Other modifications affect whether a transcript reaches the cytoplasm.

c Transport protein binding determines whether an mRNA will be delivered to a specific region of cytoplasm for local translation.

d How long an mRNA lasts depends on the proteins that are attached to it and the length of its poly-A tail.

e Translation can be blocked. mRNA cannot attach to a ribosome when proteins bind to it. Initiation factors can be inactivated.

f A new protein may be inactivated or activated. Control of enzymes and other proteins influences many cell activities.

Figure 15.3 *Animated!* Controls that influence whether, when, and how a gene in eukaryotic DNA will be expressed.

Control of Translation Many kinds of molecules function in coordinated ways during translation, and each is controlled independently. Some controls work on initiation factors and ribosome components. Others work through mRNA transcript stability. The longer a transcript lasts, the more times it can be translated. Enzymes start nibbling at the poly-A tail of a mature mRNA transcript within minutes of its appearance in the cytoplasm. How fast they digest it depends on the tail's length, its base sequences, and the proteins that have become attached to it (Section 14.1).

Controls After Translation Control is exerted over new enzymes and other proteins. For instance, Y-box proteins become activated only when enzymes attach a phosphate group to them. Other controls activate, inhibit, and stabilize diverse molecules that take part in protein synthesis. Allosteric control of tryptophan synthesis is a case in point (Section 6.4).

SAME GENES, DIFFERENT CELL LINEAGES

Later in the book, you will read about how complex organisms develop. For now, tentatively accept this premise: All cells of your body started out life with the same genes, because every one arose by mitotic cell divisions from the same fertilized egg. They all transcribe many of the same genes and are alike in most aspects of structure and housekeeping activities.

In other ways, however, *nearly all of your body cells became specialized in composition, structure, and function.*

This process—**cell differentiation**—is central to the development of all multicelled species. By selecting particular subsets of genes, specialized cells and their descendants give rise to different tissues and organs.

Here is an example: Cells generally transcribe the genes coding for enzymes of glycolysis all the time. But immature red blood cells alone transcribe genes for hemoglobin. Liver cells transcribe genes required to make enzymes that neutralize some toxins, but they are the only ones that do so. While your eyes formed, certain cells accessed genes necessary for synthesizing crystallin. No other cells in your body can activate the genes for this protein, which makes up the transparent fibers of the lens in each eye.

Figure 15.3 summarizes the main control points over gene expression in eukaryotic cells.

Gene expression is controlled by regulatory elements that interact with one another, with control elements built into the DNA, with RNA, and with newly synthesized proteins. Different forms of controls work before, during, and after transcription and translation.

Control also is exerted through chemical modifications that activate, inactivate, or restrict access to specific gene regions in DNA.

During development of all multicelled organisms, cells become different in composition, structure, and function as genes are activated and suppressed in selective ways.

15.2   A Few Outcomes of Gene Controls

LINKS TO
SECTIONS
12.1, 12.2, 12.5

The preceding section introduced an important idea. All differentiated cells in a complex, multicelled body use most of their genes the same way, but each type engages in selective gene expression that gives rise to its distinctive features. Consider two examples of the controls that guide the selections during embryonic development.

X CHROMOSOME INACTIVATION

Diploid cells of female humans and female calico cats have two X chromosomes. One is in threadlike form. The other stays scrunched up, even during interphase. This scrunching is a programmed shutdown of about 75 percent of the genes on *one* of two homologous X chromosomes. That shutdown, called **X chromosome inactivation**, happens in the female embryos of all placental mammals and their marsupial relatives.

Figure 15.4*a* shows one condensed X chromosome in the nucleus of a cell at interphase. We also call this condensed structural form a Barr body (after Murray Barr, who first identified it).

An X chromosome is inactivated when XX embryos are still a tiny ball of cells. In placental mammals, the shutdown is random, in that *either* chromosome could become condensed. The maternal X chromosome may be inactivated in one cell; the paternal or the maternal X chromosome may be inactivated in a cell next to it.

Once the random molecular selection is made in a cell, all of that cell's descendants make the exact same selection as they go on dividing to form tissues. What is the outcome? *A fully developed female has patches of tissue where genes of the maternal X chromosome are being expressed and patches of tissue where genes of the paternal X chromosome are being expressed.* She is a "mosaic" for the expression of X-linked genes.

When alleles on two homologous X chromosomes are not identical, patches of tissues through the body often show variation. Mosaic tissues can be observed in women who are heterozygous for a rare mutant allele that causes an absence of sweat glands. Sweat glands form in some patches of skin only. Where sweat glands are absent, the mutant allele is on the active X chromosome. The mosaic effect is especially apparent in females affected by *anhidrotic ectodermal dysplasia* (Figure 15.4*b*). Abnormalities in the skin and structures derived from it, including teeth, hair, nails, and sweat glands, are signs of this heritable disorder.

A different mosaic tissue effect shows up in female calico cats, of the sort shown in Figure 15.5. These cats are heterozygous for a certain coat color allele on their X chromosomes.

According to the theory of **dosage compensation**, the shutdown is not an accident of evolution; it is a gene control mechanism. In mammals, recall, males are XY, which means that females have twice as many X chromosome genes (Section 12.5). Inactivating one of their two X chromosomes balances gene expression

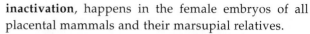

Figure 15.4   **(a)** In the somatic cell nucleus of a human female, a condensed X chromosome, also called a Barr body (*arrow*). The X chromosome in cells of human males is not condensed this way.

(b) A mosaic tissue effect that becomes apparent in women who are affected by anhidrotic ectodermal dysplasia. Some patches of skin have sweat glands, but other patches (color-coded *yellow*) have none.

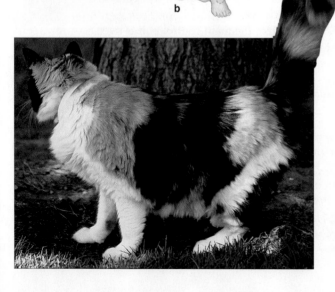

Figure 15.5 *Animated!*   Why is this female cat "calico"? In her body cells, one of her two X chromosomes has a dominant allele for the brownish-black pigment melanin. Expression of the allele on her other X chromosome codes for orange fur. When this cat was still an embryo, one X chromosome was inactivated at random in each cell that had formed by then. Patches of different colors reflect which allele was shut down in cells that formed a given tissue region. (White patches are an outcome of an interaction that involves a different gene, the product of which blocks melanin synthesis.)

petal
carpel
stamen
sepal

B

A   C

1   2   3   4

petals   carpel

c sepals   stamens

a Wild-type flower

b The abnormal flowers of four mutant plants

Figure 15.6 *Animated!* Controls over formation of flowers, based on mutations in *Arabidopsis thaliana*. This plant's flowers have four sepals, four petals, six stamens, and two fused carpels. The pattern of expression of floral identity genes affects whorls of cells that differentiate near the tip of newly forming flowers. Whorl 1 becomes sepals; whorl 2, petals; whorl 3, stamens; and whorl 4, the carpel. The above model represents the relative locations of tissues in which each set of floral identity genes—*A*, *B*, or *C*—is expressed. Gene products "tell" cells in each whorl what to do.

between the sexes. The normal development of female embryos depends on this type of control.

How, in a single nucleus, does only one of two X chromosomes get shut down? Methylation of histones and the action of *XIST*, an X-linked gene, do the trick. The *XIST* product, a large RNA molecule, sticks like masking paint to chromosomal DNA. Although we do not know why, the *XIST* gene on only one of the two chromosomes is active. That chromosome and its genes get painted with RNA. The other one remains paint-free; its genes remain available for transcription —sort of. Be sure to read *Critical Thinking* question 9 on page 241. It puts a twist on this generalized picture of X chromosome inactivation.

GENE CONTROL OF FLOWER FORMATION

Plants, too, offer fine examples of gene controls. For instance, when some plant shoots put on new growth, young plant cells right behind the tips differentiate in ways that produce flowers. Whorls of the new tissues become sepals, petals, stamens, and carpels (Figure 15.6). Studies of mutations in the common wall cress plant, *Arabidopsis thaliana*, support an **ABC model** for how all of the specialized parts of a flower develop in a predictable pattern. Three sets of master genes—*A*, *B*, and *C*—guide the process. As you will see, they are like the genes that control how body parts of animal embryos form in predictable patterns.

The cells dividing at the tip of a floral shoot form whorls of tissue, one over the other, like onion layers. What will the cells in each whorl become? It depends

on which genes of the *ABC* group are activated. In the outermost whorl, only *A* genes are switched on, and their products trigger events that cause sepals to form. Moving inward, cells in the next whorl express *A* and *B* genes; they give rise to petals. Farther in are cells that express *B* and *C* genes; they give rise to stamens (male floral structures). Cells of the innermost whorl express *C* genes only; they give rise to a fused carpel (a female floral structure).

Support for the model comes from mutations in genes of the *ABC* group (Figure 15.6*b*). Mutation in an *A* group gene alters the two outermost whorls. The flower that forms has stamens and carpels but no petals. Mutation in a *B* group gene affects the second and third whorls; sepals replace petals, and a carpel replaces stamens. Mutation in a *C* group gene alters the innermost whorls. The resulting flower is sterile (no stamens, no carpel) but has a profusion of petals.

The product of a different gene, *Leafy*, controls the activation of the sets of *ABC* genes. Certain mutations in *Leafy* keep flowers from forming on shoots where we normally expect to see them. And what switches on *Leafy*? Evidence points to a steroid hormone.

Dosage compensation in mammals is an example of gene control in eukaryotes. Most of the genes on one of the X chromosomes in females (XX) are inactivated so that early development proceeds the same as it does in males (XY).

As another example, selective expression of ABC genes controls how flowers develop.

15.3 There's a Fly in My Research

Patterns in the body plan emerge as an embryo develops, and they are both beautiful and fascinating. Researchers have correlated many of the patterns with expression of specific genes at particular times, in particular tissues. Tiny fruit flies yielded big clues to the connection.

For about a hundred years, *Drosophila melanogaster* has been the fly of choice for laboratory experiments. Why? It costs almost nothing to feed this fruit fly, which is only about 4.6 centimeters (1.8 inches) long and can live in bottles. Also, *D. melanogaster* reproduces fast and has a short life cycle, and disposing of dozens of spent bodies after an experiment is a snap. We now know how all of its 13,601 genes are distributed along the length of its four pairs of chromosomes.

Anatomical, cytological, biochemical, and genetic studies of *Drosophila* continue to reveal gene controls over development. In addition, they yield insights into evolutionary connections among groups of animals.

Discovery of Homeotic Genes   Like fruit flies, most eukaryotic species have **homeotic genes**, a class of master genes that contain information about mapping out the basic body plan. The genes code for regulatory proteins that include a "homeodomain," a sequence of about sixty amino acids. This sequence binds to control elements in promoters and enhancers.

Different homeotic genes are transcribed in specific parts of a developing embryo, so their products become concentrated in local tissue regions. Body parts form as the products interact with one another and with control elements to switch on other genes along the length of the body's main axis, according to an inherited plan.

Researchers discovered homeotic genes in mutant fruit flies that had body parts growing out of the wrong places. As an example, the *antennapedia* gene is supposed to be transcribed only in embryonic tissues that give rise to a thorax, complete with legs. This gene normally is not transcribed in cells of all other tissue regions. But Figure 15.7a shows what happened after a mutation altered

some control over transcription and the gene was wrongly transcribed in the tissue destined to become a head.

Plants, too, have master genes. You already read about how they control floral development. Similarly, a different master gene helps leaf veins in corn plants form straight, parallel lines. When the gene mutates, the veins twist.

More than 100 homeotic genes have been identified in diverse eukaryotes—and the same mechanisms control their transcription. Many of the genes are functionally interchangeable among species as evolutionarily distant as yeasts and humans, so we can expect that they evolved in the most ancient eukaryotic cells. Their protein products often differ only in modest substitutions. In other words, one amino acid has replaced another, but its chemical properties are still similar.

Knockout Experiments   *Drosophila* researchers made more discoveries about how embryos develop. For instance, with **knockout experiments**, a wild-type gene is mutated in a way that prevents its transcription or translation. If genetically engineered knockout individuals differ in form or behavior from wild-type individuals, this may be a clue to the function of the missing gene. Such experiments have yielded insights into the functions of many hundreds of genes in different organisms.

Researchers tend to name the genes based on what happens in their absence. For instance, *eyeless* is a control gene expressed in fruit fly embryos. In its absence, no eyes form. *Dunce* is a regulatory gene required for learning and memory. *Wingless, wrinkled,* and *minibrain* genes are self-explanatory. *Tinman* is necessary for heart development. Among other things, *groucho* prevents overproduction of whisker bristles. Figure 15.7 shows a few of the mutants.

In other experiments, researchers add special promoters to a gene so that they can control its expression with an external cue, such as temperature. They delete genes from one part of the *Drosophila* genome and put them back someplace else. This molecular sleight of hand revealed that expression of the *eyeless* gene can induce an eye to form not only on the fruit fly head, but also on the wings and legs (Figure 15.7c).

Figure 15.7 (**a**) Experimental evidence of controls over where body parts develop. In *Drosophila* larvae, activation of genes in one group of cells normally results in antennae on the head. A mutation that affects *antennapedia* gene transcription puts legs on the head. This is one of the genes controlled by regulatory proteins with homeodomains. (**b**) Model for a homeodomain binding to a transcriptional control site in DNA. (**c**) More *Drosophila* mutations.

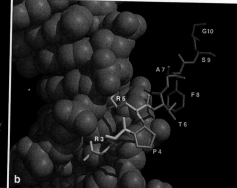

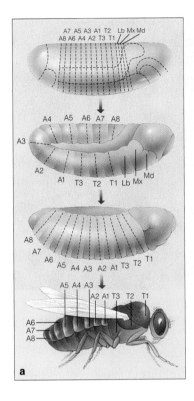

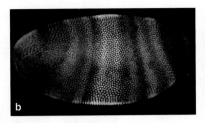

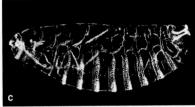

Figure 15.8 Genes and *Drosophila*'s segmented body plan. (**a**) Fate map for the surface of a *Drosophila* zygote. Such maps indicate where each differentiated cell type in the adult originated. The pattern starts with the polar distribution of maternal mRNA and proteins in the unfertilized egg. This polarity dictates the future body axis. A series of segments will develop along this axis. Genes specify whether legs, wings, eyes, or some other body parts will develop on a particular segment.

Briefly, here is how it happens: Maternal gene products prompt expression of gap genes. Different gap genes become activated in regions of the embryo with higher or lower concentrations of different maternal gene products. Gap gene products influence each other's expression as well. They form a primitive spatial map.

Depending on where they occur relative to concentrations of gap gene products, embryonic cells express different pair-rule genes. Products of pair-rule genes accumulate in seven transverse stripes that mark the onset of segmentation (**b**). They activate other genes, the products of which divide the body into units (**c**). These interactions influence the expression of homeotic genes, which collectively govern the structural and functional identity of each segment.

The *eyeless* gene even has counterparts in humans (the *PAX6* gene), mice (*Pax-6*), and squids (also *Pax-6*). Humans who have no functional *PAX6* genes have eyes with malformed irises. *PAX-6* inserted into any tissue of an eyeless mutant fly induces an eye to form wherever it is expressed. This kind of molecular evidence points to a shared ancestor among animals as evolutionarily distant as insects, cephalopods, and mammals.

Filling In Details of Body Plans Let's take stock. As an embryo develops, cells in different body regions become organized in different ways. Cells divide and differentiate. They migrate or stick to cells of the same type in tissues. They live or die after performing their function. These are genetically programmed events that fill in details of the body in orderly patterns, in keeping with the expression of master genes. Those genes are switched on in specific tissues, at specific stages of development. The products of those genes deal mainly with transcription. In effect, they form a three-dimensional map along the main body axis.

Depending on where undifferentiated cells are relative to the map, they are the start of specialized tissues and organs. That is how the sequential expression of master genes along the body axis gives rise to the body segments of fruit flies (Figure 15.8).

Pattern formation is the name for the emergence of embryonic tissues and organs in orderly patterns, at times and in places where we expect them to be. Section 43.5 offers a closer look at the controlled gene interactions that fill in details of the animal body plan.

c A few more *Drosophila* mutations that yielded clues to gene function *Left to right,* an eye that formed on a leg, yellow miniature, curly wings, vestigial wings, and a double thorax.

15.4 Prokaryotic Gene Control

LINK TO
SECTION
8.2

In prokaryotic cells, gene controls deal mainly with quickly slowing down and starting up transcription in response to short-term shifts in environmental conditions. A diversity of long-term controls is not required; none of these species slowly develops into a complex, multicelled form (Table 15.1).

When nutrients are plentiful and when other external conditions also favor growth and reproduction, all prokaryotic cells rapidly transcribe genes that specify all of the enzymes required for nutrient absorption and other growth-related tasks. Genes that are tapped most often occur one after the other as a set of genetic information in the DNA. They all can be transcribed together, which yields a single RNA strand.

NEGATIVE CONTROL OF THE LACTOSE OPERON

With this bit of background, consider an example of how one kind of prokaryote responds to the presence or absence of lactose. *Escherichia coli* lives in the gut of mammals, where it dines on nutrients traveling past. Milk typically nourishes mammalian infants. It does not contain glucose, the sugar of choice for *E. coli*. It does contain lactose, a different sugar.

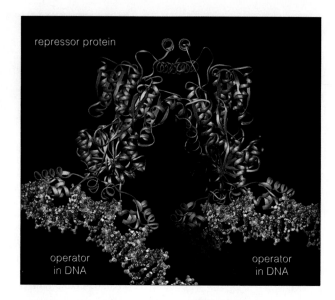

Figure 15.9 Model for the repressor protein of the lactose operon when it is bound to two operators in DNA.

After being weaned, infants of most species drink little (if any) milk. Even so, *E. coli* cells can still use lactose if and when it shows up in the gut. They can activate a set of three genes for lactose-metabolizing enzymes. In *E. coli* DNA, a promoter precedes all three genes, and two operators flank it. Each **operator** is a binding site for a type of regulatory protein known as repressor, which stops transcription (Figure 15.9).

Any arrangement in which a promoter and a set of operators control access to more than one prokaryotic gene is called an **operon**.

In the absence of lactose, a repressor molecule binds to the set of operators. Binding causes the DNA region that contains the promoter to twist into a loop, as in Figure 15.10. RNA polymerase, the workhorse that transcribes genes, is not able to bind to a looped-up promoter. The result is that operon genes are not used when they are not required.

When lactose *is* in the gut, *E. coli* converts some of it to allolactose. This sugar binds to the repressor and changes its molecular shape. The altered repressor cannot bind to operators. The looped DNA unwinds and RNA polymerase transcribes the genes, so lactose-degrading enzymes are produced when required.

POSITIVE CONTROL OF THE LACTOSE OPERON

E. coli cells pay far more attention to glucose than to lactose. Even when lactose is in the gut, the lactose operon is not used much—unless there is no glucose.

Table 15.1 Prokaryotic Versus Eukaryotic Gene Control

Prokaryotic Gene Control

1. Control mechanisms adjust enzyme-mediated reactions in response to short-term changes in nutrient availability and other environmental conditions.

2. Operons control the expression of more than one gene at a time.

3. Transcriptional controls are *reversibly* inhibited when conditions do not favor growth and reproduction.

4. Translation starts immediately; prokaryotic RNA transcripts have no introns, no processing controls.

Eukaryotic Gene Control

1. Some control mechanisms adjust enzyme-mediated reactions in response to short-term changing conditions.

2. In multicelled species, other controls activate sets of genes at different times, in different tissues. They induce generally *irreversible* events that are part of a long-term program of growth and development.

3. Diverse controls operate during gene transcription and translation, and on the gene products. mRNA transcripts are processed in the nucleus; controls govern the timing and rate of their translation in the cytoplasm.

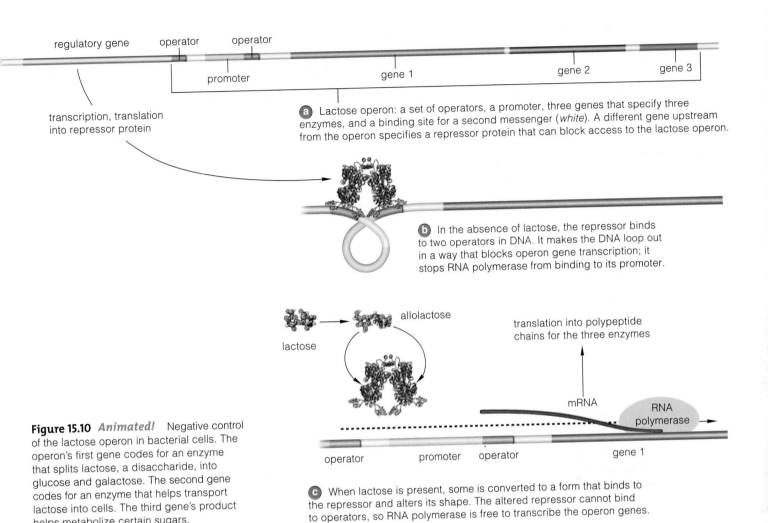

Figure 15.10 *Animated!* Negative control of the lactose operon in bacterial cells. The operon's first gene codes for an enzyme that splits lactose, a disaccharide, into glucose and galactose. The second gene codes for an enzyme that helps transport lactose into cells. The third gene's product helps metabolize certain sugars.

a Lactose operon: a set of operators, a promoter, three genes that specify three enzymes, and a binding site for a second messenger (*white*). A different gene upstream from the operon specifies a repressor protein that can block access to the lactose operon.

b In the absence of lactose, the repressor binds to two operators in DNA. It makes the DNA loop out in a way that blocks operon gene transcription; it stops RNA polymerase from binding to its promoter.

c When lactose is present, some is converted to a form that binds to the repressor and alters its shape. The altered repressor cannot bind to operators, so RNA polymerase is free to transcribe the operon genes.

When that happens, an activator called CAP (short for catabolite activator protein) exerts positive control over the lactose operon. It makes a promoter far more inviting to RNA polymerase. But CAP cannot issue the invitation until it has already become bound to a chemical messenger: cAMP (short for cyclic adenosine monophosphate). When the activator and cAMP join together as a complex to the promoter, they make it much easier for RNA polymerase to start transcribing genes. Such complexes are called transcription factors.

When glucose is plentiful, ATP forms by glycolysis (Section 8.2), but synthesis of an enzyme necessary to synthesize cAMP is blocked. The blocking ends when glucose is scarce and lactose becomes available. cAMP accumulates, the CAP–cAMP complexes form, and the lactose operon genes are transcribed fast. The gene products allow lactose to be converted to glucose, the preferred sugar of *E. coli*.

Unlike cells of *E. coli*, many of us develop *lactose intolerance*. Cells making up the lining of our small intestine make and then secrete lactase into the gut. As many people age, however, concentrations of this lactose-digesting enzyme decline. Lactose accumulates and is moved on to the large intestine, or colon. It promotes population explosions of resident bacteria. As the bacterial cells busily digest the lactose, a gaseous metabolic product accumulates, the gas distends the colon's wall and causes pain. The short fatty acid chains that form during bacterial metabolism cause diarrhea, which can be severe.

Prokaryotic cells do not require extensive controls over long-term development of complex bodies; they are small, fast reproducers. The main controls guide the transcription of enzyme-coding genes in response to short-term shifts in nutrient availability and other outside conditions.

Summary

Section 15.1 Gene expression within a cell changes in response to chemical conditions and signals from the outside. In complex multicelled species, it is subject to long-term controls over growth and development.

Control mechanisms govern whether, when, and how a gene is expressed. Hormones, activator proteins, and other regulatory elements interact with one another before, during, and after transcription and translation.

With negative control mechanisms, regulatory elements slow or stop a cell activity. With positive control mechanisms, they promote it.

Control is exerted before, during, and after gene transcription and translation. Transcription is a major control point for most eukaryotic genes because so many of the participating molecules can be controlled independently of the others.

Diverse controls guide embryonic development of multicelled eukaryotes. Each cell in an embryo inherits the same genes, but they start selectively activating and suppressing some in unique ways. The outcome of selective gene expression is called cell differentiation: cell lineages become unique in one or more aspects of composition, structure, and function. Those lineages are the start of specialized tissues and organs.

Biology⑤Now
Review the control points for gene expression with the animation on BiologyNow.

Section 15.2 Two examples are given of eukaryotic gene controls, one in mammals, the other in plants:

In the embryos of all female mammals, X chromosome inactivation is an outcome of the interactions between a product of the *XIST* gene and control elements in one of the two X chromosomes in cells. This control mechanism maintains a required balance of gene expression between the sexes while mammalian embryos are developing.

Studies of mutations in *Arabidopsis thaliana* support an ABC model for the formation of flowers. Three sets of master genes (*A, B,* and *C*) guide the differentiation of whorls of cells into sepals, petals, stamens, and carpels.

Biology⑤Now
Observe how eukaryotic gene controls influence development with the animation on BiologyNow.

Section 15.3 Many gene controls were identified through experiments with mutant forms of *Drosophila melanogaster*. Others were discovered by knockout experiments in which individual genes are deactivated before a new wild-type fly develops.

While embryos of this fruit fly and of most other eukaryotes develop, homeotic genes are activated in sequence. The protein products of this class of master genes become more or less concentrated along the body's main axis, which maps out the basic body plan. Cells differentiate according to their location along the map. Their descendants fill in the details of the body plan by forming specialized tissues and organs in patterns where we expect them to be.

Section 15.4 Prokaryotic cells do not have great structural complexity and do not undergo development. Most of the gene controls reversibly adjust transcription rates in response to environmental conditions, especially nutrient availability. Bacterial operons are examples of prokaryotic gene controls. The lactose operon controls three genes, the three products of which digest lactose. It has a promoter region in DNA (binding sites for RNA polymerase). Two operators flank it and are binding sites for a repressor protein that can block transcription.

Biology⑤Now
Explore the structure and function of the bacterial lactose operon with the animation on BiologyNow.

Self-Quiz

Answers in Appendix II

1. The expression of a given gene depends on the _____ .
   a. type and function of cell c. environmental signals
   b. chemical conditions d. all of the above

2. Control mechanisms adjust gene expression in response to changing _____ .
   a. nutrient availability c. signals from other cells
   b. solute concentrations d. all of the above

3. Regulatory elements interact with _____ .
   a. DNA c. gene products
   b. RNA d. all of the above

4. At _____ in DNA, regulatory proteins gather and control transcription of specific genes.
   a. promoters c. operators
   b. enhancers d. both a and b

5. Eukaryotic gene controls govern _____ .
   a. transcription e. mRNA degradation
   b. RNA processing f. gene products
   c. translation g. a through e
   d. RNA transport h. all of the above

6. Eukaryotic genes guide _____ .
   a. fast short-term activities c. development
   b. overall growth d. all of the above

7. Cell differentiation _____ .
   a. occurs in all complex multicelled organisms
   b. requires unique genes in different cells
   c. involves selective gene expression
   d. both a and c
   e. all of the above

8. During X chromosome inactivation _____ .
   a. many genes are shut down c. sweat glands form
   b. RNA paints chromosomes d. both a and b

9. A cell with a Barr body is _____ .
   a. prokaryotic c. from a female mammal
   b. from a male mammal d. infected by Barr virus

10. Homeotic gene products _____ .
   a. are binding sites that flank a bacterial operon
   b. map out a developing embryo's body plan
   c. control X chromosome inactivation
   d. both a and c

11. Knockout experiments mutate _____ genes.
   a. bacterial c. engineered
   b. wild-type d. both a and c

12. A(n) _____ is a promoter and a set of operators that control access to two or more prokaryotic genes.
    a. lactose molecule   c. dosage compensator
    b. operon   d. both b and c

13. Match the terms with the most suitable description.
    _____ ABC model   a. a big RNA is its product
    _____ *XIST* gene   b. binding site for repressor
    _____ operator   c. cells become specialized in
    _____ Barr body   composition, function, etc.
    _____ process of cell   d. inactivated X chromosome
           differentiation   e. how flowers develop
    _____ methylation   f. —CH$_3$ additions to DNA

Additional questions are available on Biology ⊜ Now™

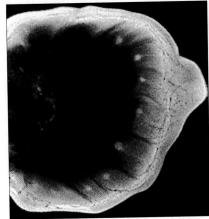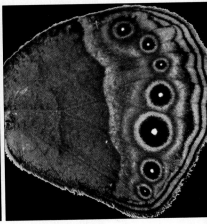

Figure 15.11 *Left*, seven spots in the embryonic wing of a moth larva identify the presence of a gene product that will induce the formation of seven "eyespots" in the wing of the adult (*right*).

Critical Thinking

1. Do all transcriptional controls operate in prokaryotic as well as eukaryotic cells? Why or why not?

2. If all cells in your body start out life with the same inherited information on how to build proteins, then what caused the differences between a red blood cell and a white one? Between a white blood cell and a nerve cell?

3. Unlike most rodents, guinea pigs are well developed at the time of birth. Within a few days, they can eat grass, vegetables, and other plant material.

    Suppose a breeder decides to separate baby guinea pigs from their mothers three weeks after they were born. He wants to raise the males and the females in different cages. However, he has trouble identifying the sex of young guinea pigs. Suggest how a quick look through a microscope can help him identify the females.

4. Calico cats are almost always female. A male calico cat is usually sterile. Find out why.

5. Reflect on the mutant *Arabidopsis thaliana* flowers in Figure 15.6. Small changes in the structure of control genes brought about those changes. Would you predict that such changes figured in the evolution of more than 295,000 kinds of plants, each with distinctive flowers?

    Also reflect on the *Drosophila melanogaster* mutants shown in Figure 15.7. Would you predict that homeotic gene mutations figured in the evolution of the more than 1.5 million known species of animals?

6. *Duchenne muscular dystrophy*, a genetic disorder, affects boys almost exclusively. Muscles begin to atrophy (waste away) in affected children, who typically die in their teens or early twenties (Section 12.7).

    Muscle biopsies of a few women who carry an allele that is associated with the disorder identified some body regions of atrophied muscle tissue. They also showed that muscles adjacent to a region of atrophy were normal or even larger and more chemically active, as if to compensate for the weakness of the adjoining region.

    Form a hypothesis about the genetic basis of Duchenne muscular dystrophy that includes an explanation of why the symptoms might appear in some body regions but not others.

7. Figure 15.11 shows seven "spots" that emerge in the wings of a developing moth larva. The spots identify where seven distinct eyespots will appear on the wings of adult moths. What is the name of the class of genes responsible for mapping out such details of the body plan of developing embryos, including insect larvae?

8. Geraldo isolated an *E. coli* strain in which a mutation has hampered the capacity of CAP to bind to a region of the lactose operon, as it would do normally. How will this mutation affect transcription of the lactose operon when the *E. coli* cells are exposed to the following conditions? Briefly state your answers:
    a. Lactose and glucose are both available.
    b. Lactose is available but glucose is not.
    c. Both lactose and glucose are absent.

9. About 300 million years ago, before mammals began their great adaptive radiation, their X and Y chromosomes were about the same in size. When paired, the two sex chromosomes typically synapsed and exchanged alleles along their length. The X chromosome now carries 1,141 genes. Over time, however, the Y chromosome lost most of itself and now contains only 255 genes. Its big claim to fame is ownership of the *SRY* gene, the master of sex determination.

    Think about the dosage compensation theory, sketched out in Section 15.2. According to this theory, *X chromosome inactivation* is nature's way of compensating for a double dose of X-linked genes in XX embryos, because there are not enough genes left on the puny Y chromosome to balance out their expression. And yet, about 15 percent of the genes on an inactivated X chromosome escape being painted to varying degrees—which means women make more copies of certain proteins than men do.

    Besides this, another 10 percent of the X-linked genes might or might not get painted in individual embryos—which means women differ significantly from one another in which X-linked genes are active.

    Now consider this: Human and chimpanzee genomes differ by 1.5 percent. Women differ from men by 1 percent! Go ahead and let your brain chew on that one.

    You may wish to start with this recent article: L. Carel and H. Willard, "X-Inactivation Profile Reveals Extensive Variability in X-Linked Gene Expression in Females," *Nature* 2005; 434(7031):400–404.

16 STUDYING AND MANIPULATING GENOMES

Golden Rice, or Frankenfood?

Not too long ago, the World Health Organization made a conservative estimate that 124 million children around the world show vitamin A deficiencies. Their skin, eyes, and mucous membranes are dry and vulnerable to infection. They do not grow and develop as they should, and they show signs of mental impairment. Each year at least a million die of malnutrition, and about 350,000 end up permanently blind.

Ingo Potrykus and Peter Beyer wanted to help. As they knew, beta-carotene is a yellow pigment in all plant leaves, and it also is a precursor for vitamin A. These geneticists borrowed three genes from garden daffodils (*Narcissus pseudonarcissus*) and a bacterium, and transferred them to rice plants. The plants transcribed the genes and did something they could not do before. They made beta-carotene not only in their leaves but also in their *seeds*—the grains of Golden Rice (Figure 16.1).

Why rice? Rice is the main food for 3 billion people in impoverished countries. There, the poor cannot afford leafy vegetables and other sources of beta-carotene. Getting beta-carotene into rice grains would be the least costly way to deliver the vitamin to those who need it the most, but doing so was beyond the scope of conventional breeding practices. Research continues, and the amount of beta-carotene in SGR1, a more recent version of Golden Rice, is twenty-three times higher than the prototype.

No one wants children to suffer or die. However, many people oppose the idea of genetically modified (GM) foods, including golden rice. Possibly they are unaware of the history of agrarian societies, because it is not as if our ancestors were twiddling their green thumbs. For thousands of years, their artificial selection practices coaxed new plants and new breeds of cattle, cats, dogs, and birds from wild ancestral stocks. Meatier turkeys, huge watermelons, big juicy corn kernels from puny hard ones—the list goes on (Figure 16.1).

And we are newcomers at this! During the 3.8 billion years before we even made our entrance, nature busily conducted uncountable numbers of genetic experiments by way of mutation, crossing over, and gene transfers between species. These processes introduced changes in the molecular messages of inheritance, and today we see their outcomes in the sweep of life's diversity.

Perhaps the unsettling thing about the more recent human-directed changes is that the pace has picked up, hugely. We are getting much better at tinkering with the genetics of many organisms. We do this for pure research and for useful, practical applications.

Figure 16.1   Where one genetic engineering success story started: (**a**) Researchers transferred genetic information from ordinary daffodils into rice plants, which then used it to stockpile beta-carotene in their seeds—rice grains. (**b**) Two successive generations of Golden Rice compared with grains from a regular rice plant at lower left. *Facing page*, an artificial selection success story—a big kernel from a modern strain of corn next to tiny kernels of an ancestral corn species discovered in a prehistoric cave in Mexico.

IMPACTS, ISSUES

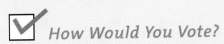

Watch the video online!

For instance, many crop plants, including corn, beets, and potatoes, have been modified. They are now widely planted. They are less temperamental about their living conditions than rice plants are, and they have not run rampant through ecosystems. After a decade-long study in the United Kingdom, researchers concluded that the new crop plants being monitored were doing no harm. Throughout Arizona, farmers grow cotton plants that are genetically engineered for pest resistance. The plantings have not put the environment at risk and might even be less disruptive compared to current agricultural practices. University of Arizona entomologist Bruce Tabashnik, who is monitoring cotton fields, notes that farmers have cut applications of chemical pesticides by 75 percent.

Take stock of how far you have come in this unit. You started with cell division mechanisms that allow parents to pass on DNA to new generations. You moved to the chromosomal and molecular basis of inheritance, then on to gene controls that guide life's continuity. The sequence parallels the history of genetics. And now, you have arrived at the point in time where geneticists hold molecular keys to the kingdom of inheritance. What they are unlocking is already having impact on life in the biosphere.

 How Would You Vote?

Nutritional labeling is required on all packaged food in the United States, but genetically modified food products may be sold without labeling. Should food distributors be required to label all products made from genetically modified plants or livestock? See BiologyNow for details, then vote online.

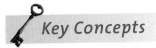 **Key Concepts**

MAKING RECOMBINANT DNA

Researchers routinely make recombinant DNA molecules. They use restriction enzymes to isolate, cut, and join gene regions from DNA of different species. They use plasmids and other vectors to insert the recombinant molecule into target cells. Section 16.1

ISOLATING AND AMPLIFYING DNA FRAGMENTS

Researchers isolate and make many copies of genes that interest them. PCR is now the gene amplification method of choice. The genes are copied in amounts large enough for research and practical applications. Section 16.2

DECIPHERING DNA FRAGMENTS

Sequencing methods reveal the linear order of bases in a sample of DNA. Automated methods complete the task with impressive speed. Sections 16.3, 16.4

MAPPING AND ANALYZING WHOLE GENOMES

Genomics is concerned with mapping and sequencing of the genomes of humans and other species. Comparative genomics yields evidence of evolutionary relationships among groups of organisms. Section 16.5

USING THE NEW TECHNOLOGIES

Genetic engineering results in transgenic organisms, which incorporate genes from another species. With gene therapy, a mutated or altered gene is isolated, modified, and copied. Copies are inserted back into the individual to cover the gene's function. The new technologies raise social, legal, ecological, and ethical questions. Sections 16.6–16.10

Links to Earlier Concepts

This chapter builds on earlier explanations of the molecular structure of DNA (Sections 3.7, 13.2), and DNA replication and DNA repair (13.4). You may wish to review quickly the nature of mRNA transcript processing (14.1) and controls over gene transcription (14.1). You will come across more uses for radioisotopes (2.2) and fluorescent light (6.6). You will be reminded of why it is useful to know about membrane proteins (5.2). You will see why the lactose operon is not necessarily of obscure interest (15.4).

16.1 A Molecular Toolkit

LINKS TO
SECTIONS
13.1, 13.3, 14.1

Analysis of genes starts with manipulation of DNA. With molecular tools, researchers can cut DNA from different sources, then splice the fragments together.

THE SCISSORS: RESTRICTION ENZYMES

In 1970, Hamilton Smith was studying viral infection of *Haemophilus influenzae*. This bacterium protects itself from infection by cutting up viral DNA before it can get inserted into the bacterial chromosome. Smith and his colleagues isolated one of the bacterial enzymes that cuts viral DNA. It was the first known **restriction enzyme**. In time, several hundred strains of bacteria and a few eukaryotic cells yielded thousands more.

A restriction enzyme cuts double-stranded DNA at a specific base sequence between four and eight base pairs in length. Most of these recognition sites contain the same nucleotide sequence, in the 5'→ 3' direction, on both strands of the DNA. For instance, the enzyme

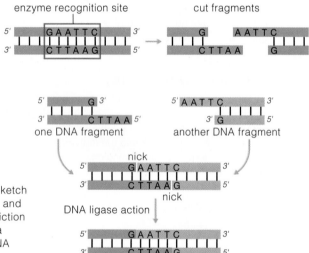

Figure 16.2 Sketch of the formation and splicing of restriction fragments into a recombinant DNA molecule.

*Eco*RI recognizes and cuts GAATTC (Figure 16.2). It makes staggered cuts that produce a "sticky end," or single-stranded "tail,"on the DNA fragments. The tail can base-pair with a tail of another fragment cut by the same enzyme, because the sticky ends of both will match up as base pairs. Tiny nicks remain when DNA fragments base-pair. Remember **DNA ligases** (Section 13.3)? They seal the nicks, which yields a recombinant molecule (Figure 16.2). We define **recombinant DNA** as any molecule consisting of base sequences from two or more organisms of the same or different species.

CLONING VECTORS

Bacterial cells, recall, have only one chromosome—a circular DNA molecule. But many also have plasmids. A **plasmid** is a small circle of extra DNA with just a few genes (Figure 16.3a). It gets replicated along with the bacterial chromosome. Bacteria normally can live without plasmids. Even so, certain plasmid genes are useful, as when they confer resistance to antibiotics.

Under favorable conditions, bacteria divide often, so huge populations of genetically identical cells form swiftly. Before each division, replication enzymes copy chromosomal DNA *and* plasmid DNA, in some cases repeatedly. This gave researchers the idea of inserting DNA fragments into a plasmid to see if a bacterial cell would replicate them right along with the plasmid.

A plasmid that has accepted foreign DNA and can slip into a host bacterium, yeast, or some other cell is a **cloning vector**. Most vectors have been engineered to incorporate multiple cloning sites, which are unique restriction enzyme sequences in one part of the vector (Figure 16.3). As you will see, cloning vectors contain genes that help researchers identify which cells take them up. Viruses also are used as cloning vectors.

Figure 16.3 (a) Plasmids (*arrows*) from a ruptured *Escherichia coli* cell. (b) A commercially available cloning vector. Its useful restriction enzyme sites are listed at right. This vector includes antibiotic resistance genes (*blue*) and the bacterial *lacZ* gene (*red*). Researchers can check for the expression of these genes as a way to identify the bacterial cells that take up recombinant molecules.

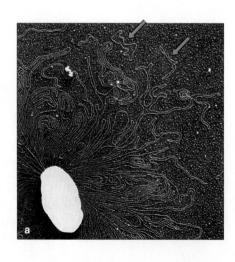

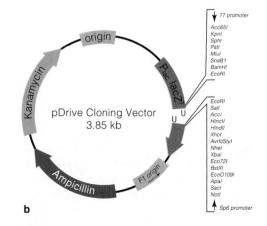

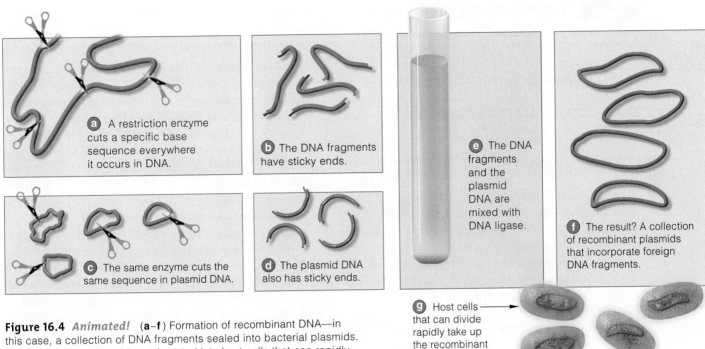

Figure 16.4 *Animated!* (**a–f**) Formation of recombinant DNA—in this case, a collection of DNA fragments sealed into bacterial plasmids. (**g**) Recombinant plasmids are inserted into host cells that can rapidly make multiple copies of the foreign DNA of interest.

Within the figure:

a A restriction enzyme cuts a specific base sequence everywhere it occurs in DNA.

b The DNA fragments have sticky ends.

c The same enzyme cuts the same sequence in plasmid DNA.

d The plasmid DNA also has sticky ends.

e The DNA fragments and the plasmid DNA are mixed with DNA ligase.

f The result? A collection of recombinant plasmids that incorporate foreign DNA fragments.

g Host cells that can divide rapidly take up the recombinant plasmids.

A cell that takes up a cloning vector may give rise to a huge population of descendant cells, each with an identical copy of the vector and the foreign DNA inserted into it. Collectively, the identical cells hold many "cloned" copies of the foreign DNA.

Such DNA cloning is a tool that helps researchers amplify and harvest unlimited amounts of particular DNA fragments for their studies (Figure 16.4).

cDNA CLONING

Remember those introns in eukaryotic DNA (Section 14.1)? Bacterial cells cannot remove introns from RNA, as eukaryotic cells do. That is why researchers often use mature mRNA transcripts. The introns already have been removed, and protein-coding sequences and a few sequences that are identifiable signals are left. Researchers also may use mRNA to study gene expression, because the cells that are actively using a gene obviously contain mRNA transcribed from it.

Restriction enzymes will not cut single-stranded molecules, so they will not cleave mRNA (which is single-stranded). However, mRNA can be cloned if it is first transcribed—in reverse. Replication enzymes isolated from viruses or bacterial cells can transcribe mRNA inside a test tube. **Reverse transcriptase** is one viral enzyme that can catalyze the bonding of free nucleotides into one strand of *complementary* DNA, or **cDNA** on an mRNA template (Figure 16.5). Base pairs

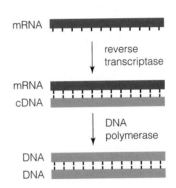

Figure 16.5 How to make cDNA. Reverse transcriptase catalyzes the assembly of a single DNA strand on an mRNA template, forming an mRNA–cDNA hybrid molecule. Next, DNA polymerase replaces the mRNA with another DNA strand. The result is double-stranded DNA.

of cDNA get hydrogen-bonded to those of mRNA, forming a hybrid molecule. Next, DNA polymerase is added to the mix. It strips RNA bases from the hybrid molecule while it copies the first strand of cDNA into a second strand. The result, a double-stranded DNA copy of the original mRNA, may be used for cloning.

Molecular biologists manipulate DNA and RNA. Restriction enzymes cut DNA from individuals of different species or the same species. DNA ligases glue the fragments into plasmids.

A recombinant plasmid is a cloning vector. It can slip into bacteria, yeast, or other cells that divide rapidly. The host cells make multiple, identical copies of the foreign DNA.

Reverse transcriptase, a viral enzyme, uses a single strand of mRNA as the template to make cDNA for cloning.

16.2 From Haystacks to Needles

LINKS TO
SECTIONS
2.1, 10.1, 13.2

*A **genome**, recall, is all the DNA in a haploid number of the chromosomes that characterize a species. To study or modify any gene, researchers must first find it among thousands of others in the genome, and it's like searching for a needle in a haystack. Once found, it must be copied many times to make enough material for experiments.*

ISOLATING GENES

A **gene library** is a collection of host cells that house different cloned fragments of DNA. We call the cloned fragments of an entire genome a *genomic* library. By contrast, a *cDNA library* is derived from mRNA.

How can a single gene of interest be isolated from thousands or millions of others in a library of clones? Clones that have the gene are mixed up with others that do not. Researchers might decide to use a **probe** to find the gene. Probes are short stretches of DNA that are complementary to a gene of interest and that are tagged with a label, such as a radioisotope, that devices can detect (Section 2.1). Probes base-pair with DNA in a gene region, then researchers pinpoint the gene by detecting the label on the probe. Any base pairing between DNA (or RNA) from more than one source is known as **nucleic acid hybridization**.

How do researchers make a probe? If they already know the gene sequence of interest, they can use it to design and assemble a **primer**, or a short stretch of synthetic, single-stranded DNA. If the sequence is not known, they can use DNA that was already isolated from the same gene in a closely related species. Even if the probe is not an exact match, it might still tag the gene by base-pairing with part of it.

Figure 16.6 shows steps of one probe hybridization technique. Bacterial cells containing a gene library are spread out on the surface of a solid growth medium, usually enriched agar, in a petri dish. Individual cells undergo repeated divisions, which result in colonies of millions of genetically identical bacterial cells.

When you press a piece of nylon or nitrocellulose filter on top of the petri dish, some cells from each colony stick to it. They mirror the distribution of all colonies on the dish. Soaking the filter in an alkaline solution ruptures the cells, which releases their DNA. The solution also denatures DNA—which separates into single strands that stick to the filter in the spots where the colonies were. When the probe is washed over the filter, it hybridizes with (sticks to) only the DNA with the targeted sequence.

The hybridized probe can be detected with x-ray film or computerized imaging devices. Its position on the film pinpoints the position of the original colony on the petri dish. Cells from that colony alone can be cultured to isolate the cloned gene of interest.

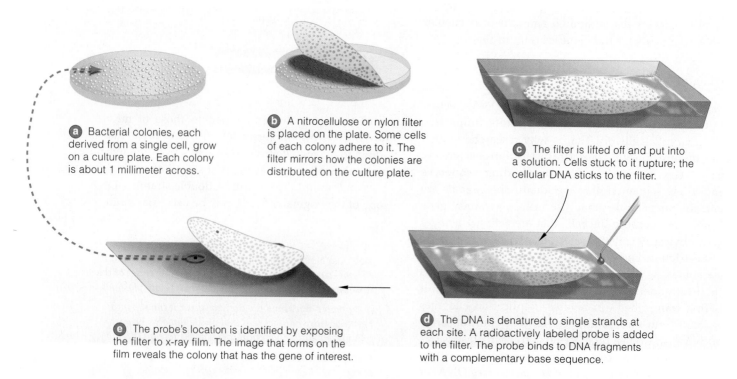

a Bacterial colonies, each derived from a single cell, grow on a culture plate. Each colony is about 1 millimeter across.

b A nitrocellulose or nylon filter is placed on the plate. Some cells of each colony adhere to it. The filter mirrors how the colonies are distributed on the culture plate.

c The filter is lifted off and put into a solution. Cells stuck to it rupture; the cellular DNA sticks to the filter.

d The DNA is denatured to single strands at each site. A radioactively labeled probe is added to the filter. The probe binds to DNA fragments with a complementary base sequence.

e The probe's location is identified by exposing the filter to x-ray film. The image that forms on the film reveals the colony that has the gene of interest.

Figure 16.6 *Animated!* How a radioactive probe helps identify a bacterial colony that contains a targeted gene.

Figure 16.7 *Animated!* Two rounds of the polymerase chain reaction, or PCR. A bacterium, *Thermus aquaticus*, is the source for the *Taq* polymerase. Thirty or more cycles of PCR may yield a billionfold increase in the number of starting DNA molecules that serve as templates.

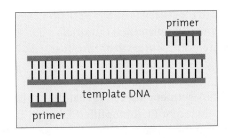

a Primers, free nucleotides, and DNA templates are mixed with heat-tolerant DNA polymerase.

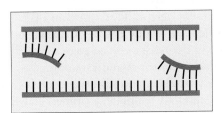

b When the mixture is heated, the DNA denatures. When it is cooled, some primers hydrogen-bond to the DNA templates.

BIG-TIME AMPLIFICATION—PCR

Researchers may replicate a gene, or part of it, with **PCR** (*Polymerase Chain Reaction*). PCR uses primers and a heat-tolerant polymerase for a hot–cold cycled reaction that replicates targeted DNA fragments. The technique can replicate the fragments by a billionfold. It can transform one needle in a haystack, that one-in-a-million DNA fragment, into a huge stack of needles with a little hay in it.

Figure 16.7 shows the reaction steps. The primers are designed to base-pair with particular nucleotide sequences on either end of the fragment of interest. Usually they are between ten and thirty bases long.

In a PCR reaction, researchers mix primers, DNA polymerase, nucleotides, and the DNA that will serve as a template for replication. Then they expose the mixture to cycles of high and low temperatures that are repeated again and again. At high temperature, the two strands of a DNA double helix separate. When the mixture is cooled, some of the primers hybridize with the DNA template.

The elevated temperatures required to separate the DNA strands destroy typical DNA polymerases. But the heat-tolerant DNA polymerase employed for PCR reactions is from *Thermus aquaticus*, a bacterium that lives in hot springs (Chapter 21). Like all other DNA polymerases, it recognizes primers bound to DNA as places to start synthesis. The temperature is raised to the optimum for this enzyme (72°C). Then synthesis occurs along the DNA template until the temperature cycles up and the DNA strands are separated again.

When the temperature cycles down, the primers rehybridize, and the reactions run once more. With each round of temperature cycling, the number of copies of targeted DNA can double. PCR quickly and exponentially amplifies even a tiny bit of DNA.

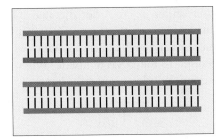

c *Taq* polymerase uses the primers to initiate synthesis. The DNA templates are copied. The first round of PCR is completed.

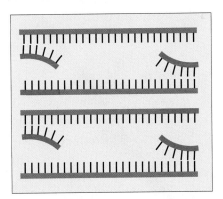

d The mixture is heated again. This denatures all the DNA into single strands. When the mixture is cooled, some of the primers hydrogen-bond to the DNA.

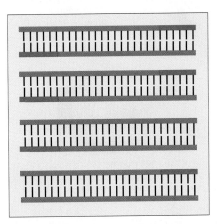

e *Taq* polymerase uses the primers to initiate synthesis, copying the DNA. The second round of PCR is complete. Each successive round of synthesis can double the number of DNA molecules.

Probes may be used to help identify one particular gene among many in gene libraries.

The polymerase chain reaction (PCR) is a method of rapidly and exponentially amplifying the number of particular DNA fragments.

16.3 Automated DNA Sequencing

LINK TO SECTION 6.6

Sequencing reveals the order of nucleotides in DNA. This technique uses DNA polymerase to partially replicate a DNA template. Automated techniques have largely replaced manual methods.

Automated DNA sequencing can reveal the sequence of a stretch of cloned or PCR-amplified DNA in just a few hours. Researchers use four standard nucleotides (T, C, A, and G). They also use four modified versions, which we represent here as T*, C*, A*, and G*. Each form of modified nucleotide has been labeled with a pigment that will fluoresce a certain color when a laser beam hits it. Each will halt strand assembly.

Researchers mix all eight kinds of nucleotides with a single-stranded DNA template, a primer, and DNA polymerase. The polymerase uses the primer to copy the template DNA into new strands of DNA. One by one, it adds nucleotides in the order dictated by the sequence of the DNA template (Figure 16.8a). Every time, the polymerase randomly attaches a standard *or* a modified nucleotide to the DNA template. When one of the modified nucleotides covalently bonds to the

forming DNA strand, no more can be added. After enough time passes, there will be some new strands that stop at each base in the DNA template sequence.

Eventually the mixture holds millions of copies of DNA fragments, all fluorescent-tagged on one end. These fragments are separated by **gel electrophoresis**, a technique that sorts fragments as they move through a semisolid slab (of polyacrylamide) in response to an electric field.

Depending on their lengths, the fragments migrate at different rates through the gel. The gel hinders the migration of longer ones more than shorter ones. By analogy, elephants running through the forest in India cannot move between the trees as fast as tigers can.

The shortest fragments migrate fastest and are first to arrive at the end of the gel. The longest fragment is last. Fragments of the same length move through the gel at the same speed, and they gather into bands.

A laser beam shines on each band when it passes through the end of the gel. The modified nucleotides attached to the fragments fluoresce in response to the light, and the sequencer detects and records the color of each band. Because each color designates one of the four particular nucleotides, the order of colored bands reveals the DNA sequence. The machine itself rapidly assembles the sequence data.

Figure 16.8b shows the partial results from one run through an automated DNA sequencer. Each peak in the tracing represents the detection of one fluorescent color as the fragments reached the end of the gel. The sequence is shown beneath the graph line.

> *DNA sequencing rapidly reveals the order of nucleotides in a cloned or amplified DNA fragment.*

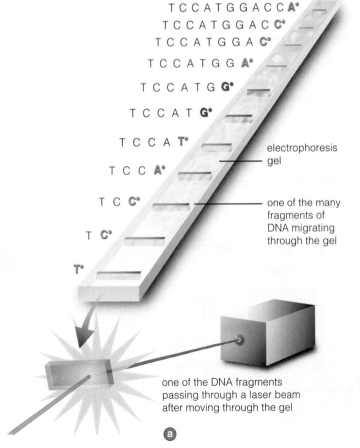

TCCATGGACC **A***
TCCATGGAC **C***
TCCATGGA **C***
TCCATGG **A***
TCCATG **G***
TCCAT **G***
TCCA **T***
TCC **A***
TC **C***
T **C***
T*

electrophoresis gel

one of the many fragments of DNA migrating through the gel

one of the DNA fragments passing through a laser beam after moving through the gel

a

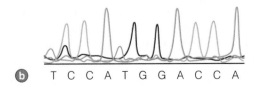

b T C C A T G G A C C A

Figure 16.8 *Animated!* Automated DNA sequencing. (**a**) Researchers synthesize DNA fragments by using a template and fluorescent nucleotides. Gel electrophoresis sorts out the fragments by length. (**b**) The order of the fluorescent bands that appear in the gel is detected by the sequencer. That order indicates the template DNA sequence. Today, researchers throughout the world use sequence databases that can be accessed via the Internet.

Except for identical twins, no two people have exactly the same sequence of bases in their DNA. One individual can be distinguished from all others on the basis of this molecular fingerprint.

Each human has a unique set of fingerprints. In addition, like other sexually reproducing species, each also has a **DNA fingerprint**—a unique array of DNA sequences that are inherited from parents in a Mendelian pattern. More than 99 percent of the DNA is the same in all humans, but the other fraction of 1 percent is unique to each individual. Some of these unique stretches of DNA are sprinkled through the human genome as **tandem repeats**—many copies of the same short base sequences, positioned one after the other along a DNA molecule.

For example, one person's DNA might contain four repeats of the bases TTTTC in a certain location. Another person's DNA might have them repeated fifteen times in the same location. One person might have ten repeats of CGG, and another might have fifteen. Such repetitive sequences slip spontaneously into DNA during replication, and their numbers grow or shrink over time. The mutation rate is relatively high in these regions.

DNA *fingerprinting* reveals differences in the tandem repeats among individuals. A restriction enzyme cuts their DNA into an assortment of fragments. The sizes of those fragments are unique to the individual. They reveal genetic differences between individuals, and they can be detected as RFLPs (*Restriction Fragment Length Polymorphisms*).

The fragments can be subjected to gel electrophoresis to form distinct bands according to their length. The banding pattern of genomic DNA fragments is the DNA fingerprint unique to the individual. For all practical purposes, it is identical only between identical twins. The odds of two unrelated people sharing an identical DNA fingerprint are 1 in 3,000,000,000,000.

PCR can be used to amplify tandem-repeat regions. Again, differences in the size of DNA fragments amplified by this technique can be detected by gel electrophoresis. A few drops of blood, semen, or cells from a hair follicle at a crime scene or on a suspect's clothing yield enough DNA to amplify with PCR, and then generate a fingerprint.

DNA fingerprints help forensic scientists identify criminals, victims, and innocent suspects. Figure 16.9 shows some tandem repeat RFLPs that were separated by gel electrophoresis. Those samples of DNA had been taken from seven people and from a bloodstain left at a crime scene. One of the DNA fingerprints matched.

Defense attorneys initially challenged the use of DNA fingerprinting as evidence in court. Today, however, the procedure has been firmly established as accurate and unambiguous. DNA fingerprinting is routinely submitted as evidence in disputes over paternity, and it is being widely used to convict the guilty and to exonerate the innocent. At this writing, DNA evidence has helped release well over 100 innocent people from prison.

DNA fingerprint analysis has even wider application. For instance, it confirmed that human bones exhumed from a shallow pit in Siberia belonged to five individuals of the Russian imperial family, all shot to death in secrecy in 1918. More recently, it was used to identify the remains of those who died in the World Trade Center on September 11, 2001.

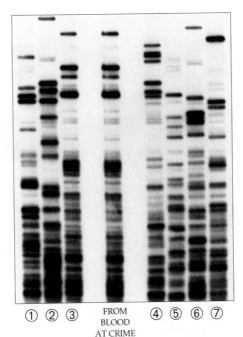

① ② ③ FROM BLOOD AT CRIME SCENE ④ ⑤ ⑥ ⑦

Figure 16.9 One case of a damning comparison of the DNA fingerprints from a bloodstain left behind at a crime scene and from blood samples of seven suspects (the series of circled numbers).

Can you point out which of the seven DNA fingerprints is an exact match?

16.5 The Rise of Genomics

LINKS TO
SECTIONS
3.7, 13.2, 14.5

The potential benefits of sequencing and analyzing the thousands of genes in the genome of selected organisms—say, the human genome—soon became apparent. Automated gene sequencing techniques were developed in response.

THE HUMAN GENOME PROJECT

By 1986, scientists were arguing about sequencing the 3 billion bases of the human genome. Many insisted that benefits for medicine and pure research would be incalculable. Others insisted that the mapping would divert funds from other work that was more urgent and had a better chance of success.

Automated sequencing had just been invented, as had PCR, the polymerase chain reaction. At the time, both techniques were cumbersome, expensive, and far from standardized, but many sensed their potential. Waiting for faster methods seemed the most efficient approach to sequencing the human genome—but who would decide when the technology was fast enough?

Several independent organizations launched their own versions of the Human Genome Project. Walter Gilbert started one company and declared he would sequence and patent the human genome. In 1988, the National Institutes of Health (NIH) annexed the entire Human Genome Project by hiring James Watson as its head and providing 200 million dollars per year to researchers. A public consortium formed between the NIH and institutions working on different versions of

the project. Watson set aside 3 percent of the funding for studies into ethical and social issues arising from the research. He then resigned in 1992 because of a disagreement with the NIH about patenting partial gene sequences. Francis Collins replaced him in 1993.

Amid ongoing squabbles over patent issues, Craig Venter started Celera Genomics (Figure 16.10). Venter cheekily declared that his new company would be the first to finish and patent the genome sequence. This prompted the public consortium to move its gene sequencing efforts into high gear.

Sequencing of the human genome was officially completed in 2003—fifty years after the discovery of the structure of DNA. About 99 percent of the coding regions in human DNA have been deciphered with a high degree of accuracy. A number of other genomes also have been fully sequenced.

What do we do with this vast amount of data? The next step is to investigate questions about precisely what each sequence means—what the genes do, what the control mechanisms are, and how they operate.

At this writing, 19,438 are confirmed as genes, and another 2,188 are probably genes. This does not mean that geneticists have learned what the genes encode.

Among the bizarre discoveries: Protein-encoding genes make up less than 2 percent of our genome. Millions of transposable elements repeated over and over make up more than half of it. There are almost as many *pseudogenes*—inactivated, nonfunctional copies of genes—as there are genes!

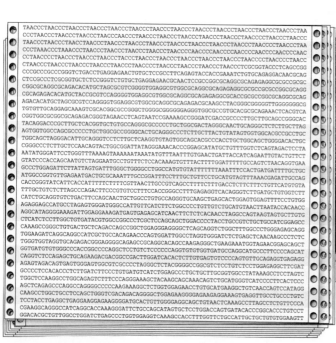

Figure 16.10 Some of the bases of the human genome—and a few of the supercomputers used to sequence it—at Celera Genomics in Maryland.

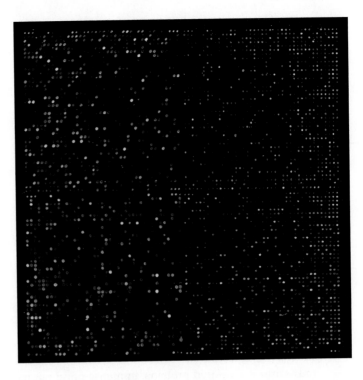

Figure 16.11 Complete yeast genome array on a DNA chip about 19 millimeters (3/4 inch) across. *Green* spots pinpoint genes that are active during fermentation. *Red* pinpoints the genes used in aerobic respiration, and *yellow*, the ones that are active in both pathways.

GENOMICS

Research into genomes of humans and other species has converged into a new research field—**genomics**. *Structural* genomics focuses on actual mapping and sequencing of the genomes of individuals. *Comparative* genomics sifts through the maps for similarities and differences that point to evolutionary connections.

Comparative genomics has practical applications as well as potential for research. The basic premise is that the genomes of all existing organisms are derived from common ancestors. For instance, pathogens share some conserved genes with human hosts even though they are only remotely related. Shared gene sequences, how they are organized, and where they differ might hold essential clues to where our immune defenses against pathogens are strongest or the most vulnerable.

Genomics has potential for **human gene therapy**—the transfer of one or more normal or modified genes into a person's body cells to correct a genetic defect or boost resistance to disease. However, even though the human genome is fully sequenced, it still is not easy to manipulate within the context of a living individual.

Today, experimenters use stripped-down viruses as vectors that inject genes into human cells. Some gene therapies deliver modified cells into a patient's tissue. In many cases, therapies make a patient's symptoms subside even when the modified cells are producing just a small amount of a required protein.

A caveat: No one can yet predict whether a virus-injected gene will be delivered to the right tissues and whether cellular mechanisms will maintain it.

DNA CHIPS

Analysis of genomes is now advancing at a stunning pace. Researchers pinpoint which genes are silent and which are being expressed with the use of **DNA chips**. These are microarrays of thousands of gene sequences representing a large subset of an entire genome—all stamped onto a glass plate that is about the size of a small business card.

A cDNA probe is built by using mRNA from, say, cells of a cancer patient. The free nucleotides used to synthesize the complementary strand of DNA have been labeled with a fluorescent pigment. Only genes that are expressed at the time the cells are harvested are making mRNA, so those genes alone make up the resulting probe population. The labeled probe is then incubated along with a chip made from genomic DNA. Wherever the probe binds with complementary base sequences on the chip, there will be a spot that glows under fluorescent light. Analysis of which spots on the chip are glowing reveals which of the thousands of genes inside the cells are active and which are not.

DNA chips are being used to compare different gene expression patterns between cells. Examples are yeasts grown in the presence and absence of oxygen, and different types of cells from the same multicelled individual. RNA from one set of cells is transformed into green fluorescent cDNA, and RNA from the other set into red fluorescent cDNA. The cDNAs are mixed and incubated with a genomic DNA chip. Green or red fluorescence indicates expression of genes in the different cell types. Yellow is a mixture of both red and green, and it indicates that both genes were being expressed at the same time in a cell (Figure 16.11).

In genomics, automated gene sequencing, the use of DNA chips, and other techniques let researchers rapidly evaluate and compare genome-spanning expression patterns.

16.6 Genetic Engineering

Genetic engineering is the deliberate modification of an individual's genome. Genes from another species may be transferred to an individual. Conversely, the individual may have its own genes isolated, modified and copied, and then receive copies of the modified genes.

Genetic engineering started with bacterial species, so consider them first. The kinds that take up plasmids are now widely used in basic research, agriculture, medicine, and industry. Plasmids, again, function as vectors for transferring fragments of foreign or modified DNA into an organism.

For instance, like you, bacterial cells have the metabolic machinery to make complex organic compounds. Genetically engineered types can be employed to transcribe genes that have been transferred to plasmids and synthesize desired proteins. Immense populations do this; they make useful amounts of medically valued proteins in huge stainless steel vats. *E. coli* cells were the first to transcribe and translate synthetic genes for human insulin. Their descendants were the first large-scale, cost-effective bacterial factory for proteins. In addition to insulin, vats of microbes churn out human somatotropin (growth hormone), hemoglobin, blood-clotting factors, interferon, and a variety of drugs and vaccines that we have come to depend upon.

Certain bacteria also hold potential for industry and for cleaning up environmental messes—that is, for *environmental remediation*. In nature, they break down organic wastes as part of their metabolic activities and help cycle nutrients through ecosystems. Modified types digest crude oil into less harmful compounds. When sprayed on oil spills, as from a shipwrecked supertanker, they can help mop up oil. Other species sponge up excess phosphates, heavy metals, and other pollutants, even radioactive wastes.

Genetic engineering refers to the directed alteration of an individual's genome. Microbes were the first targets.

In some cases, DNA is transferred between individuals of different species, the outcome being a transgenic organism.

In other cases, genes or gene regions from an individual are isolated, modified, then copied and inserted into the same individual.

16.7 Designer Plants

Think back on those Golden Rice plants described in the chapter introduction. They are a prime example of genetic engineering that can produce valuable transgenic plants. There is some urgency surrounding much of this work, as you will now read.

As crop production expands to keep pace with human population growth, it puts unavoidable pressure on ecosystems everywhere. Irrigation leaves mineral and salt residues in soils. Tilled soil erodes, taking topsoil with it. Runoff clogs rivers, and fertilizer in it causes algae to grow so much that fish suffocate. Pesticides harm humans, other animals, and beneficial insects.

Pressured to produce more food at lower cost and with less damage to the environment, some farmers are turning to genetically engineered crop plants.

Cotton plants with a built-in insecticide gene kill only the insects that eat it, so farmers that grow them are not required to use as many pesticides. Certain transgenic tomato plants can grow, develop, and bear fruit in salty soils that would wither other plants. They also absorb and store excess salt in their leaves, thus purifying saline soil for future crops.

The cotton plants in Figure 16.12a were genetically engineered for resistance to a relatively short-lived herbicide. Spraying fields with this herbicide will kill all weeds—but not the engineered cotton plants. As you read in the chapter's introduction, the practice means that farmers can use reduced amounts of less toxic chemicals. They do not have to till the soil as much to control weeds, so river-clogging runoff can be reduced. As another example, Figure 16.12b shows transgenic aspen seedlings that grow well and do not make as much lignin. Lignin-deficient trees are better for making paper and other forest products.

Engineering plant cells starts with vectors that can carry genes into plant cells. *Agrobacterium tumefaciens* is a bacterial species that infects eudicots, including beans, peas, potatoes, and other major crops plants. Genes in its plasmids cause tumors to form on these plants; hence the name Ti plasmid (*Tumor-inducing*). Researchers use the Ti plasmid to transfer foreign or modified genes into plants.

Researchers excise the tumor-inducing genes, then insert a desired gene into the plasmid (Figure 16.13). Some plant cells cultured with the modified plasmid may take it up. Whole plants may be regenerated.

Modified *A. tumefaciens* bacteria deliver genes into monocots that also are food sources, including wheat, corn, and rice. Researchers can even transfer genes into plants by way of electric shocks, chemicals, and blasts of microscopic particles coated with DNA.

Figure 16.12 (**a**) *Left*, control cotton plant. *Right*, cotton plant genetically engineered for herbicide resistance. Both plants were sprayed with a weed killer that is widely applied in cotton fields.

(**b**) Control plant (*left*) and four genetically engineered aspen seedlings. Vincent Chiang and coworkers suppressed a control gene involved in a lignin biosynthetic pathway. The modified plants synthesized normal lignin, but not as much. Lignin synthesis dropped by as much as 45 percent—yet cellulose production increased 15 percent. Root, stem, and leaf growth were greatly enhanced. Plant structure did not suffer. Wood harvested from such trees might make it easier to manufacture paper and some clean-burning fuels, such as ethanol. Lignin, a tough polymer, strengthens secondary cell walls of plants. Before paper can be made from wood, the lignin must be chemically extracted.

a   b

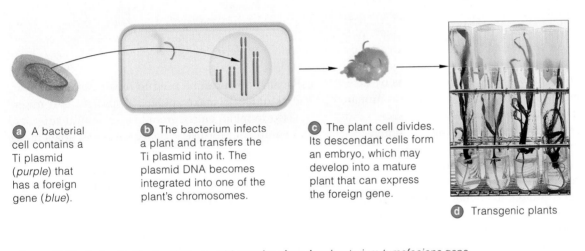

(**a**) A bacterial cell contains a Ti plasmid (*purple*) that has a foreign gene (*blue*).

(**b**) The bacterium infects a plant and transfers the Ti plasmid into it. The plasmid DNA becomes integrated into one of the plant's chromosomes.

(**c**) The plant cell divides. Its descendant cells form an embryo, which may develop into a mature plant that can express the foreign gene.

(**d**) Transgenic plants

(**e**) Example of a young plant with a fluorescent gene product.

Figure 16.13 *Animated!* (**a–d**) Ti plasmid transfer of an *Agrobacterium tumefaciens* gene to a plant cell. (**e**) A transgenic plant expressing a firefly gene for the enzyme luciferase.

Consider another compelling reason for modifying plant species: The food supply for most of the human population is extremely vulnerable. Farmers usually want to plant crops that give them the highest yields. Over time, genetically similar varieties have replaced the more diverse, older varieties. However, genetic uniformity makes food crops far more vulnerable to many pathogenic fungi, viruses, and bacteria.

That is why botanists comb the world for seeds of the older, diverse varieties of plants and of the wild ancestors of potatoes, corn, and other crop plants. They send their prizes—seeds with genes of a plant's lineage—to **seed banks**. These safe storage facilities are designed to preserve genetic diversity. They are now being tapped by genetic engineers as well as by traditional plant breeders.

Crop vulnerability is a huge problem. At one time, *Southern corn leaf blight* destroyed much of the United States corn crop. All of the plants carried the gene that conferred susceptibility to the fungal pathogen. Ever since that devastating epidemic, seed companies have been much more attentive to offering genetically diverse corn seeds. They tap seed banks, the treasure houses of plant genes.

Transgenic plants help farmers grow crops more efficiently and with less impact on the environment.

Genetic engineers as well as traditional plant breeders are tapping seed banks, which are safe storage facilities designed to preserve genetic diversity of plants.

16.8 Biotech Barnyards

LINKS TO
SECTIONS
5.2, 15.3

Laboratory mice were the first mammals to be genetically engineered. Today, featherless chickens, drug-producing goats, and transgenic pigs are part of the biotech barnyard.

TRANSGENIC ANIMALS

Traditional cross-breeding practices have produced unusual animals, including the featherless chicken in Figure 16.14. Now transgenic types are on the scene. The first ones arrived in 1982. Researchers isolated a gene for human somatotropin (growth hormone) and inserted it into a plasmid. They injected copies of the recombinant plasmids into fertilized mouse eggs that were later implanted into female mice. A third of the offspring of the surrogate mothers grew much larger than their littermates (Figure 16.15). The rat gene had become integrated into the host DNA and was being expressed in the transgenic mice.

Transgenic animals are used routinely for medical research. The functions of many gene products and how they can be controlled have been discovered by inactivating genes in "knockout mice" and analyzing the effect on phenotype (Section 15.3). Strains of mice, genetically modified mice to be susceptible to human diseases, help researchers study both the diseases and potential cures without experimenting on humans.

Genetically engineered animals also are sources of medically valued proteins. As a few examples, goats synthesize quantities of CFTR protein to treat cystic fibrosis and TPA protein to counter the bad effects of heart attacks. Rabbits make human interleukin-2, a protein that triggers divisions of immune cells called T lymphocytes. Cattle, too, may soon produce human

Figure 16.15 Evidence of a successful gene transfer. Two ten-week-old mouse littermates. *Left*, This one weighed 29 grams. *Right*, This one weighed 44 grams. It grew from a fertilized egg into which a gene for human somatotropin had been inserted.

collagen, which can be used to repair cartilage, bone, and skin. Goats make spider silk protein that might be used to make bullet-proof vests, medical supplies, and equipment for use in space. Different goats make human antithrombin, which is used to treat people with blood-clotting disorders (Figure 16.14b).

Genetic engineers have developed pigs that make environmentally friendlier manure. They have made freeze-resistant salmon, low-fat pigs, heftier sheep, and cows that are resistant to mad cow disease. Within a few years, they may give us allergen-free cats.

Figure 16.14 Genetically modified animals. (**a**) Featherless chicken developed by traditional cross-breeding methods in Israel. Such chickens survive in hot deserts where cooling systems are not an option. Chicken farmers in the United States have lost millions of feathered chickens in extremely hot weather. (**b**) Mira, a goat transgenic for human antithrombin III, an anticlotting factor. (**c**) Inquisitive transgenic pig at the Virginia Tech Swine Research facility.

Tinkering with the genetics of animals for the sake of human convenience does raise ethical questions. However, transgenic animal research may be viewed as an extension of thousands of years of acceptable barnyard breeding practices. Techniques have changed, but not the intent. Humans continue to have a vested interest in improving livestock.

KNOCKOUT CELLS AND ORGAN FACTORIES

Each year, about 75,000 people are on waiting lists for an organ transplant, but human donors are in short supply. There is talk of harvesting organs from pigs (Figure 16.14c), because pig organs function a lot like ours do. Transferring an organ from one species into another is called **xenotransplantation**.

The human immune system battles anything that it recognizes as "nonself." It rejects a pig organ at once, owing to a glycoprotein on the plasma membrane of cells that make up the blood vessels in pig organs. Antibodies circulating in human blood swiftly latch on to the sugar component and call for a response. In less than a few hours, blood inside the vessels coagulates massively and dooms the transplant. Drugs suppress this immune response, but a side effect is serious: the drugs make organ recipients vulnerable to infections.

Pig DNA contains two copies of *Ggta1*, the gene for an enzyme that catalyzes a key step in biosynthesis of alpha-1,3-galactose. This is the pig sugar that human antibodies recognize. Researchers have knocked out both copies of the *Ggta1* gene in transgenic piglets. Without the gene product, and the sugar, a pig tissue or organ may be less prone to rejection by the human immune system. Tissues and organs from such animals could help millions of people, including the ones with organs that have been severely damaged as a result of diabetes and Parkinson's disease.

Critics of xenotransplantation are concerned that, among other things, pig–human transplants would invite pig viruses to cross a species barrier and infect humans, perhaps catastrophically. Their concerns are not unfounded. In 1918, an influenza pandemic killed twenty million people worldwide. It originated with a swine flu virus—in pigs.

16.9 Safety Issues

Many years have passed since the first transfer of foreign DNA into a plasmid. That transfer ignited an ongoing debate about potential dangers of transgenic organisms entering the environment before rigorous testing.

In 1972, Paul Berg and his associates were the first to make recombinant DNA. Researchers knew that DNA was not toxic, but they could not predict what would happen every time they fused genetic material from different organisms into the recombinant molecules. Would they accidentally make superpathogens? Could they create a new form of life by the fusion of DNA from two normally harmless organisms? What if their creation escaped from the laboratory and transformed other organisms in the natural environment?

In a remarkably quick and responsible display of self-regulation, scientists reached a consensus on the safety guidelines for DNA research. Adopted at once by the NIH, their guidelines listed precautions for laboratory procedures. They covered the design and use of host organisms that could survive only under the narrow range of conditions inside the laboratory. Researchers stopped using DNA from pathogenic or toxic organisms for recombination experiments until proper containment facilities were developed.

As added precautions, "fail-safe" genes are now built into genetically engineered bacteria. They remain silent unless the bacteria escape and are exposed to environmental conditions—whereupon the genes get activated, with lethal results for the cell. Suppose that the package has a *hok* gene next to a promoter of the lactose operon (Section 15.4). Sugars are plentiful in the environment. If they were to activate the *hok* gene in a bacterial cell that escaped, the gene's product would destroy membrane function and the escapee.

Even so, does Murphy's law also apply to genetic engineering? As with any human endeavor, things can go wrong. After rabbits started taking over much of Australia, researchers were tinkering with a rabbit-killing virus in a containment laboratory on an island. Maybe the virus escaped in flying insects. However it happened, the virus is out and about, and killing lots of rabbits (Section 46.10). It is an example of why researchers are expected to expect the unexpected.

Genetic engineering started more than two decades ago. The kinds of animals being sought are beyond the scope of traditional breeding practices. Pigs engineered as donors for human organs are among the more startling cases.

Rigorous safety guidelines for DNA research have been in place for decades in the United States. They have been adopted by the NIH, and researchers are expected to comply with their stringent standards.

16.10 Modified Humans?

We as a society continue to work our way through the ethical implications of applying the new DNA technologies. Even as we are weighing the risks and benefits, however, the manipulation of individual genomes has begun.

WHO GETS WELL?

Human gene therapy is often cited as one of the most compelling reasons for embracing the new research. We already have identified more than 15,500 genetic disorders. Many are rare in the population at large. Collectively, however, they show up in 3 to 5 percent of all newborns, and they cause 20 to 30 percent of all infant deaths every year. They account for about half of mentally impaired patients and nearly a fourth of all hospital admissions. They contribute to many age-related disorders that await all of us.

Rhys Evans, shown below, was born with a severe immune deficiency known as SCID-X1, which stems from mutations in gene *IL2RG*. Children affected by this disorder can live only in germ-free isolation tents, a "bubble," because they cannot fight infections.

In 1998, doctors withdrew stem cells from the bone marrow of eleven SCID-X1 boys. Stem cells, recall, are forerunners of other cell types, including white blood cells of the immune system. The doctors used a virus to insert nonmutated copies of *IL2RG* into each boy's stem cells, which they then infused back into his bone marrow. Months later, ten of the boys left isolation tents for good; gene therapy had successfully repaired their immune system. Since then, other gene therapy trials have freed many other SCID-X1 patients from life in a bubble. Rhys Evans is one of them.

In 2002, to the shock of researchers, two boys from the 1998 trial developed leukemia and one died. The researchers had anticipated that any cancer related to the therapy would be extremely rare. The very gene targeted to do the repair work—*IL2RG*—may be a problem, especially when combined with the viral vector that delivered the gene into stem cells. One other child who took part in a gene therapy experiment for SCID-X1 has developed leukemia. That it developed at all is evidence that our understanding of the human genome lags behind our ability to modify it.

WHO GETS ENHANCED?

When all is said and done, the idea of using human gene therapy to cure genetic disorders seems like a socially acceptable goal to most of us. Now see if your comfort level can move one step further. Would it also be acceptable to modify genes of some individual who falls within the normal range if he or she simply would like to minimize or enhance a particular trait?

We have already crossed the threshold of a brave new world. Researchers who are adept at transferring genes have already engineered strains of mice with enhanced memory and improved learning abilities. Perhaps their work is a beacon to those whose very lives have been turned upside down by Alzheimer's disease. Perhaps it draws others who are enchanted with the idea of simply getting more brain power.

The idea of selecting the most desired human traits is referred to as *eugenic engineering*. Yet who decides which forms of traits are most desirable? Realistically, cures for many severe but rare genetic disorders will not happen, because the payback for research is not financially attractive. Eugenics, however, might turn a profit. Just how much would potential parents pay to engineer tall or blue-eyed or fair-skinned children? Would it be okay to engineer "superhumans" with breathtaking strength or intelligence? How about an injection that would help you lose that extra weight and keep it off permanently? Where exactly is the line between interesting and abhorrent?

In a survey conducted in the United States, more than 40 percent of those interviewed said it would be fine to use gene therapy to make smarter and cuter babies. In one poll of British parents, 18 percent would be willing to use genetic enhancement to keep their child from being aggressive, and 10 percent would use it to keep a child from growing up to be homosexual.

Some argue that we must never alter the DNA of anything. The concern is that we just do not have the wisdom to bring about any genetic changes without causing irreparable damage to ourselves and nature.

One is reminded of our peculiar human tendency to leap before we look. And yet, something about the human experience gave us the capacity to imagine wings of our own making, a capacity that carried us to the frontiers of space. It gave one individual the dream of enhancing the rice plant genome to keep millions of children from going blind.

In this brave new world, two questions are before you: Should we be more cautious, because the risk takers may go too far? And what do we stand to lose if risks are not taken?

Be engaged; our understanding of the meaning of the human genome is changing even as you read this.

Summary

Section 16.1 Recombinant DNA technology uses restriction enzymes that can cut DNA into fragments. DNA ligases can splice the fragments into plasmids or some other cloning vector. Recombinant plasmids may be taken up by rapidly dividing cells, such as bacteria. When the host cells replicate, they make multiple, identical copies of the foreign DNA as well.

Bacteria cannot correctly express eukaryotic genes, which contain introns. Reverse transcriptase, a viral enzyme, can make a complementary DNA strand on mRNA. The hybrid molecule can then be converted to cDNA for cloning.

Biology Now
Explore the tools used to make recombinant DNA with the animation on BiologyNow.

Section 16.2 A gene library is a mixed collection of cells that have taken up cloned DNA. Researchers can isolate a gene of interest from a library by using a probe, a short stretch of DNA that can base-pair with the gene and that is traceable (it is labeled with a detectable tag, such as a radioisotope). Probes can help researchers locate and base-pair with one clone among millions. Such base pairing between nucleotide sequences from different sources is known as nucleic acid hybridization.

The polymerase chain reaction (PCR) is a technique for rapidly copying DNA fragments. A sample of a DNA template is mixed with nucleotides, primers, and a heat-resistant DNA polymerase. Each round of PCR proceeds through a series of temperature changes that amplifies the number of DNA molecules exponentially.

Biology Now
Learn how researchers isolate and copy genes with the interaction on BiologyNow.

Section 16.3 Automated DNA sequencing rapidly reveals the order of nucleotides in DNA fragments. As DNA polymerase copies a template DNA, progressively longer fragments stop growing as soon as one of four different fluorescent nucleotides becomes attached to them. Electrophoresis separates the labeled fragments into bands according to length. The order of the colored bands as they migrate through the gel reflects which fluorescent base was added to the end of each fragment, and so indicates the template DNA base sequence.

Biology Now
Investigate DNA sequencing with the animation on BiologyNow.

Section 16.4 Tandem repeats are multiple copies of a short DNA sequence that follow one another along a chromosome. The number and distribution of tandem repeats, unique in each person, can be revealed by gel electrophoresis; they form a DNA fingerprint.

Biology Now
Observe the process of DNA fingerprinting with the animation on BiologyNow.

Section 16.5 The entire human genome has been sequenced and is now being analyzed. Genomes of other organisms also have been fully sequenced.

The new field of genomics is concerned with the mapping and analysis of genomes. One branch, called comparative genomics, uses similarities and differences between DNA sequences of major groups of organisms to identify their evolutionary relationships.

DNA chips are microarrays used to compare patterns of gene expression within a genome.

Sections 16.6–16.8 Recombinant DNA technology and the mapping and analysis of genomes is the basis for genetic engineering. Genetic engineering is the directed modification of the genetic makeup of an organism, often to modify its phenotype. Researchers insert normal or modified genes from one organism into another of the same or different species. Gene therapies insert copies of modified genes into individuals to cover the functions of a mutant or altered gene.

Genetically engineered bacteria that contain plasmid vectors have diverse uses in basic research, medicine, agriculture, industry, and ecology. Transgenic crop plants help farmers use less toxic pesticides and produce food more efficiently. Genetic engineering of animals allows commercial production of human proteins, as well as research into genetic disorders.

Biology Now
See how the Ti plasmid is used to genetically engineer plants with the animation on BiologyNow.

Section 16.9 There is always a risk that genetically modified experimental organisms can escape from the laboratory. Typically, potentially dangerous types have fail-safe genes built into their genome that will destroy them when exposed to conditions that exist anywhere except in the laboratory. Rigorous tests for safety must precede the release of any modified organism into the environment.

Section 16.10 The goal of human gene therapy is to transfer normal or modified genes into body cells to correct genetic defects. As with any new technology, the benefits must be weighed against potential risks.

Self-Quiz
Answers in Appendix II

1. Researchers can cut DNA molecules at specific sites by using _____ .
   a. DNA polymerase
   b. DNA probes
   c. restriction enzymes
   d. reverse transcriptase

2. Fill in the blank: A _____ is a small circle of bacterial DNA that contains only a few genes and is separate from the bacterial chromosome.

3. By reverse transcription, _____ is assembled on a(n) _____ template.
   a. mRNA; DNA
   b. cDNA; mRNA
   c. DNA; ribosome
   d. protein; mRNA

4. PCR stands for _____ .
   a. polymerase chain reaction
   b. polyploid chromosome restrictions
   c. polygraphed criminal rating
   d. politically correct research

5. Automated DNA sequencing relies on _____ .
   a. supplies of standard and labeled nucleotides
   b. primers and DNA polymerases
   c. gel electrophoresis and a laser beam
   d. all of the above

6. By gel electrophoresis, fragments of DNA can be separated according to _____ .
   a. sequence   b. length   c. species

7. _____ can be used to insert genes into human cells.
   a. PCR   c. Xenotransplantation
   b. Modified viruses   d. DNA microarrays

8. For each species, all _____ in a haploid number of chromosomes is the _____ .
   a. genomes; phenotype   c. mRNA; start of cDNA
   b. DNA; genome   d. cDNA; start of mRNA

9. Match the terms with the most suitable description.
   ____ DNA fingerprint   a. selecting "desirable" traits
   ____ Ti plasmid   b. mutations, crossovers
   ____ nature's genetic c. used in some gene transfers
        experiments   d. a person's unique collection
   ____ nucleic acid   of tandem repeats
        hybridization   e. base pairing of nucleotide
   ____ eugenic   sequences from different
        engineering   DNA or RNA source

Additional questions are available on Biology ⓔNow™

Critical Thinking

1. Lunardi's Market put out a bin of tomatoes having vine-ripened redness, flavor, and texture. A sign identified them as genetically engineered produce. Most shoppers selected unmodified tomatoes in the adjacent bin even though those tomatoes were pale pink, mealy textured, and tasteless. Which tomatoes would you pick? Why?

2. Biotechnologists envision a new Green Revolution. As they see it, designer plants hold down food production costs, reduce dependence on pesticides and herbicides, enhance crop yields, offer improved flavor and nutritional value, and often produce plants with salt tolerance and drought tolerance. Fruits and vegetables can be designed for flavor, nutritional value, and extended shelf life.

Genetically engineered food crops are widespread in the United States. At least 45 percent of cotton crops, 38 percent of soybean crops, and 25 percent of corn crops have been modified to withstand weedkillers or make their own pesticides. For years, modified corn and soybeans have been used in tofu, cereals, soy sauce, vegetable oils, beer, and soft drinks. They are fed to farm animals.

In Europe especially, public resistance to modified food runs high. Besides arguing that modified foods might be toxic and have lower nutritional value, many people worry that designer plants might cross-pollinate wild plants and produce "superweeds." The chorus of critics in Europe has forced American farmers to keep genetically engineered crops separated from traditional crops. Traditional crops only are exported to Europe. Such separation is both costly and difficult.

Read up on scientific research related to this issue and form your own opinions. The alternatives are to be swayed either by media hype (the term Frankenfood, for instance) or by sometimes biased reports from groups (such as chemical manufacturers), which have their own agendas.

3. The sequencing of the human genome is completed, and knowledge about many genes is being used to detect genetic disorders. Many insurance companies will pay for their female subscribers to take advantage of genetic testing for breast cancer and are willing to allow them to keep the results confidential.

Explain how a health insurance company might benefit financially if it were to encourage its subscribers to take confidential tests for breast cancer susceptibility.

4. Scientists at Oregon Health Sciences University produced Tetra, the first primate clone. They also made the first transgenic primate by inserting a jellyfish gene into a fertilized egg of a rhesus monkey. (The gene codes for a bioluminescent protein that fluoresces green; refer to Section 6.6). The egg was implanted in a surrogate monkey's uterus, where it developed into a male.

The long-term goal of this gene transfer project is not to make glowing-green monkeys. It is the transfer of human genes into primates whose genomes are most like ours. Transgenic primates could yield insight into genetic disorders. That insight might lead to the development of cures for those who are affected and of vaccines for those who are at risk.

Something more controversial is at stake. Will the time come when foreign genes can be inserted into human embryos? Would it be ethical to transfer a chimpanzee or monkey gene into a human embryo to cure a genetic defect? To bestow immunity against a potentially fatal disease such as AIDS? Think about it.

III Principles of Evolution

Two male frigate birds (Fregata minor) in the Galápagos Islands, far from the coast of Ecuador. Each male inflates a gular sac, a balloon of red skin at his throat, in a display that may catch the eye of a female. The males lurk together in the bushes, sacs inflated, until a female flies by. Then they wag their head back and forth and call out to her. Like other structures that males use only in courtship, the gular sac is probably an outcome of sexual selection—one of the topics you will read about in this unit.

17 EVIDENCE OF EVOLUTION

Measuring Time

How do you measure time? Is your comfort level with the past limited to your own generation? Probably you can relate to a few centuries of human events. But geologic time? Comprehending the distant past requires a huge intellectual leap from the familiar to the unknown.

Perhaps the possibility of an asteroid slamming into our planet can help you make the leap. Asteroids are rocky, metallic bodies hurtling through space. They are a few meters to 1,000 kilometers across. When our solar system's planets were forming, their gravitational force swept up most of the asteroids. At least 6,000 asteroids, including the one shown in Figure 17.1, still orbit the sun in a belt between Mars and Jupiter. Millions more frequently zip past Earth. They are hard to spot; they do not emit light. We cannot identify most of them until after they have passed close by. Some have passed too close for comfort.

We have evidence that big asteroid impacts influenced the history of life. For instance, researchers found a thin layer of iridium around the world, and it dates precisely to a mass extinction that wiped out the last of the dinosaurs (Figures 17.1 and 17.2). Iridium is rare on Earth but not in asteroids. There are plenty of fossils of dinosaurs below this layer. Above it, there are none, anywhere.

It has only been about 100,000 years since the first modern humans (*Homo sapiens*) evolved. We have fossils of dozens of humanlike species that lived in Africa during the 5 million years before our own species even showed up. So why are we the only ones left?

Unlike today's large, globally dispersed populations of humans, those early species lived in small bands. What if most were casualties of the twenty asteroids that collided with Earth while they were alive? What if *our* ancestors were just plain lucky? About 2.3 million years ago, a huge object from space hit the ocean west of what is now Chile. If it had struck the rotating Earth just a few hours earlier, it would have hit southern Africa instead of the ocean. Our ancestors could have been incinerated.

Now that we know what to look for, we are seeing more and more craters in satellite images of Earth. One crater, in Iraq, is less than 4,000 years old. Energy released during that particular impact was equivalent to the detonation of hundreds of nuclear weapons.

Watch the video online!

Figure 17.1 *Left*, an asteroid nineteen kilometers (about twelve miles) long, hurtling through space. *Right*, part of the worldwide, iridium-rich layer of sediment (*black*) that dates to the Cretaceous–Tertiary (K–T) boundary. This vertical section through stacked layers of rock is evidence of an asteroid impact. The red pocketknife gives you an idea of its thickness.

Figure 17.2 Artist's interpretation and computer-generated model for the last few minutes of the Cretaceous.

If we can figure out what an asteroid impact will do to us, then we can figure out how impacts affected life in the past. We *can* comprehend life long before our own, including its brushes with good and bad cosmic luck.

You are about to make an intellectual leap through time, to places that were not even known about a few centuries ago. We invite you to launch yourself from this premise: *Any aspect of the natural world, past as well as present, has one or more underlying causes.*

That premise is the foundation for scientific research into the history of life. It guides probes into physical and chemical aspects of Earth. It guides the studies of fossils and comparisons of species. It guides tests of hypotheses by way of experiments, models, and new technologies. This research represents a shift from experience to inference—from the known to what can only be surmised. And it has given us astonishing glimpses into the past.

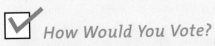

How Would You Vote?

A large asteroid could obliterate civilization and much of Earth's biodiversity. Should nations around the world contribute resources to locating and tracking asteroids? See BiologyNow for details, then vote online.

Key Concepts

EMERGENCE OF EVOLUTIONARY THOUGHT

As long ago as the 1400s, Western scientists started to learn about previously unknown species and how organisms are distributed around the world. They documented similarities and differences in the traits among living organisms and among fossil species that were being unearthed in layers of sedimentary rock. Sections 17.1, 17.2

A THEORY TAKES FORM

The emerging discoveries suggested that evolution, or changes in lines of descent, had occurred. Charles Darwin and Alfred Wallace independently developed a theory of natural selection to explain how the heritable traits that define each species might evolve. Section 17.3

EVIDENCE FROM FOSSILS

The fossil record will never be complete, so gaps are to be expected. Even so, it offers powerful evidence of change in lines of descent over great time spans. Sections 17.4, 17.5

EVIDENCE FROM BIOGEOGRAPHY

Evolutionary theories, reinforced by plate tectonics theory, help explain patterns in the distribution of species through the environment and through time. Section 17.6

EVIDENCE FROM COMPARATIVE MORPHOLOGY

The adults and embryos of different lineages often show similarities in one or more body parts that hint at descent from a common ancestor. Sections 17.7, 17.8

EVIDENCE FROM COMPARATIVE BIOCHEMISTRY

Today, researchers are using biochemical and molecular comparisons to illuminate the history of life and to clarify the evolutionary relationships among diverse species and lineages. Section 17.9

Links to Earlier Concepts

Section 1.4 sketched out key premises of the theory of natural selection. Here you will read about evidence that led to its formulation. As you read, remember that science does not deal with the supernatural, and it cannot answer subjective questions about nature (1.7).

You may wish to refresh your memory of radioisotopes (2.2), protein structure (3.5), mutation (1.4, 3.6, 14.4), nucleic acid hybridization (16.2), and automated gene sequencing (16.3). These topics are basic to understanding the biochemical and molecular comparisons that are clarifying evolutionary relationships among species.

17.1 Early Beliefs, Confounding Discoveries

LINK TO
SECTION
1.7

Prevailing beliefs can influence how we interpret clues to natural processes and their observable outcomes.

QUESTIONS FROM BIOGEOGRAPHY

Two thousand years ago the seeds of biological inquiry were taking hold in the West. Aristotle was foremost among the early naturalists. There were no books or instruments to guide him, and yet he was more than a collector of random observations. In his descriptions we see evidence that he was connecting observations in an attempt to explain the order of things. As others did, he saw nature as a continuum of organization, from lifeless matter through complex forms of plants and animals. By the fourteenth century, scholars had transformed his ideas into a rigid view of life. A Chain of Being was seen as extending from "lowest" forms to humans, and on to spiritual beings. Each kind of being, or **species**, was one separate link in the chain. All links had been designed and forged at the same time at one center of creation. They had not changed since. Once naturalists discovered and described all the links, the meaning of life would be revealed.

Then Europeans embarked on their globe-spanning explorations. They soon discovered that the world is a lot bigger than Europe. Tens of thousands of unique plants and animals from Asia, Africa, the New World, and the Pacific islands were brought back home to be carefully catalogued as one more link in the chain.

Later, Alfred Wallace and a few other naturalists moved beyond cataloguing species for its own sake. They started to identify *patterns* in where species live and how species might or might not be related. They were pioneers in **biogeography**: the study of patterns in the geographic distribution of individual species and entire communities. They were the first to think about the ecological and evolutionary forces in play.

Some patterns were intriguing. For example, many plants and animals are found only on islands in the middle of the ocean and other remote places. Many species that are strikingly similar live far apart, and vast expanses of open ocean or impassable mountain ranges keep them separated, in isolation.

Consider: Flightless, long-necked, long-legged birds are native to three continents (Figure 17.3a–c). Why are they so much alike? The plants in Figure 17.3d,e live on separate continents. Both have spines, tiny leaves, and short fleshy stems. Why are *they* so much alike?

Curiously, the flightless birds all live in the same kind of environment about the same distance from the equator. They sprint about in flat, open grasslands of dry climates, and they raise their long necks to keep an eye on predators in the distance. Both plant species also live the same distance from the equator in the

Figure 17.3 Species that resemble one another, strikingly so, even though they are native to distant geographic realms.

(**a**) South American rhea, (**b**) Australian emu, and (**c**) African ostrich. All three types of birds live in similar habitats. They are unlike most birds in several traits, most notably in their long, muscularized legs and their inability to get airborne.

(**d**) A spiny cactus native to the hot deserts of the American Southwest. (**e**) A spiny spurge native to southwestern Africa.

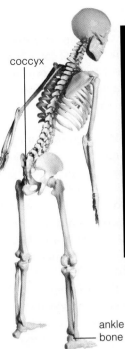

coccyx

ankle
bone

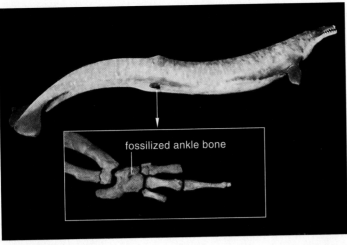

fossilized ankle bone

Figure 17.4 Body parts that have no apparent function. *Above,* reconstruction of an ancient whale (*Basilosaurus*), with a head as long as a sofa. This marine predator was fully aquatic, so it did not use its hindlimbs to support body weight as you do—yet it had ankle bones. We use our ankles, but not our coccyx bones.

Figure 17.5 Fossilized ammonites. These large marine predators lived hundreds of millions of years ago. Their shell is similar to the shell of a modern chambered nautilus.

same kind of environment—hot deserts—where water is seasonally scarce. Both species store water in their fleshy stems. Their stems have a notably thick, water-conserving cuticle and rows of sharp spines that deter thirsty, hungry herbivores.

If all birds and plants were created in one place, then how did such similar kinds end up in the same kind of environment in such distant, remote places?

QUESTIONS FROM COMPARATIVE MORPHOLOGY

The similarities and differences among species raised questions that gave rise to **comparative morphology**: the study of body plans and structures among groups of organisms. For instance, the bones in a human arm, whale flipper, and bat wing differ in size, shape, and function. As Section 17.7 explains, the different bones are located in similar body regions. They are made of the same kinds of tissues that are arranged in similar patterns. They also develop in much the same way in embryos. Naturalists who discovered the similarities wondered: Why do species that differ so much in some features look so much alike in other features?

By one hypothesis, body plans are so perfect there was no need to make a new design for each organism at the time of its creation. Yet if that were so, then why did some organisms have useless body parts? For instance, an ancient aquatic whale had ankle bones but it did not walk (Figure 17.4). Why the bones? Our coccyx is like some tailbones in many other mammals. We do not have a tail. Why do we have parts of one?

QUESTIONS ABOUT FOSSILS

About the same time, geologists were mapping layers of rock exposed by erosion or quarrying. As you will read later on, they added to the confusion when they found fossils in the same kinds of layers in different parts of the world. **Fossils** came to be recognized as the stone-hard evidence of earlier forms of life. Figures 17.4 and 17.5 have examples.

A puzzle: Many deep layers held fossils of simple marine life. Some layers above them contained fossils that were structurally similar but more intricate. In higher layers, fossils were like modern species. What did sequences in complexity among fossils of a given type mean? Were they evidence of lines of descent?

Taken as a whole, the findings from biogeography, comparative morphology, and geology did not fit with prevailing beliefs of the nineteenth century. Scholars floated novel hypotheses. If a simultaneous dispersal of all species from a center of creation was unlikely, *then perhaps species originated in more than one place.* If species had not been created in a perfect state—and fossil sequences and "useless" body parts implied they had not—*then perhaps species had become modified over time.* Awareness of evolution was in the wind.

Awareness of biological evolution emerged over centuries, through the cumulative observations of many naturalists, biogeographers, comparative anatomists, and geologists.

17.2 A Flurry of New Theories

LINK TO
SECTION
1.7

*Nineteenth-century naturalists found themselves trying
to reconcile the evidence of change with a traditional
conceptual framework that simply did not allow for it.*

SQUEEZING NEW EVIDENCE INTO OLD BELIEFS

A respected anatomist, Georges Cuvier, was among
those trying to make sense of the growing evidence for
change. For years he had compared fossils with living
organisms. He was aware of the abrupt changes in the
fossil record and was the first to recognize that they
marked times of mass extinctions.

By Cuvier's hypothesis, a single time of creation
had populated the world, which was an unchanging
stage for the human drama. Monstrous earthquakes,
floods, and other major catastrophes did happen, and
many people died. Each time, survivors repopulated
the world. By Cuvier's reckoning, there were no *new*
species. Naturalists simply had not yet found all of
the fossils that would date to the time of creation.

His hypothesis enjoyed support for a long time. It
even became elevated to the rank of theory, one that
later became known as **catastrophism**.

Still, many other scholars kept at the puzzle. For
example, in Jean Baptiste Lamarck's view, offspring
inherit traits that a parent *acquired in its lifetime.* By his
hypothesis, environmental pressure and internal needs
promote permanent changes in an individual's body
form and functions, which offspring then inherit. By

this proposed process, life was created long ago in a
simple state, and it gradually improved. The force for
change was an intense drive toward perfection, up
the Chain of Being. Lamarck thought that the force,
centered in nerves, directed an unknown "fluida" to
body parts needing change.

Try using his hypothesis to explain a giraffe's long
neck. Suppose a short-necked, hungry ancestor of the
modern giraffe kept stretching its neck in order to
browse on leaves beyond the reach of other animals.
Lengthier and lengthier stretches directed fluida into
its neck and thus made the neck permanently longer.
Offspring inherited a longer neck, and they stretched
their necks, too. Generations that strained to reach
ever loftier leaves led to the modern giraffe.

As Lamarck correctly inferred, the environment *is*
a factor in changes in lines of descent. However, his
hypothesis, and Cuvier's, has not been supported by
experimental tests. Environmental factors can alter an
individual's phenotype, as when a male builds large
muscles through strength training. But any child of a
muscle-bound parent will not be born muscle-bound.
It can inherit genes, but not increased muscle mass.

VOYAGE OF THE *BEAGLE*

In 1831, in the midst of the confusion, Charles Darwin
was twenty-two years old and wondering what to do
with his life. Ever since he was eight, he had wanted

Figure 17.6 (**a**) Charles Darwin.
(**b**) Replica of the *Beagle* sailing
off a rugged coastline of South
America. During one of his trips,
Darwin ventured into the Andes.
He discovered fossils of marine
organisms in rock layers 3.6
kilometers above sea level.

(**c–e**) The Galápagos Islands are
isolated in the ocean, far to the
west of Ecuador. They arose by
volcanic action on the seafloor
about 5 million years ago. Winds
and currents carried organisms
to the once-lifeless islands. All of
the native species are descended
from those travelers. At far right,
a blue-footed booby, one of many
species Darwin observed during
his voyage.

to hunt, fish, collect shells, or just watch insects and birds—anything but sit in school. Later, at his father's insistence, he did attempt to study medicine in college. The crude, painful procedures being used on patients in that era sickened him. His exasperated father urged him to become a clergyman, and so Darwin packed for Cambridge. His grades were good enough to earn a degree in theology. Yet he spent most of his time with faculty members who embraced natural history.

John Henslow, a botanist, perceived Darwin's real interests. He hastily arranged for Darwin to become ship's naturalist aboard the *Beagle*, which was about to leave on a five-year voyage around the world. The young man who had hated school and had no formal training quickly became an enthusiastic naturalist.

The *Beagle* sailed first to South America to finish work on mapping the coastline (Figure 17.6). During the Atlantic crossing, Darwin collected and studied marine life. He read Henslow's parting gift, the first volume of Charles Lyell's *Principles of Geology*. He saw diverse species in environments ranging from sandy shores of remote islands to high mountains. He also started circling the question of evolving life, which was now on the minds of many individuals.

Darwin started by mulling over a radical theory. As Lyell and other geologists were arguing, erosion and other gradual, natural processes of change had more impact on Earth history than rare catastrophes. Geologists for years had chipped away at sandstones,

limestones, and other rocks that form after sediments slowly accumulate in the beds of lakes, rivers, and seas. They took earthquakes and other less frequent events into account. As they knew, immense floods, more than a hundred big earthquakes, and twenty or so volcanic eruptions happen in a typical year, which means catastrophes are not that unusual.

The idea that gradual, repetitive change had shaped Earth became known as the **theory of uniformity**. It challenged the prevailing views of Earth's age.

The theory bothered scholars who firmly believed that Earth could be no more than 6,000 years old. They believed people had recorded all that had happened in those 6,000 years—and in all that time, no one had mentioned seeing a species evolve. Even so, by Lyell's calculations, it must have taken millions of years to sculpt the present landscape. *Was that not enough time for species to evolve in many diverse ways?* Later, Darwin thought so. But exactly *how* did they evolve? He would end up devoting the rest of his life to that burning question.

Prevailing beliefs can influence how we interpret clues to natural processes and their observable outcomes.

Darwin's observations during a global voyage helped him think about species in a novel way.

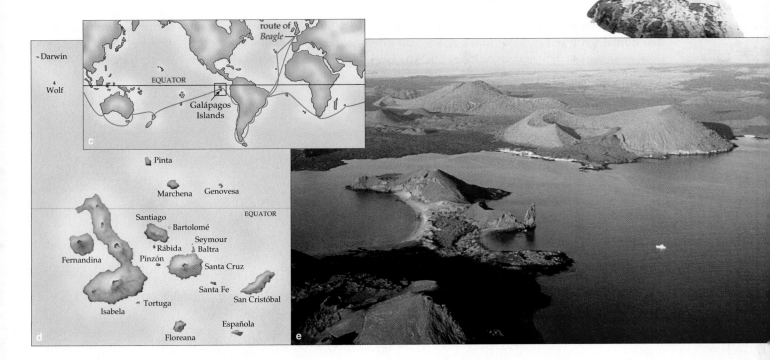

17.3 Darwin, Wallace, and Natural Selection

LINK TO SECTION 1.4

Darwin's observations of thousands of species in different parts of the world helped him see how species might evolve.

OLD BONES AND ARMADILLOS

Darwin brought thousands of specimens with him to England. Although he had page after page of notes, he had been careless about recording where each species lived and what its habitat was like. He had left much of the "geography" out of biogeography. Colleagues helped him fill in some of the blanks, and in time he was able to explain how species might evolve.

Among the specimens were fossils of glyptodonts from Argentina. Of all animals, only living armadillos are like the now-extinct glyptodonts (Figure 17.7). Of all places on Earth, armadillos live only in the places where glyptodonts once lived.

If these animals had been created at the same time, lived in the same place, and were so alike in certain odd traits—such as body armor made of overlapping scales—then why is only one still with us? What if the glyptodonts were ancient relatives of armadillos? What if some traits of their common ancestor had changed in the line of descent that led to armadillos? *Descent with modification*—it did seem possible. What, then, could be the driving force for evolution?

A KEY INSIGHT—VARIATION IN TRAITS

While Darwin assessed his notes, an essay by Thomas Malthus, a clergyman and economist, made him reflect on a topic of social interest. Malthus had correlated population size with famine, disease, and war. He said that humans run out of food, living space, and other resources because they reproduce too much. The larger a population gets, the more individuals there are to reproduce. Individuals compete with one another for dwindling resources. Many starve, get sick, or engage in war or other forms of competition.

Darwin deduced that *any* population has a capacity to produce more individuals than the environment can support. Even one sea star can produce 2,500,000 eggs per year, but the seas do not fill with sea stars. (For one thing, predators eat many of the eggs and larvae.)

Darwin also reflected on species he had observed during his voyage. Individuals of those species were not alike in their details. They varied in size, color, and other traits. *It dawned on Darwin that variations in traits influence an individual's ability to secure resources and to survive and reproduce in the environment.*

He thought about the Galápagos Islands, separated from South America by 900 kilometers of open ocean. Nearly all of their finch species live nowhere else, yet they share traits with mainland species. Perhaps fierce storms had blown a few mainland birds out to sea. Perhaps prevailing winds and currents had dispersed them to the Galápagos. Perhaps those modern species were island-hopping descendants of the colonizers.

As he knew, different species live in diverse habitats near coasts, in dry lowlands, and in mountain forests. One strong-billed type is better than others at cracking open hard seeds (Figure 17.8). A drought that lasts for several years will make soft seeds harder to find. A strong-billed individual will survive and reproduce more than the others. Its bill size has a heritable basis, so its offspring will be favored, also. Conditions in the prevailing environment "select" individuals that have strong bills, which in time become more frequent in the population. *And a population is evolving when forms of heritable traits change over the generations.*

Figure 17.7 (**a**) From Texas, a modern armadillo, about a foot long excluding the tail. (**b**) A Pleistocene glyptodont, which was about as big as a Volkswagen Beetle, and now extinct. Glyptodonts shared unusual traits and a restricted distribution with the existing armadillos. Yet the two kinds of animals are widely separated in time. Their similarities were a clue that helped Darwin develop a theory of evolution by natural selection.

a

b

Figure 17.8 Three of thirteen finch species on the Galápagos Islands. (**a**) A big-billed seed cracker, *Geospiza magnirostris*. (**b**) *G. scandens* eats cactus fruit and insects in cactus flowers. (**c**) *Camarhynchus pallidus* uses cactus spines and twigs to probe for wood-boring insects. Differences in bill shape depend in large part on when and where the signaling molecule BMP4 is switched on in bird embryos. Mutations in regulatory elements may cause the bill variations. Compare the different bills of Hawaiian honeycreepers (Chapter 19).

NATURAL SELECTION DEFINED

Let's now put Darwin's observations and conclusions in the context of what we have learned from genetics and molecular biology:

1. *Observation:* Natural populations have an inherent reproductive capacity to increase in size over time.

2. *Observation:* No population can indefinitely grow in size, because its individuals will run out of food, living space, and other resources.

3. *Inference:* Sooner or later, individuals will end up competing for dwindling resources.

4. *Observation:* Individuals share a pool of heritable information about traits, encoded in genes.

5. *Observation:* Variations in traits start with alleles, slightly different molecular forms of genes that arise through mutations.

6. *Inferences:* Some forms of traits prove better than others at helping an individual compete for resources, survive, and reproduce. In time, alleles for adaptive forms become more frequent relative to other alleles in the population. They lead to increased **fitness**—an increase in adaptation to the environment as measured by the genetic contribution to future generations.

7. *Conclusions:* **Natural selection** is the outcome of differences in reproduction among individuals of a population that vary in shared traits. Environmental agents of selection act on the range of variation, and the population may evolve as a result.

Darwin kept on looking for patterns in his data and filling in gaps in his reasoning. He also wrote out his theory but let ten years pass without publishing it. He waited too long. Alfred Wallace sent him an essay he was working on that outlined the same theory! Today, Wallace is known as the father of biogeography. He did brilliant fieldwork in the Amazon River Basin, Malay Archipelago, and elsewhere (Figure 17.9). He had written earlier letters to Lyell and Darwin about patterns in the geographic distribution of species. He, too, had connected the dots.

Figure 17.9 Alfred Wallace. For one account of the Darwin–Wallace story, read David Quammen's *Song of the Dodo*.

In 1858, just weeks after Darwin received Wallace's essay, their similar theories were presented jointly at a scientific meeting. Wallace was still in the field and knew nothing about the meeting, which Darwin did not attend. The next year, Darwin published *On the Origin of Species*, which laid out detailed evidence in support of his theory.

You may have heard that Darwin's book fanned an intellectual firestorm, but most scholars were quick to accept the idea that diversity is a result of evolution. The theory of natural selection *was* fiercely debated. Decades passed before experimental evidence from a new field, genetics, led to its widespread acceptance.

As Darwin and Wallace perceived, natural selection is the outcome of differences in survival and reproduction among traits. Natural selection can lead to increased adaptation to the environment, as measured by fitness—the relative genetic contribution to future generations.

17.4   Fossils—Evidence of Ancient Life

Turn now to fossil evidence of the connection between life's evolution and the evolution of Earth.

About 500 years ago, Leonardo da Vinci was puzzled by seashells entombed in the rocks of northern Italy's high mountains, hundreds of kilometers from the sea. How did they get there? By the prevailing belief, water from a stupendous and divinely invoked flood had surged up into the mountains, where it deposited the shells. But many shells were thin, fragile, and intact. If they had been swept across such great distances, then wouldn't they be battered to bits?

Leonardo also brooded about the rocks. They were stacked like cake layers. Some layers had shells, others had none. Then he remembered how large rivers swell with spring floodwaters and deposit silt in the sea. Did such depositions happen in ancient seasons? If so, then shells in the mountains could be evidence of layered communities of organisms that once lived in the seas!

By the 1700s, fossils were being accepted as remains and impressions of organisms that lived in the past. (*Fossil* comes from the Latin word for "something that was dug up.") People were still interpreting fossils through the prism of cultural beliefs, as when a Swiss naturalist unveiled the remains of a giant salamander and excitedly announced that they were the skeleton of a man who had drowned in the great flood.

By midcentury, naturalists were questioning these interpretations. Mining, quarrying, and excavations for canals were under way. Diggers were discovering similar rock layers and similar sequences of fossils in distant places, such as the cliffs on both sides of the English Channel. If those layers had been deposited over time, then a vertical series of fossils embedded in them might be a record of past life—*a fossil record*.

HOW DO FOSSILS FORM?

Most fossils are bones, teeth, shells, seeds, spores, and other hard parts (Figure 17.10). Even fossilized feces (coprolites) hold parts of organisms that were eaten. Indirectly, imprints of leaves, stems, tracks, burrows, and other *trace* fossils offer more evidence of past life.

Fossilization is a slow process that starts when an organism or traces of it become covered by sediments or volcanic ash. Water slowly infiltrates the remains, and metal ions and other inorganic compounds that are dissolved in it replace the minerals in bones and other hardened tissues. As sediments accumulate, they exert increasing pressure on the burial site. In time, the pressure and mineralization processes transform those remains into stony hardness.

Remains that become buried quickly are less likely to be obliterated by scavengers. Preservation is also favored when a burial site stays undisturbed. Usually, however, erosion and other geologic assaults deform, crush, break, or scatter the fossils. This is one reason fossils are relatively rare.

Figure 17.10   Two of the more than 250,000 species known from the fossil record. *Left,* fossilized parts of the oldest known land plant (*Cooksonia*). Its stems were a little taller than the length of a toothpick. *Right,* fossilized skeleton of an ichthyosaur. This marine reptile lived 200 million years ago.

Figure 17.11 A slice through time—Butterloch Canyon, Italy, once at the bottom of a sea. Its sedimentary rock layers slowly formed over hundreds of millions of years. Later, geologic forces lifted the stacked layers above sea level. Later still, the erosive force of river water carved the canyon walls and exposed the layers. Scientists Cindy Looy and Mark Sephton are climbing to reach the Permian–Triassic boundary layer, where they will look for fossilized fungal spores.

Other factors affect preservation. Organic materials cannot decompose in the absence of free oxygen, for instance. They may endure when sap, tar, ice, mud, or another air-excluding substance protects them. Insects in amber and frozen woolly mammoths are examples.

FOSSILS IN SEDIMENTARY ROCK LAYERS

Stratified (stacked) layers of sedimentary rock formed long ago from deposits of volcanic ash, silt, sand, and other materials. Sand and silt piled up after rivers transported them from land to the sea, as Leonardo suspected. Sandstones formed from sand, and shales from silt. Depositions were sometimes interrupted, in part because the sea level changed as ice ages began. Tremendous volumes of water froze in glaciers, rivers dried up, and the depositions ended in some regions. Later in time, when the climate warmed and glaciers melted, depositions resumed.

The formation of sedimentary rock layers is called **stratification**. The deepest layer was the first to form; those closest to the surface were the last. Most formed horizontally, as in Figure 17.11, because particles tend to settle in response to gravity. You may see tilted or ruptured layers, as along a road that was cut into a mountainside. Major crustal movements or upheavals disturbed them after they formed.

Most fossils are in sedimentary rock. Understand how rock layers form, and you know that fossils in them formed at specific times in the past. Specifically, *the older the rock layer, the older the fossils.*

INTERPRETING THE FOSSIL RECORD

We have fossils for more than 250,000 known species. Judging from the current range of biodiversity, there must have been many, many millions more. Yet the fossil record will never be complete. Why is this so?

The odds are against finding evidence of an extinct species. Why? At least one specimen had to be buried gently before it decomposed or something ate it. It had to escape erosion, flowing lava, and other forces of nature. The fossil had to end up where someone can find it. For instance, many have become exposed on canyon walls after a river or glacier slowly carved its way through sedimentary rock layers (Figure 17.11).

Also, most ancient species did not lend themselves to preservation. Unlike bony fishes and hard-shelled mollusks, for instance, the soft-bodied jellyfishes and worms do not show up as much in the fossil record. Probably they were just as common, or more so.

Also think about population density and body size. One plant population might release millions of spores in a single season. The earliest humans lived in small bands and raised few offspring. What are the odds of finding even one fossilized human bone compared to finding spores of plants that lived at the same time?

Finally, imagine one line of descent, a **lineage**, that vanished when its habitat on a remote volcanic island sank into the sea. Or imagine two lineages, one lasting only briefly and the other for billions of years. Which is more likely to be represented in the fossil record?

Fossils are physical evidence of organisms that lived in the remote past, a stone-hard historical record of life. In general, the oldest are in the deepest sedimentary rocks.

The fossil record is incomplete. Geologic events obliterated much of it. The record is slanted toward species that had hard parts, dense populations, and wide distribution, and that persisted a long time.

Even so, the fossil record is now substantial enough to help us reconstruct patterns and trends in the history of life.

17.5 Dating Pieces of the Puzzle

LINK TO
SECTION
2.2

How do we assign fossils to a place in time? In other words, how do we know how old fossils really are?

RADIOMETRIC DATING

At one time, people could assign only *relative* ages to their fossil treasures, not absolute ones. For instance, a fossilized mollusk embedded in a layer of rock was said to be younger than a fossil below it and older than a fossil above it, and so forth.

Things changed with **radiometric dating**. This is a way to measure proportions of a daughter isotope and the parent radioisotope of some element trapped in a rock since the time the rock formed. A radioisotope is a form of an element with an unstable nucleus (Section 2.2). Its atoms lose energy and subatomic particles—they decay—until they reach a more stable form.

We cannot predict the exact instant of one atom's decay, but a predictable number of a radioisotope's atoms decay in a characteristic time span. Like the ticking of a perfect clock, the rate of decay for each isotope is constant. Changes in pressure, temperature, or chemical state do not alter it. The time it takes for half of a quantity of a radioisotope's atoms to decay is its **half-life** (Figure 17.12*a*).

For instance, uranium 238's half-life is 4.5 billion years. It decays into thorium 234, which then decays into something else, and so on through intermediate isotopes to lead, the final, stable daughter element for this series. By measuring the uranium 238/lead ratio in the oldest known rocks, geologists figured out that Earth formed more than 4.6 billion years ago.

Radiometric dating has an error factor of less than 10 percent. Recent fossils still hold some carbon and can be dated on the basis of their carbon 14/carbon 12 ratio, as in Figure 17.12*b–d*. Older fossils are dated on the basis of isotope ratios in volcanic rocks or ashes buried with them in the same sedimentary layer.

PLACING FOSSILS IN GEOLOGIC TIME

Early geologists carefully counted backward through layers of sedimentary rock, then used their counts to construct a chronology of Earth history, or a **geologic time scale** (Figure 17.13). By comparing evidence from around the world, they found four abrupt transitions in fossil sequences and used them as boundaries for four great intervals. They named the first interval the Proterozoic, to indicate that it predates fossils of early animals. They named different intervals the Paleozoic,

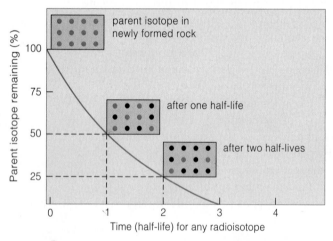

a A simple way to think about the decay of a radioisotope to a more stable form, as plotted against time.

Figure 17.12 *Animated!* (**a**) The decay of radioisotopes at a fixed rate to more stable forms. The half-life of each kind of radioisotope is the time it takes for 50 percent of a given sample to decay. After two half-lives, 75 percent of the sample has decayed, and so on.

(**b–d**) Radiometric dating of a fossil. Carbon 14 (^{14}C) forms in the atmosphere. There, it combines with free oxygen, the result being carbon dioxide. Along with far greater quantities of its more stable isotopes, trace amounts of carbon 14 enter food webs by way of photosynthesis. All organisms incorporate carbon into body tissues.

b Long ago, trace amounts of ^{14}C and a lot more ^{12}C were incorporated into the tissues of a living mollusk. Those atoms of carbon were part of organic compounds making up tissues of its prey. As long as that mollusk lived, the proportion of ^{14}C to ^{12}C in its tissues remained the same.

c When the mollusk died, it stopped gaining carbon. Over time, the proportion of ^{14}C to ^{12}C in its remains fell because of the radioactive decay of ^{14}C. Half of the ^{14}C had decayed in 5,370 years, half of what was left was gone after another 5,370 years, and so on.

d Fossil hunters find the fossil. They measure its ^{14}C/^{12}C ratio to determine half-life reductions since death. In this example, the ratio turns out to be one-eighth of the ^{14}C/^{12}C ratio in living organisms. Thus the mollusk lived about 16,000 years ago.

Eon	Era	Period	Epoch	Millions of Years Ago	Major Geologic and Biological Events That Occurred Millions of Years Ago (mya)
PHANEROZOIC	CENOZOIC	QUATERNARY	Recent	0.01	1.8 mya to present. Major glaciations. Modern humans evolve. The most recent *extinction crisis* is under way.
			Pleistocene	1.8	
		TERTIARY	Pliocene	5.3	65–1.8 mya. Major crustal movements, collisions, mountain building. Tropics, subtropics extend poleward. When climate cools, dry woodlands, grasslands emerge. *Adaptive radiations* of flowering plants, insects, birds, mammals.
			Miocene	22.8	
			Oligocene	33.7	
			Eocene	55.5	
			Paleocene	65	65 mya. Asteroid impact; *mass extinction* of all dinosaurs and many marine organisms.
	MESOZOIC	CRETACEOUS	Late		99–65 mya. Pangea breakup continues, inland seas form. Adaptive radiations of marine invertebrates, fishes, insects, and dinosaurs. Origin of angiosperms (flowering plants).
				99	
			Early		145–99 mya. Pangea starts to break up. Marine communities flourish. *Adaptive radiations* of dinosaurs.
				145	145 mya. Asteroid impact? Mass extinction of many species in seas, some on land. Mammals, some dinosaurs survive.
		JURASSIC		213	248–213 mya. *Adaptive radiations* of marine invertebrates, fishes, dinosaurs. Gymnosperms dominate land plants. Origin of mammals.
		TRIASSIC		248	248 mya. *Mass extinction*. Ninety percent of all known families lost.
	PALEOZOIC	PERMIAN		286	286–248 mya. Supercontinent Pangea and world ocean form. On land, *adaptive radiations* of reptiles and gymnosperms.
		CARBONIFEROUS		360	360–286 mya. Recurring ice ages. On land, *adaptive radiations* of insects, amphibians. Spore-bearing plants dominate; cone-bearing gymnosperms present. Origin of reptiles.
		DEVONIAN		410	360 mya. *Mass extinction* of many marine invertebrates, most fishes. 410–360 mya. Major crustal movements. Ice ages. *Mass extinction* of many marine species. Vast swamps form. Origin of vascular plants. *Adaptive radiation* of fishes continues. Origin of amphibians.
		SILURIAN		440	440–410 mya. Major crustal movements. *Adaptive radiations* of marine invertebrates, early fishes.
		ORDOVICIAN		505	505–440 mya. All land masses near equator. Simple marine communities flourish until origin of animals with hard parts.
		CAMBRIAN		544	544–505 mya. Supercontinent breaks up. Ice age. *Mass extinction*.
PROTEROZOIC				2,500	2,500–544 mya. Oxygen accumulates in atmosphere. Origin of aerobic metabolism. Origin of eukaryotic cells. Divergences lead to eukaryotic cells, then protists, fungi, plants, animals.
ARCHEAN AND EARLIER					3,800–2,500 mya. Origin of photosynthetic prokaryotic cells. 4,600–3,800 mya. Origin of Earth's crust, first atmosphere, first seas. Chemical, molecular evolution leads to origin of life (from proto-cells to anaerobic prokaryotic cells).

Figure 17.13 *Animated!* Geologic time scale. *Red* boundaries mark times of the greatest mass extinctions. If these spans were to the same scale, the Archean and Proterozoic portions would extend downward, spill off the page, and spill across the room. Compare Figure 17.14.

Mesozoic, and lastly the "modern" era, the Cenozoic. Researchers now correlate the geologic time scale with **macroevolution**, or major patterns, trends, and rates of change among lineages. Also, they have subdivided the Proterozoic into finer intervals because it was far more immense than early researchers suspected. Life originated in one of those intervals, the Archean eon.

The geologic time scale now has absolute dates assigned to its boundaries, based on radiometric dating methods. The time scale has been correlated with macroevolution: major patterns, trends, and rates of change among lineages.

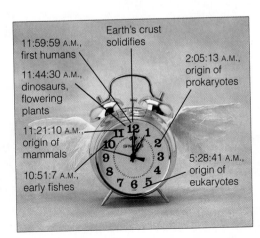

Figure 17.14 How time flies—a geologic time clock. Think of the spans as minutes on a clock that runs from midnight to noon. The recent epoch started after the very last 0.1 second before noon. And where does that put you?

Earth's crust solidifies
11:59:59 A.M., first humans
2:05:13 A.M., origin of prokaryotes
11:44:30 A.M., dinosaurs, flowering plants
11:21:10 A.M., origin of mammals
5:28:41 A.M., origin of eukaryotes
10:51:7 A.M., early fishes

17.6 Drifting Continents, Changing Seas

By clinking their hammers against the rocks, early geologists realized that "solid earth" does not stay put. It moves.

When geologists were first starting to map the vertical stacks of sedimentary rock, the theory of uniformity prevailed. They thought that mountain building and erosion had repeatedly altered Earth's surface in the same ways over time. Eventually, however, it became clear that those recurring geologic events were only part of the picture. Like life, the "unchanging" Earth had changed irreversibly.

AN OUTRAGEOUS HYPOTHESIS

For instance, the Atlantic coasts of South America and Africa seemed to "fit" like jigsaw puzzle pieces. Were all continents once part of a bigger one that had split into fragments and drifted apart? One model for the proposed supercontinent—**Pangea**—took into account the world distribution of fossils and existing species. It also took into account glacial deposits, which held clues to ancient climate zones.

Most scientists did not accept the continental drift hypothesis. Continents drifting on their own across Earth's mantle seemed to be an outrageous idea, and they preferred to think that continents did not move.

Evidence kept piling up. For example, iron-rich rocks are molten when they form, and their bits of iron become oriented toward Earth's magnetic poles. They stay that way after the rocks harden. Yet in North and South America, the tiny iron compasses in rocks that formed 200 million years ago didn't point to the north and south poles. So scientists made a map to fit the north–south alignment of their compasses. Their map put North America and western Europe right next to each other, no Atlantic Ocean between them.

Later, deep-sea probes revealed that the seafloor is spreading away from the mid-oceanic ridges (Figure 17.15). Molten rock that is spewing from a ridge flows sideways in both directions, then it hardens into new crust. The formation of more crust forces older crust into trenches elsewhere in the seafloor. These ridges and trenches are the edges of enormous crustal plates, like pieces of a gargantuan cracked eggshell. They all move at almost imperceptibly slow rates. Over great time spans, land masses end up in different locations.

These findings put continental drift into a broader explanation of crustal movements, now known as the

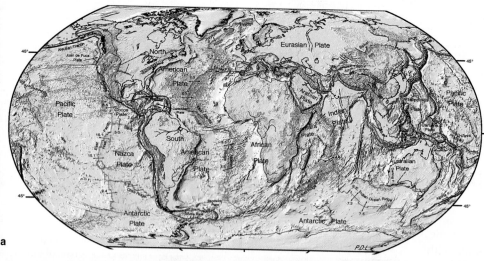

a

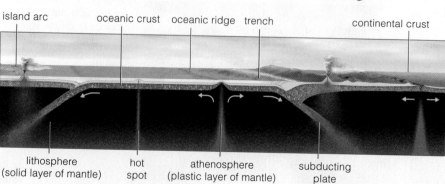

island arc   oceanic crust   oceanic ridge   trench   continental crust

lithosphere (solid layer of mantle)   hot spot   athenosphere (plastic layer of mantle)   subducting plate

b

Figure 17.15 Forces of geologic change.

(a) Present configuration of Earth's crustal plates. These immense, rigid portions of the crust split, drift apart, and collide at almost imperceptible rates. In Appendix VIII, this map is greatly enlarged to show details.

(b) Huge plumes of molten material drive the movement. They well up from the interior, then spread laterally under the crust and rupture it at deep, mid-oceanic ridges. The molten material seeps out, cools, and slowly hardens into new seafloor, which displaces plates away from the ridges.

The advancing edge of one plate can plow under an adjacent plate and lift it up. The Cascades, Andes, and other great mountain ranges paralleling the coasts of continents formed this way. When 2004 drew to a close, the Indian Plate lurched violently under the Eurasian Plate and caused huge tsunamis. These earthquake-generated ocean waves traveled 600 miles per hour across the Indian Ocean and killed more than 240,000 people.

Besides these forces, superplumes ruptured the crust at what are now called "hot spots" in the mantle. The Hawaiian Archipelago has been forming this way. Continents also can rupture in their interior. Deep rifting and splitting are happening now in Missouri, at Lake Baikal in Russia, and in eastern Africa.

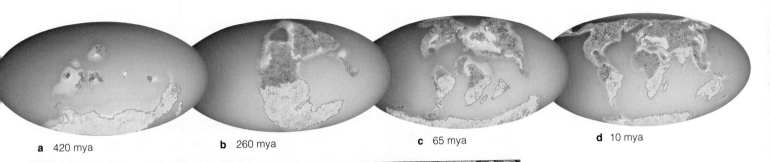

a 420 mya   **b** 260 mya   **c** 65 mya   **d** 10 mya

Figure 17.16 *Animated!* A series of reconstructions of drifting continents. (**a**) The early supercontinent Gondwana (*yellow*). (**b**) Later, all major land masses collided and formed the supercontinent Pangea. (**c**) Positions of fragments that drifted apart after Pangea split apart 65 million years ago, and (**d**) their positions 10 million years ago.

About 260 million years ago, seed ferns and other plants lived nowhere except on the area of Pangea that had once been Gondwana. So did mammal-like reptiles named therapsids. (**e**) Fossilized leaf of one of the seed ferns, *Glossopteris*. (**f**) *Lystrosaurus*, a therapsid about 1 meter (3 feet) long. This tusked herbivore fed on fibrous plants in dry floodplains.

plate tectonics theory. Researchers soon found ways to apply the new theory's predictive power.

For example, the same series of basalt formations, coal seams, and glacial deposits occurs in Africa, India, Australia, and South America. Each of these southern continents has fossils of the seed fern *Glossopteris* and of a therapsid, *Lystrosaurus* (Figure 17.16). This plant's seeds and the therapsid were too heavy to float across the ocean from one continent to the other. Researchers suspected that the organisms had evolved together on **Gondwana**, a supercontinent that preceded Pangea.

Like other land masses in the Southern Hemisphere, Antarctica formed after Gondwana broke up. Someone predicted that fossils of *Glossopteris* and *Lystrosaurus* would be discovered in a series of basalt formations, coal seams, and glacial deposits in Antarctica. In time, explorers did find the series and the fossils. Evidence supported the prediction and plate tectonics theory.

A BIG CONNECTION

Let's take stock. In the remote past, slow movements of Earth's crustal plates put immense land masses on collision courses. Over time, land masses converged and formed supercontinents, which later split at deep rifts and formed new ocean basins. Gondwana drifted south from the tropics, across the south pole, then north until it piled into other land masses. The result was Pangea, a supercontinent that extended from pole to pole with a single world ocean lapping against its coasts. All the while, erosive forces of water and wind resculpted the land surface. Asteroids and meteorites slammed into Earth's crust. The major impacts and their aftermath caused long-term changes in the global temperature, atmosphere, and regional climates.

Such changes on land and in the ocean and atmosphere influenced life's evolution. Imagine early life in shallow, warm waters along continents. Shorelines vanished as continents collided and wiped out many lineages. Yet, even as old habitats vanished, new ones opened up for survivors—and evolution took off in new directions.

Over the past 3.8 billion years, slow movements in Earth's crust as well as catastrophic events have changed the land, the atmosphere, and the ocean. Those changes have had profound effects on the evolution of life.

17.7   Divergences From a Shared Ancestor

To biologists, remember, evolution simply means heritable changes in lines of descent. Comparisons of the body form and structures of major groups of organisms yield clues to evolutionary trends.

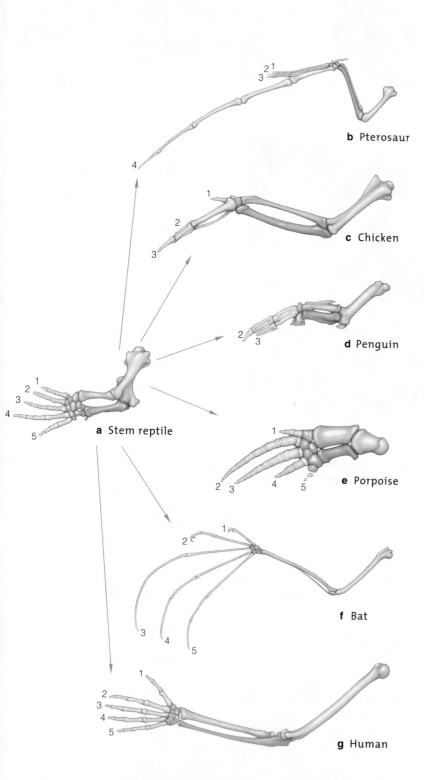

b Pterosaur

c Chicken

d Penguin

a Stem reptile

e Porpoise

f Bat

g Human

Figure 17.17 Morphological divergence among vertebrate forelimbs, starting with bones of a stem reptile (a cotylosaur). Similarities in the number and position of skeletal elements were preserved when diverse forms evolved. Some bones were lost over time (compare the numbers 1 through 5). The drawings are not to the same scale.

Comparative morphology, again, is the study of body forms and structures of major groups of organisms, such as vertebrates and flowering plants. (The Greek *morpho*– means body form.) Sometimes comparisons reveal similarities in one or more body parts between groups, which may be evidence of a common ancestor. Such body parts are **homologous structures** (*homo*– means the same). Even when different groups use the parts for different functions, the genes for constructing those parts point to shared ancestry.

MORPHOLOGICAL DIVERGENCE

Populations of a species diverge genetically after gene flow ends between them (Chapter 18). In time, some morphological traits that help to define their species commonly diverge, also. Change from the body form of a common ancestor is a major macroevolutionary pattern called **morphological divergence**.

Even if the same body part of two related species became dramatically different, some other aspects of the species may remain alike. A careful look beyond unique modifications may reveal the shared heritage.

For instance, all vertebrates on land descended from the first amphibians. Divergences led to what we call reptiles, then to birds and mammals. We know about "stem reptiles" that probably were ancestral to these groups. Fossilized, five-toed limb bones tell us that the ancestral species crouched low to the ground (Figure 17.17*a*). Later, descendants diversified into many new habitats on land. A few descendants that had become adapted for walking on land even returned to the seas after environmental conditions changed.

A five-toed limb was evolutionary clay. It became molded into different kinds of limbs having different functions. In lineages that eventually led to penguins and porpoises, it became modified into flippers used in swimming. In the lineage leading to modern horses, it became modified into long, one-toed limbs suitable for running fast. Among moles, it became stubby and useful for burrowing into dirt. Among elephants, it became strong and pillarlike, suitable for supporting a great deal of weight.

The five-toed limb also became modified into the human arm and hand. Later on, a thumb evolved in opposition to the four fingers of the hand. It was the basis of stronger and more precise motions.

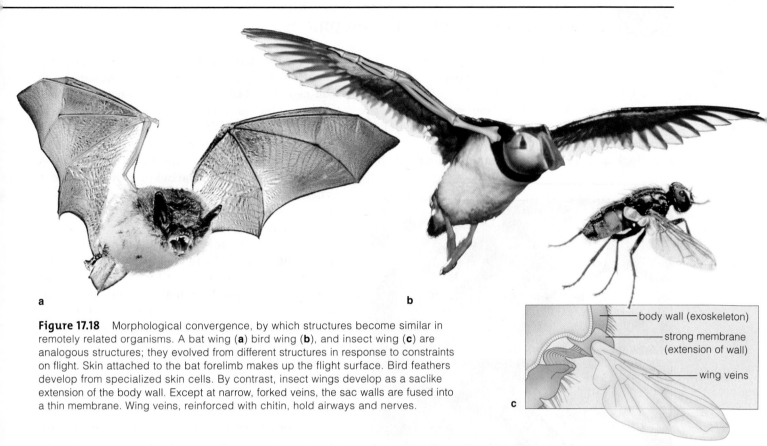

Figure 17.18 Morphological convergence, by which structures become similar in remotely related organisms. A bat wing (**a**) bird wing (**b**), and insect wing (**c**) are analogous structures; they evolved from different structures in response to constraints on flight. Skin attached to the bat forelimb makes up the flight surface. Bird feathers develop from specialized skin cells. By contrast, insect wings develop as a saclike extension of the body wall. Except at narrow, forked veins, the sac walls are fused into a thin membrane. Wing veins, reinforced with chitin, hold airways and nerves.

a

b

c

body wall (exoskeleton)
strong membrane (extension of wall)
wing veins

Even though forelimbs are not the same in size, shape, or function from one group of vertebrates to the next, they clearly are alike in the structure and positioning of their bony elements. They also are alike in the patterns of nerves, blood vessels, and muscles that develop inside them. In addition, comparisons of the early embryos of different vertebrates reveal strong resemblances in patterns of bone development. Such similarities point to a shared ancestor.

MORPHOLOGICAL CONVERGENCE

Body parts with similar form or function in different lineages are not *always* homologous. Sometimes they evolved independently in remote lineages. Parts that differed at first may have evolved in similar ways as organisms became subjected to similar environmental pressures. **Morphological convergence** refers to cases where dissimilar body parts evolved in similar ways in evolutionarily distant lineages.

For instance, you just read about the homologous forelimbs of birds and bats. Bones aside, are bird and bat wings homologous, too? No. The flight surface of birds evolved as a sweep of feathers, all derived from skin. The forelimb structurally supports it. The flight surface for bats is a thin membrane, an extension of the skin itself. The bat wing is attached to reinforcing bony elements inside the forelimb (Figure 17.18*a,b*).

The insect wing, too, resembles bird and bat wings in its function—flight. Is it homologous with them? No. This wing develops as an extension of an outer body wall reinforced with chitin. No underlying bony elements support it (Figure 17.18*c*).

The differences between bat, bird, and insect wings are evidence that each of these animal groups adapted independently to the same physical constraints that govern how a wing can function in the environment. The wings of all three are **analogous structures**. They are not modifications of comparable body parts in different lineages. They are three different responses of different body parts to similar challenges. The Greek *analogos* means similar to one another.

With morphological divergence, comparable body parts became modified in different ways in different lines of descent from a common ancestor.

Such divergences resulted in homologous structures. Even if these body parts differ in size, shape, or function, they have an underlying similarity because of shared ancestry.

With morphological convergence, dissimilar body parts became similar in lineages that are not closely related. Such body parts are analogous structures. They converged in form only as an outcome of similar pressures.

17.8 Changes in Patterns of Development

LINKS TO
SECTIONS
14.5, 15.2, 15.3

Comparing the patterns of embryonic development often yields evidence of evolutionary relationships.

Multicelled embryos of plants and animals develop step-by-step from a fertilized egg, and there are built-in constraints on how the body plan develops. Most mutations and changes in chromosomes tend to be selected against, because most mutations disrupt the inherited developmental program. Even so, a mutation with neutral or beneficial effects can move a lineage past one of the constraints.

Master gene mutations can do this. Recall, from Sections 15.2 and 15.3, that homeotic genes guide the formation of tissues and organs in orderly patterns. A mutation in a homeotic gene can disrupt the patterns, sometimes drastically. Such disruptions typically lead to huge problems, but once in a while an altered body plan proves to be advantageous.

You already saw some examples of how homeotic genes guide when and how flowers form. To reinforce the point, here is another example: A single mutation in the homeotic gene known as *Apetala1* causes male floral reproductive structures (anthers) to form where petals are supposed to form in the flowers of field mustard, *Brassica oleracea* (Figure 17.19). At least in the laboratory, such abundantly anthered mutants are exceptionally fertile plants.

Another example: The embryos of some vertebrate lineages are alike in the early stages of development. Their tissues form in similar ways when cells divide, differentiate, and interact. The gut and heart, bones, skeletal muscles, and other parts start to grow and develop in orderly spatial patterns that are strikingly similar among these groups.

How, then, did adults of different groups get to be so different? We can expect that heritable changes in the onset, rate, or completion of developmental steps led to many of the differences. Some changes could have increased or decreased relative sizes of tissues and organs. Some changes could have ended growth during a juvenile stage; the adults of certain species still do have some juvenile features.

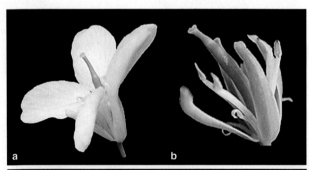

Figure 17.19 How a single mutation in a homeotic gene in many plants influences flower form and function.

(**a**) Normal flower of field mustard (*Brassica oleracea*). A mutation in the *Apetala1* gene causes a badly distorted flower (**b**) to form. (**c**) Wild-type flower of common wall cress (*Arabidopsis thaliana*). Mutation of the *Apetala1* gene in this plant causes flowers with no petals to form (**d**).

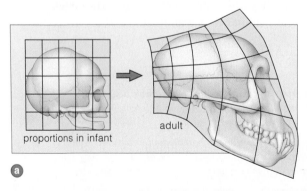
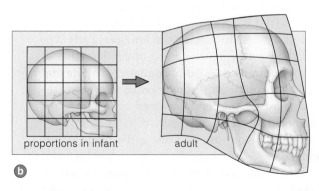

Figure 17.20 *Animated!* Differences between two primates, a possible outcome of mutations that changed the timing of steps in the body's development. The skulls are depicted as paintings on a rubber sheet divided into a grid. Stretching both sheets deforms the grid in a way that corresponds to differences in growth patterns between these primates. (**a**) Proportional changes in chimpanzee skull, and (**b**) human skull.

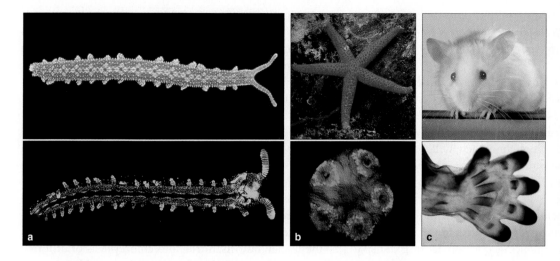
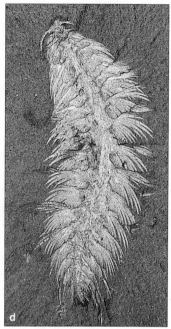

Figure 17.21 How many legs? Mutations in ancestral genes may help explain why animals differ in the number of legs and other appendages. *Dll* is a homeotic gene that initiates limb development, and other genes control its expression. Fluorescent *green* reveals *Dll* expression in (**a**) a velvet walking worm, and (**b**) a sea star; and (**c**) *blue* in a mouse embryo's foot. (**d**) Cambrian legs.

Modifications in genes that influence growth rates might have caused the major proportional differences between chimpanzee and human skull bones (Figure 17.20). For humans, the facial bones and skull bones around the brain increase in size at fairly consistent rates, from infant to adult. The rate of growth is faster for chimp facial bones, so the proportions of an infant skull and an adult skull differ significantly.

In addition, did transposons cause some variation among lineages? As Section 14.5 explains, these short DNA segments spontaneously and repeatedly slip into new places in genomes. Depending on where they end up, they can have powerful effects on gene expression.

Only primates carry the 300 base-pair transposons called *Alu* elements, and they have done so for at least 30 million years. *Alu* elements are noncoding, and yet they have sequences that resemble intron–exon splice signals. When inserted into coding regions of DNA, they promote duplications of themselves. *Alu* elements have had big effects on the expression of genes for estrogen, thyroid hormones, and other proteins that control growth and development. Were they pivotal in primate evolution? Possibly.

About 1 million *Alu* elements make up 10 percent of the human genome. The most recent shared ancestors of chimpanzees and humans diverged between 6 and 4 million years ago. More than 98 percent of human DNA is identical with chimpanzee DNA. Something in the remaining 2 percent accounts for the differences. Uniquely positioned *Alu* elements may be one factor.

As a final example, body appendages as different as crab legs, beetle legs, butterfly wings, sea star arms, fish fins, and mouse feet all start out as buds of tissue from the body surface. A bud will form wherever the *Dll* gene product is expressed. The product, a protein, is a signal for clusters of dividing embryonic cells to "stick out from the body" in an expected pattern, as in Figure 17.21. Normally, *Hox* genes help sculpt the body's details by suppressing expression of *Dll* where appendages are not supposed to form.

The *Dll* gene is expressed in similar ways across many phyla, which is strong evidence for its ancient origin. Indeed, in some Cambrian fossils, it looks like it was not suppressed at all (Figure 17.21*d*). Probably layers of gene controls evolved over time, resulting in the variable numbers and locations of appendages we observe today among all complex animals, including humans and other vertebrates.

Similarities and differences in patterns of development are often clues to shared ancestry, especially for the embryos of plants and animals.

Heritable changes that alter key steps in a developmental program may be enough to bring about major differences in the adult forms of related lineages.

Mutations in master genes and insertions of transposons into coding regions of DNA could have been enough to launch body plans in new evolutionary directions.

17.9 Clues in DNA, RNA, and Proteins

LINKS TO
SECTIONS
3.6, 14.4, 16.3,16.4

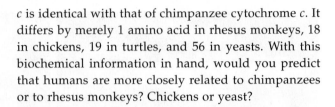

All species are a mix of ancestral and novel traits, including biochemical ones. The kinds and numbers of traits they do or do not share are clues to relationships.

Each species has its own DNA base sequence, which encodes instructions for making RNAs and proteins (Sections 3.6 and 14.4). We can expect genes to mutate in any line of descent. The more recently two lineages have diverged, the less time each will have had to accumulate unique mutations. That is why RNA and proteins of closely related species are more similar than those of more distantly related ones.

Identifying biochemical similarities and differences among species is now rapid, thanks to the methods of automated gene sequencing (Section 16.3). Extensive sequence data for numerous genomes and proteins are compiled in internationally accessible databases. With such data, we know (for example) that 31 percent of the 6,000 genes of yeast cells have counterparts in our genome. So do 40 percent of the 19,023 roundworm genes and 50 percent of the fruit fly genes.

PROTEIN COMPARISONS

Similarities in amino acids can be used to decipher connections between species and to study why certain proteins are highly conserved. When two species have many proteins with similar or identical amino acid sequences, they probably are closely related. When sequences differ considerably, many mutations have been built in, which indicates that a long time passed since the two species shared a common ancestor.

A few essential genes have evolved very little; they are highly *conserved* across diverse species. One such gene encodes cytochrome *c*. Species that range from aerobic bacteria to humans must make this protein component of electron transfer chains. In humans, its primary structure consists of only 104 amino acids. Figure 17.22 shows the striking similarity between the entire amino acid sequences for cytochrome *c* from a yeast, a plant, and an animal. And think about this: The *entire* amino acid sequence of human cytochrome

c is identical with that of chimpanzee cytochrome *c*. It differs by merely 1 amino acid in rhesus monkeys, 18 in chickens, 19 in turtles, and 56 in yeasts. With this biochemical information in hand, would you predict that humans are more closely related to chimpanzees or to rhesus monkeys? Chickens or yeast?

NUCLEIC ACID COMPARISONS

Mutations that cause differences between species are dispersed through DNA's nucleotide sequences. Some regions of those sequences are unique to each lineage. Researchers use the regions to estimate evolutionary distances. They isolate and then compare DNA from the nuclei, mitochondria, and chloroplasts of different species (Figure 17.23). They also compare DNA regions that encode ribosomal RNA (rRNA).

Nucleic acid hybridization refers to base-pairing between DNA strands from different sources (Section 16.2). In the hybrid molecule, more hydrogen bonds form between matched bases than mismatched bases. Strands with more matches associate strongly with each other. The amount of heat required to separate two strands of a hybrid can be used as a comparative measure of their similarity. Why? It takes more heat to disrupt hybrid DNA of closely related species.

Evolutionary distances are still being measured by DNA–DNA hybridizations, although automated gene sequencing now gives faster, more quantifiable results. Remember DNA fingerprinting (Section 16.4)? DNA restriction fragments from different species can be compared after gel electrophoresis has separated them.

Mitochondrial DNA (mtDNA), which mutates fast, is used to compare individuals of eukaryotic species. In sexually reproducing species, it is inherited intact from one parent—usually the mother. Thus, changes between maternally related individuals probably were caused by mutations, not by genetic recombinations.

Computer programs quickly compare collections of DNA sequencing data. Comparative analyses either reinforce or invite modification of evolutionary trees based on morphological findings and the fossil record.

$^+NH_3$-gly asp val glu lys gly lys lys ile phe ile met lys cys ser gln cys his thr val glu lys gly gly lys his lys thr gly pro asn leu his gly leu phe gly arg lys thr gly gln ala pro gly

$^+NH_3$-ala ser phe ser glu ala pro pro gly asn pro asp ala gly ala gly ala lys ile phe lys thr lys cys ala gln cys his thr val asp ala gly ala gly his lys gln gly pro asn leu his gly leu phe gly arg gln ser gly thr thr ala gly

$^+NH_3$-thr glu phe lys ala gly ser ala lys lys gly ala thr leu phe lys thr arg cys leu gln cys his thr val glu lys gly gly pro his lys val gly pro asn leu his gly ile phe gly arg his ser gly gln ala glu gly

Figure 17.22 *Animated!* Comparison of the primary structure of cytochrome *c* from a yeast (*top row*), wheat plant (*middle*), and primate (*bottom*). *Gold* highlights parts of the amino acid sequence that are identical in all three. The probability that such a pronounced molecular resemblance resulted by chance is extremely low. Cytochrome *c* is a vital component of electron transfer chains in cells. Its amino acid sequence has been highly conserved even in these three evolutionarily distant lineages.

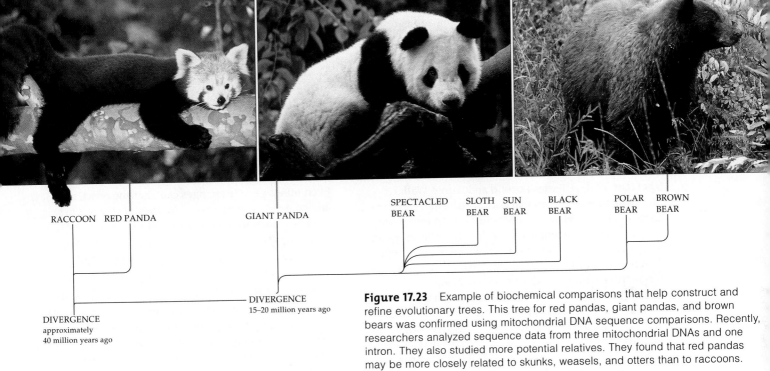

RACCOON   RED PANDA

GIANT PANDA

SPECTACLED BEAR   SLOTH BEAR   SUN BEAR   BLACK BEAR   POLAR BEAR   BROWN BEAR

DIVERGENCE
15–20 million years ago

DIVERGENCE
approximately
40 million years ago

Figure 17.23 Example of biochemical comparisons that help construct and refine evolutionary trees. This tree for red pandas, giant pandas, and brown bears was confirmed using mitochondrial DNA sequence comparisons. Recently, researchers analyzed sequence data from three mitochondrial DNAs and one intron. They also studied more potential relatives. They found that red pandas may be more closely related to skunks, weasels, and otters than to raccoons.

However, gene transfers between species can slant the results. For example, after hybridization between two different species of plants, hybrid offspring may cross back to either parental species, thus transferring genes from one species into the other. Gene swapping is rampant among prokaryotic species.

MOLECULAR CLOCKS

Some researchers estimate the timing of divergence by comparing the numbers of neutral mutations in genes that have been highly conserved in different lineages. Because the mutations have little or no effect on the individual's survival or reproduction, we can expect that neutral mutations have accumulated in conserved genes at a fairly constant rate.

The accumulation of neutral mutations to the DNA of a lineage has been likened to the predictable ticks of a **molecular clock**. Turn the hands of such a clock back, so that the total number of ticks unwinds down through past geologic intervals. Where does the last tick stop? Theoretically, it stops close to the time when molecular, ecological, and geographic events put the lineage on its unique evolutionary road.

How are molecular clocks calibrated? The number of differences in DNA base sequences or amino acid sequences between species can be plotted against a series of branch points that researchers have inferred from the fossil record. Section 19.6 will show how this is done. Such diagrams may reflect relative times of divergences among species, phyla, and other groups.

Biochemical similarity is greatest among the most closely related species and smallest among the most remote.

asn lys asn lys gly ile ile trp gly glu asp thr leu met glu tyr leu glu asn pro lys lys tyr ile pro gly thr lys met ile phe val gly ile lys lys lys glu glu arg ala asp leu ile ala tyr leu lys lys ala thr asn glu-COO⁻

asn lys asn lys ala val glu trp glu glu asn thr leu tyr asp tyr leu leu asn pro lys lys tyr ile pro gly thr lys met val phe pro gly leu lys lys pro gln asp arg ala asp leu ile ala tyr leu lys lys ala thr ser ser-COO⁻

asn ile lys lys asn val leu trp asp glu asn asn met ser glu tyr leu thr asn pro lys lys tyr ile pro gly thr lys met ala phe gly gly leu lys lys glu lys asp arg asn asp leu ile thr tyr leu lys lys ala cys glu-COO⁻

Summary

Section 17.1 Awareness of evolution, or heritable changes in lines of descent, emerged long ago through biogeography, geology, and comparative morphology.

Section 17.2 Prevailing cultural belief systems influence our interpretation of natural events. In the nineteenth century, naturalists worked to reconcile traditional belief systems with a growing body of physical evidence in support of evolution.

Biology⊛Now
Read the InfoTrac article "Typecasting a Bit Part," Stephen J. Gould, The Sciences, March 2000.

Section 17.3 Charles Darwin and Alfred Wallace proposed a novel theory that natural selection can bring about evolution. Here are the theory's main premises:

Any population tends to grow in size until resources dwindle. Its individuals must compete more for them.

Individuals with forms of traits that make them more competitive tend to produce more offspring.

Over the generations, more competitive forms of traits that have a heritable basis increase in frequency in the population relative to less competitive forms.

Thus nature "selects" variations in traits that are more effective at helping individuals survive and reproduce; such traits are more adaptive in a given environment.

Biology⊛Now
Read the InfoTrac article "What Darwin's Finches Can Teach Us About the Evolutionary Origin and Regulation of Biodiversity," B. Rosemary Grant and Peter Grant, Bioscience, March 2003.

Section 17.4 Fossils are stone-hard evidence of life in the distant past. Many fossils are embedded in stacked layers of sedimentary rock. Generally, the oldest layers are near the bottom of the sequence and more recently deposited layers are on top. Although the fossil record is not complete, it reveals much about life in the past.

Biology⊛Now
Learn more about fossil formation and the geologic time scale with the animations on BiologyNow.

Section 17.5 Fossil sequences were the basis for the first geologic time scale, which used abrupt transitions in the fossil record as boundaries for different eras. Through radiometric dating of fossils, absolute dates have since been assigned to the scale. This dating method has a relatively small margin of error.

Biology⊛Now
Learn more about the half-life of a radioisotope's atoms with the animated interaction on BiologyNow.

Section 17.6 The global distribution of land masses and fossils, magnetic patterns in volcanic rocks, and evidence of seafloor spreading from mid-oceanic ridges support the plate tectonic theory. According to this theory, slow movements of Earth's crustal plates raft land masses to new positions. Such movements had profound impacts on the directions of life's evolution.

Biology⊛Now
Learn more about drifting continents with the interaction on BiologyNow.

Section 17.7 Comparative morphology reveals evidence of evolution. Homologous structures are one of the clues. These body parts recur in different lineages, but they became modified in different ways after the lineages diverged from a shared ancestor. These parts are not the same as analogous structures. Such body parts did not start out being alike; they became similar in independent lineages as a response to similar kinds of environmental pressures.

Section 17.8 Similarities in patterns and structures of embryonic development suggest common ancestry. Even minor genetic changes can alter the onset, rate, and completion time of developmental stages. They can have major impact on the adult form.

Biology⊛Now
Explore proportional changes in embryonic development with the animated interaction on BiologyNow.

Section 17.9 We are now clarifying evolutionary relationships through comparisons of DNA, RNA, and proteins between different species. The investigative methods include nucleic acid hybridization and, more recently, automated gene sequencing and DNA fingerprinting, as explained in Chapter 16.

Some researchers estimate the times of divergences from ancestral lineages by comparing the number of neutral mutations in highly conserved genes. Such mutations alter the base sequence in DNA, but flexibility built into the genetic code keeps the change from altering the amino acid sequence of the specified protein. They may accumulate in the DNA of a species at a constant rate, like ticks of a molecular clock.

Biology⊛Now
Learn more about amino acid comparisons with the interaction on BiologyNow.

Self-Quiz
Answers in Appendix II

1. Biogeographers deal with _____ .
   a. patterns in which continents drift
   b. patterns in the world distribution of species
   c. mainland and island biodiversity
   d. both b and c are correct
   e. all are correct

2. _____ have influenced the fossil record.
   a. Sedimentation and compaction
   b. Crustal plate movements
   c. Volcanic ash deposition
   d. a through c

3. Life originated in the _____ eon.
   a. Archean   c. Phanerozoic
   b. Proterozoic   d. Cambrian

4. Which of these supercontinents formed first: Pangea or Gondwana?

5. Through _____ , the same body parts became modified differently in different lines of descent from a common ancestor.
   a. morphological convergence
   b. morphological divergence
   c. ancestral analogy
   d. ancestral homology

6. Homologous structures among major groups of organisms may differ in _____ .
   a. size   c. function
   b. shape   d. all of the above

7. By altering steps in the program by which embryos develop, _____ may lead to major differences between adults of related lineages.
   a. automated gene sequencing   c. transposons
   b. homeotic gene mutations   d. b and c

8. Molecular clocks are based on comparisons of _____ mutations in _____ genes.
   a. beneficial; moderately conserved
   b. neutral; moderately conserved
   c. neutral; highly conserved
   d. lethal; highly conserved

9. Match the terms with the most suitable description.
   ____ stratification   a. evidence of life in distant past
   ____ fossils   b. theory of repetitive change
   ____ homeotic   only in Earth history
         genes   c. body parts of similar size,
   ____ half-life   shape, or function in different
   ____ homologous   lineages with shared ancestor
         structures   d. insect wing and bird wing
   ____ uniformity   e. time it takes to decay half of a
   ____ analogous   quantity of a radioisotope's
         structures   atoms into something else
                       f. big role in development
                       g. layers of sedimentary rock

Additional questions are available on **Biology ⓔ Now™**

Critical Thinking

1. At one time, all species were ranked in a great Chain of Being, from lowly forms to Man, then to spiritual beings. Even some modern scientists still call the traits of species "rudimentary" or "advanced." Does the theory of natural selection imply that all species become more complex over time? Why or why not?

2. At the end of your backbone is a coccyx, a few small, fused-together bones (Figure 17.4). Is the human coccyx a *vestigial* structure—all that is left of the tail of some distant vertebrate ancestors? Or is it the start of a newly evolving structure?
   Formulate a hypothesis, then design a way to test the predictions you make based on the hypothesis.

3. Think about the species living around you. From the evolutionary perspective, which ones are most successful in terms of sheer numbers, geographic distribution, and how long their lineage has endured on Earth?

4. Comparative biochemistry can help us estimate evolutionary relationship and approximate times for divergences from ancestral stocks. Base sequence

Figure 17.24 Reconstruction of *Rodhocetus* based on fossils discovered in Pakistan. This cetacean lived 47 million years ago, along the shores of the Tethys Sea. Its ankle bones are strong evidence of a close evolutionary link between early whales and hoofed land mammals. Compare Figure 17.4.

comparisons and amino acid comparisons yield good estimates. Reflect on the genetic code (Section 14.2), then suggest why it may be a useful measure of mutations, mutation rates, and biochemical relatedness.

5. For some time, evolutionists accepted that the ancestors of whales were four-legged animals that walked on land, then took up life in water about 55 million years ago. Fossils reveal gradual changes in skeletal features that made an aquatic life possible. But which four-legged mammals were the ancestors?
   The answer recently came from Philip Gingerich and Iyad Zalmout. While digging for fossils in Pakistan, they found remains of early aquatic whales. Intact, sheeplike ankle bones *and* archaic whale skull bones were in the same fossilized skeletons (Figures 17.4 and 17.24).
   Ankle bones of fossilized, early whales from Pakistan have the same form as the unique ankle bones of extinct and modern artiodactyls. Modern cetaceans no longer have even a remnant of an ankle bone. Here is evidence of an evolutionary link between certain aquatic mammals and a major group of mammals on land.
   The radiometrically dated fossils are real. Yet no one was around to witness this transitional time. Because we did not see ancient life evolving, do you think there can be absolute proof of evolution in the distant past? Is the circumstantial evidence of fossil morphology enough to convince you that the theory is not wrong?

18 MICROEVOLUTIONARY PROCESSES

Rise of the Super Rats

Slipping in and out of the pages of human history are rats—*Rattus*—the most notorious of mammalian pests. One kind of rat or another has distributed pathogens and parasites that cause bubonic plague, typhus, and other deadly infectious diseases (Figure 18.1). The death toll from fleas that bit infected rats and then bit people has exceeded the dying in all wars combined.

The rats themselves are far more successful. By one estimate, there is one rat for every person in urban and suburban centers of the United States. Besides spreading diseases, rats chew their way through walls and wires of homes and cities. In any given year, they cause economic losses approaching 19 billion dollars.

For years, people have been fighting back with traps, ratproof storage facilities, and poisons, including arsenic and cyanide. During the 1950s, they used baits laced with warfarin. This synthetic organic compound interferes with blood clotting. Rats ate the baits. They died within days after bleeding internally or losing blood through cuts or scrapes.

Warfarin was extremely effective. Compared to other rat poisons, it had a lot less impact on harmless species. It quickly became the rodenticide of choice.

In 1958, however, a Scottish researcher reported that warfarin did not work against some rats. Similar reports from other European countries followed. About twenty years later, 10 percent of the urban rats caught in the United States were warfarin resistant. *What happened?* To find out, researchers compared warfarin-resistant rat populations with still-vulnerable rats. They traced the difference to a gene on one of the rat chromosomes.

Figure 18.1 *Above*, medieval attempts to deal with a bubonic plague pandemic—the Black Death—that may have killed half the people in Europe alone. Not knowing that the disease agent hitches rides on rats, Europeans tried to protect themselves by praying and dancing until they dropped. Physicians wore bird masks, such as the mask shown on the facing page. They filled the "beak" with herbs that supposedly purified the air that plague victims had breathed. For the next 300 years, anyone accused of causing an outbreak of the plague, no matter how absurd the evidence, was burned alive.

Below, example of rats in this century. Rats infest 80,000 hectares of the rice fields in the Philippine Islands. They ruin more than 20 percent of the annual crops. Rice is the main food source for people in Southeast Asia.

Today we douse agricultural land and buildings with ever more potent rat poisons. By doing so, we have unwittingly promoted the rise of super rats. Three centuries from now, how will people be viewing *our* actions?

At that gene locus, a dominant allele was common among the warfarin-resistant rat populations but rare among the vulnerable ones. The dominant allele's product actually neutralizes warfarin's effect on blood clotting.

"What happened" was evolution by natural selection. As warfarin started to exert pressure on rat populations, the rat populations changed. The previously rare dominant allele suddenly proved to be adaptive. The lucky rats that inherited the allele survived and produced more offspring. The unlucky ones that inherited the recessive allele had no built-in defense, and they died. Over time, the dominant allele's frequency increased in all rat populations exposed to the poison.

Selection pressures can and often do change. When warfarin resistance increased in rat populations, people stopped using warfarin. Not surprisingly, the frequency of the dominant allele declined. Now the latest worry is the evolution of "super rats," which the newer and even more potent rodenticides cannot seem to kill.

The point is, when you hear someone question whether life evolves, remember this: With respect to life, **evolution** simply means heritable change is occurring in some line of descent. The actual mechanisms that can bring about such change are the focus of this chapter. Later chapters highlight how these mechanisms have contributed to the evolution of new species.

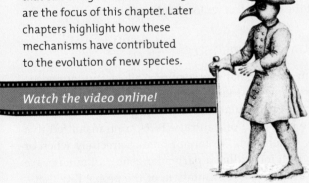

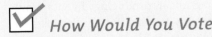
Watch the video online!

How Would You Vote?

Antibiotic-resistant strains of bacteria are becoming dangerously pervasive. Standard animal husbandry practice includes continually dosing healthy animals with antibiotics—the same antibiotics prescribed for people. Should this practice stop? See BiologyNow for details, then vote online.

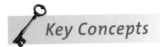

Key Concepts

WHAT IS MICROEVOLUTION?

Individuals of all natural populations share a gene pool but differ in which alleles they inherit. As a result, they show variations in phenotypes.

An individual does not evolve. Rather, a *population* evolves, which means its shared pool of alleles is changing. Over the generations, any allele may increase in its frequency among individuals, or it may become rare or lost.

Microevolution refers to changes in allele frequencies as an outcome of mutation, natural selection, genetic drift, and gene flow. Sections 18.1, 18.2

NATURAL SELECTION

Natural selection is the outcome of variation in heritable traits that influence which individuals of a population survive and reproduce in each generation. Selective agents operating in the environment can stabilize, disrupt, or cause directional shifts in the range of variation. Sections 18.3–18.6

GENETIC DRIFT

Sometimes chance events bring about random changes in allele frequencies over time. The magnitude of this genetic drift is greatest in small populations, where it can lead to a loss of genetic diversity. Section 18.7

GENE FLOW

Gene flow is the physical movement of alleles into and out of a population. It tends to oppose the effects of mutation, natural selection, and genetic drift; it keeps populations of a species similar to one another. Section 18.8

ADAPTATION AND THE ENVIRONMENT

An evolutionary adaptation is a heritable aspect of form, function, behavior, or development that contributes to the fit between an individual and its environment. The challenge is to identify environmental conditions to which a given trait is presumably adapted. Section 18.9

Links to Earlier Concepts

Before starting this chapter, review the premises of the theory of natural selection as outlined in Sections 1.4 and 17.3 as well as the definitions of basic terms in genetics (11.1).

You will be drawing upon your knowledge of mutation (14.5) and the chromosomal basis of inheritance (12.5 especially). We urge you to scan earlier sections on causes of continuous variation in populations (11.5) and on how the environment can modify gene expression (11.6).

18.1 Individuals Don't Evolve, Populations Do

*As Charles Darwin and Alfred Wallace perceived long ago, individuals don't evolve; populations do. Each **population** is a group of individuals of the same species in a specified area. To understand how it evolves, start with variation in the traits that characterize it.*

VARIATION IN POPULATIONS

The individuals of a population share certain features. Pigeons have two feathered wings, three toes forward, one toe back, and so on. These are *morphological* traits (*morpho–*, form). The individuals share *physiological* traits, including metabolic activities that help the body function in the environment. They respond the same way to certain basic stimuli, as when babies imitate adult facial expressions. These are *behavioral* traits.

However, the individuals of a population also show variation in the details of the shared traits. You know this just by thinking about the variations in the color and patterning of pigeon feathers or butterfly wings or snail shells. Figure 18.2 only hints at the range of variations in human skin color and distribution, color, texture, and amount of hair. Almost every trait of any species may vary, but variation can be dramatic among sexual reproducers.

For sexually reproducing species, at least, we may define the population as a group of individuals that are interbreeding, that are reproductively isolated from other species, and that produce fertile offspring. The offspring typically have two parents, and they have mixes of the parental forms of traits.

Many traits show *qualitative* differences; they have two or more distinct forms, or morphs. Remember the purple or white pea plant flowers that Gregor Mendel studied? The persistence of two forms of a trait in a population is a case of **dimorphism**. The persistence of three or more forms is **polymorphism**. In addition, for many traits, the individuals of a population show *quantitative* differences, a range of incrementally small variations in a specified trait (Section 11.7).

THE GENE POOL

Genes encode information about heritable traits. The individuals of a population inherit the same number and kind of genes (except for a pair of nonidentical sex chromosomes). Together, they and their offspring represent a **gene pool**—a pool of genetic resources.

For sexual reproducers, nearly all genes available in the shared pool have two or more slightly different molecular forms, or **alleles**. Any individual might or might not inherit identical alleles for any trait. This is the source of variations in *phenotype*, or differences in the details of shared traits. Whether you have black, brown, red, or blond hair depends upon which alleles you inherited from your two parents.

You read about the inheritance of alleles in earlier chapters. Here we summarize the key events involved:

Gene mutation

Crossing over at meiosis I (puts novel combinations of alleles in chromosomes)

Independent assortment at meiosis I (puts mixes of maternal and paternal chromosomes in gametes)

Fertilization (combines alleles from two parents)

Change in chromosome number or structure (loss, duplication, or repositioning of genes)

Only mutation creates new alleles. The other events shuffle existing alleles into different combinations, but what a shuffle! Each gamete gets one of many millions of possible combinations of maternal and paternal chromosomes that may or may not be identical at each locus. Unless you are an identical twin, it is extremely unlikely that another person with your precise genetic makeup has ever lived or ever will.

One other point about the nature of the gene pool: Offspring do not inherit phenotypes; they inherit *genes*. Section 11.6 describes how environmental conditions, too, bring about variation in the range of phenotypes, but the effects last no longer than the individual.

MUTATION REVISITED

Being the original source of new alleles, mutations are worth another look—this time in the context of their impact on populations. Usually, gene mutations that have beneficial or neutral effects are transmitted to a new generation. We cannot predict precisely when or in which individual a particular gene will mutate. We *can* predict rates of mutation, or the probability that a mutation will happen in a specified interval (Section 14.5). For instance, one estimated rate for mammalian genomes is 2.2^{-9} mutations per base pair per year.

Many mutations give rise to structural, functional, or behavioral alterations that reduce an individual's chances of surviving and reproducing. Even a single biochemical change may be devastating. For instance, skin, bones, tendons, lungs, blood vessels, and many other vertebrate organs incorporate collagen. Thus, when the collagen gene has mutated, drastic problems may ripple all through the body. Compare Section 11.4.

Any mutation that results in severe disruptions in phenotype usually causes death. It is a **lethal mutation**.

A **neutral mutation**, recall, alters the base sequence in DNA, but the change has no discernible effect on survival or reproduction (Section 17.9). It neither helps nor hurts the individual. For instance, if you carry a mutant gene that keeps your earlobes attached to the head instead of swinging freely, this in itself should not stop you from surviving and reproducing as well as anybody else. Therefore, natural selection does not affect the frequency of the trait in the population.

Every so often, a mutation proves useful. A mutant gene product that affects growth might make a corn plant grow larger or faster and thereby give it the best access to sunlight and nutrients. A neutral mutation might prove helpful if conditions in the environment change. Even if a mutant gene bestows only a slight advantage, natural selection or a chance event might favor its preservation in DNA and its transmission to the next generation.

Mutations are rare, so they usually have little or no immediate effect on a population's allele frequencies. But they have been slipping into genomes for billions of years. Cumulatively, they have served as reservoirs for change, for biodiversity that is staggering in its breadth. Think of it. The reason you don't look like a bacterium or an avocado or earthworm or even your neighbors down the street began with mutations that arose at different times, in different lines of descent.

STABILITY AND CHANGE IN ALLELE FREQUENCIES

Researchers typically track **allele frequencies**, or the relative abundances of alleles of a given gene among all individuals of a population. They can start from a theoretical reference point, **genetic equilibrium**, when a population is *not* evolving with respect to that locus.

Genetic equilibrium can only occur if five conditions are being met: There is no mutation, the population is infinitely large, the population is isolated from other populations of the same species, individuals mate at random, and all individuals survive and produce the same number of offspring.

If you are interested, the following section offers a closer look at the nature of genetic equilibrium—the point at which a population is not evolving.

As it happens, genetic equilibrium is exceedingly rare in nature. Why? Mutations are rare but inevitable, and they might throw a wild card in the game of who survives and reproduces. Also, three processes—called *natural selection, genetic drift*, and *gene flow*—can drive populations out of equilibrium. **Microevolution** refers to small-scale changes in allele frequencies that arise as an outcome of mutation, natural selection, genetic drift or gene flow, or some combination of these.

Figure 18.2
A sampling of the phenotypic variation in populations of humans and snails, the outcome of variations in frequencies of alleles.

We partly characterize a natural population or species by morphological, physiological, and behavioral traits, most of which are heritable.

At any gene locus, different alleles give rise to variations in individual phenotypes—to differences in the details of shared structural, functional, and behavioral traits.

The individuals of a population share a pool of genetic resources—that is, a pool of alleles.

Only mutation creates new alleles. Natural selection, genetic drift, and gene flow affect only the frequencies of various alleles at a given gene locus in the population.

Most populations are slowly evolving, which simply means that the frequencies of the alleles for a specified trait are changing from one generation to the next.

18.2 When Is A Population *Not* Evolving?

How do researchers know whether or not a population is evolving? They can start by tracking deviations from the baseline of genetic equilibrium.

The Hardy–Weinberg Formula Early in the twentieth century, Godfrey Hardy (a mathematician) and Wilhelm Weinberg (a physician) independently applied the rules of probability to sexually reproducing populations. Like the geneticists who came after them, they perceived that gene pools can remain stable only when five conditions are being met:

1. There is no mutation.
2. The population is infinitely large.
3. The population is isolated from all other populations of the species (no gene flow).
4. Mating is random.
5. All individuals survive and produce the same number of offspring.

In other words, allele frequencies for any gene in the shared pool will remain stable unless the population is evolving. Hardy and Weinberg developed a simple formula that can be used to track whether a population of any sexually reproducing species is slipping out of that state of genetic equilibrium.

Consider tracking a hypothetical pair of alleles that affect butterfly wing color. A protein pigment is specified by dominant allele *A*. If a butterfly inherits two *AA* alleles, it will have dark-blue wings. If it inherits two recessive alleles *aa*, it will have white wings. If it inherits one of each (*Aa*), the wings will be medium-blue (Figure 18.3).

At genetic equilibrium, the proportions of the wing-color genotypes are

$$p^2(AA) + 2pq(Aa) + q^2(aa) = 1.0$$

where *p* and *q* are the frequencies of alleles *A* and *a*. This is what became known as the *Hardy–Weinberg equilibrium equation*. It defines the frequency of a dominant and a recessive allele for a gene that controls a particular trait in a population.

The frequencies of *A* and *a* must add up to 1.0. To give a specific example, if *A* occupies half of all the loci for this gene in the population, then *a* must occupy the other half (0.5 + 0.5 = 1.0). If *A* occupies 90 percent of all the loci, then *a* must occupy 10 percent (0.9 + 0.1 = 1.0). No matter what the proportions,

$$p + q = 1.0$$

At meiosis, recall, paired alleles segregate and end up in different gametes. So the proportion of gametes having the *A* allele is *p*. The proportion having the *a* allele is *q*. The Punnett square on the next page reveals the genotypes possible in the next generation (*AA*, *Aa*, and *aa*).

490 *AA* butterflies
dark-blue wings

490 *AA* butterflies
dark-blue wings

490 *AA* butterflies
dark-blue wings

420 *Aa* butterflies
medium-blue wings

420 *Aa* butterflies
medium-blue wings

420 *Aa* butterflies
medium-blue wings

90 *aa* butterflies
white wings

90 *aa* butterflies
white wings

90 *aa* butterflies
white wings

Starting Population

Next Generation

Next Generation

Figure 18.3 *Animated!* How to determine whether a population is evolving. The frequencies of wing-color alleles among all individuals in this hypothetical population of morpho butterflies have not changed because all five assumptions upon which the Hardy–Weinberg rule is based are being met.

The frequencies add up to 1.0: $p^2 + 2pq + q^2 = 1.0$.

Suppose that the population has 1,000 individuals and that each one produces two gametes:

490 *AA* individuals make 980 *A* gametes
420 *Aa* individuals make 420 *A* and 420 *a* gametes
90 *aa* individuals make 180 *a* gametes

The frequency of alleles *A* and *a* among 2,000 gametes is

$$A = \frac{980 + 420}{2,000 \text{ alleles}} = \frac{1,400}{2,000} = 0.7 = p$$

$$a = \frac{180 + 420}{2,000 \text{ alleles}} = \frac{600}{2,000} = 0.3 = q$$

At fertilization, gametes combine at random and start a new generation. If the population size is still 1,000, you will find 490 *AA*, 420 *Aa*, and 90 *aa* individuals. Because the allele frequencies for dark-blue, medium-blue, and white wings are the same as they were in the original gametes, they will give rise to the same phenotypic frequencies that occurred in the preceding generation.

As long as the assumptions that Hardy and Weinberg identified continue to hold, the pattern will persist. If traits show up in different proportions from one generation to the next, however, then one or more of the five assumptions is not being met. The hunt can begin for one or more of the evolutionary forces driving the change.

Applying the Rule So how does the Hardy–Weinberg formula work in the real world? For one thing, researchers use it to estimate the frequency of carriers of alleles that cause genetic traits and disorders.

For example, about 1 percent of people of Irish ancestry are affected by *hemochromatosis*. They absorb too much iron from their food. Symptoms of this autosomal recessive disorder include liver problems, fatigue, and arthritis. We can use the number to estimate the frequency of carriers of the recessive allele. If $p^2 = 0.01$, then p is 0.1, q is 0.9, and the carrier frequency ($2pq$) must be 0.18 among Irish populations. Such information is useful to doctors and public health professionals.

Another example: A deviation from the frequencies predicted by the Hardy–Weinberg formula suggests that a mutant allele for *BRCA2* may be lethal to female embryos. The allele also has been linked to breast cancer. For one study, researchers tracked the frequency of the mutant allele among newborn girls. There were fewer homozygotes than expected, based on the number of heterozygotes and the Hardy–Weinberg formula. By itself or in combination with other alleles, a pair of mutant *BRCA2* alleles may cause the spontaneous abortion of the early embryo.

18.3 Natural Selection Revisited

Natural selection, *again, is the outcome of differences in reproduction among individuals of a population that vary in their shared traits, some of which prove more adaptive than others under prevailing environmental conditions.*

LINKS TO
SECTIONS
1.4, 17.3

Natural selection may be the most influential process of microevolution. Its impact shows up at all levels of biological organization, which is the reason you were introduced to it early on, in Chapter 1. You also came across simple examples in other chapters, and Sections 17.2 and 17.3 offered you a glimpse of the history that preceded its discovery. Turn now to major categories of selection, as sketched out in Figure 18.4.

With *directional* selection, the range of variation for a trait shifts in a consistent direction; individuals at one end of the range of variation are selected against and those at the other end are favored. With *stabilizing* selection, the forms at one or both ends of the range are selected against. With *disruptive* selection, forms at one or both ends are favored and intermediate forms are selected against.

Diverse selection pressures acting on a population might favor forms at one end in the range of variation for a trait, or intermediate forms within that range, or extreme forms at both ends of the range.

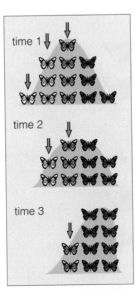

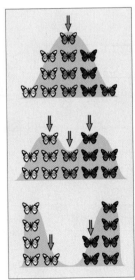

a Extreme form at one end of the range of phenotypes favored

b Intermediate form of the range of phenotypes favored

c Extreme forms at both ends of the range of phenotypes favored

Figure 18.4 Overview of the outcomes of three modes of natural selection: (**a**) directional, (**b**) stabilizing, and (**c**) disruptive.

18.4 Directional Selection

LINKS TO
SECTIONS
1.4, 16.7

*With **directional selection**, allele frequencies shift in a consistent direction, so forms at one end of a phenotypic range become more common than midrange forms, as in Figure 18.5. Directional change in the environment or novel conditions can cause the shift.*

RESPONSES TO PREDATION

The Peppered Moth Populations of peppered moths (*Biston betularia*) offer us a classic case of directional selection. The moths feed and mate at night and rest motionless on trees during the day. Their behavior and coloration (mottled gray to nearly black) camouflage them from day-flying, moth-eating birds.

In the 1850s, the industrial revolution started in England, and factory smoke altered conditions in much of the countryside. Before then, light moths were the most common form, and a dark form was rare. Also, light-gray speckled lichens had grown thickly on tree trunks. Light moths but not dark moths that rested on the lichens were camouflaged (Figure 18.6a).

Lichens are sensitive to air pollution. Between 1848 and 1898, soot and other pollutants started to kill the lichens and darken tree trunks. The dark moth form was better camouflaged (Figure 18.6b). Researchers hypothesized: If the original conditions favored light moths, then the *changed* conditions favored dark ones.

In the 1950s, H. B. Kettlewell used a *mark–release–recapture method* to test the possibility. He bred both moth forms in captivity and marked hundreds so that they could be easily identified after being released in the wild. He released them near highly industrialized areas around Birmingham and near an unpolluted part of Dorset. His team recaptured more dark moths in the polluted area and more light ones near Dorset:

	Near Birmingham (pollution high)	Near Dorset (pollution low)
Light-Gray Moths		
Released	64	393
Recaptured	16 (25%)	54 (13.7%)
Dark-Gray Moths		
Released	154	406
Recaptured	82 (53%)	19 (4.7%)

Observers also hid in blinds near moths that had been tethered to trees. They observed birds capturing more light moths around Birmingham and more dark ones around Dorset. Directional selection was in play.

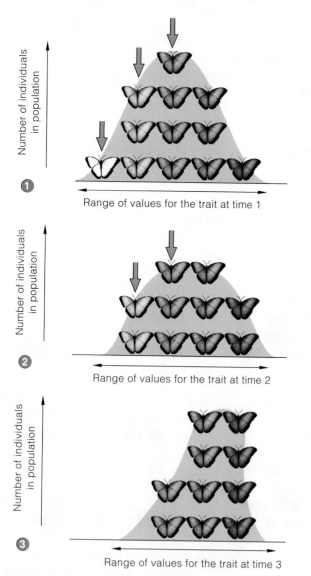

Figure 18.5 *Animated!* Directional selection. These bell-shaped curves signify a range of continuous variation in a butterfly wing-color trait. *Medium-blue* is between two phenotypic extremes—*white* and *dark purple. Orange* arrows signify which forms are being selected against over time.

Figure 18.6 Natural selection of two forms of the same trait, body surface coloration, in two settings. (**a**) Light moths (*Biston betularia*) on a nonsooty tree trunk are hidden from predators. Dark ones stand out. (**b**) The dark color is more adaptive in places where soot darkens tree trunks.

Figure 18.7 Visible evidence of directional selection in a population of rock pocket mice relative to a neighboring population, as documented by Michael Nachman, Hoi Hoekstra, and Susan D'Agostino. (**a**) Lava basalt flow at the study site. The two color morphs of rock pocket mice, each posed on two different backgrounds: (**b**) tawny fur and (**c**) dark fur.

Pollution controls went into effect in 1952. Lichens made a comeback, and tree trunks became largely free from soot. Phenotypes shifted in the reverse direction. Where pollution has decreased, the frequency of dark moths has been decreasing as well.

Pocket Mice Directional selection is at work among rock pocket mice (*Chaetodipus intermedius*) of Arizona's Sonoran Desert. Of more than eighty genes known to affect coat color in mice, researchers found a gene that governs a difference between two populations of this mouse species (Figure 18.7).

Rock pocket mice are small mammals that spend the day in underground burrows and forage for seeds at night. Some live in tawny-colored outcroppings of granite. In this habitat, individuals with tawny fur are camouflaged from predators (Figure 18.7b).

A smaller population of pocket mice lives in the same region, but these mice scamper over dark basalt of ancient lava flows. They have dark coats, so they, too, are camouflaged from predators (Figure 18.7c).

We can expect that night-flying predatory birds are selective agents that affect fur color. For instance, owls have an easier time seeing mice with fur that does not match the rocks.

Michael Nachman used genetic data on laboratory mice to formulate a hypothesis on differences in coat color in the two wild populations of pocket mice. He predicted that a mutation of either the *Mc1r* gene or *agouti* gene could cause the difference. He collected DNA from dark pocket mice at a lava flow and from light mice at adjacent granite outcroppings.

DNA analysis showed that the *Mc1r* gene sequence for all dark mice differed by four nucleotides from that of their light-furred neighbors. In the population of dark mice, the allele frequencies had evolved in a consistent direction as a result of selection pressure, so dark fur became more common.

RESISTANCE TO PESTICIDES AND ANTIBIOTICS

Pesticides can cause directional selection, as they did for the super rats. Typically, a heritable aspect of body form, physiology, or behavior helps a few individuals survive the first pesticide doses. As the most resistant ones are favored, resistance becomes more common. About 450 species of pests are now resistant to one or more types of pesticides. Also, some pesticides kill off the natural predators. Freed from natural constraints, resistant populations flourish and inflict more damage. This result of directional selection is *pest resurgence*. Some genetically engineered crop plants resist pests. In time, they too may exert selection pressure.

Antibiotics also can result in directional selection. Certain microbes produce natural antibiotics that can kill bacterial competitors for nutrients. We use natural and synthetic antibiotics to fight pathogenic bacteria. Streptomycins, for example, inhibit protein synthesis in bacterial cells. The penicillins disrupt covalent bonds that hold a bacterial cell wall together.

Yet antibiotics have been overprescribed, often for simple infections that would clear up on their own. Genetic variation in bacterial gene pools allows some cells with certain genotypes to survive as others die. So overuse of antibiotics favors the resistant bacterial populations, which will be harder to eradicate in the millions of people who contract cholera, tuberculosis, and other bacterial diseases each year. Also, healthy farm animals are routinely dosed with antibiotics to prevent infection. Consider: In eggs that look slightly fluorescent green, tetracycline is showing through.

With directional selection, allele frequencies underlying a range of variation tend to shift in a consistent direction in response to some change in the environment.

18.5 Selection Against Or in Favor of Extreme Phenotypes

Consider now two more categories of natural selection. One works against phenotypes at the fringes of a range of variation; the other favors them.

LINK TO
SECTION
17.3

STABILIZING SELECTION

With **stabilizing selection**, intermediate forms of a trait in a population are favored, and extreme forms are not. This mode of selection can counter mutation, genetic drift, and gene flow. It tends to preserve intermediate phenotypes in the population (Figure 18.8*a*).

As an example, prospects are not good for human babies who weigh far more or far less than average at birth. Also, pre-term instead of full-term pregnancies increase the risk, as Figure 18.9 indicates.

Newborns weighing less than 5.51 pounds or born before thirty-eight weeks of pregnancy are completed tend to develop high blood pressure, diabetes, and heart disease when they are adults. Researchers now suspect that the mother's blood concentration of a stress hormone, cortisol, is linked to low birth weight and illnesses that develop later in life.

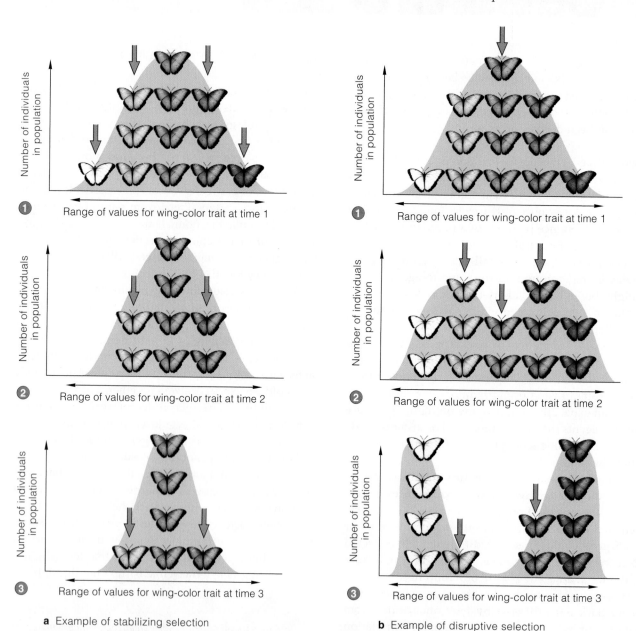

a Example of stabilizing selection

b Example of disruptive selection

Figure 18.8 *Animated!* Selection against or in favor of extreme phenotypes, with a population of butterflies as the example. (**a**) stabilizing selection and (**b**) disruptive selection. The *orange* arrows show forms of the trait being selected against.

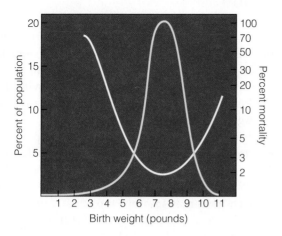

Figure 18.9 Weight distribution for 13,730 human newborns (*yellow* curve) correlated with death rate (*white* curve).

Figure 18.10 Adult sociable weaver (*Philetairus socius*), a native of the African savanna. These birds cooperate in constructing and using large communal nests in a region where trees and other good nesting sites are scarce.

Rita Covas and her colleagues gathered evidence of stabilizing selection on the body mass of juvenile and adult sociable weavers (*Philetairus socius*), as in Figure 18.10. Between 1993 and 2000, they captured, measured, tagged, released, and recaptured 70 to 100 percent of the birds living in communal nests during the breeding season. Their field studies supported a prediction that body mass is a trade-off between risks of starvation and predation. Intermediate-mass birds have the selective advantage. Foraging is not easy in this habitat, and lean birds do not store enough fat to avoid starvation. We can expect that fat ones are more attractive to predators and not as good at escaping.

DISRUPTIVE SELECTION

With **disruptive selection**, forms at both ends of the range of variation are favored and intermediate forms are selected against (Figure 18.8*b*).

Consider the black-bellied seedcracker (*Pyrenestes ostrinus*) of Cameroon. Females and males of these African finches have large or small bills—but no sizes in between (Figure 18.11). It is like everyone in Texas being four feet *or* six feet tall, with no one in between.

The pattern holds all through the geographic range. If unrelated to gender or geography, what causes it? If only two bill sizes persist, then disruptive selection may be eliminating birds with intermediate-size bills. Factors that affect feeding performance are the key. Cameroon's swamp forests flood in the wet season; lightning-sparked fires burn in the hot, dry season. Most plants are fire-resistant, grasslike sedges. One species produces hard seeds and the other, soft seeds.

Remember the bills of Galápagos finches (Section 17.3)? Here, also, the ability to crack hard seeds affects survival. All Cameroon seedcrackers prefer soft seeds,

lower bill 12 mm wide   lower bill 15 mm wide

Figure 18.11 Disruptive selection in African finch populations. Selection pressures favor birds with bills that are about 12 *or* 15 millimeters wide. The difference is correlated with competition for scarce food resources during the dry season.

but birds with large bills are better at cracking hard ones. In the dry season, the birds compete fiercely for scarce seeds. A scarcity of both types of seeds during recurring episodes of drought has a disruptive effect on bill size in the seedcracker population. Birds with intermediate sizes are being selected against, and now all bills are either 12 *or* 15 millimeters wide.

In these seedcrackers, bills of a particular size have a genetic basis. In experimental crosses between two birds with the two optimal bill sizes, all offspring had a bill of one size or the other, nothing in between.

With stabilizing selection, intermediate phenotypes are favored and extreme phenotypes at both ends of the range of variation are eliminated.

With disruptive selection, intermediate forms of traits are selected against and extreme forms in the range of variation are favored.

18.6 Maintaining Variation in a Population

LINKS TO
SECTIONS
3.6, 11.1

Natural selection theory helps explain diverse aspects of nature, including male–female differences and the relationship between sickle-cell anemia and malaria.

SEXUAL SELECTION

The individuals of many sexually reproducing species show a distinct male or female phenotype, or **sexual dimorphism** (*dimorphos,* having two forms). Often the males are larger and flashier than females. Courtship rituals and male aggression are common.

These adaptations and behaviors seem puzzling. All take energy and time away from an individual's survival activities. Why do they persist if they do not contribute directly to survival? The answer is **sexual selection**. By this mode of natural selection, winners are the ones that are better at attracting mates and successfully reproducing compared to others of the population. The most adaptive traits help individuals defeat same-sex rivals for mates or are the ones most attractive to the opposite sex.

Figure 18.12 One male bird of paradise in a flashy courtship display. He caught the eye (and, perhaps, the sexual interest) of the smaller, less colorful female. The males of this species compete fiercely for females, which function as selective agents. (Why do you suppose the females are drab-colored?)

By choosing mates, a male or female is a selective agent acting on its own species. For example, females of some species shop among a congregation of males, which vary in appearance and courtship behavior. The selected males and the females pass on their alleles to the next generation.

Flashy body parts and behaviors show up among species in which males provide little or no help with raising offspring. The female apparently chooses her partner on the basis of observable signs of health and vigor. Such traits may improve the odds of producing healthy, vigorous offspring (Figure 18.12).

You might be wondering whether we can correlate genes with specific forms of sexual behavior. The sexual deception practiced by an Australian orchid is a case in point. The flowers of *Chiloglottis trapeziformis* attract male wasps by secreting a substance that is identical with a sex pheromone—which female wasps release to attract male wasps. Flowers get pollinated as males attempt to copulate with them.

This orchid is stingy. It gives a male wasp nothing in return, not a single drop of nectar, even though it is the orchid's exclusive pollinator. The female wasps are wingless. They hatch in soil. When males do not lift and carry them to a food source, they starve to death.

When *C. trapeziformis* puts out blooms, male wasps waste precious time and metabolic energy trying to find females. Evolutionary biologist Florian Schiestl has proposed that selection pressure is afoot for wasps that can produce a new sex pheromone, one that the orchid cannot duplicate.

This interaction exploits male wasps, but Wittko Francke thinks it might put pressure on their brains to evolve. In an orchid patch, the average tiny-brained male wasp copulates blindly with whatever smells right. It will try to copulate even with the head of a pin that has a few micrograms of pheromone sprayed on it. However, a few wasps with a slightly less robotic brain might be able to identify the females by other cues, such as visual ones. Alternatively, both species could face extinction, another pattern in nature.

SICKLE-CELL ANEMIA—LESSER OF TWO EVILS?

With *balancing* selection, two or more alleles of a gene are being maintained at relatively high frequencies in the population. Their persistence is called **balanced polymorphism** (*polymorphos,* having many forms). The allele frequencies might shift slightly, but often they return to the same values over the long term. We may see this balance when conditions favor heterozygotes. In some way, their nonidentical alleles for a given trait grant them higher fitness compared to homozygotes, which, recall, have identical alleles for the trait.

Consider the environmental pressures that favor an Hb^A/Hb^S pairing in humans. The Hb^S allele codes for a mutant form of hemoglobin, an oxygen-transporting protein in blood. Homozygotes (Hb^S/Hb^S) develop the genetic disorder *sickle-cell anemia* (Section 3.6).

The Hb^S frequency is highest in both tropical and subtropical regions of Asia and Africa. Often, Hb^S/Hb^S homozygotes die in their early teens or early twenties. Yet, in these same regions, heterozygotes (Hb^A/Hb^S) make up nearly a third of the population! Why is this combination maintained at such high frequency?

The balancing act is most pronounced in areas that, historically, have had the highest incidence of *malaria* (Figure 18.13). Mosquitoes transmit the parasitic agent of malaria, *Plasmodium*, to human hosts. The parasite multiplies in the liver and then in red blood cells. The target cells rupture and release new parasites during severe, recurring bouts of infection (Section 22.7).

It turns out that Hb^A/Hb^S heterozygotes are more likely to survive malaria than people who make only normal hemoglobin. Several survival mechanisms are possible. In heterozygotes, the infected cells take on a sickle shape under normal conditions. The abnormal shape marks them as targets for the immune system, which destroys them, along with the parasites inside. In addition, heterozygotes have one functioning Hb^A allele. Although they are not completely healthy, they still produce enough normal hemoglobin to prevent sickle-cell anemia. That is why heterozygotes are more likely to survive long enough to reach reproductive age, compared to Hb^S/Hb^S homozygotes.

In short, the persistence of the "harmful" Hb^S allele may be a matter of relative evils. Malaria has been a selective force for thousands of years in tropical and subtropical areas of Asia, the Middle East, and Africa. Through that time span, natural selection has favored the Hb^A/Hb^S combination in all of the malaria-ridden regions, because heterozygotes show more resistance to the disease. In such environments, the combination has proved to have more survival value than either the Hb^S/Hb^S or the Hb^A/Hb^A combination.

With sexual selection, some version of a gender-related trait gives the individual an advantage in reproductive success. Sexual dimorphism is one outcome of sexual selection.

In a population showing balanced polymorphism, natural selection is maintaining two or more alleles at frequencies greater than 1 percent over the generations.

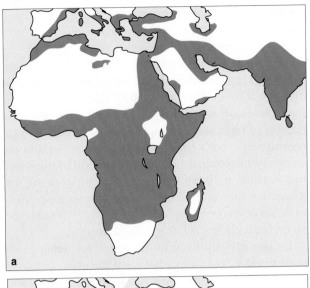

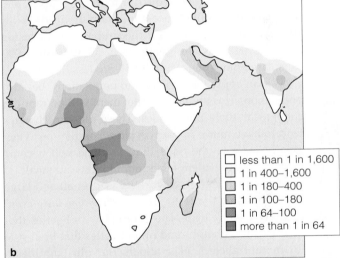

□ less than 1 in 1,600
□ 1 in 400–1,600
□ 1 in 180–400
□ 1 in 100–180
■ 1 in 64–100
■ more than 1 in 64

Figure 18.13 (**a**) Distribution of malaria cases reported in Africa, Asia, and the Middle East in the 1920s, before the start of programs to control mosquitoes, the vector for *Plasmodium*. (**b**) Distribution and frequency of people with the sickle-cell trait. Notice the close correlation between the maps. (**c**) Physician searching for *Plasmodium* larvae in Southeast Asia.

18.7 Genetic Drift—The Chance Changes

LINKS TO SECTIONS 11.2, 12.10

Especially in small populations, random changes in allele frequencies can lead to a loss of genetic diversity.

Genetic drift is a random change in allele frequencies over time, brought about by chance alone. Researchers measure it in terms of probability rules. *Probability* is the chance that something will happen relative to the number of times it could happen (Section 11.2). We can measure an event's relative frequency as a fraction on a scale from zero to 1—or 0 to 100 percent of the time. For instance, if 10 million people enter a drawing for a month-long vacation in Hawaii, all expenses paid, each has an equal chance of winning: 1/10,000,000, or an exceedingly improbable 0.00001 percent.

By one probability rule, the expected outcome of some event is less likely to occur if the event happens only rarely. Each time you flip a coin, for example, there is a 50 percent chance it will turn up heads. With 10 flips, odds are high that the proportions of heads and tails will deviate greatly from 50:50. With 1,000 flips, large deviations from 50:50 are less likely.

We can apply the same rule to populations. Because population sizes are not infinite, there will be random changes in allele frequencies. These random changes tend to have minor impact on large populations. They greatly increase the odds that an allele will become more or less prevalent when populations are small.

Steven Rich and his coworkers used small and large populations of the flour beetle (*Tribolium castaneum*) to study genetic drift. They started with beetles that bred true for allele b^+ and other beetles that bred true for mutant allele b. (The superscript plus signifies a wild-type allele.) They hybridized individuals from both groups to get a population of F_1 heterozygotes

(b^+b), which they divided into sets of twelve. Different sets consisted of 10, 20, 50, and 100 randomly selected male and female beetles, and the subpopulation sizes were maintained for twenty generations.

Figure 18.14 shows two of the test results. Drift was greatest in the sets of 10 beetles and least in the sets of 100 beetles. Notice the loss of b^+ from one of the small populations (one graph line ends at 0 in Figure 18.14*a*). Only allele b remained. When all of the individuals of a population have become homozygous for one allele only at a locus, we say that **fixation** has occurred.

Thus, *random change in allele frequencies leads to the homozygous condition and a loss of genetic diversity over time.* This is genetic drift's outcome in all populations; it simply happens faster in small ones (Figure 18.14). Once alleles from the parent population have become fixed, their frequencies will not change again unless mutation or gene flow introduces new alleles.

BOTTLENECKS AND THE FOUNDER EFFECT

Genetic drift is pronounced when a few individuals rebuild a population or start a new one. This happens after a **bottleneck**, a drastic reduction in population size brought about by severe pressure. Suppose that contagious disease, habitat loss, or hunting nearly wipes out a population. Even if a moderate number of individuals survive a bottleneck, allele frequencies will have been altered at random.

In the 1890s, hunters killed all but twenty of a large population of northern elephant seals. Government restrictions allowed the population to recover to about 130,000 individuals. Each is homozygous for all of the genes analyzed so far.

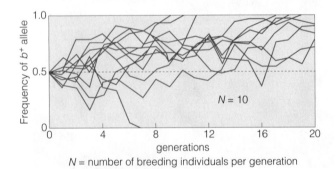

a The size of twelve populations of beetles was maintained at 10 breeding individuals per generation for twenty generations. Allele b^+ was lost and b became fixed in one population. Notice that alleles can be fixed or lost even in the absence of selection.

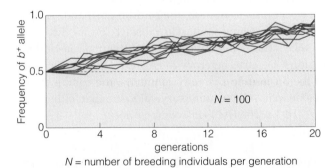

b The size of twelve populations was maintained at 100 individuals per generation for twenty generations. Allele b did not become fixed. Drift was far less in each generation than it was in the small populations tracked in (**a**).

Figure 18.14 *Animated!* Genetic drift's effect on allele frequencies in small and large populations. The starting frequency of mutant allele b^+ was 0.5.

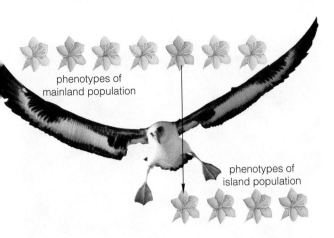

phenotypes of mainland population

phenotypes of island population

Figure 18.15 Founder effect. This wandering albatross carries seeds, stuck to its feathers, from the mainland to a remote island. By chance, most of the seeds carry an allele for orange flowers that are rare in the original population. Without further gene flow or selection for color, genetic drift will fix the allele on the island.

Unpredictable genetic shifts can occur after a few individuals establish a new population. This form of bottlenecking is a **founder effect**. Genetic diversity might be greatly reduced relative to the original gene pool, as when a lone seed founds a population on a remote island in the middle of the ocean (Figure 18.15).

INBRED POPULATIONS

Genetic drift is less pronounced in inbred populations. **Inbreeding** is nonrandom mating among very close relatives, which share many identical alleles. It leads to the homozygous condition. It also lowers fitness if harmful recessive alleles are increasing in frequency.

Most human societies forbid or discourage incest (inbreeding between parents and children or siblings). Inbreeding among other close relatives is common in geographically or culturally isolated small groups. The Old Order Amish in Pennsylvania are moderately inbred. One outcome is a rather high frequency of a recessive allele that causes *Ellis–van Creveld syndrome*. Affected individuals have extra fingers, toes, or both (Section 12.10). The allele might have been rare when a few founders entered Pennsylvania. Now, about 1 in 8 individuals of the community are heterozygous for the allele, and 1 in 200 are homozygous for it.

> *Genetic drift is the random change in allele frequencies over the generations, brought about by chance alone. The magnitude of its effect is greatest in small populations, such as one that endures a bottleneck.*

18.8 Gene Flow

Individuals, and their alleles, move into and away from populations. The physical flow of alleles counters changes introduced by other microevolutionary processes.

Individuals of the same species don't always stay put. A population loses alleles when an individual leaves it for good, an event called *emigration*. The population gains alleles when individuals permanently move in, an event called *immigration*. In both cases, **gene flow** —the physical movement of alleles into and out of a population—occurs. This microevolutionary process counters mutation, natural selection, and genetic drift.

Later chapters will give historical examples of how gene flow has kept separated populations genetically similar. For now, simply consider the acorns that blue jays disperse when they gather nuts for the winter. Each fall, jays visit acorn-bearing oak trees repeatedly, then bury acorns in the soil of home territories that may be as much as a mile away (Figure 18.16). Alleles flowing in with the "immigrant acorns" help decrease genetic differences between stands of oak trees.

Figure 18.16 Blue jay, a mover of acorns that helps keep genes flowing between separate oak populations.

Or think of the millions of people from politically explosive, economically bankrupt countries who seek a more stable home. The scale of their emigrations is unprecedented, but the flow of genes is not. Human history is rich with cases of gene flow that minimized many of the genetic differences among geographically separate groups. Remember Genghis Khan? His genes flowed from China to Vienna (Section 12.10). Similarly, the armies of Alexander the Great brought alleles for green eyes from Greece all the way to India.

> *Gene flow is the physical movement of alleles into and out of a population, through immigration and emigration. It tends to counter the effects of mutation, natural selection, and genetic drift.*

Chapter 18 Microevolutionary Processes   **295**

18.9 Adaptation to What? A Word of Caution

LINKS TO
SECTIONS
1.4, 17.3

Observable traits are not always easy to correlate with conditions in an organism's environment.

"Adaptation" is one of those words that have different meanings in different contexts. An individual plant or animal often can quickly adjust its form, function, and behavior. Junipers in inhospitably windy places grow less tall than junipers of the same species in more sheltered places. This is an example of a *short-term* adaptation, because it lasts only as long as the individual plant does.

An **evolutionary adaptation** is some aspect of form, function, behavior, or development that improves the odds for surviving and reproducing in a particular environment. This is an *outcome* of microevolution—natural selection especially—an enhancement of the fit between the individual and prevailing conditions.

SALT-TOLERANT TOMATOES

As an example of long-term adaptation, compare how tomato species handle salty water. Tomatoes evolved in Ecuador, Peru, and the Galápagos Islands. The type sold most often in markets, *Lycopersicum esculentum*, has eight close relatives in the wild. If you mix ten grams of table salt with sixty milliliters of water, then pour it into the soil around *L. esculentum*'s roots, the plant will wilt drastically in less than thirty minutes (Figure 18.17*a*). Even when the soil has only 2,500 parts per million of salt, this species grows poorly.

Yet the Galápagos tomato (*L. cheesmanii*) survives and reproduces in seawater-washed soils. We know that its salt tolerance is a heritable adaptation. How? Crosses of a wild species with the commercial species yield a small, edible F₁ hybrid. The hybrid tolerates

Figure 18.17 (**a**) Severe, rapid wilting of one commercial tomato plant (*Lycopersicum esculentum*) that absorbed salty water. (**b**) Galápagos tomato plant, *L. cheesmanii*, which stores most absorbed salts in its leaves, not in its fruits.

irrigation water that is two parts fresh and one part salty. It is getting attention in areas where fresh water is scarce and where salts have built up in croplands.

It may take modification of only a few traits to get new salt-tolerant plants. Revving up just one gene for a sodium–hydrogen ion transporter helps the tomato plants use salty water and still bear edible fruits.

NO POLAR BEARS IN THE DESERT

You can safely bet that a polar bear (*Ursus maritimis*) is finely adapted to the icy Arctic, and that its form and function would be a flop in a desert (Figure 18.18). You

Figure 18.18 Which adaptations of a polar bear (*Ursus maritimus*) won't help in a desert? Which ones help an oryx (*Oryx beisa*)? For each animal, make a tentative list of possible structural and functional adaptations to the environment. Later, after you finish reading Unit VI, see how you can expand the list.

Figure 18.19 Adaptation to what? A heritable trait is an adaptation to specific environmental conditions. Hemoglobin of llamas, which live at high altitudes, has a high oxygen-binding affinity. However, so does hemoglobin of camels, which live at lower elevations.

might be able to make some educated guesses about why that is so. However, detailed knowledge of its anatomy and physiology might make you view it—or any other animal or plant—with respect. How does a polar bear maintain its internal temperature when it sleeps on ice? How can its muscles function in frigid water? How often must it eat? How does it find food? Conversely, how can an oryx walk about all day in the blistering heat of an African desert? How does it get enough water when there is no water to drink? You will find some answers, or at least ideas about how to look for them, in the next three units of this book.

ADAPTATION TO WHAT?

Bear in mind, it is not always easy to identify a direct relationship between adaptation and the environment. For instance, the prevailing environment may be very different from the one in which a trait evolved.

Consider the llama. It is native to the cloud-piercing peaks of the Andes in western South America (Figure 18.19). The llama lives 4,800 meters (16,000 feet) above sea level. Compared to humans at lower elevations, its lungs have more air sacs and blood vessels. The llama heart has larger chambers, so it pumps larger volumes of blood. Llamas do not have to produce extra blood cells, as people do when they move permanently from lowlands to high elevations. (Extra cells make blood "stickier," so the heart has to pump harder.) But the most publicized adaptation is this: Llama hemoglobin is better than ours at latching on to oxygen. It picks up oxygen in the lungs far more efficiently.

Superficially, at least, the oxygen-binding affinity of llama hemoglobin appears to be an adaptation to thin air at high altitudes. Is it? Apparently not.

Llamas are in the same family as dromedary camels. Both share camelid ancestors that evolved in Eocene grasslands and deserts of North America. Later, the ancestors went their separate ways. Forerunners of camels reached Asia's low-elevation grasslands and deserts by a land bridge, which later submerged when the sea level rose. Forerunners of llamas moved down the Isthmus of Panama and on into South America.

Intriguingly, a dromedary camel's hemoglobin also shows a high oxygen-binding capacity. So if the trait arose in a shared ancestor, then how was it adaptive at *low* elevations? We know camels and llamas didn't just *happen* to evolve in the same way. They are close kin, and their most recent ancestors lived in very different environments with different oxygen concentrations.

Who knows why the trait was originally favored? Eocene climates were alternately warm and cool, and hemoglobin's oxygen-binding capacity does go down as temperatures go up. Did it prove adaptive during a long-term shift in climate? Or were its effects neutral at first? What if the allele for efficient hemoglobin was fixed in an ancestral population simply by chance?

Use these "what-ifs" as a reminder to think about observable traits and their presumed connection with a given environment. Identifying the connections takes a great deal of research and experimental tests.

A long-term, heritable adaptation is any aspect of form, function, behavior, or development that contributes to the fit between an individual and its environment.

An adaptive trait improves the odds of surviving and reproducing, or at least it did so under conditions that prevailed when genes for the trait first evolved.

Summary

Section 18.1 Individuals of a population generally have the same number and kinds of genes for the same traits. Alleles are different molecular forms of a gene. Individuals who inherit different allele combinations vary in details of one or more traits. An allele at any locus may become more or less common relative to other kinds or may be lost.

Mutations are rare in individuals, but they have accumulated in natural populations of all lineages. Mutations are the original source of alleles, the raw material for evolution.

Microevolution refers to changes in allele frequencies of a population brought about by mutation, natural selection, genetic drift, and gene flow (Table 18.1).

Section 18.2 Genetic equilibrium is a state in which a population is not evolving. According to the Hardy–Weinberg equilibrium formula, this occurs only if there is no mutation, the population is infinitely large and isolated from all other populations of the species, there is no natural selection, mating is random, and all individuals survive and produce the same number of offspring. Deviations from this theoretical baseline indicate microevolution is in play.

Biology⊗Now
Investigate gene frequencies and genetic equilibrium with the interaction on BiologyNow.

Section 18.3 Natural selection is the outcome of differences in reproduction among individuals of a population that show variations in their shared traits. Three major modes are directional, stabilizing, and disruptive selection. Selection pressures operating on the range of phenotypic variation shift or maintain allele frequencies in the population's gene pool.

Table 18.1	Summary Definitions for Microevolutionary Events
Mutation	A heritable change in DNA; original source of alleles in a population
Natural selection	Outcome of differences in reproduction among individuals of a population that show variation in their shared, heritable traits. Can shift the range of phenotypes in a consistent direction, disrupt it, or stabilize it
Genetic drift	Random changes in a population's allele frequencies through the generations as an outcome of chance alone
Gene flow	Individuals move their alleles into and out of a population by way of immigration and emigration; tends to counter the changes caused by mutation, natural selection, and genetic drift

Section 18.4 Directional selection shifts the range of phenotypic variation in a consistent direction. The individuals at one end of the range of variation are selected against and those at the other end are favored.

Biology⊗Now
View the animation of directional selection on BiologyNow.

Read the InfoTrac article "AIDS in Africa Has Potential to Affect Human Evolution," AIDS Weekly, June 2001.

Section 18.5 Stabilizing selection works against extremes in the range of phenotypic variation, and it favors intermediate forms. Disruptive selection favors forms at both extremes of the range; individuals in the intermediate range are selected against.

Biology⊗Now
View the animation of disruptive and stabilizing selection on BiologyNow.

Read the InfoTrac article "Portraits of Evolution: Studies of Coloration in Hawaiian Spiders," Geoffrey S. Oxford, Rosemary G. Gillespie, Bioscience, July 2001.

Section 18.6 Sexual selection, by females or males, leads to forms of traits that favor reproductive success. Persistence in phenotypic differences between males and females (sexual dimorphism) is one outcome.

Selection may result in balanced polymorphism, with nonidentical alleles for a trait being maintained over time at relatively high frequencies.

Biology⊗Now
Read the InfoTrac article "High-Risk Defenses," Gregory Cochran, Paul W. Ewald, Natural History, Feb. 1999.

Section 18.7 Genetic drift is a random change in a population's allele frequencies over time due to chance occurrences alone. It tends to lead to the homozygous condition and loss of genetic diversity.

The effect of genetic drift is most pronounced in very small populations, such as ones that have passed through a bottleneck or that arose from a small group of founders. Genetic drift has less effect on inbred populations, which are characterized by nonrandom mating of very close relatives.

Biology⊗Now
Learn more about genetic drift with the interaction on BiologyNow.

Section 18.8 Gene flow moves alleles into or out of a population by immigration or emigration. The process helps keep populations of the same species genetically alike by countering the effects of mutation, natural selection, and genetic drift.

Section 18.9 Long-term, heritable adaptations are aspects of form, function, behavior, or development that improve the chance of surviving and reproducing, or at least did so under conditions that prevailed when genes for the trait first evolved.

Often it is not easy to correlate an adaptive trait with the particular environmental conditions to which it is assumed to be adapted.

1. Individuals don't evolve, _____ do.

2. Biologists define evolution as _____ .
   a. purposeful change in a lineage
   b. heritable change in a line of descent
   c. acquiring traits during the individual's lifetime
   d. both a and b

3. _____ is the original source of new alleles.
   a. Mutation   d. Gene flow
   b. Natural selection e. All are original sources of
   c. Genetic drift   new alleles

4. Natural selection may occur when there are _____ .
   a. differences in forms of traits
   b. differences in survival and reproduction among individuals that differ in one or more traits
   c. both a and b

5. Directional selection _____ .
   a. eliminates common forms of alleles
   b. shifts allele frequencies in a consistent direction
   c. favors intermediate forms of a trait
   d. works against adaptive traits

6. Disruptive selection _____ .
   a. eliminates uncommon forms of alleles
   b. shifts allele frequencies in one direction only
   c. doesn't favor intermediate forms of a trait
   d. both b and c

7. Sexual selection, especially competition between males for access to fertile females, frequently influences aspects of body form and leads to _____ .
   a. inbreeding   c. sexual dimorphism
   b. genetic drift   d. both b and c

8. The persistence of malaria and sickle-cell anemia in a population is a case of _____ .
   a. bottlenecking   c. natural selection
   b. balanced   d. artificial selection
      polymorphism   e. both b and c

9. _____ tends to counter changes that occur in the allele frequencies among populations of a species.
   a. Genetic drift   c. Mutation
   b. Gene flow   d. Natural selection

10. Match the evolution concepts.
    ____ gene flow   a. source of new alleles
    ____ natural   b. changes in a population's allele
         selection   frequencies due to chance alone
    ____ mutation   c. allele frequencies change owing to
    ____ genetic   immigration, emigration, or both
         drift   d. outcome of differences in survival,
                           reproduction among individuals
                           of a population that vary in the
                           details of shared traits

Additional questions are available on Biology🌐Now™

Critical Thinking

1. Occasionally, a few of the families in a remote region of Kentucky produce *blue offspring*, a condition caused by an autosomal recessive disorder. Skin of affected individuals appears dark blue. Homozygous individuals do not have

Figure 18.20 Two designer dogs: the Great Dane (*legs, left*) and the chihuahua (*possibly fearful of being stepped on, right*).

the enzyme that maintains hemoglobin in its normal molecular form. Without it, a blue form of hemoglobin accumulates in blood and shows through the skin.

Formulate a hypothesis to explain the recurrence of the blue offspring trait among a cluster of families.

2. Martha is studying a population of tropical birds. The males have brightly colored tail feathers and the females don't. She suspects this difference is maintained by sexual selection. Design an experiment to test her hypothesis.

3. About 50,000 years ago, humans began domesticating wild dogs. By 14,000 years ago, they started to favor new varieties (breeds) by way of artificial selection. Individual dogs having desirable forms of traits were selected from each new litter and, later, encouraged to breed. Those with undesired forms of traits were passed over.

After favoring the pick of the litter for hundreds or thousands of generations, we ended up with sheep-herding border collies, badger-hunting dachshunds, bird-fetching retrievers, and sled-pulling huskies. And at some point we began to delight in the odd, extraordinary dog.

In practically no time at all, evolutionarily speaking, we picked our way through the pool of variant dog alleles and came up with such extreme breeds as Great Danes and chihuahuas (Figure 18.20).

Sometimes the canine designs have exceeded the limits of biological common sense. How long would a tiny, nearly hairless, nearly defenseless, finicky-eating chihuahua last in the wild? Not long. What about English bulldogs, bred for a stubby snout and compressed face? Breeders thought these traits would let the dogs get a better grip on the nose of a bull. (Why they wanted dogs to bite bulls is a story in itself.) So now the roof of the bulldog mouth is ridiculously wide and often flabby, so bulldogs have trouble breathing. Sometimes they get so short of breath they pass out.

Why do you suppose many people easily accept that artificial selection practices can produce startling diversity but will not accept that natural selection might do the same in the wild?

Last of the Honeycreepers?

More than 5 million years ago, Kauai rose above the surface of the sea. It was the first of the big islands of the Hawaiian Archipelago. Several million years later, a few quite possibly terrified finches reached it after bobbing 4,000 kilometers (2,500 miles) across the open ocean. Were they unwilling pioneers, blown away from the mainland during a fierce storm? We may never know, but their chance geographic dispersal was the start of something big.

No predatory mammals had preceded the finches onto that isolated, volcanically born island. But tasty insects and plants that bore tender leaves, nectar, seeds, and fruits were already there. The finches thrived. Their descendants quickly radiated into habitats along the coasts, through dry lowland forests, and into rain forests of the highlands.

Between 1.8 million and 400,000 years ago, volcanic eruptions created the rest of the archipelago. Generation after generation, descendants of the first finches traveled on the winds to vacant habitats in the new islands. They foraged in many shrublands and forests, each with special food sources and nesting sites. Diverse agents of natural selection operated in each place, and differences in bill sizes and shapes, feather coloration and patterns, and territorial songs evolved. In this way, a spectacular family of birds, the Hawaiian honeycreepers, originated.

One existing Hawaiian honeycreeper has a bill that fits in the long, curving nectar tubes of *Lobelia* flowers (Figure 19.1). One probes tree bark with its sickle-shaped upper bill, then scoops out beetle larvae with its shovel-shaped lower bill. Other species use a thickened, strong, parrotlike bill to crush or pry open hard seed pods. The po'-ouli (Figure 19.2) is the only species that preferentially eats native tree snails.

Ironically, the very isolation that favored specialized adaptations to conditions in unique habitats made these birds vulnerable to extinction. When conditions changed, they had nowhere to go. They had no built-in defenses against predatory mammals and avian diseases of the mainland, against humans who coveted cloaks made of their eye-catching feathers, or against climate change.

Accompanying humans to the islands were brown tree snakes, rats, cats, and other voracious predators. People also imported chickens and other birds that happened to be infected with disease agents. Over time, people cleared more and more of the forests. Imported crop plants and plant-eating mammals became established. The Hawaiian honeycreeper habitats shrank. Today, with a long-term increase in global temperatures—global warming—the forests at higher elevations are not as cool as they once were. They have been infiltrated by mosquitoes, which

Figure 19.1 *Left*, the Hawaiian honeycreeper known informally as Iiwi (*Vestiaria coccinea*). It evolved in the Hawaiian Archipelago (*right*), far from the mainland. It is a descendant of a spectacular adaptive radiation—one of the patterns explained in this chapter.

Figure 19.2 Male po'ouli—rare, old, and missing one eye. Ecologists captured this small honeycreeper on the east slope of Haleakala, Hawaii, as part of a last-ditch effort to save the remaining population of three birds. This male was already suffering the effects of avian malaria, and it died in 2004. The perpetuation of its species—which was not even known about until 1973—now rests on the two remaining birds. The two have not been seen in many months.

thrive in warm climates. Mosquitoes happen to be vectors for pathogens that cause avian malaria and other diseases.

At one time there were approximately fifty species of Hawaiian honeycreepers. As many as twenty-four species colonized a single island. Half of the known species are extinct. The initial wave of extinction followed the arrival of the first Polynesians, and another ten species are now endangered. The remaining species are being studied in earnest, and efforts are under way to protect them. It may be a case of too little, too late; but time will tell.

How do we know so much about a group of birds on an island chain in the middle of the Pacific Ocean? Scientific theories and tools, particularly radiometric dating and automated gene sequencing, helped shine light on their rise and impending fall. The age of volcanic rocks on each island, as well as the DNA of different species, were among the clues. Such clues give us glimpses into **macroevolution** —the long-term patterns, rates, and trends in the origin and ultimate fate of Earth's many millions of species.

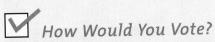

How Would You Vote?

Often, when a species is on the brink of extinction, some individuals are captured and brought to zoos for captive breeding programs. Some people object to this practice. They say keeping a species alive in a zoo is a distraction from more meaningful conservation efforts, and captive animals seldom are successfully restored to the wild. Do you support captive breeding of highly endangered species? See BiologyNow for details, then vote online.

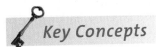

Key Concepts

HOW DO SPECIES ARISE?

All sexually reproducing species consist of one or more populations of individuals that interbreed under natural conditions, produce fertile offspring, and are reproductively isolated from other such populations.   Section 19.1

MODELS FOR SPECIATION

Speciation is a process that varies in details and duration among lineages. It starts when gene flow stops between populations of a species. Microevolutionary events occur independently in the reproductively isolated populations. The process ends when daughter species form.   Sections 19.2, 19.3

PATTERNS IN THE HISTORY OF LIFE

The timing, rate, and direction of speciation differ among branches of a lineage and between lineages. Adaptive radiations and extinction punctuate the history of life. Section 19.4

CLASSIFICATION SYSTEMS

Patterns in life's history are being identified and interpreted. Taxonomy identifies, names, and then classifies species. Systematics infers evolutionary relationships by analytical methods. Phylogenetic classification systems are efficient tools for retrieving information about the history of life. Section 19.5

PIECING TOGETHER FAMILY TREES

Biologists construct evolutionary tree diagrams that use derived traits to determine branch points. A current tree subsumes six traditionally defined kingdoms into three domains: Bacteria, Archaea, and Eukarya. It reveals how all species interconnect through shared ancestors, some remote, others recent.   Sections 19.6–19.9

Links to Earlier Concepts

Before starting this chapter, be sure you understand how gene flow can help keep populations of the same species genetically similar by countering the impact of mutation, natural selection, and genetic drift (Sections 18.1, 18.8). You will be appying your knowledge of changes in chromosome structure and function (12.8 and 15.4). Quickly review how comparisons of morphology (17.7) and of genes and proteins of different lineages (17.9) yield clues to shared ancestry.

Also reflect on the major geologic forces. They have been a factor in the origin of many species, especially on island chains (17.2, 17.6). You also will be taking a closer look at the three-domain system of classification (1.3).

19.1 Reproductive Isolation, Maybe New Species

LINKS TO
SECTIONS
11.6, 18.1, 18.8

Speciation is a macroevolutionary process. It starts when a population becomes reproductively isolated from others of the species and ends when daughter species have formed.

WHAT IS A SPECIES?

Species is a Latin word that means "kind," as in "one kind of plant." This generic definition does not help much when we are trying to figure out whether, say, a population of plants in one place belongs to the same species as a population of plants somewhere else. You may see variations in traits between the populations and variation within them, because plants can inherit diverse combinations of alleles. Also, some individuals may grow in very different environments that cause changes in gene expression (Section 11.6 and Figure 19.3). In other words, we might not be able to identify a biological species on the basis of appearance alone.

Evolutionary biologist Ernst Mayr came up with a **biological species concept**: A species is one or more groups of individuals that interbreed, produce fertile offspring, and are reproductively isolated from other such groups. This definition is reasonable for species that reproduce sexually—which most species do. It does not apply to asexual reproducers, and it cannot be used to interpret the fossil record.

A more recent definition has wider applicability: A **species** is one or more populations of individuals that share at least one structural, functional, or behavioral trait—*the legacy of a common ancestor*—that sets them apart from other species. This definition is based on comparative morphology, biochemistry, and the fossil record. It applies to sexually or asexually reproducing species. Unlike the biological species concept, it does not directly address how a species attains and then maintains its separate identity. That clue, for sexual reproducers at least, is *reproductive isolation*—the end of gene exchanges between populations.

REPRODUCTIVE ISOLATING MECHANISMS

Gene flow, recall, is the movement of alleles into and out of a population (Section 18.8). Speciation begins when gene flow, or the potential for it, ends between natural populations. Once it stops, gene pools start to change and populations undergo **genetic divergence**, because mutation, natural selection, and genetic drift are free to operate independently in each one (Section 18.8). As you will see later, speciation may result from gradual genetic divergence. It also may be completed within a few generations, as commonly occurs among flowering plants.

a

b

Figure 19.3 Morphological differences between plants of the same species (*Sagittaria sagittifolia*) growing (**a**) in water and (**b**) on land. The leaf shapes are responses to different environmental conditions, not to different genetic programs.

Figure 19.4 *Animated!* (**a**) Mechanical isolation. Few pollinating insects fit as well as wasps on a zebra flower. Petals form a landing platform below stamens.

(**b**) Temporal isolation. *Magicicada septendecim*, a periodical cicada that matures underground and emerges to reproduce every seventeen years. Its populations often overlap the habitats of a sibling species (*M. tredecim*), which reproduces every thirteen years. Adults live only a few weeks.

(**c**) Behavioral isolation. Courtship displays precede sex among many kinds of birds, including these albatrosses. Individuals recognize tactile, visual, and acoustical signals, such as a prancing dance followed by back arching, a skyward pointing bill and an exposed throat, and wing spreading.

c

Figure 19.5 *Animated!* When certain reproductive isolating mechanisms prevent interbreeding. There are barriers to (**a**) getting together, mating, or pollination, (**b**) successful fertilization, and (**c**) survival, fitness, or fertility of hybrid embryos or offspring.

Either way, **reproductive isolating mechanisms** evolve. All of these heritable aspects of body form, function, or behavior block interbreeding between populations. *Prezygotic* mechanisms, as in Figure 19.4, stop cross-pollination or cross-breeding, the formation of gametes, or fertilization. *Postzygotic* mechanisms kill hybrids or make them weak or infertile. Let us start off with the prezygotic isolating mechanisms listed in Figure 19.5*a,b*.

Mechanical isolation. The body parts of a species are not a physical match with those of a species that could otherwise serve as a mate or pollinator. Figure 19.4*a* shows the fit between a zebra plant and its preferred pollinator. Similarly, the pollen-bearing stamens of the flowers of one sage species extend above petals that act as a landing platform. Big-bodied pollinators get a dusting of pollen when they land and collect nectar. Pollen-gathering bees are not large enough to brush against these stamens. But the other sage species has its stamens poised above a bee-sized platform that is too small and fragile to hold big, heavy pollinators.

Temporal isolation. Diverging populations cannot interbreed when their timing of reproduction differs. Cicada species that differ in form and behavior often live in the same habitat in the eastern United States. They all mature underground and feed on juicy roots. Every 17 years, three species emerge and reproduce (Figure 19.4*b*). Each one has a *sibling* species of similar form and behavior. But siblings emerge on a 13-year cycle. This means that each species and its sibling do not get together except once every 221 years!

Behavioral isolation. Behavioral differences bar gene flow between related species. Before male and female birds copulate, they may engage in courtship displays (Figure 19.4*c*). A female bird is genetically prewired to recognize the singing, wing spreading, prancing, or head bobbing of a male of her species as an overture to sex. Females of different species usually do not.

Ecological isolation. Populations occupying different microenvironments may be ecologically isolated. Two manzanita species live in seasonally dry foothills of the Sierra Nevada, one at elevations between 600 and 1,850 meters, the other between 750 and 3,350 meters. They hybridize rarely, and only where the two ranges overlap. Water-conserving mechanisms operate in dry seasons. But one species is adapted to sites where water stress is not intense. The other lives in drier, exposed sites on rocky hillsides, so cross-pollination is unlikely.

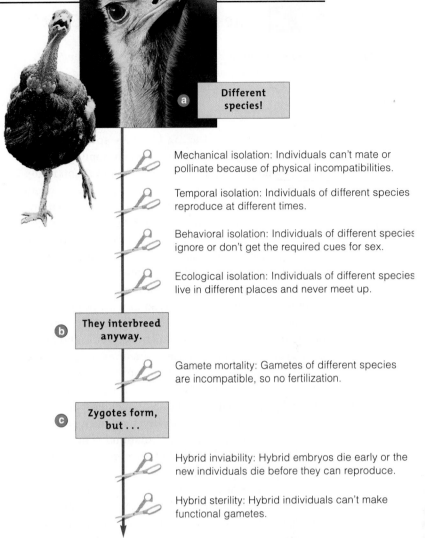

a Different species!

Mechanical isolation: Individuals can't mate or pollinate because of physical incompatibilities.

Temporal isolation: Individuals of different species reproduce at different times.

Behavioral isolation: Individuals of different species ignore or don't get the required cues for sex.

Ecological isolation: Individuals of different species live in different places and never meet up.

b They interbreed anyway.

Gamete mortality: Gametes of different species are incompatible, so no fertilization.

c Zygotes form, but . . .

Hybrid inviability: Hybrid embryos die early or the new individuals die before they can reproduce.

Hybrid sterility: Hybrid individuals can't make functional gametes.

No offspring, sterile offspring, or weak offspring that die before reproducing

Gamete mortality. Gametes of different species may have molecular incompatibilities. Example: If pollen lands on a plant of another species, it usually does not respond to the plant's molecular signals to germinate.

Postzygotic isolating mechanisms act in an embryo (Figure 19.5*c*). Unsuitable interactions among genes or gene products cause early death, sterility, or weak hybrids with low survival rates. Certain hybrids are sturdy but sterile. Mules, which are the offspring of a female horse and male donkey, are infertile hybrids.

A species is one or more populations of individuals having a unique common ancestor. Its individuals share a gene pool, produce fertile offspring, and remain reproductively isolated from individuals of other species.

Speciation is the process by which daughter species form from a population or subpopulation of a parent species. The process varies in its details and duration, but all modes of speciation are based on reproductive isolation.

19.2 The Main Model for Speciation

LINKS TO
SECTIONS
17.2, 17.6, 17.9

Three models for speciation differ in their basic premise of how populations become reproductively isolated.

START WITH GEOGRAPHIC ISOLATION

The genetic changes leading to a new species usually begin with *physical separation* between populations, so allopatry might be the most common speciation route. By a model for **allopatric speciation**, physical barriers stop gene flow among populations or subpopulations of a species. (*Allo–* means different; *patria* can be taken to mean the homeland.) In both groups, reproductive isolating mechanisms develop. In time, speciation is complete. Interbreeding is no longer possible even if daughter species come into contact with one another.

Whether a geographic barrier can block gene flow depends on an organism's means of travel (deliberate or accidental), how fast it can travel, and whether it is inclined to disperse. Populations of most species are some distance apart, and gene flow is intermittent. Barriers may arise abruptly and end the flow entirely. In the 1800s, a major earthquake buckled part of the Midwest and the Mississippi River changed course. It cut through the habitats of populations of insects that could not swim or fly. It ended the gene flow between those adjoining populations.

The fossil record suggests that geographic isolation generally happens slowly. For example, it happened after vast glaciers advanced into North America and Europe during the ice ages and cut off populations of plants and animals from one another. After glaciers retreated and the descendants of related populations met, some were no longer reproductively compatible. They were separate species. Genetic divergence was not as great between other separated populations, so descendants still interbred. In their case, reproductive isolation was incomplete; speciation did not follow.

Also, remember how Earth's crust is fractured into gigantic plates? Slow, colossal movements inevitably alter the configurations of land masses (Section 17.6). As Central America formed, part of an ancient ocean basin was uplifted, and it became a land bridge—now called the Isthmus of Panama. Some camelids crossed the bridge into South America. Geographic separation led to new species: llamas and vicunas (Figure 19.6).

THE INVITING ARCHIPELAGOS

An **archipelago** is an island chain some distance from a continent. Many chains are so close to the mainland that gene flow is more or less unimpeded, so there is little if any speciation. The Florida Keys are like this. As you read earlier, the Hawaiian Islands, Galápagos Islands, and other remote, isolated archipelagos favor adaptive radiations and speciation (Figures 17.3 and 19.1). The islands are only the tops of volcanoes that started building up on the seafloor. In time they broke the surface of the ocean. We can therefore assume that their fiery surfaces were initially barren, with no life.

In one view, winds or ocean currents carry a few individuals of some mainland species to such islands, as shown in Figure 19.7*a*. Descendants colonize other

Figure 19.6 Allopatric speciations. The earliest camelids, no bigger than a jackrabbit, evolved in the Eocene grasslands and deserts of North America. By the end of the Miocene, they included the now-extinct *Procamelus*. The fossil record and comparative studies indicate that this may have been the common ancestral stock for llamas (**a**), vicunas (**b**), and camels (**c**). One of the descendant lineages dispersed into Africa and Asia and evolved into modern camels. A different lineage, ancestral to the llamas and vicunas, dispersed into South America after gradual crustal movements formed a land bridge between the two continents.

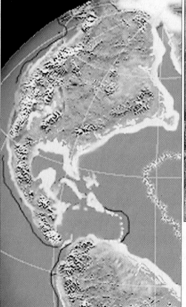

Late Eocene paleomap, before a land bridge formed between North and South America. At that time, North America and Eurasia were still connected by a land bridge

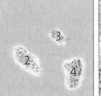

a A few individuals of a mainland species reach isolated island 1. Speciation follows genetic divergence in a new habitat.

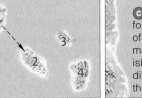

b Much later, a few individuals of the new species colonize nearby island 2. In this new habitat, speciation follows genetic divergence.

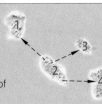

c Speciation may follow colonization of islands 3 and 4. It may follow invasion of island 1 by genetically different descendants of the ancestral species.

Akepa (*Loxops coccineus*)
Insects, spiders from buds twisted apart by bill; some nectar; high mountain rain forest

Akekee (*L. caeruleirostris*)
Insects, spiders, some nectar, high mountain rain forest

Nihoa finch (*Telespiza ultima*)
Insects, buds, seeds, flowers, seabird eggs; rocky or shrubby slopes

Palila (*Loxioides bailleui*)
Mamane seeds ripped from pods; buds, flowers, some berries, insects; high mountain dry forests

Maui parrotbill (*Pseudonestor xanthrophrys*)
Rips dry branches for insect larvae, pupae, caterpillars; mountain forest with open canopy, dense underbrush

Apapane (*Himatione sanguinea*)
Nectar, especially of ohi'a-lehua flowers; caterpillars and other insects; spiders; high mountain forests

Po'ouli (*Melamprosops phaeosoma*)
Tree snails, insects in understory; last known male died in 2004

Alauahio (*Paroreomyza montana*)
Bark or leaf insects; some nectar, high mountain rain forest

Kauai Amakihi (*Hemignathus kauaiensis*)
Bark-picker; insects, spiders; nectar; high mountain rain forest

Akiapolaau (*H. munroi*)
Probes, digs insects from big trees; high mountain rain forest

Akohekohe (*Palmeria dolei*)
Mostly nectar from flowering trees; some insects, pollen; high mountain rain forest

Iiwi (*Vestiaria coccinea*)
Mostly nectar (Ohia tree flowers lobelias, some mints); some insects, high mountain rain fores

d The ancestor of Hawaiian honeycreepers might have resembled this housefinch (*Carpodacus*), based on morphological studies, and comparisons of chromosomal DNA and mitochondrial DNA sequences for proteins, such as cytochrome *b*.

Figure 19.7 *Animated!* (**a–c**) Allopatric speciation on an isolated archipelago. (**d**) Twelve of fifty-seven known species and subspecies of Hawaiian honeycreepers, with a sampling of their dietary and habitat preferences. Honeycreeper bills are adapted to diverse foods, such as insects, seeds, fruits, and nectar in floral cups.

islands that form in the chain. Habitats and selection pressures differ within and between these islands, so allopatric speciation proceeds by way of divergences. Later, new species may even invade islands that were colonized by their ancestors. Distances between islands in archipelagos are enough to favor divergence but not enough to stop the occasional colonizers.

The big island of Hawaii formed less than 1 million years ago. Its habitats range from old lava beds, rain forests, and grasslands to snow-capped volcanoes. The first birds to colonize it found a buffet of fruits, seeds, nectars, tasty insects, and few competitors for them. The near absence of competition spurred rapid speciations into vacant adaptive zones. Figure 19.7*d*

shows some of the Hawaiian honeycreepers described earlier. Like thousands of other species of animals and plants, they are unique to this island. As still another example of their potential for speciation, the Hawaiian Islands combined make up less than 2 percent of the world's land masses. Yet they are the original home of 40 percent of all species of fruit flies (*Drosophila*).

By one allopatric speciation model, some type of physical barrier intervenes between populations or subpopulations of a species and prevents gene flow among them. Gene flow ends, and genetic divergences give rise to daughter species.

19.3 Other Speciation Models

LINKS TO SECTIONS 4.10, 12.8, 15.4, 17.9

There is evidence that some species have arisen and are being maintained by less common mechanisms in which environmental barriers do not play a role.

ISOLATION WITHIN THE HOME RANGE

By the model for **sympatric speciation**, a species may form *within* the home range of an existing species, in the absence of a physical barrier. *Sym–* means together with, as in "together with others in the homeland."

Evidence From Cichlids in Africa   In Cameroon, West Africa, many species of freshwater fishes called cichlids may have arisen by sympatric speciation. The fish live in lakes that formed in the collapsed cones of small volcanoes (Figure 19.8). The cichlids probably colonized the lakes before volcanic action severed the inflow from a nearby river system.

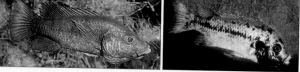

Figure 19.8   A small, isolated crater lake in Cameroon, West Africa, where different species of cichlids may have originated by way of sympatric speciation.

Figure 19.9   Love those polyploids! Among them are several cotton species (including the kind shown here), sugarcane, seedless watermelons, bananas, plums, sweet potatoes, coffee plants with 22, 44, 66, or 88 chromosomes, and marigolds, azaleas, and lilies.

Remember how gene sequences can be compared (Section 17.9)? Ulrich Schliewen looked at differences in nuclear DNA and mitochondrial DNA for eleven cichlid species in Barombi Mbo, one of the small crater lakes. He also compared the samples with DNA from cichlid species in nearby lakes and rivers. He found that cichlid species in Barombi Mbo are more closely related to one another than to neighboring species. He concluded that all of the Barombi Mbo cichlids are descended from the same ancestral species—and that speciation must have occurred *within* this lake.

What could have cause the divergences that led to speciation? The lake is only 2.5 kilometers across, so it is not likely that cichlid populations were separated from one another by any type of barrier. Also, physical and chemical conditions are uniform throughout the lake. Another point: Cichlids are good swimmers, so individuals of different species often meet up.

However, the Barombi Mbo species do show some *ecological* separation. Feeding preferences put species in different places. Some feed in open waters, others at the lake bottom. Yet they all breed close to the lake bottom, in sympatry. Was this small-scale ecological separation enough to promote sexual selection among potential mates? Possibly. Over time, it may have led to reproductive isolation, then speciation.

Polyploidy's Impact   Reproductive isolation might happen within a few generations through **polyploidy**, in which individuals inherit three or more sets of the chromosomes characteristic of their species (Section 12.8). Either a somatic cell fails to divide mitotically after its DNA is duplicated, or nondisjunction occurs at meiosis and results in an unreduced chromosome number in gametes. Offspring usually cannot breed or mate successfully with the parent species, but they may be able to reproduce asexually.

*Auto*polyploids arise by a doubling of the parental chromosome number. This event arises spontaneously in nature but can be in artificially induced in plant breeding laboratories. Breeders expose dividing plant cells to colchicine which, recall, stops microtubular spindles from forming during mitosis (Section 4.10). Without the spindle, duplicated chromosomes do not separate, and cells with the unreduced chromosome number may function as gametes.

*Allo*polyploids originate through (1) spontaneous or induced hybridization between closely related species and (2) doubling of the chromosome number. Figure 19.9 is one example. As genome studies reveal, many stable allopolyploids originated long ago. The kinds produced in the laboratory may or may not prove to

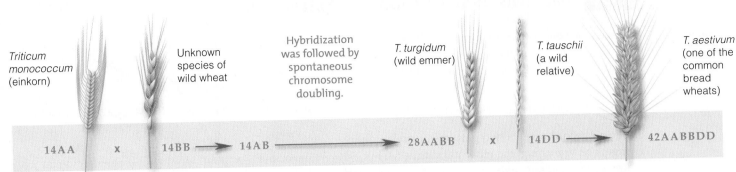

Triticum monococcum (einkorn)

Unknown species of wild wheat

Hybridization was followed by spontaneous chromosome doubling.

T. turgidum (wild emmer)

T. tauschii (a wild relative)

T. aestivum (one of the common bread wheats)

14AA   x   14BB ⟶ 14AB ⟶ 28AABB   x   14DD ⟶ 42AABBDD

a By 11,000 years ago, humans were cultivating wild wheats. Einkorn has a diploid chromosome number of 14 (two sets of 7). It probably hybridized with another wild wheat species having the same number of chromosomes.

b About 8,000 years ago, the alloploid called wild emmer originated from an AB hybrid wheat plant in which the chromosome number doubled. Wild emmer is tetraploid, or AABB; it has two sets of 14 chromosomes.

c An AABB plant probably hybridized with *T. tauschii*, a wild relative of wheat. Its diploid chromosome number is 14 (two sets of 7 DD). Common bread wheats have a chromosome number of 42 (six sets of 7 AABBDD).

be stable and fertile. Attempts are more successful if the species are close relatives.

Plant speciation is rapid when polyploids produce fertile offspring by self-fertilizing or cross-fertilizing with an identical polyploid. The ancestor of common bread wheat apparently was a wild species, *Triticum monococcum*, which spontaneously hybridized about 11,000 years ago with another wild species (Figure 19.10). Much later in time, a spontaneous chromosome doubling gave rise to *T. turgidum*, an alloploid species with two sets of chromosomes (AABB). Later still, another hybridization resulted in *T. aestivum*, a bread wheat with a chromosome number of 42.

About 95 percent of fern species and 30–70 percent of flowering plants are polyploid species. So are a few conifers, mollusks, insects, and other arthropods, as well as fishes, amphibians, and reptiles. What about mammals? In 1999, A polyploid species of rat with a chromosome number of 102 was found in Argentina.

ISOLATION AT HYBRID ZONES

Parapatric speciation might proceed when different selection pressures operating across a broad region affect populations that are in contact along a common border. Hybrids that form in the contact zone are less fit than individuals on either side of it. Because the hybrids are being selected against, they appear in the hybrid zone only (Figure 19.11).

> By a sympatric speciation model, daughter species arise from a group of individuals within an existing population. Polyploid flowering plants probably formed this way.
>
> By a parapatric speciation model, populations maintaining contact along a common border evolve into distinct species.

Figure 19.10 *Animated!* Presumed sympatric speciation in wheat. Wheat grains 11,000 years old and diploid wild wheats have been found in the Near East, and chromosome analysis indicates that they hybridized. Later, in a self-fertilizing hybrid, homologous chromosomes failed to separate at meiosis, and it produced fertile polyploid offspring. A polyploid descendant hybridized with a wild species. We make bread from grains of their hybrid descendants.

T. barretti
hybrid zone
T. anophthalmus

Figure 19.11 Example of parapatric speciation on the island of Tasmania, directly south of eastern Australia. (**a**) Giant velvet worm, *Tasmanipatus barretti* and (**b**) blind velvet worm, *T. anophthalmus*.

(**c**) Both of these rare species of velvet walking worms live in adjoining regions of northeastern Tasmania. Their habitats overlap in a hybrid zone. Hybrid offspring are sterile, which may be the main reason these two species are maintaining separate identities in the absence of an obvious physical barrier between their habitats.

19.4 Patterns of Speciation and Extinction

LINK TO SECTION 17.7

All species, past and present, are related by descent. They share genetic connections through lineages that extend back in time to the molecular origin of life.

BRANCHING AND UNBRANCHED EVOLUTION

The fossil record reveals two patterns of evolutionary change, one branching, the other unbranched. The first is known as **cladogenesis** (from *klados*, branch; and *genesis*, origin). In this pattern, a lineage splits when one or more of its populations become reproductively isolated and diverge genetically. It might be the main speciation pattern. It is the one introduced earlier, in Section 19.1.

In the second pattern, **anagenesis**, changes in allele frequencies and morphology accumulate in a single line of descent. (In this context, *ana*– means renewed.) Directional change is confined within that lineage, as gene flow continues among its populations. In time, allele frequencies and morphology shift so much that the new type differs significantly from the ancestral type, so it is classified as a separate species.

RATES OF CHANGE IN FAMILY TREES

Evolutionary trees summarize information on the relationships among groups. Figure 19.12 can start you thinking about how to construct these tree diagrams. Each branch represents one line of descent from a common ancestor. A *branch point* represents a time of genetic divergence.

When plotted against time, a branch that ends before the present (the treetop) signifies that the lineage is extinct. A dashed line signifies that we know something about the lineage but not exactly where it fits in the tree.

The **gradual model of speciation** holds that species originate by slight morphological changes over long time spans. The model fits with many fossil sequences. For example, sedimentary rock layers often hold vertical sequences of fossilized shells of foraminiferans, as in Figure 19.13. The sequence reflects gradual morphological change.

The **punctuation model of speciation** offers a different explanation for patterns of speciation. Most morphological changes are said to evolve

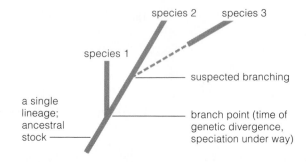

Figure 19.12 Some elements of evolutionary tree diagrams.

in a relatively brief geologic period, within the tens to hundreds of thousands of years when populations are starting to diverge. Directional selection, genetic drift, the founder effect, bottlenecks, or some combination of them favor rapid speciation. The daughter species recover fast from the adaptive wrenching, then they change very little over long periods.

The fossil record shows that stability prevailed for all but 1 percent of the history of most lineages, but it also reveals episodes of abrupt change. As it turns out, both models help explain speciation patterns. Changes have been gradual, abrupt, or both. Species originated at different times and have differed in how long they last. Some did not change much over millions of years; others were the start of adaptive radiations.

ADAPTIVE RADIATIONS

An **adaptive radiation** is a burst of divergences from a single lineage that leads to many new species. This is the pattern that gave rise to the family of Hawaiian honeycreepers. It requires **adaptive zones**, or a set of niches that come to be filled by a group of usually related species. Think of a *niche* as a way of life, such as "burrowing into seafloor sediments" or "catching winged insects in the air at night." Either the lineage enters a vacant adaptive zone or it competes with the resident species well enough to displace them.

You will read more about niches in Chapter 46, in the context of community structure. For now, be aware of two concepts. First, a species must have physical access to a niche when it opens up. Mammals were once distributed in the uniformly tropical regions of Pangea. That supercontinent broke up into huge land

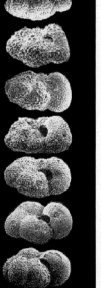

Figure 19.13 Fossilized foraminiferan shells from a vertical sequence of sedimentary rock layers. The first shell (*bottom*) is 64.5 million years old. The most recent (*top*) is 58 million years old. Analysis of shell patterns confirm that the evolutionary order matches the geological sequence.

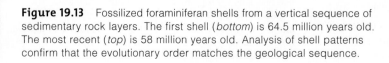

Column labels (left to right):

platypus, other monotremes · kangaroos, other marsupials · elephants, other proboscideans · manatees · anteaters · armadillos · shrews, other insectivores; bats · carnivores · whales, dolphins · deer, other artiodactyls · horses, other perissodactyls · primates · rodents · rabbits

CENOZOIC

MESOZOIC

ancestral mammal

Figure 19.14 Adaptive radiation of mammals. Branch widths indicate the range of biodiversity at different times. Mammals arose 220 million years ago but did not start a great radiation until after the K–T impact removed the last of the dinosaurs (page 260). Not all lineages are shown. The 4,000 existing species include shrews, bats, and giant whales.

The photograph shows a fossil of *Eomaia scansoria* (Greek for ancient mother climber). About 125 million years ago, this insectivore crawled on low shrubs and branches. At this writing, it is the earliest placental mammal we know about.

masses, which drifted apart. Habitats and resources changed in different ways, in different places, and set the stage for independent radiations (Figure 19.14).

Second, a species may enter an adaptive zone by a **key innovation**: A chance modification in some body structure or function gives it the opportunity to exploit the environment more efficiently or in a novel way.

Once a species has entered an adaptive zone, genetic divergences can give rise to other species, which can fill a variety of niches within the zone. For example, when the forelimbs of certain vertebrate evolved into wings, novel niches opened up for the ancestors of modern birds and bats (Section 17.7).

EXTINCTIONS—THE END OF THE LINE

An **extinction** is the irrevocable loss of a species. By some estimates, more than 99 percent of all species that ever lived are extinct. The chapter introduction gave examples of typical causes, including imports of new predators and climate change.

In addition to ongoing, small-scale extinctions, the fossil record indicates there were at least twenty or more **mass extinctions**, or catastrophic losses of entire families or other major groups. They differed in size.

For example, 250 million years ago, 95 percent of all known species were abruptly lost. At other times, fewer groups were lost. Afterward, biodiversity slowly recovered as new species filled vacant adaptive zones.

Luck, again, had a lot to do with it. Many species were wiped out by global climate change. When one asteroid struck Earth and the last dinosaurs vanished, mammals were among the survivors that could radiate into vacated adaptive zones. Asteroids, imperceptibly drifting continents, climatic change—all contributed to past patterns of major extinctions and recoveries. In the next unit, you will have plenty of examples.

Lineages have changed gradually, abruptly, or both. Their member species originated at different times and have differed in how long they have persisted.

An adaptive radiation is the rapid origin of many species from a single lineage. It happens when an adaptive zone, a set of similar niches, opens up and the lineage has physical, evolutionary, and ecological access to it.

Repeated and often large extinctions happened in the past. After times of reduced biodiversity, new species originated and occupied new or vacated adaptive zones.

19.5 Organizing Information About Species

LINK TO
SECTION
1.3

So far, you have been thinking about what a species is, how it originates, and what has become of the many, many millions of them that originated. Turn now to what taxonomists do with the information.

SETS OF ORGANISMS—THE HIGHER TAXA

One field of biology, *taxonomy*, deals with identifying, naming, and classifying species. It goes hand in hand with *systematics*, or the study of relationships among organisms. Any organism that has been identified as representing a new species is assigned a unique two-part scientific name, the first part being the genus. As outlined in Chapter 1, species are grouped into more inclusive categories, such as families, orders, classes, phyla (or divisions, which is an equivalent ranking). Figure 19.15 has a few examples.

Each set of organisms in a given category is called a **taxon** (plural, taxa). The sets above the species level are known as the higher taxa, which are the units of classification systems. Most classification systems are now phylogenic, meaning that they reflect perceived evolutionary connections within and between higher taxa as well as patterns of evolutionary change.

A **six-kingdom classification system** promoted by Robert Whittaker prevailed for some time. It assigned all of the prokaryotic species to kingdoms Eubacteria and Archaea, and all single-celled eukaryotes (as well as many multicelled species) to kingdom Protista. It

bestowed separate kingdom status on animals, plants, and fungi. Figure 19.16 shows the six kingdoms of this system. Section 1.3 sketched out a few defining traits for their representatives, which are topics of the next unit of the book.

New fossil finds, and new insights from geology, morphological studies, and biochemical comparisons, caused many researchers to rethink the six-kingdom system. Most decided to subsume the groups into a **three-domain system**, in which the three highest taxa are Bacteria, Archaea, and Eukarya (Figure 19.16).

Why the change? Ongoing research revealed that many of the taxa in earlier classification schemes are not monophyletic, or a "single tribe." A **monophyletic group** includes only the descendants from an ancestral species in which a unique feature first evolved. Said another way, the branchings in each taxon should be outgrowths from a single stem.

One problem with the six-kingdom system was that no one could find a single stem for the thousands of diverse single-celled and multicelled eukaryotic species of "kingdom Protista." Research is now clarifying their evolutionary connections with remarkable speed.

A CLADISTIC APPROACH

Think of each set of species descended from just one ancestral species as a **clade** (from *klados*, a Greek word for branch or twig). A cladistic classification system

KINGDOM	Bacteria	Plantae	Plantae	Animalia	Animalia
PHYLUM	Proteobacteria	Coniferophyta	Anthophyta	Arthropoda	Chordata
CLASS	Epsilonproteobacteria	Coniferopsida	Monocotyledonae	Insecta	Mammalia
ORDER	Campylobacterales	Coniferales	Asparagales	Diptera	Primates
FAMILY	Helicobacteraceae	Cupressaceae	Orchidaceae	Muscidae	Hominidae
GENUS	*Helicobacter*	*Juniperus*	*Vanilla*	*Musca*	*Homo*
SPECIES	*H. felis*	*J. occidentalis*	*V. planifolia*	*M. domestica*	*H. sapiens*
COMMON NAME	none	western juniper	vanilla orchid	housefly	human

Figure 19.15 Taxonomic classification of five species. Each species has been assigned to ever more inclusive sets of organisms—in this case, from species to kingdom.

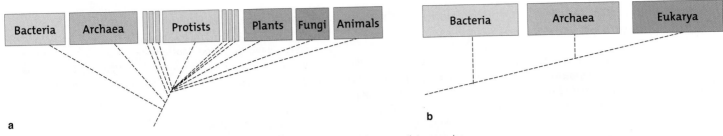

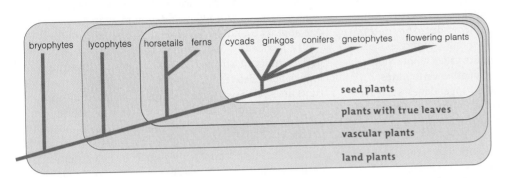

Figure 19.16 *Animated!* (**a**) Six-kingdom system of classification. In time, protists may be divided into more kingdoms. (**b**) The more recent three-domain system of classification. Protists, plants, fungi, and animals share features that unite them in domain Eukarya.

Figure 19.17 Evolutionary tree for land plants, with monophyletic groups nested as sets within sets. All but bryophytes have vascular tissues. All but bryophytes and lycophytes have true leaves. All but bryophytes, lycophytes, horsetails, and ferns produce seeds.

defines clades in terms of the history of divergences, or branch points in time. Only species that share traits derived from the last common ancestor are in the same clade. A **derived trait** is a novel feature that evolved in one species and is present only in its descendants. This emphasis means the descendants within a clade can differ—sometimes exuberantly so—in other traits.

Evolutionary tree diagrams called **cladograms** use the position of branch points from the last shared ancestor to convey inferred evolutionary relationships (phylogenies) among taxa. A cladogram is an estimate of "who came from whom." It has no time bar with absolute dates, so it cannot convey differences in rates of evolution among taxa. Even so, a cladistic approach has already reinforced part of the fossil record, and it is making us reevaluate interpretations of the past.

A tree of life only looks like a simple stick drawing. Many thousands of morphological and biochemical traits were analyzed during the attempts to make its evolutionary connections. For example, as you will see in the next unit of the book, detailed comparisons of genes and ribosomal RNAs have revealed sometimes surprising similarities and differences among groups. The evolutionary tree of life in Section 19.6 is based on such combined evidence.

The derived traits used to construct a cladogram also help us visualize different monophyletic groups as *sets within sets*. For example, Figure 19.17 shows a cladogram for major sets of land plants that have been nested into ever larger categories. We assume that the cycads, ginkgos, conifers, gnetophytes, and flowering plants form one set, because only they have a common ancestor that was the first seed-producing plant. The seed plants are nested in a larger set—plants with true leaves—that includes horsetails and ferns but excludes lycophytes and bryophytes. Only the bryophytes are not nested in the still-larger set called vascular plants; they do not have tubelike tissues that deliver water and solutes throughout the plant body.

The section to follow shows you how to construct a cladogram. It provides a closer look at the advantages and some of the pitfalls of a cladistic approach.

Taxonomists identify, name, and classify sets of organisms into ever more inclusive categories, the higher taxa.

Classification systems organize and simplify the retrieval of information about species. Phylogenetic systems attempt to reflect evolutionary relationships among species.

Reconstructing the evolutionary history of a given lineage is based on detailed understanding of the fossil record, morphology, life-styles, and habitats of its representatives, and on biochemical comparisons with other groups.

Recent evidence, especially from comparative biochemistry, favors the grouping of organisms into a three-domain system of classification—Archaea, Bacteria, and Eukarya (protists, plants, fungi, and animals).

19.6 How To Construct a Cladogram

LINK TO SECTION 17.6

In case you would like to know how a cladogram can be constructed, here is a step-by-step approach.

Suppose you want to make a cladogram for vertebrates. You select an *ingroup* of organisms with traits that suggest they might be related—in this case, jaws and paired appendages. You focus on sharks, mammals, crocodiles, and birds because they also differ clearly in some morphological, physiological, and behavioral traits, or characters. Now you must select a different vertebrate that can be used as a reference point for estimating evolutionary distances within the ingroup.

To keep things simple, you check for the presence (+) or absence (−) of seven traits and tabulate them, as in Figure 19.18a. After scanning Chapter 26, you decide that lampreys are only distantly related to the other four vertebrates. For instance, although a tubular structure called a notochord forms in its embryos, as it does for all other vertebrates, only lampreys have no jaws or paired appendages, such as lateral fins and legs. They can be the *outgroup*, the one with the fewest derived traits when compared to the others.

Derived traits, recall, are evidence of morphological divergence and branching in an evolutionary tree. In Figure 19.18b, each zero (0) across the columns of traits for each vertebrate indicates an ancestral condition. Each numeral one (1) means the vertebrate shows the derived trait.

Now you look for derived traits that the selected groups do or do not share. For example, the crocodile, mammal, and bird share five derived traits, but the bird and the shark share only three. You can now make a simple cladogram, although systematists often use many traits of many taxa. Typically they use a computer to analyze data and find the pattern that is best supported by a lot of information.

Figure 19.18c–g shows how a cladogram develops as you keep adding information to it. Start with the presence or absence of jaws and paired appendages, two traits that all

groups except lampreys derived from a common ancestor. What about lungs? Like lampreys, sharks do not have them, so you have identified another branch point in vertebrate evolution. Past that branch point, only mammals have hair, only crocodiles and birds have some form of gizzard. Only birds and their immediate ancestors have feathers.

How do you "read" the final cladogram? Remember, it is an estimate of *relative* relatedness, which implies common ancestry. Birds are more closely related to crocodiles than they are to mammals. Crocodiles are not the ancestor of birds (they are modern organisms, too), but both share a more recent common ancestor than either does with mammals. Birds, crocodiles, and mammals are closer to one another evolutionarily than they are to the shark.

The higher up a branch point is on a family tree, the more derived traits are shared. The lower the position of the branch point between two groups in the diagram, the fewer traits are shared with other groups being investigated.

A few words of caution: Interpretations of evolutionary relationships are more reliable when many traits are used, and there must be strong evidence that shared traits are derived. This helps counter the impact of a bad choice, such as including a trait that is a result of morphological convergence rather than divergence (Section 17.6).

The choice of derived traits is essential. If you were to select body size, for instance, you might wrongly perceive an evolutionary connection between *Sauroposeidon* (a dinosaur that weighed 60 tons), blue whales (mammals that weigh 200,000 pounds), quaking aspen (one plant has 50,000 stems and weighs an estimated 13 million pounds), and a honey mushroom that has been growing for 2,400 years (its underground body extends through 2,200 acres).

Cladograms are only as good as the choices made for their construction—and good choices start with a broad, deep knowledge of life.

Figure 19.18 (**a**) Charting out a selection of traits among vertebrate groups that can be used for the construction of a simple cladogram.

(**b**) A trait's absence in an outgroup or ingroup indicates an ancestral state (here indicated by a zero). Its presence in the set of vertebrates selected as the ingroup is taken to mean it is a derived trait, indicated by a numeral one.

(**c–g**) Step-by-step construction of a cladogram, as explained in the text.

a

Taxon	Traits, or Characters						
	Notochord in Embryo	Jaws	Paired Appendages	Lungs	Hair	Gizzard	Feathers
Lamprey	+	−	−	−	−	−	−
Shark	+	+	+	−	−	−	−
Crocodile	+	+	+	+	−	+	−
Mammal	+	+	+	+	+	−	−
Bird	+	+	+	+	−	+	+

b

Taxon	Traits, or Characters						
	Notochord in Embryo	Jaws	Paired Appendages	Lungs	Hair	Gizzard	Feathers
Lamprey	1	0	0	0	0	0	0
Shark	1	1	1	0	0	0	0
Crocodile	1	1	1	1	0	1	0
Mammal	1	1	1	1	1	0	0
Bird	1	1	1	1	0	1	1

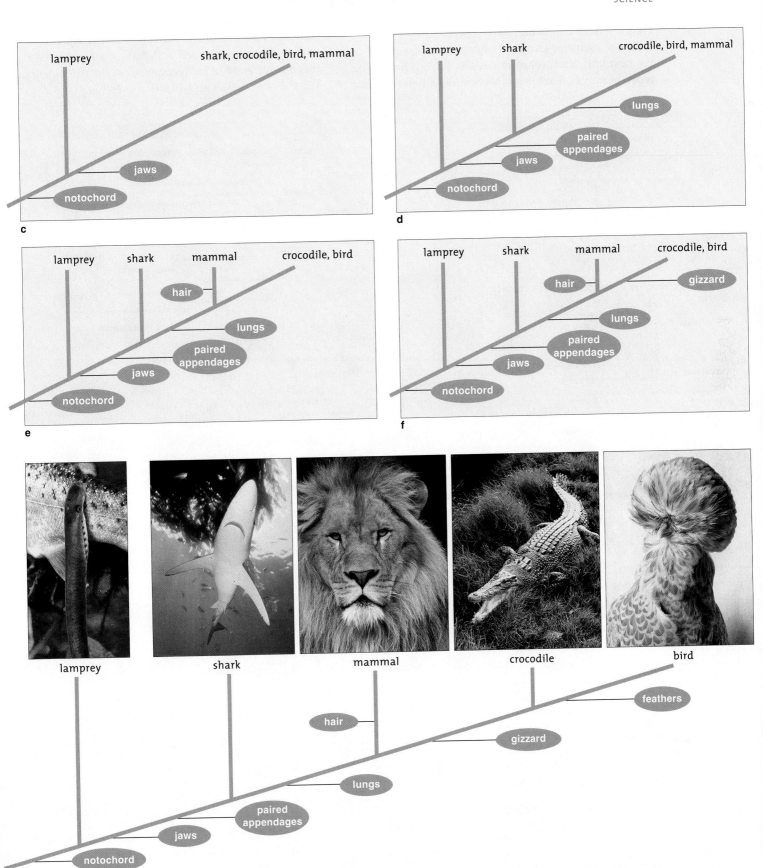

g The completed diagram, livened up with photographs of representative species.

19.7 Preview of Life's Evolutionary History

Figure 19.19, a tree of life, shows the macroevolutionary links among major groups of organisms, as described in the next unit. Each set of organisms (taxon) has living representatives. Each branch point represents the last common ancestor of the set above it. The small boxes within domains Archaea and Eukarya highlight taxa that are currently being recognized as the equivalent of kingdoms in earlier classification systems.

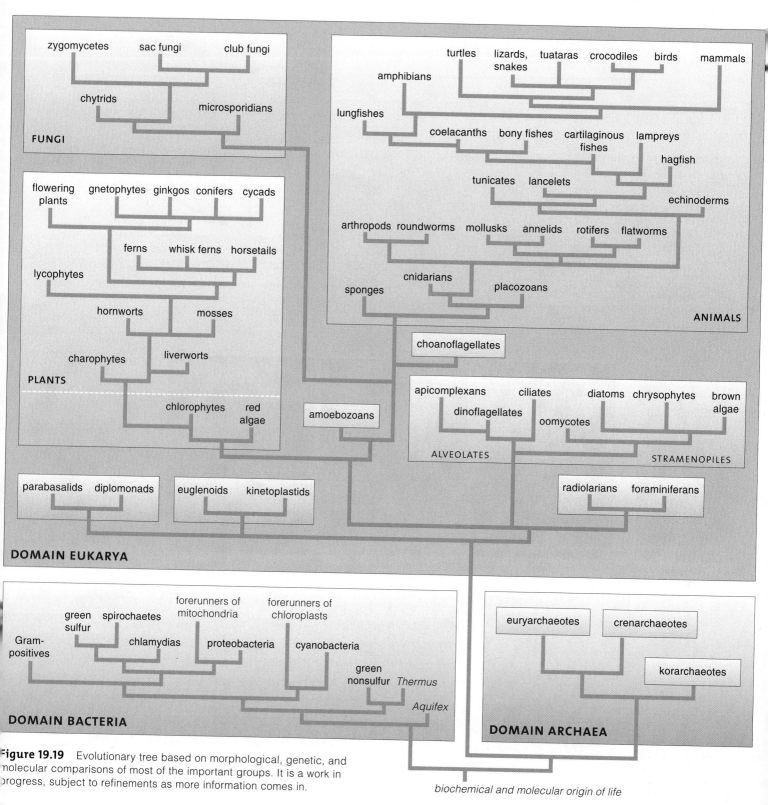

Figure 19.19 Evolutionary tree based on morphological, genetic, and molecular comparisons of most of the important groups. It is a work in progress, subject to refinements as more information comes in.

biochemical and molecular origin of life

19.8 Madeleine's Limbs

So what does macroevolution have to do with you and me? Everything.

In August of 1994, about 900 million years after the first animals appeared on Earth, Madeleine made *her* entrance. Her grandmothers and aunts made a quick count—arms, legs, ears, and eyes, two of each; fully formed mouth and nose—just to be sure these were present and accounted for. One grandmother, having been too long in the company of biologists, had an epiphany as she witnessed Madeleine's birth. In that instant she sensed ancestral connections between the distant past and, through this child, the future.

Madeleine's body plan did not emerge out of thin air. Thirty-five thousand years ago, people just like us were having children just like Madeleine. If we are reading the fossil record correctly, then five million years ago, the offspring of individuals on the road to modern humans resembled her in some respects but not others. Sixty million years ago, primate ancestors of those individuals were giving birth precariously, up in the trees. Two hundred fifty million years ago, the mammalian ancestors of those primates were giving birth—and so on back in time to the very first animals, which had no limbs or eyes or noses at all.

We know little about the very first animals. Yet one thing is clear. By the dawn of the Cambrian, they had given rise to all major groups of invertebrates and to Madeleine's backboned, jawed ancestors. We know this from fossils. For example, one Cambrian community flourished 530 million years ago in, on, and above the dimly lit mud in a submerged basin between a steep reef and the coast of an early continent. About 500 feet below the surface, the water was oxygenated and clear (Figure 19.20). Like a castle built from wet sand, their home was unstable and an underwater avalanche buried them. Over great time spans, compaction and chemical change transformed those small, flattened animals into fossils. By 1909, tectonic activity had moved the fossils high into the eastern mountains of British Columbia, and there a fossil hunter found them.

In the next unit, you will compare body plans of diverse organisms. Such comparisons give insight into evolutionary relatedness and help us construct family trees. As you poke through the tree branches, make use of the evolutionary perspective. At each branch point, the processes of microevolution gave rise to workable changes in body plans. Your collection of conserved and modified traits, and Madeleine's, evolved earlier in countless generations of vertebrates and, even before them, in ancient invertebrate forms.

Our family tree is a record of conserved and derived traits.

Figure 19.20 *Left*, reconstruction of a few Cambrian animals known from fossils of the Burgess Shale in British Columbia. *Right*, Madeleine.

Summary

Section 19.1 Populations of each species share at least one unique trait, a legacy of a common ancestor. In sexually reproducing species, individuals interbreed, produce fertile offspring under natural conditions, and are reproductively isolated from all other species.

If gene flow ends between populations, divergences may lead to new species. Mutation, natural selection, and genetic drift operate independently and may give rise to reproductive isolating mechanisms (Table 19.1). In some cases, reproductive isolation occurs in a few generations.

Prezygotic isolating mechanisms stop interbreeding. They include incompatibilities between reproductive parts or between gametes, differences in reproductive timing or behavior, and ecological restriction to different microenvironments in the same area. The postzygotic mechanisms lead to early death, sterility, or unfit hybrid offspring. They come into play after fertilization.

Biology Now
Use the animation and interaction on BiologyNow to explore how species become reproductively isolated.
Read the Infotrac article "Tracking the Red-Eyed, Sluggish, and Ear-splitting," Tabitha M. Powledge, American Scientist, July 2004.

Section 19.2 By the allopatric speciation model, a geographic barrier cuts off gene flow between two or more populations. Genetic divergence and reproductive isolation are favored and may result in a new species.

Biology Now
Learn more about speciation on an archipelago with the animation on BiologyNow.

Section 19.3 By a sympatric speciation model, populations in physical contact diverge from each other. Polyploid species of many plants and some animals have originated by chromosome doublings and hybridizations.

By a parapatric speciation model, different selection pressures across a broad region act on populations that are in contact along a common border. Unfit hybrids form in the contact zone, so populations on either side diverge independently from each other.

Biology Now
Explore the effects of sympatric speciation in wheat with the animation on BiologyNow.

Section 19.4 Macroevolution refers to the timing, duration, and direction of speciation in the history of life. These features differ among lineages. The major speciation patterns are unbranched (evolution within a single lineage) or branching (divergences from ancestral stock). Most lineages remain stable for long periods, but abrupt episodes of change also have occurred.

Radiations occur in adaptive zones, a similar set of niches that come to be filled by a (usually) related group of species. A niche is a way of life, such as catching insects in the air at night. Species must have physical, evolutionary, and ecological access to these zones.

A key innovation is a chance modification in some body structure or function that lets an organism exploit the environment more efficiently or in a novel way.

Most species are now extinct. Mass extinctions, slow recoveries, and adaptive radiations are major patterns.

Section 19.5 Each species has a unique, two-part scientific name. Taxonomy deals with identifying, naming, and classifying species. Systematics deals with reconstructing life's evolutionary history (phylogeny). In classification systems, sets of organisms (taxa) are organized into ever more inclusive categories as a way to retrieve information about species.

A current three-domain classification system is based largely on phylogenetic evidence. It recognizes three domains: Bacteria, Archaea, and Eukarya. The Eukarya includes diverse lineages known informally as protists, as well as plants, fungi, and animals.

Biology Now
Review biological classification systems with the animation on BiologyNow.

Section 19.6 A cladistic classification system recognizes monophyletic groups. Each group is a clade, a set of species that includes only descendants that display a derived trait, inherited from an ancestor in which that trait first evolved. It is the equivalent of all branches growing from the same point on a stem.

Biology Now
Read the InfoTrac article "How Taxonomy Helps Us Make Sense Out of the Natural World," Sue Hubbell, Smithsonian, May 1996.

Sections 19.7, 19.8 Representing life's history as a tree with branchings from ancestral stems brings clarity to the view that all organisms are related by descent.

Table 19.1   Summary of Processes and Patterns of Evolution

Microevolutionary Processes

Mutation	Original source of alleles	Stability or change in heritable traits that define populations, and the species, is the outcome of balances or imbalances among all of these processes. Population size and prevailing conditions in the environment influence the outcome.
Gene flow	Preserves species cohesion	
Genetic drift	Erodes species cohesion	
Natural selection	Preserves or erodes species cohesion, depending on environmental pressures	

Macroevolutionary Processes

Genetic persistence	The basis of the unity of life. The biochemical and molecular basis of inheritance extends from the origin of first cells through all subsequent lines of descent.
Genetic divergence	Basis of life's diversity, as brought about by adaptive shifts, branching, and radiations. Rates and times of change varied within and between lineages.
Genetic disconnect	End of the line for a species. Mass extinctions are catastrophic events in which major groups abruptly and simultaneously are lost.

Figure 19.21
Rama the cama displaying his unexpected short temper.

Self-Quiz

Answers in Appendix II

1. _____ can isolate one population from others.
   a. Structural traits   c. Behavioral traits
   b. Functional traits   d. all of the above

2. Reproductive isolating mechanisms _____ .
   a. stop interbreeding   c. reinforce genetic divergence
   b. stop gene flow   d. all of the above

3. Most species originate by a (an) _____ route.
   a. allopatric   c. parapatric
   b. sympatric   d. parametric

4. In evolutionary trees, a branch point represents a _____ ; and a branch that ends represents _____ .
   a. single species; incomplete data on lineage
   b. single species; extinction
   c. time of divergence; extinction
   d. time of divergence; speciation complete

5. Fossil evidence supports the _____ model of evolutionary change.
   a. punctuation   b. gradual   c. both are correct

6. *Pinus banksiana, Pinus strobus,* and *Pinus radiata* are _____ .
   a. three families of pine trees
   b. three different names for the same organism
   c. three species grouped in the same genus
   d. both a and c

7. Individuals of a monophyletic group _____ .
   a. are all descended from an ancestral species
   b. demonstrate morphological convergence
   c. have a derived trait that first evolved in their last shared ancestor
   d. both a and d

8. A(n) _____ classification system reflects presumed evolutionary relationships.
   a. epigenetic   c. phylogenetic
   b. tectonic   d. both b and c

9. In modern classification systems, groupings of sets of taxa range from _____ to _____ .
   a. kingdom; genera and species
   b. kingdom; genera and domain
   c. genera; domain and kingdom
   d. species; kingdom and domain

10. Match these terms suitably.
    ___ phylogeny   a. now the most inclusive taxon
    ___ extinction   b. tree of branching lineages
    ___ domain   c. many lineages diverge from
    ___ derived trait   one in a new adaptive zone
    ___ cladogram   d. end of a species or lineage
    ___ adaptive   e. evolutionary history of species
         radiation   f. only in descendants of ancestor
                          in which it first evolved

Additional questions are available on Biology ⊜ Now™

Critical Thinking

1. You notice several duck species in the same lake habitat, with no physical barriers hampering the ducks' movements. All the females of the various species look quite similar to one another. But the males differ in the patterning and coloration of their feathers. Speculate on which forms of reproductive isolation may be keeping each species distinct. How does the appearance of the male ducks provide a clue to the answer?

2. *Rama the cama*, a llama-camel hybrid, was born in 1997 (Figure 19.21). Camels and llamas have a shared ancestor but have been separated for 30 million years. Veterinarians collected semen from a male camel that weighed close to 1,000 pounds, then used it to artificially inseminate a female llama one-sixth his weight. The idea was to breed an animal having a camel's strength and endurance and a llama's gentle disposition.

   Instead of being large, strong, and sweet, Rama is smaller than expected and has a camel's short temper. Rama resembles both parents, with a camel's long tail and short ears but no hump, and llama-like hooves rather than camel footpads. Now old enough to mate, he is too short to get together with a female camel and too heavy to mount a female llama. He has his eye on Kamilah, a female cama born in early 2002, but will have to wait several years for her to mature. The question is, will any offspring from such a match be fertile?

   What does Rama's story tell you about the genetic changes required for irreversible reproductive isolation in nature? Explain why a biologist might not view Rama as evidence that llamas and camels are the same species.

3. Speculate on what might have been a key innovation in human evolution. Describe how that innovation might be the basis of an adaptive radiation in environments of the distant future.

4. Shannon thinks there are too many major taxa and sees no reason to make a new one for something as tiny as archaeans. "Keep them with the other prokaryotes!" she says. Taxonomists would call her a "lumper." But Andrew is a "splitter." He sees no reason to withhold separate status from archaeans simply because they are part of a microscopic world that not many people know about. Which may be the most useful: more or fewer boundaries between groups? Explain your answer.

5. Richard Lenski uses bacterial populations in culture tubes to develop model systems for studying evolution. Bacteria produce several generations in a day. Researchers can store them in the deep freeze, then bring them back to active form, unaltered, to directly compare ancestors and their descendants. Are bacterial models relevant to any evolutionary studies of sexually reproducing organisms? Before you answer, read a short article by P. Raine and M. Travisano entitled "Adaptive Radiation in a Heterogeneous Environment" (*Nature*, July 2, 1998: 69–72).

Looking for Life in All the Odd Places

In the 1960s, microbiologist Thomas Brock was looking for signs of life in the hot springs and pools in Yellowstone National Park (Figure 20.1). He found a simple ecosystem of microscopically small cells, including *Thermus aquaticus*. This prokaryote uses simple carbon compounds dissolved in the water as its energy source. It is known as one of the thermophiles, or "heat lovers," for good reason. *T. aquaticus* withstands temperatures on the order of 80°C (176°F)!

Brock's work had two unexpected results. First, it put researchers on paths that led them to a great domain of life, the Archaea. Second, it led to a faster way to copy DNA and end up with useful amounts of it. *T. aquaticus* happens to make a heat-resistant enzyme, and it can catalyze the polymerase chain reaction—PCR. Synthetic forms of the enzyme helped trigger a revolution in biotechnology.

Bioprospecting became the new game in town. Many companies started to look closely at thermal pools and other extreme environments for species that might yield valuable products. They found forms of life adapted to extraordinary levels of temperature, acidity, alkalinity, salinity, and pressure.

To extreme thermophiles on the seafloor, Yellowstone's hot water would be too cool. They live in the superheated, mineral-rich water near hydrothermal vents. One kind even grows and reproduces at 121°C (249°F). Different species live in acidic springs, where the pH approaches zero, and in highly alkaline soda lakes. In Earth's polar regions, some types cling to life in salt ponds that never freeze and in glacial ice that never melts.

Extreme environments also support some eukaryotic species of ancient lineages. Populations of snow algae tint mountain glaciers red. Another red alga, *Cyanidium caldarium,* is a resident of acidic hot springs. Free-living photosynthetic cells called diatoms live in extremely salty lakes, where the hypertonicity would make cells of most organisms shrivel and die.

What could top that? Nanobes. Australian researchers found nanobes growing 3.8 kilometers (3 miles) below Earth's surface in truly hot rocks—170°C (338°F). Being one-tenth the size of most bacteria, nanobes cannot be observed without electron microscopes. Outwardly, they look something like the simplest fungi (Figure 20.2).

Nanobes are probably too small to be alive. They do not seem to be big enough to hold all of the metabolic machinery that now runs life processes. Even so, nanobes do contain DNA. And they appear to grow. Are they like proto-cells, which preceded the origin of the first living cells? Maybe.

Watch the video online!

Figure 20.1 From a thermal pool in Yellowstone National Park, cells of *Thermus aquaticus*, a prokaryotic species that is immensely admired by recombinant DNA researchers for its heat-resistant enzymes.

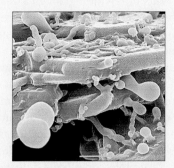

Figure 20.2 Nanobes, possibly like proto-cells. Australian researchers found them in hot rocks far beneath Earth's surface. They are only fifteen to twenty nanometers across; this image has been magnified 20,000 times. However, they do have DNA and other organic compounds enclosed within a membrane, and they grow.

What is the point of these examples? Simply this: *Life can take hold in almost any environment that has sources of carbon and energy.*

This chapter is your introduction to a sweeping slice through time, one that cuts back to Earth's formation and to life's chemical origins. The picture it paints sets the stage for the next unit, which will take you along lines of descent that led to the present range of biodiversity.

The picture is incomplete. Even so, evidence from many avenues of research points to a concept that can help us organize information about an immense journey: *Life is a magnificent continuation of the physical and chemical evolution of the universe, and of the planet Earth.*

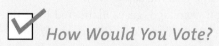

How Would You Vote?

Private companies make millions of dollars selling an enzyme first isolated from cells in Yellowstone National Park. Should the federal government let private companies bioprospect within the boundaries of national parks, as long as it shares in the profits from any discoveries? See BiologyNow for details, then vote online.

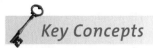

Key Concepts

ABIOTIC SYNTHESIS OF ORGANIC COMPOUNDS

The origin and early evolution of life correlate with the physical and chemical evolution of the universe, the stars, and Earth. The first step toward life was the spontaneous formation of complex organic compounds from simpler substances present on the early Earth. Section 20.1

ORIGIN AND EARLY EVOLUTION OF CELLS

Laboratory studies and computer simulations yield indirect evidence that self-assembly of membranes, combined with chemical and molecular evolution, gave rise to the structural and functional forerunners of cells.

The first cells were anaerobic prokaryotes. Some gave rise to bacteria, others to archaeans and to the ancestors of eukaryotic cells. Evolution of the noncyclic pathway of photosynthesis added oxygen to the atmosphere, which became a major selection pressure. Sections 20.2, 20.3

HOW THE FIRST EUKARYOTIC CELLS EVOLVED

Organelles help define eukaryotic cells. The nucleus and ER membranes may have evolved through infoldings of the plasma membrane. Mitochondria and chloroplasts may be descended from bacterial parasites or prey that took up permanent residence in host cells. Section 20.4

VISUAL PREVIEW OF THE HISTORY OF LIFE

A timeline for milestones in the history of life highlights the shared connections among all organisms. Section 20.5

Links to Earlier Concepts

This chapter starts your survey of the sweep of biodiversity, as introduced in Section 1.3. This is where all of those details of cell metabolism, genetics, and evolutionary theory start to converge and help you make sense of life's fabulous journey. Now you can correlate prokaryotes (4.3) and eukaryotes (4.4) with a timeline of Earth history (17.5).

You will use your knowledge of how organic compounds are assembled (3.2), and of amino acids (3.5), membranes (5.1), enzymes (6.3), and the link between photosynthesis and aerobic respiration (Chapter 7). You may find yourself referring to the sections on DNA replication (13.3), RNAs and protein synthesis (14.1), and the genetic code (14.2). You will consider how the nucleus, ER, mitochondria, and chloroplasts (4.5–4.8) may have originated.

20.1 In the Beginning . . .

LINKS TO SECTIONS 3.2, 3.5

Life originated when Earth was a thin-crusted inferno, so we may never find evidence of the first cells. Still, answers to three questions can yield clues to their origins. What were conditions like? Did cells emerge as a result of chemical and molecular evolution? Can experimental tests disprove that they did? Let's take a look.

Some clear evening, look up at the moon. *Five billion trillion times* the distance between it and you are the systems of stars, or galaxies, at the edge of the known universe. Light energy travels far faster than anything else, millions of meters a second, yet wavelengths of light that originated from faraway galaxies billions of years ago are just now reaching Earth. By all known measures, all near and distant galaxies in the space of the universe are moving away from one another. The entire universe, it seems, is expanding. One theory of how the colossal expansion started might account for every bit of matter in every living thing.

Think about how you can rewind a videotape on a VCR, then imagine "rewinding" the universe. As you do, the galaxies start moving closer together. After 12 to 15 billion years of rewinding, all galaxies, all matter and space are compressed into a hot, dense volume at one single point. You have arrived at time zero.

That incredibly hot, dense state lasted only for an instant. What happened next is called the **big bang**, the nearly instantaneous distribution of all matter and energy throughout the universe. Within minutes, the temperature dropped a billion degrees. Nuclear fusion reactions created most of the simplest elements, such as helium, which still are the most abundant kinds in the universe. Radio telescopes have detected a relic of the big bang—cooled, diluted background radiation left over from the beginning of time.

Over the next billion years, uncountable numbers of gaseous particles collided, and gravitational forces condensed them into the first stars. When stars were massive enough, nuclear reactions ignited inside them and gave off tremendous light and heat as the heavier elements formed. Stars have a life history, from birth to an often explosive death. In what might be called the original stardust memories, the heavier elements released from dying stars were swept up when new stars formed and helped form even heavier elements.

When explosions of dying stars ripped through our galaxy, they left behind a dense cloud of dust and gas that extended trillions of kilometers in space. As the cloud cooled, countless bits of matter gravitated toward one another. By 5 billion years ago, the shining star of our solar system—the sun—was born.

CONDITIONS ON THE EARLY EARTH

Figure 20.3 shows part of one of the vast clouds in the universe. It is mostly hydrogen gas, along with water, iron, silicates, hydrogen cyanide, ammonia, methane, formaldehyde, and other small inorganic and organic substances. Between 4.6 billion and 4.5 billion years ago, the cloud that became our solar system probably had a similar composition. Clumps of minerals and ice at the cloud's perimeter grew more massive. They became planets; one was the early Earth.

By four billion years ago, gases blanketed the first patches of Earth's thin, fiery crust (Figure 20.4). Most likely, this first atmosphere was a mixture of gaseous hydrogen, nitrogen, carbon monoxide, carbon dioxide. There was little free oxygen. How can we tell? When free oxygen is present, some binds to iron in rocks. However, geologists have discovered that such "rust" did not form until fairly recently in Earth's history.

Figure 20.3 Part of the Eagle nebula, a hotbed of star formation. Each pillar is wider than our solar system. New stars shine on the tips of gaseous streamers.

Figure 20.4 *Animated!* (**a**) What the cloud of dust, gases, rocks, and ice around the early sun might have looked like. (**b**) Less than 500,000 million years later, Earth was a thin-crusted inferno. (**c**) Sketch of the apparatus Stanley Miller used to test whether small organic compounds could form spontaneously in such a harsh environment.

The relatively low oxygen levels on the early Earth probably made the origin of life possible. Free oxygen is highly reactive. If it had been present, the organic compounds characteristic of life would not have been able to form and persist. Oxygen radicals would have attacked and destroyed compounds as they formed.

What about water? All of the water that fell on the molten surface would have evaporated at once. After the crust cooled and became solid, however, rainfall and runoff eroded mineral salts from rocks. Over many millions of years, salty water collected in crustal depressions and formed early seas. If liquid water had not accumulated, membranes could not have formed, because they take on their bilayer structure in water. No membrane, no cell, and no life.

ABIOTIC SYNTHESIS OF ORGANIC COMPOUNDS

Cells appeared less than 200 million years after the crust solidified, so complex carbohydrates and lipids, proteins, and nucleic acids must have formed by then. We know that meteorites, Mars, and Earth all formed at the same time, from the same cosmic cloud. Their rocks contain simple sugars, fatty acids, amino acids, and nucleotides, so we can expect that the precursors of biological molecules were on the early Earth, too.

Synthesizing organic compounds requires energy. On the early Earth, lightning, sunlight, or heat from hydrothermal vents might have fueled the reactions. Stanley Miller was the first to test the hypothesis that the simple compounds that now serve as the building blocks of life can form by chemical processes. He put water, methane, hydrogen, and ammonia in a reaction chamber. He kept circulating the mixture and zapping it with sparks to simulate lightning (Figure 20.4c). In

less than a week, amino acids and other small organic compounds had formed in the chemical brew.

Recent geologic evidence suggests that Earth's early atmosphere was not quite like the Miller mixture. But in simulations that used other gases, different organic compounds formed—including certain types that can act as nucleotide precursors of nucleic acids.

By another hypothesis, simple organic compounds formed in outer space. Researchers detect amino acids in interstellar clouds and in some of the carbon-rich meteorites that have landed on Earth. One meteorite found in Australia contains eight amino acids that are identical with those in living organisms.

What about proteins, DNA, and the other *complex* organic compounds? Where could they form? In open water, hydrolysis reactions would have broken them apart as fast as they assembled. By one hypothesis, the clay of tidal flats bound and protected the newly forming polymers. Certain clays contain mineral ions that attract amino acids or nucleotides. Experiments show that once some of these molecules stick to clay, other molecules bond to them and form chains that resemble the proteins or nucleic acids in living cells.

Another hypothesis that is currently getting a lot of attention is this: The first biological molecules were synthesized near hydrothermal vents. Certainly the ancient seafloor was oxygen-poor. Experiments show that amino acids, at least, will condense into protein-like structures when heated in water.

> *Experiments provide indirect evidence that the complex organic molecules characteristic of life could have formed under conditions that probably prevailed on the early Earth.*

20.2 How Did Cells Emerge?

LINKS TO
SECTIONS 5.1,
6.3, 13.4, 14.1, 14.3

Metabolism and reproduction are defining characteristics of life. In the first 600 million years or so of Earth history, enzymes, ATP, and other essential organic compounds assembled spontaneously. If they did so in the same places, their close association might have promoted the start of metabolic pathways and self-replicating systems.

ORIGIN OF AGENTS OF METABOLISM

Before cells appeared, chemical processes may have favored the formation of proteins and other complex organic compounds (Figure 20.5). However proteins originated, their molecular structure dictated their behavior. If some promoted reactions by acting like weak enzymes, they could interact with more amino acids and enzyme helpers, such as metal ions.

Visualize an early estuary, where seawater mixed with mineral-rich water that drained from the land. Beneath the sun's rays, organic molecules got stuck to clay in the mud (Figure 20.6a). At first, there were quantities of an amino acid; call it D. Molecules of D became incorporated into proteins—until D started to run out. Close by, however, was a weakly catalytic protein. This protein could speed the formation of D from a plentiful, simpler substance C.

By chance, clumps of organic molecules included the enzyme-like protein. Such clumps had an edge in the acquisition of starting materials. Suppose that the C molecules became scarce. The advantage tilted to

molecular clumps that promoted the formation of C from simpler substances B and A. Suppose that B and A were carbon dioxide and water. The atmosphere and seas contain unlimited amounts of both. Thus, chemical selection favored a synthetic pathway:

$$A + B \longrightarrow C \longrightarrow D$$

Were some clumps better at absorbing and using energy? Think back on chlorophyll a (Section 7.1). A group of rings in this pigment absorbs light and gives up electrons. The same kinds of ring structures occur in electron transfer chains in all photosynthetic and aerobically respiring cells. They form spontaneously from formaldehyde (Figure 20.5)—one of the legacies of cosmic clouds. Were similar structures transferring electrons in early metabolic pathways? Probably.

The point is, long before cells emerged, a form of chemical competition was under way. Enzymes and other reactive organic compounds had the competitive edge in the acquisition of energy and materials.

ORIGIN OF THE FIRST PLASMA MEMBRANES

All living cells have an outer membrane that controls which substances enter and leave the cytoplasm in a given interval (Section 5.1). By a current hypothesis, proto-cells were transitional forms between simple organic compounds and the first living cells. These **proto-cells** were no more than membrane-bound sacs

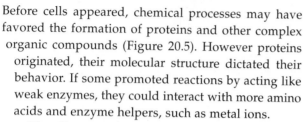

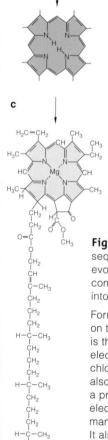

Figure 20.5 Hypothetical sequence of the chemical evolution of (**a**) an organic compound, formaldehyde, into (**c**) porphyrin.

Formaldehyde was present on the early Earth. Porphyrin is the light-absorbing and electron-donating part of chlorophyll molecules (**d**). It also is part of cytochrome, a protein component of the electron transfer chains in many metabolic pathways. It also is part of the heme of hemoglobin.

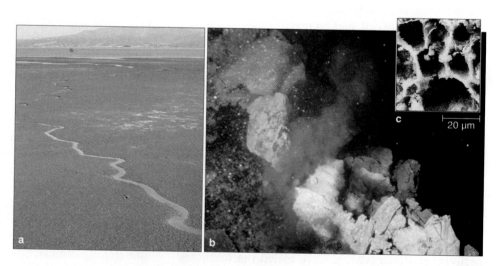

Figure 20.6 Where did the cells originate? Two likely candidates: (**a**) Clay templates in mud flats, and (**b**) iron sulfide-rich rocks at hydrothermal vents, which contain cell-sized chambers (**c**). Experiments show that such chambers are protected microenvironments in which membranes can form spontaneously. Iron sulfides projecting from the walls of such chambers catalyzed the synthesis of short peptide chains and other substances, as happens in metabolism. Many reactions in living cells use iron-sulfide cofactors. Are the cofactors a metallic legacy from a deep-sea ancestor? Perhaps.

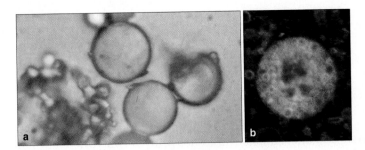
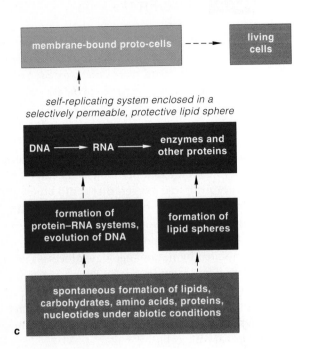

that contained systems of enzymes and other agents of metabolism, and that were self-replicating.

Experiments reveal that membrane sacs can form spontaneously. Under conditions that simulate ancient sunbaked tidal flats, amino acids do form chains that surround a volume of fluid (Figure 20.7a). Fatty acids and alcohols spontaneously form vesicles, especially when clays rich in minerals are present (Figure 20.7b).

Or did proto-cells form from organic compounds at hydrothermal vents? Cell-sized chambers occur in mineral-rich rocks at existing vents (Figure 20.6b,c). Were the chamber walls replication templates for RNA, proteins, DNA, and lipids? The molecules would have accumulated inside, favoring the chemical conditions required for the emergence of living cells.

Figure 20.7 Laboratory-grown proto-cells. (**a**) Selectively permeable sacs. Heated amino acids formed protein chains. When moistened, the chains assembled into a membrane. (**b**) A membrane of fatty acids and alcohols (*green*) enclosing RNA-coated clay (*red*). The mineral-rich clay catalyzes RNA polymerization and promotes the formation of a membrane sac. (**c**) Model for steps in the chemical processes that led to the first living, self-replicating, membrane-bound cells.

ORIGIN OF SELF-REPLICATING SYSTEMS

Life also is characterized by reproduction, which now starts with protein-building instructions in DNA. As you know from Section 14.3, it takes RNA, enzymes, and other molecules to translate DNA into proteins.

Coenzymes and metal ions assist most enzymes—and certain coenzymes are structurally identical with RNA subunits. When you mix and heat RNA subunits with very short chains of phosphate groups, they self-assemble into strands of RNA. Simple self-replicating systems of RNA, enzymes, and coenzymes have been made in laboratories. So we know RNA can serve as an information-storing template for making proteins.

Also, remember that one of the rRNA components of ribosomes catalyzes protein synthesis (Sections 14.3 and 14.4). The structure and function of ribosomes have been conserved over time; ribosomes of the most complex eukaryotes are extremely similar to those in prokaryotic cells of ancient lineages. rRNA's catalytic behavior probably evolved early in Earth history.

Did an **RNA world** *precede* the emergence of DNA? That is, were short RNA strands the first templates for protein synthesis? As you know, RNA and DNA are similar. Three of their four bases are identical. RNA's uracil differs from DNA's thymine by a single functional group. But DNA's *helically coiled, double-*

stranded structure is more stable than RNA, and it can store much more protein-building information in less space. There would have been selective advantage in functionally separating the storage of protein-building information (DNA) from protein synthesis (RNA).

Until we identify chemical ancestors of RNA and DNA, the history of life's origin will not be complete. But clues are coming in. For instance, researchers fed data about inorganic compounds and energy sources into a supercomputer. They programmed the computer to simulate random chemical reactions among organic compounds, which may well have happened untold billions of times in the distant past. Then they ran the program again and again.

The outcome of their experiment was always the same. *Simple precursors evolved. Then they spontaneously organized themselves into large, complex molecules. And they began to interact as complex systems.*

There are gaps in our knowledge of life's origin. But diverse laboratory experiments and computer simulations show that chemical processes can result in all organic molecules and structures that we think of as being characteristic of life.

20.3 The First Cells

LINKS TO
SECTIONS
4.3, 6.4, 7.8

The first cells apparently evolved during the Archaean, an eon that lasted from 3.8 billion to 2.5 billion years ago. Not long afterward, divergences gave rise to three great lineages that have persisted to the present.

THE GOLDEN AGE OF PROKARYOTES

Fossils indicate that the first cells were like existing prokaryotes; they had no nucleus (Section 4.3). There was very little free oxygen that could attack them. Its absence is a clue to their mode of nutrition. Anaerobic pathways would allow them to obtain energy from simple organic compounds and mineral ions that had accumulated by natural geologic processes in the seas.

Molecular comparisons of living prokaryotes tell us that some populations diverged not long after life originated. One lineage gave rise to the bacteria. The other gave rise to the shared ancestors of archaeans and eukaryotic cells.

Microscopically small fossils in 3.5-billion-year-old rocks give clues to what some of the first prokaryotes looked like (Figure 20.8a). Other fossils clearly show that chemoautotrophic forms had become established near deep-sea hydrothermal vents by 3.2 billion years ago. In some groups, pigments probably detected the type of weak infrared radiation (heat) that has been measured at hydrothermal vents. Pigments may have helped cells detect and avoid boiling water, as they do for some existing hydrothermal vent species.

Gene mutations arose independently in some of the prokaryotic populations. They led to modifications in radiation-sensitive pigments, electron transfer chains, and other bits of metabolic machinery that started a novel mode of nutrition. We call it the cyclic pathway of photosynthesis. Those bacterial populations were photoautotrophic; they had tapped into sunlight, an unlimited energy source (Section 7.8).

As they reproduced, those self-feeding populations of tiny cells grew on top of one another. They became flattened mats, infiltrated with calcium carbonate and other dissolved mineral ions, and fine sediments. In time, they were transformed into dome-shaped fossils known as **stromatolites**. Radiometric dating tells us that some are 3 billion years old (Figure 20.9).

When the Proterozoic dawned 2.7 billion years ago, stromatolites were abundant. By that time, a noncyclic pathway of photosynthesis had evolved in a bacterial lineage, the cyanobacteria. Cyanobacterial populations increased, and so did the pathway's waste product—free oxygen. At first, oxygen slowly accumulated in the surface waters of the seas, then in air. So now we return to events sketched out in Chapter 7.

An atmosphere enriched with free oxygen had two irreversible effects. First, *it stopped the further chemical origin of living cells.* Except in a few anaerobic habitats, complex organic compounds could no longer assemble spontaneously and stay intact; they could not escape attacks by oxygen radicals. Second, *aerobic respiration evolved and in time became the dominant energy-releasing pathway.* In many prokaryotic lineages, selection had favored this pathway, which neutralized oxygen by *using* it as an electron acceptor. Aerobic respiration was a key innovation that contributed to the rise of all complex, multicelled eukaryotes.

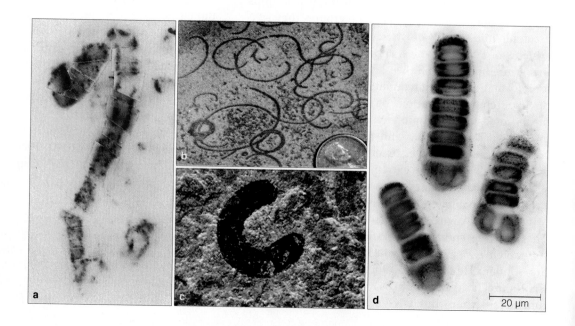

Figure 20.8 A sampling of early life. (**a**) A strand of what might be walled prokaryotic cells dates back 3.5 billion years. (**b**) One of the oldest known eukaryotic species, *Grypania spiralis*, which lived 2.1 billion years ago. Its fossilized colonies are large enough to see without a microscope. (**c**) Fossil of *Tawuia*, another early eukaryotic species that lived during the Proterozoic. (**d**) Fossils of a red alga, *Bangiomorpha pubescens*. This multicelled species lived 1.2 billion years ago, and it reproduced sexually.

20 µm

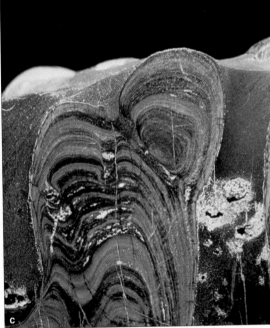

THE RISE OF EUKARYOTES

Eukaryotic cells also evolved during the Proterozoic. Traces of the kinds of lipids that existing eukaryotic cells produce have been isolated from rocks dated at 2.8 billion years old. But the first complete eukaryotic fossils are about 2.1 billion years old (Figure 20.8b,c). Those ancient species had organelles.

As you know, organelles are the defining features of eukaryotic cells. Where did they come from? The next section presents a few plausible hypotheses.

We still do not know how the earliest eukaryotes fit in evolutionary trees. The earliest known form we can assign to a modern group is the filamentous alga *Bangiomorpha pubescens*. This red alga, which lived 1.2 billion years ago, is the first multicelled eukaryotic species to be discovered. Its cells were differentiated. Some cells in its strandlike body served as anchoring structures. Others formed two types of sexual spores. Spore production certainly makes *B. pubescens* one of the earliest practitioners of sexual reproduction.

By 1.1 billion years ago the supercontinent Rodinia had formed. Stromatolites dotted its vast shorelines, but 300 million years later, they were in decline. Were the cyanobacteria a vast food source for predators and parasites? By then, protists, fungi, animals, and the algae that would later give rise to plants were sharing the shoreline with them. Also, 570 million years ago, when oxygen in the atmosphere approached modern levels, animals began their first adaptive radiations in the Cambrian seas. A coevolutionary arms race that continues to this day was off and running.

Figure 20.9 Some stromatolites. (**a**) A painting of how one shallow sea might have looked early in the Proterozoic.

(**b**) In Australia's Shark Bay are mounds that are 2,000 years old. They are structurally similar to stromatolites that formed 3 billion years ago.

(**c**) A cut stromatolite reveals many layers of fine sediments and mineral deposits. The cyanobacterial cells often were preserved as well.

The first living cells evolved by 3.8 billion years ago, in the Archaean eon. All were prokaryotic, and they obtained energy by anaerobic pathways. Not long afterward, the ancestors of archaeans and eukaryotic cells diverged from the lineage that led to modern bacteria.

After the noncyclic pathway of photosynthesis evolved, free oxygen accumulated in the atmosphere and ended the further spontaneous chemical origin of life. The stage was set for the evolution of eukaryotic cells.

20.4 Where Did Organelles Come From?

LINKS TO
SECTIONS
4.3, 4.5–4.8, 14.2

Thanks to globe-hopping microfossil hunters, we have considerable evidence of early life, including the fossil treasures shown in Sections 4.3 and 20.3. Today, most descendant species contain a profusion of organelles. Where did the organelles come from?

ORIGIN OF THE NUCLEUS AND ER

Prokaryotic cells, recall, do not have an abundance of organelles. Some do have infoldings of their plasma membrane, which incorporates many enzymes and other components used in metabolic reactions (Figure 20.10a). Applying the theory of natural selection, we may hypothesize that infoldings originated among ancestors of eukaryotic cells. What advantages did the infoldings offer? They became channels that could concentrate nutrients, organic compounds, and other substances. Also, a membrane with a greater surface area could be a physical platform for more metabolic

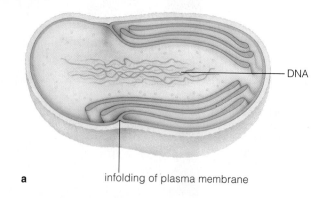

a

infolding of plasma membrane

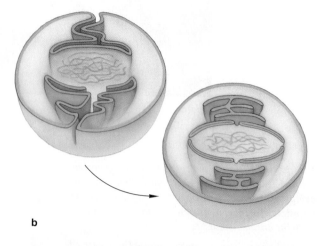

b

Figure 20.10 (a) Sketch of a bacterial cell (*Nitrobacter*) that lives in soil. Cytoplasmic fluid bathes permanent infoldings of the plasma membrane. (b) Model for the origin of the nuclear envelope and the endoplasmic reticulum. In prokaryotic ancestors of eukaryotic cells, infoldings of the plasma membrane may have evolved into these organelles.

machinery as well as transport proteins. Remember the surface-to-volume ratio?

The channels of endoplasmic reticulum (ER) may have evolved this way. They also may have protected the metabolic machinery from uninvited guests. From time to time, metabolically "hungry" foreign cells do enter the cytoplasm of existing prokaryotic cells.

Some infoldings might have extended around the DNA, the start of a nuclear envelope (Figure 20.10b). A nuclear envelope would have been favored because it helped protect the cell's hereditary material from foreign DNA. Bacteria and the simple eukaryotic cells called yeasts can transfer plasmids among themselves. Early eukaryotic cells with a nuclear envelope could copy and use their messages of inheritance, free from metabolic competition from a potentially disruptive hodgepodge of foreign DNA.

ORIGIN OF MITOCHONDRIA AND CHLOROPLASTS

Early in the history of life, cells became food for one another. Heterotrophs engulfed autotrophs and other heterotrophs. Intracellular parasites dined inside their hosts. In some cases, the engulfed meals or parasites struck an uneasy balance with the host cells. They were protected, they withdrew some nutrients from the cytoplasm, and—like their hosts—they continued to divide and reproduce. Over time, they evolved into mitochondria, chloroplasts, and some other organelles.

The novel partnerships are one premise of a theory of **endosymbiosis**, as championed by Lynn Margulis and others. (*Endo–* means within and *symbiosis* means living together.) The symbiont species lives out its life inside a host species, and the interaction benefits one or both of them.

By this theory, eukaryotic cells evolved after the noncyclic pathway of photosynthesis emerged and permanently changed the atmosphere. By 2.1 billion years ago, remember, certain prokaryotic cells had adapted to the concentration of free oxygen and were already engaged in aerobic respiration. The ancestors of eukaryotic cells preyed upon some aerobic bacteria and were parasitized by others (Figure 20.11a). At that time, endosymbiotic interactions began.

The host began to use ATP produced by its aerobic symbiont. The aerobe no longer had to spend energy on acquiring raw materials; the host did this work for it. DNA regions that specified proteins produced by both host and symbiont were free to mutate and lose their function in one partner or the other. In time, both types of cells became incapable of independent life.

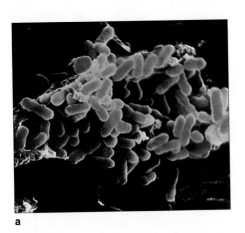

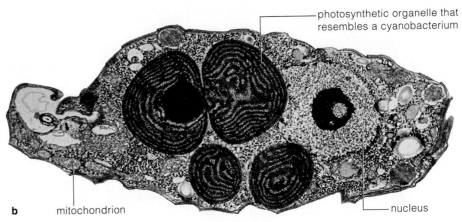

photosynthetic organelle that resembles a cyanobacterium

nucleus

a

b   mitochondrion

Figure 20.11 Clues to ancient endosymbiotic interactions. (**a**) What the ancestors of mitochondria may have looked like. The protist *Reclinomonas americana* has the structurally simplest mitochondria. The mitochondrial genes resemble genes of *Rickettsia prowazekii*, a parasitic bacterium that causes typhus. Like mitochondria, *R. prowazekii* divides only inside the cytoplasm of eukaryotic cells. Enzymes in the cytoplasm catalyze the partial breakdown of organic compounds—a task that is completed inside aerobically respiring mitochondria. (**b**) *Cyanophora paradoxa* is one of the flagellated protists called glaucophytes. Its mitochondria resemble aerobic bacteria in size and structure. Its photosynthetic structures resemble cyanobacteria—they even have a wall like that of cyanobacteria.

EVIDENCE OF ENDOSYMBIOSIS

Is such a theory far-fetched? A chance discovery in Jeon Kwang's laboratory suggests otherwise. In 1966, a rod-shaped bacterium had infected his culture of *Amoeba discoides*. Some infected cells died right away. Others grew more slowly, and they were smaller and vulnerable to starving to death. Kwang maintained the infected culture. Five years later, infected amoebas were harboring many bacterial cells, yet they were all thriving. Exposure to antibiotics killed the bacterial cells (but not the amoebas).

Infection-free cells were stripped of their nucleus and got a nucleus from an infected cell. They died. Yet more than 90 percent survived when a few bacteria were included with the transplant. As other studies showed, the infected amoebas had lost their ability to synthesize an essential enzyme. They depended on the bacterium to make it for them! Invading bacterial cells had become symbiotic with the amoebas.

When you think about it, mitochondria do resemble bacteria in size and structure. Each has its own DNA and divides independently of cell division. The inner membrane of a mitochondrion resembles a bacterial cell's plasma membrane. Its DNA has just a few genes (thirty-seven in human mitochondrial DNA). Also, a few of the codons are slightly different from those of the near-universal genetic code (Section 14.2).

We can predict that chloroplasts, too, originated by endosymbiosis. In one scenario, photosynthetic cells were engulfed by predatory aerobic bacteria, but they escaped digestion. They started to absorb nutrients in the host's cytoplasm and continued to function. They also released oxygen when they photosynthesized. By releasing oxygen inside the aerobically respiring hosts, they acted as agents favoring endosymbiosis.

In their metabolism and their overall nucleic acid sequence, existing chloroplasts resemble cyanobacteria. The chloroplast DNA replicates itself independently of cellular DNA. Chloroplasts and the cells in which they reside divide independently of each other.

Or consider the protists called glaucophytes. They have unique photosynthetic organelles that resemble cyanobacteria. These organelles even have their own cell wall (Figure 20.11b).

However they arose, the first eukaryotic cells had a nucleus, an endomembrane system, mitochondria and, in some lineages, chloroplasts. They were the world's first protists. They had efficient metabolic systems, and they evolved fast. In no time at all, evolutionarily speaking, some of their descendants evolved into the plants, fungi, and animals. The next section provides a time frame for these pivotal events.

> *A nucleus and other organelles are defining features of eukaryotic cells. The nucleus and ER may have evolved by infoldings of the plasma membrane. Mitochondria and chloroplasts may have evolved through endosymbiosis between heterotrophic host cells and their prey or parasites.*

20.5 Time Line for Life's Origin and Evolution

LINKS TO
SECTIONS
1.1, 17.5

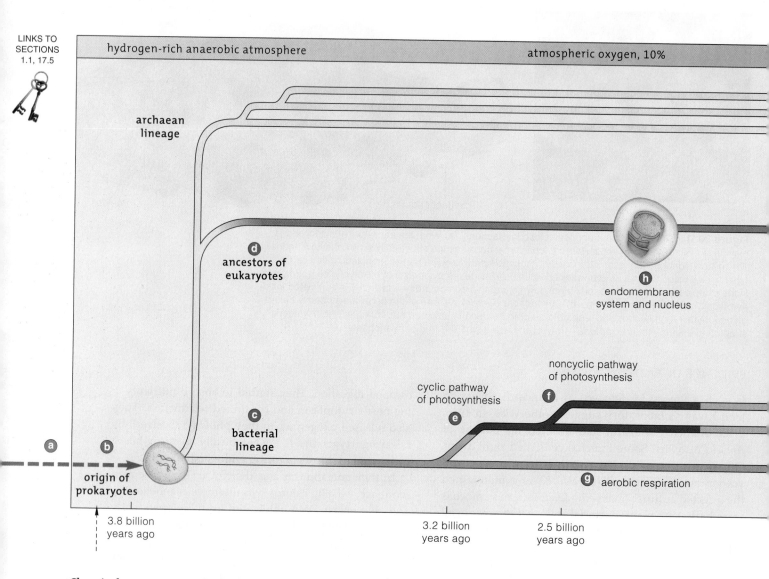

Chemical and Molecular Evolution

a Between 5 billion and 3.8 billion years ago, as an outcome of chemical and molecular evolution, complex carbohydrates, lipids, proteins, and nucleic acids formed from the simple organic compounds present on the early Earth.

Origin of Prokaryotic Cells

b The first living cells probably had evolved by 3.8 billion years ago. All were prokaryotic; they did not have a nucleus or other organelles. Atmospheric oxygen was low and the early cells made ATP by anaerobic pathways.

Three Domains of Life

c The first major divergence gave rise to bacteria and to the common ancestor of the archaeans and all eukaryotic cells.

d Not long after, the ancestors of archaeans and eukaryotic cells diverged.

Photosynthesis, Aerobic Respiration Evolve

e A cyclic pathway of photosynthesis evolved in some bacterial groups.

f An oxygen-releasing noncyclic pathway evolved later in the cyanobacteria and, over time, changed the atmosphere.

g Aerobic respiration evolved independently in many bacterial groups.

Origin of Endomembrane System, Nucleus

h Cell sizes and the amount of genetic information continued increasing in ancestors of what would become the eukaryotic cells. The endomembrane system, including the nuclear envelope, arose through the modification of cell membranes.

Figure 20.12 *Animated!* Milestones in the history of life. As you read the next unit on life's past and present diversity, refer to this visual overview. It can serve as a simple reminder of the evolutionary connections among all groups of organisms, from the structurally simple to the most complex.

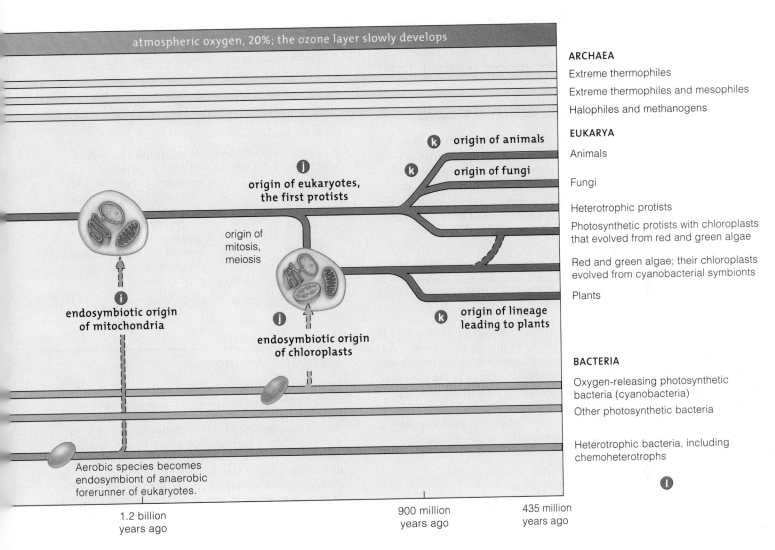

atmospheric oxygen, 20%; the ozone layer slowly develops

ARCHAEA

Extreme thermophiles

Extreme thermophiles and mesophiles

Halophiles and methanogens

EUKARYA

Animals

Fungi

Heterotrophic protists

Photosynthetic protists with chloroplasts that evolved from red and green algae

Red and green algae; their chloroplasts evolved from cyanobacterial symbionts

Plants

BACTERIA

Oxygen-releasing photosynthetic bacteria (cyanobacteria)

Other photosynthetic bacteria

Heterotrophic bacteria, including chemoheterotrophs

k origin of animals

j origin of eukaryotes, the first protists

k origin of fungi

origin of mitosis, meiosis

i endosymbiotic origin of mitochondria

j endosymbiotic origin of chloroplasts

k origin of lineage leading to plants

Aerobic species becomes endosymbiont of anaerobic forerunner of eukaryotes.

1.2 billion years ago

900 million years ago

435 million years ago

Endosymbiotic Origin of Mitochondria

i Before about 1.2 billion years ago, aerobic bacterial species and an anaerobic ancestor of eukaryotic cells entered into close symbiotic interaction. The endosymbiont evolved into the mitochondrion.

Endosymbiotic Origin of Chloroplasts

j Cyanobacteria entered into a close symbiotic interaction with early protists and evolved into chloroplasts. Later, photosynthetic protists would evolve into chloroplasts inside other protist hosts.

Plants, Fungi, and Animals Evolve

k By 900 million years ago, all major lineages— including fungi, animals, and the algae that would give rise to plants—had evolved along shorelines of the first supercontinent.

Lineages That Have Endured to the Present

l Today, organisms live in all regions of Earth's waters, crust, and atmosphere. They are related by descent and share certain traits. However, each lineage encountered different selective pressures, and each has evolved its own characteristic traits.

Summary

Section 20.1 Earth formed more than 4 billion years ago. Experimental tests, information on the formation of stars and planets, and other lines of research offer indirect evidence that the complex organic compounds characteristic of life could have formed spontaneously under the conditions that prevailed on the early Earth.

Biology Now
See experiments on how organic compounds can form spontaneously with the animation on BiologyNow.

Section 20.2 The emergence of the first cells was preceded by chemical evolution that led to enzymes and other agents of metabolism, the self-assembly of membranes on environmental templates, and a self-replicating system. RNA probably was the template for protein synthesis before DNA evolved as an efficient way to store protein-building information.

Biology Now
Read the InfoTrac article "Transitions from Nonliving to Living Matter," Steen Rasmussen et al., Science, February 2004. Also "First Cell," David Deamer, Discover, November 1995.

Section 20.3 The first cells may have originated 3.8 billion years ago. They were anaerobic prokaryotes. An early divergence separated bacteria from the ancestors of archaeans and eukaryotes. Evolution of the noncyclic pathway of photosynthesis in cyanobacteria resulted in an accumulation of free oxygen in the atmosphere, which favored aerobic respiration. This pathway was a key innovation in the evolution of eukaryotic cells.

Biology Now
Explore levels of biological organization with the interaction on BiologyNow.

Section 20.4 The internal membranes of eukaryotic cells may have evolved through infoldings of the cell membrane. Mitochondria and chloroplasts most likely evolved by endosymbiosis, at the times indicated in the Section 20.5 visual summary.

Section 20.5 Key events in life's origin and early evolution can be correlated with the geologic time scale.

Biology Now
Investigate the history of life with the animated interaction on BiologyNow.

Self-Quiz
Answers in Appendix II

1. An abundance of _____ in the atmosphere would have prevented the spontaneous (abiotic) assembly of organic compounds on the early Earth.
   a. hydrogen b. methane c. oxygen d. nitrogen

2. The prevalence of iron-sulfide cofactors in living organisms may be evidence that life arose _____ .
   a. in outer space   c. near deep-sea vents
   b. on tidal flats   d. in the upper atmosphere

3. The evolution of _____ resulted in an increase in the levels of atmospheric oxygen.
   a. sexual reproduction
   b. aerobic respiration
   c. the noncyclic pathway of photosynthesis
   d. the cyclic pathway of photosynthesis

4. Mitochondria may have evolved from _____ .
   a. chloroplasts   c. early protists
   b. bacteria   d. archaeans

5. Infoldings of the plasma membrane into the cytoplasm of some prokaryotes may have evolved into the _____ .
   a. nuclear envelope c. primary cell wall
   b. ER membranes   d. both a and b

6. Chronologically arrange the evolutionary events, with 1 being the earliest and 6 the most recent.
   ____ 1   a. emergence of the noncyclic
   ____ 2   pathway of photosynthesis
   ____ 3   b. origin of mitochondria
   ____ 4   c. origin of proto-cells
   ____ 5   d. emergence of the cyclic
   ____ 6   pathway of photosynthesis
                       e. origin of chloroplasts
                       f. the big bang

Additional questions are available on **Biology Now™**

Critical Thinking

1. Mars formed about 5 million years earlier than Earth, and it has a similar composition but is far richer in iron. It is farther from the sun and much chillier, with an average surface temperature of −63° C. Today, nearly all of the water on Mars is permanently frozen in soil. To some researchers, photographs of certain geological features indicate that liquid water might have flowed across the planet's surface during an earlier and warmer time. The Martian atmophere is now richer in carbon dioxide than Earth's, but very low in nitrogen and oxygen. Based on this information, would you rule out the possibility that life could have existed on Mars or that simple life forms could currently exist there? Explain your reasoning.

2. What if it were possible to create life in test tubes? That is the idea behind modeling and perhaps creating minimal organisms: living cells having the smallest set of genes required to survive and reproduce.

Craig Venter and Claire Fraser found that *Mycoplasma genitalium*, a bacterium that has only 517 genes (and 2,209 transposons), is a good candidate for such an experiment. By disabling its genes one at a time, they discovered it may have only 265–350 essential protein-coding genes.

What if those genes were synthesized one at a time and inserted into an engineered cell consisting only of a plasma membrane and cytoplasm? Would the cell come to life? The possibility that it might prompted Venter and Fraser to seek advice from a panel of bioethicists and theologians. No one on the panel objected to synthetic life research. They said that much good might come of it, provided scientists did not claim to have found "the secret of life." The December 10, 1999, issue of *Science* includes an essay from the panel and an article on *M. genitalium* research. Read both, then write down your thoughts about "creating" life in a test tube.

VII Principles of Ecology

Two organisms—a fox in the shadows cast by a snow-dusted spruce tree. What are the consequences of their interactions with each other, with other kinds of organisms, and with their environment? By the end of this last unit, you might find worlds within worlds in such photographs.

45 POPULATION ECOLOGY

The Numbers Game

In 1944 Allied forces invaded Normandy, which marked the beginning of the end of Hitler's "Fortress Europe." On the other side of the world, the United States Coast Guard stationed nineteen men on a remote island in the Bering Sea. The enlisted men set up long-range navigational aids for ships and aircraft. They barged in twenty-nine reindeer (*Rangifer tarandus*) as an emergency food source.

Remember, reindeer preferentially eat lichens (Chapter 24). Thick mats of lichens carpeted St. Matthew, an island where winds howl across tundra and tall cliffs above the sea. The island, which is 320 kilometers from Alaska, is only 6.4 kilometers (about 4 miles) wide and 51 kilometers long.

World War II started to wind down before any reindeer were shot. The Coast Guard pulled out, leaving behind some seabirds, arctic foxes, and voles—and a herd of healthy reindeer with nothing big enough to hunt them down.

In 1957 a biologist with the U.S. Fish and Wildlife Service, who later became a University of Alaska professor, visited St. Matthew. On a hike from one end of the island to the other, David Klein counted 1,350 well-fed reindeer. He noticed lichens that had been overgrazed and trampled.

Six years after that, Klein and three other biologists returned to the small island. They counted 6,000 reindeer. They could not help but notice the profusion of reindeer tracks and feces, and a lot of pummeled lichens.

Klein did not return to St. Matthew until the summer of 1966. Bleached-out reindeer bones littered the island. Forty-two reindeer were still alive. Only one was a male, and it had abnormally shaped antlers. There were no fawns. The population had plummeted to 1 percent of the founding herd! Apparently, thousands had starved to death during the winter of Klein's previous visit. By the time the 1980s rolled around, there were no reindeer at all.

St. Matthew Island is small, with clear boundaries, so it is easy to draw a lesson from this unintended experiment in population ecology: *A population's growth depends on environmental resources, few of which are unlimited.*

Does the lesson apply to other populations, in other places? Another case, on another isolated island, suggests that it does. Remember the Chapter 27 introduction? That human population, too, plummeted in size after growing beyond the capacity of the environment to sustain it.

What if the environment for a population is as big as a continent or a sea? Do resources still run out? Consider this: There are more whitetail deer (*Odocoileus virginianus*) in North America than there were five centuries ago. There are an estimated 20 million to 33 million. The nation's forests no longer can sustain them. Deer now overbrowse ground vegetation. They strip trees of leaves and bark. By eating so many acorns and seedlings, they have stopped the self-renewal of many oak forests. Forests remain in good shape only when there are no more than twenty deer per square mile. Today, densities are often greater than seventy deer per square mile.

Figure 45.1 What happens when you import a small herd of herbivores to a remote island where there are no natural predators and then forget about them?

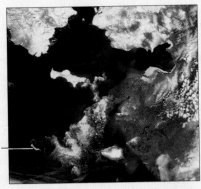

Saint Matthew
Island in the
Bering Sea,
between
Alaska and
Siberia

The rampant browsing of the whitetail deer population also is endangering nesting birds, wildflowers, and other species. Deer spill into human habitats as well. They cause highway accidents that kill 200 or so people and cost about a billion dollars' worth of property damage annually. Each year, farmers lose about 400 million dollars' worth of crops to deer. Many of us know firsthand what even a few hungry deer can do to gardens.

Fewer people are hunting deer for sport, and hunting for the commercial market is banned. Animal rights groups are pleased. They want to control local populations with birth control or other nonlethal methods. However, it is difficult and expensive to track down and treat deer with injectable birth control drugs. Efforts to introduce birth control drugs into the deer's food sources could harm other herbivores.

The point is, *certain principles govern the growth and sustainability of all populations over time.* These principles are the bedrock of **ecology**—the systematic study of how organisms interact with one another and with the physical and chemical environment. Ecological interactions start within and between populations and extend on through communities, ecosystems, and the biosphere. They are the focus of this last unit of the book. After presenting the basic principles, this chapter invites you to apply them to the past, present, and future of the human species.

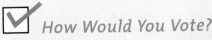

How Would You Vote?

Some people oppose any deer hunting, while others see hunters as a logical substitute for an absence of natural predators. Do you support encouraging hunting in areas where the presence of too many deer is harming the habitat? See BiologyNow for details, then vote online.

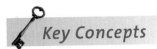

Key Concepts

WHAT ARE THE DEMOGRAPHICS?

Ecological principles govern the growth and sustainability of all populations. Genetic factors and a population's size, density, distribution, and the number of individuals in its various age categories influence patterns of growth. Sections 45.1, 45.2

EXPONENTIAL RATES OF GROWTH

Any population that is growing at a rate proportional to its size is showing exponential growth. Depending on the size of the population's reproductive base, exponential growth may be slow or fast. Section 45.3

LIMITS ON INCREASES IN SIZE

In time, exponential growth typically overshoots the carrying capacity, which is the maximum number of individuals of a population that environmental resources can sustain indefinitely. Some populations stabilize after a crash. Others never do recover. Section 45.4

PATTERNS OF SURVIVAL AND REPRODUCTION

Competition, disease, predation, and other factors that control population growth vary among species and help shape their life history patterns. Sections 45.5, 45.6

THE HUMAN POPULATION

Historically, expansion into new habitats around the world, cultural interventions, and technological innovations have allowed human populations to postpone abiotic and biotic limits to growth. However, the operative word is "postpone." Sections 45.7–45.10

Links to Earlier Concepts

Earlier chapters defined the population, a unit of biological organization that undergoes evolution (Sections 1.4, 17.3, 19.1–19.3). They introduced you to certain morphological, physiological, and behavioral traits that help characterize populations in general (17.3, 18.1, 18.8). With this chapter we turn to demographics—population size and other vital statistics—and the factors that limit increases in size.

45.1 Characteristics of Populations

LINKS TO
SECTIONS
17.3, 18.1, 18.8

*By this point in the book, you know that a population is a group of individuals of the same species. Ecological interactions begin with characteristics of populations. We call these vital statistics **demographics**.*

Each population has a gene pool and an evolutionary history, as explained in Chapters 17 and 18. It also has a characteristic size, density, distribution, and number of individuals in its various age categories.

Population size is the number of individuals that actually or potentially contribute to the gene pool. The **age structure** is the number of individuals in each of several age categories. For instance, individuals often are grouped by *pre-reproductive*, *reproductive*, and *post-reproductive* ages. Those in the first category have the capacity to produce offspring when mature. Together with individuals in the second category, they make up the population's **reproductive base**.

Population density is the number of individuals in some specified area or volume of a habitat. A *habitat*, remember, is the type of place where a species lives. We characterize a habitat by its physical and chemical features and its particular array of species. **Population distribution** is the pattern in which the individuals are dispersed in a specified area.

Crude density is a measured number of individuals in a specified area. It does not reveal how much of the habitat is actually being used for living space. Even areas that seem rather uniform, such as a long, sandy shoreline, are more like tapestries of light, moisture, temperature, composition, and many other variables. Only one portion of the habitat might be suitable for a given population. It might be suitable all of the time or only some of the time, as in summer versus winter.

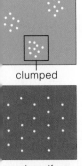

clumped

nearly uniform

random

Different species occupying the same area typically compete for energy, nutrients, living space, and other resources. Such *interspecific* interactions influence each population's density and dispersion through a habitat.

Theoretically, populations show a clumped, nearly uniform, or random distribution pattern (Figure 45.2). Clumping is the most common, for several reasons. First, each species is adapted to particular conditions and resources, which often are not uniform through a habitat. Some animals cluster by a water hole, seeds sprout only in moist soil, and so on. Second, animals may live in social groups, which offer more protection and mating opportunities. A school of fish is like this. Third, many plant seedlings and the offspring of many animals cannot disperse far from their parents.

With nearly uniform distribution, individuals are more evenly spaced than we would expect on the basis of chance alone. Uniform distribution is relatively rare in nature. It sometimes occurs when competition for resources or territory is fierce, as in a nesting colony of seabirds. Figures 45.2 and 49.16 show examples.

We observe random dispersion only when habitat conditions are nearly uniform, resource availability is fairly steady, and individuals of a population or pairs of them neither attract nor avoid one another. Each wolf spider does not hunt far from its burrow, which can be almost anywhere in forest soil (Figure 45.2).

Each population has characteristic demographics, such as size, density, distribution pattern, and age structure.

Environmental conditions and species interactions shape these characteristics, which may change over time.

Figure 45.2 Three patterns of population distribution: clumped, as in squirrelfish schools; more or less uniform, as in a royal penguin nesting colony; and random, as when wolf spiders live in randomly located burrows in forest soil.

Ecologists go into the field to test theories about species interactions and population dynamics, and to monitor the health of threatened or endangered populations.

As the chapter introduction indicated, deer are all around us in forests, grasslands, golf courses, and gardens. How would you go about counting the ones living near you?

A full count would be a measure of absolute population density. Census takers supposedly make such a count of human populations every ten years, although not everyone answers the door. Ecologists make counts of large species in small areas, such as birds in a forest, northern fur seals at their breeding grounds, and sea stars in a tidepool. More often, however, a full count is impractical, so ecologists sample part of a population and estimate its total density.

For instance, you could divide a map of your county into small plots, or quadrats. **Quadrats** are sampling areas of the same size and shape, such as rectangles, squares, and hexagons. You could count individual deer in several plots and, from that, extrapolate the average number for the county as a whole. Ecologists often conduct such counts for plants and other species that stay put (Figure 45.3). Some counts in small areas also help them estimate the population sizes of migrating animals.

Deer are among the animals that do not stay put. How can ecologists be sure that the individuals being counted in a given plot are not the same ones counted earlier in a different plot? **Capture–recapture methods** are one way to sample a population of mobile animals. Such individuals are captured and marked in some way. Deer get collars, squirrels get tattoos, salmon get tags, birds get leg rings, butterflies get wing markers, and so on (Figure 45.4). The marked animals are released at time 1. At time 2, traps are reset. When all goes well, the proportion of marked animals in the second sample is representative of the proportion marked in the whole population:

$$\frac{\text{Marked individuals in sampling at time 2}}{\text{Total captured in sampling 2}} = \frac{\text{Marked individuals in sampling at time 1}}{\text{Total population size}}$$

Ideally, both marked and unmarked individuals of the population are captured at random, none of the marked animals is overlooked, and none dies or otherwise departs during the study interval.

In the real world, recapturing marked individuals might not be random. For example, squirrels that were marked after being attracted to bait in boxes might now be trap-happy or trap-shy. Such individuals may overrepresent or underrepresent their population. Other examples: Instead of mailing tags of marked fish to ecologists, a fisherman may keep them as good-luck charms. Birds lose leg rings.

Your estimate also depends on the time of year when you make a sampling. Population distribution varies with time, as during migrations in response to environmental rhythms. Few places yield abundant resources all year long, so many populations move between habitats as seasons change. Canada geese are like this. So are deer. In such cases, capture–recapture methods might be used more than once a year, for several years.

Figure 45.3   Near the eastern base of the Sierra Nevada, a population of creosote bushes showing nearly uniform distribution. The plants compete for scarce water in this desert climate zone, which has extremely hot, dry summers and mild winters.

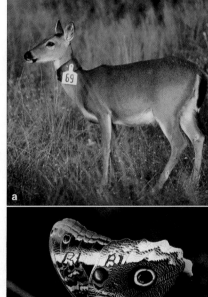

Figure 45.4   Two individuals marked for population studies. (**a**) Florida Key deer and (**b**) Costa Rican owl butterfly (*Caligo*).

45.3 Population Size and Exponential Growth

LINK TO
SECTION
18.8

Populations are dynamic units of nature. Depending on the species, they may add or lose individuals every minute of every day, season, or year. Sometimes they glut portions of their habitat with individuals. Other times, individuals are scarce. Populations even drive themselves or are driven to extinction.

GAINS AND LOSSES IN POPULATION SIZE

You can measure change in population size in terms of birth rates, death rates, and how many individuals are entering and leaving during a specified interval.

Population size increases as a result of births and **immigration**, the arrival of new residents from other populations of the same species. Its size decreases as a result of deaths and **emigration**, the departure of individuals that take up permanent residence in some other place. As one example, Arnold Schwarzenegger emigrated from Austria to the United States, where he became a celebrated immigrant. His permanent move decreased the Austrian population by 1 and increased the United States population by 1.

For many species, population size changes during seasonal or daily migrations. However, **migration** is a recurring round trip between two distinct regions, so we need not consider its transient effects in this initial look at the nature of increases in population size.

FROM ZERO TO EXPONENTIAL GROWTH

To keep things simple, assume that immigration and emigration balance each other over time so that you can ignore the effects of both on population size. By doing so, you can define **zero population growth** as an interval in which the number of births is balanced by the number of deaths. During such an interval, the population size remains stable, with no net increase or decrease in the number of individuals.

Births, deaths, and the other variables that might change population size can be measured in terms of **per capita** rates, or rates per individual. *Capita* means head, as in head counts.

Visualize 2,000 mice living in a cornfield. Twenty or so days after their eggs get fertilized, the females give birth to a litter, then they nurse the offspring for a while. Then they get pregnant again. Suppose 1,000 mice are born in one month. The birth rate is 0.5 per mouse per month (1,000 births/2,000 mice). If 200 of the 2,000 die during that interval, the death rate will be 200/2,000 = 0.1 per mouse per month.

Assume further that the birth rate and death rate remain constant. By doing so, you can combine both variables into a single variable—the **net reproduction per individual per unit time**, or *r* for short. For our mice, *r* is 0.5 – 0.1 = 0.4 per mouse per month.

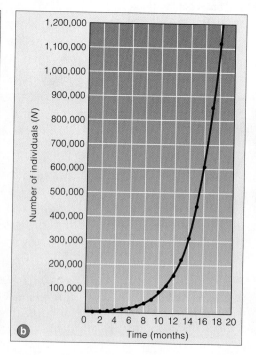

	Net Monthly Increase:	New Population Size:
$G = r \times$ 3,920 =	1,568 =	5,488
$r \times$ 5,488 =	2,195 =	7,683
$r \times$ 7,683 =	3,073 =	10,756
$r \times$ 10,756 =	4,302 =	15,058
$r \times$ 15,058 =	6,023 =	21,081
$r \times$ 21,081 =	8,432 =	29,513
$r \times$ 29,513 =	11,805 =	41,318
$r \times$ 41,318 =	16,527 =	57,845
$r \times$ 57,845 =	23,138 =	80,983
$r \times$ 80,983 =	32,393 =	113,376
$r \times$ 113,376 =	45,350 =	158,726
$r \times$ 158,726 =	63,490 =	222,216
$r \times$ 222,216 =	88,887 =	311,103
$r \times$ 311,103 =	124,441 =	435,544
$r \times$ 435,544 =	174,218 =	609,762
$r \times$ 609,762 =	243,905 =	853,667
$r \times$ 853,677 =	341,467 =	1,195,134

(a)

(b)

Figure 45.5 *Animated!* **(a)** Net monthly increases in a population of field mice living in a cornfield. Start to finish, the list shows a pattern typical of exponential growth. **(b)** Graph the numerical data and you end up with a J-shaped growth curve.

Figure 45.6 Effect of deaths on the rate of increase in two hypothetical populations of bacteria. Plot population growth for bacterial cells that reproduce every half hour and you get growth curve *1*. Plot the growth of a population of cells that divide every half hour, with 25 percent dying between divisions, and you get growth curve *2*. Deaths do slow the rate of increase, but as long as birth rate exceeds the death rate, exponential growth will continue.

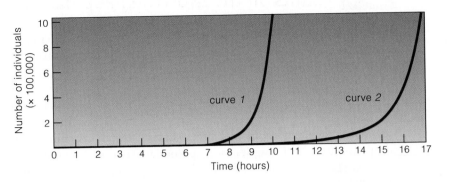

Thus the hypothetical mice in a cornfield give us a simple way to represent population growth as:

$$\begin{array}{ccc} \text{population} & & \text{net population} \\ \text{growth per} & = & \text{growth rate} \\ \text{unit time} & & \text{per individual} \\ & & \text{per unit time} \end{array} \times \begin{array}{c} \text{number of} \\ \text{individuals} \end{array}$$

or, more simply, $G = rN$.

When the next month starts, 2,800 mice are living in the cornfield. The net increase of 800 fertile mice means the reproductive base has become larger. All of these mice reproduce, so the population size expands, for a net increase of $0.4 \times 2,800 = 1,120$. Population size is now 3,920. Suppose all mice in the population reproduce month after month. As Figure 45.5*a* shows, within two years, the number of mice in the cornfield will increase from 2,000 to more than 1 million!

Plot the monthly increases against time and you end up with a graph line in the shape of a "J," as in Figure 45.5*b*. When the growth of any population over time plots out as a J-shaped curve, you know that you are tracking exponential growth.

Exponential growth refers to any quantity that is growing at a rate proportional to its size. For instance, a population that is growing by a fixed percentage every day, month, or some other specified interval is growing exponentially. This does not necessarily mean eyepoppingly fast increases; a small population can grow exponentially, too, but at a slow rate. Even so, as long as *r* remains constant, the rate of growth will be proportional to the number of individuals that make up the reproductive base. A population that has 6,000 successfully reproducing individuals will grow three times faster in a given year than a population of 2,000. *The larger a population's reproductive base, the greater will be the rate of growth in a specified interval.*

Now look at other aspects of exponential growth. Start by supplying one bacterium in a culture flask with all the nutrients required for growth. After thirty minutes, the cell divides in two. Its two daughter cells divide, and so on every thirty minutes. Assume none of the cells dies between divisions. The population size doubles in each interval—from 1 to 2, then 4, 8,

16, 32, and so on. The time it takes for a population to double in size is its **doubling time**.

After 9-1/2 hours, or nineteen doublings, there are more than 500,000 cells. Ten hours (twenty doublings) later, there are more than a million. Curve *1* in Figure 45.6 is a plot of this outcome.

Will deaths put the brakes on exponential growth? Suppose that 25 percent of the descendant cells die every half hour. It now takes about seventeen hours, not ten, for the population to reach 1 million. *Deaths slowed the rate of increase but did not stop exponential growth* (curve *2* in Figure 45.6). As long as birth rates exceed death rates, exponential growth will continue.

WHAT IS THE BIOTIC POTENTIAL?

Now visualize a population in a habitat where living conditions are ideal. Every individual has sufficient shelter, food, and other vital resources. No predators, pathogens, or pollutants lurk anywhere in the habitat. The population may well display its **biotic potential**. This term refers to the maximum rate of increase per individual for any population that is growing under ideal conditions.

Each species has a characteristic maximum rate of increase. For many bacteria, it is 100 percent each half hour or so. For humans and other large mammals, the estimated biotic potential is 2 to 5 percent per year. The *actual* rate depends on how old individuals are at the onset of reproduction, how often they reproduce, and how many offspring they produce over a lifetime. The human population is not now displaying its full biotic potential, but it still is growing exponentially.

During a specified interval, population size is generally an outcome of births, deaths, immigration, and emigration.

A population that is growing at a rate proportional to the size of its reproductive base in a given interval is showing exponential growth.

As long as the per capita birth rate remains above the per capita death rate, a population will grow exponentially.

45.4 Limits on the Growth of Populations

LINKS TO
SECTIONS
17.3, 21.8

Many complex interactions take place within and between populations in nature, and it is not always easy to identify all the factors that can restrict population growth.

DENSITY-DEPENDENT LIMITING FACTORS

Most of the time, environmental circumstances keep a population from fulfilling its biotic potential. That is why sea stars—the females of which could produce 2,500,000 eggs each year—do not fill the oceans.

To get a sense of what some of the constraints may be, start again with a bacterial cell in a culture flask, where you can control the variables. First you enrich the culture medium with glucose and other nutrients necessary for bacterial growth. Then you sit back and let bacterial cells reproduce for many generations.

At first, growth may be exponential. Then it slows, and population size remains relatively stable. After a stable period, population size plummets until all of the bacterial cells are dead. *What happened?* The larger population required more nutrients. In time, nutrient levels declined, which acted as an environmental cue for cells to stop dividing. Even when growth stopped,

the population continued to absorb nutrients until no nutrients were left, so the population died out.

Any essential resource that is in short supply is a **limiting factor** on population growth. Food, mineral ions, refuge from predators, living space, and absence of pollutants are common examples (Figure 45.7). The number of limiting factors can be extensive, and their effects vary. Even so, one factor alone is often enough to put the brakes on population growth.

Suppose you kept freshening the nutrient supply. After growing exponentially, the population collapsed anyway. Like every other organism, bacteria generate metabolic wastes. The population produced so many wastes that it drastically altered the living conditions inside the culture flask. Collectively, the bacterial cells polluted the experimentally designed habitat and put a stop to further exponential growth.

CARRYING CAPACITY AND LOGISTIC GROWTH

Think of a small population of individuals dispersed through the habitat. As it increases in size, more and more individuals must compete for nutrients, living quarters, and other resources. The share available to each diminishes, fewer offspring are born, and more die from starvation or nutrient deficiencies. Now the population's growth rate declines until the births are balanced or outnumbered by deaths.

Ultimately, the *sustainable* supply of resources will determine population size. **Carrying capacity** is the maximum number of individuals of a population that a given environment can sustain indefinitely.

We can use the pattern of **logistic growth** to show how carrying capacity may affect population size. By this pattern, a small population starts growing slowly in size, then it grows rapidly, and finally its size levels off once the carrying capacity is reached. This pattern plots out as an S-shaped curve, as in Figure 45.8 (time A to C). We also may represent the pattern of logistic growth by the following equation:

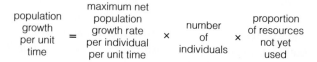

| population growth per unit time | = | maximum net population growth rate per individual per unit time | × | number of individuals | × | proportion of resources not yet used |

The S-shaped curve is only an approximation of what goes on in nature. For instance, a population that grows too fast may drastically overshoot the carrying capacity. The death rate skyrockets and the birth rate plummets, which may well drive the population far below the carrying capacity. That is what happened to the St. Matthew reindeer (Figure 45.9).

Figure 45.7 Response to a scarcity of nesting sites, a limiting factor for weaver bird populations in Africa.

(**a**) African weavers construct densely woven, cup-shaped nests that are only wide and deep enough for a hen and her nestlings. Many nests hang from the same spindly limbs. (**b**) This nest in Namibia is like an apartment house in a place where few trees are available. Between 100 and 300 pairs of sparrow weavers occupy their own flask-shaped nests, each with its own tubular entrance.

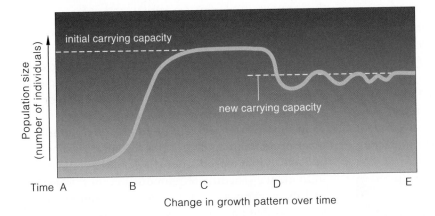

Figure 45.8 *Animated!* An idealized S-shaped curve, characteristic of logistic growth. Population growth slows after a phase of rapid increase (time A to C). The growth curve flattens as the carrying capacity is reached (time C to D). An S-shaped growth curve can show variations, as when changes in the environment lower the carrying capacity (time D to E).

Fluctuations in the pattern emerged after the bubonic plague swept through Europe's crowded cities in the fourteenth century. Remember the introduction to Chapter 18? One pandemic claimed 25 million lives.

Food and other essential resources are not the only factors that come into play when populations become too dense. When either exponential or logistic growth leads to overcrowding, many abiotic and biotic factors function as **density-dependent controls**, which means that they reduce the odds for individual survival.

For instance, interactions with predators or other species can drive the number of individuals below the maximum sustainable level. Predators, parasites, and pathogens have more intense effects in overcrowded populations of prey or host populations. In most cases, they thin out the population and thereby remove the very conditions that invited their controlling effect on population growth, as the next chapter explains.

DENSITY-INDEPENDENT LIMITING FACTORS

Density-independent factors can cause more deaths or fewer births regardless of population density. For instance, each year, millions of monarch butterflies fly from Canada to Mexico's forested mountains, where they spend the winter (Figure 45.10). Deforestation is going on in those mountains. In 2002 a sudden freeze —made worse by deforestation—killed off millions of them. That freeze would have killed them regardless of the density of the butterfly population.

> *Carrying capacity is the maximum number of individuals of a population that can be sustained indefinitely by the resources in a given environment.*
>
> *With logistic growth, population growth is fast during times of low density, then it slows as the population approaches carrying capacity, where the numbers may level off.*
>
> *Density-dependent factors, such the availability of a vital resource, exert control after populations become too dense as a result of exponential or logistic growth. Other factors exert control independently of population density.*

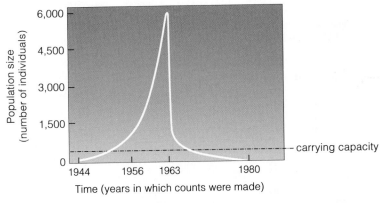

Figure 45.9 Growth curve for the reindeer herd barged over to St. Matthew Island in 1944, as described in the chapter introduction. This population did not recover after overshooting the carrying capacity.

Figure 45.10 Monarch butterflies at their wintering ground in Central Mexico. Each year these migratory insects travel hundreds of kilometers south to places that normally have been cool and humid in winter. If they were to stay in their northern breeding grounds, monarchs would risk being killed by more severe climatic conditions. Even so, deforestation and winter freezes in Mexico are now killing millions of them annually.

45.5 Life History Patterns

LINKS TO
SECTIONS 17.4,
25.11, 25.15

Researchers have identified age-specific adaptations that affect the survival, fertility, and reproduction of individuals for many kinds of species.

So far, we have looked at populations as if all of their members are identical in any given interval. For most species, however, different members are at different stages of development. Therefore, they are interacting in various ways with other organisms and with the environment. For instance, for part of their life cycle, they may be adapted to feed on a certain resource, as when larvae eat new leaves and butterflies sip nectar (Sections 25.11 and 25.15). They also may be more or less vulnerable to danger at that stage.

In short, each species has a **life history pattern**, or a set of adaptations that influence survival, fertility, and age at first reproduction. Each pattern reflects the individual's schedule of reproduction. In this section and the next, we consider a few of the environmental variables that underlie age-specific patterns.

LIFE TABLES

Each species has a characteristic life span, but few of its individuals survive to the maximum age possible. Death looms larger at particular ages. Individuals tend to reproduce during an expected age interval, and in some species they move out at an expected time.

Age-specific patterns in populations intrigue life insurance and health insurance companies as well as ecologists. Such investigators typically track a **cohort**, or a group of individuals recorded from the time of birth until the last one dies (Table 45.1). They also record the number of offspring born to individuals in each age interval. Life tables list the data for an age-specific death schedule, which are typically converted to much cheerier "survivorship" schedules that show the number of individuals actually reaching specified ages. Table 45.2 is a typical example. It lists data for the 2001 human population of the United States.

Dividing a population into age classes and noting the age-specific birth rates and mortality risks often yields useful information. Unlike a crude head count, for instance, the data can help people make decisions about pest management, endangered species habitats, or social planning for human populations. Birth and death schedules for the northern spotted owl are one case in point. They were cited in federal court rulings that halted mechanized logging in the owl's habitat—old-growth forests of the Pacific Northwest.

PATTERNS OF SURVIVAL AND REPRODUCTION

Evolution can occur by way of differences in survival and reproductive success. We measure reproductive success of individuals in terms of the number of their surviving offspring (Section 17.4). That number varies among species, which differ in how much energy and time are allocated to making gametes, securing mates, and providing parental care to offspring of one size or

Table 45.1 Life Table for a Cohort of Annual Plants (*Phlox drummondii*)*

Age Interval (days)	Survivorship (number surviving at start of interval)	Number Dying During Interval	Death Rate (number dying/ number surviving)	"Birth" Rate during interval (number of seeds from each plant)
0–63	996	328	0.329	0
63–124	668	373	0.558	0
124–184	295	105	0.356	0
184–215	190	14	0.074	0
215–264	176	4	0.023	0
264–278	172	5	0.029	0
278–292	167	8	0.048	0
292–306	159	5	0.031	0.33
306–320	154	7	0.045	3.13
320–334	147	42	0.286	5.42
334–348	105	83	0.790	9.26
348–362	22	22	1.000	4.31
362–	0	0	0	0
		996		

* Data from W. J. Leverich and D. A. Levin, 1979.

Table 45.2 Life Table for the United States Human Population in 2001

Age Interval	Number at Start of Interval	Number Dying During Age Interval	Life Expectancy at Start of Interval	Reported Live Births
0–1	100,000	684	77.2	
1–5	99,316	132	76.7	
5–10	99,184	76	72.8	
10–15	99,108	96	67.9	7,315
15–20	99,012	330	62.9	525,493
20–25	98,682	468	58.1	1,022,106
25–30	98,214	471	53.4	1,060,391
30–35	97,743	554	48.6	951,219
35–40	97,189	801	43.9	453,927
40–45	96,388	1,154	39.2	95,788
45–50	95,234	1,682	34.7	5,244
50–55	93,552	2,373	30.3	263
55–60	91,179	3,474	26.0	
60–65	87,705	5,186	21.9	
65–70	82,519	7,397	18.1	
70–75	75,122	10,018	14.6	
75–80	65,104	13,284	11.5	
80–85	51,820	15,877	8.8	
85–90	35,943	16,147	6.5	
90–95	19,796	11,906	4.8	
95–100	7,890	5,845	3.6	
100+	2,045	2,045	2.7	

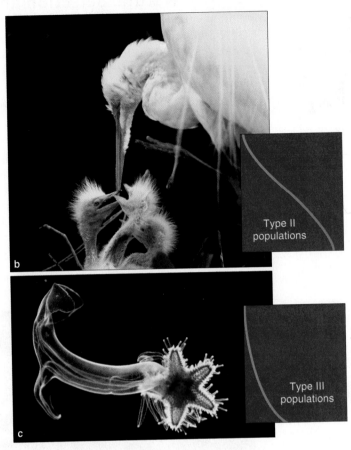

Figure 45.11 Three generalized survivorship curves. (**a**) Elephants are Type I populations. They have high survivorship until some age, then high mortality. (**b**) Snowy egrets are Type II populations. They have a fairly constant death rate. (**c**) Sea star larvae represent Type III populations, which show low survivorship early in life.

another. It seems that trade-offs have been made in response to selection pressures, such as the conditions prevailing in the habitat and species interactions.

A **survivorship curve** is a graph line that emerges when ecologists plot a cohort's age-specific survival in the habitat. Each species has a characteristic curve, and three types of curves are common in nature.

Type I curves reflect high survivorship until fairly late in life, then a large increase in deaths. Like many annual plants, the phlox species tracked in Table 45.1 show this type of pattern. So do large mammals that bear one or at most a few large-bodied offspring at a time, then engage in extended parental care (Figure 45.11*a*). For example, a female elephant gives birth to four or five calves in her lifetime and devotes several years to parenting each one.

Type I curves are typical of human populations in which the individuals have access to good health care services. However, in parts of the world where health care is poor, a sharp drop at the start of a survivorship curve reflects many infant deaths. After this, the curve levels off from childhood to early adulthood.

Type II curves reflect a fairly constant death rate at all ages. They are typical of organisms just as likely to be killed or die of disease at any age, such as lizards, small mammals, and large birds (Figure 45.11*b*).

Type III curves signify a death rate that is highest early in life. They characterize species that produce many small offspring and do little, if any, parenting.

Figure 45.11*c* shows how the curve plummets for sea stars. Sea stars release mind-boggling numbers of eggs. The tiny larvae must eat fast, grow, and finish developing on their own without support, protection, or guidance from parents. Corals and other animals quickly eat most of them, so their survivorship curve plummets. Such a curve is common for many marine invertebrates, insects, fishes, plants, and fungi.

At one time, ecologists thought selection processes favored *either* early, rapid production of many small offspring *or* late production of a few large offspring. They now see that the two patterns are only extremes at opposite ends of a range of possible life histories. Also, both patterns—as well as intermediate ones—sometimes unfold among different populations and at different times in the life cycle.

Tracking a cohort (a group of individuals) from birth until the last one dies reveals patterns of reproduction, death, and migration that typify the populations of a species.

Survivorship curves can reveal differences in age-specific survival among species. In some cases, such differences exist even between populations of the same species.

45.6 Natural Selection and Life Histories

LINKS TO
SECTIONS
1.4, 18.3, 26.2

Earlier you read that jaws evolved among certain fishes during the Cambrian. This key innovation led to adaptive radiations among predators and diverse defenses among prey. No one witnessed that coevolutionary arms race. However, experimental studies show that predators are still acting as selective agents, and prey are still evolving.

Several years ago, with fishnets in hand and drenched in sweat, two evolutionary biologists conducted fieldwork in the mountains of Trinidad, an island in the southern Caribbean Sea. They wanted to capture small fishes that live in the shallow freshwater streams (Figure 45.12). The

fish were guppies (*Poecilia reticulata*). David Reznick and John Endler were starting an eleven-year study of the variables that help shape guppy life history patterns.

Male guppies are generally smaller and have brighter fish scales than females of the same age. The colors serve as visual signals for mating during the guppy's complex courtship rituals. Females are drab colored. Unlike males, they continue to grow after they reach sexual maturity.

Reznick and Endler were interested in the effects of predation on guppy evolution. They chose their study site because different predators act on different populations of guppies in the mountain streams of Trinidad. Different predators are present even along the length of the same

a *Right*, guppy that shared a stream with killifishes (*below*).

b *Right*, guppy that shared a stream with pike-cichlids (*below*).

Figure 45.12 (**a,b**) Two guppies (*Poecilia reticulata*) and two guppy eaters. (**c**) Biologist David Reznick contemplating interactions among guppies and their predators in a freshwater stream in Trinidad.

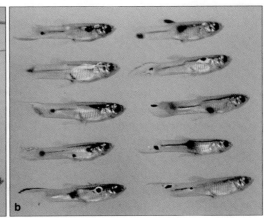

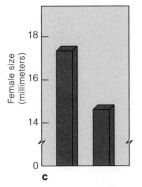
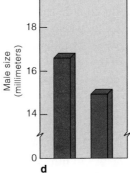
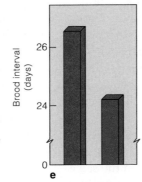
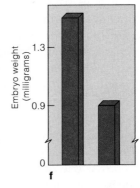

Figure 45.13 Typical size differences between (**a**) guppies that were preyed upon by killifishes and (**b**) guppies that were preyed upon by pike-cichlids.

(**c–f**) Graphs of some of the experimental evidence of natural selection among guppy populations that experimenters subjected to different predation pressures.

Compared to the guppies raised with killifish (*red* bars), guppies raised with pike-cichlids (*green* bars) differed in body size and length of time between broods. Killifish are small and prey on smaller guppies. Pike-cichlids are large fish and prey on larger guppies. The two predators select for differences in guppy life histories.

stream, because waterfalls prevent them from moving upstream or downstream from their habitat (Figure 45.12c).

Two major predators of guppies are killifishes (*Rivulus hartii*) and pike-cichlids (*Crenicichla*), as shown in Figure 45.12a,b. A killifish is not a very big fish. It preys efficiently on small, immature guppies but not on the larger adults. Pike-cichlids live in other streams. They prey on larger and sexually mature guppies and tend to ignore small ones.

Reznick and Endler hypothesized that predation is a selective agent that has shaped guppy life history patterns. As they knew, guppies in pike-cichlid streams grow faster and are smaller at maturity, compared with the guppies in killifish streams (Figure 45.13a,b). Also, guppies hunted by pike-cichlids reproduce earlier and more often, and they have more offspring per brood (Figure 45.13c–f).

Were these differences genetic, or did other variables influence life history patterns in killifish and pike-cichlid streams? To find out, the researchers shipped live guppies from each stream back to their laboratory in the United States. They allowed the guppies to reproduce in separate, predator-free aquariums for two generations. All other physical and chemical conditions in the artificial habitats were identical for the different experimental groups.

As it turned out, the experimental guppy populations displayed the same differences that the researchers saw in natural populations. The conclusion? *Differences between guppies preyed upon by different predators have a genetic foundation and therefore are subject to natural selection.*

What would happen if the selective pressure on a guppy population were to change? Reznick and Endler answered the question with sets of field experiments. For one set, they introduced guppies upstream from a small waterfall. Before the experiment, the waterfall had barred guppies and large pike-cichlids from emigrating upstream, where killifish were in the stream. Guppies introduced to the upstream experimental site were taken from a population that had evolved with pike-cichlids downstream from the waterfall.

Eleven years later, after thirty to sixty generations of guppies had been born, researchers revisited the stream. The experimental population had evolved. Guppies now had traits like those of guppies that had been living with killifishes for a longer time. The difference in the type of predator had influenced guppy body size, the frequency of reproduction, and other aspects of the life history patterns. Laboratory experiments with two generations of guppies confirmed that the differences have a genetic basis.

Reznick and Endler showed that life history traits, like other characteristics, can be inherited. They demonstrated that these traits can evolve. Traits that affect life history can be altered in a surprisingly short time in response to particular selection pressures.

45.7 Human Population Growth

Human population size surpassed 6.4 billion in 2005. Take a look now at what the number means.

LINKS TO
SECTIONS
21.8, 26.15

THE HUMAN POPULATION TODAY

Worldwide, the average rate of increase for the human population in 2004 was 1.3 percent. As long as birth rates continue to exceed death rates, annual additions to the population will drive a *larger* absolute increase each year into the foreseeable future.

Human population size is expanding even though more than 1 billion people are already confronted by limits to growth. They are malnourished or starving (Figure 45.14). They do not have clean drinking water, adequate shelter, access to health care systems, and sewage treatment facilities. Most of the population is expanding in already overcrowded parts of the world. Figure 45.15 is a graphic clue to what the expansion means with respect to the carrying capacity.

Even if it were possible to double food supplies to keep pace with growth, living conditions would still be marginal for most people. At least 10 million would continue to die each year from starvation.

For a time, it will be like the Red Queen's garden in Lewis Carroll's *Through the Looking Glass*, where one is forced to run as fast as one can to stay in the same place. What happens when our population doubles again? Can you brush the doubling aside as being too

far in the future? *It is no farther removed from you than the sons and daughters of the next generation.*

EXTRAORDINARY FOUNDATIONS FOR GROWTH

How did we get into this predicament? For most of its history, the human population grew slowly. Things started to pick up about 10,000 years ago, and in the past two centuries, growth rates skyrocketed. Three trends promoted the rates of increase. First, humans gradually developed the capacity to expand into new habitats and climate zones. Second, humans increased the carrying capacity of their existing habitats. Third, human populations sidestepped limiting factors that tend to restrain the growth of other species.

Reflect on the first point. Early humans evolved in woodlands, then in savannas. They were vegetarians, mostly, but they also scavenged bits of meat. Bands of hunter–gatherers moved out of Africa about 2 million years ago. By 40,000 years ago, their descendants were established in much of the world (Section 26.15).

Few species can expand into such a broad range of habitats. Having a truly complex brain, early humans drew on learning and memory to figure out how to build fires, make shelters, make clothing, make tools, and cooperate in hunts. With the advent of language, knowledge did not die with the individual. It spread quickly among groups. *The human population expanded into diverse environments far more rapidly compared to the long-term geographic dispersals of other species.*

Reflect on the second point. Starting about 11,000 years ago, many bands of hunter–gatherers shifted to agriculture. Instead of simply following the migratory game herds, they settled in fertile valleys and other regions that favored seasonal harvesting of fruits and grains. In this way, they developed a more dependable basis for life. A pivotal factor was the domestication of wild grasses, including species ancestral to modern wheat and rice. People harvested, stored, and planted seeds all in one place. They domesticated animals for food and pulling plows. They dug irrigation ditches and diverted water to croplands.

Agricultural productivity was a basis for increases in population growth rates. Towns and cities formed. Later in time, food supplies increased again, and yet again, by the use of chemical fertilizers, herbicides, and pesticides. Transportation improved, as did food distribution. *Thus, even at its simplest, management of food supplies through agriculture increased the carrying capacity for the human population.*

What about sidestepping of limiting factors? Until about 300 years ago, poor hygiene, malnutrition, and

Figure 45.14 Far from well-fed humans who live in the highly developed countries, an Ethiopian showing some morphological outcomes of starvation. Ethiopia is one of the poorest developing countries, with an annual per capita income of 120 dollars. Average caloric intake is more than 25 percent below the minimum required to maintain good health. The population has one of the highest annual rates of increase—about 2.7 percent in 2003. In that year Ethiopia's total fertility rate was 5.9 children per woman. In addition, Ethiopia is being torn apart by prolonged civil war. Even so, in 2003, its population of 74 million was expected to double in less than twenty-five years.

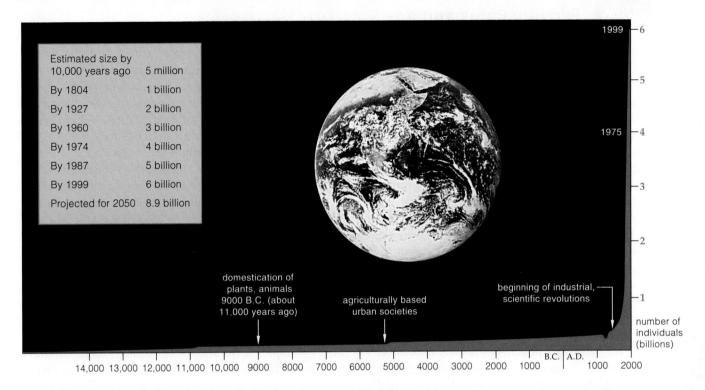

Estimated size by 10,000 years ago	5 million
By 1804	1 billion
By 1927	2 billion
By 1960	3 billion
By 1974	4 billion
By 1987	5 billion
By 1999	6 billion
Projected for 2050	8.9 billion

domestication of plants, animals 9000 B.C. (about 11,000 years ago)

agriculturally based urban societies

beginning of industrial, scientific revolutions

number of individuals (billions)

14,000 13,000 12,000 11,000 10,000 9000 8000 7000 6000 5000 4000 3000 2000 1000 | B.C. | A.D. | 1000 2000

Figure 45.15 Growth curve (*red*) for the world human population. The *blue* box indicates how long it took for the human population to increase from 5 million to 6 billion. The dip between years 1347 and 1351 marks the time when 60 million people died during a bubonic plague, as explained in the Chapter 18 introduction.

infectious diseases kept death rates high enough to more or less balance birth rates. Infectious diseases became density-dependent controls. Epidemics swept through overcrowded settlements and cities that were infested with fleas and rodents. Then came plumbing and new methods of sewage treatment. Over time, vaccines, antibiotics, and other drugs were developed as weapons against many pathogens. The death rates dropped sharply. Births began to exceed deaths—and rapid population growth was under way.

In the industrial revolution of the mid-eighteenth century, people discovered how to harness the energy stored in fossil fuels, starting with coal. Within a few decades, large industrialized societies began to form in western Europe and North America. The urgency of World War I sparked the development of even more technologies. After the war, factories mass-produced cars, tractors, and other affordable goods. Advances in agriculture meant that fewer farmers were required to support a larger population.

In sum, by controlling disease agents and tapping into fossil fuels—forms of energy already concentrated for the taking—the human population has managed to sidestep big factors that had previously limited its rate of increase.

Where have the far-flung dispersals and stunning advances in agriculture, industrialization, and health care taken us? Starting with *Homo habilis*, it took about 2.5 million years for human population size to reach 1 billion. As Figure 45.15 shows, it took just 123 years to reach 2 billion, 33 more to reach 3 billion, 14 more to reach 4 billion, and then 13 more to get to 5 billion. It

took only 12 more years to arrive at 6 billion! Given the principles governing population growth, we may expect the rate of increase to decline as birth rates fall or death rates rise. Alternatively, the rates of increase may continue to rise if breakthroughs in technology expand the carrying capacity. *Even so, continued growth cannot be sustained indefinitely.*

Why? Continuing increases in population size are invitations to certain density-dependent controls. For instance, globe-hopping travelers introduce pathogens to dense urban areas all around the world in a matter of weeks (Section 21.8). Also, emigration away from economic hardship and civil strife have put 50 million individuals on the move within and between nations. Will relocations of so many individuals be peaceable? How much food, clean water, and other resources will become available to them, wherever they end up?

Through expansion into new habitats, cultural interventions, and technological innovations, the human population has temporarily skirted environmental resistance to growth.

As population increases, density-dependent controls, such as disease and competition for resources, may slow growth.

45.8 Fertility Rates and Age Structure

LINK TO
SECTION
39.10

Acknowledgment of the risks posed by rising populations has resulted in increased family planning in almost every region. Putting the brakes on population growth is not easy, and numbers are expected to continue increasing.

Most governments recognize that population growth, resource depletion, pollution, and the quality of life are interconnected. Most are working to lower long-term birth rates, as with family planning programs. Details vary among countries, but most are offering information on available methods of fertility control.

The attempts are having impact. Birth rates are now slowing worldwide. Death rates are declining, mainly because improved diets and health care are lowering infant mortality rates: the number of infants per 1,000 who die in their first year. However, AIDS sent death rates soaring in some African countries (Section 39.10).

We still expect the world population to peak at 8.9 billion by 2050 and possibly to decline near the end of the century. Think about all the resources that will be required. We will have to boost food production and find more sources of energy and fresh water to meet even basic needs, something that still eludes close to half of the population. The large-scale manipulations of resources will intensify pollution.

We expect to see the most growth in India, China, Pakistan, Nigeria, Bangladesh, and Indonesia, in that order. China (with 1.3 billion people) and India (with 1.09 billion) dwarf other countries; together, they make up 38 percent of the world population. Next in line is the United States, with 294 million.

The **total fertility rate** (TFR) is the average number of children born to the women of a population during their reproductive years. TFR estimates are based on current age-specific rates. In 1950, the worldwide TFR averaged 6.5. Currently it is 2.8, which is still far above the replacement level of 2.1—or the average number of children a couple must bear to replace themselves.

These numbers are averages. TFRs are at or below replacement levels in many developed countries; the developing countries in western Asia and Africa have the highest. Figure 45.16 has some examples of the disparities in demographic indicators.

Comparing the age structure diagrams for different populations is revealing. In Figure 45.17, focus on the reproductive age category for the next fifteen years. The average range for childbearing years is 15–49. We can expect populations with a broad base to increase in size at a faster rate. The United States population has a relatively narrow base and is undergoing slow growth, which has implications for 78 million *baby-boomers* (Figure 45.18). This cohort started forming in 1946 when American soldiers came home after World War II and began to raise families. The cohort is big, and the workforce must sustain their retirement.

Even if every couple decides to bear no more than two children, world population growth will not slow for sixty years, because 1.9 billion are about to enter the reproductive age bracket. *More than one-third of the world population is in the broad pre-reproductive base.*

China has the most wide-reaching family planning program. Its government discourages premarital sex; it urges people to delay marriage and limit families to one or two children. It offers abortions, contraceptives, and sterilization at no cost to married couples. Even in remote rural areas, paramedics and mobile units offer access to these measures. Couples who follow these guidelines receive more food, free medical care, better housing, and salary bonuses. Their offspring receive free tuition and preferential treatment when they are old enough to enter the job market. Parents who have more than two children lose government benefits and pay more taxes.

Although the policy might sound harsh, it works. Since 1972, China's TFR has fallen sharply, from 5.7 to 1.8. An unintended consequence has been a shift in the country's sex ratio. Traditional cultural preference

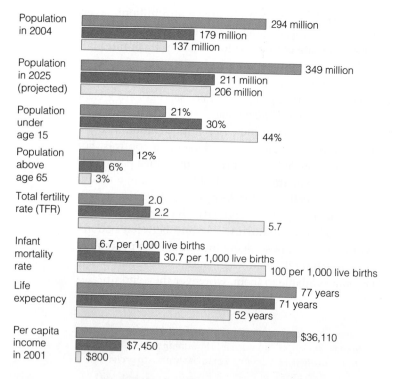

Figure 45.16 Key demographic indicators for three countries, mainly in 2004. The United States (*brown* bar) is highly developed, Brazil (*red* bar) is moderately developed, and Nigeria (*gold* bar) is less developed.

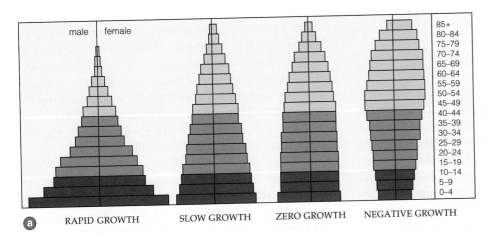

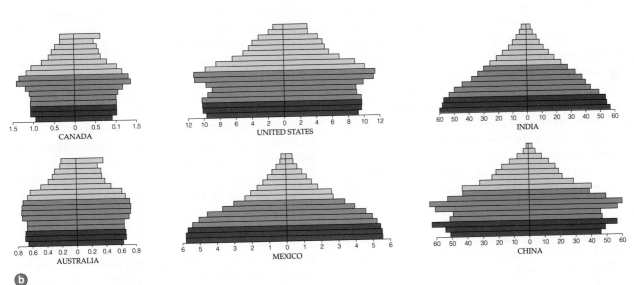

Figure 45.17 *Animated!* (a) General age structure diagrams for countries with rapid, slow, zero, and negative rates of population growth. The pre-reproductive years are *green* bars; reproductive years, *purple;* and the post-reproductive years, *light blue.* A vertical axis divides each graph into males (*left*) and females (*right*). Bar widths correspond to proportions of individuals in each age group.

(b) 1997 age structure diagrams for a few representative countries. Population sizes are measured in millions.

for sons, especially in the rural areas, has led some parents to abort developing females or even commit infanticide. Worldwide, 1.06 boys are born for every girl, but in China the latest census reports 1.19 boys per girl. Also, more than 100,000 girls are abandoned each year. The government now is offering additional cash and tax incentives to the parents of girls. In the meantime, China's population time bomb continues to tick. About 150 million Chinese girls are now in the pre-reproductive age category.

The worldwide total fertility rate has been dropping, but it is still above the replacement level that would move the population growth rate close to zero.

Most countries support family planning programs of some sort. Even with the slowdowns, the human population will continue to increase; its pre-reproductive base is immense.

At present, more than one-third of the human population is in a very broad pre-reproductive base.

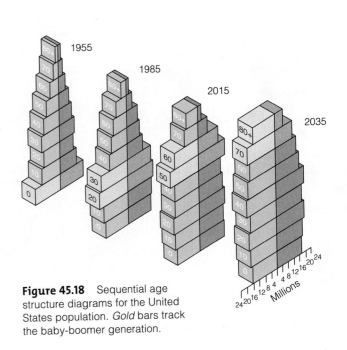

Figure 45.18 Sequential age structure diagrams for the United States population. *Gold* bars track the baby-boomer generation.

45.9 Population Growth and Economic Effects

LINK TO
SECTION
39.10

The most highly developed countries have the slowest growth rates and use the most resources.

DEMOGRAPHIC TRANSITIONS

Changes in population growth rates often correlate with four stages of economic development, the heart of the **demographic transition model**. By this model, living conditions are harshest in a *preindustrial* stage, before technology and medical advances spread. Birth and death rates are high, so the rate of growth is low. In the *transitional* stage, industrialization begins. Food production and health care improve and death rates slow. Birth rates stay high in the agricultural societies, where big families provide help in the fields. Annual growth rates are between 2.5 and 3 percent. As living conditions improve and birth rates begin to decline, growth generally starts to level off (Figure 45.19).

In the *industrial* stage, industrialization is in full swing and growth slows. People move to cities, and couples often want small families. As they accumulate goods, many decide the time and cost of raising more than a few children conflict with their goals.

In the *postindustrial* stage, population growth rates become negative. The birth rate falls below the death rate, and population size slowly decreases.

The United States, Canada, Australia, and most of western Europe, Japan, and much of the former Soviet Union are in the industrial stage. Most developing countries, such as Mexico, are now in the transitional stage, without enough skilled workers to complete the transition to a fully industrial economy.

By some projections, many developing countries will make the demographic transition to an industrial stage in the next few decades. However, there also are signs that the still-rapid population growth in many of those countries will overwhelm economic growth, food production, and health care systems. If that were to happen, they would be trapped demographically, unable to pass through the transition stage.

Africa and some other developing countries already are caught in the demographic trap. Here you might wish to reflect again on the magnitude of the AIDS pandemic that is wreaking havoc on populations, as in sub-Saharan Africa (Section 39.10). One outcome is that many African populations are being driven back to the lowest stage of economic development.

The demographic transition model might not apply to many developing countries, because the conditions on which it is based no longer prevail in some places. For instance, how many can compete in a new global economy without a base of high-tech workers? How many have funds for fast economic growth? How much of what they do have is used to pay interest on debts already owed? Recognizing the problem, in 2004, the world's richest nations agreed to write off 40 billion dollars owed to them by the poorest nations.

A QUESTION OF RESOURCE CONSUMPTION

The industrialized nations use the most resources. For example, the United States has about 4.6 percent of the world's population and produces about 21 percent of all goods and services. Yet it requires thirty-five times

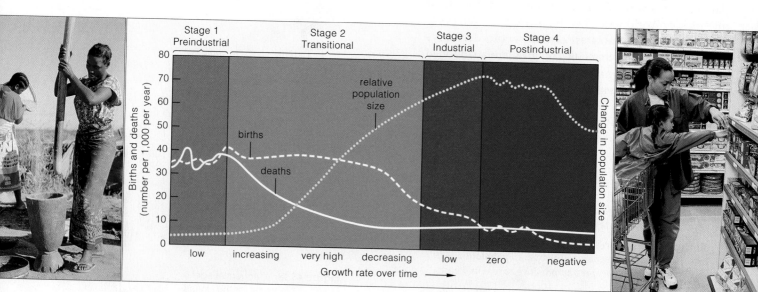

Figure 45.19 *Animated!* Demographic transition model for changes in population growth rates and sizes, correlated with long-term changes in the economy.

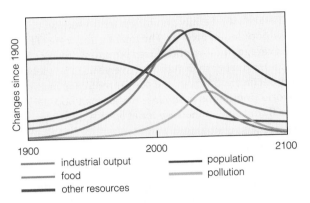

For humans, as for all species, the biological implications of exponential population growth are sobering. However, so are the social implications of what would happen if human population growth were to approach zero.

In a growing population, most of the individuals are in lower age brackets. When living conditions favor moderate growth, then the age distribution should guarantee a future workforce. But the distribution has social implications. Why? It takes a large workforce to support individuals in the higher age brackets.

In the United States, most seniors who have retired expect the government to subsidize their medical care and provide low-cost housing as well as many other social programs. Remember the baby-boomers?

However, as one outcome of better medicine and hygiene, people in these brackets are living far longer than seniors did when the nationwide social security program was established. Cash benefits now exceed contributions that individuals made to the program when *they* were younger.

If the human population does reach and maintain zero growth, a larger proportion of individuals will end up in higher age brackets. Even slower growth poses problems. Will these people continue to receive goods and services as the workforce carries more and more of the economic burden? Put it to yourself. How much economic hardship are you willing to bear for the sake of your parents? Your grandparents? How much will your children bear for you?

We have arrived at a turning point, not only in our biological evolution but in our cultural evolution as well. The decisions awaiting us are among the most pressing and difficult we will ever have to make.

All species face limits to growth. We might think we are different from the rest, and in some respects we are. The uniquely human capacity to undergo rapid cultural evolution has helped us postpone the action of most factors that limit growth. However, the crucial word is *postpone*. On the basis of all the models that are available to us, we can be fairly sure of this: Much of the human population will not escape the impact of limiting factors in the environment.

Figure 45.20 Computer-based projection of what might happen if human population size continues to skyrocket without dramatic policy changes and technological innovation. The assumptions were that the population has already overshot the carrying capacity and current trends will continue unchanged.

more goods and services than India. It uses 25 percent or so of the world's processed minerals and much of the available energy supplies. The United States is not alone in this. China and India are now demanding an ever increasing share of the economic pie.

G. Tyler Miller once estimated that it would take 12.9 billion impoverished individuals living in India to have as much impact on the environment as 284 million people living at the time in the United States. He pointed out that the projected increase in human population growth rates raises serious questions. Will there be enough food, energy, water, and other basic resources to sustain so many people? Will regional governments be able to provide adequate education, housing, medical care, and other social services for them? Computer models suggest not (Figure 45.20). Even so, some analysts claim we can adapt politically and socially to a more crowded world if innovative technologies improve harvests, if food resources are distributed more equitably, and if dietary preferences are shifted away from animal products.

There are no easy answers. If you have not been doing so, start following the arguments in the media. It is a good idea to become an informed participant in a debate that will have impact on your future.

Differences in population growth and resource consumption among countries can be correlated with levels of economic development. Growth rates are typically greatest during the transition to industrialization.

Global conditions have so changed that the demographic transition model may no longer apply to many nations.

The human population has sidestepped a number of the constraints that typically restrict the population growth of other species.

By doing so, staggering numbers of individuals have now become more vulnerable to the laws of nature that cannot be repealed.

Summary

Sections 45.1, 45.2   A population is a group of individuals of the same species in a specified area. It is characterized in part by size, density, distribution, and age structure, which are measurable. Most populations in nature have a clumped distribution pattern.

Counting the number of individuals in quadrats is one way to estimate the density of a population in a specified area. Using capture–mark–recapture methods is a way to estimate the density for mobile animals.

Biology⊗Now
Learn how to estimate population size with the interaction on BiologyNow.

Section 45.3   The growth rate for a population in a specified interval depends on the rates of birth, death, immigration, and emigration. By putting aside the effects of immigration and emigration, we may then represent population growth (*G*) as

$$G = rN$$

where *r* is the net reproduction per individual per unit time and *N* is the number of individuals.

In cases of exponential growth, a population's rate of growth is proportional to its size. The reproductive base, and population size, increases at a fixed rate in a given interval. This trend plots out as a J-shaped growth curve. The rate of growth may be slow or rapid. As long as the population's per capita birth rate remains above its per capita death rate, it shows exponential growth.

Biology⊗Now
Observe a pattern of exponential growth with the animation on BiologyNow.

Section 45.4   The maximum number of individuals of a population that can be sustained indefinitely by the resources in their environment is called the carrying capacity. Food and other essential resources, disease, competition, and predation are examples of density-dependent factors that can limit population growth. Density-independent factors affect growth regardless of how crowded the individuals are.

Unlike exponential growth, a logistic growth pattern plots out as an S-shaped curve. As one example, a small population increases slowly in size, then rapidly, then levels off once the carrying capacity is reached.

Biology⊗Now
Learn about logistic growth on BiologyNow.

Sections 45.5. 45.6   Each species has a life history pattern characterized by the age at first reproduction, number of offspring per generation, life span, and other traits. Three general types of survivorship curves are common: a high death rate late in life, a constant rate at all ages, or a high rate early in life. Many aspects of life histories have a genetic basis, are subject to natural selection, and differ among populations and species.

Section 45.7   The human population has surpassed 6.4 billion. Its rapid growth in the past two centuries

occurred through expansion into many diverse habitats and through agricultural, medical, and technological developments that raised carrying capacity.

Section 45.8   Family planning refers to societal efforts to slow population growth. The total fertility rate (TFR) is the average number of children born to women of a population during their reproductive years. The global TFR is declining. Even so, the pre-reproductive base of the world population is so large that human population size will continue to increase for at least sixty years.

Biology⊗Now
Compare age structure diagrams with the interaction on BiologyNow.

Section 45.9   The demographic transition model correlates industrial and economic development with changes in population growth rates, although global conditions have changed so much that the model may no longer apply to many of the developing nations. Per capita consumption of resources in developed nations is far higher than it is in developing nations.

Biology⊗Now
Learn about the demographic transition model with the animation on BiologyNow.

Section 45.10   Zero population growth has social repercussions, as when a population's age structure is such that the number of older individuals exceeds the number of young workers that must support them.

Self-Quiz   *Answers in Appendix II*

1. The rate at which a population grows or declines depends on the rate of _____ .
    a. births   c. immigration   e. a and b
    b. deaths   d. emigration   f. all of the above

2. Populations grow exponentially when _____ .
    a. its rate of increase is proportional to the size of its reproductive base in a given interval
    b. the size of a low-density population increases slowly, then quickly, then levels off once the carrying capacity is reached
    c. a and b are characteristics of exponential growth

3. For a given species, the maximum rate of increase per individual under ideal conditions is its _____ .
    a. biotic potential   c. environmental resistance
    b. carrying capacity   d. density control

4. Resource competition, disease, and predation are _____ controls on population growth rates.
    a. density-independent   c. age-specific
    b. population-sustaining   d. density-dependent

5. A life history pattern for a population is a set of adaptations that influence the individual's _____ .
    a. longevity   c. age at reproductive maturity
    b. fertility   d. all of the above

6. In 2004, the worldwide average rate of increase for the human population at midyear was _____ percent.
    a. 0   c. 1.3   e. 3.8
    b. 0.5   d. 2.7   f. 4.6

Figure 45.21 Saguaros (*Canegiea gigantea*) growing very slowly in Arizona's Sonoran desert.

Figure 45.22 A young Malian, with a 10 percent chance of becoming a mother by age fifteen, and a 50 percent chance before nineteen. Mali's TFR, about 7, is one of the world's highest.

7. Match each term with its most suitable description.

_____ carrying capacity
_____ exponential growth
_____ biotic potential
_____ limiting factor
_____ logistic growth

a. maximum rate of increase per individual under ideal conditions
b. population growth plots out as an S-shaped curve
c. maximum number of individuals sustainable by the resources in a given environment
d. population growth plots out as a J-shaped curve
e. essential resource that restricts population growth when scarce

Additional questions are available on Biology ⒺNow™

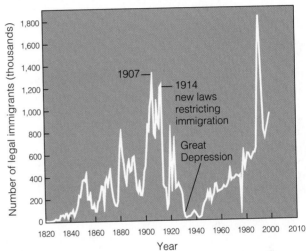

Figure 45.23 Chart of legal immigration to the United States between 1820 and 2000.

Critical Thinking

1. If house cats that have not been neutered or spayed live up to their biotic potential, two can be the start of many kittens—12 the first year, 72 the second year, 429 the third, 2,574 the fourth, 15,416 the fifth, 92,332 the sixth, 553,019 the seventh, 3,312,280 the eighth, and 19,838,741 kittens the ninth year. Is this a case of logistic growth? Exponential growth? Irresponsible cat owners?

2. Reflect on Section 45.6. When researchers moved guppies from populations that were prey of pike-cichlids to a habitat with killifish, the life histories of the transplanted guppies evolved. They came to resemble those of guppy populations that had been preyed upon by killifish. The age of first reproduction increased, as did body size. The males became gaudier. Some of their scales formed larger, more colorful spots. How could a decrease in predation pressure on sexually mature fish influence male guppy coloration?

3. Each summer, a giant saguaro cactus produces tens of thousands of tiny black seeds. Most die, but a few land in a sheltered spot and sprout the following spring. The saguaro is a slow-growing CAM plant (Section 7.7). After fifteen years, it may be only knee high, and it will not flower for another fifteen years. It may live for 200 years. Saguaros share their habitat with annuals, such as poppies, that sprout, form seeds, and die in just a few weeks (Figure 45.21). Speculate on how these different life histories can both be adaptive in the same desert environment.

4. A third of the world population is younger than fifteen (Figure 45.22). Describe the effect this age distribution will have on the human population's growth rate. If you suspect it will have severe impact, what humane recommendations would you make to encourage individuals of this age group to limit their family size? What are some social, economic, and environmental factors that might prevent them from following the recommendations?

5. Figure 45.23 charts the legal immigration to the United States between 1820 and 2000. The greatest increase came after the Immigration Reform and Control Act of 1986 gave legal status to undocumented immigrants who proved they had lived in the country for years. Economic downturns in the 1980s and 1990s fanned resentment against immigrants.

Many people in the United States would like to limit legal immigration to 300,000–450,000 per year and to deport undocumented individuals. Others would like to have open borders; they say a rigidly enforced documentation policy would discriminate against legal immigrants of the same ethnic background. Do some research, then write an essay on the arguments on both sides of this volatile issue, which has social and economic ramifications.

6. Write a short essay about a population having one of the age structures signified by the diagrams at right. Speculate on that population's current economic status and the social and economic problems it may face in the future.

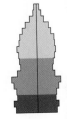

46 COMMUNITY STRUCTURE AND BIODIVERSITY

Fire Ants in the Pants

Solenopsis richteri and *S. invicta* entered the United States in the 1930s, probably as stowaways on cargo ships. These two species of Argentine fire ants infiltrated communities throughout the Northern Hemisphere, starting with the southeastern states. *S. invicta*, the imported red fire ant, recently colonized Southern California and New Mexico.

Disturb a fire ant that crawled onto your skin and it will bite down even as it pumps venom into you through a stinger. Searing pain follows, then a pus-filled bump forms where you were bitten (Figure 46.1). At one time or another, about half of all the Americans who live where fire ants are common have been stung. More than eighty people have died from the attacks.

Imported fire ants menace more than people. These insects attack just about anything that disturbs them, including livestock, pets, and wildlife. They also are more competitive than native ant species and other animals that feed on insects. The imports may be contributing to the declines of some native wildlife species.

To give an example, the Texas horned lizard (*Phrynosoma cornutum*) vanished from most of its home range when red fire ants moved in and displaced the native ants. To the Texas horned lizard, native ants are the food of choice, and it cannot tolerate eating the invaders.

The young of other lizard species are worse off. So are the hatchlings of quail and other ground-nesting birds. Fire ants swarm all over them and kill them directly.

Invicta means "invincible" in Latin. So far, *S. invicta* is living up to its species name. Pesticides have not slowed its invasions of new habitats. To the contrary, they might even be facilitating the invasions by wiping out most of the native ant populations.

Ecologists are enlisting biological controls. Two phorid fly species attack *S. invicta* in its native habitat. Both are parasitoids, a specialized type of parasite that kills its host in a rather gruesome way. A female fly pierces the cuticle of an adult ant, then lays an egg in the ant's soft tissues. The egg hatches into a larva, which grows and then eats

Figure 46.1 Fire ant mounds in west Texas, and agitated fire ants swarming over a leather boot. *Facing page*, skin eruptions that typically follow a concerted attack by these exotic imports.

IMPACTS, ISSUES

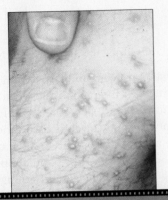

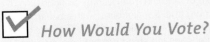

Watch the video online!

its way through tissues to the ant's head. After it gets big enough, the larva secretes an enzyme that makes the head fall off. The larva, sheltered inside the detached, cuticle-covered head, undergoes metamorphosis into an adult.

The flies are choosy about where they lay their eggs. Native ants are not candidates. Knowing this, ecologists released one of the parasitic fly species in Florida in 1997. They released a second species in other southern states in 2001. It is too soon to know whether these biological controls are working.

As ecologists wait for results, they are exploring other options. One idea is to use imported, pathogenic fungi or protists that will infect *S. invicta* but not the native ants. Another idea is to introduce a parasitic ant species that invades *S. invicta* colonies and decapitates the queens.

This example invites you into the sometimes rough-and-tumble aspects of **community structure**, or patterns in the number of species and their relative abundances. As you will see, species interactions and disturbances to the habitat shift community structure in small and large ways—some predictable, others unexpected.

How Would You Vote?

Currently, only a fraction of the crates being imported into the United States are inspected for the inadvertent or deliberate presence of exotic species. Would the cost of added inspections be worth it? See BiologyNow for details, then vote online.

Key Concepts

COMMUNITY CHARACTERISTICS

A community consists of all species in a habitat. Each species has a niche—the sum of activities and relationships in which its individuals take part as they secure and use vital resources. The habitat's history and characteristics, resource availability over time, and the history, adaptations, and interactions of its array of species shape community structure. Section 46.1

FORMS OF SPECIES INTERACTIONS

Commensalism, mutualism, competition, predation, and parasitism are forms of symbiotic interactions that directly involve two or more species. Sections 46.2–46.7

COMMUNITY STABILITY AND CHANGE

By an older model, a predictable succession of species in a habitat stabilizes as a climax community, which thereafter does not change much. It now appears that abiotic and human-created disturbances are more significant factors in shaping community structure. Sections 46.8–46.10

GLOBAL PATTERNS IN COMMUNITY STRUCTURE

Biogeographers identify patterns in species richness of mainland and island communities around the world. Two of the most striking patterns correlate with distance from the equator and from colonizing sources. Section 46.11

Links to Earlier Concepts

In this chapter, you will see how studies from diverse fields of inquiry often converge to explain big patterns in life. You will draw on the Unit IV survey of biodiversity. You will deepen your sense of the challenges facing conservation biology, as by species introductions (Chapter 27). You will revisit biogeography and take a closer look at global patterns in species richness (Sections 17.1, 17.3). You also will see how microevolutionary processes and population dynamics can influence community structure (18.4, 18.7, 45.1, 45.5). You will come across modern expressions of evolutionary arms races that started in the Cambrian seas (26.2).

46.1 Which Factors Shape Community Structure?

*The type of place where each organism normally lives is its **habitat**. All species that directly or indirectly associate with one another in a habitat represent a **community**.*

Each community has a characteristic structure, which we define by **species richness**—the number of species —and their relative abundances. That structure arises largely in response to these abiotic and biotic factors:

1. The physical and chemical conditions that prevail in the habitat, such as temperature, rainfall, soil type, size, and annual incoming solar radiation.

2. The type, amount, and seasonal availability of food and other resources, as in Figure 46.2.

3. The evolutionary history of the habitat and of each resident species.

4. The morphological, physiological, and behavioral traits that help species survive in the habitat.

5. Interactions among species.

6. Natural and human-induced physical disturbances that vary unpredictably in magnitude and frequency.

It will take more than one chapter to survey these factors. Chapter 47, for example, focuses on energy flow and nutrient cycling among species. Here we start with the niche of each species in the community.

THE NICHE

All species of a community share the same habitat— the same "address"—but each has a "profession" that sets it apart. It has a distinct **niche**, the sum of its activities and interactions as it goes about acquiring and using the resources it must have to survive and reproduce. Its *fundamental* niche would prevail even in the absence of competition or any other factors that might limit how individuals get and use resources.

However, constraining factors come into play, and they tend to bring about a more limited, *realized* niche. The realized niche is dynamic. It shifts over time, in small or large ways, in response to a mosaic of changes.

CATEGORIES OF SPECIES INTERACTIONS

Even in the simplest communities, dozens to hundreds of species interact. Interactions between two species may have indirect effects on others, but focus now on five forms of *symbiosis*, or close associations between two or more species during part or all of the life cycle. Each can promote or suppress population growth of a participating species. Let's simplify things by casting the definitions in terms of two-species interactions.

Commensalism directly helps one species but affects the other little, if at all. A bird may get a roosting site from a tree, which gets no benefit but is not harmed. In **mutualism**, both species benefit. Don't think of this as cozy cooperation; the benefits flow from a two-way exploitation. In **interspecific competition**, one species wins or loses with respect to access to some resource. **Predation** and **parasitism** directly benefit one species. Predators typically kill and eat prey. Parasites live in or on hosts and weaken but rarely kill them outright.

A habitat is the type of place where individuals of a species normally live. All of its species form a community. The community's structure arises from a habitat's physical and chemical features, resource availability over time, adaptive traits of its species, how its species interact, and the history of the habitat and its occupants.

A niche is the sum of all activities and relationships in which individuals of a species engage as they secure and use the resources necessary to survive and reproduce.

Commensalism, mutualism, competition, predation, and parasitism are all forms of symbiotic interactions.

Figure 46.2 Three of twelve fruit-eating pigeon species in Papua New Guinea's tropical rain forests. *Left to right,* the tiny pied imperial pigeon, the superb crowned fruit pigeon, and the turkey-sized Victoria crowned pigeon. The forest's trees differ in the size of fruit and fruit-bearing branches. The big pigeons eat big fruit. Smaller ones, with smaller bills, cannot peck open big, thick-skinned fruit. They eat small, soft fruit on branches too spindly to hold big pigeons.

Trees feed the birds, which help the trees. Seeds in fruit resist digestion in the bird gut. Flying pigeons disperse seed-rich droppings, often some distance from tall, mature trees that are established competitors for water, minerals, and sunlight. With dispersal, some seedlings have a better chance to take hold.

46.2 Mutualism

In a mutualistic interaction, two species take advantage of their partner in ways that benefit both, as when one withdraws nutrients from the other while sheltering it.

Interactions in which positive benefits flow both ways abound in nature. Remember Section 31.2? Flowering plants and the insects, birds, bats, and other animals that pollinate them are vivid examples. Similarly, rain forest trees give pigeons food, and pigeons disperse seeds from the trees to new sites (Figure 46.2).

In *facultative* mutualism, the interaction is helpful but not vital. Ants and aphids get along well without each other, but ants do protect aphids as they feed on sugar droplets exuding from aphids (Figure 31.14).

With *obligatory* mutualism, each species must have access to the other in order to complete its life cycle and reproduce. Yucca plants and the yucca moths that pollinate them are obligatory mutualists (Figure 46.3). So are fungi that interact with a photobiont in lichens or with plant roots in mycorrhizae (Section 24.6). In a mycorrhiza, fungal hyphae penetrate root cells or form a dense, velvety mat around them. The plant pilfers mineral ions from the fungus, which absorbs far more ions than the plant could do on its own. The fungus pilfers a few photosynthetic products—sugars—from the plant. The fungus depends on the plant mutualist for its reproductive success. It will stop making spores if the plant stops photosynthesizing.

Anemone fishes can hide out among the tentacles of one or more species of sea anemones; a thick coat of mucus makes them impervious to nematocysts. In one mutualistic interaction, the sea anemone benefits, too. An aggressive anemone fish chases off another kind of fish that likes to eat the tentacles (Figure 46.4).

Or reflect on the apparent endosymbiotic origin of eukaryotes (Section 20.4). Long ago, phagocytes were engulfing aerobic bacterial cells—but some resisted digestion, tapped into host nutrients, and then kept reproducing independently of the host cell body. In time, the hosts came to depend on the ATP produced by the guests—which evolved into mitochondria and chloroplasts. If those ancient prokaryotic cells had not coevolved as mutualists, you and all other eukaryotic species would not be around today.

> *Mutualism is a common form of symbiosis. Each species benefits as it exploits a partner in some way that helps assure its own reproductive success. In cases of obligatory mutualism, one or both partners cannot complete its life cycle in the absence of the interaction.*

LINKS TO SECTIONS 20.4 24.6, 28.5, 31.2

Figure 46.3 Mutualism on a rocky slope of the high desert in Colorado.

Only one yucca moth species pollinates plants of each *Yucca* species; it cannot complete its life cycle with any other plant. The moth matures when yucca flowers blossom. The female has specialized mouthparts that collect and roll sticky pollen into a ball. She flies to another flower and pierces its ovary, where seeds will form and develop, and lays eggs inside. As she crawls out, she pushes a ball of pollen onto the flower's pollen-receiving platform.

After pollen grains germinate, they give rise to pollen tubes, which grow through the ovary tissues and deliver sperm to the plant's eggs. Seeds develop after fertilization.

Meanwhile, moth eggs develop into larvae that eat a few seeds, then gnaw their way out of the ovary. Seeds that larvae do not eat give rise to new yucca plants.

Figure 46.4 The sea anemone *Heteractis magnifica*, which shelters about a dozen fish species. It has a mutualistic association with the pink anemone fish (*Amphiprion perideraion*). This tiny but aggressive fish chases away predatory butterfly fishes that bite off the tips of its partner's tentacles. In return, the fish and its eggs get protection and shelter—scarce commodities on tropical reefs (Section 27.5).

46.3 Competitive Interactions

LINKS TO
SECTIONS
29.5, 45.4

Where you come across limited supplies of energy, nutrients, living space, and other natural resources, there you are likely to find organisms competing for a share of them.

Competition for resources is typically intense between individuals of the same species (Chapters 45 and 49). At the community level, competition between species usually is not as intense. Why not? *The requirements of two species may be similar but are never as close as they are among individuals of the same species.* Let's consider two forms of interspecific competition.

In **interference competition**, one species controls or blocks access of another species to some resource, regardless of its abundance. The leaves of some plant species exude aromatic compounds that taint soil and prevent potential competitors from taking root. A few aggressive chipmunk species keep others out of their habitats (Figure 46.5). In spring and early summer, a male broadtailed hummingbird evicts birds of its own species from its richly flowered territory in the Rocky Mountains. In August, however, *rufous* hummingbirds migrate through the Rockies on their way to Mexico. Until they fly on, the stronger, more aggressive rufous males force the male broadtails to give up territory.

In **exploitative competition**, different species have equal access to a resource, but one is better at using it. In one experiment, a large and a small species of water flea (*Daphnia*) that feed on the same alga were grown together in an alga-enriched culture flask. The larger species increased in body mass. Also, its population expanded. The smaller species lost body mass, and its population shrank—which leads us to a theory.

THEORY OF COMPETITIVE EXCLUSION

Any two species differ to a greater or lesser extent in their capacity to secure and use resources. The more they overlap in these respects, the less likely they are to coexist in the same habitat.

Years ago, G. Gause found evidence of this when he grew two species of *Paramecium* separately and then together (Figure 46.6). Both of these ciliated protozoans hunt the same prey—bacteria—and compete intensely for it. Gause's species, which use identical resources, could not coexist indefinitely. Later experiments with water fleas and many other species yielded the same results, in support of what ecologists now call the theory of **competitive exclusion**.

Gause also studied two other *Paramecium* species that did not overlap much in requirements. He grew them together. One species tended to feed on bacteria suspended in culture tube liquid. The other ate yeast cells near the bottom of the tube. Population growth rates slowed for both species—but the overlap in use

Figure 46.5 Example of interspecific competition in nature. On the slopes of the Sierra Nevada, competition helps keep nine species of chipmunks (*Tamias*) in different habitats.

The alpine chipmunk (**a**) lives in the alpine zone, the highest elevation. Below it are the lodgepole pine, piñon pine, and then sagebrush habitat zones. Lodgepole pine chipmunks (**b**), least chipmunks (**c**), and other species live in the forest zones. Merriam's chipmunk (**d**) lives at the base of the mountains, in sagebrush. Its traits would allow it to move up into the pines, but the aggressively competitive behavior of forest-dwelling chipmunks won't let it. Food preferences keep the pine forest chipmunks out of the sagebrush habitat.

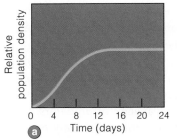

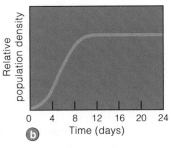

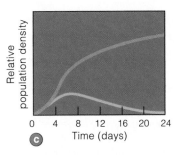

Paramecium caudatum

P. aurelia

Figure 46.6 *Animated!* Results of competitive exclusion between two protozoan species that compete for the same food. (**a**) *Paramecium caudatum* and (**b**) *P. aurelia* were grown in separate culture flasks and established stable populations. The S-shaped graph curves indicate logistic growth and stability.

(**c**) Then the two species were grown together. *P. aurelia* (*brown* curve) drove *P. caudatum* toward extinction (*green* curve in **c**). This experiment and others suggest that two species cannot coexist indefinitely in the same habitat *when they require identical resources*. If their requirements do not overlap much, one might influence the population growth rate of the other, but they may still coexist.

Figure 46.7 Two coexisting species of salamanders: (**a**) *Plethodon glutinosus* complex and (**b**) *P. jordani*.

of resources was not enough for one species to fully exclude the other. The two continued to coexist.

Field experiments also reveal effects of competition. For instance, N. Hairston studied salamanders in the Balsam Mountains and Great Smoky Mountains. One species, *Plethodon glutinosus*, lives at lower elevations than its relative *P. jordani*, but the home ranges overlap in some areas (Figure 46.7). Hairston removed one or the other species from test plots in the overlap areas. He left some plots untouched as controls. Five years later, nothing had changed in those control plots; the species were coexisting. Population sizes in test plots were growing. Plots cleared of *P. jordani* had a greater proportion of *P. glutinosus*. In addition, plots cleared of *P. glutinosus* had a greater proportion of *P. jordani*.

Hairston concluded that, where populations of the two salamander species coexist in nature, competitive interactions suppress the growth rate of both.

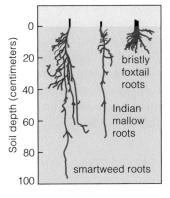

bristly foxtail

Indian mallow   smartweed

Figure 46.8 Resource partitioning among three annual plant species in an abandoned field. The plants differ in how they are adapted to secure soil water and mineral ions. The roots of each species tap into different depths of soil.

RESOURCE PARTITIONING

Think back on those fruit-eating pigeon species. They all use the same resource: fruit. Yet they overlap only a bit in their use of it, because each prefers fruits of a certain size. They are a case of **resource partitioning** —a *subdividing* of some category of similar resources, which allows competing species to coexist.

Similarly, three annual plant species live in the same plowed, abandoned field. All require sunlight, water, and minerals. Each exploits a slightly different part of the habitat (Figure 46.8). Bristly foxtail grasses have a shallow, fibrous root system that absorbs water fast during rains. They grow where moisture shifts daily, and are drought-tolerant. Indian mallow has a taproot

system in deeper soil that is moist early in spring and drier later. The taproot system of smartweed branches in topsoil and soil below the roots of other species. It grows where soil is perpetually moist (Section 29.5).

In some competitive interactions, one species controls or blocks access to a resource, regardless of whether it is scarce or abundant. In other interactions, one is better than another at exploiting a shared resource.

When two species overlap too much in their requirements, they cannot coexist in the same habitat unless they share required resources in different ways or at different times.

46.4 Predator–Prey Interactions

LINKS TO
SECTIONS
1.5, 1.6, 26.2

Predators are consumers that obtain energy and nutrients from living organisms—their prey—which they generally capture and kill. The quantity and types of prey species affect predator diversity and abundances, and the types of predators and their numbers do the same for prey.

COEVOLUTION OF PREDATORS AND PREY

Coevolution influences predator and prey interactions. The term refers to species that evolve jointly as their close ecological interaction exerts selection pressure on each other over the generations. If a gene mutation in a prey organism leads to a more effective defense against predators, the mutant allele will increase in frequency in the prey population. Its bearers and their offspring will tend to survive in greater numbers. If a gene mutation in a predator leads to a better way to overcome the novel prey defense, its bearers and their offspring will eat better; they will tend to survive and leave more descendants in the predator population.

Thus, over time, the predators are selective agents that favor improved prey defenses in prey. The prey with better defenses are selective agents that favor more effective predators. This type of coevolutionary arms race started among vertebrate predators and their prey when jawed fishes emerged (Section 26.2).

MODELS FOR PREDATOR–PREY INTERACTIONS

The extent to which predators limit numbers of prey depends on several factors. A key factor is the response of individual predators to increases or decreases in prey density. Figure 46.9*a* is an overview of the three general patterns of functional responses.

By the type I model, a predator removes a constant proportion of prey over time, regardless of levels of prey abundance. The number of prey killed in a given interval depends only on the prey density. This model applies to passive predators, such as web spiders. The more flies there are, the more get caught in webs.

By the type II model, the capacity of predators to consume and digest prey determines how many prey they capture. When prey density rises, the proportion captured rises steeply at first, then slows as predators are exposed to more prey than they can deal with at one time. Figure 46.9*b* offers an example. A wolf that just killed a caribou will not hunt another until it has eaten and digested the first one.

By the type III model, predator response is lowest when prey density is low. It is highest at intermediate prey densities, then levels off. This type of response is observed for predators that can switch to other prey when individuals of a prey species are scarce and hard to find. Predators that can make the type I and type II responses can limit prey at a stable equilibrium point.

Other factors besides individual predator response to prey density are at work. For example, predator and prey reproductive rates affect the interaction. So do hiding places for prey, the presence of other prey or predator species, and carrying capacities.

THE CANADIAN LYNX AND SNOWSHOE HARE

In some cases, shifts in environmental conditions can cause predator and prey densities to oscillate. At the lowest level, predation will strongly depress the prey density. At the highest level, predation is absent and the prey population nears the carrying capacity.

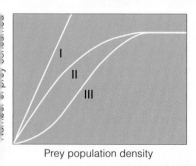

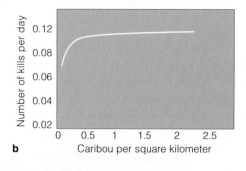

Figure 46.9 *Animated!* (**a**) Three models for responses of predators to prey density. Type I: Prey consumption rises linearly as prey density rises. Type II: Prey consumption is high at first, then levels off as predator bellies stay full. Type III: When prey density is low, it takes longer to hunt prey, so the predator response is low. (**b**) A type II response in nature. For one winter month in Alaska, B. W. Dale and his coworkers observed four wolf packs (*Canis lupus*) feeding on caribou (*Rangifer tarandus*). The interaction fit the type II model for the functional response of predators to the prey density.

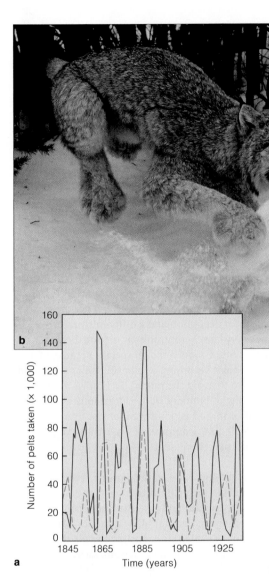

Figure 46.10 (a) Correspondence between abundances of Canadian lynx (*dashed* line) and snowshoe hares (*solid* line), based on counts of pelts sold by trappers to Hudson's Bay Company during a ninety-year period. (b) Charles Krebs observed that predation causes heightened alertness among snowshoe hares, which continually look over their shoulders during the declining phase of each cycle. (c) This photograph supports the Krebs hypothesis that there is a three-level interaction going on, one that involves plants.

The graph may be a good test of whether you tend to accept someone else's conclusions without questioning their basis in science. Remember those sections in Chapter 1 that introduced the nature of scientific methods?

What other factors may have had impact on the cycle? Did the weather vary, with more severe winters imposing greater demand for hares (to keep lynx warmer) and higher death rates? Did the lynx compete with other predators, such as owls? Did the predators turn to alternative prey during low points of the hare cycle? When fur prices rose in Europe, did the trapping increase? When the pelt supply outstripped the demand, did trapping decline?

Consider a ten-year oscillation in populations of a predator, the Canadian lynx, and the snowshoe hare that is its main prey (Figure 46.10). To identify the causes of this pattern, the ecologist Charles Krebs and his coworkers tracked hare population densities for ten years in Alaska, in the Yukon River Valley. They set up 1-square-kilometer control plots and experimental plots. Electric fences kept predatory mammals out of some plots. Extra food or fertilizers that fanned plant growth were placed in other plots. The team captured and released more than a thousand snowshoe hares, lynx, and other animals, giving each a radio collar.

In predator-free plots, the hare density doubled. In plots with extra food, it tripled. In plots having extra food and fewer predators, it increased elevenfold.

The experimental manipulations delayed the cyclic declines in population density but did not stop them.

Why not? Owls and other raptors flew over the fences. Only 9 percent of the collared hares starved to death; predators devoured most of the rest. Krebs concluded that a simple predator–prey or plant–herbivore model cannot fully explain his Yukon River Valley results. For the Canadian lynx and snowshoe hare cycle, other variables are at work, during multilevel interactions.

Predator and prey populations tend to exert coevolutionary pressures on one another.

Predators may affect prey density. There are three general patterns of response to changes in prey density. Population levels of prey may also show periodic oscillations.

Predator and prey numbers often vary in complex ways that reflect the multiple levels of interaction in a community.

46.5 An Evolutionary Arms Race

LINKS TO
SECTIONS 1.6,
18.4, 26.8, 33.1

As explained in the preceding section, predators and prey exert selective pressure on one another. One defends itself and the other must overcome defenses. Such interactions are often evidence of a coevolutionary arms race.

PREY DEFENSES

Camouflage Many heritable traits help an organism hide in the open; they function in **camouflaging**. Body form, patterning, color, behavior, or some combination of these blend with the surroundings and help the organism avoid detection. Consider Figure 46.11. Some nesting birds thrust their beak upward and sway slightly, like the plants around them. A caterpillar with special color patterns passes itself off as a bird dropping. When a certain desert plant (*Lithops*) is not flowering, it looks like a rock. It flowers only during a brief rainy season, when herbivores are more likely to be distracted by the profuse growth of other plants. Section 18.4 explains the genetic basis for camouflage among rock pocket mice as part of an example of natural selection.

Mimicry Many prey species closely resemble a hard-to-catch, dangerous, or unpalatable species. **Mimicry** is the name for an ecological association between one species that is a *model* for deception and a different species—a *mimic*, which very closely resembles it in form, behavior, or both. Predators often avoid a model species because of a repellent taste, toxic secretion, or painful bite or sting, and so they tend also to avoid the mimic. Section 1.6 offers an experimental test of mimicry. Here, Figure 46.12 shows the deceptive look of three tasty but weaponless mimics. All strongly resemble a very aggressive wasp that can sting repeatedly, with painful results.

Chemical Defenses The leaves, flowers, and seeds of many plants contain bitter, hard-to-digest, or dangerous repellents. Peach, apricot, and rose seeds are loaded with cyanide. Remember the Chapter 14 introduction? The castor bean plant did not develop its capacity to make the lethal chemical ricin in an evolutionary vacuum. Ricin protects this plant from herbivores that would otherwise eat it.

Many prey species that taste bad or that make toxins announce their unpalatability with **warning coloration**. They have conspicuous patterns and colors that predators learn to recognize as avoidance signals. For instance, a young, inexperienced bird might eat an orange-and-black patterned monarch butterfly once. It quickly learns to associate the butterfly's coloration and patterning with "Eat me and you will vomit foul-tasting toxins."

Figure 46.11 Prey camouflage. (**a**) What bird??? When a predator approaches its nest, the least bittern stretches its neck (which is colored like the surrounding withered reeds), points its bill upward, and sways like reeds in the wind. (**b**) An inedible bird dropping? No. This caterpillar's body coloration and its capacity to hold its body in a rigid position help camouflage it from predatory birds. (**c**) Find the plants (*Lithops*) hiding in the open from herbivores with the help of their stonelike form, pattern, and coloration.

a A dangerous model   **b** One of its edible mimics   **c** Another edible mimic   **d** And another edible mimic

Figure 46.12 An example of mimicry. Edible insect species often resemble toxic or unpalatable species that are not at all closely related. (**a**) A yellowjacket can deliver a painful sting. It might be the model for nonstinging wasps (**b**), beetles (**c**), and flies (**d**) of strikingly similar appearance.

Truly dangerous or repugnant species often make little or no attempt to conceal themselves. Remember the vividly colored and poisonous frogs (Section 33.1)? Or think about skunks, which spray one of the most odious repellents.

Moment-of-Truth Defenses When luck runs out and an animal is cornered or under attack, survival may turn on a last-chance trick. Many animals try to startle predators. For instance, some hiss, puff up, flash big eye-shaped spots on their body, bare sharp teeth, or flare neck ruffs (Figure 26.17*d*). Opossum and hognose snakes make a big show of pretending to be dead. Many cornered animals, including hognose snakes and certain beetles, secrete or squirt out irritating chemical repellents or toxins (Figure 46.13*a*).

ADAPTIVE RESPONSES OF PREDATORS

Again, predators tend to counter prey defenses with their own adaptations. Stealth, camouflage, and ingenious ways of avoiding repellents are some countermeasures. Consider the edible beetles that direct sprays of noxious chemicals at attackers. A grasshopper mouse grabs the beetle and plunges the sprayer end into the ground, and then chews on the tasty, unprotected head (Figure 46.13*a,b*).

Some prey can outrun even cheetahs when they get a head start. But the cheetah is the world's fastest land animal. One was clocked at 114 kilometers (70 miles) per hour. Compared to other big cats, the cheetah has longer legs relative to its body size and nonretractable claws that act like cleats to increase traction. Thomson's gazelle, its main prey, can run longer but not as fast (80 kilometers per hour). Without a head start, it is toast, so to speak.

Camouflaging helps predators as well as prey. Think of white polar bears stalking seals over ice, striped tigers crouched in tall-stalked, golden grasses, and scorpionfish hidden on the seafloor (Figure 46.13*c*). Camouflage is often stunning among predatory insects (Figure 46.13*d*). With camouflaging, predators select for enhanced sensory systems in prey. By one theory, primate color vision may have evolved in part to enhance detection of predators.

Figure 46.13 Predator responses to prey defenses. (**a**) Some beetles spray noxious chemicals at attackers, which deters them some of the time. (**b**) At other times, grasshopper mice plunge the chemical-spraying tail end of their beetle prey into the ground and feast on the head end. (**c**) Find the scorpionfish, a venomous predator with camouflaging fleshy flaps, multiple colors, and profuse spines. (**d**) Where do the pink flowers end and the pink praying mantis begin?

46.6 Parasite–Host Interactions

LINKS TO
SECTIONS 21.8,
25.5, 25.10, 25.16

Parasites spend all or part of their life cycle in or on other living organisms, from which they draw nutrients. They weaken a host but usually do not kill it outright. Different kinds complete their life cycle in one or more host species.

PARASITES AND PARASITOIDS

Parasites have pervasive impacts on populations. By draining nutrients from hosts, they alter the amount of energy and nutrients the host population demands from a habitat. Also, weakened hosts are usually more vulnerable to predation and less attractive to potential mates. Some parasite infections cause sterility. Others shift the ratio of host males to females. In such ways, parasitic infections lower birth rates, raise death rates, and affect intraspecific and interspecific competition.

Sometimes the gradual drain of nutrients during a parasitic infection indirectly leads to death. The host becomes so weakened that it can't fight off secondary infections. Nevertheless, in evolutionary terms, killing a host too quickly is bad for a parasite's reproductive success. A parasitic infection must last long enough to give the parasite time to produce some offspring. The longer it lives in the host, the more offspring. We may therefore expect selective agents to favor parasites that have less-than-fatal effects on hosts (Section 21.8).

Usually, death occurs only when a parasite attacks a novel host—one with no coevolved defenses against it—or when too many parasitic individuals attack at the same time and collectively overwhelm the body.

You looked at many parasites in the diversity unit, especially in Chapters 21, 24, and 25. You saw how some species require a single host and how others are free-living some of the time or residents of different hosts at different times. Many types ride inside insects and other arthropods, which are vectors between one host organism and the next (Section 25.16).

All viruses and some bacteria, protists, and fungi are parasites. Figure 46.14 shows a young trout that was parasitized by *Myxobolus cerebralis,* a protist.

Even a few plants are parasitic. Nonphotosynthetic types, such as dodders, obtain energy and nutrients from other plants (Figure 46.15). Other types carry out photosynthesis but still tap into the nutrients and water in tissues of a host plant. Mistletoe is like this; its modified roots invade the sapwood of host trees.

Many tapeworms, flukes, and certain roundworms are well-known invertebrate parasites (Figure 46.16). So are ticks, many insects, and many crustaceans.

You already read about **parasitoids**. An immature stage of these insects matures in a different insect's body, which they devour from the inside out. Unlike parasites, parasitoids always kill their hosts directly. About 15 percent of all insects may be parasitoids.

Social parasites are animals that take advantage of the social behavior of a host as a way to complete the life cycle. The cuckoos and North American cowbirds, described shortly, are like this.

Figure 46.14 (a) A young trout with a twisted spine and darkened tail caused by whirling disease, which damages cartilage and nerves. Jaw deformities and whirling movements are other symptoms. (b) Spores of *Myxobolus cerebralis,* the introduced protist that causes the disease. It is now in many lakes and streams in Western and Northeastern states.

Figure 46.15 Dodder (*Cuscuta*), also known as strangleweed or devil's hair. This parasitic flowering plant's sporophytes have no chlorophylls. They wind around a host plant during growth. Modified roots penetrate the host's vascular tissues and absorb water and nutrients from them.

Figure 46.16 Adult roundworms (*Ascaris*), an endoparasite, packed inside the small intestine from a host pig. Sections 25.5 and 25.10 give more examples of parasitic worms.

Figure 46.17 Biological control agent: a commercially raised parasitoid wasp about to deposit an egg in an aphid. This wasp reduces aphid populations. It stops the aphid from laying eggs even before the wasp egg develops into a larva that will eat it.

USES AS BIOLOGICAL CONTROLS

Parasites and parasitoids are commercially raised and released in target areas as *biological controls*. They are promoted as a workable alternative to pesticides. The chapter introduction and Figure 46.17 give examples.

Effective biological controls display five attributes. The agents are adapted to a specific host species and to its habitat; they are good at locating hosts; their population growth rate is high compared to the host's; their offspring are good at dispersing; and they make a type III functional response to prey, without much lag time after shifts occur in the host population size.

Biological control is not without risks of its own. Releasing more than one kind of biological control agent in an area may invite competition among them, which can lower their effectiveness against an intended target. In addition, an introduced parasite sometimes parasitizes nontargeted species as well as—or instead of—the species they were expected to control.

In Hawaii, the introduction of several parasitoids to control an imported stink bug resulted in the decline of the koa bug, the state's largest native bug. Few koa bugs have been collected since 1978. Apparently the koa bugs, which congregate in big groups, were more tempting to parasitoids. Also, introduced parasitoids have been implicated in the ongoing decline of many native Hawaiian butterflies and moths.

Natural selection favors parasitic species that temper their attacks in ways that ensure an adequate supply of hosts.

Parasitic species belong to many groups, including bacteria, protists, invertebrates, and plants. Parasitoids are insects that feed on and kill other insects. Social parasites use the social behavior of another species to their own benefit.

The brown-headed cowbird's genus name (Molothrus) means "intruder" in Latin. This bird intrudes, sneakily, into the life cycle of other species. Let us ask: Why?

Brown-headed cowbirds (*Molothrus ater*) evolved in the Great Plains of North America. They lived as commensalists with bison. Great herds of these hefty ungulates stirred up plenty of insects as they migrated through the grasslands, and, being insect-eaters, the cowbirds wandered around with them (Figure 46.18a).

A vagabond way of life did not lend itself to nesting in any one place. However it happened, cowbirds learned to lay eggs in nests constructed by other species, then leave them and move on with the herds. Many species became "hosts"; they did not have the neural wiring to recognize the differences between cowbird eggs and their own eggs. Concurrently, cowbird hatchlings became innately wired for hostile takeovers. Even before hatchlings open their eyes, they shove the owner's eggs out of the nest and demand to be fed as rightful occupants (Figure 46.18b). Thus, for thousands of years, cowbirds have perpetuated their genes by way of parasitic chutzpah.

When American pioneers moved west, many cleared swaths of woodlands for pastures. Cowbirds now moved in the other direction. They adapted easily to a life with new ungulates—cattle—in the manmade grasslands; hence their name. They started to penetrate adjacent woodlands and exploit novel species. Today, brown-headed cowbirds parasitize at least fifteen species of native North American birds. Some of those birds are threatened or endangered.

Besides being successful opportunists, cowbirds are big-time reproducers. A female can lay an egg a day for ten days, give her ovaries a rest, do the same again, and then again in one season. As many as thirty eggs in thirty nests—that is a lot of cowbirds.

Figure 46.18 Oh give me a home, where the buffalo roam—brown-headed cowbirds (*Molothrus ater*) originally evolved as commensalists with bison and as social parasites of other bird species of the North American Great Plains. When conditions changed, they expanded their range. They became nest usurpers in woodlands as well as grasslands in much of the United States.

46.8 Ecological Succession

LINKS TO
SECTIONS
17.4, 23.11

*By an older model for **ecological succession**, a community comes into being through competition and other species interactions and in time stabilizes into a predictable array of species. However, abiotic forces, including fire, storms, and human-created disturbances, may be more important in shaping community structure.*

SUCCESSIONAL CHANGE

A concept of "nature in balance" once guided studies in community ecology. Researchers knew that **pioneer species** are the start of community structure. These are opportunistic colonizers of new or newly vacated habitats. They have high dispersal rates, they grow and mature quickly, and they produce many offspring. In time, more competitive species replace them. Then the replacements are replaced.

Primary succession is a process that begins when pioneer species colonize a barren habitat, such as a new volcanic island and land exposed when a glacier retreats (Figure 46.19). Pioneers include lichens and plants, such as club mosses, that are small, have short life cycles, and can survive intense sunlight, extreme temperature changes, and nutrient-poor soil. Early on, hardy annual flowering plants put out many small seeds, which are quickly dispersed.

Established pioneers often improve soil and other conditions. In doing so, they typically set the stage for their own replacement. Many of the new arrivals are mutualists with nitrogen-fixing bacteria, so they can grow in nitrogen-poor habitats. Seeds of later species find shelter inside mats of the pioneers, which do not grow high enough to shade out the new seedlings.

Organic wastes and remains accumulate over time, which add volume and nutrients to soil, which favors invasions by other species. Later successional species crowd out earlier ones, whose spores and seeds travel as fugitives on wind and water—destined, perhaps, for another new but temporary habitat.

In **secondary succession**, a disturbed area within a community recovers. If improved soil is still present, secondary succession can be fast. It commonly occurs in abandoned fields, burned forests, and tracts of land cleared by volcanic eruptions.

INTERMEDIATE DISTURBANCE HYPOTHESIS

In a traditional view, a predictable array of species in the habitat stabilizes as the *climax* community, after which not much changes. The community is adapted to many factors, such as topography, climate, soil, and species interactions, and it may show some variation

Figure 46.19 In Alaska's Glacier Bay region, one pathway of primary succession. (**a**) As a glacier retreats from the sea, meltwater leaches minerals from the glacial till. (**b**) Lichens, horsetails, mosses, fireweed, and mountain avens are pioneer species; some are mutualists with nitrogen-fixing microbes. Within twenty years, alder, cottonwood, and willow seedlings take hold. Alders have nitrogen-fixing symbionts. (**c**) Within fifty years, they form dense, mature thickets in which cottonwood, hemlock, and a few evergreen spruce grow fast. (**d**) After eighty years, western hemlock and spruce crowd out mature alders. (**e**) In areas deglaciated for more than a century, forests of Sitka spruce dominate.

Figure 46.20 A natural laboratory for succession after the 1980 Mount Saint Helens eruption (**a**). The community at the base of this Cascade volcano was destroyed. (**b**) In less than a decade, pioneer species took hold. (**c**) Twelve years later, seedlings of the dominant species, Douglas firs, were taking hold.

along gradients of environmental conditions. In this view, even after a disturbance, the community reverts to a climax state. Later, Henry Gleason proposed that most communities are *not* stable, that unpredictable disturbances can alter the direction of succession.

It turned out that the magnitude and frequency of disturbances may be more important than interactions among species in defining the community. According to the **intermediate disturbance hypothesis**, species richness of a community becomes greatest in between disturbances of moderate intensity or frequency. There is enough time for many colonizing species to enter the habitat but not enough time for many species to be competitively excluded from it:

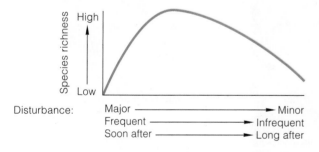

Tolerance, inhibition, and facilitation may be three successional mechanisms. In cases of *tolerance*, an early colonizer has no effect on which species will colonize the habitat after it. In *inhibition*, the early colonizer changes conditions of the habitat in specific ways that bar colonization by later species. In *facilitation*, early colonizers improve conditions for later ones.

Ecologists documented inhibition and facilitation in intertidal zone succession. After Wayne Sousa cleared algae from an intertidal zone in Southern California, different algae moved in. After Teresa Turner removed attached algae from plots in an Oregon intertidal zone, surf grass could not move in, because they use algae as anchoring sites. Experimental studies in old fields, temperate forests, and other land regions where major disturbances have occurred also give evidence of these three mechanisms of succession.

For instance, after Washington state's Mount Saint Helens erupted in 1980, the blast wave, superheated mudslides, and floods obliterated approximately 600 square kilometers of forests (Figure 46.20). Afterward, ecologists moved in to monitor succession first-hand. They observed and recorded in detail natural patterns of colonization. They also manipulated plots inside the blast zone. William Morris and David Wood showed that facilitation and inhibition were factors in plant succession. By adding seeds of certain plant species to some plots and keeping some other plots barren, they demonstrated that early colonizers helped several other species of colonizing plants move in. They also found that earlier colonizers kept some plant species out.

A community develops through a succession of stages, starting with pioneer species that are replaced by others. Biotic (biological) and abiotic (physical and chemical) factors affect community structure.

Disturbances are unpredictable and vary in magnitude and frequency. By an intermediate disturbance hypothesis, species richness is greatest between moderate disturbances.

46.9 Species Interactions and Community Instability

LINKS TO
SECTIONS
17.4, 23.11

*The loss or addition of even one species may destabilize the
number and relative abundances of species in a community.*

As you read earlier, short-term physical disturbances
can knock a community out of equilibrium. Long-term
changes in climate or another environmental variable
also have destabilizing effects. Besides this, a shift in
species interactions also can tip a community out of
its uneasy balance. Remember, resources are sustained
as long as populations do not flirt dangerously with
the carrying capacity. Predators and their prey coexist
as long as neither wins. Competitors have no sense of
fair play. Mutualists are stingy, as when plants make
as little nectar as necessary to attract pollinators and
the pollinators take as much nectar as they can for the
least possible effort.

Whether biotic or abiotic, a disturbance sometimes
causes the number and relative abundances of species
to shift irrevocably. For instance, if some occupants of
the habitat happen to be rare or do not compete well
with the others, they might be driven to extinction.

THE ROLE OF KEYSTONE SPECIES

The uneasy balancing of forces in a community comes
into focus when we observe the effects of a **keystone
species**. Such a species has a disproportionately large
effect on a community relative to its abundance. Robert
Paine was the first to describe the role of a keystone
species after his experiments on the rocky shores of
California's coast. Species in this rocky intertidal zone
survive by clinging to rocks, and access to spaces to
cling to is a limiting factor. Paine set up control plots
with the sea star *Pisaster ochraceus* and its main prey—
chitons, limpets, barnacles, and mussels. He removed
all sea stars from his experimental plots.

Mussels (*Mytilus*) happen to be the prey of choice
for sea stars. In the absence of sea stars, they took over
Paine's experimental plots; they became the strongest
competitors and crowded out seven other species of
invertebrates. In this intertidal zone, predation by sea
stars normally keeps the number of prey species high
because it restricts competitive exclusion by mussels.

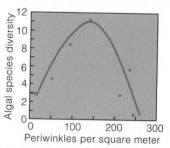

d Algal diversity in tidepools

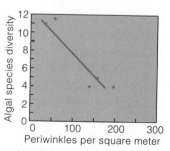

e Algal diversity on rocks that
become exposed at high tide

Figure 46.21 Effect of competition and predation in an intertidal zone. (**a**) Grazing periwinkles
(*Littorina littorea*) affect the number of algal species in different ways in different marine habitats.
(**b**) *Chondrus* and (**c**) *Enteromorpha*, two kinds of algae in their natural habitats. (**d**) By grazing
on the dominant alga in tidepools (*Enteromorpha*), the periwinkles promote the survival of less
competitive algal species that would otherwise be overgrown. (**e**) *Enteromorpha* doesn't grow
on rocks. Here, *Chondrus* is dominant. Periwinkles find *Chondrus* tough and dine instead on less
competitive algal species. By doing so, periwinkles decrease the algal diversity on the rocks.

Table 46.1	Adverse Effects of Some Species Introduced Into the United States		
Species Introduced	Origin	Mode of Introduction	Outcome
Water hyacinth	South America	Intentionally introduced (1884)	Clogged waterways; other plants shaded out
Dutch elm disease:			
Ophiostoma ulmi (fungus)	Asia (by way	Accidental; on infected elm timber (1930)	Millions of mature elms destroyed
Bark beetle (vector)	of Europe)	Accidental; on unbarked elm timber (1909)	
Chestnut blight fungus	Asia	Accidental; on nursery plants (1900)	Nearly all eastern American chestnuts killed
Zebra mussel	Russia	Accidental; in ballast water of ship (1985)	Clog pipes and water intake valves of power plants; displacing native Great Lake bivalves
Japanese beetle	Japan	Accidental; on irises or azaleas (1911)	Close to 300 plant species (e.g., citrus) defoliated
Sea lamprey	North Atlantic	Ship hulls, through canals (1860s, 1921)	Trout, other fish species destroyed in Great Lakes
European starling	Europe	Intentional release, New York City (1890)	Outcompete native cavity-nesting birds; crop damage; swine disease vector
Nutria	South America	Accidental release of captive animals being raised for fur (1930)	Crop damage, destruction of levees, overgrazing of marsh habitat

Remove all the sea stars, and the community shrinks from fifteen species to eight.

The impact of a keystone species can vary between habitats that differ in their species arrays. Periwinkles (*Littorina littorea*) are alga-eating snails of intertidal zones. Jane Lubchenco showed that their removal can increase *or* decrease the diversity of algal species in different habitats (Figure 46.21).

In tidepools, the periwinkles prefer to eat the alga *Enteromorpha*, which can outgrow other algal species. By keeping *Enteromorpha* in check, periwinkles help less competitive algal species survive. However, on exposed rocks in the lower intertidal zone, they avoid *Chondrus* and other tough, unpalatable red algae that persist as the dominant species. Periwinkles on these rocks graze on competitively weaker algal species. In short, they help *maintain* the number of algal species in tidepools but *reduce* it on exposed rock surfaces.

HOW SPECIES INTRODUCTIONS TIP THE BALANCE

Instabilities also are set in motion when residents of established communities move out from their home range and successfully take up residence elsewhere. This type of directional movement, called **geographic dispersal**, happens in three ways.

First, over a number of generations, a population might expand its home range by slowly moving into outlying regions that prove hospitable. Second, some individuals might be rapidly transported across great distances, an event called *jump* dispersal. This often takes individuals across regions where they could not survive on their own, as when insects travel from the mainland to Maui in a ship's cargo hold. Third, some population might be moved away from a home range by continental drift, at an almost imperceptibly slow pace over long spans of time.

Successful dispersal and colonization of a vacant adaptive zone can be remarkably rapid. Consider one of Amy Schoener's experiments in the Bahamas. She set out plastic sponges on barren sand at the bottom of Bimini Lagoon. How fast did aquatic species take up residence on or in the artificial habitats? Schoener recorded occupancy by 220 species within thirty days.

When you hear someone bubbling enthusiastically about an exotic species, you can safely bet the speaker isn't an ecologist. An **exotic species** is a resident of an established community that dispersed from its home range and became established elsewhere. Unlike most imports, which never do take hold outside the home range, an exotic species permanently insinuates itself into a new community.

Following jump dispersal, more than 4,500 exotic species have become established in the United States. We put some of the new arrivals, including soybeans, rice, wheat, corn, and potatoes, to use as food crops.

Accidental imports also alter community structure. You learned about imported fire ants in the chapter introduction. Table 46.1 lists others, and the section to follow describes the unintended impact of a few more.

A keystone species is one that has a major effect on species richness and relative abundances in particular habitats.

Species introductions and other biotic disturbances can permanently alter community structure.

46.10 Exotic Invaders

LINKS TO
SECTIONS
17.4, 23.11

Nonnative species are on the loose in communities on every continent. They can alter habitats; they often outcompete and displace native species.

THE ALGA TRIUMPHANT

They looked so perfect in saltwater aquariums, those long, green, feathery branches of *Caulerpa taxifolia*. So Stuttgart Aquarium researchers in Germany developed a hybrid, sterile strain of this green alga and magnanimously shared it with other marine institutions. Was it from Monaco's Oceanographic Museum that the hybrid strain escaped into the wild? Some say yes, Monaco says no.

The aquarium strain grows asexually by runners, just a few centimeters a day, but boat propellers and fishing nets dispersed it. Between 1984 and 2000, this alga blanketed over 30,000 hectares of seafloor near the Mediterranean coast (Figure 46.22a). Scuba divers found it growing off the Southern California coast. Someone might have drained water from a home aquarium into a storm drain or into the lagoon itself. Governmental and private groups sprang into action. They tarped over the area to shut out sunlight, pumped chlorine into the mud to poison the alga, and used welders to boil it. So far, eradication and surveillance programs have worked, but they have cost more than 3.4 million dollars.

It is now illegal to import the harmful strain into the United States. Interstate sale also is prohibited. Some still slip into the country because the aquarium industry has successfully lobbied against a ban on all *Caulerpa* species,

and it is difficult to distinguish the invasive strain without genetic analysis.

Just how bad is it? The aquarium strain of *C. taxifolia* thrives on sandy or rocky shores and in mud. It can live ten days after being discarded in meadows. Unlike its tropical parents, it survives in cool water and polluted water. It also displaces endemic algae. Its toxin poisons invertebrates and fishes, including herbivorous types that might keep it in check. It has the potential to overgrow reefs and destroy marine food webs. Can you sense why this algal strain has been nominated as one of the 100 worst exotic invaders?

THE PLANTS THAT ATE GEORGIA

One more of the infamous 100: In 1876, kudzu (*Pueraria montana*) from Japan was introduced to the United States. In its native habitat—temperate regions of Asia—this vine is a well-behaved legume with a strong root system. It *seemed* like a good idea to use it for forage and to control erosion. But kudzu grew faster in the Southeast, where herbivores, pathogens, and less competitive plants posed no serious threat to it.

With nothing to stop it, kudzu shoots grow sixty meters per year. Its vines now blanket streambanks, trees, telephone poles, houses, and almost everything else in their path (Figure 46.22b). It withstands burning, and its deep roots resist being dug up. Grazing goats and herbicides help. But goats eat most other plants along with it, and herbicides taint water supplies. Kudzu invasions now stretch from Connecticut down to Florida and are reported in Arkansas. It has crossed

Figure 46.22 (a) Aquarium strain of *Caulerpa taxifolia* suffocating yet another richly diverse marine ecosystem.

(b) Kudzu (*Pueraria montana*) taking over part of Lyman, South Carolina. This vine has become invasive in many states from coast to coast. Ruth Duncan of Alabama, who makes 200 kudzu vine baskets a year, just can't keep up.

Figure 46.23 Rabbit-proof fence? Not quite. This is part of a fence built to hold back the 200 million to 300 million rabbits that are wreaking havoc with the vegetation in Australia. It didn't work.

the Mississippi River into Texas, and thanks to jump dispersal, it is now an invasive species in Oregon.

On the bright side, Asians use a starch extracted from kudzu in drinks, herbal medicines, and candy. A kudzu processing plant in Alabama may export this starch to Asia, where the demand currently exceeds the supply. Also, kudzu may help save trees; it can be an alternative source for paper. Today, about 90 percent of Asian wallpaper is kudzu-based.

THE RABBITS THAT ATE AUSTRALIA

During the 1800s, British settlers in Australia just couldn't bond with koalas and kangaroos, and so they imported familiar animals from home. In 1859, in what would be the start of a major disaster, a landowner in northern Australia imported and then released two dozen European rabbits (*Oryctolagus cuniculus*). Good food and sport hunting—that was the idea. An ideal rabbit habitat with no natural predators—that was the reality.

Six years later, the landowner had killed 20,000 rabbits and was besieged by 20,000 more. The rabbits displaced livestock and caused the decline of native wildlife. Now 200 to 300 million are hippity-hopping through the southern half of the country. They graze on grasses in good times and strip bark from shrubs and trees during droughts. Thumping hordes turn shrublands as well as grasslands into eroded deserts. Their burrows undermine the soil and set the stage for widespread erosion.

Rabbit warrens have been shot at, fumigated, plowed under, and dynamited. The first all-out assaults killed 70 percent of them, but the rabbits rebounded in less than a year. When a fence 2,000 miles long was built to protect western Australia, rabbits made it from one side to the other before workers could finish the job (Figure 46.23).

In 1951, the government introduced a myxoma virus that normally infects South American rabbits. The virus causes *myxomatosis*. This disease has mild effects on its coevolved host but nearly always kills *O. cuniculus*. Mosquitoes and fleas transmit the virus to new host. Having no coevolved defenses against the import, European rabbits died in droves. But natural selection has since favored a rise in rabbit populations resistant to the imported virus.

In 1991, on an uninhabited island in Australia's Spencer Gulf, researchers released rabbits that were injected with a calicivirus. The rabbits died from blood clots in their lungs, heart, and kidneys. The test virus escaped from the island in 1995, perhaps on insect vectors.

By 2001, the rabbit population sizes were staying 80 to 85 percent below their peak values. Grasses, nonwoody shrubs, and woody shrubs are rebounding. Different kinds of herbivores are increasing in density.

The rabbit calicivirus was discovered in China in 1984 and is now found in Europe and other countries as well. To date, tests on more than forty animal species indicate that it replicates in rabbits alone. However, other caliciviruses can and do cross species barriers. The jury is still out on the long-term impact of the viral releases.

As you might have deduced, *O. cuniculus* is another one of the 100 worst exotic invaders. Also on the list are two *Anopheles* species, the vectors for malaria. So is the cane toad (*Bufo marinus*). It was introduced as a biological control of pests in fields of sugarcane and other crops all over the world, but it eats almost everything. Despite its catchy name, the banana bunchy top virus is another one of the worst. So is the house cat (*Felis catus*) turned feral. Finally, the house mouse (*Mus musculus*) probably has a greater distribution than any other mammal except humans. Populations of this prolific breeder destroy crops and consume or contaminate much of our food supplies. They are implicated in the extinction of many species. Interested in learning more? Go to http://www.issg.org/ for some eye-openers.

46.11 Biogeographic Patterns in Community Structure

LINKS TO
SECTIONS 17.1,
17.3, 18.7, 26.15,
45.3, CHAPTER 27

The richness and relative abundances of species differ from one habitat or one world province to another. Often these differences correspond to predictable patterns that have biogeographic and historical foundations.

Unit IV gave you a sense of the sweep of biodiversity, and Chapter 27 placed it in evolutionary perspective. Starting with Alfred Wallace and other naturalists of the 1800s, it became apparent that communities show *patterns* in biodiversity, as measured by the richness and relative abundances of species. Certain patterns follow environmental gradients in sunlight intensity, temperature, rainfall, and other factors that differ by latitude, elevation, and depth. Other patterns have their roots in the history of a habitat and its species, which vary in their resource requirements, physiology, capacity for dispersal, and the specific ways in which they interact with one another.

MAINLAND AND MARINE PATTERNS

Perhaps the most striking pattern of species richness corresponds with distance from the equator. *For most groups of plants and animals, the number of coexisting species on land and in the seas is greatest in the tropics, and it systematically declines from the equator to the poles.* Figure 46.24 shows two clear examples of this pattern. Consider just a few factors that help bring about such a pattern and maintain it.

First, for reasons explained in Section 46.1, tropical latitudes intercept more intense sunlight and receive more rainfall, and their growing season is longer. As one outcome, resource availability tends to be greater and more reliable in the tropics than elsewhere. This favors a degree of specialized interrelationships not possible where species are active for shorter periods.

Second, tropical communities have been evolving for a longer time than temperate ones, some of which did not start forming until the end of the last ice age.

Third, species richness may be self-reinforcing. The number of species of trees in tropical forests is much greater than in comparable forests at higher latitudes. When more plant species compete and coexist, so will more species of herbivores, partly because no single herbivore species can overcome all chemical defenses of all plants. Also, more predatory and parasitic species evolve in response to more kinds of prey and hosts. The same effect applies to the number of species on tropical reefs.

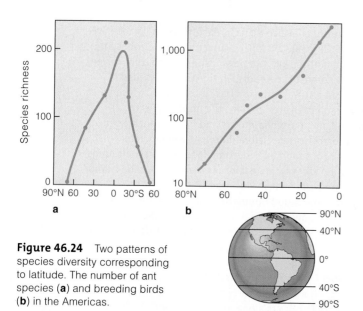

Figure 46.24 Two patterns of species diversity corresponding to latitude. The number of ant species (**a**) and breeding birds (**b**) in the Americas.

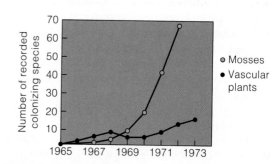

Figure 46.25 Surtsey, a volcanic island, at the time of its formation. Newly formed, isolated islands are natural laboratories for ecologists. The chart gives the number of colonizing species between 1965 and 1973.

Species richness (number of species)
1,000
500
100
50
10
5

Area (square kilometers)
5 10 50 100 500 1,000 5,000 10,000 50,000 100,000 500,000 1,000,000

islands less than 300 kilometers from source

islands more than 300 kilometers from source

a

b

ISLAND PATTERNS

As you saw in Chapter 45, islands are laboratories for population studies. They also have been laboratories for community studies. For instance, a 1965 volcanic eruption quickly formed Surtsey, an island southwest of Iceland. Within six months, bacteria, fungi, seeds, flies, and seabirds were established on it. A vascular plant appeared two years after the island formed; the first mosses came along two years after that (Figure 46.25). As the island soil became enriched, more and more plant species began to take hold.

As is the case for other islands, the number of new species on Surtsey will not increase indefinitely. Why not? Models based on studies of island communities around the world suggest some answers.

First, larger islands tend to support more species than smaller ones the same distance from a colonizing source. This is the **area effect** (Figure 46.26a). Larger islands generally have more varied habitats, and more of them. Most have complex topography and higher elevations. Such variations promote species richness. Also, being bigger, the larger islands intercept more of the accidental tourists that winds and ocean currents move from the mainland but offer no way back.

Second, islands that are far away from a source of potential colonists receive fewer colonizing species. The few that do arrive naturally are adapted for long-distance dispersal (Figure 46.26a). This is the **distance effect**. Remember the nature of individual extinctions (Section 27.1)? Extinctions are more prevalent on the small islands. Because immigration rates are low and extinction rates are high, small islands support fewer species once the balance is struck. Island populations are far more vulnerable to famine, storms, droughts, disease and genetic drift. Remember the account of St. Matthew Island that opened Chapter 45?

Figure 46.26 (**a**) Two island biodiversity patterns. Distance effect: Species richness on islands of a specified size declines with increasing distance from a source of colonizing species. *Green* circles signify islands less than 300 kilometers from the colonizing source. *Orange* triangles signify islands more than 300 kilometers from the source areas. Area effect: Among islands the same distance from a source of colonizing species, the larger ones support more species.

(**b**) Wandering albatross, one travel agent for jump dispersals. Seabirds that island-hop long distances often have seeds stuck to their feathers. Seeds that successfully germinate in a new island community may give rise to a population of new immigrants.

One more island pattern: Remember the miniature *Homo* species that was discovered on the Indonesian island Flores (Section 26.15)? There is a trend, among new arrivals, for the big to get smaller and the small to get bigger. They adapt to fewer or different resources than in the place left behind. Biogeographers know more about patterns of diversity and the disruptions of them. If you wish to learn more, David Quammen's *Song of the Dodo* is a good place to start.

Species richness shows global patterns, as when it correlates with environmental gradients in latitude, elevation, and depth. Microenvironments along these gradients often introduce variations in the overall patterns.

Species richness in a given area also is an outcome of the evolutionary history of each species, its requirements for resources, its physiology, its capacity for dispersal, and its rates of birth, death, immigration, and emigration.

Generally, species richness is highest in the tropics and lowest at the poles. The number of species on an island also depends on its size and distance from a colonizing source.

Summary

Section 46.1 A habitat is the type of place where individuals of a species normally live. A community is an association of all populations of species that occupy a habitat. Each species in a community has a niche, the sum of all of the activities and relationships in which its individuals engage as they secure and use the resources required for their survival and reproduction.

Community structure arises from a habitat's physical and chemical features, resource availability over time, adaptive traits of its species, how its species interact, and the history of the habitat and its occupants.

Direct symbiotic interactions help shape community structure. They include commensalism, mutualism, competition, predation, and parasitism.

Section 46.2 Mutualism is a species interaction that benefits both participants. Some mutualists cannot complete their life cycle without the interaction.

Section 46.3 By the competitive exclusion theory, when two (or more) species require identical resources, they cannot coexist indefinitely. Species may coexist when they differ in their use of a resource, share it in different ways, or share it at different times.

Biology⊗Now
Learn about competitive interactions with the animation on BiologyNow.

Sections 46.4, 46.5 Predators and prey exert selection pressure on each other. Densities of predator and prey populations often oscillate. The carrying capacity, density dependencies, refuges, predator efficiency, and often alternative prey sources affect the cycles. Threat displays, chemical weapons, camouflage, stealth, and mimicry may be outcomes of coevolution between predators and their prey.

Biology⊗Now
Compare the three alternative models for predator responses to prey density with the animation on BiologyNow.

Read the InfoTrac article "How the Pufferfish Got Its Puff," Carl Zimmer, Discover, September 1997.

Sections 46.6, 46.7 Parasites live in or on other living hosts and withdraw nutrients from host tissues for part of their life cycle. Hosts may or may not die as a result. Parasitoids kill their hosts, and social parasites take over some aspect of a host's life cycle.

Section 46.8 By a model for ecological succession, a community develops in predictable sequence, from its pioneer species to a climax community—a stable, self-perpetuating array of species that are in equilibrium with one another and the environment. However, abiotic and biotic disturbances have destabilizing effects. They are unpredictable and vary in magnitude and frequency. By an intermediate disturbance hypothesis, species richness is greatest between moderate disturbances.

Sections 46.9, 46.10 Community structure reflects an uneasy balance between biotic as well as abiotic forces, including predation and competition, that can shift over time. Species introductions can change the structure.

Section 46.11 Many studies of mainland and island communities reveal global patterns in species richness.

Biology⊗Now
Learn about the area effect and distance effect with the interaction on BiologyNow.

Read the InfoTrac article "Island Biogeography's Lasting Impact," Fred Powledge, Bioscience, November 2003.

Self-Quiz   *Answers in Appendix II*

1. A habitat _____ .
   a. has distinguishing physical and chemical features
   b. is where individuals of a species normally live
   c. is occupied by various species
   d. all of the above

2. A niche is _____ .
   a. the sum of activities and relationships by which individuals of a species secure and use resources
   b. unvarying for a given species
   c. something that shifts in large and small ways
   d. both a and c

3. Two species may coexist indefinitely in some habitat when they _____ .
   a. differ in their use of resources
   b. share the same resource in different ways
   c. use the same resource at different times
   d. all of the above

4. A predator population and prey population _____ .
   a. always coexist at relatively stable levels
   b. may undergo cyclic or irregular changes in density
   c. cannot coexist indefinitely in the same habitat
   d. both b and c

5. Parasites _____ .
   a. weaken their hosts   c. feed on host tissues
   b. can kill novel hosts   d. all of the above

6. By a currently favored hypothesis, species richness of a community is greatest between physical disturbances of _____ intensity or frequency.
   a. low   b. intermediate   c. high   d. variable

7. Match the terms with the most suitable descriptions.
   ____ geographic   a. opportunistic colonizer of
         dispersal   barren or disturbed habitat
   ____ area effect   b. greatly affects other species
   ____ pioneer   c. individuals leave home range,
         species   become established elsewhere
   ____ climax   d. more species on large islands
         community   than small ones at same distance
   ____ keystone   from the source of colonists
         species   e. array of species at the end of
   ____ exotic   successional stages in a habitat
         species   f. allows competitors to coexist
   ____ resource   g. often outcompete, displace native
         partitioning   species of established community

Additional questions are available on **Biology⊗Now™**

Figure 46.27 Phasmids. (**a**) South African stick insect. (**b**) Leaf insect from Java. (**c**) Phasmid eggs often look like seeds.

Figure 46.28 One of the nominations for the worst 100 invaders: water hyacinths (*Eichhornia crassipes*) choking a Florida waterway.

Critical Thinking

1. With antibiotic resistance rising, researchers are looking for ways to reduce use of antibiotics. Cattle were once fed antibiotic-laced food but now get *probiotic feeds* that contain cultured bacteria that can establish or bolster populations of helpful bacteria in the animal's gut. The idea is that if a large population of beneficial bacteria is in place, then the harmful bacteria cannot become established or thrive. Which ecological theory is guiding this research?

2. Most phasmids resemble sticks or leaves (Figure 46.27). All are herbivorous insects. Most are motionless in the day, and move and feed only at night. If disturbed, a phasmid will fall to the ground, as if dead. Speculate on the selective pressures that may have shaped phasmid morphology and behavior. Suggest an experiment with one species to test whether its appearance and behavior may be adaptive.

3. The water hyacinth (*Eichhornia crassipes*) is an aquatic plant native to South America. Today, this plant lives in nutrient-rich waters from Florida to San Francisco. It has displaced many native species, and choked rivers and canals (Figure 46.28). Research and write a brief account of how it got from one continent to another.

4. Answering this question well should earn you big points. Long ago, Alfred Wallace puzzled over an odd pattern in the distribution of organisms in the islands of Indonesia. Deep water separates Bali and Lombok and, farther north, the larger islands of Borneo and Sulawesi (Figure 46.29). Most major groups on the Asian mainland had representative species on Borneo and Bali—but few or none on Lombok and Sulawesi. The boundary he had identified came to be called *Wallace's Line*, and his explanation for it is still valid.

In Wallace's time, geologists had already discovered evidence of past ice ages, when much of the ocean's waters became locked up in vast ice sheets. Wallace's line marks the boundary of the Asian continent when the sea level fell 75 fathoms (450 feet). All of the shallow seas and straits from the Asian mainland to Borneo and Bali became dry land. Wallace inferred that many species dispersed to the east. When the sea level rose again, they became cut off from the mainland. Some survived; others vanished.

Even during the ice ages, Lombok and Sulawesi never were connected to the Asian mainland. If a plant or animal could not fly, swim, or be blown or rafted across an expanse of deep water, then they never got across Wallace's line. An expanse of deep water also separates Lombok and Sulawesi from Australia and Papua New Guinea.

Sulawesi is famous for its remarkably high percentage of endemic bird species. About one-third are endemic or close to it. By comparison, Borneo is home to relatively few endemic species of birds. Section 19.2 presents a model for speciation on island archipelagos. Review this section, and then formulate a hypothesis to explain why there are more endemic bird species on Sulawesi than on Borneo.

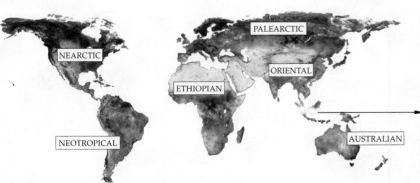

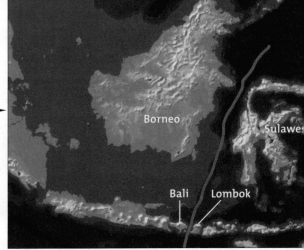

Figure 46.29 Wallace's Line (*red*), which helped nineteenth-century naturalists mark a boundary between two biogeographic realms (Oriental and Australian). The other realms shown were identified later. They have since become subdivided into biomes and then into ecoregions, which include the water provinces.

Bye-Bye, Blue Bayou

Each Labor Day, the coastal Louisiana town of Morgan City celebrates the region's economic mainstays with the Louisiana Shrimp and Petroleum Festival. The state is the nation's third-largest petroleum producer and the leader in shrimp harvesting. But the petroleum industry's success may be contributing indirectly to the possible disappearance of the state's fisheries.

The global air temperature is rising, and fossil fuel burning is a contributing factor. Warmer air heats water near the sea surface, heated water expands, and so the sea level is rising. Warmer air also is melting ancient glaciers and ice caps, and meltwater is adding to the sea volume.

Since the 1940s, Louisiana has lost an area the size of Rhode Island to the sea. Low elevations along the United States coastline—including *14,720,000 acres* next to the Gulf of Mexico and Atlantic Ocean—may be one to three feet under water within fifty years.

Given that it has more than 40 percent of the nation's saltwater marshes, Louisiana has the most to lose (Figure 47.1). Its wetlands are already sinking, because extensive dams and levees interfere with the deposition of sediments that could replace those washed out to sea. In time, a rise in sea level will make 70 percent of the nation's wetlands *really* wet, with no land at all.

Are ecological and economic disasters now unfolding? What will happen to the livelihoods of people who harvest more than 3 billion dollars' worth of shellfish and fish from Louisiana's wetlands each year? What will happen to the more than 5 million birds—about 40 percent of North America's migratory ducks—that overwinter here? What will happen to villages, cities, and natural ecosystems at the low inland elevations, which Louisiana's wetlands buffer from storm surges and hurricanes?

More bad news: Warmer water may promote algal blooms and huge fish kills. Also, populations of many pathogenic bacteria increase in warmer water, so more people might get sick after swimming in contaminated water or eating contaminated shellfish.

Inland, heat waves and wildfires will become more intense. Deaths related to heat stroke will climb. Warmer temperatures will permit mosquitoes to extend their inland ranges. Some mosquitoes are vectors for agents of malaria, West Nile virus, and other diseases.

For some time, researchers have been predicting that global warming will raise evaporation rates, alter weather patterns, and cause prolonged drought for some regions and severe flooding for others, including Louisiana. They worry that 3 billion people may run out of fresh drinking

Figure 47.1
Cypress swamp in Louisiana. Inland saltwater intrusions threatening these trees, which are actually adapted to freshwater habitats. *Facing page*, Dawn on the bayou.

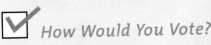
Watch the video online!

water within twelve years. Reflect on Katrina, the category 5 hurricane that made a direct hit on Gulf Coast lowlands in 2005. Reflect on the devastation, flooding, contaminated freshwater sources, displaced populations, and impact on the nation's economy. Are predictions becoming reality?

This chapter can get you thinking about energy flow through ecosystems, starting with energy inputs from the sun. It will show how ecosystems depend on inputs, cycling, and outputs of nutrients—and how nutrients are cycled on a global scale.

The chapter also can get you thinking more about a related concept of equal importance. We have become players in the global flows of energy and nutrients even before we fully comprehend how the game plans work. Decisions we make today about global warming and other environmental issues may affect the quality of human life and the environment far into the future.

How Would You Vote?

Emissions from motor vehicles are a major source of greenhouse gases. Many people buy large vehicles that use more fuel but are viewed as safer and more useful. Should such vehicles be additionally taxed to discourage sales and offset their environmental costs? Can we expect better fuels as well as more of the fuel-efficient, larger vehicles that are becoming available? See BiologyNow for details, then vote online.

Key Concepts

ORGANIZATION OF ECOSYSTEMS

An ecosystem is a community and its physical environment. It is maintained by a one-way flow of energy and a cycling of materials through its interacting participants. It is an open system, with inputs, internal transfers, and outputs of both energy and nutrients. Section 47.1

FOOD WEBS

Food chains are linear sequences of feeding relationships, from producers through consumers, decomposers, and detritivores. The chains cross-connect, as food webs.

Most of the energy that enters a food web returns to the environment, mainly as metabolic heat. Most of the nutrients are cycled, but some are lost to the environment.

Biological magnification is the increasing concentration of a substance in the tissues of organisms as it moves up food chains. Sections 47.2, 47.3

PRIMARY PRODUCTIVITY

An ecosystem's primary productivity is the rate at which its producers capture and store energy in their tissues during a given interval. The amount stored depends on the number of producers and on the balance between photosynthesis and aerobic respiration. Section 47.4

CYCLING OF WATER AND NUTRIENTS

Primary productivity is influenced by the availability of water, carbon, nitrogen, phosphorus, and other substances, the ions or molecules of which move slowly from environmental reservoirs, among organisms of food webs, then back to the reservoirs. Human activities intervene in these cycles in measurable ways. Sections 47.5–47.12

Links to Earlier Concepts

This chapter takes a closer look at the main participants in ecosystems, especially the autotrophs (Sections 1.2, 7.8). It builds on your understanding of how the one-way flow of energy in nature shapes the organization of life (6.1, 6.2). You will place nitrogen-fixing microbes as well as soil erosion and leaching in the context of a global nitrogen cycle (30.1, 30.2). You will revisit pesticides (32.2), algal blooms (22.6), and methane hydrates (Chapter 3 introduction). You will come across more effects of deforestation (23.10).

47.1 The Nature of Ecosystems

LINKS TO
SECTIONS
1.2, 6.1, 7.8, 46.1

In the preceding chapter, you focused on the dynamic nature of community structure. Turn now to the ways in which the energy and raw materials available in the physical environment help organize the interactions among species in that community. By identifying these interactions, ecologists can make predictions about whether they will remain stable and how they might change over the long term.

OVERVIEW OF THE PARTICIPANTS

Diverse natural systems abound on Earth's surface. In climate, landforms, soil, vegetation, animal life, and other features, deserts differ from hardwood forests, which differ from tundra and the prairies. Reefs differ from the open ocean, which differs from streams and lakes. *Even so, despite their differences, all of the systems are alike in many aspects of their structure and function.*

These systems run on energy that autotrophs—the self-feeders—capture. The most familiar autotrophs, remember, are plants and phytoplankton (Sections 7.8 and 22.6). As you know, both convert energy from the sun to chemical bond energy and use it to synthesize organic compounds from simple inorganic materials. These photoautotrophs are the **primary producers** for the system (Figure 47.2).

All other organisms in the system are **consumers**. They are different kinds of heterotrophs that feed on the tissues, products, and remains of other organisms. We may describe consumers by their diets. *Herbivores* eat plants. *Carnivores* eat flesh. *Parasites* live in or on a host and feed on its tissues. Earthworms, crabs, and other **detritivores** eat particles of decomposing organic matter (detritus), such as decaying bits of fallen leaves. **Decomposers** break down organic remains and wastes of all organisms. Hundreds of thousands of species of bacteria, protists, and fungi are decomposers.

Bear in mind, we cannot place some consumers in simple categories. Different kinds are *omnivores*, which may feed on animals, plants, fungi, protists, and even bacteria. A red fox is an example (Figure 47.3). It also scavenges when the opportunity presents itself. In the natural world, a full-time *scavenger* is a type of animal that feeds on the flesh of dead and decaying animals. Vultures are full-time scavengers. Hyenas hunt to kill but, like foxes, are opportunistic scavengers.

How does a system cycle nutrients? First, primary producers get hydrogen, oxygen, and carbon atoms from water and carbon dioxide in their environment. They also take up minerals, such as phosphorus and nitrogen. These are materials for biosynthesis. Later on, decomposition of organic wastes and remains releases

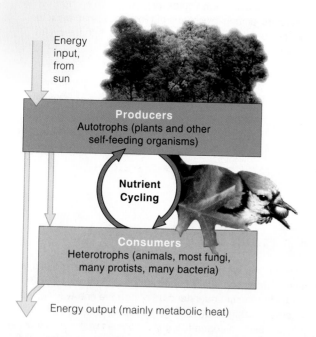

Figure 47.2 *Animated!* Model for ecosystems. Energy flows one way: into an ecosystem and out from it. Nutrients are cycled among autotrophs and heterotrophs. In nearly all ecosystems, energy flow starts with autotrophs that capture energy from the sun.

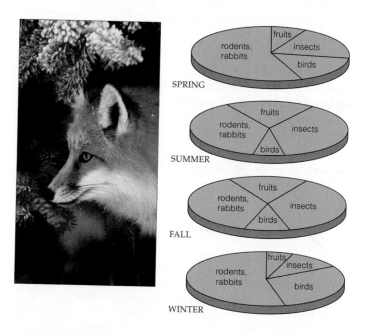

Figure 47.3 Red fox, an omnivore. Its diet shifts with seasonal changes in available food. Rodents, rabbits, and some birds make up the bulk of its diet in spring and winter. It eats more fruits and insects in the summer and fall.

nutrients back into the environment. Unless released substances move out of the system, as when mineral ions become dissolved in a stream that flows from a meadow, producers usually take them up again.

What we have just outlined is the **ecosystem**. We define each ecosystem as an array of organisms and their physical environment, all interacting through a one-way flow of energy and a cycling of the materials required to sustain life. It is an open system, in that it cannot sustain itself.

Energy inputs to most ecosystems are in the form of sunlight. There may be *nutrient inputs*, as from a creek delivering dissolved minerals to a lake. There are also *energy outputs* and *nutrient outputs*.

Energy transfers, remember, cannot be 100 percent efficient (Section 6.1). Over time, the energy originally harnessed by producers escapes to the environment, mainly as metabolically generated heat.

STRUCTURE OF ECOSYSTEMS

We can classify all organisms of an ecosystem by their functional roles in a hierarchy of feeding relationships called **trophic levels** (*troph*, nourishment). "Who eats whom?" we might ask. If organism B eats organism A, energy is transferred from A to B. All organisms at a given trophic level are the same number of transfer steps away from the energy input into an ecosystem.

As one example, think about some organisms of a tallgrass prairie ecosystem. The flowering plants and other producers that tap energy from the sun are at the first trophic level. Plants are eaten by herbivores, such as cutworms, which are at the next trophic level. Cutworms are one of the primary consumers that are eaten by carnivores at the third trophic level, and so on up through tiers of trophic levels.

At each trophic level, organisms interact with the same sets of predators, prey, or both. Omnivores feed at several levels, so we would partition them among different levels or assign them to a level of their own.

A **food chain** is a straight-line sequence of steps by which energy originally stored in autotroph tissues moves to higher trophic levels. In one tallgrass prairie food chain, for instance, energy from a plant flows to a cutworm that eats its juicy parts and on to a garter snake that eats the cutworm, to a crow that eats snake eggs and hatchlings, and finally to a marsh hawk that eats crow eggs and hatchlings (Figure 47.4).

Identifying a food chain is a simple way to start thinking about who eats whom in ecosystems. Bear in mind, many different species are usually competing for food in complex ways. Tallgrass prairie producers

Figure 47.4 *Animated!* Example of a simple food chain and its corresponding trophic levels in a tallgrass prairie.

fifth trophic level
top carnivore
(fourth-level consumer)

fourth trophic level
carnivore
(third-level consumer)

third trophic level
carnivore
(second-level consumer)

second trophic level
herbivore
(primary consumer)

first trophic level
autotroph
(primary producer)

marsh hawk

crow

garter snake

cutworm

flowering plant

(mainly flowering plants) feed grazing mammals and herbivorous insects. But many more species interact in the tallgrass prairie and nearly all other ecosystems, particularly at the lower trophic levels. A number of food chains *cross-connect* with one another—as **food webs**—and that is the topic of the next section.

An ecosystem is a community of organisms that interconnect with one another and with their physical environment by a one-way energy flow and a cycling of materials.

Autotrophs tap into an environmental energy source and make their own organic compounds from inorganic raw materials. They are the ecosystem's primary producers.

Autotrophs are at the first trophic level of a food chain, a straight-line sequence of feeding relationships that proceeds through one or more levels of heterotrophs, or consumers.

In ecosystems, food chains cross-connect, as food webs.

47.2 The Nature of Food Webs

LINKS TO
SECTIONS
6.1, 6.2

Food chains cross-connect with one another in food webs. By untangling the chains of many food webs, ecologists discovered patterns of organization. Those patterns reflect environmental constraints and the inefficiency of energy transfers from one trophic level to the next.

Recall, from Section 6.1, that energy concentrated in one place tends to spread out, or disperse, on its own. The collective strength of chemical bonds resists this spontaneous direction of energy flow. Every organism in an ecosystem must tap into a concentrated energy source and use it to build complex molecules even as they continually lose energy, as metabolic heat.

Plants capture energy that is concentrated in rays from the sun. They use some of it to drive metabolism, store about half of it in new plant tissues, and lose the rest as heat. Consumers tap into energy that became stored in plant tissues, remains, and wastes. They too, lose metabolic heat. *Taken together, all of the heat losses represent a one-way flow of energy out of the ecosystem.*

HOW MANY TRANSFERS?

When ecologists compared food chains in different kinds of food webs, a pattern emerged. In most cases, energy initially captured by producers passes through no more than four or five trophic levels. Even the rich ecosystems with complex food webs, such as the one in Figure 47.5, do not have lengthy food chains. The inefficiency of energy transfers may limit the sequence.

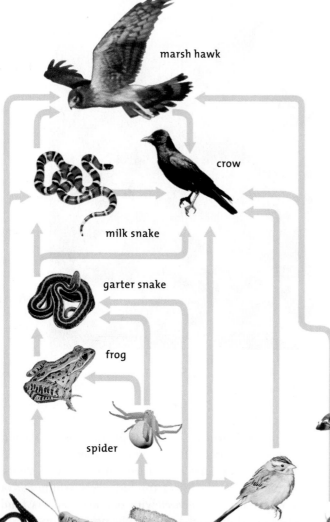

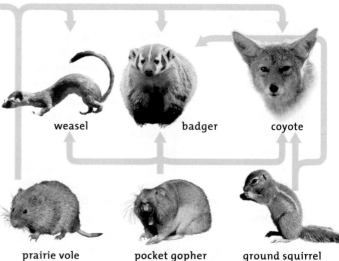

higher trophic levels

Complex array of carnivores, omnivores, parasites, detritivores, decomposers, and other consumers. Many feed at more than one trophic level all the time, seasonally, or whenever an opportunity presents itself.

second trophic level

Primary consumers (e.g., herbivores, detritivores, and decomposers)

first trophic level

Primary producers

marsh hawk

crow

milk snake

garter snake

frog

spider

weasel   badger   coyote

clay-colored sparrow

prairie vole   pocket gopher   ground squirrel

earthworms, insects (e.g., grasshoppers, cutworms)

grasses, composites

Figure 47.5 *Animated!* A small sampling of the organisms at successively higher trophic levels for a tallgrass prairie food web.

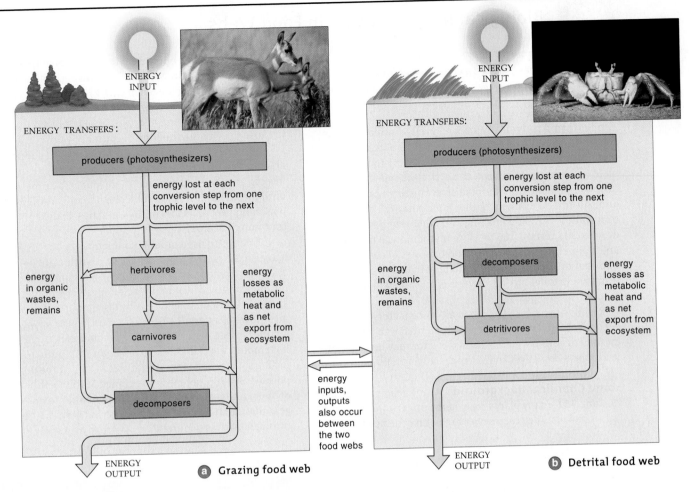

Figure 47.6 Generalized sketches of the one-way flow of energy through the participants of (**a**) a grazing food web and (**b**) a detrital food web.

Field studies and computer simulations of aquatic and land food webs reveal more patterns. Chains in food webs tend to be shortest where environmental conditions usually vary widely over time. Food chains tend to be longer in habitats that are more stable, such as ocean depths. The most complex webs tend to have many herbivorous species, as happens in grasslands. By comparison, the food webs with fewer connections tend to have more carnivores.

TWO CATEGORIES OF FOOD WEBS

Energy from producers—the organisms closest to a primary source—flows in one direction through two kinds of webs. In a **grazing food web**, energy flows mostly into herbivores, carnivores, then decomposers. In a **detrital food web**, energy from producers flows mainly into detritivores and decomposers. Figure 47.6 summarizes the flow through these food webs.

In nearly all ecosystems, both kinds of webs cross-connect. For example, in a rocky intertidal ecosystem, energy captured by algae flows to snails, which are eaten by herring gulls as part of a grazing food web. However, gulls also hunt crabs, which are among the primary consumers in the detrital food web.

The amount of energy that moves through the two kinds of food webs differs among ecosystems, and it often varies with the seasons. In most cases, however, most of the energy stored in producer tissues moves through *detrital* food webs. Think of cattle that graze heavily in a pasture. About half the energy stored in the grass plants enters the grazers. But cattle cannot access all of the stored energy. A lot is still present in undigested plant parts and in feces, and decomposers and detritivores go to work. Similarly, in marshes, most of the energy initially stored in the marsh grass tissues enters detrital food webs when the plants die.

The inherent inefficiency in energy transfers between trophic levels limits the length of food chains.

Tissues of living photosynthetic organisms are the basis for grazing food webs. Remains and wastes of these organisms are the basis for detrital food webs. In nearly all ecosystems, both types of food webs prevail and interconnect.

47.3 Biological Magnification in Food Webs

LINKS TO
SECTIONS 27.3,
28.4, 32.2, 46.5

We turn now to a premise that opened this chapter—that disturbances to one part of an ecosystem often can have unexpected effects on other, seemingly unrelated parts.

Ecosystem Analysis Many programs in ecology devise models as a way to monitor and predict the outcome of disturbances to ecosystems. Researchers work to identify all of the interacting biological, physical, chemical, and geologic factors that determine an ecosystem's processes and patterns. They might gather information by direct observations, satellite imaging and other remote sensing devices, and tests. Often they use mathematical models and computer programs to integrate pieces of available information on how the factors interact. Analysis of the results help them predict how the ecosystem will react to forces of change.

Results are most useful when all of the factors have been identified and accurately incorporated into a model for the ecosystem. The most crucial factor may be one that researchers do not yet know. A case in point follows.

Some Chemical Background As you read in Sections 28.4 and 46.5, many plants repel herbivorous animals with natural toxins. They themselves are not harmed by these organic compounds, but the chemical effects may repel or kill individuals of a different species. We encounter traces of natural plant toxins, even in such familiar foods as hot peppers, potatoes, figs, celery, rhubarb, and alfalfa sprouts. We do not get sick or die in droves from hot peppers, often because toxicity is a function of concentration.

Just a few thousand years ago, farmers used sulfur, lead, arsenic, and mercury to help protect crop plants against insects. They freely dispensed these highly toxic metals until the late 1920s, when someone figured out they were poisoning people. Traces of toxic metals still turn up in contaminated croplands.

Farmers also used organic compounds extracted from leaves, flowers, and roots as natural pesticides. In 1945, scientists started to make synthetic toxins and to identify mechanisms by which toxins attack pests. *Herbicides*, such as synthetic auxins, kill weeds by disrupting metabolism and growth (Section 32.2). *Insecticides* clog the airways of a target insect, disrupt its nerves and muscles, or prevent its reproduction. *Fungicides* work against harmful fungi, including a mold that makes aflatoxin, one of the deadliest poisons. By 1995, people in the United States were spraying or spreading more than 1.25 billion pounds of toxins each year through fields, gardens, homes, and industrial and commercial sites (Figure 47.7).

a *2,4-D* (2,4-dichlorophenoxyacetic acid), a synthetic auxin widely used as a herbicide. Enzymes of weeds and microbes cannot easily degrade 2,4-D, compared to natural auxins.

b *Atrazine*, the best-selling herbicide, kills weeds within a few days, as do glyphosate (Roundup), alachlor, (Lasso), and daminozide (Alar). It now appears that atrazine causes abnormal sexual development in frogs, even in trace amounts below the level allowed in drinking water.

c Dichlorodiphenyltrichloroethane, or *DDT*. It takes two to fifteen years for this nerve cell poison to break down. Chlordane, another type of insecticide, also persists for a long time in the environment.

d *Malathion*. Like other organophosphates, it is cheap, breaks down faster than chlorinated hydrocarbons, and is more toxic. Organophosphates represent half of all insecticides used in the United States. Some are now banned for crops; application of others must end at least three weeks before harvest. Farmers who contest this policy want the Environmental Protection Agency to consider economic and trade issues as well as human health.

Figure 47.7 A few pesticides, some more toxic than others. The photograph shows one of the crop dusters that intervene in the competition for nutrients between crop plants and pests, including weeds.

DDT Residues (ppm wet weight of whole live organism)	
Ring-billed gull fledgling (*Larus delawarensis*)	75.5
Herring gull (*Larus argentatus*)	18.5
Osprey (*Pandion haliaetus*)	13.8
Green heron (*Butorides virescens*)	3.57
Atlantic needlefish (*Strongylura marina*)	2.07
Summer flounder (*Paralichthys dentatus*)	1.28
Sheepshead minnow (*Cyprinodon variegatus*)	0.94
Hard clam (*Mercenaria mercenaria*)	0.42
Marsh grass shoots (*Spartina patens*)	0.33
Flying insects (mostly flies)	0.30
Mud snail (*Nassarius obsoletus*)	0.26
Shrimps (composite of several samples)	0.16
Green alga (*Cladophora gracilis*)	0.083
Plankton (mostly zooplankton)	0.040
Water	0.00005

Figure 47.8 Biological magnification in an estuary on the south shore of Long Island, New York, as reported in 1967 by George Woodwell, Charles Wurster, and Peter Isaacson. The researchers knew of broad correlations between the extent of DDT exposure and mortality. For instance, residues in birds known to have died from DDT poisoning were 30–295 ppm, and they were 1–26 ppm in several fish species. Some DDT concentrations measured during this study were below lethal thresholds but were still high enough to interfere with reproductive success.

Figure 47.9 Peregrine falcon, a top carnivore in some food webs. This raptor almost became extinct as a result of biological magnification of DDT. A wildlife management program successfully brought back its population sizes. Peregrine falcons were reintroduced into wild habitats. They have adapted to cities. There, they hunt pigeons, large populations of which are a messy nuisance.

DDT in Food Webs The DDT molecule highlighted in Figure 47.7c is a fairly stable hydrocarbon that is nearly insoluble in water. Therefore, you might think—as many others did—that it would exert its toxic effects only where it was applied. However, winds can easily disperse DDT in vapor form, and water can disperse fine particles of it.

Given its molecular properties, DDT is highly soluble in fats, and so it can accumulate in the tissues of organisms. That is why DDT can show **biological magnification**. By this occurrence, a substance that degrades slowly or not at all becomes ever more concentrated in tissues of organisms at higher trophic levels of a food web.

Most of the DDT that becomes concentrated in all of the organisms that a consumer eats during its lifetime ends up in the consumer's own tissues. DDT and its modified forms disrupt metabolic activities and are toxic to many aquatic and terrestrial animals.

Several decades ago, DDT started to infiltrate food webs and exert its effects on diverse organisms in ways that no one had predicted. Where people sprayed DDT to control Dutch elm disease, songbirds died (Section 27.3). In forests where DDT was sprayed to kill budworm larvae, fish in the forest streams died. In fields sprayed to control one kind of pest, new pests moved in. *DDT was indiscriminately killing the natural predators that keep pest populations in check.*

Then side effects of biological magnification started to show up in habitats far removed from where the DDT had been applied—*and much later in time*. Most vulnerable were brown pelicans, bald eagles, peregrine falcons, and other top carnivores of some food webs (Figures 47.8 and 47.9). Why? A product of DDT breakdown interferes with some physiological processes. As one outcome, bird eggs developed brittle shells; many chick embryos did not even hatch. Some species were facing extinction.

In the United States, DDT has been banned since the 1970s except where necessary to protect public health. Many species hit hardest have recovered. Some birds still lay thin-shelled eggs because they pick up DDT at their winter ranges in Latin America. As late as 1990, a fishery near Los Angeles was closed. DDT from industrial waste discharges that had stopped twenty years earlier was still contaminating that ecosystem.

Today, ecologists are monitoring more than pesticides in ecosystems. Radiosotopes and heavy metals, including copper, zinc, lead, and mercury, also can become ever more concentrated in organisms. For example, in fields near heavily trafficked highways, ecologists found out that the soil concentration of lead can be as high as 1,200 parts per million (ppm)—and it gets magnified as it moves up food chains. The longer the chain, the greater the magnification.

47.4 Studying Energy Flow Through Ecosystems

LINKS TO
SECTIONS
7.8, 8.7

Ecologists measure the amount of energy and nutrients entering an ecosystem, how much is captured, and the proportion stored in each trophic level.

WHAT IS PRIMARY PRODUCTIVITY?

The rate at which producers capture and store energy in their tissues during a given interval is the **primary productivity** of an ecosystem. How much energy gets stored depends on (1) how many producers there are and (2) the balance between photosynthesis (energy trapped) and aerobic respiration (energy used). *Gross primary production* is all energy initially trapped by the producers. *Net* primary production is the fraction of trapped energy that producers funnel into growth and reproduction. **Net ecosystem production** is the gross primary production *minus* the energy used by the producers and soil detritivores and decomposers. That amount of energy is subtracted because it cannot be transferred to herbivores at the next trophic level.

On land and in the water provinces, many factors impact net production, its seasonal patterns, and its distribution through a habitat (Section 7.8 and Figure 47.10). For instance, the size and form of the primary

producers, the temperature range, the availability of mineral ions, and the amount of sunlight and rainfall in each growing season affect energy acquisition and storage. The harsher the conditions are, the less new growth plants add in a given season, and the lower the primary productivity.

ECOLOGICAL PYRAMIDS

Ecologists often represent the trophic structure of an ecosystem in the form of an ecological pyramid. In such pyramids, all primary producers form a base for successive tiers of consumers above them.

A **biomass pyramid** depicts the dry weight of all of an ecosystem's organisms at each tier. Figure 47.11 shows a biomass pyramid for one aquatic ecosystem. The amounts measured are grams per square meter at some specified time. Most commonly, the primary producers have most of the biomass in pyramids like this, and top carnivores are few. But some biomass pyramids are "upside-down," in that the smallest tier is on the bottom. This happens in springtime blooms of phytoplankton, which grow and reproduce quickly. The primary producers of these aquatic communities support a larger biomass of zooplankton, which eat them about as fast as they can reproduce.

An **energy pyramid** illustrates how the amount of usable energy diminishes as it is transferred through an ecosystem. Sunlight energy is captured at the base (first trophic level) and declines through successive levels to its tip (the top carnivores). Energy pyramids have a large energy base at the bottom, so they are always "right-side up." Such pyramids can provide a clear picture of energy flow from an outside source

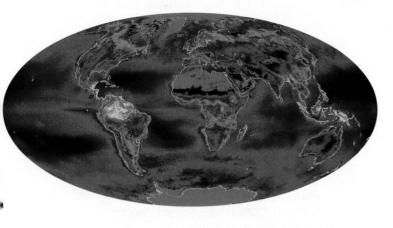

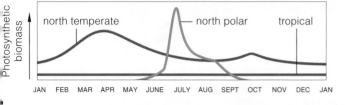

Figure 47.10 (a) Summary of satellite data on net primary productivity during 2002. Productivity is coded as *red* (highest) down through *orange*, *yellow*, *green*, *blue*, and *purple* (lowest). Although average productivity per unit of sea surface is lower than it is on land, total productivity on land and in seas is about equal, because most of Earth's surface is covered by water. (b) Examples of seasonal shifts in net primary productivity for three categories of ocean ecosystems.

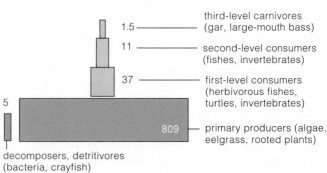

Figure 47.11 Biomass pyramid for Silver Springs, a small aquatic ecosystem in which biomass decreases in successively higher tiers. In different ecosystems, autotrophs are eaten almost as fast as they grow and reproduce. In such cases, biomass accumulates faster in consumers, so the biomass pyramid would be upside down.

Figure 47.12 *Animated!* Breakdown of the annual energy flow through Silver Springs, Florida, as measured in kilocalories/square meter/year. Most of the primary producers in this small spring are aquatic plants. Most carnivores are insects and small fishes; the top carnivores are larger fishes. The original energy source, sunlight, is available all year. Detritivores and decomposers cycle organic compounds from the other trophic levels.

Producers trapped 1.2 percent of the incoming solar energy, and only a little more than a third of that became fixed in new plant biomass. The producers used more than 63 percent of the fixed energy for their own metabolism.

About 16 percent of the fixed energy was transferred to herbivores. Most was used for metabolism or transferred to detritivores and decomposers. Of the energy that transferred to herbivores, only 11.4 percent reached the next trophic level (carnivores). About 5.5 percent of the energy in the lower-level carnivores flowed to the top carnivores.

By the end of the specified interval, all 20,810 kilocalories of energy that flowed through the system appeared as metabolically generated heat.

and on through its departure, mainly by losses of the metabolic heat that each organism generates.

ENERGY FLOW THROUGH SILVER SPRINGS

Visualize yourself with ecologists who are gathering data to construct an energy pyramid for a freshwater spring over the course of one year. They measure how much energy one individual of each species takes in, loses as metabolic heat, stores in its body tissues, and then loses as wastes. They multiply the energy per individual by population size, then calculate energy inputs and outputs. Then they express the energy flow per unit of water (or land) per unit of time. Figure 47.12 was constructed from data that were gathered this way during a long-term study of a grazing food web in this type of aquatic ecosystem. It shows some calculations that ecologists used to depict the energy flow in pyramid form in Figure 47.13.

Based on many such studies, ecologists arrived at this generalization: Given the metabolic demands of organisms and the amount of energy lost in organic wastes, only 6 to 16 percent of the energy entering one trophic level is available for organisms at the next.

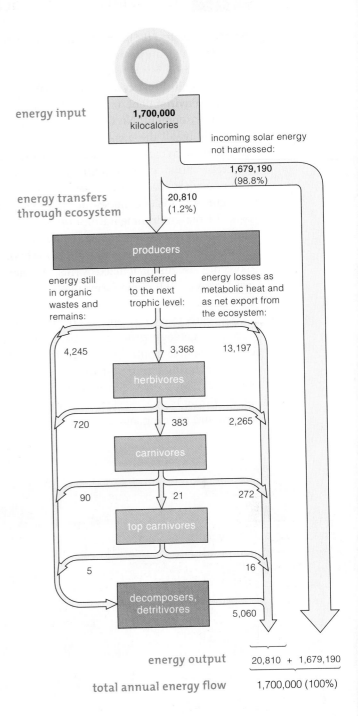

Gross primary productivity is an ecosystem's total rate of photosynthesis during a specified interval. The net amount is the rate at which primary producers store energy in tissues in excess of their rate of aerobic respiration. Heterotrophic consumption affects the rate of energy storage.

The trophic structure of an ecosystem may be represented by an ecological pyramid. Biomass pyramids may be top- or bottom-heavy depending on the ecosystem. In contrast, an energy pyramid always has the largest tier on the bottom.

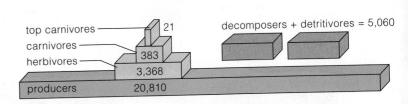

Figure 47.13 Pyramid of energy flow through Silver Springs, in kilocalories/square meter/year. This is a summary of the data used to construct Figure 47.12. Compare Figure 47.11, the biomass pyramid for this same ecosystem.

47.5 Overview of Biogeochemical Cycles

Without water and the nutrients dissolved in it, there would be no primary productivity, and no life.

In a **biogeochemical cycle**, an essential element moves from the environment, through ecosystems, then back to the environment. No other element can directly or indirectly fulfill the metabolic role of such elements, or **nutrients**, which is why we call them essential. As you read earlier, oxygen, hydrogen, carbon, nitrogen, and phosphorus are among them.

Figure 47.14 is one model for these cycles. Transfers to and from environmental reservoirs are usually far slower than rates of exchange among organisms of an ecosystem. Water is the main source for hydrogen and oxygen. Gaseous or ionized forms of other elements are dissolved in it. Solid forms of elements are tied up in rocks or sediments.

Nutrients move into and out of ecosystems by way of natural geologic processes. Weathering of rocks is a common source of nutrient inputs into an ecosystem. Erosion and runoff put nutrients into streams that carry them away. Most often, the quantity of a nutrient being cycled through an ecosystem each year is greater than the amount entering and leaving.

Decomposers help cycle the nutrients in ecosystems. Various prokaryotic species help transform solids and ions into gases, then back again. Through their action, they convert some elements that function as nutrients to forms that primary producers can take up.

In three types of biogeochemical cycles, portions of the environment are reservoirs for specific elements. In the *hydrologic* cycle, oxygen and hydrogen move, on a grand scale, in molecules of water. In *atmospheric* cycles, some gaseous form of the nutrient is the one available to ecosystems. Carbon and nitrogen cycles are examples. Phosphorus and other solid nutrients that have no gaseous form move in *sedimentary* cycles. They accumulate on the seafloor and eventually return to land through geological uplifting, which typically has taken millions of years. Earth's crust is the biggest reservoir for nutrients that have sedimentary cycles.

Primary productivity depends on water and nutrients that become dissolved in it. In a biogeochemical cycle, a nutrient moves slowly through the environment, then rapidly among organisms, and back to environmental reservoirs.

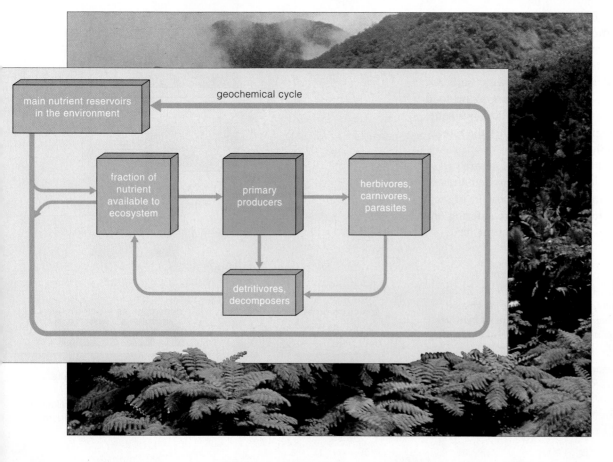

Figure 47.14 One generalized model of nutrient flow through an ecosystem on land. The overall movement of nutrients from the physical environment, through organisms, and then back to the environment is a biogeochemical cycle.

47.6 Hydrologic Cycle

On land, the availability of water, and nutrients dissolved in it, is not plentiful all of the time in all ecosystems. The variation affects primary productivity.

Driven by solar energy, Earth's waters slowly move from the ocean into the atmosphere, to land, and back to the ocean—the main reservoir. Figure 47.15 shows this **hydrologic cycle**. Water that evaporates into the lower atmosphere stays aloft as vapor, clouds, and ice crystals, then falls mainly as rain and snow. Ocean circulation and wind patterns influence the cycle.

Water moves nutrients into and out of ecosystems. A **watershed** is any region where precipitation flows into a single stream or river. Watersheds may be as small as the area that drains into a stream or as vast as the Amazon River or Mississippi River basin. Most water entering a watershed seeps into soil or joins surface runoff into streams. Plants take up water from soil and lose it by transpiration (Figure 47.16).

> *In the hydrologic cycle, water slowly moves on a global scale from the world ocean—the main reservoir—through the atmosphere, onto land, then back to the ocean.*

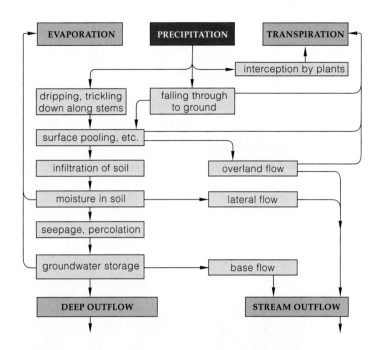

Figure 47.16 Model for how water moves through watersheds in general. *Dark blue* box is the input to the watershed; *light blue*, the distribution within it; and *medium blue*, outputs from it. Transpiration is the name for evaporation of water from leaves and other plant parts exposed to air (Section 30.3). Plants absorb water from soil and groundwater stores.

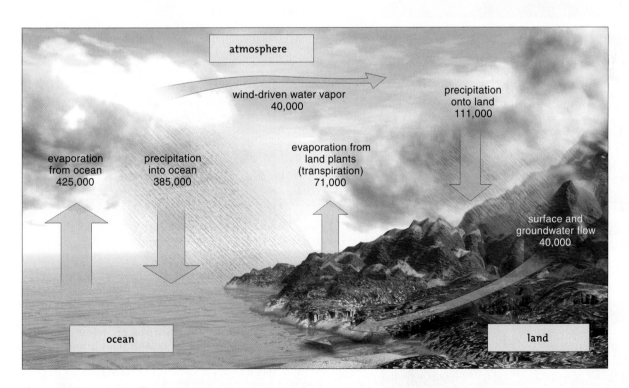

Figure 47.15 *Animated!* Hydrologic cycle. Water moves from the ocean to the atmosphere, land, and back. Arrows identify processes that move water, as measured in cubic kilometers per year. With 1,370,000,000 cubic kilometers, the ocean is the main reservoir. The next largest, polar ice and glaciers, locks up 29,000,000. Groundwater makes up only 4,000,000, lakes and rivers only 241,000, soil 67,000, and the atmosphere 14,000 cubic kilometers.

47.7 Watershed Experiments

LINKS TO
SECTIONS
23.10, 30.1

Water is vital for all organisms. It also is a transport medium; it moves nutrients into and out of ecosystems. Its role in moving nutrients became clear in long-term studies of watersheds.

A watershed, again, is any region in which the precipitation becomes funneled into just one stream or one river. Figure 47.17a shows part of an experimental forest in the Hubbard Brook Valley of New Hampshire. The watersheds in this forest have a surface area of 14.6 hectares (36 acres), on average. Over the years, ecologists have painstakingly measured nutrient inputs and outputs in this forest. Such measurements have many practical applications.

For instance, cities that draw from a watershed's supply of surface water can adjust their usage in compliance with seasonal shifts in the volume of water. Measurements also reveal the extent to which vegetation cover influences the movement of nutrients through the ecosystem phase of biogeochemical cycles.

For example, you might think that surface runoff in a watershed would swiftly leach out calcium ions and other minerals dissolved in soil water. (Here you may wish to review the Section 30.1 explanation of leaching.) However, in the young, undisturbed forests of the Hubbard Brook watersheds, each hectare lost only eight kilograms or so of its calcium. The weathering of rocks and rainfall were replacing the lost calcium. In addition, tree roots were "mining" the soil by absorbing dissolved mineral ions, so calcium was being stored in a growing biomass of tree tissues.

In experimental watersheds in the Hubbard Brook Valley, deforestation caused a shift in nutrient outputs. The results, summarized in Figure 47.17d, are sobering. Calcium and other nutrients cycle very slowly, which means that deforestation may disrupt the availability of nutrients for an entire ecosystem. This is especially the case for forests that cannot regenerate themselves over the short term because of their soil properties and other characteristics. As you will see in the next chapter, the northern coniferous forests and tropical rain forests require long recovery times.

a

b

c

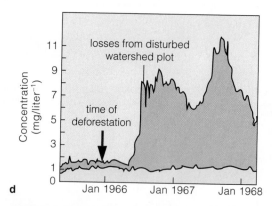

d

Figure 47.17 (**a**) Experimental deforestation in the Hubbard Brook watershed of New Hampshire. Researchers monitor surface runoff flowing over concrete catchments (**b**) on its way to a stream below. For some experiments, they stripped vegetation from forest plots but did not disturb the soil. They applied herbicides for three years to prevent regrowth. (**c**) They compared concentrations of calcium ions and other minerals in runoff over a control catchment against concentrations in runoff from an undisturbed area.

(**d**) Calcium losses were *six times* greater in deforested plots. Removing all vegetation from such forests clearly alters nutrient outputs in ways that can disrupt nutrient availability for an entire ecosystem.

47.8 A Global Water Crisis

Most of Earth's water is too salty to drink or use for agriculture. The skyrocketing increases in human population size make this a big problem.

Two-thirds of the fresh water that humans use goes directly into irrigating fields (Figure 47.18). Ironically, irrigation makes the land less suitable for agriculture. Piped-in water commonly has high concentrations of mineral salts. Where soil drains poorly, evaporation results in **salinization**, or a build-up of salt in soil that stunts crop plants and decreases yields.

Soil and aquifers hold **groundwater**. About half of the United States population taps into groundwater as a source of drinking water. Chemicals leached from landfills, hazardous waste dumps, and underground tanks that store gasoline, oil, and some solvents often contaminate it. Unlike flowing streams, which recover fast, polluted groundwater is difficult and expensive to clean up.

Groundwater overdrafts, or the amount that nature has not replenished, are high in many areas. Figure 47.19 shows some regions of aquifer depletion in the United States. Overdrafts have now depleted half of the great Ogallala aquifer, which supplies irrigation water for 20 percent of the Midwest's croplands.

Inputs of sewage, animal wastes, and many toxic chemicals from power-generating plants and factories make water unfit to drink. Sediments and pesticides run off from fields into water, along with phosphates and other nutrients that promote algal blooms. The pollutants accumulate in lakes, rivers, and bays before reaching the ocean. Many cities all over the world are still dumping untreated sewage into coastal waters.

If current rates of human population growth and water depletion continue, the amount of fresh water available for everyone will soon be 55 to 66 percent less than it was in 1976. In this past decade, thirty-three nations have already engaged in conflicts over reductions in water flow, pollution, and silt buildup in aquifers, rivers, and lakes. Among the squabblers are the United States and Mexico, Pakistan and India, and Israel and the Palestinian territories.

Could we meet our water needs by **desalinization**, or removal of salt from seawater? Salt can be removed by distillation or pushing water through membranes. The processes require fossil fuels, which makes them more feasible in Saudi Arabia and other countries with small populations and big fuel reserves. Most likely, desalinization will not be cost-effective for large-scale agriculture. It also produces mountains of salts.

We may be in for upheavals and wars over water rights. Does this sound far-fetched? Consider the new dam across the Euphrates River. By building immense irrigation systems and dams at the headwaters of the Tigris and Euphrates rivers, Turkey can, in the view of one of its dam site managers, shut off water flow into Syria and Iraq for as long as eight months "to regulate their political behavior." One might say that regional, national, and global planning is overdue.

Figure 47.18 If the world has so little fresh water, why are we irrigating deserts?

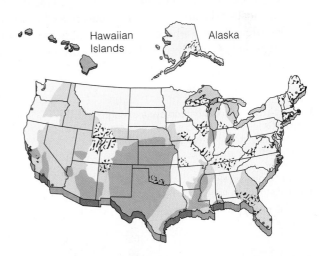

Figure 47.19 Aquifer depletion, seawater intrusion, and groundwater contamination in the United States. *Green* signifies high overdrafts, *gold*, moderate overdrafts, and *pale yellow*, insignificant withdrawals. Shaded areas are sites of major groundwater pollution. *Blue* squares indicate saltwater intrusion from nearby seas.

Agriculture accounts for about two-thirds of the human population's use of freshwater.

Aquifers that supply much of the world's drinking water are becoming polluted and depleted. Regional conflicts over access to clean, drinkable water are likely to increase.

LINKS TO
SECTIONS
7.8, 23.10,
NTRODUCTIONS
CHAPTERS 3, 22

47.9 Carbon Cycle

Most of the world's carbon is locked in ocean sediments and rocks. It moves into and out of ecosystems in gaseous form, so its movement is said to be an atmospheric cycle.

In the **carbon cycle**, carbon moves through the lower atmosphere and all food webs on its way to and from its large reservoirs (Figure 47.20). Earth's crust holds the most carbon—66 million to 100 million gigatons, of which 4,000 are present in fossil fuels. (One gigaton is a billion tons.) Remember Chapter 22? Many single-celled organisms of ancient aquatic habitats, including foraminiferans and coccolithophores, formed shells of calcium carbonate. Uncountable numbers of cells died, sank, and were buried in seafloor sediments. Carbon in their remains have been cycled exceedingly slowly, after geologic forces uplift part of the seafloor. Such cycling cannot be measured in years, obviously.

Most of the annual cycling takes place between the ocean and atmosphere. The ocean holds 38,000–40,000 gigatons of dissolved carbon, primarily in the form of bicarbonate and carbonate ions. The atmosphere holds about 766 gigatons of carbon, mainly combined with oxygen in the form of carbon dioxide (CO_2).

Detritus in soil holds another 1,500–1,600 gigatons of carbon atoms. Another 540–610 gigatons is present in biomass. Methane hydrates form a huge reservoir that was, oddly, overlooked in the past. Between 10,000 and 11,000 gigatons are sequestered off the coasts of continents and in permafrost. As explained in Section 48.10, permafrost consists of perpetually frozen peat bogs that are sometimes more than 500 meters thick. You read about methane hydrates in the introduction to Chapter 3. Also, on page 865 of this chapter, you are invited to consider how unstable deposits on the seafloor can have big impact on the carbon cycle.

Why doesn't all of the CO_2 dissolved in warm sea surface waters escape into the atmosphere? Driven by winds and regional differences in water density, ocean water makes a gigantic loop from the surface of the Pacific and Atlantic oceans down to the Atlantic and

Figure 47.20 *Animated!* Global carbon cycle through typical marine ecosystems (**a**) and land ecosystems (**b**). *Gold* boxes show the main carbon reservoirs. The vast majority of carbon atoms are in sediments and rocks, followed by ever lesser amounts in ocean water, soil, the atmosphere, and biomass. Here are typical annual fluxes in the global distribution of carbon, in gigatons:

From atmosphere to plants by carbon fixation	120
From atmosphere to ocean	107
To atmosphere from ocean	105
To atmosphere from plants	60
To atmosphere from soil	60
To atmosphere from fossil fuel burning	5
To atmosphere from net destruction of plants	2
To ocean from runoff	0.4
Burial in ocean sediments	0.1

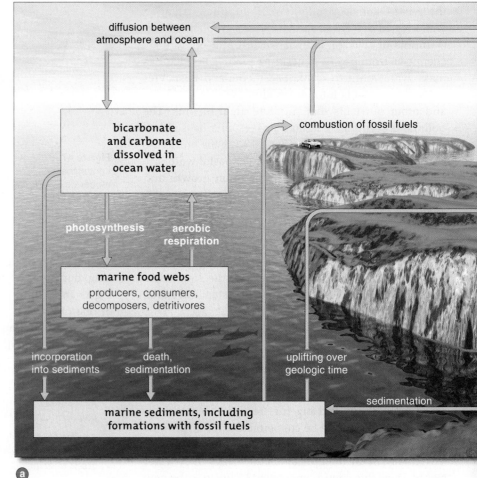

diffusion between
atmosphere and ocean

combustion of fossil fuels

bicarbonate
and carbonate
dissolved in
ocean water

photosynthesis   aerobic
respiration

marine food webs
producers, consumers,
decomposers, detritivores

incorporation
into sediments

death,
sedimentation

uplifting over
geologic time

sedimentation

marine sediments, including
formations with fossil fuels

a

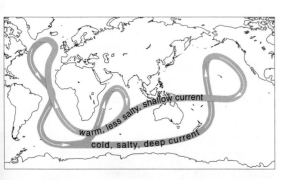

warm, less salty, shallow current

cold, salty, deep current

Figure 47.21 Ocean loop that moves carbon dioxide to carbon's deep ocean reservoir. It sinks in the cold, salty North Atlantic and rises in the warmer Pacific.

Antarctic seafloors. The CO_2 moves into deep storage reservoirs before water loops back up (Figure 47.21). The loop effectively mediates the annual fluxes in the global distribution of carbon.

As you know, CO_2 is the key source of carbon for autotrophs, and for food webs in ecosystems on land and in the seas. That is why biologists often refer to the glocal cycling of carbon as the *carbon–oxygen cycle*. When photosynthetic autotrophs fix carbon, they lock up billions of metric tons of carbon atoms in organic compounds annually (Section 7.8). When aerobic cells engage in aerobic respiration, they release CO_2. More CO_2 is released when fossil fuels or forests burn and when volcanoes erupt.

The average time that an ecosystem holds a given carbon atom varies. As examples, organic wastes and remains decompose so fast in tropical rain forests that carbon does not build up at the soil surface. Bogs and other anaerobic habitats do not favor decomposition, so the organic material is not degraded to smaller bits and carbon accumulates in peat. Humans withdraw 4 to 5 gigatons from fossil fuel reservoirs every year. At the same time, human activities put about 6 gigatons more carbon in the atmosphere than can be cycled to the ocean reservoirs by natural processes.

Only about 2 percent of the excess carbon entering the atmosphere will become dissolved in ocean water. Most researchers now suspect that the carbon build-up in the atmosphere is amplifying the greenhouse effect. In other words, the increase might be contributing to global warming. The next section takes a look at this possibility and its environmental implications.

> *Earth's crust holds the vast majority of carbon. The ocean is the next largest reservoir. Most of the annual cycling of carbon occurs between the ocean and atmosphere.*
>
> *Carbon moves into and out of ecosystems mainly when combined with oxygen, as in carbon dioxide, bicarbonate, and carbonate. We refer to this as the carbon–oxygen cycle.*

b

47.10 Greenhouse Gases, Global Warming

LINKS TO
SECTIONS
7.1, 21.5, 23.10

The atmospheric concentrations of gaseous molecules help determine the average temperature near Earth's surface. Human activities are contributing to increases that may cause dramatic climate change.

Concentrations of a variety of gaseous molecules in Earth's atmosphere profoundly influence the average temperature near its surface. Temperature, in turn, has far-reaching effects on global and regional climates.

Atmospheric molecules of carbon dioxide, water, nitrous oxide, methane, and chlorofluorocarbons are among the main players in interactions that affect global temperature. Collectively, these gases function like the panes of glass in a greenhouse—hence their name, "greenhouse gases." The wavelengths of visible light pass through these gases to Earth's surface, which absorbs them and then emits longer, infrared wavelengths—heat. Greenhouse gases impede the escape of heat energy from Earth into space. How? The gaseous molecules absorb the longer wavelengths, then radiate much of it back toward Earth (Figure 47.22).

Constant reradiation of heat by greenhouse gases occurs lockstep with the constant bombardment and absorption of wavelengths from the sun. As heat builds up in the lower atmosphere, the air temperature near Earth's surface rises. The warming action is known as the **greenhouse effect**. Without it, Earth's surface would be so cold that it could not support life.

In the 1950s, laboratory researchers on Hawaii's highest volcano set out to measure the atmospheric concentrations of greenhouse gases. That remote site is almost free of local airborne contamination; it is also representative of overall atmospheric conditions for the Northern Hemisphere. What did they find? Briefly, carbon dioxide concentrations follow annual cycles of primary production. They drop during the summer, when photosynthesis rates are highest. They rise

Figure 47.23 *Facing page*, graphs of recent increases in four categories of atmospheric greenhouse gases. A key factor is the sheer number of gasoline-burning vehicles in large cities. *Above*, Mexico City on a smoggy morning. With 10 million residents, it is the world's largest city.

in winter, when photosynthesis rates decline but aerobic respiration is still going on.

Alternating troughs and peaks along the graph line in Figure 47.23*a* are annual lows and highs of global carbon dioxide concentrations. For the first time, we could see the integrated effects of carbon balances for an entire hemisphere. Notice the midline of the troughs and peaks in the cycle. It shows that carbon dioxide concentration is steadily increasing—as are the concentrations of other major greenhouse gases.

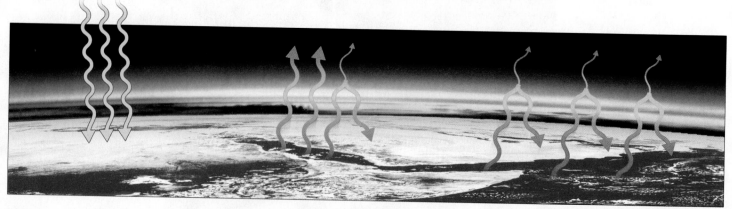

ⓐ Wavelengths in rays from the sun penetrate the lower atmosphere, and they warm the Earth's surface.

ⓑ The surface radiates heat (infrared wavelengths) to the atmosphere. Some heat escapes into space. But greenhouse gases and water vapor absorb some infrared energy and radiate a portion of it back toward Earth.

ⓒ Increased concentrations of greenhouse gases trap more heat near Earth's surface. Sea surface temperatures rise, so more water evaporates into the atmosphere. Earth's surface temperature rises.

Figure 47.22 *Animated!* The greenhouse effect.

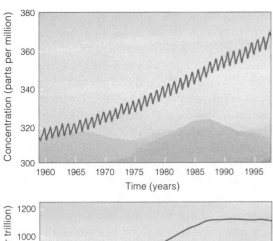

a Carbon dioxide (CO$_2$). Of all human activities, the burning of fossil fuels and deforestation (Section 23.10) contribute the most to rising atmospheric levels.

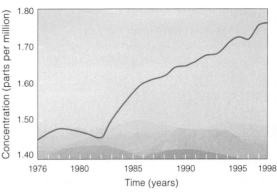

c Methane (CH$_4$). Production and distribution of natural gas as fuel adds to methane released by some bacteria that live in swamps, rice fields, landfills, and in the digestive tract of cattle and other ruminants (Section 21.5).

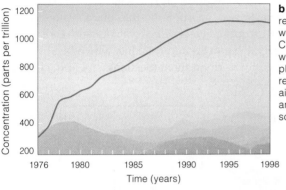

b CFCs. Until restrictions were in place, CFCs were widely used in plastic foams, refrigerators, air conditioners, and industrial solvents.

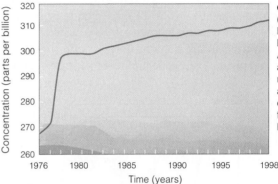

d Nitrous oxide (N$_2$O). Denitrifying bacteria produce N$_2$O in metabolism. Also, fertilizers and animal wastes release enormous amounts; this is especially so for large-scale livestock feedlots.

Figure 47.24 Recorded changes in global temperature between 1880 and 2000. At this writing, the hottest year on record was 1998.

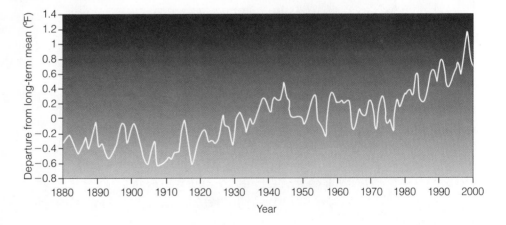

Atmospheric levels of greenhouse gases are far higher than they were in most of the past. Carbon dioxide may be at its highest level since 420,000 years ago, and possibly since 20 million years ago. There is a growing consensus that the rise in greenhouse gases is caused by some human activities, mainly burning of fossil fuels. The big worry is that the increase may have far-reaching environmental consequences.

The increase in greenhouse gases may be a factor in **global warming**, a long-term increase in temperature near Earth's surface. Since direct atmospheric readings started in 1861, the lower atmosphere's temperature has risen by more than 1°F, mostly since 1946 (Figure 47.24). Also since then, nine of the ten hottest years on record occurred between

1990 and the present. Data from satellites, weather stations and balloons, research ships, and supercomputer programs suggest that irreversible climate changes are already under way. Polar ice is melting; glaciers are retreating. This past century, the sea level may have risen as much as twenty centimeters (eight inches).

We can expect continued temperature increases to have drastic effects on climate. As evaporation increases, so will global precipitation. Intense rains and flooding are expected to become more frequent in some regions.

It bears repeating: As investigations continue, a key research goal is to investigate all of the variables in play. With respect to the consequences of global warming, the most crucial variable may be the one we do not know.

47.11 Nitrogen Cycle

LINKS TO
SECTIONS 21.4,
22.6, 24.6, 30.2

Gaseous nitrogen makes up about 80 percent of the lower atmosphere. Successively smaller reservoirs are seafloor sediments, ocean water, soil, biomass on land, nitrous oxide in the atmosphere, and marine biomass.

INPUTS INTO ECOSYSTEMS

Gaseous nitrogen (N_2) travels in an atmospheric cycle called the **nitrogen cycle**. Triple covalent bonds join its two atoms ($N\equiv N$). Volcanic action and lightning convert some N_2 into forms that enter food webs. Far more enters by **nitrogen fixation**. With this metabolic process, bacteria split all three bonds in N_2 and use the atoms to form ammonia (NH_3). Later, ammonia is converted to ammonium (NH_4^+) and nitrate (NO_3^-). Most plants easily take up these two forms of nitrogen.

Figure 47.25 shows the nitrogen cycle. Its nitrogen fixers include cyanobacteria in aquatic habitats and in many lichens. *Rhizobium* is a nitrogen fixer in nodules on legume roots (Sections 24.6 and 30.2). Collectively, these photoautotrophic bacteria fix about 200 million metric tons of nitrogen each year. The plants do pay a high metabolic cost for the interaction. They give up sugars and other photosynthetic products that take large investments of ATP and NADPH. Such plants have a competitive edge in nitrogen-poor soil. Other plants that do not pay the metabolic price commonly displace them in nitrogen-rich soil.

The nitrogen incorporated into plant tissues moves through trophic levels of ecosystems and ends up in nitrogen-rich wastes and remains, where bacteria and fungi go to work on them (Sections 21.4 and 24.6). By

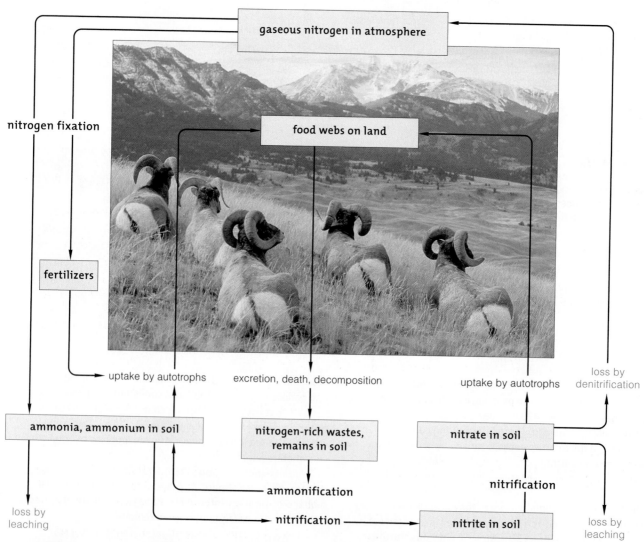

nitrogen fixation

fertilizers

food webs on land

gaseous nitrogen in atmosphere

uptake by autotrophs

excretion, death, decomposition

uptake by autotrophs

loss by denitrification

ammonia, ammonium in soil

nitrogen-rich wastes, remains in soil

nitrate in soil

ammonification

nitrification

loss by leaching

nitrification

nitrite in soil

loss by leaching

Figure 47.25 *Animated!* The nitrogen cycle in an ecosystem on land. Activities of nitrogen-fixing bacteria make nitrogen available to plants. Other bacterial species cycle nitrogen to plants. They break down organic wastes to ammonium and nitrates.

the process of **ammonification**, these microbes break down nitrogenous materials, and ammonium forms. They use some of the ammonium and release the rest to soil. Plants take it up, as do some nitrifying bacteria. In the first step of **nitrification**, certain bacteria cause nitrite (NO_2^-) to form when they strip electrons from ammonium. Different nitrifying bacteria use the nitrite in reactions that form nitrate (NO_3^-).

NATURAL LOSSES FROM ECOSYSTEMS

Ecosystems lose nitrogen through **denitrification**. By this process, denitrifying bacteria convert nitrate or nitrite to gaseous nitrogen or to nitrogen oxide (NO_2). Most denitrifying bacteria are anaerobic; they live in waterlogged soils and aquatic sediments.

Ammonium, nitrite, and nitrate are also lost from a land ecosystem in runoff and by leaching, the removal of some nutrients as water percolates through the soil (Section 30.1). Leaching removes nitrogen from land ecosystems and adds it to aquatic ones.

DISRUPTIONS BY HUMAN ACTIVITIES

Deforestation and grassland conversion for agriculture also cause big nitrogen losses. With each clearing and harvest, nitrogen in plant tissues is removed. Soil also becomes more vulnerable to erosion and leaching.

Many farmers counter nitrogen losses by rotating crops, as by alternating wheat with legumes. Rotation can help keep soil stable and productive. In developed countries, farmers also spread nitrogen-rich fertilizers. They even select new strains of crop plants that have a greater capacity to take up fertilizers from soil. By such practices, crop yields per hectare have doubled and sometimes quadrupled over the past forty years.

High temperature and pressure converts nitrogen and hydrogen gases to ammonia fertilizers. The use of these manufactured fertilizers greatly increases crop yields. It also can alter soil chemistry by disrupting a pH-dependent process called **ion exchange**. By this process, ions dissociate from soil particles, and then other ions in soil water replace them (Section 30.2). The most abundant exchangeable ions are calcium and magnesium. The hydrogen ions in nitrogen fertilizers makes soil water more acidic, and they displace other ions from binding sites on soil particles. Too many calcium and magnesium ions, which also are required for plant growth, trickle away in soil water.

Deposition of nitrogen in acid rains can have the same effect as overfertilization. Fossil fuel burned in power plants and vehicles releases nitrogen oxides,

Figure 47.26 Dead and dying trees in Smoky Mountain National Park. Forests are among the casualties of nitrogen oxides and other forms of air pollution.

which contribute to global warming and to acid rain. Winds often carry these air pollutants far from their sources (Figure 47.26). By some estimates, pollutants are putting ten times the normal amounts of nitrogen into certain forests in eastern Europe.

Different plant species respond in different ways to high nitrogen levels. Increases in nitrogen can disrupt the balance among competing species in a community (Section 46.1), and diversity may decline. The impact can be pronounced in forests at high elevations and high latitudes, which have nitrogen-poor soils.

Some human activities disrupt aquatic ecosystems through nitrogen enrichment. Crop plants cannot take up all of the nitrogen in fertilizers. About half of the nitrogen applied to fields runs off into rivers, lakes, and estuaries. Sewage from cities and animal wastes puts even more nitrogen into the water provinces. As one outcome, nitrogen inputs promote algal blooms. So does the phosphorus in fertilizers, as explained in Sections 22.6 and 47.12.

The ecosystem phase of the nitrogen cycle starts with nitrogen fixation. Bacteria convert gaseous nitrogen in the air to ammonia and then to ammonium, which is a form that plants easily take up.

By ammonification, bacteria and fungi make additional ammonium available to plants when they break down nitrogen-rich organic wastes and remains.

By nitrification, bacteria convert nitrites in soil to nitrate, which also is a form that plants easily take up.

The ecosystem loses nitrogen when denitrifying bacteria convert nitrite and nitrate back to gaseous nitrogen, and when nitrogen is leached from soil.

47.12 Sedimentary Cycles

LINKS TO
SECTIONS
3.8, 22.6

Unlike carbon and nitrogen, phosphorus does not cycle into and out of ecosystems in gaseous form. Like nitrogen, phosphorus can be taken up by plants only in ionized form, and it, too, is often a limiting factor on plant growth.

In the **phosphorus cycle**, phosphorus passes quickly through food webs as it moves from land to ocean sediments, then slowly back to dry land. Earth's crust is the largest reservoir of phosphorus.

The phosphorus in rock formations is mainly in the form of phosphate (PO_4^{3-}). Weathering and erosion deliver these ions to streams and rivers, which move them onward to the sea (Figure 47.27). The phosphates gradually accumulate and form insoluble deposits on submerged continental shelves. After many millions of years, crustal movements might uplift part of the seafloor and expose the phosphates on land surfaces. There, weathering and erosion will release phosphates from exposed rocks and start the cycle over again.

Phosphates are required building blocks for ATP, phospholipids, nucleic acids, and other compounds. Plants take up dissolved phosphates from soil water. Herbivores get them by eating plants; carnivores get them by eating herbivores. Animals lose phosphate in urine and in feces. Bacterial and fungal decomposers release phosphate from organic wastes and remains, then plants take them up again.

The hydrologic cycle helps move phosphorus and other minerals through ecosystems. Water evaporates from the ocean and falls on land. As it flows back to the ocean, it transports silt and dissolved phosphates that the primary producers require for growth.

Of all minerals, phosphorus is often the limiting factor in ecosystems. Only newly weathered, young soils are high in phosphorus. In aquatic habitats, most phosphorus is locked up in sediments. Not much is in gaseous form, so little is lost to the atmosphere.

Phosphorus is being lost from many tropical and subtropical ecosystems, many of which already have phosphorus-poor soils. Phosphorus stored in biomass and released from decomposing organic matter can sustain undisturbed forests or grasslands. As trees are harvested or land is cleared, phosphorus is lost. Crop yields start out low and soon are nonexistent. After fields are abandoned, natural regrowth is sparse. In developing countries especially, 1 to 2 billion hectares may be already depleted of phosphorus.

What about the developed countries? After years of fertilizer applications, many soils have phosphorus overloads. It is concentrated in eroded sediments and

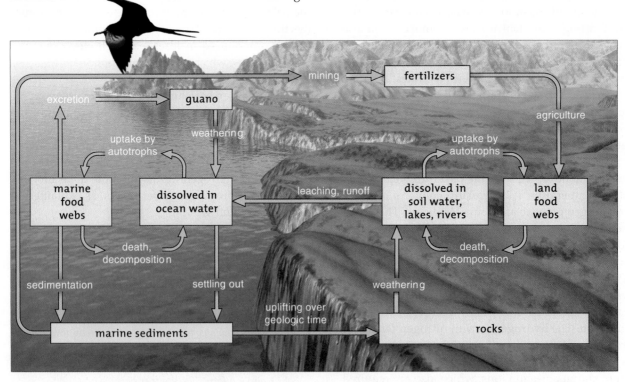

Figure 47.27 *Animated!* Phosphorus cycle. In this sedimentary cycle, phosphorus moves mainly in the form of phosphate ions (PO_4^{3-}) to the ocean. It moves through phytoplankton of marine food webs, then to fishes that eat plankton. Seabirds eat the fishes, and their droppings (guano) accumulate on islands. Humans collect and use guano as a phosphate-rich fertilizer.

runoff from agricultural fields. Phosphorus also is a waste in the outflows from sewage treatment plants and factories, and in the runoff from fields. Dissolved phosphorus that gets into streams, rivers, lakes, and estuaries can promote destructive algal blooms. Like plants, all photosynthetic algae require phosphorus, nitrogen, and other ions to grow. In many freshwater ecosystems, nitrogen-fixing bacteria keep the nitrogen levels high, so phosphorus becomes the limiting factor. When phosphate-rich pollutants pour in, populations of algae soar. As aerobic decomposers break down the remains of the algae, the water becomes depleted of the oxygen that fishes and other organisms require.

Eutrophication refers to the nutrient enrichment of any ecosystem that is otherwise low in nutrients. It is a process of natural succession. Phosphorus inputs as from agriculture can accelerate it, as the experiment shown in Figure 47.28 demonstrated.

Sedimentary cycles, in combination with the hydrologic cycle, move most mineral elements, such as phosphorus, through terrestrial and aquatic ecosystems.

Agriculture, deforestation, and other human activities upset the nutrient balances of ecosystems.

Figure 47.28 One of the eutrophication experiments. Researchers put a plastic curtain across a channel between two basins of a natural lake. They added nitrogen, carbon, and phosphorus on one side of the curtain (here, the *lower* part of the lake) and added nitrogen and carbon on the other side. Within months, the phosphorus-rich basin was eutrophic, with a dense algal bloom (green) covering its surface.

Summary

Section 47.1 An ecosystem consists of an array of organisms together with their physical and chemical environment. There is a one-way flow of energy into and out of an ecosystem, and a cycling of materials among the organisms. All ecosystems have inputs and outputs of energy and nutrients.

Sunlight is the initial energy source for almost all ecosystems. Primary producers capture energy from the sun. They also assimilate nutrients that they, and all consumers, require. Consumers include herbivores, carnivores, omnivores, decomposers, and detritivores.

Organisms in an ecosystem are classified by trophic levels. Those at the same level are the same number of steps away from the energy input into the ecosystem.

Biology⊘Now
Learn about energy flow and material cycling with the animation on BiologyNow.

Section 47.2 Linear sequences by which energy and nutrients move through ever higher trophic levels are food chains, which interconnect as food webs. The efficiency of energy transfers is always low, so most ecosystems support no more than four or five trophic levels away from an original energy source. In a grazing food web, energy captured by producers flows directly to consumers. In a detrital food web, it flows directly to detritivores and decomposers. In nearly all ecosystems, both types of food webs interconnect.

Biology⊘Now
Explore a food web with the animation on BiologyNow.

Section 47.3 By biological magnification, some chemical substance is passed from organisms at one trophic level to those above and becomes increasingly concentrated in body tissues. DDT is an example.

Section 47.4 A system's primary productivity is the rate at which producers capture and store energy in their tissues. It varies with climate, season, nutrient availability, and other factors.

Ecologists construct energy pyramids and biomass pyramids to show how energy and organic compounds are distributed in an ecosystem. Energy pyramids are largest at their base. The lowest trophic level has the greatest proportion of the energy in an ecosystem.

Long-term studies of the Silver Springs ecosystem in Florida illustrate the inefficiency of energy transfers. At each trophic level, far more energy was lost to the environment or in wastes and remains than was passed on to the next trophic level.

Biology⊘Now
See how energy flows through one ecosystem with the animation on BiologyNow.

Section 47.5 In a biogeochemical cycle, water or a nutrient moves through the environment, then through organisms, then back to an environmental reservoir.

Sections 47.6–47.8 In the hydrologic cycle, water moves from the ocean into the atmosphere, to land, and back to the ocean—the main reservoir. Human actions are disrupting the cycle in ways that result in shortages and pollution of water.

Biology⊗Now
Learn about the hydrologic cycle with the animation on BiologyNow.

Section 47.9 The carbon cycle moves carbon from its main reservoirs in rocks and seawater, through its gaseous form (carbon dioxide) in the atmosphere, and then through ecosystems. Deforestation and the burning of wood and fossil fuels are adding more carbon dioxide to the atmosphere than the oceans can absorb.

Biology⊗Now
Observe the flow of carbon through its global cycle with the animation on BiologyNow.

Section 47.10 Collectively, greenhouse gases trap heat in the lower atmosphere, which helps make Earth's surface warm enough to support life. Natural processes and human activities are adding more greenhouse gases, including carbon dioxide, CFCs, methane, and nitrous oxide, to the atmosphere. The rise correlates with a rise in global temperatures and other climate changes.

Biology⊗Now
Explore the causes of the greenhouse effect and global warming with the animation on BiologyNow.

Section 47.11 The atmosphere is the main reservoir for N_2, a gaseous form of nitrogen that plants cannot use. In nitrogen fixation, some soil bacteria degrade N_2 and assimilate the two nitrogen atoms into ammonia. Other reactions convert ammonia to ammonium and nitrate, which plants are able to take up. Some nitrogen is lost to the atmosphere by the action of denitrifying bacteria.

Human activities add nitrogen to ecosystems; for example, through fertilizer applications and fossil fuel burning, which releases nitrogen oxides.

Biology⊗Now
Learn how nitrogen is cycled with the animation on BiologyNow.

Section 47.12 The phosphorus cycle is the main sedimentary cycle. Earth's crust is the largest reservoir. Phosphorus is often the limiting factor on the population growth of producers. Excess inputs of phosphorus to aquatic ecosystems contribute to eutrophication.

Biology⊗Now
Learn how phosphorus is cycled with the animation on BiologyNow.

Self-Quiz

Answers in Appendix II

1. Ecosystems have _____ .
   a. energy inputs and outputs
   b. one trophic level
   c. no nutrient outputs; all nutrients are cycled
   d. a and b

2. Organisms at the lowest trophic level in a tallgrass prairie are all _____ .
   a. at the first step away from the original energy input
   b. autotrophs
   c. heterotrophs
   d. both a and b
   e. both a and c

3. Decomposers are commonly _____ .
   a. fungi   b. animals   c. bacteria   d. a and c

4. Trophic levels are _____ .
   a. structured feeding relationships
   b. a case of who eats whom in an ecosystem
   c. a hierarchy of energy transfers
   d. all of the above

5. Primary productivity on land is affected by _____ .
   a. nutrient availability   c. temperature
   b. amount of sunlight   d. all of the above

6. If biological magnification occurs, the _____ will have the highest levels of toxins in their systems.
   a. producers   c. primary carnivores
   b. herbivores   d. top carnivores

7. Disruption of the _____ cycle is depleting aquifers.
   a. hydrologic   c. nitrogen
   b. carbon   d. phosphorus

8. Earth's largest carbon reservoir is _____ .
   a. the atmosphere   c. seawater
   b. sediments and rocks   d. living organisms

9. The _____ cycle is a sedimentary cycle.
   a. hydrologic   c. nitrogen
   b. carbon   d. phosphorus

10. _____ is often a limiting factor for plant growth.
    a. Nitrogen   d. both a and c
    b. Carbon   e. all of the above
    c. Phosphorus

11. Nitrogen fixation converts _____ to _____ .
    a. nitrogen gas; ammonia   d. ammonia; nitrates
    b. nitrates; nitrites   e. nitrites; nitrogen oxides
    c. ammonia; nitrogen gas

12. Match the terms with suitable descriptions.
    ____ producers   a. feed on plants
    ____ herbivores   b. feed on small bits of organic matter
    ____ decomposers   c. degrade organic wastes and remains to inorganic forms
    ____ detritivores   d. capture sunlight energy

Additional questions are available on Biology⊗Now™

Critical Thinking

1. Visualize and then describe an extreme situation in which you are a participant in a food chain rather than a food web.

2. Marguerite is growing a vegetable garden in Maine. Eduardo is growing arugula in Spain. What are some of the variables that influence primary production in each of these locations?

3. Look around you and name all of the objects, natural or manufactured, that might be contributing to amplification of the greenhouse effect.

4. Polar ice shelves are vast, thickened sheets of ice that float on seawater. In March 2002, 3,200 square kilometers (1,410 square miles) of Antarctica's largest ice shelf broke free from the continent and shattered into thousands of icebergs (Figure 47.29). Scientists knew the ice shelf was shrinking and breaking up, but this was the single largest loss ever observed at one time. Why should this concern people who live in more temperate climates?

5. Fishes are a fine source of protein and of *omega-3 fatty acids*, which are necessary for the normal development of the nervous system. This would seem to make fish a good choice for pregnant women. But coal-burning power plants put mercury into the environment, and some of it ends up in fish. Eating mercury-tainted fish during pregnancy can adversely affect development of a fetal nervous system.

Tissues of predatory marine fishes, such as swordfishes, tunas, marlins, and sharks, have especially high levels of mercury. The Environmental Protection Agency has issued health advisories to pregnant women, suggesting that they limit their consumption of fish species most likely to be tainted with mercury. Although sardines are harvested from the same ocean, they have lower mercury levels and are not on the warning list. Explain why two species of fishes that live in the same place can have very different levels of mercury in their tissues.

6. Methane, remember, is a gaseous molecule of one carbon atom to which four hydrogens are attached (Section 3.1). *Methane hydrate* is a methane molecule surrounded by an icelike lattice of water molecules, and it forms only at low temperatures, high pressures, and high concentrations of methane. Such conditions prevail beneath the seafloor and in the arctic tundra, where vast deposits of methane hydrate have formed in frozen peat bogs. The deposits typically are hundreds of meters thick.

Over millions of years, ancient organisms that died and sank to the ocean floor were buried in sediments. Their carbon-rich remains are food for anaerobic archaeans living far beneath the seafloor. The archaeans produce methane, which bubbles up to the seafloor. There, the high pressures and low temperatures freeze the methane into solid blocks of methane hydrates (Figure 47.30).

Again, ocean deposits of methane hydrate hold 10,000 to 11,000 gigatons of methane. The next largest deposit, in arctic regions, only amounts to hundreds of gigatons. Significant amounts of carbon continually enter and leave the deposits. For instance, bacterial activity continually converts some of the methane to carbon dioxide, which helps control the amount of methane that can escape into the atmosphere.

The oceanic reservoir of methane hydrates may contain more carbon than all of the known reserves of oil, coal, and natural gas. However, the deposits are highly unstable; ice fills spaces in sediments, so increases in pressure or ocean water temperature can trigger catastrophic landslides and tsunamis. Reflect again on the global carbon cycle, then list some of the consequences of a catastrophic release of methane in terms of global temperature, climate, glaciation and sea level changes, and the composition of ocean water.

7. Reflect once more on Figure 47.30. The methane-eating and sulfate-eating bacteria near seeps on the seafloor are the start of food webs. Do some research and identify the producers and consumers in these deep-sea communities. Before you start, would you expect the food chains to be short or long? Make a list that organizes the participants by trophic levels.

Figure 47.29 Antarctica's Larson B ice shelf in (**a**) January and (**b**) March 2002. About 720 billion tons of ice broke from the shelf, forming thousands of icebergs. (**c**) These are the just the tips of the icebergs, projecting twenty-five meters (eighty-two feet) above the sea surface.

methane-eating archaeans (*red*) and sulfate-eating bacteria (*green*) near seeps

methane-producing archaeans

methane hydrates

Figure 47.30 Methane cycling on the seafloor. Archaeans beneath the seafloor produce methane that seeps out from seafloor sediments. There, methane-eating microbes release carbon dioxide as well as hydrogen sulfide as metabolic products that become the basis of deep-sea food webs.

Surfers, Seals, and the Sea

The stormy winter of 1997–1998 was a very good time for surfers on the lookout for the biggest waves, and a very bad time for seals and sea lions. As Ken Bradshaw rode a monster wave (Figure 48.8), half of the population of sea lions on the Galápagos Islands were dying, including nine of every ten sea lion pups. In California, the number of liveborn Northern fur seals plummeted. Most of the ones that made it through birth were dead within a few months. Diverse forms of life in distant parts of the world were connected by the full fury of El Niño—a recurring event that ushers in an often spectacular seesaw in the world climate.

That winter, a massive volume of warm water from the southwestern Pacific moved east. It piled into coasts from California down through Peru and displaced currents that otherwise would have churned up tons of nutrients from the deep. Without a replenishment of nutrients, primary producers for marine food webs declined in numbers. The scarcity of producers, in combination with the warmer water temperature, drove away consumers. The great populations of anchovies and some other fishes dispersed elsewhere. Fishes and squids that could not do so starved to death. So did many seals and sea lions, because fishes and squids are the mainstay of their diet.

Marine mammals did not dominate the headlines, because the 1997–1998 El Niño gave humans plenty of other things to worry about. It battered Pacific coasts with fierce winds and torrential rains that resulted in massive flooding and landslides. As another rippling effect, an ice storm in New York, New England, and central and eastern Canada crippled regional electrical grids. Three weeks later, 700,000 people still had no electricity. Meanwhile, the global seesaw caused drought-driven crop failures and raging wildfires in Australia and Indonesia.

Figure 48.1 Ken Bradshaw surfing a monster wave, more than twelve meters high, during the most powerful El Niño of the past century. In January 1998, a storm formed off the Siberian coast. It generated an ocean swell that, at the time, was the biggest wave known to hit Hawaii.

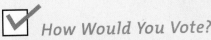
All told, that one El Niño episode killed thousands of people and drained away tens of billions of dollars from economies around the world.

The impact of El Niño on diverse communities invites us back to **biogeography**—the study of factors that give rise to patterns in the distribution of organisms through the environment. This chapter invites you to reflect on how climate, topography, human activities, and other factors influence that distribution in the space of the biosphere.

The **biosphere**, again, is the sum of all places where we find life on Earth. Organisms live in the *hydrosphere*—the ocean, ice caps, and other bodies of water, liquid and frozen. They live on and within sediments and soils of the *lithosphere*—Earth's outer, rocky layer. Many lift off into the lower region of the *atmosphere*—the gases and airborne particles that envelop Earth.

☑ How Would You Vote?

We cannot stop an El Niño from happening, but we might be able to minimize its environmental, social, and economic impacts. Would you support the use of taxpayer dollars to fund research into the causes and effects of El Niño? See BiologyNow for details, then vote online.

🔑 Key Concepts

AIR CIRCULATION PATTERNS

Indirectly, energy inputs from the sun are the starting point for the global distribution of communities and ecosystems. Its continual inputs of heat energy warm the atmosphere and drive Earth's weather systems. Sections 48.1, 48.2

OCEAN CIRCULATION PATTERNS

Atmospheric and ocean circulation patterns interact with topography and cause regional variations in temperature and rainfall. The interactions influence soils and sediments, which in turn affect the population growth and distribution of primary producers. Section 48.3

LAND PROVINCES

A biome is a vast region of land characterized partly by its distinctive, dominant vegetation. The global distribution of biomes is an outcome of Earth's physical history as well as climate, topography, soil type, and species interactions. Sections 48.4–48.11

WATER PROVINCES

Water provinces cover more than 71 percent of Earth's surface. Freshwater and marine ecosystems have gradients in light availability, temperature, and dissolved gases that vary daily and seasonally. Primary productivity shifts with the variations. Sections 48.12–48.15

APPLYING THE CONCEPTS

Understanding the interactions among the atmosphere, ocean, and land can lead to discoveries about specific events—in this case, recurring cholera epidemics—that impact human life. Section 48.16

 ## Links to Earlier Concepts

With this chapter, you have arrived at the highest level of organization in nature (Section 1.1). You will draw on earlier topics, from acid rain (2.6) to eutrophication (47.12), the ozone layer (7.1), soils (30.1), the carbon cycle (47.9), and ecosystem productivity (7.8, 47.4, 47.6). You will revisit agricultural practices (45.7), deforestation (23.10, 27.7, 47.7), coral reefs (27.5), and hydrothermal vents (20.2, 21.5). You will deepen your knowledge of biogeography (17.1, 27.6, 46.1, 46.11). The chapter ends with an example of the power of a scientific approach to problem solving (1.5, 1.6).

48.1 Global Air Circulation Patterns

LINKS TO
SECTIONS
7.1, 23.5

The biosphere encompasses ecosystems that range from continent-straddling forests to rainwater pools in cup-shaped clusters of leaves. Except for a few ecosystems at hydrothermal vents, climate influences all of them.

CLIMATE AND TEMPERATURE ZONES

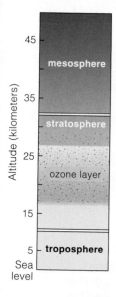

Climate refers to average weather conditions, such as cloud cover, temperature, humidity, and wind speed, over time. It arises from variations in solar radiation, Earth's daily rotation and annual path around the sun, the distribution of land masses and seas, and land elevations. Interactions among these factors are the source of prevailing winds and ocean currents, even the composition of soils.

First, sunlight warms air near Earth's surface (Figure 48.2). The sun's rays are spread out over a greater area near the poles (which intercept them at an angle) than they are at the equator (which intercepts them head-on). The intense light at the equator warms air a lot more. Warm air rises, then spreads north and south toward cooler regions—and so begins a global pattern of air circulation.

Earth's rotation and its curvature alter the initial air circulation pattern. Air masses moving north or south are not attached to Earth—which, like any ball, spins fastest at its equator during each spin around its axis. Air masses moving north or south from a given point *seem* to be deflected east or west relative to the curve of the surface spinning under them. This is the basis of prevailing east and west winds (Figure 48.3).

Also, land absorbs and gives up heat faster than the ocean, so air parcels above it sink and rise faster. Warm air expands, so its pressure is lower where it rises and greater where it cools and sinks. The uneven distribution of land and water between regions causes pressure differences. Regional winds arise and disrupt the overall flow of air from the equator to the poles.

In short, *latitudinal variations in solar heating cause a north–south pattern of air circulation, and then east–west deflections and air pressure differences over land and water introduce variations in the pattern.*

Differences in rainfall by latitude accompany the air circulation patterns. Warm air holds more moisture than cool air does. At the equator, warm air masses pick up moisture from the ocean, then rise and cool.

Figure 48.2 *Above*, Earth's atmosphere. Air circulates mainly in the lower atmosphere, or troposphere, where temperatures cool rapidly with increases in altitude. An ozone layer between 17 and 27 kilometers above sea level absorbs most of the ultraviolet (UV) wavelengths in the sun's rays. Ozone and oxygen in the atmosphere absorb most of the incoming UV light.

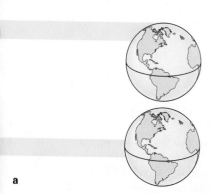

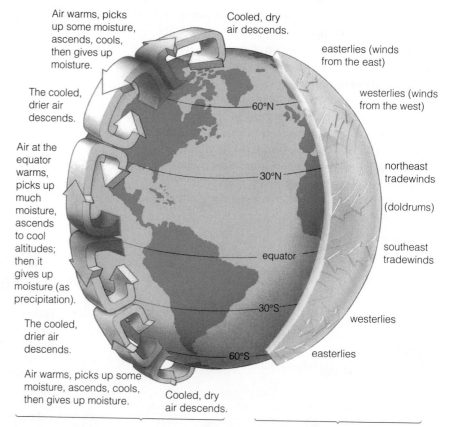

Figure 48.3 *Animated!* (**a**) Concentration of rays from the sun, by latitude. (**b,c**) Global air circulation patterns. Latitudinal differences in the solar heating start a north–south air circulation pattern. As Earth's rotation and its curvature deflect the pattern, prevailing east and west winds arise.

Air warms, picks up some moisture, ascends, cools, then gives up moisture.

Cooled, dry air descends.

easterlies (winds from the east)

westerlies (winds from the west)

The cooled, drier air descends.

Air at the equator warms, picks up much moisture, ascends to cool altitudes; then it gives up moisture (as precipitation).

northeast tradewinds

(doldrums)

southeast tradewinds

60°N

30°N

equator

30°S

60°S

westerlies

easterlies

The cooled, drier air descends.

Air warms, picks up some moisture, ascends, cools, then gives up moisture.

Cooled, dry air descends.

b Initial pattern of air circulation as air masses warm and rise, then cool and fall.

c Deflections in the initial pattern near Earth's surface.

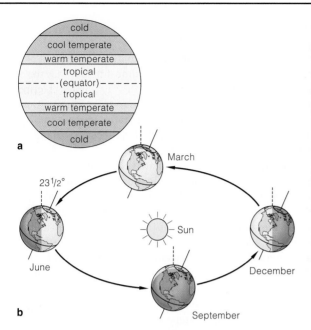

Figure 48.4 (a) World temperature zones. (b) Incoming solar radiation varies annually. The northern end of Earth's fixed axis tilts toward the sun in June and away from it in December, changing the equator's position relative to the day–night boundary of illumination. Variations in sunlight intensity and daylength cause seasonal temperature shifts.

Figure 48.5 (a) Large arrays of electricity-producing photovoltaic cells in panels that collect solar energy. (b) In California, a field of turbines harvesting wind energy.

They give up some moisture as rain, which supports forest ecosystems. The now-drier air moves north or south. It warms and loses more moisture as it descends at latitudes 30°, where deserts typically form. Farther north and south, air picks up moisture, ascends, and gives up rain near latitudes 60°. It descends in polar regions, where cold temperatures and a near-absence of precipitation result in cold, dry polar deserts.

We divide the temperature gradients from Earth's equator to the poles into **temperature zones** (Figure 48.4a). Temperatures shift in the zones as Earth's orbit puts it closer to and farther from the sun during each annual cycle (Figure 48.4b). Temperatures, the hours of daylight, and winds change with the seasons. The changes are far greater inland (away from the ocean's moderating effects) and farther from the equator. The more pronounced the change, the more that primary productivity rises and falls on land and in the seas.

HARNESSING THE SUN AND WIND

Paralleling the human population's J-shaped growth curve is a steep rise in its total and per capita energy consumption. You may think we have an abundance of energy, but there is a big difference between total and net amounts. *Net* is what is left after subtracting the energy it takes to find, extract, transport, store, and deliver energy to consumers. Some sources, such

as coal, are not renewable (Section 23.5), but solar and wind energy are another matter. Every year, incoming solar energy surpasses, by about ten times, the energy that is stored in all known fossil fuel reserves.

We already know how to get *solar–hydrogen energy*. Photovoltaic cells (Figure 48.5a) hold electrodes that, when exposed to the sun's rays, generate an electric current that splits water molecules into oxygen and hydrogen gas, which can be stored efficiently. The gas can directly fuel cars. It can heat and cool buildings. Water is the only waste. It also costs less to distribute hydrogen gas than electricity. Space satellites run on it.

Unlike fossil fuels, the sun's energy and seawater are unlimited. A solar–hydrogen age might end smog, oil spills, acid rain, and a reliance on nuclear energy, and it might help reduce global warming.

Solar energy also is converted into the mechanical energy of winds. Turbines at "wind farms" exploit the wind patterns that arise from latitudinal variations in sunlight intensity. Wind power provides California with 1 percent of its electricity. Winds of North and South Dakota might meet 80 percent of the current energy needs of the United States. Winds do not blow constantly, but when they do, wind energy can be fed into utility grids. Wind power also has potential for islands and other areas remote from utility grids.

Major temperature zones and climates start with global patterns of circulation, which arise through interacting factors: latitudinal variations in incoming solar radiation, Earth's rotation and annual path around the sun, and the distribution of land masses and seas.

48.2 Circulating Airborne Pollutants

LINKS TO
SECTIONS 2.6,
7.1, 42.9, 47.9

Through activities that pollute the air, human populations interact with global air circulation patterns in unexpected ways, with unintended consequences. **Pollutants** *are any natural or synthetic substances that have accumulated in harmful or disruptive amounts because organisms have had no prior evolutionary experience with them.*

A Fence of Wind and Ozone Thinning

The ozone layer (Figure 48.2) is nearly twice as high above sea level as Mount Everest. From September to October, it thins above both poles. Seasonal **ozone thinning** is so vast that it was once called an "ozone hole" in the stratosphere. Figure 48.6 has an example. With a decline in the ozone concentration, far more UV radiation reaches Earth's surface. That is why the declining concentration correlates with increasing cases of skin cancers, cataracts, and weakened immunity. It also alters the atmosphere's composition indirectly. UV radiation kills phytoplankton, which results in drastic declines in their oxygen-releasing activity (Section 7.8).

Chlorofluorocarbons (CFCs) are major ozone destroyers. These odorless gases have been used as propellants in aerosol cans, coolants in refrigerators and air conditioners, and in solvents and plastic foam. They slowly seep into the air, and they resist breakdown. A free CFC molecule gives up a chlorine atom when it absorbs UV light. Reaction of this atom with ozone yields oxygen and chlorine monoxide. Chloride monoxide in turn reacts with free oxygen and releases another chlorine. Each chlorine atom can break apart more than 10,000 ozone molecules!

Chlorine monoxide concentrations above polar regions are 100 to 500 times higher than at midlatitudes. Why? Like a dynamic fence, winds rotate around the poles for most of the winter. Chlorine compounds are split apart on ice crystals in the clouds. After the almost perpetually dark polar winter ends, UV light in the sun's rays invites chlorine to start destroying ozone. Methyl bromide is worse for the ozone layer. Each year in the United States, farmers spray about 60 million pounds of this fumigant over croplands to kill insects, nematodes, and other pests.

Developed countries phased out CFC production. The developing countries may phase it out by 2010. Methyl bromide production is expected to end at that time as well. Even so, it will be one or two centuries before the ozone layer fully recovers.

In 2004 the destruction of ozone reached near-record levels, with close to a 50 percent loss in some parts of the stratosphere. However, in 2005, it became apparent that global forces can mediate the impact. Stratospheric wind patterns shifted and transported ozone-rich air northward from the midlatitudes. Ozone levels in polar regions were restored to near-normal levels.

No Wind, Lots of Pollutants, and Smog

Certain weather conditions trap a layer of cool, dense air under a warm air layer. This is a *thermal inversion*. It intensifies **smog**, an atmospheric condition in which winds cannot disperse air pollutants that have accumulated and are trapped under a thermal inversion layer (Figure 48.7). Thermal inversions in certain parts of the world have contributed to some of the worst air pollution disasters.

Where winters are cold and wet, *industrial* smog forms as a gray haze over cities that burn a lot of coal and other fossil fuels. Burning releases smoke, soot, ashes, asbestos, oil, particles of lead and other heavy metals, and sulfur oxides. If winds and rain do not disperse them, these air

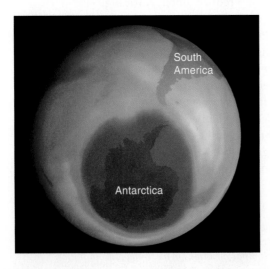

Figure 48.6 Seasonal ozone thinning above Antarctica during 2001. *Darkest blue* indicates the area with the lowest ozone level, at that time the largest recorded.

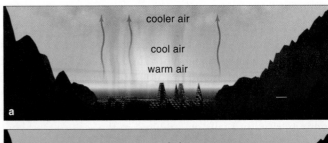
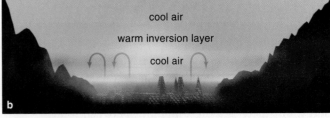

Figure 48.7 (**a**) Normal pattern of air circulation in smog-forming regions. (**b**) Air pollutants are trapped under a thermal inversion layer.

pollutants can reach lethal concentrations. Most industrial smog now forms in China, India, and eastern Europe.

Big cities in warm climate zones are bathed in a brown haze called *photochemical* smog. This type of smog is most dense when the city is in a natural topographic basin. Los Angeles and Mexico City are two classic cases (Figure 47.23). Exhaust fumes from vehicles contain nitric oxide, a major pollutant that forms nitrogen dioxide by combining with oxygen. When sunlight strikes it, nitrogen dioxide reacts with hydrocarbon gases to form photochemical oxidants. Most hydrocarbon gases are released from spilled or partly burned gasoline.

Winds and Acid Rain Coal-burning power plants, smelters, and factories emit sulfur dioxides. Vehicles, power plants that burn gas and oil, and nitrogen-rich fertilizers all emit nitrogen oxides. In dry weather, airborne oxides fall as dry acid deposition. In moist air, they form nitric acid vapor, sulfuric acid droplets, and sulfate and nitrate salts. Winds typically disperse them far from their source. They fall to Earth in rain and snow. We call this wet acid deposition, or **acid rain**.

The pH of typical rainwater is 5 or so (Section 2.6). Acid rain can be 0 to 100 times more acidic, as potent as lemon juice! It corrodes metals, marble, rubber, plastics, nylon stockings, and other materials. It harms organisms, and it can alter the chemistry of ecosystems.

Depending on the soil type and vegetation cover, some regions are more sensitive to acid rain (Figure 48.8). Highly alkaline soil neutralizes acids before they enter streams and lakes. Also, highly alkaline water can neutralize the acid inputs. But many of the watersheds of northern Europe, southeastern Canada, and regions throughout the United States have thin soil layers on top of solid granite. These soils cannot buffer much of the acidic inputs.

Rain in much of eastern North America is thirty to forty times more acidic than it was even a few decades ago. Crop yields are declining. Fish populations have disappeared from more than 200 lakes in the Adirondack Mountains of New York. Air pollutants from distant industrial regions are changing the acidity of rainfall. The change is contributing to the decline of forest trees and mycorrhizae that support new growth.

As Harvard and Brigham Young University researchers report, living with airborne particles of dust, soot, smoke, or acid droplets shortens the human life span by a year or so. Smaller airborne particles damage lung tissues. High levels of ultrafine particles can increase the risk of lung cancer (Figure 48.9).

At one time, the world's tallest smokestack, in the Canadian province of Ontario, produced 1 percent by weight of the world's annual emissions of sulfur dioxide. Today, however, Canada gets more acid deposition from the midwestern United States than it sends across its southern border. *Prevailing winds—hence air pollutants— do not stop at national boundaries.*

pH	
	>5.3
	5.2–5.3
	5.1–5.2
	5.0–5.1
	4.9–5.0
	4.8–4.9
	4.7–4.8
	4.6–4.7
	4.5–4.6
	4.4–4.5
	4.3–4.4
	<4.3

Figure 48.8 (**a**) The average 1998 precipitation acidities in the United States. *Red* dots mark large coal-burning power and industrial plants. (**b**) Biologist measuring the pH of New York's Woods Lake during a spring melt of acidified snow. Acid rain has already altered the lake.

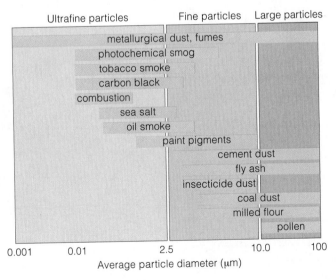

Figure 48.9 Suspended particulate matter. These solids and liquid droplets are small enough to stay aloft for variable intervals.

Ultrafine particles contribute to respiratory disorders. Carbon black is a powdered form of carbon used in paints, tires, and other goods. About 6 million tons are manufactured annually. About 45 million tons of fly ash are generated annually by coal combustion.

48.3 The Ocean, Landforms, and Climates

LINKS TO
SECTIONS
26.13, 47.10

The ocean is a continuous body of water that covers more than 71 percent of Earth's surface. Driven by solar heat and wind friction, its upper 10 percent moves in currents that distribute nutrients through marine ecosystems.

OCEAN CURRENTS AND THEIR EFFECTS

Latitudinal and seasonal variations in sunlight warm and cool water. At the equator, where vast volumes of water warm and expand, the sea level is about eight centimeters (three inches) higher than at either pole. The volume of water in this "slope" is enough to get sea surface water moving in response to gravity, most often toward the poles. The moving water warms air parcels above it. At midlatitudes it transfers *10 million billion* calories of heat energy per second to the air!

Ocean currents are large volumes of water flowing in response to the tug of trade winds and westerlies. Their direction and properties are outcomes of Earth's rotation and topography. They circulate clockwise in the Northern Hemisphere and counterclockwise in the Southern Hemisphere (Figure 48.10).

Swift, deep, and narrow currents of nutrient-poor water parallel the east coast of continents. Along the eastern coast of North America, warm water moves northward, as the Gulf Stream. Slower, shallow, broad currents of cold water paralleling the western coast of continents flow toward the equator.

These currents affect climate zones. Why are Pacific Northwest coasts cool and foggy in summer? The cold California Current is giving up moisture; warm winds by the coast are transferring heat to it. Why are Boston and Baltimore muggy in summer? Air masses pick up heat and moisture from the warm Gulf Stream, then southerly and easterly winds put them over the cities. Why are the winters milder in London and Edinburgh than they are in Ontario and central Canada—which are at the same latitude? Warm water from the Gulf Stream flows into the North Atlantic Current (Figure 48.10). That current gives up heat to prevailing winds, which warm northwestern Europe.

The patterns changed in the past. They may change again if global warming disrupts ocean currents and climate zones (Sections 26.13 and 47.10).

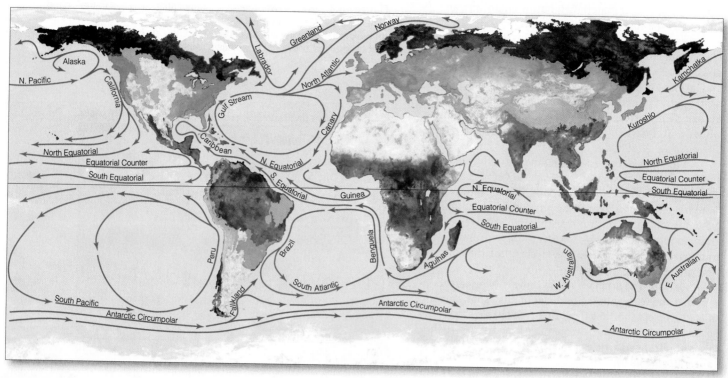

Figure 48.10 *Animated!* Major climate zones correlated with surface currents and surface drifts of the world ocean. The warm surface currents start moving from the equator toward the poles, but prevailing winds, Earth's rotation, gravity, the shape of ocean basins, and land masses all influence the direction of flow. Water temperatures, which differ with latitude and depth, contribute to differences in air temperature and in rainfall patterns.

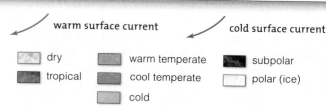

warm surface current   cold surface current

dry   warm temperate   subpolar
tropical   cool temperate   polar (ice)
cold

a Prevailing winds move moisture inland from the Pacific

b Clouds pile up and rain forms on side of mountain range facing prevailing winds

c Rain shadow on side facing away from the prevailing winds makes arid conditions

4,000/ 75
3,000/ 85   2,000/ 25
1,800/ 125   1,000/ 25
1,000/ 85
moist habitats
15/ 25

Figure 48.11 *Animated!* Rain shadow effect and the Sierra Nevada. On the side of mountains facing away from the prevailing winds, rainfall is light. *Black* numbers signify annual precipitation, in centimeters, averaged on both sides of this mountain range. The *white* numbers signify elevations, in meters.

RAIN SHADOWS AND MONSOONS

Mountains, valleys, and other topographical features affect regional climates. *Topography* refers to a region's surface features, such as elevation. Track a warm air mass after it picks up moisture off California's coast. It moves inland, as wind from the west, and piles up against the Sierra Nevada. This high mountain range parallels the distant coast. The air cools as it rises in altitude and loses moisture as rain (Figure 48.11). The result is a **rain shadow**—a semiarid or arid region of sparse rainfall on the leeward side of high mountains. *Leeward* is the side facing away from the wind. The Himalayas, Andes, Rockies, and other great mountain ranges cause vast rain shadows on continents.

Belts of vegetation at different elevations relate to differences in temperature and moisture. Grasslands form at the western base of the Sierra Nevada. Higher up, in the cooler air, deciduous and evergreen species reign. Higher still are a few evergreen species that are adapted to the cold habitat. Above the subalpine belt, hardy, dwarfed plants are all that can withstand even more extreme temperatures.

There are rain shadows on the leeward side of the Andes, Rockies, Himalayas, and other great mountain ranges. On the side of Hawaii's high volcanic peaks facing into the wind (*windward*), lush tropical forests flourish. Desert conditions prevail on the other side.

Air circulation patterns called **monsoons** influence continents that lie north or south of warm oceans. The land near these oceans heats intensely in summer, and vast, low-pressure air parcels form above it. The low pressure draws moisture-laden air from the ocean, as from the Bay of Bengal into Bangladesh. Trade winds converge here. Together with the equatorial sun, they invite intense heating and heavy rainfall. Air moving northward and southward across the continents gives rise to alternating dry and wet seasons, to alternating drought conditions and flooding.

Recurring coastal breezes are like mini-monsoons. Water and coastal land have different heat capacities. In the morning, water does not warm as fast as land. When warm air above land rises, cooler marine air moves in. After sunset, the land loses heat faster than water, so land breezes flow in the reverse direction.

Surface ocean currents influence regional climates and help distribute nutrients in marine ecosystems.

Air circulation patterns, ocean currents, and landforms interact in ways that influence regional temperatures and moisture levels. Thus they also influence the distribution and dominant features of ecosystems.

48.4 Biogeographic Realms

LINKS TO
SECTIONS 17.1,
27.6, 46.11

Differences in physical and chemical properties, and in evolutionary history, help explain why deserts, grasslands, forests, and tundra form where they do, and why some water provinces are richer than others in biodiversity.

Suppose you live in the coastal hills of California and decide to tour the Mediterranean coast, the southern tip of Africa, and central Chile. In each region, you see highly branched, tough-leafed woody plants that look a lot like the highly branched, tough-leafed chaparral plants back home. Vast geographic and evolutionary distances separate the plants. Why are they alike?

You decide to compare their locations on a global map. You discover that American and African desert plants live about the same distance from the equator. Chaparral plants and their distant look-alikes all grow along the western and southern coasts of continents positioned between latitudes 30° and 40°. As Alfred

Wallace, Charles Darwin, and other naturalists did so long ago, you have just stumbled onto one of many biogeographic patterns.

Those naturalists divided Earth's land masses into six **biogeographic realms**—vast expanses where they could expect to find communities of certain types of plants and animals, such as palm trees and camels in the Ethiopian realm (Section 46.11 and Figure 46.29). In time, the classic realms shown in Figure 48.12 were subdivided, as when Hawaii, parts of Indonesia and Japan, and Polynesia, Micronesia, Papua New Guinea, and New Zealand became the Oceania realm.

Biomes are finer subdivisions of the great realms, but they are still identifiable on a global scale. Their distribution has been shaped partly by evolutionary processes and events, as when evolving species were slowly rafted about on different land masses after the splitting of Pangea (Chapter 17). They also owe their

desert

dry shrubland, dry woodland

warm grassland (e.g., savanna)

temperate grassland

mountain grassland

tropical broadleaf forest

temperate deciduous forest

tropical coniferous forest

temperate coniferous forest (e.g., rain forest)

northern coniferous forest (boreal forest)

tropical dry forest

tundra

mountains, complex zonation

mangrove swamp

perpetual ice cover

marine ecoregions

Figure 48.12 *Animated!* Global distribution of major categories of biomes and marine ecoregions.

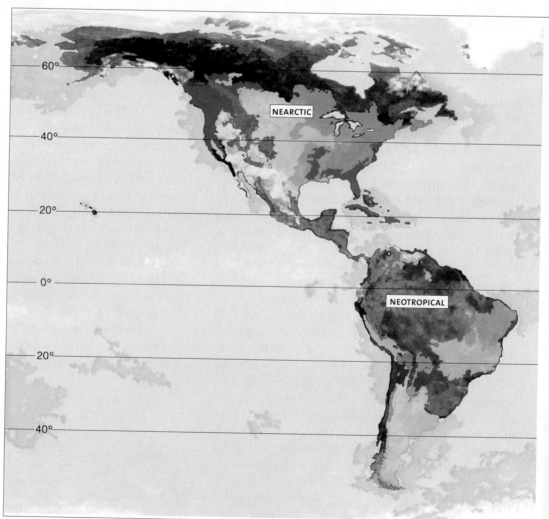

distribution to topography, climate, and interactions among species. Some biomes extend across more than one continent, and their communities, although similar in many ways, consist of unique species. Notice, in Figure 48.12, the distribution of dry shrublands and woodlands (coded dark brown). Chaparral is part of that biome. Similarly, the temperate grassland biome occurs in North America (the prairie), South America (pampa), southern Africa (veld), and Eurasia (steppe). In each case, the community is dominated by grasses that can tolerate strong winds and drought.

In general, communities that characterize a biome are arrays of species adapted to specific temperatures, patterns of rainfall, soil type, and one another. The community's consumers are adapted to the dominant vegetation, as when tall forest trees invite competitive birds to partition resources between the forest floor and the canopy (Sections 46.1 and 46.3). Adaptations,

recall, extend from the form, function, and behavior of each species to its life-history pattern.

Evolutionary events and environmental conditions also underlie the distribution of communities in the seas. Figure 48.12 shows the main marine ecoregions.

Remember Section 27.6? It sketches out the sweep of conservation biology. Conservationists are working to locate, inventory, and protect the world's **hot spots**, portions of biomes and ecoregions that are richest in biodiversity and the most vulnerable to species losses. There are 150 hot spots in North America alone.

> Biomes are vast expanses of land dominated by distinct kinds of communities. Marine ecoregions are realms of biodiversity in the seas. Their distribution is an outcome of evolutionary history, topography, climate, and species interactions, which vary in different parts of the world.

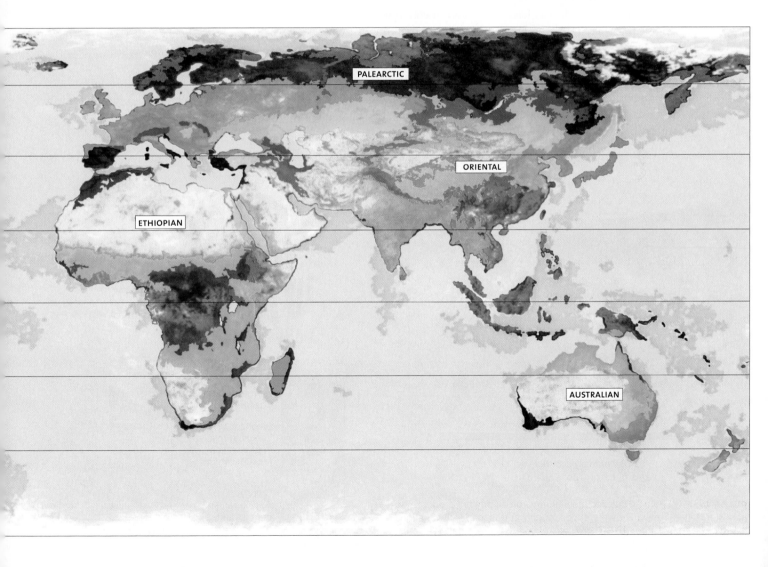

48.5 Availabililty of Sunlight, Soils, and Moisture

LINKS TO
SECTIONS 23.10,
24.6, 30.1, 47.11

Biomes differ in their soil profiles. They differ in their daily and seasonal supplies of water and other resources, and therefore in their primary productivity.

Soils are mixtures of mineral particles and varying amounts of the decomposing organic material we call humus. When rocks are weathered and broken down, they form coarse-grained gravel, then sand, silt, and finely grained clay. Water and air fill spaces between soil particles. As explained in Section 30.1, the types, proportions, and compaction of particles differ within and between regions. Clay is richest in minerals, but its fine, closely packed particles drain poorly. It also does not have enough air spaces for roots to take up oxygen. Gravelly or sandy soils invite leaching, which depletes them of water and mineral ions.

Biome soils differ in their layered structure, or *soil profile*, which reflects how they formed (Figure 48.13). Natural grasslands and then deciduous forests tend to have the most topsoil. Topsoil is richest in humus but is easily eroded. It is less than 1 centimeter thick on steep slopes. It can be more than 1 meter thick in grasslands, which is why former grasslands are the top choice for agriculture. Tropical forests also are cleared for agriculture, but little topsoil accumulates above their poorly draining layers. Clearing exposes topsoil to rains that leach nutrients, so crops perform poorly unless heavily fertilized, as Section 47.11 explains.

Reflect on the map in Figure 48.13a. Where there is plenty of moisture, competition for sunlight influences community structure. That is why the sun-drenched deciduous forests have an obvious vertical structure. As you will see, dense stands of trees form a canopy high above the ground. Shorter, understory trees and shrubs compete for light filtering through the canopy.

Where desert biomes have formed, you seldom find competition for sunlight. Water is the key limiting factor in deserts. As you saw in Section 45.2, widely spaced desert plants are evidence of root systems that compete for this scarce resource.

Some parts of desert biomes are monotonously low in biodiversity. Figure 48.14a shows part of hundreds of square kilometers of the Sonoran Desert in Arizona, where you see little more than widely spaced creosote bushes. Add some moisture and a higher elevation to the mix, and you see more diversity, as in this desert's wetter uplands (Figure 48.14b). The caption to Figure 48.15 offers a glimpse into how desert soils form.

A biome's soil profile and its proportions of sand, silt, clay, gravel, and humus influence its primary productivity.

Even within the boundaries of the same biome, differences in water availability and temperature can bring about big differences in species richness.

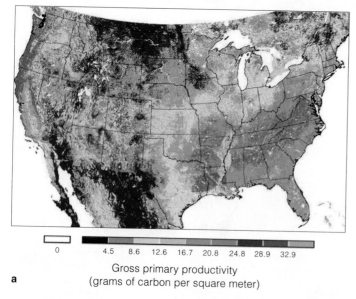

a

Gross primary productivity
(grams of carbon per square meter)

0   4.5   8.6   12.6   16.7   20.8   24.8   28.9   32.9

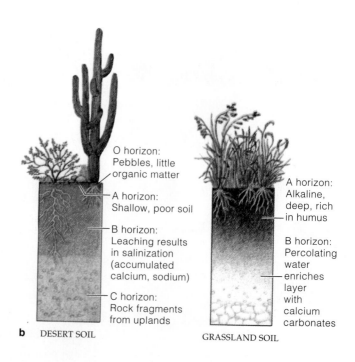

O horizon:
Pebbles, little
organic matter

A horizon:
Shallow, poor soil

B horizon:
Leaching results
in salinization
(accumulated
calcium, sodium)

C horizon:
Rock fragments
from uplands

b DESERT SOIL

A horizon:
Alkaline,
deep, rich
in humus

B horizon:
Percolating
water
enriches
layer
with
calcium
carbonates

GRASSLAND SOIL

Figure 48.13   (**a**) Remote satellite monitoring of gross primary productivity across the United States. The differences roughly correspond with variations in soil types and moisture. (**b**) Soil profiles from a few representative biomes.

a

b

Figure 48.14 Two views of a single biome—the Sonoran Desert of Arizona. Sunlight is equally intense in the lowlands (**a**) and uplands (**b**), but differences in water availability, temperature, and soil types influence plant growth.

Compared to wetter biomes, deserts are low in primary productivity. All desert soils are mineral-rich, but they are in an early stage of development. Particles in the upper horizons are loose and not yet stabilized. Little organic matter accumulates at the surface, so decomposers cannot form much humus. The soils cannot hold on to water, which falls only in intense pulses during a brief rainy season. Also, evaporative water loss from desert soils is high, so dissolved salts rise to the soil surface. Extensive saltpans form, and they support little to no plant growth.

The uplands rarely frost over. Also, they get heavy pulses of rain in summer and light but prolonged rain in winter. Annuals and perennials that bloom in summer and winter are not as water-stressed in the uplands. In hotter, drier, flat valley floors, temperatures are extremely high, rainfall is sparse, and woody plants are widely spaced. Creosote bush (*Larrea*), sometimes mixed with bursage (*Ambrosia*), dominates.

Figure 48.15 How desert soils start. Over millions of years, rain, wind, freezes and thaws, and chemical processing erode mountain ranges. Runoff moves small, loose rocks and particles toward the floor of adjoining valleys. Gravel, sand and silt collect in lowland deserts. *Cryptobiotic crusts* may form. These desert encrustations are mainly lichens, which slowly enrich the soil (Section 24.6). Where a thin humus layer forms, as in the Sonoran uplands, the soil stabilizes and holds some water. When dune buggies race across "empty" deserts, they destroy the crusts.

The photograph shows debris in a gully at the base of some mountains in the Chihuahuan Desert in Texas. The gully channels water draining from the slopes, and accumulated debris has stabilized enough to support woody shrubs and herbaceous plants. Plants are sparse on the gully's right slope. They are less water-stressed on the left side, which is shaded during the hottest time of day.

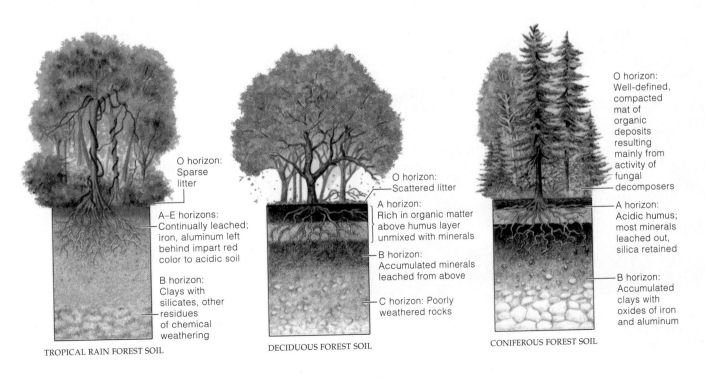

O horizon: Sparse litter

A–E horizons: Continually leached; iron, aluminum left behind impart red color to acidic soil

B horizon: Clays with silicates, other residues of chemical weathering

TROPICAL RAIN FOREST SOIL

O horizon: Scattered litter

A horizon: Rich in organic matter above humus layer unmixed with minerals

B horizon: Accumulated minerals leached from above

C horizon: Poorly weathered rocks

DECIDUOUS FOREST SOIL

O horizon: Well-defined, compacted mat of organic deposits resulting mainly from activity of fungal decomposers

A horizon: Acidic humus; most minerals leached out, silica retained

B horizon: Accumulated clays with oxides of iron and aluminum

CONIFEROUS FOREST SOIL

48.6 Moisture-Challenged Biomes

LINK TO
SECTION
27.4

At certain latitudes with sparse rainfall and high rates of evaporation, drought-tolerant plants predominate.

DESERTS

Deserts tend to form near latitudes 30° north and south. Annual rainfall is less than ten centimeters or so, and evaporation rates are high. Brief, infrequent pulses of rain swiftly erode the topsoil. Humidity is so low that the sun's rays easily penetrate air masses. The ground heats fast, then cools fast at night. The arid or semiarid conditions do not support large, leafy plants, but, as the preceding section explained, the species richness is often high where moisture is available in more than one season. Figure 48.16 shows another example.

DRY SHRUBLANDS, WOODLANDS, AND GRASSLANDS

Dry shrublands receive less than 25 to 60 centimeters of rain a year. They dominate Mediterranean, South African, and California regions that are vulnerable to lightning-sparked, wind-driven firestorms in summer.

DESERTS

Figure 48.16 From the Mojave Desert of California, cactus (cholla), golden poppies, and—in the distance—tall saguaro cacti. The inset shows flowers of a claret cup cactus.

The shrubs have highly flammable leaves and quickly burn to the ground. They are adapted to episodes of fire and resprout from the root crowns. Trees do not fare as well during firestorms. Shrubs that withstand the fires have a competitive edge (Figure 48.17).

Dry woodlands prevail where annual rainfall is 40 to 100 centimeters. Trees are often tall, but they do not provide a continuous canopy. Eucalyptus-dominated areas of southwestern Australia and oak woodlands of California and Oregon are examples.

Grasslands form in the interior of continents in the zones between deserts and temperate forests (Figure 48.18). Summers are warm; winters are cold. Annual rainfall of 25 to 100 centimeters prevents deserts from forming, but this is not enough to support forests. The primary producers tolerate strong winds, sparse and infrequent rain, rapid evaporation, and drought. The dominant animals are grazing and burrowing species. Their activities, combined with infrequent fires, help stop shrublands and forests from encroaching on the fringes of many grasslands.

Between the tropical forests and the hot deserts of Africa, South America, and Australia are savannas—broad belts of grasslands with a few shrubs and trees (Figure 48.18a). Rainfall averages 90–150 centimeters per year. Droughts are seasonal. Where rainfall is low, fast-growing grasses prevail. The savannas grade into tropical woodlands, where low trees and shrubs, and coarse grasses, die and often burn in the dry season.

On flat or rolling land in North America, native shortgrass and tallgrass prairie once prevailed (Figure 48.18b,c). Roots of perennial grasses extended deep into rich topsoil. In the 1930s, shortgrass prairie in the Great Plains was overgrazed. It also was plowed to grow wheat. Prolonged droughts killed this crop, and strong winds stripped away the topsoil. The region became "the Dust Bowl." John Steinbeck's novel *The Grapes of Wrath* is a glimpse into the human tragedies that unfolded because of this environmental disaster.

Grasses two meters tall gave the tallgrass prairie its name. Legumes and composites, including daisies, thrived amidst the grasses in the continent's eastern interior. Nearly all of the original tallgrass prairie has now been converted to cereal croplands (Section 27.4). A few patches that did escape the plow are protected reserves; some others are being restored.

Deserts, dry shrublands, dry woodlands, and grasslands form in regions of sparse rainfall, dry air, strong winds, and recurring episodes of drought and fire.

Figure 48.17 *Above*, two views of California chaparral. The dominant plants are multibranched, woody, and typically only a few meters tall. They are adapted to periodic fires; some produce seeds that germinate only after a fire. This fire raced through chaparral-choked canyons above Malibu. California has 2.4 million hectares (6 million acres) of this dry shrubland.

Figure 48.18 *Right*, (**a**) scarce water in the African savanna, attracting a big herd of wildebeest. Other herbivores of this immense grassland include Cape buffalos, zebras, impalas, giraffes, and Thomson's gazelles.

(**b**) Shortgrass prairie, east of the Rocky Mountains, that once sustained an estimated 60 million bison.

(**c**) A rare patch of natural tallgrass prairie in eastern Kansas.

48.7 More Rain, Broadleaf Forests

LINKS TO
SECTIONS
23.10, 30.1

In forest biomes, tall trees grow close together and form a fairly continuous canopy over a broad region. Rainfall and distance from the equator influence which trees dominate.

TROPICAL RAIN FORESTS

Evergreen broadleaf forests form between latitudes 10° north and south—equatorial zones of Africa, the East Indies, Malaysia, Southeast Asia, South America, and Central America. Rainfall is a whopping 130 to 200 centimeters per year. Regular rains, an annual mean temperature of 25°C, and at least 80 percent humidity support tropical rain forests of the sort shown on the facing page. In structure and diversity, these biomes are the most complex. Some trees are 30.5 meters (100 feet) tall. Many form a closed canopy that stops much of the sunlight from reaching the forest floor. Hence we see a profusion of epiphytes, vines, and climbers.

Decomposition and mineral cycling are rapid in these forests, so litter does not accumulate. The soils are highly weathered, heavily leached, and very poor nutrient reservoirs. You read about the consequences in earlier chapters (Sections 23.10 and 30.1).

SEMI-EVERGREEN AND DECIDUOUS BROADLEAF FORESTS

Away from the equatorial forests, between latitudes 10° to 25°, the dry season grows longer, and broadleaf forests are less and less complex. In humid, tropical regions of Southeast Asia and India, decomposition is slow, and *semi-evergreen forests* form. Where less than 2.5 centimeters (1 inch) of rain falls in the dry season, *tropical deciduous broadleaf* forests form.

Broadleaf deciduous forests form in warm or humid subtropical parts of eastern North America, western and central Europe, and eastern Asia, including Japan. There is a six-month growing season. About 50–150 centimeters (about 20–60 inches) of precipitation fall throughout the year. Oak, hickory, maple, beech, elm, basswood, sweet gum, chestnut, and walnut trees are dominant. Rhododendrons, azaleas, mountain laurel, lichens, club mosses, and mosses thrive in the forests.

Particularly in undisturbed forests of eastern North America, leaves turn almost fluorescent red, orange, and yellow before dropping in autumn (Figure 48.19). The leaf drop is considerable from these fast-growing trees, and it starts decaying into rich humus in spring. Soils of temperate deciduous forests in the Northern Hemisphere rank among the most fertile. That is why vast tracts have been cleared for agriculture. In some parts of the world, the cleared tracts have been under cultivation for thousands of years.

Conditions in broadleaf forest biomes favor dense stands of trees that form a continuous canopy over broad regions. As in other forest biomes, tree structure and growth patterns are adapted to patterns in rainfall and temperature.

BROADLEAF FORESTS

Figure 48.19 North American temperate deciduous forest. The series above shows changes in one deciduous tree's foliage from fall (*far left*) through winter, spring, and summer.

48.8 You and the Tropical Forests

You read about economic aspects of the destruction of tropical rain forests in earlier chapters. We invite you to reflect on a few more consequences of deforestation.

Developing nations in Latin America, Southeast Asia, and Africa have the fastest-growing populations but not enough food, fuel, and lumber. Of necessity, they turn to their forests for growth-sustaining resources. Most of the forests may disappear within your lifetime. That possibility elicits the most outcries from concerned groups in highly developed nations—which happen to use most of the world's resources, including forest products.

For purely ethical reasons, many people condemn the destruction of so much biodiversity. Tropical rain forests have the greatest variety and numbers of insects, and the world's largest ones. They are homes to the most species of birds and to plants with the largest flowers (*Rafflesia*). The forest canopy and understory support monkeys, tapirs, and jaguars in South America and apes, okapi, and leopards in Africa. Massive vines twist around trees. Orchids, mosses, lichens, and other organisms grow on branches, absorbing minerals that rains deliver to them. Entire communities of microbes, insects, spiders, and amphibians live, breed, and die in small pools of water that collect in furled leaves.

Their disappearance will have repercussions on your life. The few strains of crop plants and livestock that sustain most human populations are vulnerable to ever evolving pathogens. Tissue-culture specialists and genetic engineers use genes of forest species to develop new or hybrid strains that can make our food base less vulnerable. Geneticists use them to develop better antibiotics and vaccines. Aspirin, the most widely used painkiller, is based on a chemical blueprint of an extract from tropical willow leaves. Many ornamental plants, spices, and foods, including cinnamon, cocoa, and coffee, originated in tropical forests. So did the latex, gums, resins, dyes, waxes, and oils used in tires, shoes, toothpaste, ice cream, shampoo, compact discs, condoms, and perfumes. And think about this: The burning of tropical forests around the world is releasing enough air pollutants to change the air you breathe and possibly to help overheat the planet in your lifetime.

And so conservation biologists rightly decry the mass extinction, the assaults on species diversity, the depletion of much of the world's genetic reservoir. Yet something else is going on here. Too many of us grow uneasy when we pass through obliterated forests in our own country. Is it because we are losing the comfort of our heritage—a connection with our evolutionary past? Many millions of years ago, our earliest primate ancestors moved into the trees of tropical forests. Through countless generations, their nervous and sensory systems evolved and became highly responsive to information-rich, arboreal worlds.

Does our neural wiring still resonate with rustling leaves, with shafts of light and mosaic shadows? Are we innately attuned to the forests of Eden—or have time and change buried recognition of home?

Rafflesia

48.9 Wet Summers, Cold Winters, and Conifers

LINKS TO
CHAPTER 23
INTRODUCTION
AND SECTION 23.10

Conifers—cone-bearing trees—are primary producers of *coniferous* forests. Most have thick cuticles, needle-shaped leaves, and recessed stomata, adaptations that help conserve water through droughts and snows. They dominate the boreal forests, montane coniferous forests, temperate rain forests, and pine barrens.

Boreal forests of mostly pine, fir, and spruce stretch across northern Europe and Asia, and North America. They are known as *taigas*, meaning "swamp forests." Most form in glaciated regions with cold lakes and streams (Figure 48.20). Most rain falls in the summer, and little water evaporates into the cool summer air. Winters are cold, dry, and far more severe in eastern parts of these biomes than in the west, where ocean winds moderate climate. Spruce and fir dominate the boreal forests of North America. Forests of pine, birch, and aspen form in burned or logged areas. In poorly drained soil, acidic bogs prevail. Farther to the north, boreal forests thin and grade into arctic tundra.

Coniferous forests also form in high mountains. At high northern elevations, too, spruce and fir dominate.

The montane coniferous forests give way to pine forests in the south and at lower elevations, where the winters are milder. Coniferous forests also flourish in some temperate lowlands and near the Pacific coast from Alaska into northern California. The tallest trees in the world are in these forests—Sitka spruce to the north and coast redwoods to the south. Large tracts have been logged over (Chapter 23).

Coniferous forests also endure in warmer regions. For instance, forests of pine and scrub oak thrive in New Jersey. Southern pine forests dominate coastal plains of the southern Atlantic and Gulf states. In the Deep South, palmettos grow beneath loblolly pines. Many species are adapted to dry, sandy, nutrient-poor soil and to periodic, lightning-sparked fires.

> Coniferous forests prevail across the Northern Hemisphere in regions where wet summers alternate with cold, dry winters. They also prevail at high elevations.

CONIFEROUS FORESTS

Figure 48.20 (a) Taiga in Alberta, Canada. (b) Montane coniferous forest near Mount Ranier, Washington.

48.10 Brief Summers and Long, Icy Winters

Tundra lies between the polar ice cap and belts of boreal forests in the Northern Hemisphere. It is the youngest biome, having first evolved about 10,000 years ago.

The Northern Hemisphere's treeless plain, the *arctic tundra*, is extremely cold. Annual snowmelt and rain are usually less than 25 centimeters. Plants grow fast in the nearly continuous sunlight of a brief growing season (Figure 48.21).

Not much more than the surface soil thaws during summer. Just below is **permafrost**, a frozen layer 500 meters thick in some places. It prevents drainage, so the soil above is perpetually waterlogged (page 865). The cool, anaerobic conditions do not favor nutrient cycling. Plant remains accumulate in soggy masses and decay slowly. The accumulation of undecayed organic matter in permafrost makes the arctic tundra one of Earth's greatest stores of carbon. However, the frozen layer is starting to thaw. Global warming is melting ice and snow, which reflect sunlight. Newly exposed soil is absorbing heat from the sun's rays.

Alpine tundra is a similar biome, but it develops in high mountains throughout the world (Figure 48.22). At night, the below-freezing temperatures make it too

Figure 48.22
Compact, low-growing, hardy plants typical of alpine tundra in the Washington Cascade range.

difficult for trees to grow. Even in summer, shaded patches of snow persist in this biome, but there is no permafrost. Alpine soil is thin and well drained, but it is nutrient-poor. As a result, primary productivity is low. Grasses, heaths, and small-leafed shrubs grow in patches where better soil has formed. These low plant species are adapted to withstand strong winds.

Arctic tundra prevails at high latitudes, where short, cold summers alternate with long, cold winters. Alpine tundra prevails in high, cold mountains regardless of seasonal differences in latitude.

Figure 48.21 (**a**) Arctic tundra in the summer. Hardy lichens and shallow-rooted, low-growing plants are a base for food webs that include voles, arctic hares, caribou, arctic foxes, wolves, and polar bears. Great numbers of migratory birds nest here in summer, when the air is thick with mosquitoes and other kinds of flying insects.

(**b**) Arctic tundra makes up about 4 percent of Earth's land mass. It is blanketed with snow for as long as nine months of the year. Most occurs in northern Russia and Canada, followed by Alaska and Scandinavia. Bands of humans have herded reindeer, hunted, and fished in these sparsely populated regions for hundreds of thousands of years. More people, and machines, are moving in to extract mineral and fossil fuels. If the operations alter the vegetation and soils, it might take decades for a region to recover. Why? Tundra plants grow very slowly, and their seasonal growth is limited to just a few months of each year.

48.11 Converting Marginal Land for Agriculture

LINKS TO
SECTIONS 23.10,
30.1, 32.9, 45.8

Desertification has become one of the most far-reaching environmental challenges facing us today. If it continues unchecked, gains in human well-being in marginal lands will be arrested and, in some cases, reversed.

What Is Desertification? The conversion of large tracts of land to a more desertlike condition is known as **desertification**. The term applies as well when a similar conversion of rain-fed or irrigated croplands results in a 10 percent or greater decline in agricultural productivity. Over the past fifty years, about 9 million square kilometers worldwide have become desertified.

Each year, on all continents except Antarctica, natural processes and human activities are converting at least 200,000 square kilometers to deserts. Humans contribute to desertification by cutting dryland shrubs for firewood, allowing livestock to overgraze on marginal rangelands, and by other destructive agricultural practices. Prolonged droughts accelerate the process, just as one did years ago in the Great Plains of the American Midwest (Section 30.1).

This is a huge problem, because human populations already use nearly 21 percent of Earth's land surfaces for cropland or for grazing. Another 28 percent of the surface is said to be potentially suitable for agriculture, but the primary productivity would be so low that the conversion may not be worth the cost (Figure 48.23). As you know from Section 45.8, the human population size is far from

stabilized; it is expected to increase to 8.9 billion within the next fifty years. You do the math.

Impact on Human Populations Severe, recurring food shortages are common in heavily populated regions of Asia, Central and South America, Africa, and the Middle East. In these regions, people already have 80 percent of the productive land under cultivation, and pressure is on to expand into marginal drylands.

More than 500 million of the most impoverished people live on marginal lands in the Sahel and at high watershed elevations in the Andes and Himalayas. Under current policies and conditions, that number is expected to rise to 800 million by 2020. Their lives are directly and acutely impacted by the deterioration of natural resources.

About 1.5 billion people around the world are now living in deserts, dry shrublands, and dry woodland. In China, nearly all of the 65 million people who are officially recognized as income-poor live in remote mountains with poor soils.

Scientists continue to make valiant efforts to improve production on existing cropland. Under the banner of the *green revolution*, their research has been directed toward (1) improving the genetic traits of crop plants for higher yields and (2) exporting modern agricultural practices and equipment to the developing countries. Here you may wish to refer to the Section 32.9 case study on quinoa cultivation.

Many of these countries rely on subsistence agriculture, which runs on energy inputs from sunlight and human labor. They also rely heavily on animal-assisted agriculture, with energy inputs from oxen and other draft animals. By contrast, mechanized agriculture requires massive inputs of fertilizers, pesticides, and ample irrigation to sustain high-yield crops. It requires fossil fuel energy to drive farm machines. Crop yields are four times as high. However, the modern practices require a hundred times more energy and soil nutrients. Also, there are signs that limiting factors may be about to come into play. If so, they will slow down additional increases in crop yields.

Impact on Biodiversity As Figure 48.24 indicates, effects of desertification are not confined to local regions. Desertification invites immense dust storms, as in Figure 48.25. The loss of vegetation cover results in downstream flooding and sedimentation. It also disrupts the global cycling of carbon. Such factors have adverse impact on the stability of communities—and species richness—throughout the world.

With a little ingenuity, it may be possible to maintain biodiversity and meet human needs. In Africa, imported livestock—cattle, sheep, and goats—are a major factor in desertification. These domesticated animals evolved in areas where water is plentiful and so require more water than native African herbivores do. The introduced species continually move back and forth between their grazing areas and watering holes. As they do, they trample grasses and compact the soil surface (Figure 48.26). By contrast,

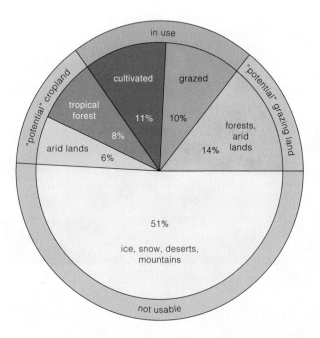

Figure 48.23 Classification of land in terms of its suitability for agriculture. Theoretically, clearing vast tracts of tropical forests and irrigating marginal lands could more than double the world's cropland. Doing so would destroy valuable forest resources, damage the environment, cause severe losses in biodiversity, and possibly cost more than it is worth.

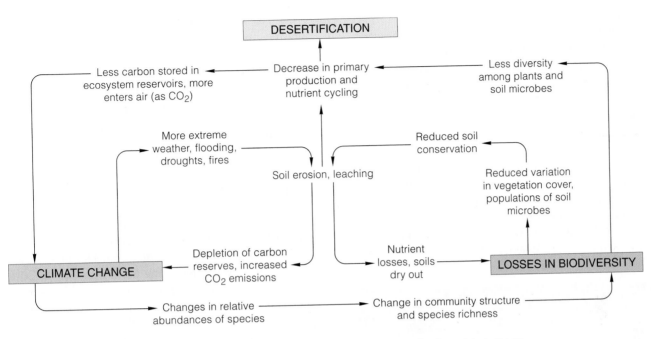

DESERTIFICATION

Less carbon stored in ecosystem reservoirs, more enters air (as CO_2)

Decrease in primary production and nutrient cycling

Less diversity among plants and soil microbes

More extreme weather, flooding, droughts, fires

Reduced soil conservation

Soil erosion, leaching

Reduced variation in vegetation cover, populations of soil microbes

CLIMATE CHANGE

Depletion of carbon reserves, increased CO_2 emissions

Nutrient losses, soils dry out

LOSSES IN BIODIVERSITY

Changes in relative abundances of species

Change in community structure and species richness

Figure 48.24 Model for the connections, including feedback loops, among desertification, global climate change, and losses in biodiversity. After Millenium Ecosystem Assessment's Desertification Synthesis.

gazelles and other wild herbivores get most (if not all) of their water from plants. They also are better at conserving water; they lose little in feces, compared to imported livestock.

In 1976 a biologist, David Hopcraft, began rearing gazelles, antelopes, giraffes, wildebeasts, ostriches, and other native herbivores on a ranch in Kenya. In one study, he compared the meat yield and evironmental impact of raising cattle versus gazelles in two adjacent study areas. Compared to

cattle, the gazelles left much more of the vegetation intact, which helped maintain plant biodiversity. In addition, the gazelles yielded almost twice the amount of meat per acre.

Similar ranches are now being set up in other parts of Africa, but there are obstacles. Such ranches are more expensive to set up and they require specialized butchering, packing, and marketing efforts. Also, most Africans prefer the taste of imported cattle to that of native animals, which tends to be very lean.

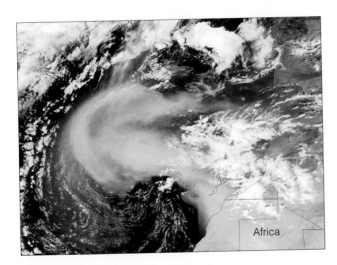

Figure 48.25 Satellite image of an immense dust storm that formed in the hot, dry Sahara Desert, then continued past the west coast of Africa, and is well on its way across the Atlantic Ocean.

Figure 48.26 Desertification in the Sahel, a region of West Africa that forms a belt between the hot, dry Sahara Desert and tropical forests. This savanna area is undergoing rapid desertification due to overgrazing, overfarming, and prolonged drought.

48.12 Standing Freshwater Ecosystems

LINKS TO
SECTIONS
47.11, 47.12

Freshwater and saltwater provinces cover more of Earth's surface than all biomes combined. They include the world ocean, lakes, ponds, wetlands, and coral reefs. There are no "typical" regions. Ponds are shallow; Siberia's Lake Baikal is 1.7 kilometers deep. All aquatic ecosystems have gradients in light penetration, temperature, and dissolved gases, but values differ greatly. All we can do here is sample the diversity, starting with freshwater provinces called lakes.

A lake is a body of standing freshwater, as in Figure 48.27. Over time, erosion and sedimentation alter its dimensions; it usually ends up filled in or drained. A young lake has littoral, limnetic, and profundal zones (Figure 48.28a). Its littoral zone extends all around the shore to the depth where rooted aquatic plants cannot

Figure 48.27 Lake in Chile's Torres del Paine National Park.

grow. The well-lit, shallow, warm water supports high biodiversity. The limnetic zone encompasses the sunlit, open water away from shore to depths where light and photosynthesis are limited. Its *phyto*plankton includes cyanobacteria, green algae, and diatoms. *Zoo*plankton includes rotifers and copepods. The profundal zone is all open water at depths that are impenetrable to the most efficient wavelengths for photosynthesis. Below it, sediments house communities of decomposers.

SEASONAL CHANGES IN LAKES

In temperate regions, many lakes undergo seasonal changes in density and temperature gradients, from surface to bottom. In midwinter, a surface layer of ice often forms. Water under the ice is near the freezing point and is the least dense. Water at 4°C is the most dense; it forms deeper layers that are a bit warmer.

In spring, there are more daylight hours and the air warms. The ice melts, the temperature of the surface layer rises to 4°C, and temperature gradients vanish. Winds blowing across the lake surface cause a **spring overturn**, in which strong vertical movements deliver dissolved oxygen from surface waters to the depths. At the same time, nutrients released by decomposers of the lake bottom sediments move to the surface.

In summer, the lake develops a *thermocline*, which means it becomes thermally stratified in between the surface and its depths. The midlayer cools, which stops the vertical mixing between the warmer, oxygen-rich surface layer and the cold, oxygen-poor layer below it (Figure 48.28b). Decomposers now deplete the oxygen dissolved near the lake bottom.

In autumn, the upper layer cools and gets denser. It sinks and the thermocline vanishes. During this **fall overturn**, water mixes vertically, and again dissolved oxygen moves down and nutrients move up.

Primary productivity is seasonal. After the spring overturn, longer daylengths and the cycled nutrients

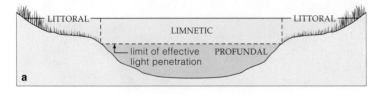
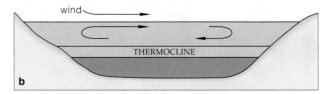

Figure 48.28 **(a)** Lake zonation. A lake's littoral zone extends all around the shore to a depth where aquatic plants stop growing. Its profundal zone is all water below the depth of light penetration. Above the profundal are the open, sunlit waters of a limnetic zone. **(b)** In temperate regions, thermal layering occurs in many lakes during the summer.

Figure 48.29 Crater Lake, Oregon, a collapsed volcanic cone filled with rainwater and snowmelt. Like the rest of the volcanoes of the Cascade Range, it started forming at the dawn of the Cenozoic.

The chart compares the main characteristics of oligotrophic and eutrophic lakes. Some lakes fall in a category that is intermediate between these two groups; they are called mesotrophic lakes. In which category would you place Crater Lake?

Oligotrophic Lake	Eutrophic Lake
Deep, steeply banked	Shallow with broad littoral
Large deep-water volume relative to surface-water volume	Small deep-water volume relative to surface-water volume
Highly transparent	Limited transparency
Water blue or green	Water green to yellow- or brownish-green
Low nutrient content	High nutrient content
Oxygen abundant through all levels throughout year	Oxygen depleted in deep water during summer
Not much phytoplankton; green algae and diatoms dominant	Abundant, thick masses of phytoplankton; and cyanobacteria dominant
Abundant aerobic decomposers favored in profundal zone	Anaerobic decomposers
Low biomass in profundal	High biomass in profundal

favor increased primary productivity. Phytoplankton and aquatic plants take up phosphorus, nitrogen, and other nutrients. During the growing season, vertical thermocline mixing ends. Nutrients do not move up, and photosynthesis slows. By late summer, shortages of nutrients limit growth. The fall overturn does cycle nutrients back to the surface, and there is a sudden burst of primary productivity. But a sustained burst is not possible, given the fewer daylight hours. Primary productivity will not rise again until spring.

TROPHIC NATURE OF LAKES

Each lake's topography, climate, and geologic history affect the number and relative abundances of species, how they are dispersed through the lake, and how they cycle nutrients. Soils of the region and sediments in the lake basin contribute to the type and amount of nutrients available. Oxygen, phosphorus, and nitrogen dissolved in the water influence primary production (Sections 47.11 and 47.12). So does the water volume and how long it has been standing in the lake.

Interplays among climate, soil, basin shape, and metabolic activities of the lake's residents contribute to a lake's trophic status. *Oligotrophic* lakes typically are newly formed, deep, clear, and nutrient-poor, with low primary productivity. *Eutrophic* lakes are older, shallower, nutrient-rich, and higher in their primary productivity (Figure 48.29). As a lake ages, sediments accumulate, water becomes opaque and shallow, and phytoplankton come to dominate the community. A filled-in basin is the final successional stage.

In Section 47.12, you read about an experiment in **eutrophication**. The term refers to natural or artificial processes that enrich a body of water with nutrients. Here is an another example:

Human activities caused eutrophication of Seattle's Lake Washington. From 1941 to 1963, phosphate-rich sewage drained into the lake. This made nitrogen the major limiting factor for the photosynthetic species. Cyanobacteria dominate when nitrogen is scarce; they can fix gaseous nitrogen (N_2). They became dominant and formed slimy mats in summer, which made the lake completely useless for recreation. Sewage inputs were stopped. By 1975, the lake neared full recovery.

Water provinces are far more extensive than the biomes. Like the other aquatic ecosystems, lakes show gradients in light penetration, temperature, and dissolved gases.

48.13 Flowing Freshwater Ecosystems

The composition of streams, rivulets, and rivers becomes altered as water drains away from watersheds on its journey to the sea.

tissues of migratory fishes and other animals. They spiral between aquatic organisms and the water as it flows on a one-way course to the sea.

STREAM ECOSYSTEMS

Flowing-water ecosystems called **streams** start out as freshwater springs or seeps. As they flow downslope, they grow and merge, then often converge as a river. Between a river's headwaters and end, we find riffles, pools, and runs (Figure 48.30). The *riffles* are shallow, turbulent stretches where the water flows swiftly over a rough, sandy and rocky bottom. In *pools*, deep water flows slowly over a smooth, sandy, or muddy bottom. *Runs* are smooth-surfaced, rapidly flowing stretches above bedrock or rock and sand.

Rainfall, snowmelt, geography, altitude, even the shade cast by plants influence a stream's average flow volume and its temperature. Streambed composition, along with agricultural, industrial, and urban wastes, shape the solute concentrations in the water.

A stream imports organic matter into food webs, especially in forest ecosystems. Trees cast shade and thus hamper photosynthesis, but their litter is the start of detrital food webs (Section 47.2). Aquatic species take up and then release nutrients as the water flows downstream. Nutrients move upstream only inside the

RIVER SYSTEMS

More than 250,000 rivers drain the watersheds of the United States. The Mississippi River drains the largest watershed. Each second, its flow volume into the Gulf of Mexico is about 16,792 cubic meters (593,000 cubic feet). It is not the longest river in the United States. From its headwaters high in the Rocky Mountains to its convergence with the Mississippi, the Missouri River flows for more than 4,000 kilometers (2,500 miles). The shortest river in the United States is Oregon's Devil River. It moves water 36.5 meters (120 or so feet) from Devil's Lake to the Pacific Ocean.

More and more sediments accumulate in the water of long rivers during the journey to the sea. Figure 48.31 shows the Mississippi River Delta, formed from sediments as far away as the Missouri's headwaters.

Water flows downhill. By the time it has moved as rivulets and streams to a river, its composition reflects that of the watersheds it drained. Nutrients in fallen leaves alter the composition. So do mudslides, heavy rains, debris from fires, and other natural events. So do human activities.

WATER POLLUTION

Ever since cities formed, streams and rivers have been sewers for the wastes from agriculture, industry, and cities. Runoff from poorly managed agricultural fields contains silt, animal wastes, pesticides, and nutrients such as phosphates, which promote algal blooms that choke streams. Power-generating plants and factories add toxic chemicals to the water.

Figure 48.30 Stream habitats in North Carolina and Virginia. (**a**) Rapids, where rocks break up a swift current. Leaves add nutrients to the stream's water. (**b**) Pool in autumn. Pools have a smooth surface; water is streaming slowly over a fine substrate. (**c**) A run, Sinking Creek. Runs also are smooth surfaced, but they flow faster over rock and sand. (**d**) A riffle. Water flow is swift and turbulent over a rough stretch of the streambed.

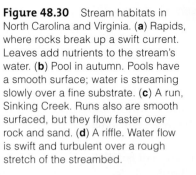

Unlike lakes, streams are resilient. They can recover fairly quickly when pollution is controlled. However, pollutants make streamwater unfit to drink.

Water pollutants collect in lakes, rivers, and bays before water gets to the sea. Many cities throughout the world dump untreated sewage into their coastal waters. The cities along rivers and harbors maintain shipping channels by dredging the polluted muck and barging it out to sea. They also barge out sewage sludge—coarse, settled solids enriched with bacteria, viruses, and toxic metals.

In the United States, 15,000 or so facilities partially treat liquid wastes from 70 percent of the population and 87,000 industries. Wastes from suburban and rural populations are treated in septic tanks or lagoons, but much is discharged, untreated, into waterways.

There are three levels of *wastewater treatment*. With primary treatment, screens and settling tanks remove sludge, which is dried, burned, dumped in landfills, or treated further. Chlorine kills most pathogens but forms carcinogens by reacting with some chemicals. In secondary treatment, microbial populations break down organic matter after the primary treatment but before water is chlorinated. The two treatments get rid of most of the solids and oxygen-demanding wastes —but not all nitrogen, phosphorus, toxins, and heavy metals. Tertiary treatment cleanses the water but is still largely experimental and expensive. Only 5 percent of the nation's wastewater gets this level of treatment.

Thus, most wastewater is not treated adequately. A pattern gets repeated thousands of times along the waterways. The water for drinking is drawn upstream from a city, and the wastes from industry and sewage treatment are discharged downstream. That is how pollution intensifies as rivers flow down to the sea. In Louisiana, waters drained from the central states flow toward the Gulf of Mexico. Its high pollution levels threaten public health as well as ecosystems.

This picture might be bleak to most of us, but not to biologist John Todd. He constructed experimental wastewater treatment facilities in several greenhouses and artificial lagoons (Figure 48.32). When it works properly, his solar–aquatic treatment system produces water fit to drink. Such natural alternatives cannot work for the large urban areas. They are an attractive alternative for small towns and rural areas.

You may wish to investigate where the drinking water for your own city comes from, and what it has picked up from its surroundings.

Figure 48.31 Satellite image of the Mississippi River Delta, where the biggest river in North America empties into the Gulf of Mexico. The Mississippi is not the world's largest river. The flow volume at the mouth of the Amazon River is far greater; it is close to 220,000 cubic meters (7 million cubic feet) per second.

Figure 48.32 An experimental wastewater treatment facility in Rhode Island. Treatment begins when sewage flows into rows of large water tanks in which water hyacinths, cattails, and other aquatic plants are growing. Decomposers inside the tanks degrade wastes—which contain nutrients that promote plant growth. Heat from incoming sunlight speeds the decomposition.

From these tanks, water flows through an artificial marsh of sand, gravel, and bulrushes that filter out algae and organic wastes. Then it flows into aquarium tanks where zooplankton and snails consume microorganisms suspended in the water. There also, zooplankton become food for crayfishes and fishes, such as tilapia, that can be sold as bait. After ten days, the now-clear water flows into a second artificial marsh for final filtering and cleansing.

48.14 Life at Land's End

LINKS TO
SECTIONS
22.8, 25.17, 27.5

Near the coasts of continents, around islands and reefs, concentrations of nutrients support some of the world's most productive ecosystems.

WETLANDS AND THE INTERTIDAL ZONE

Like freshwater ecosystems, estuaries and mangrove wetlands have distinct physical and chemical features that include depth, water temperature, salinity, and the light penetration. **Estuaries** are partly enclosed coast regions where seawater mixes with nutrient-rich fresh water from rivers, streams, and runoff (Figure 48.33a). The confined region, slow mixing of water, and tidal action combine to trap dissolved nutrients. Water flow continually replenishes nutrients, which is one reason estuaries can support highly productive ecosystems.

Primary producers are phytoplankton, plants that tolerate submergence at high tide, and algae. Detrital food webs are common. So many larval and juvenile stages of invertebrates and some fishes develop here that estuaries are sometimes called marine nurseries. Many migratory birds use the estuaries as rest stops.

Estuaries range from broad, shallow Chesapeake Bay, Mobile Bay, and San Francisco Bay to the narrow, deep fjords of Norway and others like them in Alaska and British Columbia. Many estuaries are in decline because fresh water is being diverted upstream, and agricultural runoff and wastes are flowing in.

In tidal flats at tropical latitudes, we find nutrient-rich *mangrove wetlands*. "Mangrove" refers to forests of salt-tolerant plants in sheltered areas along tropical coasts. These plants have shallow or branching prop roots that extend from the trunk (Figure 48.33b). Many have root extensions that take up oxygen. Mangrove trees germinate while still attached to the parent tree. Seedlings drop to the water and float upright until the currents deposit them in the mud of shallow water.

Net primary productivity of a mangrove wetland depends partly on the tidal volume and flow rate, as well as on salinity and nutrient availability. But tidal circulation and nutrient input combined can support notable biomass. Especially along the Gulf of Mexico and the Malaysian peninsula, currents carry nutrient-rich detritus away from mangrove wetlands and into the neighboring estuarine ecosystems.

ROCKY AND SANDY COASTLINES

Rocky and sandy coastlines support ecosystems of the intertidal zone, which is not renowned for creature comforts. Waves batter its residents; tides alternately submerge and expose them. The higher up they are, the more they dry out, freeze in winter, and bake in summer, and the less food comes their way. The lower they are, the more they compete in limited spaces. At low tides, birds, rats, and raccoons move in and feed on them. High tides bring the predatory fishes.

Generalizing about coastlines is not easy, for waves and tides continually resculpt them. One feature that rocky and sandy shores share is vertical zonation.

Rocky shores have three zones. Their *upper* littoral zone is submerged only at the highest tide of the lunar cycle and is sparsely populated (Figure 48.34a). The *mid*littoral is submerged at the highest regular tide and exposed at the lowest. Its tidepools hold algae, fishes, hermit crabs, nudibranchs, sea urchins, and sea

Figure 48.33 (**a**) South Carolina salt marsh. A marsh grass (*Spartina*) is a major producer.
(**b**) In the Florida Everglades, a mangrove wetland lined with red mangroves (*Rhizophora*).

— upper littoral of intertidal zone; submerged only at highest tide of lunar cycle

— midlittoral; submerged at each highest regular tide and exposed at lowest tide

— lower littoral; exposed only at lowest tide of lunar cycle

a   b

Figure 48.34 (a) Tidepool on a rocky shore of the Pacific Northwest, with algae and invertebrates. (b) In this coastal region, you are likely to come across pronounced vertical zonation, as shown here.

Around the world, the difference between the high and low tide marks ranges from a few centimeters in the Mediterranean Sea to about fifteen meters in the Bay of Fundy, near Nova Scotia.

Figure 48.35 Coral fragment washed up on the sandy shore of Heron Island, part of Australia's Great Barrier Reef.

Figure 48.36 Two inhabitants of coral reefs. *Left*, clownfish with sea anemone. Compare Section 47.2. *Right*, sea fan (*Gorgonia*), one of the corals.

stars (Sections 22.8 and 25.17). The *lower* littoral zone is exposed only during the lunar cycle's lowest tide. It has the greatest diversity. In all three zones, erosion is so swift that detritus cannot build up, so grazing food webs prevail (Figure 48.34*b*).

Waves and currents continually rearrange the loose sediments of *sandy* and *muddy* shores. Few big plants can grow in unstable places, so you will not discover grazing food webs here. Detrital food webs start with inputs from land or offshore (Figure 48.35).

CORAL REEFS

As Section 27.5 explains, *coral reefs* develop in clear, warm waters near coasts or around volcanic islands,

mainly between latitudes 25° north and south. Each is a wave-resistant formation of the slowly accumulated remains of marine organisms. Hard corals as well as mineral-hardened cell walls of red algae, cemented together, formed the reef spine. Figure 48.36 shows two more examples of the wealth of warning colors, tentacles, and stealth of reef species—signs of danger and fierce competition for resources by individuals that must interact in a limited space.

Life thrives where land meets the sea. Wetlands and coral reefs show high primary productivity. Rocky and sandy shores are not renowned for their creature comforts.

48.15 The Open Ocean

LINKS TO
SECTIONS 7.8,
20.2, 20.3, 25.4

The world ocean consists of two vast provinces (Figure 48.37). Its benthic (bottom) province starts at continental shelves and extends to deep-sea trenches. Its pelagic province is the full volume of ocean water. The neritic zone is the volume above continental shelves, and the oceanic zone is the volume above the ocean basins.

SURPRISING DIVERSITY

Photosynthesis is seasonal and intense near the ocean surface. Drifting in seawater are phytoplankton, the "pastures" that feed copepods, krill, whales, squids, fishes, and other members of marine food webs. Also near the surface, photoautotrophs account for most of the ocean's primary productivity. They range in size from bacterial cells less than five micrometers across (ultraplankton) to coccolithophores and other types of cells as much as fifty micrometers (nannoplankton).

Deeper ocean water is too dark for photosynthesis. There, food webs start with **marine snow**. These tiny bits of organic matter drift down from communities above. They are the base for staggering biodiversity; midoceanic water may be home to 10 million species!

Also, in what might be the greatest of all circadian migrations, a number of species rise thousands of feet to feed in upper waters at night and move down the next morning. Carnivores at the top of the food webs range from familiar types, including sharks and giant squids, to the visually jarring deep-sea angler fishes and immense siphonophores.

The benthic province includes largely unexplored ecosystems on seamounts and at hydrothermal vents (Figure 48.38). *Seamounts* are extinct volcanoes that rise at least 1,000 meters from the seafloor but are far below the ocean surface. At *hydrothermal vents*, near-freezing water seeps into fissures in the seafloor and becomes superheated. As it spews back out, it leaches mineral ions from rocks. Dissolved in the outpouring are iron, zinc, copper sulfides, and sulfates of calcium and magnesium. The minerals settle out and form rich deposits, which are an energy source for bacterial and archaean chemoautotrophs. These prokaryotes are the primary producers for rich food webs, which include a variety of fishes, crustaceans, clams, and tube worms, such as those shown in Figure 48.38b.

Many biologists suspect that life originated in such hot, nutrient-rich places on the seafloor. Sections 20.2 and 20.3 offer some evidence of this possibility.

UPWELLING AND DOWNWELLING

As you read earlier, prevailing winds that parallel the western coasts of continents tug on the ocean surface. Wind friction gets the surface waters moving. Earth's rotational force deflects masses of slow-moving water away from the coasts. Cold, deep, often nutrient-rich

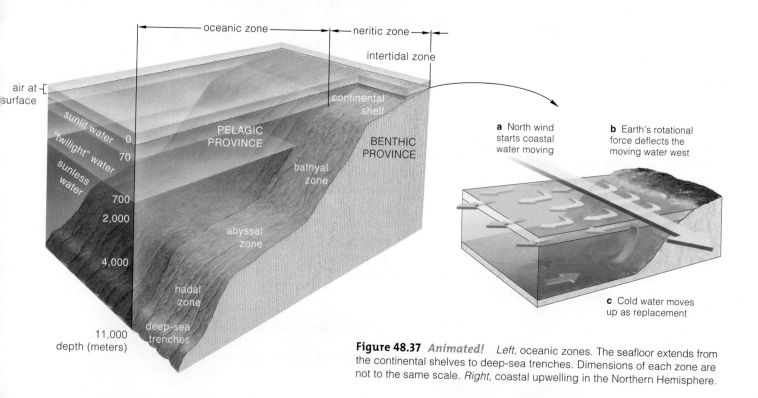

Figure 48.37 *Animated!* *Left*, oceanic zones. The seafloor extends from the continental shelves to deep-sea trenches. Dimensions of each zone are not to the same scale. *Right*, coastal upwelling in the Northern Hemisphere.

water moves in vertically in its place (Figure 48.37). Cold, deeper water moving up this way is called an **upwelling**. Upwelling occurs in equatorial currents and along continents, and it cools air masses above it. When thick fogbanks form near California's coast, an upwelling of cold water is interacting with warm air.

In the Southern Hemisphere, commercial fisheries depend on wind-induced upwelling along Peru and Chile. Prevailing coastal winds blow from the south and southeast, tugging surface water away from the shore. Cold, deeper water carried to the continental shelf by the Humboldt Current moves up near the surface. Large quantities of nitrate and phosphate are pulled up and carried north by the cold Peru Current. The nutrients sustain phytoplankton that are the basis of one of the world's richest fisheries.

Every three to seven years, warm surface waters of the western equatorial Pacific Ocean move eastward. This massive displacement of warm water acts on the prevailing wind direction. The eastward flow speeds up so much that it hampers the vertical movement of water along the coasts of Central and South America.

Surface water piling into a coast is forced down and flows away from it. Near Peru's coast, prolonged **downwelling** of nutrient-poor water displaces cooler waters of the Humboldt Current and puts a stop to upwelling. The warm current typically arrives around Christmas. Fishermen in Peru named it **El Niño** ("the little one," in reference to the baby Jesus). The name became incorporated into a more inclusive, scientific explanation called the El Niño Southern Oscillation, or ENSO. The next section takes a closer look at some of the consequences of this recurring event.

OCEAN AS GARBAGE DUMP

The North Pacific is the largest ocean realm, about the size of Africa, in the Northern Hemisphere. Circular winds above it drag the surface in an ever tightening spiral, the north central Pacific gyre. This gyre is the most stable feature of Earth's weather systems. It also has become a self-perpetuating garbage dump.

Anything that remains afloat on the North Pacific ocean ends up here. Organic debris breaks down, but plastics do not. Bacterial decomposers cannot degrade the synthetic compounds. Sunlight breaks them down into individual molecules. By one estimate, there may be 2.7 kilograms (6 pounds) of plastic debris for every .45 kilograms (1 pound) of plankton in this continent-sized stretch of floating plastic sand. To field biologist Shawn Farry, the sight of floating plastic, light bulbs, shoes, bottles, and discarded or lost fishing lines and

Figure 48.38 What lies beneath—a vast, largely unexplored world of marine life. (**a**) Flytrap anemone on Davidson seamount, off the California coast. There are an estimated 30,000 seamounts. They may be home to rich marine ecosystems that also may be resting stops for hammerhead sharks and other marine vertebrates that migrate across the open ocean.

(**b**) Tube worms, part of a hydrothermal vent ecosystem on the ocean floor.

(**c**) *Praya dubia*, a relative of the Portuguese man-of-war. This stinging, bioluminescent siphonophore (a type of cnidarian) is one of the longest existing animals. Some specimens have measured fifty meters, from a mouthless, pulsating swimming bell to the tip of a narrow stem to which reproductive medusae, tentacles, and feeding polyps connect. *P. dubia* moves vertically in a circadian migration. (**d**) Deep-sea angler fish.

nets floating around even the most remote islands is nothing new. What was shocking to him was the vast concentration anywhere he dove in the middle of the ocean. Even at depths of about 30.5 meters (100 feet), researchers aboard the research vessel *Alguita* watched invertebrate filter-feeders consuming debris and also becoming entangled in it. Think about that the next time you see a piece of Styrofoam bobbing along.

From the ocean's coral reefs down to hydrothermal vents, throughout the pelagic province, we find astounding levels of primary productivity and biodiversity.

48.16 Rita in the Time of Cholera

LINKS TO
SECTIONS
7.8, 22.8. 25.13

We turn now to an application that reinforces a unifying ecological concept. Events in the atmosphere and ocean, and on land, interconnect in ways that can profoundly influence the world of life.

An El Niño Southern Oscillation, or **ENSO**, is defined by changes in sea surface temperatures and in the air circulation patterns. "Southern oscillation" refers to a seesawing of the atmospheric pressure in the western equatorial Pacific—the world's greatest reservoir of warm water and warm air. It is the source of heavy rainfall, which releases enough heat energy to drive global air circulation.

Between ENSOs, the warm waters and heavy rains move westward (Figure 48.39a). *During* an ENSO, the prevailing surface winds over the western equatorial Pacific pick up speed and "drag" surface waters east (Figure 48.39b). As they do, the westward transport of water slows down. Sea surface temperatures rise, evaporation accelerates, and air pressure falls. These changes have global repercussions.

El Niño episodes usually persist for six to eighteen months. Then another oscillation called **La Niña** starts up, and the weather seesaws again.

As you read in the chapter opening, 1997 ushered in the most powerful ENSO event of the century. The average sea surface temperatures in the eastern Pacific rose 9°F (about 5°C). The warmer water extended 9,660 kilometers west from the coast of Peru.

The 1997–1998 El Niño/La Niña rollercoaster had record-breaking impact on primary productivity in the equatorial Pacific. With the massive eastward flow of nutrient-poor warm water, photoautotrophs were almost undetectable (Figure 48.40a).

During the La Niña rebound, cooler, nutrient-rich water welled up to the sea surface and was displaced westward all along the equator. As satellite images clearly revealed, the upwelling had sustained a vast algal bloom, one that stretched across the equatorial Pacific (Figure 48.40b; also compare Section 7.8).

During the 1997–1998 El Niño event, 30,000 cases of *cholera* were reported in Peru alone, compared to only 60 cases from January to August in 1997. People knew that water contaminated by *Vibrio cholerae* causes epidemics of cholera (Figure 48.41). The disease agent triggers severe diarrhea, and it thereby enters water supplies in feces. Individuals who are forced to use the tainted water become infected.

Figure 48.39 *Animated!* (**a**) Westward flow of cold, equatorial surface water between ENSOs. (**b**) Eastward dislocation of warm water during an ENSO.

Figure 48.39a labels:
warm, moist, ascending air masses, low pressure, storms in western Pacific
high winds blow west to east
clear skies, dry descending air masses, high pressure
equatorial trade winds blow east to west
warming water
upwelling of cold water to 30–160 feet below surface

Figure 48.39b labels:
clear skies, descending air masses, high pressure
high winds blow west
warm, moist, ascending air masses, low pressure, storms
rain falls in central Pacific
trade winds weaken; warm water flows east
no upwelling; cold water as deep as 500 feet below surface

a Near-absence of phytoplankton in the equatorial Pacific during an El Niño.

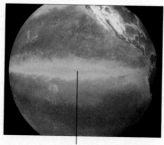

b Huge algal bloom in the equatorial Pacific in the La Niña rebound event.

Figure 48.40 Satellite data on primary productivity in the equatorial Pacific Ocean. The concentration of chlorophyll was used as the measure. (**a**) During the 1997–1998 El Niño episode, a massive amount of nutrient-poor water moved to the east, and so photosynthetic activity was negligible. (**b**) During a subsequent La Niña episode, massive upwelling and westward displacement of nutrient-rich water led to a vast algal bloom that stretched all the way to the coast of Peru.

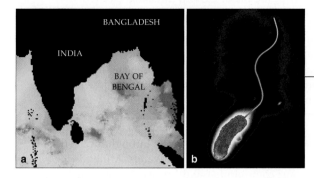

What people did *not* know was where *V. cholerae* remained between cholera outbreaks. It could not be found in humans or in water supplies. Even so, the pathogen would show up simultaneously in places that could be far apart—usually coastal cities where the urban poor draw water from rivers to the sea.

Marine biologist Rita Colwell had been thinking about the fact that humans are not the host between outbreaks. Was there an environmental reservoir for the pathogen? Maybe. But nobody had detected it in water samples subjected to standard culturing.

Then Colwell had a flash of insight: What if no one could find the pathogen because it changes its form and enters a dormant stage between outbreaks?

During one cholera outbreak in Louisiana, Colwell realized that she could use an antibody-based test to detect a protein unique to *V. cholerae*'s surface. Later, tests in Bangladesh revealed bacteria in fifty-one of fifty-two samples of water. Standard culture methods had missed it in all but seven samples.

V. cholerae lives in rivers, estuaries, and seas. As Colwell knew, plankton also thrive in these aquatic environments. She decided to restrict her search for the unknown host to warm waters near Bangladesh, where outbreaks of cholera occur seasonally (Figure 48.41*c*). It was here that she discovered the dormant *V. cholerae* stage inside copepods. These tiny marine crustaceans graze on algae and other phytoplankton species (Figure 48.41*b*). The number of copepods— and of the *V. cholerae* cells inside them—rises and falls with shifts in phytoplankton abundances.

Colwell already knew about seasonal variations in sea surface temperatures. Remember the old saying, *Chance favors the prepared mind*? In one sense, she was prepared to recognize a connection between cholera cases and seasonal temperature peaks in the Bay of Bengal. She compared data from the 1990–1991 and 1997–1998 El Niño episodes. Her correlation held. Four to six weeks after the sea surface temperatures go up, so do cases of cholera!

Figure 48.41 (**a**) Satellite data on rising sea surface temperatures in the Bay of Bengal correlated with cholera cases in the region's hospitals. *Red* signifies warmest summer temperatures. (**b**) *Vibrio cholerae*, agent of cholera. Copepods host a dormant stage of this bacterium that waits out adverse environmental conditions that do not favor its growth and reproduction. (**c**) A typical Bangladesh waterway from which water samples were drawn for analysis. (**d**) In Bangladesh, Rita Colwell comparing samples of unfiltered and filtered drinking water.

Today, Colwell and Anwarul Huq, a Bangladeshi scientist, are investigating salinity and other factors that may influence outbreaks. Their goal is to design a model for predicting where cholera will break out next. They have advised women in Bangladesh to use sari cloth as a filter to remove *V. cholerae* cells from the water (Figure 48.41*d*). Copepod hosts are too big to pass through the thin cloths, which can be rinsed in clean water, sun-dried, and used again and again. This simple and inexpensive method has cut cholera outbreaks by half.

Combine knowledge about life with knowledge about the physical and chemical aspects of the biosphere, and who knows what you may discover.

Summary

Sections 48.1, 48.2 Global air circulation patterns affect climate and the distribution of communities. The patterns start with latitudinal variations in incoming solar radiation. The basic patterns are influenced by Earth's daily rotation and annual path around the sun, the distribution of continents and seas, and elevations of land masses. Solar energy, and the winds it drives, are renewable, clean sources of energy.

Human activities alter the atmosphere. The use of CFCs and methyl bromide depletes ozone in the upper atmosphere. With seasonal ozone thinning, more UV radiation reaches Earth's surface.

Smog, a form of air pollution, arises in areas where large amounts of fossil fuels are burned. Coal-burning power plants are also the main contributors to acid rain, which alters habitats and kills many organisms.

Biology ⑤ Now
Learn how sunlight energy drives global patterns of air circulation with the interaction on BiologyNow.

Section 48.3 Latitudinal and seasonal variations in sunlight warm ocean water and set currents in motion. The currents distribute heat energy around the seas and affect weather patterns. Ocean currents, air currents, and topography interact to shape global climate zones.

Biology ⑤ Now
See the patterns of major ocean currents with the animation on BiologyNow.

Section 48.4 The world's land masses are realms of biodiversity, each with an evolutionary history and a tapestry of physical and chemical conditions. Biomes are vast expanses characterized by specific arrays of species, mainly plants and animals. Regional variations in climate, landforms, and soils influence them. Marine ecoregions are comparable realms of biodiversity.

Biology ⑤ Now
Examine the distribution of biomes with the animation on BiologyNow.

Section 48.5 Soil characteristics vary among biomes and help determine their primary productivity.

Sections 48.6–48.10 Deserts form near latitudes 30° north and south if annual rainfall is sparse. Slightly moister southern or western coastal regions support dry woodlands and shrublands. In the interior of midlatitude continents, vast deserts or grasslands form.

From the equator to latitudes 10° north and south, evergreen tropical forests grow in regions of high rainfall, high humidity, and mild temperatures. Semi-evergreen and deciduous broadleaf forests form between latitudes 10°–25°, depending on how much of the annual rainfall occurs in a prolonged dry season.

Where a cold, dry season alternates with a cold, rainy season, coniferous forests dominate.

Low-growing, hardy plants of the tundra dominate at high latitudes and high altitudes.

Section 48.11 Desertification, the conversion of marginally productive lands to desertlike conditions, is one of the major current threats to biodiversity.

Sections 48.12–48.14 Lakes, streams, and other aquatic ecosystems show gradients in penetration of sunlight, water temperature, salinity, and dissolved gases. These factors vary over time and affect primary productivity. Coastal zones and tropical reefs support diverse ecosystems. Primary productivity is high in coastal wetlands and on coral reefs.

Section 48.15 Life persists throughout the ocean. Diversity is highest in sunlit waters. Mineral-rich waters support communities at deep-sea hydrothermal vents. Upwelling is an upward movement of deep, cool, often nutrient-rich ocean water, typically along the coasts of continents. An El Niño event disrupts upwelling, and it triggers massive, reversible changes in rainfall as well as other weather patterns around the world.

Biology ⑤ Now
Learn about the oceanic zones with the animation on BiologyNow.

Section 48.16 Drawing on knowledge of microbial ecology as well as biogeographic patterns, Rita Colwell found a crucial bit of information that led to effective countermeasures against cholera outbreaks.

Biology ⑤ Now
Observe how an El Niño event affects ocean currents and upwelling with the animation on BiologyNow.

Self-Quiz

Answers in Appendix II

1. Solar radiation drives the distribution of weather systems and so influences _____ .
   a. temperature zones   c. seasonal variations
   b. rainfall distribution   d. all of the above

2. _____ shields life against the sun's UV wavelengths.
   a. A thermal inversion   c. The ozone layer
   b. Acid precipitation   d. The greenhouse effect

3. Regional variations in the global patterns of rainfall and temperature depend on _____ .
   a. global air circulation   c. topography
   b. ocean currents   d. all of the above

4. A rain shadow is a reduction in rainfall _____ .
   a. on the leeward side of a mountain range
   b. during an El Niño event
   c. that occurs seasonally in the tropics

5. Acid rain is one outcome of _____ .
   a. coal burning   c. nitrogen-rich fertilizers
   b. gas and oil burning   d. all of the above

6. Biomes are _____ .
   a. water provinces   d. partly characterized
   b. water and land zones   by dominant plants
   c. vast expanses of land   e. both c and d

7. Biome distribution depends on _____ .
   a. climate   c. soils
   b. topography   d. all of the above

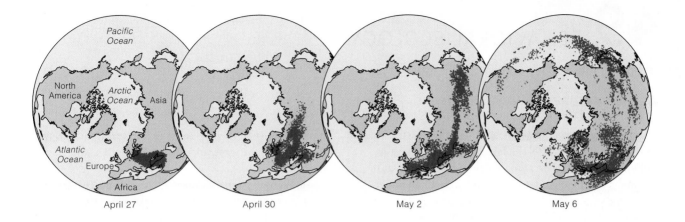

Pacific
Ocean

North
America   Arctic
Ocean   Asia

Atlantic
Ocean
Europe

Africa

April 27   April 30   May 2   May 6

8. Grasslands most often predominate _____ .
   a. near the equator   c. in interior of continents
   b. at high altitudes   d. b and c

9. During _____ , deeper, often nutrient-rich water moves to the surface of a body of water.
   a. spring overturns   c. upwellings
   b. fall overturns   d. all of the above

10. Match the terms with the most suitable description.
    ____ tundra   a. equatorial broadleaf forest
    ____ chaparral   b. partly enclosed by land; where
    ____ desert   freshwater and seawater mix
    ____ savanna   c. type of grassland with trees
    ____ estuary   d. has low-growing plants at
    ____ boreal forest   high latitudes or elevations
    ____ tropical rain   e. at latitudes 30° north and south
         forest   f. mineral-rich, superheated water
    ____ hydrothermal   supports communities here
         vents   g. conifers dominate
                          h. dry shrubland

Additional questions are available on Biology ⒺNow™

Critical Thinking

1. On April 26, 1986, in Ukraine, a meltdown occurred at the Chernobyl nuclear power plant. Nuclear fuel burned for nearly ten days and released 400 times more radioactive material than the atomic bomb that dropped on Hiroshima. Winds carried radioactive fallout around the globe (Figure 48.42). Thirty-one people died right after the meltdown. Thousands more are still likely to die from cancers and other harmful effects of radiation.

The Chernobyl accident stiffened opposition to *nuclear power* in the United States, but recent developments have some people reconsidering. Increasing the use of nuclear energy would diminish the country's dependence on oil from the politically unstable Middle East. Nuclear power does not contribute to global warming, acid rain, or smog. It does produce highly radioactive wastes. Investigate the pros and cons of nuclear power, and decide if you think the environmental benefits outweigh the risks. Would you feel differently if a nuclear power plant were about to be built ten kilometers upwind from your home?

2. Use of off-road recreational vehicles may double over the next twenty years. Many off-road enthusiasts would like increased access to government-owned desert areas.

Figure 48.42 Global distribution of radioactive fallout after the 1986 meltdown of the Chernobyl nuclear power plant in Ukraine. The meltdown put 300 million to 400 million people at risk for leukemia and other radiation-induced disorders. By 1998, the rate of thyroid abnormalities in children living downwind from the site was nearly seven times as high as for those upwind; their thyroid gland concentrated the iodine radioisotopes.

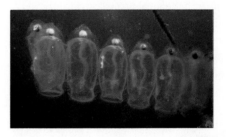

Figure 48.43 Chain of salps (*Thalia democratica*). Like you, salps have a nerve cord. The cord's anterior end develops into a rudimentary brain, with a light-sensitive eyespot.

Some argue that it's just the perfect place for off-roaders because "There's nothing there." Do you agree? If not, how would you counter this argument?

3. Write a short description of how global warming may affect spring overturn and thermocline formation in a Minnesota lake. What would be some ecological effects?

4. *Thalia democratica*, a salp, is one of our remote chordate relatives (Figure 48.43). This urochordate is part of marine plankton, usually in warm and temperate seas but also in cold, deep water. Salps swim, separately or in loose chains, in vast numbers. Salps range in size from 1.5 centimeters to a reported tubular specimen (*Pyrostremma*) that was 20 meters long and wide enough for a scuba diver to swim through. Refer to Section 25.1, on the feeding mode of urochordates. Then formulate a hypothesis on how the deep curtain of plastic debris in the ocean may adversely affect the vast salp populations and, through them, marine food webs.

5. *Southern pine forests* dominate the coastal plains of the southern Atlantic and Gulf states. Many pine species are adapted to the periodic, lightning-sparked fires, but fires are suppressed where buildings are encroaching on the forests. Suppression results in an accumulation of dry undergrowth that can fuel uncontrollable wildfires, such as the one shown at right. Do some research on whether and how Florida and other vulnerable states carry out controlled burns. How many acres are at risk?

My Pheromones Made Me Do It

A few years ago, as Toha Bererub walked down a street near her Las Vegas home, she felt a sharp pain above her right eye. Then another, and then another. Seconds later, hundreds of stinging bees covered the upper half of her body. Firefighters in protective gear rescued her, but not before she had been stung more than 500 times.

Bererub's tiny attackers were Africanized honeybees, a hybrid between the mild-tempered European honeybee and an African strain that is easy to provoke (Figure 49.1). Breeders had imported African bees to Brazil in the 1950s. They thought cross-breeding experiments would result in a mild-tempered but zippier pollinator for commercial orchards. However, some of the captive imports escaped and started mating with the locals.

Then, in a grand example of geographic dispersal, some descendant bees buzzed all the way from Brazil to Mexico and on into the United States. So far, the Africanized bees have established themselves in Texas, New Mexico, Nevada, California to the west, and Alabama, Virginia, and Florida to the east.

Honeybees sting only once. All species make the same kind of venom. Africanized bees make a bit less venom, but they get riled up faster and mount collective attacks. One squadron reportedly chased a perceived threat for a quarter of a mile.

The Africanized bees became known as "killer bees," although they rarely kill their target. Their stings are extremely painful, but adults in good health usually can survive a collective attack. Bererub was seventy years old when attacked, and she recovered fully after spending a week in the hospital.

What makes the Africanized bees so testy? Isopentyl acetate. This chemical, which smells like bananas, is a key component of honeybee alarm pheromone.

A **pheromone**, remember, is a chemical signal released by one individual that may cause another individual of the species to alter its behavior. A honeybee releases an alarm pheromone when it recognizes and stings a perceived threat. The signaling molecules diffuse through air and form a concentration gradient, which guides other bees to the individual sounding the alarm.

Researchers once studied hundreds of colonies of Africanized honeybees and European honeybees to compare their responses to alarm pheromone. They positioned a tiny target in front of each colony and then released a small quantity of an artificial pheromone. The Africanized bees flew out of the colony and zeroed in on the perceived threat much faster. They also plunged six to eight times as many stingers into it.

Figure 49.1 Good bee, bad bee. At left, a European honeybee about to pollinate a flower. *Facing page*, two of its aggressive relatives, Africanized honeybees, that stand guard at the entrance to their hive. If a potential intruder appears, they will release an alarm pheromone that stimulates hivemates to join an attack.

Watch the video online!

The two kinds of honeybees show other differences in their behavior. Compared to European bees, Africanized bees are less picky about where they establish a colony. They are more likely to abandon their colony after being disturbed. Of more concern to beekeepers, they are less interested in stashing large amounts of honey.

Such differences among honeybees lead us into the world of **animal behavior**, to the coordinated responses that animal species make to stimuli. We invite you to reflect on the genetic basis of behavior before turning to the instinctive and learned mechanisms that arise from it. Along the way, we also will consider the adaptive value of behavior.

 How Would You Vote?

Africanized bees are slowly expanding their range in North America. Some think the more we know about them, the better we will be able to protect ourselves. Should we fund more research into the genetic basis of their behavior? See BiologyNow for details, then vote online.

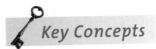 **Key Concepts**

FOUNDATIONS FOR BEHAVIOR

An individual's behavior starts with interactions among gene products, such as hormones and pheromones. Most behavior has innate components but can be modified by environmental factors.

Behavioral traits that have a heritable basis and that enhance the individual's reproductive success can evolve by natural selection.   Sections 49.1–49.3

CUES FOR SOCIAL BEHAVIOR

Evolved modes of communication underlie social behavior. Communication signals hold clear meaning for both the sender and the receiver of signals.   Section 49.4

COSTS AND BENEFITS OF BEHAVIOR

Life in social groups has reproductive benefits and costs. Not every environment favors the evolution of such groups. Self-sacrificing behavior has evolved among a few kinds of animals that live in large family groups.   Sections 49.5–49.7

FOUNDATIONS FOR HUMAN SOCIAL BEHAVIOR

The social behavior of all primates, including humans, has evolved in complex ways. Only humans consistently make moral choices about their behavior.   Sections 49.8, 49.9

Links to Earlier Concepts

This chapter builds on your understanding of the nervous system and sensory systems (Sections 34.1, 35.1). You will consider the functions of neurotransmitters, hormones, and pheromones in behavior (36.1, 36.2). You will revisit the social parasites (46.7).

Be sure you understand the concepts of directional selection (18.4), sexual selection (18.6), and adaptation (18.9). You will see how predation (46.4) can exert selection pressure on the evolution of behavior. You may wish to review the sections on the evolution of primates and modern humans (26.12, 26.15).

49.1 Behavior's Heritable Basis

LINKS TO
SECTIONS
34.1, 35.1, 36.1

The nervous and endocrine systems govern behavioral responses to stimuli. Because genes specify the substances required for constructing and operating those systems, they are the heritable foundation for animal behavior.

GENES AND BEHAVIOR

Before an animal is even born or hatched, the nervous system becomes prewired to detect, interpret, and then issue commands for response to stimuli. A **stimulus**, recall, is a piece of information about the external or internal environment that a specific type of sensory receptor has detected. It takes gene products to build and operate sensory receptors, nerves and, in most

Figure 49.2 (**a**) Banana slug, food for (**b**) an adult garter snake of coastal California. (**c**) Newborn garter snake from a coastal population, tongue-flicking at a cotton swab drenched with tissue fluids from a banana slug.

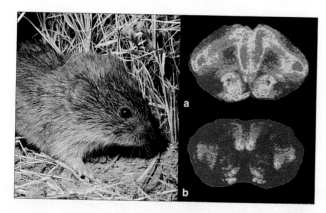

Figure 49.3 Distribution of oxytocin receptors (*red*) inside the brain of (**a**) a mate-for-life prairie vole and (**b**) a promiscuous mountain vole.

species, a brain. Gene products also affect behavioral responses to stimuli.

Stevan Arnold found experimental evidence of the genetic basis for behavior in the feeding preferences of coastal and inland snake populations in California. Garter snakes living near the coast hunt banana slugs (Figure 49.2*a*). Snakes living inland hunt tadpoles and fishes. Offer them a banana slug and they ignore it.

Arnold offered captive newborn snakes a bit of slug as a first meal. Newborn coastal snakes usually ate it and flicked their tongue at cotton swabs drenched in essence of slug. (Snakes "smell" by tongue-flicking, which pulls odors into the mouth.) Newborn inland snakes ignored the swabs and rarely ate bits of slug. Here was a big difference between captive snakes that had no prior experience with slugs. These snakes are programmed before hatching to accept or reject slugs; they did not learn feeding preferences by taste trials.

Did allelic differences influence how odor-detecting mechanisms form in the garter snake embryo? Arnold crossed coastal with inland snakes. He predicted that hybrid offspring would make an *intermediate* response to slug chunks and odors, and they did. Many hybrid baby snakes tongue-flicked at slug-perfumed swabs more often than newborn inland snakes did—but not as often as newborn coastal snakes did (Figure 49.2*c*).

Some genes have been linked to specific behaviors. The *fruitless* gene controls male fruit fly courtship. A female will not mate unless a male waves his wings and licks and taps her body. Male flies that researchers induced to make the female version of the fruitless protein became more attracted to males than females. Female flies induced to make the male version of the protein waved their wings at females. These altered flies had no interest in ordinary males, but they did court males who had been made to smell like females.

This gene product is a master switch in the nervous system, with far-reaching effects on complex behavior.

HORMONES AND BEHAVIOR

Some hormones are behavior-guiding gene products. For instance, all mammals make and secrete oxytocin, which affects more than labor and lactation (Section 44.14). In many species, it guides social behavior, such as pair bonding, aggression, and territoriality.

In prairie voles (*Microtus ochrogaster*), oxytocin is the hormonal key that unlocks the female's heart. The female of these small rodents bonds with a male after a night of repeated matings, and she mates for life. To test oxytocin's impact, researchers kept a female vole with a male for a few hours but blocked mating. They

Figure 49.4 Instinctive behavior of the European cuckoo. (**a**) This social parasite lays eggs in the nests of other birds. Even before a cuckoo hatchling opens its eyes, it reacts instinctually to anything round—typically the host bird's egg—and shoves it from the nest. (**b**) The clueless foster parents instinctually respond to a gaping mouth, not to a usurper's size or other traits that differ from their own species.

Figure 49.5 Instinctive behavior of a human baby who is imitating an adult's facial expression.

injected oxytocin into the female, and the pair bonded without the normally required sex act. By contrast, pair-bonded female prairie voles that were injected with an oxytocin blocker immediately dumped their former partners.

Whether a vole species is monogamous depends on the number and distribution of receptors for oxytocin. Monogamous prairie voles have more receptors than highly promiscuous mountain voles (Figure 49.3).

Monogamous voles also have more receptors in the brain for antidiuretic hormone (ADH). As you know, kidney cells have receptors for this hormone, but so do cells in the brain. Researchers isolated the gene for an ADH receptor in monogamous prairie voles. They transferred copies of the gene into some forebrain cells of male meadow voles (*M. pennsylvanicus*). Afterward, the males of this more promiscuous species showed an increased tendency to partner with one female only.

Male meadow voles used as a control group also got copies of the gene, but in a brain region not known to be involved in pair-bonding. Unlike the experimental group, the males retained their promiscuous ways.

INSTINCTIVE BEHAVIOR

Like many other animals, slug-loving garter snakes, wing-waving fruit flies, and pair-bonding voles offer us evidence of **instinctive behavior**—they perform a behavior without having first learned it through actual experience in the environment. They are prewired to recognize sign stimuli before being born or hatched. *Sign stimuli* are one or two simple, well-defined cues that trigger a suitable response. For garter snakes, the cue is a specific slug scent that calls for a *fixed action pattern*—a stereotyped motor program of coordinated muscle activity that runs to completion independently of feedback from the environment. The baby snake is compelled to strike, capture, and eat a slug.

Or consider cuckoos, a type of social parasite. Like cowbirds, the females lay eggs in nests of other birds.

A newly hatched cuckoo is blind; skin covers its eyes. But contact with an egg (or any round object) triggers a fixed action pattern. That hatchling maneuvers the egg onto its back, then pushes it from the nest (Figure 49.4*a*). Its behavior helps the hatchling get undivided attention. Its "foster parents" are oblivious to the odd color and size of the usurper. They respond only to one sign stimulus—the gaping mouth of a chick—and continue with their parenting (Figure 49.4*b*).

Humans, too, display instinctive behavior. Three days after birth, a human infant already displays a capacity to mimic facial expressions of an adult who comes close to it (Figure 49.5). The infant cannot see its own face, nor can it feel which facial muscles the adult is using. Somehow it is able to open its mouth, protrude its tongue, or rotate its head the same way as the adult. Infants will also respond to a simplified stimulus—a flat, face-sized mask with two dark spots for eyes. One "eye" won't do the trick.

Behavior, or coordinated responses to stimuli, starts with genes. Some gene products construct and operate the nervous system, which governs behavior. Other products, such as hormones, help control the mechanisms required for specific forms of behavior.

Animals start out life neurally wired to recognize vital cues and to make an instinctively suitable response, one that has not been learned through actual experience.

Many animals execute a fixed action pattern, a stereotyped program of coordinated muscle activity in response to one or two simple, well-defined environmental cues.

49.2 Learned Behavior

*With **learned behavior**, an individual draws from past experiences and varies or changes its response to stimuli. A classic example, imprinting, occurs early in life, during a genetically determined period.*

Animals process information about experiences and then use it to change or adjust responses to stimuli. Learned behavior arises as the environment directly or indirectly influences gene expression. Sensory input and good or bad nutrition are typical factors that lead to alterations in how and what an animal learns.

Birdsong (Figure 49.6) is an instinctive behavior. Even so, songbirds can learn variations, or dialects, of the species song in different habitats. As Peter Marler demonstrated, many male birds learn the full song ten to fifty days after hatching by listening to other birds sing it. The male nervous system is prewired to recognize the species song; a learning mechanism is primed to select and respond to acoustical input. But what the male bird hears during a sensitive period shapes his *rendition* of the song.

In one study, Marler raised white-crown nestlings to maturity in soundproof chambers so they could not hear adult males. Their songs did not have the exact structure of a typical adult song. Marler also isolated captive nestlings and let them hear recorded songs of white-crown sparrows *and* song sparrows. When the captives matured, they sang just the white-crown song and mimicked the species dialect of the unseen tutor.

In another experiment, Marler did not use taped songs. He let young, hand-reared male white-crowns interact with a "social tutor" of the different species. The males tended to learn the tutor's song.

Results from many such experiments support this hypothesis: Birdsong starts with the genetically based capacity to learn from acoustical cues.

Imprinting is a classic case of learned behavior. This time-dependent form of learning is triggered by exposure to a sign stimulus. Exposure normally takes place during a sensitive period when the animal is young. Imprinting of baby geese on their mother is a favorite example of animal behaviorists (Figure 49.7).

> *Animals process information about experiences in the environment and use it to change or vary their response to a stimulus. This learned behavior involves interactions between gene products and environmental inputs.*

Figure 49.6 Male marsh wren belting out a territorial song that has been likened to a loud gurgle. Males of this species start to imitate their species song when they are about fifteen days old. Unlike many species, marsh wrens continue to learn songs throughout their life.

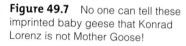

Figure 49.7 No one can tell these imprinted baby geese that Konrad Lorenz is not Mother Goose!

(**a**) In response to a moving object and probably acoustical cues, baby geese imprint on the mother goose and follow her during a short, sensitive period right after hatching. They are neurally wired to learn crucial information—the identity of the one individual that will be most likely to protect them in the months ahead. Usually that will be their mother.

(**b**) Konrad Lorenz, one of the early investigators of animal behavior, presented these baby geese with sign stimuli that made them form an attachment to him.

49.3 The Adaptive Value of Behavior

If forms of behavior have a genetic basis, then they may evolve in various ways through natural selection. Alleles that encode the most adaptive versions of a trait tend to to increase in frequency in a population, and alternative alleles do not. In time, genetic changes in behavior that yield greater reproductive success are favored.

Natural selection theory helps us develop and test explanations of why some behavior persists and how it offers reproductive benefits that offset reproductive costs (disadvantages) associated with it. If a behavior is adaptive, it promotes the *individual's* production of offspring. Here are five definitions to keep in mind:

1. **Reproductive success.** An individual reproduces, and at least some offspring survive.

2. **Adaptive behavior.** A form of behavior that helps perpetuate the individual's genes. Its frequency in a population is maintained or increases over time.

3. **Social behavior.** Behavior expressed in the context of interactions among individuals of the same species.

4. **Selfish behavior.** Form of behavior that improves an individual's chance to produce or protect its own offspring regardless of the impact on the population.

5. **Altruism.** Self-sacrificing behavior. An individual behaves in a way that helps others in the population but reduces its own chance of producing offspring.

When biologists speak of selfish or altruistic behavior, they do not mean that the individual is consciously aware of some behavior or its reproductive goal. A hungry lion does not have to know that eating zebras is good for reproductive success. Its nervous system simply calls for *HUNTING BEHAVIOR!* when that lion sees a zebra. Hunting behavior persists in lion populations because genes for neural mechanisms that command hunting behavior are persisting.

To assess the adaptive value of any behavior, look for how it might promote reproductive success. For example, starlings (*Sturnus vulgaris*) nest in cavities of trees and decorate the nest bowl with sprigs of fresh leaves of pungent plants, such as wild carrot (*Daucus carota*). Larry Clark and Russell Mason hypothesized that nest decorating behavior suppresses populations of mites that infest nests and parasitize birds. Even a few mites produce thousands of descendants. In large numbers, mites suck enough blood from a nestling to weaken it and affect its growth and survival.

Clark and Mason tested their hypothesis with a set of experimental nests, some with fresh-cut wild carrot leaves and some without. They removed natural nests that starlings were using. Half of the nesting starling

Figure 49.8 Experimental test of the adaptive value of starling nest-decorating behavior (**a**). Nests designated *A* did not have fresh sprigs of wild carrot (**b**) and other plants that make aromatic compounds. Nests designated *B* had fresh sprigs added every seven days. (**c**) Twenty-one days after the experiment started, the chicks left and researchers made counts of the mites (*Ornithonyssus sylviarum*) infesting each nest. The test results supported the hypothesis that aromatic compounds suppress development of juvenile mites into (**d**) adult mites.

pairs got new nests with wild carrot sprigs. Swapped nests for the other pairs were sprigless. Figure 49.8c gives the results. Sprig-free nests had more mites than sprig-festooned nests. At the end of one experiment, sprig-free nests teemed with an average of 750,000 mites. Nests with sprigs had 8,000 mites. Why? Wild carrot sprigs contain an aromatic steroid compound that repels herbivores and helps plants survive. By coincidence, it prevents mites from maturing sexually.

Selection theory continues to guide experiments on this behavior. For instance, other researchers did not yield the same evidence that greenery reduces mite populations. Rather, their test results indicate that the decorating behavior may be adaptive either because it deters different kinds of parasites or because it boosts the immune function of the nestlings.

A genetically determined behavior may persist or increase in frequency in a population when it is adaptive. A behavior is adaptive when it increases the number of descendants that an individual successfully produces.

49.4 Communication Signals

LINKS TO
SECTIONS
18.6, 35.1, 36.1

Competing for food, defending territory, alerting others to danger, advertising sexual readiness, forming bonds with a mate, caring for the offspring—such intraspecific behaviors require unambiguous forms of communication.

THE NATURE OF COMMUNICATION SIGNALS

Communication signals are unambiguous cues sent and received among individuals of a species, and they involve instinctive and learned forms of behavior. Information-laden cues from a signaler are meant to change the behavior of receivers. Chemical, acoustical, and visual cues are among the most common.

Pheromones, again, are communication signals. The *signaling* pheromones induce the receiver to respond fast. They include chemical alarms, such as honeybee calls to action against potential threats. They include sex attractants. Bombykol is one of them. Bombykol molecules released by a female silk moth can attract males that are kilometers away. *Priming* pheromones bring about physiological (not behavioral) responses. As one example, a volatile odor in the urine of certain male mice can trigger and enhance estrus in female mice of the same species.

Acoustical signals are common. Male birds, frogs, grasshoppers, whales, and many other animals make sounds that attract females. Prairie dogs bark alarms. Wolves howl and kangaroo rats drum their feet on the ground when advertising possession of territory.

Some signals never vary. Zebra ears pressed flat to the head convey hostility; ears pointing up convey its absence. Different signals convey the intensity of the message. A zebra with ears laid back is not too riled up as long as its mouth is open only a bit. When the ears are laid back and its mouth gapes, watch out. That combination is a type of *composite* signal. Such signals have information encoded in two or more cues.

Signals often take on different meaning in different contexts. A lion emits a spine-tingling roar to keep in touch with its pride *or* to threaten rivals. Also, a signal can convey information about signals to follow. Dogs and wolves solicit play behavior with their play bow, as in Figure 49.9*a*. Without the bow, the signal receiver may construe the behaviors that follow as aggressive, sexual, or even exploratory—but not playful.

Signals evolve or persist in a population when they promote reproductive success of both the sender *and* receiver. If a signal is harmful, natural selection will favor individuals that don't send it or respond to it.

COMMUNICATION DISPLAYS

The play bow is a *communication* display, a pattern of behavior that is a social signal. The *threat* display is another common pattern. It announces that a signaler is prepared to attack a signal receiver. If a rival for a receptive female confronts a dominant male baboon, the dominant animal will roll his eyes upward and "yawn," which exposes sharp canines (Figure 49.9*b*). The signaler can benefit when the rival backs down, because he can control access to the female without having to fight. The signal receiver benefits because he can avoid a serious beating, infected wounds, and possibly death.

Figure 49.9 Communication displays. (**a**) Play bow of a young male wolf soliciting a romp. (**b**) Part of a male baboon's threat display: exposed canines. (**c**) Courtship display of Adelé penguins.

Figure 49.10 *Animated!* Honeybee dances, a classic example of a tactile display. (**a**) Honeybees that have visited a source of food close to their hive return and perform a *round* dance on the hive's honeycomb. Worker bees that maintain contact with the foraging bee throughout the dance will fly out and search for food near the hive.

(**b**) A bee that visits a feeding station more than 100 meters distant from the hive performs a *waggle* dance. During the dance, it makes a straight run and waggles its abdomen. A waggle dancer also varies the dance speed to convey more information about distance to a food source. For example, when food is 150 meters away, a bee dances much faster, and with more waggles per straight run, compared to a dance about a food source that is 500 meters away.

(**c**) As Karl von Frisch discovered, a *straight* run's orientation varies, depending on the direction in which a food source is located. He put one dish of honey on a direct line between a hive and the sun. Foragers that located it returned to the hive and oriented their straight runs right up the honeycomb. He put another dish of honey at right angles to a line between the hive and the sun. Foraging bees made their straight runs 90 degrees to vertical on the honeycomb. Thus, a honeybee "recruited" into foraging orients its flight *with respect to the sun and the hive*. By doing so, it wastes less time and energy during its food-gathering expedition.

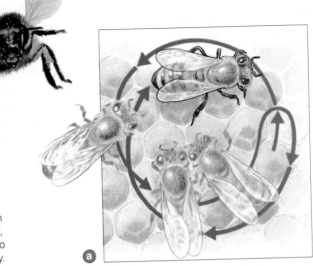

When bee moves straight down comb, recruits fly to source directly away from the sun.

When bee moves to right of vertical, recruits fly at 90° angle to right of the sun.

When bee moves straight up comb, recruits fly straight toward the sun.

Such displays are ritualized, with intended changes in the function of common behavior patterns. Normal movements might be exaggerated or frozen. Feathers, manes, claws, and other body parts are often notably enlarged, patterned, and colored. Ritualization is well developed in *courtship* displays—the steps that must precede pair formation. Courtship displays are well developed among birds (Section 18.6 and Figure 49.9c).

With *tactile* displays, a signaler touches the receiver in ritualized ways. After locating a source of pollen or nectar, a foraging honeybee returns to its colony (the hive) and performs a complex dance. It moves in a defined pattern, jostling a crowd of workers that stay in close physical contact with it. Its signals give other bees information about the general location, distance, and direction of a food source (Figure 49.10).

ILLEGITIMATE SIGNALERS AND RECEIVERS

Unintended recipients can intercept communication signals. Male tungara frogs make two kinds of calls—one simple, the other complex. The calls mean "come on over" to female frogs, but they mean "dinner over here" to fringe-lipped bats. Complex calls are more inviting to females but make it easier for bats to find the caller. When bats are near, male frogs vocalize less and are more likely to make the simpler call.

There are illegitimate signalers, too. Some assassin bugs can borrow the scent of their prey—termites—by hooking a dead termite on their back. By signaling that they "belong" to a termite colony, they can more easily hunt termites. As another example, if a female of certain predatory firefly species sees a flash from a male of a different species, she will flash back. If she lures him into attack range, she will capture and eat him. Getting eaten is an evolutionary cost of having an otherwise useful response to a come-hither signal.

A communication signal transfers information from one individual to another individual of the same species. Such signals benefit both the signaler and the receiver.

Some individuals of a different species act illegitimately as a communication signaler or receiver.

49.5 Mates, Offspring, and Reproductive Success

LINKS TO
SECTIONS
18.6, 26.10

For reasons we need not explore here, many people find mating and parenting behaviors of animals fascinating. How useful is selection theory in helping us interpret such behavior? Take a look.

SEXUAL SELECTION AND MATING BEHAVIOR

Competition among members of one sex for access to mates is common. So is choosiness in selecting a mate. Such activities, recall, are forms of **sexual selection**. This microevolutionary process favors traits that give the individual a competitive advantage in attracting and often holding on to mates (Section 18.6).

But *whose* reproductive success is it—the male's or the female's? Male animals, remember, produce many tiny sperm, and females produce far larger but fewer eggs. For the male, success generally depends on how many eggs he can fertilize. For the female, it depends more on how many eggs she produces or how many offspring she can raise. Usually, the most important factor in a female's sexual preference is the quality of the mate, not the quantity of partners.

Female hangingflies (*Harpobittacus apicalis*) provide an instructive example. They choose males that offer superior food. A male hunts and kills a moth or some other insect. Then he releases a sex pheromone, which attracts females to him and his "nuptial gift" (Figure 49.11*a*). A female tends to select the male that offers a large calorie-rich gift. Only after the female has been eating the gift for five minutes or so does she start to accept sperm from her partner. She lets the male continue inseminating her—but only for as long as it takes for her to devour the gift.

Before twenty minutes are up, a female hangingfly can break off the mating at any point. If she does, she might well mate with a different male hangingfly and accept his sperm. Doing so dilutes the reproductive success of her first partner.

Females of different species shop around for males with the best burrows. Consider the fiddler crabs that live along muddy shores from Massachusetts down to Florida. In males, one of the two claws is enlarged. Some of those claws are enlarged enough to make up more than half the body weight (Figure 49.11*b*). When spring tides are favorable, the male crabs build their elaborate mating burrows in the same area. Each male stands beside his burrow, waving his oversized claw. Females stroll by, checking out details of the burrows. When a female likes what she sees, she will follow the male into his burrow and engage in sex.

Many female birds are choosy. Male sage grouse (*Centrocercus urophasianus*) converge at a **lek**, a type of communal display ground. Each male stakes out a few square meters. With tail feathers erect, males use their large, puffed-out neck pouches to emit booming calls (Figure 49.11*d*). As they do, they stamp about on

Figure 49.11 (**a**) Male hangingfly dangling a moth as a nuptial gift for a potential mate. Females of some hangingfly species choose sexual partners that offer the largest gift to them. By waving his enlarged claw, a male fiddler crab (**b**) may attract the eye of a female fiddler crab (**c**). A male sage grouse (**d**) showing off as he competes for female attention at a communal display ground.

their patch of prairie, a bit like wind-up toys. Females tend to select and mate with one male sage grouse. Afterward, they go off to nest and raise the young by themselves. Many females often select the same male, so most of the males never do mate.

In another behavioral pattern, sexually receptive females of some species cluster in defendable groups. Where you come across such a group, you are likely to observe males competing for access to clusters. The competition for ready-made harems has resulted in combative male lions, sheep, elk, elephant seals, and bison, to name a few types of animals (Figure 49.12).

PARENTAL CARE

When females fight for males, then we can expect that the males provide more than sperm delivery. Some help with parenting. Midwife toads are an example. A male wraps strings of fertilized eggs around his legs until the eggs hatch (Figure 49.13a). With her eggs being cared for, a female can mate with other males, if she can find some that are not already caring for eggs. Late in the breeding season, unencumbered males are rare, and female toads fight for access to them. The females even attempt to pry mating pairs apart.

Parental behavior uses up time and energy, which parents otherwise might spend on living long enough to reproduce again. However, for many species, the benefit of immediate reproductive success outweighs the cost of parenting. Reproductive success might be more chancy later on.

For amphibians and reptiles, parenting is rare once the young are hatched. Crocodilians are an exception. Crocodilian parents construct a nest, as birds do. Their young call out when they are ready to hatch. Parents dig up the young and care for them for some time.

Most birds are monogamous, and both parents often care for the young (Figure 49.13b). In mammals, males typically leave after mating. Females raise the young alone, and males attempt to mate again or conserve energy for the next breeding season (Figure 49.13c). Mammalian species in which males do help care for the young tend to be monogamous. About 5 percent of all mammals fall into this category.

Researchers use selection theory to explain some aspects of mating behavior.

Male or female preferences for certain behavioral traits can provide the individual with a competitive edge and promote its reproductive success.

Figure 49.12 Male bison locked in combat during the breeding season.

Figure 49.13 (a) Male midwife toad with developing eggs wrapped around his legs. (b) Male and female Caspian terns cooperate in the care of their chick. (c) A female grizzly will care for her cub for as long as two years. The male takes no part in its upbringing.

49.6 Costs and Benefits of Social Groups

LINKS TO
SECTIONS
45.1, 46.4

*Survey the animal kingdom and you will find a range
of social groups, with evolutionary costs and benefits.*

COOPERATIVE PREDATOR AVOIDANCE

Cooperative responses to predators help some groups reduce the net risk to all. Vulnerable individuals, too, can be on the alert for predators, join a counterattack, or engage in more effective defenses (Figure 49.14).

Vervet monkeys, meerkats, prairie dogs, and many other mammals cooperate with their alarm calls, as in Figure 49.14a. A prairie dog makes a particular bark when it sights an eagle and a different signal when it sights a coyote. Others dive into burrows to escape an eagle's attack or they stand erect, the better to scan the horizon and zero in on the threat.

Ecologist Birgitta Sillén-Tullberg observed group benefits for Australian sawfly caterpillars that live in clumps on branches (Figure 49.14b). When disturbed, individuals collectively rear back, writhe, and vomit partly digested eucalyptus leaves, which are toxic to songbirds and other animals that prey on them.

As Sillén-Tullberg hypothesized, individual sawfly caterpillars benefit from their coordinated repulsion of predatory birds. She used her hypothesis to predict that birds are more likely to eat a lone caterpillar. She tested her prediction with young hand-reared birds. Birds that were offered one caterpillar at a time ate an average of 5.6 caterpillars. Birds that were offered a clump of caterpillars ate an average of 4.1. Individuals were safer in a group, as predicted.

THE SELFISH HERD

Simply by their physical position in the group, some individuals form a living shield against predation on others. They belong to a **selfish herd**, a simple society that benefits their reproductive self-interest. Selfish-herd behavior has been studied in bluegill sunfishes. Male sunfishes build adjacent nests on the bottom of a lake. Then females deposit their eggs where males have used their fins to scoop out depressions in mud.

If a colony of bluegill males is a selfish herd, then we can predict competition for the "safe" sites—at the center of a colony. Compared to eggs at the periphery, eggs in nests at the center are less likely to be eaten by snails and largemouth bass. Competition does indeed occur. The largest, most powerful males tend to claim centermost locations. Other, smaller males assemble around them and bear the brunt of predatory attacks. Even so, they are better off in the group than on their own, fending off a bass single-handedly, so to speak.

COOPERATIVE HUNTING

Many predatory mammals, including wolves, lions, and wild dogs, live in social groups and cooperate in hunts (Figure 49.15). Are group hunts more successful than solitary hunts? Often they are not. Researchers observed a solitary lion that captured prey about 15 percent of the time. Two lions hunting together did capture prey twice as often, but they had to share it, so the number of successful hunts per lion balanced

Figure 49.14 Group defenses. (**a**) Black-tailed prairie dogs bark an alarm call that warns others of predators. Does this put the caller at risk? Not much. Prairie dogs usually act as sentries only if they are done feeding and are standing beside their burrows. (**b**) Australian sawfly caterpillars form clumps and collectively regurgitate a fluid (the yellow blobs) that is toxic to most predators. (**c**) Musk oxen adults (*Ovibos moshatus*) form a ring of horns, often around the young.

Figure 49.15 Members of a wolf pack (*Canis lupus*). Wolves cooperate in hunting, caring for the young, and defending a territory. Benefits are not distributed equally. Only the highest ranking individuals, the alpha male and alpha female, breed.

out. When more lions joined the hunt, the success rate per lion fell. Wolves show a similar pattern. Among many cooperative hunters, hunting success in itself might not explain group living. Individuals do hunt together, but they also may fend off scavengers, care for one another's young, and protect territory.

DOMINANCE HIERARCHIES

Many social groups share resources unequally among some individuals that are subordinate to others. Most wolf packs, for instance, have one dominant male that breeds with just one dominant female. Other wolves in the pack are nonbreeding brothers and sisters, or aunts and uncles. They all hunt and bring food to the individuals that guard the young in their den.

Baboons live in large troops. A female stays with the group into which she was born and inherits social standing from her mother. Dominant females get more food, water, and grooming. Their young grow and mature faster than those of lower-ranking females.

Why would a subordinate give up resources and, often, breeding privileges? It might get injured or die if it challenges a strong individual. It might not be able to survive on its own. A subordinate might even get a chance to reproduce if it lives long enough or if its dominant peers are taken out by a predator or old age. Some subordinate wolves and baboons do move up the social ladder when the opportunity arises.

REGARDING THE COSTS

If social behavior is advantageous, *then why are there so few social species?* In most habitats, the costs outweigh benefits. For instance, packed-together individuals do compete more for a share of resources (Section 45.1). Cormorants, puffins, and many other seabirds form dense breeding colonies, as in Figure 49.16. All must compete for a share of the same ecological pie.

Figure 49.16 Nearly uniform spacing in a crowded cormorant colony.

Large social groups also attract more predators. If individuals are crowded together, they invite parasites and contagious diseases that jump from host to host. The individuals may also be at risk of being killed or exploited by others. Given the opportunity, breeding pairs of herring gulls cannibalize a neighbor's eggs and any chicks that wander away from their nest.

Living in a social group can provide benefits, as through cooperative defenses or shielding against predators.

Group living has costs, in terms of increased competition, increased vulnerability to infections, and exploitation by others of the group.

49.7 Why Sacrifice Yourself?

LINK TO
CHAPTER 46
INTRODUCTION

Extreme cases of sterility and self-sacrifice have evolved in only two groups of insects and one group of mammals. How are genes of the nonreproducers perpetuated?

SOCIAL INSECTS

Honeybees and fire ants (Chapter 46) are among the true social (eusocial) insects. Like termites, they stay together for generations in a group that has a division of labor. Many permanently sterile individuals care cooperatively for the offspring of just a few breeding individuals. Often they are highly specialized in form and function (Figure 49.17).

Consider a honeybee hive. The only fertile female, a queen, secretes a pheromone that other female bees distribute through the hive. This signaling molecule suppresses the development of ovaries in all the other females, which makes them sterile. The queen bee is larger than worker bees partly because of her enlarged egg-producing ovaries (Figure 49.18*a*).

About 30,000 to 50,000 female workers feed larvae, clean and maintain the hive, and build honeycomb from waxy secretions. Adult worker bees live for about six weeks in the spring and summer. When foragers return to the hive after finding a rich source of nectar or pollen, they engage others in a dance. This tactile display recruits more foragers (Figure 49.10). Workers also cooperate through the transfer of food from one to another. They guard the entrance to the hive and will sacrifice themselves to repel intruders.

Males, the stingless drones, develop only in spring and in summer. They have no part in the day-to-day work and subsist on food gathered by their worker sisters. Drones live for sex. Each day, they fly out in search of a mate. If one is lucky, he will find a virgin queen on her single flight away from her colony. The sole function of her flight is to meet up with and mate with a drone. A drone dies right after he inseminates a virgin queen, which then founds a new colony. She will store and use his sperm for years, perpetuating his genes and those of his original colony.

Like honeybees, termites live in enormous family groups with a queen specialized for producing eggs (Figure 49.18*c*). Unlike a honeybee hive, each termite colony holds sterile individuals of both sexes. A king supplies the female with sperm. Winged reproductive termites of both sexes develop seasonally.

SOCIAL MOLE-RATS

Vertebrates are not known for sterility and extreme self-sacrifice. The only eusocial mammals are African mole-rats. The best studied is *Heterocephalus glaber*, the naked mole-rat. Clans of this nearly hairless rodent build and occupy burrows in arid parts of East Africa.

A reproducing female dominates the clan, and she mates with one to three males (Figure 49.18*b*). Other, nonbreeding members live just to protect and care for the "queen" and "king" (or kings) and their offspring. The sterile diggers excavate subterranean tunnels and chambers that are living rooms or dumps for wastes. When a digger comes across a tasty tuber or root, it hauls some back to the main chamber, where it emits a series of chirps. Its chirps recruit others, which help carry the tuber back to the chamber. In this way, the queen, her retinue of males, and her offspring get fed. Digger mole-rats also deliver food to other helpers that seem to loaf about, shoulder to shoulder and belly to back, with the reproductive royals. These "loafers" actually spring to action when a snake or some other enemy threatens the clan. Collectively, and at great risk, they chase away or attack and kill the predator.

Figure 49.17 Specialized ways of serving and defending the colony. (**a**) An Australian honeypot ant worker. This sterile female is a living container for her colony's food reserves. (**b**) Army ant soldier (*Eciton burchelli*) with formidable mandibles. (**c**) Eyeless soldier termite (*Nasutitermes*). It bombards intruders with a stream of sticky goo from its nozzle-shaped head.

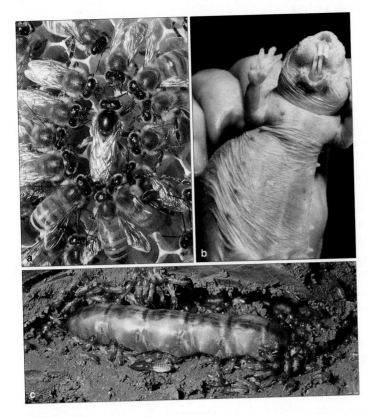

Figure 49.18 Three queens. (**a**) A queen honeybee with her court of sterile worker daughters. (**b**) This queen naked mole-rat has twelve mammary glands, the better to feed her many offspring. In a laboratory colony at Cornell University, one female produced a litter of twenty-eight pups. She gave birth to more than 900 offspring during her lifetime. (**c**) A termite queen (*Macrotermes*) dwarfs her offspring and her mate. Her body pumps out thousands of eggs a day.

Figure 49.19 Damaraland mole-rats in a burrow. Like their relatives, the naked mole-rats, they live in colonies having nonbreeding workers. Unlike naked mole-rats, these fuzzy burrowers are not highly inbred.

INDIRECT SELECTION FOR ALTRUISM

None of the altruistic individuals of a honeybee hive, termite colony, or naked mole-rat clan directly passes genes to the next generation. So how are genes that underlie altruistic behavior perpetuated? According to William Hamilton's theory of **inclusive fitness**, genes associated with altruism can be favored by selection if they lead to behavior that will increase the number of offspring produced by an altruist's closest relatives.

A sexually reproducing, diploid parent caring for offspring is not helping exact genetic copies of itself. Each of its gametes, and each of its offspring, inherits one-half of its genes. Other individuals of the social group that have the same ancestors also share genes with their parents. Two siblings (brothers or sisters) are as genetically similar as a parent and its offspring. Nephews and nieces share about one-fourth of their uncle's genes.

Sterile workers may be indirectly promoting genes for "self-sacrifice" through altruistic behavior that will benefit their close relatives. All of the individuals in honeybee, termite, and ant colonies are members of a great extended family. Nonbreeding family members support siblings, a few of which are future kings and queens. Although a guard bee dies after driving her stinger into a bear, siblings in the hive will perpetuate some of her genes.

Does close kinship explain why naked mole-rats are the only eusocial mammals? DNA fingerprinting studies of one naked mole-rat clan revealed that all of the individuals are *very* close relatives and genetically different from individuals of other clans. Each clan is highly inbred after many generations of brother–sister, mother–son, and father–daughter matings.

However, inbreeding might not even be necessary for mole-rat eusociality. The social organization of the Damaraland mole-rat (*Cryptomys damarensis*) resembles that of *H. glaber* (Figure 49.19). Nonbreeding members of both sexes cooperatively assist one breeding pair. Even so, breeding pairs of wild Damaraland mole-rat colonies usually are unrelated.

Researchers are now searching for other factors that select for eusocial behavior in mole-rats. According to one hypothesis, arid habitats and patchy food sources favor mole-rat genes that give rise to cooperation in digging burrows, searching for food, and fending off competitors of other species for resources.

Altruistic behavior may persist when individuals pass on genes indirectly, by helping relatives survive and reproduce.

By the theory of inclusive fitness, genes associated with altruistic behavior that is directed toward relatives may spread through a population in certain situations.

49.8 A Look at Primate Social Behavior

LINKS TO
SECTIONS
26.12, 26.15

Primates, especially chimpanzees and bonobos, live in groups. Their social environment is a significant factor in determining an individual's reproductive success.

In the 1960s Jane Goodall, a young primatologist, set out on her lifelong study of chimpanzees in Tanzania. One of her earliest discoveries was the chimpanzee's capacity to make and use simple tools—"fishing sticks"—by stripping leaves from branches. The long, flexible sticks are inserted into a termite mound, as shown in Figure 49.20*a*, which agitates the termites. The stick is carefully withdrawn after termites swarm on it, and the chimpanzee gets a high-protein snack. Thicker sticks are used to make holes in the mound, then the fishing sticks are inserted into the holes.

Different chimpanzee groups use slightly different tool-shaping and termite-fishing methods. Youngsters of each group learn by imitating the adults.

Male chimpanzees spend their lives in the group in which they are born and form strong social bonds. The females are often unrelated and interact little with one another. A female's status is dictated mostly by how she gets along with the males. Before the rainy season, mature females that are entering their fertile cycle go through hormone-driven physiological and behavioral changes. Their external genitalia become swollen and vivid pink. The swellings are strong visual signals to males. They are flags for sexual jamborees—for great gatherings of highly stimulated chimpanzees in which any males present may have a turn at copulating with the same female.

Male chimpanzees cooperatively hunt for monkeys, small pigs, and antelopes. They may also cooperate in attacks on neighboring groups. Males sometimes even kill infants. By one hypothesis, infanticidal behavior of males may exert selection pressure for promiscuity in females. A female who mates with many males might protect her offspring by obscuring their paternity. A male would be expected to avoid killing an infant that might carry his genes.

Comparative studies of the closely related bonobo reveal contrasting sexual and social behavior (Figure 49.20*b*). As with chimpanzees, adult males are related and females are not. Yet bonobo females form strong social bonds. Unlike female chimpanzees, they can be receptive to sex at any time, not just during the fertile cycle. Male bonobos display less social cohesion than male chimpanzees do. They do not hunt together, and no one has come across an infanticidal male.

What explains the differences? Does a higher level of interaction help female bonobos deter potentially infanticidal males? Does unlimited access to sexually receptive females interfere with male–male bonding or diffuse male aggression? We do not know. Hormones that affect pair bonding may play a role. Like prairie voles and mountain voles, chimpanzees and bonobos differ in a regulatory region near a gene that encodes one ADH receptor. In voles, a longer sequence in this region correlates with more family-oriented behavior. Interestingly, the bonobo sequence for this region is about 360 bases longer than the chimpanzee sequence. What about humans? Our sequence in this region is nearly identical to that of the bonobos—and with this in mind, we turn briefly to human behavior.

Chimpanzees and bonobos both live in social groups. They differ in the details of social organization, degree of female cooperation, and extent of male aggression.

Figure 49.20 (**a**) Chimpanzees (*Pan troglodytes*) using sticks as tools for extracting tasty termites from a nest.

(**b**) Female bonobo (*Pan paniscus*) with her offspring. Like humans, bonobos are bipedal; they often walk on two legs. Also like humans, and unlike chimpanzees, the bonobo females have sexual organs that allow them to copulate facing their partner, and they can be sexually receptive at any time of year. They use sex as a means of strengthening social bonds.

49.9 An Evolutionary View of Human Social Behavior

Evolutionary forces shaped animal behavior—but humans alone consistently make moral choices about their behavior.

LINK TO
CHAPTER 43
INTRODUCTION

EXAMPLES OF BEHAVIORAL CUES

Is it possible that molecular cues help humans form social attachments, as they do in other animals? Think of how oxytocin and ADH help control pair bonding in voles. Now think about *autism*. Someone affected by this behavioral disorder cannot enter normal social relationships. An autistic child has significantly low levels of oxytocin in blood. Also, a control sequence near the gene for one ADH receptor is shorter than normal. This same sequence is shorter in chimpanzees than in bonobos and humans.

Researchers are studying how hormones influence mother–infant bonding and romantic bonds. Nursing stimulates oxytocin secretion. So does orgasm, even a friendly massage. Does the brief increase in oxytocin or other hormonal responses contribute to what we perceive as love? That is an open question.

Also, human pheromones may be present in sweat or other secretions. When females live in proximity, as they do in college dormitories, their menstrual cycles typically become synchronized. Martha McClintock and Kathleen Stern demonstrated that one woman's menstrual cycle will lengthen or shorten after she has become exposed to sweat secreted by a woman who was in a different phase of the cycle.

Men and women secrete different chemicals and respond differently to them. PET scans reveal that one chemical component in male sweat activates certain brain areas in women but not in most men. Similarly, a chemical component of female urine activates brain areas in most males more than it does in females. Intriguingly, male homosexuals show the same brain response to male sweat as women do.

In most mammals, pheromones bind to receptors in a vomeronasal organ, or VNO. Neurons connect it to parts of the brain that control behavior. In humans, the VNO is a tiny, ductlike structure on the septum, a tissue that divides the nose into two nostrils. Many scientists hypothesize that human VNOs are vestigial structures—no longer functional. Others suspect that the human VNO does connect to the brain, by way of some pathway that has not yet been discovered.

EVOLUTIONARY QUESTIONS

If we are comfortable with studying the evolutionary basis of the behavior of termites, naked mole-rats, and other animals, why do so many people resist the idea of analyzing human behavior in the same way? Often they fear that attempts to identify the adaptive value of some human trait will be used to define its morality. However, there is a clear difference between trying to explain behavior in terms of its evolutionary history and attempting to justify it. To a biologist, "adaptive" does not mean "morally right." It simply means useful in perpetuating an individual's genes.

An example: Infanticide is morally repugnant. Is it unnatural? No. It happens in many animal groups and all human cultures. Male lions often kill the offspring of other males when they take over a pride. Doing so frees up the lionesses to breed with them, which can increase the infanticidal male's reproductive success.

Biologists may predict that unrelated human males are a threat to infants, and evidence supports this. The absence of a biological father and the presence of an unrelated male increases risk of death for an American child under age two by seventy times.

What about parents who kill their own offspring? In her book on maternal behavior, primatologist Sarah Blaffer Hrdy cites a study of a village in Papua New Guinea in which about 40 percent of the newborns were killed by parents. She argues that when resources or social support are hard to come by, a mother might increase her fitness by killing a newborn. She can then allocate child-rearing energy to her other offspring or save it for children she may have in the future.

Do most of us find such behavior appalling? Yes. Does such behavior warrant attention? Think about all you have learned in this book, then decide.

A behavior that might be adaptive in the evolutionary sense may still be judged by society to be morally wrong.

Summary

Section 49.1 Animal behavior starts with genes that specify products required for development of the nervous, endocrine, and muscular systems. Hormones are among the gene products that affect behavior.

Instinctive behavior is performed without having been learned by experience in the environment. It is a prewired response to one or two simple, well-defined environmental cues.

Section 49.2 An animal learns when it processes and integrates information from experiences, then uses that information to vary or change responses to stimuli. Imprinting is one form of learning that happens only during a sensitive period early in life.

Section 49.3 A behavior that has a genetic basis is subject to evolution by natural selection. Adaptive forms of behavior evolved as a result of individual differences in reproductive success in past generations. A behavior persists when its reproductive benefits exceed the reproductive costs.

Section 49.4 Communication signals are meant to change the behavior of individuals of the same species. Pheromones are signaling molecules that have roles in social communication.

Visual signals are key components of courtship displays and threat displays. Acoustical signals are sounds that have precise, species-specific information. Tactile signals are specific forms of physical contact between a signaler and a receiver.

Biology⊗Now
Explore the honeybee dance language with the animation on BiologyNow.

Section 49.5 Sexual selection favors traits that give an individual a competitive edge in attracting and often holding on to mates. Females of many species select for males that have traits or engage in behaviors they find attractive. When large numbers of females cluster in defensible areas, males may compete with one another to control the areas.

Parental care has reproductive costs in terms of future reproduction and survival. It is adaptive when benefits to a present set of offspring offset the costs.

Biology⊗Now
Read the InfoTrac article "Something Fishy in the Nest," Bryan Neff, Natural History, February 2004.

Section 49.6 Animals that live in social groups may benefit by cooperating in predator detection, defense, and rearing the young. Benefits of group living are often distributed unequally. Species that live in large groups incur costs, including increased disease and parasitism, and increased competition for resources.

Biology⊗Now
Read the InfoTrac article "Caterpillars as Social Insects," James Costa, American Scientist, March–April 1997.

Section 49.7 Ants, termites, and some other insects as well as two species of mole-rats are eusocial. They live in colonies with overlapping generations and have a reproductive division of labor. Most colony members do not reproduce; they assist their relatives and rear their offspring.

According to the theory of inclusive fitness, such extreme altruism is perpetuated because altruistic individuals have some number of genes in common with their reproducing relatives. Altruistic individuals in the social group pass on "by proxy" the genes that underlie this behavior.

Sections 49.8, 49.9 Researchers are identifying the mechanisms and adaptive significance of primate social behavior. With respect to humans, a behavior that is adaptive in the evolutionary sense may still be judged by society to be morally wrong.

Self-Quiz
Answers in Appendix II

1. Genes affect the behavior of individuals by _____ .
   a. influencing the development of nervous systems
   b. affecting the kinds of hormones in individuals
   c. governing development of muscles and skeletons
   d. all of the above

2. A behavior is defined as adaptive if it _____ .
   a. varies among individuals of a population
   b. occurs without prior learning
   c. increases an individual's reproductive success
   d. is widespread across a species
   e. benefits unrelated members of the species

3. Steven Arnold offered slug meat to newborn garter snakes from different populations to test his hypothesis that the snakes' response to slugs _____ .
   a. was shaped by indirect selection
   b. is an instinctive behavior
   c. is based on pheromones
   d. is adaptive

4. Generally, living in a social group costs the individual, in terms of _____ .
   a. competition for food, other resources
   b. vulnerability to contagious diseases
   c. competition for mates
   d. all of the above

5. Social behavior evolves because _____ .
   a. social animals are more advanced than solitary ones
   b. under some conditions, the costs of social life to individuals are offset by benefits to the species
   c. under some conditions, the benefits of social life to an individual offset the costs to that individual
   d. under most conditions, social life has no costs to an individual.

6. Eusocial insects _____ .
   a. live in extended family groups
   b. are found among almost all insect orders
   c. show a reproductive division of labor
   d. a and c
   e. all of the above

7. Helping other individuals at a reproductive cost to oneself might be adaptive if those helped are _____ .
   a. members of another species
   b. competitors for mates
   c. close relatives
   d. illegitimate signalers

8. Match the terms with their most suitable description.
   ____ fixed action pattern
   ____ altruism
   ____ basis of instinctive and learned behavior
   ____ imprinting
   ____ pheromone

   a. time-dependent form of learning requiring exposure to key stimulus
   b. genes plus actual experience
   c. stereotyped motor program that runs to completion independently of feedback from environment
   d. assisting another individual at one's own expense
   e. one communication signal

Additional questions are available on Biology ⑤ Now™

Critical Thinking

1. Sexual imprinting is common in birds. During a short sensitive period in early life, the bird learns features that it will seek later, when ready to mate. Figure 49.21 shows an amorous rooster wading into the water after ducks. Speculate on what might have caused this behavior.

2. Nazca boobies (*Sula granti*) lay two eggs, several days apart. No matter how much food is available, only one chick survives to adulthood (Figure 49.22). The first chick to hatch pushes its younger sibling from the nest, and that sibling dies of starvation and neglect. Formulate a hypothesis on how it might be adaptive for parents of this species to lay two eggs if one of the hatchlings tends to kill the other. Design an experiment to test your hypothesis.

3. In 2002 Svante Paabo proposed how one gene, *FOXP2,* might have been pivotal in the evolution of *language.* Humans who have a base-pair substitution in this gene cannot speak intelligibly, understand complex sentences, or make certain movements of the mouth and face.

   All mammals have the *FOXP2* gene, which has a 715 base-pair sequence. The gene has mutated very little over evolutionary time. The one in chimpanzees differs from the one in mice by a single base pair. But two more base pairs mutated after the ancestors of humans diverged from the lineage that led to chimpanzees. This altered version of the gene became fixed in the lineage that led to modern humans. Why? By one hypothesis, language-related traits that arose from the two recent substitutions were favored by directional selection. Speculate on how a capacity to make and comprehend more complex auditory signals shaped the social behavior of the forerunners of humans.

4. A cheetah scent-marks plants in its territory with certain exocrine gland secretions. What evidence would you require to demonstrate that the cheetah's action is an evolved communication signal?

5. Among primates, differences in sexual behavior tend to be related to the size of a male's gonads. Gorillas have relatively tiny testicles. In a 450-pound male, they may weigh about an ounce. Gorillas live in groups consisting of a male, a few females, and offspring. This is the most typical kind of primate social group. When a female is ready to mate, there usually is only one adult male around to inseminate her.

   In contrast, a female chimpanzee advertises her fertile period and mates with many males (Section 49.8). A 100-pound chimpanzee male has testicles about four times as weighty as a gorilla's. By making far more sperm, a male chimpanzee increases the odds that his sperm, not a rival's, will fertilize a female's egg.

   An adult human male is larger than a chimpanzee, but his testicles are only about half the weight. What might this suggest about female promiscuity and male competition to fertilize eggs in the lineage that led to humans?

6. In moths and many other insects, potential mates find one another with the help of species-specific pheromones. The pheromones are usually mixes of chemicals derived from fatty acids. Explain how a mutation could result in a change in the mix of chemicals in a moth pheromone. How might such mutations encourage speciation?

Figure 49.21 Behaviorally confused rooster.

Figure 49.22 A Nazca booby attends to its single surviving chick.

Epilogue

BIOLOGICAL PRINCIPLES AND THE HUMAN IMPERATIVE

Molecules, single cells, tissues, organs, organ systems, multicelled organisms, populations, communities, ecosystems, and the biosphere. These are architectural systems of life, assembled in increasingly complex ways over the past 3.8 billion years. We are latecomers to this immense biological building program. And yet, within the relatively short span of 10,000 years, many of our activities have been changing the character of the land, ocean, and atmosphere, even the genetic character of species.

It would be presumptuous to think that we alone have had profound impact on the world of life. As long ago as the Proterozoic, photosynthetic organisms were irrevocably changing the course of biological evolution by enriching the atmosphere with oxygen. During the past as well as the present, competitive adaptations led to the rise of some groups, whose dominance assured the decline of others. Change is nothing new. What *is* new is the capacity of one species to comprehend what might be going on.

We now have the population size, technology, and cultural inclination to use up energy and modify the environment at rapid rates. Where will this end? Will feedback controls operate as they do, for instance, when population growth exceeds carrying capacity? In other words, will negative feedback controls come into play and keep things from getting too far out of hand?

Feedback control will not be enough, for it does not get under way until the deviation has reached a critical

threshold. Our patterns of resource consumption and our population growth are founded on an illusion of unlimited resources and a forgiving environment. A prolonged, global shortage of food or the passing of a critical threshold for the global climate can come too fast to be corrected; in which case the impact of the deviation may be too great to be reversed.

What about feedforward mechanisms, which might serve as early warning systems? For example, when sensory receptors near the surface of skin detect a drop in outside air temperature, each sends messages to the nervous system. That system responds by triggering mechanisms that raise the body's core temperature before the body itself becomes dangerously chilled. Extrapolating from this, if we develop feedforward control mechanisms, would it not be possible to start corrective measures before we do too much harm?

Feedforward controls alone will not work, for they operate after change is under way. Think of the DEW line—the Distant Early Warning system. It is like a vast sensory receptor for detecting missiles launched against North America. By the time it does what it is supposed to, it may be too late to stop widespread destruction.

It would be naive to assume we can ever reverse who we are at this point in evolutionary time, to de-evolve ourselves culturally and biologically into becoming less complex in the hope of averting disaster. Yet there is reason to believe we can avert disaster by

using a third kind of control mechanism—a capacity to anticipate events even before they happen. We are not locked into responding only after irreversible change has begun. We have the capacity to anticipate the future—it is the essence of our visions of utopia and hell. *We all have the capacity to adapt to a future that we can partly shape.*

For instance, we can stop trying to "beat nature" and learn to work with it. Individually and collectively, we can work to develop long-term policies that take into account biotic and abiotic limits on population growth. Far from being a surrender, this would be one of the most intelligent behaviors of which we are capable.

Having a capacity to adapt and using it are not the same thing. We have already put the world of life on dangerous ground because we have not yet mobilized ourselves as a species to work toward self-control.

Our survival depends on predicting possible futures. It depends on preserving, restoring, and constructing ecosystems that fit with our definition of basic human values and available biological models. Human values can change; our expectations can and must be adapted to biological reality. *For the principles of energy flow and resource utilization, which govern the survival of all systems of life, do not change.*

It is our biological and cultural imperative that we come to terms with these principles, and ask ourselves this: What will be our long-term contribution to the world of life?

Appendix I. Classification System

This revised classification scheme is a composite of several that microbiologists, botanists, and zoologists use. The major groupings are agreed upon, more or less. However, there is not always agreement on what to name a particular grouping or where it might fit within the overall hierarchy. There are several reasons why full consensus is not possible at this time.

First, the fossil record varies in its completeness and quality. Therefore, the phylogenetic relationship of one group to other groups is sometimes open to interpretation. Today, comparative studies at the molecular level are firming up the picture, but the work is still under way. Also, molecular comparisons do not always provide definitive answers to questions about phylogeny. Comparisons based on one set of genes may conflict with those comparing a different part of the genome. Or comparisons with one member of a group may conflict with comparisons based on other group members.

Second, ever since the time of Linnaeus, systems of classification have been based on the perceived morphological similarities and differences among organisms. Although some original interpretations are now open to question, we are so used to thinking about organisms in certain ways that reclassification often proceeds slowly.

A few examples: Traditionally, birds and reptiles were grouped in separate classes (Reptilia and Aves); yet there are compelling arguments for grouping the lizards and snakes in one group and the crocodilians, dinosaurs, and birds in another. Many biologists still favor a six-kingdom system of classification (archaea, bacteria, protists, plants, fungi, and animals). Others advocate a switch to the more recently proposed three-domain system (archaea, bacteria, and eukarya).

Third, researchers in microbiology, mycology, botany, zoology, and other fields of inquiry inherited a wealth of literature, based on classification systems that have been developed over time in each field of inquiry. Many are reluctant to give up established terminology that offers access to the past.

For example, botanists and microbiologists often use *division*, and zoologists *phylum*, for taxa that are equivalent in hierarchies of classification.

Why bother with classification frameworks if we know they only imperfectly reflect the evolutionary history of life? We do so for the same reasons that a writer might break up a history of civilization into several volumes, each with a number of chapters. Both are efforts to impart structure to an enormous body of knowledge and to facilitate retrieval of information from it. More importantly, to the extent that modern classification schemes accurately reflect evolutionary relationships, they provide the basis for comparative biological studies, which link all fields of biology.

Bear in mind that we include this appendix for your reference purposes only. Besides being open to revision, it is not meant to be complete. Names shown in "quotes" are polyphyletic or paraphyletic groups that are undergoing revision. For example, "reptiles" comprise at least three and possibly more lineages.

The most recently discovered species, as from the mid-ocean province, are not listed. Many existing and extinct species of the more obscure phyla are also not represented. Our strategy is to focus primarily on the organisms mentioned in the text or familiar to most students. We delve more deeply into flowering plants than into bryophytes, and into chordates than annelids.

PROKARYOTES AND EUKARYOTES COMPARED

As a general frame of reference, note that almost all bacteria and archaea are microscopic in size. Their DNA is concentrated in a nucleoid (a region of cytoplasm), not in a membrane-bound nucleus. All are single cells or simple associations of cells. They reproduce by prokaryotic fission or budding; they transfer genes by bacterial conjugation.

Table A lists representative types of autotrophic and heterotrophic prokaryotes. The authoritative reference, *Bergey's Manual of Systematic Bacteriology*, has called this a time of taxonomic transition. It references groups mainly by numerical taxonomy (Section 19.1) rather than by phylogeny. Our classification system does reflect evidence of evolutionary relationships for at least some bacterial groups.

The first life forms were prokaryotic. Similarities between Bacteria and Archaea have more ancient origins relative to the traits of eukaryotes.

Unlike the prokaryotes, all eukaryotic cells start out life with a DNA-enclosing nucleus and other membrane-bound organelles. Their chromosomes have many histones and other proteins attached. They include spectacularly diverse single-celled and multicelled species, which can reproduce by way of meiosis, mitosis, or both.

DOMAIN BACTERIA	DOMAIN ARCHAEA	DOMAIN EUKARYA
Kingdom Bacteria	Kingdom Archaea	Kingdom Protista / Kingdom Fungi / Kingdom Plantae / Kingdom Animalia

DOMAIN OF BACTERIA

KINGDOM BACTERIA

The largest, and most diverse group of prokaryotic cells. Includes photosynthetic autotrophs, chemosynthetic autotrophs, and heterotrophs. All prokaryotic pathogens of vertebrates are bacteria.

PHYLUM AQIFACAE Most ancient branch of the bacterial tree. Gram-negative, mostly aerobic chemoautotrophs, mainly of volcanic hot springs. *Aquifex.*

PHYLUM DEINOCOCCUS-THERMUS Gram-positive, heat-loving chemoautotrophs. *Deinococcus* is the most radiation resistant organism known. *Thermus* occurs in hot springs and near hydrothermal vents.

PHYLUM CHLOROFLEXI Green nonsulfur bacteria. Gram-negative bacteria of hot springs, freshwater lakes, and marine habitats. Act as nonoxygen-producing photoautotrophs or aerobic chemoheterotrophs. *Chloroflexus.*

PHYLUM ACTINOBACTERIA Gram-positive, mostly aerobic heterotrophs in soil, freshwater and marine habitats, and on mammalian skin. *Propionibacterium, Actinomyces, Streptomyces.*

PHYLUM CYANOBACTERIA Gram-negative, oxygen-releasing photoautotrophs mainly in aquatic habitats. They have chlorophyll *a* and photosystem I. Includes many nitrogen-fixing genera. *Anabaena, Nostoc, Oscillatoria.*

PHYLUM CHLOROBIUM Green sulfur bacteria. Gram-negative nonoxygen-producing photosynthesizers, mainly in freshwater sediments. *Chlorobium.*

PHYLUM FIRMICUTES Gram-positive walled cells and the cell wall-less mycoplasmas. All are heterotrophs. Some survive in soil, hot springs, lakes, or oceans. Others live on or in animals. *Bacillus, Clostridium, Heliobacterium, Lactobacillus, Listeria, Mycobacterium, Mycoplasma, Streptococcus.*

PHYLUM CHLAMYDIAE Gram-negative intracellular parasites of birds and mammals. *Chlamydia.*

PHYLUM SPIROCHETES Free-living, parasitic, and mutualistic gram-negative spring-shaped bacteria. *Borelia, Pillotina, Spirillum, Treponema.*

PHYLUM PROTEOBACTERIA The largest bacterial group. Includes photoautotrophs, chemoautotrophs, and heterotrophs; free-living, parasitic, and colonial groups. All are gram-negative.

Class Alphaproteobacteria. *Agrobacterium, Azospirillum, Nitrobacter, Rickettsia, Rhizobium.*

Class Betaproteobacteria. *Neisseria.*

Class Gammaproteobacteria. *Chromatium, Escherichia, Haemopilius, Pseudomonas, Salmonella, Shigella, Thiomargarita, Vibrio, Yersinia.*

Class Deltaproteobacteria. *Azotobacter, Myxococcus.*

Class Epsilonproteobacteria. *Campylobacter, Helicobacter.*

DOMAIN OF ARCHAEA

KINGDOM ARCHAEA

Prokaryotes that are evolutionarily between eukaryotic cells and the bacteria. Most are anaerobes. None are photosynthetic. Originally discovered in extreme habitats, they are now known to be widely dispersed. Compared with bacteria, the archaea have a distinctive cell wall structure and unique membrane lipids, ribosomes, and RNA sequences. Some are symbiotic with animals, but none are known to be animal pathogens.

PHYLUM EURYARCHAEOTA Largest archean group. Includes extreme thermophiles, halophiles, and methanogens. Others are abundant in the upper waters of the ocean and other more moderate habitats. *Methanocaldococcus, Nanoarchaeum.*

PHYLUM CRENARCHAEOTA Includes extreme theromophiles, as well as species that survive in Antarctic waters, and in more moderate habitats. *Sulfolobus, Ignicoccus.*

PHYLUM KORARCHAEOTA Known only from DNA isolated from hydrothermal pools. As of this writing, none have been cultured and no species have been named.

DOMAIN OF EUKARYOTES

KINGDOM "PROTISTA"

A collection of single-celled and multicelled lineages, which does not constitute a monophyletic group. Some biologists consider the groups listed below to be kingdoms in their own right.

PARABASALIA Parabasalids. Flagellated, single-celled anaerobic heterotrophs with a cytoskeletal "backbone" that runs the length of the cell. There are no mitochondria, but a hydrogenosome serves a similar function. *Trichomonas, Trichonympha.*

DIPLOMONADIDA Diplomonads. Flagellated, anaerobic single-celled heterotrophs that do not have mitochondria or Golgi bodies and do not form a bipolar spindle at mitosis. May be one of the most ancient lineages. *Giardia.*

EUGLENOZOA Euglenoids and kinetoplastids. Free-living and parasitic flagellates. All with one or more mitochondria. Some photosynthetic euglenoids with chloroplasts, others heterotrophic. *Euglena, Trypanosoma, Leishmania.*

RHIZARIA Formaminiferans and radiolarians. Free-living, heterotrophic amoeboid cells that are enclosed in shells. Most live in ocean waters or sediments. *Pterocorys, Stylosphaera.*

ALVEOLATA Single cells having a unique array of membrane-bound sacs (alveoli) just beneath the plasma membrane.

Ciliata. Ciliated protozoans. Heterotrophic protists with many cilia. *Paramecium, Didinium.*

Dinoflagellates. Diverse heterotrophic and photosynthetic flagellated cells that deposit cellulose in their alveoli. *Gonyaulax, Gymnodinium, Karenia, Noctiluca.*

Apicomplexans. Single-celled parasites of animals. A unique microtubular device is used to attach to and penetrate a host cell. *Plasmodium.*

STRAMENOPHILA Stramenophiles. Single-celled and multicelled forms; flagella with tinsel-like filaments.

Oomycotes. Water molds. Heterotrophs. Decomposers, some parasites. *Saprolegnia, Phytophthora, Plasmopara.*

Chrysophytes. Golden algae, yellow-green algae, diatoms, coccolithophores. Photosynthetic. *Emiliania, Mischococcus.*

Phaeophytes. Brown algae. Photosynthetic; nearly all live in temperate marine waters. All are multicellular. *Macrocystis, Laminaria, Sargassum, Postelsia.*

RHODOPHYTA Red algae. Mostly photosynthetic, some parasitic. Nearly all marine, some in freshwater habitats. Most multicellular. *Porphyra, Antithamion.*

CHLOROPHYTA Green algae. Mostly photosynthetic, some parasitic. Most freshwater, some marine or terrestrial. Single-celled, colonial, and multicellular forms. Some biologists place the chlorophytes and charophytes with the land plants in a kingdom called the Viridiplantae. *Acetabularia, Chlamydomonas, Chlorella, Codium, Udotea, Ulva, Volvox.*

CHAROPHYTA Photosynthetic. Closest living relatives of plants. Include both single-celled and multicelled forms. Desmids, stoneworts. *Micrasterias, Chara, Spirogyra.*

AMOEBOZOA True amoebas and slime molds. Heterotrophs that spend all or part of the life cycle as a single cell that uses pseudopods to capture food. *Amoeba, Entoamoeba* (amoebas), *Dictyostelium* (cellular slime mold), *Physarum* (plasmodial slime mold).

KINGDOM FUNGI

Nearly all multicelled eukaryotic species with chitin-containing cell walls. Heterotrophs, mostly saprobic decomposers, some parasites. Nutrition based upon extracellular digestion of organic matter and absorption of nutrients by individual cells. Multicelled species form absorptive mycelia and reproductive structures that produce asexual spores (and sometimes sexual spores).

PHYLUM CHYTRIDIOMYCOTA Chytrids. Primarily aquatic; saprobic decomposers or parasites that produce flagellated spores. *Chytridium.*

PHYLUM ZYGOMYCOTA Zygomycetes. Producers of zygospores (zygotes inside thick wall) by way of sexual reproduction. Bread molds, related forms. *Rhizopus, Philobolus.*

PHYLUM ASCOMYCOTA Ascomycetes. Sac fungi. Sac-shaped cells form sexual spores (ascospores). Most yeasts and molds, morels, truffles. *Saccharomyces, Morchella, Neurospora, Claviceps, Candida, Aspergillus, Penicillium.*

PHYLUM BASIDIOMYCOTA Basidiomycetes. Club fungi. Most diverse group. Produce basidiospores inside club-shaped structures. Mushrooms, shelf fungi, stinkhorns. *Agaricus, Amanita, Craterellus, Gymnopilus, Puccinia, Ustilago.*

"IMPERFECT FUNGI" Sexual spores absent or undetected. The group has no formal taxonomic status. If better understood, a given species might be grouped with sac fungi or club fungi. *Arthobotrys, Histoplasma, Microsporum, Verticillium.*

"LICHENS" Mutualistic interactions between fungal species and a cyanobacterium, green alga, or both. *Lobaria, Usnea.*

KINGDOM PLANTAE

Most photosynthetic with chlorophylls *a* and *b*. Some parasitic. Nearly all live on land. Sexual reproduction predominates.

BRYOPHYTES (NONVASCULAR PLANTS)

Small flattened haploid gametophyte dominates the life cycle; sporophyte remains attached to it. Sperm are flagellated; require water to swim to eggs for fertilization.

PHYLUM HEPATOPHYTA Liverworts. *Marchantia.*

PHYLUM ANTHOCEROPHYTA Hornworts.

PHYLUM BRYOPHYTA Mosses. *Polytrichum, Sphagnum.*

SEEDLESS VASCULAR PLANTS

Diploid sporophyte dominates, free-living gametophytes, flagellated sperm require water for fertilization.

PHYLUM LYCOPHYTA Lycophytes, club mosses. Small single-veined leaves, branching rhizomes. *Lycopodium, Selaginella.*

PHYLUM MONILOPHYTA

Subphylum Psilophyta. Whisk ferns. No obvious roots or leaves on sporophyte, very reduced. *Psilotum.*

Subphylum Sphenophyta. Horsetails. Reduced scalelike leaves. Some stems photosynthetic, others spore-producing. *Calamites* (extinct), *Equisetum.*

Subphylum Pterophyta. Ferns. Large leaves, usually with sori. Largest group of seedless vascular plants (12,000 species), mainly tropical, temperate habitats. *Pteris, Trichomanes, Cyathea* (tree ferns), *Polystichum.*

SEED-BEARING VASCULAR PLANTS

PHYLUM CYCADOPHYTA Cycads. Group of gymnosperms (vascular, bear "naked" seeds). Tropical, subtropical. Compound leaves, simple cones on male and female plants. Plants usually palm-like. Motile sperm. *Zamia, Cycas.*

PHYLUM GINKGOPHYTA Ginkgo (maidenhair tree). Type of gymnosperm. Motile sperm. Seeds with fleshy layer. *Ginkgo.*

PHYLUM GNETOPHYTA Gnetophytes. Only gymnosperms with vessels in xylem and double fertilization (but endosperm does not form). *Ephedra, Welwitchia, Gnetum.*

PHYLUM CONIFEROPHYTA Conifers. Most common and familiar gymnosperms. Generally cone-bearing species with needle-like or scale-like leaves. Includes pines (*Pinus*), redwoods (*Sequoia*), yews (*Taxus*).

PHYLUM ANTHOPHYTA Angiosperms (the flowering plants). Largest, most diverse group of vascular seed-bearing plants. Only organisms that produce flowers, fruits. Some families from several representative orders are listed:

BASAL FAMILIES

Family Amborellaceae. *Amborella.*
Family Nymphaeaceae. Water lilies.
Family Illiciaceae. Star anise.

MAGNOLIIDS

Family Magnoliaceae. Magnolias.
Family Lauraceae. Cinnamon, sassafras, avocados.
Family Piperaceae. Black pepper, white pepper.

EUDICOTS

Family Papaveraceae. Poppies.
Family Cactaceae. Cacti.
Family Euphorbiaceae. Spurges, poinsettia.
Family Salicaceae. Willows, poplars.
Family Fabaceae. Peas, beans, lupines, mesquite.
Family Rosaceae. Roses, apples, almonds, strawberries.
Family Moraceae. Figs, mulberries.
Family Cucurbitaceae. Squashes, melons, cucumbers.
Family Fagaceae. Oaks, chestnuts, beeches.
Family Brassicaceae. Mustards, cabbages, radishes.
Family Malvaceae. Mallows, okra, cotton, hibiscus, cocoa.
Family Sapindaceae. Soapberry, litchi, maples.
Family Ericaceae. Heaths, blueberries, azaleas.
Family Rubiaceae. Coffee.
Family Lamiaceae. Mints.
Family Solanaceae. Potatoes, eggplant, petunias.
Family Apiaceae. Parsleys, carrots, poison hemlock.
Family Asteraceae. Composites. Chrysanthemums, sunflowers, lettuces, dandelions.

MONOCOTS

Family Araceae. Anthuriums, calla lily, philodendrons.
Family Liliaceae. Lilies, tulips.
Family Alliaceae. Onions, garlic.
Family Iridaceae. Irises, gladioli, crocuses.
Family Orchidaceae. Orchids.
Family Arecaceae. Date palms, coconut palms.
Family Bromeliaceae. Bromeliads, pineapples.
Family Cyperaceae. Sedges.
Family Poaceae. Grasses, bamboos, corn, wheat, sugarcane.
Family Zingiberaceae. Gingers.

KINGDOM ANIMALIA

Multicelled heterotrophs, nearly all with tissues and organs, and organ systems, that are motile during part of the life cycle. Sexual reproduction occurs in most, but some also reproduce asexually. Embryos develop through a series of stages.

PHYLUM PORIFERA Sponges. No symmetry, tissues.

PHYLUM PLACOZOA Marine. Simplest known animal. Two cell layers, no mouth, no organs. *Trichoplax.*

PHYLUM CNIDARIA Radial symmetry, tissues, nematocysts.
Class Hydrozoa. Hydrozoans. *Hydra, Obelia, Physalia, Prya.*
Class Scyphozoa. Jellyfishes. *Aurelia.*
Class Anthozoa. Sea anemones, corals. *Telesto.*

PHYLUM PLATYHELMINTHES Flatworms. Bilateral, cephalized; simplest animals with organ systems. Saclike gut.

  Class Turbellaria. Triclads (planarians), polyclads. *Dugesia.*
  Class Trematoda. Flukes. *Clonorchis, Schistosoma.*
  Class Cestoda. Tapeworms. *Diphyllobothrium, Taenia.*

PHYLUM ROTIFERA Rotifers. *Asplancha, Philodina.*

PHYLUM MOLLUSCA Mollusks.

  Class Polyplacophora. Chitons. *Cryptochiton, Tonicella.*
  Class Gastropoda. Snails, sea slugs, land slugs. *Aplysia, Ariolimax, Cypraea, Haliotis, Helix, Liguus, Limax, Littorina.*
  Class Bivalvia. Clams, mussels, scallops, cockles, oysters, shipworms. *Ensis, Chlamys, Mytelus, Patinopectin.*
  Class Cephalopoda. Squids, octopuses, cuttlefish, nautiluses. *Dosidiscus, Loligo, Nautilus, Octopus, Sepia.*

PHYLUM ANNELIDA Segmented worms.

  Class Polychaeta. Mostly marine worms. *Eunice, Neanthes.*
  Class Oligochaeta. Mostly freshwater and terrestrial worms, many marine. *Lumbricus* (earthworms), *Tubifex.*
  Class Hirudinea. Leeches. *Hirudo, Placobdella.*

PHYLUM NEMATODA Roundworms. *Ascaris, Caenorhabditis elegans, Necator* (hookworms), *Trichinella.*

PHYLUM ARTHROPODA

  Subphylum Chelicerata. Chelicerates. Horseshoe crabs, spiders, scorpions, ticks, mites.
  Subphylum Crustacea. Shrimps, crayfishes, lobsters, crabs, barnacles, copepods, isopods (sowbugs).
  Subphylum Myriapoda. Centipedes, millipedes.
  Subphylum Hexapoda. Insects and sprintails.

PHYLUM ECHINODERMATA Echinoderms.

  Class Asteroidea. Sea stars. *Asterias.*
  Class Ophiuroidea. Brittle stars.
  Class Echinoidea. Sea urchins, heart urchins, sand dollars.
  Class Holothuroidea. Sea cucumbers.
  Class Crinoidea. Feather stars, sea lilies.
  Class Concentricycloidea. Sea daisies.

PHYLUM CHORDATA Chordates.

  Subphylum Urochordata. Tunicates, related forms.
  Subphylum Cephalochordata. Lancelets.

CRANIATES

  Class Myxini. Hagfishes.

VERTEBRATES (SUBGROUP OF CRANIATES)

  Class Cephalaspidomorphi. Lampreys.
  Class Chondrichthyes. Cartilaginous fishes (sharks, rays, skates, chimaeras).
  Class "Osteichthyes." Bony fishes. Not monophyletic (sturgeons, paddlefish, herrings, carps, cods, trout, seahorses, tunas, lungfishes, and coelocanths).

TETRAPODS (SUBGROUP OF VERTEBRATES)

  Class Amphibia. Amphibians. Require water to reproduce.
  Order Caudata. Salamanders and newts.
  Order Anura. Frogs, toads.
  Order Apoda. Apodans (caecilians).

AMNIOTES (SUBGROUP OF TETRAPODS)

  Class "Reptilia." Skin with scales, embryo protected and nutritionally supported by extraembryonic membranes.

  Subclass Anapsida. Turtles, tortoises.
  Subclass Lepidosaura. *Sphenodon*, lizards, snakes.
  Subclass Archosaura. Crocodiles, alligators.

Class Aves. Birds. In some classifications birds are grouped in the archosaurs.

  Order Struthioniformes. Ostriches.
  Order Sphenisciformes. Penguins.
  Order Procellariiformes. Albatrosses, petrels.
  Order Ciconiiformes. Herons, bitterns, storks, flamingoes.
  Order Anseriformes. Swans, geese, ducks.
  Order Falconiformes. Eagles, hawks, vultures, falcons.
  Order Galliformes. Ptarmigan, turkeys, domestic fowl.
  Order Columbiformes. Pigeons, doves.
  Order Strigiformes. Owls.
  Order Apodiformes. Swifts, hummingbirds.
  Order Passeriformes. Sparrows, jays, finches, crows, robins, starlings, wrens.
  Order Piciformes. Woodpeckers, toucans.
  Order Psittaciformes. Parrots, cockatoos, macaws.

Class Mammalia. Skin with hair; young nourished by milk-secreting mammary glands of adult.

  Subclass Prototheria. Egg-laying mammals (monotremes; duckbilled platypus, spiny anteaters).
  Subclass Metatheria. Pouched mammals or marsupials (opossums, kangaroos, wombats, Tasmanian devils).
  Subclass Eutheria. Placental mammals.
  Order Edentata. Anteaters, tree sloths, armadillos.
  Order Insectivora. Tree shrews, moles, hedgehogs.
  Order Chiroptera. Bats.
  Order Scandentia. Insectivorous tree shrews.
  Order Primates.
  Suborder Strepsirhini (prosimians). Lemurs, lorises.
  Suborder Haplorhini (tarsioids and anthropoids).
    Infraorder Tarsiiformes. Tarsiers.
    Infraorder Platyrrhini (New World monkeys).
      Family Cebidae. Spider monkeys, howler monkeys, capuchin.
    Infraorder Catarrhini (Old World monkeys and hominoids).
      Superfamily Cercopithecoidea. Baboons, macaques, langurs.
      Superfamily Hominoidea. Apes and humans.
        Family Hylobatidae. Gibbon.
        Family "Pongidae." Chimpanzees, gorillas, orangutans.
        Family Hominidae. Existing and extinct human species (*Homo*) and humanlike species, including the australopiths.
  Order Lagomorpha. Rabbits, hares, pikas.
  Order Rodentia. Most gnawing animals (squirrels, rats, mice, guinea pigs, porcupines, beavers, etc.).
  Order Carnivora. Carnivores (wolves, cats, bears, etc.).
  Order Pinnipedia. Seals, walruses, sea lions.
  Order Proboscidea. Elephants, mammoths (extinct).
  Order Sirenia. Sea cows (manatees, dugongs).
  Order Perissodactyla. Odd-toed ungulates (horses, tapirs, rhinos).
  Order Tubulidentata. African aardvarks.
  Order Artiodactyla. Even-toed ungulates (camels, deer, bison, sheep, goats, antelopes, giraffes, etc.).
  Order Cetacea. Whales, porpoises.

Appendix II. Answers to Self-Quizzes

Italicized numbers refer to relevant section numbers

CHAPTER 1

1. cell — *1.1*
2. energy — *1.2*
3. homeostasis — *1.2*
4. domains — *1.3*
5. d — *1.2, 1.4*
6. d — *1.2*
7. mutation — *1.4*
8. adaptive — *1.4*
9. a — *1.6*
10. c — *1.1*
    e — *1.4*
    d — *1.5*
    b — *1.5*
    b — *1.5*

CHAPTER 2

1. False — *2.1*
2. b — *2.1*
3. d — *2.2*
4. c — *2.4*
5. a — *2.4*
6. e — *2.5*
7. f — *2.6*
8. acid, base — *2.6*
9. c — *2.6*
10. e — *Introduction*
    d — *2.6*
    b — *2.4*
    c — *2.5*
    a — *2.1*

CHAPTER 3

1. complex carbo-
   hydrates:
   simple sugars — *3.3*
   lipids; fatty acids
   or sterol rings — *3.4*
   proteins; amino
   acids — *3.5*
   nucleic acids;
   nucleotides — *3.7*
2. d — *3.1*
3. c — *3.2*
4. f — *3.3*
5. b — *3.4*
6. b — *3.4*
7. e — *3.4*
8. d — *3.5, 3.7*
9. d — *3.6*
10. d — *3.7*
11. b — *3.7*
12. c — *3.5*
    e — *3.7*
    b — *3.4*
    d — *3.7*
    a — *3.3*

CHAPTER 4

1. c — *4.1*
2. See Figure 4.15
3. d — *4.4*
4. d — *4.9*
5. False — *4.9*
6. c — *4.3*
7. e — *4.7*
   d — *4.8*
   a — *4.1, 4.4*
   a — *4.6*
   c — *4.6*

CHAPTER 5

1. c — *5.1*
2. c — *5.1*
3. a — *5.1*
4. d — *5.2*
5. d — *5.3*
6. d — *5.3*
7. b — *5.4*
8. a — *5.5*
9. c — *5.6*
10. d — *5.6*
    g — *5.4*
    a — *5.2*
    e — *5.4*
    c — *5.1*
    b — *5.3*
    f — *5.2*

CHAPTER 6

1. c — *6.1*
2. d — *6.1*
3. b — *6.1*
4. d — *6.3*
5. d — *6.4*
6. b — *6.5*
7. c — *6.2*
   g — *6.2*
   a — *6.2*
   d — *6.2*
   e — *6.2*
   b — *6.3*
   f — *6.2*

CHAPTER 7

1. carbon dioxide,
   sunlight — *Introduction*
2. b — *7.1*
3. a — *7.4*
4. b — *7.4*
5. c — *7.4*
6. d — *7.4*
7. c — *7.6*
8. b — *7.6*
9. d — *7.6*
10. c — *7.5*
    a — *7.6*
    b — *7.6*

CHAPTER 8

1. d — *8.1*
2. c — *8.2*
3. b — *8.4*
4. c — *8.4*
5. See Figure 8.3
6. c — *8.5*
7. b — *8.5*
8. d — *8.6*
9. b — *8.2*
   c — *8.5*
   a — *8.3*
   d — *8.4*

CHAPTER 9

1. d — *9.1*
2. b — *9.1*
3. c — *9.1*
4. d — *9.2*
5. a — *9.2*
6. c — *9.2*
7. a — *9.3*
8. b — *9.3*
9. d — *9.3*
   b — *9.3*
   c — *9.3*
   a — *9.3*

CHAPTER 10

1. c — *10.1*
2. b — *10.2*
3. a — *10.2*
4. d — *10.1*
5. d — *10.2*
6. b — *10.2*
7. d — *10.3*
8. Sister chromatids
   remain attached. — *10.3*
9. d — *10.3*
10. e — *10.4*
11. d — *10.2*
    a — *10.1*
    c — *10.3*
    b — *10.3*

CHAPTER 11

1. a — *11.1*
2. b — *11.1*
3. a — *11.1*
4. b — *11.1*
5. c — *11.2*
6. a — *11.2*
7. d — *11.3*
8. c — *11.5*
9. a — *11.5*
10. b — *11.3*
    d — *11.2*
    a — *11.1*
    c — *11.1*

CHAPTER 12

1. d — *12.2*
2. c — *12.5*
3. b — *12.3*
4. b — *12.3*
5. b — *12.3*
6. False — *12.7*
7. d — *12.7*
8. e — *12.8*
9. d — *12.9*
10. False — *12.9*
11. c — *12.9*
12. a — *12.10*
13. c — *12.9*
    e — *12.8*
    d — *12.9*
    b — *12.8*
    a — *12.2*
    f — *12.9*

CHAPTER 13

1. c — *13.2*
2. d — *13.2*
3. c — *13.2*
4. a — *13.3*
5. d — *13.3*
6. b — *13.2*
7. b — *13.4*
8. c — *13.1*
   e — *13.4*
   a — *13.2*
   b — *13.3*
   d — *13.3*
   f — *13.3*

CHAPTER 14

1. c — *14.1*
2. b — *14.1*
3. c — *14.1*
4. c — *14.1*
5. d — *14.2*
6. a — *14.3*
7. f — *14.5*
8. e — *14.5*
   c — *14.4*
   a — *14.1*
   f — *14.2*
   d — *14.3*
   g — *14.1*
   b — *14.2*

CHAPTER 15

1. d — *15.1*
2. d — *15.1*
3. d — *15.1, 15.4*
4. d — *15.1*
5. h — *15.1*
6. d — *15.1*
7. d — *15.1*
8. d — *15.2*
9. c — *15.2*
10. b — *15.3*
11. b — *15.3*
12. b — *15.4*
13. e — *15.2*
    a — *15.2*
    b — *15.4*
    d — *15.2*
    c — *15.1*
    f — *15.1*

CHAPTER 16

1. c — *16.1*
2. plasmid — *16.1*
3. b — *16.1*
4. a — *16.2*
5. d — *16.3*
6. b — *16.3*
7. b — *16.5*
8. b — *16.5*
9. d — *16.4*
   c — *16.7*
   b — *Introduction*
   e — *16.2*
   a — *16.10*

CHAPTER 17

1. d — *17.1*
2. d — *17.4*
3. a — *17.5*
4. Gondwana — *17.6*
5. b — *17.7*
6. d — *17.7*
7. d — *17.8*
8. c — *17.8*
   g — *17.4*
   a — *17.4*
   f — *17.8*
   e — *17.5*
   c — *17.7*
   b — *17.2*
   d — *17.7*

CHAPTER 18

1. populations — *18.1*
2. b — *Issues, Impacts*
3. a — *18.1*
4. c — *18.1, 18.3*
5. b — *18.4*
6. c — *18.5*
7. c — *18.6*
8. e — *18.6*
9. a — *18.7*
10. c — *18.8*
    d — *18.1, 18.3*
    a — *18.1*
    b — *18.7*

CHAPTER 19

1. d — *19.1*
2. d — *19.1*
3. a — *19.2*
4. c — *19.4*
5. c — *19.4*
6. c — *19.5*
7. d — *19.5*
8. c — *19.6*
9. d — *19.5*
10. e — *19.5*
    d — *19.4*
    a — *19.5*
    f — *19.5*
    b — *19.5, 19.6*
    c — *19.4*

CHAPTER 20

1. c — *20.1*
2. c — *20.2*
3. c — *20.3*
4. b — *20.4*
5. d — *20.4*
6. f — *20.1*
   c — *20.2*
   d — *20.3*
   a — *20.3*
   b — *20.5*
   e — *20.5*

CHAPTER 21

1. d — *21.1*
2. c — *21.2*
3. c — *21.1*
4. d — *21.4*
5. b — *21.4*
6. c — *21.4*
7. d — *21.2*
8. b — *21.6*
9. false — *21.6*
10. d — *21.7*
11. d — *21.5*
    e — *21.4*
    b — *21.6*
    f — *21.1*
    g — *21.5*
    a — *21.8*
    c — *21.1*

CHAPTER 22

1. f — *22.3*
2. a — *22.4*
3. d — *22.5*
4. a — *22.8*
5. b — *22.8*
6. d — *22.12*
7. e — *22.3*
   a — *22.3*
   b — *22.9*
   c — *22.6*
   f — *22.4*
   d — *22.11*

CHAPTER 23

1. c — *23.1*
2. a — *23.2*
3. b — *23.3*
4. c — *23.4*
5. a — *23.5*
6. e — *23.3, 23.4*
7. b — *23.6*
8. c — *23.2*
9. c — *23.7*
   e — *23.2*
   g — *23.4*
   h — *23.8*
   f — *23.3*
   a — *23.2*
   b — *23.2*
   d — *23.8*

CHAPTER 24

1. b — *24.6*
2. a — *24.1*
3. a — *24.1*
4. c — *24.1*
5. c — *24.1, 24.3*
6. e — *24.2*
   c — *24.6*
   d — *24.1*
   g — *24.1, 24.3*
   b — *24.4*
   f — *24.4*
   a — *24.1*

CHAPTER 25

1. a — *25.1*
2. a — *25.2*
3. a — *25.4*
4. a — *25.5*
5. b — *25.15*
6. c — *25.5, 25.6*
7. b — *25.17*
8. i — *25.1*
   c — *25.3*
   h — *25.4*
   b — *25.5*
   a — *25.10*
   f — *25.6*
   d — *25.11*
   e — *25.8*
   g — *25.17*

CHAPTER 26
1. b — 26.1
2. a — 26.2
3. d — 26.3
4. b — 26.6
5. f — 26.6
6. a — 26.8
7. c — 26.9
8. f — 26.10, 26.12
9. c — 26.15
10. g — 26.3
    a — 26.4
    e — 26.8
    b — 26.9
    c — 26.10
    f — 26.10
    d — 26.12

CHAPTER 27
1. b — 27.1
2. f — 27.4
3. d — 27.4
4. a — 27.4
5. d — 27.6
6. d — 27.6
7. d — 27.7

CHAPTER 28
1. a — 28.1
2. c — 28.1
3. d — 28.2
4. d — 28.5
5. b — 28.4
   c — 28.3
   a — 28.5
   d — 28.3

CHAPTER 29
1. Eudicot above, with blue vascular bundles separating ground tissue into outer cortex and inner pith. Dicot, below, with vascular bundles dispersed in ground tissue. — 29.1, 29.3
2. a — 29.1
3. d — 29.1, 29.6
4. eudicot, monocot — 29.1
5. c — 29.2
6. c — 29.4
7. b — 29.2
8. b — 29.2
9. d — 29.7
10. b — 29.1
    d — 29.1
    e — 29.2
    c — 29.2
    f — 29.5
    a — 29.6

CHAPTER 30
1. a — 30.1
2. c — 30.2
3. b — 30.2
4. c — 30.3
5. d — 30.3
6. a — 30.4
7. b — 30.4
8. c — 30.4
   g — 30.1
   e — 30.5
   b — 30.2
   d — 30.3
   a — 30.3
   f — 30.5

CHAPTER 31
1. a — 31.1
2. d — 31.1, 31.3
3. b — 31.1
4. c — 31.4
5. b — 31.3
6. b — 31.3
7. a — 31.4
8. b — 31.4
9. d — 31.4
10. d — 31.4
11. c — 31.7
12. c — 31.1
    f — 31.1
    a — 31.3
    e — 31.1
    d — 31.1
    b — 31.3

CHAPTER 32
1. c — 32.1
2. c — 32.2
3. e — 32.2
4. d — 32.1
5. d — 32.4
6. a — 32.5, 32.6
7. c — 32.6
8. a — 32.7
9. d — 32.6
   e — 32.3
   a — 32.1
   b — 32.4
   c — 32.2

CHAPTER 33
1. (a) epithelium, sheetlike with one free surface 33.1; (b) skeletal muscle, striated contractile cells 33.3; (c) loose connective tissue, scattered cells and fibers in a extracelluar matrix of their own secretions 33.2; (d) adipose tissue, cells swollen with stored fat, nuclei pushed to the side 33.2.
2. a — 33.1
3. c — 33.1
4. a — 33.1
5. b — 33.1, 33.2
6. b — 33.2
7. c — 33.2
8. c — 33.3
9. d — 33.3
10. d — 33.4
11. b — 33.1
    g — 33.1
    a — 33.2
    c — 33.5
    d — 33.3
    f — 33.2
    e — 33.1

CHAPTER 34
1. a — 34.1
2. d — 34.2
3. d — 34.3
4. a — 34.4
5. c — 34.6
6. c — 34.8
7. b — 34.8
8. a — 34.5
9. a — 34.9
10. f — 34.7
    d — 34.4, 34.5
    g — 34.11
    b — 34.9
    h — 34.10
    a — 34.9
    e — 34.6
    i — 34.8
    c — 34.9

CHAPTER 35
1. a — 35.1
2. c — 35.1
3. c — 35.2
4. e — 35.3
5. a — 35.2
6. b — 35.4
7. b — 35.5
8. See Figure 35.17
9. d — 35.8
   g — 35.5
   f — 35.6, 35.7
   a — 35.4, 35.5
   c — 35.8
   e — 35.3
   b — 35.4
   h — 35.2

CHAPTER 36
1. f — 36.1
2. b — 36.3
3. a — 36.3
4. e — 36.2
5. b — 36.6
6. b — 36.4
7. b — 36.6
8. d — 36.8
   f — 36.4
   c — 36.4
   e — 36.6
   a — 36.10
   b — 36.1

CHAPTER 37
1. d — 37.4
2. b — 37.5
3. b — 37.6
4. b — 37.6
5. d — 37.6
6. d — 37.8
7. e — 37.4
   f — 37.9
   g — 37.9
   h — 37.4
   a — 37.6
   c — 37.4
   b — 37.3
   i — 37.6
   d — 37.9

CHAPTER 38
1. c — 38.1
2. b — 38.1
3. d — 38.2
4. b — 38.4
5. d — 38.2
6. b — 38.6
7. c — 38.7
8. a — 38.7
9. c — 38.8
10. d — 38.10
11. f — 38.8
    a — 38.10
    e — 38.2
    g — 38.7
    b — 38.6
    c — 38.8
    d — 38.5
12. See Figure 38.13
13. artery, high speed transport away from the heart; vein; transport to the heart and blood reservoir; arteriole, adjusts blood distribution; capillary, diffusion zone

CHAPTER 39
1. f — 39.2
2. e — 39.3
3. d — 39.4
4. d — 39.5
5. e — 39.4
6. e — 39.5
7. b — 39.7
8. c — 39.3
   b — 39.5, 39.6
   a — 39.1
   e — 39.6
   d — 39.9

CHAPTER 40
1. a — 40.1
2. d — 40.1, 40.5
3. c — 40.2
4. a — 40.3
5. c — 40.4, 40.5
6. d — 40.6
7. a — 40.6
8. a — 40.5
9. d — 40.4
   h — 40.4
   f — 40.4
   e — 40.1
   g — 40.4
   c — 40.4
   b — 40.4
   a — 40.6

CHAPTER 41
1. d — 41.1
2. b — 41.4
3. c — 41.5
4. b — 41.4, 41.5
5. a — 41.5
6. c — 41.6
7. b — 41.9
8. f — 41.4
   b — 41.6
   d — 41.4
   e — 41.5
   c — 41.2, 41.4

CHAPTER 42
1. c — 42.1
2. a — 42.2
3. b — 42.2
4. See Figures 42.5 and 42.6
5. d — 42.3
6. b — 42.3
7. a — 42.4
8. a — 42.4
9. c — 42.2
   a — 42.2
   b — 42.2
   d — 42.4
   d — 42.4
10. d — 42.8
11. d — 42.8
12. False — 42.4
13. b — 42.7
    a — 42.7
    d — 42.7
    c — 42.7
    e — 42.7

CHAPTER 43
1. d — 43.1
2. c — 43.2
3. c — 43.2
4. b — 43.3
5. c — 43.4
6. d — 43.4
7. c — 43.5
8. d — 43.5
9. b — 43.5
10. a — 43.3
11. c — 43.2
    d — 43.2
    a — 43.2, 43.3
    b — 43.2, 43.4
    f — 43.4
    e — 43.4

CHAPTER 44
1. See Figure 44.4
2. Figure 44.11
3. d — 44.2
4. c — 44.4
5. c — 44.4
6. e — 44.8
7. c — 44.9
8. a — 44.9, 44.12
9. c — 44.6
10. c — 44.9
11. c — 44.11
12. f — 44.10
13. e — 44.12
14. c — 44.2
    h — 44.3
    a — 44.11
    g — 44.14
    e — 44.4
      — 44.6
    b — 44.1
    f — 44.3

CHAPTER 45
1. f — 45.3
2. a — 45.3
3. a — 45.3
4. d — 45.4
5. d — 45.5
6. c — 45.7
7. c — 45.4
   d — 45.3
   a — 45.3
   e — 45.4
   b — 45.4

CHAPTER 46
1. d — 46.1
2. d — 46.1
3. d — 46.3
4. b — 46.4
5. d — 46.6
6. b — 46.8
7. c — 46.9
   d — 46.11
   a — 46.8
   e — 46.8
   b — 46.9
   g — 46.9
   f — 46.3

CHAPTER 47
1. a — 47.1
2. d — 47.1
3. d — 47.1
4. d — 47.1
5. d — 47.4
6. d — 47.3
7. a — 47.6, 47.8
8. b — 47.9
9. d — 47.12
10. b — 47.11, 47.12
11. a — 47.11
12. d — 47.1
    a — 47.1
    c — 47.1
    b — 47.1

CHAPTER 48
1. c — 48.1
2. c — 48.2
3. d — 48.1, 48.3
4. a — 48.3
5. d — 48.2
6. d — 48.4
7. d — 48.4
8. c — 48.6
9. d — 48.12, 48.15
10. d — 48.10
    h — 48.4
    e — 48.6
    c — 48.6
    b — 48.14
    g — 48.9
    a — 48.7
    f — 48.15

CHAPTER 49
1. d — 49.1
2. c — 49.3
3. b — 49.1
4. d — 49.6
5. b — 49.6
6. d — 49.7
7. c — 49.7
8. c — 49.1
   d — 49.3, 49.7
   b — 49.1
   a — 49.2
   e — 49.4

Appendix III. Answers to Genetics Problems

CHAPTER 11

1. a. Both parents are heterozygotes (*Aa*). Their children may be albino (*aa*) or unaffected (*AA* or *Aa*).

b. All are homozygous recessive (*aa*).

c. Homozygous recessive (*aa*) father, and heterozygous (*Aa*) mother. The albino child is *aa*, the unaffected children *Aa*.

2. Possible outcomes of an experimental cross between F_1 rose plants heterozygous for height (*Aa*):

	(A)	(a)
(A)	AA climber	Aa climber
(a)	Aa climber	aa shrubby

3:1 possible ratio of genotypes and phenotypes in F_2 generation

Possible outcomes of a testcross between an F_1 rose plant heterozygous for height and a shrubby rose plant:

Gametes F_1 hybrid:

Gametes shrubby plant:

	(A)	(a)
(a)	Aa climber	aa shrubby
(a)	Aa climber	aa shrubby

1:1 possible ratio of genotypes and phenotypes in F_2 generation

3. a. *AB*

b. *AB, aB*

c. *Ab, ab*

d. *AB, Ab, aB, ab*

4. a. All offspring will be *AaBB*.

b. 1/4 *AABB*   (25% each genotype)
1/4 *AABb*
1/4 *AaBB*
1/4 *AaBb*

c. 1/4 *AaBb*   (25% each genotype)
1/4 *Aabb*
1/4 *aaBb*
1/4 *aabb*

d. 1/16 *AABB* (6.25% of genotype)
1/8 *AaBB*   (12.5%)
1/16 *aaBB*   (6.25%)
1/8 *AABb*   (12.5%)
1/4 *AaBb*   (25%)
1/8 *aaBb*   (12.5%)
1/16 *AAbb*   (6.25%)
1/8 *Aabb*   (12.5%)
1/16 *aabb*   (6.25%)

5. a. *ABC*

b. *ABC, aBC*

c. *ABC, aBC, ABc, aBc*

d. *ABC*
aBC
AbC
abC
ABc
aBc
Abc
abc

6. A mating of two M^L cats yields 1/4 *MM*, 1/2 M^LM, and 1/4 M^LM^L. Because M^LM^L is lethal, the probability that any one kitten among the survivors will be heterozygous is 2/3.

7. Yellow is recessive. Because F_1 plants have a green phenotype and must be heterozygous, green must be dominant over the recessive yellow.

8. a. *RR* and *rr*

b. all *Rr*

9. Because all F_1 plants of this dihybrid cross had to be heterozygous for both genes, then 1/4 (25%) of the F_2 plants will be heterozygous for both genes.

10. A mating between a mouse from a true-breeding, white-furred strain and a mouse from a true-breeding, brown-furred strain would provide you with the most direct evidence. Because true-breeding strains of organisms typically are homozygous for a trait being studied, all F_1 offspring from this mating should be heterozygous. Record the phenotype of each F_1 mouse, then let them mate with one another. Assuming only one gene locus is involved, these are possible outcomes for the F_1 offspring:

a. All F_1 mice are brown, and their F_2 offspring segregate: 3 brown : 1 white. *Conclusion:* Brown is dominant to white.

b. All F_1 mice are white, and their F_2 offspring segregate: 3 white : 1 brown. *Conclusion:* White is dominant to brown.

c. All F_1 mice are tan, and the F_2 offspring segregate: 1 brown : 2 tan : 1 white. *Conclusion:* The alleles at this locus show incomplete dominance.

11. The data reveal that these genes do not assort independently because the observed ratio is very far from the 9:3:3:1 ratio expected with independent assortment. Instead, the results can be explained if the genes are located close to each other on the same chromosome, which is called linkage.

12. Fred could use a testcross to find out if his pet's genotype is *WW* or *Ww*. He can let his black guinea pig mate with a white guinea pig having the genotype *ww*.

If any F_1 offspring are white, then the genotype of his pet is *Ww*. If the two guinea pig parents are allowed to mate repeatedly and all the offspring of the matings are black, then there is a high probability that his pet guinea pig is *WW*.

(For instance, if ten offspring are all black, then the probability that the male is *WW* is about 99.9 percent. The greater the number of offspring, the more confident Fred can be of his conclusion.)

13. a. $\underline{1/2}$ red $\underline{1/2}$ pink $\underline{}$ white
    b. $\underline{}$ red $\underline{All}$ pink $\underline{}$ white
    c. $\underline{1/4}$ red $\underline{1/2}$ pink $\underline{1/4}$ white
    d. $\underline{}$ red $\underline{1/2}$ pink $\underline{1/2}$ white

14. 9/16 walnut
    3/16 rose
    3/16 pea
    1/16 single

15. Because both parents are heterozygotes (Hb^AHb^S), the following are the probabilities for each child:
    a. 1/4 Hb^SHb^S
    b. 1/4 Hb^AHb^A
    c. 1/2 Hb^AHb^S

16. 2/3

17. The smooth rind/furrowed rind ratio is 230:230, which is exactly 1:1. The nonexplosive rind/explosive rind ratio is 227:233, which is close to a 1:1 ratio.

The overall ratio is close to a 1:1 ratio, which indicates that the genes are assorting independently.

18. See the percentages in the graph below. The varied colors in wheat kernels are due to the combined effects of incomplete dominance of alleles of two genes that influence the same phenotype.

CHAPTER 12

1. a. Human males (XY) inherit their X chromosome from their mother.

b. A male can produce two kinds of gametes. Half carry an X chromosome and half carry a Y chromosome. All the gametes that carry the X chromosome carry the same X-linked allele.

c. A female homozygous for an X-linked allele produces only one kind of gamete.

d. Fifty percent of the gametes of a female who is heterozygous for an X-linked allele carry one of the two alleles at that locus; the other fifty percent carry its partner allele for that locus.

2. Because Marfan syndrome is a case of autosomal dominant inheritance and because one parent bears the allele, the probability that any child of theirs will inherit the mutant allele is 50 percent.

3. a. Nondisjunction might occur during anaphase I or anaphase II of meiosis.

b. As a result of translocation, chromosome 21 may get attached to the end of chromosome 14. The new individual's chromosome number would still be 46, but its somatic cells would have the translocated chromosome 21 in addition to two normal chromosomes 21.

4. A daughter could develop this muscular dystrophy only if she inherited two X-linked recessive alleles— one from each parent. Males who carry the allele are unlikely to father children because they develop the disorder and die early in life.

5. In the mother, a crossover between the two genes at meiosis generates an X chromosome that carries neither mutant allele.

6. The phenotype appeared in every generation shown in the diagram, so this must be a pattern of autosomal dominant inheritance.

7. There is no scientific answer to this question, which simply invites you to reflect on the difference between a scientific and a subjective interpretation of this individual's condition.

Genotype	Phenotype	Number Displaying the Trait	Percent of Population
$A^1A^1B^1B^1$	Dark red	181	9.05
$A^1A^1B^1B^2$ or $A^1A^2B^1B^1$	Red	360	18.00
$A^1A^2B^1B^2$ or $A^1A^1B^2B^2$ or $A^2A^2B^1B^1$	Salmon	922	46.10
$A^1A^2B^2B^2$ or $A^2A^2B^1B^2$	Pink	358	17.90
$A^2A^2B^2B^2$	White	179	8.95
	Totals	2,000	100

Appendix IV. Periodic Table of the Elements

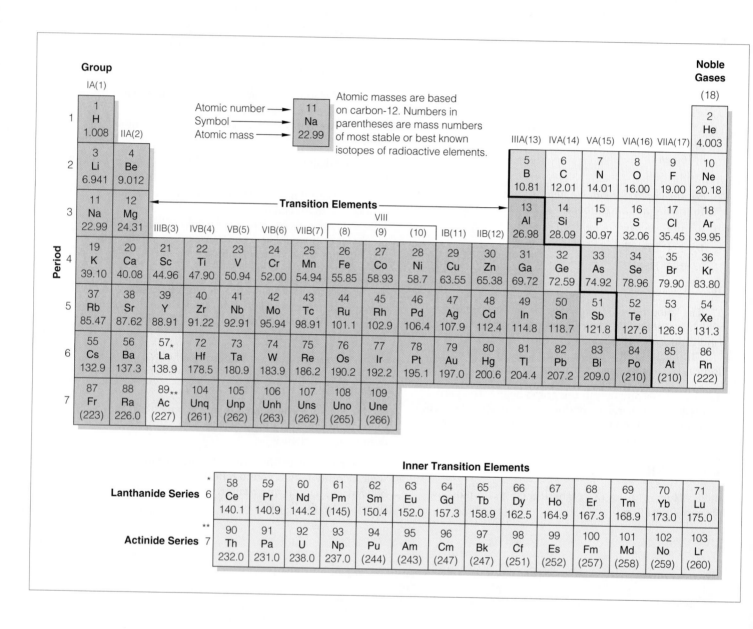

Appendix V. The Amino Acids

Neutral, nonpolar side group

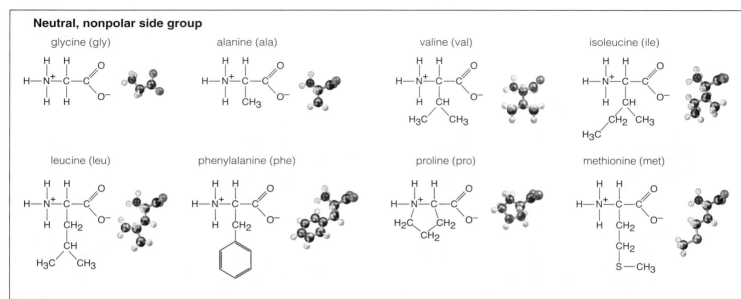

glycine (gly)   alanine (ala)   valine (val)   isoleucine (ile)

leucine (leu)   phenylalanine (phe)   proline (pro)   methionine (met)

Neutral, polar side group

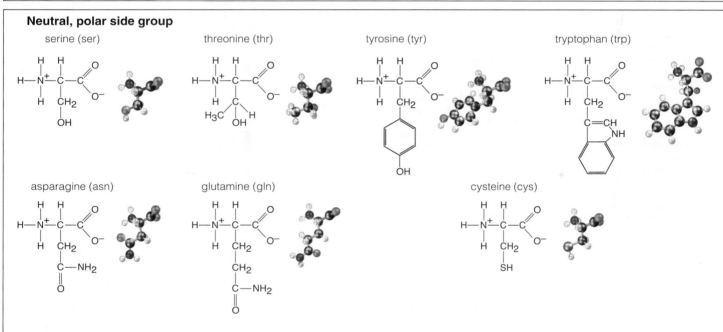

serine (ser)   threonine (thr)   tyrosine (tyr)   tryptophan (trp)

asparagine (asn)   glutamine (gln)   cysteine (cys)

Acidic side group

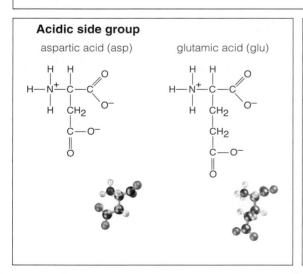

aspartic acid (asp)   glutamic acid (glu)

Basic side group

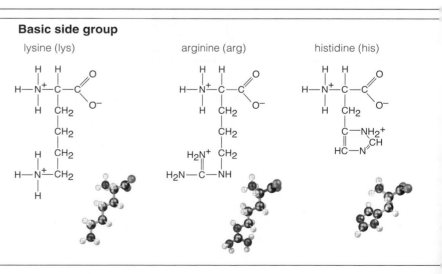

lysine (lys)   arginine (arg)   histidine (his)

Metric-English Conversions

Length

English		Metric
inch	=	2.54 centimeters
foot	=	0.30 meter
yard	=	0.91 meter
mile (5,280 feet)	=	1.61 kilometer

To convert	multiply by	to obtain
inches	2.54	centimeters
feet	30.00	centimeters
centimeters	0.39	inches
millimeters	0.039	inches

Weight

English		Metric
grain	=	64.80 milligrams
ounce	=	28.35 grams
pound	=	453.60 grams
ton (short) (2,000 pounds)	=	0.91 metric ton

To convert	multiply by	to obtain
ounces	28.3	grams
pounds	453.6	grams
pounds	0.45	kilograms
grams	0.035	ounces
kilograms	2.2	pounds

Volume

English		Metric
cubic inch	=	16.39 cubic centimeters
cubic foot	=	0.03 cubic meter
cubic yard	=	0.765 cubic meters
ounce	=	0.03 liter
pint	=	0.47 liter
quart	=	0.95 liter
gallon	=	3.79 liters

To convert	multiply by	to obtain
fluid ounces	30.00	milliliters
quart	0.95	liters
milliliters	0.03	fluid ounces
liters	1.06	quarts

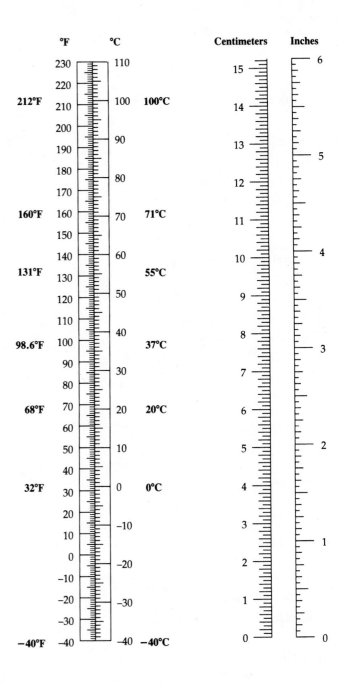

Appendix VII. Closer Look at Some Major Metabolic Pathways

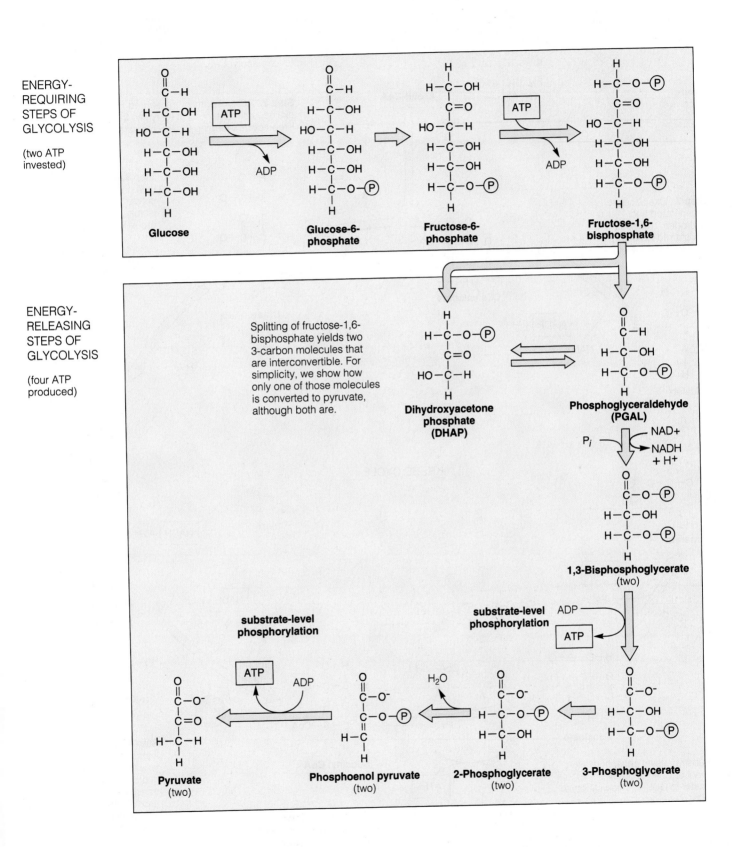

ENERGY-REQUIRING STEPS OF GLYCOLYSIS

(two ATP invested)

Glucose → Glucose-6-phosphate → Fructose-6-phosphate → Fructose-1,6-bisphosphate

ENERGY-RELEASING STEPS OF GLYCOLYSIS

(four ATP produced)

Splitting of fructose-1,6-bisphosphate yields two 3-carbon molecules that are interconvertible. For simplicity, we show how only one of those molecules is converted to pyruvate, although both are.

Dihydroxyacetone phosphate (DHAP)

Phosphoglyceraldehyde (PGAL)

P_i → NAD+ → NADH + H+

1,3-Bisphosphoglycerate (two)

substrate-level phosphorylation

ADP → ATP

3-Phosphoglycerate (two)

2-Phosphoglycerate (two)

H$_2$O

Phosphoenol pyruvate (two)

substrate-level phosphorylation

ATP ← ADP

Pyruvate (two)

Figure A Glycolysis, ending with two 3-carbon pyruvate molecules for each 6-carbon glucose molecule entering the reactions. The *net* energy yield is two ATP molecules (two invested, four produced).

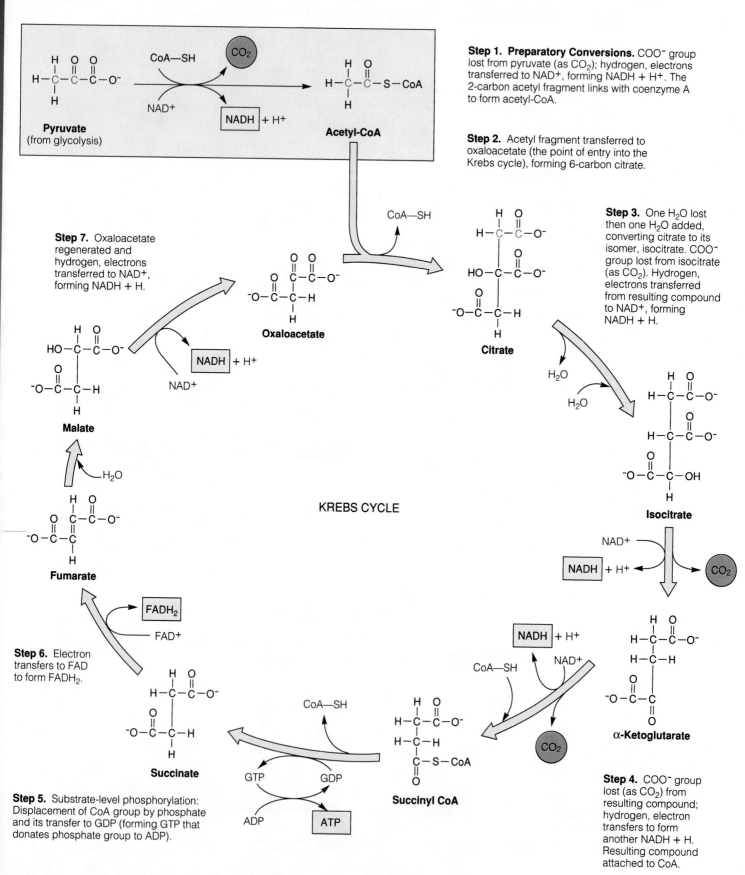

Step 1. Preparatory Conversions. COO⁻ group lost from pyruvate (as CO_2); hydrogen, electrons transferred to NAD⁺, forming NADH + H⁺. The 2-carbon acetyl fragment links with coenzyme A to form acetyl-CoA.

Step 2. Acetyl fragment transferred to oxaloacetate (the point of entry into the Krebs cycle), forming 6-carbon citrate.

Step 3. One H_2O lost then one H_2O added, converting citrate to its isomer, isocitrate. COO⁻ group lost from isocitrate (as CO_2). Hydrogen, electrons transferred from resulting compound to NAD⁺, forming NADH + H.

Step 7. Oxaloacetate regenerated and hydrogen, electrons transferred to NAD⁺, forming NADH + H.

Step 6. Electron transfers to FAD to form $FADH_2$.

Step 5. Substrate-level phosphorylation: Displacement of CoA group by phosphate and its transfer to GDP (forming GTP that donates phosphate group to ADP).

Step 4. COO⁻ group lost (as CO_2) from resulting compound; hydrogen, electron transfers to form another NADH + H. Resulting compound attached to CoA.

KREBS CYCLE

Figure B Krebs cycle, also known as the citric acid cycle. *Red* identifies carbon atoms entering the cyclic pathway (by way of acetyl-CoA) and leaving (by way of carbon dioxide). These cyclic reactions run twice for each glucose molecule that has been degraded to two pyruvate molecules.

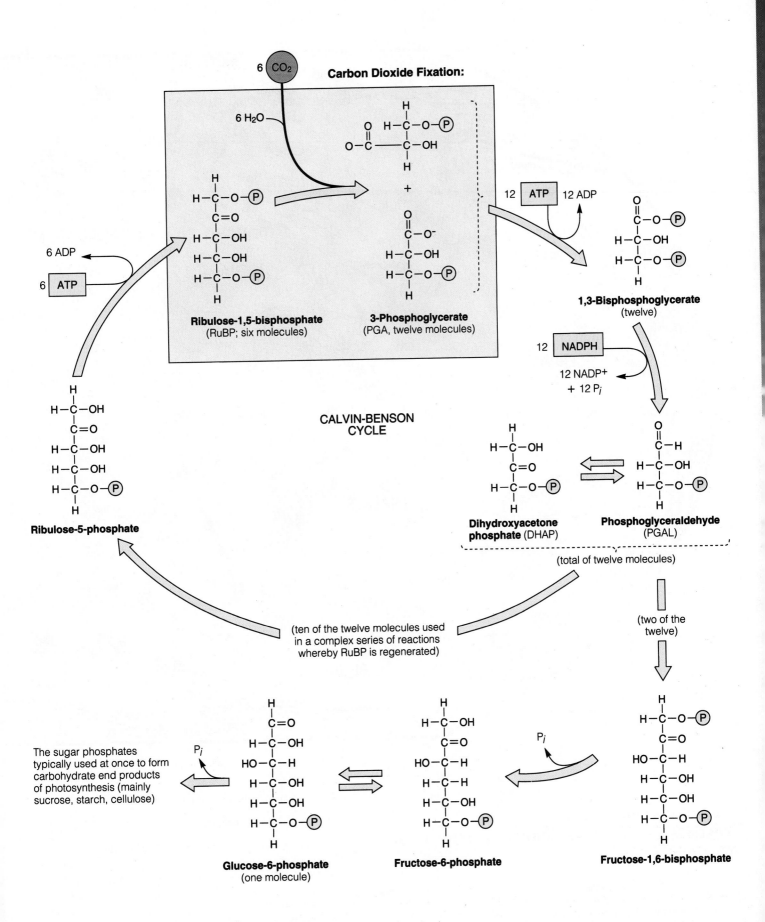

Figure C Calvin–Benson cycle of the light-independent reactions of photosynthesis.

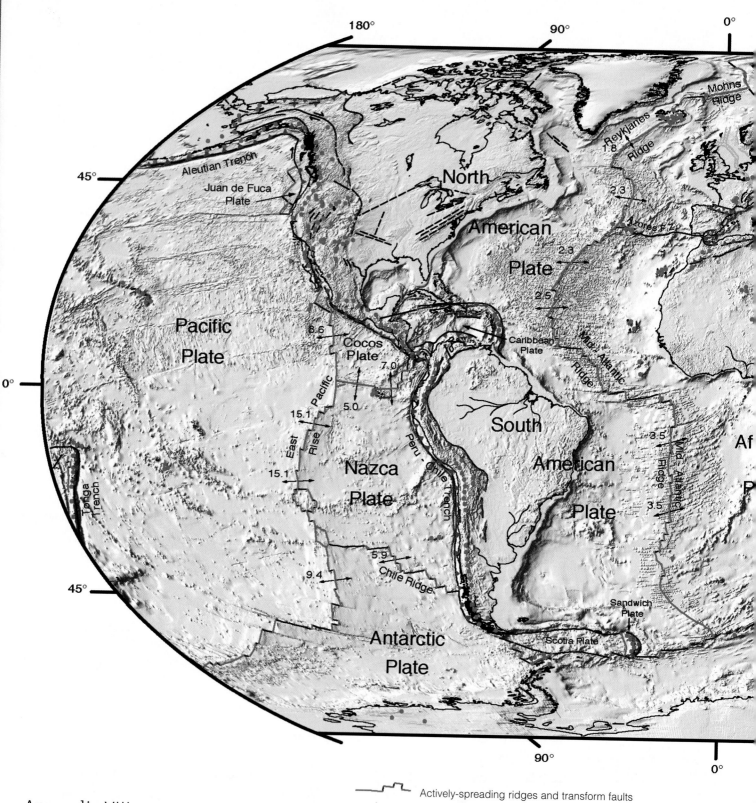

180° **90°** **0°**

Mohns Ridge

Reykjanes 7.8 Ridge

45°

Aleutian Trench

Juan de Fuca Plate

North

2.3

Azores F.Z.

American

2.3

Plate

2.5

0°

Pacific

Plate

8.6

Cocos Plate 7.0

Caribbean Plate

Mid-Atlantic Ridge

5.0

East Pacific Rise

15.1

3.5

Nazca

Plate

Peru - Chile Trench

South

Mid-Atlantic Ridge

15.1

American

3.5

Tonga Trench

Plate

Af

P

5.9

9.4

Chile Ridge

45°

Sandwich Plate

Antarctic

Scotia Plate

Plate

90° **0°**

Appendix VIII.
Restless Earth—Life's Changing
Geologic Stage

This NASA map summarizes the tectonic and volcanic
activity of Earth during the past 1 million years. The
reconstructions at far right indicate positions of Earth's
major land masses through time.

Actively-spreading ridges and transform faults

Total spreading rate, cm/year

1.4

Major active fault or fault zone; dashed where nature,
location, or activity uncertain

Normal fault or rift; hachures on downthrown side

Reverse fault (overthrust, subduction zones); generalized;
barbs on upthrown side

Volcanic centers active within the last one million years;
generalized. Minor basaltic centers and seamounts omitted.

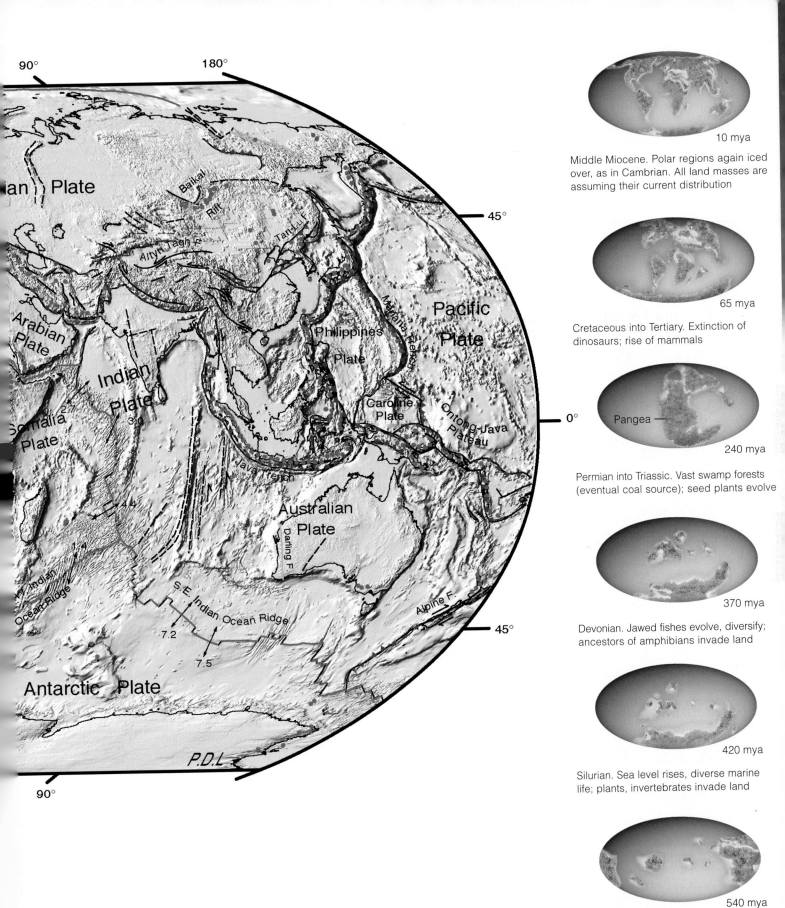

90°　　　　180°

45°

an Plate

Baikal
Rift

Altyn Tagh F.

Tan-Lu F.

Arabian
Plate

Indian
Plate

Mariana Trench

Pacific
Plate

45°

Philippines
Plate

Somalia
Plate

Caroline
Plate

Ontong-Java
Plateau

0°

Java Trench

Australian
Plate

Darling F.

Alpine F.

S.E. Indian Ocean Ridge

Mid Indian
Ocean Ridge

7.2

7.5

45°

Antarctic　Plate

P.D.L

90°

10 mya

Middle Miocene. Polar regions again iced over, as in Cambrian. All land masses are assuming their current distribution

65 mya

Cretaceous into Tertiary. Extinction of dinosaurs; rise of mammals

Pangea —

240 mya

Permian into Triassic. Vast swamp forests (eventual coal source); seed plants evolve

370 mya

Devonian. Jawed fishes evolve, diversify; ancestors of amphibians invade land

420 mya

Silurian. Sea level rises, diverse marine life; plants, invertebrates invade land

540 mya

Cambrian. Fragments of Rodinia, the first supercontinent. Major adaptive radiations in equatorial seas; icy polar regions

Appendix VIII

Appendix IX. Annotations to A Journal Article

This journal article reports on the movements of a female wolf during the summer of 2002 in northwestern Canada. It also reports on a scientific process of inquiry, observation and interpretation to learn where, how and why the wolf traveled as she did. In some ways, this article reflects the story of "how to do science" told in section 1.5 of this textbook. These notes are intended to help you read and understand how scientists work and how they report on their work.

---

(1) ARCTIC

(2) VOL. 57, NO. 2 (JUNE 2004) P. 196–203

(3) Long Foraging Movement of a Denning Tundra Wolf

(4) Paul F. Frame,[1,2] David S. Hik,[1] H. Dean Cluff,[3] and Paul C. Paquet[4]

(5) *(Received 3 September 2003; accepted in revised form 16 January 2004)*

---

(6) **ABSTRACT** Wolves (*Canis lupus*) on the Canadian barrens are intimately linked to migrating herds of barren-ground caribou (*Rangifer tarandus*). We deployed a Global Positioning System (GPS) radio collar on an adult female wolf to record her movements in response to changing caribou densities near her den during summer. This wolf and two other females were observed nursing a group of 11 pups. She traveled a minimum of 341 km during a 14-day excursion. The straight-line distance from the den to the farthest location was 103 km, and the overall minimum rate of travel was 3.1 km/h. The distance between the wolf and the radio-collared caribou decreased from 242 km one week before the excursion to 8 km four days into the excursion. We discuss several possible explanations for the long foraging bout.

(7) *Key words:* wolf, GPS tracking, movements, *Canis lupus*, foraging, caribou, Northwest Territories

(8) **RÉSUMÉ** Les loups (*Canis lupus*) dans la toundra canadienne sont étroitement liés aux hardes de caribous des toundras (*Rangifer tarandus*). On a équipé une louve adulte d'un collier émetteur muni d'un système de positionnement mondial (GPS) afin d'enregistrer ses déplacements en réponse au changement de densité du caribou près de sa tanière durant l'été. On a observé cette louve ainsi que deux autres en train d'allaiter un groupe de 11 louveteaux. Elle a parcouru un minimum de 341 km durant une sortie de 14 jours. La distance en ligne droite de la tanière à l'endroit le plus éloigné était de 103 km, et la vitesse minimum durant tout le voyage était de 3,1 km/h. La distance entre la louve et le caribou muni du collier émetteur a diminué de 242 km une semaine avant la sortie à 8 km quatre jours après la sortie. On commente diverses explications possibles pour ce long épisode de recherche de nourriture.

Mots clés: loup, repérage GPS, déplacements, *Canis lupus*, recherche de nourriture, caribou, Territoires du Nord-Ouest

Traduit pour la revue *Arctic* par Nésida Loyer.

---

(9) Introduction

Wolves (*Canis lupus*) that den on the central barrens of mainland Canada follow the seasonal movements of their main prey, migratory barren-ground caribou (*Rangifer tarandus*) (Kuyt, 1962; Kelsall, 1968; Walton et al., 2001). However, most wolves do not den near caribou calving grounds, but select sites farther south, closer to the tree line (Heard and Williams, 1992). Most caribou migrate beyond primary wolf denning areas by mid-June and do not return until mid-to-late July (Heard et al., 1996; Gunn et al., 2001). Conse-

quently, caribou density near dens is low for part of the summer.

During this period of spatial separation from the main caribou herds, wolves must either search near the homesite for scarce caribou or alternative prey (or both), travel to where prey are abundant, or use a combination of these strategies.

Walton et al. (2001) postulated that the travel of tundra wolves outside their normal summer ranges is a response to low caribou availability rather than a pre-dispersal exploration like that observed in terri torial wolves (Fritts and Mech, 1981; Messier, 1985). The authors postulated this because most such travel was directed toward caribou calving grounds. We report details of such a long-distance excursion by a breeding female tundra wolf wearing a GPS radio collar. We discuss the relationship of the excursion to movements of satellite-collared caribou (Gunn et al., 2001), supporting the hypothesis that tundra wolves make directional, rapid, long-distance movements in response to seasonal prey availability.

[1] Department of Biological Sciences, University of Alberta, Edmonton, Alberta T6G 2E9, Canada
[2] Corresponding author: pframe@ualberta.ca
[3] Department of Resources, Wildlife, and Economic Development, North Slave Region, Government of the Northwest Territories, P.O. Box 2668, 3803 Bretzlaff Dr., Yellowknife, Northwest Territories X1A 2P9, Canada; Dean_Cluff@gov.nt.ca
[4] Faculty of Environmental Design, University of Calgary, Calgary, Alberta T2N 1N4, Canada; current address: P.O. Box 150, Meacham, Saskatchewan S0K 2V0, Canada

196

---

1 Title of the journal, which reports on science taking place in Arctic regions.

2 Volume number, issue number and date of the journal, and page numbers of the article.

3 Title of the article: a concise but specific description of the subject of study—one episode of long-range travel by a wolf hunting for food on the Arctic tundra.

4 Authors of the article: scientists working at the institutions listed in the footnotes below. Note #2 indicates that P. F. Frame is the *corresponding author*—the person to contact with questions or comments. His email address is provided.

5 Date on which a draft of the article was received by the journal editor, followed by date one which a revised draft was accepted for publication. Between these dates, the article was reviewed and critiqued by other scientists, a process called peer review. The authors revised the article to make it clearer, according to those reviews.

6 ABSTRACT: A brief description of the study containing all basic elements of this report. First sentence summarizes the *background* material. Second sentence encapsulates the *methods* used. The rest of the paragraph sums up the *results*. Authors introduce the main *subject* of the study—a female wolf (#388) with pups in a den—and refer to later *discussion* of possible explanations for her behavior.

7 Key words are listed to help researchers using computer databases. Searching the databases using these key words will yield a list of studies related to this one.

8 RÉSUMÉ: The French translation of the abstract and key words. Many researchers in this field are French Canadian. Some journals provide such translations in French or in other languages.

9 INTRODUCTION: Gives the background for this wolf study. This paragraph tells of known or suspected wolf behavior that is important for this study. Note that (a) major species mentioned are always accompanied by scientific names, and (b) statements of fact or *postulations* (claims or assumptions about what is likely to be true) are followed by references to studies that established those facts or supported the postulations.

10 This paragraph focuses directly on the wolf behaviors that were studied here.

11 This paragraph starts with a statement of the *hypothesis* being tested, one that originated in other studies and is supported by this one. The hypothesis is restated more succinctly in the last sentence of this paragraph. This is the *inquiry* part of the scientific process—asking questions and suggesting possible answers.

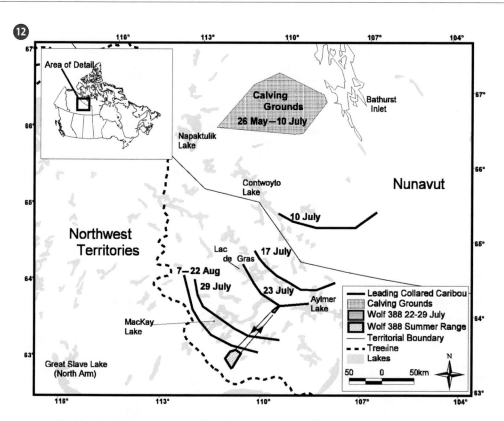

Figure 1. Map showing the movements of satellite radio-collared caribou with respect to female wolf 388's summer range and long foraging movement, in summer 2002.

12 This map shows the study area and depicts wolf and caribou locations and movements during one summer. Some of this information is explained below.

13 STUDY AREA: This section sets the stage for the study, locating it precisely with latitude and longitude coordinates and describing the area (illustrated by the map in Figure 1).

14 Here begins the story of how prey (caribou) and predators (wolves) interact on the tundra. Authors describe movements of these nomadic animals throughout the year.

15 We focus on the denning season (summer) and learn how wolves locate their dens and travel according to the movements of caribou herds.

🔢13 Study Area

Our study took place in the northern boreal forest–low Arctic tundra transition zone (63° 30′ N, 110° 00′ W; Figure 1; Timoney et al., 1992). Permafrost in the area changes from discontinuous to continuous (Harris, 1986). Patches of spruce (*Picea mariana*, *P. glauca*) occur in the southern portion and give way to open tundra to the northeast. Eskers, kames, and other glacial deposits are scattered throughout the study area. Standing water and exposed bedrock are characteristic of the area.

🔢14 *Details of the Caribou-Wolf System*

The Bathurst caribou herd uses this study area. Most caribou cows have begun migrating by late April, reaching calving grounds by June (Gunn et al., 2001; Figure 1). Calving peaks by 15 June (Gunn et al., 2001), and calves begin to travel with the herd by one week of age (Kelsall, 1968). The movement patterns of bulls are less known, but bulls frequent areas near calving grounds by mid-June (Heard et al., 1996; Gunn et al., 2001). In summer, Bathurst caribou cows generally travel south from their calving grounds and then, parallel to the tree line, to the northwest. The rut usually takes place at the tree line in October (Gunn et al., 2001). The winter range of the Bathurst herd varies among years, ranging through the taiga and along the tree line from south of Great Bear Lake to southeast of Great Slave Lake. Some caribou spend the winter on the tundra (Gunn et al., 2001; Thorpe et al., 2001).

In winter, wolves that prey on Bathurst caribou do not behave territorially. Instead, they follow the herd throughout its winter range (Walton et al., 2001; Musiani, 2003). However, during denning (May– 🔢15

16 Other variables are considered—prey other than caribou and their relative abundance in 2002.

17 METHODS: There is no one scientific method. Procedures for each and every study must be explained carefully.

18 Authors explain when and how they tracked caribou and wolves, including tools used and the exact procedures followed.

19 This important subsection explains what data were calculated (average distance ...) and how, including the software used and where it came from. (The calculations are listed in Table 1.) Note that the behavior measured (traveling) is carefully defined.

20 RESULTS: The heart of the report and the *observation* part of the scientific process. This section is organized parallel to the Methods section.

21 This subsection is broken down by periods of observation. Pre-excursion period covers the time between 388's capture and the start of her long-distance travel. The investigators used visual observations as well as telemetry (measurements taken using the global positioning system (GPS)) to gather data. They looked at how 388 cared for her pups, interacted with other adults, and moved about the den area.

Table 1. Daily distances from wolf 388 and the den to the nearest radio-collared caribou during a long excursion in summer 2002.

Date (2002)	Mean distance from caribou to wolf (km)	Daily distance from closest caribou to den
12 July	242	241
13 July	210	209
14 July	200	199
15 July	186	180
16 July	163	162
17 July	151	148
18 July	144	137
19 July[1]	126	124
20 July	103	130
21 July	73	130
22 July	40	110
23 July[2]	9	104
29 July[3]	16	43
30 July	32	43
31 July	28	44
1 August	29	46
2 August[4]	54	52
3 August	53	53
4 August	74	74
5 August	75	75
6 August	74	75
7 August	72	75
8 August	76	75
9 August	79	79

[1] Excursion starts.
[2] Wolf closest to collared caribou.
[3] Previous five days' caribou locations not available.
[4] Excursion ends.

August, parturition late May to mid-June), wolf movements are limited by the need to return food to the den. To maximize access to migrating caribou, many wolves select den sites closer to the tree line than to caribou calving grounds (Heard and Williams, 1992). Because of caribou movement patterns, tundra denning wolves are separated from the main caribou herds by several hundred kilometers at some time during summer (Williams, 1990:19; Figure 1; Table 1).

16 Muskoxen do not occur in the study area (Fournier and Gunn, 1998), and there are few moose there (H.D. Cluff, pers. obs.). Therefore, alternative prey for wolves includes waterfowl, other ground-nesting birds, their eggs, rodents, and hares (Kuyt, 1972; Williams, 1990:16; H.D. Cluff and P.F. Frame, unpubl. data). During 56 hours of den observations, we saw no ground squirrels or hares, only birds. It appears that the abundance of alternative prey was relatively low in 2002.

17 ## Methods

Wolf Monitoring

18 We captured female wolf 388 near her den on 22 June 2002, using a helicopter net-gun (Walton et al., 2001). She was fitted with a releasable GPS radio collar (Merrill et al., 1998) programmed to acquire locations at 30-

minute intervals. The collar was electronically released (e.g., Mech and Gese, 1992) on 20 August 2002. From 27 June to 3 July 2002, we observed 388's den with a 78 mm spotting scope at a distance of 390 m.

Caribou Monitoring

In spring of 2002, ten female caribou were captured by helicopter net-gun and fitted with satellite radio collars, bringing the total number of collared Bathurst cows to 19. Eight of these spent the summer of 2002 south of Queen Maud Gulf, well east of normal Bathurst caribou range. Therefore, we used 11 caribou for this analysis. The collars provided one location per day during our study, except for five days from 24 to 28 July. Locations of satellite collars were obtained from Service Argos, Inc. (Landover, Maryland).

Data Analysis

19 Location data were analyzed by ArcView GIS software (Environmental Systems Research Institute Inc., Redlands, California). We calculated the average distance from the nearest collared caribou to the wolf and the den for each day of the study.

Wolf foraging bouts were calculated from the time 388 exited a buffer zone (500 m radius around the den) until she re-entered it. We considered her to be traveling when two consecutive locations were spatially separated by more than 100 m. Minimum distance traveled was the sum of distances between each location and the next during the excursion.

We compared pre- and post-excursion data using Analysis of Variance (ANOVA; Zar, 1999). We first tested for homogeneity of variances with Levene's test (Brown and Forsythe, 1974). No transformations of these data were required.

Results **20**

Wolf Monitoring

Pre-Excursion Period: Wolf 388 was lactating when **21** captured on 22 June. We observed her and two other females nursing a group of 11 pups between 27 June and 3 July. During our observations, the pack consisted of at least four adults (3 females and 1 male) and 11 pups. On 30 June, three pups were moved to a location 310 m from the other eight and cared for by an uncollared female. The male was not seen at the den after the evening of 30 June.

Before the excursion, telemetry indicated 18 foraging bouts. The mean distance traveled during these bouts was 25.29 km (± 4.5 SE, range 3.1–82.5 km). Mean greatest distance from the den on foraging

198 *P.F. Frame, et al*

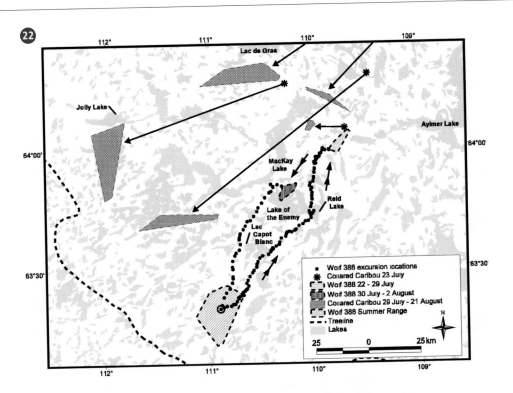

Figure 2. Details of a long foraging movement by female wolf 388 between 19 July and 2 August 2002. Also shown are locations and movements of three satellite radio-collared caribou from 23 July to 21 August 2002. On 23 July, the wolf was 8 km from a collared caribou. The farthest point from the den (103 km distant) was recorded on 27 July. Arrows indicate direction of travel.

22 The key in the lower right-hand corner of the map shows areas (shaded) within which the wolves and caribou moved, and the dotted trail of 388 during her excursion. From the results depicted on this map, the investigators tried to determine when and where 388 might have encountered caribou and how their locations affected her traveling behavior.

23 The wolf's excursion (her long trip away from the den area) is the focus of this study. These paragraphs present detailed measurements of daily movements during her two-week trip—how far she traveled, how far she was from collared caribou, her time spent traveling and resting, and her rate of speed. Authors use the phrase "minimum distance traveled" to acknowledge they couldn't track every step but were measuring samples of her movements. They knew that she went at least as far as they measured. This shows how scientists try to be exact when reporting results. Results of this study are depicted graphically in the map in Figure 2.

bouts was 7.1 km (± 0.9 SE, range 1.7–17.0 km). The average duration of foraging bouts for the period was 20.9 h (± 4.5 SE, range 1–71 h).

The average daily distance between the wolf and the nearest collared caribou decreased from 242 km on 12 July, one week before the excursion period, to 126 km on 19 July, the day the excursion began (Table 1).

23 **Excursion Period:** On 19 July at 2203, after spending 14 h at the den, 388 began moving to the northeast and did not return for 336 h (14 d; Figure 2). Whether she traveled alone or with other wolves is unknown. During the excursion, 476 (71%) of 672 possible locations were recorded. The wolf crossed the southeast end of Lac Capot Blanc on a small land bridge, where she paused for 4.5 h after traveling for 19.5 h (37.5

km). Following this rest, she traveled for 9 h (26.3 km) onto a peninsula in Reid Lake, where she spent 2 h before backtracking and stopping for 8 h just off the peninsula. Her next period of travel lasted 16.5 h (32.7 km), terminating in a pause of 9.5 h just 3.8 km from a concentration of locations at the far end of her excursion, where we presume she encountered caribou. The mean duration of these three movement periods was 15.7 h (± 2.5 SE), and that of the pauses, 7.3 h (± 1.5). The wolf required 72.5 h (3.0 d) to travel a minimum of 95 km from her den to this area near caribou (Figure 2). She remained there (35.5 km2) for 151.5 h (6.3 d) and then moved south to Lake of the Enemy, where she stayed (31.9 km²) for 74 h (3.1 d) before returning to her den. Her greatest distance from the den, 103 km, was recorded 174.5 h (7.3 d) after the excursion

24 Post-excursion measurements of 388's movements were made to compare with those of the pre-excursion period. In order to compare, scientists often use *means*, or averages, of a series of measurements—mean distances, mean duration, etc.

25 In the comparison, authors used statistical calculations (F and df) to determine that the differences between pre- and post-excursion measurements were *statistically insignificant*, or close enough to be considered essentially the same or similar.

26 As with wolf 388, the investigators measured the movements of caribou during the study period. The areas within which the caribou moved are shown in Figure 2 by shaded polygons mentioned in the second paragraph of this subsection.

27 This subsection summarizes how distances separating predators and prey varied during the study period.

28 DISCUSSION: This section is the *interpretation* part of the scientific process.

29 This subsection reviews observations from other studies and suggests that this study fits with patterns of those observations.

30 Authors discuss a prevailing *theory* (CBFT) which might explain why a wolf would travel far to meet her own energy needs while taking food caught closer to the den back to her pups. The results of this study seem to fit that pattern.

---

began, at 0433 on 27 July. She was 8 km from a collared caribou on 23 July, four days after the excursion began (Table 1).

The return trip began at 0403 on 2 August, 318 h (13.2 d) after leaving the den. She followed a relatively direct path for 18 h back to the den, a distance of 75 km.

The minimum distance traveled during the excursion was 339 km. The estimated overall minimum travel rate was 3.1 km/h, 2.6 km/h away from the den and 4.2 km/h on the return trip.

24 **Post-Excursion Period:** We saw three pups when recovering the collar on 20 August, but others may have been hiding in vegetation.

Telemetry recorded 13 foraging bouts in the post-excursion period. The mean distance traveled during these bouts was 18.3 km (+ 2.7 SE, range 1.2–47.7 km), and mean greatest distance from the den was 7.1 km (+ 0.7 SE, range 1.1–11.0 km). The mean duration of these post-excursion foraging bouts was 10.9 h (+ 2.4 SE, range 1–33 h).

When 388 reached her den on 2 August, the distance to the nearest collared caribou was 54 km. On 9 August, one week after she returned, the distance was 79 km (Table 1).

Pre- and Post-Excursion Comparison

25 We found no differences in the mean distance of foraging bouts before and after the excursion period (F = 1.5, df = 1, 29, p = 0.24). Likewise, the mean greatest distance from the den was similar pre- and post-excursion (F = 0.004, df = 1, 29, p = 0.95). However, the mean duration of 388's foraging bouts decreased by 10.0 h after her long excursion (F = 3.1, df = 1, 29, p = 0.09).

26 *Caribou Monitoring*

Summer Movements: On 10 July, 5 of 11 collared caribou were dispersed over a distance of 10 km, 140 km south of their calving grounds (Figure 1). On the same day, three caribou were still on the calving grounds, two were between the calving grounds and the leaders, and one was missing. One week later (17 July), the leading radio-collared cows were 100 km farther south (Figure 1). Two were within 5 km of each other in front of the rest, who were more dispersed. All radio-collared cows had left the calving grounds by this time. On 23 July, the leading radio-collared caribou had moved 35 km farther south, and all of them were more widely dispersed. The two cows closest to the leader were 26 km and 33 km away, with 37 km between them. On the next location (29 July), the most southerly caribou were 60 km

farther south. All of the caribou were now in the areas where they remained for the duration of the study (Figure 2).

A Minimum Convex Polygon (Mohr and Stumpf, 1966) around all caribou locations acquired during the study encompassed 85 119 km^2.

Relative to the Wolf Den: The distance from the **27** nearest collared caribou to the den decreased from 241 km one week before the excursion to 124 km the day it began. The nearest a collared caribou came to the den was 43 km away, on 29 and 30 July. During the study, four collared caribou were located within 100 km of the den. Each of these four was closest to the wolf on at least one day during the period reported.

28 **Discussion**

Prey Abundance

Caribou are the single most important prey of tundra **29** wolves (Clark, 1971; Kuyt, 1972; Stephenson and James, 1982; Williams, 1990). Caribou range over vast areas, and for part of the summer, they are scarce or absent in wolf home ranges (Heard et al., 1996). Both the long distance between radio-collared caribou and the den the week before the excursion and the increased time spent foraging by wolf 388 indicate that caribou availability near the den was low. Observations of the pups' being left alone for up to 18 h, presumably while adults were searching for food, provide additional support for low caribou availability locally. Mean foraging bout duration decreased by 10.0 h after the excursion, when collared caribou were closer to the den, suggesting an increase in caribou availability nearby.

Foraging Excursion

One aspect of central place foraging theory (CPFT) **30** deals with the optimality of returning different-sized food loads from varying distances to dependents at a central place (i.e., the den) (Orians and Pearson, 1979). Carlson (1985) tested CPFT and found that the predator usually consumed prey captured far from the central place, while feeding prey captured nearby to dependants. Wolf 388 spent 7.2 days in one area near caribou before moving to a location 23 km back towards the den, where she spent an additional 3.1 days, likely hunting caribou. She began her return trip from this closer location, traveling directly to the den. While away, she may have made one or more successful kills and spent time meeting her own energetic needs before returning to the den. Alternatively, it may have taken several attempts to make a kill, which she then fed on before beginning her return trip. We do not know if she returned food to the pups, but such behavior would be supported by CPFT.

Other workers have reported wolves' making long round trips and referred to them as "extraterritorial" or "pre-dispersal" forays (Fritts and Mech, 1981; Messier, 1985; Ballard et al., 1997; Merrill and Mech, 2000). These movements are most often made by young wolves (1–3 years old), in areas where annual territories are maintained and prey are relatively sedentary (Fritts and Mech, 1981; Messier, 1985). The long excursion of 388 differs in that tundra wolves do not maintain annual territories (Walton et al., 2001), and the main prey migrate over vast areas (Gunn et al., 2001).

Another difference between 388's excursion and those reported earlier is that she is a mature, breeding female. No study of territorial wolves has reported reproductive adults making extraterritorial movements in summer (Fritts and Mech, 1981; Messier, 1985; Ballard et al., 1997; Merrill and Mech, 2001). However, Walton et al. (2001) also report that breeding female tundra wolves made excursions.

Direction of Movement

Possible explanations for the relatively direct route 388 took to the caribou include landscape influence and experience. Considering the timing of 388's trip and the locations of caribou, had the wolf moved northwest, she might have missed the caribou entirely, or the encounter might have been delayed.

A reasonable possibility is that the land directed 388's route. The barrens are crisscrossed with trails worn into the tundra over centuries by hundreds of thousands of caribou and other animals (Kelsall, 1968; Thorpe et al., 2001). At river crossings, lakes, or narrow peninsulas, trails converge and funnel towards and away from caribou calving grounds and summer range. Wolves use trails for travel (Paquet et al., 1996; Mech and Boitani, 2003; P. Frame, pers. observation). Thus, the landscape may direct an animal's movements and lead it to where cues, such as the odor of caribou on the wind or scent marks of other wolves, may lead it to caribou.

Another possibility is that 388 knew where to find caribou in summer. Sexually immature tundra wolves sometimes follow caribou to calving grounds (D. Heard, unpubl. data). Possibly, 388 had made such journeys in previous years and killed caribou. If this were the case, then in times of local prey scarcity she might travel to areas where she had hunted successfully before. Continued monitoring of tundra wolves may answer questions about how their food needs are met in times of low caribou abundance near dens.

Caribou often form large groups while moving south to the tree line (Kelsall, 1968). After a large aggregation of caribou moves through an area, its scent can linger for weeks (Thorpe et al., 2001:104). It is conceivable that 388 detected caribou scent on the wind, which was blowing from the northeast on 19–21 July (Environment Canada, 2003), at the same time her excursion began. Many factors, such as odor strength and wind direction and strength, make systematic study of scent detection in wolves difficult under field conditions (Harrington and Asa, 2003). However, humans are able to smell odors such as forest fires or oil refineries more than 100 km away. The olfactory capabilities of dogs, which are similar to wolves, are thought to be 100 to 1 million times that of humans (Harrington and Asa, 2003). Therefore, it is reasonable to think that under the right wind conditions, the scent of many caribou traveling together could be detected by wolves from great distances, thus triggering a long foraging bout.

Rate of Travel

Mech (1994) reported the rate of travel of Arctic wolves on barren ground was 8.7 km/h during regular travel and 10.0 km/h when returning to the den, a difference of 1.3 km/h. These rates are based on direct observation and exclude periods when wolves moved slowly or not at all. Our calculated travel rates are assumed to include periods of slow movement or no movement. However, the pattern we report is similar to that reported by Mech (1994), in that homeward travel was faster than regular travel by 1.6 km/h. The faster rate on return may be explained by the need to return food to the den. Pup survival can increase with the number of adults in a pack available to deliver food to pups (Harrington et al., 1983). Therefore, an increased rate of travel on homeward trips could improve a wolf's reproductive fitness by getting food to pups more quickly.

Fate of 388's Pups

Wolf 388 was caring for pups during den observa- tions. The pups were estimated to be six weeks old, and were seen ranging as far as 800 m from the den. They received some regurgitated food from two of the females, but were unattended for long periods. The excursion started 16 days after our observations, and it is improbable that the pups could have traveled the distance that 388 moved. If the pups died, this would have removed parental responsibility, allowing the long movement.

Our observations and the locations of radio-collared caribou indicate that prey became scarce in

31 Here our authors note other possible explanations for wolves' excursions presented by other investigators, but this study does not seem to support those ideas.

32 Authors discuss possible reasons for why 388 traveled directly to where caribou were located. They take what they learned from earlier studies and apply it to this case, suggesting that the lay of the land played a role. Note that their description paints a clear picture of the landscape.

33 Authors suggest that 388 may have learned in traveling during previous summers where the caribou were. The last two sentences suggest ideas for future studies.

34 Or maybe 388 followed the scent of the caribou. Authors acknowledge difficulties of proving this, but they suggest another area where future studies might be done.

35 Authors suggest that results of this study support previous studies about how fast wolves travel to and from the den. In the last sentence, they speculate on how these observed patterns would fit into the theory of evolution.

36 Authors also speculate on the fate of 388's pups while she was traveling. This leads to . . .

Glossary of Biological Terms

ABC model Model for the genetic basis of flower formation; products of three master genes (*A, B, C*) control the development of sepals, petals, and stamens and carpels from meristematic tissue.

ABC transporter One of a distinct class of membrane proteins, each a channel or pump for a specific hydrophobic substance (e.g., ions, sugars, amino acids).

ABO blood typing Method of identifying which self-recognition proteins of types A and B are at the surface of an individual's red blood cells; the absence of either type is designated O.

abortion Premature expulsion of embryo or fetus from the uterus; called miscarriage when spontaneous rather than induced.

abscisic acid Plant hormone; stimulates stomatal closure in response to water stress, protein storage in seeds, maturation of embryo sporophyte; possibly induces and maintains dormancy in some plants.

abscission (ab-SIH-zhun) The dropping of leaves, flowers, fruits, or other parts from a plant in response to seasonal change, drought, injury, or nutrient deficiencies.

absorption Of pigments, interception of photon energy. Of cells, uptake of water and solutes from the surroundings. Of digestion, uptake of water and solutes into the internal environment.

absorption spectrum Range of wavelengths that a given type of pigment can absorb.

accessory pigment A pigment that absorbs and transfers light energy to a photosystem; extends the range of light wavelengths for photosynthesis; e.g., a carotenoid.

acclimatization Processes by which the body adjusts in physiology and behavior to a new environment; e.g., after moving from sea level to a high-altitude habitat.

acetylation The attachment of an acetyl group (CH3CO) to an organic compound.

acetylcholine (ACh) Neurotransmitter with stimulatory or inhibitory effects in the brain, spinal cord, glands, and muscles.

acetyl–CoA Coenzyme A bound to a two-carbon fragment from pyruvate, which it transfers to oxaloacetate for Krebs cycle.

acid [L. *acidus*, sour] Any water-soluble substance that releases hydrogen ions (H$^+$) in water, yielding a pH below 7.0.

acid–base balance Outcome of control over solute concentrations; extracellular fluid is neither too acidic nor too basic (alkaline).

acidity A solution with a pH of less than 7.

acid rain Acidic precipitation; rain or snow with high levels of sulfur and nitrogen oxides.

acoelomate animal Any invertebrate with no fluid-filled cavity between its gut and body wall; e.g., a flatworm.

acoustical receptor Any mechanoreceptor sensitive to sound.

acoustical signal A sound or sounds used in intraspecific communication.

actin Protein monomer of microfilaments that functions in contraction, cell division, and reinforcing or reconfiguring the shape of a cell or its contents.

action potential Of excitable cells, a self-propagating, abrupt reversal in the voltage difference across the plasma membrane.

activation energy Minimum amount of energy required to start a reaction; enzyme action lowers this energy barrier. Reactions differ in the amount required.

activator A regulatory molecule that binds to specific sequences in DNA and thereby promotes transcription.

active site Chemically stable crevice in an enzyme where substrates bind and a reaction can be catalyzed repeatedly.

active transport Pumping of a specific solute across a cell membrane against its concentration gradient, through the interior of a transport protein. Requires energy input, as from ATP.

adaptation, evolutionary [L. *adaptare*, to fit] Any long-term, heritable aspect of form, function, or behavior that improves an individual's chances of surviving and reproducing; outcome of natural selection and other microevolutionary processes.

adaptation, sensory Of sensory neurons, a decline or cessation of action potentials when a stimulus of constant strength does not end.

adaptive immunity The mechanisms that defend the vertebrate body against specific threats to health, as characterized by self/nonself recognition, specificity, diversity, and memory. All antibody-mediated and cell-mediated responses to antigen.

adaptive radiation A macroevolutionary pattern. A burst of genetic divergences from a lineage that gives rise to many species, each able to use a novel resource or to move into a new, or newly vacated, habitat.

adaptive trait An aspect of form, function, or behavior that helps an individual survive and reproduce under prevailing conditions.

adaptive zone A set of different niches that become be filled by a group of species.

adenine One of four nitrogen-containing bases in nucleotide monomers of DNA or RNA; also refers to a nucleotide having an adenine base component.

ADH Antidiuretic hormone. Hypothalamic hormone released by the posterior pituitary that induces water conservation by kidneys.

adhering junction Complex of adhesion proteins that anchors cells to each other and to extracellular matrixes.

adhesion protein Of multicelled species, a plasma membrane protein that helps cells stick together in tissues and to extracellular matrixes such as basement membrane.

adipose tissue Type of connective tissue having an abundance of fat-storing cells.

ADP Adenosine diphosphate (ah-DEN-uh-seen die-FOSS-fate). A nucleotide with an adenine base and two phosphate groups.

adrenal cortex Outer zone of the adrenal gland; secretes cortisol and aldosterone.

adrenal gland Endocrine gland located on top of the kidney; regulates stress reponses and influences glucose metabolism.

adrenal medulla Inner zone of adrenal gland that secretes epinephrine and norepinephrine.

aerobic respiration (air-OH-bik) [Gk. *aer*, air, + *bios*, life] Oxygen-requiring pathway of ATP formation in mitochondria: from glycolysis, to Krebs cycle and electron transport phosphorylation. Typical net energy yield: 36 ATP per glucose molecule.

African emergence model Model for the origin of modern humans; *Homo sapiens* is said to have originated in Africa, then replaced archaic *Homo* populations in different parts of the world.

age structure Of a population, the number of individuals in each age category.

agglutination (ah-glue-tin-AY-shun) A vertebrate defense response; antibodies bind antigen and form insoluble clumps that attract phagocytes.

aging Of complex multicelled organisms, a time-dependent progressive deterioration of molecules, cells, tissues, and organs that weakens the body's capacity to function.

AIDS Acquired immune deficiency syndrome. A set of chronic disorders that develops after prolonged infection by HIV has weakened the immune system.

alcohol Organic compound having one or more hydroxyl groups that dissolves easily in water; e.g., ethanol.

alcoholic fermentation An anaerobic ATP-forming pathway using pyruvate and NADH from glycolysis. NADH transfers electrons to an intermediate, acetaldehyde, forming ethanol. Occurs in cytoplasm only. The net yield is 2 ATP from glycolysis; the steps remaining only regenerate NAD$^+$.

which she then fed on before beginning her return trip. We do not know if she returned food to the pups, but such behavior would be supported by CPFT.

31 Other workers have reported wolves' making long round trips and referred to them as "extraterritorial" or "pre-dispersal" forays (Fritts and Mech, 1981; Messier, 1985; Ballard et al., 1997; Merrill and Mech, 2000). These movements are most often made by young wolves (1–3 years old), in areas where annual territories are maintained and prey are relatively sedentary (Fritts and Mech, 1981; Messier, 1985). The long excursion of 388 differs in that tundra wolves do not maintain annual territories (Walton et al., 2001), and the main prey migrate over vast areas (Gunn et al., 2001).

Another difference between 388's excursion and those reported earlier is that she is a mature, breeding female. No study of territorial wolves has reported reproductive adults making extraterritorial movements in summer (Fritts and Mech, 1981; Messier, 1985; Ballard et al., 1997; Merrill and Mech, 2001). However, Walton et al. (2001) also report that breeding female tundra wolves made excursions.

Direction of Movement

32 Possible explanations for the relatively direct route 388 took to the caribou include landscape influence and experience. Considering the timing of 388's trip and the locations of caribou, had the wolf moved northwest, she might have missed the caribou entirely, or the encounter might have been delayed.

A reasonable possibility is that the land directed 388's route. The barrens are crisscrossed with trails worn into the tundra over centuries by hundreds of thousands of caribou and other animals (Kelsall, 1968; Thorpe et al., 2001). At river crossings, lakes, or narrow peninsulas, trails converge and funnel towards and away from caribou calving grounds and summer range. Wolves use trails for travel (Paquet et al., 1996; Mech and Boitani, 2003; P. Frame, pers. observation). Thus, the landscape may direct an animal's movements and lead it to where cues, such as the odor of caribou on the wind or scent marks of other wolves, may lead it to caribou.

33 Another possibility is that 388 knew where to find caribou in summer. Sexually immature tundra wolves sometimes follow caribou to calving grounds (D. Heard, unpubl. data). Possibly, 388 had made such journeys in previous years and killed caribou. If this were the case, then in times of local prey scarcity she might travel to areas where she had hunted successfully before. Continued monitoring of tundra wolves may answer questions about how their food needs are met in times of low caribou abundance near dens.

34 Caribou often form large groups while moving south to the tree line (Kelsall, 1968). After a large aggregation of caribou moves through an area, its scent can linger for weeks (Thorpe et al., 2001:104). It is conceivable that 388 detected caribou scent on the wind, which was blowing from the northeast on 19–21 July (Environment Canada, 2003), at the same time her excursion began. Many factors, such as odor strength and wind direction and strength, make systematic study of scent detection in wolves difficult under field conditions (Harrington and Asa, 2003). However, humans are able to smell odors such as forest fires or oil refineries more than 100 km away. The olfactory capabilities of dogs, which are similar to wolves, are thought to be 100 to 1 million times that of humans (Harrington and Asa, 2003). Therefore, it is reasonable to think that under the right wind conditions, the scent of many caribou traveling together could be detected by wolves from great distances, thus triggering a long foraging bout.

Rate of Travel

35 Mech (1994) reported the rate of travel of Arctic wolves on barren ground was 8.7 km/h during regular travel and 10.0 km/h when returning to the den, a difference of 1.3 km/h. These rates are based on direct observation and exclude periods when wolves moved slowly or not at all. Our calculated travel rates are assumed to include periods of slow movement or no movement. However, the pattern we report is similar to that reported by Mech (1994), in that homeward travel was faster than regular travel by 1.6 km/h. The faster rate on return may be explained by the need to return food to the den. Pup survival can increase with the number of adults in a pack available to deliver food to pups (Harrington et al., 1983). Therefore, an increased rate of travel on homeward trips could improve a wolf's reproductive fitness by getting food to pups more quickly.

Fate of 388's Pups

36 Wolf 388 was caring for pups during den observations. The pups were estimated to be six weeks old, and were seen ranging as far as 800 m from the den. They received some regurgitated food from two of the females, but were unattended for long periods. The excursion started 16 days after our observations, and it is improbable that the pups could have traveled the distance that 388 moved. If the pups died, this would have removed parental responsibility, allowing the long movement.

Our observations and the locations of radio-collared caribou indicate that prey became scarce in

31 Here our authors note other possible explanations for wolves' excursions presented by other investigators, but this study does not seem to support those ideas.

32 Authors discuss possible reasons for why 388 traveled directly to where caribou were located. They take what they learned from earlier studies and apply it to this case, suggesting that the lay of the land played a role. Note that their description paints a clear picture of the landscape.

33 Authors suggest that 388 may have learned in traveling during previous summers where the caribou were. The last two sentences suggest ideas for future studies.

34 Or maybe 388 followed the scent of the caribou. Authors acknowledge difficulties of proving this, but they suggest another area where future studies might be done.

35 Authors suggest that results of this study support previous studies about how fast wolves travel to and from the den. In the last sentence, they speculate on how these observed patterns would fit into the theory of evolution.

36 Authors also speculate on the fate of 388's pups while she was traveling. This leads to . . .

37 Discussion of cooperative rearing of pups and, in turn, to speculation on how this study and what is known about cooperative rearing might fit into the animal's strategies for survival of the species. Again, the authors approach the broader theory of evolution and how it might explain some of their results.

38 And again, they suggest that this study points to several areas where further study will shed some light.

39 In conclusion, the authors suggest that their study supports the hypothesis being tested here. And they touch on the implications of increased human activity on the tundra predicted by their results.

40 ACKNOWLEDGEMENTS: Authors note the support of institutions, companies and individuals. They thank their reviewers ad list permits under which their research was carried on.

41 REFERENCES: List of all studies cited in the report. This may seem tedious, but is a vitally important part of scientific reporting. It is a record of the sources of information on which this study is based. It provides readers with a wealth of resources for further reading on this topic. Much of it will form the foundation of future scientific studies like this one.

---

the area of the den as summer progressed. Wolf 388 may have abandoned her pups to seek food for herself. However, she returned to the den after the excursion, where she was seen near pups. In fact, she foraged in a similar pattern before and after the excursion, suggesting that she again was providing for pups after her return to the den.

37 A more likely possibility is that one or both of the other lactating females cared for the pups during 388's absence. The three females at this den were not seen with the pups at the same time. However, two weeks earlier, at a different den, we observed three females cooperatively caring for a group of six pups. At that den, the three lactating females were observed providing food for each other and trading places while nursing pups. Such a situation at the den of 388 could have created conditions that allowed one or more of the lactating females to range far from the den for a period, returning to her parental duties afterwards. However, the pups would have been weaned by eight weeks of age (Packard et al., 1992), so nonlactating adults could also have cared for them, as often happens in wolf packs (Packard et al., 1992; Mech et al., 1999).

Cooperative rearing of multiple litters by a pack could create opportunities for long-distance foraging movements by some reproductive wolves during summer periods of local food scarcity. We have recorded multiple lactating females at one or more tundra wolf dens per year since 1997. This reproductive strategy may be an adaptation to temporally and spatially unpredictable food resources. All of these **38** possibilities require further study, but emphasize both the adaptability of wolves living on the barrens and their dependence on caribou.

Long-range wolf movement in response to caribou **39** availability has been suggested by other researchers (Kuyt, 1972; Walton et al., 2001) and traditional ecological knowledge (Thorpe et al., 2001). Our report demonstrates the rapid and extreme response of wolves to caribou distribution and movements in summer. Increased human activity on the tundra (mining, road building, pipelines, ecotourism) may influence caribou movement patterns and change the interactions between wolves and caribou in the region. Continued monitoring of both species will help us to assess whether the association is being affected adversely by anthropogenic change.

40 Acknowledgements

This research was supported by the Department of Resources, Wildlife, and Economic Development, Government of the Northwest Territories; the Department of Biological Sciences at the University of Alberta; the Natural Sciences and Engineering Research Council of Canada; the Department of Indian and Northern Affairs Canada; the Canadian Circumpolar Institute; and DeBeers Canada, Ltd. Lorna Ruechel assisted with den observations. A. Gunn provided caribou location data. We thank Dave Mech for the use of GPS collars. M. Nelson, A. Gunn, and three anonymous reviewers made helpful comments on earlier drafts of the manuscript. This work was done under Wildlife Research Permit – WL002948 issued by the Government of the Northwest Territories, Department of Resources, Wildlife, and Economic Development.

41 References

BALLARD, W.B., AYRES, L.A., KRAUSMAN, P.R., REED, D.J., and FANCY, S.G. 1997. Ecology of wolves in relation to a migratory caribou herd in northwest Alaska. Wildlife Monographs 135. 47 p.

BROWN, M.B., and FORSYTHE, A.B. 1974. Robust tests for the equality of variances. Journal of the American Statistical Association 69:364–367.

CARLSON, A. 1985. Central place foraging in the red-backed shrike (Lanius collurio L.): Allocation of prey between forager and sedentary consumer. Animal Behaviour 33:664–666.

CLARK, K.R.F. 1971. Food habits and behavior of the tundra wolf on central Baffin Island. Ph.D. Thesis, University of Toronto, Ontario, Canada.

ENVIRONMENT CANADA. 2003. National climate data information archive. Available online: http://www.climate.weatheroffice.ec.gc.ca/Welcome_e.html

FOURNIER, B., and GUNN, A. 1998. Musk ox numbers and distribution in the NWT, 1997. File Report No. 121. Yellowknife: Department of Resources, Wildlife, and Economic Development, Government of the Northwest Territories. 55 p.

FRITTS, S.H., and MECH, L.D. 1981. Dynamics, movements, and feeding ecology of a newly protected wolf population in northwestern Minnesota. Wildlife Monographs 80. 79 p.

GUNN, A., DRAGON, J., and BOULANGER, J. 2001. Seasonal movements of satellite-collared caribou from the Bathurst herd. Final Report to the West Kitikmeot Slave Study Society, Yellowknife, NWT. 80 p. Available online: http://www.wkss.nt.ca/HTML/08_ProjectsReports/PDF/Seasonal MovementsFinal.pdf

HARRINGTON, F.H., and ASA, C.S. 2003. Wolf communication. In: Mech, L.D., and Boitani, L., eds. Wolves: Behavior, ecology, and conservation. Chicago: University of Chicago Press. 66–103.

HARRINGTON, F.H., MECH, L.D., and FRITTS, S.H. 1983. Pack size and wolf pup survival: Their relationship under varying ecological conditions. Behavioral Ecology and Sociobiology 13:19–26.

HARRIS, S.A. 1986. Permafrost distribution, zonation and stability along the eastern ranges of the cordillera of North America. Arctic 39(1):29–38.

HEARD, D.C., and WILLIAMS, T.M. 1992. Distribution of wolf dens on migratory caribou ranges in the Northwest

Territories, Canada. Canadian Journal of Zoology 70:1504–1510.

HEARD, D.C., WILLIAMS, T.M., and MELTON, D.A. 1996. The relationship between food intake and predation risk in migratory caribou and implication to caribou and wolf population dynamics. Rangifer Special Issue No. 2:37–44.

KELSALL, J.P. 1968. The migratory barren-ground caribou of Canada. Canadian Wildlife Service Monograph Series 3. Ottawa: Queen's Printer. 340 p.

KUYT, E. 1962. Movements of young wolves in the Northwest Territories of Canada. Journal of Mammalogy 43:270–271.

———. 1972. Food habits and ecology of wolves on barren-ground caribou range in the Northwest Territories. Canadian Wildlife Service Report Series 21. Ottawa: Information Canada. 36 p.

MECH, L.D. 1994. Regular and homeward travel speeds of Arctic wolves. Journal of Mammalogy 75:741–742.

MECH, L.D., and BOITANI, L. 2003. Wolf social ecology. In: Mech, L.D., and Boitani, L., eds. Wolves: Behavior, ecology, and conservation. Chicago: University of Chicago Press. 1–34.

MECH, L.D., and GESE, E.M. 1992. Field testing the Wildlink capture collar on wolves. Wildlife Society Bulletin 20:249–256.

MECH, L.D., WOLFE, P., and PACKARD, J.M. 1999. Regurgitative food transfer among wild wolves. Canadian Journal of Zoology 77:1192–1195.

MERRILL, S.B., and MECH, L.D. 2000. Details of extensive movements by Minnesota wolves (Canis lupus). American Midland Naturalist 144:428–433.

MERRILL, S.B., ADAMS, L.G., NELSON, M.E., and MECH, L.D. 1998. Testing releasable GPS radiocollars on wolves and white-tailed deer. Wildlife Society Bulletin 26:830–835.

MESSIER, F. 1985. Solitary living and extraterritorial movements of wolves in relation to social status and prey abundance. Canadian Journal of Zoology 63:239–245.

MOHR, C.O., and STUMPF, W.A. 1966. Comparison of methods for calculating areas of animal activity. Journal of Wildlife Management 30:293–304.

MUSIANI, M. 2003. Conservation biology and management of wolves and wolf-human conflicts in western North America. Ph.D. Thesis, University of Calgary, Calgary, Alberta, Canada.

ORIANS, G.H., and PEARSON, N.E. 1979. On the theory of central place foraging. In: Mitchell, R.D., and Stairs, G.F., eds. Analysis of ecological systems. Columbus: Ohio State University Press. 154–177.

PACKARD, J.M., MECH, L.D., and REAM, R.R. 1992. Weaning in an arctic wolf pack: Behavioral mechanisms. Canadian Journal of Zoology 70:1269–1275.

PAQUET, P.C., WIERZCHOWSKI, J., and CALLAGHAN, C. 1996. Summary report on the effects of human activity on gray wolves in the Bow River Valley, Banff National Park, Alberta. In: Green, J., Pacas, C., Bayley, S., and Cornwell, L., eds. A cumulative effects assessment and futures outlook for the Banff Bow Valley. Prepared for the Banff Bow Valley Study. Ottawa: Department of Canadian Heritage.

STEPHENSON, R.O., and JAMES, D. 1982. Wolf movements and food habits in northwest Alaska. In: Harrington, F.H., and Paquet, P.C., eds. Wolves of the world. New Jersey: Noyes Publications. 223–237.

THORPE, N., EYEGETOK, S., HAKONGAK, N., and QITIRMIUT ELDERS. 2001. The Tuktu and Nogak Project: A caribou chronicle. Final Report to the West Kitikmeot/Slave Study Society, Ikaluktuuttiak, NWT. 160 p.

TIMONEY, K.P., LA ROI, G.H., ZOLTAI, S.C., and ROBINSON, A.L. 1992. The high subarctic forest-tundra of northwestern Canada: Position, width, and vegetation gradients in relation to climate. Arctic 45(1):1–9.

WALTON, L.R., CLUFF, H.D., PAQUET, P.C., and RAMSAY, M.A. 2001. Movement patterns of barren-ground wolves in the central Canadian Arctic. Journal of Mammalogy 82:867–876.

WILLIAMS, T.M. 1990. Summer diet and behavior of wolves denning on barren-ground caribou range in the Northwest Territories, Canada. M.Sc. Thesis, University of Alberta, Edmonton, Alberta, Canada.

ZAR, J.H. 1999. Biostatistical analysis. 4th ed. New Jersey: Prentice Hall. 663 p.

Glossary of Biological Terms

ABC model Model for the genetic basis of flower formation; products of three master genes (*A*, *B*, *C*) control the development of sepals, petals, and stamens and carpels from meristematic tissue.

ABC transporter One of a distinct class of membrane proteins, each a channel or pump for a specific hydrophobic substance (e.g., ions, sugars, amino acids).

ABO blood typing Method of identifying which self-recognition proteins of types A and B are at the surface of an individual's red blood cells; the absence of either type is designated O.

abortion Premature expulsion of embryo or fetus from the uterus; called miscarriage when spontaneous rather than induced.

abscisic acid Plant hormone; stimulates stomatal closure in response to water stress, protein storage in seeds, maturation of embryo sporophyte; possibly induces and maintains dormancy in some plants.

abscission (ab-SIH-zhun) The dropping of leaves, flowers, fruits, or other parts from a plant in response to seasonal change, drought, injury, or nutrient deficiencies.

absorption Of pigments, interception of photon energy. Of cells, uptake of water and solutes from the surroundings. Of digestion, uptake of water and solutes into the internal environment.

absorption spectrum Range of wavelengths that a given type of pigment can absorb.

accessory pigment A pigment that absorbs and transfers light energy to a photosystem; extends the range of light wavelengths for photosynthesis; e.g., a carotenoid.

acclimatization Processes by which the body adjusts in physiology and behavior to a new environment; e.g., after moving from sea level to a high-altitude habitat.

acetylation The attachment of an acetyl group (CH_3CO) to an organic compound.

acetylcholine (ACh) Neurotransmitter with stimulatory or inhibitory effects in the brain, spinal cord, glands, and muscles.

acetyl–CoA Coenzyme A bound to a two-carbon fragment from pyruvate, which it transfers to oxaloacetate for Krebs cycle.

acid [L. *acidus*, sour] Any water-soluble substance that releases hydrogen ions (H^+) in water, yielding a pH below 7.0.

acid–base balance Outcome of control over solute concentrations; extracellular fluid is neither too acidic nor too basic (alkaline).

acidity A solution with a pH of less than 7.

acid rain Acidic precipitation; rain or snow with high levels of sulfur and nitrogen oxides.

acoelomate animal Any invertebrate with no fluid-filled cavity between its gut and body wall; e.g., a flatworm.

acoustical receptor Any mechanoreceptor sensitive to sound.

acoustical signal A sound or sounds used in intraspecific communication.

actin Protein monomer of microfilaments that functions in contraction, cell division, and reinforcing or reconfiguring the shape of a cell or its contents.

action potential Of excitable cells, a self-propagating, abrupt reversal in the voltage difference across the plasma membrane.

activation energy Minimum amount of energy required to start a reaction; enzyme action lowers this energy barrier. Reactions differ in the amount required.

activator A regulatory molecule that binds to specific sequences in DNA and thereby promotes transcription.

active site Chemically stable crevice in an enzyme where substrates bind and a reaction can be catalyzed repeatedly.

active transport Pumping of a specific solute across a cell membrane against its concentration gradient, through the interior of a transport protein. Requires energy input, as from ATP.

adaptation, evolutionary [L. *adaptare*, to fit] Any long-term, heritable aspect of form, function, or behavior that improves an individual's chances of surviving and reproducing; outcome of natural selection and other microevolutionary processes.

adaptation, sensory Of sensory neurons, a decline or cessation of action potentials when a stimulus of constant strength does not end.

adaptive immunity The mechanisms that defend the vertebrate body against specific threats to health, as characterized by self/nonself recognition, specificity, diversity, and memory. All antibody-mediated and cell-mediated responses to antigen.

adaptive radiation A macroevolutionary pattern. A burst of genetic divergences from a lineage that gives rise to many species, each able to use a novel resource or to move into a new, or newly vacated, habitat.

adaptive trait An aspect of form, function, or behavior that helps an individual survive and reproduce under prevailing conditions.

adaptive zone A set of different niches that become be filled by a group of species.

adenine One of four nitrogen-containing bases in nucleotide monomers of DNA or RNA; also refers to a nucleotide having an adenine base component.

ADH Antidiuretic hormone. Hypothalamic hormone released by the posterior pituitary that induces water conservation by kidneys.

adhering junction Complex of adhesion proteins that anchors cells to each other and to extracellular matrixes.

adhesion protein Of multicelled species, a plasma membrane protein that helps cells stick together in tissues and to extracellular matrixes such as basement membrane.

adipose tissue Type of connective tissue having an abundance of fat-storing cells.

ADP Adenosine diphosphate (ah-DEN-uh-seen die-FOSS-fate). A nucleotide with an adenine base and two phosphate groups.

adrenal cortex Outer zone of the adrenal gland; secretes cortisol and aldosterone.

adrenal gland Endocrine gland located on top of the kidney; regulates stress reponses and influences glucose metabolism.

adrenal medulla Inner zone of adrenal gland that secretes epinephrine and norepinephrine.

aerobic respiration (air-OH-bik) [Gk. *aer*, air, + *bios*, life] Oxygen-requiring pathway of ATP formation in mitochondria: from glycolysis, to Krebs cycle and electron transport phosphorylation. Typical net energy yield: 36 ATP per glucose molecule.

African emergence model Model for the origin of modern humans; *Homo sapiens* is said to have originated in Africa, then replaced by archaic *Homo* populations in different parts of the world.

age structure Of a population, the number of individuals in each age category.

agglutination (ah-glue-tin-AY-shun) A vertebrate defense response; antibodies bind antigen and form insoluble clumps that attract phagocytes.

aging Of complex multicelled organisms, a time-dependent progressive deterioration of molecules, cells, tissues, and organs that weakens the body's capacity to function.

AIDS Acquired immune deficiency syndrome. A set of chronic disorders that develops after prolonged infection by HIV has weakened the immune system.

alcohol Organic compound having one or more hydroxyl groups that dissolves easily in water; e.g., ethanol.

alcoholic fermentation An anaerobic ATP-forming pathway using pyruvate and NADH from glycolysis. NADH transfers electrons to an intermediate, acetaldehyde, forming ethanol. Occurs in cytoplasm only. The net yield is 2 ATP from glycolysis; the steps remaining only regenerate NAD^+.

aldosterone (al-DOSS-tuh-rohn) Adrenal cortex hormone; acts in kidneys to promote sodium retention.

alga, plural **algae** Informal term for groups of single-celled or multicelled eukaryotic photoautotrophs, mostly aquatic; e.g., kelps.

algal bloom Rapid, huge increases in algal population sizes after nutrient enrichment of an aquatic habitat.

alkylation Of a molecule, replacement of a hydrogen atom by a hydrocarbon group.

allantois (ah-LAN-twahz) [Gk. *allas*, sausage] One of four extraembryonic membranes of amniote eggs. In reptiles, birds, and some mammals, it exchanges gases and stores metabolic wastes; in humans, it helps form placental blood vessels, urinary bladder.

allele One of two or more molecular forms of a gene at a given locus; alleles arise by mutation and encode slightly different versions of the same trait.

allele frequency Abundance of one allele relative to others at a gene locus among individuals of a population.

allergen A normally harmless substance that can provoke immune responses.

allergy Hypersensitivity to an allergen.

allopatric speciation [Gk. *allos*, different, + L. *patria*, native land] Speciation model. A physical barrier arises and separates populations or subpopulations of a species, ends gene flow, and so favors divergences that result in new species.

alternation of generations The alternation of haploid (gamete-producing) and diploid (spore-producing) phases in the life cycle of an organism.

alternative splicing Event by which the same gene can specify two or more slightly different proteins. All exons in a pre-mRNA transcript of the gene are retained or some are removed and the rest spliced in various combinations for the mature transcript.

altruism (AL-true-IZ-um) Social behavior that decreases the individual's chance of reproductive success while improving the chances for others of its species.

alveolate A type of single-celled eukaryote that has many tiny, membrane-bound sacs just beneath the plasma membrane; e.g., a ciliate, apicomplexan, or dinoflagellate.

alveolus (ahl-VEE-uh-lus), plural **alveoli** At the endings of respiratory bronchioles, one of great numbers of thin-walled, cup-shaped outpouching where air in the lungs exchange gases with blood.

amino acid (uh-MEE-no) A small organic compound with a carboxylic acid group, an amino group, and a characteristic side group (R); monomer of polypeptide chains.

ammonification (uh-moan-ih-fih-KAY-shun) Part of the nitrogen cycle; soil fungi and bacteria decompose nitrogen-containing compounds, the result being ammonia and ammonium ions that plant roots can absorb.

amnion One of the four extraembryonic membranes of amniote eggs; the boundary layer of a fluid-filled, cushioning sac in which the embryo develops.

amniote Type of tetrapod that produces amniote eggs. Major groups are synapsids (mammals and early mammal-like reptiles) and sauropsids ("reptiles" and birds).

amniote egg An egg, often shelled, with four extraembryonic membranes (amnion, chorion, yolk sac, allantois). Pivotal factor in the early evolution of reptiles, birds, and mammals in habitats on land.

amoeba A single-celled amoebozoan that moves on pseudopods. All are predatory or parasitic; none forms colonies.

amphibian A tetrapod, or a descendant of one, having a body plan and reproductive mode between fishes and reptiles.

anaerobic electron transfer (an-uh-ROW-bik) [Gk. *an*, without, + *aer*, air] Of some bacteria and archaeans, ATP formation by way of a flow of electrons through transfer chains in the plasma membrane to a final electron acceptor that is not oxygen.

anaerobic pathway Any set of metabolic reactions for which a substance other than oxygen is the final acceptor of electrons stripped from substrates.

anagenesis A major pattern of speciation. Directional changes in allele frequencies and morphology are confined within a single lineage, and in time a new type differs so much from the ancestral type that it is classified as a separate species.

analogous structures (an-AL-uh-gus) [Gk. *analogos*, similar to one another] Dissimilar body parts that have become similar in structure, function, or both in lineages that are not closely related but were subjected to similar pressures.

anaphase, meiosis Nuclear division stage. In anaphase I, each chromosome and its homologue move to opposite poles; both are still duplicated. In anaphase II, sister chromatids of each chromosome separate from each other, move to opposite poles.

anaphase, mitosis (AN-uh-faze) Nuclear division stage. Sister chromatids of each chromosome are separated from each other and move to opposite spindle poles.

anatomy Study of the internal parts of an organism to ascertain their structure and positions relative to one another. Now conducted at levels of organization from molecules through organ systems.

anemia Type of disorder resulting from having too few functional red blood cells.

aneuploidy (AN-yoo-ploy-dee) A type of chromosome abnormality in which body (somatic) cells have one extra or one less chromosome relative to the parental chromosome number.

angiosperm [Gk. *angeion*, vessel + *spermia*, seed] A flowering plant; its egg-containing ovules mature into seeds within closed, protected chambers called ovaries.

angiotensin II Plasma protein that helps constrict arterioles and stimulates ADH and aldosterone secretion.

animal Any multicelled heterotroph that ingests other organisms or their tissues, develops through a series of embryonic stages, and is motile during part or all of the life cyle. Most species have epithelial tissues and extracellular matrixes.

animal behavior A coordinated response to stimuli that involves motor, neural, and endocrine components. Animal behavior has a genetic basis, it can evolve, and it can be modified by learning.

Animalia Kingdom of animals.

annelid A bilateral invertebrate having a highly segmented body; major groups are polychaetes, oligochaetes, and leeches. Except in leeches, segments have clusters of chitin-reinforced bristles.

annual A plant having a life cycle that starts and ends in one growing season.

anthocyanin One of a class of accessory pigments that reflect red to blue light.

anthropoid One of a group of primates; a monkey, ape, or human.

antibiotic [Gk. *anti*, against] In nature, a metabolic product of certain bacteria and fungi in soil that is toxic to their microbial competitors for nutrients.

antibody Antigen-binding glycoprotein made and secreted only by B cells; during adaptive immunity, activates complement, neutralizes toxins, enhances phagocytosis, immobilizes internal pathogens or parasites.

antibody-mediated immune response One of two arms of adaptive immunity in which antibodies are produced in response to a specific antigen; mediated by B cells.

anticodon Series of three nucleotide bases in tRNA that can base-pair with mRNA codons.

antigen (AN-tih-jen) Any molecular pattern that triggers an immune response.

antigen–MHC complex Fragment(s) of antigen bound to MHC markers at a cell's plasma membrane; recognized by T cells.

antigen-presenting cell Lymphocyte that binds and processes antigen to present to T cells as antigen–MHC complexes; secretes cytokines that stimulate proliferation and differentiation of lymphocytes.

antioxidant Any enzyme or cofactor that helps neutralize free radicals before they damage tissues.

anus The terminal opening of a complete digestive system.

aorta (ay-OR-tah) Of vertebrates, the main artery of systemic circulation.

apical dominance (AY-pih-kul) Growth-inhibiting effect on lateral (axillary) buds, caused by auxin diffusing down a shoot tip from the terminal bud.

apical meristem (MARE-ih-stem) [L. *apex*, top, + Gk. *meristos*, divisible] Mass of dividing cells at root tips and shoot tips.

apicomplexan A parasitic alveolate having a unique microtubular device at its anterior end; the device attaches to and penetrates a host cell.

apoptosis (APP-oh-TOE-sis) Programmed cell death. A cell is induced to commit suicide as part of growth, development, and maintenance of a multicelled body.

appendicular skeleton (ap-en-DIK-yoo-lahr) Bones of limbs, hips, and shoulders.

appendix Small, narrow outpouching from the cecum, vulnerable to infection.

aquaporin A type of passive transporter that assists diffusion of water molecules across the plasma membrane.

Archaea Domain of prokaryotic species; one of two lineages that evolved shortly after life originated. Archaeans have many unique molecular and biochemical traits but also share some traits with bacteria and other traits with eukaryotic species.

Archean Eon extending from the time that life originated, 3.8 billion years ago, to 2.5 billion years ago.

archipelago A chain or cluster of islands, often of volcanic origin in the open ocean.

area effect Biogeographical pattern; larger islands support more species than smaller ones at equivalent distances from sources of colonizer species.

arteriole (ar-TEER-ee-ole) The type of blood vessel in between arteries and capillaries. Selectively distributing more of the total blood volume to different organs in a given interval requires controls over dilation and constriction of the diameter of arterioles.

arteriosclerosis Chronic disease in which the wall of arteries thickens abnormally, hardens, and loses its elasticity.

artery A thick-walled, muscular, rapid-transport vessel that smooths out pulses of pressure generated by heartbeats.

arthropod Type of invertebrate having a hardened exoskeleton and specialized segments with jointed appendages; e.g., millipedes, spiders, lobsters, insects.

artificial selection Manipulation of the reproduction of a species as by breeding practices. Only individuals of a captive population that display a valued trait are allowed to reproduce, the goal being to increase the trait's magnitude and frequency over the generations.

ascospore Sexual spore of sac fungi.

asexual reproduction Any reproductive mode by which offspring arise from one parent and inherit that parent's genes only; e.g., prokaryotic fission, transverse fission, budding, vegetative propagation.

atherosclerosis A medical condition in which arteries narrow in diameter as lipids and other deposits accumulate in their wall.

atmosphere, Earth's The volume of gases, water vapor, and airborne particles that envelopes Earth's surface.

atom The smallest unit of an element that still retains the element's properties.

atomic number The number of protons in the nucleus of atoms of a given element.

ATP Adenosine triphosphate (ah-DEN-uh-seen try-FOSS-fate). A type of nucleotide that functions as the main energy carrier between reaction sites in cells. Consists of the base adenine, the five-carbon sugar ribose, and three phosphate groups.

ATP/ADP cycle How a cell regenerates its ATP supply. ADP forms when ATP gives up a phosphate group, then ATP forms as ADP binds to inorganic phosphate or a phosphate group split from a molecule.

ATP synthase A type of membrane-bound active transport protein that also catalyzes the formation of ATP.

australopith (OHSS-trah-low-pith) [L. *australis*, southern, + Gk. *pithekos*, ape] One of the early hominids of Africa.

autoimmune response Inappropriate lymphocyte attack on normal body cells.

automated DNA sequencing Extremely rapid, robotic method of identifying the nucleotide sequence of a region of DNA. Gel electrophoresis and laser detection of fluorescent tracers are part of method.

autonomic nerve (AH-toe-NOM-ik) One of the nerves from the central nervous system that helps control smooth muscle, cardiac muscle, and glands of viscera.

autosome Of a sexually reproducing species, any chromosome of a type that is the same in both males and females.

autotroph [Gk. *auto*, self, and *trophos*, feeder] An organism that synthesizes its own food from simple inorganic compounds in its environment with energy captured from the sun or from oxidizing inorganic substances; e.g., a photoautotroph or chemoautotroph.

auxin (OX-in) A type of plant hormone that stimulates lengthening of shoots and coleoptiles, vascular cambium activity, and vascular tissue differentiation; also inhibits lateral bud formation, abscission, and fruit formation; responsive to gravity and light.

axial skeleton (AX-ee-uhl) Skull, backbone, ribs, and breastbone (sternum).

axon A neuron's signal-conducting zone; action potentials typically self-propagate away from the cell body on this slender, typically long process.

B lymphocyte B cell. Type of white blood cell central to immune responses; only cell that makes antibodies.

bacillus Rod-shaped prokaryotic cell.

Bacteria Domain of prokaryotic species; the first kinds of cells that formed after life originated. Collectively, bacteria are the most metabolically diverse organisms. Most kinds are chemoheterotrophs.

bacterial chromosome A circular, double-stranded molecule of prokaryotic DNA.

bacteriophage (bak-TEER-ee-oh-fahj) One of a class of viruses that infects bacteria.

balanced polymorphism An outcome of natural selection against homozygotes, so that two or more alleles for a trait are being maintained in the population.

bark Of woody plants, all tissues that are external to the vascular cambium.

Barr body Of the two X chromosomes in the somatic cells of female mammals, the one that has been condensed.

basal body An organelle that started out as a centriole, the source of a 9+2 array of microtubules in a cilium or flagellum. It remains below the finished array.

base Any water-soluble substance that releases hydroxyl ions in water to yield a pH greater than 7.0. Also the nitrogen-containing component of a nucleotide.

base-pair substitution Mutation in which one nucleotide is wrongly substituted for another during DNA replication.

base sequence Linear order of nucleotides that compose a DNA or RNA strand.

basidiospore Sexual spore of club fungi.

basophil White blood cell circulating in blood that secretes histamine and other substances with roles in inflammation.

bell curve Idealized statistical distribution of the continuous variation in a population for a trait of interest.

biennial (bi-EN-yul) A flowering plant that requires two growing seasons to complete its life cycle; flowers and fruits form in the second season.

big bang Model for the origin of universe, by a nearly instantaneous distribution of all matter and energy through all of space.

bilateral symmetry Body plan in which the main axis divides the body into two halves that are mirror images of one another.

bile Mix of salts, cholesterol, and pigments made by the liver and used in fat digestion.

binary fission Asexual reproductive mode of certain invertebrates; the body splits spontaneously, then both parts grow what is missing. *See also* Prokaryotic fission.

binding energy Energy released as weak bonds form between a substrate, enzyme, and any cofactor.

binomial system A scientific system of naming species, whereby each kind of organism receives a two-part name. The first part indicates the genus; the second part is the species epithet (descriptor).

biodiversity [Gk. *bios*, life] Biological diversity in an environment, as measured by the number of species and their relative abundances.

biofilm Large microbial populations that anchored themselves to epithelium, rocks, or other surfaces by their own secretions.

biogeochemical cycle Slow movement of an element from environmental reservoirs, through food webs, then back.

biogeographic realm [Gk. *bios*, life, + *geographein*, to describe Earth's surface] One of many vast expanses of land where one can expect to find communities of certain types of plants and animals.

biogeography Scientific study of patterns in the geographic distribution of species and communities.

biological clock Internal time-measuring mechanism by which individuals adjust their activities seasonally, daily, or both in response to environmental cues.

biological magnification Ever increasing concentration of a slowly degradable or nondegradable substance in body tissues as it is passed along food chains.

biological species concept Definition of a sexually reproducing species as one or more populations of individuals that interbreed under natural conditions, produce fertile offspring, and are reproductively isolated from other such populations.

biology The scientific study of life.

bioluminescence Fluorescent light formed when certain organisms convert chemical bond energy to photon energy.

biomass Of an ecosystem, the combined weight of all organisms at a trophic level.

biomass pyramid Chart in which the size of successive tiers depicts the measured

biomass (dry weight) of an ecosystem's producers, consumers, and decomposers.

biome One of the finer subdivisions of a biogeographic realm.

biosphere [Gk. *bios*, life, + *sphaira*, globe] All regions of Earth's waters, crust, and atmosphere in which organisms live.

biosynthetic pathway Any metabolic pathway by which one or more organic compounds are synthesized.

biotic potential The maximum rate of increase per individual for any population that is growing under ideal conditions.

bipedalism Habitually walking upright on two feet, as by ostriches and hominids.

bipolar spindle Of eukaryotic cells, a dynamic array of microtubules that moves chromosomes with respect to its two poles during mitosis or meiosis.

bird A warm-blooded, feathered amniote classified as a sauropsid; the dinosaurs and crocodilians are its closest relatives.

blastocyst (BLASS-tuh-sist) A type of blastula with a surface layer of blastomeres, a cavity filled with their secretions, and an inner cell mass; e.g., a human blastocyst.

blastomere One of the small, nucleated cells that forms during the cleavage stage of animal development.

blastula A ball of blastomeres and a cavity filled with their own secretions; outcome of the cleavage stage of animal development.

blood A fluid connective tissue that is the transport medium of circulatory systems. Mostly water in which ions, molecules, blood cells, and platelets are dissolved.

blood–brain barrier Specialized blood capillaries that protect the brain and spinal cord by exerting some control over which solutes enter the cerebrospinal fluid.

blood pressure Fluid pressure generated by heartbeats that causes blood circulation.

bone Type of vertebrate organ consisting of mineral-hardened connective tissue. Functions in movement, mineral storage, and protection; blood cells form in some.

bone remodeling Ongoing depositions and withdrawals of mineral ions from bone by certain bone cells; their antagonistic actions adjust bone strength as well as calcium and phosphorus levels in blood.

bone tissue Of vertebrate skeletons, a tissue of osteoblast secretions, which have become hardened with mineral ions.

bony fish Aquatic vertebrate that has an endoskeleton, including a cranium, mostly of bone tissue.

boreal forest *Taiga*. One of the extensive northern coniferous forests of Europe, Asia, and North America.

bottleneck Severe reduction in the size of a population, brought about by intense selection pressure or a natural calamity.

Bowman's capsule First part of a nephron, where its wall balloons back on itself in the shape of a double-layer cup; under the force of blood pressure, water and solutes are filtered out of blood and into the cup.

brain Of most nervous systems, a major integrating center that receives, processes, and often stores sensory input, and issues coordinated commands for responses.

brain stem The most ancient nerve tissue in all three divisions of a vertebrate brain.

bronchiole Finely branched airway that is part of the bronchial tree inside a lung.

bronchus, plural **bronchi** (BRONG-cuss, BRONG-kee) [Gk. *bronchos*, windpipe] A tubular airway that starts at the trachea and becomes the main branch into a lung.

brown alga A stramenopile; a multicelled marine photoautotroph with an abundance of the pigment fucoxanthin; e.g., kelps.

bryophyte Nonvascular land plant. The haploid stage dominates its life cycle, and its sperm require standing water to reach eggs. A moss, liverwort, or hornwort.

bud A dormant shoot, mostly meristematic tissue and often sheathed in small, young leaves. A lateral (axillary) bud forms in a leaf axil; a terminal bud forms at a shoot tip and is the main zone of primary growth.

buffer system A weak acid and the salt that forms when it dissolves. The two work as a pair to counter slight shifts in pH.

bulk Of the vertebrate gut, the volume of undigested material in the small intestine that cannot be decreased by absorption.

bulk flow The mass movement of one or more substances in the same direction, most often in response to pressure.

C3 plant Type of plant in which three-carbon PGA is the first stable intermediate to form after carbon fixation.

C4 plant Type of plant in which four-carbon oxaloacetate is the first stable intermediate to form after initial carbon fixation; in these plants, carbon is fixed twice, in two different types of photosynthetic cells.

calcium pump Active transport protein; pumps calcium ions across a cell membrane against their concentration gradient.

Calvin–Benson cycle Cyclic reactions that form sugar and regenerate RuBP in the second stage of photosynthesis. The reactions require carbon (from carbon dioxide). They use energy from ATP and hydrogens and electrons from NADPH, both of which form in the first stage.

CAM plant Type of plant that conserves water by opening stomata only at night, when it fixes carbon by repeated turns of the C4 pathway; stands for crassulacean acid metabolism.

camera eye A camera-like eyeball having an inner darkened chamber, one opening for light, and a retina (like film) on which visual stimuli are focused. Cephalopods and vertebrates have camera eyes.

camouflage Body coloration, patterning, form, or behavior that helps predators or prey blend with the surroundings and possibly escape detection.

cancer A malignant neoplasm; a mass of abnormally dividing cells that can leave their home tissue and invade and form new masses in other parts of the body.

capillary, blood Smallest diameter blood vessel; the exchanges between interstitial fluid and blood occur across its wall, which is only one cell thick.

capillary bed One of the diffusion zones for circulatory systems; great numbers of blood capillaries exchange substances with interstitial fluid.

capture–recapture method Individuals of a mobile species are captured (or selected) at random, marked, then released so they can mix with unmarked individuals. One or more samples are taken. The ratio of marked to unmarked individuals is used for estimating the size of the population.

carbamino hemoglobin $HbCO_2$, the form in which 30 percent or so of the CO_2 in blood is transported.

carbohydrate Any molecule of carbon, hydrogen, and oxygen typically in a 1:2:1 ratio. Main kinds are monosaccharides, oligosaccharides, and polysaccharides. They serve as structural materials, energy stores, and transportable energy forms.

carbon cycle Atmospheric cycle. Carbon moves from its environmental reservoirs (sediments, rocks, the ocean), through the atmosphere (mostly as CO_2), food webs, and back to the reservoirs.

carbon fixation Process by which any autotrophic cell incorporates carbon atoms into a stable organic compound. Different cells get carbon dioxide from the air or dissolved in water.

carbonic anhydrase Enzyme in red blood cells that speeds formation of bicarbonate from CO_2 and water.

carcinogen (kar-SIN-uh-jen) Any agent or substance that can cause cancer.

cardiac conduction system [Gk. *kardia*, heart, + *kyklos*, circle] A set of specialized cardiac muscle cells that initiate and send signals that make regular cardiac muscle cells contract. The SA node, AV node, and junctional fibers that link them.

cardiac cycle A recurring sequence of muscle contraction and relaxation that corresponds to one heartbeat.

cardiac muscle tissue A contractile tissue present only in the heart wall.

cardiac pacemaker Sinoatrial (SA) node; a cluster of self-excitatory cardiac muscle cells that spontaneously started contracting first; they continue to set the normal rate of heartbeat.

carnivore An animal that eats primarily the flesh of other animals.

carnivorous plant A plant that traps and digests insects and other small animals, and absorbs the released nutrients, which are otherwise scarce in its habitat.

carotenoid One of a class of accessory pigments in photosynthesis that reflect red, orange, and yellow light. One kind, beta-carotene, is a precursor of vitamin A.

carpel (KAR-pul) Female reproductive parts of flowers; a sticky or hairlike stigma, often stalked, above a chamber (ovary) in which one or more ovules mature into seeds.

carrying capacity Maximum number of individuals in a population or species that a given environment can sustain indefinitely.

cartilage Connective tissue consisting of fine collagen fibers packed in a secreted, rubbery matrix that resists compression.

cartilaginous fish Jawed fish having an endoskeleton, including a cranium, of cartilage and large fins; e.g., sharks.

Casparian strip A waxy, impermeable band that seals abutting cell walls of endodermis (and exodermis) in roots; forces water and solutes to pass through cells, which helps control the type and amount of solutes that enter the vascular cylinder.

catastrophism Idea that abrupt changes in the geologic and fossil records are evidence of divinely invoked catastrophes.

cDNA DNA synthesized from an mRNA transcript through the use of the enzyme reverse transcriptase.

cell Smallest unit that still displays the properties of life; it has the capacity to survive and reproduce on its own.

cell communication How free-living cells or cells of a multicelled species coordinate activities; they send, receive, transduce, and respond to signaling molecules.

cell cortex A dynamic mesh of crosslinked cytoskeletal elements just underneath the plasma membrane and attached to it.

cell count The number of cells of a given type present in one microliter of blood.

cell cycle Of eukaryotic cells, a series of events from the time a cell forms until it reproduces. A cycle consists of interphase, mitosis, and cytoplasmic division.

cell differentiation In developing embryos of multicelled organisms, the process by which different cell lineages selectively express a different fraction of their genome and thereby become specialized in their composition, structure, and function.

cell junction Of a tissue, any molecular structure that connects adjoining cells physically, chemically, or both at their plasma membranes.

cell-mediated immune response Actions of sensitized phagocytes and cytotoxic T cells that directly destroy infected or cancerous body cells.

cell plate formation The mechanism of cytoplasmic division in plant cells. After nuclear division, vesicles derived from Golgi bodies deposit the material for a cross-wall that cuts through the cytoplasm and connects to the parent cell wall.

cell theory All organisms consist of one or more cells, the cell is the smallest unit of organization still displaying the properties of life, and life's continuity arises directly from growth and division of single cells.

cell wall Of many cells (not animal cells), a semirigid but permeable structure that surrounds the plasma membrane; helps a cell retain its shape and resist rupturing.

Cenozoic The modern geologic era, from 65 million years ago to the present.

centipede Venomous predatory arthropod with many segments having paired legs.

central nervous system Of vertebrates, the brain and spinal cord.

central vacuole In many mature, living plant cells, an organelle that stores amino acids, sugars, and some wastes; when it enlarges during growth, it forces the cell to enlarge and increase its surface area.

centriole A barrel-shaped structure that arises from a centrosome and organizes newly forming microtubules into a 9+2 array inside a cilium or flagellum.

centromere Of a eukaryotic chromosome, a constricted region having binding sites (kinetochores) for spindle microtubules.

centrosome Dense mass of material in the cytoplasm of eukaryotic cells from which microtubules start to grow.

cephalization (SEF-ah-lah-ZAY-shun) [Gk. *kephalikos*, head] During the evolution of most kinds of animals, the increasing concentration of sensory structures and nerve cells at the anterior end of the body.

cephalochordate Lancelet. A filter-feeding invertebrate chordate with tapered ends.

cephalopod Soft-bodied mollusk with a closed circulatory system. Moves by jet propulsion of water from a siphon; e.g., squids, octopuses, chambered nautilus.

cerebellum (ser-ah-BELL-um) Hindbrain region with reflex centers that maintain posture and smoothing limb movements.

cerebral cortex Thin surface layer of two cerebral hemispheres; its interneurons receive, integrate, and store sensory information and coordinate responses.

cerebrospinal fluid Clear extracellular fluid that bathes and protects the brain and spinal cord; contained in a system of canals and chambers.

cerebrum (suh-REE-bruhm) A forebrain region concerned with olfactory input and motor responses. In mammals, it evolved into the most complex integrating center.

charophyte A type of photoautotroph once grouped with other green algae but now known to be more closely related to land plants; e.g., desmids, stoneworts.

checkpoint gene A gene that encodes a protein that can help delay, advance, or block the cell cycle when something goes wrong during DNA replication or repair.

chemical bond A union between the electron structures of two or more atoms.

chemical energy Potential energy in the bonds between atoms in molecules.

chemical equilibrium No net change in concentrations of reactants and products in a reversible chemical reaction.

chemical synapse (SIN-aps) A cleft between a presynaptic neuron and postsynaptic cell that neurotransmitters diffuse across.

chemiosmotic theory Well-supported but confusingly named theory of ATP formation by way of an electrochemical gradient. The action of electron transfer chains causes H+ to accumulate inside a membrane-bound compartment. ATP forms as H+ follows the resulting concentration/electric gradients across the membrane through ATP synthases.

chemoautotroph (KEE-moe-AH-toe-trofe) Any prokaryotic cell that makes its own food by oxidizing inorganic substances.

chemoreceptor Sensory receptor; detects dissolved ions or molecules in fluid.

chlamydia A group of bacteria; all are intracellular parasites that cannot make ATP; they pilfer it from animal cells.

chlorofluorocarbon (KLORE-oh-FLOOR-oh-car-bun) CFC; an organic compound that contains chlorine and fluorine; contributes to ozone thinning in the atmosphere.

chlorophyll *a* (KLOR-uh-fill) [Gk. *chloros*, green, + *phyllon*, leaf] In plants and algae, a pigment that is a receptor for the photon energy required to start photosynthesis; it absorbs mainly violet and red light and reflects or transmits green light.

chlorophyll *b* An accessory pigment that absorbs mainly blue and orange light.

chlorophyte Formal taxon for most species of green algae. Single-celled, multicelled, and colonial photoautotrophs of mostly aquatic habitats, closely related to land plants; e.g., *Ulva, Chlamydomonas, Chlorella.*

chloroplast Organelle of photosynthesis in plants and algae. Two outer membranes enclose a semifluid interior, the stroma. A third membrane forms a compartment inside that functions in ATP and NADPH formation; sugars form in the stroma.

choanoflagellate Single-celled eukaryote having a microvilli collar around a single flagellum at their anterior end. A sister taxon of animals and fungi.

cholecystokinin (CCK) A hormone that stimulates gallbladder contractions and the secretion of pancreatic enzymes; also may suppress appetite.

chordate Animal with a notochord, dorsal hollow nerve cord, pharynx, gill slits in the pharynx wall, and a tail that extends past the anus. These traits develop in embryos but some may not persist in the adult form.

chorion (CORE-ee-on) An extraembryonic membrane of amniote eggs; becomes part of the placenta. Villi form at its surface and facilitate the exchange of substances between the embryo and mother.

chromatid One of the two DNA molecules of a duplicated chromosome that remain attached to each other at the centromere region during nuclear division.

chromatin All of the DNA molecules and associated proteins in a nucleus.

chromosome In eukaryotic cells, a linear DNA double helix with many histones and other proteins attached. *See also* Bacterial chromosome.

chromosome number The sum of all of the chromosomes in cells of a given type.

chrysophyte One of the stramenopiles; most are single-celled photoautotrophs and components of phytoplankton; e.g., coccolithophores, diatoms.

chyme Semidigested food in the gut.

chytrid A flagellated intracellular parasite of a fungal group, the microsporidians.

ciliate An alveolate having arrays of cilia at its surface; traditionally called a ciliated protozoan. Most are free-living predators.

cilium, plural **cilia** A motile structure with a 9+2 array of microtubules that projects from the plasma membrane of certain eukaryotic cells. Modified cilia, such as those of hair cells, have sensory functions.

circadian rhythm (ser-KAYD-ee-un) [L. *circa*, about, + *dies*, day] Any biological activity repeated in cycles, each about twenty-four hours long, independently of any shifts in environmental conditions.

circulatory system Organ system that rapidly transports substances to and from cells; typically consists of a heart, blood vessels, and blood. Helps stabilize body temperature and pH in some animals.

clade [Gk. *klados*-, branch] All species that share a unique trait, being descended from an ancestral species in which the trait first evolved.

cladogenesis One speciation pattern. A lineage branches when one or more of its populations or subpopulations become reproductively isolated, and then genetic divergences result in new species.

cladogram Evolutionary tree diagram that depicts relative relatedness among groups. Each branch is monopyletic; it includes only an ancestral species in which a unique trait first evolved and all of its descendants.

classification system A way to organize and retrieve information about species.

cleavage Early stage of development in animals. Mitotic cell divisions cut up a fertilized egg into many smaller, nucleated cells (blastomeres); the original volume of egg cytoplasm does not increase.

climate Prevailing weather conditions of a region; e.g., temperature, cloud cover, wind speed, rainfall, and humidity.

climax community An array of species that develops by ecological succession. By a traditional model, it has stabilized under prevailing habitat conditions.

cloaca (kloe-AY-kuh) Last gut chamber or duct of some animals, roles in excretion, reproduction, and sometimes respiration.

clone A genetically identical copy of DNA, a cell, or a multicelled organism.

cloning A method used in recombinant DNA technology to make multiple copies of a DNA fragment. Also, manipulated reproductive interventions that bypass sexual reproduction; e.g., embryo cloning, adult cloning, and therapeutic cloning.

cloning vector Any DNA molecule that can accept foreign DNA and that can be replicated inside a host cell.

club fungus Fungus that produces sexual spores in a club-shaped cell, a basidium.

cnidarian (nye-DAR-ee-un) A type of radial invertebrate having epithelial tissues and a saclike gut. The only animal that makes nematocysts.

coal A nonrenewable energy source that formed more than 280 million years ago from submerged, undecayed, and slowly compacted plant remains.

coccolithophore A single-celled marine autotroph having calcium carbonate plates; one of the chrysophytes that are abundant in phytoplankton and the leading source of calcium deposits on the seafloor.

coccus A spherical prokaryotic cell.

cochlea [Gk. *koklias*, snail] A fluid-filled, coiled structure in the inner ear; transduces sound waves into action potentials.

codominance A condition in which a pair of nonidentical alleles that influence two different phenotypes are expressed at the same time in heterozygotes.

codon A base triplet; a linear sequence of three nucleotides in an mRNA transcript; a code for an amino acid or a termination signal that gets translated during protein synthesis.

coelom (SEE-lum) Between the gut and body wall, a cavity lined with peritoneum.

coenzyme An organic molecule that is a necessary participant in some enzymatic reactions; helps catalysis by donating or accepting electrons or functional groups; e.g., a vitamin, ATP, NAD$^+$.

coevolution The joint evolution of two species interacting so closely that a change in the structure, function, or behavior of one exerts selection pressure on the other over the generations.

cofactor A metal ion or a coenzyme that assists an enzyme in catalysis by accepting or donating electrons or functional groups.

cohesion A capacity to resist rupturing when placed under tension (stretched).

cohesion–tension theory Explanation of how water is transported from roots to leaves in plants. Water evaporation from leaves pulls water up in xylem by creating a continuous negative pressure (tension) that extends to roots.

cohort Group of individuals of the same age.

coitus Sexual intercourse.

coleoptile A thin tissue sheath that forms in embryo sporophytes of grasses; protects a primary shoot while growth is pushing it through soil after a seed germinates.

collar cell A sponge cell having a ring of food-trapping villi around a flagellum.

collecting duct A small tube into which as many as eight nephrons drain and that in turn drains into the renal pelvis.

collenchyma (coll-ENG-kih-mah) One of three simple plant tissues. Flexibly supports rapidly growing plant parts. Its elongated cells, alive at maturity, have a pectin-rich primary wall that is thickened where three or more collenchyma cells abut.

colon (CO-lun) Large intestine.

commensalism An ecological interaction in which one species benefits directly and one or more others are affected little, if at all.

communication display A social signal, often ritualized with intended changes in functions of common patterns.

communication protein A membrane protein that helps form an open channel between the cytoplasm of adjoining cells.

communication signal A social cue that is encoded in stimuli, such as the body's surface coloration or patterning, odors, sounds, and postures.

community All populations of all species in a habitat.

community structure The number of species and their relative abundances in a habitat, which shift over time.

companion cell Specialized parenchyma cell that helps load sugars into conducting cells of phloem.

comparative morphology [Gk. *morph*, form] Scientific study of comparable external body parts of embryonic stages and adult forms of major lineages.

compartmentalization In some plants, a defense response to attack, including secretion of sticky resins and toxins.

competition, exploitative An ecological interaction in which different species have equal access to a resource but one is better at exploiting it.

competition, interference An ecological interaction in which one species restricts or blocks access of another species to a resource regardless of its abundance.

competition, interspecific An ecological interaction in which the individuals of different species are competing for a share of resources.

competition, intraspecific An ecological interaction in which individuals of a population compete for resources.

competitive exclusion Theory that two or more species that require identical resources cannot coexist indefinitely.

complement system Set of proteins that circulate in inactive form in blood. Active kinds attract phagocytes and enhance their binding to antigen, promote inflammation, and induce lysis of pathogens during both innate and adaptive immune responses.

complete digestive system A tubular digestive system having a mouth at one end and an anus at the other.

composite signal A communication signal with more than one information-laden cue.

compound Molecule consisting of two or more elements in proportions that do not vary, as they can in mixtures.

compound eye Crustacean or insect eye having multiple rodlike units, each of which samples part of the visual field.

concentration gradient Difference in the number of molecules or ions of any one substance between two adjoining regions.

condensation reaction Type of chemical reaction in which two molecules become covalently bonded as a larger molecule; water often forms as a by-product.

conduction, heat Of two objects in contact with each other, an exchange of heat as a result of a thermal gradient between them.

cone Reproductive structure of certain seed-bearing plants; has clusters of scales with exposed ovules on their surface.

cone cell A vertebrate photoreceptor that responds to intense light and contributes to sharp daytime vision and color perception.

conifer A type of gymnosperm adapted to conserve water through droughts and cold winters. Cone-producing woody trees or shrubs with thickly cuticled needlelike or scalelike leaves.

conjugation Among prokaryotic species, a mode of gene transfer that is possible when one of the cells has an F plasmid. Also a sexual reproductive mode among some single-celled eukaryotes.

connective tissue Most abundant type of animal tissue. Soft connective tissues differ in the amounts and arrangements of fibroblasts, fibers, ground substance. Adipose tissue, cartilage, bone tissue, and blood are specialized types.

conservation biology An international field of inquiry. Biodiversity, as measured by species richness and abundances, is being surveyed and its evolutionary and ecological origins are being identified. Methods to maintain and use biodiversity for the benefit of the human population are being identified.

conservation of mass, law of The total mass of all substances entering a reaction equals the total mass of all products.

consumer Type of heterotroph that feeds on the tissues of other organisms as its source of carbon and energy.

continuous variation Of individuals of a population, a range of small differences in the phenotypic expression of a trait.

contractile cell A cell having cytoskeletal elements that help it contract (shorten) in response to stimulation and then lengthen (relax) and return to a resting position.

contractile ring mechanism Mechanism of cytoplasmic division of animal cells. Just beneath the plasma membrane, a thin band of contractile filaments around the cell midsection contracts and pinches the cytoplasm in two.

contractile vacuole [L. *contractus*, to draw together] Organelle in some single-celled eukaryotes that collects excess water in the cell body and then expels it.

control group In experimental tests, a group used as a standard for comparison against one or more experimental groups.

convection Air or water movement driven by a temperature gradient; also the transfer of heat by moving molecules.

convergent evolution In response to similar environmental pressures, evolutionarily distant lineages slowly evolve in similar ways and end up alike in some aspect of biochemistry, morphology, or behavior.

coral reef A formation of accumulated hard parts of corals and other organisms in warm, clear waters between latitudes 25° north and south.

core temperature The internal temperature of a large-bodied animal.

cork Tissue component of bark with many suberized layers; waterproofs, insulates, and protects woody stem and root surfaces.

cork cambium A lateral meristem, the descendants of which replace epidermis with cork on woody plant parts.

cornea Transparent, light-admitting part of the outer layer of a vertebrate eyeball.

corpus luteum (CORE-pus LOO-tee-um) A glandular structure that forms from cells of a ruptured follicle after ovulation; its progesterone and estrogen secretions help thicken the endometrium in preparation for a pregnancy.

cortex Generally, a rindlike layer. In cells, a mesh of cytoskeletal elements beneath the plasma membrane. In vascular plants, a ground tissue, mostly parenchyma, that supports parts and stores food.

cortisol A hormone that helps maintain the blood level of glucose between meals; its level rises when the body is stressed.

cotyledon (KOT-uhl-EE-dun) Seed leaf; part of a flowering plant embryo. In eudicots, two cotyledons absorb nutrients from endosperm, emerge aboveground as the seed germinates, and transfer nutrients that sustain early growth; photosynthetic before true leaves form. In most monocots, one small cotyledon helps transfer nutrients from endosperm to the embryo, but it remains underground when a seed germinates and is never photosynthetic.

countercurrent exchange In fish gills, the exchange of gases between blood flowing one way in blood vessels and water that is flowing over the vessels in the opposite direction. At membrane proteins of the ascending and descending limbs of the loop of Henle of a nephron, the pumping of specific solutes into and out of interstitial fluid in ways that alter its composition.

countercurrent flow Any movement of two fluids in opposing directions.

courtship display A pattern of ritualized social behavior between potential mates.

covalent bond (koe-VAY-lunt) [L. *con*, together, + *valere*, to be strong] A sharing of one or more electrons between two atoms. In a polar covalent bond, the atoms share electrons unequally; in a nonpolar covalent bond, each atom gets an equal share of the electrons.

craniate A vertebrate that has its brain protected inside a cranium; all modern fishes, amphibians, reptiles, birds, and mammals are craniates.

creatine phosphate Organic compound that can transfer phosphate to ADP in a fast, short-term, ATP-generating pathway.

CRH Corticotropin-releasing hormone; a hypothalamic releaser that stimulates the secretion of ACTH from the adrenal gland.

cross-bridge formation In sarcomeres of muscle fibers, a reversible, ATP-driven interaction between an actin filament and myosin head that results in a short power stroke; the basis of muscle contraction.

crossing over At prophase I of meiosis, reciprocal exchange of segments between two nonsister chromatids of a pair of homologous chromosomes. Puts novel combinations of alleles in gametes.

crust, Earth's Outer zone of low-density rocks resting on Earth's mantle.

crustacean One of the abundant "insects of the seas," mostly marine arthropods having a hardened, flexible exoskeleton and pairs of jointed appendages.

culture Sum of behavior patterns of a social group, passed between generations by learning and symbolic behavior.

cuticle (KEW-tih-kull) Of plants, a cover of transparent waxes and cutin on the outer wall of epidermal cells. Of annelids, a thin, flexible coat. Of arthropods, a lightweight exoskeleton hardened with chitin.

cutin Lipid polymer synthesized by land plants and deposited in cell walls and on the outer surface of epidermal cells.

cyanobacterium A type of single-celled photoautotroph; the first to use a noncyclic pathway of photosynthesis, which slowly enriched the early atmosphere with oxygen.

cycad A gymnosperm of subtropical or tropical habitats; pollen-bearing and seed-bearing strobili on separate plants.

cyclic AMP (SIK-lik) A nucleotide that is often a second messenger; relays a signal from outside through the cytoplasm.

cyclic pathway of ATP formation Oldest photosynthetic pathway. Photon energy forces electrons out of membrane-bound photosystems to transfer systems, which return them to the photosystems. Electron flow across the membrane sets up H^+ gradients that drive ATP formation.

cyst Of many microbes, a resting stage with a secreted cover. Also an abnormal, fluid-filled sac in skin with no opening.

cytochrome (SIGH-toe-krome) An iron-containing protein molecule of electron transfer systems.

cytokinesis (SIGH-toe-kih-NEE-sis) [Gk. *kinesis*, motion] Cytoplasmic division.

cytokinin (SIGH-toe-KYE-nin) A type of plant hormone; promotes cell division and leaf expansion, and retards leaf aging.

cytoplasm (SIGH-toe-plaz-um) All cell parts, particles, and semifluid substances between the plasma membrane and the nucleus or nucleoid.

cytoplasmic division Cytokinesis. After nuclear division, a splitting of the parent cell cytoplasm that completes formation of daughter cells.

cytoplasmic localization The accumulation of different kinds of proteins or RNAs in specific regions of the egg cytoplasm. These "maternal messages" are partitioned into different blastomeres at the cleavage stage of animal development.

cytosine (SIGH-toe-seen) One of the four nitrogen-containing bases in nucleotide monomers of DNA or RNA; also applies to a nucleotide that contains a cysteine base.

cytoskeleton In a eukaryotic cell, the dynamic framework of diverse protein filaments that structurally support, organize, and move the cell and internal structures. Prokaryotic cells have a few similar protein filaments.

cytotoxic T cell T lymphocyte that acts in adaptive immune responses; touch-kills infected or cancerous body cells.

day-neutral plant A plant that flowers when mature, independently of seasons.

decomposer [L. *dis*–, to pieces] One of the prokaryotic or fungal heterotrophs that obtains carbon and energy by breaking down wastes or remains of organisms. The collective action of decomposers helps cycle nutrients to producers in ecosystems.

deforestation Removal of all trees from a large tract of land.

degradative pathway Any of the stepwise series of metabolic reactions that break down organic compounds.

deletion Loss of a chromosome segment; often leads to genetic disorders. Also the loss of one or more nucleotide bases from a DNA molecule.

demographics The vital statistics of a population; e.g., size, age structure.

demographic transition model Model that correlates changes in population growth with stages of economic development; may no longer apply to developing countries, which now compete in a global market.

denaturation (deh-NAY-chur-AY-shun) Disruption of hydrogen bonds and other interactions holding a molecule in its three-dimensional shape, which thereby changes. Increases in temperature, shifts in pH, and detergents can cause it.

dendrite (DEN-drite) [Gk. *dendron*, tree] Short, slender extension from cell body of a neuron; commonly a signal input zone.

dendritic cell Phagocytic white blood cell; mainly presents antigen to naive T cells.

denitrification (DEE-nite-rih-fih-KAY-shun) Conversion of nitrate or nitrite to gaseous nitrogen (N_2) or nitrogen oxide (NO_2) by metabolic activity of certain bacteria in soil.

dense, irregular connective tissue A type of animal tissue with fibroblasts and many fibers asymmetrically arrayed in a matrix. In skin and some capsules around organs.

dense, regular connective tissue A type of animal tissue with rows of fibroblasts between parallel bundles of fibers. In tendons, elastic ligaments.

density-dependent control Any factor that comes into play in an overcrowded population; reduces birth rate or raises death and dispersal rates, as by intensified predation, parasitism, disease, competition.

density-independent factor Any factor that causes fewer births or more deaths in a population regardless of its density; e.g., a severe storm or flood.

dentition (den-TIH-shun) The type, size, and number of an animal's teeth.

deoxyribonucleic acid *See* DNA.

derived trait A novel feature shared only by descendants of an ancestral species in which it originated.

dermal tissue system Tissues that cover and protect all exposed plant surfaces.

dermis Skin layer beneath the epidermis; mostly dense connective tissue.

desalinization Removal of salt from water.

desert Biome of areas where the potential for evaporation greatly exceeds rainfall, where soil is thin and vegetation sparse.

desertification (dez-urt-ih-fih-KAY-shun) Conversion of grassland or irrigated or rain-fed cropland to desertlike conditions.

detrital food web (dih-TRY-tul) Cross-connecting food chains in which energy flows mainly from plants through arrays of detritivores and decomposers.

detritivore Any animal that feeds on decomposing particles of organic matter; e.g., a crab, earthworm, or roundworm.

deuterostome (DUE-ter-oh-stome) [Gk. *deuteros*, second, + *stoma*, mouth] A bilateral animal of a lineage characterized in part by events of embryonic development, as when the second indentation to appear on the early embryo's surface becomes the mouth; e.g., an echinoderm or a chordate.

development Of complex multicelled species, a series of stages from formation of gametes, then fertilization, and on through embryonic and adult forms.

diaphragm [Gk. *diaphragma*, to partition] A muscular partition between the thoracic and abdominal cavities. Also a fertility control device inserted into the vagina to prevent sperm from entering uterus.

diatom A single-celled photoautotroph with a perforated silica shell, which has two overlapping parts that fit together like a pillbox; one of the chrysophytes.

dicot *See* eudicot.

diffusion Net movement of like ions or molecules from a region where they are most concentrated to an adjoining region where they are less concentrated; they move down their concentration gradient.

digestive system Body sac or tube, often having specialized regions where food is ingested, digested, and absorbed, and undigested residues expelled. Incomplete systems have one opening; the complete systems have two (mouth and anus).

dihybrid experiment Type of experiment that starts with a cross between two true-breeding, homozygous parents that differ in two traits governed by alleles of two genes. The actual experiment is a cross between two of their F_1 offspring that are identically heterozygous for alleles of the two genes; e.g., *AaBb* x *AaBb*.

dimorphism Persistence of two forms of the same trait in a population.

dinoflagellate One of the alveolates that deposits cellulose in alveoli, often as thick protective plates. Predators, parasites and photoautotrophs; some cause red tides.

dinosaur One of a group of reptiles that arose in the Triassic and became dominant land vertebrates for 125 million years.

diploid chromosome number (DIP-loyd) Of many sexually reproducing species, having two chromosomes of each type, or pairs of homologues, in somatic cells.

diplomonad A flagellated heterotroph with no mitochondria and three flagella at its anterior end and one at its trailing end. Belongs to one of earliest lineages of single-celled eukaryotes; e.g., *Giardia*.

directional selection Mode of natural selection by which forms at one end of a range of phenotypic variation are favored.

disaccharide (die-SAK-uh-ride) [Gk. *di*, two, + *sakcharon*, sugar] A carbohydrate composed of two sugar monomers.

disease Condition that arises when the body's defenses cannot overcome infection and activities of the pathogen or parasite interfere with normal body functions.

disruptive selection Mode of natural selection that favors different forms of a trait at both ends of a range of variation; intermediate forms are selected against.

distal tubule Tubular part of nephron where water and sodium reabsorption are adjusted by hormonal controls.

distance effect A major biogeographic pattern. Only species adapted for long-distance dispersal are potential colonists of islands far from their home range.

diversity of life Sum of all variations in form, function, and behavior in all lineages, from life's origin to the present.

division of labor Of multicelled species, a splitting up of tasks among different types of cells, tissues, and often organs, and organ systems, which collectively help the whole organism survive. Also a splitting up of tasks among different stages of the life cycle, as in insects.

DNA Deoxyribonucleic acid (dee-OX-ee-RYE-bow-new-CLAY-ik). Double-stranded nucleic acid twisted into a helical shape; its base sequence encodes the primary hereditary information for all living organisms and many viruses.

DNA chip Microarray of thousands of gene sequences that represents a large subset of a genome; stamped onto a glass plate and used to study gene expression.

DNA clone Fragment of DNA inserted into a vector such as a plasmid and introduced into a host organism; used to make many copies of a particular segment of DNA.

DNA fingerprinting A way to distinguish one individual from all others based on unique differences in parts of their DNA; fragments cut from an individual's DNA (RFLPs) have a unique pattern of sizes.

DNA ligase (LYE-gaze) Type of enzyme that catalyzes the sealing of short stretches of DNA into a continuous strand during replication; also seals strand breaks.

DNA polymerase Type of enzyme that catalyzes the addition of free nucleotides to new DNA strands during replication; also proofreads and corrects mismatches.

DNA proofreading mechanism Any enzyme-mediated process that fixes DNA replication errors or strand breaks.

DNA replication Process by which a cell duplicates its DNA molecules before it divides into daughter cells.

domain Of protein structure, part or all of a polypeptide chain that is a structurally stable, functional unit. Of one classification system, the most inclusive taxon.

dominance hierarchy Social organization in which some individuals of the group have a subordinate status to others.

dominant allele Of diploid cells, an allele that masks the phenotypic effect of any recessive allele paired with it.

dopamine Neurotransmitter that affects fine motor control, pleasure-seeking behavior.

dormancy [L. *dormire*, to sleep] Of many spores, cysts, seeds, perennials, and some animals, a predictable time of metabolic inactivity during the life cycle.

dosage compensation A gene control mechanism in female mammals in which most genes on one of two X chromosomes in somatic cells are inactivated; ensures that X chromosome genes are expressed at the same levels as in males (XY).

double-blind study A study in which neither the subjects nor the experimenter know if any particular subject is in the experimental group or the control group; minimizes bias.

double fertilization Of flowering plants only, fusion of a sperm and egg nucleus, and the fusion of another sperm nucleus with nuclei of a cell that gives rise to the endosperm, a nutritive tissue in seeds.

doubling time The time it takes for a population to double in size.

downwelling Water forced down and away from a coast after winds shift and make a surface current pile into the coast.

drug addiction Dependence on a drug, which assumes an "essential" biochemical role following habituation and tolerance.

dry acid deposition Airborne oxides of sulfur, nitrogen fall during dry weather.

dry shrubland Biome of areas that get less than 25 to 60 centimeters of rain; short, multibranched woody shrubs dominate.

dry woodland Biome of areas that get about 40 to 100 centimeters of rain may have many tall trees but no dense canopy.

duplication Base sequence in DNA that has been repeated two or more times.

ecdysone Hormone of many insect life cycles; roles in metamorphosis, molting.

echinoderm One of the protostomes; a radial invertebrate with some bilateral features and calcified spines or plates on the body wall; e.g., sea stars.

echolocation Use of echoes from self-generated ultrasounds as a navigational mechanism, as by bats and dolphins.

ecological succession Traditional view that a community arises by species interactions and in time forms a stable array of species, a climax community. Primary succession starts with pioneer species that colonize a barren habitat; secondary succession is the recovery of a disturbed climax community. *See* Intermediate disturbance hypothesis.

ecology [Gk. *oikos*, home, + *logos*, reason] Scientific study of how organisms interact with one another and the environment.

ecoregion Broad land or ocean province influenced by abiotic and biotic factors.

ecosystem Array of organisms, together with their environment, interacting by a flow of energy and cycling of materials.

ecosystem modeling Analytical method; computer programs and models predict effects of disturbances to an ecosystem.

ectoderm [Gk. *ecto*, outside, + *derma*, skin] First-formed, outer primary tissue layer of animal embryos; gives rise to nervous tissues and outer layer of the integument.

ectotherm An animal that can stay warm mainly by absorbing environmental heat, as from the sun's rays.

Ediacaran One of a diverse collection of tiny multicelled precambrian species having a highly flattened body, sometimes with many unspecialized segments.

effector Muscle (or gland); helps bring about movement (or chemical change) in response to neural or endocrine signals.

effector cell Antigen-sensitized B cell or T cell that carries out adaptive immunity.

egg Mature female gamete, or ovum.

El Niño Massive eastward flow of warm surface waters of the western equatorial Pacific that displaces cool water off South America. Recurs, disrupts global climates.

electric gradient A difference in electric charge between adjoining regions.

electromagnetic spectrum All wavelengths of photon energy from gamma rays less than 10^{-5} nanometers long to radio waves more than 10 kilometers long.

electron Negatively charged subatomic particle. Electrons occupy orbitals around the atomic nucleus.

electron transfer chain Array of enzymes and other molecules in a cell membrane that accept and give up electrons in sequence; operation of chain releases the energy of the electrons in small, usable increments.

electron transfer phosphorylation Final stage of aerobic respiration; electron flow through electron transfer chains in inner mitochondrial membrane sets up H^+ concentration and electric gradients that drives ATP formation. Oxygen accepts electrons at the end of the chain.

element Fundamental form of matter that cannot be degraded to a simpler form by ordinary means. All atoms of an element have the same atomic number.

embryo Of animals, a new individual that forms by cleavage, gastrulation, and other early stages of development. Of plants, a young sporophyte until germination.

embryonic induction A change in the composition, structure, or both of cells in an embryo by exposure to signals from cells of nearby tissues; basis of pattern formation.

emergent property With respect to life's levels of organization, a new property that emerges through interactions of entities at lower levels, none of which displays the property; e.g., living cells that emerge from "lifeless" molecules.

emerging pathogen A newly mutated or opportunistic strain of a deadly pathogen.

emigration Permanent move of one or more individuals out of a population.

emulsification In the gut, the coating of fat droplets with bile salts so that fats remain suspended in chyme.

encapsulated receptor A type of skin mechanoreceptor that detects pressure, temperature, and low vibrations.

endangered species A species endemic (native) to a habitat, found nowhere else, and highly vulnerable to extinction.

endergonic reaction (en-dur-GONE-ik) A chemical reaction that requires a net energy input and converts more stable reactants into less stable products; not spontaneous.

endocrine gland A ductless gland that secretes hormone molecules, which typically travel in blood to target cells.

endocrine system Control system of cells, tissues, and organs that interacts intimately with the nervous system; secretes hormones and other signaling molecules.

endocytosis (EN-doe-sigh-TOE-sis) Cell uptake of substances by forming vesicles from patches of plasma membrane. Three modes are receptor-mediated endocytosis, phagocytosis, and the bulk transport of extracellular fluid.

endoderm Inner primary tissue layer of animal embryos; source of the inner gut lining and organs derived from it.

endodermis Cylindrical, sheetlike cell layer around the root vascular cylinder; helps control water and solute uptake.

endomembrane system Endoplasmic reticulum, Golgi bodies, and transport vesicles concerned with modification of many new proteins, lipid assembly, and their transport within the cytoplasm or to the plasma membrane for export.

endometrium [Gk. *metrios*, of the womb] Inner lining of the uterus.

endophytic fungus A fungal symbiont in leaves and stems of most plants. Helpful, neutral, or sometimes harmful effects.

endoplasmic reticulum ER. Organelle that extends from the nuclear envelope through cytoplasm. Ribosomes coat the cytoplasmic side of rough ER, which modifes many new polypeptide chains in its lumen. Membrane lipids are assembled, fatty acids are broken down, and some toxins are inactivated in the lumen of smooth ER.

endorphin One of the neuromodulators that is a natural painkiller.

endoskeleton Of chordates, an internal framework consisting of cartilage, bone, or both; works with skeletal muscle to position, support, and move the body.

endosperm Nutritive tissue in the seeds of flowering plants only.

endospore Of certain bacteria, a resting structure enclosing a bit of cytoplasm and the DNA; resists heat, irradiation, drying, acids, disinfectants, and boiling water. It germinates when conditions favor growth and a bacterium emerges from it.

endosymbiosis [*Endo–*, within + *symbiosis*, living together] An intimate, permanent ecological interaction in which one species lives and reproduces in the other's body to the benefit of one or both.

endotherm An animal that can stay warm mainly by metabolically generated heat.

energy A capacity to do work.

energy carrier A molecule that delivers chemical energy from one reaction site to another; mainly ATP.

energy pyramid Diagram that depicts the energy stored in the tissues of organisms at each trophic level in an ecosystem. Lowest tier of the pyramid, consisting of primary producers, is always the largest.

enhancer A small sequence in DNA that binds transcription-regulating molecules; enhances transcription rates.

enkephalin A neuromodulator that is a natural painkiller.

ENSO El Niño Southern Oscillation. A recurring seesaw of atmospheric pressure in the western equatorial Pacific that has global repercussions on climates.

entropy Measure of how much and how far a concentrated form of energy has been dispersed after an energy change.

enzyme A type of protein that catalyzes (speeds) a chemical reaction. Some RNAs also show catalytic activity.

eosinophil A white blood cell that, during inflammatory responses, secretes enzymes and toxins that target extracellular parasites too large for phagocytosis.

epidemic Rapid spread, then subsidence, of a disease within a population.

epidermis Outermost tissue layer of plants and nearly all animals.

epiglottis Flaplike structure between the pharynx and larynx; controlled positional changes direct air into the trachea or food into the esophagus.

epinephrine (ep-ih-NEF-rin) A signaling molecule of the adrenal medulla that acts as a hormone or neurotransmitter on different targets; affects metabolism, heart function; works with norepinephrine in the fight–flight response. Also known as adrenaline.

epistasis (eh-PISS-tah-sis) An interaction among products of two or more gene pairs that influence the same trait.

epitheliomuscular cell Of structurally simple invertebrates, an epithelial cell with elongated extensions that contain parallel arrays of contractile filaments. Muscle fibers evolved from such cells.

epithelium (EP-ih-THEE-lee-um) Animal tissue covering external and internal body surfaces. A key innovation that favored larger, more complex bodies; cells started interacting as functional units.

EPSP Excitatory postsynaptic potential. Graded potential that drives an excitable cell's membrane toward threshold.

equilibrium model of island biogeography A model describing the number of species expected to inhabit a habitat island of a particular size and distance from colonists.

ER *See* endoplasmic reticulum.

erosion, soil Wearing away of land surface by wind, running water, and ice.

erythropoietin Kidney hormone; induces stem cells in bone marrow to give rise to red blood cells.

esophagus (ee-SOF-uh-gus) A muscular tube between the pharynx and stomach.

essential amino acid Any amino acid that an organism cannot synthesize for itself and must obtain from food.

essential fatty acid Any fatty acid that an organism cannot synthesize for itself and must obtain from food.

estrogen A female sex hormone. It helps oocytes mature and prime the endometrium for pregnancy; affects growth, development, and female secondary sexual traits.

estuary Partly enclosed coastal region where seawater mixes with fresh water and runoff from land, as in rivers.

ethylene Plant hormone; promotes fruit ripening and leaf, flower, fruit abscission.

eudicot (YOO-dih-kot) Flowering plant characterized by having embryos with two cotyledons; net-veined leaves; and floral parts in fours, fives, or multiples of these.

euglenoid A single eukaryotic cell with a crystalline rod reinforcing a thick flagellum. Different kinds are colorless heterotrophs or photoautotrophs of aquatic habitats.

Eukarya Domain of eukaryotic species; all "protists," plants, fungi, and animals.

eukaryotic cell Type of cell that starts life with a nucleus and other membrane-bound organelles.

eutherian Placental mammal.

eutrophication Nutrient enrichment of a body of water that promotes population growth of phytoplankton and opacity.

evaporation Process of conversion of a liquid to a gas; requires energy input.

evolution, biological [L. *evolutio*, an unrolling] Genetic change in a line of descent by microevolutionary events (gene mutation, natural selection, genetic drift, and gene flow); basis of large-scale patterns, rates, and trends in the history of life.

evolutionary tree A treelike diagram in which each branch point represents a divergence from a shared ancestor; each branch is a separate line of descent.

excretion Removal of excess water and solutes by urinary system or glands.

exercise Increased contractile activity.

exergonic reaction (EX-ur-GONE-ik) Any chemical reaction with a net energy loss.

exocrine gland Glandular structure that secretes products, usually through ducts or tubes, to a free epithelial surface.

exocytosis Fusion of a cytoplasmic vesicle with the plasma membrane; as it becomes part of the membrane, its contents are released to extracellular fluid.

exodermis Cylindrical sheet of cells close to root epidermis of most flowering plants; helps control uptake of water and solutes.

exon A base sequence in eukaryotic DNA that is part or all of a protein-encoding gene; may or may not be excised from a pre-mRNA during transcript processing.

exoskeleton [Gk. *skléros*, hard, stiff] An external skeleton; e.g., a hardened cuticle.

exotic species Species that has become established in a new community after dispersing from its home range.

experiment, scientific A test that simplifies observation in nature or the laboratory by manipulating and controlling conditions under which observations are made.

experimental group A group of objects or individuals that display or are exposed to the variable under investigation. Test results for this group are compared against the results for a control group.

exponential growth (EX-po-NEN-shul) Any quantity that is growing at a rate proportional to its size. For populations, it plots out as a J-shaped curve.

external ear The sound-collecting flap of cartilage-reinforced skin of many ears.

extinction Irrevocable loss of a species.

extracellular digestion, absorption Mode of nutrition; the organism grows in or on organic matter, digests it with secreted enzymes, and absorbs digested bits.

extracellular fluid All fluid not in cells; e.g., blood's plasma and interstitial fluid.

extracellular matrix Secretions and other deposits on or between cells of a tissue.

extreme halophile Bacterium or archaean adapted to an extremely salty habitat.

extreme thermophile Bacterium or archaean adapted to a hot aquatic habitat; e.g., a hot spring or hydrothermal vent.

eye Sensory organ that incorporates a dense array of photoreceptors.

F₁, F₂ The first and second generation offspring of experimental crosses.

FAD Flavin adenine dinucleotide. A type of nucleotide coenzyme; transfers electrons and H^+ from one reaction site to another.

fall overturn Vertical mixing of a body of water in fall. Its upper oxygenated layer cools, gets dense, and sinks; nutrient-rich water from the bottom moves up.

fat Type of lipid with one, two, or three fatty acid tails attached to a glycerol head.

fate map Surface diagram of certain early embryos (e.g., *Drosophila*) showing where differentiated cells of the adult originate.

fatty acid Organic compound having a carboxyl group and a backbone of as many as thirty-six carbon atoms; saturated types have single bonds only; unsaturated types include one or more double covalent bonds.

feather Of birds, lightweight structures used in flight, as body insulation, and often in courtship displays.

feedback inhibition Mechanism by which a change that results from some cellular activity triggers responses that decrease or shut down the activity.

fermentation *See* alcoholic fermentation, lactate fermentation.

fern A seedless vascular plant having fronds that often are divided in leaflets.

fertilization Fusion of a sperm nucleus and an egg nucleus, the result being a single-celled zygote.

fetus In mammalian development, the stage after all major organ systems have formed until time of birth.

fever An internally induced rise in core body temperature above a set point in the hypothalamic temperature control center.

fibrous, irregular connective tissue One of the soft connecive tissues; its matrix is packed with fibroblasts and collagen fibers oriented in all directions.

fibrous, regular connective tissue One of the soft connective tissues, with orderly rows of fibroblasts in between parallel, tightly packed bundles of fibers.

fibrous root system Lateral branchings of adventitious roots arising from a new stem.

Fick's law The rate at which a gas will diffuse across a respiratory surface is proportional to its partial pressure and the surface area.

filter feeder Animal that filters food from a current of water that flows through pores or slits of some body structure.

filtration *See* Glomerular filtration and Ultrafiltration.

fin An appendage that helps stabilize, orient, and propel most fishes in water.

first law of thermodynamics Energy cannot be created or destroyed.

fish An aquatic animal of the oldest and most diverse vertebrate lineage; a jawless, jawed cartilaginous, or jawed bony fish.

fitness The degree of adaptation to the environment, as measured by the relative genetic contribution to future generations.

fixation Of a population, the loss of all alleles but one at a gene locus; all individuals have become homozygous for the allele.

fixed action pattern Instinctual program of coordinated, stereotyped movements that runs its course independently of any feedback from environment.

flagellum, plural flagella Of many eukaryotic cells, a long, whip-like motile structure with an inner 9 + 2 array of microtubules. Prokaryotic flagella do not have this array and are not whiplike; they rotate like a propeller.

flatworm One of the simplest existing animals with organ systems that form from three primary tissue layers.

flavoprotein A plant pigment that absorbs blue light and can induce phototropism.

flower A reproductive structure of fertile parts (stamens, carpels) nonfertile parts (sepals, petals), and a receptacle (modified base of floral shoot).

flowering plant A magnoliid, eudicot, or monocot. The most successful group of plants; most coevolved with pollinators.

fluid mosaic model A cell membrane has a mixed composition (mosaic) of lipids and proteins, the interactions and motions of which impart fluidity to it.

fluorescence Light that may become visible after a molecule has absorbed a photon, then emits another photon of lower energy.

folate Water-soluble B vitamin especially essential for embryonic development.

follicle (FOLL-ih-kul) Small sac, pit, or cavity, as around a hair; a mammalian oocyte with its surrounding layer of cells.

food chain Linear sequence of steps by which energy stored in autotroph tissues enters higher trophic levels.

food pyramid Chart of a purportedly well-balanced diet; continually updated.

food web Cross-connecting food chains consisting of producers, consumers, and decomposers, detritivores, or both.

foramen magnum Opening in the skull where the spinal cord and brain connect. Its position relative to the skull's base helps researchers determine whether a fossilized animal was bipedal or a tetrapod.

foraminiferan Single-celled, predatory eukaryote with a richly perforated shell through which thin pseudopods project.

forebrain Part of vertebrate brain that includes the cerebrum, olfactory lobes, and hypothalamus.

forest A community in which tall trees grow close enough together to form a fairly continuous canopy.

fossil Recognizable, physical evidence of an organism that lived in the distant past.

fossil fuel Coal, petroleum, or natural gas; nonrenewable energy source that formed long ago from remains of swamp forests.

fossilization How fossils form over time. An organism or evidence of it gets buried in sediments or volcanic ash; water slowly infiltrates the remains, and metal ions and other inorganic compounds dissolved in it replace the minerals in bones and other hardened tissues.

founder effect A form of bottlenecking. By chance, a few individuals that establish a new population differ in allele frequencies relative to the original population.

free nerve ending One of the simplest sensory receptors in skin, internal tissues; unmyelinated or thinly myelinated.

free radical Any unbound molecular fragment with an unpaired electron.

fruit [L. after *frui*, to enjoy] Mature ovary, often with accessory parts, from a flower.

fruiting body Spore-bearing structures formed by some bacteria, fungi.

FSH Follicle-stimulating hormone of the anterior lobe of pituitary gland; has reproductive roles in both sexes.

functional group An atom or a group of atoms with characteristic properties that is covalently bonded to the carbon backbone of an organic compound.

functional-group transfer One molecule donates a functional group to another.

Fungi Kingdom of fungi.

fungus, plural **fungi** Type of eukaryotic heterotroph that obtains nutrients by extracellular digestion and absorption; fungi are notable for being prolific spore producers and major decomposers.

GABA Gamma amino butyric acid. A neuromodulator that blocks neurotransmitter release by other neurons in the brain.

gallbladder Organ that stores bile from the liver; its duct connects to the small intestine.

gamete (GAM-eet) Haploid cell formed by meiotic cell division of a reproductive cell; required for sexual reproduction.

gamete formation Formation of cells used in sexual reproduction; e.g., sperm or eggs.

gametophyte (gam-EET-oh-fite) [Gk. *phyton*, plant] A haploid multicelled body in which haploid gametes form during the life cycle of plants and some algae.

ganglion (GANG-lee-on), plural **ganglia** Distinct cluster of cell bodies of neurons.

gap junction Cylindrical arrays of proteins in the plasma membrane of adjoining cells; they pair up as open channels for rapid flows of ions and small molecules.

gastric fluid Extremely acidic mixture of secretions from the stomach lining.

gastrodermis Glandular epithelium that lines the gut of many invertebrates.

gastrula Early animal embryo with two or three primary tissue layers (germ layers).

gastrulation (gas-tru-LAY-shun) Stage of animal development; the reorganization of embryonic cells that formed by cleavage into two or three primary tissue layers.

gel electrophoresis Method of separating DNA molecules according to length, or protein molecules according to size and charge. The molecules move apart while migrating through a gel matrix in response to a weak electric current.

gene Unit of heritable information in DNA, transmissable from parents to offspring.

gene control A molecular mechanism that governs if, when, or how a specific gene is transcribed or translated.

gene expression Conversion of heritable information in a gene into a product; e.g., from DNA to mRNA to a structural or functional protein.

gene flow Microevolutionary process; alleles enter and leave a population by immigration and emigration. Counters mutation, natural selection, and genetic drift, hence reproductive isolation.

gene library Collection of host cells that contain different cloned DNA fragments representing all or most of a genome.

gene locus A gene's location along the length of a chromosome.

gene mutation Small-scale change in the nucleotide sequence of a gene; can result in an altered protein product.

gene pair Two alleles at the same locus on a pair of homologous chromosomes.

gene pool All genotypes in a population; a pool of genetic resources.

gene therapy Generally, a transfer of one or more normal genes into an organism to correct or minimize a genetic disorder.

genetic abnormality A less common or rare version of a heritable trait.

genetic code Correspondence between triplets of nucleotides in DNA and mRNA, and specific sequences of amino acids in a polypeptide chain; near-universal language of protein synthesis; mitochondria and a few species have a few variant code words.

genetic disorder An inherited condition causing mild to severe medical problems.

genetic divergence An accumulation of differences in the gene pools of two or more populations or subpopulations of a species after gene flow stops entirely; mutation, natural selection, and genetic drift operate independently in each one.

genetic drift Change in allele frequencies over generations due to chance alone. Most pronounced effects in small populations.

genetic engineering Manipulation of an organism's DNA, usually to alter at least one aspect of phenotype.

genetic equilibrium In theory, a state in which a population is not evolving with respect to a specified gene locus. *Compare* Hardy–Weinberg rule.

genetic recombination Outcome of any process that puts new genetic information in a DNA molecule; e.g., by crossing over.

genome All DNA in a haploid number of chromosomes for a species.

genomics The study of genes and gene function in humans and other organisms.

genotype (JEEN-oh-type) Genetic makeup of an individual; a single gene pair or the sum total of an individual's genes.

genus, plural **genera** (JEEN-US, JEN-er-ah) [L. *genus*, race or origin] A grouping of species more closely related to one another in morphology, ecology, and history than to others at the same taxonomic level.

geographic dispersal A movement of individuals out of their home range and their integration in a new community.

geologic time scale Time scale for Earth's history; major subdivisions correspond to mass extinctions. Dates are now absolute as a result of radiometrically dating.

germ cell Animal cell set aside for sexual reproduction; gives rise to gametes.

germination (jur-mih-NAY-shun) Of a seed or a spore, the resumption of growth after dormancy, dispersal, or both.

ghrelin Hormone secreted from cells of the stomach lining that stimulates an appetite control center.

gibberellin (JIB-er-ELL-un) Plant hormone; induces stem elongation, helps seeds break dormancy, role in flowering in some species.

gill Respiratory organ with a thin, moist, vascularized layer for gas exchange.

gill slit One of the openings in a thin-walled pharynx that functions in food-trapping, respiration, or both.

ginkgo A deciduous gymnosperm; its ancestors were diverse in dinosaur times.

gland A saclike, secretory organ that opens onto a free epithelial surface. Hormone-secreting endocrine glands have ducts; exocrine glands are ductless.

gland cell A cell that secretes products unrelated to its own metabolism.

global broiling hypothesis An asteroid impact caused the K–T mass extinction, the debris from which raised the global air temperature by thousands of degrees.

global warming Long-term increase in temperature of Earth's lower atmosphere.

glomerular capillary (glow-MARE-you-lar) [L. *glomus*, ball] A set of blood capillaries in Bowman's capsule of nephron.

glomerular filtration First step in urine formation, when blood pressure forces water out of glomerular capillaries.

glomerulus Bowman's capsule and the glomerular capillaries that it cups around.

glottis Opening between the vocal cords.

glucagon Pancreatic hormone; stimulates conversion of glycogen and amino acids to glucose when blood glucose levels fall.

glyceride (GLISS-er-ide) Molecule of one, two, or three fatty acid tails attached to a glycerol backbone; one of the fats or oils.

glycerol Three-carbon compound having three hydroxyl groups; in fats and oils.

glycocalyx Sticky meshlike capsule or slime layer around a prokaryotic cell wall.

glycogen (GLY-kuh-jen) Highly branched polysaccharide of glucose monomers; the main storage carbohydrate in animals.

glycolysis Breakdown of glucose or another organic compound to two pyruvates. First stage of aerobic respiration, fermentation, or anaerobic electron transfer. Oxygen has no role in glycolysis, which takes place in the cytoplasm of all cells. Two NADH form. Net yield: 2 ATP per glucose molecule.

glycoprotein Protein with linear or branched oligosaccharides covalently bonded to it.

gnetophyte A type of woody, vinelike or shrubby gymnosperm.

GnRH Gonadotropin-releasing hormone, induces the anterior pituitary to release LH and FSH.

golden alga A chrysophyte with silica scales or other hard parts and fucoxanthin.

Golgi body Organelle of endomembrane system; its enzymes modify many new polypeptide chains, assemble lipids, and package both inside vesicles for secretion or for use inside cell.

gonad (GO-nad) Primary reproductive organ in animals; produces gametes.

Gondwana Paleozoic supercontinent that later became part of Pangea.

graded potential Of excitable cells, a change in the resting membrane potential at an input zone; can vary in magnitude.

gradual model, speciation Addresses the rate of speciation and cites fossil evidence that morphological changes accumulate slowly over great time spans.

Gram-positives Informal name for mostly chemoheterotrophic bacteria that have a multilayered wall; not a monophyletic group.

Gram stain Microbiology diagnostic tool. Cells are exposed to purple dye, iodine, an alcohol wash, and then counterstain. Cell walls of Gram-positive species stay purple; Gram-negative species turn pink.

granum, plural **grana** Of chloroplasts, one portion of the thylakoid membrane in the shape of a stack of flattened disks.

grassland Biome in flat or rolling interiors of continents with warm summers, 25–100 centimeters of rain, and recurring natural fires that regenerate the dominant plants.

gravitropism (GRAV-ih-TROPE-izm) Growth in a direction influenced by gravity.

gray crescent Of amphibian eggs, partially pigmented region of cell cortex; establishes the embryo's anterior–posterior axis.

gray matter Areas of neuron cell bodies, dendrites, and unmyelinated axons, plus neuroglia, in the brain and spinal cord.

grazing food web Cross-connecting food chains in which energy flows from plants to an array of herbivores, then carnivores.

green alga *See* charophyte; chlorophyte.

green revolution Use of improved crop strains and modern equipment to increase crop yields in the developing countries.

greenhouse effect Trapping of heat near Earth's surface by the action of atmospheric gases. The gases absorb infrared wavelengths (heat) from the sun-warmed surface, and then radiate some wavelengths downward.

ground tissue system Parenchyma and other tissues; the bulk of a plant body.

groundwater Water in soil and aquifers.

growth Of multicelled species, increases in the number, size, and volume of cells. Of single-celled prokaryotes, increases in the number of cells of a population.

growth factor A protein that stimulates increases in size; e.g., by inducing mitosis.

growth ring One of the alternating bands of early and late wood; a "tree ring."

growth, tissue specialization Stage of animal development; new organs enlarge and assume specialized functions. This stage continues into adulthood.

guanine One of four nitrogen-containing bases in nucleotide monomers of DNA or RNA; also may refer to a nucleotide that contains a guanine base.

guard cell One of two cells that define a stoma across leaf or stem epidermis.

gut A sac or tube in which food is digested. Also the gastrointestinal tract from the stomach onward.

gymnosperm (JIM-noe-sperm) [Gk. *gymnos*, naked, + *sperma*, seed] A vascular plant that forms seeds on exposed surfaces of spore-producing structures; e.g., conifers, cycads.

habitat [L. *habitare*, to live in] The place where an organism or species normally lives, characterized by its physical and chemical features and its array of species.

habitat fragmentation The break-up of a habitat into patches too small to support successful breeding; may make species more vulnerable to losses.

habitat island An area of endemic species that is surrounded by a "sea" of habitats unsuitable for sustaining the species; e.g., a lake surrounded by a forest.

habitat loss Reduction in suitable living space and closure of part of a habitat as an outcome of chemical pollution.

hair A flexible structure rooted in skin, with a shaft above the skin's surface.

hair cell Hairlike mechanoreceptor; it is activated when sufficiently bent or tilted.

half-life The unvarying time it takes for half of a quantity of any radioisotope to decay into a more stable form.

haploid chromosome number The sum of all chromosomes in cells with one of each type of chromosome characteristic of the species; e.g., in a gamete.

hardwood Strong, dense wood with many vessels, tracheids, and fibers in xylem.

Hardy–Weinberg rule Theoretical baseline for tracking changes in allele frequencies over the generations. Frequencies do not change as long as there is no mutation, the population is infinitely large and isolated from other populations, and all individuals are reproducing equally and randomly.

HCG Human chorionic gonadotropin; secreted by blastocyst; helps maintain the endometrium until placenta secretes it, about eleven weeks later.

HDL A high-density lipoprotein in blood; it transports dietary cholesterol to the liver, which metabolizes it.

hearing Perception of sound.

heart Muscular pump; its contractions circulate blood through the animal body.

heartwood Dense, dry tissue at the core of aging tree stems and roots; helps trees defy gravity and store metabolic wastes.

heat A transfer of thermal energy.

HeLa cell Cancer cell of a lineage used in research laboratories around the world.

helicase Type of enzyme that catalyzes breaking of hydrogen bonds during DNA replication so the two strands of double helix can unwind from each other.

helper T cell CD4 lymphocyte. Central to adaptive immunity; induces responsive T and B cells to form antigen-sensitive armies.

heme Oxygen-transporting cofactor of many enzymes and pigments; one iron atom at the center of an organic ring structure.

hemoglobin (HEEM-oh-glow-bin) [Gk. *haima*, blood, + L. *globus*, ball] A heme-containing protein produced by red blood cells; carries most of the oxygen in blood.

hemostasis (HEE-mow-STAY-sis) [Gk. *stasis*, standing] Process that stops blood loss from a damaged blood vessel by coagulation, spasm, and other mechanisms.

herbicide Natural or synthetic toxin that can kill or inhibit growth of target plants.

herbivore [L. *herba*, grass, + *vovare*, to devour] Plant-eating animal.

hermaphrodite (her-MAH-froe-dyte) An individual with male and female gonads.

heterocyst (HET-er-oh-sist) Self-modified cyanobacterial cell; synthesizes nitrogen-fixing enzyme when nitrogen is scarce.

heterotherm An animal that maintains its core temperature by controlling metabolic activity some of the time and allowing it to rise or fall at other times.

heterotroph (HET-er-oh-trofe) [Gk. *heteros*, other, + *trophos*, feeder] Organism that cannot make its own food; feeds on other organisms, their wastes, or their remains.

heterozygous condition (HET-er-oh-ZYE-guss) [Gk. *zygoun*, join together] Having nonidentical alleles at a given gene locus on a pair of homologous chromosomes.

higher taxon, plural **taxa** One of ever more inclusive groupings of species; e.g., family, order, class, phylum, kingdom.

hindbrain Medulla oblongata, cerebellum, and pons. Its reflex centers are vital for respiration and other basic functions, and for coordinating motor responses.

histamine Local signaling molecule that stimulates inflammation; makes arterioles vasodilate and capillaries more permeable.

histone Type of structural protein that helps organize and condense eukaryotic chromosomes and control access to genes during interphase.

HLA Human leukocyte antigens. *See* MHC.

homeostasis (HOE-me-oh-STAY-sis) [Gk. *homo*, same, + *stasis*, standing] State in which physical and chemical aspects of internal environment (blood, interstitial fluid) are being maintained within ranges that are tolerable for cell activities.

homeotic gene One of a class of master genes; helps determine identity of body parts during embryonic development.

hominid [L. *homo*, man] All humanlike and human species.

hominoid Apes, humans, and their most recent ancestors.

homologous chromosome (huh-MOLL-uh-gus) [Gk. *homologia*, correspondence] One of a pair of chromosomes in body cells of diploid organisms; except for a pairing of nonidentical sex chromosomes, a pair has the same size, shape, and gene sequence.

homozygous dominant condition Having a pair of dominant alleles at a gene locus on homologous chromosomes; e.g., *AA*.

homozygous recessive condition Having a pair of recessive alleles at a gene locus on homologous chromosomes; e.g., *Aa*.

hormone [Gk. *hormon*, stir up] Signaling molecule secreted by one cell that can alter activities of any cell with receptors for it.

hornwort Bryophyte having a horn-shaped sporophyte attached to a flat gametophyte.

horsetail Seedless vascular plant having rhizomes, scale-like leaves, and hollow stems with silica-reinforced ribs.

host, of parasite Living organism in or on which a parasite must complete its life cycle. A definitive host harbors the mature stage. Intermediate hosts harbor immature stages.

host, of symbiont The larger, stronger, or more dominant partner of two symbionts.

hot spot A region where human activities are driving many species to extinction. Also

a region where superplumes have ruptured the crust; e.g., at the Hawaiian Archipelago.

human Primate of species *Homo sapiens*.

human gene therapy The transfer of one or more normal or modified genes into a person to correct a genetic defect, or to boost resistance to a disease.

humus Variably thick layer of organic matter that is decomposing in soil.

hybrid Individual having a nonidentical pair of alleles for a trait being studied.

hydrocarbon Organic compound with only hydrogen bonded to its carbon backbone.

hydrogen bond A weak attraction that has formed between a covalently bonded hydrogen atom and an electronegative atom taking part in another covalent bond.

hydrogen ion Free (or unbound) proton; one hydrogen atom that lost its electron and now bears a positive charge (H^+).

hydrologic cycle Biogeochemical cycle driven by solar energy; water moves through atmosphere, on or through land, to the ocean, and back to the atmosphere.

hydrolysis (high-DRAWL-ih-sis) [L. *hydro*, water, + Gk. *lysis*, loosening] A cleavage reaction; an enzyme splits a molecule, then the components of water (—OH and —H) are attached to the fragments.

hydrophilic substance [Gk. *philos*, loving] A polar molecule that dissolves easily in water; e.g., glucose.

hydrophobic substance [Gk. *phobos*, dreading] A nonpolar molecule that resists dissolving in water; e.g., oil.

hydrostatic pressure Pressure exerted by a volume of fluid against a cell wall, membrane, or some other structure that contains it; also called turgor pressure.

hydrostatic skeleton A fluid-filled cavity against which a contractile force can act.

hydrothermal vent A steaming fissure on the ocean floor; has unique ecosystems.

hypertonic solution Of two fluids, the one with the higher solute concentration.

hypha (HIGH-fuh), plural **hyphae** Fungal filament having chitin-reinforced walls; component of a mycelium.

hypothalamus [Gk. *hypo*, under, + *thalamos*, inner chamber] Forebrain region; a center of homeostatic control of internal environment (e.g., salt–water balance, core temperature); influences hunger, thirst, sex, other viscera-related behaviors, and emotions.

hypothesis, scientific An explanation of a phenomenon, one that has the potential to be proven false by experimental tests.

hypotonic solution Of two fluids, the one with the lower solute concentration.

imbibition Water molecules move into a seed, attracted by hydrophilic groups of proteins; assists in germination.

immigration One or more individuals move and take up residence in another population of its species.

immune system White blood cells and signaling molecules of vertebrate adaptive immunity; they recognize self and nonself and have the potential to target a billion specific antigens, with lasting effect.

immunity The body's ability to resist and combat infections.

immunization A process that promotes immunity from disease; e.g., vaccination.

immunoglobulin One of five classes of antibodies, each with antigen-binding and class-specific structural components.

implantation A process in pregnancy; a blastocyst burrows into the endometrium; it establishes connections by which the embryo that forms from its inner cell mass will exchange substances with the mother.

imprinting A form of learning triggered by exposure to sign stimuli; time-dependent, often in a young animal's sensitive period.

in vitro fertilization Conception outside the body, "in glass" petri dishes or tubes.

inbreeding Nonrandom mating among very close relatives that share many identical alleles; may fix harmful alleles.

inclusive fitness theory Idea that genes associated with caring for relatives may be favored in some situations.

incomplete digestive system Saclike gut in which both food intake and waste output occur through a single opening.

incomplete dominance Condition in which one allele of a pair is not fully dominant; the heterozygous phenotype is somewhere between both homozygous phenotypes.

independent assortment An outcome of random alignments at metaphase I of meiosis. Each homologous chromosome and its partner—and the genes they carry —are assorted into different gametes independently of the other pairs. Crossing over can affect the outcome.

indicator species Any species which, by its abundance or scarcity, is a measure of the health or degradation of its habitat.

induced-fit model Explanation of how some enzymes work; their shape changes and fits a bound substrate more closely, and the tension destabilizes substrate bonds so that they can break.

infection Invasion and multiplication of a pathogen or parasite in a host. Disease follows if defenses are not mobilized fast enough against the tissue disruptions.

inflammation, acute Rapid, nonspecific response to tissue invasion or injury. White blood cells release the cytokines that attract phagocytes and cause local vasodilation. Signs include redness, heat, swelling, pain.

inheritance Transmission, from parents to offspring, of genes that underlie the traits characteristic of their species.

inhibin Hormone that inhibits secretion of GnRH and FSH from the hypothalamus and pituitary gland.

inhibiting hormone Signaling molecule from the hypothalamus that suppresses release of an anterior pituitary hormone.

inhibitor Any substance that binds to a molecule and interferes with its function.

innate immunity Immediate, off-the-shelf set of responses to tissue invasion that rid the body of most pathogens. Recognition of a fixed set of conserved pathogen-associated molecular patterns triggers phagocytosis, inflammation, and complement activation.

inner ear Of vertebrates, the primary organ of equilibrium and hearing; includes a vestibular apparatus and cochlea.

insertion A mutation by which one or more bases are introduced into a DNA strand. Also a movable attachment of muscle to bone.

instinctive behavior Behavior performed without having first been learned through actual experience in the environment.

insulin Pancreatic hormone. Its actions lower the blood level of glucose.

integrator A control center that receives, processes, and stores sensory input, and coordinates the responses; e.g., a brain.

integument Of animals, a protective body covering; e.g., skin. Of seed-bearing plants, one of the layers around an ovule that mature into a seed coat.

integumentary exchange Of some animals, gas exchange across thin, moistened skin or some other external body surface.

interleukin A type of cytokine; a signaling molecule of cells of immune system.

intermediate A substance formed between the start and end of a metabolic pathway.

intermediate disturbance hypothesis An explanation of community structure; holds that species richness is greatest in between disturbances that are moderate in intensity, frequency, or both.

intermediate filament Cytoskeletal element that mechanically strengthens some cells.

internal environment The body fluid *not* inside cells, or extracellular fluid; in most animals, blood and interstitial fluid.

interneuron Any of the diverse neurons of the brain or spinal cord.

internode Plant stem between two nodes.

interphase In a eukaryotic cell cycle, the interval between mitotic divisions when a cell grows in mass, roughly doubles the number of its cytoplasmic components, and replicates its DNA.

interstitial fluid (IN-ter-STISH-ul) All fluid in spaces between cells of all tissues except the connective tissue called blood.

intertidal zone Between low and high water marks of a rocky or sandy shore.

intervertebral disk In between vertebrae, a cartilaginous flex point and shock absorber.

intron One of the noncoding sequences in eukaryotic genes; it is excised from the pre-mRNA transcripts before translation.

inversion A chromosomal alteration; part of the DNA sequence gets oriented in the reverse direction, with no molecular loss.

invertebrate Animal without a backbone.

ion Atom having an unequal number of protons and electrons; it carries a positive or negative electric charge.

ion exchange pH-dependent process; ions dissociate from soil particles, then other ions dissolved in soil water replace them.

ionic bond Ions interacting through the attraction of their opposite charges.

ionizing radiation Form of radiation with enough energy to eject electrons from atoms.

IPSP An inhibitory postsynaptic potential; a type of graded potential at an input zone of an excitable cell that drives its membrane away from threshold.

isotonic solution Any fluid having the same solute concentration as another fluid to which it is being compared.

isotope One of two or more atoms of the same element (same number of protons) that differ in their number of neutrons.

jaw Paired, hinged cartilaginous or bony feeding structures of most chordates. Many invertebrates have hinged feeding structures but not of bone or cartilage.

joint Area of contact between bones.

J-shaped curve Diagrammatic curve that emerges as unrestricted exponential growth of a population is plotted against time.

juvenile Post-embryonic stage of certain animals; it changes in size and proportion before adulthood, with no metamorphosis.

karyotype Preparation of an individual's metaphase chromosomes arranged by length, centromere location, and shape.

keratinocyte Skin cell that makes keratin, a tough, water-insoluble protein.

key innovation A chance modification in some body structure or function that gives a species the opportunity to exploit the environment more efficiently or in a novel way; e.g., modifications of the forelimbs of amniotes into diverse legs and wings during radiations into adaptive zones.

keystone species A species that influences community structure in disproportionally large ways relative to its abundance.

kidney One of a pair of vertebrate organs that filter ions and other substances from blood; it controls the amounts returned to help maintain the internal environment.

kilocalorie 1,000 calories of heat energy; amount needed to raise the temperature of 1 kilogram of water by 1°C. Standard unit of measure for food's caloric content.

kinase Type of enzyme that transfers a phosphate-group to an organic molecule.

kinetic energy Energy of motion.

kinetochore A mass of protein and DNA in the centromere to which microtubules of the spindle attach.

kinetoplastid A colorless flagellate; the only eukaryote with mitochondrial DNA massed inside a mitochondrion almost as long as the cell; e.g., *Trypanosoma*.

knockout experiment An experiment in which a living organism is engineered so that one of its genes does not function.

Krebs cycle The second stage of aerobic respiration in which many coenzymes form as pyruvate from glycolysis is fully broken down to CO_2 and H_2O. Two ATP also form. Occurs only in mitochondria.

K–T asteroid impact theory A massive asteroid struck Earth 65 million years ago and caused a mass extinction; casualties included the last of the dinosaurs.

K–T boundary The boundary between the Cretaceous and Tertiary periods.

La Niña Cooler climatic event between ENSOs; disrupts global climates.

labor Time of childbirth.

lactate fermentation One of the anaerobic pathways of ATP formation. NADH from glycolysis donates hydrogen and electrons to pyruvate, converting it to three-carbon lactate, and regenerating NAD^+. The net energy yield is 2 ATP (from glycolysis).

lactation Milk production and secretion by hormone-primed mammary glands.

lake A body of standing fresh water in a basin characterized by light penetration, temperature gradients, and other features.

Langerhans cell Antigen-presenting cell in skin; engulfs viruses and bacteria.

large intestine Colon. The bacteria-rich region of the vertebrate gut that absorbs water and mineral ions and also compacts undigested food residues for elimination.

larva, plural **larvae** An immature stage between the embryo and adult in the life cycle of many animals.

larynx (LARE-inks) Tubular airway leading to lungs; has vocal cords in some animals.

lateral bud Axillary bud. A dormant shoot that forms in a leaf axil.

lateral meristem Vascular cambium or cork cambium. A sheetlike cylinder of meristem inside older stems and roots.

lateral root Outward branching from the first (primary) root of a taproot system.

LDL Low-density lipoprotein; transports cholesterol; excess amounts in blood may contribute to atherosclerosis.

leaching Removal of some nutrients from soil as water percolates through it.

leaf Chlorophyll-rich plant organ of sunlight interception and photosynthesis.

learned behavior Enduring modification of a behavior as an outcome of experience in the environment.

lek A communal courtship display ground.

lens Of camera eyes, a transparent body that bends light rays so they all converge suitably onto photoreceptors of a retina.

leptin An appetite-suppressing hormone produced mainly by adipose tissue.

lethal mutation Mutation having drastic effects on phenotype; usually causes death.

Leydig cell Testosterone-secreting cell in mammalian testes.

LH Luteinizing hormone. An anterior pituitary hormone; roles in reproductive function of male and female mammals.

lichen (LY-kun) Mutualism between a fungus and one or more photoautotrophs.

life cycle A series of stages through which an individual passes from the time it forms by way of a mode of sexual or asexual reproduction until its own reproduction. Among complex species, the individual typically ages and dies at some time after it has reproduced.

life history pattern Of many species, the pattern of when and how many offspring are produced during a typical lifetime.

ligament A strap of dense connective tissue that bridges a skeletal joint.

light-dependent reactions First stage of photosynthesis. Pigments trap photon energy, which is transduced to ATP chemical energy. In a noncyclic pathway, a reduced coenzyme, NADPH, also forms.

light-independent reactions Second stage of photosynthesis. Involves carbon fixation and cyclic reactions that form sugars and regenerate an organic compound that is the cycle's entry point. ATP from the first stage delivers energy that drives the reactions. NADPH from the first stage donates electrons and hydrogen building blocks. The carbon and nitrogen come from CO_2.

lignin Gluelike polymer deposited in secondary cell walls; makes some plant parts stronger, more waterproof, and less vulnerable to attacks.

limbic system Centers in cerebrum that govern emotions; roles in memory.

limiting factor Any essential resource that limits population growth when scarce.

lineage (LIN-ee-edge) Line of descent.

linkage group All genes on a chromosome.

lipid One of the nonpolar hydrocarbons; e.g., a fat, oil, wax, sterol, phospholipid, or glycolipid. Cells use as storage forms of energy and building blocks.

lipid bilayer Structural basis of all cell membranes; mainly phospholipids arranged tail-to-tail in two layers, with hydrophilic heads of one dissolved in cytoplasmic fluid and heads of the other in extracellular fluid.

lipoprotein A protein complexed with cholesterol, triglycerides, or phospholipids that were absorbed from the small intestine.

liver A large gland that stores, converts, and helps maintain blood levels of organic compounds; also inactivates most hormone molecules after signaling ends as well as compounds that are toxic at high levels.

liverwort One of the bryophytes.

loam Soil best for plant growth; roughly the same proportions of sand, silt, clay.

lobe-finned fish Only bony fish having ventral fins with fleshy extensions and internal skeletal elements.

local signaling molecule One of many cell secretions into extracellular fluid. All have potent effects but are inactivated so fast that the signal is confined to local tissues; e.g., prostaglandins.

logistic growth (low-JISS-tik) Population growth pattern. A low-density population slowly increases in size, enters a phase of rapid growth, then levels off in size once the carrying capacity has been reached.

long-day plant A plant that flowers in spring, when nights are shorter (and days longer) than some critical value.

loop of Henle Hairpin-shaped, tubular part of a nephron where water and solutes are reabsorbed from interstitial fluid.

loose connective tissue Animal tissue with fibers and fibroblasts loosely arrayed in a semifluid matrix of cell secretions.

lung One of a pair of internal sac-shaped respiratory surfaces that originated in oxygen-poor aquatic habitats. Exclusive organs of respiration in birds, reptiles, and mammals; supplements respiration in some fishes and most amphibians.

lungfish A type of bony fish having both gills and one or two lung-like outpouchings of the gut wall that assist in respiration.

lycophyte A type of seedless vascular plant, typically with true leaves, roots, and stems; e.g., a club moss.

lymph Interstitial fluid that has entered vessels of the lymphatic system.

lymph node Lymphoid organ that is a key site for immune responses, as executed by its organized arrays of lymphocytes.

lymph vascular system The portion of the lymphatic system that takes up and conducts excess tissue fluid, absorbed fats, and reclaimable solutes to blood.

lymphatic system Organ system with vessels that return excess interstitial fluid and reclaimable solutes to blood and with lymphoid organs that function in defense.

lymphocyte A class of white blood cells. *See* B lymphocyte, T lymphocyte, NK cell.

lysis Gross damage to a cell wall, plasma membrane, or both that lets cytoplasm leak out; causes cell death.

lysogenic pathway A latent period that extends many viral replication cycles. Viral genes are integrated into host chromosome and may remain inactivated through many host cell divisions before being replicated.

lysosome Vesicle filled with enzymes that functions in intracellular digestion.

lysozyme Infection-fighting enzyme in mucous membranes; e.g., of mouth.

lytic pathway A rapid viral replication pathway that ends with lysis of host cell.

macroevolution Large-scale patterns, rates of change, and trends among lineages.

macrophage Phagocytic white blood cell; in vertebrates, it takes part in nonspecific defenses and adaptive immunity.

magnoliid One of three major flowering plant groups; e.g., magnolias, avocados.

malpighian tubule One of many small tubes that help insects on land dispose of toxic wastes without losing body water.

mammal Only amniote that makes hair and nourishes offspring with milk from the female's mammary glands.

mangrove wetland Tidal flat community at tropical latitudes; rich in nutrients.

mantle Of mollusks, a tissue draped over the visceral mass. Of Earth, a rocky zone of intermediate density under the crust.

marine snow Organic matter drifting down from ultraplankton to mid-oceanic water; supports food webs and marine biodiversity only now being explored.

marsupial Pouched mammal.

mass extinction Catastrophic event or phase in geologic time when families or other major groups are lost.

mass number Sum of protons and neutrons in the nucleus of an element's atoms.

mast cell White blood cell in connective tissue; secretes most of the cytokines during an innate immune response.

master gene One of the genes encoding products that map out the body plan in developing embryos. Gene products form gradients by diffusing from a source tissue. Cells along the gradient differentiate in ways that give rise to tissues and organs in expected places.

mechanoreceptor Sensory cell that detects mechanical energy (a change in pressure, position, or acceleration).

medulla oblongata Hindbrain region. Its reflex centers control respiration and other basic tasks; coordinate motor responses with complex reflexes; e.g., coughing.

medusa (meh-DOO-sah) [Gk. *Medousa*, one of three sisters in Greek mythology with snake-entwined hair] Of cnidarian life cycles, a free-swimming, bell-shaped stage, often with oral lobes and tentacles.

megaspore Haploid meiotic spore in ovary of seed-bearing plants; gives rise to a female gametophyte with egg cell.

meiosis (my-OH-sis) [Gk. *meioun*, to diminish] A nuclear division process that halves the parental chromosome number, to a haploid (n) number. Prerequisite to the formation of gametes and sexual spores.

melanin A brownish-black pigment.

melanocyte A skin cell that produces and releases melanin to keratinocytes.

memory A capacity to store and retrieve information about sensory experiences.

memory cell A sensitized B or T cell that forms in a primary immune response but is reserved for recurrence of the same antigen.

menstrual cycle Recurring cycle in adult human females and some other primates. A secondary oocyte is released from an ovary and the uterine lining is primed for pregnancy, all under hormonal control.

meristem [Gk. *meristos*, divisible] One of the localized zones where dividing cells gives rise to differentiated cell lineages that form all mature plant tissues.

mesoderm (MEH-zoe-derm) Primary tissue layers gives rise to many internal organs and part of the integument; pivotal in the evolution of large, complex animals.

mesoglea Of cnidarians, a gelatinous matrix with scattered cells between the epidermis and gastrodermis; functions as a buoyant, deformable skeleton.

mesophyll (MEH-zoe-fill) Photosynthetic parenchyma with many air spaces.

Mesozoic Era of spectacular expansion in the range of global diversity; lasted from 240 million to 65 million years ago.

messenger RNA mRNA. A single strand of ribonucleotides transcribed from DNA; the only type of RNA that carries protein-building information to ribosomes.

metabolic pathway A stepwise sequence of enzyme-mediated reactions.

metabolism (meh-TAB-oh-lizm) All the controlled, enzyme-mediated chemical reactions by which cells acquire and use energy as they synthesize, store, degrade, and eliminate substances.

metamorphosis (me-tuh-MOR-foe-sis) [Gk. *meta*, change, + *morphe*, form] Major changes in body form of certain animals. Hormonally controlled growth, tissue reorganization, and remodeling of body parts leads to adult form.

metaphase Of meiosis I, stage when all pairs of homologues are positioned at the equator of a bipolar spindle. Of mitosis or meiosis II, the stage when all duplicated chromosomes are positioned at the equator.

metastasis Abnormal migration of cancer cells that break away from home tissues and may start colonies in other tissues.

methanogen Any bacterium or archaean that produces methane gas as by-product of anaerobic reactions.

methylation Attachment of a methyl group to an organic compound; also a common gene control mechanism.

MHC molecule Also called HLA. Type of proteins at the surface of body cells that T cells recognize as self-markers. Sounds the immune alarm when it becomes complexed with antigen fragments.

micelle formation The combining of bile salts with fatty acids into tiny droplets.

microevolution Of a population, a small-scale change in allele frequencies resulting from mutation, genetic drift, gene flow, natural selection, or a combination of them.

microfilament The thinnest cytoskeletal element; consists of actin subunits that function in cell contraction, movement, and structural support.

micrograph Photograph of an image formed with the aid of a microscope.

microorganism Microbe. Any organism, usually single celled, that is too small to be observed without a microscope.

microspore Type of walled haploid spore of gymnosperms and angiosperms that gives rise to pollen grains.

microsporidian Intracellular fungal parasite of aquatic habitats that forms flagellated spores; belongs to one of the most ancient eukaryotic lineages.

microtubular spindle *See* Bipolar spindle.

microtubule Largest cytoskeletal element; a filament of tubulin subunits. Contributes to cell shape, growth, and motion.

microtubule organizing center MTOC. Of eukaryotic cells, a mass of cytoplasmic substances, the number, type, and location of which dictate how microtubules will be organized and oriented in a given type of cell; e.g., a centrosome.

microvillus (MY-crow-VILL-us) [L. *villus*, shaggy hair] Slender extension from free surface of certain cells; arrays of many microvilli greatly increase the absorptive or secretory surface area of a cell.

midbrain A vertebrate brain region with centers for coordinating reflex responses to visual and auditory input; also relays signals to forebrain.

middle ear The eardrum and ear bones that transmit air waves to the inner ear.

migration Of many animals, a recurring pattern of movement between two or more regions in response to seasonal change or other environmental rhythms.

millipede An arthropod with a great many unspecialized segments and paired legs; scavenges decaying plant material.

mimicry (MIM-ik-ree) A case of one species (the mimic) closely resembling another (its model) in form, behavior, or both.

mineral Element or inorganic compound required for normal cell functioning.

mitochondrion (MY-toe-KON-dree-on) Double-membraned organelle of ATP formation; only site of the second and third stages of aerobic respiration.

mitosis (my-TOE-sis) [Gk. *mitos*, thread] Type of nuclear division that maintains the parental chromosome number. The basis of growth in size, tissue repair, and often asexual reproduction for eukaryotes.

mixture Two or more types of molecules intermingled in proportions that can and usually do vary.

model Theoretical explanation of any object or event that has not been or cannot be directly observed.

molar Tooth with cusps that crush, grind, and shear food; one of the cheek teeth.

molecular clock Model used to calculate the time of origin of one lineage relative to others; assumes that a group of genes accumulates mutations at a constant rate, measurable as a series of predictable ticks back through time. The last tick stops close to the time the lineage originated.

molecule Two or more covalently bonded atoms of the same or different elements.

mollusk Only invertebrate with a mantle draped over a soft, fleshy visceral mass; most have an external or internal shell; e.g., gastropods, bivalves, cephalopods.

molting Periodic shedding of worn-out or too-small body structures. Permits an animal to grow in size or renew parts.

monocot (MON-oh-kot) Monocotyledon; flowering plant characterized by embryo sporophytes having one cotyledon; floral parts usually in threes (or multiples of three); and often parallel-veined leaves.

monohybrid experiment An experiment that starts with a cross between two true-breeding, homozygous parents that differ in a trait governed by alleles of one gene. The experiment is a cross between two F₁ offspring that are identically heterozygous for the two genes; e.g., *Aa* x *Aa*.

monomer Any small molecule that is a repeating subunit in a polymer; e.g., the sugar monomers of starch.

monophyletic group A set of species that share a derived trait, a novel feature that evolved in one species and is present only in its descendants; all of the evolutionary branchings from a single stem.

monosaccharide [Gk. *monos*, alone, single, + *sakcharon*, sugar] A simple sugar.

monotreme Egg-laying mammal.

monsoon Air circulation pattern; moves moisture-laden air above warm oceans to continents north or south of them.

morphogen An inducer molecule. Diffuses through embryonic tissues; the resulting gradient sequentially activates master genes.

morphogenesis (MORE-foe-JEN-ih-sis) [Gk. *morphe*, form, + *genesis*, origin] Orderly, genetically programmed changes in size, proportion, and shape of body parts of an animal embryo through which specialized tissues and organs form.

morphological convergence A pattern of macroevolution. In response to similar environmental pressures, body parts of evolutionarily distant lineages slowly evolve in similar ways and end up being alike in function, appearance, or both.

morphological divergence Pattern of macroevolution. One or more body parts of genetically diverging lineages undergo structural and functional changes from the parts in the common ancestor.

mosaic tissue effect In female mammals, an outcome of random X chromosome inactivation; different patches of tissue are expressing different X-linked alleles.

mosaicism Two or more genetically distinct cell lineages in an individual.

moss Most common kind of bryophyte.

motor neuron Neuron that relays signals from the brain or spinal cord to muscle cells or gland cells.

motor protein A type of accessory protein that interacts with microfilaments or with microtubules to move cell structures or the whole cell; e.g., myosin.

motor unit One motor neuron and all muscle cells that form junctions with its axon endings.

multicelled organism Organism that consists of many cells that, at the least, have formed layers; most have many differentiated cells that have formed true tissues, organs, and organ systems.

multiple allele system Three or more slightly different molecular forms of a gene that persists among the individuals of a population.

multiregional model Idea that modern humans evolved from *Homo erectus* groups that spread through much of the world by about 1 million years ago and evolved into regionally distinctive "races."

muscle fatigue Decline in muscle tension when tetanic contraction is continuous.

muscle fiber A group of muscle cells in parallel array. Each large, multinucleated fiber of skeletal and cardiac muscles formed when a group of undifferentiated muscle cells fused during embryonic development. Smooth muscle fibers are shorter, and each cell has retained its own nucleus.

muscle spindle A sensory organ that detects muscle stretching; its input zones are enclosed in a sheath that runs parallel with the muscle.

muscle tension Mechanical force exerted by a contracting muscle; resists opposing forces; e.g., weight of an object being lifted.

muscle tissue Tissue with muscle fibers arranged in parallel to bring about the directional contraction of a body part.

muscle twitch A sequence of muscle contraction and relaxation in response to a brief stimulus.

mushroom Aboveground reproductive structure produced by many club fungi.

mutation [L. *mutatus*, a change, + *-ion*, act, result, or process] Heritable change in DNA's molecular structure. Original source of new alleles and life's diversity.

mutation rate Of a given gene locus, the probability that a spontaneous mutation will happen in a specified interval.

mutualism [L. *mutuus*, reciprocal] A type of symbiotic interaction that benefits both participants.

mycelium (my-SEE-lee-um), plural **mycelia** [Gk. *mykes*, fungus] Underground mesh of tiny, branching filaments (hyphae); the food-absorbing portion of most fungi.

mycorrhiza (MY-coe-RIZE-uh) "Fungus-root." A form of mutualism between a fungus and young plant roots. Hyphae withdraw some carbohydrates from the plant, which withdraws some absorbed mineral ions from hyphae.

myelin sheath Lipid-rich wrappings of oligodendrocytes around axons of many sensory and motor neurons; enhances long-distance propagation of action potentials.

myofibril (MY-oh-FY-brill) One of many long, thin structures divided into contractile units that run parallel with the long axis of a muscle fiber.

myoglobin A pigment that is structurally similar to a hemoglobin chain but stores oxygen; abundant in some muscle fibers.

myosin (MY-uh-sin) An ATP-energized motor protein that moves cell components on cytoskeletal tracks. Interacts with actin in sarcomeres to bring about contraction.

NAD⁺ Nicotinamide adenine dinucleotide. A nucleotide coenzyme; after it accepts electrons and H⁺, abbreviated as NADH.

NADP⁺ Nicotinamide adenine dinucleotide phosphate. A phosphorylated nucleotide coenzyme; after it accepts electrons and H⁺, abbreviated NADPH₂.

nannoplankton Coccolithophores and other marine photoautotrophs from five to fifty micrometers across.

natural selection Microevolutionary process; the outcome of differences in survival and reproduction among individuals of a population that differ in the details of their heritable traits.

necrosis (neh-CROW-sis) Passive death of many cells after severe tissue damage.

nectar Dilute, sucrose-rich fluid secreted from a nectary that connects to phloem; attracts pollinators.

negative control Control mechanism by which one or more regulatory proteins slow down a cell activity.

negative feedback mechanism A main homeostatic mechanism by which some activity changes conditions in a cell or multicelled organism and thereby triggers a response that reverses the change.

nematocyst (NEM-at-uh-sist) [Gk. *nema*, thread + *kystis*, pouch] A fluid-filled, jack-in-the-box capsule housed in one of three types of sensory–effector cells in cnidarians. It has a mechanoreceptor projecting above the cell surface and a dischargeable, tubular thread, often with barbs or toxin-drenched. Only cnidarians make nematocysts.

neoplasm Mass of cells (tumor) that lost control over the cell cycle.

nephridium, plural **nephridia** Of some invertebrates, one of many water-regulating units that help control the composition and volume of tissue fluid.

nephron (NEFF-ron) [Gk. *nephros*, kidney] One of millions of tubules in kidneys; it filters water and solutes from blood, then reabsorbs adjusted amounts of both.

nerve A sheathed, cordlike communication line that holds bundled fibers of sensory neurons, motor neurons, or both.

nerve cell A neuron.

nerve cord Of bilateral animals, a line of communication, usually paired, that runs parallel with the anterior–posterior axis. In large or long invertebrates, it often has one or more large axons. In chordates, it develops as a hollow, neural tube that gives rise to the spinal cord and brain.

nerve net Nervous system of cnidarians and some other invertebrate groups; an asymmetrical mesh of sensory and motor neurons that controls simple movements. It activates epitheliomuscular cells arrayed as sheets or rings in the body wall.

nervous system Organ system of neurons and, in many animals, neuroglia. Detects, distributes, processes, and issues signals for responses to sensory information; also stores information in complex species.

nervous tissue Tissue consisting of neurons and often neuroglia.

net ecosystem production All the energy the primary producers have accumulated during growth, reproduction in a specified interval (net primary production), *minus* energy that producers, and decomposers, have used.

neural tube Embryonic and evolutionary forerunner of the brain and spinal cord.

neuroglia (NUR-oh-GLEE-uh) Collectively, cells that structurally and metabolically support neurons; about half the volume of nervous tissue in vertebrates.

neuromodulator Any signaling molecule that reduces or magnifies the influence of a neurotransmitter on target cells.

neuromuscular junction A chemical synapse between a motor neuron's axon endings and a muscle fiber.

neuron (NUR-on) A nerve cell; the basic communication unit in nervous systems.

neurotransmitter Any of a diverse class of signaling molecules that are secreted by neurons. It acts in a synaptic cleft, then is rapidly degraded or recycled.

neutral mutation A mutation with no effect on phenotype; natural selection thus cannot change its frequency in a population.

neutron Type of subatomic particle in the nucleus of all atoms except hydrogen; has mass but no charge.

neutrophil Abundant circulating white blood cell; mainly phagocytic in innate immunity; its enzymes kill extracellular microbes and stimulate inflammation.

niche (NITCH) [L. *nidas*, nest] Sum total of all activities and relationships in which individuals of a species engage as they secure and use the resources required to survive and reproduce.

nitrification (nye-trih-fih-KAY-shun) One stage of the nitrogen cycle. Soil bacteria break down ammonia or ammonium to nitrite, then other bacteria break down nitrite to nitrate, which plants can absorb.

nitrogen cycle An atmospheric cycle. Nitrogen moves from its largest reservoir (atmosphere), then through the ocean, ocean sediments, soils, and food webs, then back to the atmosphere.

nitrogen fixation One stage of the nitrogen cycle process. Bacteria convert gaseous nitrogen to ammonia, which dissolves in their cytoplasm to form ammonium for use in biosynthesis.

NK cell Natural killer cell. One of the cytotoxic lymphocytes of innate and adaptive immunity; touch-kills tumor cells and virus-infected cells.

node A location along the length of a stem where one or more leaves form.

noncyclic pathway of ATP formation (non-SIK-lik) [L. *non*, not, + Gk. *kylos*, circle] The light-dependent reactions of photosynthesis that produce both ATP and NADPH; its oxygen by-product is the basis of Earth's oxygen-rich atmosphere.

nondisjunction Failure of sister chromatids or homologous chromosomes to move apart in meiosis or mitosis. Daughter cells get too many or too few chromosomes.

nonionizing radiation Form of radiation that carries enough energy to boost electrons to higher energy levels but not enough to eject them from an atom.

nonshivering heat production Increase in metabolically generated heat in response to prolonged or severe cold exposure.

norepinephrine (NOR-epih-NEF-rin) A stress hormone released from the adrenal medulla and released as a neurotransmitter from sympathetic neurons and the brain. Affects metabolic rates, heart function; acts with epinephrine in the fight–flight response.

notochord (KNOW-toe-kord) A rod of stiffened tissue, neither cartilage nor bone, that develops in chordate embryos and that may or may not persist as a supporting structure for the adult body.

nuclear envelope A double membrane that is the outer boundary of the nucleus.

nucleic acid Single-stranded or double-stranded molecule of nucleotides joined at phosphate groups; e.g., DNA, RNA.

nucleic acid hybridization Any base-pairing between DNA or RNA strands from different sources.

nucleoid (NEW-KLEE-oid) The portion of a prokaryotic cell where DNA is physically organized but not enclosed in a membrane.

nucleolus (new-KLEE-oh-lus) [L. *nucleolus*, tiny kernel] In an interphase nucleus, a mass of material from which RNA and proteins are assembled into the subunits of ribosomes.

nucleosome Small stretch of eukaryotic DNA wound twice around a spool of proteins called histones.

nucleotide Small organic compound with a five-carbon sugar, a nitrogen-containing base, and a phosphate group. Functions as coenzymes or monomers of nucleic acids.

nucleus Large organelle with an outer envelope of two pore-ridden lipid bilayers that separates eukaryotic chromosomes from the cytoplasm.

numerical taxonomy In microbiology, a method of classifying an unidentified microbe by comparing it with a known group on the basis of shape, wall staining attributes, and other observable traits; the more traits shared, the closer is the inferred relatedness.

nutrient Any element having a direct or indirect role in metabolism that no other element can fulfill.

nutrition Collectively, processes by which an organism takes in, digests, absorbs, and converts food into organic compounds.

nymph Immature, post-embryonic stage of some insect life cycles.

obesity Having an excessive amount of fat in adipose tissue; caloric intake has exceeded the body's energy output.

ocean A continuous body of water that covers more than 71 percent of Earth; its currents distribute nutrients in marine ecosystems and affect regional climates.

olfactory receptor Chemoreceptor for a water-soluble or volatile substance.

oligosaccharide (oh-LIG-oh-SAC-uh-rid) Short-chain carbohydrate of two or more covalently bonded sugar monomers; e.g., sucrose and other disaccharides.

omnivore [L. *omnis*, all, + *vovare*, to devour] A type of animal that eats other organisms at more than one trophic level.

oncogene (ON-koe-jeen) A gene which, when mutated or expressed at abnormal levels, is associated with cancer.

oocyte A type of immature egg.

oomycote "Egg fungus." Heterotrophic stramenopile, once wrongly grouped with fungi. Many are pathogens of plants; e.g., water molds, downy mildews.

operator Part of an operon; a DNA binding site for a regulatory protein.

operon Group of bacterial genes together with a promoter–operator DNA sequence that controls their transcription.

organ Body structure with definite form and function made of more than one tissue.

organ formation Developmental stage in which primary tissue layers give rise to differentiated cell lineages, the descendants of which form all organs of the adult.

organ system A set of organs that are interacting chemically, physically, or both in a common task.

organelle One of the membrane-bound compartments that carry out specialized metabolic functions in eukaryotic cells; e.g., a nucleus, mitochondria.

organic compound Any carbon-based molecule that also incorporates atoms of hydrogen and, often, oxygen, nitrogen, and other elements; e.g., fats, proteins.

osmoreceptor Type of sensory receptor that detects shifts in water volume.

osmosis Diffusion of water across a selectively permeable membrane from a region where the water concentration is higher to a region where it is lower.

osmotic pressure The amount of pressure which, when applied to a hypertonic fluid, will stop osmosis from occurring across a semipermeable membrane.

osteoblast Bone-forming cell; it secretes organic substances that get mineralized.

osteoclast Bone-digesting cell; it secretes enzymes that digest bone's organic matrix, which releases calcium and phosphorus for uptake by blood when metabolism requires more of these ions.

osteocyte A mature bone cell, imprisoned in its own secretions.

ostracoderm An early craniate; a filter-feeding bottom-dwelling jawless fish that became extinct after jawed fishes evolved.

ovary (OH-vuh-ree) Of animals, a female gonad. Of flowering plants, the enlarged base of a carpel in which one or more ovules develop into seeds.

oviduct (OH-vih-dukt) Duct between the ovary and uterus where fertilization most often occurs. Also called a Fallopian tube.

ovulation (OHV-you-LAY-shun) Release of a secondary oocyte from an ovary.

ovule (OHV-youl) [L. *ovum*, egg] Of seed-bearing plants, an egg-containing female gametophyte surrounded by tissue layers; a mature ovule is a seed.

ovum Mature secondary oocyte.

oxaloacetate (ox-AL-oh-ASS-ih-tate) A four-carbon compound with roles in metabolism; e.g., the point of entry into the Krebs cycle.

oxidation–reduction reaction Transfer of electrons between reactant molecules.

oxidized molecule A molecule that has lost one or more electrons.

oxygen debt A lower O_2 level in blood after muscle cells use up more ATP than they have formed by aerobic respiration.

oxyhemoglobin In red blood cells only, oxygen bound to hemoglobin; HbO_2.

oxytocin Animal hormone with roles in labor, lactation, and recovery of uterus after pregnancy. In many animals, also guides social behavior; e.g., pair bonding.

ozone thinning Pronounced seasonal thinning of the atmosphere's ozone layer.

P$_i$ Abbreviation for inorganic phosphate.

pain Perception of injury to a body region.

pain receptor A nociceptor; a sensory receptor that detects tissue damage.

Paleozoic Era from 544 million to 248 million years ago; Cambrian through Permian.

PAN Peroxylacyl nitrate. An oxidant in photochemical smog.

pancreas (PAN-cree-us) Glandular organ. Secretes enzymes and bicarbonate that help digestion in the small intestine; secretes insulin and glucagon that have central roles in organic metabolism, glucose especially.

pancreatic islet Any of 2 million or so clusters of endocrine cells of the pancreas.

pandemic An epidemic that breaks out in several countries at the same time.

Pangea Paleozoic supercontinent; the first land plants and animals evolved on it.

parabasalid A flagellated heterotroph with bundled microtubules as long as the cell and giving rise to four to thousands of flagella; one of the earliest lineages of single-celled eukaryotes; e.g., *Trichomonas*.

parapatric speciation A speciation model. Populations in contact along a common border evolve into new species; hybrids that form in the contact zone are less fit than individuals on either side of it and thereby act as a reproductive isolating mechanism.

parasite [Gk. *para*, alongside, + *sitos*, food] Organism that withdraws nutrients from a living host, which it usually does not kill outright.

parasitism Symbiotic interaction in which a parasitic species benefits as it exploits and harms (but usually does not kill) the host.

parasitoid A type of insect that, in a larval stage, grows inside a host (usually another insect), feeds on its soft tissues, and kills it.

parasympathetic neuron A neuron of the autonomic nervous system. Its signals slow overall activities and divert energy to basic tasks; also works in opposition with sympathetic neurons to make small ongoing adjustments in the activities of internal organs that they both innervate.

parathyroid gland One of four small glands embedded in the back of the thyroid gland; their secretions trigger increases in blood calcium levels.

parenchyma (par-EN-kih-mah) One of the simple plant tissues; makes up the bulk of the plant. Its living cells have roles in photosynthesis, storage, and other tasks.

parthenogenesis (par-THEN-oh-GEN-uh-sis) The development of an embryo from an unfertilized egg.

partial pressure Contribution of one gas to the total pressure of a mixture of gases.

passive transport Diffusion of a solute across a cell membrane, through the interior of a transport protein.

pathogen [Gk. *pathos*, suffering, + *genēs*, origin] A virus, bacterium, fungus, protist, or parasitic worm that infects an organism and multiplies in it, thus causing disease.

pattern formation In animal embryonic development, the sculpting of specialized tissues and organs from clumps of cells in the proper places, in the proper order by way of embryonic induction.

PCR Polymerase chain reaction. A method to rapidly copy DNA fragments.

peat bog Compressed, soggy, acidic mat of accumulated remains of peat mosses.

pedigree Chart of connections among individuals related by descent.

pellicle A thin, flexible, protein-rich body covering of some single-celled eukaryotes.

peptide hormone A hormone that binds to a membrane receptor, which activates enzymes and often a second messenger in the cytoplasm.

per capita [L. *capita*, head] A term used in head counts of a population.

perception Understanding of a stimulus.

perennial [L. *per-*, throughout, + *annus*, year] Plant having a life cycle that extends through three or more growing seasons.

pericarp The fleshy part of a fruit; the endocarp, mesocarp, and exocarp.

pericycle (PARE-ih-sigh-kul) [Gk. *peri-*, around, + *kyklos*, circle] One or more cell layers inside the endodermis; gives rise to lateral roots and also contributes to secondary growth.

periderm Protective cover that replaces plant epidermis on older stems and roots.

periodic table of the elements Tabular arrangement of elements in order of their increasing atomic number.

peripheral nervous system (per-IF-ur-uhl) [Gk. *peripherein*, to carry around] All nerves leading into and out of the spinal cord and brain, plus their ganglia.

peripheral vasoconstriction Diameters of arterioles constrict, decreasing blood's delivery of heat to body surface.

peripheral vasodilation Blood vessels in the skin dilate; more blood flows to skin, which then dissipates excess body heat.

peristalsis (pare-ih-STAL-sis) Recurring waves of contraction of muscles in the wall of a tubular or saclike organ.

peritoneum (pare-ih-tuh-NEE-um) The membrane that lines the coelom.

peritubular capillaries A set of blood capillaries around the tubular parts of a nephron that reabsorbs water and solutes; and that excretes excess H^+, other solutes.

permafrost An impermeable, perpetually frozen layer, sometimes 500 meters thick, that underlies arctic tundra.

peroxisome Enzyme-filled vesicle that breaks down amino acids, fatty acids, and toxic substances such as ethanol.

PGA Phosphoglycerate. During glycolysis, the intermediate that results after ATP has formed by substrate-level phosphorylation; also the first stable intermediate of the Calvin–Benson cycle of photosynthesis.

PGAL Phosphoglyceraldehyde. During glycolysis, the intermediate that gives up electrons and hydrogen to form NADH. During turns of the Calvin–Benson cycle, two PGALs form one sugar; rearrangements of ten others regenerate a compound that is the entry point for the cycle.

pH scale Measure of the H^+ concentration of a solution. pH 7 is neutral.

phagocytosis [Gk. *phagein*, to eat] "Cell eating," a common endocytic pathway by which various cells engulf food bits, microbes, and cellular debris.

pharynx A muscular tube. Invertebrate chordates use theirs in filter-feeding and respiration. In land vertebrates, it is the entrance to the esophagus and trachea.

phenotype (FEE-no-type) [Gk. *phainein*, to show + *typos*, image] Observable trait or traits of an individual.

pheromone Nearly odorless exocrine gland secretion. A hormone-like signaling molecule between individuals of the same species that integrates social behavior.

phloem (FLOW-um) Plant vascular tissue that distributes photosynthetic products through the plant body. Its conducting tubes are interconnecting, living cells assisted by companion cells that help load solutes into the tubes.

phospholipid A lipid with a phosphate group in its hydrophilic head. The main constituent of cell membranes.

phosphorus cycle A sedimentary cycle. Phosphorus (mainly phosphate) moves from land, through food webs, to ocean sediments, then back to land.

phosphorylation Enzyme-mediated transfer of a phosphate group to an organic compound.

photoautotroph Any photosynthetic autotroph; e.g., nearly all plants, most algae, and a few bacteria.

photolysis (foe-TALL-ih-sis) [Gk. *photos*, light, + *-lysis*, breaking apart] Reactions that split water molecules, which release electrons for the noncyclic pathway of photosynthesis; oxygen is a by-product.

photon Unit of electromagnetic energy; has wave-like and particle-like properties.

photoperiodism Biological response to change in the relative lengths of daylight and darkness.

photoreceptor A light-sensitive sensory cell of invertebrates and vertebrates.

photosynthesis The process by which photoautotrophs capture sunlight energy and use it in the formation of ATP and NADPH, then in the formation of sugars from carbon dioxide and water. ATP gives up energy that drives the sugar-building reactions, and NADPH donates electrons and hydrogen building blocks.

photosystem In photosynthetic cells, a cluster of membrane-bound pigments and other molecules; it converts light energy to chemical energy.

phototropism Change in the direction of cell movement or growth in response to a light source.

photovoltaic cell Unit in a device that converts sunlight energy into electricity.

phycobilin One of a class of accessory pigments in cyanobacteria and red algae that reflects red to blue light.

phylogeny Evolutionary relationships among species.

physiology Study of how the multicelled body functions in its environment; more specifically, of the mechanisms by which its component parts grow, develop, and are maintained and reproduced.

phytochrome A light-sensitive pigment that helps set plant circadian rhythms based on length of night. Influences stem lengthening and branching, leaf expansion, and often flowering.

phytoplankton (FIE-toe-PLANK-tun) [Gk. *phyton*, plant, + *planktos*, wandering] An aquatic community of floating or weakly swimming photoautotrophs.

pigment Any light-absorbing molecule.

pilomotor response Formation of a layer of still air next to skin as hairs or feathers become erect.

pilus Among prokaryotic cells, a short, filamentous protein that projects above the cell wall and can adhere to surfaces; a sex pilus functions in conjugation.

pineal gland Light-sensitive, melatonin-secreting endocrine gland. Seasonal change in melatonin levels affect biological clocks, overall activity, and reproductive cycles.

pioneer species An opportunistic colonizer of barren or disturbed habitats. Adapted for rapid growth and dispersal.

pith Of most eudicot stems, ground tissue inside the ring of vascular bundles.

pituitary gland Vertebrate endocrine gland; interacts with the hypothalamus to control many physiological functions, including activity of many other glands. Its posterior lobe stores and secretes hormones from the hypothalamus; its anterior lobe produces and secretes its own hormones.

placenta (plah-SEN-tuh) Of pregnant female placental mammals, a blood-engorged organ that forms from endometrial tissue and extraembryonic membranes. Lets a mother exchange substances with a fetus but keeps their blood circulation separate.

placoderm An early jawed craniate with paired fins, armor plates on head; extinct.

placozoan An asymmetric, soft-bodied animal with two simple tissues around a thin, inner matrix.

plankton Aquatic community of mostly microscopic autotrophs and heterotrophs.

plant A multicelled photoautotroph, most with well-developed roots and shoots (e.g., stems, leaves), as well as photosynthetic cells that include starch grains as well as chlorophylls *a* and *b*, and polysaccharides such as cellulose, pectin, and lignin in cell walls. The primary producers on land.

Plantae Kingdom of plants.

planula Of cnidarians, a type of swimming or creeping larva, usually with a ciliated epidermis.

plasma (PLAZ-muh) Liquid portion of blood; mainly water and dissolved ions, proteins, sugars, gases, and other solutes.

plasma membrane Outer cell membrane; the structural and functional boundary between cytoplasm and extracellular fluid.

plasmid A small, circular bacterial DNA molecule having a few genes; replicated independently of the bacterial chromosome.

plasmodesma (PLAZ-moe-DEZ-muh), plural **plasmodesmata** A plant cell junction that connects the cytoplasm of adjoining cells.

plasmodium Of plasmodial slime molds, a multinucleated mass that forms when a single diploid cell undergoes rounds of mitosis without cytoplasmic division.

plate tectonics Theory that great slabs or plates of Earth's outer layer float on a hot, semi-molten mantle. All plates are moving slowly and have rafted continents to new positions over time.

platelet A megakaryocyte fragment; it releases substances that help form clots.

pleiotropy A case of alleles at a single gene locus having positive or negative impact on two or more traits.

polar body One of four cells that form by meiotic cell division of an oocyte but that does not become the ovum.

pollen grain [L. *pollen*, fine dust] A tiny structure that forms from microspores; consists of a sturdy wall around a few cells that will develop into a mature, sperm-bearing, male gametophyte.

pollination Arrival of pollen on a carpel's stigma in a flower of the same species.

pollinator Any agent that delivers pollen grains to the egg-containing structures in flowers of the same species; e.g., wind, water, or birds, bats, and other animals.

pollutant Natural or synthetic substance of types or in amounts that are novel in the history of an ecosystem, so there is no evolved mechanism that can prevent the substance from accumulating to harmful or disruptive levels.

polygenic inheritance Inheritance of multiple genes that affect the same trait.

polymer Large molecule of multiple linked monomers.

polymorphism (poly-MORE-fizz-um) [Gk. *polus*, many, + *morphe*, form] Persistence of two or more qualitatively different forms of a trait, or morphs, in a population.

polyp (POH-lip) Vase-shaped, sedentary stage of cnidarian life cycles.

polypeptide chain Three or more amino acids linked by peptide bonds.

polyploidy A case of somatic cells having three or more of each type of chromosome characteristic of the species.

polysaccharide [Gk. *polus*, many, + *sakcharon*, sugar] Straight or branched chain of covalently bonded monomers of the same or different kinds of sugars; e.g., cellulose, starch, and glycogen.

polysome A series of ribosomes that are all translating the same mRNA molecule at the same time.

polytene chromosome Of some insects, a chromosome consisting of many parallel copies of the same DNA molecule.

pons Hindbrain traffic center for signals between the cerebellum and forebrain.

population All individuals of the same species living in a specified area.

population density Count of individuals of a population in a specified area or volume of a habitat.

population distribution The pattern in which individuals of a population are dispersed through their habitat.

population size The total number of individuals that make up a population.

positive control Use of regulatory proteins to promote gene expression.

positive feedback mechanism Major form of homeostatic control; initiates a chain of events that intensify a change in conditions; e.g., a complement cascade.

potential energy A object's capacity to do work owing to its position in space or the arrangement of its parts.

predation Ecological interaction in which a predator feeds on a prey organism.

predator [L. *prehendere*, to grasp, seize] A heterotroph that eats other living organisms (its prey), does not live in or on them, and most often kills them.

prediction A statement, based on a hypothesis, about what you expect to observe in nature; the "if-then process."

pressure flow theory In vascular plants, organic compounds flow through phloem in response to pressure and concentration gradients between sources (e.g., leaves) and sinks (use or storage in growing parts).

pressure gradient Difference in pressure between two adjoining regions.

prey Any organism that another organism captures as a food source.

primary growth Plant growth originating at root tips and shoot tips.

primary oocyte Of human females, an immature egg that is arrested in prophase I of meiosis until eight to ten hours before being released from an ovary.

primary producer An autotroph at the first trophic level of an ecosystem.

primary productivity The rate at which an ecosystem's primary producers secure and store energy in tissues in a given interval.

primary root First root of a seed plant.

primary succession *See* ecological succession.

primary wall The first thin, pliable wall of young plant cells.

primate A type of mammal; a prosimian, a tarsioid, or an anthropoid.

primer Short nucleotide sequence that researchers design as an initiation site for synthesis of a DNA strand on a DNA or RNA template.

prion A type of protein particle normally in vertebrate nervous systems that turns infectious when its shape changes.

probability The odds that each outcome of an event will occur is proportional to the total number of ways in which that outcome can be reached.

probe Short nucleotide sequence that has been labeled with a tracer; designed to hybridize with part of a gene or mRNA.

producer An autotrophic organism.

product A substance remaining at the end of a reaction.

progesterone (pro-JESS-tuh-rown) One of the sex hormones; ovaries and the corpus luteum secrete it.

proglottid One of many tapeworm body units that bud behind the scolex.

progymnosperm Among earliest plants to produce seedlike structures or seeds.

prokaryotic cell [L. *pro*, before, + Gk. *karyon*, kernel] A single-celled organism, often walled, that does not have the organelles characteristic of eukaryotic cells. Only bacteria and archaeans are prokaryotic.

prokaryotic fission Cell reproduction mechanism of prokaryotic cells only.

prolactin Hormone that induces synthesis of enzymes used in milk production.

promoter Short stretch of DNA to which RNA polymerase binds. Transcription then begins at the gene closest to the promoter.

prophase, meiosis In prophase I in a germ cell, all duplicated chromosomes condense, typically undergo crossing over with their homologue, then get tethered to a spindle and move to its equator. In prophase II, one member of each pair of homologous chromosomes is tethered to the opposite spindle pole and moved to the equator.

prophase, mitosis All of the duplicated chromosomes in a cell condense and get attached to a newly forming spindle.

protein Organic compound consisting of one or more polypeptide chains. Diverse kinds have structural, functional, and regulatory roles in all organisms.

proteobacteria A group of Gram-negative bacteria; the most diverse monophyletic group of prokaryotic cells.

Proterozoic Era between 2.5 million to 544 million years ago. An oxygen-rich early atmosphere formed, sparking the Cambrian explosion of biodiversity.

"protist" Informal name for all structurally simple eukaryotes, which are now being classified as monophyletic groups.

proto-cell Presumed stage of chemical evolution that preceded living cells.

proton Positively charged subatomic particle in the nucleus of all atoms.

protostome (PRO-toe-stome) [Gk. *proto*, first, + *stoma*, mouth] A bilateral animal of a branching lineage characterized partly by events in embryonic development, as when the first indentation to form on the early embryo's surface becomes a mouth; e.g., mollusks, annelids, arthropods.

protozoan Traditional name for one of the motile predatory or parasitic species of single-celled eukaryotes.

proximal tubule Tubular portion of a nephron closest to Bowman's capsule.

pseudocoel False coelom; a main body cavity incompletely lined with tissue derived from mesoderm.

pseudopod A dynamic lobe of membrane-enclosed cytoplasm; functions in motility and phagocytosis by amoebas, amoeboid cells, and many white blood cells.

puberty Of humans, the post-embryonic stage when gametes start to mature and secondary sexual traits emerge.

pulmonary circuit Cardiovascular route in which oxygen-poor blood flows to lungs from the heart, gets oxygenated, then flows back to the heart.

punctuation model, speciation Addresses the rate of speciation; cites fossil evidence that morphological changes required for reproductive isolation evolve in a relatively brief time span, within the tens to hundreds of thousands of years when two or more populations are diverging from each other.

Punnett-square method A simple way to predict the probable outcomes of a genetic cross by constructing and filling in a diagram of all possible combinations of genotypes, phenotypes, or both.

pupa, plural **pupae** An immature, post-embryonic stage of many insect life cycles.

purine A nucleotide base with a double ring structure; e.g., adenine or guanine.

pyrimidine A nucleotide base with a single ring structure; e.g., cytosine, thymine, uracil.

pyruvate Three-carbon compound that forms as an end product of glycolysis.

quadrat One of a number of sampling areas of the same size and shape used to estimate population size.

r Net reproduction per individual per unit time; a variable in population growth equations for which birth and death rates are assumed to remain constant.

radial symmetry Animal body plan with four or more roughly equivalent parts around an anterior–posterior axis.

radiation Any form of radiant energy.

radioactive decay Natural, inevitable process by which an atom emits energy as subatomic particles and x-rays as its unstable nucleus spontaneously breaks apart; transforms one element into another in a predictable time span.

radioisotope Any isotope that has an unstable nucleus.

radiolarian A single-celled predatory eukaryote that has pseudopods projecting from a perforated shell and a cell cortex with buoyancy-imparting vacuoles.

radiometric dating Method of measuring proportions of a radioisotope in a mineral trapped long ago in newly formed rock and a daughter isotope that formed from it by radioactive decay in the same rock. Used to assign absolute dates to fossil-containing rocks and to the geologic time scale.

rain shadow Reduction in rainfall on the leeward side of a high mountain range that results in arid or semiarid conditions.

ray-finned fish A bony fish having fin supports derived from skin, a swim bladder, and thin, flexible scales.

reabsorption At a capillary bed, osmotic movement of some interstitial fluid into plasma. *See also* tubular reabsorption.

reactant Substance that enters a reaction.

reaction center At a photosystem's center, a special pair of chlorophyll *a* molecules; the center loses electrons on absorption of photon energy, thereby initiating the light-dependent reactions of photosynthesis.

rearrangement, molecular Conversion of one organic compound to another through changes in its internal bonds.

receptor, molecular A protein or some other molecule with a binding site for a specific signaling molecule.

receptor, sensory Sensory cell or a specialized ending of one that detects a particular kind of stimulus.

recessive allele Allele whose expression in heterozygotes is fully or partially masked by expression of a dominant partner allele. It is fully expressed only in homozygous recessives.

reciprocal cross A paired cross that may identify the role of parental sex on the inheritance of a trait. In the second cross, a trait characteristic of each sex is reversed compared to the original cross.

recognition protein One of a class of glycoproteins or glycolipids that project above the plasma membrane and that identify a cell as *nonself* (foreign) or *self* (belonging to one's own body tissue).

recombinant DNA A DNA molecule that contains genetic material from more than one organism of the same species or from different species.

recombinant DNA technology Techniques by which DNA molecules from different species can be cut into fragments, spliced together into cloning vectors, and then amplified to useful quantities.

recombination, genetic Introduction of nonparental combinations of alleles in chromosomes, as by crossing over.

rectum Last part of the mammalian gut that briefly stores feces before their expulsion.

red alga An aquatic, mostly multicelled photoautotroph having an abundance of phycobilins that masks its chlorophyll *a*.

red blood cell Erythrocyte; functions in the efficient transport of oxygen in blood.

red marrow Site of blood cell formation in the spongy tissue of many bones.

red tide An algal blood that turns the water near coasts rust-red or brown.

reduced molecule A molecule to which one or more electrons were transferred.

reflex [L. *reflectere*, to bend back] Simple, stereotyped movement in response to a stimulus; sensory neurons synapse on motor neurons in the simplest reflex arcs.

regulatory protein Part of mechanisms that control transcription, translation, and gene products by interacting with DNA, RNA, new polypeptide chains, or proteins such as enzymes.

releaser Hypothalamic signaling molecule that enhances or slows the secretion of a specific anterior pituitary hormone.

renal corpuscle Bowman's capsule and the glomerular capillaries it cups around.

renal failure Condition in which nephrons of both kidneys no longer function.

repair enzyme Type of enzymes that repairs nucleotide mismatches in a DNA strand.

repressor Type of protein that can block transcription of a prokaryotic gene by binding to an operator.

reproduction Any asexual or sexual process by which a parent cell or organism produces offspring.

reproductive base The number of actually and potentially reproducing individuals of a population.

reproductive isolating mechanism Any heritable feature of body form, function, or behavior that prevents interbreeding between two or more populations; sets the stage for genetic divergences.

reproductive success Of individuals, the production of viable, fertile offspring.

"reptile" No longer a formal taxon; not a monophyletic group. The name persists as a means to refer to sauropsid lineages other than birds that show basic amniote features but not derived traits that define birds or mammals; e.g., a turtle, crocodile.

resource partitioning The sharing of a resource in different ways or at different times that permits two or more species to coexist in a habitat.

respiration [L. *respirare*, to breathe] The sum of physiological processes that move O_2 from the surroundings to metabolically active tissues in the animal body and CO_2 from tissues to the outside.

respiratory cycle One in-and-out breath.

respiratory membrane Fused-together alveolar and blood capillary epithelial and the basement membrane in between; a respiratory surface in the human lung.

respiratory pigment A protein complexed with one or more metal ions that binds O_2 in oxygen-rich animal tissues and gives it up where O_2 levels are lowest.

respiratory surface Any thin, moist body surface that functions in gas exchange.

respiratory system Animal organ system that takes in O_2 for aerobic respiration and rids the body of its CO_2 wastes.

resting membrane potential The voltage difference across the plasma membrane of a neuron or other excitable cell that is not receiving outside stimulation.

restoration ecology Work to reestablish biodiversity in ecosystems severely altered by mining, agriculture, other disturbances.

restriction enzyme One of hundreds of proteins that recognize and cut specific base sequences in double-stranded DNA.

reticular formation Mesh of interneurons that is a low-level pathway of information flow through the upper spinal cord, brain stem, and cerebral cortex.

retina Of vertebrate and many invertebrate eyes, a tissue packed with photoreceptors and interwoven with sensory cells.

reverse transcriptase A viral enzyme that catalyzes the assembly of free nucleotides into a strand of DNA on an RNA template.

Rh blood typing Method of determining whether Rh+, a type of surface recognition protein, is present on an individual's red blood cells; if absent, the cell is Rh−.

rhizoid A rootlike absorptive structure.

rhizome A short absorptive stem that grows underground in a horizontally branching pattern, most often.

rhyniophyte The first seedless vascular plants; originated in Gondwana lowlands.

ribosomal RNA rRNA. A class of RNA that becomes complexed with proteins to form ribosomes; some catalyze assembly of polypeptide chains.

ribosome The site of polypeptide chain synthesis in all cells. An intact ribosome has two subunits of rRNA and proteins.

riparian zone The narrow corridor of vegetation along a stream or river.

RNA Ribonucleic acid. Any of a class of single-stranded nucleic acids involved in gene transcription and translation; some RNAs show enzyme activity.

RNA polymerase Enzyme that catalyzes transcription of DNA into RNA.

RNA world Model for a time prior to the evolution of DNA; a self-replicating system chemically evolved in which RNA strands were templates for protein synthesis.

rod cell Vertebrate photoreceptor that detects very dim light; contributes to the coarse perception of movement.

root Typically belowground plant part. It absorbs water and dissolved minerals, often anchors aboveground parts and stores food.

root hair Hairlike, absorptive extension of a young, specialized root epidermal cell.

root nodule Mutualistic association of nitrogen-fixing bacteria and roots of some legumes and other plants; infection leads to a localized tissue swelling.

root system Underground vascular plant structures that absorb water, mineral ions.

rotifer Bilateral, cephalized animal with a false coelom and a crown of cilia.

roundworm Bilateral invertebrate with a false coelom and complete digestive system in a cylindrical body. Most are decomposers; many are parasites.

rubisco RuBP carboxylase. Carbon-fixing enzyme of the C3 photosynthesis pathway.

RuBP Ribulose bisphosphate. A five-carbon organic compound; the entry point for the Calvin–Benson cycle, which regenerates it.

ruminant Hoofed, herbivorous mammal that has multiple stomach chambers.

sac fungus Fungus that produces sexual spores in sac-shaped cells; e.g., truffles.

salinization Salt buildup in soil by poor drainage, evaporation, or heavy irrigation.

saliva Salivary gland secretion into the mouth that starts starch breakdown.

salt Any compound that releases ions other than H+ and OH− in solution.

saltatory conduction Of a myelinated neuron, a rapid form of action potential propagation. Excitation hops node to node between jellyrolled membranes of neuroglial cells of the myelin sheath.

sampling error Using a sample or subset of a population, an event, or some other aspect of nature as an experimental group that is not large enough to be representative of the whole.

saprobe Heterotroph that extracts energy and carbon from nonliving organic matter and so causes its decay.

sapwood Of an older stem or root, the moist secondary growth between the vascular cambium and heartwood.

sarcomere (SAR-koe-meer) One of many basic units of contraction, defined by Z lines, along the length of a muscle fiber. It shortens by ATP-driven interactions between its parallel arrays of actin and myosin components.

sarcoplasmic reticulum Specialized ER that forms flattened, membrane-bound chambers around muscle fibers; takes up, stores, and releases Ca++ for contraction.

sauropsid A "reptile" or a bird.

savanna Broad belt of warm grassland with a smattering of shrubs and trees.

scale Of a fish, one of a number of small, bony plates that protect the body without weighing it down.

Schwann cell Type of neuroglial cell that myelinates many axons.

scientific theory *See* Theory, scientific.

sclerenchyma (skler-ENG-kih-mah) One of three simple plant tissues; supports mature parts and often protects seeds. Lignin often thickens and reinforces its cell walls.

second law of thermodynamics Energy tends to flow from concentrated to less concentrated forms.

second messenger Molecule in a cell that relays a hormonal signal; e.g., cyclic AMP.

secondary growth A thickening of older stems and roots; wood when extensive.

secondary oocyte A haploid cell which, with a first polar body, is produced by the first meiotic division of a primary oocyte; the cell released from the ovary of a female vertebrate at ovulation.

secondary sexual trait A trait associated with maleness or femaleness but with no direct role in reproduction (e.g., body hair distribution). The primary sexual trait is the presence of male or female gonads.

secondary succession *See* Ecological succession.

secondary wall A rigid, permeable wall inside the primary wall of many plant cells; forms after the first growing season.

secretion Release of a substance from a cell or gland to its surroundings.

sedimentary cycle Any biogeochemical cycle in which an element having no gaseous phase moves from land, through food webs, to the seafloor, then back to land through long-term uplifting.

seed A mature ovule.

seed bank A storage facility where genes of diverse plant lineages are preserved.

seed fern One of the earliest plants to make seedlike structures, or seeds.

segmentation Of animal body plans, a series of units that may or may not be similar in appearance. Of tubular organs, an oscillating movement produced by rings of circular muscle in the tube wall.

segregation, theory of Mendelian theory that two genes of a pair on homologous chromosomes are separated from each other at meiosis, eventually to end up in different gametes.

selective gene expression Outcome of controls over which gene products a cell makes or activates in a specified interval. Basis of cell differentiation.

selective permeability Built-in capacity of a cell membrane to prevent or allow specific substances from crossing it at certain times, in certain amounts.

selfish behavior An individual increases its own chance to reproduce regardless of the biological costs to its social group.

selfish herd Social group held together by reproductive self-interest.

semen (SEE-mun) Sperm-bearing fluid expelled from a penis during sex.

semiconservative replication [Gk. *semi–*, half, + L. *conservare*, to keep] Mechanism by which a DNA molecule is duplicated. The double helix unzips along its length, exposed bases of each strand are a template upon which a new strand is assembled, then each conserved strand and its new partner wind up in a double helix. Two double helixes, each with a parental strand and new strand of DNA, result.

seminiferous tubule One of the coiled tubes in testes where sperm start forming.

senescence (sen-ESS-cents) [L. *senescere*, to grow old] Of differentiated multicelled organisms, the phase in a life cycle from maturity until death; also applies to death of parts, such as plant leaves.

sensation Conscious awareness of a stimulus.

sensory neuron Type of neuron that detects a stimulus and relays information about it toward an integrating center.

sensory system Collectively, all sensory cells of a nervous system that detect and report information about external and internal stimuli to integrating centers.

serotonin A neurotransmitter that affects mood, memory, and sleep behavior.

Sertoli cell A type of cell in seminiferous tubules with FSH receptors; helps nourish and support developing sperm.

sessile animal (SESS-ihl) Animal that is attached to a substrate during part of the life cycle; e.g., an adult barnacle.

sex chromosome One of two kinds of homologous chromosomes that, in certain combinations, dictate the gender of the new individual. Also has genes unrelated to sexual traits.

sexual dimorphism A notable difference between female and male phenotypes of a population.

sexual reproduction Production of genetically variable offspring by meiosis, gamete formation, and fertilization.

sexual selection A category of natural selection; an outcome of differences in success at attracting mates and reproducing among individuals of a population.

shell model Model for how electrons are distributed in an atom; all of the orbitals are shown as a nested series of shells.

shifting cultivation A practice of cutting and burning trees, then tilling ashes into the soil of a small plot of land. Once called slash-and-burn agriculture.

shivering response Rhythmic tremors in response to cold; raises heat production.

shoot system Aboveground plant parts; e.g., stems, leaves, flowers.

short-day plant Plant that flowers in late summer or early fall, when night length is longer than a critical value.

sieve tube A conducting tube in phloem.

sieve-tube member A living cell that helps form a conducting tube in phloem.

sign stimulus Simple environmental cue that triggers a response to a stimulus; the nervous system is prewired to recognize it.

signal reception Activation of a molecular or sensory receptor when a hormone or another signaling molecule binds to it.

signal transduction Conversion of an extracellular signal into a molecular or chemical form that causes a change in some activity inside a target cell.

signaling molecule Any secretion from one cell type that can alter the behavior of a different cell that bears a receptor for it; a means of cell communication.

sister chromatid (CROW-mah-tid) One of the two attached members of a duplicated eukaryotic chromosome.

six-kingdom classification system The grouping of all organisms into kingdoms Bacteria, Archaea, Protista, Fungi, Plantae, and Animalia.

skeletal muscle Organ of many muscle fibers bundled inside a connective tissue sheath and attached to bone by tendons.

skeletal muscle tissue Contractile tissue that is the functional partner of bone.

skin Vertebrate integument and diverse structures derived from it.

sliding-filament model Model for how the sarcomeres of muscle fibers contract. ATP-activated myosin heads repeatedly bind actin filaments (tethered to Z lines) and tilt in short power strokes that slide the actin toward the sarcomere's center.

slime mold An amoebozoan; one of the free-living, amoebalike cells that also cluster into a migrating mass, differentiate, and form reproductive structures.

small intestine Part of the vertebrate gut in which digestion is completed and from which most dietary nutrients are absorbed.

smog Atmospheric condition in which winds cannot disperse airborne pollutants that have become trapped under a thermal inversion.

smooth muscle tissue Contractile tissue in the wall of soft internal organs.

social behavior Interacting individuals of a species that display, send, and respond to shared forms of communication.

social parasite Species that completes its life cycle by taking advantage of the social behavior of a host species, thus harming it.

sodium–potassium pump Cotransporter that, when energized, actively transports sodium out of a cell and helps potassium passively diffuse into it at the same time.

softwood Wood with tracheids, no fibers or vessels; less dense than hardwood.

soil Mix of mineral particles of variable sizes, decomposing organic material, and air and water in spaces between particles.

solar-hydrogen energy Sunlight energy is used to convert water to H_2 as a fuel source.

solar tracking A photoperiodic response to sun's changing angle through the day.

solute (SOL-yoot) [L. *solvere*, to loosen] Any substance dissolved in a solution.

solvent Any fluid (e.g., water) in which one or more substances are dissolved.

somatic cell (so-MAT-ik) [Gk. *soma*–, body] Any body cell that is not a germ cell.

somatic nervous system The nerves that connect the vertebrate central nervous system and skeletal muscles.

somatic sensation Perception of touch, pain, pressure, temperature, motion, or positional changes of body parts.

somatosensory cortex Part of the outer gray matter of the cerebral hemispheres.

somite One of many paired segments in a vertebrate embryo that gives rise to most bones, skeletal muscles of the head and trunk, and the dermis.

special sense Vision, hearing, olfaction, or another sensation involving receptors that are restricted to certain body parts.

speciation (spee-see-AY-shun) One of the macroevolutionary processes; formation of daughter species from a population or subpopulation of a parent species; the routes vary in their details and duration.

species (SPEE-sheez) [L. *species*, a kind] Of sexually reproducing species, one or more natural populations of individuals that successfully interbreed and are isolated reproductively from other such groups. By a cladistic definition, one or more natural populations of individuals with at least one unique trait derived a common ancestor that occurs in no other groups.

specific epithet The last part of a two-part species name; the genus is first.

sperm Mature male gamete.

sphere of hydration A clustering of water molecules around molecules or ions of a solute by positive and negative interactions.

sphincter A ring of muscles that alternately contract and relax, which closes and opens a passageway between two organs.

spinal cord The part of a central nervous system inside a vertebral canal. Basic reflex centers, and tracts to and from the brain.

spindle, microtubular *See* Bipolar spindle.

spirillum A spiral-shaped prokaryotic cell.

spirochaete A motile, parasitic or symbiotic bacterium that looks like a stretched spring.

spleen The largest lymphoid organ, with phagocytic white blood cells and B cells; filters antigen and used-up platelets and worn-out or dead red blood cells. In embryos only, a site of red blood cell formation.

sponge Structurally, the simplest existing animal. Its asymmetrical body has a spicule-reinforced matrix in two cell layers (not epithelium). Its phagocytic collar cells trap food from water flowing through pores in its wall.

spore A structure of one or a few cells, often walled or coated, that protects and/or disperses a new sexual or asexual generation. Many bacteria as well as apicomplexans, fungi, and plants form spores.

sporophyte [Gk. *phyton*, plant] A spore-producing vegetative body of a plant or multicelled alga that grows by mitotic cell divisions from a zygote.

sporozoan *See* Apicomplexan.

spring overturn Of large bodies of water, a downward movement of oxygenated surface water and an upward movement of nutrient-rich water from below during spring; fans primary productivity.

S-shaped curve Type of diagrammatic curve that emerges when plotting logistic population growth against time.

stabilizing selection Mode of natural selection; intermediate phenotypes are favored over extremes at both ends of the range of variation.

stamen (STAY-mun) An anther, typically raised on a stalked filament.

statolith A cluster of particles that acts as a gravity-sensing mechanism.

STD A sexually transmitted disease.

stem cell Self-perpetuating, undifferentiated animal cell. A portion of its daughter cells becomes specialized; e.g., red blood cells from stem cells in bone marrow.

steroid hormone Cholesterol-derived, lipid-soluble hormone.

sterol Any lipid consisting of a rigid backbone of four fused carbon rings.

stigma Sticky or hairy surface tissue on the top of a carpel or fused carpels; captures pollen and promotes its germination.

stimulus [L. *stimulus*, goad] A specific form of energy that activates a sensory receptor able to detect it; e.g., pressure.

stoma, plural **stomata** A gap between two plumped guard cells that lets water vapor and gases diffuse across the epidermis of a leaf or primary stem; diffusion stops when the cells lose water and collapse.

stomach Muscular, stretchable sac; mixes and stores ingested food and helps break it apart mechanically and chemically.

strain A type of organism which, when compared against an organism of known type, has differences that are too minor to classify it as a separate species.

stramenopile A single-celled or multicelled eukaryote with four outer membranes and thin tinsel-like filaments projecting from one of two flagella; e.g., a photosynthetic chrysophyte or a colorless oomycote.

stratification Stacks of sedimentary rock layers, built up by deposition of silt and other materials over time.

stream A flowing-water ecosystem that starts out as a freshwater spring or seep.

strip logging A way to minimize erosion from deforestation; a narrow corridor that parallels contours of sloped land is cleared; the upper part is used as a log-hauling road then is reseeded from intact forest above it.

strobilus Of certain nonflowering plants, a cluster of spore-producing structures.

stroma The semifluid matrix between the thylakoid membrane system and two outer membranes of a chloroplast where sucrose, starch, cellulose, and other end products of photosynthesis are built.

stromatolite Fossilized remains of dome-shaped mats of shallow-water communities, cyanobacterial species especially, that were infiltrated with dissolved minerals and fine sediments. Some are 3 billion years old.

substance P A neuromodulator that enhances pain perception.

substrate A reactant molecule that is specifically acted upon by an enzyme.

substrate-level phosphorylation Direct, enzyme-mediated transfer of a phosphate group from a substrate to another molecule.

succession *See* ecological succession.

suppressor T cell Type of lymphocyte that helps end an immune response.

surface-to-volume ratio A relationship in which the volume of an object increases with the cube of the diameter, but the surface area increases with the square.

survivorship curve Plot of age-specific survival of a cohort, from the time of birth until the last individual dies.

swim bladder Adjustable flotation sac that helps many fishes maintain neutral buoyancy in water; its volume changes as it exchanges gases with blood.

symbiosis [Gk. *sym*, together, + *bios*, life, mode of life] An ecological interaction in which one or more individuals interact closely with individuals of a different species for some or all of the life cycle; e.g., mutualism, predation, parasitism.

sympathetic neuron A neuron of the autonomic nervous system. Its signals cause increases in overall activities in times of stress or heightened awareness. Also works in opposition with sympathetic neurons to make small ongoing adjustments in activities of internal organs they both innervate.

sympatric speciation [Gk. *sym*, together, + *patria*, native land] A speciation model. Occurs inside the home range of a species in the absence of a physical barrier; e.g., by way of polyploidy in flowering plants.

synapsid An amniote lineage of early mammal-like reptiles and mammals.

synaptic integration (sin-AP-tik) The summation of excitatory and inhibitory signals that are arriving at an excitable cell's input zone at the same time.

syndrome The set of symptoms that characterize a medical condition.

system acquired resistance Of many plants, a mechanism that induces cells to produce and release compounds that will protect tissues from attack.

systemic circuit Cardiovascular route in which oxygenated blood flows from the heart through the rest of the body, where it gives up oxygen and takes up carbon dioxide, then flows back to the heart.

T lymphocyte T cell. White blood cell that regulates vertebrate immune responses by way of cytokines; cytotoxic T cells carry out cell-mediated immunity.

tactile display A type of ritualized social interaction involving physical contact.

tandem repeat One of many copies of short base sequences positioned one after another on a chromosome; used in DNA fingerprinting.

taproot system A primary root and all of its lateral branchings.

target cell Any cell that has molecular receptors for a signaling molecule.

taste receptor A type of chemoreceptor that detects solutes in the fluid bathing it.

taxon, plural **taxon** A set of organisms of a given type.

taxonomy Field of biology that identifies, names, and classifies species.

TCR Antigen-binding receptor of T cells.

tectum Midbrain's roof. In fishes and amphibians, coordinates most sensory inputs and initiates motor responses. In most vertebrates (not mammals), a reflex center; relays sensory input to forebrain.

telomere A cap of repetitive DNA sequences on the end of a chromosome. Each nuclear division, enzymes digest a bit of it; cells stop dividing when only a nubbin remains.

telophase (TEE-low-faze) Of meiosis I, a stage when one member of each pair of homologous chromosomes has arrived at a spindle pole. Of mitosis and of meiosis II, the stage when chromosomes typically decondense into threadlike structures and two daughter nuclei form.

temperature Measure of molecular motion.

temperature zone Globe-spanning bands of temperature defined by latitude; e.g., cool temperate, equatorial.

tendon A cord or strap of dense connective tissue that attaches a muscle to bone.

terminal bud *See* Bud.

territory An area that an animal defends against competitors for food, water, living space, mates, and other resources.

test, scientific Any standardized or innovative means by which a prediction based on a hypothesis might be disproved; often requires designing and conducting experiments, making observations, or developing models.

testcross A cross that might reveal the (unknown) genotype of an individual showing dominance for a trait; the individual is crossed with a known homozygous recessive individual.

testis, plural **testes** A type of gonad where male gametes and sex hormones form.

testosterone (tess-TOSS-tuh-rown) A sex hormone necessary for the development and functioning of the male reproductive system of vertebrates.

tetanus (TET-uh-nuss) A large muscle contraction. Repeated stimulation of a motor unit causes muscle twitches to run together. In the disease tetanus, muscles cannot be released from contraction.

tetrapod A vertebrate that is a four-legged walker or a descendant of one.

thalamus (THAL-uh-muss) Forebrain region; a coordinating center for sensory input and a relay station for signals to the cerebrum.

theory, scientific A time-tested, widely accepted intellectual framework used to interpret a broad range of observations and data about some aspect of nature. Tested rigorously but is still open to tests, revision, and tentative acceptance or rejection.

thermal inversion A layer of dense, cool air trapped beneath a layer of warm air.

thermal radiation Emission of radiant energy (heat) from any object.

thermocline Thermal stratification in a large body of water; a cool midlayer stops vertical mixing between warm surface water above it and cold water below it.

thermoreceptor Type of sensory cell that detects radiant energy (heat).

thigmotropism (thig-MOE-truh-pizm) [Gk. *thigm*, touch] Redirected growth in response to physical contact with a solid object; e.g., a vine curling around a post.

thirst center Part of the hypothalamus; promotes water-seeking behavior when osmoreceptors in the brain detect a rise in the blood level of sodium.

threat display Ritualized intraspecific signal conveying intent to attack.

three-domain system A classification system that groups all organisms into domains Bacteria, Archaea, and Eukarya.

thylakoid membrane A chloroplast's inner membrane system, often folded as flattened sacs, that forms a continuous compartment in the stroma. In the first stage of photosynthesis, pigments and enzymes in the membrane function in the formation of ATP and NADPH.

thymine (THY-meen) One of four nitrogen-containing bases in nucleotide monomers of DNA; also applies to a nucleotide with a thymine base component.

thymus gland Lymphoid organ; secretes hormones that influences the maturation of T cells that circulate to this gland right after they have formed in bone marrow.

thyroid gland Endocrine gland; secretes hormones that influence overall growth, development, and rates of metabolism.

tidal volume Volume of air flowing in and out of lungs in one respiratory cycle.

tight junction An array of many strands of fibrous proteins collectively joining the sides of cells that make up an epithelium; the array prevents solutes from leaking between the cells.

tissue Of multicelled organisms, a group of cells and matrixes interacting in the performance of one or more tasks.

tissue culture propagation Inducing the vegetative growth of a plant fragment or cell in a culture medium.

titin Elastic protein that keeps myosin filaments centered in a sarcomere and lets relaxed muscles passively resist stretching.

tongue A vertebrate organ of membrane-covered skeletal muscles used to position food and swallow, also to make sounds.

tonicity (toe-NISS-ih-TEE) Relative solute concentrations of two fluids.

tooth A hardened appendage used to cut, shred, pierce, or pummel food.

topsoil Uppermost soil layer with the most nutrients for plant growth.

torsion A drastic twisting of the body, including the visceral mass, as certain molluscan embryos develop.

total fertility rate TFR. Of humans, the average number of children born to females during their reproductive years.

touch-killing Mechanism by which a cytotoxic T cell kills target cells; it directly releases perforins and toxins onto them.

toxin Normal metabolic product that can damage or kill cells of a different species.

trace element Any element making up less than 0.01 percent of body weight.

tracer Any substance with a radioisotope attached; researchers can track it after delivering it into a cell, a multicelled body, ecosystem, or some other system.

trachea (TRAY-kee-uh), plural **tracheae** An air-conducting tube used in respiration. Of land vertebrates, the windpipe.

tracheal system Finely branching tubes for respiration that start at openings across the integument and dead-end in body tissues of arthropods; e.g., grasshoppers.

tracheid (TRAY-kid) A type of cell in xylem that conducts water and mineral ions.

tract Cordlike bundle of axons of sensory neurons, motor neurons, or both in the brain or spinal cord.

transcription [L. *trans*, across, + *scribere*, to write] First stage of protein synthesis. An RNA strand is assembled from nucleotides using a gene region in DNA as a template.

transfer RNA tRNA. One of a class of small RNA molecules that delivers amino acids to a ribosome. Its anticodon pairs with an mRNA codon during translation.

transition state A fleeting point when a chemical reaction can run to product or back to reactant.

translation Second stage of protein synthesis. At ribosomes, information encoded in an mRNA transcript guides the synthesis of a new polypeptide chain from amino acids.

translocation Attachment of a piece of a broken chromosome to another chromosome. Also, a mechanism by which organic compounds are conducted in phloem.

transpiration Evaporative water loss from a plant's aboveground parts.

transport protein Membrane protein that passively or actively assists specific ions or molecules into or out of a cell. The solutes move through the protein's interior.

transposon Transposable element. A stretch of DNA that jumps spontaneously and randomly to a different location in the genome and may mutate a gene.

triglyceride A lipid with three fatty acid tails attached to a glycerol backbone.

trisomy Having one extra chromosome in somatic cells; e.g., trisomy 21 ($2n + 1$).

trophic level (TROE-fik) All organisms the same number of transfer steps away from the energy input into an ecosystem.

tropical rain forest A biome in regions of regular, heavy rainfall, an annual mean temperature of 25°C, and humidity greater than 80 percent. Rich in biodiversity but low in topsoil; decomposition is too fast.

tropism (TROE-pizm) Directional growth response to an environmental factor; e.g., a shoot bending toward a light source.

true breeding lineage A group consisting of parents and their offspring in which only one version of a trait persists over time.

tubular reabsorption A process by which peritubular capillaries reclaim water and solutes that leak or are pumped out of a nephron's tubular regions.

tubular secretion Transport of H^+, urea, other solutes out of peritubular capillaries and into nephrons for excretion.

tumor Tissue mass of cells dividing at an abnormally high rate. Benign tumor cells stay in their home tissue; malignant ones metastasize, or slip away and invade other places in the body, where they may start new tumors. *See also* neoplasm.

tundra Biome of high-latitudes or high elevations with poor drainage, very little decomposition, very low temperatures, and a short growing season.

tunicate One of the baglike, filter-feeding urochordates.

turgor pressure (TUR-gore) Hydrostatic pressure. The pressure that any volume of fluid exerts against a wall, membrane, or some other structure containing it.

ultrafiltration Bulk flow of some protein-free plasma out of a blood capillary when outward-directed blood pressure exceeds the inward-directed osmotic movement of interstitial fluid.

ultraplankton Photosynthetic bacteria less than five micrometers across that help form "pastures of the seas."

uniformity theory Theory that Earth's surface has changed in slow, uniformly repetitive ways except for expected annual catastrophes, such as big floods. Changed Darwin's view of evolution; has since been discredited by plate tectonics theory.

upwelling Upward movement of deep, often nutrient-rich water near a coastline; replaces a mass of surface ocean water forced away by prevailing winds.

uracil (YUR-uh-sill) One of four nitrogen-containing bases in nucleotide monomers of RNA; also applies to a nucleotide with a uracil base component. Like thymine, uracil can base-pair with adenine.

urea Waste product formed in the liver from ammonia (derived from protein breakdown) and CO_2; excreted in urine.

ureter A urine-conducting tube from each kidney to the urinary bladder.

urethra A tube that drains the urinary bladder and opens at the body surface.

urinary bladder Distensible sac in which urine is stored before being excreted.

urinary excretion Mechanism by which excess water and solutes are removed from the body by the urinary system.

urinary system Vertebrate organ system that adjusts blood's volume and composition; helps maintain extracellular fluid.

urine Fluid consisting of excess water, wastes, and solutes that forms in kidneys by filtration, reabsorption, and secretion.

urochordate A bag-shaped chordate with larvae that have a firm, flexible notochord extending through a tail; e.g., a tunicate.

uterus (YOU-tur-us) [L. *uterus*, womb] Of a female placental mammal, a muscular, pear-shaped organ in which embryos are housed and nurtured during pregnancy.

vaccination Immunization procedure against a specific pathogen.

vaccine A type of antigen-containing preparation introduced into the body to prime the immune system to recognize the threat before actual infection.

vagina Of female mammals, the organ that receives sperm, forms part of birth canal, and channels menstrual flow.

variable Of experimental tests, a specific aspect of an object or event of interest that may differ over time and among individuals. A single variable is directly manipulated in an experimental group.

vascular bundle Multistranded, sheathed bundle of primary xylem and phloem in the ground tissue system of a stem or leaf.

vascular cambium A lateral meristem that forms in older stems or roots.

vascular cylinder Multistranded, sheathed, cylindrical array of primary xylem and phloem inside a root.

vascular plant Plant with xylem, phloem, and usually well-developed roots, stems, and leaves.

vascular tissue system All xylem and phloem in plants that are structurally more complex than bryophytes.

vasoconstriction A decrease in blood vessel diameter, arterioles especially.

vasodilation An increase in blood vessel diameter, arterioles especially.

vegetative growth Growth of a new plant from an extension or fragment of another.

vein Of a cardiovascular system, any of the large-diameter vessels that lead back to the heart. Of leaves, a vascular bundle threading through photosynthetic tissue.

venule A small blood vessel that connects several capillaries to a vein.

vernalization Stimulation of flowering in spring by low temperature in the season preceding it.

vertebra, plural **vertebrae** One of a series of hard bones that protects the spinal cord and forms the structural backbone for the anterior–posterior body axis.

vertebrate Animal having a backbone.

vesicle A small, membrane-bound sac in the cytoplasm; different sacs transport or store substances or hold enzymes that digest their contents.

vessel member Type of cell in xylem, dead at maturity; its wall becomes part of a water-conducting vessel.

vestibular apparatus Of vertebrates, an organ of equilibrium.

vestigial (ves-TIDJ-ul) A small body part, tissue, or organ that developed abnormally or degenerated over the generations and is unable to function as it normally might; e.g., vestigial wings of mutant fruit flies and human "tail bones."

villus (VIL-us), plural **villi** A fingerlike absorptive structure projecting from the free surface of some epithelia; e.g., the profusion of intestinal villi.

viroid Infectious particle of short, tightly folded strands or circles of RNA.

virus A noncellular infectious agent of DNA or RNA, a protein coat and, in some types, an outer lipid envelope; it can be replicated only after its genetic material enters a host cell and subverts the host's metabolic machinery.

viscera All soft organs inside an animal body; e.g., heart, lungs, and stomach.

vision Perception of visual stimuli based on light focused on a retina and image formation in the brain.

visual accommodation Light-focusing adjustments in a lens position or shape.

visual field The portion of the outside world that an animal sees.

visual signal An observable action or cue that functions as a communication signal.

vital capacity Air volume leaving lungs in one breath after maximum inhalation.

vitamin Any organic substance that an organism requires in trace amounts for metabolism but that it generally cannot synthesize for itself. Many coenzymes function as vitamins.

vitamin D A fat-soluble vitamin; helps the body absorb dietary calcium.

vocal cord One of the thick, muscular folds of the larynx that help some animals produce sound waves for vocalization.

warning coloration Of many toxic species and their mimics, strong colors, patterns, and other signals that predators learn to recognize and avoid.

wastewater treatment Removal of toxins, sludge, organic matter from liquid wastes.

water mold A stramenopile; most are saprobic decomposers or opportunistic parasites, of aquatic habitats.

water table Upper limit at which ground in a region is fully saturated with water.

watershed A region of any specified size in which all precipitation drains into one stream or river.

water–vascular system Of echinoderms, a system of tube feet connected to canals, through which controlled water flow can extend the feet in coordinated ways.

wavelength The distance between the crests of two successive wavelike forms of energy in motion.

wax A lipid with long-chain fatty acids attached to an alcohol other than glycerol.

whisk fern Seedless vascular plant having a branching form and no true roots; e.g., *Psilotum*.

white blood cell Leukocyte. A participant in innate or adaptive immunity, or both; e.g., an eosinophil, neutrophil, basophil, macrophage, T cell, B cell.

white matter Tracts of myelinated axons in the brain and spinal cord.

wild-type allele Of a given gene locus, the allele that occurs normally or with the greatest frequency among individuals of a population.

wind farm Collection of turbines used to convert mechanical energy into electricity.

wing A body part that functions in flight, as among birds, bats, and many insects.

X chromosome A type of sex chromosome that influences sex determination; e.g., XX mammalian embryo becomes female; an XY pairing causes it to develop into a male.

X chromosome inactivation In a female mammalian embryo, the programmed painting of special RNAs over most of one of the two X chromosomes, which cuts off access to the majority of its genes. Which X chromosome gets painted in each cell is a random event, so tissues of adult female mammals are a mosaic of traits. *See also* Dosage compensation.

xanthophyll One of a class of accessory pigments in photosynthesis that reflects yellow to orange light.

xenotransplantation Surgical transfer of an organ from one species to another.

X-linked gene Any gene on an X chromosome.

X-linked recessive inheritance Recessive condition in which the responsible, mutated gene is on the X chromosome.

x-ray diffraction image Film image of x-rays scattered by a crystalline sample; the resulting pattern of streaks and dots can be used to calculate the spacing between the atoms in the crystal lattice.

xylem (ZYE-lum) [Gk. *xylon*, wood] Of vascular plants, a complex tissue that conducts water and solutes through tubes of interconnected walls of cells that are dead at maturity.

Y chromosome Distinctive chromosome in males or females of many species (not both); e.g., human males XY, females, XX.

yellow-green alga A chrysophyte that does not make fucoxanthin; species are common in salt marshes.

yellow marrow Of most mature bones, a fatty tissue that produces red blood cells when blood loss from the body is severe.

Y-linked gene Gene on a Y chromosome.

yolk Protein- and lipid-rich substance that nourishes embryos in animal eggs.

yolk sac Extraembryonic membrane. In most shelled eggs, it holds nutritive yolk; in humans, part becomes a blood cell formation site, and some cells give rise to forerunners of gametes.

zero population growth No net increase or decrease in population size during a specified interval.

zooplankton A community of mostly microscopic heterotrophs suspended or weakly swimming in an aquatic habitat.

zygomycetes Type of parasitic or saprobic fungus in which diploid zygotes develop into zygospores, a type of thick-walled sexual spore in a thin, clear covering.

zygospore Sexual spore of zygomycetes.

zygote (ZYE-goat) A fertilized egg.

Art Credits and Acknowledgments

Page iii, v Photographer Russ Lowgren.

TABLE OF CONTENTS **Page vii** From left, © University of California Museum of Paleontology; Jeremy Pickett-Heaps, School of Botany, University of Melbourne; Jeremy Pickett-Heaps, School of Botany, University of Melbourne; Armed Forces Institute of Pathology. **Page viii** From left, Larry West/FPG/Getty Images; © Professors P. Motta and T. Naguro/SPL/Photo Researchers, Inc. **Page ix** From left, Dr. Pascal Madaule, France; © Tom and Pat Leeson/Photo Researchers, Inc.; Raychel Ciemma. **Page x** From left, Lisa Starr; Photo by Victor Fisher, courtesy Genetic Savings & Clone. **Page xi** From left, Courtesy of Professor Martin F. Yanofsky, UCSD; © Visuals Unlimited; Christopher Ralling; bottom left, Lisa Starr; bottom right, Courtesy of John McNamara, www.paleodirect.com. **Page xii** From left, © Francois Gohier/Photo Researchers, Inc.; © David Parker/SPL/Photo Researchers, Inc.; © Jack Jeffrey Photography. **Page xiii** Clockwise from top left, © David Lees/Getty Images; Lisa Starr; © Dr. Dennis Kunkel/Visuals Unlimited; © Stem Jems/Photo Researchers, Inc. **Page xiv** Clockwise from top left, © Gregory G. Dimijian/Photo Researchers, Inc.; © Sanford/Agliolo/Corbis; © Brandon D. Cole/Corbis; © 2002/Photodisc/Getty Images; Jane Burton/Bruce Coleman, Ltd.; Robert C. Simpson/Nature Stock. **Page xv** From left, © Karen Carr Studio/www.karencarr.com; © James Marshall/Corbis. **Page xvi** From left, © Cory Gray; © Photodisc/Getty Images. **Page xvii** Clockwise from top left, © Andrew Syred/Photo Researchers, Inc.; © Dr. Jeremy Burgess/SPL/Photo Researchers, Inc.; © Cathlyn Melloan/Stone/Getty Images; Robert E. Basye Rose Breeding and Genetics Research Program, Department of Horticultural Sciences, Texas A&M University. **Page xviii** From left, © John D. Cunningham/Visuals Unlimited; © Triarch/Visuals Unlimited; Kenneth Garrett/National Geographic Image Collection. **Page xix** From left, Eric A. Newman; © David Aubrey/Corbis; Ed Reschke; Bone Clones®, www.boneclones.com. **Page xx** From left, © David Scharf/Peter Arnold, Inc.; © NSIBC/SPL/Photo Researchers, Inc.; © NIBSC/Photo Researchers, Inc. **Page xxi** From left, © Dr. Richard Kessel and Dr. Randy Kardon/Tissues & Organs/Visuals Unlimited; Micrograph, Ed Reschke; Gunter Ziesler/Bruce Coleman, Inc. **Page xxii** From left, © Archivo Iconografico, S.A./Corbis; © Don W. Fawcett/Photo Researchers, Inc.; © Science Photo Library/Photo Researchers, Inc. **Page xxiii** From left, © Minden Pictures; © Eric and David Hosking/Corbis; © Thomas W. Doeppner. **Page xxiv** Clockwise from top left, R. Barrick/USGS; © W. Perry Conway/Corbis; © Hank Fotos Photography; © C. James Webb/Phototake USA. **Page xxv** From left, Robert Vrijenhoek, MBARI; Gerry Ellis/The Wildlife Collection; NASA.

INTRODUCTION NASA Space Flight Center

CHAPTER 1 **1.1** John McColgan/Bureau of Land Management, Alaska Fire Service; (inset) © Peter Turnley/CORBIS. **1.2** (a) Rendered with Atom In A Box, copyright Dauger Research, Inc.; (b, above left) PDB file courtesy of Dr. Christina A. Bailey, Department of Chemistry & Biochemistry, California Polytechnic State University, San Luis Obispo, CA.; (b, above center) PDB ID: 1BBB; Silva, M. M., Rogers, P. H., Arnone, A.; A third quaternary structure of human hemoglobin A at 1.7-A resolution; J Biol Chem 267 pp. 17248 (1992); (b, above right) PDB file from Klotho Biochemical Compounds Declarative Database; Photographs: (d) © Science Photo Library/CORBIS; (h) © Jeffrey L. Rotman/CORBIS; (i) Peter Scoones; (j–k) NASA. **1.3** David Neal Parks. **1.4** © Y. Arthus-Bertrand/Peter Arnold, Inc. **1.6** Photographs by Jack de Coningh. **1.8** Page 8, Clockwise from above left, © P. Hawtin, University of Southampton/SPL/Photo Researchers, Inc.; CNRI/SPL/Photo Researchers, Inc.; © Dr. Harald Huber, Dr. Michael Hohn, Prof. Dr. K. O. Stetter, University of Regensburg, Germany; R. Robinson/Visuals Unlimited; Page 9, Clockwise from above left, © Lewis Trusty/Animals Animals; John Lotter Gurling/Tom Stack & Associates; Edward S. Ross; © Stephen Dalton/Photo Researchers, Inc.; Edward S. Ross; Robert C. Simpson/Nature Stock; © Oliver Meckes/Photo Researchers, Inc.; Courtesy © James Evarts; Emiliania Huxleyi. Photograph by Vita Pariente. Scanning electron micrograph taken on a Jeol T330A instrument at the Texas A & M University Electron Microscopy Center; Carolina Biological Supply Company. **1.9** Left, Photographs courtesy Derrell Fowler, Tecumseh, Oklahoma; right, © Nick Brent. **Page 11** © LWA-Stephen Welstead/CORBIS. **Page 12** © SuperStock. **1.11** (a–b) © Chris D. Jiggins; (c) Background, © Kevin Schafer/Peter Arnold, Inc.; (d) © Martin Reid. **1.12** © Gary Head. **Page 16** © Digital Vision/PictureQuest.

Page 17 Unit I © Wim van Egmond, Micropolitan Museum

CHAPTER 2 **2.1** © Owaki-Kulla/CORBIS. **2.2** (c) Rendered with Atom In A Box, copyright Dauger Research, Inc. **2.4** (a) © CC Studio/Photo Researchers, Inc.; (d) Harry T. Chugani, M.D., UCLA School of Medicine. **Page 22** © Michael S. Yamashita/CORBIS. **2.5** Rendered with Atom In A Box, copyright Dauger Research, Inc. **2.8** Photographs (a) below, Micrograph © Bruce Iverson; (c, page 25) PDB ID:IBNA; H.R. Drew, R. M. Wing, T. Takano, C. Broka, S. Tanaka, K. Itakura, R. E. Dickerson; Structure of a B-DNA Dodecamer. Conformation and Dynamics, PNAS. **2.9** (a,b,c, left) PDB file from NYU Scientific Visualization Lab; (b, right) © Steve Lissau/Rainbow; (c, right) © Mark Newman/Bruce Coleman USA. **2.11** (a) © Lester Lefkowitz/CORBIS. **2.13** Michael Grecco/Picture Group. **2.14** © National Gallery Collection; by kind permission of the Trustees of the National Gallery, London/CORBIS. **2.15** © H. Eisenbeiss/Frank Lane Picture Agency.

CHAPTER 3 **3.1** Left, © 2002 Charlie Wait/Stone/Getty Images; right, © Dr. W. Michaelis/Universitat Hamburg. **Page 33** © John Collier. Great Britain, 1850–1934, *Priestess of Delphi*, 1891, London, oil on canvas, 160.0 x 80.0 cm. Gift of the Rt. Honourable, the Earl of Kintore, 1893. **Page 34** (right, top) PDB file from NYU Scientific Visualization Lab; (right, center), PDB file from NYU Scientific Visualization Lab; (right bottom), PDB file from Klotho Biochemical Compounds Declarative Database. **3.5** Photograph, Tim Davis/Photo Researchers, Inc. **3.9** © Steve Chenn/CORBIS. **3.10** © David Scharf/Peter Arnold, Inc. **3.11** (a) PDB file courtesy of Dr. Christina A. Bailey, Department of Chemistry and Biochemistry, California Polytechnic State University, San Luis Obispo, CA. **3.12** Left, © Kevin Schafer/CORBIS. **3.13** (a) PDB file courtesy of Dr. Christina A. Bailey, Department of Chemistry. **3.14** (a) © Scott Camazine/Photo Researchers, Inc. **3.15** (b–e) PDB files from NYU Scientific Visualization Lab. **3.16** (b, right) After: *Introduction to Protein Structure*, 2nd ed., Branden & Tooze, Garland Publishing, Inc.; (c, left) PDB ID: 1BBB; Silva, M. M., Rogers, P. H., Arnone, A.; A third quaternary structure of human hemoglobin A at 1.7-Å resolution; J Biol Chem 267 pp. 17248 (1992); (c, right) After: *Introduction to Protein Structure*, 2nd ed., Branden & Tooze, Garland Publishing, Inc. **3.17** PDB ID: 1BBB; Silva, M. M., Rogers, P. H., Arnone, A.; A third quaternary structure of human hemoglobin A at 1.7-Å resolution; J Biol Chem 267 pp. 17248 (1992). **3.18** (a,b) PDB files from New York University Scientific Visualization Center; (c) © Dr. Gopal Murti/SPL/Photo Researchers, Inc.; (d) Courtesy of Melba Moore. **3.19** PDB files from Klotho Biochemical Compounds Declarative Database. **3.21** PDB ID:1BNA; H. R. Drew, R. M. Wing, T. Takano, C. Broka, S. Tanaka, K. Itakura, R. E. Dickerson; Structure of a B-DNA Dodecamer. Conformation and Dynamics; PNAS V. 78 2179, 1981. **3.22** © ThinkStock/SuperStock. **3.23** Left, PDB ID: 1AKJ; Gao, G. F., Tormo, J., Gerth, U. C., Wyer, J. R., McMichael, A. J., Stuart, D. I., Bell, J. I., Jones, E. Y., Jakobsen, B. K.; Crystal structure of the complex between human CD8alpha(alpha) and HLA-A2; Nature 387 pp. 630 (1997); right, Al Giddings/Images Unlimited.

CHAPTER 4 **4.1** © Tony Brian and David Parker/SPL/Photo Researchers, Inc. **4.2** Left, National Library of Medicine; right, Armed Forces Institute of Pathology. **4.7** Leica Microsystems, Inc., Deerfield, IL. **4.8** © Geoff Tompkinson/SPL/Photo Researchers, Inc. **4.9** Photographs: (hummingbird) © Robert A. Tyrrell; (human) © Pete Saloutos/CORBIS; (redwood) © Sally A. Morgan, Ecoscene/CORBIS. **4.10** Photographs by Jeremy Pickett-Heaps, School of Botany, University of Melbourne. **4.11** (a) K. G. Murti/Visuals Unlimited; (b) R. Calentine/Visuals Unlimited; (c) Gary Gaard and Arthur Kelman. **4.12** (a) © University of California Museum of Paleontology; (b) © University of California Museum of Paleontology; (c) © Russell Kightley/SPL/Photo Researchers, Inc. **4.13** M. C. Ledbetter, Brookhaven National Laboratory. **4.14** Micrograph, G. L. Decker. **4.16** Stephen L. Wolfe. **4.17** Left micrograph, Don W. Fawcett/Visuals Unlimited; center micrograph, A. C. Faberge, *Cell and Tissue Research*, 151: 403–415, 1974. **4.18** Micrographs: (a) Stephen L. Wolfe; (c,d) Don W. Fawcett/Visuals Unlimited, computer enhanced; (e) Gary Grimes, computer enhanced. **4.19** Right micrograph, Keith R. Porter. **4.20** © Dr. Jeremy Burgess/SPL/Photo Researchers, Inc. **4.21** Micrograph, © Ray F. Evert. **4.22** (a) George S. Ellmore; (b left) © Science Photo Library/Photo Researchers, Inc.; (b right) Bone Clones®, www.boneclones.com. **4.25** (a) © J. W. Shuler/Photo Researchers, Inc.; (b) Courtesy Dr. Vincenzo Cirulli, Laboratory of Developmental Biology, The Whittier Institute for Diabetes University of California-San Diego, La Jolla, California; (c) Courtesy of Mary Osborn, Max Planck Institute for Biophysical Chemistry, Goettingen FRG. **4.26** (a) John Lonsdale, www.johnlonsdale.net; (b) David C. Martin, Ph.D. **4.28** (a) © CNRI/SPL/Photo Researchers, Inc.; (b) © Dow W. Fawcett/Photo Researchers, Inc.; (c) © Mike Abbey/Visuals Unlimited. **4.29** Left, © Don W. Fawcett/Photo Researchers, Inc.; right, After Stephen L. Wolfe, *Molecular and Cellular Biology*,

Wadsworth, 1993. **4.30** Right, (a–b) From *Tissue and Cell*, Vol. 27, pp. 421–427, Courtesy of Bjorn Afzelius, Stockholm University.

CHAPTER 5 **5.1** © Abraham Menashe **5.6** Left, with integrin: PDB ID:1JV2; Xiong, J. P., Stehle, T., Diefenbach, B., Zhang, R., Dunker, R., Scott, D. L., Joachimiak, A., Goodman, S. L., Arnaout, M. A.: *Crystal Structure of the Extracellular Segment of Integrin*; right, Chris Keeney with Human growth hormone: PDB ID:1A22; Clackson, T., Ultsch, M. H., Wells, J. A., de Vos, A. M.: Structural and functional analysis of the 1:1 growth hormone: receptor complex reveals the molecular basis for receptor affinity. J Mol Biol 277 pp. 1111 (1998); HLA: PDB ID: 1AKJ; Gao, G. F., Tormo, J., Gerth, U. C., Wyer, J. R., McMichael, A., Stuart, D. I., Bell, J. I., Jones, E. Y., Jakobsen, B. K.; Crystal structure of the complex between human CD8alpha(alpha) and HLA-A2; *Nature* 387 pp. 630 (1997); glut1: PDB ID:1JA5; Zuniga, F. A., Shi, G., Haller, J. F., Rubashkin, A., Flynn, D. R., Iserovich, P., Fischbarg, J.: A Three-Dimensional Model of the Human Facilitative Glucose Transporter Glut1 J.Biol.Chem. 276 pp. 44970 (2001); calcium pump: PDB ID:1EUL; Toyoshima, C., Nakasako, M., Nomura, H., Ogawa, H.: Crystal Structure of the Calcium Pump of Sarcoplasmic Reticulum at 2.6 Angstrom Resolution. *Nature* 405 pp. 647 (2000); ATPase: PDB ID:1BHE; Menz, R. I., Walker, J. E., Leslie, A. G. W.: Structure of Bovine Mitochondrial F1-ATPase with Nucleotide Bound to All Three Catalytic Sites: Implications for the Mechanism of Rotary Catalysis. Cell (Cambridge, Mass.) 106 pp. 331 (2001). **5.7** Photograph, © Andrew Lambert/SPL/Photo Researchers, Inc. **5.10** PDB files from NYU Scientific Visualization Lab. **5.11** After: David H. MacLennan, William J. Rice and N. Michael Green, "The Mechanism of Ca2+ Transport by Sarco (Endo) plasmic Reticulum Ca2+-ATPases." JBC Volume 272, Number 46, Issue of November 14, 1997 pp. 28815–28818. **Page 84** © Hubert Stadler/CORBIS **5.13** Micrographs, M. Sheetz, R. Painter, and S. Singer, *Journal of Cell Biology*, 70:193 (1976) by permission of The Rockefeller University Press. **5.16** © R. G. W. Anderson, M. S. Brown and J. L. Goldstein. *Cell* 10:351 (1977) **5.17** (a) © Juergen Berger/Max Planck Inst./SPL/Photo Researchers, Inc. **5.20** © Prof. Marcel Bessis/SPL/Photo Researchers, Inc. **5.21** © Frieder Sauer/Bruce Coleman Ltd. **5.22** Dr. Peter Agre, M.D., Johns Hopkins University School of Medicine.

CHAPTER 6 **6.1** Left, Model by Dr. David B. Goodin, The Scripps Research Institute; right, © Stockbyte/SuperStock. **6.2** © Vandystadt/Photo Researchers, Inc. **6.3** NASA. **6.4** Above, © Craig Aurness/CORBIS; below, © William Dow/CORBIS. **6.6** PDB file from Klotho Biochemical Compounds Declarative Database. **6.10** Left, Models by Dr. David B. Goodin, The Scripps Research Institute; (a-c) PDB ID: 1DGF; Putnam, C. D., Arvai, A. S., Bourne, Y., Tainer, J. A.: Active and Inhibited Human Catalase Structures: Lingand Nadph Binding and Catalytic Mechanism J Mol Biol. 296, p. 295 (2000). **6.13** (b) © Scott McKiernan/ZUMA Press. **6.14** (b) © Foodpix/Bill Boch. **6.17** From B. Alberts, et al., *Molecular Biology of the Cell*, 1983, Garland Publishing. **6.18** (a) © Frank Borges Llosa/www.frankley.com; (b) Sara Lewis, Tufts University. **6.19** Prof. J. Woodland Hastings, Harvard University. **6.20** C. Contag, *Molecular Microbiology*, November 1985, Vol. 18, No. 4, pp. 593-603. "Photonic Detection of Bacterial Pathogens in Living Hosts." Reprinted by permission of Blackwell Science. **6.21** (a) Models by Dr. David B. Goodin, The Scripps Research Institute; (b) © Gary Head.

CHAPTER 7 **7.1** © Richard Uhlhorn Photography. **Page 107** NASA. **7.2** Left, © 2002 PhotoDisc/Getty Images. **7.3** (a) Larry West/FPG/Getty Images. **7.6** (a) Left, © Craig Tuttle/CORBIS. **7.5** © Jason Sonneman. **7.7** (a) Harindar Keer, Thorsten Ritz Laboratory at UC Irvine, Dept. of Physic and Astronomy, using VMD proprietary software. **7.8** Light Harvesting Complex PDB ID: 1RWT; Liu, Z., Yan, H., Wang, K., Kuang, T., Zhang, J., Gui, L., An, X., Chang, W.: Crystal Structure of Spinach Major Light-Harvesting Complex at 2.72 A Resolution Nature 428 pp. 287 (2004). **7.11** (a) Top, Courtesy of John S. Russell, Pioneer High School; (a) center, micrograph by Bruce Iverson, computer-enhanced; (b) top, © Foodpix/Bill Boch; (b) center, micrograph by Ken Wagner/Visuals Unlimited, computer-enhanced; (c) top, © Chris Hellier/CORBIS; (c) center, micrograph by James Mauseth, University of Texas, Mauseth Lab. **7.13** NASA. **7.15** © E. R. Degginger. **7.16** (a) Douglas Faulkner/Sally Faulkner Collection; (b) Herve Chaumeton/Agence Nature.

CHAPTER 8 **8.1** © Louise Chalcraft-Frank and FARA. **Page 123** © Professors P. Motta and T. Naguro/SPL/Photo Researchers, Inc. **8.2** Photographs: Clockwise from above left, © Jim Cummins/CORBIS; John Lotter Gurling/Tom Stack & Associates; © Chase Swift/CORBIS. **8.5** Right, © Professors P. Motta and T. Naguro/SPL/Photo Researchers, Inc. **8.10** (a) Adrian Warren/Ardea London; (b–c) © Foodpix/Ben Fink. **8.12** © Randy Faris/CORBIS; Inset, © Gladden Willis, MD/Visuals Unlimited. **Page 134** © Lois Ellen Frank/CORBIS. **8.13** © Gary Head. **Page 136** © R. Llewellyn/SuperStock, Inc.

Page 139 Unit II © Francis Leroy, Biocosmos/SPL/Photo Researchers, Inc.

CHAPTER 9 **9.1** Dr. Pascal Madaule, France. **9.2** Courtesy of The Family of Henrietta Lacks. **9.3** © Divital Vision/Getty Images. **9.4** (a) Left, C. J. Harrison et al, *Cytogenetics and Cell Genetics*, 35:21–27, 1983, S. Karger, and A. G. Basel; (c) B. Hamkalo; (d) O. L. Miller, Jr., Steve L. McKnight. **9.6** Left, © L. Willatt, East Anglian Regional Genetics Service/SPL/Photo Researchers, Inc. **9.7** (b–g, above) © Jennifer W. Shuler/Science Source/Photo Researchers, Inc. **9.8** Above, micrograph, © D. M. Phillips/Visuals Unlimited; below, micrograph, © R. Calentine/Visuals Unlimited. **9.9** © Jennifer W. Shuler/Science Source/Photo Researchers, Inc. **9.10**, Lennart Nilsson from *A Child Is Born* ©1966, 1967 Dell Publishing Company, Inc. **9.11** © Phillip B. Carpenter, Department of Biochemistry and Molecular Biology. **9.12** © Science Photo Library/Photo Researchers, Inc. **9.14** (a) Ken Greer/Visuals Unlimited; (b) © Biophoto Associates/Science Source/Photo Researchers, Inc.; (c) © James Stevenson/SPL/Photo Researchers, Inc. **9.15** Micrographs by A. S. Bajer, University of Oregon.

CHAPTER 10 **10.1** (a) © Dan Kline/Visuals Unlimited; (b) AP/Wide World Photos; (c) © George D. Lepp/CORBIS; (d) © Andrew Syred/Photo Researchers, Inc. **10.2** Image courtesy of Carl Zeiss MicroImaging, Thornwood, NY. **10.4** © L. Willatt, East Anglian Regional Genetics Service/SPL/Photo Researchers, Inc. **10.5** Micrographs, (a–h) above, with thanks to the John Innes Foundation Trustees. **10.8** Seth Gold. **10.10** © Francis Leroy, Biocosmos/SPL/Photo Researchers, Inc. **10.11** Photographs (page 165), left, Dr. Stan Erlandsen, University of Minnesota; right, Cytographics. **10.13** © Ron Neumeyer, www.microimaging.ca. **10.14** © Lisa O'Connor/ZUMA/CORBIS.

CHAPTER 11 **11.1** Left, Robert E. Basye, Rose Breeding and Genetics Research Program, Department of Horticultural Sciences, Texas A&M University; right, Department of Horticultural Sciences, Texas A&M University. **Page 169** Bob Cerasoli. **11.2** Moravian Museum, Brno. **11.3** (a) Jean M. Labat/Ardea, London. **11.10** © David Scharf/Peter Arnold, Inc. **11.11** Photographs: above, William E. Ferguson; below, © Francesc Muntada/CORBIS. **11.12** Tedd Somes. **11.13** (a–b) Michael Stuckey/Comstock, Inc.; (c) Bosco Broyer, photograph by Gary Head. **11.14** © Bettmann/CORBIS. **11.17** Left, © Pamela Harper/Harper Horticultural Slide Library; right, from Prof. Otto Wilhelm Thomé, Flora von Deutschland Österreich und der Schweiz. 1885, Gera, Germany. **11.18** Left (Down from top), Frank Cezus/FPG/Getty Images; Frank Cezus/FPG/Getty Images; Ted Beaudin/FPG/Getty Images; © Michael Prince/CORBIS; right, © Lisa Starr. **11.20** Courtesy of Ray Carson, University of Florida News and Public Affairs. **11.21** Left, © Tom and Pat Leeson/Photo Researchers, Inc.; right, © Rick Guidotti, Positive Exposure. **11.22** (a) Courtesy of Wayside Gardens/www.waysidegardens.com; (b) © Gene Ahrens/SuperStock; (c) © Karen Tweedy-Holmes/CORBIS; (d) © Clay Perry/CORBIS. **11.23** Leslie Falteisek/Clacritter Manx. **Page 185** Tedd Somes. **11.24** © Maximilian Stock Ltd./Foodpix.

CHAPTER 12 **12.1** Left, © Reuters/CORBIS; center, Gene Griessman/www.presidentlincoln.com; right, © Hulton-Deutsch Collection/CORBIS. **12.2** Andrew Syred/Photo Researchers, Inc. **12.3** (b) right, © Charles D. Winters/Photo Researchers, Inc.; (f) © Omikron/Photo Researchers, Inc. **12.4** From *Multicolor Spectral Karyotyping of Human Chromosomes*, by E. Schrock, T. Ried, et al, *Science*, 26 July 1996, 273:495. Used by permission of E. Schrock, T. Reid and the American Association for the Advancement of Science. **12.5** Above, © Frank Trapper/CORBIS Sygma. **12.6** © Lois Ellen Frank/CORBIS. **12.7** Eddie Adams/AP Wide World Photos. **Page 192** Above, © 2001 PhotoDisc, Inc.; below, © 2001 EyeWire. **12.8** (b) from M. Cummings, *Human Heredity: Principles and Issues*, 3rd Edition, p. 126. © 1994 by Brooks/Cole. All rights reserved; (c) after Patten, Carlson & others. **Page 193** Top right, Carolina Biological Supply Company. **12.9** Left, © Carolina Biological/Visuals Unlimited; right, © Terry Gleason/Visuals Unlimited. **12.11** Art, After V. A. McKusick, *Human Genetics*, 2nd Ed., © 1969. Reprinted by permission of author; photograph Bettmann/CORBIS. **12.12** Left, photos by Gary L. Friedman, www.FriedmanArchives.com. **Page 195** © Russ Schleipman/CORBIS. **12.13** Courtesy G. H. Valentine. **12.14** From *Multicolor Spectral Karyotyping of Human Chromosomes*, by E. Schrock, T. Ried, et al, *Science*, 26 July 1996, 273:496. Used by permission of E. Schrock and T. Reid and the American Association for the Advancement of Science. **12.16** (a) © CNRI/Photo Researchers, Inc. **Page 199** UNC Medical Illustration and Photography. **12.18** © Stapleton Collection/CORBIS. **12.19** Dr. Victor A. McKusick. **12.20** Steve Uzzell. **12.21** © Saturn Stills/SPL/Photo Researchers, Inc. **12.22** From Lennart Nilsson, *A Child is Born*, © 1966, 1977 Dell Publishing Company, Inc. **12.23** © Matthew Alan/CORBIS; Inset, Fran Heyl Associates © Jacques Cohen, computer-enhanced by © Pix Elation. **12.24** Stefan Schwarz.

CHAPTER 13 **13.1** PA News Photo Library. **13.2** A. C. Barrington Brown © 1968 J. D. Watson. **13.4** (c) photograph, Eye of Science/Photo Researchers, Inc. **13.6** PDB ID: 1BBB; Silva, M. M., Rogers, P. H., Arnone, A.: A third quaternary structure of human hemoglobin A at 1.7-Å resolution. J Biol Chem 267 pp. 17248 (1992). **13.9** (1–3) © James King-Holmes/ SPL/Photo Researchers, Inc.; (4) © McLeod Murdo/CORBIS Sygma. **13.10** Photos by Victor Fisher, courtesy Genetic Savings & Clone. **13.12** © SPL/Photo Researchers, Inc. **13.13** Right, Shahbaz A. Janjua, MD/Dermatlas; http://www.dermatlas.org.

CHAPTER 14 **14.1** Left, © Vaughan Fleming/ SPL/Photo Researchers, Inc.; right, PDB ID: 2AAI; Rutenber, E., Katzin, B.J., Ernst, S., Collins, E.J., Mlsna, D., Ready, M. P., Robertus, J. D., Crystallographic Refinement of ricin to 2.5 A. Proteins 10pp.240 (1991). **14.7** Above, tRNA model by Dr. David B. Goodin, The Scripps Research Institute. **14.8** Courtesy of Thomas A. Steitz from *Science*. **14.11** Left, Nik Kleinberg; right, P. J. Maughan. **14.12** © John W. Gofman and Arthur R. Tamplin. From *Poisoned Power: The Case Against Nuclear Power Plants Before and After Three Mile Island*, Rodale Press, PA, 1979. **14.14** © Dr. M. A. Ansary/SPL/Photo Researchers, Inc.

CHAPTER 15 **15.1** From the archives of www.breastpath.com, courtesy of J. B. Askew, Jr., M.D., P. A. Reprinted with permission, copyright 2004 Breastpath.com. **Page 231** Courtesy of Robin Shoulla and Young Survival Coalition. **15.2** (b) From the collection of Jamos Werner and John T. Lis. **15.4** (a) Dr. Karen Dyer Montgomery. **15.5** Jack Carey. **15.6** (a) Above, Juergen Berger, Max Planck Institute for Developmental Biology–Tuebingen, Germany; (a) below, © Jose Luis Riechmann; (b) below, © Jose Luis Riechmann. **15.7** (a) Left, © Visuals Unlimited; (a) right, UCSF Computer Graphics Laboratory, National Institutes, NCRR Grant 01081; (c) from left, © Walter J. Ghering/ University of Basel, Switzerland; © Carolina Biological/Visuals Unlimited; © Carolina Biological/Visuals Unlimited; © Carolina Biological/Visuals Unlimited; Courtesy of Edward B. Lewis, California Institute of Technology **15.8** (a) Palay/Beaubois after Robert F. Weaver and Philip W. Hedrick, *Genetics*. © 1989 W. C. Brown Publishers; (b–c) © Jim Langeland, Jim Williams, Julie Gates, Kathy Vorwerk, Steve Paddock, and Sean Carroll, HHMI, University of Wisconsin-Madison. **15.9** PDB ID: 1CJG; Spronk, C. A. E. M., Bonvin, A. M. J. J., Radha, P. K., Melacini, G., Boelens, R., Kaptein, R.: The Solution Structure of Lac Repressor Headpiece 62 Complexed to a Symmetrical Lac Operator. Structure (London) 7 pp. 1483 (1999). Also PDB ID: 1LBI; Lewis, M., Chang, G., Horton, N. C., Kercher, M. A., Pace, H. C., Schumacher, M. A., Brennan, R. G., Lu, P.: Crystal structure of the lactose operon repressor and its complexes with DNA and inducer. *Science* 271 pp. 1247 (1996); lactose pdb files from the Hetero-Compound Information Centre - Uppsala (HIC-Up). **15.11** © Jim Langeland, Jim Williams, Julie Gates, Kathy Vorwerk, Steve Paddock, and Sean Carroll, HHMI, University of Wisconsin-Madison.

CHAPTER 16 **16.1** (a) Per Hardestam/ www.hardestam.se; (b) Dr. Jorge Mayer, Golden Rice Project. **Page 243** ScienceUV/Visuals Unlimited. **16.3** (a) Dr. Huntington Potter and Dr. David Dressler; (b) with permission of © QIAGEN, Inc. **Page 248** © TEK IMAGE/Photo Researchers, Inc. **16.9** Left, © David Parker/SPL/Photo Researchers, Inc.; right, Cellmark Diagnostics, Abingdon, UK. **16.10** Right, © Volker Steger/SPL/ Photo Researchers, Inc. **16.11** Courtesy of Joseph DeRisa. From *Science*, 1997 Oct. 24; 278 (5338) 680–686. **Page 252** © Professor Stanley Cohen/ SPL/Photo Researchers, Inc. **16.12** (a) Courtesy Calgene, LLC; (b) Dr. Vincent Chiang, School of Forestry and Wood Products, Michigan Technology

University. **16.13** (d) © Lowell Georgis/CORBIS; (e) Keith V. Wood. **16.14** (a) © Adi Nes, Dvir Gallery Ltd.; (b) Transgenic goat produced using nuclear transfer at GTC Biotherapeutics. Photo used with permission; (c) © Matt Gentry/Roanoke Times. **16.14** R. Brinster, R. E. Hammer, School of Veterinary Medicine, University of Pennsylvania. **Page 256** © Jeans for Gene Appeal.

Page 259 UNIT III © Wolfgang Kaehler/Corbis.

CHAPTER 17 **17.1** Left, NASA Galileo Imaging Team; Right © David A. Kring, NASA/Univ. Arizona Space Imagery Center. **17.2** Art by Don Davis. **17.3** (a, c) © Wolfgang Kaehler/Corbis; (b) © Earl & Nazima Kowall/Corbis; (d, e) Edward S. Ross. **17.4** right, © Bruce J. Mohn; (inset) Phillip Gingerich, Director, University of Michigan. Museum of Paleontology. **17.5** © Jonathan Blair/ Corbis. **17.6** (a) Courtesy George P. Darwin, Darwin Museum, Down House; (b) © Christopher Ralling; (e) Dieter & Mary Plage/Survival Anglia. **Page 265** Heather Angel. **17.7** (a) © Joe McDonald/Corbis; (b) © Karen Carr Studio/www.karencarr.com. **17.8** (a) © Gerra and Sommazzi/www.justbirds.org; (b) © Kevin Schafer/Corbis; (c) © Alan Root/Bruce Coleman Ltd. **17.9** Down House and The Royal College of Surgeons of England. **17.10** Left, H. P. Banks; Right, Jonathan Blair. **17.11** © Jonathan Blair/Corbis. **17.12** (b) © 2001 Photodisc, Inc. **17.14** © Corbis. **17.16** © NASA/GSFC. **17.16** (a–d) After A.M. Ziegler, C.R. Scotese, and S.F. Barrett, "Mesozoic and Cenozoic Paleogeographic Maps," and J. Krohn and J. Sundermann (Eds.), Tidal Frictions and the Earth's Rotation II, Springer-Verlag, 1983; (e) © Martin Land/Photo Researchers, Inc.; (f) © John Sibbick. **17.18** (a) J. Scott Altenbach, University of New Mexico, computer enhanced by Lisa Starr; (b) Frans Lanting/Minden Pictures; computer enhanced by Lisa Starr; (c) above, © Stephen Dalton/Photo Researchers, Inc.); (c bottom) Natural History Collection, Royal BC Museum. **17.19** (a, b) Courtesy of Professor Richard Amasino, University of Wisconsin-Madison; (c) Juergen Berger, Max Planck Institute for Developmental Biology—Tuebingen, Germany; (d) Courtesy of Professor Martin F. Yanofsky, UCSD. **17.21** (a) above, Tait/Sunnucks Peripatus Research; (a) below, © Jennifer Grenier, Grace Boekhoff-Falk and Sean Carroll, HMI, University of Wisconsin-Madison; (b) above, Herve Chaumeton/Agence Nature; (b) below, © Jennifer Grenier, Grace Boekhoff-Falk and Sean Carroll, HMI, University of Wisconsin-Madison; (c) above, © Peter Skinner/ Photo Researchers, Inc.; (c) below, Courtesy of Dr. Giovanni Levi; (d) Dr. Chip Clark. **Page 278** © TEK IMAGE/Photo Researchers, Inc. **17.23** Left, Kjell B. Sandved/Visuals Unlimited; Center, Jeffrey Sylvester/FPG/Getty Images; Right, Thomas D. Mangelsen/Images of Nature. **17.24** John Klausmeyer, University of Michigan Exhibit of Natural History.

CHAPER 18 **18.1** Above, © Bettmann/Corbis; Below, © Reuters NewMedia, Inc./Corbis. **Page 283** © St. Bartholomew's Hospital/Science Photo Library/Photo Researchers, Inc. **18.2** Clockwise from left, © Peter Bowater/Photo Researchers, Inc.; © Owen Franken/Corbis; © Sam Kleinman/ Corbis; Alan Solem; Christopher Briscoe/Photo Researchers, Inc.; © Jim Cornfield/Corbis. **18.3** © 2002/Photodisc/ Getty Images. **18.6** J. A. Bishop, L. M. Cook. **18.7** Courtesy of Hopi Hoekstra, University of California, San Diego. **18.10** © Peter Chadwick/Science Photo Library/Photo Researchers, Inc. **18.11** Thomas Bates Smith. **18.12** Bruce Beehler. **18.13** (a–b) After Ayala and others; (c) © Michael Freeman/Corbis. **18.14** Adapted from S. S. Rich, A. E. Bell, and S. P. Wilson, "Genetic

drift in small populations of Tribolium," *Evolution* 33:579-584, Fig. 1, p. 580, 1979. Used by permission of the publisher. **Page 294** © Steve Bronstein/The Image Bank/Getty Images. **18.15** Frans Lanting/ Minden Pictures (computer-modified by Lisa Starr). **18.16** Left, David Neal Parks; right W. Carter Johnson. **18.17** (b) John W. Merck, Jr., University of Maryland. **18.18** Left, © Thomas Mangelsen; right © Theo Allofs/Corbis. **18.19** Left, © Francois Gohier/ Photo Researchers, Inc.; right © David Parker/ SPL/Photo Researchers, Inc.. **18.20** Elliot Erwitt/ Magnum Photos, Inc..

CHAPTER 19 **19.1** Left, © Jack Jeffrey Photography; Right, Image courtesy of the Image Analysis Laboratory, NASA/Johnson Space Center. **19.2** Bill Sparklin/Ashley Dayer. **19.4** (a) John Alcock, Arizona State University; (b) © Alvin E. Staffan/Photo Researchers, Inc.; (c) G. Ziesler/ ZEFA. **19.5** Left © Digital Vision/PictureQuest; (a) © Joe McDonald/Corbis. **19.6** (a) © Graham Neden/Corbis; (b) © Kevin Schafer/ Corbis; Center, © Ron Blakey, Northern Arizona University; (c) © Rick Rosen/Corbis SABA. **19.7** Po' ouli, Bill Sparklin/Ashley Dayer; All others, © Jack Jeffrey Photography. **19.8** Above, Steve Gartlan; Below, © Below Water Photography/www.belowwater.com. **19.9** Jean-Claude Carton/Bruce Coleman, Inc. **19.10** After W. Jensen and F. B. Salisbury, Botany: An Ecological Approach, Wadsworth, 1972. **19.11** Courtesy of Dr. Robert Mesibov. **19.13** Courtesy of Daniel C. Kelley, Anthony J. Arnold, and William C. Parker, Florida State University Department of Geological Science. **19.14** © Carnegie Museum of Natural History. **19.15** From left, © Science Photo Library/Photo Researchers, Inc.; © Galen Rowell/ Corbis; © Kevin Schafer/Corbis; Courtesy of Department of Entomology, University of Nebraska-Lincoln; Bruce Coleman, Ltd. **19.18** From left, © Hans Reinhard/Bruce Coleman, Inc; © Phillip Colla Photography; © Randy Wells/Corbis; © Cousteau Society/The Image Bank/Getty Images; © Robert Dowling/Corbis. **19.20** Left, Courtesy of Department of Library Services, American Museum of Natural History (Neg. #K10273); Right, Photo by Lisa Starr. **19.21** © Gulf News, Dubai, UAE.

CHAPTER 20 **20.1** Left, Courtesy of Agriculture Canada; Right, © Raymond Gehman/Corbis. **20.2** © Philippa Uwins/The University of Queensland. **20.3** Jeff Hester and Paul Scowen, Arizona State University, and NASA. **20.4** Left, Painting by William K. Hartmann; Right, Painting by Chesley Bonestell. **20.6** (a) Eiichi Kurasawa/Photo Researchers, Inc.; (b) © Dr. Ken MacDonald/ SPL/Photo Researchers, Inc.; (c) © Micheal J. Russell, Scottish Universities Environmental Research Centre. **20.7** (a) Sidney W. Fox; (b) From Hanczyc, Fujikawa, and Szostak, Experimental Models of Primitive Cellular Compartments: Encapsulation, Growth, and Division; www. sciencemag.org, *Science* 24 October 2003; 302;529, Figure 2, page 619. Reprinted with Permission of the authors and AAAS. **20.8** (a) Stanley M. Awramik; (b-c) © Bruce Runnegar, NASA Astrobiology Institute; (d) © N. J. Butterfield, University of Cambridge. **20.9** (a) © Chase Studios/ Photo Researchers, Inc.; (b) © John Reader/SPL/ Photo Researchers, Inc.; (c) © Sinclair Stammers/ SPL/Photo Researchers, Inc. **20.10** (a) © CNRI/ Photo Researchers, Inc.; (b) © Robert Trench, Professor Emeritus, University of British Columbia.

Page 331 UNIT IV © Layne Kennedy/Corbis.

CHAPTER 21 **21.1** © David Lees/Getty Images. **Page 333** © R. Sorensen/J. Olsen/Photo Researchers, Inc. **21.3** (a) P. Hawtin, University of Southampton/SPL/Photo Researchers, Inc.; (b) ©

Dr. Manfred Schloesser, Max Planck Institute for Marine Microbiology; (c) CNRI/SPL/Photo Researchers, Inc.; (d) © Dr. Dennis Kunkel/Visuals Unlimited. **21.4** L. J. LeBeau, University of Illinois Hospital/BPS; **21.5** Micrograph L. Santo. **21.7** Electron micrograph of Aquifex pyrophilus, platinum shadowed. Bar: 1 micrometer. Image by R. Rachel and K. O. Stetter, University Regensburg, Germany. **21.8** (a) P. W. Johnson and J. MeN. Sieburth, Univ. Rhode Island/BPS; (b) © Dr. Jeremy Burgess/SPL/ Photo Researchers, Inc.; (c) © Stem Jems/Photo Researchers, Inc.; (d) Dr. Terry J. Beveridge, Department of Microbiology, University of Guelph, Ontario, Canada. **21.9** Richard Blakemore. **21.11** (a) Courtesy Jack Jones, *Archives of Microbiology*, Vol. 136, 1983, pp. 254-261. Reprinted by permission of Springer-Verlag; (b) © Dr. John Brackenbury/ Science Photo Library/Photo Researchers, Inc. **21.12** (a) © Martin Miller/Visuals Unlimited; (b) © Alan L. Detrick, Science Source/Photo Researchers, Inc.; (c) © Dr. Harald Huber, Dr. Michael Hohn, Prof. Dr. K.O.Stetter, University of Regensburg, Germany. **21.13** After Stephen L. Wolfe. **21.14** (a) © CAMR/A. B. Dowsett/SPL/Photo Researchers, Inc.; (b) © Dr. Linda Stannard, UCT/SPL/Photo Researchers, Inc.; (c-d) Kenneth M. Corbett. **21.15** © Science Photo Library/Photo Researchers, Inc. **Page 346** Left, above, © CAMR, Barry Dowsett/ Science Photo Library/Photo Researchers, Inc.; below © Sercomi/Photo Researchers, Inc.; right, © Camr/B. Dowsett/SPL/Photo Researchers, Inc. **21.17** (a) © Lily Echeverria/Miami Herald; (b) © APHIS photo by Dr. Al Jenny; (bottom) PDB ID: 1QLX; Zahn, R., Liu, A., Luhrs, T., Riek, R., Von Schroetter, C., Garcia, F.L., Billeter, M., Calzolai, L., Wider, G., Wuthrich, K.: NMR Solution Structure of the Human Prion Protein, Proc. Nat. Acad. Sci. USA 97 pp. 145 (2000). **21.18** right, E. A. Zottola, University of Minnesota.

CHAPTER 22 **22.1** Wim van Egmond/Visuals Unlimited. **Page 351** Above, © Adam Woolfitt/ Corbis: below, © Ric Ergenbright/Corbis. **22.3** (a) © Dr. Dennis Kunkel/Visuals Unlimited; (b-c) Dr. Stan Erlandsen, University of Minnesota. **22.4** (a) P. L. Walne and J. H. Arnott, Planta, 77:325-354, 1967; (b) Photo by Stephen Durr. **22.5** (a) After Prescott et al., Microbiology, third edition; (b) © Oliver Meckes/Photo Researchers, Inc. **22.6** (a) Courtesy of Allen W. H. Bé and David A. Caron; (b) © Wim van Egmond; (c) © G. Shih and R. Kessel/Visuals Unlimited. **22.7** (a) Above, Courtesy Professor Steve Beck, Nassau Community College; (a) Below, Courtesy James Evarts; (b) Gary W. Grimes and Steven L'Hernault; (c) Redrawn from V. & M. Pearse and M. & R. Buchsbaum, Living Invertebrates, The Boxwood Press, 1987. Used by permission. **22.8** © John Walsh/SPL/Photo Researchers, Inc. **22.9** (a) © Wim van Egmond/Micropolitan Museum; (b) © Dr. David Phillips/Visuals Unlimited. **22.10** © Lexey Swall/Staff from article, " Deep Trouble: Bad Blooms" October 3, 2003 by Eric Staats. **22.11** Left (mosquito), © Sinclair Stammers/Photo Researchers, Inc.; top right, © London School of Hygiene & Tropical Medicine/Photo Researchers, Inc.; bottom right © Moredum Animal Health, Ltd./ Photo Researchers, Inc.; center bottom (gametocyte), Micrograph Steven L'Hernault. **22.12** (a-b) Ron Hoham, Dept. of Biology, Colgate University; (c) Emiliania huxleyi. Photograph by Vita Pariente. Scanning electron micrograph taken on a Jeol T330A instrument at the Texas A & M University Electron Microscopy Center; (d) Greta Fryxell, University of Texas, Austin. **22.13** Left (background) Steven C. Wilson/Entheos; (a) © Jeffrey Levinton, State University of New York, Stony Brook; (b) © Lewis Trusty/Animals Animals; (c) From T. Garrison, Oceanography: An Invitation to Marine Science, Brooks/Cole, 1993. **22.14** Claude Taylor and the

University of Wisconsin Dept. of Botany. **22.15** (a) Heather Angel; (b) International Potato Center, Lima, Peru. **22.16** Left, © Susan Frankel, USDA-FS; right, Dr. Pavel Svihra. **22.17** © Photodisc/Getty Images. **22.18** © Wim van Egmond. **22.19** (a) © Lawson Wood/Corbis; (b) Monterey Bay Aquarium; (c) Courtesy of Professor Astrid Saugestad; (d) Courtesy of Knut Norstog and the Botanical Society of America; (e) D. S. Littler. **22.20** (b) Courtesy of Professeur Michel Cavalla. **22.21** © Astrid Hanns-Frieder Michler/SPL/Photo Researchers, Inc. **22.22** (a) Edward S. Ross; (b) Courtesy of www.hiddenforest.co.nz. **22.23** (b) M. Claviez, G. Gerish, and R. Guggenheim; (c-e) Carolina Biological Supply Company; (f) Courtesy Robert R. Kay from R. R. Kay, et al., Development, 1989 Supplement, pp. 81-90, (c) The Company of Biologists Ltd., 1989. **Page 351** Above right, Nature Publishing Group, www.nature.com. 1: Figure, Number 1 from Nature, Vol. 410, pp. 430, *Asexual reproduction: 'Midwives' assist dividing aboebae* by David Biron, Pazit Libros, Dror Sagi, David Mirelman, Ellisha Moses, et al. **22.24** © W. P. Armstrong; inset, Courtesy Brian Duval. **22.25** Lauren and Homer, Photography by Gary Head. **23.1** © T. Kerasote/Photo Researchers, Inc. **Page 371** © Craig Allikas/www.orchidworks.com.

CHAPTER 23 **23.3** (a) © Wim van Egmond; (b) Courtesy Microbial Culture Collection, National Institute for Environmental Studies, Japan. **23.4** (a) © Reprinted with permission from Elsevier; (b) Patricia G. Gensel; (c) Illustration by Zdenek Burian, © Jeri Hochman and Martin Hochman; (d) © Karen Carr Studio/www.karencarr.com. **23.6** (b) After E.O. Dodson and P. Dodson, Evolution: Process and Product, Third Ed., p. 401, PWS. **23.7** Robert Potts, California Academy of Sciences. **23.8** (a) Craig Wood/Visuals Unlimited; (b) Jane Burton/Bruce Coleman Ltd. **23.9** (a) Fred Bavendam/Peter Arnold, Inc.; (b) John D. Cunningham/Visuals Unlimited. **23.10** (a) © University of Wisconsin-Madison, Department of Biology, Anthoceros CD; (b) Left, National Park Services, Paul Stehr-Green; (b) Right, National Park Services, Martin Hutten; (c) © Wayne P. Armstrong, Professor of Biology and Botany, Palomar College, San Marcos, California. **23.11** (a) Gerald D. Carr; (b) Ed Reschke/Peter Arnold, Inc.; (c) © Colin Bates, www.coastalimage-works.com; (d) Left, Photo by A. Murray, University of Florida, Center for Aquatic and Invasive Plants. Used with permission; (e) Derrick Ditlchburn/ Visuals Unlimited. **23.12** (a) Above right, A. & E. Bomford/Ardea, London; (b) © Klein, Hubert/ Peter Arnold, Inc. **23.13** Above, Brian Parker/Tom Stack & Associates; Below Field Museum of Natural History, Chicago (Neg. #7500C). **23.14** (a) Ralph Pleasant/FPG/Getty Images; (b) © Earl Roberge/ Photo Researchers, Inc.; (c) George Loun/Visuals Unlimited; (d) Courtesy of Water Research Commission, South Africa. **Page 381** Above right, © George J. Wilder/Visuals Unlimited, computer enhanced by Lachina Publishing Services, Inc. **23.15** (a) © Dave Cavagnaro/Peter Arnold, Inc.; (b) © Robert & Linda Mitchell Photography; (c) © E. Webber/Visuals Unlimited; (d) © Michael P. Gadomski/Photo Researchers, Inc.; (e) © Sinclair Stammers/Photo Researchers, Inc.; (f) Courtesy of Wayside Gardens/www.waysidegardens.com; (g) © Gerald & Buff Corsi/Visuals Unlimited; (h) © Fletcher and Baylis/Photo Researchers, Inc. **23.16** Left, Robert Potts, California Academy of Sciences; (a) Robert & Linda Mitchell Photography; (b) © R. J. Erwin/Photo Researchers, Inc. **23.17** From top, Ed Reschke; Lee Casebere; Robert & Linda Mitchell Photography; Runk & Schoenberger/Grant Heilman, Inc. **23.18** (a) © Michelle Garrett/Corbis; (b) © Sanford/Agliolo/Corbis; (c) © Gregory G. Dimijian/Photo Researchers, Inc.; (d) © Darrell

Gulin/Corbis; (e) Photo provided by DLN/ Permission by Dr. Daniel L. Nickrent. **23.21** Gerry Ellis/The Wildlife Collection. **23.22** © William Campbell/TimePix/Getty Images. **23.23** Left, © 1989 Clinton Webb.

CHAPTER 24 **24.1** © Charles Lewallen. **Page 391** © Jacques Langevin/Corbis Sygma. **Page 392** Micrograph Garry T. Cole, University of Texas, Austin/BPS. **24.3** (a-e) Robert C. Simpson/Nature Stock. **24.4** (a) Courtesy of Ken Nemuras; (b) CDC. **24.5** N. Allin and G. L. Barron. **24.6** (a-b) Micrographs Ed Reschke; Below right, Micrograph J. D. Cunningham/Visuals Unlimited. **24.7** Left, Micrograph Garry T. Cole, University of Texas, Austin/BPS; right, © Michael W. Clayton/ University of Wisconsin-Madison, Department of Biology; art, After T. Rost, et al., *Botany*, Wiley 1979. **24.9** (a) Above, © North Carolina State University, Department of Plant Pathology; (a) below, © Michael Wood/mykob.com; (b) © Fred Stevens/ Mykoweb.com; (c) © Dennis Kunkel Microscopy, Inc.; (d) Garry T. Cole, University of Texas, Austin/ BPS. **24.10** (a) © Dr. P. Marazzi/SPL/Photo Researchers, Inc.; (b) Eric Crichton/Bruce Coleman; (c) © Harry Regin. **24.11** (b) Mark Mattock/Planet Earth Pictures; (c) © Mark E. Gibson/Visuals Unlimited; (d) After Raven, Evert, and Eichhorn, *Biology of Plants*, 4th ed., Worth Publishers, New York, 1986. **24.12** (a) Prof. DJ Read, University of Sheffield; (b) © 1990 Gary Braasch; (c) F. B. Reeves. **24.13** John Hodgin. **24.14** Robert C. Simpson/ Nature Stock. **24.15** (a) Jane Burton/Bruce Coleman, Ltd.; (b) © Chris Worden.

CHAPTER 25 **25.1** © K.S. Matz. **Page 403** © Callum Roberts, University of York. **25.2** © David Aubrey/Corbis. **25.4** David Patterson, courtesy micro*scope/http://microscope.mbl.edu. **25.8** (a-b) Neville Pledge/South Australian Museum; (c) Dr. Chip Clark. **25.9** (a) Marty Snyderman/Planet Earth Pictures; (b) Bruce Hall; (c) © David Aubrey/ Corbis; (d) Don W. Fawcett/Visuals Unlimited. **25.11** (a) © Robert Brons/livingreefimages.com; (b left) After Laszlo Meszoly, in L. Margulis, *Early Life*, Jones and Bartlett, 1982. **25.12** (c) © Brandon D. Cole/Corbis; (d) © Jeffrey L. Rotman/Corbis. **25.13** (a) After Eugene Kozloff; (b) Courtesy of Dr. William H. Hamner. **25.14** (a) Kim Taylor/Bruce Coleman, Ltd.; (b) © A.N.T./Photo Researchers, Inc. **25.15** (Above) After T. Storer, et al., *General Zoology*, Sixth Edition; Right, © Wim van Egmond/ Micropolitan Museum. **25.17** (a) © James Marshall/ Corbis. **25.18** Right © Andrew Syred/SPL/Photo Researchers, Inc. **25.19** (a) J. Solliday/BPS; (b) Jon Kenfield/Bruce Coleman Ltd.; (c-d) Adapted from Rasmussen, "Ophelia," Vol. 11, in Eugene Kozloff, Invertebrates, 1990. **25.20** J. A. L. Cooke/Oxford Scientific Films. **25.21** (g) © Cabisco/Visuals Unlimited; (h) © Science Photo Library/Photo Researchers, Inc. **Page 416** Danielle C. Zacherl with John McNulty. **25.24** (a) © B. Borrell Casals/Frank Lane Picture Agency/Corbis; (b) Jeff Foott/Tom Stack & Associates; (c) © Joe McDonald/Corbis; (d) © Reinhard Dirscherl/Visuals Unlimited; (e) Alex Kirstitch. **25.25** (a) Herve Chaumeton/Agence Nature. **25.26** (a) Illustrations by Zdenek Burian, © Jeri Hochman and Martin Hochman; (c) Alex Kirstitch; (d) Bob Cranston. **25.27** Below, Micrograph, J. Sulston, MRC Laboratory of Molecular Biology. **25.28** (a) © Sinclair Stammers/ SPL/Photo Researchers, Inc.; (b) © L. Jensen/ Visuals Unlimited; (c) Dianora Niccolin. **25.29** Jane Burton/Bruce Coleman, Ltd. **25.30** (a) © Angelo Giampiccolo/FPG/Getty Images; (b) © Frans Lemmens/The Image bank/Getty Images. **25.31** (a) Redrawn from Living Invertebrates, V. & J. Pearse/M. & R. Buchsbaum, The Boxwood Press, 1987. Used by permission; (b) © Corbis; (c) ©

Andrew Syred/Photo Researchers, Inc. **25.32** (a) © Jeff Hunter/The Image Bank/Getty Images; (b) © Peter Parks/Imagequestmarine.com; (c) © Science Photo Library/Photo Researchers, Inc.; d-e) After D.H. Milne, Marine Life and the Sea, Wadsworth, 1995. **25.34** (a) © Michael & Patricia Fogden/Corbis; (b) Steve Martin/Tom Stack & Associates. **25.37** (a) David Maitland/Seaphot Limited/Planet Earth Pictures; (b-g) Edward S. Ross; (h) © Mark Moffett/Minden Pictures; (i) Courtesy of Karen Swain, North Carolina Museum of Natural Sciences; (j) Chris Anderson/Darklight Imagery; (k) Joseph L. Spencer. **25.38** (a) John H. Gerard; (b) © D. Suzio/Photo Researchers, Inc. **25.39** (a) © Stem Jems/Photo Researchers, Inc.; (b) © California Department of Health Services; (c) © Bernard Cohen, M.D., Dermatlas; http:// www.dermata-las.org. **25.40** William Dow/Corbis. **25.41** (a) Marlin E. Rice, Iowa State University; (b-c) John Obermeyer, Purdue University, Dept of Entomology. **25.42** Photo by James Gathany, Centers for Disease Control. **25.44** (a) Herve Chaumeton/Agence Nature; (b) © Fred Bavendam/Minden Pictures; (c) © George Perina, www.seapix.com; (d) Jan Haaga, Kodiak Lab, AFSC/NMFS; (e) Herve Chaumeton/Agence Nature; (g) Jane Burton/Bruce Coleman, Ltd. **25.45** (a) Walter Deas/Seaphot Limited/Planet Earth Pictures; (b) © E. Webber/Visuals Unlimited. **25.46** Jane Burton/Bruce Coleman, Ltd. **26.1** © Karen Carr Studio/www.karencarr.com. **Page 433** P. Morris/Ardea London.

CHAPTER 26 **26.3** (a) © 2002 Gary Bell/Taxi/Getty Images; (b-c) Redrawn from Living Invertebrates, V. & J. Pearse and M. & R. Buchsbaum. The Boxwood Press, 1987. Used by permission. **26.5** © Brandon D. Cole/Corbis. **26.6** (a) © John and Bridgette Sibbick; (b-c) © Jenna Hellack, Department of Biology, Univerisy of Central Oklahoma. (a–c) Adapted from A.S. Romer and T.S. Parsons, The Vertebrate Body, Sixth Edition, Saunders, 1986; Left, Photo by Lisa Starr; right, Courtesy of John McNamara, www.paleodirect.com. **26.9** (a) © Jonathan Bird/Oceanic Research Group, Inc.; (b) © Gido Braase/Deep Blue Productions, (c) © Tom McHugh/Photo Researchers, Inc.; (d) Robert & Linda Mitchell Photography; (e) © Ivor Fulcher/Corbis; (f) Patrice Ceisel/© 1986 John G. Shedd Aquarium. **26.10** (a) © Norbert Wu/Peter Arnold, Inc.; (b) Wernher Krutein/photovault.com; (c) © Alfred Kamajian. **26.11** (left) Adapted from A.S. Romer and T.S. Parsons, The Vertebrate Body, Sixth Edition, Saunders, 1986. (a) © Bill M. Campbell, MD; (b) © Stephen Dalton/Photo Researchers, Inc.; (c) John Serrano/Visuals Unlimited. **26.12** Juan M. Renjifo/Animals Animals. **26.13** (a) Pieter Johnson; (b) Stanley Sessions/Hartwick College. **26.14** © 1989 D. Braginetz. **26.15** © Karen Carr Studio/www.karencarr.com. **Page 443** Bottom right, © Julian Baum/SPL/Photo Researchers, Inc. **Page 444** Left, S. Blair Hedges. **26.17** (a) © Kevin Schafer/Corbis; (c) © Joe McDonald/Corbis; (d) © David A. Northcott/Corbis; (e) © Pete & Judy Morrin/Ardea London; (f) © Stephen Dalton/Photo Researchers, Inc.; (g) Kevin Schafer/Tom Stack & Associates. **26.18** © James Reece, Nature Focus, Australian Museum. **26.19** (a) From The Life of Birds, fourth edition, L. Baptista and J.C. Whelty, 1988, Saunders; (b-c) Courtesy of Dr. M. Guinan, University of California-Davis, Anatomy, Physiology and Cell Biology, School of Veterinary Medicine. **26.21** (a) Gerard Lacz/ANT Photolibrary; (b) © Kevin Schafer/Corbis. **26.23** (a) Sandy Roessler/FPG/Getty Images; (b) After M. Weiss and A. Mann, Human Biology and Behavior, 5th Edition, HarperCollins, 1990 **26.24** Painting © Ely Kish. **26.25** (a) Painting © Ely Kish; (b) © Karen Carr Studio/www.karencarr.com. **26.26** (e) D. & V. Blagden/ANT Photo Library; (f) © Nigel J. Dennis/

Gallo Images/Corbis; (g) © Tom Ulrich/Visuals Unlimited. **26.27** (a) © Tom McHugh/Photo Researchers, Inc.; (b) Corbis Images/PictureQuest; (c) Mike Jagoe/Talune Wildlife Park, Tasmania, Australia. **26.28** (b) © Mike Johnson. All rights reserved, www.earthwindow.com; (c) © Marine Themes Stock Photo Library; (d) © Douglas Faulkner/Photo Researchers, Inc.; (e) © David Parker/SPL/Photo Researchers, Inc.; (f) Bryan and Cherry Alexander Photography; (g) © Stephen Dalton/Photo Researchers, Inc.; (h) © Merlin D. Tuttle/Bat Conservation International; (i) Alan and Sandy Carey. **26.30** (a) Larry Burrows/Aspect Photolibrary; (c) Allen Gathman, Biology department, Southeast Missouri State University; (d) © Dallas Zoo, Robert Cabello; (e) Bone Clones®, www.boneclones.com; (g) Courtesy of Dr. Takeshi Furuichi, Biology, Meiji-Gakuin University-Yokohama. **26.31** © Utah's Hogle Zoo; left, Gerry Ellis/The Wildlife Collection. **26.32** After National Geographic, February 1997, p. 82. **26.33** Left, MPFT/Corbis Sygma; (all others) National Museum of Ethiopia, Addis Ababa. © 1985 David L. Brill. **26.34** (a) Dr. Donald Johanson, Institute of Human Origins; (b) Kenneth Garrett/National Geographic Image Collection; (c) Louise M. Robbins; (d) Kenneth Garrett/National Geographic Image Collection. **26.35** Kenneth Garrett/National Geographic Image Collection. **26.36** Left, Jean Paul Tibbles; right, National Museum of Ethiopia, Addis Ababa. © 1985 David L. Brill. **26.37** Left, Elizabeth Delaney/Visuals Unlimited; right, John Reader © 1981. **26.39** National Museum of Ethiopia, Addis Ababa. © 1985 David L. Brill. **26.41** Left, National Museum of Ethiopia, Addis Ababa. © 1985 David L. Brill; right, NASA. **26.43** Left, Sandak/FPG/Getty Images; right, Douglas Mazonowicz/Gallery of Prehistoric Art. **26.44** © California Academy of Sciences. **26.45** © Jean Phillipe Varin/Jacana/Photo Researchers, Inc. **26.47** Z. Leszczynski/Animals Animals.

CHAPTER 27 **27.1** © David Nunuk/PhotoResearchers, Inc. **27.3** (a) Painting by Charles Knight/American Museum of Natural History; (b) Mansell Collection/Time, Inc./Getty Images. **27.4** Photo, Gary Head; Topographic maps, U.S. Geological Survey. **27.5** Eric Hartmann/Magnum Photos. **27.6** © James Marshall/Corbis. **27.7** © Greenpeace/Cunningham. **27.8** © Bagla Pallava/Corbis Sygma; inset, © A. Bannister/Photo Researchers, Inc. (b) From T. Garrison, Oceanography: An Invitation to Marine Science, Third Edition, Brooks/Cole, 2000. All rights reserved. **27.10** (a) C. B. & D. W. Frith/Bruce Coleman, Ltd.; (b) © Douglas Faulkner/Photo Researchers, Inc.; (c) Douglas Faulkner/Sally Faulkner Collection; (d) Sea Studios/Peter Arnold, Inc.; (e) From left, top Douglas Faulkner/Sally Faulkner Collection; Peter Scoones; center, Jeff Rotman; Alex Kirstitch; Douglas Faulkner/Sally Faulkner Collection; bottom (all), Douglas Faulkner/Sally Faulkner Collection. **27.11** © Greenpeace/Grace. **27.14** Hans Renner. **27.15** Above, © R. Bieregaard/Photo Researchers, Inc.; below, photo © 2000 Photodisc, Inc. **27.16** Bureau of Land Management. **27.17** Left, Peter Scoones; right, NASA **27.18** Courtesy of Eternal Reefs, Inc., www.eternalreefs.com.

Page 477 UNIT INTRODUCTION © 2002 Stuart Westmorland/Stone/Getty Images.

CHAPTER 28 **28.1** Star Tribune/Minneapolis-St. Paul. **Page 479** (Left) © VVG/Science Photo Library/Photo Researchers, Inc.; (right) © Michael Davidson/Mortimer Abramowitz Gallery of Photomicrography/www.olympusmicro.com **28.2** Top Courtesy of Charles Lewallen; Center & bottom, © Bruce Iverson. **28.3** Left (Art by Lisa Starr with) ©

2000 Photodisc, Inc; Right, above, © CNRI/SPL/Photo Researchers, Inc.; below, Dr. Robert Wagner/University of Delaware, www.udel.edu/Biology/Wags. **28.4** Left © Pat Johnson Studios Photography; Right © Darrell Gulin/The Image Bank/Getty Images. **28.5** (a) © Cory Gray; (b) © Photodisc/Getty Images; (c) Heather Angel; (d) © Biophoto Associates/Photo Researchers, Inc. **28.6** (a) © Geoff Tompkinson/SPL/Photo Researchers, Inc.; (b) © John Beatty/SPL/Photo Researchers, Inc. **28.8** © VVG/Science Photo Library/Photo Researchers, Inc. **28.9** Galen Rowell/Peter Arnold, Inc.. **28.10** © Niall Benvie/Corbis. **28.11** Left © Kennan Ward/Corbis; Right G. J. McKenzie (MGS). **28.12** Frank B. Salisbury. **28.14** (a) Courtesy of Dr. Kathleen K. Sulik, Bowles Center for Alcohol Studies, the University of North Carolina at Chapel Hill. **28.15** John DaSiai, MD/Custom Medical Stock Photo. **28.16** (a) Courtesy of Dr. Consuelo M. De Moraes; (b–d) © Andrei Sourakov and Consuelo M. De Moraes.

Page 503 Unit V © Jim Christensen, Fine Art Digital Photographic Images

CHAPTER 29 **29.1** (a) © Michael Westmoreland/Corbis; (b) © Charles O'Rear/Corbis. **Page 493** © Reuters/Corbis. **29.4** (a) From top, © Bruce Iverson; © Ernest Manewal/Index Stock Imagery; © Simon Fraser/Photo Researchers, Inc.; © Andrew Syred/Photo Researchers, Inc.; (b) From top, © Mike Clayton/University of Wisconsin Department of Botany; © Darrell Gulin/Corbis; Gary Head; © Andrew Syred/Photo Researchers, Inc. **29.6** Left, © Donald L. Rubbelke/Lakeland Community College; right, © Andrew Syred/Photo Researchers, Inc. **29.7** (a) © Dr. Dale M. Benham, Nebraska Wesleyan University; (b) D. E. Akin and I. L. Risgby, Richard B. Russel Agricultural Research Center, Agricultural Research Service, U.S. Dept. Agriculture, Athens, GA; (c) Kingsley R. Stern. **29.8** Below, © Andrew Syred/Photo Researchers, Inc. **29.9** George S. Ellmore. **29.10** (a) Below, © Dr. Dale M. Benham, Nebraska Wesleyan University. **29.11** (a) Left, Ray F. Evert; (a) right, James W. Perry; (b) Left, Carolina Biological Supply Company; (b) right, James W. Perry. **29.13** David Cavagnaro/Peter Arnold, Inc. **Page 500** Right, © 2001 Photodisc, Inc. **29.14** (a) © N. Cattlin/Photo Researchers, Inc.; (c) C. E. Jeffree, et al., Planta, 172(1):20-37, 1987. Reprinted by permission of C. E. Jeffree and Springer-Verlag; (d) Jeremy Burgess/SPL/Photo Researchers, Inc. **29.15** (a) © Simon Fraser/Photo Researchers, Inc. **29.16** (a) Left, John Limbaugh/Ripon Microslides, Inc.; (a right) After Salisbury and Ross, Plant Physiology, Fourth Edition, Wadsworth; (b) © Mike Clayton/University of Wisconsin Department of Botany. **29.17** Carolina Biological Supply Company. **29.18** © Omikron/Photo Researchers, Inc.. **29.21** Alison W. Roberts, University of Rhode Island. **29.23** John Lotter Gurling/Tom Stack & Associates. **29.24** (b) H. A. Core, W. A. Cote, and A. C. Day, Wood Structure and Identification, 2nd Ed., Syracuse University Press, 1979. **29.25** (a) © Peter Ryan/SPL/Photo Researchers, Inc.; (b) © Jon Pilcher; (c) © George Bernard/SPL/Photo Researchers, Inc. **29.26** Edward S. Ross. **29.27** © NOAA; (b) © USDA/Forestry Service; (c) © David W. Stahle, Department of Geosciences, University of Arkansas.

CHAPTER 30 **30.1** (a) © OPSEC Control Number #4 077-A-4; (b) © Billy Wrobel, 2004; (c) © Keith Weller/USDA-ARS. **30.2** William Ferguson. **30.3** (a) © Robert Frerch/Stone/Getty Images; (b) Courtesy of NOAA. **30.4** (a) Mark E. Dudley and Sharon R. Long; (b) Adrian P. Davies/Bruce Coleman, Ltd; (c) NifTAL Project, Univ. of Hawaii, Maui. **30.5** Left, © Andrew Syred/Photo Researchers, Inc.; right, Courtesy of Mark Holland,

Bergman & Associates, Inc. **38.9** (a–b) After G. J. Tortora and N. Anagnostakos, *Principles of Anatomy and Physiology*, 6th ed. © 1990 by Biological Sciences Textbooks, Inc., A&P Textbooks, Inc., and Ellia-Sparta, Inc. Reprinted by permission of John Wiley & Sons, Inc. **38.13** (b) C. Yokochi and J. Rohen, Photographic Anatomy of the Human Body, 2nd Ed., Igaku-Shoin, Ltd., 1979. **38.15** (b) Dr. Richard Kessel/Visuals Unlimited. **38.19** © Jose Pelaez, Inc./Corbis. **38.20** © Sheila Terry/SPL/Photo Researchers, Inc.; inset, Courtesy of Oregon Scientific, Inc. **38.21** © Biophoto Associates/Photo Researchers, Inc. **38.22** (a) Left, Lisa Starr, using © 2001 Photodisc, Inc. photograph; Right, Dr. John D. Cunningham/Visuals Unlimited. **38.23** © Professor P. Motta/Department of Anatomy/University La Sapienca, Rome/SPL/Photo Researchers, Inc. **38.24** (a) Ed Reschke; (b) © Biophoto Associates/Photo Researchers, Inc. **38.25** © Lester V. Bergman/Corbis. **38.28** Lennart Nilsson from *Behold Man*, © 1974 by Albert Bonniers Forlag and Little, Brown and Company, Boston.

CHAPTER 39 **39.1** © Lowell Tindell. **39.2** The Granger Collection, New York; inset, © NIBSC/Photo Researchers, Inc. **39.3** After *Bloodline Image Atlas*, University of Nebraska-Omaha, and Sherri Wicks, *Human Physiology and Anatomy*, University of Wisconsin Web Education System, and others. **39.4** © Biology Media/Photo Researchers, Inc. **39.5** © David Scharf, 1999. All rights reserved. **Page 682** Right, © Larry Williams/Corbis. **39.6** Dr. Richard Kessel and Dr. Randy Kardon/*Tissues & Organs*/Visuals Unlimited. **39.7** (a) © Kwangshin Kim/Photo Researchers, Inc. **39.8** (c) Robert R. Dourmashkin, courtesy of Clinical Research Centre, Harrow, England. **39.9** © NSIBC/SPL/Photo Researchers, Inc. **39.10** Photograph, David Scharf/Peter Arnold, Inc. **39.13** (Top) From Harris, L.J.; Larson, S.B.; Hasel, K.W.; McPherson, A.; *Biochemistry* 36, p. 1581 (1997). Structure rendered with RIBBONS. **39.19** © Dr. A. Liepins/SPL/Photo Researchers, Inc. **39.20** © Simon Fraser/Photo Researchers, Inc. **39.21** © Lowell Georgia/Science Source/Photo Researchers, Inc. **39.22** Left, David Scharf/Peter Arnold, Inc.; right, © Kent Wood/Photo Researchers, Inc. **39.23** Greg Ruffing. **39.24** © Zeva Oelbaum/Peter Arnold, Inc. **39.25** Left, © NIBSC/Photo Researchers, Inc.; (a–e) After Stephen Wolfe, *Molecular Biology of the Cell*, Wadsworth. 1993 **39.26** Photo courtesy of MU Extension and Agricultural Information.

CHAPTER 40 **40.1** Left, © Ariel Skelley/Corbis; right, Courtesy of Dr. Joe Losos. **40.4** (a) Peter Parks/Oxford Scientific Films; (b) Herve Chaumeton/Agence Nature. **40.5** Above, Micrograph Ed Reschke; (bottom) Redrawn from *Living Invertebrates*, V & J Pearse/M & R Buchsbaum, The Boxwood Press, 1987. **40.9** Micrograph H. R. Duncker, Justus-Liebig University, Giessen, Germany. **40.11** Photographs, Courtesy of Kay Elemetrics Corporation; (bottom) Modified from A. Spence and E. Mason, *Human Anatomy and Physiology*, Fourth Edition, 1992, West Publishing Company. **40.12** (a) © R. Kessel/Visuals Unlimited. **40.13** (a) PDB ID: 1BBB; Silva, M. M., Rogers, P. H., Arnone, A; A third quaternary structure of human hemoglobin A at 1.7-A resolution; J Biol Chem 267 pp. 17248 (1992). (b) PDB ID: 1A6M: Vojtechovsky, J., Berendzen, J., Chu, K., Schlichting, I., Sweet, R. M.: Implications for the Mechanism of Ligand Discrimination and Identification of Substates Derived from Crystal Structures of Myoglobin-Ligand Complexes at Atomic Resolution. To Be Published. **40.15** (a) © 2000 Photodisc, Inc. (with art by Lisa Starr); (b–c) SIU/Visuals Unlimited. **Page 711** © Joe McBride/Getty Images. **40.17** C. Yokochi and J. Rohen, Photographic Anatomy of

the Human Body, 2nd Ed., Igaku-Shoin, Ltd., 1979. **40.18** (a) Micrograph, Lennart Nilsson from *Behold Man*, © 1974 by Albert Bonniers Forlag and Little, Brown and Company, Boston; (b) CNRI/SPL/Photo Researchers, Inc. **40.19** O. Auerbach/Visuals Unlimited. **40.20** © Francois Gohier/Photo Researchers, Inc. **40.21** (a) Christian Zuber/Bruce Coleman, Ltd.; (b) © 2002 Stuart Westmorland/Stone/Getty Images. **40.22** (a) © David Nardini/Getty Images; (b) © John Lund/Getty Images.

CHAPTER 41 **41.1** Left, Jean Paul Tibbles; right, Courtesy of Kevin Wickenheiser, University of Michigan. **41.2** Courtesy of Lisa Hyche. **41.4** © W. Perry Conway/Corbis; (a–b art) Adapted from A. Romer and T. Parsons, *The Vertebrate Body*, Sixth Edition, Saunders Publishing Company, 1986. **41.7** After A. Vander et al., *Human Physiology: Mechanisms of Body Function*, Fifth Edition, McGraw-Hill, 1990. Used by permission. **41.8** (a) Microslide courtesy Mark Nielsen, University of Utah; (b) After A. Vander et al., *Human Physiology: Mechanisms of Body Function*, Fifth Edition, McGraw-Hill, 1990. Used by permission. **41.9** Photos, (a) Right, Microslide courtesy Mark Nielsen, University of Utah; (b) Right, © D. W. Fawcett/Photo Researchers, Inc.; Art, After Sherwood and others. **41.12** Ralph Pleasant/FPG/Getty Images. **41.13** From top left, Ralph Pleasant/FPG/Getty Images; Ralph Pleasant/FPG/Getty Images; © 2001 Photodisc, Inc.; © Paul Poplis Photography, Inc./Stockfood America; © 2001 Photodisc, Inc.; © 2001 Photodisc, Inc. **41.15** Dr. Douglas Coleman, The Jackson Laboratory. **41.16** © Reuters NewsMedia/Corbis. **41.17** Gunter Ziesler/Bruce Coleman, Inc.

CHAPTER 42 **42.1** © Archivo Iconografico, S.A./Corbis. **Page 739** Ed Kashi/Corbis. **42.3** From T. Garrison, *Oceanography: An Invitation to Marine Science*, Brooks/Cole, 1993. All rights reserved. **42.4** Right, above, David Noble/FPG/Getty Images; below, Claude Steelman/Tom Stack & Associates. **42.9** Evan Cerasoli. **42.10** © Air Force News/Photo by Tech. Sgt. Timothy Hoffman. **42.11** (a) © Bob McKeever/Tom Stack & Associates; (b) © S. J. Krasemann/Photo Researchers, Inc. **42.12** © David Parker/SPL/Photo Researchers, Inc. **42.13** Above, © Dan Guravich/Corbis; below, Corbis-Bettmann. **Page 753** Right, Claude Steelman/Tom Stack & Associates.

CHAPTER 43 **43.1** © Minden Pictures. **Page 755** © Charles Michael Murray/Corbis. **43.2** (a) © Fred SaintOurs/University of Massachusetts-Boston; (b) © Photo Researchers, Inc.; (c) © Doug Wechsler/VIREO; (d) © Marc Moritsch. **43.3** (a) Frieder Sauer/Bruce Coleman, Ltd; (b) Matjaz Kuntner; (c) © Ron Austing/Frank Lane Picture Agency/Corbis; (d) © Doug Perrine/seapics.com; (e) © Carolina Biological Supply Company; (f) Fred McKinney/FPG/Getty Images. **43.5** (b–i) Carolina Biological Supply Company; (j–k) © David M. Dennis/Tom Stack & Associates, Inc.; (l) © John Shaw/Tom Stack & Associates, Inc. **43.7** (d) Charles B. Kimmel, William W. Ballard, Seth R. Kimmel, Bonnie Ullmann, and Thomas F. Schilling. *Developmental Dynamics* 203:253-310 (1995). Copyright © 1995 Wiley-Liss, Inc. Reprinted only by permission of Wiley-Liss, a subsidiary of John Wiley & Sons, Inc. **43.9** Dr. Maria Leptin, Institute of Genetics, University of Koln, Germany. **43.10** (b) After B. Burnside, *Developmental Biology*, 1971, 26:416-441. Used by permission of Academic Press. **43.11** Left, Carolina Biological Supply Company; far right, Peter Parks/Oxford Science Films/Animals Animals. **43.13** (a–b) After S. Gilbert, *Developmental Biology*, Fourth Edition; (c) © Professor Jonathon Slack. **43.14** Peter Parks/Oxford Science Films/Animals Animals. **Page 766** © Denis Scott/Corbis.

Page 767 © David Seawell/Corbis. **Page 769** Left, Micrograph, by J. B. Morrill. **43.3** (a) © David M. Parichy; (b–c) © Dr. Sharon Amacher.

CHAPTER 44 **44.1** © 1999 Dana Fineman/Corbis Sygma. **Page 771** Lennart Nilsson from *A Child is Born*, © 1966, 1977 Dell Publishing Company, Inc. **Table 44.1** © Laura Dwight/Corbis. **44.4** (b) © Ed Reschke. **44.8** Right, Photograph Lennart Nilsson from *A Child is Born*, (c) 1966, 1977 Dell Publishing Company, Inc. **44.13** Heidi Specht, West Virginia University. **44.14** (a) © Dr. E. Walker/Photo Researchers, Inc.; (b) © Western Ophthalmic Hospital/Photo Researchers, Inc.; (c) Kenneth Greer/Visuals Unlimited; (d) © CNRI/Photo Researchers, Inc. **44.15** (a) David M. Phillips/Visuals Unlimited; (b) © CNRI/SPL/Photo Researchers, Inc.; (c) John D. Cunningham/Visuals Unlimited. **44.16** © Todd Warshaw/Getty Images. **44.20** Lennart Nilsson, *A Child is Born*, © 1966, 1977 Dell Publishing Company, Inc. **44.21** Modified from K.L. Moore, *The Developing Human: Clinically Oriented Embryology*, Fourth Edition, Philadelphia: W.B. Saunders Co., 1988. **44.22** Left, © Zeva Oelbaum/Corbis; right, James W. Hanson, M.D. **44.25** (top) Adapted from L.B. Arey, *Developmental Anatomy*, Philadelphia, W.B. Saunders Co., 1965; photograph, Lisa Starr.

Page 799 **UNIT VII** Photograph by Alan and Sandy Carey.

CHAPTER 45 **45.1** © Peter Lija/The Image Bank/Getty Images. **Page 801** NASA/Jacques Descloitres, MODIS Land Rapid Response Team. **45.2** Left, © Amos Nachoum/Corbis; center, A. E. Zuckerman/Tom Stack & Associates; right, © Corbis. **45.3** E. R. Degginger; inset, Jeff Foott Productions/Bruce Coleman, Ltd. **45.4** (a) © Cynthia Bateman, Bateman Photography; (b) © Tom Davis. **45.5** © Jeff Lepore/Photo Researchers, Inc. **45.7** © Lilliam Lampas/Omni-Photo. **45.10** © Danny Lehman/Corbis. **45.11** (a) © Joe McDonald/Corbis; (b) © Wayne Bennett/Corbis; (c) © Douglas P. Wilson/Corbis. **45.12** (a–b) Above, David Reznick/University of California-Riverside; computer enhanced by Lisa Starr; (a–b) below, Hippocampus Bildarchiv; (c) Helen Rodd. **45.13** John A. Endler. **45.14** AP/Wide World Photos. **45.15** NASA. **45.18** Data from Population Reference Bureau after G.T. Miller, Jr., *Living in the Environment*, Eighth Edition, Brooks/Cole, 1993. All rights reserved. **45.19** Left © Adrian Arbib/Corbis; right, © Don Mason/Corbis. **45.20** After G. T. Miller, Jr., *Living in the Environment*, Eighth Edition, Brooks/Cole, 1993. All rights reserved. **45.21** John Alcock/Arizona State University. **45.22** © Wolfgang Kaehler/Corbis. **45.23** After G. T. Miller, Jr., *Living in the Environment*, Eighth Edition, Brooks/Cole, 1993. All rights reserved.

CHAPTER 46 **46.1** Photography by B. M. Drees, Texas A&M University. Http://fireant.tamu. **Page 821** © Daniel Wojak/USDA. **46.2** From top left, Donna Hutchins; © B. G. Thomson/Photo Researchers, Inc.; © Len Robinson, Frank Lane Picture Agency/Corbis; © Martin Harvey, Gallo Images/Corbis. **46.3** Above, Harlo H. Hadow; below, Bob and Miriam Francis/Tom Stack & Associates. **46.4** © Thomas W. Doeppner. **46.5** Left, © Richard Cummins/Corbis; (a, d) © Don Roberson; (b) © Kennan Ward/Corbis; (c) © D. Robert Franz/Corbis. **46.6** Photos, left, © Michael Abbey/Photo Researchers, Inc.; right, © Eric V. Grave/Photo Researchers, Inc. **46.7** Stephen G. Tilley. **46.8** Art, After N. Weldan and F. Bazazz, *Ecology*, 56:681-688, © 1975 Ecological Society of America; Above photo, © Joe McDonald/Corbis; below left, © Hal Horwitz/Corbis; below right, © Tony Wharton, Frank Lane Picture Agency/Corbis.

46.9 (a–b) After Rickleffs & Miller, *Ecology*, Fourth Edition, page 459 (Fig. 23.13a) and page 461 (Fig. 23.14); photo, © W. Perry Conway/Corbis. **46.10** (b) © Ed Cesar/Photo Researchers, Inc.; (c) © Kennan Ward. **46.11** (a) © JH Pete Carmichael; (b) Edward S. Ross; (c) W. M. Laetsch. **46.12** (a–c) Edward S. Ross; (d) © Nigel Jones. **46.13** (a–b) Thomas Eisner, Cornell University; (c) © Jeffrey Rotman Photography; (d) © Bob Jensen Photography. **46.14** (a) MSU News Service, photo by Montana Water Center; (b) Karl Andree. **46.15** Left, © The Samuel Roberts Noble Foundation, Inc.; right, Courtesy of Colin Purrington, Swarthmore College. **46.16** © C. James Webb/Phototake USA. **46.17** © Peter J. Bryant/Biological Photo Service. **46.18** (a) © Richard Price/Getty Images; (b) © E.R. Degginger/ Photo Researchers, Inc. **46.19** (a) © Doug Peebles/ Corbis; (b) © Pat O'Hara/Corbis; (c–d) © Tom Bean/Corbis; (e) © Duncan Murrell/Taxi/Getty Images. **46.20** (a) R. Barrick/USGS; (b–c) © 1980 Gary Braasch. **46.21** (a, c) Jane Burton/Bruce Coleman, Ltd.; (b) Heather Angel; (d–e) Based on Jane Lubchenco, *American Naturalist*, 112:23-19, © 1978 University of Chicago Press. Used with permission. **46.22** Above left and (b) © Angelina Lax/Photo Researchers, Inc.; (a) © Dr. Alexande Meinesz, University of Nice-Sophia Antipolis; right, © The University of Alabama Center for Public TV. **46.23** Peter Bird/Australian Picture Library/ Westlight. **46.24** After W. Dansgaard et al., *Nature*, 364:218-220, July 15 1993; D. Raymond et al., *Science*, 259:926-933, February 1993; W. Post, *American Scientist*, 78:310-326, July-August 1990. **46.25** © Pierre Vauthey/Corbis Sygma; art, After S. Fridriksson, *Evolution of Life on a Volcanic Island*, Butterworth, London 1975. **46.26** (a) © Susan G. Drinker/Corbis; (b) Frans Lanting/Minden Pictures. **46.27** (a) © Anthony Bannister, Gallo Images/Corbis; (b) © Bob Jensen Photography. **46.28** Heather Angel/Biofotos. **46.29** Photograph NASA.

CHAPTER 47 **47.1** LA Wildlife & Fisheries, Natural Heritage Program, Patti Faulkner. **Page 843** NOAA, photo by Commander Grady Tuell. **47.2** Above, Photodisc, Inc.; below, David Neal Parks. **47.3** Photograph Alan and Sandy Carey; (right) After R.L. Smith, *Ecology and Field Biology*, Fifth Edition. **47.4** Field of flowers, © Frank Oberle/ Stone/Getty Images; marsh hawk, © J. Lichter/ Photo Researchers, Inc.; crow, © Ed Reschke; garter snake, Michael Jeffords; cutworm, © Nigel Cattlin/ Holt Studios International/Photo Researchers, Inc. **47.5** Field of flowers, © Frank Oberle/Stone/ Getty Images; marsh hawk, © J. Lichter/Photo Researchers, Inc.; crow, © Ed Reschke; milk snake, Mike Pingleton/www.pingleton.com; garter snake and spider, Michael Jeffords; frog, John H. Gerard; Earthworm, grasshopper, badger, coyote, and ground squirrel, Photodisc/Getty Images; cut-worm, © Nigel Cattlin/Holt Studios International/ Photo Researchers, Inc.; clay-colored sparrow, © Rod Planck/Photo Researchers, Inc.; weasel, Courtesy of Biology Department, Loyola Marymount University; prairie vole and pocket gopher, © Tom McHugh/ Photo Researchers, Inc. **47.6** Left, D. Robert Franz; right, Frans Lanting/ Bruce Coleman, Ltd.; art, After Paul Hertz. **47.7** Right, Inga Spence/Tom Stack & Associates. **47.9** © David T. Grewcock/Corbis. **47.10** (a) NASA's Earth Observatory. **47.14** Gerry Ellis/The Wildlife Collection. **47.17** (a) www .hubbardbrook.org; (b) © Hubbard Brook Experimental Forest, www.hubbardbrook.org; (c) Gene E. Likens from G. E. Likens, et. al., *Ecology Monograph*, 40(1):23-47, 1970; (d) After G.E. Likens and F. H. Bormann, "An Experimental Approach to New England Landscapes," In A. D. Hasler (ed.), *Coupling of Land and Water Systems*, Chapman & Hall, 1975. **47.18** © Craig Aurness/Corbis. **47.20**

(wolf) © 2000 Photodisc, Inc. **47.22** NASA photograph from JSC Digital Image Collection. **47.23** © Yann Arthus-Bertrand/Corbis. **47.24** (a) Compilation of data from Mauna Loa Observatory, Keeling and Whorf, Scripps Institute of Oceanography; (b) Compilation of data from Prinn, et al., CDIAC, Oak Ridge National Laboratory, World Resources Institute; Khalil and Rasmussen, Oregon Graduate Institute of Science and Technology, CDIAC DB-1010; Liefer and Chan, CDIAC DB-1019; (c,d) Compilation of data from World Resources Institute; Law Dome ice core samples, Etheridge, Pearman, and Fraser, Commonwealth Scientific and Industrial Research Organization; Prinn et al., CDIAC, Oak Ridge National Laboratory; Leifer and Chan, CDIAC DB-1019. **47.25** © Jeff Vanuga/Corbis. **47.26** © Frederica Georgia/Photo Researchers, Inc. **47.27** Above, © 2000 Photodisc, Inc. **47.28** Fisheries & Oceans Canada, Experimental Lakes Area. **47.29** (a–b) Courtesy of NASA's Terra satellite, supplied by Ted Scambos, National Snow and Ice Data Center, University of Colorado, Boulder; (c) Courtesy of Keith Nicholls, British Antarctic Survey. **47.30** Left, above, © Boetius et al. 2000, *Nature* 407, 623-626; below, Courtesy of K. O. Stetter & R. Rachel, University of Regensburg.

CHAPTER 48 **48.01** © Hank Fotos Photography. **Page 867** NASA. **48.5** Alex MacLean/Landslides. **48.06, 48.10** NASA. **48.8** (a) Adapted from *Living in the Environment* by G. Tyler Miller, Jr., p. 428. © 2002 by Brooks/Cole, a division of Thomson Learning; (b) © Ted Spiegel/Corbis. **48.11** Left, © Sally A. Morgan, Ecoscene/Corbis; right, © Bob Rowan, Progressive Image/Corbis. **48.12** NASA. **48.13** NASA's Earth Observatory; (Art) After Whittaker, Bland, and Tilman. **48.14, 48.15** Courtesy of Jim Deacon, The University of Edinburgh. **48.16** © George H. Huey/Corbis; inset, © John M. Roberts/ Corbis. **48.17** Left, © John C. Cunningham/Visuals Unlimited; right, AP/Wide World Photos. **48.18** (a) Jonathan Scott/Planet Earth Pictures; (b) © Tom Bean Photography; (c) Ray Wagner/Save the Tall Grass Prairie, Inc. **48.19** Left © James Randklev/ Corbis; trees, © Randy Wells/Corbis. **Page 867** Above, Gerry Ellis/The Wildlife Collection; below © 1991 Gary Braasch; inset Edward S. Ross. **48.20** (a) © Raymond Gehman/Corbis; (b) © Thomas Wiewandt/ChromoSohm Media, Inc./Photo Researchers, Inc. **48.21** (a) © Darrell Gulin/Corbis; (b) © Paul A. Souders/Corbis. **48.22** © Pat O'Hara/ Corbis. **48.23** Based on data from G.T. Miller, Jr. **48.25** © Orbimage Imagery. **48.26** U.S. Agency for International Development. **48.27** © Onne van der Wal/Corbis. **48.28** (b) After E.S. Deevy, Jr., *Scientific American*, October 1951. **48.29** Jack Carey. **48.30** (a) Bruce M. Herman/Photo Researchers, Inc.; (b–d) E. F. Benfield, Virginia Tech. **48.31** Image courtesy of the Image Analysis Laboratory, NASA Johnson Space Center. **48.32** Ocean Arks International. **48.33** (a) © Annie Griffiths Belt/Corbis; (b) © Douglas Peebles/Corbis. **48.34** (a) © Nancy Sefton; (b) Courtesy of J. L. Sumich, Biology of Marine Life, 7th ed., W. C. Brown, 1999. **48.35** © Paul A. Souders/ Corbis. **48.36** Left © Amos Nachoum/Corbis; right, © Corbis. **48.38** (a) Image courtesy of NOAA and MBARI; (b) Robert Vrijenhoek, MBARI; (c) Steven Haddock, MBARI; (d) © Peter David/FPG/Getty Images. **48.40** (a) NASA–Goddard Space Flight Center Scientific Visualization Studio. **48.41** (a) CHAART, at NASA Ames Research Center; (b) © Eye of Science/Photo Researchers, Inc.; (c) Courtesy of Dr. Anwar Huq and Dr. Rita Colwell, University of Maryland; (d) Raghu Rai/Magnum Photos. **48.42** After M. H. Dickerson, "ARAC: Modeling an Ill Wind," in *Energy and Technology Review*, August 1987. Used by permission of University of California Lawrence Livermore National Laboratory and U.S.

Dept. of Energy. **48.43** © Lawson Wood/Corbis. **Page 987** Right, © Nigel Cook/Dayton Beach News Journal/Corbis Sygma.

CHAPTER 49 **49.1** © Stephen Dalton/Photo Researchers, Inc. **Page 899** © Scott Camazine. **49.2** (a) Eugene Kozloff; (b–c) Stevan Arnold. **49.3** (a) © Robert M. Timm & Barbara L. Clauson, University of Kansas; (b) Reprinted from Trends in Neuroscience, Vol. 21, Issue 2, 1998, L. J. Young, W. Zuoxin, T. R. Insel, "Neuroendocrine bases of monogamy", Pages 71 – 75, ©1998, with permission from Elsevier Science. **49.4** (a) Eric Hosking; (b) © Stephen Dalton/Photo Researchers, Inc. **49.5** © Jennie Woodcock, Reflections Photolibrary/Corbis. **49.6** © James Zipp/Photo Researchers, Inc. **49.7** © Nina Leen/TimePix/Getty Images; inset, © Robert Semeniuk/Corbis. **49.8** © Robert Maier/Animals Animals; (b) © John Bova/Photo Researchers, Inc.; (d) Jack Clark/Comstock, Inc. **49.9** (a) © Monty Sloan, www.wolfphotography.com; (b) © Tom and Pat Leeson, leesonphoto.com; (c) © Kevin Schafer/ Corbis. **49.10** © Stephen Dalton/Photo Researchers, Inc. **49.11** (a) John Alcock, Arizona State University; (b–c) © Pam Gardner/Frank Lane Picture Agency/ Corbis; (d) © D. Robert Franz/Corbis. **49.12** Michael Francis/The Wildlife Collection. **49.13** (a) © B. Borrell Casals/Frank Lane Picture Agency/ Corbis; (b) © Steve Kaufman/Corbis; (c) © John Conrad/Corbis. **49.14** (a) © Tom and Pat Leeson, leesonphoto.com; (b) John Alcock, Arizona State University; (c) © Paul Nicklen/National Geographic/Getty Images. **49.15** © Jeff Vanuga/ Corbis. **49.16** © Eric and David Hosking/Corbis. **49.17** (a) © Australian Picture Library/Corbis; (b) © Alexander Wild; (c) © Professor Louis De Vos. **49.18** (a) Kenneth Lorenzen; (b) © Nicola Kountoupes/Cornell University; (c) © Peter Johnson/Corbis. **49.19** © Dr. Tim Jackson, University of Pretoria. **49.20** (a) Steve Bloom Images/www.stevebloom.com; (b) © Gallo Images/Corbis. **Page 913** © Matthew Alan/ Corbis. **49.22** F. Schutz. **49.23** © Brad Bergstrom. **Page 916** © Joseph Sohm, Visions of America/ Corbis.

Index
The letter i *designates illustration;* t *designates table;* **bold** *designates defined term;*
■ *highlights the location of applications contained in text.*

A

Aardvark, 449, 449i, 450t
Abalone, 608, 608i
ABC model, flowering, **235**, 235i, 240
ABC transporters, 74, 75i
Abdominal aorta, 742i
Abdominal cavity, 566i, 628, 664i, 703, 703i, 707, 711, 717, 717i, 728, 742, 742i
Abiotic synthesis, 321, 323i
■ ABO blood typing, **176**, 176i, 182, 459i, **662**–663, 663i, 675
■ Abortion, 199, **203**, 287, 558, **783**–784, 796, 814–815
Abscisic acid (ABA), 519, 519i, 541, 544–**545**, 544t, 545t, 553, 555–556
Abscission, **544**–545, 544t, **552**, 555–556
Absorption, heat, 487, 487i, 500
Absorption, light, 338, 387. *See also* Photosynthesis
Absorption, nutrients
  by animals, 718–721, 722i, 723, 725–729, 725i, 726i, 736, 740–741, 752
  by fungi, 335, 392
  by mycorrhiza, 399
  by plants, 494–495, 502–503, 511–512, 514–515, 514i, 515i, 523
Absorption, water
  plants, 377, 493, 494, 495, 502, 511–512, 514–517, 514i, 515i, 516i, 517i, 522
  vertebrates, 740–741, 740i, 741i, 752
Absorption spectrum, **110**, 110i
■ Abstinence, sexual, 153, **782**, 782i, 797
Abyssal zone, ocean, 892i
Acacia tortilis, 490
Acanthostega, 439i
Acceleration, force of, 599–600, 605, 615
Accessory fruit, **532**–533, 533t
Accessory pigment, **108**–110, 109i, 120–121
Acclimatization, **714**–716
Acer, 500i, 534, 534i
Acetabularia, 352i, 364i
Acetaldehyde, 90, 132–133, 132i, 137
Acetate (acetic acid), 90, 340
Acetyl–CoA, 128–129, 129i, 131i, 134, 137–138
Acetyl group, 128, 232, 232i
Acetylation, **232**
Acetylcholine (ACh), 77, **581**–583, 585–587, 585i, 594, 650, 650i, 653–654, 729i
Acetylcholinesterase, 583
■ Achondroplasia, 190, 190i, 201t
Acid, **28**–29, 28i, **30**–31, 30t, 132, 604
Acid/base balance, 29, 31, 706–707, 733t, 745, **747**, 752
■ Acid deposition, 871, 871i
■ Acid rain, 28i, 29, 29i, 399, 861, 869, **871**, 871i, 896–897
■ Acid stomach, **28**
Acidic solution, **28**, 29, 31, 36i, 99, 99i, 318, 377, 724–725, 728, 737–738, 747, 772, 871, 882
Acne, 568, 638, **683**
Acoelomate animal, 406i, 430
Acorn, 295, 295i, 532
Acoustical signal, 302i, 303, 598–599, 902, 904, 914
Acquired characteristics theory, Lamarck, 264
Acquired immunodeficiency syndrome. *See* AIDS

■ Acromegaly, **625**
Acrosome, 774, 775i
Actin (microfilament), 68–69, 68i, 69i, 83, 148–149, 148i, 149i, 564–565, 639–640, **648**–650, 648i, 649i, 650i, 651i, 653–654
Actinomyces, 338i
Action potential, **576**–581, 578i, 579i, 580i, 582, 584–585, 584i, 585i, 589, **596**, 624i, **650**, 712
  contraction and, 650–651, 650i, 654, 667, 676
  recordings, 578–579, 579i, 656i
  in sensory pathways, 599–601, 601i, 605–607, 612–613, 613i, 615
Activated complement, 684, 684i
Activation energy, **94**–96, 96i, **97**–98, 104
Activator, 98, 98i, 99, 239–240
Active immunization, **694**
Active site, **96**–99, 98i, 104–105
Active transport, 75, **77**–78, 77i, **79**, 79i, **81**, 81i, **82**–83, 83i, 88, 88i, 95i, 104t, 482–483, 745i
  by Na^+/K^+ pump, 727, 727i, 736
  nature of, 95, 520, 520i, 547, 547i
  stomatal function and, 518–519, 519i, 521i
■ Acute inflammation, 346t, **684**–685, 685i, 692
■ Acyclovir, 784
Adam. *See* MDMA
Adaptation, 154, 221, **296**, 326, 414–415, 437, 511, 602, 617, 703, 756, 822, 829, 849i
  arthropod, 420, 425
  Darwin's view, 267, 280
  environmental, 297–298, 326, 438, 461, 469, 749, 753
  of Hawaiian honeycreepers, 300–301, 300i, 301i
  in human evolution, 433, 452–453, 458–459, 569, 718, 718i
  life history patterns, **808**–809, 875
  long-term, 296–298, 301, 630–631, 631i
  natural selection and, 282–283
  plant, 296, 296i, 371, 373, 375, 388–389, 550, 553, 819, 876, 882
  short-term, 296, 631, 755–756, 768
  in vertebrate evolution, 437, 642–643, 642i, 643i, 654, 720–721
Adaptive behavior, 899, **903**, 903i, 906, 913–915
Adaptive immunity, 679–**680**, 680t, 681, 681i, 684–687, 686i, 687i, 696, 698–699, 698t
Adaptive radiation, 271i, 301, **308**, 325, 409, 433, 463, 464t, 475
  on archipelagoes, 300, 300i, 304
  fishes, 271i, 418, 436–437, 460, 810
  mammals, 241, 271i, 308–309, 309i, 433, 448–449, 449i, 452
  nature of, 308–309, 316–317, 316t
  plants, 370–373, 373i, 375, 378, 381, 384, 384i, 388
  reptiles and birds, 271i, 433, 442–443, 446
Adaptive trait, 297, 298
Adaptive zone, 305, **308**, 309, 316, 443, 454, 464, 835
■ Addison's disease, **637**
Adductor longus, 647i
Adenine (A), 46, 46i, 95, 95i, 218–221, 220i, 223, 226, 228, 248, 248i
  DNA base pairing rule, 207, 210–212, 210i, 211i, 212i, 213i, 216

Adenosine, 695i
■ Adenosine deaminase (ADA), 695, 695i
Adenosine diphosphate (ADP), 48t, 83i, 95, 95i, 104, 126, 127i, 129i, 130, 130i, 131i, 132i, 137
  in photosynthesis, 111i, 112, 113i, 115i, 120, 120i
  sarcomere contraction role, 649, 649i, 651, 651i
Adenosine monophosphate (AMP), 95i
Adenosine triphosphate (ATP). *See* ATP
■ Adenovirus, 342i, 343t
Adenylate cyclase, 622
Adhering junction, **67**, 67i, **561**, 561i, 564, 564i, 568, 570, 667i
Adhesion protein, **77**–**78**, 77i, 78i, 88, 88i, 151, 404–405, 560, 763–764
Adipose tissue, 40–41, 134, 138, 559, 562–**563**, 563i, 568, 570–571, 718–719, 734, 751, 751i, 776
  characteristics, 729–730, 794i, 795
  in endocrine function, 620, 621i, 628i, 630, 635t
Adrenal cortex, **630**, 630i, 634t, 635t, 636, 752, 794
Adrenal gland, 484i, 586i, 587, 620, 624, 625i, 630, 631i, 630i, 634t, 636–637, 742i, 747
Adrenal medulla, **630**, 630i, 635t, 636
Adrenaline, 582, 635t
Adrenocorticotropin (ACTH), 621i, 624–625, 625i, 630–631, 630i, 634t, 636
■ Adult cloning, 206, 206i, **214**–216, 214i, 214t, 763
Adult stage, 420, 424, 424i, 795–797, 795i, 903i
Adventitious root, **503**, 536, 536t, 543
Aedes triseriatus, 427i
Aegyptopithecus, 454i
AER cell, 765i
Aerobic respiration, 122–**124**, 125, 125i, 132, 136–137, 187, 251i, 339, 354, 368t, 404, 434, 482, 565, 715, 751
  carbon cycle and, 117, 117i, 857, 856i–857i
  in ecosystems, 843, 850, 858
  energy for contraction, 651, 651i, 654
  evolution and, 107, 118, 120
  as metabolic pathway, 100–101, 100i, 104–105
  in organic metabolism, 59i, 64, 72, 124, 135i, 137, 420, 630, 660, 729, 887i
  origin, 271i, 322, 324, 326, 327i, 328i–329i, 330
  photosynthesis and, 96, 107, 110, 110i, 118i, 120, 322, 327, 328i, 480, 542, 545, 546i
  plant cells, 503, 506, 512, 518
  vs. respiration, 701–702, 707–708, 716
  stages, 123, 124i, 125–126, 125i, 126i, 128–131, 128i, 129i, 130i, 131i, 135i, 137
Aesclepias, 539
Aesculus, 500i, 552i
Afferent, **575**, 587
Afferent arteriole, **743**–744, 743i, 744i
Aflatoxin, 848

Africa, 93, 260, 289i, 513i
■ AIDS in, 678, 814, 816
  animals, 291, 291i, 618, 627, 677, 806i, 910
  human population, 814, 814i, 816
African emergence model, **458**–459, 460
■ African sleeping sickness, 354–355
African violet, 536, 536t
Africanized bee, 898–899, 899i
Afterbirth, 794, 794i, 797
Agar, 193, 246, 363, 546i
Agaricus brunnescens, 395
■ Age determination, 21, 507, 507i
Age of Cycads, 381
■ Age spots, 105, 105i
Age structure, populations, **802**, 814–815, 815i, 817–819, 819i
Agglutination, **662**, 662i
Aggregate fruit, **532**, 533t
Aggressive behavior, 900, 904, 912
Aging, 122, 199i, 203, 206, 239, 545, 603, 673, 683, 755, **766**, 768
■ diet and, 554, 719, 733
■ exercise, muscles and, 639, 652–653
■ free radicals and, 99, 105, 105i
■ human life cycle, 771, 795, 795i, 795t
  plants, 544t, 552, 555
■ in progeria, 191, 191i, 201t
■ related disorders, 256, 614–615, 657, 728, 773
■ skin, 569, 766
■ Agriculture, 170, 289, 462, 464t, 486
■ artificial selection and, 168, 168i
■ cultivated land, 387, 880, 884, 884i
■ environmental impact, 119, 252, 393i, 492–493, 492i–493i, 618, 618i, 862–863, 862i, 863i
■ erosion, 252, 618, 638i
■ fertilizer use, 876, 884
■ genetic engineering in, 242–243, 252, 254, 254i, 257
■ herbicide, 252, 545, 545t, 618, 618i
  history, 812–813
■ hormone usage, 545, 545t
■ irrigation, 116, 252, 855, 855i, 884
■ on marginal land, 472, 554, 884
■ mechanized, 466, 884
■ pesticides, 252, 289, 391, 427, 618, 884
  pests, 419, 427, 427i
■ population growth and, 473, 812–813, 813i, 816
■ runoff, 252, 852–855, 854i, 861–863, 862i, 888, 890
■ salinization, 252
■ seed banks and, 253
■ soils and, 252, 861, 876, 880
Agrobacterium, 252, 253i, 338
■ AIDS pandemic, 2, 258, 342, 343t, 346, 346t, 402, 571, 594, 695–697, 784t, 814, 816
  HIV and, 678, 679i, 696, 696i, 696t, 697i
■ opportunistic pathogens and, 393, 397, 397t, 785
■ social behavior and, 785, 785i
Air, transpiration, **516**–517, 517i
Air circulation, 449, 867–870, 868i, 873, 894, 896
  as pollination vector, 393, 395, 396i, 525, 527–528, 534, 538
■ Air pollution, 391, 510, 861, 861i, 871
■ fossil fuels. *See* Fossil fuel
■ impact, 377, 871, 881
■ lungs and, 700, 706–707, 712–713

smog, 519, 519i, 869–**870**, 870i, 896
sources, 119, 881
Air (atmospheric) pressure, 702, 702i, 716
air circulation patterns and, 714, 868–869, 868i, 873, 893–894, 894i
in respiration, 702, 702i, 710–711, 710i, 711i, 714, 716
Air sac, 560i, 703, 703i, 705, 705i, **706**–709, 706i, 708i, 716
Aix sponsa, 36i
Ajellomyces capsulatus, 397, 397t
Alachlor, 848i
Alanine, 42i, 222i
Alar (herbicide), 848i
Alarm signal, intraspecific, 898, 898i, 904, 908, 908i
Albatross, 133, 295i, 302i, 447i, 839i
Albinism, 183, 183i, 201t
Albumin, 44–45, 446, 660i
Alchemist, 31, 31i
Alcohol, **36**, 36i, 41, 48t, 91, 105, 132, 323, 323i, 490, 533i, 589, 594–595, 645
effects on liver, 63, 90, 90i, 729
pregnancy and, 793, 793i, 795, 797
Alcohol dehydrogenase, 90
Alcoholic cirrhosis, 90
Alcoholic fermentation, 123, **132**–133, 132i, 137
Alcoholic hepatitis, 90
Aldehyde group, 36i, 38, 38i, 48t
Alder, 832i
Aldosterone, 621i, 622, 622t, 635t, 739, 746–**747**, 746i, 752–753
Aleurone, 546, 546i
Alexander the Great, 295, 332, 332i
Alfalfa, 499i, 524, 848
Alga (algae), 53, 102, 164, 252, 356, 374i, 375, 414i, 824, 833, 834i, 835–836, 836i, 847, 889i
brown, 314i, 351, 352i, 361, 361i, 368
golden, 355, 355i, 360–361, 360i, 368
green, 55i, 70i, 110i, 121, 121i, 298, 329i, 351, 352i, 354, 358, 364–365, 364i, 365i, 369, 372–373, 372i, 388, 400, 842, 849i, 850, 850i, 855, 861, 863, 863i, 886, 887i
haploid dominance among, 374, 388
intertidal zone species, 890, 891i, 895
in lakes, 886, 887i
origin, 325, 329i
photosynthetic, 110, 110i, 115
red, 109, 121, 121i, 314i, 318, 324i, 325, 329i, 341, 351, 352i, 358, **363**, 363i, 369, 470, 470i, 835, 891
reef-forming, 363
yellow-green, 360–361, 360i, 368
Algal bloom, 119, 119i, **358**, 358i, 360, 369, 842, 850, 850i, 855, 861, 863, 863i, 888, 894, 894i
Algin, 361
Alguita research vessel, 893
Alkaline soda lake, 318
Alkaline solution, 28, 31, 246, 318, 738, 747
Alkaloid, 381, 397, 398, 604
Alkalosis, 29
Alkylating agent, **227**
Allantois, 446i, **787**, 787i, 787t, **797**
Allele, 155–**156**, 160–161, 160i, 166, **171**, 177i, **182**, 184, 232, 234, 241, **284**, **298**
autosomal dominant, 187, 190–191, 190i, 193–195, 200, 201i, 204
autosomal recessive, 187, 190–191, 190i, 193–194, 193i, 200–202, 204
codominant, 169, 176, 176i, 182

dominant, 169, 171–174, 172i, 173i, 174i, 176–177, 182–185, 234i, 283, 286
in heterozygous condition, 171, 184, 234
in homozygous condition, 171–172, 179, 184, 234
incomplete dominance, 176, 177, 182, 184–185
mutant, 179–180, 179i, 183–185, 190–191, 193–195, 193i, 201, 205, 229, 234, 241, 267, 284–285, 287, 293–294, 294i, 737, 826
recessive, 169, 172, 173i, 174, 174i, 176–177, 182–185, 283, 286, 295
recessive x-linked, 195, 205
wild-type, 193, 193i, 294
Allele frequency, 178, 178i, 202, **285**, 285i
balancing selection, 292–293, 293i
directional selection and, 283, 287i, 288–289, 289i, 298, 308, 316
disruptive selection, and 283, 287i, 290i, 291, 291i, 298
genetic drift, 283, 285, 294, 294i, 295i, 298, 298t, 308
Hardy–Weinberg rule, 286–287, 286i, 298
in microevolution, 283–287, 286i, 298
natural selection and, 283, 285–291, 298, 298t
Allergen, 254, 397t, 680, **694**–695, 694i, 699
Allergy, 527, 689, **694**, 698t, 699, 713
dust mites and, 421i, 426
Alligator, 333, 444i, 445, 589i, 618–619
Allolactose, 238, 239i
Allopatric speciation, **304**–305, 304i, 305i, 316
Allopolyploid, **306**–307, 307i
Allosteric control, enzyme activity, 98, 98i, 233
Aloe vera, 381
Alpha cell, pancreas, **628**, 628i, 636
Alpha globin, 44, 44i, 709i
Alpha-1, 3-galactose, 255
Alpha rhythm, 591
Alpine tundra, 883, 883i
Alternative splicing, **221**
Altitude sickness, 138, 714
Altruism, 899, **903**, 910–911, 910i, 911i, 914
Alu transposon, 277
Aluminosilicate, 512
Aluminum, 877i
Alvarez, Luis, 443
Alvarez, Walter, 443
Alveolar sac, 706i, 707–710, 708i, 709i, 716
Alveolate, 314i, 351, 352i, **356**–358, 356i, 357i, 368
Alveolus (alveoli), 356, 356i, 358, 368, 703, 703i, 705–**706**, 705i, 706i, 707–710, 708i, 712–714, 716
Alzheimer's disease, 122, 256, **593**, 766
Ama (Asian divers), 715
Amacrine cell, retina, 612, 612i
Amanita, 397t, 401i
Amborella, 385, 385i
Ambrosia, 877i
Amine hormone, 622, 622t, 626, 632, 636
Amino acid, **42**, 42i, 44, 45i, 48t, 56, 65, 97–98, 97i, 105, 115, 281, 321, 323, 323i, 382, 604, 622, 638, 680, 708
absorption from gut, 724t, 725–727, 727i, 736
blood transport, 660–660i
essential, human diet, 554, **730**

in filtrate, 744–745
metabolism, 63, 134, 135i, 137, 202, 630, 630i, 729, 729i, 732t
molecular structure of, 35, 47
neurotransmitters from, 582–583
organic compound role, 36–37, 36i
protein structure and, 7, 36i, 47, 49, 74, 236, 278, 278i, 280, 546
in protein synthesis, 62, 208, 218–220, 222–226, 222i, 223i, 224i, 225i, 226i, 228–229, 228i, 568, 569i, 730
Amino group, 36i, 37, 42, 42i
Aminopeptidase, 724t
Ammonia, 25i, 99i, 134, 135i, 320, 321, 321i, 338, 514, 729, 729i, 731, 741, 747, 753, 860, 860i, 864
Ammonification, 860–**861**, 860i
Ammonite, 263i, 443i
Ammonium, 860–861, 860i, 864
Amnesia, **593**
Amniocentesis, 202i, **203**
Amnion, 203, 446i, **786**–788, 787i, 787t, 790i, 794, **797**
Amniote, 433, 437i, **442**–446, 442i, 446i, 448, 452, 460–461, 461i
Amniotic cavity, 203, **786**, 787i, 788i
Amniotic fluid, 202i, 203, 793–794
Amoeba, 68, 70i, 71–72, 86–87, 144, 167i, 327, 352i, 356–357, **366**, 366i, 369, 409, 608
Amoebic dysentery, 346t, 366
Amoeboid cell, 351, 366–367, 367i, 369, 392, 392i, 400, 405, 408, 409i
Amoebozoan, 314i, 351, 352i, **366**–367, 369
Amphetamine, 572–573, 594
Amphibian, 53, 232, 314i, 444, 464i, 523, 881, 907
catastrophic declines in, 393, 393i, 397t, 441, 473
characteristics, 307, 440–441, 587–588, 589i, 658–659, 659i, 720i, 740, 749
deformities, 618–619, 618i, 627, 627i, 636
development, 761, 764, 764i
evolution, 271i, 274, 404i, 428i, 433, 434i, 436–437, 437i, 439i, 441–442, 460, 642, 642i, 654, 659
respiration, 704–705, 705i, 716–717
Amphiprion perideraion, 823i
Ampicillin, 244i
Amplitude, **606**–607, 606i, 615
Ampulla, 429i
Amputation, 629, 629t
Amygdala, 591, 591i, 593, 593i
Amylase, 546, 546i
Amyloplast, 65
Amylose, 38i, 39i
Amyotrophic lateral sclerosis (ALS) (Lou Gehrig's disease), 122, 382
Anabaena, 338, 338i, 339i
Anabolic pathway, **100**
Anabolic steroid, 638–639, 645
Anaerobic electron transfers, **133**, 137, 353–354, 368t
Anaerobic energy-releasing pathways, 118, 123–126, 124i, 126i, 131–133, 132i, 133i, 137, 271i, 319, 338–341, 651, 715, 883, 887i. See also Fermentation
origin of, 324–325, 328i, 329i, 330
photoautotroph, 107–108, 114, 120
Anagenesis, **308**
Analogous structure, **275**, 275i, 280
Ananas, 533i
Anaphase, mitosis, 141, 144i, 145, **147**–148, 147i, 152, 153i, 157i, 158i, 159i, 164i, 165i, 166
Anaphase I, meiosis, 157i, 158i, 164i, 166, 198i

Anaphase II, meiosis, 157i, 159i, 165i, 198i
Anaphylactic shock, **695**
Anapsid, 442i
Anatomy, **479**, **489**, 558
Andes, 272i, 297, 554, 873, 884
Androgen, 622t, 635t, 636
Androgen insensitivity syndrome, 201t, **622**
Androstenedione ("andro"), 638
Anemia, 45, 201t, **662**, 732t, 733t
Anemone fish, 823, 823i
Aneuploidy, **198**–199, 204
Angina pectoris, **672**
Angiosperm, 375, 375i, **464**, 464i
coevolution, 384, 389
evolution, 271i, 370–371, 374i, 384–385, 384i, 385i, 388–389, 388t
Angiotensin, 635t
Angler fish, 892, 893i
Angraecum sesquipedale, 529, 529i
Anhidrotic ectodermal dysplasia, 234, 234i
Animal (Animalia), 6, 6i, **9**, 9i, 65, 138, 231, 241, 368t, **404**, 640, 767, 862
characteristics, 9, 39–**41**, 41i, 53, 106, 188, 236–237, 237i, 403–407, 406i, 407i, 480–481, 488–489, 489i, 559, 741, 741i
classification, 8–9, 8t, 14, 310–311, 310i, 311i, 314i, 316, 392, 400, 404, 404i
domestication, 812–813, 813i, 884
evolution, 269, 271i, 278, 325, 327, 329i, 351, 352i, 402–405, 464, 464t, 566, 574, 640, 765, 768
family trees, 403–404, 404i, 407i, 434–435, 434i
genetic engineering of, 254–255, 254i, 257–258
life cycle, 155, 162i, 167, 755, 758, 768
origins, 325i, 404–405, 405i
pollinator, 525, 528–529, 538
vectors, 534, 534i, 538
Animal behavior, **899**. See also Behavior
Animal cell, 58, 58i, 59i, 77i, 81i, 152
characteristics, 51, 52i, 55i, 64i, 66–69, 71, 142, 146, 148–149, 149i, 158i–159i
Animal pole, **760**–761
Animal rights, 801
Animal tissue, 50, 67, 67i, 76i, 122, 128i, 214t, 215, 231, 255, 368t, 403, 407i, 558
formation, 403–405, 405i
lab-grown, 569, 571
types of, 558–559, 560i, 562–565, 562i, 563i, 564i, 565i
Animalcules, 50
Annelid, 314i, 404i, 407, 407i, **414**–415, 414i, 415i, 428, 428i, 430–431, 608, 702, 761
Annual plant, **504**, 808t, 809, 825, 825i, 832, 877i
Anomaluridae, 450t
Anopheles, 359, 837
Anorexia nervosa, **737**, 737i
Ant, 424, 449–450, 524, 820–821, 820i, 821i, 823, 838i, 910–911, 910i, 914
Antacid, 28, 335i
Antarctica, 118, 273, 336, 340, 376, 408, 449, 449i, 865, 865i
Anteater, 309i, 449–450, 449i, 450t
Antelope, 721, 721i, 756
Antenna, 236, 236i, 420, 424, 424i, 604, 633i, 769
Antennapedia gene, 236, 236i
Anterior (directional term), 406, 406i, 413, **566**, 566i, 626i

Anterior lobe, pituitary, **624**–627, 625i, 626i, 630–631, 630i, 634t, 636–637
Anterior–posterior axis, animals, 406, 406i, 760, 762, 764–765, 769, 788
Anther, 156i, 276, 526, 526i, 527i, 530, 530i, 538
Anthocyanin, **108**
Anthozoan, **410**
■ Anthrax, 339, 679
Anthropoid, **452**, 454, 454i, 460
■ Anti-acne drug, 793
■ Antibiotic, 11, 102–103, 103i, 289, 327, 335i, 348, 390, 396, 441, 683, 737, 784–785, 813, 841, 881
Antibiotic resistance, 57, 74, 244, 244i, 289, 347, 348, 841
Antibody, 48t, 79i, 255, 626, 662, 674i, 675, 677, 684i, **688**, 688i, 689i, 693–695, 693i, 698, 785, 792, 895
  B lymphocytes and, 679, 688–689, 691i, 698, 698t
  classes (immunoglobin), 688–689
  Rh markers and, 663, 663i
Antibody-mediated immune response, 679, 684i, **687**, 687i, 690–692, 690i, 691i, 698
Anticodon, **223**–225, 223i, 224i, 228
■ Antidepressant, 582, 747, 793
Antidiuretic hormone (ADH), 621i, 622t, 624–625, 624i, 634t, 635–636, 739, **746**–747, 746i, 752, 901, 912–913
Antigen, 679–**680**, 680t, 681, 683–684, 686–694, 686i, 687i, 688i, 689i, 690i, 691i, 692i, 692t, 696, 698
Antigen–MHC complex, 686, 686i, 690–693, 691i, 692i, 698, 698t
■ Antihistamine, 695
■ Antioxidant, **99**, 766
■ Antisense drug, 229
Antithamnion plumula, 352i, 363i
■ Antithrombin III, 254, 254i
■ Antitoxin, 653
Antitrypsin, 713
■ Antivenin, 427i
■ Antiviral drug, 348, 784
Anus, 206, 671, 703i, 720–721, 722i, **723**, 728, 736, 736t, 762, 773i, 777i, 784
  chordate, 433–434, 435i, 460
  invertebrate, 406–407, 407i, 416–417, 416i, 419, 419i, 421i, 428, 430
Anvil, ear, 606, 606i
Aorta, 177, 177i, 435i, 658i, **664**, 664i, 665i, 666–667, 666i, 667i, 673, 673i, 676, 742i
Aortic body, 665i, 712
Apatosaurus, 432i
Ape, 197, 197i, **452**–456, 455i, 460, 881
Apetala 1 gene, 276, 276i
Aphid, 154, 154i, 156, 362, 520, 520i, 823, 831, 831i
Apical dominance, **544**–545, 544t
Apical meristem, 542i, 544, 544t, 547, 547i
Apicomplexan, 314i, 351, 352i, 356, **358**, 363, 368, 687
Aplysia, 597, 597i, 703, 703i
■ Apnea, 711
Apneustic center, **712**, 712i
ApoA1, 49
Apolemichthys xanthurus, 717i
Apoptosis, **488**–490, 489i, 692i, 693, 698, **763**, 793
■ Appendicitis, 419i, 728
Appendicular skeleton, human, 642, 643i

Appendix, 674i, 675, **728**, 728i
Appetite, hormones controlling, 718–719, 722i, 728, 735–736, 735i
Apple, 105–106, 532–533, 533i, 539, 545
■ Apple scab, 397, 397i, 397t
Apricot, 532, 828
Aquaporin, 79i, 81, 81i, 88–89, 89i, **746**–747
Aqueous humor, 610i, 611, 615
Aquifer, 855, 855i
Aquifex, 314i, 338, 338i
Aquificales, 338i
Aquilegia, 385i
Arabian oryx, 490
Arabidopsis thaliana, 235, 235i, 240–241, 276i, 551, 556
Arachnid, 421, 421i, 430
Arceuthobium, 385i
Archaea, **8**, 8t, 14, 51–52, **56**–57, 57i, 69, 72, 73t, 301, 318, **337**, 340–341, 368t, 472, 892
  characteristics, 32, 32i, 106, 109, 118, 133, 142, 142t, 333–334, 336i, 348–349, 865, 865i
  classification, 310–311, 311i, 314, 314i, 316, 340, 340i
  origin, 319, 324–325, 328i, 329i, 330
Archaean eon, 271, 271i, 324–325, 709i
Archaeanthus linnenbergeri, 373i
Archaefructus sinensis, 384i
Archaeopteryx, 432–433, 432i, 433i, 446, 446i
Archenteron, 759i
Archipelago, 300, 300i, **304**, 841
  allopatric speciation on, 304–305, 305i
Architectural constraints, body plan, **765**
Archosaur, 442i
Arctic tundra, 390, 473i, 865, 883, 883i
  animals, 447, 753, 800, 883i
Area effect, **839**, 839i
■ Arenavirus infection, 343t
Argentine fire ant, 820, 820i, 821i, 835
Arginine, 49, 96, 222i, 226i
Aristotle, 262
Armadillo, 266, 266i, 309i, 769
Arnold, Stevan, 900
9+2 array, 71, 71i, 73t
■ Arrhythmia, **673**, 673i, 676
Arsenic, 18, 18i, 282, 510, 748, 848
Artemesia, 359
Artemisinin, 359
Arteriole, 664–665, 665i, **668**–669, 668i, 669i, 670i, 676, 726, 742, 744, 750–752
  controls over, 630, 635t, 668, 685, 685i
■ Arteriosclerosis, **672**
Artery, 49, 201t, **668**–669, 669i, 726i, 746
■ atherosclerotic plaque, 672–673, 672i
  function, 666–668, 667i
  in human, 657, 664, 664i, 665i, 666–668, 666i, 676
  renal, 742, 742i, 752
  structure, 564, 565, 668i, 670i, 700
■ Arthritis, 206, 287, 645
Arthrobotrys dactyloides, 393i
Arthropod, 314i, **420**, 430, 696
  ancestry, 403, 404i, 407, 407i, 428, 428i, 761
  characteristics, 307, 606, 608–609, 633, 636, 641, 654, 658, 703
  harmful, 422i, 423, 426–427, 426i, 427i
Artificial hive, 524
Artificial insemination, 317

■ Artificial selection, **10**, 10i, 168, 168i, 242, 242i, 299, 299i
Artificial twinning, 214
Artiodactyl, 281, 309i, 449
Asbestos, 870
■ *Ascaris*, 419, 419i, 830, 830i
Ascomycete, 391, **393**, 396, 396i, 400
Ascorbic acid, 732t
Ascospore, **396**, 396i
Ascus (asci), 396, 396i, 400
Asexual reproduction, 142–143, 152, 154–**156**, 154i, 164, 166, 227, 302, 306, 354, 377i, 755–**756**, 756i, 768, 836, 836i
  animals, 404, 409i, 411i, 412, 413i
  flowering plant, 525, 536–538, 536i, 537i
  fungal, 391, 393–394, 394i, 396, 396i, 400
  prokaryotic, 142, 142t, 238t, 336
  protistan, 354, 357, 359, 359i, 361, 363, 365–366, 365i
■ Aspergilloses, 397t
Asparagine, 222i
Aspartame, 202
Aspartate, 222i
Aspen, 252, 253i, 371, 536, 537i, 882
■ *Aspergillus*, 393, 396–397, 397t
■ Aspirin, 545, 748, 881
Assassin bug, 905
■ Asteroid, **260**, 260i, 271i, 273, 309, 309i, 440, 443, 464t, 465, 468
■ Asthma, **695**, 700
■ Astigmatism, 614
Astrocyte, 583, 583i
Ataxia, 122
Atelopus varius, 393i
Athenosphere, 272i
■ Atherosclerosis, 49, 122, 629t, **672**–673, 672i, 676, 766
Athlete's foot, 397, 397i, 397t
Atlantic needlefish, 849i
Atmosphere, 32, 34, 124, 270i, 273, 330, 443, 465–466, 511, 600i, **867**. *See also* Global warming
  circulation patterns, 867–870, 868i, 873, 894, 896
  formation of early, 106–107, 116, 118, 136, 270i, 271i, 273, 319–320, 322, 324, 326, 328i–329i, 330, 338, 371–372
Atmospheric cycle, 852, 856–857, 856i–857i, 860–861, 860i, 864
Atoll, 470i
Atom, 3, **4**–5, 4i, 9, **18**–19, **20**–24, 20i, 22i, 23i, **30**, 30t
Atomic number, 20, 20i, 31
ATP (adenosine triphosphate), **46**–47, 46i, **95**, 239, 322, 649, 649i, 666, 860, 733t, 862
  function, 36i, 37, 46–48, 48t, 64, 64i, 91–92, 94–95, 95i, 102, 104–105, 104t, 124, 126, 127i, 131i, 135i, 137, 622–623, 623i, 639, 741i
  function in photosynthesis, 107, 111, 111i, 115, 118i
  membrane transporters, 81i, 83, 83i, 88, 577
  metabolism and, 95, 95i, 104, 134, 135i
  in mitochondrion, 58, 59i, 64, 72, 73t
  motor proteins and, 69–71, 71i, 75, 75i, 146, 148, 212t
  sliding-filament model role, 649, 649i, 651, 651i, 654
  ATP formation, 57, 64, 73t, 80, 151, 239, 321, 326, 328i, 522, 522i, 729, 732t, 823
  in aerobic respiration, 59i, 64, 72, 100–101, 118i, 123–126, 124i, 125i, 126i, 127i, 128i, 129–131, 129i, 130i, 131i, 133–134,

137–138, 187, 341, 354, 404, 420, 503, 518, 542, 546i, 565, 630, 702, 708, 751
  in anaerobic electron transfers, 126, 126i, 127i, 132–133, 132i, 340, 348, 354
  in chloroplast, 58, 65, 113–114, 113i, 114, 114i
  in mitochondrion, 122, 122i, 123, 124i
  in photosynthesis, 107, 111, 111i, 112–115, 113i, 114i, 118i, 120, 120i, 124, 137
  role of electron transfers in, 91, 92, 105, 107, 111–114, 111i, 113i, 114i, 118i, 120, 120i
ATP synthase, 79i, **112**, 113i, 120, 130–131, 130i, 131i, 133, 137, 212t, 341
ATP/ADP cycle, **95**, 95i, 733t
ATPase pump, 77i, 79i, 81i
■ Atrazine, 618, 618i, 848i
Atrial fibrillation, **673**
Atrial natriuretic hormone, 635t
Atrioventricular node, 667, 667i, 676
Atrioventricular valve, 666, 666i, 667i
Atrium (atria) (heart), 657, 659, 659i, 666–667, 666i, 667i, 673, 676
Atrophy, **241**
Attack complex, complement, 684, 684i
Attalea, 500
Auditory canal, 558, 606, 606i, 615
Australia, 449, 449i, 815i, 816, 875i
  insects, 908, 908i, 910i
  reef biodiversity, 470–471, 470i, 837
Australian lungfish, 439i
Australopith, **455**, 456i, 458, 460
Australopithecus, 455, 455i, 457i
■ Autism, 186, 913
Auto-antibody, 695
Autoimmune response, 584, 629, 645, 679, **695**, 699, 766
Automated DNA sequencing, **248**, 248i, 250–251, 257, 278, 280, 301, 337
Automated external defibrillator (AED), 657
Autonomic nerve, 575i, **586**–587, 586i, 596, 728
Autopolyploid, **306**, 306i
Autosomal aneuploidy, 198, 204
Autosomal dominant inheritance, 177, 190–191, 190i, 200, 201t, 204–205, 229, 229i
Autosomal recessive inheritance, 190, 190i, 191, 200, 201t, 204, 205, 217, 287, 299, 637
Autosome, 178, 187–**188**, 189i, 191, 198–199, 204, 459
Autotroph, **106**, 106i, 118–121, 118i, 119i, 326, 482
  ecosystem roles, 844–845, 844i, 845i, 857, 860i, 862, 862i
Auxin (IAA), 541, **544**–545, 544t, 545i, 545t, 546i, 547–549, 547i, 548i, 549i, 552, 555–556, 848, 848i
Avery, Oswald, 208
Axial development, 236–237, 237i, 240
Axial skeleton, human, 642, 643i, 706i
Axolotl, 441, 764, 764i
Axon, **576**, 579, 581, 588, 592, 597, 695
  endings, 345, 576i, 580, 580i, 581i, 585–586, 585i, 586i, 620, 624, 624i, 630, 650i, 652
  myelinated, 583–587, 584i, 585i, 586i, 587i, 596
  sensory, 600–601, 601i, 604, 604i, 612i, 613, 615

Azospirillum, 338i
Azotobacter, 338i
■ AZT, 697

B

B lymphocyte (B cell), 79i, 661, 661i, 679, 680t, **681**, 681i, 686–689, 687i, 689i, 690i, 691–693, 691i, 695–696, 698–699, 698t
■ Babesiasis, 426
Baboon, 631, 631i, 904i, 909
Baby-boomer population, 814, 815i, 817
Bacillus (bacilli), **334**, 335i, 338i, 339, 348
■ *Bacillus*, 336i, 339, 679
Backbone, 315, 353, 433–434, 436, 452, 642, 643i, 645–646, 647i, 653, 742
Backflow, valves, 671, 671i, 674i, 675
Bacterial chromosome, 57, 334t, **336**, 348
■ Bacterial endocarditis, 682
Bacterial flagellum, 334i, **335**, 335i, 348
Bacteriochlorophyll, 338
Bacteriophage, 55i, **208**, 209i, 210, **342**
multiplication cycle, 344–345, 348
Bacteriorhodopsin, 109, 341
Bacterium (bacteria), **8**, 14, **56**, 98, 109, 223i, 226, 242, 244i, 301, **337**, 341, 349, 356, 368t, 709i, 712, 889, 892
aerobic, 110, 110i, 124, 278, 326–327, 327i, 328i, 329i, 358, 823
anaerobic, 124, 132, 133, 653–654, 861
bioluminescence, 102–103
characteristics, 8, 8i, 8t, 50–52, 50i, 52i, 55i, 57, 57i, 64, 69, 72, 73t, 84, 89, 106, 114, 164, 238–240, 238t, 244, 327, 340, 348, 511, 522, 798, 860, 865, 865i
classification, 310i, 311, 311i, 314i, 316–317
competitive exclusion, 824–825, 825i
decomposers, 6i, 33, 252, 358, 377, 390–392, 844, 844i, 893
defense against, 49i, 86, 87i
■ genetic engineering of, 252, 253i, 255, 257
immune response to, 678, 680–682, 681i, 683i, 684i, 685i, 686–688, 690, 691i, 692, 698t
metabolism, 118, 238–240, 239i
nitrifying, 514, 514i, 523, 832, 832i, 859i, 860–861, 863–864
origins, 319, 324–326, 326i, 328i, 329i, 330
pathogenic, 57, 70, 73–74, 102–103, 208, 209i, 217, 252–253, 289, 319, 326–327, 327i, 333, 335i, 346, 346t, 348–349, 481i, 568–569, 615, 661–662, 677, 784–785, 841–842, 895, 895i
photosynthetic, 56i, 65, 107, 114, 329i
plasmids, 244, 245i, 252, 257
population studies of, 805–806, 805i
reproduction, 142, 142t, 244–247, 336–337, 336i
Bahama woodstar, 528i
Bakane, 540
Baking soda, pH of, 28, 28i
Balance, sense of, 440, 448, 582, 589, 599, 600t, 601, 604–605, 605i, 615, 617
Balanced polymorphism, **292**–293, 298
■ Balloon angioplasty, **673**

Banana, 306i, 462, 545
Banana bunchy top virus, 837
Banana slug, 900, 900i
Bangiomorpha pubescens, 324i, 325
Bangladesh, 814, 895, 895i
■ Barbiturate, 594, 793
Barbule, 446i
Bark, 486, **506**–509, 506i, 507i
Bark beetle, 835t
Bark scorpion, 427
Barley seed, 546, 546i
Barnacle, 422–423, 422i, 430, 834
Baroreceptor, 600t, 665i, 669, 746
Barr, Murray, 234
Barr body, 234, 234i
Barrier reef, 470i
Basal body, **70**, 71, 354, 356i
■ Basal cell carcinoma, 151i
Basal ganglion, 593, 593i
Base, **28**–29, 28i, **30**–31, 30t
nucleotide, 36i, 207, 210–212, 210i, 213i, 216, 222–223, 222i, 227–228
Base pair, 278, 284, 915
Base-pair substitution, **226**, 226i, 227, 228, 915
Base pairing, 220i, 227, 250i
DNA, 207, 210, 211, 211i, 212, 212t, 213, 213i, 216
recombinant, 244–247, 257
in transcription, 220–221, 220i–221i, 223, 229
Base sequence, 220–222, 220i, 221i, 222i, 226, 228, 677
DNA, 207, 211, 216–217, 219, 232, 243–244, 245i, 246i, 248–249, 251, 257, 278, 280, 285
RNA, 232–233, 340
Base sequencing, automated, **248**, 248i, 250–251, 257, 278, 280–281
Base triplet, 219, 222–223, 222i, 226
Basement membrane, 67i, 404, 560, 560i, 668i, 670, 708, 708i, 716, 743i, 744
Basic (alkaline) solutions, **28**–29, 31
Basidiomycete, 391, **393**, 395, 395i, 400
Basidiospore, **395**
Basidium (basidia), 395, 395i
Basilar membrane, cochlea, 606–607, 607i
Basilosaurus, 263, 263i
Basophil, 660i, 661, 661i, **681**, 681i, 689, 696, 698t
Basswood, 116, 116i, 518i, 880
Bat, 274i, 309i, 446–447, 451i, 616–617, 617i, 904–905
as pollinator, 384, 389, 525, 528–529, 528i, 535, 538–539, 823
wing, 263, 275, 275i, 309, 616
Bathyal zone, ocean, 892i
■ *Batrachochytrium*, 393i, 397t
Bay of Bengal, 895, 895i
Bayliss, W., 620
Bayou, 842, 842i, 843i
bcl-2 gene, 489
Beagle, Darwin and, 264–265, 264i, 265i
Bean plant, 116, 252, 487, 487i, 495, 501i, 543i, 730–731, 731i
Bear, 279i, 468–469, 469i, 751, 751i, 753, 829, 883i, 907i
Becquerel, Henri, 21
Bedstraw, 534
Bee, 41, 41i, 694–695, 829i, 900, 911i
Africanized, 898–899, 899i
colony (hive), 529, 898–899, 899i, 905, 905i, 910–911, 910i
■ dance, 425i, 905, 905i, 910
as pollinators, 303, 384, 389, 524, 528–529, 528i, 539, 898, 898i, 905
Beer, 90, 90i, 258, 734

Beeswax, 41, 41i
Beet plant, 243, 554
Beetle, 154i, 277, 425i, 765, 829, 829i
as pollinators, 524, 529, 538
Behavior, 8, 463, 470, 528–529, 538, 575, 747, 754, 767, 774, 897, **899**, 901, 903
adaptive value, 433, 442, 442i, 467, 899, 903, 903i, 906, 913–915
altruistic, 899, 903, 910–911, 910i, 911i, 914
communication, 300, 425i, 447, 632, 632i
courtship, 259, 292, 292i, 302i, 303, 446, 632, 756, 900, 904i, 905–906, 914
defensive, 898, 898i, 904, 904i, 908–910, 908i, 914–915
feeding, 409, 409i, 411, 411i, 640, 640i, 720–721, 720i, 721i, 897, 900
instinctive, 899, 901–902, 901i
learned, 448, 452–453, 461i, 899–900, 902, 902i
mating, 444–445, 754, 756–757, 808–810, 900–901, 906–907, 912–915
migration, 447, 617, 883i, 888, 890, 892, 893i
■ parental, 445, 448, 453, 460, 461i, 754, 754i, 808–809, 899, 901, 901i, 904, 907, 907i, 908i, 910–911, 914
play, 904, 904i
sexual, 453, 631–632, 635, 771, 783–785, 797, 903–904, 906–907, 912, 914
social, 447, 453, 456, 604, 620, 631–632, 631i, 635, 899–900, 904, 908–910, 908i, 912–915, 912i
in temperature regulation, 445–446, 749–752, 750t
Behavioral flexibility, **448**, 459
Behavioral isolation, 302i, **303**, 303i
Behavioral trait, **284**–285, 312
Bell-shaped curve, 180i, **181**, 181i, 288i
■ Belladonna, humans and, 389
Benaron, David, 103
■ Bends, the, 714
Bengal cat, 215i, 469i
Benthic province, 892, 892i
Bermuda grass, 527, 536t
Berry, 532–533, 533t, 732t
Beta-carotene, 109i, 110i, 121, 242, 732t
Beta cell, pancreas, **628**–629, 628i, 636
Beta hemoglobin, 44, 44i, 45i, 226, 226i, 709i
Bicarbonate (HCO_3^-), 29, 69i, 77, 79i, 360, 708–709, 716, 723, 725–726, 728, 752
in carbon cycle, 856–857, 856i–857i
Bicarbonate-carbonic buffer system, 747
Biceps, 585, 585i, 646, 646i, 647i, 648i
Biennial plant, **504**, 544, 551
Big bang, 320
Bilateral symmetry, 403, **406**, 573–575, 596, 665i, 788
invertebrate, 406i, 407, 407i, 412, 414–417, 419–420, 428, 430, 434
vertebrate, 434, 437i
Bile, 722i, **725**, 730, 736, 736t
Bile salt, 41, 672, 682, 725, 727, 727i
Bill, bird, 266, 267i, 291, 291i, 300, 305, 446i, 528i, 539, 720i, 721
■ Billings Rhythm Method, 782i
Binary fission, **336**, **354**, 357, 368t
Binding energy, 97–98, 97i, 98i, 104–105
■ Binge–purge cycle, 737
Biochemistry, 209, 261, 310, 337–338, 679

Biodiversity, 464i, 820–841, 875, 886, 892–893, 896. *See also* Diversity of life
competition and, 834–835, 834i, 876
global distribution, 472–**473**, 473i, 874, 896
■ loss of, 269, 283, 294–295, 298, 309, 462i, 463–475, 464i, 464t, 471, 835, 861, 881, 884, 884i, 885i, 896
nature of, 8–9, 15t, 209, 211
patterns, 483, 821, 838–840, 838i, 839i
■ Bioethics, 243, 250, 255–256, 330, 463
■ abortion, 203, 783, 796
■ of cloning, 206, 215, 215i
competition in science, 207, 211, 216
■ human impact on biosphere, 869, 877i, 881
■ in vitro fertilization, 770, 783
■ organ selling, 748
■ Biofilm, **74**, 700
Biogeochemical cycle, 848, **852**, 852i, 854, 863
Biogeographic realm, **874**
Biogeography, **262**, 468–469, 475, **867**
evolution and, 261, 263, 267, 280
global patterns, 267, 281, 821, 838–840, 838i, 839i, 867, 874–875, 874i–875i
island patterns, 267, 459, 459i, 821, 838i, 839–840, 839i
mainland patterns, 821, 838, 838i, 840
Biological clock, 447, **550**, 555, 608, 621i, **632**, 636, 766, 768
Biological control, 821, 830–831, 830i, 831i
Biological magnification, **843**, 848–849, 848i, 849i, 863
Biological molecule, 19, 24–25, 24i, 25i, 29, 31, 34–37, 36i, 47, 321
Biological species concept, **302**
Biology, 2, 2i, **3**, 11
■ Bioluminescence, **102**–103, 103i, 105, 248, 248i, 251, 251i, 253i, 257–258, 358, 893
Biomass, 424, 854, 856, 856i–857i, 860, 862, 887i, 890
Biomass pyramid, **850**–851, 850i, 863
Biome, 841, 841i, 867, **874**, 876, 876i, 877i, 896
boreal forest, 874i–875i, 881–883
broadleaf forest, 873, 874i–875i, 876, 877i, 880, 896
coniferous forest, 874i–875i, 877i, 882, 882i, 896
desert, 873–875, 874i–875i, 877i, 878, 878i, 884, 896
distribution, 867, 869, 874–875, 896
grassland, 873–876, 874i–875i, 878, 879i, 896
shrubland, 874i–875i, 875, 878, 879i, 884, 896
tundra, 874, 874i–875i
woodland, 874i–875i, 877i, 878, 880, 896
■ Bioprospecting, 318–319
Biosphere, 3, **5**, 5i, 14, 100, 118–119, 119i, 136, 243, **867**–868
autotroph impact on, 118–119, 119i
human impact on. *See* Human impact on biosphere
Biosynthetic pathway, 82, 98, 98i, **100**–101, 104, 134, 144, 253i, 255, 844
■ Biotech barnyards, 254–255, 254i
■ Biotechnology, 169, 318, 545t
■ Bioterrorism, 2, 218
Biotic potential, **805**–806, 819
Biotin, 732t

Bipedalism, 443, 446, 448, **452**–453, 455–456, 455i, 458, 460, 642–643, 654, 912i
Bipolar cell, retina, 612, 612i
Bipolar disorder, 186, 187, 191
Birch, 500, 882
Bird, 41, 53, 121, 154, 188, 291, 312, 312i, 313i, 314i, 331i, 464i, 469, 534, 755, 767, 844i, 881
  ancestry, 262, 271i, 274, 309, 404i, 428i
  behavior, 302i, 427, 456, 842, 883i, 890, 902–905, 902i, 903i, 914–915
  characteristics, 275, 275i, 299, 446–447, 446i, 447i, 460–461, 465, 465i, 474, 589i, 602, 610–611, 626, 658–660, 659i, 705, 705i, 716, 720–721, 720i, 749–750, 749i, 753, 820, 835t
  DDT and, 467, 849i
  development, 446, 761
  diseases, 332–333
  endangered species, 473, 524
  evolution, 432–433, 434i, 436–437, 437i, 442–443, 442i, 445, 452, 460, 465, 465i
  as pollinators, 384, 389, 524, 528–529, 528i, 538–539, 823
  reproduction, 757, 757i, 787–788, 838i
  species distribution, 262–263, 262i, 462, 468, 841
  survivorship, 473, 803, 809, 809i
Birdsong, 300, 447, 632, 632i, 902, 902i
Bird of prey, 469i, 610, 610i, 617, 908
Birth, live, 757i, 770, 804–805, 818
  human, 140, 347, 770, 770i, 793–794, 794i, 796, 808, 808t, 812–816, 814i, 815i, 816i, 818, 830, 839
Birth control, 754, 782, 814–815, 815i
Birth control patch, 782i, **783**
Birth control pill, 618, 782i, **783**
Bison, 831, 831i, 879i, 907, 907i
Biston betularia, 288, 288i
Bitter sensation, 604, 616
Bivalve, 416–417, 417i
Black Death, 3, 282i
Black locust, 500i
Black market, 469, 469i
Black rain, 2
Black Sea, methane gas, 32i
Black spot, 168, 168i, 397
Black stem wheat rust, 397t
Black-tailed prairie dog, 908
Black widow spider bite, 426, 426i
Bladder, 361, 586i
  urinary, 415, 415i, 564i, 565, 739, 742–743, 742i, 752, 772i, 773i, 776i, 777i, 787, 787t
Bladder cancer, 713i, 738
Blade, 361, 361i, 364, 500–501, 500i, 501i
Blastocoel, 758, 759i, 768, 786, 786i
Blastocyst, **761**, 769, 771, 776, 777i, 779, 780i, 786–787, 786i, 787i, 795i, 797
Blastomere, **758**, 760–761, 760i, 761i, 768–769, 788, 798i
Blastopore, 407i
Blastula, **758**, 758i, 759i, 761, 762i, 768–769, 795t
Blending theory of inheritance, 170, 176
Blennies, 439
Blind spot, 610i
Blind staggers, 397
Blind velvet worm, 307i
Blindness, 122i, 242, 256, 615, 629t, 732t
Blood, 6, 39, 82, 84, 134, 229, 424i, 481i, 570, 589, **658**, 671, 677, 701, **740**

characteristics, 559, 562–563, 563i, 571, 681, 798
composition, 484–485, 489, 644, 654, 657, 660–661, 660i, 661i, 669, 675
crime scene, 249, 249i
filtration in kidney, 731, 738i, 739, 741–745, 742i, 743i, 744i, 745i, 748, 752
function, 562i, 563, 564i, 567i, 657–658, 660–661, 660i, 727, 736
glucose level, 622, 628–631, 628i, 629i, 630i, 631, 635t, 636, 729–730
hormone levels/transport, 620, 623i, 626, 630, 634, 636, 638–639
pH of, 28–29, 28i, 660, 660i, 709, 747
Blood–brain barrier, **588**–589, 595–597, 604, 712
Blood cell. See specific types
Blood cell disorders, 189i, 193–194, 194i, 197, 201t, 203, 657, 662, 675
Blood circulation, 90, 478, 620, 624, 653, 658–659, 685, 715
  flow characteristics, 602, 630, 635t, 657–660, 659i, 665i, 668–669, 668i, 671, 676, 744, 746i, 751–752
  human embryo, 789, 789i, 797
  pulmonary circuit, 657, **659**, 659i, 664, 664i, 668, 675–676
  systemic circuit, 657, **659**, 659i, 664, 664i, 668, 668i, 669i, 675–676
  vertebrate, 433, 566, 644–645, 657, 704–705, 708, 714, 716
Blood clot, **672**–673, 672i, 677, 685, 783
Blood clotting, 90, 255, 282–283, 402, 478, 563, 627, 660–661, 660i, 672, 672i, 676–677, 700, 732t, 733t
  factors, 96, 192–193, 252, 254, 254i, 680t, 685, 685i
  in hemophilia, 193–194, 201t
Blood doping, **662**
Blood fluke, infection, 412, 413i, 441i
Blood letting, 414i
Blood loss, 644, 662, 672, 672i
Blood pressure, 478, 572, 587, 594, 657–659, 662, 666, 668–669, 668i, 670i, 671i, 676, 695, 700, 744
  at glomerulus, 744–746, 752
  high, 671, 733t, 744, 747–748, 753, 798
  hormones affecting, 631, 635, 635t
  measuring, 665i, 669, 669i
Blood transfusion, 662–663, 675
Blood typing, 176, 176i, 182, 662–663, 662i, 663i, 675
Blood vessel, 78i, 255, 414, 420, 434, 437, 446i, 484i, 559, 568–569, 568i, 584i, 594, 600t, 629t, 635t, 700, 714, 798
  bone tissue and, 644, 644i, 645i
  function, 657, 676
  major, human, 665i
  in nephron, 743, 743i
  ruptured/clogged, 657, 671–672, 672i, 673i, 700
  structure, 657–659, 658i, 668–669, 668i, 676–677, 677i
Blue-footed booby, 264i, 265i
Blue jay, 295, 295i
Blue offspring, 201t, 299
Blueberry plant, 524
Bluegill sunfish, 908
Bluegrass, 116i
BMP4 signaling molecule, 267i
Body axis, animal, 236–237, 237i, 240, 403, 407, 415i, 430, 566i, 759i, 760–761, 761i, 764–765, 788, 788i, 797
Body-building, 638–639, 638i, 647i
Body mass, 291, 291i
Body mass index (BMI), **734**
Body piercing, 571, 571i
Body plan. See Pattern formation
Body size, 404–405, 414, 420, 430

Bog, 99i, 132, 512, 523
Bombykol, 904
Bone, 4i, 67–68, 67i, 480, 566, 588, 631, **639**–640, 654, 713i
  abnormalities, 229, 627, 635t, 636, 732t
  bird, 446–447, 447i
  characteristics, 563–564, 563i, 564i, 623–624, 634t, 644–645, 654
  evolution of, 263, 263i, 274–275, 274i, 281, 281i, 434, 439, 439i, 452, 455, 460, 642–643, 642i, 643i
  function, 563, 563i, 644–645, 644t, 654
  structure, 41–42, 47, 48t, 644, 644i
  vertebrate skeleton, 249, 642–645, 642i, 643i, 644i, 644t, 645i
  vitamins, minerals, and, 732t, 733t
Bone cancer, 693
Bone formation, 644–645, 645i, 732t, 733t, 758, 769i, 788, 788i, 795, 795t, 797
Bone marrow, 144, 150, 188, 201t, 256, 635t, 644–645, 644i, 645i, 695, 714
  blood cell formation in, 661i, 662, 674i, 675, 689, 698
  stem cells in, 558, 563, 660, 661i, 675, 680t, 681
Bone remodeling, **644**–645
Bone tissue, 67, 67i, 189i, 405, **436**, 558–559, 562–**563**, 563i, 570, 644–645, 644i, 645i, 655, 655i
Bonobo, 452–454, 912–913, 912i
Bony fish, 314i, 438i, 439, 439i, 460
  characteristics, 740, 740i, 757
  evolution, 404i, 428i, 433, 434i, 568
Book lung, 421, 421i, **703**, 716
Boreal forest, 390, 874i–875i, 881–883
Boron, plant growth and, 512, 512t
Borrelia infection, 338i
B. burgdorferi, 338, 339i, 426, 426i
Botox injection, 655
Bottleneck, **294**–295, 298, 308
Bottlenose dolphin, 358, 477i, 715, 715i
Botulism, 132, 218, 339, 349, **653**
Bovine spongiform encephalopathy (BSE), 347, 349
Bowman's capsule, **743**–744, 743i, 744i, 752
53BP1 protein, 150i
Brachial artery, 665i, 669, 669i
Bradycardia, **673**, 673i
Bradykinin, 603
Bradyrhizobium, 514i
Brain, 43, 45i, 89, 144, 582, 681, 739, 741
  blood flow to, 656, 665i, 669i, 670
  development, 762i, 763i
  disorders, 187, 190–191, 201t, 202, 478–479, 792
  energy requirements, 122, 134–135, 629–630, 630i, 729
  evolution, 406, 418, 421i, 433–435, 440, 442, 452–454, 593, 762
  function, 484–485, 484i
  homeostasis and, 629, 630
  infections, 332, 355, 682
  inflammation, 343t, 347–348
  as integrator, 484–485, 484i
  invertebrate, 435, 574i, 575, 596
  reptile, 444i, 445
  rudimentary, 412i, 414, 415i, 897i
  sensory pathways to, 599–602, 601i, 605, 609, 612–613, 613i, 615–616
  vertebrate, 436, 440, 442, 455, 455i, 460, 572, 575–576, 575i, 576i, 586–589, 588i, 589i, 596

Brain, human, 179, 576, 583i, 584, 587, 589, 596, 653, 711, 715, 812
  development, 595, 788, 790i, 791–793, 792i, 797
  divisions, 588, 588i, 589i, 596t
  drugs and, 572–573, 583, 594–595, 594t, 595i, 597, 700
  evolution, 456, 456i, 458, 460
  neurons and, 565, 565i, 583
  PET scans, 582, 582i, 590i, 595i
  split-brain experiments, 592, 592i
  structure, 586i, 670
Brain stem, **588**–589, 591, 596, 712, 712i, 716
Branch point, **308**, 308i, 311–312, 315, 375i, 402–403
Branched evolution, 279, 308, 308i, 309i, 310, 312, 316, 316i
Brassica oleracea, 276i
Brassinosteroid, **545**, 555
BRCA1 gene, 150i, 230
BRCA2 allele, 287
BRCA2 gene, 230
Bread mold, 394, 394i
Breast cancer, 153, 230–231, 230i, 258, 287, 693, 700, 734, 783
Breast tissue, 199, 448i, 632, 635t, 637–638, 637i, 777, 794i, 795
Breastbone, 446–447, 642, 643i, 645
Breastfeeding, 754, 794i, 795
Breathing, 397, 485, 485i, 573, 583, 587, 596, 653, 701, 705–708, 706i, 707i, 710–712, 710i, 711i, 714–716
  smoking and, 700, 700i, 711
Brittle star, 428, 428i
Broadleaf deciduous forest, **880**, 896
Broca's area, 590, 590i, 592
Bronchiole, 560i, 683i, 706i, **707**, 712, 715–716
Bronchitis, 700, 712, 712i, 713i, 716
Bronchus (bronchi), 560i, 586i, 706i, **707**, 712, 712i, 716
Brown, Robert, 50
Brown alga, 314i, 351, 352i, **361**, 361i, 368
Brown recluse spider bite, 426, 426i
Brundtland, G. H., 713
Brush border cell, 726–727, 726i, 727i, 736
Bryophyte, 311, 311i, 371–373, 373i, 374i, 375, 375i, **376**–378, 376i, 377i, 388, 388t
"Bubble boys," gene therapy for, 256
Bubonic plague, 2–3, 282, 807i
Buckeye, 500i
Bud, 498, 500i, 504, 512t, 520, 550, 552
  dormancy, 540, 552–553, 553i, 555
  lateral (axillary), 494i, 498–499, 498i, 500i, 504i, 536t, 544, 544t
  terminal, 494i, 498–499, 504i
Budding, 154, 277, 277i, 336, 342, 345, 345i, 348, 368t, 409, 413, 763i, 765, 765i, 790, 790i
  sac fungi, 396, 396i
  viral, 696, 697i
Budworm, 849
Buffer, **709**, 722i, 723, 728, 736t, 747, 773, 871
Buffer system, 19, **29**, 31, **747**
Bufo marinus, 837
Bulb of Krause, 602, 603i
Bulbourethral gland, 772t, 773, 773i, 774i
Bulimia, **737**
Bulk, dietary, **728**
Bulk flow, **84**, 85i, 670i, **671**
Bulk-phase endocytosis, **87**
Bullet-proof vest, 254
Bulrush, 889i

Bundle-sheath cell, **116**, 117i
Bunkley–Williams, Lucy, 470
■ Bunyamwera virus, 343t
Buoyancy, 361, 438, 642–643, 654
■ Burkitt's lymphoma, 343t
Bursa, 647i
Butorides virescens, 849i
Butterfly, 12–13, 13i, 188, 284, 420, 424i, 425i, 609i, 765–766, 803, 803i, 808, 831
 allele frequency example, 286–287, 287i, 288i, 290i
 as pollinator, 524–525, 528–529, 538–539
Butterfly fish, 823i

C

C3 plant, **116**–117, 116i, 117i, 120–121
C4 plant, **116**–117, 117i, 120–121
Cacao tree, 524, 534
Cactus, 116i, 117, 117i, 262–263, 262i, 267i, 385, 469i, 483, 483i, 500, 502, 878i
Cadherin, 79i, 404–405, 560, 764
Cadmium ion, 510
Caecilian, 440i, 441
Caenorhabditis elegans, 419, 419i
■ Caesarian section, 770
Caffeine, 589, 594, 597
CAG nucleotide repeat, 190
Caimen, 445, 445i
Calamite, 380, 380i
Calcitonin, 622t, 627, 635t, 645
Calcitrol, 635t
Calcium, 18, 18i, 19i, 22, 34, 95i, 356, 550i, 569, 580, 580i, 621i, 626, 636, 861
 bones and, 420, 428, 567i, 644–645, 644t, 654, 732t, 733
 cross-bridge formation role, 649, 649i, 651, 651i
 dietary, 554, 627, 733t, 748
 ions, 29, 79i, 81i, 83, 83i
 muscle function and, 650, 650i, 651i
 plant function and, 512, 512t, 519, 519i
 in soil, 854, 854i, 876i
Calcium carbonate, 350, 360, 411, 856, 876i
Calcium pump, 77i, 79i, **83**, 83i, 95i, 580
Calcium sulfate, 892
Calicivirus, 837
■ California Current, 872, 872i
■ California encephalitis, 343t
California poppy, 503, 503i, 540i
Callinectes sapidus, 637
Calisher, Charles, 332
Callus, 536, 537i, 629t
■ Caloric intake, human, 718–719, 730, 734–736, 812i
Calvaria major, 465i
Calvin, Melvin, 21, 364
Calvin–Benson cycle, **115**–117, 115i, 116i, 117i, 120, 120i
Calyx, 526, 527i
CAM plant, 116i, **117**, 117i, 120, 518, 819
Camarhynchus pallidus, 267i
Cambrian period, 271i, 277, 277i, 314, 314i, 325, 355, 409, 436–437, 464, 464t, 568, 810, 821
Camel, 297, 297i, 304i, 317, 449, 451i, 874
Camelid, 297, 304i
■ *Camellia sinensis,* 381i
Camera eye, **609**–610, 610i
Camouflaging, 288, 288i, **828**–829, 828i, 829i, 840
■ Camptodactyly, **180**, 201t
Camptosaurus, 432i
■ *Campylobacter,* 338t, 347

■ Cancer, **151**, 153, 488i, 489, 747, 767
Aspergillus flavus, 397t
 basal cell carcinoma, 151i
 bladder, 713i, 738
 bone, 693
 breast, 153, 230–231, 230i, 258, 287, 693, 700, 734, 783
 causes, 2, 188, 227, 229–231, 718, 730, 766
 cervix, 150i, 153, 343t, 783–784
 Chernobyl and, 897, 897i
 colon, 616, 682, 728, 734
 diagnosing, 69, 773
 duodenal, 682
 esophagus, 595, 713i
 gastric, 682
 HeLa cells, 140, 140i, 151
 immune response to, 86–87, 661, 679, 680t, 681, 692–693, 698t
 Kaposi's sarcoma, **696**, 696i
 kidney, 738
 larynx, 713i
 leukemia, 256, 662, 662i, 897i
 liver, 343t, 783
 lung, 229, 595, 700, 713i, 773, 871
 malignant melanoma, 151i, 343t
 mouth, 595, 713i
 nature of, 141, 144, 150–152
 ovarian, 153, 783
 pancreas, 713i
 pharynx, 343t
 prostate gland, 738, **773**
 screening, 153, 258
 skin, 217, 217i, 569, 693, 870
 squamous cell carcinoma, 151i
 stomach, 335i
 testicular, **773**
 therapies, 103, 151, 153, 229–230, 251, 381, 402, 632, 662, 693, 699, 773
 viruses and, 342
■ *Candida albicans,* 393, 396, 396i, 397t
Canegiea gigantea, 819, 819i
Canidae, 450t
Canine, tooth, 448i, 453, 571, 723, 723i, 904i
Canis lupus, 826, 826i
■ Cannibalism, 463, 909
Cannabis, 595, 713i
Canopy, 474, 505
 forest, 875–876, 878, 880–881
CAP–cAMP complex, 239
Capillary, 151, 589, 596, 653, 657–659, **668**, 668i, 675–676, 704i, 705–706, 706i, 708
 blood, 478, 481i, 482, 483i
 function, 670–671, 670i, 676
 glomerular, 742–743, 743i, 748, 752
 in intestinal villi, 726i, 727
 "leaky," 685, 685i, 695, 698, 752
 lymphatic, 674–676, 674i
 pulmonary, 664, 664i
Capillary bed, 624, 658–659, 659i, 715
 exchanges, 561, 664i, 666, 670–671, 670i, 675–676
 function, 670–671, 674, 676
 gills, 704, 704i
 lungs, 664, 664i
Capillary reabsorption, 670i, **671**, 676
Capita, **804**, 818
Capsella, 532, 532i
Capture–recapture method, **803**, 818
Carapace, 421
Carbaminohemoglobin, 708
Carbohydrate, 6, 33, 38–39, 48t, 49, 78, 87i, 323i, 399–400, 536t, 563
 digestion, 63, 719–720, 724, 724t, 736, 741i
 function, 34–37, 38, 47
 human dietary, 730–731, 736
 metabolism, 90, 124, 134–135, 137, 630, 722i, 723, 729, 729i, 731, 732t, 736t

 storage in plants, 115, 115i, 520–521
 synthesis, 90, 94, 100, 107, 111, 124, 144
Carbon, 32, 843, 852, 856–857, 856i–857i, 863, 863i, 865, 883
 in aerobic respiration, 126, 127i, 128–129, 128i, 129i, 137
 backbone bonding behavior, 33–35, 36i, 37–38, 40–41, 40i, 41i, 43, 47, 47i, 76, 124, 126, 132, 135i, 137, 210, 211i, 212, 213i
 central role in life, 18–22, 18i, 19i, 319, 335–336, 348, 394
 function in organic compounds, 34, 36, 38, 42, 47
 plant growth and, 106, 106i, 111, 111i, 115–116, 116i, 118, 118i, 120–121, 512, 512t, 522
 ring structure, 34, 36i, 38, 38i, 40–41, 46–47, 46i, 48t
Carbon 12, 21, 23i
Carbon cycle, 118–120, 136, 338, 340, 360, 387, 389, **856**–857, 856i–857i, 864–865, 884, 885i
Carbon dioxide, 9, 21, 29, 36, 104, 229, 336, 348, 545i, 589, 600t
 in aerobic respiration, 123, 125, 125i, 128–129, 128i, 129i, 131i, 132, 135i, 136–137, 434, 437, 741
 in anaerobic pathways, 132, 132i, 137
 atmospheric, 33, 106, 116, 119, 270i, 320, 322, 330, 387, 511, 856–857, 856i–857i, 864–865
 in blood, 485, 489, 563, 563i, 567i, 659–660, 660i, 664, 665i, 669–670, 675, 708–709, 712, 716
 as greenhouse gas, 858–859, 858i, 859i, 864
 lichen symbiont, 391, 399–400
 membrane crossing by, 52, 441, 658, 670, 789, 789i
 as metabolic byproduct, 94–96, 100i
 from methane cycling, 865, 865i
 partial pressure, 708–709, 709i, 712, 716
 in photosynthesis, 6, 94–95, 106–107, 111, 111i, 115–117, 115i, 116i, 117i, 118i, 120, 120i, 270i, 518
 in respiration, 340, 481i, 482, 567i, 701–702, 701i, 704–705, 707–708, 711, 714, 716, 720i, 740i, 741, 747
 uptake by plants, 81i, 88, 371, 374, 480, 482, 493, 497, 501, 501i, 506, 508, 512, 512t, 518–519, 522
Carbon 14 dating, 270, 270i
Carbon fixation, **115**–117, 116i, 117i, 119–121, 360, 856–857, 856i–857i
 rubisco and, 115–116, 115i, 116i, 120
Carbon monoxide, 320, 709i, 717, 793
■ Carbon monoxide poisoning, 709i, 717
Carbon–oxygen cycle, 856–857, 856i–857i
Carbonate (carbonic acid), 747, 856–857, 856i–857i
Carbonic acid, 28–29, 708–709
Carbonic anhydrase, 709, 716
Carboniferous period, 271i, 370, 370i, 373, 373i, 378, 380, 380i, 388, 437, 442, 442i, 448, 449i, 464t
Carbonyl, functional group, 36i, 37
Carboxy peptidase, 724t
Carboxyl group, 36i, 37, 40, 42, 42i
■ Carcinogen, 229, 700, 889
■ Carcinoma, 230i
Cardiac conduction system, **667**, 667i, 676
Cardiac cycle, **666**–669, 667i, 669i, 676
Cardiac (heart) muscle, 78i, 122, 214t, 215, 559, 561, 581, 586–587,

646, 649, 653–654, 656i, **666**, 677, 708
 characteristics, 564–565
 contraction, 564, 564i, 582, 656, 664, 666–667, 667i, 675–676
 function, 564i, 565
 gap junctions in, 561, 564i, 565
Cardiac muscle tissue, **564**–565, 564i, 570
Cardiac output, 669
Cardiac pacemaker, 656, **667**, 667i, 673, 676
■ Cardiopulmonary resuscitation (CPR), 656–657
Cardiovascular risk factor, 673, 677
Cardiovascular system, 631, 664–665, 664i–665i, 672–673, 672i, 673i, 676, 734t, 783
Carel, L., 241
Caribou, 390, 826, 826i, 883i
Carica papaya, 539, 539i
Carnivore, 9, 309i, 410–411, 430, 432i, 441, 444, 446, 448, 450, 450t, 456–457, 461, 721
 food webs and, **844**–845, 845i, 846i, 847, 847i, 849–850, 849i, 850i, 851i, 852i, 862–863, 892
Carnivorous plant, 523, 523i
Carotene, 569
Carotenoid, 65, **108**, 121, 354, 360, 369
Carotid body, 600t, 665i, 669, 712
Carpal (wrist bone), 643i
Carpel, 170i, 235, 235i, 240, 384i, **526**–527, 526i, 527i, 530, 532–533, 533t, 534i, 538
Carpodacus, 305i
■ Carrageenan, 363
Carrot, 65, 503, 536, 903, 903i
Carrying capacity, **801**, **806**–807, 813i, **818**, 826, 834, 840
 habitat, human increase of, 812–813, 817–818, 817i
 logistic growth and, 801, 806–807, 806i, 807i, 818
■ Carson, Rachel, 467, 467i
Cartilage, 43, 67, 190, 434–436, 436i, 460, 558–559, **562**–564, 562i, 563i, 570, 639, 715, 732t
 skeletons, 438, 562, 642–645, 642i, 643i, 645i, 654
Cartilaginous fish, 314i, 404i, 428i, 433, 434i, 437i, **438**, 438i, 460, 642, 642i, 644
Cascade mountain range, 272i, 883i, 887i
Casparian strip, **515**, 515i, 522
Castanea, 505
Castor oil, plant, 218, 218i, 828
Cat, 99i, 121, 179, 300, 613i, 819, 829, 837
 calico, 234, 234i, 241
■ clone, 206, 215, 215i
■ genetically engineered, 242, 254
 Manx, 184, 184i
Catabolic pathway, **100**
Catabolite activator protein (CAP), 239, 240
Catalase, 90, 90i, 99, 105
■ Cataract, eye, 89, **615**, 766, 870
Catastrophism, **264**, 265
Caterpillar, 7i, 121, 420, 490, 490i, 828, 828i
Cattail, 534, 889
Cattle, 32, 353, 474, 475i, 831, 841, 847
 digestive tract, 859i
 diseases, 347, 347i, 349
 environmental impact of, 878, 884–885, 885i
■ genetically engineered, 214, 242, 254
Caudate nucleus, 593i

Caulerpa species, ban on, 836
C. taxifolia, aquarium strain, 836, 836i
Cave painting, Lascaux, 459i
Cebidae, 450t
Cecum, 728, 728i
Celera Genomics, 250, 250i
Celery, 496i, 540, 848
Cell, 4–5, 4i, 6–7, 14, 17i, 35–37, 51–52, **54**, 69i, 85, 85i, **144**, 406, 680t, 693. *See also* specific types
    appearance, 564, 564i
    branched vs. unbranched, 464–465, 464i
    early observations of, 50–51, 51i
    energy changes, 93–95, 93i, 104
    energy input, 6–7, 14
    function, 58, 135i, 231, 672
    heritable information for, 46–47
    metabolism. *See* Metabolism
    origin and evolution, 319, 322–323, 322i, 323i, 328i, 330
    plant, 510–511
    reproduction, 51–52, 141, 144, 150
    shape, 43, 53, 53i, 57, 66, 68–69, 71–72, 763
    size, 50, 50i, 52–53, 53i, 55i, 66, 72, 328i, 405, 542, 763
    structure, 26, 39, 52, 231, 672
    undifferentiated, 203, 558, 760i, 774
Cell communication, 38, 67, 367, 402, 479, 483, 490, 584–585, 667i
    in animal growth and development, 755, 758, 763
    gap junctions, 67, 67i, 88, 561, 561i, 564i, 565, 570, 667, 667i, 786i
    at heart contraction, 564–565, 564i
    hormones in, 544, 622
    in immune system, 680t, 681
    nature of, 576–577, 576i
    in nervous system, 559, 565, 565i, 570, 576–581, 576i, 577i, 578i, 579i, 580i, 581i, 600, 615
    proteins of, 42, 75, 77–**78**, 78i, 88, 88i
    signal reception, transduction and responses, 78i, 488–489, 488i, 489i, 540–541, 544, 546–547, 546i, 549, 550i, 555, 622–623, 623i, 764–765, 764i, 765i, 768
Cell cortex, **68**, 69, 148, 152, 195
Cell count, human blood, **661**–662
Cell cycle, 141, **144**–145, 144i, 164, 655
    controls, 141, 144, 150–152, 188, 189i, 212–213, 230–231
Cell death, 150, 218, 218i, 226, 680t
    programmed, **488**–490, 489i
Cell differentiation, 231, **233**, 237, 237i, 240, 325, 583, 660, 755, **762**
    animal, 231, 233–234, 233i, 404, 409i, 656, 755, 762–764, 768
    cloning and, 214–215
    in immune response, 679, 680t, 690i, 691, 691i, 692i, 693, 698
    nature of, 558, 558i, 762–765, 763i, 768
    plants, 231, 235, 235i, 498, 498i, 504i, 536, 536i, 537i, 542, 545, 555
    selective gene expression, 231, 233–234, 233i, 240, 367, 367i, 369, 786i
Cell division, 51–52, 140, 140i, 142, 142t, 144, 152, 243, 360i, 537–538, 537i, 583, 655, 758i, 763–764, 766, 768
    controls, 68, 78, 78i, 141, 149–151, 151i, 230, 237, 622, 633, 634t, 635t
    DNA duplication in, 212–213
    embryonic, 788, 788i
    eukaryotic, 66, 68, 142, 142t, 143, 152, 207, 225, 327, 368t
    meiotic. *See* Meiosis
    meristematic, 502i, 504, 504i, 505i, 506, 508, 542, 544–545, 544t, 555
    mitotic. *See* Mitosis
    prokaryotic, 142, 142t, 336–337, 336i, 337i, 344i, 348, 368i
Cell elongation, 544–545, 544t, 546i, 547–550, 548i, 553, 555
Cell junction, **67**, 67i
    in animal tissue, 561, 561i, 570
    in cardiac muscle, 561, 564–565, 564i, 667, 667i
Cell lineage, 140, 233, 240
Cell-mediated immune response, 679, 680t, 681, 681i, **687**, 687i, 690i, 691–693, 691i, 692i, 698
Cell membrane, 4i, 51, 52i, 53, 58, 75–77, 79i, 109i, 579–581, 714
    components, 76–77, 76i, 79i, 112
    crossing mechanisms, 81–83, 81i, 83i
    origin of, 326, 328i, 330
    proteins, 52, 52i, 53, 59i, 61–62, 61i, 63i, 68, 72, 78, 79i, 88, 88i, 402
    selective permeability, 75, 80–81, 81i, 84–85, 84i, 85i
    solute crossing at, 66, 75, 80, 82, 104
    structure, 33, 41, 41i, 47, 48t, 75–76, 321, 672
Cell memory, in development, 764, 764i
Cell migration, 69i, 70–71, 569, 763
    abnormal, 151–152, 151i
    in animal development, 237, 405i, 758i, 759i, 762–764, 762i, 768
    dendritic cells, 691i, 692, 692i
    Dictyostelium, 367, 367i, 369
    embryonic, 786, 788, 788i
Cell plate formation, 148i, **149**, 152
Cell rearrangement, 758i, 759i, 762, 788
Cell suicide, 488–490, 488i, 489i, 622, 763, 768
Cell theory, 51, **54**
Cell wall, **66**, 72, 73t, 84, **334**, 496
    algal, 470
    archaean, 340
    bacterial, 56i, 57, 73t, 84, 684, 684i
    eukaryote, 368t, 369
    plant, 59i, 66, 66i, 72, 73t, 84–85, 343, 374, 497, 497i, 518, 518i, 537i, 544, 546i, 547, 547i, 552, 555
    prokaryotic, **334**–335, 334i, 334t, 336i, 339, 348, 368t
    protistan, 327, 327i, 360i, 362, 364–365, 369
Cellular slime mold, **366**–367, 367i
Cellular work, energy for, 93i, 94i, 95, 95i, 101i, 104
Cellulose, 38–39, 38i, 39i, 48t, 368t, 369, 514i
    digestion, 338, 721, 721i, 728
    plant cell, 66, 66i, 94, 496, 518, 547, 547i, 552, 555
    protistans, 358, 362, 364, 367i
    synthesis, 115i, 120, 120i, 253i
Cenozoic era, 271, 271i, 309i, 464i, 464t, 887i
Centers for Disease Control, 347
Centers for Disease Control and Prevention, 694i
Centipede, 420, 420i, 423, 423i, 430, 703
Central nervous system, 573, **575**, 575i, 586, 596, 596t, 792i
Central vacuole, 59i, 63, **65**, 65i, 73t, 85, 401, 510, 518i
Centriole, 59i, **70**, 146, 146i, 158i, 159i, 166, 781
Centrocercus urophasianus, 906
Centrofugation, 188–**189**, 189i
Centromere, **143**, 143i, 146, 152, 157, 157i, 158i, 189i, 204
Centrosomes, 68, **146**, 146i

Centruroides sculpturatus, 427, 427i
Cephalization, **406**–407, 412–413, 416, 430, 574–**575**
Cephalochordate, **435**
Cephalopod, 237, 416, **418**, 418i, 430, 575, 609–610, 609i
Cephalothorax, 426, 641, 641i
Cercopithecidae, 450t
Cerebellum, 448, **588**–589, 588i, 589i, 593, 596i
Cerebral cortex, 589–**590**, 591, 591i, 593, 593i, 596–597, 596t, 746
    drug effects on, 573, 594
    functional divisions, 590–591, 590i, 613
    sensory pathways to, 590–591, 597, 602, 602i, 604, 604i, 613, 615–616
Cerebrospinal fluid, 588–589, 588i, 695, 712, 714, 716
Cerebrum, **588**–591, 588i, 596t, 602, 604
Cervical cancer, 150i, 153, 783–784
Cervical cap, in fertility control, 782i
Cervical nerve, 575i, 586i
Cervix, 776, 776i, 777i, 781i, 783–785, 794, 794i, 796
Cestode, 412
Cetacean, 281, 281i
CFTR gene, mutant, 75
CFTR protein, 74, 75i, 254
Chaetae, 414
Chaetodipus intermedius, 289
Chagas disease, 355
Chain fern, 379, 379i
Chain of Being, 262, 264, 281
Chalk deposit, 350, 350i, 351i
Chambered nautilus, 263i, 418i, 431i, 471i
Chameleon, 444, 565i
Chancre, 784i, 785
Chaos carolinense, 70i
Chapparal plant, 874–875, 879i
Chara, 372i
Chargaff, Erwin, 210
Charophyte, 314i, **364**, **372**, 372i, 375i
Chase, Martha, 208
Checkpoint gene, 150, 150i, 164, 405
Cheek tooth, 721
Cheetah, 829, 915
Chelicerate, 420–421, 421i, 430
Chemical agent, 712
Chemical attack, toxicity, 196, 213, 228–230
Chemical barrier, 682t, 698
Chemical bond, 19, **22**–25, 23i, 24i, 25i, 30, 30t, 91–94, 97–98, 97i, 104, 111, 122–124, 126, 137. *See also* specific types
Chemical burn, 28
Chemical defense, 483, 680–681, 680t, 688, 698
Chemical energy, **92**–95, 104, 107, 112
Chemical equilibrium, **100**, 100i
Chemical formula, 23, 23i
Chemical gradient, 763, 765, 768
Chemical selection, 322, 324–325, 328i, 330
Chemical sense, 599, 600t, 615
Chemical signal, 762i, 904, 915
Chemical soup habitat, 119, 252, 441, 467, 475, 582, 618, 627, 627i, 636–637, 713, 888
Chemical synapse, **580**–581, 580i, 581i, 596
Chemical terms, 30t
Chemical weapon, 483, 828, 840
Chemiosmosis, 130, 137
Chemoautotroph, 106–107, 118, 120, 324, **335**, 348, 892
Chemoheterotroph, 329i, **335**, 339, 348
Chemoreceptor, 598–**600**, 600t, 604, 604i, 615, 712, 716, 723
Chemotactic effect, 680t, 684, 690

Chemotherapy, 151, 230, 662, 693
Chenopodium quinoa, 554, 730
Chernobyl meltdown, 897, 897i
Cherry tree (*Prunus*), 108, 195i, 526i, 527i, 530, 530i–531i, 532, 539
Chesapeake Bay, 510, 890
Chestnut blight, 397t, 835t
Chestnut tree, 505, 835t, 880
Chiang, Vincent, 253i
Chicken, 133, 254, 254i, 176, 177i, 185, 274i, 278, 300, 677, 731, 731i, 763i, 765i
Chicken pox, 343t, 699
Childbirth, 353, 397, 621i, 634t, 663, 663i
Children's Rainforest, 473
Chiloglottis trapeziformis, 292
Chimaera, 438, 438i
Chimpanzee, 167i, 258, 241, 454i, 455–456, 455i, 456i, 461i, 468, 469i, 915
    characteristics, 145, 197, 197i, 204, 276i, 277–278, 452
    social behavior, 912–913, 912i, 915
Chin, dimple, 156, 167, 167i
China, human population, 814, 815i, 817
Chinese traditional medicine, 753
Chipmunk, 824, 824i
Chironix, 410i
Chitin, 39, 39i, 275, 275i, 368t, 392, 414, 420, 703i
Chiton, 416–417, 417i, 834
Chlamydia, 314i, **338**, 338i, 348, 615
C. trachomatis, 615, 784, 784t
Chlamydial infection, **784**, 784i, 784t, 785i
Chlamydomonas, 164, 352i, 365, 365i
C. nivalis, 369, 369i
Chlordane, 848i
Chlorella, 352i, 364
Chloride, 24, 24i, 27–28, 74, 77, 79i, 81i, 733t, 745, 745i
Chlorinated hydrocarbon, 848i
Chlorine, 23i, 24, 24i, 34, 218, 512, 512t, 836, 870, 889
Chlorine monoxide, 870
Chlorobium, 338i
Chloroflexus, 338i
Chlorofluorocarbon (CFC), 870, 896
    as greenhouse gas, 858, 859i, 864
Chlorophyll, 65, 107, 109–110, 109i, 112–113, 119i, 121, 338, 894i
    a, **108**, 109i, 110i, 112, 114i, 120, 322, 322i, 354, 363–364, 368–369
    b, **108**, 109i, 110i, 354, 364, 369
    c_1, 360, 368
    c_2, 360, 368
Chlorophyte, 314i, 352i, **364**, 364i
Chloroplast, **39**, 39i, 55i, **65**, 65i, 68, 70, **111**, 122, 278, 314i, 519i, 823
    function, 39i, 58, 65, 72, 73t
    origin, 319, 326–327, 329i, 330
    photosystems, 57, 72, 73t
    plant, 59i, 65, 70, 72, 107, 111–112, 111i, 112i, 115, 115i, 120, 335, 338i
    protistan, 107, 111, 352, 354, 354i, 356, 358, 360, 363–364, 368–369
Chlorosis, 512t
Choanoflagellate, 314i, 404i, **405**, 408, 408i, 428i
Chocolate, 524, 524i
Choking, 717, 723
Cholecalciferol, 569
Cholecystokinin (CCK), **719**, 725
Cholera, 2, 289, 347, 867, **894**–896, 895i
Cholesterol, 41, 41i, 43, 48t, 49, 201t, 615, 622, 636, 638, 725, 730
    cardiovascular disorders and, 672–673
    in cell membranes, 76i, 77i, 86i
    dietary, 730–731
Cholla, 878i

Chondrichthyes, 438
Chondrin, 562
Chondrocyte, 562i
Chondrus, 834i, 835
Chordate, 403, 404i, 407, 407i, 428, 433–**434**, 434i, 435, 435i, 437, 437i, 460, 699, 761
Chorion, 203, 446i, 786i, **787**–788, 787i, 787t, **797**
Chorionic villus (villi), 787i, 789, 789i
  sampling (CVS), **203**
Choroid, 610–611, 610i
Chriacus, 448i
Chromatid, 142i, 143, 145–146, 152, 157i, 159i, 160, 160i, 166
  sister, **142**, 142i, 145–147, 146i, 147i, 150, 152, **157**, 157i, 159i, 160i, 166, 166i
Chromatin, **60**–61, 60i, 60t, 62i
Chromatium, **338**, 338i
Chromoplast, 65
Chromosome, eukaryotic, **60**–61, 60t, 142i, 230, 232, 244, 253i, 257
  abnormalities, 149, 150, 150i, 187, 188, 226, 227i, 228, 276
  banding, 188i, 197, 197i
  duplication, 141–143, 142i, 143i, 145–147, 145i, 152, 154, 157, 158i–159i, 160–161, 160i, 164, 165i, 166–167, 166i, 187, **196**–197, 197i, 204, 766
  homologous, 156–157, 157i, 158i, 160–161, 160i, 161i, 164, 164i, 166, 166i, 169, 171–173, 171i, 174i, 175, 177–178, 180, 182, 188, 196, 198, 204
  maternal/paternal, 156, 158i, 160i, 161, 161i, 163, 164i, 166–167
  organization, 142–143, 143i, 146i, 152, 206
  polytene, 232, 232i
  sex, 156, 187–189, 189i, 192–194, 192i, 193i, 194i, 195i, 231, 241
  structure, 61, 142–143, 143i, 152, 187–188, 196–197, 197i, 204, 284
Chromosome, human, 160, 160i, 163, 164i, 166–167, 196–197, 197i, 201t, 204
  disorders, 150, 187–188, 194–199, 194i, 195i, 196i, 199i, 204
  X, 157i, 160i, 166, 187–188, 192–195, 192i, 193i, 194i, 195i, 199, 204, 771
  Y, 157i, 160i, 166, 187–188, 192, 192i, 194, 199, 204, 771–772
Chromosome, prokaryotic (bacterial), 57, 334t, 336–337, 337i
Chromosome, protistan, 352
Chromosome number, **145**–147, 145i, 152, **156**, 162, 166–167, 166i, 167i
  altered, 187–188, 198–199, 198i, 201t, 204–205
  changes, 284, 306–307, 306i, 307i, 316
  diploid, 145, 145i, 147, 147i, 152, 154, **156**–157, 162, 164i, 166, 166i, 167–168, 781
  haploid, 157, 158i–159i, 162, 162i, 164i, 166, 166i, 170, 246
■ Chronic anemia, 662
■ Chronic depression, 179, 186, 186i, 191, 572, 582, 594, 653, 793–794
■ Chronic inflammatory disorders, 347
■ Chronic myelogenous leukemia (CML), 189i, 201t, 662i
■ Chronic viral hepatitis, 571
■ Chronic viral infection, 693
Chrysophyte, 314i, 351, 352i, **360**, 360i, 368
Chylomicron, 727, 727i
Chyme, 724–727, 725i

Chymotrypsin, 724t, 725
Chytrid, 314i, 391, 392i, **393**, 393i, 397t, 400
■ Chytridomycosis, 393i
Cicada, 302i, 303
Cichlid, 306, 306i
Ciliary body, 610, 610i
Ciliary muscle, 611, 611i, 614
Ciliary photoreceptor, **608**, 612
Ciliated protozoan (ciliate), 314i, 351, 352i, **356**–357, 356i, 368
Cilium (cilia), 17i, **70**–71, 70i, 71i, 73t, 74, 146, 356–357, 356i, 481i, 560i, 640, 683
  in airways, 682–683, 682t, 683i, 700, 707, 712, 712i
  invertebrate, 405, 408–409, 413i, 417, 417i, 435
  rotifer, 416, 416i, 430
  sensory, 607–608
Cingulate gyrus, **591**, 591i
Ciona savignyi, 461, 461i
Circadian cycle, **550**, 555
Circadian rhythm, **487**, 489–490, 596t, 892, 893i
Circulatory system, 405, 657, **658**–659, 665i, 675, 740
  bird, 446–447
  closed, 414–415, 415i, 418, 657–**658**, 658i, 659, 659i, 675
  function, 561, 567i, 657–658, 665i
  human, 490, 567i, 700, 790
  lymphatic system and, 657, 680
  open, 420–421, 657–**658**, 658i, 675, 677
  organ system links, 719–720, 740, 740i
  vertebrate, 564i, 566, 567i, 701i, 707, 758
Cis fatty acid tails, 49, 49i
Citrate, 128, 129i, 137
Citric acid, 128, 396
Citrullus, 185, 185i
Citrus fruit, 533, 545t, 732t
Clade, **310**–311, 316, 365
Cladogenesis, **308**
Cladogram, **311**–313, 312i, 375i
Cladonia rangiferina, 390, 390i
Cladophora, 110, 110i, 849i
■ *Cladosporium*, 397
Clam, 416, 417i, 849i, 892
Clark, Larry, 903
Class (taxon), 310, 310i
Classification system, **311**
  taxonomic, 301, 310, 310i, 316
  three-domain, 8, 8t, 14, 310–311, 311i, 316
Clavaria, 392i
■ *Claviceps purpura*, 397, 397i, 397t
Clavicle, 642, 643i
Claw, 69, 422, 829, 906, 906i
Clay, 321–323, 322i, 323i, 512–514, 876, 877i
  as biosynthetic template, 321–323, 322i, 323i
Clay-colored sparrow, 846i
Cleavage, animal development, 755, **758**
  mechanisms, 755, 758, 758i, 760–761, 760i, 762i, 763i, 768–769
  patterns, 755, 758, 759i, 761, 761i, 768–769
Cleavage, human embryo, 771, 783, 786–788, 792i, 795t, 797, 798i
Cleavage furrow, 148, 786i
Cleavage reaction, 37, 37i, **97**
Climate, 107, 138, 433, 465, 472, 509, 822, 865–866, **868**
  air circulation and, 867–869, 868i, 896
  biome distribution, 867, 873, 875, 896

C3 vs. C4 adaptations to, 116–117, 116i, 117i
  changes in, 300–301, 309, 355, 359, 409, 441, 443, 449, 454–455, 454i, 492–493, 507i, 834, 843, 858–859, 858i, 859i, 863–864, 885i, 917
  El Niño, 866, 866i
  global, 118–120, 119i, 269, 271i, 273, 280, 309, 370, 373, 375, 380, 443, 454i, 455, 917
  ice ages, 269, 271i, 304, 355, 449, 458, 464, 464t
  ocean currents and, 454i, 872, 872i, 896
  Paleocene, 448, 448i
  zones, 272, 469, 812, 868–869, 868i, 872, 872i, 896
Climax community, 821, 832–833, 840, 867, 875
Clitoris, 776, 777i, 781
Cloaca, 416i, 444, 444i, 446, 720i, **721**
Clonal selection, **690**–691, 690i, 691i, 692i, 693, 698, 698t
■ Clone, **156**, 164, 167, 179, **206**, 206i, 214–215, 215i, 536
■   aspen, 371, 536
■   sheep, 206, 206i, 214i, 215
■ Cloning, 206, **216**
■   adult, 206, 206i, **214**–216, 214i, 214t, 763
■   embryo, **214**, 214t, 216
    immune function, 686, 690–691, 691i, 692i, 693, 698, 698t
■   mammals, 206, 215, 225
    plants, 536–539, 537i
■   therapeutic, 214, 214t, **215**–216
■ Cloning vector, 243, **244**–245, 244i, 256–257
  Closed circulatory system, 414–415, 415i, 418, 657–**658**, 658i, 659, 659i, 675
  Clostridium, 338i, 339, 339i, 653, 653i, 682
  Cloud forest, 473, 473i
  Clover, 534
  Club fungus, 314i, 391, 392i, **393**, 395–396, 395i, 397t, 399–401
  Club moss, 370, 378, 380, 380i, 388t, 832, 880
  Cnidarian, 314i, **410**, 417
    ancestry, 403, 404i, 407i, 408i, 428i
    characteristics, 410–411, 410i, 411i, 430–431, 608, 640–641, 640i
    nervous system, 574, 574i
  Coal, 273, **380**, 865
■   burning, 29i, 377i, 391, 813, 870–871, 871i, 896
■   original sources of, 380, 380i, 388
  Coast redwood, 370, 505, 506i, 556, 882
  Coca plant, 381, 401
■ Cocaine, 381, 401, 594, 595i, 738
■   pregnancy and, 793, 797
■ *Coccidioides immitis*, 397t
  Coccolithophore, 350, **360**–361, 360i, 368, 856, 892
  Coccus (cocci), **334**, 335i, 348
  Coccygeal nerve, 575i
  Coccyx bone, 263, 263i, 281
  Cochlea, **606**, 606i, 607i, 615
  Cochlear duct, 606–607, 607i, 615, 617
  Cocklebur, 534, 534i, 550
  Cocoa bean, 524i, 881
  Coconut palm, 534, 537
■ Codeine, 595
  Codium, 121i, 352i, 364, 364i
  Codominant allele, 169, **176**–177, 182
  Codon, **222**–226, 222i, 224i, 225i, 228, 327, 340
  Coelocanth, 314i, 424i, 428i, 434i, 439, 439i, 468

Coelom, 406i, **407**, 407i, 412, 414–416, 415i, 420, 429i, 430, 434, 437i, 640, 707
Coenzyme, 46–47, **99**
  in aerobic respiration, 125, 125i, 128–130, 128i, 129i, 131i, 137
  in anaerobic pathways, 132–133
  dietary supplements, 732, 732t, 733t
  function, 46, 48, 48t, 94, 99, 101, 104t, 105, 323
  in photosynthesis, 107, 111–113, 111i, 118i, 120
Coenzyme A, 128, 129i
Coevolution, 154, 346, **384**, 469, 810, **826**
  animal/plant, 465, 465i
  brain/behavior/culture, 453
  brain/sensory organs, 440–441
  lungs/circulatory system, 437
  myxoma virus/rabbit, 837
  parasite/host, 409
  pathogen/host, 327, 346, 348, 680
  plant/pollinator, 384–385, 389, 525, 528–529, 528i, 529i
  predator/prey, 364, 409, 828, 840
Cofactor, **94**, 99, 104–105, 104t, 322i
  enzyme, 107, 111
Coffee, 28, 306i, 597, 881
Cohesion, **27**, **516**, 517i, 522, 710
  of water molecule, 19, 27, 27i, 30
Cohesion–tension theory, 516–517, 516i, 517i, 522–523
Cohort, **808**–809, 808t, 814
Coitus, 781
Colchicine, 68, 188, 189i, 306
Colchicum autumnale, 68, 69i
■ Cold sore, 343t, 345, 569
Cold stress, 750–751, 750t, 751i, 751t
Coleoptera, 425i
Coleoptile, 542i, 543i, 544, 544t, 546i, 547–549, 549i, 555
Coleus, 498i
■ Colitis, 682
Collagen, 48t, 78i, 209–210, 254, 284, 610, 655, 655i, 666, 672, 732t, 766
  bone, 644–645, 654, 713i
  connective tissue, 405, 562, 562i, 563i, 568–569, 685, 794
Collar (marker), 803, 803i, 827
Collar cell, 405–406, 405i, 408, 409i, 430
Collarbone, 642, 643i
Collecting duct, 743, 743i, 744i, 745i, 746–747, 746i, 752
Collenchyma, 495–**496**, 496i, 497, 499i, 508, 508t
Colon, 239, 586i, 616, 722i, 723, 726, **728**, 728i, 730, 736, 736t. *See also* Large intestine
■ Colon cancer, 616, 682, 728, 734
  Colonial theory, **405**, 430
  Colonizer species, 304–306, 305i, 335i, 356, 360i, 364, 364i, 374, 377, 398, 411, 411i, 459i, 486, 821, 832–833, 835, 838i, 839, 839i
■ Colonoscopy, **728**
  Colony
    ant, 820, 820i, 910–911, 910i, 914
    bacterial, 103, 103i, 246, 246i
■   cancer cell, 151–152, 151i
    cnidarian, 410i, 411, 411i
    cormorant, 909, 909i
    honeybee, 898–899, 899i, 905, 905i, 911
    mole-rat, 910, 911i, 914
    resident microbial, 679, 682–683, 682t, 698
    royal penguin, 802i
    sponge, 405
    termite, 910–912, 910i, 911i, 912i, 914
  Color, 54, 99i, 168, 184–185, 284, 295i, 447

as attractant, 528, 528i, 539i
basis of, 108–110, 110i, 120–121, 177, 177i, 193, 193i
- blindness, **195**, 195i, 205, 614
perception of, 452, 612, 616
prey, 828, 828i
Coloration
camouflage, 288, 288i
warning, 828–829, 828i, 829i
Colwell, Rita, 895–896, 895i
- Coma, 29, 401i, 594, 714
Comb shape, poultry, 176, 177i, 185
Combustion, 101, 101i
Commensalism, 821–**822**, 831, 831i, 840
- Common cold, 342, 343t, 700, 713
Communal display ground, 906, 906i
Communication, 598
behavior, 425i, 447, 458, 589–590, 899, 904–905, 904i, 905i
cell. See Cell communication
Communication signal, **904**–905, 904i, 905i, 914–915
Community, **5**, 5i, **821**–**822**, **840**
Community structure
abiotic factors in, 821, 822, 834, 841
biogeographic patterns in, 820, 838–840, 838i, 839i, 841, 841i, 867, 874-875
biotic factors in, 822–834
climax, 821, 832–833, 840, 867, 875
factors shaping, 821–822, 832–833, 840
habitat and, 468–469, 471, 822, 824–825, 838
human impact on, 466–474, 820, 820i, 821i, 832, 834–835, 834i, 835t, 836–837, 840
interactions, 820–821, 826–833, 826i, 827i, 828i, 829i, 830i, 831i, 832i, 833i, 840
intermediate disturbance hypothesis, 832–833, 833i
keystone species in, **834**–835, 834i
niches, 821–822, 840
restoration of disturbed, 832–833, 833i, 840
species introductions and, 468, 469, 820, 820i, 821i, 834–835, 834i, 835t, 836–837, 838–839, 840
stability, 821, 833–835, 834i, 835t, 840
structure, 820–841, **821**, 875–876, 885i
successional models, 832–833, 832i, 833i
tropical forest, 822, 838
Compact bone tissue, 563i, 644, 644i
Compaction, 380
Companion cell, 497, 497i, 499i, 508, **520**–522, 520i, 521i
Comparative anatomy, 263, 263i
Comparative biochemistry, 278, 368
Alu transposon, 277
by automated DNA sequencing, 278, 337
cytochrome *c*, 278, 278i
in evolutionary systematics, 261, 278, 281, 302, 310, 314i, 433
mitochondrial DNA, 278
nature of, 261, 278–279, 279i
Comparative genomics, 243, **251**, 257, 352i, 353, 368
Comparative morphology, **263**, **274**
in evolutionary systematics, 261, 263, 278, 280, 302, 302i, 310, 314i, 433
of protistans, 352, 352i, 368
vertebrates, 274–275, 274i
Compartmentalization, 403, **405**, 429i, 430, **486**–**487**, 486i, 489, 507
Competition, interspecific, 308, **802**, 821–**822**, 824, 824i, 830, 840, 904
early fish, 437

early mammals, 449–450
in ecosystems, 845, 878, 891
Hawaiian archipelago, 305
insect/humans, 424–425, 427, 430
intertidal zone, 834, 834i, 890–891
population growth and, 266–267, 280
resource partitioning in, 266–267, 291, 908–909, 914
Competition, intraspecific, 830
parent plant/seedling, 534, 534i, 538
population growth and, 806–807, 813, 818
sexual selection, 906–907, 907i, 914–915
in social groups, 908–909
Competitive exclusion, 824–825, 825i, 833–834, 840
Complement system, 680–681, 680t, 684–685, 684i, 685i, 687, 687i, 690–691, 691i, 698
activated, 684–685, 684i, 687i
cascading reaction, 684, 684i, 688, 690, 695
Complementary DNA (cDNA), **245**, 245i, 246, 251, 257, 697
Complete digestive system, **406**, 414–415, 424, 430, 719–**720**, 720i, 721–723, 736
Complete metamorphosis, 424i
Complete protein, **730**
Complex carbohydrate, 7, 33, 38–40, 47, 48t, 135i, 321, 328i
characteristics, 4–5, 4i, 38–39, 47
in human diet, 719–720, 730
Complex lipid, 5, 7
Complex plant tissue, 495–497, 496i, 497i, 508, 508t
Complex virus, 342i
Composite signal, **904**
Compound, **23**, 29, 30t, 31
Compound eye, 420, 424i, **608**–609, 609i
Compound light microscope, 51, **54**, 54i, 55i, 72
Computer applications, 246, 476
- automated DNA sequencing, 278
- biomolecules, simulated origin, 319, 323
- DNA double helix, 211
- karyotyping, 188, 189i
- population growth modeling, 817, 817i
- virtual colonoscopy, 728
Concentration gradient, 75, **80**, **88**, 123, 482, 684, 749
diffusion and, 83–84, 83i, 84i, 88, 482, 727i, 764, 898
gas exchange and, 482–483, 702
neuron membrane, 577, 577i, 579i, 596
osmosis and, 75, 84–85, 84i, 85i, 88, 670i, 726
in plant function, 112, 490, 518i, 520, 521i, 528, 544, 547, 547i, 555
in solute-water balance, 75, 79i, 80–84, 80i, 81i, 84i, 88, 482–483, 670i, 726–727, 727i, 736, 744i, 745, 745i
thykaloid membrane, 112, 113i, 114i, 120
transport proteins in, 81–83, 81i, 82i, 88, 94, 95i, 112, 726–727, 727i
Conch, 608, 608i
Condensation reaction, **37**, 37i, 38i, 40i, **97**, 210
Condenser lens, 54i
- Condom, in fertility control, 782–**783**, 782i, 785
Conducting zone, neuron, **576**, 576i, 596
Conduction, **749**
Cone, 271i, **382**–383, 383i, 388t, 389

Cone cell, 600t, 609i, **612**, 612i, 614, 616
Confusiusornis sanctus, 446, 446i
- Congenital rubella syndrome (CRS), 798
Conidiospore, 396, 396i
Conifer, 271, 307, 370, 372i, 373, 373i, 375, 375i, 381–**382**, 383, 383i, 384i, 388t, 389, 389i, 507, **882**
classification, 311, 311i, 314i
Coniferous forest, 854, 854i, 874i–875i, 877i, **882**, 882i, 896
Conjugation, **337**, **357**
bacterial, 333, 335, 335i, **337**, 337i, 348
protozoan, **357**, 357i
Conjugation tube, 337, 337i
Conjunctiva, 615
- Conjunctivitis, 343t
Connective tissue, 47, 177, 201t, **405**, 430, 481i, 558, 560i, **562**–563, 584, 640, 645–646, 654, 657, 660–661, 667, 675, 677, 684, 724i, 732t, 742, 758, 766
characteristics, 559, 563i, 570–571
components, 559, 562
soft, 562–563, 562i, 570
specialized, 562–563, 562i–563i, 570
Conotoxin, 402, 402i
Conraua goliath, 642i
Consciousness, state of, 591–592, 597
Conservation biology, 463, 467, **472**–473, 475–476
- deforestation and, 387, 389
- hot spots, 875
species diversity chart, 472i
Conserved trait, 278, 278i, 280, 315, 434–435
- Constipation, **728**, 730
Consumer, **6**–7, 6i, 8, 93, 93i, 866
in community structure, 822, 826, 875
in food web, 844–846, 844i, 845i, 846i, 849–850, 850i, 863, 866
Contag, Christopher, 103
Contag, Pamela, 103
Contagious disease, 294, **346**, 662
Continental drift, 272, 272i, 273i, 280, 309, 835
Continental shelf, 470i, 892–893, 892i
Continuous variation, **180**–182, 180i, 181i, 288i
students' heights, 458, 458i
- wing color, 287, 287i, 288i
- Contraceptive, 782–783, 782i, 814
Contractile cell, 409i, 410i, 411, 435, 564–565, 564i, 639–641, 640i, 654, 667
Contractile ring mechanism, **148**–149, 148i, 149i, 152
Contractile vacuole, 89, 89i, **354**, 356, 356i
Contraction, 70, 71, 92, 232, 437, 558, 570, 639, 641, 677, 715, 742
ACh in, 581, 654
cardiac. See Cardiac muscle
controls over, 795, 797
cytoskeletal elements in, 62, 68–69, 703, 703i
in digestive system, 722i, 723–725, 724i, 725i, 728
directional, 646–647, 646i, 647i, 654
earthworm, 415, 415i, 430
involuntary, 672
isometric vs. isotonic, 652, 652i
reproductive organ muscles, 485, 489, 772, 781, 794, 797
sarcomere, 649, 649i
skeletal. See Skeletal muscle
sliding-filament model, 70, 649, 649i, 654, 666–667
- tetany, 29, 652, 652i, 653i
Control group, **12**–13, 12i, 13i, 15

Conus geographicus, 402, 402i
C. magnus, 402
Convection, **749**, 751
Convergent evolution, 361, 449–450, 449i, 450t, 456–457, 609
Cooksonia, 268i, 372, 372i
Cooperative defense behavior, 908–912, 908i, 914
Copepod, 422i, 423, 430, 886, 892, 895, 895i
Copernicus, Nikolaus, 14
Copper, 512, 512t, 702, 733t, 849
Copper sulfide, 892
Coprolite, 268
Coral, 154, 358, 410, 430–431, 431i, 809, 891, 891i
reef building, 410, 410i
Coral grouper, 438i
Coral polyp, 470
Coral reef, 1, 3, 5i, 358, 363, 471i, 474–475, 475i, 838, 886, **891**, 891i, 893, 896
Burgess Shale community, 315, 315i
- destruction, 2, 470–471, 470i
Corallina, 470, 470i
Core temperature, body, 602, 739, 749–752, 750i, 750t, 782, 782i, 794, 917
Cork, 50, 51i, **506**, 507i, 508t
Cork cambium, 494i, 504i, 506, 507i, 508t, 509
Corm, 536t
Cormorant, 909, 909i
Corn (*Zea mays*), 65i, 167i, 178, 227i, 285, 385, 397, 495, 499i, 526, 534, 835
ancestral species, 242i, 253
atrophied, 492i–493i
carbon fixation, 116, 116i, 117i
characteristics, 514, 532, 536t
crops, 509, 537, 618, 618i
development, 236, 543i
direction of growth, 548, 548i
genetic engineering, 242–243, 242i, 252, 258
grain, 542, 542i, 543i
leaf, 117i, 543i
pests, 427, 427i
root, 427, 427i, 503, 503i, 543i, 548i
- smut, 397t
Corn oil, 730
Cornea, 180, **608**, 609i, 610–611, 610i, 611i, 614–615
Corolla, 526, 527i
Coronary artery, 665i, 666, 672–673, 673i, 713i
- Coronary bypass surgery, **673**, 673i
Coronavirus, 343t, 346
Corpus callosum, 589, 589i, 591–592, 592i
Corpus luteum, 634t, 776t, **777**, 777i, 778i, 779, 779i, 780i, 783, 787, 797
Corpus striatum, **593**, 593i
Cortex, 195, 760, 760i
adrenal, 621i
kidney, **742**–743, 742i, 743i, 744i, 745–746, 746i, 752
Cortex, plant, 506, 508, 517i
root, 499, 502i, 503, 503i, 505i, 515, 515i, 547i
stem, 498i, 499, 499i
Corticotropin releasing hormone (CRH), 630, 630i, 794
Cortisol, 290, 621i, 622t, 623–624, 630–631, 630i, 634, 634t, 635t, 636–637, **794**
Cosmetic product testing, 571
Costa Rica, conservation biology, 472–473
Cotransporter, 79i, 726–727, 736, 744
Cotton, 243, 252, 253i, 258, 306i, 553
Cotyledon, 384–385, **495**, 495i, **532**, 532i, 533i, 538, 542, 543i, 546i
Cotylosaur, 274i

Coughing, 588, 682, 713
Countercurrent flow, **704**–705, 704i, 716, 745
Coupling reactions, **95**, 104t
Courtship behavior, 900, 904i, 906, 906i
Courtship display, 259, 292, 292i, 302i, 303, 446, 632, 756, 808–810, 900, 904i, 905–906, 906i, 914
Covalent bond, 19, **24**–25, 25i, 30–31, 44–45, 94, 109, 248, 289
  in DNA replication, 213, 216–217
  in organic compounds, 34, 36–38, 37i, 38i, 43, 47, 47i, 48t, 76
  in RNA molecule, 221i, 228
Cowbird, 830–831, 831i, 901
■ Cowpox, 343t, 678
Coyote, 846i, 908
Crab, 39, 277, 404i, 422, 422i, 423i, 430–431, 633, 633i, 637, 637i, 740, 765, 844, 847, 906, 906i
Cranial bone, 456, 461, 643i
Cranial nerve, 575, 575i, 586
Craniate, **436**–437, 436i, 452, 460, 642
Cranium, 434, 460, 566i
Crassulacean Acid Metabolism (CAM), plant, 116i, **117**, 117i
Craterellus, 392i
Crayfish, 162, 422i, 574i, 575, 889i
■ Creatine phosphate, 638–639, 651, 651i, 654–655
■ Creatine supplement, 638–639
Crenarchaeote, 314i, 340, 340i, 348
Crenicichla, 810i, 811, 811i
Creosote bush, 536, 803i, 876, 877i
Cretaceous period, 271i, 372i, 373, 373i, 442i, 444, 449i, 464t, 465i
Cretaceous–Tertiary asteroid impact, 260, 260i, 271i, 443, 443i
■ Cri-du-chat syndrome, 196, 196i, 201t
Cricetidae, 450t
Crick, Francis, 207i, 211–212, 215–216
Crinoid, 418i, 428
Crocodilian (crocodile), 312, 312i, 313i, 314i, 404i, 428i, 434i, 442i, 443–446, 444i, 445i, 460, 907
Crocus, 68, 69i
Crop, animal, 415i, 720i, 721, 884
Crop, plant, 116, 534, 537, 556, 855
  dicot vs. monocot, 385
■ genetic engineering, 242–243, 242i, 252–253, 257
■ hybridizations, 185, 296, 881
■ infections, 343, 350
  introduced species and, 835t
  protection, 486, 848
■ rotation, 861
■ vulnerability, 362, 362i, 419, 524
■ Crop dusting, 848i
Crop production, 65, 106, 111, 120, 462, 835, 866, 871
■ drought, 492–493, 492i–493i
■ El Niño and, 866
■ fertilizers. See Fertilizer
■ fungal pathogens, 397, 397i, 397t
■ genetic engineering, 252–253, 253i, 257–258, 289
■ genetic uniformity in, 253
  insects and, 424–425, 425i, 427
■ irrigation, 884, 884i
  land available for, 379i, 878, 884, 884i
  major world crops, 282i
■ pesticides and, 282i, 425, 427, 870, 884
■ salt tolerance and, 296, 296i
■ seed banks for, 253
■ yields, 861–862, 884
Croplands, soil erosion, 513, 513i
Cross-bridge formation, 639, 649–651, 649i, 651i, 654
Cross-fertilization, 303

animal, 185, 254, 254i, 898
plant, 168, 170i, 171, 175i, 176, 182–185
Cross-pollination, 258, 303, 307
Crossing over, **160**, 160i, 163, 164i, 166–167, 196, 242, 284
gene linkage and, 178, 178i, 182
Crosswall, 141, 148i, 149, 152
Crow, 332, 332i, 845, 845i, 846i
Crown, tooth, 721, 721i, 723, 723i
Crude density, **802**
Crustacean, 118, 358, 420, **422**–423, 422i, 423i, 430, 472i, 608, 633, 633i, 702, 769, 830, 892, 895
■ Cryophile, 340i, 341
Cryphonectria parasitica, 397, 397t
Cryptobiotic crust, 877i
Cryptomys damarensis, 911
■ Cryptosporidiosis, 346t
Crystal meth, 594
Crystallin, 233, 609i, 762
Ctenomyidae, 450t
Cuckoo, 830, 901, 901i
Cultivar, 168, 168i
■ Culture, human, 433, **452**–453, 458–459, 459i
Cumulative assaults hypothesis, 766, 768
Curcumbitacin, 427
Cuscuta, 830, 830i
■ Cushing's syndrome, **631**
Cuticle, animal, 41, 404, 568i, 640
  annelid, 414
  arthropod, 420, 422, 633
  fire ant, 820–821
  invertebrate, 608i
  roundworm, 419, 430
Cuticle, plant, 66, 67i, 116, 117i, 388t, 497, 497i, 500, 501i, 508, 511
  function, 263, 374–377, 381, 388
  water conservation features, 487, 518–519, 518i, 519i, 522
Cutin, 41, 48t, 497, **518**
Cutting, plant, 179, 179i, 536, 545i, 545t
Cutworm, 845, 845i, 846i
Cuvier, Georges, 264
Cyanide, 105, 138, 828
■ Cyanide poisoning, 105, 138, 282
Cyanidium caldarium, 318
Cyanobacterium (Cyanobacteria), 57, 109, 114, 314i, 324, 325i, 327, 327i, 328i, 329i, 330, 335, **338**, 338i, 339i, 348, 860, 886–887, 887i
  in lichen, 338, 390, 398–400
  pigments, 363, 369
Cyanophora paradoxa, 327i
Cyathea, 379i
Cycad, 370, 372i, 373i, 375, 375i, 381, 382i
  evolution, 311, 311i, 314i, 382–383, 384i, 388t, 389
Cyclic adenosine monophosphate (cAMP), 46, 48t, 238, 367, 367i, 622–623, 623i, 636
Cyclic guanine monophosphate (cGMP), 798
Cyclic metabolic pathway, photosynthesis, 100, **113**–115, 114i, 120, 324, 328i
Cyclommatus, 425i
Cypress, 382, 509, 509i, 842i
Cyprinodon variegatus, 849i
Cyst, **353**, 369, 413i, 419, 441i
■ Cystic fibrosis (CF), 74, 74i, 177, 201t, 203, 254
Cytochrome, 138, 322i, 733t
  b, 305i
  c, 278, 278i
Cytokeratin, 69, 69i
Cytokine, **680**–681, 680t, 684–686, 689, 691, 691i, 692i, 693–694, 696, 698–699, 698t

Cytokinesis, 148
Cytokinin, 541, **544**–545, 544t, 545t, 552, 555
■ Cytomegalovirus, 343t
Cytoplasm, **52**, 77–78, 77i, 78i, 81, 82i, 83, 85–88, 87i, 88i, 151, 322, 488i, 501, 503, 515, 515i, 518i, 519i, 522, 650
  eukaryotic cell, 51–53, 52i, 53i, 58, 59i, 60–63, 60i, 62i, 63i, 64i, 65i, 66i, 69, 71i, 72, 219, 221, 223, 224i, 225, 225i, 228, 228i, 232–233, 233i, 238t, 392
  main energy-releasing pathways and, 124–125, 124i
  neural membrane, 576–578, 576i, 578i, 580, 584
  prokaryotic cell, 51–52, 52i, 56i, 57, 72, 222, 228, 228i, 334, 334i, 336, 336i, 348
  role in aerobic respiration, 124i, 125i, 126i, 129–130, 134
Cytoplasmic division, 68, 142
  in animal cells, 148–149, 148i, 149i, 152, 162, 163i. See also Cleavage, animal development
  in cell cycle, 141, 144–145, 152
  eukaryotic cell, 142–143, 142t, 152, 357i, 367, 368t
  in gamete formation, 155, 158i, 162, 163i, 165i, 530, 530i, 531i, 759–760, 779i, 781, 796–797
  after meiosis, 142–143, 142t, 155, 157, 158i–159i, 163i, 165i, 166
  after mitosis, 142–144, 142t, 145i, 148, 152, 165i
  nature of, 148–149, 152
  in plant cells, 148–149, 148i, 152, 530, 530i, 531i
  prokaryotic fission, 142, 142t, 152
Cytoplasmic fusion, 357i, 365i, 395, 395i, 396i, 398
Cytoplasmic localization, 755, **760**–761, 765, 768–769
  frog, 760, 760i
Cytoplasmic streaming, **68**, 366–367, 367i
Cytoplasmic vesicle, 87, 88
Cytosine (C), 46, 46i, 219–220, 220i, 223, 227–228, 248, 248i
  DNA base pairing rule, 207, 210–212, 210i, 211i, 212i, 213i, 216
Cytoskeletal protein, 488
Cytoskeleton, 51, **68**–69, 69i, 72, 73t, 151, 352, 356, 640, 764
  components, 41–42, 47, 58, 59i, 68–69, 68i, 77i, 88i, 148, 561i, 763
Cytotoxic T cell, 679, 687, 687i, 692–693, 692i, 693i, 696, 698, 698t

D

■ 2,4–D, 848i
D11 gene, 277, 277i, 423
da Vinci, Leonardo, 268, 269
Daisy, 529, 878
Daisy coral, 471i
Dale, B. W., 826i
Damaraland mole-rat, 911, 911i
Daminozide, 848i
Danio rerio, 769
Daphnia, 824
Darlingtonia californica, 500i
Darwin, Charles, 3, 10–11, 14, 170, 186, 274i, 432, 529, 535, 874
  Beagle voyage, 264–266, 264i, 265i
  biogeography and, 267
  on natural selection, 261, 267, 280, 284, 432, 535
  on phototropism, 548
Dasypus novemcinctus, 769
Database, international, gene sequence data, 278
Daucus carota, 536, 903
■ Day care center infections, 353

Day-neutral plant, 550, 555
Daylength, 756
  plants and, 540–542, 550–553, 550i, 551i, 553i, 555–556
  seasonal variations in, 444, 447, 632, 635t, 867, 869, 869i, 886–887
■ DDT, 467, 619, 848i, 849, 849i, 863
Dead Sea, 341
■ Deafness, 122i, 714, 792
Death, 151, 206, 256, 478–479, 484i, 518, 812–814, 816, 820, 830, 839
  human perspectives on, 766–767
  population growth and, 804–805, 805i, 812, 818
  premature, 303, 303i, 316
Decibel, 606, 607i
Deciduous forest, 528, 873, 874i–875i, 876, 877i, 880, 896
Deciduous plant, 108, **382**, 500, 552
Declarative memory, 593, 593i
Decomposer, **6**, 8, 9i, 425, 486, **844**, 846i, 847, 847i, 850–852, 850i, 851i, 852i, 857, 856i–857i, 862–863, 862i
  bacterial, 6i, 3i, 252, 335, 348, 358, 377, 390–392, 844, 844i, 893
  ecosystem role, 377, 380, 387, 886, 887i, 889i, 893
  fungal, 362, 377, 391–393, 397, 400, 844, 844i, 877i
  protist, 350, 352, 362, 362i, 368
  roundworms as, 419, 430
Decomposition, 269, 513i, 844–845, 857, 862, 862i, 880, 883
■ Decompression sickness, 714
Deer, 309i, 800–801, 800i, 803, 803i
Deer tick, 426, 426i
Defense mechanisms, plant, 482–483, 483i, 486, 489
■ Defibrillator, 656, 656i, 657i, 667, 673
Definitive host, **412**
■ Deforestation, 370, **387**, 389–391, 462–463, 464t, 468, 473, 486, 854, 854i, 856i–857i, 857, 859i, 861, 864, 881, 884i
■ tropical forests, 387i, 393i, 881
Degradative pathway, **100**–101, 104
Dehiscent fruit, **532**, 533t
Dehydration, 478–479, 478i, 490, 652, 738
Delbrück, Max, 208
Deletion, **226**–228
  chromosomal, 187, **196**–197, 204, 236
Delphi oracle, 32, 32i
Delta cell, pancreas, **628**
Demographic transition model, **816**, 816i, 818
Demographics, 802, 814, 814i
Denaturation, 44–45, 347
Dendrite, **576**, 576i, 584, 587, 587i
Dendritic cell, 661, 661i, **681**, 681i, 686i, 687i, 689–690, 691i, 692–693, 692i, 696, 698, 698t
Dendrobates, 561i
Dendroclimatology, **509**
■ Dengue fever, 343t, 427
Denitrification, 859i, 861
Density-dependent control, 806–807, 813
Density-independent factor, **807**
Dentin, tooth, 436, 438, 723, 723i
Deoxyribonucleic acid (DNA). See DNA
Deoxyribose, 38, 46, 46i, 210, 210i, 211i, 212, 216, 220i
■ Depo-Provera, 783, 783i
Depolarization, membrane, 581
■ Depressant, 594–595
Derived trait, **311**–312, 312i, 315–316, 442

Dermal tissue system, plants, 493, 494i, 495–499, 498i, 502, 508, 526
Dermatitis, 732t
Dermis, **568**, 568i, 602, 603i, 788, 788i, 797
echinoderm, 641, 654
Dermochelys coriacea, 715, 715i
Desalinization, 252, **855**
Desert, 56, 117, 296–297, 296i, 304i, 334, 336, 376, 387, 449, 451i, 473i, 490, 803i, 819, **878**, 884, 884i
characteristics, 876, 876i, 877i, 878, 878i, 896–897
distribution, 873–875, 874i–875i, 896
plant adaptations, 500, 502, 507
Desertification, **884**, 885i, 896
Designer animals, 242, 299i
Designer plants, 242, 252, 258
Desmid, 372, 372i
Desmin, 69
Detrital food web, **847**, 847i, 863, 888, 890–891
Detritivore, **844**, 846i, 847, 847i, 850–852, 850i, 851i, 863
Detritus, 414, **844**, 847i, 856, 865, 888, 890–891
Deuterostome, 403, **407**, 407i, 428, 428i, 430, 434, 434i, 761–762, 761i
Development, 3, **7**, 7i, 9, 237, 237i, 387i, **480**–481, 489
constraints on, 276–277, 280
controls, 231, 233, 233i, 234–236, 236i, 238t, 240
Development, animal, 9, 63, 276–277, 276i, 416, 416i, 436–437, 442
embryonic, 234–236, 234i, 236i, 240
hormones in, 619–620, 621i, 622, 627, 635t
metamorphosis in, 420, 424, 424i
pattern formation, 236–237, 237i, 240, 761, 761i, 765
primary tissue layers, 404–405, 405i, 412–413
stages of, 403–404, 420, 423–424, 424i, 430, 632, 758, 758i, 759i, 764, 768–769, 769i
Development, human, 792–793, 795t, 798
brain, 190–191, 788, 790i, 797
embryonic, 203, 203i, 234–236, 234i, 461i, 761, 769, 771, 783, 788, 788i, 790, 790i, 792
fetal, 790, 792–794, 797
genetic disorders, 191, 194–199, 201t
postnatal, 461, 461i, 754, 754i, 772, 793, 795, 795i, 795t, 797
proportional changes during, 276i, 277, 280, 786
Development, plant, 66, 252–253, 253i, 537i, **542**, 550, 550i
flower formation in, 235, 235i, 240, 276, 276i
fruit formation in, 525, 532–535, 533i
hormones, 540–542, 540i, 555
seed formation in, 525, 526i, 527, 530
Devonian period, 271i, 372i, 373, 373i, 378, 381, 418, 421, 437, 439–440, 460, 464t, 704
Diabetes, 6, 255, 290, 615, **629**, 629t, 631, 673, 718, 730, 738
insipidus, 89, **625**, 747
Type 1 (mellitus), 122, 122i, 629, 629i
Type 2 (mellitus), 629, 730, 734, 738, 748
Diabrotica virgifera, 427, 427i
Dialysis, 278
Diaphragm, 664i, 665i, 666i, 706i, **707**, 710–711, 710i, 717, 742i

Diaphragm, birth control, **782**–783, 782i
Diarrhea, 191, 239, 343t, 346t, 393, 397, 397t, 401i, 595, 682, 682t, 732t, 733t
Diastole, cardiac cycle, **666**, 668i, 669, 669i, 676
Diatom, 314i, 318, 351, 352i, 355, **360**–361, 360i, 368, 886, 887i
Dichlorophenoxyacetate (2,4–D), 545
Dickensonia, 407i
Dicot (eudicot), 385, 388t, 483i, 494–495, 495i, 498, 498i, 503, 503i, 507
Dictyostelium, 352i, 366–367, 367i, 488
Didinium, 352i, 356i
Diet, 638–639, 673, 713, 731. *See also* Nutrition, human
early primate, 453, 455, 718i, 719, 726, 728, 792
human, 456–457, 629, 629i, 631, 719, 726, 728, 792
omnivore, 844, 844i
vegetarian, 677, 733, 817
Dieting, 734
Diffusion, 80, 405, 413, 420, 486, 562, 620, 630, 675, 744, 764, 898
capillary bed, 561, 624, 624i, 625i, 658, 668, 670–671, 676
across cell membranes, 75, 78, 79i, **80**–85, 80i, 81i, 84i, 85i, 88–89, 565, 580–581, 580i, 581i, 583, 596, 622, 623i, 658, 727, 727i, 746
at placental membrane, 789, 789i, 797
in plants, 482, 497, 501, 501i, 503, 518–519, 518i, 519i, 522
at respiratory surfaces, 434, 482, 602–703, 705, 708–709, 716, 740
Digestion, animal, 64, 73t, 87, 406, 586, 628, 719–721, 723, 724i, 725, 736
Digestion, carnivorous plant, 523, 523i
Digestive enzyme, 57, 62–63, 109, 391–392, 682, 686, 733t
in human reproduction, 774, 781, 781i
plant, 488, 488i, 537i, 546, 546i, 552
seeds and, 534–535
vertebrate, 561, 627–628, 720, 722, 722i, 723–725, 724t, 736
Digestive system, 74, 135i, 406, 480, 567i, 688, **720**, 728–729, 736
accessory organs, 719–720, 722–723, 722i, 726, 736, 736t
flatworm, 412, 720
functional links with organ systems, 664, 665i, 719–720, 722i, 740, 740i
human, 567i, 719, 722–723, 722i, 725–727, 736, 736t
incomplete vs. complete, 406, 414, 424, 719–**720**, 720i, 721–723, 736
invertebrate, 414–416, 415i, 416i, 424, 429i
ruminant, 721i
vertebrate, 566, 701i, 720, 720i
Digitalin, 381
Dihybrid experiment, **174**–175, 174i–175i, 178, 180, 182, 185
Dihydroxyacetone phosphate (DHAP), 126, 127i
Dikaryotic cell, 395, 395i, 400
Dimethyl sulfide, 360
Dimorphism, **284**
Dinoflagellate, 102i, 314i, 351, 352i, 355–356, **358**, 358i, 363, 368, 411, 470
Dinosaur, 312, 372i, 373i, 446, 465, 468
extinctions, 260, 271i, 309i, 443

origin/evolution, 271i, 432–433, 432i, 433i, 442–443, 442i
Dionaea muscipula, 523, 523i
Dioon, 382i
Diphtheria, 694i
Diploid chromosome number (2n), **145**, 145i, 146i, 147, 147i, 152, 154, **156**, 162i, 164i, 166–168, 166i, **171**, 174i, 182, 188, 192i, 307i, 536
fungal, 394, 394i, 395i, 396i
Diploid dominance, 374, 374i, 388, 388t
Diplomonad, 314i, 352i, **353**, 368
Directional movement, animal, 639–641, 640i, 641i
Directional selection, 283, **287**, 287i, **288**–289, 288i, 289i, 298, 308, 316, 915
Disaccharide, 38, 38i, 48t, 239i, 724t
Disease, 168, 168i, 251, 254, 294, **346**, 348
agents of, 282, 300–301, 835t
Disruptive selection, 283, **287**, 287i, 290i, 291, 291i, 298
Dissolved substance, 19, **27**, 29–31, 30t, 37–38, 40–41, 47, 48t, 77
Distal tubule, nephron, **743**, 743i, 744i, 746–747, 746i, 752
Distance effect, **839**, 839i
Disulfide bridge, 36i, 568i, 569i
Diversity, adaptive immunity, **686**–687
Diversity of life, 3, **6**, 14, 243, 253, 285, 309, 309i, 316t, 319, 471, 483
basis of, 8–9, 15t, 209, 211
early naturalist views of, 262
evolutionary view, 10–11, 14, 267, 464i, 464t
extinctions, 269, 283, 294–295, 298, 309, 463–475, 462i, 464i, 464t
visual overview, 328i–329i
Diving, deep-sea, 701, 714–715, 751
Division of labor, 368t, 405, 430, 480, **566**, 570, 910, 910i, 914
Dixon, Henry, 516
DNA (deoxyribonucleic acid), 3, 4i, 5, 7, 44, **46**, 103, 136, 167–168, **208**, 223–224, 246, 246i, 247i, 277, 280, 306, 327, 680, 724t, 764
base pairing, 46, 46i, 47i
as basis of life, 318, 319i, 321, 323, 323i, 326, 760
chromosomal, 60t, 61, 150, 150i, 152, 156, 164, 171, 213–214, 232, 232i, 235, 244, 305i, 345
damaged, 153, 226–227, 227i, 230, 233i, 569
double helix, 46–47, 47i, 143, 143i, 207, 211–213, 211i, 212i, 216, 219–220, 220i, 228, 247, 323
eukaryotic. *See* Eukaryotic DNA
function, 19, 33, 36i, 37, 43, 46–47, 48t, 73t, 206–207, 209, 219
"heavy" vs. "light," 217
human, 178, 250, 774, 775i, 796
human vs. chimpanzee, 277–278
hydrogen bonds in, 210i, 220, 220i, 278
methylation, 232
model, 207i, 211i, 216
mutation. *See* Mutation
nucleotides, 25, 25i, 220, 220i, 228
plasmid, 243–**244**, 244i, 245i, 252, 253i
prokaryotic, 50–52, 56i, 57, 72, 238, 238i, 239i, 240, 334i, 336i
structure, 19, 37–38, 46–48, 46i, 60–61, 206–207, 207i, 209–211, 209i, 210i, 211i, 213i, 216, 219–220, 220i, 250, 323, 488
synthesis, 213, 213i, 247, 247i, 251, 345

transcription of, 59i, 219–222, 220i, 221i, 222i, 228, 228i, 243, 252, 344, 345i, 348, 689
viral, 208, 209i, 244, 333, 342–345, 342i, 343t, 344i, 345i, 348
DNA amplification, 243, 245, 249, 341
by PCR, 243, 247, 247i, 248, 257
DNA chip, **251**, 251i, 257
DNA cloning, 206, 206i, 214, 214i, 214t, 216, 244i, 245–246, 245i, 248, 252, 257
DNA–DNA hybridization, 278
DNA fingerprint, **249**, 257, 280, 911
forensics, 249, 249i
DNA ligase, **212**–213, 212t, 216, 226, **244**–245, 244i, 245i, 257
DNA polymerase, **212**–213, 212t, 216, 220, 226–227, 229, 232, 245, 245i, 247–248, 247i, 248i, 257, 341
DNA proofreading mechanism, **213**, 216–217
DNA repair, 155, 164, 207, 212–213, 212t, 216–217, 227, 229–230
aging and, 99, 105, 766, 768
DNA replication (duplication), 152–153, 191, **212**–213, 212i, 213i, 216–217, 226, 244, 245i, 247–249, 247i, 318, 323
in cell cycle, 141, 150, 152
control of, 150, 152, 231–233, 232i, 233i
before meiosis II, 142, 157, 159i, 160, 164, 165i, 178, 760
mitosis, 142, 144, 144i, 146i
mutation during, 226–229, 227i
nature of, 207, 212–213, 212i, 212t, 213i, 219–221, 220i–221i
prokaryotic, 333, 336–337, 336i, 337i, 348
DNA research, safety guidelines, 255, 256
DNA sequencing, 196, 214, 216, 243, 258, 278, 279i, 280, 352, 428
automated, 248, 248i, 250–251, 257
DNA-to-RNA-to protein, 219–221, 220i–221i, 228, 228i, 233i, 323, 323i, 330
Dodo, 465, 465i
Dog, 299, 396, 419, 702, 717, 717i, 766, 904, 908
artificial selection, 242, 299
Doldrum, 868i
Dolly, the sheep, 206, 206i, 214i, 215
Dolphin, 309i, 462–463, 477i, 617, 617i, 715, 715i
Domain, 8, **43**, 43i, 45, 47, 49, 78, 102i
evolutionary, 301
Dominance hierarchy, 631, 631i, 909–910, 909i
Dominant allele, 169, **171**–174, 172i, 173i, 174i, 176–177, 182–185, 229, 283, 286
autosomal inheritance, 187, 190–191, 190i, 193–195, 200, 201i, 204
Dopamine, **582**–583, 582i, 594–595, 597
Dormancy, 365, 374, 381, 394i, 540–541, 544t, 545, 545t, 550i, **552**–553, 552i, 553i, 555–556
Vibrio cholerae, 895, 895i
Dorsal lip, 759i, 764, 764i
Dorsal surface, 406, 406i, 409, 422, 433–434, 435i, 460, **566**, 566i
Dorsal–ventral axis, 765
Dosage compensation, **234**–235, 241
Dosidicus, 418i
Double-blind study, 16
Double covalent bond, **25**, 25i
Double fertilization, 386i, **530**, 531i, 538
Doubling time, **805**

- Douching, **782**, 782i
- Douglas fir, 362i, 552, 553i, 833i
- Dove, 467, 535
- Down syndrome, **198**, 199i, 201t, 203–205, 778
- Downwelling, 892–**893**
- Downy mildew, 362
- Drew-Baker, Kathleen, 363i
- Drinking, culture of, 91
- *Dromaeosaurus*, 432i
- Dromedary camel, 297, 750, 750i
- *Drosophila melanogaster* (fruit fly), 167i, 178, 193, 193i, 305, 677
  - development, 231, 232i, 236–237, 236i, 237i, 240–241, 761, 761i, 762i, 764–765, 769
- Drought, 2, 117, 266, 365, 399, 474, **492**–493, 492i–493i, 507, 507i, 509, 509i, 513i, 516i, 839, 843, 866, 873, 875, 878, 884, 885i
- Drought tolerance, 254, 254i, 258
- Drug, 91, 103, 151, 695, 738, 798
- development/testing, 343, 359, 402, 408, 813
- elimination/excretion, 738–739
- genetic engineering, 252, 254, 254i
- pregnancy and, 793, 795
- Drug abuse, 572, 582–583, 594–595, 594t, 595i, 597, 697, 700
- addiction, 583, **594**–595, 594t, 595i, 597, 700
- testing for, 738–739, 739i
- Drupe, **532**, 533t
- Dry acid deposition, 871
- Dry fruit, 532–533, 532i, 533i, 533t, 534i, 538, 542
- Dry shrubland, 874i–875i, 875, **878**, 879i, 884, 896
- Dry woodland, 874i–875i, **878**, 884, 896
- Dryopith, 454i
- DTP vaccination, 694i
- Duchenne muscular dystrophy (DMD), 195, 205, 241, 652–653
- Duck, 36i, 133, 317, 842, 915
- Duck-billed dinosaur, 442i
- Duck-billed platypus, 450, 450i, 450t, 461, 461i
- Duck louse, 425i
- Duckweed, 384, 500
- *Dugesia*, 756i
- *Dunce* gene, 236
- *Dunkleosteus*, 436i
- Duodenal cancer, 682
- Duodenum, 722i, 724i, 725, 737
- Duplication, chromosomal, 187, **196**–197, 197i, 204
- Dust Bowl, 513, 878
- Dust mite, 421, 421i, 426, 694
- Dust storm, 878, 884, 885i
- Dutch elm disease, 397t, 835t, 849
- Dwarfism, 190, 190i, 201t, 544, 545t, 625, 637, 637i
- Dynamic equilibrium, **605**, 605i, 617
- Dynamiting, coral reefs, 471, 475
- Dynein, 70–73, 71i, 73i, 146
- Dystrophin, 195

E

- Eagle, 468, 469i, 476, 842, 849, 908
- Eagle nebula, 320i
- Ear, 179, 588, 600t, 607i, 615–617
  - human, 606, 606i, 617, 644, 790i, 792, 792i
- Eardrum, 606, 606i, 607i
- Earlobe trait, 285
- Early wood, 507, 507i
- Earth, 5i, 18–19, 19i, 31, 270, 883i
  - air circulation, 868–869, 868i
  - crust, 269, 271i, 272–273, 272i, 280, 320–321, 321i, 329i, 852, 856–857, 856i–857i, 862, 864

- history, 260–261, 265, 269–273, 272i, 273i, 280, 319–320, 322–323, 328i
- origin, 319–321, 320i, 321i, 322i, 330
- plate tectonics. See Plate tectonics
- rotation, 868, 868i, 872, 872i, 892, 892i, 896
- temperature zones, 868–869, 868i, 869i
- water provinces, 872, 896
- Earthquake, 92–93, 93i, 265, 272i, 304
- Earthworm, 39, 167i, 404i, 414, 423, 430, 574i, 575, 608, 640–641, 654, 658, 658i, 844, 846i
- Earwig, 425i
- East African Rift Valley, 456–457
- Easter Island, 462–463, 462i
- Eating disorder, 737
- *Ebola* virus, 343t, 346–347, 346i
- Ecdysone, 232i, **633**, 633i, 636–637
- Echinoderm, 314i, 403, 404i, 407, 407i, **428**, 428i, 429i, 431, 434, 434i, 608, 641, 654, 761
- Echolocation, **598**
- *Eciton burchelli*, 910i
- Ecological isolation, **303**, 303i
- Ecological pyramid, **850**–851, 850i, 851i
- Ecological separation, **306**, 316
- Ecological succession, **832**–833, 832i, 833i, 840
- Ecology, 333, **801**
- Economy-class syndrome, **677**
- Ecoregion, **472**–473, 473i, 476, 841, 841i, 875, 896
- *EcoRI* enzyme, 244
- Ecosystem, **5**, 5i, 9i, 11, 14, 29, 243, 252, 799i, 842–**843**, 844–**845**, 846–**863**, 917
  - Antarctica, 865, 865i
  - aquatic, 836, 850–851, 850i, 851i, 861–864, 862i, 863i, 873, 874i–875i, 875
  - biogeochemical cycles of, 848, **852**, 852i, 854, 863
  - city as, 854–855, 858–859, 858i, 859i
  - dry woodland, 476
  - endangered, 119, 370, 389, 871
  - energy flow, 93i, 843–844, 844i, 846–847, 847i, 850–851, 850i, 851i, 863
  - energy pyramids, **850**–851, 851i, 863
  - energy transfers within, 133, 845–846, 846i, 847i, 850–851, 851i, 863
  - estuarine, 849i, 863, 890
  - forest, 390, 849, 854, 854i, 856i–857i, 857, 861–862, 862i
  - global distribution, 843, 850, 850i, 852–853, 853i, 855–857, 855i, 856i–857i, 868, 896
  - hydrothermal vent, 318, 324
  - kelp bed as, 361, 361i
  - lake, 853i, 863, 863i, 886–887, 886i, 887i
  - on land, 845, 850–851, 850i, 852–853, 852i, 853i, 856–857, 856i–857i, 860i, 861
  - materials cycling within, 843–845, 844i, 852, 852i, 856–857, 856i–857i, 860i, 863–864, 863i
  - participants, 844–847, 844i, 845i, 846i, 847i
  - Silver Springs, 850–851, 850i, 851i, 863
  - stream, 852–855, 853i, 863, 863i, 888–889, 888i
- Ecosystem modeling, 844, 844i, 848, 853, 853i
- Ecotourism, 472–473
- Ecstasy. *See* MDMA

- Ectoderm, **404**, 412, 430, 559–560, **566**, 570, **758**, 759i, 762–763, 762i, 765, 768, 797
- Ectomycorrhizae, **399**, 399i
- Ectotherm, **749**, 749i, 753
- Edema, 419, 419i, 427, **671**, 685, 685i
- Ediacaran, 407i, **409**
- *Edotea*, 364
- Effector, **484**, 484i, 489
  - nervous systems, 574, 574i, 596, 752
- Effector cell, immune response, **686**–687, 687i, 690i, 691, 691i, 692i, 693–694, 698, 698t
- Efferent, **575**, 587
- Efferent arteriole, **743**, 743i, 744i, 747, 752
- Egg, 42, 44–45, **160**, 225, 237i, 362, 362i, 536, 536i, 635t, 764, 787
  - amniote, 442–444, 446, 446i, 461, 461i
  - amphibian, 53, 232, 441, 769
  - animal, 142, 149, 163i, 167, 566
  - animal, formation of, 756–758, 758i, 760, 768
  - armadillo, 769
  - bird, 446, 757i, 761
  - bryophyte, 371
  - chicken, 763i
  - cortex, 760, 760i
  - cowbird, 831, 831i
  - crow, 845
  - dinosaur, 442–443, 442i
  - fertilized, 154, 163i, 233, 755, 757–758, 758i, 760i, 761i, 763, 768–769, 781, 781i, 906–907, 915
  - fish, 761
  - flowering plant, 525–528, 526i, 530–531, 531i, 533i, 535, 538
  - frog, 55i, 441, 758i, 759i, 760i, 761i, 762–763, 762i
  - fruit fly (*Drosophila*), 761, 761i
  - human, 70i, 73, 139, 140, 142, 156i, 161, 163i, 192, 199, 203, 214, 558i, 567i, 738, 757, 757i, 770–772, 776–777, 777i, 778i, 781, 781i, 795t, 796–797
  - insect, 7i, 761
  - invertebrate, 408, 413, 413i, 417i, 419i, 421, 423
  - mammal, 214i, 215, 632, 634t
  - Mendelian genetics and, 170i, 171–172, 174–175
  - ostrich, 162
  - parasitoid fly, 820–821
  - phasmid, 841, 841i
  - plant, 170, 170i, 371, 375, 376i, 379, 379i, 381, 383, 383i, 386, 386i, 388
  - platypus, 450
  - reptile, 444, 761
  - sea anemone, 823i
  - sea star, 806, 809, 809i
  - sea turtle, 715
  - sea urchin (roe), 428, 761, 761i
  - snail, 757i
  - snake, 444–445, 845
  - spider, 421, 757i
  - spiny anteater, 450
  - turtle, 444
  - wasp, 490, 490i, 831i
  - yucca moth, 823i
  - zebrafish, 761, 769
- Egg-laying mammal, 448–450, 460–461
- Egg sac, spider, 757i
- Egg white, 28, 28i, 44–45, 446i, 732t
- *Eichhornia crassipes*, 841, 841i
- Einkorn, 307i
- Ejaculation, 781–782, 796
- Ejaculatory duct, 772–773, 772t, 796
- El Niño, 866, 866i, **893**–896, 894i
- El Niño/La Niña episode, 894i, 894i
- El Niño Southern Oscillation (ENSO), 893–**894**, 894i
- Elastin, 177, 562, 568–569, 666

- Electric gradient, 79i, **80**–82, 88, 101, 112, 113, 114i, 120, 123, 125, 125i, 130–131, 130i, 131i, 137, 576
- Electrocardiogram (ECG), **656**, 673, 673i
- Electrochemical gradient, 745
- Electroencephalogram (EEG), 591
- Electromagnetic spectrum, **108**, 108i
- Electron, 10, 19, **20**, 22–25, 23i, **30**, 30t, 101
  - excitation, 22, 102, 109, 111–112, 114, 227
  - orbitals, 22–23, 22i, **30**, 109
- Electron microscope, 51, **54**, 54i, 55i, 72, 318, 349
- Electron transfer, 22, 37, 48t, 94, **97**, 99, 105
  - in aerobic respiration, 123–126, 125i, 127i, 128–131, 129i, 130i, 131i, 137–138
  - in anaerobic pathways, 132–133, 137
- Electron transfer chain, **101**, 101i, 104–105, **112**, 118, 122–123, 125, 125i, 130–131, 130i, 131i, 133, 137–138, 278, 278i, 335, 733
  - in origin of life, 322, 322i, 324
  - in photosynthesis, 107, 111–114, 111i, 113i, 114i, 115i, 118i, 120
- Electron transfer phosphorylation, **125**, 125i, **130**, 130i, 131i, 135i, 187
- Electron transfer system, in mitochondria, 122–123
- Electrophoresis, gel, 248–249, 248i, 257
- Element, **18**, 18i, 19–**20**, 19i, 20i, 21, 23, **30**, 30t, 512–513, 522, 522i
- Elephant, 274, 309i, 468, 469i, 767, 809, 809i
- Elephant seal, 907, 907i
- Elephantiasis, 419, 419i, 427, **671**
- Elimination, from gut, 719–720, 720i, 728–729, 729i, 736
- Ellis–van Creveld syndrome, 200i, 201t, 295
- Elm tree, 385, 507i, 835t, 880
- *Elodea*, 121i
- Elongation stage, 224–225, 224i, 225i, 228
- Embolus, **672**
- Embryo, animal, **202**, 481, 755, 758, 760, 768, 797, 849
  - axolotl, 764i
  - biological costs of producing, 757
  - bird, 267i, 303i, 446i
  - chick, 763i
  - chordate, 588
  - development, 231, 234, 240–241, 276–277, 280, 486, 489, 489i, 574–575
  - *Drosophila*, 235–237, 235i–236i, 237i, 240–241
  - earliest known, 261, 263, 266, 266i, 407
  - frog, 759i, 760, 760i, 764, 764i
  - guppy, 811, 811i
  - human, 69i, 149i, 190–192, 192i, 202, 204, 258, 287, 407, 461i, 757, 761, 763, 769–772, 771i, 776–777, 776t, 777i, 783, 784i, 786–789, 786i–787i, 787t, 788i, 791i, 792, 795i, 795t, 796–797
  - invertebrate, 403, 405i, 406–407, 416, 430, 640, 757i
  - mammal, 154, 231, 234–235, 234i, 312, 449–450, 451i, 461i, 757
  - marsupial, 757i
  - reptile, 461, 757i
  - sea urchin, 769
  - shark, 757i
  - vertebrate, 276, 312, 312i, 407, 407i, 433–435, 441–442, 460, 559–560, 588, 588i, 596, 644, 645i, 757i, 763

zebrafish, 769
Embryo, plant, 170i, 253i, 495, 495i
  development, 276–277, 280
■ Embryo cloning, **214**, 214t, 216
Embryo sac, 530, 531i, 536t
Embryo sporophyte, 377, 381,
  383i, 385–386, 386i, 525, 531i,
  532–534, 532i, 533i, 536, 536t,
  538, 541
  growth and development, 542,
    542i, 544t, 545, 546i, 547, 555
Embryonic disk, 761, 761i, 786, 787i,
  788, 788i
Embryonic induction, **764**, 764i,
  765i, 768–769
Embryonic period, **786**, 786i,
  788–789, 788i, 791i
Emergent property, **5**
Emigration, **295**, 298, 298t, **804–805**,
  813, 818, 839
Emiliania huxleyi, 352i, 360i
Emmer, 307i
Emotion, 179, 527, 588, 591, 593, 597,
  603–604, 784
Emotional–visceral brain, 591
Emperor penguin, 40i, 41, 753
■ Emphysema, 712–713, 713i, 716
Emulsification, **725**, 727i
Enamel, tooth, 438–439, 455–456,
  723, 723i
■ Encapsulated receptor, **602**, 615
■ Encephalitis, 332, 332i, 343t,
  426–427
■ Endangered species, 206, 463, **468**,
  471–473, **475**, 715, 715i, 801, 831
■ extinction crisis, 301, 333, 370
  flowering plants, 524–525, 524i
■ humans as agents, 428, 438i, 441,
    444, 444i, 460
  mammals, 450i
■ *oryx leucoryx*, 490
Endemic species, **468–469**, 474–**475**
Endergonic reaction, 94i, **95**, 104
Endler, John, 810–811
Endocrine disrupter, **618**–619
Endocrine gland, **561**, 570, 589, 620,
  625i, 628, 633i, 636
Endocrine system, 485, 567i, 589,
  618–**620**, 620i, 621i, 900
  links with circulatory system,
    669, 740i
  links with digestive system, 725,
    729, 736, 740i
  links with nervous system, 567i,
    620, 621i
  links with respiratory system, 740i
  links with urinary system, 740i
  pituitary/hypothalamus link, 619
Endocytic pathway, cells, **58**, 63i
Endocytic vesicle, 63, 63i, 86–87,
  86i, 87i
■ Endocytosis, 75, **81**, 81i, **86–89**, 86i,
  345, 348, 670, 690
Endoderm, **404**–405, 412, 430,
  559, **566**, 570, **758**, 762, 768,
  788, 797
Endodermis, 502i, **503**, 503i, 515,
  515i, 517i, 522
Endomembrane system, **62–63**, 62i,
  63i, 72, 74–75, 176, 225, 225i
  possible origin of, 326–327, 328i
■ Endometriosis, **777**
Endometrium, **776–777**, 776t, 777i,
  779, 779i, 780i, 786i, 787, 789,
  796–797
Endomycorrhizae, **399**
Endoparasite, 830, 830i
Endophytic fungus, **398**–400
Endoplasmic reticulum (ER), 58, 59i,
  60, **62–63**, 63i, 72, 73t, 74, 83, 86i,
  87, 87i
  possible origin, 319, 326–327, 326i
  protistan, 352, 355i, 368
Endorphin, **583**, 595, 603

Endoskeleton, 435, 439, 639–**640**,
  641–642, 641i, 642i, 654
Endosperm, 386, 386i, 530–**531**, 531i,
  532, 532i, 538, 542, 542i, 546–547,
  546i, 555
Endospore, **339**, 339i, 349, 653
Endosymbiosis, 64–65, 326–**327**,
  327i, 329i, 330, 354, 356, 358, 360,
  363, 368–369
Endothelium, 78i, **666**, 666i, 668i,
  670, 672, 675, 685, 708i
Endotherm, **749**, 749i, 753
Energy, **6**, 6i, 14, 19, 64, **92–93**, 105,
  130, 466, 507, 507i, 514, 529
  of activation, enzymes, 91, 94–98,
    96i, 104
  for cellular work, 6, 36–37, 48t, 93i,
    94i, 95, 95i, 101i, 104, 292, 405,
    649, 651, 651i, 654
  chemical bonds and, 91, 93–95,
    104, 844, 846
  coupling, 91, 95, 104t
  for early life, 335, 348
  ecosystem roles, 843–844, 844i,
    846, 850–851, 850i, 851i, 863
  electrochemical, 580, 600, 608, 615
  forms of, 91–93, 93i, 104, 109,
    112–113, 113i, 122, 138
  input/output ratio, 405
  levels in atom, 22–23, 22i, 23i,
    25i, 30
  mechanical, 484, 606–607, 615
  for origin of life, 106, 106i, 319,
    321, 757
  photon, 608, 613i
  release, 91, 95, 95i, 96i, 97, 100,
    104–105, 126, 126i, 127i, 129, 131
  reproduction, 154, 166, 535,
    756, 756i
  stored, 39–41, 47, 48t, 93–94, 93i,
    123, 130, 134, 136, 138, 563, 563i
  sunlight as source of, 6, 6i, 9, 36,
    65, 73t, 93–94, 93i, 100, 104, 106,
    108, 112, 124, 335, 348, 371–372,
    374, 494, 505, 612, 844–845, 844i,
    850–851, 851i, 863, 867
  transfer, 845–846, 846i, 847i, 863
  translocation in plants, 521–522, 521i
  transportable, 39, 47, 48t, 123,
    126, 129
Energy, for human body, 629–630,
  630i, 635t, 729–730, 729i, 736, 772
■ alternatives, 134–135, 135i, 137–138
  instant burst of, 38–39, 47, 82, 138
Energy-acquiring pathway, 107, 118i
Energy carrier, 46–47, 48t, 94–95, 104
  ATP as, 64, 64i, 95, 95i, 104, 104t
Energy conversion, 52, 73t
  nature of, 91–93, 93i, 95, 104
Energy flow, 917
  ecosystem, 843–844, 844i, 846–847,
    847i, 863
  one-way, 6, 6i, 7, 92–93, 93i, 104,
    107–108, 118–119, 123, 135
  in photosynthesis, 107, 114, 119
  principles, 92–94, 118, 136,
    846, 917
Energy hill, 94–96, 96i, 101
Energy pyramid, **850–851**, 851i, 863
Energy-releasing pathway, 107, 118i,
  123. *See also* Aerobic respiration,
  Anaerobic energy-releasing
  pathway, Fermentation
  overview, 124–125, 125i
Energy source, human population,
  380, 638–639, 814, 817, 869, 869i,
  896–897
Energy transfer, nature of, 6, 6i, 91,
  92–95, 104
Engelmann, Wilhelm Theodor,
  110, 110i
Enhancer, **232**, 236
Enkephalin, **583**, 595, 603
Enriquez, Carlos, 349

■ *Entamoeba histolytica*, 366–367
Enterobacteria, 728, 732t
■ *Enterobius vermicularis*, 419
■ *Enterocytozoon bieneusi*, 393, 397t
Enteromorpha, 834i, 835
■ Enterovirus, 343t
Entropy, **92–93**, 93i, 104
Enveloped virus, 333, 342i, 343, 343i,
  345, 345i, 696, 697i
Environment, 14, 15t, 52, 479, 483,
  483i, 485, 489, 766, 806, 807i
  effects on phenotype, 154–155,
    167, 264, 280, 458, 458i
  effects on wood formation,
    506–507, 507i
  enzyme activity and, 98–99, 99i
  evolution and, 261–263, 266–267,
    274, 280, 283, 287–289, 289i, 293,
    405, 458–459, 464
  extreme, 8, 56, 57i, 318, 318i, 321,
    321i, 377
  gene expression and, 169, 179–182,
    179i, 186, 191, 231, 240
  hormonal secretion and, 540–541,
    556, 623, 631–633, 632i, 633i, 636
  human impact. *See* Human impact
    on biosphere
  impacts of genetic engineering,
    242, 252–253, 255, 257, 401
  natural selection in. *See* Natural
    selection
  plant responses to, 116–117, 116i,
    117i, 120, 168, 302, 302i, 375,
    375i, 381, 391, 399, 482, 512i,
    540–542, 548–553, 549i, 550i,
    551i, 555–556
  pollution of. *See* Pollution
  protistan response to, 365–366
  reproductive timing and, 154,
    154i, 756
  seasons, 374–376, 374i, 381, 383,
    399, 420, 447, 454, 461, 507, 540,
    550–551, 550i, 551i, 553, 555–556,
    632, 635t
  short-term shifts in, 238–240, 238t
Environmental agents, toxic
  chemicals, 228–230, 240
Environmental gradient,
  community structure and,
  832–833, 838–840
Environmental movement, 467
Environmental Protection Agency,
  510, 510i, 618, 848i, 865
■ Environmental remediation, **252**
Enzyme, 33, **37**, 77–78, 79i, **94**, **96**,
  255, 478, 489, 644, 712–713, 798
  activation mechanisms, 97, 104,
    498, 582–583
  in aerobic respiration, 123,
    125–126, 125i, 128
  antimicrobial, 680t, 681, 681i, 698t
  of bioluminescence, 102, 102i, 253i
  carbonic anhydrase, 709, 716
  controls over, 90–91, 98–99, 104,
    151, 232–233, 232i
  digestive, 58, 62–63, 63i, 74,
    208, 238–239, 239i, 339, 365,
    368, 391–392, 400, 409, 409i,
    411, 416, 488, 488i, 500i,
    534–535, 537i, 546, 546i,
    552, 627, 720, 722–723, 722i,
    725, 736
  digestive, in immune response,
    682, 686
  functions, 7, 36–37, 37i, 39, 39i,
    45–46, 48t, 90, 94–97, 95i, 96i,
    104, 104t, 134, 136, 142–144, 150,
    176–177, 179, 179i, 179i, 183, 202,
    220–221, 220i, 224–225, 228–229,
    622, 623i, 627–628, 636
  maternal message, 760–761, 768
  metabolic pathway, 90, 90i,
    176–177, 179–182, 323, 327,
    330, 762

pH effects on, 28–29, 91, 98–99,
  99i, 104
plant, 106, 112, 115, 120, 500i,
  547i, 555
protein role of, 218–221, 228
reaction rate, 37, 44, 47, 48t, 95,
  95i, 97–101, 103–105, 238t, 580
repair, 185, **213**, 216–217
replication, 207, 212, 213i, 216,
  244–245, 653, 766
restriction, 243, **244**, 244i, 245,
  245i, 249, 257
shapes, 43, 47, 98, 98i
temperature and, 91, 98–99,
  99i, 104, 179, 179i, 318,
  318i, 685
viral, 245, 257, 344–345
Eocene epoch, 271i, 297, 304i, 331i,
  449, 449i, 452i, 454–455
Eomaia scansoria, 309i
Eosinophil, 660i, 661i, **681**, 681i, 698t
Ephedra viridins, 382
Ephedrine, 572
■ Epidemic, 140, **346**, 349–350, 362,
  397, 678, 867
Epidermal growth factor, 150, 405
Epidermis, animal, 410i, 434, 435i,
  446i, 566, **568–570**, 568i, 603i,
  633, 641
  characteristics, 99i, 105, 406i, 411,
    430, 608, 608i
  specialization, 483, 483i
Epidermis, plant, 487, 494i, 495–**497**,
  496i, 497i, 504, 506, 508, 508t,
  515i, 517i, 521i, 523, 523i
  leaves, 111i, 116i, 117i, 480, 499,
    499i, 501, 501i
  root, 502i, 503, 503i, 505i, 514,
    514i, 547i
  specialization, 483, 483i, 526
  water conservation, 518–519, 518i,
    519i, 522
■ *Epidermophyton floccosum*, 397i, 397t
Epididymis, 772–773, 772t, 773i,
  774i, 784, 796
Epiglottis, 626i, 706i, **707**, 707i, 715,
  717, 723
■ Epilepsy, 402, 592
Epinephrine, **582–583**, 587, 593, 621i,
  622t, 630–631, 634, 635t, 636
Epiphyte, **379**, 880
Epistasis, **177**, 177i, **185**
Epithelial cell, evolution,
  639–640, 654
Epithelial tissue, 481i, 558–561, 560i,
  561i, 570
Epithelium, 67i, 69i, 74, 150, 177,
  409, 410i, 411, 430, **560–561**, 640,
  640i, 654, 682, 682t, 697–698,
  732t, 776
  alveolar, 708, 708i, 712, 712i
  characteristics, 404–405,
    560–561, 560i
  cnidarian, 574, 574i
  glandular, 560–561, 561i, 683, 698
  intestinal, 620, 722, 722i, 724–726,
    726i, 727i, 728, 736
  pigmented, 612, 612i
  simple, **560**, 560i
  stratified, **560**, 560i, 568
■ Epstein–Barr virus, 343t, 662
Equator, biodiversity pattern role,
  821, 838–839
Equilibrium, 615
  dynamic, 605, 605i, 617, 617i
  island biogeography, 468–469, 475
  sense of, 605
  static, 605, 605i, 617, 617i
Equisetum, 167i, 378–379, 378i
ERBB2, 230
■ Erectile dysfunction, 798
Erectile tissue, 773i
Erethizon dorsatum, 483i
■ Ergotism, 397, 397t

■ Erosion, 263, 265, 268–269, 269i, 272–273, 321, 387, 462, 473, 836–837, 842, 852, 861–862, 877i, 878, 885–886, 891
■ *Erythroblastosis fetalis*, **663**
Erythrocyte, 660, 661i, 675
Erythropoietin, 635t, **714**
■ *Escherichia coli*, 56i, 209i, 217, 238–239, 238i, 239i, 241, 244i, 252, 334, 335i, 337, 338i, 349, 728
  strain 0157:H7, 347
Eschscholzia californica, 540i
Esophagus, 444i, 706i, **707**, 713i, 720i, 721i, **723**, 736t
  human, 722i, **723**, 724i
  invertebrate, 415i, 416, 416i, 529
Essential amino acid, **730**
Essential fatty acid, **730**
Estrogen, 36i, 37, 192, 199, 277, 618, 632, 634, 634t, 635t, 636, 777, 777i, 779, 779i, 780i, 787, 789, 795–797
  characteristics, 619, 621i, 622t
  effects on fish, amphibian, 618
  receptor, 695
  sexual trait and, 637i
  synthesis and hormones, 638–639
■ Estrogen-like chemicals, 618–619, 637i
Estrous cycle, **776**, 904
Estuary, 322, 454–455, 637, **890**
Ethane, 32
Ethanol (ethyl alcohol), 90, 132, 132i, 137, 253i
Ethiopian realm, 874, 875i
Ethyl group, 227, 595
Ethylene, 32, 541, 544–**545**, 544t, 545t, 549, 552, 555
Eubacterium, classification, 310
Eucalyptus tree, 384, 450i, 878, 908
Euchlanis, 416i
Eudicot, 252, **385**, 385i, 386i, 388t, 389, 483i, 493–495, 495i, 498–499, 498i, 499i, 500i, 501, 501i, 502–504, 503i, 507–508, 525, 531i, 532, 532i, 538, 543i, 545, 554
■ Eugenic engineering, **256**
Euglena gracilis, 352i, 354, 354i
Euglenoid, 314i, 352i, **354**–357, 354i, 368
Eukarya, 8–9, 8i, 8t, 9i, 14, 301, 823
  archaeans and, 340–341
Eukaryotic cell, **52**, 164, 244–245, 318
  characteristics, 50–53, 52i, 56, 60–61, 64–67, 66i, 67i, 69, 72, 124, 126i, 128i, 766, 769
  classification, 310–311, 311i, 314, 314i, 316
  components, 41, 58, 59i, 60i, 60t, 70, 70i, 72, 73t, 74–75, 325, 327
  cytoskeleton. See Cytoskeleton
  division, 61, 142–143, 142t, 146i–147i, 152
  evolution, 278, 301, 319, 323, 325–326, 326i, 327i, 328i–329i, 330, 337, 368t, 392, 464
  gene control, 231–236, 233i, 240
  origin of, 271i, 319, 324–325, 324i, 327, 328i, 329i, 330, 351, 353, 823
  prokaryotic vs., 56–57, 60, 69, 72, 238i, 333–336, 368, 368t
  reproduction, 140–152, 142t, 154–165
  single-celled protists, 351–355, 368
Eukaryotic DNA, 352
  characteristics, 47, 51–53, 52i, 59i, 60–61, 60i, 60t, 72, 73t, 207–213
  genes, expression, 231, 233, 233i, 240
  organization in chromosomes, 142–143, 142i, 143i, 146i, 152, 231–232, 245, 257

RNA transcription, 219, 221, 221i, 223, 224i, 228, 228i
Eupenicillium, 396i
Euplectella, 408i
Eurasian Plate, 272i
European starling, 835t
Euryarchaeote, 314i, 340, 340i, 348
Eusocial behavior, 910–911, 914
Eutherian, **448**, 460
■ Eutrophic lake, 887, 887i
Eutrophication, **863**–864, 863i, **887**
Evaporation, **27**, 27i, 511, 522, **749**, 894
  body temperature and, 478–479, 478i, 490
  in hydrologic cycle, 843, 853, 853i, 862
  transpiration, **516**–517, 517i
Evaporative heat loss, **750**, 750t
Evaporative water loss, 877–878, 882
  animals, 741, 741i, 749–752
  deforestation and, 387
  plants, 487, 487i, 518
Evergreen, 116i, **382**, 388t, 500, 832i
Evergreen broadleaf forest, 873, 874i–875i, **880**, 896
Evolution, biochemical, 107, 121, 271i, 278–279, 279i, 319, 322, 322i, 324–325, 328i, 330
  evidence of, 458–460
Evolution, biological, **10**–11, **283**, 296, 333, 346, 480, 488, 498, 758, 761, 810. *See also* Natural selection
  bacterial model, 317
  branched, 308, 308i, 309i, 311–312, 311i, 313i, 316, 403, 436
  comparative genomics and, 251, 257
  convergent, 361, 449, 449i, 457, 609
  deuterostome divergence, 428, 428i
  early theories of, 262–266, 272, 280–281
  endoskeleton, 642, 642i
  by endosymbiosis, 64–65, 326–327, 327i
  evidence of, 236–237, 243, 261–263, 263i, 273, 273i, 280, 432–433, 433i, 443, 458–460
  first cells, 319, 322–323, 322i, 323i, 325–326, 326i, 327i, 330
  mutation and, 45, 217, 227, 241, 276–277, 283–285, 295, 298, 417
  nervous systems, 574–575, 574i, 575i
  of organelles, 319, 325–327, 326i
  of parasites/hosts, 326–327
  patterns, 310–312, 316t, 327, 765, 769
  perspective on, 916
  unbranching, 308, 316
  vertebrate skeletons, 642–643, 642i, 643i
  visual/summary, 328i–329i, 330
Evolution, geologic (of Earth), 867
  evidence of, 261–263, 272–273, 272i, 273i, 280
  life's history and, 260–263, 263i, 308, 316, 321, 373i, 388, 456–457, 867, 896
  time scale for, 270–271, 271i
Evolution, human, 197, 204, 317, 456, 573, 812. *See also* Human history
  asteroids and, 260
  brain and spinal cord, 456, 456i, 458
  perspective on, 881, 916
Evolutionary adaptation, 197, 204, 283, **296**
Evolutionary tree, 278, 279i, 301, **308**. *See also* Tree of life; Pedigree
  amniote, 442i

animal, 403
  chordate, 434i, 437i
  cladogram, 311–312, 312i, 313i
  domain archaea, 340i
  domain bacteria, 338i
  early primates to humans, 197, 204
  eukaryote, 325
  flowering plants, 385, 385i
  fungal, 392, 392i
  Homo sapiens, 459i
  how to read, 301, 308, 308i, 312, 316
  major lineages, 311, 313i, 314i, 328i–329i
  mammals, 309i
  plants, 311i, 372i, 375i
  protistan, 327, 352, 352i
  vertebrates, 312, 312i, 313i, 437i
Evolutionary trend, 300
  plants, 388t
  primate, 197, 197i, 204, 479
  vertebrates, 274, 274i, 309, 642–643, 705i
Excitable cell, 565, 576–577, 596, 650
Excitation, waves of, 667, 667i, 676
Excitatory postsynaptic potential (EPSP), 573, 580i, **581**, 581i, 594
Excretion, 229, 444, 446, 559, 567i, 729, 729i, 731, 736, 738
  urinary, **741**, 741i, 743, 745, 747, 752–753
Excretory system, invertebrate, 415, 415i
■ Exercising, 39, 133–134, 133i, 138, 629, 638–639, 651–653, 651i, 676, 750
  body weight and, 719, 734
  heart and, 673, 673i
  kidneys and, 744
  muscles and, 638–639, 652
  respiration and, 711, 711i
  veins and, 671
Exergonic reaction, 94i, **95**, 100, 104
Exhalation, **710**–712, 710i, 711i, 716, 741, 741i, 752
Exocrine gland, **561**, 561i, 568, 628, 688, 915
Exocytic vesicle, 63, 63i, 86, 727
Exocytosis, 75, **81**, 81i, **86**–88, 86i, 580, 580i, 727, 727i
Exodermis, **515**, 515i, 522
Exon, **221**, 221i, 228, 689i
Exoskeleton, 39, 39i, **420**, 428, 639–**640**, 641, 641i, 654
  arthropod, 420, 420i, 423, 425
  insect, 275i, 404
  movement, 639, 654
Exotic species, **835**, 838–840, 838i, 839i
Expansion mutation, **190**
Experiment, 3, **11**, **12**–13, 12i, 15
Experiment, examples
  action potential recordings, 578–579, 579i
  appetite suppression, 735
  artificial, sponge colonization, 835
  artificial selection, roses, 168–169, 168i
  auxin effects, 546i, 548, 548i, 556
  bacterial population growth, 806
  bacterial transformation, 208, 208i
  bee dance, 905
  behavior, migratory, 617
  bioluminescence, 103, 103i
  birdsong, 902
  cancer immune response, 693
  carbon fixation, 121
  caterpillar defensive behavior, 908, 908i
  cell differentiation, 762–763
  cell fusion, 76–77, 77i
  cell memory, 764
  cephalopod eyes, 609i

cloning, 248, 248i
  competitive exclusion, 824–825, 825i
  computer simulation of origin of biological molecules, 319, 323, 330
  creatine, muscular dystrophy and, 638–639
  cross-breeding Africanized bee, 898
  cytoplasmic localization, 760i
  dicer-free mice, 769
  dihybrid cross, 174, 174i–175i, 178, 182
  DNA function, 208–209, 208i, 209i, 216
  DNA replication, 244–245, 244i
  dormancy, fir seedlings, 552–553, 553i
  dormancy, lilac, 551, 551i
  Down syndrome/maternal age, 199i
  Drosophila development, 236, 236i, 237i, 240
  Drosophila recombinants, 178, 193, 193i
  early Earth conditions, 321
  effect of intense sound on inner ear, 607i
  embryonic induction, 764, 764i, 765i
  environmental effects, genes, 179, 179i
  eutrophication, 863, 863i, 887
  experimental overeating, 735
  feeding behavior, garter snake, 900
  flower/set fruit ratio, 535
  flowering plant design, 509
  flowering response, 551, 551i, 556, 556i
  free radicals, antioxidants and, 766
  frog neural function, 582
  fungal pest control, 401
  fused mouse eggs, 154, 154i
  gene therapy, 833
  gene transfers, 251–255, 253i
  genetic engineering, 236, 247, 247i, 252–255, 253i
  ghrelin production, dieting and, 718
  gibberellin effects, 540, 540i, 544, 544i
  gravitropism, 548, 548i
  guppy life history patterns, 811
  heartbeat recording, 656–657
  imprinting, 902i
  insects, carbohydrate transport, 520, 520i
  intermediate disturbance hypothesis, 833
  isolating genes, 246, 246i
  keystone species, 834–835, 834i, 835i
  knockout, 236–237, 240
  life span extension, 766
  lymphocytic expansion/stimulation, 693
  marker-assisted selection, 169
  Mendel's, 170–175, 182
  monohybrid cross, 172–173, 172i, 182
  mycorrhizae and plant growth, 399i
  natural selection among *Heliconius* butterflies, 12–13, 13i
  natural selection among peppered moths, 288, 288i
  nature of photosynthesis, 110, 110i, 121
  nest decorating behavior, 903, 903i
  obese mice, 718, 718i, 735i
  Olestra causing intestinal cramps, 12, 12i, 16

organic molecule formation, 321, 330
oxytocin role, mating, 900–901, 900i
pancreatic secretion, 620
plant defense mechanisms, 490
plant nutrients/deficiencies, 512, 512t
plant wilting, 518–519, 518i, 519i, 523
poplars for phytoremediation, 510, 510i
population ecology, 800
prayer, effects of, 16
predator–prey interaction, 827, 827i
protein synthesis, 321
receptive fields, visual stimuli, 613i
reciprocal crosses, 193
restriction enzyme, 244
senescence, 552i
siRNA importance, 769
soil erosion control, 513, 513i
split-brain, 592, 592i
spontaneous cell membrane formation, 322i
symbiosis, 327
test-tube life, 330
testcross, 173, 173i
tissue culture propagation, 536–537
topsoil depth, 513i
toxin-storing capacity of plants, 510–511, 511i
transpiration rate, tomato plant, 523
tree compartmentalization, 486, 486i
vernalization, 551, 551i
viral/bacterial/algal interactions, 349
water absorption in corn plant, 514
water flea exploitative competition, 824
water transport in plants, 516–517, 517i
watermelon rind, 185
watershed disturbance, 853–854, 854i
wilting tomato plants, 252
yeast genomic expression, 251
Experimental design, 12, 16
Experimental group, **12**–13, 12i, 13i, 15
Exploitative competition, **824**
Exponential growth, 801, 804–**805**, 804i, 805i, 806–807, 817–819
Extinction, 8, 153, 217, 271i, 292, 300–301, 308–**309**, 316, 370–371, 373, 373i, 388, 420, 525, 834, 837, 839, 849. *See also* Mass extinction
crisis, 463–464, 475
■ Extracellular digestion and absorption, **392**–393, 400
Extracellular fluid, 52i, 53i, 77, 77i, 82i, 87–88, 88i, 479, 481, **484**, 489, 588–589, 660i, 720, **740**, 749, 766
acid-base balance in, 747
composition, 600t, 740, 746, 752
water-solute balance in, 739–742, 740i, 746–748, 746i, 752
Extracellular matrix, 78i, 88, 403–404, 430, 562–563, 568, 570, 763
Extraembryonic membrane, 786–787, 787i, 787t, 789, 797
Extreme environment, life in, 318, 318i, 341, 341i, 349, 701, 892
Extreme halophile, **340**–341, 340i, 341i, 348
Extreme thermophile, 318, 329i, 338, **340**–341, 340i, 341i, 349
Eye, 602i, **608**–609, 608i, 616, 633i, 765

arthropod, 420, 421i, 424
cephalopod, 599, 609–610, 609i
compound, 420, 424, **608**
fruit fly, 193, 193i, 236–237, 237i
insect, 609i, 765
invertebrate, 237, 414i, 416, 418, 608–609, 608i, 641i, 765
octopus, 609, 609i, 616
photoreceptors, 195, 599, 601, 608–609, 616
simple, **608**
third, in Tuatara, 444
vertebrate, 215i, 237, 454, 599, 609–611, 610i, 611i, 617, 765
Eye, human, 452, 528, 572, 584, 586i, 588, 591, 640, 655, 682, 682t
  ■ color, 170, 180–181, 180i, 295
  components, 610–611, 610i
  ■ disorders, 191, 195, 198, 201t, 611, 614–615, 614i, 616, 629t, 765
  formation, 233, 237, 762, 765, 791, 792i
  structure, 54, 54i, 55i, 610i
  tears, 682, 682t, 688, 698
Eye color, 193, 193i, 215i
Eyeless gene, 236–237, 765
Eyespot, 241, 241i, 354, 354i, 412, 429i, 435i, 575, 897i

F

F (Fertility) plasmid, 337
F$_1$ (first-generation offspring), 171–174, 173i, 175i, 176, 176i, 178i, 182–184, 193, 193i
F$_2$ (second-generation offspring), 171–173, 172i, 173i, 174i, 175, 176i, 178, 182, 184, 193, 193i
Facial bone, human, 454–456, 458, 643i
Facilitated diffusion, **81**, 82, 747. *See also* Passive transport
Factor X, 672i
Facultative mutualism, **823**
FAD (flavin adeninedinucleotide), 46, 48t, **125**, 125i, 129–131, 129i, 130i, 137
FADH$_2$, 125, 125i, 128i, 129–131, 129i, 130i, 131i, 135i, 137
"Fail-safe" gene, 255, 257
Fall overturn, **886**–887
Fallopian tube, 776, 796
False coelom, 416, 419, 419i, 430
False feet, 70, 71
■ Familial hypercholesterolemia, 201t
■ Family (taxon), 310, 310i
■ Family planning, 814–815, 815i, 818–819
Family tree diagram. *See* Evolutionary tree, Pedigree
Farmland, 296, 884
■ Farsightedness, 611, 614, 614i
Fast food, "super-sized," 735
Fast-twitch muscle fibers, 133, 133i, 137–138
Fat (lipid), 5–6, **40**, 138, 558, 674–676, 683, 772, 777
dietary, 729i, 730, 736–737
digestion, 41, 105, 722i, 724i, 725, 727, 727i, 736
function, 37, 41, 41i, 48t, 683, 730, 749
hormones acting on, 628–630, 628i
human body, 134, 192, 734–736, 735i, 772
metabolism, 134–135, 135i, 137, 630, 630i, 635t, 729–730, 729i, 732t, 736i
saturated, 730–731, 736
storage, 121, 134, 563, 563i, 718, 718i, 729–730, 729i, 734, 795
■ triglycerides, 134, 724t, 725, 727, 727i, 729–730, 736
Fate map, 237i

Fatty acid, 33, 36i, **40**, 239, 321, 323, 323i, 455, 545, 683, 730, 863, 915
blood glucose and, 630, 729
characteristics, **40**, 40i, 48t
from fat digestion, 724–725, 727, 727i, 736
metabolism, 59i, 62–63, 134, 135i, 137–138, 651
organic compounds role and, 33, 36–37, 36i
saturated/unsaturated, 40, 40i, 41i
structure, 40–41, 40i, 48t, 49, 76
synthesis, 721i, 732t
Feather, 36i, 41–42, 121, 254, 254i, 312, 312i, 313i, 432, 443, **446**–447, 460, 749, 749i, 751, 906
characteristics, 275i, 446, 446i, 460
color/pattern, 284, 300, 317, 447, 756
Feces, 390, 413i, 424, 534, 722i, 728, 730, 736, 736i, 741, 741i, 847, 859, 860i, 861–862, 885, 894
Feedback loop
climate change/desertification/biodiversity losses, 885i
kidney/hypothalamus, 746i
ovaries/hypothalamus pituitary, 777, 779, 779i, 796
testes/hypothalamus, 774–775, 775i, 796
thermoreceptor/hypothalamus, 750
tryptophan synthesis, 98, 98i
Feedback mechanism, **484**–485, 489, 901
homeostasis and, 478–479, 746i
hormone control, 619, 623, 626, 630, 636, 695
inhibition, **98**, 98i, 104
negative, 619, 626–627, 626i, 630, 630i, 636, 645, 746i, 750, 774–775, 775i, 779i, 916
positive, 684, 779i, 794
Feedforward mechanism, 917
Felis catus, 837
■ Feminization, 199, 201t, 618–619
Femoral artery, 665i
Femoral vein, 665i
Femur (thighbone), 458i, 643i, 644i
■ Fentanyl, 595
Fermentation pathway, 124, 353, 396, 682–683, 721, 721i
alcoholic, 123, **132**, 132i, 137, 396
lactate, 123, **132**–133, 133i, 137, 399, 651, 747
nature of, 123, 126i, 132, 137
Fern, 307, 311, 311i, 314i, 371, 372i, 373i, 374i, 375, 375i, **378**–379, 378i, 379i, 381, 384i, 388, 388t, 544
Fertility, human, 197, 199, 199i, 770–771, 776, 796, 812, 814–815, 814i, 815i
  ■ interventions, 782–783, 782i, 814–815, 815i
■ Fertility drug, 770, 770i
Fertilization, 7i, **162**, 303, 303i, 316, 446, 460, **758**
in animals, 162, 162i, 167, 413i, 417i, 566, 755–**758**, 757i, 759i, 760, 768
double, 386i
frog, 758i, 759i, 760
human, 139–140, 192i, 198, 214, 567i, 770–771, 776, 776t, 781, 781i, 783, 786–788, 786i, 787i, 795t, 796–797
  ■ in vitro, 203, 214, 770, 783, 783i
plant, 162, 162i, 170i, 172, 172i, 174, 276, 374, 374i, 376i, 379i, 381, 383, 383i, 386, 386i, 388i, 512t, 525–527, 526i, 530–531, 530i, 531i, 533i, 535, 538, 823i
reptile, 444–445
role in variation of traits, 163, 166–167, 170, 284, 287

in sexual reproduction, 155–156, 166, 166i, 170, 906, 912
  ■ Fertilizer, 119, 252, 361, 369, 469, 512t, 523, 812, 827, 864, 884
  ■ nitrogen-containing, 29, 859i, 860i, 861
  ■ phosphorus cycle and, 862–863, 862i
  ■ *Festuca arundinacea*, 398
  ■ Fetal alcohol syndrome (FAS), 793, 793i
Fetal period, **786**, 790–791, 791i
Fetus, **202**–203, 202i, 353, 485, 489, 688, 783, **786**
development, 645i, 777i, 786, 789i, 791–794, 791i, 792i, 795t, 797
  ■ prenatal diagnosis of, 663, 675
  ■ Fever, 98, 595, 679, 680t, 681, 683, **685**–686, 698, **750**
  ■ Fever blister, 345
Fiber, 462, 507, 508t
connective tissue, 562–563, 562i, 568, 568i, 667, 676
plant, **497**, 506, 730
  ■ Fiber optics, 202i, 203
Fibrillin, 177
Fibrin, 672i, 685
Fibrinogen, 660i, 672, 672i
Fibroblast, 562–563, 562i
Fibrous, irregular connective tissue, **562**, 562i
Fibrous, regular connective tissue, **562**, 562i
Fibrous protein, 48t
Fibrous root system, 503, 503i, 508
Fibrous tunic, 610i
Fibula, 643i
Fick's law, **702**
Fig, 532, 848
  ■ Fight–flight response, 587, **630**–631
  ■ Filovirus, 343t
Filter feeder, 408, 409i, 422i, **434**–437, 435i, 460, 893
Filtrate, 742–743, **744**–745, 745i, 747
Filtration, blood, at nephrons, 738i, 739, 741–745, 742i, 748, 752
Fin, 312, 433, 436–**437**, 438–439, 439i, 440i, 642, 654
Finch, 266, 267i, 291, 291i, 300, 305i
Finger, 180, 198, 200i, 201t, 203, 452, 602, 602i, 643i, 645
formation, 489, 489i, 790–791, 790i, 791i
Fir, 382, 882
Fire, 94, 468, 486, 832, 878, 879i, 881–882, 885i, 897
Fire ant, 820, 820i, 821i, 835, 910
Firefly, 102, 102i, 253i, 905
Fireweed, as pioneer species, 832i
First law of thermodynamics, **92**, 94, 104–105
Fish, 5, 118, 188, 361, 423, 455, 462–463, 731, 731i, 732t, 733t, 842, 889i, 892, 900
armor-plated, 436–437, 568
bony, 269, 404i, 433, 434i, 438i, 439, 439i, 460, 464i, 740, 740i, 757
cartilaginous, 404i, 433, 434i, 437i, 438, 438i, 440i, 441, 460, 462, 888
characteristics, 102, 588, 589i, 605–606, 608, 611, 658, 749
cichlid, 306, 306i
coral reef inhabitants, 470–471, 471i
deformities, 618–619
development, 277, 761, 761i, 765, 769
evolution, 271i, 436–437, 608, 642, 810
freshwater, 740, 740i, 769
jawed, 404i, 436–439, 436i, 452, 680, 809–810, 826
jawless, 404i, 435–436, 436i, 452, 464t

phosphorus cycle and, 862–863, 862i
pollution and, 252, 849, 849i, 871
polyploid, 198, 204
population dispersal, 802i, 866
predatory, 851, 851i, 890
reproduction, 53, 154, 757
respiration, 704, 704i, 705i
speciation among, 307
water-solute balance, 740, 740i
Fish gill, 437, 439, 701, 703–705, 704i, 716, 717i, 740, 740i
Fish kill, 358, 358i, 360, 431, 842
Fishing, commercial, 468, 471, 475, 849, 893
Fitness, evolutionary, **267**
Five-toed limb, 274, 274i
Fixation, **294**, 294i, 295i
Fixed action pattern, **901**
Flabellina iodinea, 417i
Flagellate, 351, 353–354, 368–369, 403, 405–406, 430
Flagellum (flagella), **70**–72, 71i, 73i, 73t, 146, 361, 368, 393, 640
bacterial, 56i, 57, 73t, 334i, 335, 335i, 348
collar cell, 405, 405i, 430
protist, 351, 353–355, 354i, 355i, 358, 360–363, 366, 368, 784
sperm, 377, 388, 774, 796
sponge, 408–409, 409i, 430
Flame cell, 412, 412i
Flatworm, 314i, **412**, 482, 483i
characteristics, 412–413, 430, 608
digestive system, 407, 412, 412i, 720, 720i
evolution, 404i, 407, 407i, 428i
nervous system, 412, 412i, 574, 574i
parasitic, 412–413, 413i, 431
reproduction, 154, 336, 412, 412i, 756, 756i
respiration, 702, 703i
Flavavirus, 332, 343t
Flavoprotein, **549**, 555
Flax, 496i
Flea, 282, 425i, 837
Fleshy fin, 437, 439, 452
Fleshy fruit, 532–534, 533i, 533t, 538, 540
Flight, 275, 275i, 420, 446–447, 446i, 447i, 451i, 460–461
Flooding, 387, 474, 843, 859, 873, 884–885
global warming effect, 866, 885i
Floral identity gene, 235i, 241
Floral spur, 529, 529i
Florida, 304, 471, 803i, 890i
Flounder, 849i
Flour beetle, 294, 294i
Flower, 162, **384**, 480i, 493, 508, 509i, 520–521, **526**–527, 532, 881
characteristics, 384, 495–496, 495i, 529, 533t, 538, 550–552
color, 65, 108, 121, 168, 170i, 171–172, 172i, 174–175, 174i, 175i, 176i, 179, 184, 295i, 384, 385i, 528, 528i, 539i
components, 170i, 183, 183i, 235, 235i, 240, 526, 527i, 538
development, 276, 276i
examples, 170i, 171, 183, 183i, 385, 385i
formation controls, 235–236, 235i, 240–241, 498
function, 371, 384, 385i, 525–528, 528i, 533t, 535, 538
in life cycle, 526i, 538
nectar guide, 384, 528, 528i
perfect vs. imperfect, 526
structure, 384, 384i, 385i, 388t, 494, 494i, 525–527, 527i, 533t

Flowering plant, 184, 375, **384**, 464i, 491i, 493, 508t, 544, 823, 845, 845i
adaptive radiation, 271i
asexual, 525, 536–538, 536t, 537i
bloom schedule, 168, 544, 551–552
body plan, 494, 494i, 496, 542, 555
classification, 311, 311i, 314i
coevolution, pollinators, 384–385, 389, 425, 525, 528–529, 528i
development, 276, 276i
disease resistant, 168, 168i, 183
diversity, 384–385, 388t, 389
evolution, 241, 271i, 274, 276, 370, 372i, 373, 373i, 375, 375i, 381, 384–385, 384i, 388–389, 388t
evolutionary tree diagram, 385i
hormones. *See* Hormone, plant
human uses of, 381, 381i
life cycle, 504, 525–527, 526i, 538, 545, 552, 555
parasitic, 384, 830, 830i
polyploidy, 198, 204, 307
primary/secondary growth, 540
root systems, 502–503, 502i, 503i, 515i
seed dispersal, 832, 832i
sexual reproduction, 292, 525–526, 528–531, 528i–531i, 533t, 535, 541–542, 555
shoots, 525–527, 538
structure, 498–499, 498i, 499i
Flowering response, 541, 544–545, 544t, 550–551, 550i, 551i, 553, 555–556
"Flu shot," 342, 699
Fluid mosaic model, **76**, 77i, 78
Fluke, 404i, 412–413, 413i, 430, 441i, 830
Fluorescence, 54, 188, 248, 248i, 251, 251i, 253i, 257–258
Fluorescent light, 102–103, 105, 217
Fluoride, 19
Fluorine, dietary, 733t
Fluoxetine, 582
Fly, 424i, 565i, 761, 762i, 764–765, 767, 826, 829i, 849i
as pollinator, 524, 529
Flying fish, 439
Flying squirrel, 450t, 451i
Focusing, eye, 605, 611, 611i, 614–616, 614i
Folate (folic acid), 569, 732t, 792
Follicle, 446, 776t, 778–779, 778i, 779i, 780i, 781i, 796–797
Follicle-stimulating hormone (FSH), 621i, 622t, 624–625, 625i, 633, 634t, 636, 774–**775**, 775i, 777, 779, 779i, 780i, 796, 798
Follicular phase, 776t, **777**, 780i, 796
Food and Drug Administration (FDA), guidelines, 12, 638, 732t, 735
Food chain, 347, 382, **843**, **845**–847, 845i, 846i, 847i, 849, **863**
Food irradiation, 347–**349**
Food poisoning, 335i, 339, 347–349, 369, 653
Food supply, 291, 495, 822, 837
genetic engineering and, 242–243, 253, 257, 881
genetic uniformity, 253, 881
human population, 252, 812–814, 816–817, 817i, 917
pathogenic attacks on, 132, 253, 347, 394, 395i, 396–397, 397t, 400
Food web, 106i, 133, 270i, 341, 422, 427, **845**–847, 857, 860, 860i, 865, 865i, 883i
aquatic, 118–119, 119i, 121, 836, 866, 892, 897
carbon cycle and, 856, 856i
characteristics, 843, 847, 846i, 847i, 849, 849i, 862, 862i

detrital, **847**, 847i, 863, 888, 890–891
grazing, **847**, 847i, 851, 863, 891
"Foolish seedling" effect, 540, 544i
Foot, 390, 428, 429i, 461, 629t
human, 198, 200, 200i, 201t, 203, 790i
molluskan, 416–417, 416i, 417i
Foot and mouth disease, 349
Foramen magnum, **452**
Foraminiferan, 308, 308i, 314i, 350–351, 350i, 352i, **355**, 355i, 368, 856
Forebrain, 444i, 588–589, 588i, 589i, 596t, 624, 636
Forensic science, 249, 249i
Forest, 5, 341, 350, 366, 452, 473i, 513
aspen, 536, 537i
boreal, 390, 874i–875i, 881–883
burning, 856–857i, 857, 881
canopy, 875–876, 878, 880–881
Carboniferous, 370, 370i, 380, 380i
coniferous, 874i–875i, 877i, 882, 882i
deciduous, 528, 873, 874i–875i, 876, 877i, 880, 880i, 896
deforestation, 387, 389, 389i, 881, 884i
ecosystem, 849, 854, 854i, 856–857i, 857, 861–862, 862i, 888
evergreen broadleaf, 874i–875i, 880, 896
global distribution, 371, 874–875, 874i–875i
old-growth, 390, 468, 808
Paleocene, 448, 448i
regeneration, 387, 387i, 800–801
resource partitioning, 825, 825i
semi-evergreen, 873, 880, 896
temperate, 387, 399, 878, 880i, 882
tree fern, 379, 379i
tropical, 387, 387i, 432, 432i, 449, 528, 557, 873, 874i–875i, 878, 896
tropical rain forest, 874i–875i, 877i, 896
understory, 876, 881
underwater, 361, 361i, 368
Forest fire, 2, 2i, 387, 881–882, 897
Forest zone, 824i
Formaldehyde, 320, 322, 322i
Formylmethionine, 56, 340, 680
Fossil, **263**, 266, 268–**269**, 273–274, 273i, 274i, 280–281, 281i, 330i, 371, 443, 448i, 457
Fossil, example
African hominids, 455i
ammonite, 263i
Archaeopteryx, 432, 432i, 433i
Australopithecus afarensis, 454i
Bangiomorpha pubescens, 324i
Basilosaurus ankle bone, 263, 263i
bipedal hominid footprints, 455i
Cambrian, 277i
Cooksonia, 268i, 372, 372i
Dickensonia, 407i
earliest known eukaryote, 324i, 325
Ediacarans, 407i
Eocene bird, 331i
Eomaia scansoria, 309i
foraminiferan shell, 308, 308i
ginkgo, 382i
Glossopteris, 273, 273i
Grypania spiralis, 324i
Homo erectus, 458i
H. habilis, 456i
H. neanderthalensis, 458i
H. rudolfensis, 456i
H. sapiens, 459i
Ichthyolestes, 617i
ichthyosaur, 268i
Psilophyton, 372i
Spriggina, 407i
stromatolite, 324, 325i
Tawuia, 324i

trilobite, 407i
walled prokaryotic cells, 324i
Fossil fuel, 29, 29i, 32, 34, 514, 709i, 855, 859i, 869, 883
carbon cycle and, 856–857, 856i–857i, 864
coal, 377i, 380, 391, 813, 870–871, 871i, 896
combustion, 2, 2i, 119, 391, 861, 864
energy source, 869, 881, 884
oil, 2, 871, 871i, 897
pollution, 288–289, 288i, 377i, 391, 491, 870, 870i, 881
population growth and, 813, 816–817
Fossil record, 33, 57i, 168, **268**, 280, 302, 308–309, 311, 393
analysis of, 261, 268–269, 272, 278–279, 281, 308, 315, 368, 439, 443, 446i, 456
Burgess Shale, 315
early view of, 263–264, 264i, 268
interpreting, 260, 263, 268–269, 279, 281, 304, 304i, 311
nature of, 268–269, 268i, 337
radiometric dating, 270, 270i, 280–281, 432–433
transitional forms, 432, 432i
vertebrate skeletons, 642, 642i
Fossilization, **268**
in limestone beds, 432–433
Founder effect, 294–**295**, 295i, 298, 308
Fovea, 610i, 612, 613i, 615
Fox, 451i, 799i, 844, 844i, 883i
FOXP2 gene, 915
Frageria, 533i
Fragile X syndrome, 201t
Fragmentation, 409
Frameshift mutation, 226, 226i
Frankenfood, 247, 258
Franklin, Rosalind, 210–211, 216, 216i
Fraser, Claire, 330
Fraternal twin, **798**
Free nerve ending, 600t, **602**, 603i, 615
Free radical, **99**, **105**, 105i, 150, 226, 572, **733**
aging and, 766
concentration, 122
human diet and, 731, 732t, 733
Frequency, **600**, **606**
of action potentials, **600**–601, 615
sound, **606**–607, 606i, 617i
Freshwater ecosystem, 360, 364, 365i, 366, 366i, 368, 408, 473i, 855, 855i, 863, 867, 886–887, 886i, 887i, 890
Freshwater spring ecosystem, 850–851, 850i, 851i, 888
Friedreich's ataxia, 122, 122i
Frigate bird, 259
Frog, 55i, 63, 167i, 404i, 405i, 440i, 441, 460, 462i, 646, 646i, 755, 846i, 904–905
deformities, 441i, 618, 618i, 619i, 627, 627i, 848i
development, 758, 758i, 759i, 761, 761i
digestive system, 720, 720i
heart, 582, 589i
neural function, 582, 587
poisonous, 561i, 829
reproduction, 756, 762
respiration, 704–705, 705i, 707
Frontal lobe, cerebral cortex, 590–592, 590i
Fructose, 38, 38i, 727, 730, 772, 773i
Fructose-6-phosphate, 126, 126i
Fruit, 65, 108, 385–386, 389, 465i, 520–521, **533**, 552, 812, 822i, 825, 844i

categories, 532–533, 533t, 538–539
formation, 493, 532–533, 532i, 533i, 535, 535i, 538, 541, 542i, 544, 544t, 550, 555
function, 381i, 386, 524–525, 534, 534i, 538
in human nutrition, 453, 730–731, 731i, 732t, 733t
ripening, 540, 544t, 545, 545t, 555
■ seedless production, 540, 540i, 545, 545t
structure, 525, 532, 533t
Fruit fly, 167i, 178, 278, 305, 402, 425i, 677, 703, 900. *See also Drosophila melanogaster*
chromosomes, 188, 193, 193i, 200, 204
development, 231, 240, 424i, 761, 762i, 764–765, 769
experiments, 193, 193i, 236–237, 236i–237i, 240
Fruiting body, protist, 366–367, 366i, 367i
Fruitless gene, 900
Fucoxanthin, 360–361, 368
■ Fuel, clean-burning, 253i
Full count, **803**
■ Fumigant, 870, 903
Functional group, **34**, **36**–37, 36i, 41, 44i, 47, 48t, 94, 99, 105
Functional-group transfer, 37, 37i, 46, 83, 83i, **97**
Fungicide, 168, **848**
Fungus (Fungi), 132i, 368t, 390–**392**, 393–399, 835t
cell walls, 39, 39i, 66, 67, 72, 73t, 84
characteristics, 6i, **8**, 9i, 51, 106, 122, 335, 384, 392–393, 392i, 393i, 398, 514, 544, 860
classification, 8t, 9i, 14, 310–311, 311i, 314i, 316, 392–393
as decomposer, 362, 377, 391–393, 397, 400, 844, 844i, 877i
evolution, 269i, 271i, 325, 327, 329i, 351, 352i, 391, 464, 809
immune response to, 680, 682, 686–687, 692
of lichens, 390–391, 398–399, 398i
life cycle, 142, 391, 394i, 395i, 396i, 400
major groups, 391, 393, 400
origins, 329i
parasitic, 392–394, 393i, 397, 399–401, 830
pathogenic, 168, 253, 339, 346, 391, 397, 397i, 397t, 400, 401i, 497, 540, 821
reproduction, 142, 154, 392–393
saprobic, 391–394, 397
species diversity, 393, 472i
spores, 142, 269i, 391–393, 678, 694
symbionts, 374, 391, 396, 398–401, 398i, 399i, 514, 823
■ toxic, 396i, 397–401, 397t
Fur. *See also* Hair
characteristics, 749–750
color, 99i, 177, 177i, 179, 179i, 182, 184, 234, 234i, 289, 289i, 624
examples, 99i, 177, 177i, 179, 179i, 184, 451i, 461, 751i
■ *Fusarium oxysporum*, 401
Fusiform initial, 504, 505i

G

G1, interphase, 655
G1 Interval, 144, 144i, 153
G2 Interval, 144–145, 144i
GAATTC, 244
Galactose, 38, 190, 191i, 239i, 727
Galactose–1–phosphate, 191, 191i
■ Galactosemia, 190–191, 191i, 201t
Galápagos Islands, 259, 264i, 265i, 304, 471, 866

animals, 266, 267i, 291, 438i, 444, 445i
tomato plant, 296, 296i
Galelei, Galileo, 14, 50
Gallbladder, 635t, 720, 720i, 722i, 723, 725, 736, 736t
■ Gallstone, 734
Gamete, 41, 164, 166–167, 227, 306, 481, 808–809
plant, 169, 171, 172i, 173, 174i, 175
protist, 362, 362i, 363i, 364i, 365i
Gamete formation, 174, 214, 394i, **758**
animals, 162, 162i, 163i, 632, 636, 755–758, 758i, 911
human, 157, 163, 163i, 192i, 198, 770–772, 774i, 787, 796
meiosis and, 142–143, 152, 158i, 160–162, 162i, 165i, 166, 169, 171, 172i, 173, 174i, 175, 178, 178i, 184, 192i, 193, 194i, 196, 199, 284, 286–287, 756
plant, 156i, 162, 162i, 371, 374–375, 374i, 376i, 377, 388t, 525–527, 526i, 530, 541
preventing, 303, 316
sex hormones, 632, 636
sexual reproduction and, 142–143, 155–156, 158i, 160, 166–167, 166i, 624, 757
Gamete mortality, **303**, 303i, 316, 770
Gametocyte, sporozoan, 359, 359i
Gametophyte, **162**, 162i, 167, **361**, **374**, 378, **526**
bryophyte, 376i, 377, 388
female, 375, 377i, 383, 383i, 386i, 388, 525–528, 526i, 530–531, 531i, 538
flowering plant, 381, 388, 525–**526**, 526i, 527, 530, 536
in life cycles, 374, 374i
male, 375, 377i, 381, 383i, 386i, 388, 525–527, 526i, 530i, 531, 538
in plant evolution, 374–375
seedless vascular plants, 378–379, 379i
Gamma amino butyric acid (GABA), 582–583, 595, 653
Gamma-glutamyl carboxylase (GGC), 402
Gamma ray, 108, 108i, 227i
Ganglion, **412**, 412i, 414–416, **574**–**575**, 574i, 587i, 612–613, 613i, 615
in *Herpes simplex* infection, 345
human, **586**, 586i
Gangrene, 397
Gap gene, 237i
Gap junction, **67**, 67i, 78i, 144, 488, **561**, 561i, 564i, 570, 667, 667i, 786i
Garden pea, 167i, 185, 200, 252, 338
chromosome number, 171i
Mendel's experiments, 170–172, 170i, 172i, 174i–175i, 175, 182, 184, 193, 284, 544
Garter snake, 845, 845i, 846i, 900–901, 900i
Gas, natural, 865, 871
Gas exchange, 438, 489, 657, 670
across skin, 441–442, 478–479
double flow circuit, 659, 659i, 675
factors influencing, 701–702, 710, 712
gills, 437, 701, 703–704, 703i, 704i, 716
invertebrate, 414, 417i, 701, 703, 703i
lungs, 437, 481–483, 481i
plant adaptations to, 493, 496, 500–501, 508, 511, 519, 522
respiratory surface, 701–702, 707, 710–711, 710i, 711i, 716
vertebrate, 433, 566, 701, 704–716, 704i, 705i

■ Gastric bypass surgery, **718**, 719i
■ Gastric cancer, 682
Gastric fluid, 28, 28i, 67, 99, 682, 724–725, 736–737, 736t
ingested pathogens, 682, 682t, 698, 722i, 724, 736t
Gastric gland, 416, 416i
Gastric inhibitory peptide (GIP), 725
Gastrin, 635t, 724–725, 729
■ Gastritis, 335i
Gastrocnemius, 647i
Gastrodermis, 410i, 411, 430
■ Gastroenteritis, 343t, 346t
Gastrointestinal tract, 723. *See also* Gut
Gastropod, 416, 416i, 430, 703i
Gastrula, **758**, 758i, 762, 762i, 764, 769
Gastrulation, **758**, 759i, 760, 771–788, 788i, 797
stage, in life cycle, 755, 758, 758i, 759i, 762, 762i, 764, 764i, 768
Gated membrane protein, 79i, 83, 88, 577–580, 577i, 578i, 579i, 580i, 582, 584, 584i
Gause, G., 824
Gazania, hybrid Fiesta Red, 539i
Gazelle, 879i, 885
Gel electrophoresis, **248**–249, 248i, 257, 278
Gemma (gemmae), 377i
Gemmule, 409, 409i
Gender determination, 187–188
Gene, **44**, **156**, **171**, 175, **182**, 237i, 254, 284, 489
chromosomal location, 168–169, 174, 182
for conserved trait, 168–169, 278, 278i, 280
master, 193, 235–237, 237i, 240, 276, 404, 551, 755, **765**
maternal/paternal, 155–156, 166
pair, 169, 171, 171i, 172i, 173–177, 180, 182, 185
Gene amplification, 243
Gene control, eukaryotic, 164, 230, **231**, 235, 238t, 240–241, 368t
in animal development, 206, 232–233, 232i–233i, 235, 240, 241, 277
cancer and, 150–151, 150i, 230–231
checkpoint mechanisms, 150, 150i, 152, 164
mechanisms, 150, 152, 232, 232i, 234, 240, 243
in plant development, 174, 235–236, 235i, 240–241, 253i, 540, 540i, 555
points of, 232–233, 233i, 240
signaling mechanisms, 150, 231, 232, 540, 765
Gene control, prokaryotic, 238–241, 238t, 239i, 368t
Gene duplication, 633
Gene expression, 215, **232**, 245, 488
cell differentiation and, 367
in continuous variation, 155–156, 166
control of, 231–233, 233i, 235i, 236, 240, 695
dominance relations in, 169, 182
environment and, 155, 169, 179–182, 179i, 236, 902
factors influencing, 176–177, 187, 189i
hormones and, 620, 622–623
in human development, 190, 192, 786
for language, 915
in mosaic tissue, 199, 201t, 205, 234, 234i
patterns, 251, 251i, 257
in plant development, 235i, 240, 253, 302, 488i, 542, 546, 549, 555

selective. *See* Selective gene expression
silent, 251, 255, 760
transposons and, 277
Gene flow, **283**, 285–286, 294–**295**, 298, 298t, 301–**302**
barriers to, 303–305, 316
effects, 308, 316t
Gene isolation, 246, 252, 257
Gene library, **246**–247, 257
Gene linkage, 178, 178i, 182
Gene locus, **171**–172, 171i, 176–178, 177i, 178i, **182**, 185, 193, 193i, 232
alleles at, 283, 285–286, 294, 298
Gene map, of human X chromosome, 195
Gene map, of rose chromosome, 168–169
Gene mutation, 122, 122i, 156, 222, **226**–**227**, 226i, 227i, **228**–229, 242, 324, 622, 695i, 765–766, 769, 915
allele frequency, 284–285
cancer and, 230–231
checkpoint, 150–152
Drosophila, 236–237, 236i, 237i, 240–241
effects on development, 454–455
evolutionary, 197, 204, 278, 280
flower formation, 235, 235i, 241
■ neurobiological disorder (NBD), 186
for variation in traits, 179–180
Gene pool, 284–285, 289, 295, 298, 302–303, 458, 460, 802
Gene sequence, 188, 189i, 232, 238, 240, 251, 277, 306, 349, 366, 461, 622
African emergence model and, 458–459
for antigen receptor, 689, 698
automated, 248, 248i, 250–251
expressed sequence tags for, 680t
of human genome, 250–251
prokaryotic, 238
shared, 251
Gene splicing, 243–244, 244i, 257, 689
■ Gene therapy, 103, 243, **251**
■ bioethics of, 203, 256
■ bubble boys, 256
■ early applications, 695i
■ human, **251**, 257
■ leukemia, 256, 662
■ somatic cell nuclear transfer (SCNT), 215
Gene transcription. *See* Transcription
■ Gene transfer, 242, 279
■ bacterial factories and, 252, 257
■ for bioluminescence, 102–103, 103i, 105, 248, 248i, 251, 251i, 253i, 257–258
■ crop plants, 170i, 252, 257–258
early in life history, 366
■ eugenic engineering, 256
■ medical applications, 252, 254
■ pharmaceuticals and, 252, 254, 254i, 257
■ plants, 169, 252, 253i
■ safety issues, 255
Genetic abnormality, 122, 122i, 188, 190–191, 196, 196i, 198–**200**, **201**, 201t, 204
Genetic analysis, 187, 193
human, 193, 194i, 200–201
Genetic code, 116, 179, 183, 219–220, **222**, 222i, 227i, 230, 233, 234i, 236, 239i, 250, 258, 280–281, 327, 645, 689
for protein, 220–221, 220i–221i, 226, 228, 245, 250, 330
■ Genetic counseling, 203–204
Genetic disconnect, 316t

- Genetic disorder, 74, 89, 177i, 183, **200**, 201t, 204, 677, 694–695, 695i. *See also* specific types
- diagnosing/treating, 187–188, 188i, 189i, 200–**201**, 202–204, 202i, 629
- genomics potential for, 251

inheritance patterns for, 44, 47, 72–73, 89, 149, 190–191, 190i, 194–196, 194i, 195i, 196i, 199i, 200, 204–205, 213, 217, 217i, 235, 241, 287, 293, 299, 622
- muscles and, 652–653, 655, 655i
- nature of, 44, 177, 183, 185, 571
- phenotypic treatment, 202, 204
- research into, 256–258
- screening/counseling, 202–204, 258

Genetic divergence, 251, 253, **302**, 316t, 464

adaptive radiation. *See* Adaptive radiation

allopatric speciation, 304–305, 304i, 305i, 316

animal lineages, 428

biochemical evidence of, 278–279, 633

chimpanzee/human lineage, 276i, 277–278, 915

eukaryotic lineages, 271i, 278, 328i, 330

in evolutionary tree diagrams, 279i, 308, 308i, 309, 309i, 316, 459i

extent of, variation in, 633

gradual vs. abrupt, 308

origin of species and, 324–325, 328i

panda/bear lineages, 279

plant lineages, 276, 276i, 278, 371–372

primate lineages, 276–278, 276i, 278i

prokaryotic lineages, 279, 337

reproductive isolating mechanism, 302–305, 305i, 308, 316

source of morphological divergence, 274–275, 274i, 280

time of, molecular time clock, 279–281

Genetic drift, 290, **294–295**, 839

allele frequencies, 283, 294, 294i, 295i

in diverging populations, 283, 285, 298, 298t, 302, 308, 316, 316t

effect, 294–295, 298

nature of, 283, 294
- Genetic engineering, **252**, **257**
- ADA gene, 695i
- applications, 252–255, 253i, 254i, 257
- bacteria, 252, 338, 342
- crop plants, 242–243, 242i, 252–253, 253i, 289, 881
- Frankenfood and, 242–243, 258
- of immunotoxins, 693
- knockout individuals, 236
- mammals, 206, 254, 254i
- plants, 169, 510–511, 510i, 511i
- safety issues, 255, 257, 401
- transgenic pigs, 699, 699i, 748
- yeast cells, 251, 251i, 396

Genetic equilibrium, 285–287, **298**

Genetic modification (GM), 242–243, 246, 251–253, 253i, 257–258

Genetic persistence, 316t

Genetic predisposition, 673, 694, 748

for weight control, 735–737, 735i

Genetic recombination, 156, 164, 278

crossing over, 160–161, 160i, 178, 178i, 182

virus/bacterium, 344–345, 680t

Genetic Savings and Clones, 215, 215i

Genetic uniformity, dangers of, 253, 283, 769

Genetics, modern, 170i, 171, 171i, 175
- Genital herpes, 343t, 784, 784t

Genital organ, 586i, 776, 777i, 784–785, 792i, 912
- Genital wart, 153, 784, 784i

Genome, 226, **246**, 252, 256, 536

animal, 284, 409, 764

automated DNA sequencing of, 250–251, 257

Caenorhabditis elegans, 419

chimpanzee vs. human, 241, 277, 277i

Ciona savignyi, 461, 461i

Drosophila, 236

Entamoeba histolytica, 366

human, 243, 249–251, 250i, 256–258, 278, 461

Nanoarchaeum equitans, 341

Trichoplax adhaerens, 409i

yeast, 251, 251i

Genomic library, 246
- Genomics, 243, 249, **251**, 257

Genotype, **171**, 173, 173i, 179, **182**, 184, 203, 798

variations in, 175–176, 175i, 176i, 178i, 183–185, 286, 289

Genus (genera), **8**, 310, 310i

Geographic dispersal, 433, **835**, 898

Geographic isolation, 304–306, 316

Geologic evolution. *See* Evolution, geologic

Geologic time, 118, 260, **270**–271, 271i, 280, 315, 330, 463

Geomyidae, 450t

Geospiza, 267i

Germ cell, **142**, 149, 157, 160, 162, 163i, 164i, 166i, 192i, 199, 227, 566, 766, 774i, 787, 787t, 797

Germ layer, 403–**404**, 407i, 758, 768
- German measles, 792

Germination, 339, **542**, 879i

endospores, 653

pollen grain, 303, 527, 530, 530i, 538

protistan spore, 360i, 365–367, 365i

seed, plant, 375, 381, 383i, 465i, 495, 498, 502, 504, 531–532, 534, 538, 541–542, 543i, 544–546, 544t, 546i, 550i, 553, 555–556, 839i, 890

spore, 374, 376i, 379, 393, 394i, 395, 395i, 396i, 397, 400–401

Gestational period, human, 786

Gey, George, 140

Gey, Margaret, 140

Ggta1 gene, 255

Ghrelin, **718**, 718i, 722i, 730, 736

Giant anteater, 449, 449i, 450t

Giant horsetail, 380, 380i

Giant kelp, 361, 361i, 368

Giant saguaro, 528i, 535, 535i

Giant velvet worm, 307i

Giardia, 164, 352i, 353, 353i, 368
- Giardiasis, 353

Gibberella fujikuroi, 540

Gibberellin, 540, 540i, **544–547**, 544i, 544t, 545i, 546i, 550, 552–553, 555–556

Gibbon, 197, 197i, 204, 452, 461i
- Gigantism, 625, 625i

Gill, **437**, 701, **703–704**, 703i, 704i, 716–717

amphibian, 440–441, 627

arthropod, 420

fish, 437, 439, 701, 703–705, 704i, 716, 717i, 740, 740i

function, 658–659

lungs vs., 433, 441, 658

molluscan, 416–418, 416i, 418i

mushroom, 391, 395, 395i, 400

vertebrate, 658–659, 704–705, 704i

Gill slit, 433–**434**, 434i, 435–436, 435i, 436i, 438, 460, 704

Gingerich, Philip, 281

Gingiva, 723i

Ginkgo, 311, 311i, 314i, 370, 372i, 373i, 375, 375i, **382–383**, 382i, 384i, 388t, 389

Giraffe, 563i, 597, 879i, 885

"Giraffe rhinoceros," 448i, 449

Girdling, **509**

Gizzard, 312, 312i, 313i, 415i, 465i, 720i, **721**

Glaciation (ice age), 269, 271i, 304, 865, 882

global warming and, 842, 853, 853i, 858–859, 859i

Glacier, 272–273, 318, 369, 832, 832i

life in, 334, 336

Glacier Bay, Alaska, 832i
- Glacier melting, 2, 269, 373, 390

Gland, 4i, 90, 234, 234i, 484, 559, 560i, **561**, 565, 569–570, 574, 574i, 582, 596, 619

neural signals, 580–581, 581i, 586–587

Gland cell, 232, 560–561, 570, 620, 772

cnidarian, 411, 430

Trichoplax, 409, 409i

Glandular epithelium, 560–561, 561i, 620, 621i, 683i, 698, 724–725, 735–736
- Glaucoma, **615**

Glaucophyte, 327, 327i

Gleditsia, 500i

Gleebruk village, Indonesia, 93i

Glia, **583**, 762i, 763

Global broiling hypothesis, **443**
- Global warming, 2, 300, 469, 842–843, 853, 853i, 857–**859**, 858i, 859i, 861, 869, 883, 897

autotrophs and, 107, 119
- climate change and, 2, 881
- greenhouse gases and, 26i, 32
- ocean currents and, 872

seawater, 470, 475

Global water cycle, 387, 389

Globin, 44, 44i, 197, 662, 702

Globular protein, 48t

Globulin, 660i

Glomerular capillary, **743–744**, 743i, 744i, 748, 752

Glomerular filtration, 739, 743–**744**, 744i, 745, 748, 752

Glossopteris, 273, 273i

Glottis, **704–705**, 705i, **707**, 707i, 717

Glucagon, 134, 621i, 622, 623i, 628–629, 628i, 634, 635t, 636

Glucan, 680

Glucocorticoid, 635t
- Glucometer, 629i

Glucose, 21, 48t, 124, 190, 604, 629

absorption from gut, 724t, 725, 727

activation, 622, 623i, 635t, 636

alcoholic fermentation, 132–133

blood transport, 660, 660i, 664, 729–730

bonding patterns, 38i, 39i

energy content, 94–95, 94i

in filtrate, 744–745, 745i

function, 729–730

how animals use, 134

how bacteria use, 238–239, 239i, 241, 806

insulin and, 144, 621i, 622, 628, 628i

membrane crossing, 79i, 82, 82i, 84, 84i, 88, 589

metabolism, 621i, 634t, 651, 651i

molecular structure, 34, 38, 38i

phosphorylated, 95i, 115, 115i, 120, 120i, 134

storage, 39, 39i, 144–145, 622, 628, 628i

uptake by cells, 144–145, 622, 628–630, 628i, 635t, 636, 727

Glucose formation, 104, 107

by photosynthesis, 94–95, 100, 100i, 107, 111, 115, 115i, 118i, 120

Glucose metabolism, 48t, 95–96, 95i, 101, 722i, 762

Giraffe, — aerobic respiration, 100i, 118i, 122–126, 125i, 126i–127i, 129, 129i, 131–132, 131i, 134, 135i, 137

diet and, 719, 730, 732t

Glucose–1–phosphate, 190, 191i

Glucose–6–phosphate, 127i, 134, 135i, 191i

Glucose–6–1–phosphate, 115i

Glucose transporter, 82, 82i, 88, 727

GluT1, 79i

Glutamate, 44, 45i, 222, 222i, 225i, 226i, 228i, 582, 604

Glutamine, 222i, 225i, 228i

Gluteus maximus, 647i

Glyceride, 48t, 683

Glycerol, 38, 40–41, 40i, 48t, 76, 134, 135i, 137, 729

Glycine, 96, 222, 225i, 226i, 228i, 653

Glycocalyx, **334**, 348

Glycogen, 38–39, 39i, 48t, 134, 135i, 190, 565, 729, 732t

glucose and, 622, 623i, 628, 628i, 630, 635t, 729

muscle cells, 651–652, 651i

Glycolipid, 76, 79i, 88, 176, 680

Glycolysis, **124**, 134, 190, 191i, 233, 239, 565, 651, 651i, 653–655

in aerobic respiration, 101, 123–126, 125i, 126i–127i, 128i, 129, 135i, 137

energy-releasing/requiring steps, 126, 126i, 127i, 130, 132i, 133i

fermentation and, 123, 124i, 132–133, 132i, 137

Glycophorin, 77

Glycoprotein, 43, 79i, 255, 682–683, 696, 779

viral coat, 342, 343i, 348

Glycosylase, 213

Glycyrrhiza, 753

Glyocalyx, **334**, 348

Glyphosate, 848i

Gnetophyte, 311, 311i, 314i, 372i, 375, 375i, **382–383**, 382i, 388t, 389, 530

GnRH, 774–**775**, 775i, 778, 779i, 780i, 796

Goat, 254, 254i, 884

Goblet cell, 683i
- Goiter, **626–627**, 733t

simple, **626**, 627i
- toxic, **626**

Golden alga, 355, 355i, **360–361**, 360i, 368
- Golden rice, 242, 242i, 252

Golgi body, 58, 62–**63**, 72, 74

function, 59, 63, 63i, 72, 73t, 86i, 87, 87i

plant cell division, 148i, 149, 152

protist, 352–353, 355i

Gonad, 411–412, 419i, 429i, 435i, 444i, 620, **632**, 635t, 915

hormone control, 632

human female, 192, 192i, 621i, 632, 635t, 636, 770–771, 776, 776i, 776t, 796

human male, 192, 192i, 621i, 632, 635t, 636, 770–773, 772i, 796

Gondwana, **273**, 273i, 372, 373i
- Gonorrhea, 784–785, 784i, 785i

Gonyaulax, 352i, 358

Goodall, Jane, 912

Goose, 124i, 138, 589i, 803, 902

Goose barnacle, 422i

Gorgonia, 891i

Gorilla, 452, 453i, 468, 469i, 915

chromosome, 145, 197, 197i, 204

Graded potential, **578**, 580i, 581

Gradient, **80**, 84, 88, 404, 406

chemical, 763, 765, 768

dissolved gases, 867, 886–887, 887i, 890, 896

light availability, 867, 886–887, 886i, 887i, 890, 896

salinity, 890, 895–896
temperature, 867, 869, 886–887, 886i, 887i, 890, 896
Gradual model of speciation, **308**
Grafting, plant, 536
Grain, 532, 730–731, 732t, 733t, 812
Gram-negative species, **334**, 335i, 338, 338i
Gram-positive species, 314i, **334**, 335i, **338**, 338i, 339, 348
■ Gram staining, **334**, 335i
Granum (grana), 65
Grape, 362, 533, 540, 540i, 545t
Grapevine, 536
Grass, 58i, 116i, 241, 462–463, 474, 501, 503, 503i, 509, 812, 825, 825i, 846i, 847, 883
pollen, 527, 527i
Grasshopper, 424i, 574i, 575, 658i, 703, 703i, 846i, 904
Grasshopper mouse, 829, 829i
Grassland, 271i, 297, 304i, 305, 341, 387, 449, 473i, 513, 528, 831, 831i, 837, 847, **878**
characteristics, 876, 876i, 878, 879i
distribution, 873–875, 874i–875i, 896
Gravel, in soil, 876, 877i
■ Grave's disorder, 626, 695
Gravitropism, **548**, 548i, 555
Gravity, force of, 599, 605, 615
plant response to, 541–542, 548, 548i, 555
Gray crescent, 759i, **760**, 760i, 769
Gray matter, 587, 587i, 590–591
Grazing animal, 449, 474, 475i, 653, 878, 884, 884i
Grazing food web, **847**, 847i, 851, 863, 891
Great Barrier Reef, Australia, 470, 470i, 608i, 891i
Great Dane, 299, 299i
The Great Dying, 33
Great Lakes, 341, 436i
Great Plains, 878, 884
Great Salt Lake, 341, 341i
Green alga, 329i, 351, 352i, 354, 358, 364–365, 364i, 365i, 369, 372–373, 372i, 374i, 388, 398, 400, 842, 849i, 850, 850i, 855, 861, 863, 863i
aquarium strain, 836, 836i
characteristics, 364, 364i
ecosystem and, 886, 887i
pigments, 121, 121i
■ Green Belt Movement, 389
Green nonsulfur bacteria, 314i, 338i
■ Green Revolution, 258, **884**
Green River formation, 331
Green sulfur bacteria, 314i, 338i
Greenhouse, 549, 551i, 889, 889i
Greenhouse effect, 387, 857, **858**–859, 858i, 859i, 864
Greenhouse gas, 26i, 32, 843, **858**–859, 858i, 864
Griffith, Frederick, 208, 208i
Grizzly bear, 469i, 907i
Gross primary production, **850**
Groucho gene, 236
Ground substance, 562i
Ground tissue, plant, 493, 526
body plan, 493–497, 494i, 495i, 508
characteristics, 500–501, 501i, 508
from root, 502–503, 503i
of stems, 493, 498–499, 498i, 499i
Groundwater, **855**, 855i
■ Groundwater, contamination, 510, 618, 855, 855i
Groundwater overdraft, 855, 855i
Growth, 7, 284, 318, 319i, **336**, **480**–481, 489, **542**
bacterial, 238, 238i
cell division in. *See* Cell division
nature of, 68, 238t

Growth, animal, 9, 68, 118, 276i, 277, 558, 631, 733t
gene control mechanisms, 232i, 240
hormones and, 619–620, 621i, 622, 625i, 634t, 635t
human embryo, 191, 198, 771, 792–793, 792i, 797
tissue specialization during, 755, 758, 758i, 759i, 763, 768, 771
Growth, plant, 116, 118, 401, **542**
cell elongation, 544–545, 544t, 546i, 547–550, 548i, 553, 555
environment and, 116–117, 116i, 375, 381, 449, 540, 542, 548–553, 548i, 549i, 550i, 551i
hormones in. *See* Hormone, plant
inhibitors, 544–545, 544t, 548–550, 548i, 549i, 555
nature of, 65–67, 66i
patterns, 363, 363i, 364i, 374, 398–399, 398i, 399i, 540–542, 540i, 544, 548–550, 555
primary, 493, 540, 547i, 555–556
secondary, 540, 556
tropisms, 548–549, 548i, 549i, 553, 555
Growth factor, **150**, **583**, 693
Growth hormone (GH), 622t, 624, 625i, 634t, 636. *See also* Somatotropin, human
■ genetically engineered, 252, 254, 254i
plant, 545–546, 555
Growth layer, 507, 507i, 509, 509i
Growth ring, **507**, 507i, 509, 509i
Guanine (G), 46, 46i, 219–221, 220i, 223, 228, 248, 248i
DNA base pairing rule, 207, 210–212, 210i, 211i, 212i,213i, 216
Guano, 862, 862i
Guar (cloned), 206
Guard cell, 497, 508, **518**–519, 519i, 522
Guard hair, 751i
Guillemin, Roger, 625
Guinea pig, 184, 241, 607
■ Guinea worm, 419
Gular sac, 259
Gulf of Aqaba, 5i, 474, 475i
Gulf of Mexico, 889–890, 889i
Gulf of Panama, reef biodiversity, 471
Gulf Stream, 872, 872i
Gull, 847, 849i, 909
Gullet, 356, 356i
Gum (gingival), 629t, 683, 699, 723i, 881
Gurdon, John, 762
Gut, 134, 238–239, **406**–407, 411–414, 412i, 416, 420, 429i, 430, 434, 587, 602, 645, 653, 682, 682i, **723**, 724i, 729, 758, 762, 841
calcium absorption, 645
dodo, 465i
sea anemone, 640, 640i
specie examples, 520i, 574, 822i
Gut cavity, 406i, 411, 658i, 720–721, 720i, 759i
Gymnast, 600i, 601
Gymnodinium, 352i, 358
Gymnophilus, 392i
Gymnosperm, 375, **382**, 464i, 504, 544
evolution, 271i, 370–371, 374i, 375i, 381, 384i, 388–389, 388t
examples, 382, 382i
Gypania spiralis, 324i

🅷
H band, 648i
Habitat, 56–57, 57i, 468, 468i, 474, **483**, 500, 505, 511, 513i, **802**, 808, **822**, 824i, **840**, 847, 850
anaerobic, 107, 118, 353
aquatic, 115, 167, 480, 842i

characteristics, 56, 133, 486, 703, 705, 705i, 716, 802, 811, 822, 835, 835t, 839
colonization, 832, 835
elevation, 179, 179i
hot spot, 118, 472
■ human, 466–467, 466i, 467i, 812
sandy shore, 486, 487i
species relationships and, 262–263, 262i, 266, 269
■ Habitat fragmentation, 463, **468**, **475**
Habitat island, 468–469, **475**
Habitat loss, 294, 390, 463, 466–**468**, 469, **475**, 487
Habitats for Humanity, 473
Habropoda laboriosa, 524
Hadal zone, ocean, 892i
Haemophilia, 338i
Haemophilus influenzae, 244, 694i
Hagar Qim temple, 350, 350i, 351i
Hagfish, 314i, 404i, 428i, 434i, 435, 435i, 437i
Hair, 42–43, 47, 48t, 69, 170, 234, 568, 569i, 751i, 791
■ color, 284
follicle, 249, 568i, 602, 603i, 683
growth, 568, 638
mammalian trait, 192, 312, 312i, 313i, 448–450, 448i
structure, 568i, 569i, 751i
■ thinning/loss, 199, 568–569, 638, 732t
Hair cell, 600t, 605, **607**, 607i, 615
Hairston, N., 825
Half-life, **270**, 270i, 280
■ Hallucinogen, 32, 401i, 595
Halobacterium, 109, 340i
Halophile, 329i
Hamilton, William, 911
Hammer, ear, 606, 606i
Hamstring, 647i
Hand, 602i, 629, 629t
bones, 274, 274i, 452
evolution, 452–453, 456, 460
formation, 488–489, 489i, 763
human, 790i
opposable movement by, 274, 452–453
prehensile movement, 452–453
pressure receptors in, 601i, 602
tetanus, 653
Hangingfly, 906, 906i
■ Hantavirus, 343t
Haploid number (*n*), chromosome, **157**, 159i, 162, 162i, 164i, 166, 166i, 246
fungal, 394–395, 394i, 395i, 396i
Haploid dominance, 374, 388, 388t
Hardwood, **507**, 507i, 539
Hardy, Godfrey, 286–287
Hardy–Weinberg equilibrium equation (rule), 286–287, 286i, 298
Hare, 826–827, 827i
Harpobittacus apicalis, 906
Hartshorn, Gary, 475
Harvesting, 370, 462, 473, 812, 817
Harvesting/shipping fruit, 545, 545t
Hatchling, 820, 831, 831i, 845
Hauhau tree, 462–463
Hawaiian Archipelago, 272i, 300, 300i, 304–305, 305i, 470i, 471
Hawaiian honeycreeper, 267i, 300–301, 300i, 301i, 305, 305i, 308
Hawkmoth, 528–529, 529i, 538
■ Hay fever, 527, **695**
Hayes, Tyrone, 618, 618i
Hayflick, Leonard, 766
Hb^A allele, 293
Hb^S allele, 293
HbS. *See* Hemoglobin, HbS
HDL. *See* High-density lipoprotein
Head, animal, 236, 236i, **406**, 424, 435, 574i, 575

invertebrate, 412i, 415i, 416, 416i, 430
Head, human, 790, 790i
Health care system, population growth and, 812–814, 813i, 816–817
Hearing, sense of, 343t, 440, 591, 593i, 604, 606–607, 615
■ Hearing loss, 607, 607i
Heart, 19, 78i, 92, 131, 437, 485, 558–559, 560i, 563, **658**, 675, 742
■ abnormalities, 45i, 122, 122i, 177, 177i, 195, 198, 201t, 673, 747, 793
accessory (booster), 418, 418i
ACh and, 582
amphibian, 659, 659i
chambers, 440, 445–446, 658–659, 659i, 666–667, 666i, 667i, 676
development, 236, 656, 663i, 790i, 792i
diet and, 730–731
endocrine roles, 620, 621i, 635t
fish, 658–659, 659i
function, 657–659, 664, 665i, 675–677
human, 572, 582, 586i, 657, 700
invertebrate, 405, 414, 415i, 416, 416i, 420–421, 658i
mammal, 659, 659i
muscle tissue. *See* Cardiac muscle
nerves servicing, 667, 676
pressure generated by, 744–745
shocks, 656–657, 656i
structure, 657, 664, 666, 666i, 673, 675–676
vertebrate, 444i, 445, 582, 642, 643i, 659, 659i
■ Heart attack (failure), 49, 191, 254, 558, 565, 594, 603, 629t, 656, 671–673, 676, 699–700, 733t, 737
Heart cell. *See* Cardiac muscle cell
■ Heart disease, 49, 290, 718, 730–731, 734, 734i
Heartbeat, 478, 586i, 587, 592, 656–657, 668–669, 676, 711, 714, 791
abnormal, 656–657, 673, 673i
■ Heartburn, 629t
Heartwood, 506–507, 507i
Heat (estrous), 776
Heat energy, 91, **92**–94, 101, 101i, 109, 112, 320–321, 734, 846, 847i, 889i
absorbed, environmental, 739, 749
color sensitivity, 99i
conservation of, 446–447, 458i
dispersed, 80, 92–94, 104
dissipating metabolic, 478, 478i, 568, 660
global climate and, 867–868, 868i, 873, 896
at hydrothermal vents, 324
leaf folding response, 487, 487i
loss, environmental, 118, 739, 749, 750t, 753, 872, 894
mammalian body, 567i, 739, 749–750, 750t
metabolic, 6, 6i
Heat index, 478–479
Heat loss-gain balance, 749, 752
Heat-shock protein, 685
■ Heat stress, 479, 750–751, 750i, 750t
■ Heat stroke, **478**–479, 842
■ Heat wave, 2, 490, 842
Heavy metal, 252, 849, 870, 889
Height, variation in, 174–175, 174i, 175i, 180–181, 180i, 181i, 184
■ Heimlich maneuver, **717**, 717i
HeLa cells, 140, 140i, 151, 343
Helianthus, 553i
Helical virus, 342i
Helicase, **212**–213, 212t, 216, 766
Helicobacter, 335i, 338i, 737
Heliconius, 12–13, 13i
Helium, 20, 22, 23i, 320

van Helmont, Jan Baptista, 121
Helper T lymphocyte (T cell), 687i, **690**–691, 691i, 692i, 693, 696–698, 698t
Hematopoietic growth factor, 693
Heme group, 35, 35i, **44**, 44i, 97i, 99, 109i, 322i, 571, **708**, 709i, 716
Hemerythrin, 702
Hemlock tree, 399i, 832i
■ Hemochromatosis, 287
■ Hemocyanin, 702
■ Hemodialysis, **748**
Hemoglobin, 226i, 359, 569, 571, 661–663, 702, 708–709, 709i, 714–716, 714i, 741, 793
■ blue form, 299
camel/llama, 297, 297i
dietary minerals and, 733, 733t
evolution of, 197, 322i
Hb^A, 185
Hb^S, 185
■ HbS, 44, 45i
mutation, 44–45, 293
oxygen-binding capacity, 297, 297i, 660–661
oxygen-transporting function of, 35, 35i, 44–45, 48t, 677
structure, 35, 35i, 43–45, 47
■ synthesis, 233, 252
Hemolymph, 677
■ Hemolytic anemia, **662**–663
■ Hemophilia, 193–**194**, 201t, 203
■ Hemophilia A, **194**, 194i, 205
■ Hemophilia B, 205
■ Hemorrhage, 343t, 397, 732t
■ Hemorrhagic anemia, **662**
■ Hemorrhoid, **671**
■ Hemorrhagic fever, 343t, 346
Hemostasis, **672**, 672i, 676
Henbane, humans and, 389
Henslow, John, 265
■ Hepadnavirus, 343t
■ Hepatic portal vein, 665i
■ Hepatitis
■ A virus, 343t, 694i
■ B virus, 343t, 346t, 594, 694, 694i
■ C virus, 594
HER2 surface protein, 693
Herbaceous plant, 385, 474, 877i
■ Herbicide, 252, 253i, 258, 370, 545, 545t, 618, 618i, 812, **848**, 848i
Herbivore, 9, 273i, 364, 398, 400, 442, 444, 448–449, 461, 800–801, 800i, 828, 837–838, **844**–845, 845i, 846i, 847, 847i, 851, 851i, 852i, 862–863, 879i, 884–885, 903
■ Herceptin, 693
Heritable trait, 10, 14, 155–156, 161, 207, 230, 642, 828
evolution of, 261, 266–267
■ Hermaphrodite, 412–413, 417i, 419, 423, 618
■ Herniated disk, 643
■ Heroin, 582, 595
■ Herpes infection, 342
■ Herpes virus, 343i, 343t, 345
■ *Herpes simplex*, 615
■ *H. simplex* Type 1, 343t, 345
■ *H. simplex* Type 2, 343t, 784
Hershey, Alfred, 208
Hesperidium, 533t
Heteractis magnifica, 823, 823i
Heterocephalus glaber, 910–911
Heterocyst, 338, 339i
Heterospory, **375**, 388
Heterotherm, **749**–750, 750i
Heterotroph, **106**, 124, 329i, 392–393, 400, 482, 844, 844i, 851
animals as, 403–405, 430
dependence on autotrophs, 106, 118, 119i, 121, 326–327
protist, 353–356, 358, 368–369

Heterozygous condition, **171**, 172i, 173–174, 175i, 176, 176i, **182**, 184–185, 234, 287, 292–295
human, 190, 190i, 194, 195, 201, 204
Hexose, 528i
■ HiB vaccination, 694i
■ Hibernation, 751
Hiccup, **717**
High altitude, 712, 714–716
■ High blood pressure, 290, 629t, 671–673, 676, 733t, 744, 747–748, 753, 798
■ High-density lipoprotein (HDL), 49, 638, **672**, 700
High-frequency sound, 598
High glycemic index, **730**
■ High protein diet, 748
■ Higher order multiple birth, 770
Higher taxon, 310–311
Himalaya range, 873, 884
Hindbrain, 444i, 588–589, 588i, 589i, 596t
Hip joint, 645
Hippocampus, 591, 591i, 593, 593i, 631
Hirudo medicinalis, 414i
Histamine, 602–603, **684**–685, 685i, 689, 694, 696, 698, 698t
Histidine, 45i, 97i, 222i
Histone, 56, 143, 143i, 232, 232i, 235, 340, 368, 762
■ Histoplasmosis, 397, 397t, 615
■ HIV (human immunodeficiency virus), 342–343, 343t, 345, 693
■ infection, 393, 678, 689, 696–697, 699, 784–785, 785i
■ micrographs, 679i
■ replication, 696, 697i
■ HIV–I, 696
■ HIV–II, 696
hok gene, 255
Holdfast, **361**, 361i
Homeodomain, 236, 236i
Homeostasis, 7, 14, **478**–479, 481, **484**, 489, **559**, 570, **701**
ADH/kidney cells, 635
in animals, 484–485, 484i, 740
circulatory system and, 664, 665i
controls over digestion and, 628, 628i
core temperature, 749
digestive system and, 664, 665i, 720, 736
ecstasy effect, 572
glucose, 629
gonadal hormones and, 632
hypothalamus and, 588–589, 624, 625i, 636
maintenance, organ system interaction, 740, 740i
in plants, 486–487, 486i, 487i, 489, 553
respiratory system and, 664, 665i, 701, 701i, 706–707, 706i
urinary system and, 664, 665i, 740, 744, 746, 752
water-solute balance, 629, 634t
Homeotic gene, **236**, 237i, 240–241, 276, 276i, 277i, **765**
Hominid, **452**–456, 455i, 460, 642, 718, 718i
Hominid timeline, 457i
Hominoid, **454**–455, 460
Homo erectus, 381, 457i, 458–460, 458i
Homo ergaster, 457i
H. floresiensis, 458–459
H. habilis, 456–457, 456i, 457i, 718i, 813
H. heidelbergensis, 457i
H. neanderthalensis, 457i, 458i
H. rudolfensis, 456i, 457i
H. sapiens, 10, 167i, 260, 457i, 458–461, 459i. *See also* Human; Human history

Homo species, 839
Homologous chromosome, **156**–157, 157i, 158i, 160–161, 160i, 161i, 164, 164i, 166, 166i, 188, 198i, 204, 234, 307i
duplication in, 196–197
in inheritance patterns, 169, 171–173, 171i, 174i, 175, 177–178, 182
Homologous structures, **274**–275, 280
Homosexuality, 256, 913
Homosporous, **375**
Homozygous condition, **171**–172, 174, 176, 176i, 179, 179i, 183–185, 190, 193, 204, 287, 293, 419
in population, 294–295, 298–299
Homozygous dominant, **171**–173, 172i, 173i, 174i, **182**, 193i
Homozygous recessive, **171**–173, 172i, 173i, 174i, **182**, 184–185, 190, 202
Honey, 41, 529, 899
Honey locust, 500i
Honeybee, 425i, 524, 529, 898–899, 898i, 904
Africanized, 898–899, 899i
colony (hive), 898–899, 899i, 905, 905i, 910–911
■ dance, 905, 905i, 910
division of labor, 910, 910i
Honeycomb, 41, 41i, 905, 910
Hooke, Robert, 50, 51i
Hookworm, 404i, 419
Horizon (soil), 513, 513i, 876i–877i
Horizontal cell, eye, 612, 612i
Hormone, animal, 52, 134, 290, 556, 589, 619–**620**, 636–637, 680t, 714
behavior and, 620, 631–632, 631i, 632i, 900–901, 912–913
blood transport, 660, 660i
categories, 622t
environmental cues and, 632–633, 632i, 636
feedback controls, 485, 619, 623, 626–627, 626i, 630, 630i, 636, 645
gastrointestinal, 620, 725–726, 726i, 729, 736
human female reproductive, 567i, 618–619, 621i, 622t, 632, 636, 777, 777i, 779–780, 779i, 780i, 787, 794, 796–797
human male reproductive, 567i, 618, 621i, 622t, 632, 636, 772, 773i, 774
invertebrate, 232i, 420, 619, 633
nature of, 622–623, 622t, 623i
protein, 45, 48t, 622, 622t
receptors for, 78, 79i, 86, 619–620, 622–623, 623i, 630, 633–634, 636
sex. *See* Sex hormones
in sex determination, 756–757
as signaling mechanisms, 232, 232i, 240, 479, 482, 619–620, 622–623, 623i, 636
in solute-water balance, 675, 738–739, 746–747, 746i
sources, 561, 570, 619–620, 621i, 635t
steroid, 41, 622–623, 622t, 623i
■ synthetic, 638, 783, 794
thermoregulation, 751
in weight control, 718–719, 722i, 728, 735–736, 735i
Hormone, plant, 235, 479, 482, **540**–553, 544t, 545t, 547i, 555–556
abscisic acid, 541, 544–**545**, 544t, 545t, 555
auxins, 541, **544**–545, 544t, 545t, 555
cytokinin, 541, **544**–545, 544t, 545t, 555
ethylene, 541, **544**–545, 544t, 545t, 555
gibberellin, 540–541, 540i, **544**–547, 544t, 545t, 546i, 555

Hormone–receptor complex, 622, 623i, 695, 783
■ Hormone replacement therapy, 202
Horn, animal, 69, 446i, 469i
Hornwort, 314i, 372i, 376–377, 377i, 388
Horse, 170, 274, 303, 309i, 332, 401, 449
Horse chestnut tree, 552i
Horseshoe crab, 421, 421i, 430–431
Horsetail, 167i, 311, 311i, 314i, 370–371, 372i, 373i, 375, 375i, **378**–380, 378i, 388, 388t, 832i
■ Hospital-acquired disease, 682
Host, 64, 245–246, 245i, 251, 254–255, 257, 326–327, 369, 822–823, 831, 837–838, 840
viral particles and, 342–345, 345i, 348
■ Hot spot, **472**, 476, **875**
■ chemical, 627, 627i
in Earth's mantle, 272i
frog deformities, 627, 627i
■ for global diversity, 118
Hot spring, life in, 118, 247, 318, 318i, 334, 341, 341i, 472
House centipede, 423
Houseplant propagating, 536
Hox gene, 277
■ HPV 16 infection, 784
■ HPV 18 infection, 784
Hubbard Brook watershed, 854, 854i
Hubel, David, 613
Hughes, Sarah, 605, 605i
Human, **452**, **456**, 468
chromosome, 149, 197, 197i, 204
chromosome number, **145**–147, 145i, 147i, 167i, 187–188, 188i
classification, 310i, 452, 460
cloning, possibility of, 206, 215
embryonic stem cell research, 558
genetic disorders. *See* Genetic disorders
genome, 241, 249–250, 278, 461, 677
life cycle, 771, 795, 795i, 795t
life span, 461i, 766–767, 871
Human behavior, 913
capacity to adapt, 917
hormones and, 620, 631–632, 631i, 635, 913
instinctive, 901, 901i
limbic system and, 604
moral choice, 899, 913, 917
sexual, 604, 912–913
■ symbolic, 452–453. *See also* Language
Human body
bone, 249, 645i
brain, 587–589, 588i, 589i, 596t
breast, 230–231, 230
circulatory system, 567i
composition, 18–19, 18i, 19i
development. *See* Development, human
digestive system, 567i, 719, 722–723, 722i
ear, 606, 606i
endocrine system, 567i, 621i, 637i
■ energy for, 123–126, 129–131, 134–135, 137
■ eye, 54, 54i, 55i, 108, 233, 237, 605, 762
■ forelimb ancestry, 149i, 263, 274–275, 274i, 763
■ growth, 142–143, 142t, 150, 152, 276i, 277
■ height, 55i, 458, 458i
■ immune system, 255
integumentary system, 567i
■ lymphatic system, 230, 567i
major cavities in, 566i
muscular system, 567i
nervous system, 567i, 572–573
organ systems, overview, 567i

reproductive system. *See* Human reproduction

respiratory system, 124i, 481i, 567i, 705–707, 705i, 706i, 716

sensory systems, 599, 604–605, 604i, 605i

sex determination, 192, 192i

skeletal/muscular system, 230, 276i, 277, 281, 567i

skin, 334

solute-water balance, 741–742, 741i, 742i

temperature control by, 478–479, 478i, 750

urinary system, 567i, 739, 741, 741i

weight, 192, 199, 642, 660i, 671, 676, 718–719, 734–735, 734i

Human chorionic gonadotropin (HCG), 787, 797

Human gene therapy, **251**, 257

Human Genome Project, 250

Human history, 295, 678

body weight and, 718, 718i

early dispersals, 458–460, 459i, 462–463, 462i

Easter Island, 462–463

emergence of culture during, 458–459, 459i, 817

evolution, 260, 269, 271i, 277, 452–453, 456–461, 917

food sources in, 456–457

fossil record, 260

fungi and, 397

language and, 915

origins, 433, 456, 458–460

peat bogs, 377, 377i

plant domestication during, 381, 381i, 387, 389

subpopulations (race), 458, 460

Human immunodeficiency virus. *See* HIV

Human impact on biosphere, 466, 836, 852, 856i–857i, 857, 863, 916–917

agriculture, 119

atmosphere, 119–120, 391, 870–871, 870i, 871i, 896

bioethics of, 881

carbon cycle, 119–120

deforestation, 391

dune buggies and desert biomes, 877i, 897

endangered species, 463, 539, 881

energy extraction costs, 869, 881

habitat losses, 390, 466–467, 881, 884i

land conversions, 119, 390, 876, 878, 880–881, 884, 884i

nuclear waste disposal, 252

per capita energy consumption, 869

pesticides and, 252, 257, 391

phosphorus cycle and, 252

population growth and, 252, 881, 884

sewage, 119, 252

species introduction, 884–885, 885i

Human leukocyte antigen (HLA), 49, 49i, 79i, 686

Human papillomavirus (HPV), 153, 784, 784t

Human population, 464t

adaptation to climate, 138

as agent of dispersal, 534, 539

density in habitats, 466–467

Easter Island, 462–463, 462i

food supply, 252–253, 257, 884

growth, 252, 783, 869

resource consumption and, 266, 884, 884i

size, 463, 466

Human reproduction, 156, 202, 249, 567i, 795

accessory glands, 772–773, 772t

egg formation, 162, 163i, 770

female reproductive function, 773, 776–777, 777i, 781

female reproductive organs, 156i, 192, 192i, 770–771, 776i, 776t, 777i, 796

fertility control, 771, 782–783, 782i, 796

fertilization, 139–140, 755, 770–771, 776, 776t, 781, 781i, 783, 786–788, 786i, 787i, 797

gamete formation, 162–163, 163i, 770

hormones in, 771–772, 773i, 774, 777, 777i, 779–780, 779i, 780i, 787

male reproductive function, 772t, 781, 781i

male reproductive organs, 156i, 192, 192i, 770–773, 772t, 773i, 781, 796

menstrual cycle, 771, **776–780**, 776t, 778i, 779i, 780i, 796

pregnancy, 770

sexual intercourse, 771–772, 772t, 773i, 781, 783, 796

sperm formation, 139, 162, 163i, 771–775, 774i–775i, 796

Human somatotropin (GH), 252, 254, 254i

Human T-cell leukemia virus I (HTLV-I), 343t

Human T-cell leukemia virus II (HTLV-II), 343t

Humboldt Current, 893

Humerus, 447i, 643i

Humidity, 168, 473, 473i, 478–479, 868, 878, 880, 896

body temperature and, 749–750

heat-related illness, 478–479, 490

Hummingbird, 55i, 385i, 447, 525, 528i, 529, 749, 757, 824

Humus, **512–513**, 876, 876i, 877i, 880

Hunting behavior, 294, 459, 469, 469i, 472, 475, 801, 812, 903, 908–909, 909i, 912

Huntington's disease, 122, 190, 201i, 201t

Huq, Anwarul, 895

Husky, 299, 655, 655i

Hutchinson–Gilford progeria syndrome, 191, 191i, 201t

Hybrid, 77, **171**, 182, 217, 245, 245i, 294, 307, 537, 693

poplars, 510, 510i

sterility/inviability, 303, 303i, 316

Hybrid zone, 307, 307i

Hybridization, 278

in animals, 303, 317, 317i, 898, 900

in crop plants, 296, 307, 307i, 881

DNA-DNA, 278–279

Drosophila, 193, 193i

in plants, 279, 296, 307, 307i, 881

and sympatric speciation, 307, 307i, 316

Hydra, 404i, 411i

Hydraulic pressure, **641**, 641i, 654

Hydrocarbon, 32, 32i, **34**, 36–37, 41, 48t, 109i, 871

Hydrocarbon gas, 871

Hydrochloric acid, 28–29, 28i, 682

in gut, 722i, 724–725, 733t, 736t

Hydrogen, 4i, 18–25, 20i, 30, 32, 32i, 97i, 101, 101i, 320, 861

aerobic pathways, 709, 712, 716

in anaerobic pathways, 132

in atmosphere, 136

in first atmosphere, 320–321, 321i

in human body, 18, 18i, 19i

molecular, 24–25, 25i

in organic compounds, 34, 38, 40, 40i, 42, 47, 118, 669

in photosynthesis, 107, 111–112, 111i, 114–115, 115i, 118i, 120, 512, 512t, 522

Hydrogen bonding, 19, 22, 23i, **25–27**, 25i, 26i, 27i, 30, 99

cohesion–tension theory, 517

denaturation, 44

in DNA molecule, 46–47, 46i, 47i, 207, 210–213, 210i, 212t, 216, 220, 220i, 245, 247i, 278

nature of, 37, 39, 39i, 43, 43i, 44i

transpiration and, 516, 522

in water, 136, 844, 850

Hydrogen cyanide, 320

Hydrogen gas, as energy source, 869

Hydrogen ion (H+), 29, 30t, 99, 105

in acid-base reactions, 28–29, 28i, 747

ATP formation, 58, 64, 130–131, 130i, 131i, 133, 137–138

electron transfers and, 101, 101i, 122–123, 125–126, 125i, 129, 129i, 131, 131i

excretion, 745, 745i, 747, 752

from glucose breakdown, 118i

membrane crossings by, 79i, 81i, 547, 547i

pH and, 19, 28–29, 28i, 31

in photosynthesis, 112–113, 113i, 114i, 120

Hydrogen peroxide, 63, 97i, 99, 105

Hydrogen sulfide, 106, 118, 133, 683, 865i

Hydroid, 410–411, 411i, 430

Hydrologic cycle, **852–853**, 853i, 862–863

Hydrolysis, **37**, 37i, 39, 321, 546

Hydrophilic substances, **26–27**, **30**, 30t, 41i, 52i, 76–78, 76i, 88, 97, 542

Hydrophobic substances, **26–27**, **30**, 30t, 41, 41i, 49, 52i, 74, 76–78, 76i, 81, 86, 88

Hydrosphere, **867**

Hydrostatic pressure, **85**, 670i

Hydrostatic skeleton, **411**, 415, 639, **640–641**, 640i, 654

Hydrothermal vent, 133, 318, **892**

characteristics, 868, 892–893, 896

inhabitants, 8i, 57i, 118, 121, 318, 324, 340i, 341, 341i, 892, 893i

possible origin of life at, 321, 322i, 323–324, 341

Hydroxide ion, 19, 28–29, 30t, 31, 747

Hydroxyl group, 36–39, 36i, 37i, 39i, 48t, 94, 127i, 212, 213i, 216

1, 25-hydroxyvitamin D6, 635t

Hydrozoan, 410–411, 411i

Hygrophorus, 392i

Hyperaldosteronism, **747**

Hyperalgesia, **603**

Hypercortisolism, 631

Hypericum, 509i

Hyperopia, 614

Hyperosmotic cell, 747

Hyperpolarization, membrane, 581

Hypertension, 631, **673**, 676, 730, 734

Hyperthermia, 595, **750**

Hyperthyroidism, **626**

Hypertonic solution, **84–85**, 85i, 89, 318, 745

Hyperventilation, **485**, 714

Hypha (hyphae), **391–392**, 393–396, 393i, 394i, 395i, 396i, 397i, 398–401, 398i, 399i, 823

Hypodermis, 568, 568i

Hypoglycemia, **629**

Hypothalamus, 484i, **588–589**, 588i, 589i, 591, 591i, 593, 593i, 595, 596t, 600t, **621**, 621i, **624**, 685

in body temperature regulation, 750–752, 750i

endocrine role, 620, 621i, 625, 634t, 636

in female reproductive function, 771, 778–779, 779i, 780i, 794, 796

in male reproductive function, 771, 774–775, 775i, 781, 796

pituitary link, 619, 621i, 624–627, 624i, 625i, 626i, 630, 630i, 634, 634t, 636–637

roles in thirst, 746, 746i, 752

sex hormones in, 782, 794

Hypothermia, **751**, 751i

Hypothesis, **11–13**, 15

Hypothyroidism, **626**

Hypotonic solution, **84–85**, 85i, 89, 188, 189i, 518i

Hypoxia, **714**, 716

Hyracotherium, 449

Hysterectomy, 153

I

i allele, 176, 176i

I^A allele, 176, 176i

I^B allele, 176, 176i

Ice, 26i, 27, 56, 318, 321i, 454i, 866

Antarctica, 449, 865, 865i

Ice age (glaciation), 269, 271i, 304, 355, 438, 449, 464t, 838, 841

Ice cap, arctic, 26i, 867, 883, 884i

melting, 2, 842, 883

Ichthyolestes, 617i

Ichthyosaur, 268i, 442i, 443, 443i

Ichthyostega, 439i

Identical twin, 10, 214, 214t, 216, 249, 284, 763, 769, **798**, 798i

IgA, 688, 691, 691i

IgD, 688–689

IgE, 688–689, 691, 691i, 694, 696

IgG, 688, 690i, 691, 691i, 695–696, 792

IgM, 688–689, 691

Ignicoccus, 341i

Ileum, 722i, 725, 728

Iliac artery, 665i

Iliac vein, 665i

Illegitimate signal receiver, 905

Illegitimate signaler, 905

IL2RG gene, 256

Immigration, **295**, 298, 298t, **804–805**, 818, 839

United States, 819, 819i

Immune deficiency, 256, 695, 697, 733t

Immune response, 251, 569, 583, 660i, 661, 684, 684i, 698t, 750, 785

against self, 679, 766. *See also* Autoimmune response

allergies and, 679, 694

antibody-mediated, 79i, 255, 662–663, 663i, 674i, 675, 677, 679, 684i, 687, 687i, 690–692, 690i, 691i, 698

antigen recognition and, 686, 691–692, 691i

cell-mediated, 254, 679, 681, 681i, 687, 687i, 692–693, 692i, 698

deficient, 679, 695, 695i, 699

heightened, 694–695, 699

inflammation in, 679, 680t, 681, 683–686, 685i, 688, 690, 698, 698t

nonself recognition, 679–680, 698

pathogen-specific, 686–687, 699

primary, 680–681, 690i, 691–693, 698

secondary, 681

Immune system, 49, 342, 662–663, 681, 713i, 772

adaptive, 679–681, 680t, 681i, 684–687, 686i, 687i, 696, 698–699, 698t

innate, 679–681, 680t, 681i, 684–685, 698, 698t

lines of defense, 680–681

pathogens and, 359, 397, 569, 785

sporozoans and, 293

suppression, 215, 255, 630–631, 699

surface protection, 680–683, 682i, 682t, 683i

thymus gland and, 674i, 675

weakened, infections and, 342, 347, 369, 696, 785, 870

Immunity, 38, 678, **680**–681, 680t, 694–695, 699
Immunization, **694**–695, 694i, 699. *See also* Vaccination
Immunoglobin (Ig), **688**–691, 688i, 694–696, 698t, 795
Immunological comparison, 459, 459i
Immunotherapy, **693**, 693i, 699
Immunotoxin, **693**
Impatiens capensis, 534
Imperfect flower, 526
Imperfect fungi, 393, 393i, 400
Impetigo, 346
Implantation, 214i, 771, **786**–787, 786i, 787i, 792i, 797
Imprinting, **902**, 902i, 914–915
In vitro fertilization (IVF), **203**, 558, 770, **783**, 783i
Inbreeding, **295**, 298, 911
Incest, 295
Incisor, tooth, 448i, 723, 723i
Inclusive fitness, theory of, **911**, 914
Incomplete cleavage, 761, 761i, 763i, 768
Incomplete digestive system, **406**, 719–**720**, 720i, 721, 736
Incomplete dominance, **176**–177, 182, 184–185
Incomplete metamorphosis, 424i
Incomplete protein, **730**
Indehiscent fruit, **532**, 533t
Independent assortment, theory of, 174–**175**, 174i, 178, 182, 184–185, 284
India, human population, 814, 815i, 816–817
Indian corn, 178, 227i. *See also* Corn
Indian Plate, 272i
Indicator species, **469**, **475**–476
Indirect selection, 911
Indocetus, 617i
Indoleacetic acid (IAA), 544
Indonesia, 93, 93i, 465i, 814, 841, 841i
Indricotherium, 448i
Indriidae, 450t
Induced-fit model, **97**
Industrial smog, **870**–871, 871i, 896
Industrial stage, 390, 466, **816**, 816i
pollution, 252, 618, 637, 637i
population growth and, 813, 813i, 816–817
wastes, 252, 618, 849, 888
Infant mortality rate, 814–815, 814i, 815i
Infanticide behavior, 814–815, 912–913
Infection, 74, 202–203, **346**, 348, 481i, 488i, 527
plant, 483, 486, 489, 512t
Infection, bacterial agent, 102–103, 103i, 561, 571, 629t, 645, 738, 792
Bacillus anthracis, 339, 679
Borrelia burgdorferi, 338, 339i, 426, 426i
Chlamydia trachomatis, 615, 784, 784t, 785i
cholera, 289
Clostridium tetani, 339, 682
Escherichia coli, 349
Haemophilus influenzae, 244
Helicobacter pylori, 335i, 737
Mycobacterium tuberculosis, 102–103
Neisseria gonorrhea, 784, 784t, 785i
Pneumococcus, 694i
Propionibacterium acnes, 683, 683i
Pseudomonas, 349
P. aeruginosa, 74
Rickettsia prowazekii, 327i
Salmonella, 103, 349
Staphylococcus, 349
S. aureus, 690–691
S. epidermidis, 682, 682i
Streptococcus mutans, 683
S. pneumoniae, 208, 347

S. pyrogenes, 677
S. sanguis, 683
Treponema pallidum, 784i, 784t, 785, 785i
tuberculosis, 289
Infection, flatworm agent
Schistosoma, 412
Taenia saginata, 413i
Infection, fungal agent, 441, 615, 629t
Ajellomyces capsulatus, 397, 397t
Amanita, 397t
A. phalloides, 401i
Aspergillus, 397
A. flavus, 397
Batrachochytrium dendrobatidis, 393i, 397t
Candida albicans, 396, 396i, 397t
Cladosporium, 397
Claviceps purpura, 397, 397t
Coccidioides immitis, 397t
Cryphonectria parasitica, 397, 397t
Enterocytozoon bieneusi, 397t
Epidermophyton floccosum, 397i
Fusarium oxysporum, 401
Gibberella fujikuroi, 540
Memnoliella, 397
Microsporum, 397t
Monilinia fructicola, 397t
Ophiostoma ulmi, 397t
Penicillium, 397
Phytophthora, 398
Puccinia graminis, 397t
Rhizopus oryzae, 394
Stachybotrys, 397
Tilletia indica, 397t
Trichophyton, 397t
Ustilago maydis, 397t
Venturia inaequalis, 397i, 397t
Verticillium, 397t
Infection, prion agent
bovine spongiform encephalopathy (BSE), 347, 347i
scrapie, 347
variant Creutzfeldt–Jakob disease, 347, 347i
Infection, protistan agent
Entamoeba histolytica, 366
Phytophthora infestans, 350, 362, 362i
P. ramorum, 350, 362, 362i
Plasmopara viticola, 362
Saprolegnia, 362
Infection, protozoan agent
Giardia lamblia, 352i, 353, 353i
Leishmania, 354
L. donovani, 355
L. mexicana, 355
Trichomonas vaginalis, 8, 353, 353i, 784, 784t
Trypanosoma, 354
T. brucei, 354, 355i
T. cruzi, 355
Vibrio cholerae, 894–895, 895i
Infection, roundworm agent
Ascaris lumbricoides, 419
elephantiasis, 671
Enterobius vermicularis, 419
guinea worm, 419
hookworm, 419
pinworm, 404i, 419
Trichinella spiralis, 419, 419i
Wuchereria bancrofti, 419, 419i
Infection, sporozoan agent
plasmodium, 293, 293i, 358
Pneumocystis carinii, 397, 397t, 696
Toxoplasma, 369, 369i
Infection, viral agent, 645, 680, 693, 792
adenovirus, 343t
arenavirus, 343t
bunyamwera virus, 343t
bunyavirus, 343t
calicivirus, 837
coronavirus, 343t
cytomegalovirus, 343t

enterovirus, 343t
Epstein–Barr, 343t
filovirus, 343t
flavivirus, 343t
Haemophilus influenzae, 694i
hantavirus, 343t
hepadnavirus, 343t
hepatitis A virus, 343t, 571
herpes virus, 343i, 343t, 569, 615, 784, 784t
human immunodeficiency virus (HIV), 785
human papillomavirus (HPV), 153, 784, 784t
multiple sclerosis, 584
myxoma virus, 837
orthomyxovirus, 343t
orthopoxvirus, 343t
papovavirus, 343t
paramyxovirus, 343t
parvovirus, 343t
phlebovirus, 343t
picornavirus, 343t, 349
reovirus, 343t
retrovirus, 343t, 345
rhabdovirus, 343t
rhinovirus, 343t
togavirus, 343t
varicella–zoster, 343t, 694i
West Nile, 332–333, 332i
Infectious disease, 208, 334, 346–347, 441, 615, 631, 637, 792, 839
deadliest worldwide, 255, 346t
group living and, 909, 914
human history and, 282, 282i, 678, 812–813
lymphoid organs and, 674i, 675
opportunistic, 393, 397, 397t
Infectious hepatitis, 343t
Infectious mononucleosis, 343t, **662**
Infectious prion, 347–348, 347i
Inferior vena cava, 665i, 742i
Infertility, human, 73, 777, 782–784
Inflammation, 73, 195, 332, 343t, 408, 568, 584, 589, 626, 630–631, 645, 660i, 661, 672, 677, 695, 712, 784
acute, 684–685, 685i, 692
as immune response, 603, 679, 680t, 681, 683, 686, 688, 690, 694, 698, 698t
Influenza, 2, 255, 342, 343i, 343t, 346t, 694i, 699
Infrared radiation, 108i, 324
Ingroup, cladistics, **312**, 312i
Inhalation, **710**–712, 710i, 711i, 716–717
Inheritance, **7**, 208–209, 243, 277
blending theory of, 170, 176
of body plan, 237, 237i, 240–241, 274–275, 277
chromosomal basis of, 168–170, 193, 207, 243
continuous variation in, 180–182, 180i, 181i
environmental effect on, 179, 179i, 182, 283
impact of crossing over on, 178, 178i, 182
Lamarck's hypothesis, 264
plant, 168–169, 168i, 172
pleiotropy, 177, 177i
variation of traits in, 172–177, 175i, 176i, 177i, 182
Inheritance pattern, human, 141, 178
analysis, 194i, 196, 200–201
autosomal dominant, 177, 182, 187, 190, 190i, 200
autosomal recessive, 187, 190–191, 190i, 200
chromosomal basis, 170, 187, 193, 196–201, 196i, 197i, 199i, 204
in sex determination, 187–188, 192, 192i
X-linked gene, 193–194, 193i, 194i

Inheritance pattern, Mendelian, 169–172, 172i, 182, 190, 193–194, 200–201
Inhibin, 775, 775i
Inhibitor, 98–99, 98i, 621i, **624**, 625i, 626, 626i, 628, 630, 630i, 633i, 635t, 636
Inhibitory postsynaptic potential (IPSP), 573, 580–**581**, 581i
Initiation factor, 233, 233i
Initiation stage, 224, 224i, 225, 228
Innate immunity, 679–**680**, 680t, 681, 681i, 684–685, 698, 698t
Inner cell mass, 786, 786i, 788, 795t
Inner ear, 605–**606**, 606i, 607i, 615, 617
Inoculation, 514i, 678. *See also* Vaccination
Input zone, neuron, **576**, 576i, 578, 578i, 581, 581i, 585, 596
Insect, 343i, 420, 440, 472i, 512t, 520, 534–535, 835, 844i, 881
beneficial vs. harmful, 252, 427
biodiversity, 464i, 465
carnivore, 425, 851, 851i
characteristics, 89, 424–425, 424i, 430, 446, 608, 609i, 769, 828, 829i
cuticle, 640–641, 641i
development, 7i, 232, 232i, 424–425, 424i
diversity, 403, 424–425, 424i, 425i
evolution, 237, 271i, 402, 404i, 464i, 809
exoskeleton, 39, 641, 641i
herbivorous, 500i, 523, 523i, 845, 846i
life cycle, 424–425, 424i
life span, 766–767
molting, 633
parasitoid, 425, 830–831, 831i
pesticides, 848, 849i
as pollinator, 384, 388t, 528–529, 528i, 823
polyploidy, 198, 204, 307
respiration, 703, 703i
social, 910, 910i, 911i, 914
Venus flytrap attraction, 523, 523i
wing, 275, 275i, 424–425, 430
Insecticide, 252, 619, 633, **848**, 848i, 871i
"Insects of the sea," 422
Insertion (base pair), **226**–228
Instinctive behavior, 899, **901**–902, 901i, 904
Insulin, 6, 48t, 134, 252, 622t, 628i, 629, 634, 635t, 636
endocrine source, 621i, 628, 636
in organic metabolism, 722i, 725, 730
Insulin shock, 629
Integral protein, 78
Integration, nature of, 403, 405, 429i, 430, 605, 609i, 680
Integrator, **484**, 484i, 486, 489, 574i, 575
Integrin, 78i, 404, 560, 764
Integument, 530, 531i, 532, 568, 571i, 608, 634t, 701, 703, 758
Integumentary exchange, 701, **703**–704, 716
Integumentary system, 4i, 559, 567i
Intelligence, human, 186–187, 186i, 199
Interbreeding, 301–304, 303i, 316, 458
in defining species, 284
Intercostal muscle, 706i, 710–711, 710i
Interference competition, **824**, 824i
Interferon, 252, 680t, 681, 693
Interglacial, 449
Interleukin, 680i, 681, 691, 693
Interleukin-2, 254
Interleukin-4 (IL-4), 696

Intermediary molecule, 113, 113i, 115–116, 115i, 120
Intermediate disturbance hypothesis, **832–833**, 833i
Intermediate filament, 59i, **68–69**, 68i, 71–72, 565
Intermediate host, 354, 359, 359i, 369, **412**–413, 413i, 419
Intermediate lobe, pituitary, 624, 634t
Intermediate metabolic reaction, **94**, 99–100, 104, 104t, 126, 126i, 127i, 129i, 131, 132i, 133–134, 137, 229, 729
Internal clock, 632, 636
Internal environment, 6–7, 14, 91, 488, 619, 633, **658**–659, 727i, 749
 blood circulation, 90, 658, 664
 chemical sense, 599, 600t, 602
 digestive system and, 720–722, 736
 feedback mechanisms, 484–485, 490
 homeostasis, 74, 89, 478–479, 481–485, 481i, 484i, 489–490, 559, 635, 664, 665i, 719–720, 740i, 744, 749, 752
 human lungs, 701, 706–707, 709i, 716
 immune system and, 680, 682–683, 682i, 690
 nature of, 566, 567i, 570
 pH of, 28, 701–702
 of plants, 486–487, 486i, 487i, 489
 urinary system, 444i
 water-solute balance, 629, 634t, 740–742, 740i, 741i, 744, 747, 752
Internal transport, 482–483
Interneuron, 565, 565i, **574**, 574i, **576**–577, 581, 584–585, 587, 589, 591, 596, 601i, 602, 615
Internode, 494i, 498, 540, 552
Interphase, 141, **144**–146, 144i, 145i, 146i, 150, 152, 153i, 212, 217, 227i, 232, 234
 germ cell at, 157, 157i, 160i, 164i, 165i, 166, 166i
Interstitial fluid, 482, **484**–485, 559, 622, 623i, 627, 644, 650, **658**–659, 675, 727, 736, 738i, **740**–741, 744i, 745, 745i, 747, 752
 antigens in, 684–685, 687–688, 690–693, 691i, 692i
 exchanges at capillary beds, 670–671, 670i, 674, 674i, 676
 neural membrane, 577i, 578i
 respiration and, 701, 705, 707, 709, 714, 716
Intertidal zone, 833–835, 834i, 890–891, 891i, 892i
Intervertebral disk, 587i, **642**–643, 643i
Intestinal infection, 343t
Intestinal nuclease, 724i
Intestinal parasite, 353, 353i, 419, 419i
Intestine, 334, 339, 444i, 564i, 620, 627
 blood circulation and, 664, 664i, 665i, 675
 comparisons, 720i, 721
 invertebrate, 416, 416i, 419i
Intracellular pathogen, **687**
Intrapleural pressure, 711i
Intrapulmonary pressure, 711i
Intrauterine device (IUD), 782i
Intravenous drug abuse, 697
Intron, **221**, 221i, 228, 232, 238i, 245, 257, 277, 279i, 633, 689i
Inuit skeleton, 458i
Inversion, chromosomal, 187, **196**–197, 204
Invertebrate, 390, 402–403, 440, 468, 523, 757, 836
 annelids, 414–415, 414i, 415i
 arthropod, 420–427, 633
 characteristics, 154, 658, 658i, 893
 chordates, 404i, 434–435, 434i, 452, 460

cnidarians, 403, 410–411, 410i, 411i
crustaceans, 422–423, 422i, 423i, 633, 633i
evolution, 271i, 315
eyes, 608–609, 608i
flatworms, 412–413, 412i, 413i
hormones, 619, 633, 633i
insect, 424–425, 424i, 425i
intertidal zone, 834, 890, 891i
marine, 464t, 740, 809, 809i
mollusk, 416–418, 416i, 417i, 418i
parasites, 423, 830, 830i
placozoans, 403, 408–409, 409i
respiration, 76, 702–703, 703i
rotifer, 416, 416i
roundworm, 419, 419i
skeleton, 639–641, 640i, 641i
spiders, 421, 421i, 426, 426i
sponges, 403, 408–409, 408i, 409i
vertebrate vs., 633, 636, 699, 740
Involuntary muscle action, 190, 565
Iodine, 626–627, 636, 733t, 897i
Iodized salt, 733t
Ion, 19, **24**–25, 27, 27i, 29–**30**, 30t, 65, 75, 94, 514, 514i, 644t
 blood transport, 660, 660i, 669–670
 membrane crossing, 52, 58, 61, 64, 79i, 80–82, 81i, 85, 87–88, 112, 130, 137, 561, 570, 577–578, 577i, 580, 580i, 583–584, 584i, 589, 596
 metal, 99, 105
Ion exchange, 268, **861**
Ion-selective channels, 75i, 79i
Ionic bonding, 19, **24**, 24i, 25, 30
Ionization, 36i, 547, 547i
Ionizing radiation, 105, 213, **226**–228, 227i
Iridium, 260, 260i, 443
Iris, 509i
Iris, eye, 180, 180i, 609–611, 610i, 616, 640
Iris, monocot, 237, 509i, 518i, 551i
Iron, 34, 44, 97i, 118, 122, 320, 330, 335, 702, 708, 877i
 dietary, deficiency or excess, 662, 667, 733, 733t
 on early Earth, 272, 320, 322i
 in human body, 569
 plant nutrient, 109i, 512, 512t, 522, 554
Iron-deficiency anemia, **662**, 733t
Irrigation, 116, 252, 296, 812, 855, 855i, 884, 884i
Isaacson, Peter, 849i
Island biodiversity pattern, 838–840, 838i, 839i
Island biogeography, 468–469, 475
Isoleucine, 222i, 223, 225i, 228i, 730
Isometric vs. isotonic contraction, 652, 652i
Isopentyl acetate, 898
Isotonic solution, 84–85, 85i, 89, 745
Isotope, 19, **21**, 30, 30t, 270, 270i
IUD. *See* Intrauterine device
Ixodes, 426, 426i

J
J-Field, 510, 510i
J-shaped growth curve, 804–805, 804i, 805i, 818
Janis, Christine, 448
Janzen, David, 476
Japanese beetle, 835t
Jasmonates, **545**
Jaw, 312, 312i, 313i, **436**, 444, 448, 460, 598, 602i, 653
 evolution, 433, 436–437, 436i, 441, 568
 human, 315, 453, 458, 642, 643i, 723
 invertebrate, 414i, 416, 416i, 418i, 422, 422i
 mammal, 312i, 313i, 448, 453–455
 reptile, 444–445, 444i, 448, 737, 737i

Jawed fish, 404i, 436–439, 436i, 437i, 452, 568, 680, 810, 826
Jawless fish, 404i, 435–436, 436i, 452
Jejunum, 722i, 725
Jellyfish, 258, 269, 404i, 405, 410, 430, 432, 574
Jenner, Edward, 678, 679i, 699
Jerzy Boyz organic farm, 106i
Jet lag, 632
Jet propulsion, cephalopod, 418
Jimmie the bulldog, 656–657, 656i
Joey (kangaroo), 757i
Joint, 590, 601–602, 605, **645**, 695
 crustacean, 769
 skeletal, 562, 639, 643i, 644–645, 654
Jointed appendage, 420–421, 422i, 425, 430
Jugular vein, 230, 665i
Jump dispersal, **835**–837, 839i
Juniper, 296, 310i, 382, 399i
Jurassic period, 271i, 373, 373i, 432–433, 432i, 442i, 443i, 448, 449i, 464t, 642i
Juvenile stage, 441, 461i, 627, 633, 757i, 890, 903i
 arthropod, 420, 423i
Juvenile-onset diabetes, 629

K
K–12 strain, *Escherichia coli*, 336
K–T asteroid impact, 260, 260i, 271i, 309, 443, 464t, 465
K–T asteroid impact theory, **443**
Kamilah the cama, 317
Kanamycin, 244i
Kangaroo, 309i, 757i, 837
Kangaroo rat, 69i, 741, 741i, 753, 904
Kaposi's sarcoma, **696**, 696i
Karenia brevis, 352i, 358, 358i
Karyotype, 187–**188**, 189i, 196–199, 198i, **204**–205
Kartagener syndrome, 72–73, 73i
Kelp, 361, 361i, 364i, 368, 468
Kepone, 619
Keratin, 48i, 69i, 568–569, 568i, 569i
Keratinocyte, 489, **568**–569
Kereru, 539
Ketamine, 572, 595
Ketoacidosis, 629
Ketone, 36i, 38, 38i, 48t, 529, 731
Kettlewell, H. B., 288
Key innovation, **309**, 316
 aerobic respiration as, 324
 coelom, 407
 division of labor, 566
 human evolution, 317, 452–453
 jaws, 436–437, 460
 jointed exoskeleton, 420
 lungs, 437, 437i, 460
 mesoderm, 758
 paired lobed fins, 439, 439i, 460
 pollen grains, 375
 "self vs. nonself" recognition, 680
 tissue formation, 404
Keystone species, **834**–835
Kidney, 483, 560i, 563, 563i, 586i, 594, 639, 645, 665i, 669, 681, 714, 738i, **740**–743, 742i, 745, 746i, 752
 damage/disorders, 45i, 343t, 401i, 629, 732t, 738, 747–748
 endocrine role, 620, 621i, 622–624, 624i, 627, 630, 630i, 634t, 635–636, 635t
 energy source, 131, 134
 failure, 343t, 478, 595, 629t, 737, 748, 752
 function, 63, 89, 442, 729, 731, 732t, 738i, 739, 741–743, 742i, 743i, 748, 752
 hormones and, 738–739, 746i, 901
 structure, 739, 742i, 743
Kidney cancer, 738
Kidney cortex, **742**–743, 742i, 743i, 744i, 745, 746i, 752

Kidney dialysis, 748, 752
Kidney failure, 343t, 478, 595, 629t, 737, 748, 752
Kidney medulla, **742**, 742i, 743i, 744i, 745, 745i, 746i, 752
Kidney stone, 731, 733t, 748
Kidney transplant, 748, 752
"Killer bee," 898
Killifish, 810i, 811, 811i, 819
Kilocalorie, 92, **734**–735, 737
Kinase, **150**, 518–519, 622, 623i
Kinesin, 69–70, 70i, 146, 148i
Kinetic energy, 92, 104
Kinetochore, **143**, 146–147, 152
Kinetoplastid, 314i, 352i, **354**–355, 368
Kingdom (taxon), 8, 301, 310, 310i, 311i, 317
Kiss, 484
Kissing, AIDS and, 785
Kitti's hog-nosed bat, 451i
Klinefelter syndrome, **199**, 201t, 205i
Knee-jerk reflex, 585
Knee joint, 643i, 645
Knight, Charles, 465i
Knockout experiment, **236**, 240, 254
Koala, 450i, 450t, 837
Koch, Robert, 678–679
Komodo dragon, 444, 465i
Korana, Gobind, 222
Korarchaeotes, 314i, 340, 340i, 348
Krebs, Charles, 827, 827i
Krebs cycle, **125**, 125i, 126i, 128–129, 128i, 129i, 131, 134, 135i, 137–138
Krill, 118–119, 892
Kubicek, Mary, 140
Kudzu, 836–837, 836i
Kurosawa, Ewiti, 540
Kwashiorkor, **554**

L
La Niña, 894, 894i
Lab-grown epidermis, **569**, 571
Labium, 424i
Labium majora, 776, 777i
Labium minora, 776, 777i
Labor, human birth, 794, 794i, 797, 900
 contraction, 485, 489
Lacks, Henrietta, 140, 140i, 141i, 150i
Lactase, 239
Lactate, 132–133, 133i, 137, 583, 715
Lactate fermentation, 123, **132**–133, 133i, 137, 651, 747
Lactation, 794i, **795**, 900, 913
Lactic acid, 132, 682
Lactobacillus, 132, 338i, 339, 682
Lactose, 38, 190, 238–241, 239i, 737, 795
Lactose intolerance, 190–191, 239
Lactose operon, 238–241, 238i, 239i, 255
lacZ gene, 244i
Ladybird beetle, 425i
Lagoon, 470i, 889
Lake, 384i, 454–455, 469, 886, 886i, 889
 contamination, 618, 887
 ecosystem, 360, 364
 seasonal change, 886, 886i, 897
 trophic nature of, 887, 887i
 zonation, 886, 886i
Lake Baikal rift, 272i
Lamarck, Jean Baptiste, 264
Lamella, middle, 66i, 552
Lamin, 69, 191
Laminaria, 352i, 361
Lamprey, 312, 312i, 313i, 314i, 404i, 428i, 434i, 436–437, 436i, 437i
Lancelet, 314i, 404i, 428i, 434i, 435–436, 435i, 437i, 460, 699
Land plant, 311, 311i, 364, 369, 374–375, 374i, 375i, 388
Land snail, 417i, 608, 608i

Landfill, 859i
Langerhans cell, 569, 686i
■ Language, human, 453, 458, 589–590, 592, 812, **915**
Lanugo, 791
Large intestine, 239, 682, 720, 720i, 722i, **723**, 728, 728i, 736, 736t. *See also* Colon
Larrea, 536, 877i
Larus, 849i
Larva (larvae), 232, 232i, 241, 241i, **408**, 640, 808, 890
 amphibian, 441, 704, 759i
 budworm, 849
 cnidarians, 574
 crab, 423
 echinoderm, 428, 428i
 fish, 704
 insect, 424, 424i, 425i, 427, 427i, 769
 lamprey, 436, 436i
 molluscan, 417
 parasitic worms, 413, 413i
 parasitoid, 820–821, 831i
 planula, 411, 411i
 sea star, 809, 809i
 sea urchin, 757
 sponge, 408
 tunicate, 434–435, 434i
 wasp, 490, 490i
 yucca moth, 823i
■ Laryngitis, 707
Larynx, 196, 201t, 586i, 704, 706–**707**, 713i, 716, 788, 788i
■ Laser angioplasty, **673**
Laser beam, 248, 248i
■ Laser coagulation surgery, 153
■ Laser surgery, 614
■ Laser therapy, 615
■ LASIK, 614
■ Lasso (herbicide), 848i
■ Late blight, 362
Late wood, 507, 507i
Latency, 345, 348
Lateral (axillary) bud, 494i, 498–499, 498i, 504i, 526, 536t, 544, 544t
Lateral geniculate nucleus, 613, 613i
■ Latex, 783, 785, 881
Latimeria, 439, 439i
Latissimus dorsi, 647i
Latrodectus, 426
Leaching, 387, **513**, 854–855, 856i–857i, 861, 862i, 876, 876i, 877i, 880, 885i, 892
Lead, 18, 18i, 20i, 31, 270, 510, 848–849
■ in air pollution, 870
■ in renal failure, 748
Leaf, 9i, 27, 67i, 162, 168i, 302i, 375, 379, 480, 482–483, 493, **500**–501, 500i, 501i, 506, 508, 513i, 526, 538, 548, 550, 844
 abscission (drop), 541, 544, 544t
 cohesion–tension theory, 516–517, 516i, 517i, 522
 color, 65, 108, 109i, 500, 552i, 880
 and deficiencies, 512, 512t
 development, 236, 543i, 544t
 diffusion, 80
 evolution, 374, 388, 388t
 folding/unfolding, 487, 487i, 489–490
 formation, 498, 542, 542i
 function, 39i, 115, 511, 518, 520–521, 521i
 growth, 253i, 496, 498i, 550, 552
 photosynthesis in. *See* Photosynthesis
 primary, 543i, 544
 rhythmic movements, 487, 487i, 489–490, 500
 seed (cotyledon), 532, 532i, 538
 stomata, 116, 116i, 374, 388t, 518–519, 518i, 519i, 522

structure, 67i, 493–495, 494i, 497, 497i
 vein, 388t, 483i, 495i
Leaf insect from Java, 841, 841i
Leaflet, 487i, 500, 500i
Leafy gene, 235
Leakey, Mary, 455i
Learned behavior (learning), 199, 204, 236, 256, 631, 754, 795, 812, 899, **902**, 902i, 904, 912, 914
 vs. instinct, 900–901
Leatherback sea turtle, 468, 701, 715–716, 715i
Lecithin, 725, 730
Leder, Philip, 222
Leech, 404i, 414, 414i, 430
van Leeuwenhoek, Antoni, 50
Leeward side, **873**
Leg, 277i, 604, 617, 655
 animal, 277, 277i
 arthropod, 420–421, 423, 430
 human, 67, 458, 458i, 655
 master genes and, 236, 236i, 237i, 277i
 vertebrate, 312, 312i, 313i
Legume, 486–487, 487i, 860–861, 878
 in diet, 730–731, 731i, 732t, 733t
 root nodules, 338
■ *Leishmania*, 87i, 352i, 354–355, 368
■ Leishmaniasis, 87i, 355
Lek, **906**
Lemon, 28, 28i, 105, 533, 871
Lemon shark, 757i
Lemur, 450t, 461i
Lens, eye, 233, 444, **608**, 608i, 609i, 610–611, 610i, 611i, 614–616, 762, 765, 790i
Lenticel, **506**
Lentiform nucleus, 593i
Lepidodendron, 380i
Leptin, **718**, 718i, 730, 735i, 736
Leptonychotes weddelli, 715
Lethal allele, 184
Lethal mutation, **284**, 287
Leucine, 42i, 45i, 222i, 730
Leucocyte. *See* White blood cell
■ Leukemia, 188, 189i, 197, 201t, 256, 558, **662**, 662i, 897i
Levels of biological organization, 404–405
Leydig cell, 774–775, 774i, 775i, 796, 798
Libido, **632**, 782
Lichen, 364, **390**, 390i, 398–399, 398i, 400, 800, 860, 880–881
 air pollution and, 288–289, 391
 characteristics, 338, 390–391, 400
 known types of, 398, 398i
 mutualism, 823
 as pioneer species, 390, 398, 832, 832i, 877i, 883i
Life, 3, 5, 5i, 11, 255, **344**
 biochemical basis, 319, 337
 characteristics of, 7, 14, 106, 106i, 322
 diversity of. *See* Diversity of life
 evolution. *See* Evolution, biological
 history, 261, 269, 280–281, 433
 history timeline, 319, 328i–329i, 330
 levels of organization, 3–5, 4i–5i, 7, 14
 origin, 19, 26–27, 30, 51, 106–107, 136, 271, 271i, 308, 318–327, 328i–329i, 330, 337, 341, 796
 perspective on, 136, 771
 three domains of, 310, 311i, 328i
 unity of. *See* Unity of life
Life cycle, example
 amphibian, 441
 beef tapeworm (*Taenia saginata*), 413i
 bryophyte (*Polytrichum*), 376i, 377
 chain fern (*Woodwardia*), 379i
 cherry tree, 526i, 531i

of *Chlamydomonas* (green alga), 365, 365i
 club fungi, 395, 395i, 400
 cnidarian (*Obelia*), 411, 411i
 conifer (ponderosa pine), 382–383, 383i
 crab, 423i
of *Dictyostelium discoideum* (cellular slime mold), 367i
 flatworm (beef tapeworm; blood fluke), 413i
 flowering plant, 526i, 531i
 flowering plant/lily, 386, 386i, 389
 fluke (*Schistosoma*), 413i
 frog (*Rana pipiens*), 758i, 759i
 gymnosperm (conifer), 382–383, 383i
 HIV virus, 696, 697i
 hydrozoan (*Obelia*), 411i
 insect, 424, 424i
 land plant (generalized), 374i
 monocot, 386, 386i, 389
 moss (*Polytrichum*), 376i, 377
 Neurospora crassa, 396, 396i, 400
 plants, generalized, 142
 plasmodium, 359i
 red alga, 363i
 Rhizopus stolonifer, 394, 394i, 400
 seedless vascular plant (chain fern), 379, 379i
Life history pattern, 301, 316, 801, **808**–809, 818, 875
 guppy, 810–811, 810i, 811i
 natural selection and, 809–811, 810i, 811i, 818
Life span, 199, 461, 461i, 766
 human, 736, 766–767, 808, 808t, 814–815, 814i, 817–818
 survivorship, 808, 808t
Ligament, 587, 601, 639, 643i, **645**, 654
 function, 562, 562i
Light, 21, 94, 108, 320, 452, 480. *See also* Sunlight
 bioluminescent, 102, 102i, 358, 358i
 conversion by cells, 57, 93, 93i
 fluorescent, 54i, 251
 properties, 108, 108i, 110, 608–609
 wavelength. *See* Wavelength
Light-dependent reactions, 108, **111**–114, 111i, 112i–113i, 118i, 120, 120i, 322i, 480
Light-harvesting complex, 110–113, 110i, 112i, 113i, 114i, 120
Light-independent reaction, **111**, 111i, 115, 115i, 120, 120i, 364
Light microscope, 146
Light penetration, lake depth, 886, 886i
Lightning, 321, 860, 882, 897
Lignin, 66–67, 252, 253i, 480, 496–497, 496i, 508, 516, 721
 in plant evolution, 374–375, 380
Lilium, 306i, 385, 386i, 495, 536t, 537
Lily pad, 482, 483i
Limb, 231, 439, 442, 602
 amphibian, 433, 439i, 440, 440i, 441i, 759i
 bones, 439i, 440, 562–563, 563i
 formation, 790, 790i, 792i
 human, 200i, 201t
 skeletal muscle attachments, 646, 646i, 647i
 vertebrate, 309, 642, 643i, 654
Limbic system, 588i, **591**, 591i, 595, 596t, 597, 604, 604i, 615, 782
Limestone bed, 350, 360, 432–433
 Limestone bed, 350, 360, 432–433
Limiting factor, **806**–807, 806i, 807i, 812–813, 818
Limnetic zone, lake, 886, 886i
Limpet, 416, 608i, 834
Lineage, 261, **269**, 273, 283, 285, 298, 301, 464–465

evolutionary relationships and, 261, 263–264, 266, 269, 271, 274–281, 278i
Linear metabolic pathway, 100
Linkage group, **178**, 178i, 182
Linoleic acid, 730
Linolenic acid, 40i
Lion, 6i, 721, 754–755, 754i, 903–904, 907–909, 913
Lip, 484, 590, 590i, 602, 602i, 707
Lipase, 724t, 725
Lipid, 47, 87i, 115, 563, 622, 680
 blood transport, 660, 660i, 672
 characteristics, 4i, 5, **40**, 43, 47, 48t, 55i
 function of, 33, 36–37, 40–41, 47, 48t, 49, 52–53, 52i, 176
 in human nutrition, 719–720, 723
 metabolism, 90, 124, 729, 729i
 in origin of life, 321, 323, 323i, 325, 328i
 structure, 38, 40i–41i, 105
 synthesis, 59i, 62–63, 62i, 63i, 72, 73t, 144, 336
 viral, 342i, 348
Lipid bilayer, **52**, 72, 109i, 714
 diffusion across, 81, 81i, 82i, 89, 130, 622, 670, 727, 727i, 736
 neural membrane, 577, 577i, 596
 plant, 109i, 112
 structure, 52–53, 52i, 53i, 57, 60–61, 61i, 62i, 75, **76**–78, 76i, 77i, 79i, 86, 88, 684i, 689
Lipopolysaccharide, 683
Lipoprotein, 43
■ Liposuctioning, 558
Liriodendron, 534
■ *Listeria*, 338i, 347
Lithops, 828, 828i
Lithosphere, 272i, **867**
Littoral zone
 intertidal, 890–891, 891i
 lake, 886, 886i, 887i
Littorina littorea, 834i, 835
Liver, 92, 510, 586i, 681, 732i, 732t
 animal, 58i, 444i
 blood flow through, 664, 664i, 665i, 676
■ diseases, 90–91, 191, 201t, 293, 343t, 359i
■ disorders, 150, 287, 401i, 638, 732t, 733t, 747
 drugs and, 90, 594, 729, 738
 endocrine role, 620, 621i
 energy source, 131, 134
 function, 39, 39i, 41i, 49, 62, 86, 90, 134, 233, 664, 672, 676, 684, 687, 720, 720i, 722i, 723, 725, 729, 729i, 731, 736t, 741
 hormones and, 622, 623i, 624, 628, 628i, 630, 635t, 636, 729
 structure, 64
■ Liver cancer, 783
 Liver cell, 90, 214–215
■ Liver failure, 595
Liverwort, 314i, 372, 372i, 373i, 376–377, 377i, 388
Liwi, 300i, 305i
Lizard, 31, 314i, 404i, 428i, 434i, 442i, 443–**444**, 460, 557, 565i, 705i, 749, 757i, 809, 820
 characteristics, 444, 445i
 marine, 465, 465i
Llama, 297, 297i, 304i, 317, 714, 714i
Loam, **512**
Lobaria, 390
Lobe-finned fish, 437i, **439**, 439i, 452, 460
Lobelia, 300, 300i
Lobster, 422, 422i, 430–431, 617, 641
Local signaling molecule, **620**, 630, 636, 750
■ Lockjaw, 653
Locomotion, 70i, 71, 73t

animal trait of, 403–404, 406, 408, 430
  arthropod walking legs, 422–423, 422i, 430
  cephalopod, 418, 418i, 430
  earthworm, 415, 415i, 430
  fish, 438, 440i, 441
  insect, winged, 420, 424–425, 430
  lancelet, 435
  mollusk foot, 416
  reptile, 442, 444
  salamander, 440i, 441
  scallop, 417
  sea star, 428, 429i
  shark, 438
  vertebrate, 433, 564i, 566
■ Logging, 387, 389, 389i, 475, 882
■ mechanized, halting of, 808
■ strip, 474, 474i, 882
Logistic population growth, 801, 806–807, 806i, 807i, 818, 825i
Loligo, 579i
Long-day plant, 550–551, 550i, 551i, 555–556
Long-term memory, 593, 593i, 597
Longitudinal fission, 357
Loop of Henle, 743, 743i, 744i, 745, 745i, 752–753
Loose connective tissue, 562, 562i, 568, 570
Lorenz, Konrad, 902i
■ Low-carb diet, 731
■ Low-density lipoprotein (LDL), 49, 672, 730–731
Low-frequency sound, 599, 602
Lower littoral zone, 891, 891i
Loxosceles laeta, 426
LSD (lysergic acid diethylamide), 595
Lubchenco, Jane, 835
Luciferase, 102–103, 102i, 253i
Luciferin, 102
■ Luft's syndrome, 122
Lumbar nerve, 575i, 586i
Lumbricus terrestris, 167i
Lumen, 588–589, 671–672, 672i, 682, 703, 720, 722–729, 726i, 727i, 736, 745i, 775i
Lumper vs. splitter, 317
Lung, 70, 437, 510, 560i, 701–702, 704, 706i, 716, 723, 741
  air pollution and, 700, 706–707, 712
  blood flow through, 658–659, 664, 664i, 665i, 668, 669i
  "book," 421, 421i, 703, 716
■ diseases, 45i, 206, 397, 397t, 615, 682, 712–713, 713i
■ disorders, 72–74, 794, 871
  evolution of, 433, 437, 437i, 440–442, 460, 658, 675, 704
  human, 70, 70i, 73, 481i, 482
  immune response, 681–682, 683i
  reptile, 444i, 446, 705, 705i
  structure, 70, 70i, 89, 705, 705i
  vertebrate, 312, 312i, 313i, 642, 643i, 705, 705i, 715
Lung, human, 586i, 706i, 707–708, 708i, 710–712, 710i, 711i, 712i, 716
  drug addiction and, 594
  volume, 710–711, 710i, 711i
■ Lung cancer, 595, 700, 713t, 773, 871
Lungfish, 314i, 404i, 428i, 434i, 437i, 439, 439i, 717
Lupinus arboreus, 486–487, 487i
Luria, Salvador, 208
Lutcavage, Molly, 715i
Luteal phase, 776t, 777, 780i, 797
Luteinizing hormone (LH), 621i, 622t, 624–625, 625i, 633, 636, 738, 774–775, 775i, 777, 779, 779i, 780i, 796
Lycopersicon, 296, 296i, 494i
Lycopersicum, 296, 296i
Lycophyte, 311, 311i, 314i, 371, 372i, 375, 375i, 378–379, 378i, 388

carboniferous, 373i, 378, 380, 380i
Lycopodium, 378, 378i
Lyell, Charles, 265, 267
■ Lyme disease, 338, 339i, 426, 426i
Lymph, 674–676, 674i, 681
Lymph capillary, 674–676
Lymph node, 230, 419i, 661, 674–675, 674i, 676, 681, 687, 687i, 690, 691i, 692, 692i, 696, 773
Lymph vascular system, 657, 674–676, 674i, 687i
Lymph vessel, 560i, 568, 659, 671, 674–676, 674i, 687, 690
  food absorption, 726–727, 726i, 736
Lymphatic system, 567i, 574i, 657, 659, 661, 675–676, 687i
  circulatory system linkage, 657, 659, 670i, 671, 674–676, 674i
  function, 567i, 674, 674i
Lymphocyte, 674i, 680
  immune response by, 660i, 661–662, 675, 679, 680t, 681, 681i, 685–687, 686i, 696, 697i, 698, 698t
Lymphoid organ, 657, 675–676
■ Lymphoma, 197
Lynx, 826–827, 827i
Lysine, 222i, 226i, 554, 730
Lysis, 344, 344i, 348–349, 662, 680t, 684, 684i, 732t
Lysogenic pathway, 344–345, 344i, 348
Lysosome, 58, 59i, 63, 73t, 86i, 87, 87i, 353, 488, 686
Lysozyme, 682–683, 682t, 698, 726, 726i, 736
Lystrosaurus, 273, 273i, 442
Lytechinus, 769
Lytic pathway, 344–345, 344i, 348

Ⓜ
Maathai, Wangari, 387i, 389
MacArthur, Robert, 468
McCain, Garvin, 16
McClintock, Barbara, 226, 227i
McClintock, Martha, 913
Macrocystis, 352i, 361, 361i
Macroevolution, 271, 301–302, 302i, 310, 316
  evolutionary tree diagrams for, 301, 314, 314i
  in morphology, 274–275, 274i–275i
  trends. See Evolutionary trends
Macronucleus, 356i, 357, 357i
Macronutrient, 512–513, 512t, 522, 522i
Macrophage, 71, 86, 355, 661i, 681, 696
  in immune response, 335, 397, 681, 681i, 686, 687i, 693, 698, 698t, 750
  in inflammation, 684–685, 685i
  phagocytosis by, 660i, 661
Macrotermes, 911i
■ Macular degeneration (AMD), 615
■ Mad cow disease, 254, 347, 347i
Magicicada, 302i
Magnesium, 34, 109i, 512, 512t, 861
  dietary, 733t
Magnesium sulfate, 892
Magnetic field, sense of, 617
Magnetic pattern, volcanic rock, 272
Magnetic resonance imaging (MRI), 631
Magnetotactic bacterium, 339, 339i
Magnoliid, 385, 385i, 388t, 389, 494, 499, 504
Maiasaura, 442i
Mainland biodiversity pattern, 838, 838i, 840
■ Malaria, 293, 293i, 301, 301i, 346t, 368, 427, 837, 842
■ sporozoan agent of, 358–359, 359i
Malate, 116–117, 117i, 519, 519i
Malathion, 848i
■ Malibu firestorm, 879i

■ Malignancy, 693
■ Malignant melanoma, 151i
■ Malignant neoplasm, 151, 151i
■ Malnutrition, 191, 242, 397, 554, 718, 737i, 812–813, 812i
Malpighian tubule, 421i, 424
Malthus, Thomas, 266
Malus, 533i
Mammal, 164, 196, 238, 282, 307, 333–334, 431, 448, 464i, 468, 534, 718
  adaptive radiation, 241, 271i, 308–309, 309i, 390
  biotic potential, 805
  brain, 576, 576i, 589i
  characteristics, 41, 188, 300, 312, 312i, 313i, 448–449, 448i, 460–461, 596t, 642i, 845, 907–909
  circulatory system, 658–660, 659i
■ cloning, 206, 214–215
  current diversity, 450, 450i, 450t, 451i, 473
  development, 760–761
  dosage compensation in, 234–235
  evolution, 237, 241, 271i, 274, 281, 281i, 284, 312, 312i, 313i, 314i, 404i, 407, 407i, 428i, 432i, 433, 434i, 436–437, 437i, 442–443, 442i, 448–449, 448i, 449i, 452, 454–455, 460, 642–643, 643i, 809, 809i
  genetically engineered, 254, 254i
  glucose, body use of, 134–135, 135i
  hormones, 619, 626, 632, 635
  major groups, 404i
  marine, 469, 715–716, 715i, 866
  reproduction, 154, 632, 754, 757i, 772, 776, 787–788, 794, 837
  respiration, 701, 705, 705i, 716
  sensory systems, 602, 604, 606, 611–612, 616–617, 617i
  sex chromosomes, 231, 240
  specie convergences, 450t
  temperature regulation, 449, 478, 749–751, 750i, 751i, 751t
  urinary system, 741–742, 753
Mammary gland, 448–449, 460, 624, 624i, 625i, 634t, 636, 640, 757i, 794i, 795, 797, 911
  human (breasts), 448i, 638
Manatee, 309i, 358, 451i
Mandible, 422i, 424i, 910i
Manduca sexta, 528
Manganese, plant growth and, 512, 512t
Mangrove wetland, 473i, 874i–875i, 890, 890i
Mantle, 416, 703i
  Earth, 272, 272i
  molluscan, 416–418, 416i, 417i, 418i, 430
Maple tree, 385, 495, 500i, 506, 532, 534, 534i, 880
Marchantia, 377i
■ Marfan syndrome, 177, 177i, 201t, 205
Margulis, Lynn, 326
■ Marijuana, 381, 401, 595, 713, 738
Marine biodiversity pattern, 838, 838i
Marine ecoregion, 875, 896
Marine ecosystem, 118–119, 468–469, 473i, 850–851, 850i, 851i, 861–862, 862i, 864, 867, 892, 893i, 896
Marine nurseries, 890
Marine Peace Park, 474, 475i
Marine sanctuary, 469, 469i
Marine snow, 892
Mark–release–recapture method, 288, 291, 803
Marker-assisted selection, 168
Marler, Peter, 902
Marsh, 132, 510, 835t, 847, 889i
Marsh grass, 847, 849i, 890i
Marsh hawk, 845, 845i, 846i

Marsupial, 234, 309i, 448–450, 448i, 449i, 450i, 460, 757i
Masai skeleton, 458i
Mason, Russell, 903
Mass extinction, 33, 118, 309, 316, 316i, 446, 476
  Cambrian, 271i
  competitive exclusion, 824–825, 825i
  Cretaceous, 271i, 443
  Cretaceous–Tertiary (K–T) impact, 260, 260i, 271i
■ current, 444, 463, 468–469, 475
  Devonian, 271i, 373, 440
  early placental mammals, 449, 449i
  fossil record of, 264
  through geologic time, 464i, 464t
  hot spots, 472
■ human-induced, 271i, 444, 458, 463, 475
  Jurassic, 271i, 443
■ K–T impact and, 443
  Permian, 271i, 373, 448
  recoveries from, 464, 464i
  Triassic, 271i
Mass number, atomic, 20–21
Mast cell, 661i, 681, 681i, 684, 685i, 689, 694, 696, 698, 698t
Master gene, 235, 404, 433, 440, 551, 574, 765, 900
  Arabidopsis thaliana, 235, 240
  homeotic, 236, 240, 276, 765
  in pattern formation, 276–277, 276i, 404, 755, 765, 768, 788
  plant (A,B,C), 236, 240
  in sex determination, 192, 241, 771
Maternal chromosome, 156, 158i, 160i, 161, 161i, 163, 164i, 166–167
Maternal effect gene, 237i
Maternal message, 232, 237i, 760–761, 760i, 764, 768
Mating behavior, 417, 417i, 444–445, 588, 620, 756, 808–810, 900, 906–907, 915
Mayr, Ernst, 302
Mc1r gene, 289
■ MDMA (Ecstasy), 572–573, 572i, 573i, 582–583, 594, 738
■ Measles, 343t, 346t, 694i
Mechanical energy, 93, 93i
Mechanical isolation, 302i, 303, 303i
Mechanical processing, digestion, 719–721, 723–724, 736
Mechanical stress, 667i
  connective tissue and, 562
  plant response to, 545, 548–549, 549i, 555
■ Mechanized logging, 387
Mechanoreceptor, 599–600, 600t, 602, 605, 615, 725
Medicago, 499i
■ Mediterranean diet pyramid, 731
Medulla oblongata, 586i, 588, 588i, 589i, 591, 596t, 621i
Medullary center, 712, 712i
Medullosa, 380i
Medusa, 410–411, 410i, 411i, 893i
Medusazoan, 410
Meerkat, 571, 571i, 908
Megachile rotundata, 524
Megakaryocyte, 661, 661i
Megaspore, 375, 380–381, 383, 383i, 384i, 386i, 388, 525, 526i, 530, 531i
Meiosis, 142–143, 142t, 156, 188, 214, 329i, 368t
  abnormalities during, 190i, 196–199, 204–205
  characteristics, 142–143, 152, 155, 158i–159i, 166
  chromosome number and, 156–157, 162, 166
  crossing over during, 160, 160i, 169–170, 172–173, 172i, 175, 178, 178i, 182, 184, 284

division stages, 155, 157i, 158i–159i, 164i–165i, 166
in egg formation, 162, 163i, 778i, 779, 781, 781i, 796–797
in fungi, 394i, 395i, 396i, 400
gamete formation in, 192i, 193, 194i, 196, 198i, 286–287
independent assortment in, 284
metaphase I alignment, 174, 174i, 182
mitosis vs., 142, 155–157, 164, 164i–165i, 167
nondisjunction during, 306, 307i
in plants, 162, 162i, 374, 374i, 376i, 379i, 386i, 526i, 530, 530i, 531i, 538
random alignment of chromosomes, 160, 161i, 166
sexual reproduction role, 142, 152, 155–156, 158i–159i, 160, 166, 756, 759i
in sperm formation, 162, 163i, 774, 775i
Meiosis I, 157, 157i, 158i, 162, 163i, 166, 166i, 205
Meiosis II, 157, 157i, 159i, 162, 163i, 164, 165i, 166, 166i, 205
Meiotic cell division
gamete formation, 158i, 160–162, 162i, 165i, 166
in protists, 352, 357i, 365, 365i, 368
spore formation, 155, 158i, 162i, 164i, 165i, 166
Meissner's corpuscle, 602, 603i
Melanin, 99i, 177, 179–181, 179i, 180i, 183, 234i, 569, 733t
Melanocyte, **569**
Melanocyte-stimulating hormone (MSH), 634t
Melatonin, 621i, 622t, 632, 632i, 635t, 636
Melosh, H., 443
■ *Memnoliella*, 397
Memory, 199, 205i, 236, 256, 572, 812
brain function, 581–583, 591, 596t, 597, 604, 631
Memory cell, immune response, 680t, 681, **686**–687, 687i, 690i, 691, 691i, 692i, 694, 698, 698t
Mendel, Gregor, 176, 284, 544
inheritance patterns, 187, 190–191, 193–194, 200–201, 204–205
studies of inheritance, 169–175, 170i, 172i, 173i, 174i–175i, 182, 184, 249
Mendeleyev, Dmitry, 20, 20i
Meninges, 587–588, 587i, 589i
■ Meningitis, 347, **587**, 682
Menopause, 645, 738, **777**
Menstrual cycle, 631, 638, 738, 771, **776**–780, 776t, 778i, 779i, 780i, 782, 788, 796, 913
Menstruation, 568, 776t, 777, 780i, 783–784, 787
Mental impairment, 186–187, 196, 198–199, 201t, 343t, 626
Mercenaria mercenaria, 849i
Mercury, 18, 18i, 510, 589, 795, 848–849, 865
Meristem, **493**, 494i, **495**, 508, 532, 536, 542, 552
apical, 493, 494i, 495, 498, 498i, 502–503, 502i, 508, 542i, 544
lateral, 493, 494i, 495, 504, 504i, 508
nature of, 493, 494i, 495–496, 498, 502
Merozoite, 359, 359i
Mescaline, 572
Mesoderm, **405**, 407, 412, 430, 559, **566**, 570, **758**, 762, 765, 768, 788, 788i, 797
Mesoglea, 410i, **411**
Mesophile, 329i

Mesophyll, 116i, 496, 500–501, 501i, 508, 517i, 520–521, 523i
Mesophyll cell, **116**–117, 116i, 117i
Mesotrophic lake, 887i
Mesozoic era, 271, 271i, 309i, 384, 384i, 442i, 446, 452, 464i, 464t
Messenger RNA (mRNA), 62i, 219–**220**, 226i, 229, 345, 348
cDNA formed on, 245–246, 245i, 251, 257
eukaryotic, 219, 221, 223, 232, 237i, 238t
inactivation, 232–233, 233i
prokaryotic, 219
transcript formation, 220–226, 221i, 222i, 223i, 224i, 225i, 228–229, 228i, 689i
transcript processing, 221, 221i, 228i, 232, 233i, 760–761, 768–769
translation, 219, 223–225, 224i, 225i, 228, 228i, 232, 233i, 239i, 689i, 769
■ Metabolic acidosis, **747**
Metabolic heat, 26, 91–94, 122, 179, 446, 739, 749–752, 751i, 751t, 843, 844i, 845–846, 847i, 850–851, 851i
blood-borne, 685, 685i
nature of, 478, 484i, 485
Metabolic pathway, 91, **100**, 100i, 104, 122, 651, 651i, 702
function, 91, 98, 98i, 101
genetic disorders, 190–191, 191i, 202
mutations and, 118, 179–181, 179i, 202
origin of, 322, 322i, 326–327
Metabolic rate, 734, 749, 751–752
Metabolic reaction, 37, 37i, 482
coenzyme role in, 37, 99, 104, 104t
energy changes in, 91, 94–97, 94i, 96i–97i, 104
participants in, 91, 92–99, 104, 104t
reversible, 100–101, 100i, 104
Metabolic waste, 32, 480–481, 660, 664, 669, 672, 731, 741–742, 745, 745i, 747, 752, 806
Metabolic water, 741, 741i
Metabolism, 26, **90**, 103, 136, 162, 240, 284, 582, 582i, 849
ATP and, 46, 48, 91, 95
bacterial, 118, 239
blood calcium level, 644–645
blood flow and, 669, 669i, 676
carbohydrate, 719–720
core temperature and, 685, 698
■ disorders, 21, 21i, 30t, 629, 631, 733t, 738–739, 747–748
electron transfers in, 91, 101, 104, 122–123, 125
fat (lipid), 719–720
genetic basis of, 455, 735–736
glucose, 48t, 126, 127i, 239i, 621i, 628, 636, 719
hormonal control, 619–620, 621i, 626–627, 633, 635t, 636, 735–736, 735i, 764i
human, 478–479, 481, 489
nature of, 51–53, 58, 72, 75, 88, 91, 94, 104
nucleic acid and, 719–720
organic. *See* Organic metabolism
origin of agents of, 322–323, 322i, 327, 330
prokaryotic, 56–57, 72, 333–334, 334t
protein, 719–720
rates, 443, 445–446, 695
Metabolism, plant, 117, 481, 487–489, 488i, 505, 512–513, 516, 522, 522i, 846, 851, 851i
Metacarpals, 643i
Metal ion, function of, 322–324
Metamorphosis, **420**, 424, 424i, 434i, **627**, 821
frog, 441i, 627, 627i, 636, 759i

Metaphase, mitosis, 141, 144i, 145–**146**, 145i, 146i, 147, 147i, 152, 153i, 157, 158i, 160–161, 160i, 161i, 163, 164i, 166, 174, 174i, 182, 188, 189i, 204
Metaphase I, meiosis, 157i, 158i, 160–161, 161i, 163, 164i, 166, 174, 174i, 182, 198i
Metaphase II, meiosis, 157i, 159i, 165i, 198i
Metastasis, **151**–152, 151i, 152i, 693, 773
Metatarsals, 643i
Meteorite, 273, 321, 338, 464t
Methamphetamine, 572, 594
Methamphetamine hydrochloride, 594
Methane, 8i, 25, 26i, 32, 32i, 34, 106, 320–321, 321i, 340, 348, 858, 859i, 864–865
Methane cycling, 865, 865i
Methane hydrate, 32, 341, 440
in carbon cycle, 856, 865, 865i
Methanobacterium, 340i
Methanocaldococcus jannaschii, 340i
Methanococcus, 340i
Methanogen, 329i, **340**–341, 340i, 348
Methionine, 42i, 56, 222, 222i, 224i, 225i, 228i, 340, 730
Methyl, functional group, 36i, 227, 232
Methyl bromide, air pollutant, 870, 896
Methylation, **232**, 235
MHC (Major Histocompatibility Complex) marker, **686**, 686i, 689–690, 691i, 692i, 693, 698, 698t
Micelle formation, **727**, 727i
Micrasterias, 372i
Microevolution, 282–283, **285**, **298**, 298t, 315, 336, 821
directional selection, 283, 287–289, 287i, 288i, 289i, 298, 308, 316t
disruptive selection, 283, 287, 287i, 290i, 291, 291i, 298, 298t
gene flow in, 283, 286, 290, 294–295, 295i, 298, 298t, 301–302, 308, 316t
gene pool for, 284, 298
genetic drift, 283, 290, 294–295, 298, 298t, 302, 308, 316t
Hardy-Weinberg rule, 286–287, 286i, 298
mutations and, 283–287, 290, 298, 298t, 302, 306, 307i, 316t
natural selection, 283, 287–291, 298, 298t, 906
population as a unit of, 284–285, 285i, 298
speciation and, 301, 316
stabilizing selection, 283, 285, 290–291, 290i, 298
variation in traits, 283–284, 292–293, 298
Microfibril, 568i
Microfilament, **68**–72
in animal cell, 59i, 68, 760, 762i
in plant cell, 59i
Microglia, 583
Micrograph, **54**, 55i, 58i, 72
Micronucleus, 356i, 357, 357i
Micronutrient, **512**–513, 512t, 522, 522i
Microscope, 50–51, 51i, 54i, 55i, 72
Microscopy, 50–51, 54, 55i, 72, 188, 189i, 204, 648, 679
Microspore, 375, 380–**381**, 383, 383i, 384i, 386i, 388, 525, 526i, 530, 530i
Microsporidian, 314i, 391, 392i, **393**, 397t, 400
Microtubular spindle, 141, 145–147, 145i, 146i, 147i, 148i, 151–153,

157, 158i–159i, 164, 164i–165i, 166–167, 306, 760–761, 768
equator, 146i, 147–148, 148i, 158i, 161, 165i, 166
Microtubule, 57, **68**–69, 69i, 72, 143, 152
in animal cell, 59i, 68
colchicines and, 188, 189i
function, 68–71, 70i
in meiosis, 157, 158i–159i, 161, 164i
in mitosis, 145–147, 145i, 146i, 147i, 148i, 153, 164i, 166
in plant cell, 59i, 66i, 68
protist, 352–353, 358, 366
structure, 68, 68i, 71, 71i, 73i, 73t, 760, 762i
Microtus ochrogaster, 900
M. pennsylvanicus, 901
Microvillus (microvilli), **405**–406, 408, 409i, 560i, 608–609, **726**–727, 726i
Microwave, 108i
Midbrain, 444i, 586i, 588, 588i, 589i, 596t
Middle ear, 598, **606**, 606i, 615, 644
■ Middle ear infection, 347, 700
Middle East conservation effort, 474, 475i
Midline, embryo, 763
Midlittoral zone, **890**, 891i
Midsagittal plane, 566i
Miescher, Johann, 208
■ Mifepristone (RU 486), 783
Migration, **447**, 449i, 617, 803–**804**, 807i
animal, 390, 390i, 715
bird, 133, 138, 447, 824, 842, 883i, 890
circadian, open ocean, 892, 893i
fish, 360, 888
human, 459, 569, 812
intracellular, 248, 248i, 257, 530
monarch butterfly, 525
■ Mildew, 168, 183
Milk, 238, 335i, 448–449, 448i, 460–461, 554, 561, 570, 621i, 624, 634t, 636, 677, 688, 794–795, 794i, 797
human dietary, 730, 732t, 737
■ lactose intolerance, 190–191, 239
Milk of magnesia, 28, 28i
Millenium Ecosystem Assessment's Desertification Synthesis, 885i
Miller, G. Tyler, 817
Miller, Stanley, 321, 321i
Millipede, 420, 420i, 423, 423i, 430, 703
Mimicry, **12**–13, 13i, **828**, 829i, 840
Mineral, 86, 268, 644–645, 654, **732**, 736–737, 850
in human diet, 719, 728, 730, 732–733, 733t, 736, 792
in plant nutrition, 371, 374, 493–494, 494i, 502–503, 508, 512–513, 512t, 513t, 520–523, 520i, 521i, 522i, 529, 876, 877i
Mineral cycling, 880, 892
Mineralocorticoid, 635t
Minibrain gene, 236
■ Miscarriage, 198, 203, 347, 369, 770, 793
Mischococcus, 352i, 360i
"Missing links," 432, 435
Mississippi River Delta, 888, 889i
Missouri rift, 272i
Missouri River, 888
Mite, 421, 421i, 426, 426i, 430, 524, 694, 903i, 903i
Mitochondrial DNA (mtDNA), 222, 278, 279i, 305i, 306, 327, 345, 348, 354, 458–459, 459i

Mitochondrion (mitochondria), **64**, 64i, 138, 164, 278, 314i, 368t, 714, 823
  aerobic respiration and, 123–125, 125i, 128, 128i, 130–131, 131i, 133, 137–138, 708, 751, 753
  characteristics, 64–65, 72, 327
  dysfunction, 122, 122i
  eukaryotic cell, 222, 228
  function, 58, 59i, 64, 72, 73t, 122
  human sperm, 774, 775i
  micrographs, 55i, 64i
  muscle cell, 564i, 565, 653, 655, 667, 677
  origin, 319, 326–327, 327i, 329i, 330, 338i
  protist, 352–354, 354i, 355i, 368
  structure, 64, 64i, 128i, 129i, 130–131, 130i, 131i, 137, 766
Mitosis, **142**, 329i, 775i
  cell cycle and, 141, 144–145, 188, 189i
  chromosome number and, 145–146, 145i, 152
  cytoplasmic division, 141, 142t, 145, 152
  in fungi, 394i, 395i, 396i, 400
  meiosis vs., 142, 154–157, 164, 164i–165i, 167
  stages, 141, 145–147, 146i–147i, 152–153, 153i, 165i
Mitotic cell division, 189i, 196, 203, 214i, 368t, 583, 660
  abnormalities, 191, 196, 198–199, 306
  animals, 146, 405i, 420, 566, 568, 633, 758, 758i, 760, 768
  in asexual reproduction, 142–143, 142t, 152, 336, 338, 536, 537i, 756
  bodily growth, 142–143, 142t, 150, 152
  in cell replacement, 142–143, 142t, 150, 152
  eukaryotic cells, 142, 142i, 143, 152, 233
  in immune responses, 686, 690
  plants, 162, 374i, 386i, 496, 526, 526i, 530, 530i, 531i, 542
  in protists, 352–353, 365i, 366–368, 367i
  in sexual reproduction, 156, 166
Mixture, **23**, 30, 30t, 40, 47
■ MMR vaccination, 694i
Models, **11**, 15
Molar, tooth, 448i, 455, 721, 721i
Mold, household, 397
■ Mole, skin, 150, 274
Mole-rat, 450t, 910, 911i
Molecular clock, **279**–280
Molecule, 3, **4–8**, 4i, **22–23**, 23i, 25i, 30t, 37, 245, 245i
Molecules of life, **4–5**, 4i, 7, 32–49, 94
Mollusk, 307, 314i, 402, 402i, **416–417**, 416i, 417i, 430–431, 438, 470, 472i, 597, 597i, 608, 658, 702
  evolution, 269–270, 270i, 404i, 407, 428, 428i, 761
Molothrus ater, 830–831, 831i
Molt-inhibiting hormone (MIH), 633i
Molting, 407i, **420**, 420i, 423–424, 424i, 619, **633**, 633i, 636–637, 637i
Molybdenum, plant growth and, 512, 512t
Moment-of-truth defense, 829, 829i
Monarch butterfly, 525, 807, 807i, 828
■ *Monilinia fructicola*, 397t
Monkey, 258, 346, 450t, **452–454**, 453i, 460, 461i, 631, 663, 881
■ Monkeypox, 343t
Monoclonal antibodies, **693**, 693i, 699
Monocot, 252, **385**, 385i, 386i, 388t, 389, 493–495, 495i, 499, 499i, 500i, 501, 501i, 508, 543i, 544, 618
  characteristics, 503, 503i, 532, 538

  vs. eudicot, 495, 495i
Monocyte, 660i, 661i, 662, 681, 689, 696
Monoglyceride, 724t, 725, 727, 727i, 736
Monohybrid experiment, 169, **172**–173, 172i, 173i, 175, 182
Monomer, **36**, 38–39, 46, 68–69, 216, 546, 546i
  glucose, 623i, 628, 628i
Monophyletic group, **310–311**, 311i, 316, 338, 338i, 351–352, 364, 366–369, 375i, 392, 442
Monosaccharide, 38, 38i, 48t, 724t, 725, 727i
Monosodium glutamate (MSG), 604
Monotreme, 309i, **448–450**, 449i, 450i, 460
Monsoon, **873**
Montane coniferous forest, 882, 882i
Monteverde Cloud Forest Reserve, 472–473, 473i
Moorhead, Paul, 766
Moral choice, 14, 899, 913–914
Morchella esculenta, 396i
Morgan, Thomas, 193
■ Morning-after pill, **783**
Morphine, 402, 583, 595
Morphogen, **764**–765
Morphogenesis, 755, 762–**763**, 762i, 763i, 764, 768, 788i
Morphological convergence, **275**, 275i
  vs. divergence, 312
Morphological divergence, **274**, 308, 312
  vertebrate forelimb, 274–275, 274i
Morphological trait, **284**–285, 286i, 289i, 311–312
Morphology, comparative. See Comparative morphology
Mortality risk, 808, 808t
Morula, 786i, 795t
Mosaic theory of image formation, 609
■ Mosaic tissue effect, 199, 201t, 205, 234, 234i
Mosasaur, 465, 465i
Mosquito, 300–301, 424i, 837, 842, 883i
  as disease vector, 293, 293i, 301, 332, 359, 359i, 842
  as intermediate host, 419, 427, 427i
Moss, 314i, 372i, 376–377, 376i, 388, 544, 832, 832i, 880–881
Moth, 188, 241, 241i, 288–289, 288i, 524, 538, 604, 620, 904, 906, 906i, 915
  Hawaiian, 831
Mother–infant bonding, 913
■ Motion sickness, **605**
Motor area, brain, 589–591, 590i, 593i
Motor neuron, 565, 565i, **574–577**, 574i, 575i, 576i, 580–581, 581i, 584–587, 585i, 587i, 596–597, 601i, 650, 650i, 652–654
Motor protein, 69–71, 70i, 82–83, 146–147, 147i, 152, 158i
Motor unit, **652**, 654
Mount Saint Helens, 833, 833i
Mountain aven, as pioneer species, 832i
Mountain vole, 900i, 901, 912
Mouse, 154, 154i, 184, 237, 277, 277i, 677, 749, 765, 837, 904, 915
  ■ bioluminescence, 102–103, 103i
  ■ as experimental organism, 206, 208, 208i, 215, 254, 254i, 256, 769
  exponential population growth, 804–805, 804i
  mitosis stages, 146i–147i
  obesity, 718, 718i
Mouth, 604, 615–616, 633i, 682, 683i, 706i, 707, 716, 750, 762, 762i
  ■ cancer, 595, 713t

  digestion and, 720–721, 720i, 723–724, 736, 736t
  invertebrate, 406–407, 407i, 416i, 417, 417i, 421i, 428, 430
■ Mouth-to-mouth respiration, 656
MreB protein monomer, 69
mRNA. See Messenger RNA
mtRNA. See Mitochondial RNA
Mucin, 682, 723
Mucosa, 724i, 725–727, 725i, 726i, 736
Mucous membrane, 334, 397t, 696, 784
  defense against pathogens, 679
Mucus, 72, 73, 74, 74i, 561, 682–683, 682i, 683i, 688, 694, 698, 707, 712, 712i, 823
  in digestive system, 722–724, 722i, 726, 726i, 736, 736t
  function, 772t, 773, 773i, 776, 776t, 777i, 779
Mucus gland, 561i
■ Mule, 303
Multicelled organism, 4i, **5–8**, 5i, 9i, 14, 35, 47, 142t, 162i, 233, 367
■ Multiple allele system, **176**, 182
■ Multiple birth, 770
■ Multiple fruit, **532**, 533i, 533t
■ Multiple sclerosis (MS), 584, 695
Multiplication cycle, viral, 333, 344–345, 344i, 345i, 348
Multiregional model, **458**
■ Mumps, 343t, 694i
Mus musculus, 837
Muscle, 92, 241, 484, 566, 574, 574i, 596, 602, 642, 643i, 644, 702, 758
  abdominal, 703, 703i, 711
  body builder, 264, 638–639, 638i
  contraction. See Contraction
  disorders, 195, 201t, 205, 229, 638–639
  flight, 446, 447i, 461
  longitudinal, 415, 415i
  mechanoreceptors, 599, 601i, 602
  neural signals, 580–581, 581i, 596
  segmented, 414–415, 415i, 435–437, 435i, 759i
  voluntary/involuntary, 464, 565
Muscle cell, 29, 53, 69, 79i, 134, 565, 565i, 622, 628i
  ■ cloning, 214t, 215
  components, 39, 39i, 43, 47
■ Muscle cramp, **652**, 733t
Muscle fatigue, 602, **652**–653
Muscle fiber, 83, **564**, 564i, 565i, 580–582, 581i, 585i, **646**, 648–655, 648i, 649i
Muscle sense, 599, 602
Muscle spindle, **585**, 585i, 588, 600t, 601–602
Muscle tension, 639, **652**, 654
Muscle tissue, 558–559, 564–565, 564i, 565i, 570, 638–639, 638i, 651, 653–654
  contraction. See Contraction
Muscle twitch, 652, 652i
■ Muscular dystrophy, 195, 201t, 203, 205, 638–639, 652–653
Muscular system, human, 567i
Mushroom, 8, 312, 391, 392i, 393–395, 395i, 396i, 400
  ■ poisoning, 397t, 401, 401i
Mussel, 417, 417i, 428, 640, 834
■ Mustard gas, 218
Mutation, **10**, 14, 49, **171**, 286, 290, **298**, 529, 544, 545t, 655, 697, 709i, 711
  allele frequencies, 283–285, 295, 298
  allele source, 229, 284, 294, 298, 298t, 316t, 737, 826
  Arabidopsis thaliana, 235, 235i, 240–241
  base-pair substitution, 226–228, 226i, 340
  beneficial, 284–285, 537

  cancer-causing, 150, 227, 230–231, 489
  causing agents, 226–227, 230, 346
  deletion, 187, 196–197, 226–228, 226i
  DNA, 10, 44–45, 47, 138, 150, 188, 190, 249
  DNA repair and, 213, 217, 230
  Drosophila, 193, 193i, 236–237, 236i, 237i, 240–241
  in duplication, 187, 196–197, 197i
  effects on development, 74, 150, 276–278, 407, 416, 416i, 454–455, 548, 551
  evolution and, 197, 227, 276, 278, 281
  frameshift, 226, 226i
  gene, 89, 150, 156, 219, 222, 228, 235, 235i, 241–242, 257, 582, 677, 695, 765–766, 769, 915
  genetic disorders, 72–73, 177, 183, 185–186, 188, 190–191, 191i, 194–195, 195i, 201, 204–205, 256, 622, 637, 653, 662
  genetic divergence and, 276, 276i, 281, 302, 316, 404, 536, 633, 637
  in human evolution, 680
  insertion, 226–228
  in inversion, 187, 196–197
  lethal, 74, 184, 197–199, 204, 208, 284, 287, 693
  master gene, 276–277, 276i, 281, 433, 440, 755, 765, 768
  natural selection and, 10
  nervous system, 574–575
  neutral, 279–280, 284–285, 297
  spontaneous, 190–191, 196, 226, 228, 306, 307i
  transposon, 197, 226, 227i, 228
  variation in traits and, 179–181, 179i, 267, 267i, 280, 765
  viral, 230, 342, 785
Mutation rate, 227
Mutualism, **390**, 400, **822**, **840**
  dinoflagellate/coral, 411
  fungus, 390, 399–400
  nature of, 821–823, 823i, 832, 834, 840
  obligatory, **823**
  pioneer species/nitrogen fixers, 832, 832i
  plant/fungus (mycorrhizae), 391, 399–400, 399i
Mycelium (mycella), **392–395**, 394i, 395i, 397, 399–400
Mycobacterium, 338i
■ *Mycobacterium tuberculosis*, treatment, 102–103
Mycobiont, **398**–399
■ Mycoherbicide, 401
Mycoplasma, 330, 338i
Mycorrhiza (mycorrhizae), 384, 391, **399–400**, 399i, 511, **514–515**, 522, 823, 871
Myelin, **583**
Myelin sheath, **584**–585, 584i, 585i, 587, 596, 602, 672, 695
■ Myeloma, 197
Myllokunmingia, 436i
Myocardium, **666**, 666i
Myofibril, 564, 639, **648**–650, 648i, 649i, 650i, 654
Myoglobin, 133, 702, 708, 709i, 715
Myometrium, 776, 777i
■ Myopia, 614
Myosin, 68–70, 83, 564–565, 639–640
  role in contraction, **648**–650, 648i, 649i, 651i, 654
Myosin head, 649–650, 649i, 651i, 654
■ Myotonic muscular dystrophy, 652
Myrmecophagidae, 450t
Mytilus, 834
Myxobacteria, 339
Myxobolus cerebralis, 830, 830i

reptile, 444i
structure, 587, 587i
vertebrate, 573, 575, 575i, 596
■ Spinal fusion, 122i
Spinal nerve, 575, 575i, 586, 587i
Spindle, microtubular, 68, 141,
  145–147, 145i, 146i, 147i, 148i,
  149i, 151–153, 157, 158i–159i,
  164, 164i, 165i, 166–167, 188,
  760–761, 768
  equator, 146i, 147–148, 148i, 149i,
  158i, 161, 164i–165i, 166
Spindle poles, 174, 174i
Spiracle, 436i, 703, 703i
Spiral cleavage, 761, 761i
Spirillum (spirilla), 334, 338i, 348
Spirochaete group, 314i, 338, 338i,
  339i, 348
Spirochete, 426, 785
Spiroloculina, 350i, 352i
Spleen, 45i, 586i, 661, 674i,
  675–676, 681
■ infection, 343t, 687, 687i, 692i
Split-brain experiment, 592, 592i
Sponge, 314i, 403, 408, 408i, 641, 765
  ancestry, 404–405, 407i, 408,
  408i, 428i
  characteristics, 405, 408–409, 409i,
  430–431, 641
  reproduction, 408–409, 409i,
  756, 758
Spongy bone tissue, 563i, 644, 644i
Spontaneous fission, 756i
Sporangium (sporangia), 378i, 394
Spore, 162, 235, 393, 823
  formation during meiosis, 155,
  158i, 162i, 164i, 165i, 166–167
  fungal, 391–396, 392i, 393i, 394i,
  395i, 396i, 400
  meiotic formation of, 142–143, 152
  protist, 352, 360i, 361i, 362, 365–367,
  365i, 366i, 367i, 830, 830i
Spore, plant, 162, 166, 374, 392, 488,
  525–527, 530, 530i, 538
  evolution, 269, 271i, 371, 374–375,
  380, 388
  megaspore, 525, 526i, 530, 531i, 538
  microspore, 525, 526i, 530, 530i, 538
  seedless plants, 371, 378–380, 379i
Spore sac, 394, 394i, 401, 401i
Sporophyte, 162, 162i, 167, 361, 361i,
  363i, 374, 374i, 376i, 526–527,
  526i, 531, 531i, 538, 830i
  development, 374–375, 381, 388,
  541–542
  examples, 375i, 377i, 379i, 386,
  386i, 388t
  nature of, 377–378, 382–383, 388
■ Sporozoan infection, 293, 346t, 359
Sporozoite, 359, 359i
Sprain, joint, 645
Spriggina, 407i
Spring overturn, 886, 897
Spruce, 382, 451i, 799i, 832i, 882
Spurge, 262–263, 262i
■ Squamous cell carcinoma, 151i
Squid, 237, 418, 418i, 430, 443i, 579i,
  609, 616, 866, 892
Squirrel, 767, 803, 846i
Squirrelfish, 802i
SRY gene, 192, 192i, 204, 241
Stabilizing selection, 285–287, 287i,
  290–291, 290i, 298
■ Stachybotrys, 397
Stahl, Franklin, 217
Staining, microscopy, 54
Stalk, 395i, 400, 531i
Stamen, 170i, 171, 235, 235i, 240,
  302i, 303, 384i, 526–527, 527i,
  528–529, 538
■ Staphylococcus, 335i, 347, 349, 682,
  682i, 690–691
Star anise, 385, 385i
Starch, 21, 38–40, 39i, 48t, 394, 837

in diet, 723, 730
formation, 37, 38i, 39, 115, 115i,
  120, 120i
storage in plants, 65, 73t, 520–521,
  546, 546i
synthesis, 65, 100
Starch grain, 65, 115, 364, 369, 548
Starling, 903, 903i
Starling, E., 620
Starvation, 266, 291, 492, 754, 796,
  800, 806, 812, 812i, 827
Static equilibrium, 605, 605i, 617
Statolith, 548, 548i, 555
Stearic acid, 40i
Stegosaurus, 432i
Steller nerve, 579i
Stem, 9i, 65, 115–116, 162, 253i, 375,
  378, 480, 508, 516, 517i, 520–521
  decay, 486, 486i
  evolution of, 374, 380
  formation, 498, 498i
  functions, 496–497, 496i, 497i, 529
  growth, 498–499, 498i, 499i,
  536, 536t
  plant, 378, 382, 493–500, 494i, 496i,
  498i, 499i, 500i, 540, 542, 543i,
  544, 548, 555
  primary growth, 504
  woody, 497, 504–507, 504i,
  505i, 507i
Stem cell, 188, 558, 563, 644, 660, 714
  bone marrow, 660, 661i, 680t, 681
  embryonic, 558, 558i
  platelet progenitor, 660–661, 661i,
  674i, 675
  red blood cell progenitor, 188, 660,
  661i, 674i, 675
■ research, 256, 558
■ in therapeutic cloning, 214t,
  215–216
  white blood cell progenitor, 189i,
  660, 661i, 674i, 675
Stem node, 544
"Stem reptile," 274, 274i, 442i, 448
Steppe, 449, 875
■ Sterility, 241, 766, 783, 785, 830
■ CFTR mutation and, 74
■ in genetic disorders, 199, 201t, 235
  hybrid, 303, 303i, 307i, 316
■ in vitro fertilization and, 783, 783i
■ self-sacrificing behavior, 910–911,
  910i, 911i
■ Sterilization, 814
Sternum, 446, 447i, 642, 643i
■ Steroid hormone, 41, 48t, 545,
  622–623, 622t, 623i, 633, 634t,
  636, 645, 672, 729i, 730, 774
■ synthetic (anabolic), 638–639, 732t
■ urine test for, 738
Sterol, 40–41, 41i, 47, 48t, 76, 76i,
  88, 730
Stethoscope, 669i, 791
Steward, Frederick, 536–537
Stigma, 526–528, 527i, 530–531, 530i,
  531i, 536, 538
Stillbirth, 713i
Stimulant, 594, 700
Stimulus, 6, 484, 484i, 559, 565, 565i,
  567i, 578, 579i, 580–581, 584–585,
  585i, 596, 599–600, 601–604, 601i,
  615, 899–900, 901–902, 914
  hormonal, 626, 626i, 628i, 630–631,
  633, 633i, 634t
  nervous, 630–631, 633i, 636
  split-brain experiments, 592, 592i
  visual, 608, 609i, 610–613, 611i, 613i
Stingray, 438
Stinkbug, 425i, 831
Stipes, 361, 361i
Stirrup, ear, 606, 606i
■ Stockyards, 34
Stoma (stomata), 116, 116i, 117, 117i,
  120, 480, 482–483, 497, 500–501,
  501i, 508, 508t, 511, 518, 522

abscisic acid and, 544t, 545
function, 553, 555
in plant evolution, 374–375, 388t
transpiration, 516–517, 517i
and water conservation, 487, 487i,
  493, 518–519, 518i, 519i, 522
water loss at, 374, 388
Stomach, 67, 69i, 90, 98–99, 416,
  416i, 564i, 565, 646, 720, 720i, 723
  endocrine roles, 620, 621i, 628, 635t
  function, 724–726, 736, 736i
  glandular secretions in, 718,
  724, 724t
  human, 586i, 722i, 723–725, 724i,
  736, 736t
  lining, 561, 682
  multi-chambered, 721, 721i
  reptile, 444i
  structure, 724–725, 724i
■ Stomach cancer, 335i
■ Stomach stapling, 737
Stone tool, 457, 457i, 459
Stonewort, 372, 372i
Stork, 7
Storm, 474, 839, 842
■ Strain, 337, 346–349, 365i, 645
Stramenopile, 314i, 351, 352i,
  360–362, 362i, 368
Strangleweed, 830, 830i
Stratification, 269
Stratified epithelium, 560
Stratosphere, 870
Strawberry, 532, 533i, 536, 536t
Stream ecosystem, 888–889, 888i
■ Strength training, 264, 653
■ Streptococcus, 337i, 338i, 677, 683
■ S. pneumoniae, 208, 208i, 347
Streptomyces, 338i
■ Streptomycin, 289
Stress marker, 693, 698t
Stress reaction, 694
Stress response, 179, 290, 527, 545,
  548–549, 568–569, 621i, 630–631,
  636–637, 643i, 673, 694, 725, 729,
  744, 766, 787
  cold stress, 750, 750t
  heat stress, 750, 750i, 750t
  long-term (chronic), 630–631, 631i
  short-term, 631
Stretch receptor, 600t, 601–602, 601i,
  615, 794
Stretch reflex, 585, 585i, 587
Stringer, Korey, 478, 478i, 490
■ Strip logging, 474, 474i
■ Strip mining, 883
Strobilus (strobili), 378–380, 378i,
  382–383, 382i, 383i, 389
Stroke, brain, 49, 191, 605, 629t,
  672–673, 676, 700, 730
Stroma, 65, 65i, 111–115, 111i, 113i,
  115i, 120
Stromatolite, 325, 325i, 337
Strongylura marina, 849i
Structural formula, 24, 40i, 41i, 46,
  46i, 76i
  numbering, ring structure, 38i
  for organic compounds, 34
Structural genomics, 251
Structural organization, 480–481, 489
Structural protein, 191, 195, 223,
  223i, 225, 228
Sturgeon, 439, 468
Sturnis vulgaris, 903
Style, 526, 527i, 530, 531i, 536
Stylonychia, 352i
Stylosphaera, 352i, 355i
Subalpine plant, 873
Subatomic particle, 20–21
Suberin, 506, 552
Suberized layer, 552, 552i
Submucosa, 724i, 725i
Subpopulation (race), 304–305,
  458, 460
■ Subsistence farming, 473

Substance P, 583, 603
Substrate, 96–98, 97i, 98i, 104–105,
  361i, 390, 394, 399, 416, 439
  as anchor, 376, 434i, 438i
Substrate-level phosphorylation,
  126, 127i, 129i, 137
Succession, ecological, 832–833,
  832i, 833i
Succulent, 116i, 117
Sucrose, 38–39, 38i, 48t, 85i
  synthesis, 115, 115i, 120, 120i
  transport in plant, 115, 484, 511,
  520–522, 520i, 522i, 528i, 529
Sudden cardiac arrest, 656, 656i
■ Sudden infant death syndrome
  (SIDS), 711
Sudden oak death, 350, 362i
Sugar (deoxyribose), 210, 210i, 211i,
  212, 216
Sugar, simple, 6–7, 23, 26, 38, 48t, 93,
  176, 321, 381i, 394, 508, 604, 860
  absorption in gut, 726–727,
  729–730, 736
  glycolysis and, 126, 132, 132i
  human dietary, 730
  insect facultative mutualism, 823
  metabolism, 93, 95i, 135i, 137
  organic compound role, 33, 36–37,
  46–48, 46i
  in photosynthesis, 21
  plant storage, 65, 364, 506, 511, 514
  structure, 36–38, 36i, 63
  synthesis, 57, 65, 106–107, 111,
  114–116, 115i, 116i, 120
  transport in plants, 493, 497, 497i,
  501, 501i, 520–522, 520i,
  546, 546i
  in urine, 738
Sugar maple, 506
Sugarcane, 381i, 385, 462, 837
Suicidal cell, 150
■ Suicide, 186
Sula granti, 915
Sulawesi, island realm, 841, 841i
Sulfate, 133, 137, 871
Sulfate-reducing euryarchaeote, 340i
Sulfhydryl group, 36i, 37
Sulfolobus, 340i, 341
Sulfur, 18, 18i, 19i, 34, 335, 338,
  341, 848
  dietary, 733t
  metabolism, bacterial, 133
  in organisms, 209i
  plant growth and, 512, 512t
Sulfur dioxide, 29i, 871
■ Sulfur oxide, 391, 870
Sulfur shelf fungus, 401, 401i
Sulfuric acid, 28, 417, 871
Sun, 260, 320, 320i, 321i
■ Sunburn, 345
Sunflower, 532, 553, 553i, 608
Sunlight, 387, 565, 632, 883, 893. See
  also Light
  chloroplast response to, 65, 70
  climate and, 867–868
  endospores in soil, 653
  as energy source, 6, 6i, 9, 22, 23i,
  65, 72, 93, 93i, 94, 100i, 104,
  106–111, 108i, 112, 112i, 113i,
  118i, 120, 120i, 124, 136, 321–322,
  324, 341, 348, 371–372, 374, 494,
  749, 844–845, 844i, 850–851, 851i,
  863, 867, 889i
  hormone secretion and, 632,
  632i, 636
  intensity, 444, 868–869, 869i, 877i
  interception by autotrophs,
  106, 112i
  light-absorbing mechanisms and,
  180–181
  photosynthesis. See Light-
  dependent reactions
  phototropism and, 548–549,
  549i, 555

plant adaptations to, 116, 480, 493, 500–501, 505, 508, 518, 519i, 541, 543i, 553, 556, 876
porphyria and, 571
skin and, 151i, 217, 227, 569, 569i
as stimulus, 565
in tropics, 838
wavelengths of, 320
■ Suntan, 569
■ Super rat, 282–283, 282i, 289
Supercontinent, 271i, 272–273, 273i, 308, 325, 329i, 388, 449i
■ Superhuman, 256
Superior vena cava, 665i
Supernatural vs. science, **12**, 14, 32
Superoxide dismutase, 105, 105i
■ Superpathogen, 255
Superplume, 272i
Supertaster, 616
■ Superweed, 258
Surface tension, 27, 27i
Surface barrier to pathogen, 568, 679, 682–683, 682i, 682t, 683i, 686, 698
Surface-to-volume ratio, **53**, 53i, 326, 374, 482, 489, 500, 708, 765
and animal body plans, 53, 72, 405, 563i
fungal mycellium, 392
gas exchange and, 702, 716
intestinal function and, 726
mycorrhiza, 399
Suricata suricatta, 571i
■ Surrogate, 214–215
Surtsey, 838–839, 838i
Surveillance program, 836
Survival, 3, 10, 13–14, 17i
Survivorship curve, **809**, 809i, 818
Survivorship schedule, 808, 808t
Sushi, 428
Suspended particulate matter, 871i
Sustainable development vs. biodiversity, 387i
Swallowing, 717, 723
Swallowtail butterfly, 425i
Swamp, 34, 443, 473i, 509i, 512, 842i, 859i
plant growth in, 372–373, 378, 388t
Swamp forest, 291, 370, 373, 373i, 378, 380, 388, 440, 454, 882
Sweat, 568, 570, 741–742, 750, 913
Sweat gland, 74, 201t, 234, 234i, 484i, 568, 568i, 640, 741i, 750, 752
■ Sweating mechanism, 27, 478, 478i, 587–588, 741, 746i, 750t, 752–753
Sweet gum tree, 880
Sweet pea plant, 184
Sweet sensation, 604
Sweet wormwood, 359
Swim bladder, 437i, **438**
■ Swimming bell, 893i
■ Swine disease, 835t
■ Swine flu virus, 255
Swordfish, 865
Sycamore tree, 385i
Symbiosis, 355, 355i, 486–487, 510–511, 795, 821–822, 840. *See also* Mutualism
alder and nitrogen-fixing bacteria, 832i
bacteria/amoeba, 327
ciliate/bacterial, 356
dinoflagellate/coral reef, 358, 411, 470
dinoflagellate/red alga, 363
in eukaryotic origins, 326, 327, 329i
fungal, 391, 396, 398–401, 398i, 399i
fungus/cyanobacterium, 338
green alga/fungi, 364
lichen, 398–400, 398i
plant/bacterium, 338
plant/fungus, 374, 511
protistan engaged in, 350
ruminant/microbe, 721i
termite/archaean, 340

Symmetry, animal body, 566i
Sympathetic nerve, 575i, 586–587, 586i, 596, 621i, 630, 725, 744
Sympathetic neuron, **586–587**
Sympatric speciation, **306–307**, 306i, 307i, 316
■ Sympto-Thermal Rhythm method, 782i
Synapse
chemical, 580–581, 580i, 581i, 585, 587, 596, 604
chromosome, 188, 241
Synapsid, **442–443**, 442i, 448
Synaptic cleft, 580–581, 580i
drug action at, 594–595, 597
neurotransmitter in, 580–581, 580i, 581i, 583, 585i, 596, 620, 630, 650, 652
Synaptic integration, **581**
neural system, 581, 581i, 584, 587, 596
in visual pathway, 612–613, 613i
Synaptic nerve signaling, 798
Synchronization, 754–756, 767, 913
Syndrome, **201**
Synura, 352i, 360i
■ Syphilis, 784i, 784t, 785, 785i
Syringia, 551i
System acquired resistance, **486–487**
Systematic classification, 301
Systematic observation, 3, 11–13, 15
Systematics, **310**, 312, 316
Systemic circuit, 657, **659**, 659i, 664, 664i, 668, 668i, 669i, 675–676, 709i, 744
Systemic resistance, 489
Systemin, **545**
Systole, cardiac cycle, **666**, 668i, 669, 669i, 676
Systolic blood pressure, 669, 669i

T

T cell. *See* T lymphocyte
T-even bacteriophage, 342i
T lymphocyte (T cell), 254, 635t, 661, 661i, 675, 680t, **681**, 681i, 686–687, 686i, 687i, 689–690, 695–696, 698–699, 698t, 766
cytotoxic, 687, 687i, 692–693, 692i, 693i, 698, 698t
helper, 687i, 690–691, 691i, 692i, 693, 696, 698, 698t
T lymphocyte (T cell) receptor (TCR), **686**, 689–690, 691i, 692i, 693, 698t
T tubule, 650, 650i
Table salt (NaCl), 24, 24i, 27, 733t
■ Table sugar, 38, 381i
■ Tachycardia, **673**, 673i
Tachyglossidae, 450t
Tactile display, **905**, 905i, 914
Tactile signal, 302i, 303
Tadpole, 63, 441, 441i, 759i, 760i, 762, 764i, 900
■ deformities, 618, 627, 627i
■ *Taenia saginata,* 413i
Tagging, 803
Taiga, 882, 882i
Tail, 184, 184i, 627, 759i, 763i
amphibian, 63, 441
chordate, 433–435, 434i, 435i, 460
dinosaur, 432
human vestigial, 263, 263i, 281, 790i, 791i
sperm cell, 774, 775i, 781i
Tall fescue, 398
Tallgrass prairie, 468, 529i, 845, 846i, 878, 879i
Tandem repeat, **249**, 257
Tangential section, plant, 496i
Tannin, 506

Tapeworm, 404i, 412–413, 413i, 430, 830
Tapir, 881
Taproot system, 382, 503, 503i, 508, 825, 825i
Taq polymerase, 247i
Tarantula, 421i
Target cell, 150–151, 243, 489–490, 763–764
hormone action at, 540, 545–547, 546i, 555, 561, 565, 619–620, 622–624, 623i, 625i, 627–631, 635t, 636, 746, 746i, 751
in immune response, 679, 684i, 685i, 687, 692–693, 698
membrane, 580–581, 583
Tarnias, 824, 824i
Taro, 462
Tarsals, 643i
Tarsier, 452, 453i, 460
Tasmanian devil, 450, 450i
Tasmanian wolf, 450t
Tasmanipatus, 307i
Taste, sense of, 590–591, 599, 600t, 604, 615, 723, 733t
Taste bud, 604, 604i, 615
Taste receptor, **604**, 604i, 615–616
■ Tattooing, **571**, 803
Tawuia, 324i
Taxodium distichum, 509
■ Taxol, 68, 151, 153
Taxon (taxa), **310–312**, 312i, 314, 314i, 316, 351, 405, 442, 464, 468, 475
Taxonomy, 301, **310**, 316–317, 340, 393
numerical, 337
Taxus brevifolia, 68, 69i, 153
TCE. *See* Trichloroethylene
■ Tea plant, leaf harvesting, 381i
Tears, 89, 561, 682, 682t, 688, 698
Technology, 813, 813i, 816–817, 817i
in human evolution, 456, 459
Tectonic change, 465
Tectorial membrane, **607**, 607i
Tectum, 588i, 596t
Teenager, 782, 793, 795i, 795t
Teleost, 439
Telesto, 431i
Telomerase, 766
Telomere, 206, **766**
Telophase, mitosis, 141, 144i, 145, **147**–148, 147i, 148i, 152–153, 153i, 157i, 158i, 159i, 164i, 165i, 166
Telophase I, meiosis, 157i, 158i, 164i, 166
Telophase II, meiosis, 157i, 159i, 165i, 166
Temnodontosaurus, 443
Temperate forest, 399, 473i
Temperate grassland, 473i
Temperate rain forest, 874i–875i, 882
Temperate zone, 116i, 507, 552, 869i
Temperature, **26**
Temperature, body, 478, 599, 750
blood circulation and, 660
changes in, 600t, 602
control of. *See* Temperature regulation
core, 602, 739, 749–752, 750i, 750t, 782, 782i, 794, 917
diffusion and, 80–81
ecstasy impact, 572
enzyme function and, 91, 98–99, 99i, 104, 179, 179i, 182
fever, 685
fur and, 99i
homeostasis, 739, 749, 752
malaria and, 359
regulation. *See* Temperature regulation
sensory receptors, 484–485, 484i, 489–490
skin and, 559, 567i, 570

for sperm formation, 772
Temperature, environmental, 446, 468–469, 484–485, 489, 694, 850
air circulation, 868, 872–873, 872i
as allergen trigger, 527
in animal evolution, 440, 443
asteroid impact and, 273
climate and, 273, 380, 399, 822, 858–859, 858i, 859i, 864
ectotherms and, 749, 749i, 752–753
endotherms and, 749, 749i, 752–753
flowering response and, 541, 550i, 551, 551i
gene expression and, 236
genetic engineering for, 247, 254, 254i
global, 273, 842, 858–859, 858i, 859i, 864–865, 867–868, 875
global broiling, 443
global cooling, 464t, 465
heterotherms, 749, 752
hormonal response to, 633
monarch butterflies and, 807, 807i
ocean circulation and, 867, 872, 872i
plant development and, 116–117, 116i, 117i, 120, 518, 541–542, 542i, 550, 550i, 555
plant dormancy and, 540–542, 550i, 552–553, 555–556
rain shadows and, 873, 873i
sea surface, 865, 894–895, 895i
seawater, 470, 475
thermophiles and, 318
■ Temperature regulation, 572
■ adaptation to, 138
■ mammals, 138, 446, 449, 478, 559, 567i, 632, 660, 749–752, 750i, 750t, 751t
■ mechanisms, 478, 489, 749–752, 750t, 751t
reptile, 445, 749
water and, 19, 26–27, 30–31
Temperature zone, **869**, 869i
Temporal isolation, 302i, **303**, 303i
Temporal lobe, 590i, 591–592
Tendon, 562, 562i, 586, 601–602, 605, 639, 645–**646**, 647i, 653–654
Tendril, 549
Tension, 652
plant, **516–517**, 516i, 517i, 522
Tentacle, 410–411, 410i, 411i, 414i, 418i, 428, 435, 435i, 574–575, 604, 823, 823i, 893i
■ Teratogen, 792i
Terminal bud, 494i, **498**–499, 504i
Termination stage, 224–225, 225i, 228
Termite, 32, 34, 338, 340, 424, 905, 910–914, 910i, 911i, 912i
Territoriality behavior, 900, 902i, 904, 915
Tertiary period, 260i, 271i, 442i, 464t
Tertiary structure, protein, 43, 43i
■ Tertiary wastewater treatment, 889
Test, observational, 535. *See also* Experiment, examples
algal sporophytes, 363i
■ biological clock, cell division, 766
■ blood, prostate cancer, 773
breast cancer, 230i
butterfly wing color, 286, 286i
■ chronic social stress, 631
for color blindness, 195, 195i
directional selection by moth color, 288
DNA replication, 208–209, 208i, 209i
■ drug testing, urine, 738–739, 739i
flower production for pollen export, 535, 538
■ hippocampus reduction, 631
■ for HIV exposure, 785
■ hormone levels, menopause, 738

natural selection among rock pocket mice, 289, 289i
pap smear, 784
phthalate effects on humans, 637
precocious breast development, 637
pregnancy, urine, 738, 787
rhythmic leaf movements, 487, 487i
skin, for allergies, 695
stabilizing selection and bird body mass, 291
sugar in urine, diabetes, 738
tropisms in plants, 548, 548i, 549i
UV levels/skin color, 569
Vibrio cholerae life cycle, 895
weight/heart disease link, 734i
XYY and criminal behavior, 199
Test, scientific, 3, **11–13**, 15
Test-tube baby, 203, 783
Testcross, **173**, 185
Testicle, 638, 915
anabolic steroids and, 638
Testicular cancer, **773**
Testis (testes), 156i, 192, 192i, 199, 412i, 560i, 621i, 622, 625i, 632, 634t, 635t, 638, 770–**772**, 772t, 773–774, 773i, 774i, 782, 796, 798, 915
function, 774–775, 775i, 796
Testosterone, 36i, 37, 595, 618, 621i, 622t, 632, 634, 634t, 635t, 636, 638, 773i, **774**–775, 775i, 796, 798
androgen insensitivity syndrome, 622
red blood cell production, 714
secondary sexual traits and, 192, 199, 204, 621i, 622
Testosterone patch, 632
Tetanus, 346t, 652–654, 652i, 653i, 694, 694i
Tetany, 29
Tethys Sea, 281i
Tetra, 258
Tetracycline, 289
Tetraploid, 307i
Tetrapod, **439**, 440i, 441, 642, 654, 704
origins, 433, 437i, 438–440, 439i, 452, 460
Texas horned lizard, 820
TFR. *See* Total fertility rate
Thalamus, **588**, 588i, 589i, 591, 591i, 593, 593i, 596t, 604
Thalassemia, 226i, **662**
Thalasseosira, 352i, 360i
Thalia democratica, 897, 897i
Thalidomide, 793
Thallus, 377i
Theobroma cacao, 524, 524i
Theory, scientific, 94
Therapeutic cloning, 214, 214t, **215**–216
Therapeutic vaccine, 699
Therapod dinosaur, 442i, 446
Therapsid, 273, 273i, 442, 442i, 448, 460
Thermal energy, **80**, **92**
Thermal gradient, 749
Thermal inversion, **870**, 870i
Thermal radiation, **749**
Thermocline, lake, **886**, 886i, 897
Thermogenesis, 138
Thermometer, 782
Thermoplasma, 340i
Thermoproteus, 340i
Thermoreceptor, **600**, 600t, 602–603, 615–616, 617i, 750–752
Thermotoga maritima, 349
Thermus, 314i, 338i
Thermus aquaticus, 247, 247i, 318, 318i, 341
Thiamin, 732t
Thighbone, 643i, 644i
Thigmotropism, **549**, 549i, 555
Thiomargarita, 338i

T. namibiensis, 335i, 338
Thirst behavior, 747
Thirst center, brain, 739, 741, **746**
Thistle, 534
Thlaspi caerulescens, 510–511, 511i
Thomas, Lewis, 767
Thomson's gazelle, 829, 879i
Thoracic cavity, human, 566i, 664i, 707, 710–711, 710i, 716
Thoracic duct, 674i
Thoracic nerve, 575i, 586i
Thoracic segment, arthropod, 422, 424
Thorax, 236, 237i, 641i, 646, 647i
Thorium, 270
Thorn, 168, 490
Threat display, 444, 445i, 450, 840, **904**, 904i, 914
Three-domain classification system, **310**–311, 311i, 316, 328i, 340
Threonine, 45i, 222i, 226i, 730
Threshold level, action potential, **578**–582, 578i, 579i, 581i, 589
Throat, 590, 706i, 707, 713
cancer, 595
Thrombin, 96, 672i
Thrombus, **672**
Thumb, 602, 602i
Thunderstorm, 507
Thykaloid compartment, 111–113, 111i, 113i, 114i, 120
Thykaloid membrane, **65**, 65i, **111**–113, 111i, 112i, 113i, 114i, 120
Thylacinidae, 450i
Thymine (T), 46–47, 46i, 219–220, 220i, 226–227, 226i, 248, 248i, 323
DNA base pairing rule, 207, 210–212, 210i, 211i, 212i, 213i, 216–217, 217i
Thymine dimer, 217, 217i
cancer and, 227
Thymopoietin, 635t
Thymosin, 621i, 689
Thymus gland, 620, 621i, 635t, 661i, 674i, 675, 689, 698
Thyroid gland, 19, 484i, 620, 621i, 624, 625i, **626**–627, 626i, 634t, 635t, 636, 645, 751
abnormalities, 627, 627i, 636
disorders, 695, 733t, 897i
frog deformities and, 627, 627i
Thyroid hormone, 277, 622–624, 622t, **626**–627, 626i, 634, 634t, 636, 695, 733t
Thyroid-stimulating hormone (TSH), 621i, 625–626, 625i, 626i, 633, 634t, 636
Thyrotoxicosis, 695
Thyrotropin (TSH), 621i, 624–625, 625i, 634t, 636
Thyroxine, 621i, 622t, 626, 635t
Ti plasmid. *See* Tumor-inducing plasmid
Tibia (shinbone), 458i, 643i
Tibialis anterior, 647i
Tick, 39, 39i, 338, 421, 430–431, 830
bites, 426, 426i
Tidal flat, 890
Tidal volume, **711**, 711i
Tide pool, 834i, 890, 891i
Tiger, 468, 469i, 829
Tight junction, **67**, 67i, **561**, 561i, 570, 670, 727, 761, 786i
Tilapia, 889i
Tilia americana, 116i
Tilletia indica, 397t
Timbre, sound, 606
Time, geologic, 260
Timothy grass cell, 58i
Tinman gene, 236, 677
Tissue, 4, 4i, 5i, 6–7, 9, 14, 236, **480**, 489, **558**–559, 558i, 570, 634t
animal. *See* Animal tissue
cell adhesion in, 151, 151i, 763

culture propagation, 140
damage, 558, 600, 600t, 602–603, 679, 680t, 681, 683–685, 685i, 698
defense, 42, 48t, 49i, 74
formation, 566, 763–765, 768, 792i
invasion, 151, 151i
malignant, 230, 230i
in metamorphosis, 420, 434i
mosaic effect, 234, 234i
nervous, 634t
plant. *See* Plant tissue
regeneration, 215–216
repair, 142–143, 142t, 152, 685, 685i, 766
specialization, 233, 237, 240, 374, 558, 755, 758, 758i, 759i, 762, 764–765, 768, 771
transplant, 215, 693
Tissue, plant, vascular, 544, 544t
Tissue culture propagation, 525, **536**–538, 536t, 537i, 545t, 881
Tissue web, 489i
Toad, 440, 441, 460, 627, 677, 704, 907, 907i
Tobacco mosaic virus, 342i, 343
Tobacco plant, 343, 490, 490i, 551, 709i
Tobacco smoking. *See* Smoking
Todd, John, 889
Tofu, 258, 731
Togavirus infection, 343t
Tomato plant, 258, 480i, 489, 494, 494i, 508, 533, 545t, 732t
body plan, 494, 494i
salt-tolerant, 252, 258, 296, 296i
Tongue, 441, 444, 565i, 590, 590i, 600t, 602, 602i, 604, 604i, 615, 707, 707i, 720i, 723, 750
Tonicity, **84**, 85i
Tonsil, 674i, 675
Tool making, 456, 912
early human, 453, 456–459, 457i
Tooth (dentition), 41, 50, 57, 234, 406, 452–454, 460, 683, 707, 723
calcium and, 645, 723, 723i, 733t
decay (caries), 683
dietary vitamins, minerals and, 732t
formation, 732t, 733t, 792i
human, 456–458
mammalian trait, 448, 448i, 461
molar, 721, 721i, 723, 723i
plaque, 683, 683i
primate, 454, 454i
shark, 438
Tooth decay, 733t, 737
Topography, 822, 839, 867, 872–**873**, 875, 896
Topsoil, 252, 387, **513**, 513i, 876, 878
Toromino shrub, 462
Torres del Paine National Park, 886i, 887
Torsion, **416**–417, 416i, 430
Tortoise, 465i
Total fertility rate (TFR), **814**–815, 814i, 817–**818**, 819, 819i
Touch, sense of, 441, 593i, 599, 600t, 602–603, 615
Touch-kill mechanism, 692, 692i, 693i, 698, 698t
Toxic goiter, **626**, 733t
Toxin, 90, 218, 339, 729, 744, 795, 889
arachnid, 426, 426i
botulinum, 653–655
Caulerpa taxifolia, 836
cnidarian, 410i
Conus, 402, 402i
dinoflagellate, 358, 358i
effect on muscles, 653–654, 653i
elimination/excretion, 739
and immune response, 680–681, 680t, 681i, 686–688, 690–693, 698
inactivation, 59i, 62–63, 63i, 90, 105

lichen, 390
neutralization, 233
neutralization in liver, 664, 676
nudibranch, 417
plant, 486, 489–490, 500, 510–511, 510i, 511i, 604, 848
prey, 828–829
and renal failure, 748
sponge, 408
synthetic, 848
Toxoplasma species, 369, 369i
Toxoplasmosis, 369
TPA protein, 254
Trace element, 18–19, 18i
Trace fossil, 268
Tracer, **21**, 21i, **30**, 30t, 209i
Trachea, 420, 626, 626i, 703, 703i, 705i, 706i, **707**, 716–717, 717i, 723
Tracheal system, **703**, 703i, 716
Tracheid, **497**, 497i, 505i, 507–508, 508i, 515i, 516, 516i, 522
Trachoma, 615
Tract, 587
Tradewinds, 868i, 872–873, 894i
Trait. *See also* Variation in traits
adaptive forms, 10, 14
control over, 232
hereditary, 145
heritable, 44, 155–156, 161
male vs. female, 37
natural vs. artificial selection, 10, 10i
observable differences in, 36i
secondary sexual, 41
shared heritable, 3, **10**, 14
Tranquilizer, 793
Trans-fatty acid, 730
Trans fatty acid tail, 49, 49i
Transcript processing, 232, 233i
Transcription, 189i, **219**–221, 220i, 221i, 228, 228i, 232, 252
B or T cell, 689–690, 689i
controls, 230–233, 232i, 233i, 235–237, 238i, 239i, 240–241, 340, 348
eukaryotic, 238t, 241
gene modification, 242
growth factors and, 150
hormones and, 232i, 240, 541–542, 544, 546–547, 546i, 550, 550i, 555
mRNA, hormones and, 622, 623i
nature of, 220–221, 220i, 229
prokaryotic, 231, 238–241, 238t, 239i
reversible, 238t, 240
RNA, 219–221, 220i, 769
Transcription factors, 239
Transduction, 519i, 549, 600, 606–607, 615–616, 619, 622, 636
of photon energy to action potentials, 610, 612–613, 613i
Transfer RNA (tRNA), 219–**220**, 228i
as initiator, 224–225, 224i, 225i, 228
structure, 223, 223i, 228
Transformation, bacterial, 208
Transgenic organisms, 243, 252
animals, 254–255, 254i, 257–258, 699, 699i, 748
plants, 252–253, 253i, 257
safety of, 255, 257
Transition state, **97**, 104
Transitional stage, **816**–817, 816i
Translation, **219**–**220**, 223, 228, 228i, 238t, 239i, 622, 623i, 693
control of, 230–233, 233i, 236, 238t, 240
of mRNA, genetic code and, 344, 348, 542, 546i
stages, 224–225, 224i–225i, 228
Translocation, **511**, **520**–521, 521i, **522**
chromosomal, 187–188, **196**–197, 204
pressure flow theory and, 521, 521i

Transmission electron microscope (TEM), **54**, 54i, 55i, 58i, 60i, 65i
Transpiration, 511, **516–517**, 517i, 519, **522**, **853**, 853i
Transport protein, 57, 61, 72, 77–**78**, 81i, 86–87, **94**, 104, 104t, 112, 179, 233i, 239i, 293, 547, 547i, 548i, 555
ABC transporter, 74–75
active, 75, 77i, 78–**79**, 79i, **81**, 81i, **82**–83, 83i, 88, 88i, 94, 95i, 104t, 547i, 745i
in food absorption, 726–728, 727i, 737
function, 94, 125, 130–131, 326, 561, 561i, 622
for glucose, 82, 82i, 88
neural membrane, 577–578, 577i, 578i, 579i, 583, 589, 596
for oxygen, 293
passive, 75, 77i, 78–**79**, 79i, **81–82**, 81i, 82i, 83, 88, 88i, 104t, 547i, 744–746, 745i
plant, 503, 522, 547, 547i
plasma membrane, 515, 515i, 740, 744
selective permeability, 84, 84i, 744, 746
Transporters, proteins as, 33, 35, 42–45, 44i, 48t, 179
Transposon, 197, **226**, 227i, 228, 330
in primate evolution, 277
Transverse fission, 357, **412**
Transverse plane, animal, 566i
Transverse section, plant, 496i
Trapezius, 647i
Trapping, 827i
Trapping fungus, 393, 393i
Trastuzumab, 693
Trauma, 589, 593
Tree, 374, 388t, 486, 486i
burning of biomass, 387
harvesting, 387
pigeon adaptation to, 822i, 823
structure/growth pattern, 875–876, 878, 880
transgenic, 252, 253i
Tree farm, 387
Tree fern, 373i, 379, 379i
Tree of life, 8i, 314, 314i, 328–329i
animals, 404i, 407i, 428i
archaeans, 337i, 340i
bacteria, 337i, 338i
fungi, 392i
hominids, 457i
human populations, 459i
plants, 373i, 375i
plotted against time, 328i–329i
protist groups, 352i
"reptiles," 442i
vertebrates, 437i
Tree ring, **507**, 507i, 509, 509i
Tree shrew, 454–455, 454i
Trematode, 412, 441i
Tremor, 582
Treponema, 338i, 784i, 784t, 785, 785i
Treponeme, 785
TRH, 626, 626i
Triassic period, 269i, 271i, 373i, 442, 442i, 444–445, 448, 449i, 461, 464t
Tribolium, castaneum, 294
Triceps brachii, 646i, 647i
Trichinella spiralis, 419, 419i
Trichinosis, 419
Trichloroethylene (TCE), 510
Trichocyst, 356, 356i
Trichoderma, 401
Trichomonas vaginalis, 352i, 353, 353i, 368, 784
Trichomoniasis, 353, 353i, 784, 784t
Trichonympha campanula, 352i, 353
Trichophyton, 397t
Trichoplax adhaerens, 404i, 409, 409i
Trigger zone, **576–579**, 576i, 578i, 579i, 581, 584i, 596

Triglyceride, **40**–41, 41i, 43, 47, 134, 724t, 725, 727, 727i, 729–730, 736
Triiodothyronine, 621i, 622t, 626, 635t
Trilobite, 407i, 418i, 420, 464i, 464t
Trimester, in human pregnancy, 786, 790–791, 793
Trinidad guppy, 810–811, 810i, 811i
Triple covalent bond, **25**
Triplet, 770
Triploid number (*3n*), 530
Trisomy 21, 198, 198i, 199i, 204
Triticum, 381, 307, 307i
tRNA. *See* Transfer RNA
Trophic level (feeding level), **845–846**, 845i, 846i, 847i, 849–851, 850i, 851i, 860, 863
Trophoblast, 786, 786i
Tropical forest, 469, 473i, 474, 822, 838, 873, 874i–875i, 876, 878, 884i, 896
deforestation, 119, 876, 881, 884i
Tropical grassland and savanna, 473i
Tropical rain forest, 473i, 476, 509, 528, 822i, 823, 854, 857, 862, 896
biodiversity, 881
deforestation, 370, 524
distribution, 874i–875i, 880
mimicry in, 12
soils, 370, 876, 877i
species, 300, 305, 393
Tropical zone, climate, 116i, 121i, 869i
Tropics, 468, 507, 838
Tropism, 548–549, 548i, 549i
Tropomyosin, 650, 651i
Troponin, 232, 650, 651i
Troposphere, 868i
Trout, 436i, 438, 830, 830i, 835t
True-breeding lineage, 171–172, 172i, 173i, 174, 174i, 176, 182–185, 193, 294
True fruit, **532–533**, 533t
Truffle, 396, 399–400
Trumpet chanterelle, 392i
Trypanosoma, 352i, 354–355, 355i, 368
Trypanosome, 354–355
Trypsin, 98, 724t, 725
Tryptophan, 42i, 98, 98i, 222i, 233, 582, 730
Tsetse fly, 354, 355i
TSH. *See* Thyroid-stimulating hormone
Tsunami, 93, 93i, 272i, 865
Tuatara, 314i, 404i, 428i, 434i, 442i, 443–445, 445i, 460–461
Tubal ligation, 782, 782i
Tubal pregnancy, 784, 784i, 798
Tube (floral), 528i, 529, 529i
Tube foot, 428, 429i, 641, 641i
Tube worm, 892, 893i
Tuber, 536t
Tuberculosis, 289, 346–347, 346i, 637
Tubular gut, 406, 430
Tubular reabsorption, 627, 739, 743–**744**, 744i, 745–747, 745i, 746i, 752–753
Tubular secretion, 739, 743–**745**, 744i, 747, 752
Tubulin, 68, 69, 145–146, 760–761, 768
Tuco-tuco, 450t
Tularemia, 426
Tulip, 343i, 536t, 556
Tulip tree, 534
Tumor (neoplasm), 141, **150**, 152–153, 343t, 408, 626, 629, 631
adrenal gland, 747
benign, 150–151, 151i
flowering plant, 338
malignant, 151, 151i, 343t
of nervous system, 201t
skin, 201t, 229, 229i
taxol and, 68
testicular, 798
Tumor cell, 150, 687, 697

antigens, 680, 693, 699
immune response to, 679–680, 680t, 693, 693i, 699
Tumor-inducing gene, 252
Tumor-inducing plasmid (Ti plasmid), 252, 253i, 257
Tumor necrosis factor (TNF), 680t, 681, 696
Tumor suppressors, **150**
Tuna, 439, 865
Tundra, 341, 378, 390, 473i, 874, 874i–875i, 883, 883i, 896
Tunicate, 314i, 404i, 428i, 434–435, 434i, 437i, 460
Tuning fork, 606
Tupaia, 454i
Turbellarian, 404i, 412–413, 430
Turgor, **85**
Turgor pressure, 401, **518**, 518i, 519i, 521i, **542**
carnivorous plant, 523i
nematocyst, 410i
in plant cell growth, 542, 547, 547i, 553, 555
plasmolysis, 518i
Turkey, 242, 465i
as parable, 16, 16i
Turner, Teresa, 833
Turner syndrome, **199**, 201t
Tursiops truncatus, 715, 715i
Turtle, 278, 314i, 404i, 428i, 434i, 442i, 443–445, 445i, 468
Tusk, elephant, 469i
Twin, 798
artificial, 214, 214t
identical, 10, 214, 214t, 216, 249, 284, 763, 769
Tylosaurus, 465i
Type 1 diabetes, **629**, 629i
Type 2 diabetes, **629**
Typhoid fever, 362
Typhus, 282, 327i
Tyrosinase, 99i, 179, 179i
Tyrosine, 202, 222i, 582, 730
Tyser, Robin, 476

U
Udder, 215
Udotea cyathiformis, 352i, 364i
Ulcer, 615, 629t, 662, 682, 724, 737, 785
Ulna, 447i, 643i
Ulnar nerve, 575i
Ultrafiltration, 670i, **671**, 676
Ultraplankton, 892
Ultrasound, 202i, 600t, 616–617, 617i
Ultraviolet (UV) radiation, 108i, 227, 466, 528, 528i, 600, 868i
effects on organisms, 107–108, 121, 230, 372, 441
harmful effects, 150, 150i, 227
ozone thinning and, 372, 870, 870i, 896
skin and, 217, 217i, 569
Ulva, 352i, 364, 364i
Umbilical cord, 202i, 203, 558, 789–790, 789i, 790i, 794, 794i
Umbrella thorn tree, 490
Unbranched evolution, 308, 316
Underhair, mammalian, 751i
Understory tree, 876, 881
Undifferentiated cells, 497, 508t, 760i, 774
Ungulate, 831, 831i
Uniformity, theory of, **265**, 272
United States
air pollution, 870–871
conservation efforts, 474, 475i
energy consumption, 869
gross primary productivity, 876i
human population, 814, 814i, 815i, 816–817, 819, 819i
species introductions, 820, 820i, 821i, 834–835, 834i, 835t, 840

watershed, 888
U.S. Army, repair of J-Field, 510, 510i
U.S. Department of Agriculture (USDA), nutritional guidelines, 730, 731i
Unity of life, 211
cellular organization and, 123, 136–137
molecular organization and, 123, 136–137
nature of, 3, 6–9, 6i, 14, 15t
Unsaturated fatty acid, **40**, 40i, 49, 76
Upper littoral zone, **890**, 891i
Upwelling, 892–**893**, 892i, 894, 894i, 896
Uracil (U), 47, **220**, 220i, 223, 228, 323
Uranium, 21, 270
Urban waste, 888–889
Urea, 135, 729, 729i, 731, **741**, 745, 745i, 752–753
Ureter, 739, 742–743, 742i, 748, 752
Urethra, 739, 742–743, 742i, 748, 752, 772–773, 773i, 774i, 776, 777i, 781, 784, 796
Uric acid, 424, 748, 753
Urinary excretion, 390, **741**, 741i, 743, 745, 747–748, 752–753, 772, 773i, 777
Urinary system, 719, **740**
acid–base balancing, 747, 752
function, 567i, 664, 665i, 739, 742, 742i, 752
functional links with organ systems, 740, 740i, 747, 752
human, 567i, 739, 741–743, 741i, 742i, 752
infection, 393, 682–683, 682t
kangaroo rat, 741, 741i
solute-water balance, 738–741, 741i
structure, 739, 742–743, 742i
urine formation in, 586, 739, 740i, 742–745, 742i, 744i, 745i, 747, 752
vertebrate, 566, 701i, 740, 740i
Urination, 682t, 683, 742
Urine, 89, 191, 624–625, 629, 682t, 729, 729i, 731, 738–**740**, 740i, 741–747, 746i, 752, 787, 862, 904, 913
drug effects on, 572
tests, 738–739, 738i, 739i
Urochordate, **434–435**, 897
Ursus maritimus, 296, 296i, 751i
Usnea, 398i
Ustilago maydis, 397t
Uterus, 192i, 203, 450, 451i, 485, 560i, 565, 586i, 624, 624i, 632, 634t, 635t, 636, **776–777**, 776t, 777i, 781i, 783, 784i, 786, 789, 789i, 794, 797
diseases of, 153
function, 757, 757i
in menstrual cycle, 771, 776–777, 776t, 779–780, 780i, 796
post-delivery, 397, 794–795, 794i
Utricle, 605, 605i

V
Vaccination, **678**, 694i, 699, 792
Vaccine, 140, 208, 252, 258, 349, **359**, 693–**694**, 699, 813, 881
against HIV, 678, 696–697
malaria, 359
recombinant, 697
recommended childhood, 694i
smallpox, 678, 679i
tetanus, 653
Vacuole, 63, 335i, 355, 355i, 356i
Vagina, 57, 192i, 334, 339, 396i, 682, 682t, 697, 737, 776, 776t, 777i, 781–782, 781i, 785, 794, 796
infections, 353
Vaginal sponge, in fertility control, 782i
Vagus nerve, 586i

Valine, 44, 45i, 222i, 224i, 225i, 226i, 228i, 730
■ Valley fever, 397t
Valve, 217, 217i
  heart, 666, 666i, 667i, 676–677
  lymph node, 674i, 675
  vein, 671, 671i
Vampire stories, porphyria and, 571
Van Tilburg, Jo Anne, 462
Vanilla orchid, 310i
Varanus komodoensis, 444
Variability, **12–13**, 15–16
■ Variant Creutzfeldt–Jakob disease (vCJD), 347, 347i
Variation in traits, 3, 6–9, 14, 45, 170, 222, 284, 483
  asexual vs. sexual reproduction, 154–156, 166
  continuous, 180–182, 180i, 181i
  crossing over and, 160–161, 160i, 178, 178i, 180, 182, 284
  environment and, 154–155, 179, 179i, 182, 266–267, 283–284
  eugenic engineering for, 256
  fertilization and, 155, 163, 166–167
  during meiosis, 160–161, 160i, 161i, 167
  Mendelian patterns, 169–172, 172i, 180, 182
  metaphase I and, 161, 161i
  in plant species, 302
  by sexual reproduction, 214, 214t
  sexual vs. asexual reproduction, 756
  tight linkage, 178, 178i, 180
■ Varicella–zoster infection, 343t, 694i
■ Varicose vein, **671**
Vas deferens (vasa deferentia), 772, 772t, 773i, 774i, 782, 796
Vascular bundle, 495, 495i, 498–**499**, 499i, 501, 501i, 508
Vascular cambium, 494i, 544, 544t
  activity at, 504–507, 504i, 505i, 507i
Vascular cylinder, 502i, **503**, 503i, **515**, 515i, 517i, 522, 547i
Vascular plant, 311, 311i, 371, **375**, 388t, 399, 493
  evolutionary trends, 271i, 361, 371, 375, 375i, 384i
Vascular ray, 505i
Vascular spasm, 672, 672i
Vascular system, 668
Vascular tissue, 27, 374–375, 480i, 482, 508, 526. *See also* Phloem; Xylem
  differentiation, 544, 544t
  early vs. late wood, 507, 507i
  evolution of, 371, 374–375, 388
  functions, 482–483, 493–494, 494i, 511, 520, 521i
  meristematic sources, 498–499, 498i, 499i, 502
  penetration by parasites, 830i
  plant body plan, 494–499, 494i, 495i, 497i, 498i, 499i
  primary, 494i, 495, 499
  secondary, 494i, 505
  structure, 511
Vascular tunic, 610i
■ Vasectomy, 782, 782i
Vasoconstriction, 669, 669i, 744, 750t, **751**, 751t, 781
Vasodilation, **669**, 669i, 685i, 694, 744, **750**–751, 750t, 781, 798
Vasopressin, 634t, 635
Vegan diet, 677
Vegetable, 108, 241–242, 730–731, 731i, 732t, 733t
Vegetable oil, 40, 48t, 49, 258, 732t
Vegetal pole, 759i, **760**–761
Vegetarian, 733
Vegetative growth, 525, **536**, 536t, 538
Vegetative propagation, 536t

Vegetative reproduction, 536, 536t, 537i
Vein, 275i, **668**, 726i
  function, 671, 671i, 676
  human, 202i, 482, 657, 665i, **668**, 668i, 671i, 675–677
  renal, 742–743, 742i
Vein, plant, 116i, 117i, 236, 483i, 495i, 500i, **501**, 501i, 508, 512t, 521, 521i
  tension, 516–517, 517i
Veld, 875
Velocity, force of, 599, 605
Velvet walking worm, 277i, 307
Vena cava, 742i
Venom, 421, 423, 426, 438, 441, 444, 445i, 461i
  examples, 694, 820, 829, 829i, 898
Venter, Craig, 250, 330
Ventilation, in gas exchange, 702–705, 703i, 704i, 705i, 710, 716
Ventral fin, 437i, 439
Ventral horn, 587i
Ventral root, 587, 587i
Ventral surface, 406, 406i, **566**, 566i
Ventricle (heart), 657, 659, 659i, 666–669, 666i, 667i, 669i, 673, 676, 714
Ventricle, brain, 588, 588i
■ Ventricular fibrillation, **673**, 673i, 751t
■ *Venturia inaequalis*, 397i, 397t
Venule, **668**, 668i, 670i, 671, 676, 726, 742–743
Venus flytrap, 523, 523i
Venus's flower basket, 408i
Vernalization, **551**
Vertebra (vertebrae), **436**, **642**, 643i, 645
Vertebral column, 436–437, 444i, 445i, 460, 562, 587, 587i, 642, 642i, 643i, 742i, 788
Vertebrate, 40, 67i, 312, 312i, 342, 433–**434**, 460, 472i, 566i, 642, 826, 893i
  blood circulation, 657–659, 675
  chordates, 404i, 407i
  circulatory system, 701i, 707
  connective tissue, 562–563, 562i–563i
  defining characteristics, 606–608, 610–611, 615, 788, 788i, 790–791
  development, 758, 762–763, 765, 769
  digestive system, 701i
  endocrine systems, 619–620, 621i, 624–636, 634t–635t
  epithelial tissue, 560–561
  evolution, 274–277, 274i, 281, 309, 315, 402, 404i, 407, 407i, 433, 435–436, 442, 442i, 588, 619, 642–643, 642i, 643i, 658–659, 787
  evolutionary trends, 433, 435–437, 436i, 437i
  immune system, 681–687, 698
  invertebrate vs., 633, 636, 699, 740
  muscle tissue, 564–565
  organ systems, 565–566, 566i, 570, 573, 701i, 740, 752
  respiratory system, 701, 701i, 704–705, 704i, 705i
  sense of hearing, 599
  skeleton, 639, 642–645, 642i, 643i, 644i, 644t, 645i, 654
  skin, 568–569, 568i
■ *Verticillium*, 297t
■ Vertigo, **605**
Vervet monkey, 908
Vesicle, **58**, 59i, 63, 63i, 68, 70, 70i, 72, 81, 81i, 85–88, 86i, 87i, 146–147, 323, 356, 686, 726i
  chemical synapse, 580, 580i
  cytoplasmic, 746–747
  endomembrane system, 62–63, 62i, 63i, 72

fungal, 401
  Golgi-derived, 148i, 149
Vessel, xylem, 497, 497i, 507, 507i, 515i
Vessel member, **497**, 497i, 499i, 502i, 508, 508t, 516, 516i, 522
Vestiaria coccinea, 300i, 305i
Vestibular apparatus, **605**–606, 605i, 606i, 615, 617
Vestibular nerve, 605
Vestigial structure, 263, 263i, 281, 913
■ Viagra, 798
■ *Vibrio*, 338i, 894–895, 895i
Victoria crowned pigeon, 822i
Vicuna, 304i
Vieques Island, Puerto Rico, 102i
Villus (villi), **726**–727, 726i, 736
Vimentin, 69
Vine, 549, 880–881
Viola, 385i
Virchow, Rudolf, 51
■ Virtual colonoscopy, **728**
Virus, 140, 208, 230, 332–**333**, **342–343**, 343i, 346, 346t, 348, 408, 661, 785, 889
  classifications, 343t
  as cloning vector, 244–245, 251, 256
  DNA, 208, 209i, 244, 333, 342, 342i, 344–345, 345i, 348, 697i
  enveloped, 86, 333, 342i, 343, 343i, 345, 345i, 348, 696, 697i
  immune response to, 569, 680–681, 680t, 686–688, 692i, 695–696, 785
  multiplication cycles, 333, 344–345, 344i, 345i, 348
  plant, 253, 343, 343i
  replication cycle, 696, 697i
  RNA, 333, 342, 342i, 344–345, 344i, 348, 680, 697i
  species barrier, 255
  structure, 342i, 697i
Viscera, 416, **586**
Visceral pain, **602**–603
Visible light, 54, 107–110, 108i, 110i, 120–121, 195, 600
Vision, sense of, 122, 122i, 440, 454, 528, 528i, 593i, 599, 604, **608**–612, 613i, 615–616
  balance, 440, 448
  primate evolution, 452–454, 460
■ Vision impairment, 714
Visual cortex, 590i, 591–592, 592i, 599, 613, 613i
Visual cues, 12, 13, 528–529, 528i, 538
Visual field, 420, 605, **608**–609, 609i, 611–613, 615
Visual receptor, 600t
Visual signal, 302i, 303, 904, 912, 914
Vital capacity, **711**, 711i
■ Vitamin, 99, 529, 554, 568, 615, 719, 721i, 730, **732**–733, 732t
■ A, 121, 242, 569, 732t, 733
■ B, 569, 732, 732t, 792
  biotin, 732t
  blood transport, 660, 660i
■ C (ascorbic acid), 38, 49, 568, 713i, 732t, 733, 793
■ D, 41, 48t, 568–570, 645, 732t, 733
  deficiency, 732t
  E, 732t, 733
  fat-soluble, 660, 730, 732t, 733
  folate (folic acid), 732t
  functions, 732t
  K, 732t, 733
  pregnancy and, 792
■ receptors for, 86
  synthesis, 728, 736–737
Vitex lucens, 539
Vitis, 540
Vitreous body, 610i, 611
Vocal cord, 707, 707i, 723
Voice box, 199

Volatile substance, 604
Volcanic island, 470i, 838–839, 838i
Volcano, 264i, 265, 305–306, 306i, 338, 833
  eruption, 32, 268–269, 280, 300, 857, 856i–857i, 860
  extinct, 887, 892
  magnetic pattern, 272, 280
Vole, 800, 846i, 883i, 900–901, 900i, 913
Voluntary muscle, 564, 570
Volvox, 352i, 364, 364i
Vomeronasal organ, **604**, 620, 913
■ Vomiting, 191, 397, 485, 588, 595, 714, 733t, 737, 746
von Frisch, Karl, 905i
Vulture, 844
Vulva, 784

Ⓦ

Waggle dance, 905i
Wakefulness, 591
Walking, 439, 582
  bipedalism, 443, 446, 448, 452–453, 455–456, 455i, 458, 460
  four-legged, 439–442, 439i, 452, 617
Walking legs, arthropod, 422–423, 422i
Wall cress plant, 235, 235i, 276i
Wallace, Alfred, 261–262, 280, 284, 838, 874
  natural selection theory and, 267, 267i
  study of biogeographic patterns, 267, 841, 841i
Wallace's Line, 841, 841i
Waller, Augustus, 656, 656i
Walnut tree, 504i, 505i, 545t, 880
Wandering albatross, 839i
Warbler, 447
■ Warfarin, 282–283
Warning coloration, **828**–829, 828i, 829i
■ Wart, 342
Wasp, 292, 302i, 490, 490i, 694–695, 829i, 831, 831i
■ Wastewater treatment, 618, **889**, 889i
Water, 26–27, 34, 36, 74, 320, 374, 512
  absorption from gut, 726–728, 736, 736t
  DDT residue, 849i
  as dispersal agent, 525
  distribution through plants, 374, 492–493, 492i–493i, 497, 497i, 500, 512, 512t, 520–522, 520i, 521i, 522i
  drinking, 889, 895, 895i
  elimination/excretion, 739, 741, 741i, 745
  fish adaptations to, 438
■ fluoridated, 733t
  global cycling, 387, 389
  global distribution of, 5i, 843, 850, 850i, 852, 855, 855i
  as greenhouse gas, 858
  human body, 660i, 665i, 671, 733t
  hydrologic cycle, 852–**853**, 853i, 863
  leaching, 513
  membrane organization and, 52, 65–66
  odors in, 600t
  origin of life and, 19, 26, 107, 321–322, 321i
  pH, 28–29, 28i
  poles in life, 110
  population growth and, 814, 817
  properties of, 19, 26–27, 27i, 30, 30t
  shortages, 843, 853, 855, 855i, 863
  soil erosion, 513
  solubility, 36i, 37–38, 41, 48t, 76i, 78
  supply, 492–493, 492i–493i
  uptake by cells, 746
  uptake in plants, 493–494, 502–503, 507–508, 514–518, 515i, 516i, 517i

volume, 853–854, 853i, 864
water-solute balance, 482–483, 489
Water conservation
  amniote, 442
  animal, 741, 753, 885
  human, 744–747, 746i, 752
  human body, 559, 567i, 568, 621i, 634t
  insects, 420, 703
  plant, 66, 117, 120, 263, 303, 374, 381, 388, 480, 487, 493, 497, 500–501, 518–519, 518i, 519i, 522, 545, 552, 555
■ riparian zone, 474
■ Water contamination, groundwater, 510, 510i
Water flea, 824
Water hyacinth, 835t, 841, 841i, 889
■ Water intoxication, **753**, 753i
Water lilies, 385, 385i
Water mold, 350, **362**
Water molecule, 6, 23, 25–26, 25i, 26i, 63, 104, 107, 136, 371, 513
  aerobic respiration and, 125, 125i, 127i, 130, 130i, 132, 135i, 136–137
  cohesion–tension theory, 516–517, 516i, 517i, 522
  hydrogen bonding, 37, 37i, 94, 96–97, 122
  membrane crossing by, 80–81, 81i, 89
  as metabolic byproduct, 94–97, 97i, 99, 100i
  osmosis, 84–85, 84i, 85i
  in photosynthesis, 6, 9, 107, 111–112, 113i, 114i, 120, 120i
  polarity, 26–27, 26i, 30, 81, 81i, 136
Water mouse, 450t
Water percolation, 876, 876i
■ Water pollution, 467, 889
■ agriculture and, 618, 618i, 627, 888. See also Agricultural runoff
  ecosystems, 842, 849, 849i, 852, 855, 863
■ groundwater, 353, 413, 510, 855
■ by H. pylori, 335i
■ industrial waste, 888
■ wastewater treatment, 353, 888
Water province, 867, 896
  freshwater, 867, 886–889, 886i, 887i, 888i
  marine, 867, 874, 874i–875i, 886
Water repellant, 41, 41i, 76, 97, 104
Water-salt balance, 635t, 733t
Water shrew, 450t
Water-solute balance, 74–75, 84–85, 84i, 85i, 88–89, 482–483, 670i, 671, 675, 738–739
  vertebrate, 629, 634t, 740–742, 740i, 741i, 746–748, 752–753, 753i
Water stress, 544t, 545, 555, 877i
Water strider, 31, 31i
Water transport, plants, 480, 480i, 482, 486, 489, 503, 505, 508, 511–512, 516–517, 516i, 517i, 522, 522i, 540, 542
  cohesion–tension theory, 516–517, 516i, 517i
  nature of, 512i, 518–519, 518i, 519i, 522
  tracheids and, 497, 497i
  vascular tissue, 493–494, 494i
Water–vascular system, **428**, 429i
Waterlily, 482, 483i
Watermelon, 53, 185, 185i, 242, 306i, 532–533
Waterproofing, 568
Watershed, 387, **853–854**, 853i, 854i, 871, 884, 888
Watson, James, 207i, 211–212, 215–216, 250
■ Watson–Crick model of DNA, 207i, 211i, 212, 216

Waveform, 591
  action potential, 579i, 581i
Wavelength, **54**, 72, **108**, 320, 886
  in photoperiodism, 550, 555
  in photosynthesis, 107, 110, 110i, 121
  in phototropism, 549, 555
  visible spectrum, 107–110, 108i, 110i, 120–121, 181, 195, 600t, 608
Wax, 40–**41**, 41i, 47, 48t, 116, 420, 682t, 683, 881
  in plant cell wall, 66, 67i, 497, 515, 515i, 518–519, 522, 534
Weapons testing and disposal site, 510–511, 510i
Weasel, 279i, 846i
Weathering of rocks, 852, 854, 862, 862i
Web site, extinct/endangered species, 837
Weed, 545, 848, 848i
Weight, human, 642, 719
■ body, 206
  diet and, 718–719, 731, 734–736
  guidelines, 734i
■ ideal, 734, 734i
■ newborn, 290, 290i, 713i, 770
■ related disorders, 74, 629, 718, 734
Weight lifting, 652–653, 655
Weight loss, 594
Welwitschia mirabilis, 382, 382i
Went, Fritz, 548
■ Werner's syndrome, **766**
Wernike's area, 592
■ West Nile virus, 332, 333i, 427, 427i, 431, 842
■ Wet acid deposition, 871
■ Wetlands, 468, 842, 886, 890–891
Wexler, Nancy, 201
Whale, 118–119, 263, 263i, 281, 281i, 309i, 312, 422–423, 451i, 598–599, 598i, 617, 617i, 715, 892, 904
■ black market, 468–469, 469i
Wheat, 185, 252, 278i, 307, 307i, 370, 381, 385, 397, 495, 536t, 537, 554, 731, 812, 835, 861, 878
■ export, and drought, 492–493
Whirling disease, 830, 830i
Whisk fern, 314i, 371, 372i, 378, 378i, 388, 388t
White blood cell, 241, 483, 563i, 584, 645, 660–661, 661i, 675, 681, 684, 695i, 728. See also Lymphocyte
  characteristics, 670, 674i, 676, 681
  disorders, 189i, 201t, 631, 662, 662i, 675
  function, 562–563, 568, 621i, 657, 660i, 661, 675, 681, 685, 698
  immune response, 79i, 86–87, 89i, 629, 674i, 680–681, 695
  respiratory system lining, 700
  virus attack, 342
White Cliffs of Dover, 350, 350i, 351i
White-crown sparrow, 902
White matter, 587, 587i
■ White rust, 362
White-throated sparrow, 632i
Whitetail deer, 426, 800–801
Whittaker, Robert, 310
■ Whooping cough, 346, 346t, 682, 694i
Whooping crane, 468
Wiesel, Torsten, 613i
Wild-type allele, **193**, 193i
Wild-type gene, 235i, 236, 240
Wildebeest, 879i, 885
Wildfire, 842, 866, 878, 897
Wildflower, 525
Wildlife management program, 849, 849i
■ Wildlife trade, illegal, 463, 468–469, 469i, 475
Wilkins, Maurice, 210–211, 216
Williams, Ernest, 470

Willow, 832i
Wilmut, Ian, 206
Wilson, Edward, 468
Wilting, 296, 296i, 397t, 512t, 518–519, 518i, 523
Wind, 468, 486–487, 487i, 513, 513i, 868
  prevailing, 549, 555, 868, 870–872, 872i, 873i, 892–894, 896
■ Wind farm, 869, 869i
Wind friction, 872, 892–894
Windpipe. See Trachea
Windward side, **873**
Wine, 90
Wing, 241, 241i, 309, 765i
  arthropod, 420, 424–425
  bat, 275, 275i, 616
  bird, 275, 275i, 446–447, 446i, 447i
  Drosophila, 236, 237i
  fruit/seed, 534, 534i, 538
  insect, 275, 275i, 277, 284, 286, 286i, 288i, 290i, 424–425, 430, 529, 641, 641i, 765
Wing marker, 803, 803i
Wingless gene, 236
Winter blues, 632
■ Witch hunt, ergotism and, 397
■ Withdrawal, in fertility control, **782**, 782i
Wobble effect, 223
Woese, Carl, 340, 341
Wolf, 450t, 468, 476, 826, 826i, 883i, 904, 904i, 908–909, 909i
Wood, 32, 39i, 253i, 480, 486, 493, 497, 506–508, 506i, 507i, 709i
  in carbon cycle, 856–857, 856i–857i, 864
■ deforestation, 370, 387, 389, 881
  hardwood vs. softwood, 507, 539
  heartwood vs. sapwood, 506–508, 507i
  meristematic sources, 497, 504–505, 504i, 505i
■ products, 387, 389, 389i, 424, 881
■ strip logging, 474, 474i
  toromino, 462
■ uses, 370, 387, 389, 389i, 881, 884
Woodlands, 271i, 449, 452, 454–457, 456i, 812, 831, 831i
Woodwardia, 379i
Woodwell, George, 849i
Woody plant, 536, 874–875, 877i, 879i
Woolly mammoth, 217
World Health Organization, 242, 713
World Heritage site, 350
World Trade Center, 2, 249
Worm, 269, 640–641, 696, 765
Wren, 467
Wrinkled gene, 236
Wrinkling, 569
■ Wuchereria bancrofti infection, 419, 419i
Wurster, Charles, 849i

X
X chromosome, 145i, 157i, 160i, 166, 193, 231, 234–235, 234i, 240–241, 459, 653
  human, 187–188, 192–195, 192i, 193i, 194i, 195i, 199, 204–205, 771
■ X chromosome inactivation, **234**–235, 240–**241**
■ X-linked anhidrotic displasia, 201t
■ X-linked gene, 193, 193i, 194i, 195, 205, 234–235, 241, 653
■ X-linked recessive inheritance, 194–195, 194i, 195i, 201t, 205, 614, 622
X organ, 633i
■ X-ray, 21, 54, 108i, 210, 246, 246i, 728
■ exposure damage, 105, 153, 226–227
■ osteogenesis imperfecta, 655i
X-ray diffraction image, **210**, 211i, 216, 216i

Xanthopan morgani praedicta, 529, 529i
Xanthophyll, **108**
Xenopus laevis, 618, 627
■ Xenotransplation, **255**, **748**
■ Xeroderma pigmentosum (XP), 217, 217i
XIST gene, 235, 240
■ XO condition, 199
■ XXX syndrome, 199, 201t, 204
■ XXY condition, 199, 204
Xylem, **374**, 482, 489, 495, 496i, **497**–498, 497i, 499i, 501i, 507–508, 507i, 508t, 511, 516–517, 516i, 517i, 522
  function, 378–379, 388, 520, 544–545, 544t
  primary, 498–499, 498i, 502i, 503–504, 503i, 504i, 505i
  secondary, 504–506, 504i, 505i
  structure, 501, 502i, 504, 504i, 506, 515, 515i
■ XYY condition, **199**, 201t, 204

Y
Y-box proteins, 232, 233
Y chromosome, 145, 145i, 157i, 160i, 166, 187–188, 192, 192i, 194, 199, 204, 234–235, 241, 459, 771–772
Y organ, 633i
Yam, 462
Yarrow plant, 179, 179i
■ Yeast, 64, 193, 236, 244–245, 251, 251i, 278, 278i, 326, 337, 400, 732t
■ baking and, 132, 132i, 396
■ infections, 396, 396i, 681i, 696
■ wine production and, 132, 132i
Yellow bush lupine, 486–487, 487i
■ Yellow fever, 343t, 427
Yellow-green alga, **360–361**, 360i, 368
' Yellow marrow, **644**, 644i
Yellowjacket, 829i
Yellowstone National Park, 318, 318i, 341i, 472
Yersinia, 338i
Yew, 68, 69i, 153
■ Yogurt production, 399
Yolk, **757**, 757i, 759i, 760–761, 760i, 761i, 763, 768
Yolk sac, 446i, **787**–788, 787i, 787t, 788i, 790i, **797**
Yucca moth, 823, 823i
Yucca plant, 823, 823i

Z
Z band, **648**–649, 648i, 649i, 650i, 653–654
Zalmont, Iyad, 281
Zea mays, 65i, 167i, 227i, 542, 542i, 543i. See also Corn
Zebra, 879i, 903–904
Zebra flower, 302i, 303
Zebra mussel, 835t
Zebrafish, 677, 761i, 769, 769i
Zero population growth, **804**, 814–815, 815i, 817–818
Zinc, 512, 512t, 733t, 849, 892
Zinc ions, 510
Zona pellucida, 778i, 779, 781, 781i
Zonation, 886, 886i, 890–891, 891i, 893
Zoo breeding program, 301
Zooplankton, 849i, 850, 850i, 886, 889i
Zygomycete, 314i, 391, 392i, **393–394**, 394i, 397t, 399–401
■ Zygomycosis, 394
Zygospore, **394**, 394i, 400
Zygote, 166i, 237, 303i
  animal, 162i, 167, 411i
  formation, 566, 756, 758, 758i, 759i, 761–762, 768, 781, 787, 795t, 796
  frog, 759i, 760, 760i, 763
  fungal, 394i, 395, 395i
  human, 781, 781i, 786, 797, 798i
  plant, 162i, 374, 374i, 376i, 379i, 383, 383i, 526, 530, 532, 538, 542
  protistan, 359, 359i, 363i, 365, 365i